P9-EEK-471

Nineteenth-Century
Literature Criticism

Guide to Gale Literary Criticism Series

When you need to review criticism of literary works, these are the Gale series to use:

If the author's death date is: **You should turn to:**

After Dec. 31, 1959
(or author is still living)

CONTEMPORARY LITERARY CRITICISM

for example: Jorge Luis Borges, Anthony Burgess,
William Faulkner, Mary Gordon,
Ernest Hemingway, Iris Murdoch

1900 through 1959

TWENTIETH-CENTURY LITERARY CRITICISM

for example: Willa Cather, F. Scott Fitzgerald,
Henry James, Mark Twain, Virginia Woolf

1800 through 1899

NINETEENTH-CENTURY LITERATURE CRITICISM

for example: Fyodor Dostoevsky, Nathaniel Hawthorne,
George Sand, William Wordsworth

1400 through 1799

LITERATURE CRITICISM FROM 1400 TO 1800
(excluding Shakespeare)

for example: Anne Bradstreet, Daniel Defoe,
Alexander Pope, François Rabelais,
Jonathan Swift, Phillis Wheatley

SHAKESPEAREAN CRITICISM

Shakespeare's plays and poetry

Antiquity through 1399

CLASSICAL AND MEDIEVAL LITERATURE CRITICISM

for example: Dante, Homer, Plato, Sophocles, Vergil,
the Beowulf Poet

Gale also publishes related criticism series:

CHILDREN'S LITERATURE REVIEW

This series covers authors of all eras who have written for the preschool through high school audience.

SHORT STORY CRITICISM

This series covers the major short fiction writers of all nationalities and periods of literary history.

POETRY CRITICISM

This series covers poets of all nationalities and periods of literary history.

DRAMA CRITICISM

This series covers dramatists of all nationalities and periods of literary history.

ISSN 0732-1864

Volume 31

Nineteenth-Century Literature Criticism

Excerpts from Criticism of the
Works of Novelists, Poets, Playwrights,
Short Story Writers, Philosophers, and Other
Creative Writers Who Died between 1800
and 1899, from the First Published Critical
Appraisals to Current Evaluations

Paula Kepos
Editor

**Jelena O. Krstović
Marie Lazzari
Thomas Ligotti
Joann Prosyniuk**
Associate Editors

 Gale Research Inc. · DETROIT · LONDON

STAFF

Paula Kepos, *Editor*

Jelena O. Krstović, Marie Lazzari, Thomas Ligotti, Joann Prosyniuk, *Associate Editors*

John P. Daniel, Ian A. Goodhall, Tina Grant, Alan Hedblad, Grace Jeromski, Andrew M. Kalasky, Jim Poniewozik, Mark Swartz, Debra A. Wells, *Assistant Editors*

Jeanne A. Gough, *Permissions & Production Manager*
Linda M. Pugliese, *Production Supervisor*
Maureen Puhl, Jennifer VanSickle, *Editorial Associates*
Donna Craft, Paul Lewon, Lorna Mabunda, Camille Robinson, Sheila Walencewicz, *Editorial Assistants*

Maureen Richards, *Research Supervisor*
Paula Cutcher-Jackson, Judy L. Gale, Robin Lupa,
Mary Beth McElmeel, *Editorial Associates*
Jennifer Brostrom, Tamara C. Nott, *Editorial Assistants*

Sandra C. Davis, *Permissions Supervisor (Text)*
Josephine M. Keene, Denise Singleton, Kimberly F. Smilay, *Permissions Associates*
Maria L. Franklin, Michele Lonoconus, Shelly Rakoczy, Shalice Shah, Nancy Sheridan, Rebecca A. Stanko, *Permissions Assistants*

Patricia A. Seefelt, *Permissions Supervisor (Pictures)*
Margaret A. Chamberlain, Pamela A. Hayes, *Permissions Associates*
Keith Reed, *Permissions Assistant*

Mary Beth Trimper, *Production Manager*
Mary Winterhalter, *External Production Assistant*

Arthur Chartow, *Art Director*
C. J. Jonik, *Keyliner*

Contents

Preface vii

Acknowledgments xi

Preface

Since its inception in 1981, *Nineteenth-Century Literature Criticism* has been a valuable resource for students and librarians seeking critical commentary on writers of this transitional period in world history. Designated an "Outstanding Reference Source" by the American Library Association with the publication of its first volume, *NCLC* has since been purchased by over 6,000 school, public, and university libraries. The series has covered more than 300 authors representing 22 nationalities and over 15,000 titles. No other reference source has surveyed the critical reaction to nineteenth-century authors and literature as thoroughly as *NCLC*.

Scope of the Series

NCLC is designed to serve as an introduction for students and advanced readers to the authors of the nineteenth century, and to the most significant interpretations of these authors' works. The great poets, novelists, short story writers, dramatists, and philosophers of this period are frequently studied in high school and college literature courses. By organizing and reprinting the enormous amount of commentary written on these authors, *NCLC* helps students develop valuable insight into literary history, promotes a better understanding of the texts, and sparks ideas for papers and assignments. Each entry in *NCLC* presents a comprehensive survey of an author's career or an individual work of literature and provides the user with a multiplicity of interpretations and assessments. Such variety allows students to pursue their own interests; furthermore, it fosters an awareness that literature is dynamic and responsive to many different opinions.

Every fourth volume of *NCLC* is devoted to literary topics that cannot be covered under the author approach used in the rest of the series. Such topics include literary movements, prominent themes in nineteenth-century literature, literary reaction to political and historical events, significant eras in literary history, prominent literary anniversaries, and the literatures of cultures that are often overlooked by English-speaking readers.

NCLC continues the survey of criticism of world literature begun by Gale's *Contemporary Literary Criticism (CLC)* and *Twentieth-Century Literary Criticism (TCLC)*, both of which excerpt and reprint commentary on authors of the twentieth century. For additional information about *TCLC, CLC,* and Gale's other criticism series, users should consult the Guide to Gale Literary Criticism Series preceding the title page in this volume.

Coverage

Each volume of *NCLC* is carefully compiled to present:

- criticism of authors, or literary topics, representing a variety of genres and nationalities
- both major and lesser-known writers and literary works of the period
- 8-12 authors or 4-6 topics per volume
- individual entries that survey critical response to each author's work or each topic in literary history, including early criticism to reflect initial reactions; later criticism to represent any rise or decline in reputation; and current retrospective analyses.

Organization of This Book

An author entry consists of the following elements: author heading, biographical and critical introduction, list of principal works, excerpts of criticism (each preceded by an annotation and followed by a bibliographic citation), and a bibliography of further reading.

- The **author heading** consists of the name under which the author most commonly wrote, followed by birth and death dates. If an author wrote consistently under a pseudonym, the pseudonym will be listed in the author heading and the real name given in parentheses on the first line of the biographical and critical introduction. Also located at the beginning of the introduction to the author entry are any name variations under which an author wrote, including transliterated forms for authors whose languages use nonroman alphabets.

- The **biographical and critical introduction** outlines the author's life and career, as well as the critical issues surrounding his or her work. References are provided to past volumes of *NCLC* and to other biographical and critical reference series published by Gale, including *Short Story Criticism, Poetry Criticism, Children's Literature Review, Contemporary Authors, Dictionary of Literary Biography,* and *Something about the Author.*

• Most *NCLC* entries include **portraits** of the author. Many entries also contain reproductions of materials pertinent to an author's career, including manuscript pages, title pages, dust jackets, letters, and drawings, as well as photographs of important people, places, and events in an author's life.

• The list of **principal works** is chronological by date of first book publication and identifies the genre of each work. In the case of foreign authors with both foreign-language publications and English translations, the title and date of the first English-language edition are given in brackets. Unless otherwise indicated, dramas are dated by first performance, not first publication.

• **Criticism** is arranged chronologically in each author entry to provide a perspective on changes in critical evaluation over the years. All titles of works by the author featured in the entry are printed in boldface type to enable the user to easily locate discussion of particular works. Also for purposes of easier identification, the critic's name and the publication date of the essay are given at the beginning of each piece of criticism. Unsigned criticism is preceded by the title of the journal in which it appeared. Some of the excerpts in *NCLC* also contain translated material. Unless otherwise noted, translations in brackets are by the editors; translations in parentheses or continuous with the text are by the critic. Publication information (such as publisher names and book prices) and parenthetical numerical references (such as footnotes or page and line references to specific editions of works) have been deleted at the editors' discretion to provide smoother reading of the text.

• Critical excerpts are prefaced by **annotations** providing the reader with information about both the critic and the criticism that follows. Included are the critic's reputation, individual approach to literary criticism, and particular expertise in an author's works. Also noted are the relative importance of a work of criticism, the scope of the excerpt, and the growth of critical controversy or changes in critical trends regarding an author. In some cases, these annotations cross-reference excerpts by critics who discuss each other's commentary.

• A complete **bibliographic citation** designed to facilitate location of the original essay or book follows each piece of criticism.

• An annotated list of **further reading** appearing at the end of each author entry suggests secondary sources on the author. In some cases it includes essays for which the editors could not obtain reprint rights.

Cumulative Indexes

• Each volume of *NCLC* contains a cumulative **author index** listing all authors who have appeared in the following Gale series: *Contemporary Literary Criticism, Twentieth-Century Literary Criticism, Nineteenth-Century Literature Criticism, Literature Criticism from 1400 to 1800,* and *Classical and Medieval Literature Criticism.* Topic entries devoted to a single author, such as the entry on James Joyce's *Ulysses* in *TCLC* 26, are listed in this index. Also included are cross-references to the Gale series *Poetry Criticism, Short Story Criticism, Children's Literature Review, Authors in the News, Contemporary Authors, Contemporary Authors Autobiography Series, Dictionary of Literary Biography, Concise Dictionary of American Literary Biography, Something about the Author, Something about the Author Autobiography Series,* and *Yesterday's Authors of Books for Children.* Useful for locating authors within the various series, this index is particularly valuable for those authors who are identified by a certain period but who, because of their death dates, are placed in another, or for those authors whose careers span two periods. For example, Fyodor Dostoevsky is found in *NCLC,* yet Leo Tolstoy, another major nineteenth-century Russian novelist, is found in *TCLC* because he died after 1899.

• Each *NCLC* volume includes a cumulative **nationality index** which lists all authors who have appeared in *NCLC* volumes, arranged alphabetically under their respective nationalities, as well as Topics volume entries devoted to particular national literatures.

• Each new volume in Gale's Literary Criticism Series includes a cumulative **topic index,** which lists all literary topics treated in *NCLC, TCLC, LC 1400-1800,* and the *CLC* Yearbook.

• Each new volume of *NCLC,* with the exception of the Topics volumes, contains a **title index** listing the titles of all literary works discussed in the volume. The first volume of *NCLC* published each year contains an index listing all titles discussed in the series since its inception. Titles discussed in the Topics volume entries are not included in the *NCLC* cumulative index.

A Note to the Reader

When writing papers, students who quote directly from any volume in Gale's Literary Criticism Series may use the following general forms to footnote reprinted criticism. The first example pertains to material drawn from periodicals, the second to material reprinted from books.

[1] T. S. Eliot, "John Donne," *The Nation and the Athenaeum,* 33 (9 June 1923), 321-32; excerpted and reprinted in *Literature Criticism from 1400 to 1800,* Vol. 10, ed. James E. Person, Jr. (Detroit: Gale Research, 1989), pp. 28-9.

[2] Clara G. Stillman, *Samuel Butler: A Mid-Victorian Modern* (Viking Press, 1932); excerpted and reprinted in *Twentieth-Century Literary Criticism,* Vol. 33, ed. Paula Kepos (Detroit: Gale Research, 1989), pp. 43-5.

Suggestions Are Welcome

In response to suggestions, several features have been added to *NCLC* since the series began, including annotations to excerpted criticism, a cumulative index to authors in all Gale literary criticism series, entries devoted to criticism on a single work by a major author, more extensive illustrations, and a title index listing all literary works discussed in the series since its inception.

Readers who wish to suggest authors or topics to appear in future volumes, or who have other suggestions, are cordially invited to write the editors.

ACKNOWLEDGMENTS

The editors wish to thank the copyright holders of the excerpted criticism included in this volume, the permissions managers of many book and magazine publishing companies for assisting us in securing reprint rights, and Anthony Bogucki for assistance with copyright research. We are also grateful to the staffs of the Detroit Public Library Complex, and University of Michigan Libraries for making their resources available to us. Following is a list of copyright holders who have granted us permission to reprint material in this volume of *NCLC*. Every effort has been made to trace copyright, but if omissions have been made, please let us know.

COPYRIGHTED EXCERPTS IN *NCLC*, VOLUME 31, WERE REPRINTED FROM THE FOLLOWING PERIODICALS:

The American Poetry Review, v. 2, March-April, 1973 for "Whitman's Indicative Words" by Galway Kinnell. Copyright © 1973 by World Poetry, Inc. Reprinted by permission of the author.—*The American Society Legion of Honor Magazine,* v. 48, 1977. © copyright by The American Society of the French Legion of Honor Magazine 1977. Reprinted by permission of the publisher.—*Books and Bookmen,* v. 17, July, 1972 for "Towards Eros: The Machinery of Masochism" by Raymond Durgnat. © copyright the author 1972. Reprinted by permission of the author.—*California Slavic Studies,* v. V, 1970 for "Portrait of Gogol as a Word Glutton" by Simon Karlinsky. © 1970 by the Regents of the University of California. Reprinted by permission of the publisher and the author.— *Critical Inquiry,* v. 1, June, 1975 for "Walt Whitman: Man and Myth" by Jorge Luis Borges. Copyright © 1975 by The University of Chicago. Reprinted by permission of the publisher and the Literary Estate of Jorge Luis Borges.—*Encounter,* v. XXXVIII, May, 1972 for "Letters from the Underworld" by Graham Parry; v. XLI, August, 1973 for "The Invisible Mayhew" by Jonathan Raban. © 1972, 1973 by Encounter Ltd. Both reprinted by permission of the respective authors.—*French Historical Studies,* v. VII, Spring, 1971 for "Symbol, Legend, and History: Michelet as Folklorist-Historian" by Charles Rearick. © 1971 by the Society for French Historical Studies. Reprinted by permission of the publisher and the author.—*University of Hartford Studies in Literature,* v. 14, 1982. Copyright © 1982 by the University of Hartford. Reprinted by permission of the publisher.—*The Journal of British Studies,* v. XVII, Spring, 1978 for "Henry Mayhew and the Life of the Streets" by Richard Maxwell. Copyright 1978 by the Conference on British Studies at Trinity College, Hartford, Connecticut. Reprinted by permission of the publisher and the author.—*Journal of Canadian Fiction,* v. 2, n. 3, Summer, 1973 which presents a revised version first appearing in v. 1, n. 2, and v. 1, n. 4. Reprinted by permission from *Journal of Canadian Fiction,* 2050 Mackay St., Montreal, Quebec H3G 2J1, Canada.—*Modern Language Quarterly,* v. XXV, March, 1964. © 1966 University of Washington. Reprinted by permission of the publisher.—*The New Criterion,* v. VII, December, 1988 for "The Canonization of Susan Warner" by D. G. Myers. Copyright © 1988 by The Foundation for Cultural Review. Reprinted by permission of the author.—*The New Republic,* v. 114, March 18, 1946 for "Walt Whitman: The Miracle" by Malcolm Cowley. Copyright 1946 The New Republic, Inc. Renewed 1973 by Malcolm Cowley. Reprinted by permission of the Literary Estate of Malcolm Cowley.—*The New York Review of Books,* v. VI, March 17, 1966. Copyright © 1966 Nyrev, Inc. Reprinted with permission from *The New York Review of Books.*—*The New Yorker,* v. XLIV, February 24, 1968 for "A Very Inquisitive Old Party" by W. H. Auden. © 1968 by the author. Reprinted by permission of the Literary Estate of W. H. Auden.—*Partisan Review,* v. XLII, 1975 for "Whitman's Song of Myself: Homosexual Dream and Vision" by Robert K. Martin. Copyright © 1975 by *Partisan Review.* Reprinted by permission of the publisher and the author.—*Raritan: A Quarterly Review,* v. IV, Fall, 1984. Copyright © 1984 by *Raritan: A Quarterly Review.* Reprinted by permission of the publisher.—*Saturday Review,* v. XLIX, September 3, 1966. © 1966 *Saturday Review* magazine.—*The Sewanee Review,* v. LXXX, Spring, 1972; v. XCII, Fall, 1984. © 1972, 1984 by The University of the South. Both reprinted by permission of the editor of *The Sewanee Review.*—*Teaching Language through Literature,* v. XXVI, April, 1987. Copyright © 1987, *Teaching Language through Literature.* Reprinted by permission of the publisher.—*The Times Literary Supplement,* n. 3424, October 12, 1967. © Times Supplements Ltd. (London) 1967. Reproduced from *The Times Literary Supplement* by permission.—*The Village Voice,* v. XXXIII, February 23, 1988 for "Bound for Glory" by John Ash. Copyright © News Group Publications, Inc., 1988. Reprinted by permission of *The Village Voice* and the author.—*The Wordsworth Circle,* v. XIX, Winter, 1988. © 1988 Marilyn Gaull. Reprinted by permission of the editor.

COPYRIGHTED EXCERPTS IN *NCLC*, VOLUME 31, WERE REPRINTED FROM THE FOLLOWING BOOKS:

Adams, Robert Martin. From *NIL: Episodes in the Literary Conquest of Void During the Nineteenth Century.* Oxford University Press, 1966. Copyright © 1966 by Robert Martin Adams. Reprinted by permission of Oxford

Emile Augier

1820-1889

(Full name Guillaume Victor Emile Augier) French dramatist.

Augier is acknowledged as one of the foremost play-wrights of the nineteenth-century French stage and is known in particular for his incisive portrayals of the middle-class society of his time. Building upon the principles of the French *pièce bien faite,* or well-made play, which stressed clear and logical plot construction, Augier created depth and power in his dramas through greater attention to social issues, character portrayal, and realistic dialogue. As a result, he has been credited with significantly advancing the development of literary Realism. However, Augier differed from many exponents of Realism in his explicit and consistent endorsement of traditional values, and Allardyce Nicoll asserted that "Augier's stress on moral ideas is perhaps his greatest contribution to [the] mid-nineteenth-century Realistic movement."

Augier was born to middle-class parents in Valence in the south of France. When he was eight years old, he moved with his family to Paris. Augier's father encouraged him to pursue a career in law, and he accordingly agreed to attend the University of Paris. However, after receiving his law degree in 1844, he chose to follow in the footsteps of his grandfather, Charles Pigault-Lebrun, who had been a popular writer in his day.

Augier's first work, a play entitled *La ciguë,* was classical in both subject and form and was warmly received at the Théâtre de l'Odéon by audiences tired of the Romantic dramas that had dominated the stage during the previous decades. After the success of *La ciguë,* Augier devoted himself to writing dramas, and his works continued to enjoy great popularity throughout the rest of the nineteenth century. In 1857, he was elected to the prestigious Academie Français. He stopped writing for the theater in 1878 and, eleven years later, he died at his home in Croissy.

Critics generally divide Augier's works into three groups: verse plays, comedies of manners, and social comedies. The verse plays, written between 1844 and 1853, demonstrate Augier's youthful uncertainty in their varying styles and subject matter. *La ciguë* and *Le joueur de flûte,* for example, are based on classical Greek themes, while *Gabrielle* (*Good for Evil; or, A Wife's Trial*) and *Philiberte* are domestic comedies. Although these works were generally popular when they were performed, critics agree that Augier was not adept in the creation of verse, and they consider his adoption of the prose form after 1853 a major development in his work.

Augier's comedies of manners were written between 1853 and 1861, most in collaboration with other writers. Like his predecessors in this style, Augier used these works to communicate clear moral messages, often concerning the

sanctity and rectitude of the traditional family structure. The setting for most of these plays is therefore typically a domestic scene. In *Le gendre de Monsieur Poirier,* his best-known work of this period, comedy is derived from the conflict between Monsieur Poirier, a wealthy, middle-class businessman, and his impoverished but aristocratic son-in-law, while a moral lesson is conveyed by the ultimate affirmation of the marital bond between Poirier's daughter and her husband. Poirier is often cited as one of the best examples of Augier's ability to create complex, realistic characters. A hard-working, shrewd individual, he hopes to improve his social standing by marrying his daughter to a member of the nobility, but he is completely unable to understand the aristocratic values of his son-in-law. Critics frequently praise Poirier as a perfect demonstration of the industriousness, pragmatism, and tenacity of the typical French businessman of the nineteenth century.

With the production of *Les éffrontés* in 1861, Augier began the third stage of his career, during which he wrote primarily social comedies. These plays concentrate on what Augier viewed as the moral malaise of the French Second Empire, especially its increasing materialism and the breakdown of traditional social stratifications. For example, in *Les éffrontés* and *Le fils de Giboyer,* the most widely praised works of this period, Augier addresses a topic approached indirectly in the earlier *Gendre de Monsieur Poirier:* the inability of members of the middle and lower classes to transcend their origins. In both plays, Augier presents the story of the journalist Giboyer, who is raised in poverty but improves his station through education. Giboyer accepts work on the basis of purely financial considerations without regard for the moral implications of the job, in one instance designing a propaganda campaign for a political cause that he personally finds offensive. In *Maître Guérin,* another highly regarded play of this period, Augier emphasizes the importance of honesty and integrity through his portrayal of the downfall of a greedy, opportunistic businessman.

During his lifetime Augier was enormously popular in France, and his plays dominated the French stage throughout the latter half of the nineteenth century. Due to the difficulty of translating his dialogue, which relies heavily on the vernacular for its realistic effect, his popularity has been limited outside of France. However, drama scholars have noted the influence of his theatrical innovations in the works of many subsequent playwrights, including such major international figures as Henrik Ibsen and Bjørnstjerne Bjørnson.

PRINCIPAL WORKS

La ciguë   (drama)   1844
L'homme de bien   (drama)   1845
L'aventuriére   (drama)   1848
  [*The Adventuress,* 1888]
Gabrielle   (drama)   1849
  [*Good for Evil; or, a Wife's Trial,* 1860]
Le joueur de flûte   (drama)   1850
La chasse au roman [with Jules Sandeau]   (drama) 1851
Diane   (drama)   1852
Philiberte   (drama)   1853
La pierre de touche [with Jules Sandeau]   (drama)   1853
Le gendre de Monsieur Poirier [with Jules Sandeau]
  (drama)   1854
  [*Monsieur Poirier's Son-in-Law* published in *Four Plays,*
  1915]
La ceinture dorée   (drama)   1855
Le mariage d'Olympe   (drama)   1855
  [*Olympe's Marriage* published in *Four Plays,* 1915]
La jeunesse   (drama)   1858
Les lionnes pauvres [with Edouard Foussier]   (drama)
  1858
Un beau mariage [with Edouard Foussier]   (drama)
  1859
Les éffrontés   (drama)   1861
Le fils de Giboyer   (drama)   1862
Maître Guérin   (drama)   1864
La contagion   (drama)   1866
Paul Forestier   (drama)   1868
  [*Paul Forrester,* 1871]
Lions et renards   (drama)   1869
Le postscriptum   (drama)   1869
  [*The Post-Script,* 1915]

Jean de Thommeray [with Jules Sandeau]   (drama)
  1873
Madame Caverlet   (drama)   1876
Le prix Martin [with Eugene Labiche]   (drama)   1876
Les Fourchambault   (drama)   1878
  [*The House of Fourchambault,* 1915]
Théâtre complet de Emile Augier. 7 vols.   (dramas)
  1889
Four Plays   (dramas)   1915

Henry James   (essay date 1878)

[*James was an American-born English novelist, short story writer, critic, and essayist of the late nineteenth and early twentieth centuries. He is regarded as one of the greatest novelists of the English language and admired as a lucid and insightful critic. As a young man he traveled extensively throughout Great Britain and Europe and benefited from the friendship and influence of many of the leading figures of nineteenth-century art and literature: in England he met John Ruskin, Dante Gabriel Rosetti, William Morris, and Leslie Stephen; in France, where he lived for several years, he was part of the literary circle that included Gustave Flaubert, Émile Zola, Edmond de Goncourt, Guy de Maupassant, and Ivan Turgenev. Thus, his criticism is informed by his sensitivity to European culture, particularly English and French literature of the late nineteenth century. James was a frequent contributor to several prominent American journals including the* North American Review, *the* Nation, *and the* Atlantic Monthly. *In the following excerpt from a review of* Les Fourchambault, *James judges Augier to be one of the most significant French dramatists of his time.*]

M. Emile Augier has just published his drama of **Les Fourchambault,** which is at present in the enjoyment of high success at the Théâtre Français, and forms, obviously, the most important contribution to the French stage—in other words, to the contemporary stage—during the present year. If to see a play from one of the best French hands acted as such things are acted at the Maison de Molière is one of the greatest possible pleasures, we may perhaps say that in the case of this pleasure being inaccessible by reason of remoteness, a fair substitute for the entertainment may be found in reading the published drama. **Les Fourchambault,** at any rate, reads extremely well, and forms a worthy supplement to that collective edition of the author's works which has been issued during the past year, in seven substantial volumes, by Calmann Lévy. In these seven volumes, by the way, M. Emile Augier makes a very honorable show; the modern theatre has few stronger pieces than **L'aventurière** and **Le mariage d'Olympe, Les lionnes pauvres** and **Maître Guérin,** just as it has nothing more charming than **Philiberte.** Alexander Dumas the younger, alone, can contest the supremacy on their common line of the author of these masterly dramas. The two writers have many points of contact. The list of their works is of about equal length; both are members of the Academy; both are would-be moralists; both attempt the social, it may even be said the didactic, rather than the romantic or the simply entertaining, drama. In Paris there is scarcely any event so important as the appearance of a new play by one of these gentlemen, unless it be the production of a piece by the other. M. Emile Augier, on his social side, is preoccupied with the sanctity of the family, as they say in France; he "goes in," as they say in England, for the importance of the domestic affections. This is his most frequent thesis. He does not wage war quite so unremittingly as his brilliant rival upon misplaced gallantry and the encroachments of mercenary wiles; but the most earnest effort of his muse may be said to be to keep the family well together. In *Les Fourchambault,* thanks to a variety of causes, it is in terrible danger of falling apart; but cohesion is ultimately restored—the manner in which it is restored forming the subject of the play. In French plays these results are sometimes brought about very oddly. Here, for instance, the good example is set to the household of M. Fourchambault by a lady who has been M. Fourchambault's mistress and by her son, who is also that of M. Fourchambault. This is a curious example of the assumption, so frequent in French novels and plays, that to take a high attitude one must have done something very improper. Upon the didactic properties of these productions English readers are always certain to make their own reflections; they think it strange to see so much pleading of causes which, among themselves, are not in the way of being lost. They reflect, too, doubtless, upon some of their other properties—their finish and shapeliness, their neat, artistic, scientific form. Only, if on one side they feel no need of learning the lesson, on the other, too often, they seem unable to apply it.

> *Henry James, in a review of "Les Fourchambault," in* The Nation, New York, *Vol. XXVI, No. 678, June 27, 1878, p. 419.*

J. Brander Matthews   (essay date 1880)

[*An American critic, playwright, and novelist, Matthews wrote extensively on world drama and served as professor of dramatic literature at Columbia University, the first person to hold that title at an American university. He was also a founding member and president of the National Institute of Arts and Letters. In the following excerpt, Matthews argues that despite evidence of influence by Hugo, Dumas (fils) and others, Augier's plays are original and "self assertive" and contain more complex characters than the works of his predecessors.*]

In criticism, as in astronomy, we must needs allow for the personal equation; and I am proud to confess a hearty admiration for the sincere and robust dramatic works of M. Émile Augier, to my mind the foremost of the French dramatists of our day, with the possible exception only of Victor Hugo. M. Augier inherits the best traditions of French comedy. He is a true child of Beaumarchais, a true grandchild of Molière. He has the Gallic thrust of the one, and something of the broad utterance of the other and greater. One of the best actors in Paris told me that he held the *Gendre de M. Poirier* to be the finest comedy since the *Mariage de Figaro.* It would be hard to gainsay him; and

in the *Fils de Giboyer* there is more than one touch which recalls the hand of the great master who drew *Tartuffe.*

It is not a little curious that, while the plays of M. Alexandre Dumas and M. Victorien Sardou are familiar to the American theatregoer, M. Augier's virile works are here but little known. Two or three years ago the case was the same in Germany; and in an appreciative study of M. Augier's career, published in *Nord und Süd,* Herr Paul Lindau asked the reason of this, and gave the answer,—which is simply that M. Augier appeals to a higher (and smaller) class than either M. Dumas or M. Sardou. It is much easier to transfer to an alien soil the situations of M. Sardou or the emotions of M. Dumas than the social studies of M. Augier, in whose plays plot and passion are subordinate and subservient to the development of character.

That M. Augier's plays, in spite of their lack of sensational scenes, should not have found favor in the eyes of Anglo-Saxon managers, is the more remarkable because he is the most moral of modern French dramatists. He is not one of "them that call evil good, and good evil; that put darkness for light, and light for darkness; that put bitter for sweet, and sweet for bitter." Unlike M. Dumas, he does not let his emotions run away with him. It is not that the moral is violently thrust through each play, as a butterfly is impaled on a pin,—to use Hawthorne's apt figure. No, the morality in M. Augier, as in all really great authors, is "simply a part of the essential richness of inspiration,"—to quote from that other American writer who has recently taken Hawthorne's life.

Although the French drama of to-day is not so bad as many believe it to be, still the dramatists, like the novelists, of France have not taken to heart Dr. Johnson's warning: "Sir, never accustom your mind to mingle vice and virtue." Mr. Matthew Arnold quotes with approval Michelet's assertion that the Reformation failed in France because France did not want a moral reform; and he adds that the French are lacking in the "power of conduct." Admitting the rule, M. Augier is a noble exception: he has an abiding sense of the importance of conduct in life, and he strenuously seeks to strengthen that sense in others by dwelling on the influences which make for it. The name which the English dramatist Robertson gave to the English comedy (for which he had borrowed the plot of M. Augier's *Aventurière*) *Home* is characteristic of all M. Augier's work. Home in his eyes is a sacred thing; and throughout his plays we can see a steadfast setting forth of the holiness of home and the sanctity of the family. This feeling will not let him be a passive spectator of assaults on what he cherishes. His is a militant morality, ever up in arms to fight for the fireside. The insidious success of the *Dame aux camélias*—in which a courtesan's love purified her so far as it might—drew from him the indignant *Mariage d'Olympe,* and gave him the opportunity of showing what might be expected when the courtesan wormed her way into an honorable household. The *Third Person* is as important to many French dramas of this century as was the "Third Estate" to the nation in the last century; but he is in no way aided and abetted by M. Augier: there is one French dramatist who can always be counted on for the husband and the home.

This love for the fireside is not merely literary capital; it is part of his actual life. In the preface to one of his plays he explains how it happens that he has written more than once in collaboration: it is owing to his fondness for chat by the hearth with a friend; and if in course of talk they start a subject for a piece and run it down, to which of the two does it belong? M. Augier's whole life has been given to literature; his career is that of a true man of letters, passing his time quietly by his fireside or in his garden in the study of men and things. Herr Lindau quotes his answer to a would-be biographer, perhaps the German critic himself, who asked for adventure or anecdote: "My life has been without incident." And an English writer has pointed out that M. Augier's love for the family can be seen even in the externals of his works,—in the dedication of his collected plays to his mother's memory and of individual pieces to his sisters and to other intimate friends. There is in all this nothing namby-pamby; on the contrary, his manly tenderness is joined to a hearty scorn of sentimentality. Indeed, the first tribute he paid to his family was an act of courage: he inscribed his earliest play to the memory of his maternal grandfather, Pigault-Lebrun. This gentleman, who ran a very mottled career, was also an author; he wrote for the stage, and produced certain free-and-easy tales. His dominant quality was what the French call "verve" and the English "go." His grandson seems to have inherited his independence and his frank gayety; perhaps, also, a portion of his imperative will.

M. Augier began modestly. A two-act comedy of antique life called the *Ciguë*—from the draught of hemlock which the hero has determined to take—was tendered first to the Théâtre Français, and was finally brought out at the Odéon, in May, 1844. It met with instant success, ran three months, and has since been taken into the repertory of the Comédie-Française. In classic purity of form, this first of his plays remains the best; it is a picture of self-seeking greed, treated with a firmness of touch and a masculine irony unusual in a young writer. M. Augier, born in 1820, was not twenty-four when the *Ciguë* first saw the light of the lamps. He had studied for the bar, but the enticements of poetry were irresistible, and after the success of the *Ciguë* he devoted himself wholly to the drama. He had come upon the stage just in the nick of time; both play-goers and professional critics accepted him as the most promising of a new school of dramatists.

Coincident with the political revolution which in 1830 drove the Bourbons from the throne of France, there was an uprising in literature and art against the cast-iron canons of critics, who in the lapse of years had learned nothing and forgotten nothing; and after this furious fight between the young blood, which was called "Romantic," and the old bones, who called themselves "Classic," there was a lull for a while, and the school of common-sense came into being. A year before the *Ciguë,* the Odéon had acted *Lucrèce,* a tragedy by François Ponsard, a classic tale told in verses of romantic variety and color. The unwitting poet was hailed at once as the chief of a new school, which was to seek safety in the middle path and to join the good qualities of both the opposing styles, without the failings of either. The *Ciguë,* on its appearance, was claimed as the second effort in the new manner. Nei-

ther Ponsard nor M. Augier, warm personal friends and both men of modesty, ever set up as leaders of a new departure,—just as it has been said that John Wilkes was never a Wilkite. M. Augier gave in no adhesion to the school of common-sense, yet was tacitly accepted as its lieutenant: when its day had passed, he stepped out of its narrow limits, and walked on toward his own goal with a sturdy tread. But for convenience, and not inaccurately, we may consider his earlier work as belonging to this school. Beautiful as much of it is, taken by itself, we see at once, when we survey his writings as a whole, that the earlier ones were only tentative, and that he had not yet discovered where his real strength lay. In the first ten years after the *Ciguë* was acted, he brought out six other plays in verse,—in 1845, the *Homme de bien;* in 1848, the *Aventurière,* the finest and firmest of all his metrical comedies; in 1849, *Gabrielle,* a noteworthy success; in 1850, the *Joueur de flute,* a weaker return to the classic and akin in subject to the *Ciguë;* in 1852, *Diane,* a romantic drama written for Rachel [pseudonym of Elisa Félix, a French actress], and acted by her without any great effect, owing perhaps to its use of the historical material which had already served Victor Hugo in *Marion Delorme;* and in 1853, *Philiberte,* a charming comedy of life in the last century. All these comedies belonged to the new school, in that they had common-sense without commonplace. In the best of them were to be seen simplicity, without the weakness of the classicists; and vigor, without the brutality of the romanticists.

Gabrielle, as we consider it now after thirty years, does not seem the best even of these earlier attempts; yet so noble was its intention and so clean its execution that, in spite of its vulnerable points, it created a profound sensation, enjoyed success beyond its fellows, and received from the Academy the Montyon prize of virtue. In it we have, briefly, a young husband devoted to his wife and child, and toiling unceasingly for their future; therefore is he unable to divine, much less to satisfy, the somewhat sentimental aspirations of his wife. Unfortunately, a friend of his falls in love with her, and tenders the ideal passion her heart craves. Fortunately, the husband is warned in time, and he fights bravely for his home,—not with his hands, but with his brain. Giving no sign of suspicion, he appeals to the lover to help him loyally to win back his wife's heart; then getting them both together, he seizes an occasion to set before them with heartfelt eloquence the consequences of a false step. So persuasive and so powerful is he that, when they are left alone for a moment, the wife dismisses the lover, who accepts his sentence without a murmur. By herself, she compares the two men: how small looks the lover by the side of her husband, on whose return she confesses! Thereupon he declares the fault to be his own, in that he has neglected her, and asks if he may hope to win back her love. Conquered by his strength and his tenderness, the wife seizes his hand, and, as the curtain falls, exclaims,—

"O père de famille! ô poëte! je t'aime!"

To understand the startling effect of such a comedy, we must consider the state of the stage in France at the time. It was a cutting rebuke to the followers of Scribe and to the disciples of Dumas. "There is something about murder," Mr. Howells tells us, "some inherent grace or refinement perhaps, that makes its actual representation upon the stage more tolerable than the most diffident suggestion of adultery." M. Scribe and the crowd of collaborators who encompassed him about were of another opinion. The fracture of the seventh commandment, actual or imminent, was to be seen at the centre of all pieces of the Scribe type. "There was a need of hearing something which had common-sense, and which should lift up, encourage, or console mankind, not so egotistic or foolish as M. Scribe declares it," wrote the younger Dumas; adding that a writer "robust, loyal, and keen presented himself, and *Gabrielle,* with its simple and touching story, with its fine and noble language, was the first revolt against the conventional comedy."

M. Dumas saw distinctly the blow M. Augier gave to Scribe; but he did not acknowledge that at the same time were shaken the foundations of the school in which his father was a leader. As M. Émile Montégut has said, only once did M. Augier take up arms against the romanticists: "The reaction of the school of commonsense had as a whole but little success, because it especially attacked the literary doctrines of romanticism, which were sufficiently solid to resist. But romanticism presented more vulnerable points than its doctrines; for example, the false ideals of sentimentality it made fashionable, and the brilliant immorality of its works, which had again and again exalted the superiority of passion over duty." With this feeling M. Augier had no sympathy; he is always for duty against passion, and *Gabrielle* was a curt rebuke to *Antony.* Yet one can but regret, with M. Montégut, that the object was attained by this mild piece in the author's earlier and gentler manner, rather than by a true comedy in the hardy and satiric style of his later work. Sham sentimentality and misplaced yearnings call for the hot iron of satire; and the weapon which M. Augier soon forged for use against the hypocrites and schemers of the *Effrontés* and the *Fils de Giboyer* would have served effectively against personified romanticism. But, like many another young warrior, M. Augier was a long time finding his right weapon. After writing without aid the seven plays in verse which have been grouped together, he changed about and took to prose and to collaboration. In *Pierre de touche,* in which M. Jules Sandeau was a partner, and in *Ceinture dorée,* in which M. Foussier was a half-partner, a distinct advance can be noted toward what was soon seen to be M. Augier's true road; and in the *Gendre de M. Poirier* he struck the path and walked straight to the goal.

To my mind the *Gendre de M. Poirier* is the model modern comedy of manners; its one competitor for the foremost place, the *Demi-Monde* of M. Dumas, is fatally weighted by its subject. M. Augier gives us a picture of the real world and not of the half-world. M. Montégut truly calls it "not only the best comedy of our time, but the only one which satisfies the idea formerly held as to what a comedy should be." Most modern French comedies are melodramatic, and many a successful play by Dumas or Sardou is but a Bowery drama in a dress-coat. But the *Gendre de M. Poirier* is pure comedy; and would be recognized as such by Congreve and Sheridan, Regnard and

Beaumarchais. The subject is the old, old strife between blood and wealth, between high birth and a full purse. M. Poirier is a shopkeeper, who, having made a fortune, has political aspirations, which he seeks to advance by an alliance with the aristocracy. The Marquis de Presles is a young nobleman, without money, but with blood and to spare. The daughter of M. Poirier becomes the wife of M. de Presles, and is the innocent victim of both father and husband; and the situations of the play are called forth by the unexpected development of her character under the pressure of suffering,—a character which M. de Presles, although they have been married three months, has hitherto held to be colorless. From idle carelessness the husband gets into trouble, and the young and plebeian wife has twice a chance of saving his patrician honor. There is no palliation of his vice, still less any pandering to it. Nakedly it stands before us, and we see the pain which the empty pursuit of pleasure may bring even on the innocent. A chance of reconciliation is offered to the marquis at a heavy cost of honor; and this brings about the beautiful scene—one of the most pathetic known to the modern stage, and ending in a truly dramatic surprise—where the wife nobly rejects the sacrifice and sends her husband forth to battle for his name. Besides these three characters there are but two others; and to carry through a full four-act comedy with but five parts is an instance of that calm simplicity which only a very high art can attain.

It may be observed that although I have hitherto spoken of the *Gendre de M. Poirier* as M. Augier's, it is signed also by M. Jules Sandeau. However, no substantial injustice is done; for while there is nothing else of M. Sandeau's which will bear comparison with the *Gendre de M. Poirier,* it is but the best expression of M. Augier's genius. Both M. Augier and M. Sandeau are men of too marked individuality to gain by collaboration, although in this play the manly vigor of the former and the caressing gentleness of the other blend harmoniously. Not always has the union been so easy. In *Pierre de touche,* for instance, as it has been neatly said, the characters are by the author of the *Effrontés,* and the situations and scenery are by the author of *Mlle. de la seiglière;* and in their latest joint-production, *Jean de Thommeray,* M. Augier had obviously only borrowed the idea of M. Sandeau's charming tale and had himself written the whole play, stamped throughout by his muscular hand. "Dans tout *concubitus,*" wrote M. Augier in regard to M. Labiche's collaborations, "il y a un mâle et une femelle." Now, it is not to be doubted that M. Augier is the *mâle.* To him that hath shall be given; *on ne prête qu' aux riches.* So much the worse for M. Sandeau.

To the partnership with M. Foussier we owe one at least of M. Augier's most important plays,—the *Lionnes pauvres.* I can but think that the play would have been better had M. Augier written it alone. M. Sandeau's gentleness may have corrected M. Augier's occasional acerbity, and the *Gendre de M. Poirier* is artistically a finer piece of work than anything M. Augier did by himself; but M. Foussier simply says "ditto" to M. Augier, and so their joint work shows an over-accentuation and almost a harshness of tone not to be found in the other plays of the author of the *Fils de Giboyer.* A comparison of the *Mari-*

age d'Olympe, written alone, with the Lionnes pauvres, written with M. Foussier, will show what I mean. In the latter there is an over-emphasis not to be detected in the former; and the conception and dramatic construction is feebler in the joint work than when M. Augier relied on himself alone. These two plays are linked together here, because, although a comedy in verse intervened, in them M. Augier came before the public in an entirely new manner. The Dame aux camélias, first acted in 1852, changed the whole aspect of contemporary dramatic literature. The merely amusing comedy was pushed from the front rank to which the skill of Scribe had advanced it; and as Scribe fell from his high estate M. Dumas came to the front as the demonstrator of social science set forth upon the stage. A quarter of a century ago M. Dumas had not developed into the moral philosopher who now so calmly surveys mankind from the summit of a preface; and the morality of his earlier plays was easy, to say the least. The success of these pieces of M. Dumas's was the one thing needful to the full fruition of M. Augier's genius. Orderly, fond of home, full of love for the family, and a bitter foe to any insidious attack on these ideals, he saw in the Dame aux camélias, its successors and its rivals, formidable adversaries with whom to do battle. The school of easy morality offered a shining mark for his satire; and in the new dramatic form which Dumas had introduced Augier found a sure weapon, ready to his hand. In the Mariage d'Olympe and in the Lionnes pauvres he first showed his willingness to sound a note of warning against social dangers, and displayed a power of grappling with social problems. In both plays the subject is repulsive, and of a kind not now tolerated on the English-speaking stage. An adaptation of the Lionnes pauvres, called A False Step, and made with due decorousness of expression, was refused a license in London, in 1878. Plays written in English, like novels written in English, must be made virginibus puerisque; and so only half of life gets itself into our literature. In France, fortunately or unfortunately, the dramatic moralist labors under no such limitations. Yet it is to be recorded that the French censors tried to prevent the production of the Lionnes pauvres unless it were made more moral,—one of their suggestions, as M. Augier tells us in his preface, being that the vicious woman should, between the fourth and fifth acts, have an attack of small-pox as a "natural consequence of her perversity."

The late G. H. Lewes, one of the best of dramatic critics, writes of a revival of this play in 1867: "The comedy—or shall I not rather call it tragedy?—was terribly affecting; the authors have shown us what comedy may be, should be. They have boldly laid bare one of the hideous sores of social life, and painted the consequences of the present rage for dress and luxury which is rapidly demoralizing the middle classes of Europe." The hideous sore was the possible change from passionate adultery to salaried prostitution for the continuance of luxury and extravagance. The scene is laid in two households; and we see in one the wife awakening to desertion, and in the other a husband discovering his dishonor. The subject was indeed a bold one; and if the play had succeeded, it would go far to contradict the assertion, made now and again in Théophile Gautier's dramatic criticisms, that the stage never becomes possessed of any idea until it has been worn threadbare in print. Unfortunately, the play, although more than once revived and always well received, never makes a long stay on the stage. It owes this lack of stability, perhaps, to the very boldness of its subject: this, at least, is the suggestion of M. Sarcey, formulated when the play was last revived, in the fall of 1879. The subject was so novel in 1858, and so hazardous, that the authors did not dare to paint the wicked woman in the vivid colors which the situation demanded; they attenuated the drawing, and filled it in with half-tints, to the obvious weakening of the effect. But in spite of this blemish the Lionnes pauvres remains a work of extraordinary vigor and value,—one which the future historian of Parisian society under the Second Empire cannot afford to neglect. Yet as a work of art it is inferior to the Mariage d'Olympe, which M. Augier wrote alone, and which had no success at all. Olympe is a courtesan who tricks an inexperienced young man into a marriage, and by a skillful comedy gets herself recognized by his family. Once sure of her position in an honorable household, she is seized by the "nostalgie de la boue,"—the longing for the mud, the homesickness for the gutter from which she has been lifted and in which she had her natural growth. A lover appears, and she sells herself to him from mere wantonness. Brought to bay by her husband's grandfather, the head of his noble house, she threatens to publish a scandal about an innocent young girl, the youngest member of the family. Unable to buy her off, the old marquis shoots her down like a dog. While this was a fit solution of the situation, so violent a method of meting out poetic justice revolted the play-going public; and the final pistol-shot killed the play as well as the heroine.

The heroine of the Mariage d'Olympe is not so vicious as the heroine of the Lionnes pauvres, for whom there is no excuse to be made; and the sudden taking off of the former is more merciful than the awful perspective opened before us as the certain course of the latter. In each play we have a sickening picture of depravity; and the stronger the artist's hand and the finer his art, the more we wish that he had chosen another subject. The orgy in the second act of the Mariage d'Olympe is as typical in its way as Couture's picture of the Romans of the decadence; but it is set forth with a decorous pen, by an author who respects himself. There is nothing in it of the unspeakable filth of M. Zola's Nana; besides, Olympe is true and in the highest degree artistic, and Nana is conventional in spite of her minute "naturalism." One feels that the mere mention of M. Augier in the same breath with M. Zola is a mistake in taste; yet in the portrait of Olympe there is an impression of main strength, which one feels M. Zola must appreciate. I should be tempted to characterize it as violent and brutal, if these were not altogether too harsh words to apply to a writer so well-bred and so keen as M. Augier. It is perhaps safe to say that had it been treated by another hand, "violent and brutal" would surely be the exact words to employ. It is not that the note is forced, or that there is anything false in the treatment; on the contrary, no work of M. Augier is more sober or direct. The painful impression is no doubt due to the repulsion inherent in the subject.

Between the Mariage d'Olympe and the Lionnes pauvres,

M. Augier had reverted to verse in *La jeunesse,* acted in 1857. Eleven years later, in 1868, came *Paul Forestier,* another poetical play. These two are his latest attempts in verse, and may therefore be considered together. *La jeunesse* is closely akin to Ponsard's *L'honneur et l'argent,* in subject and style. Its verse is not so academic in its elegance as Ponsard's, but it is fresher and it has more freedom: the flowers of M. Augier's poesy always have their roots in the soil. In spite of the dates, it seems as though *La jeunesse* must have been written just after *Gabrielle;* they are informed by the same spirit, and in each is a warning to be seen.

In as marked contrast as may be to both of these is *Paul Forestier,* M. Augier's last drama in verse. Indeed, it is so unlike the rest of his plays that it might almost be taken for the work of another. It is a play of pure passion, surcharged with hurrying emotion, and culminating in what one cannot but think, in spite of all the skill with which it is done, is a conventional conclusion, caused only by a wrenching of the logic of the characters, wherein vice is punished and virtue rewarded in spite of themselves. M. Augier's comedies are generally moral in another and nobler manner than this. Here one feels that, given the characters and situation, the outcome would have been different. In general, M. Augier's logic is so inexorable and the moral so entirely a part of the essence of his story, that to come upon this play, in which the moral seems merely tacked on, is something of a shock. The only excuse at hand is that the poet had run away with the moralist, and that the latter got the upper hand only in time to pull up as best he might.

In America the divorce between poetry and the stage seems to be as final and as unhealthy for both parties as the divorce between politics and society. In France one has a chance, now and then, of hearing an actor speak the language of the gods. The habit of writing in verse is dying out slowly; yet, as M. Augier has shown us, the poetic attitude is possible even to those who use the language of men. Style is generally on a level with the thought it clothes. In M. Augier's poetry we find none of the haziness of expression which results from weakness of conception. He sees clearly and speaks frankly; his verse is flexible, full, and direct. In his antique and mediæval plays, especially in the *Aventurière,* it abounds in grace and color; and the metre helps to keep up the artificial remoteness of the illusion.

But well as M. Augier could handle the Alexandrine, his admirable artistic instinct told him that it could only be used to great disadvantage in attacking the weak points of a more modern and complex civilization. In a play of passion like *Paul Forestier,* or in a more or less didactic and idealized comedy like *La jeunesse,* it might serve; but in a direct assault on a crying evil, as in the *Mariage d'Olympe* or the *Lionnes pauvres,* metre would hamper rather than help; and so verse was discarded for a prose as pointed and as nervous as any dramatist could wish. M. Augier's practice as a poet was of great aid in giving to his prose its form and color; it is a true poet's prose,—a prose lifted at times on the wings of poetry, but never to soar out of sight. M. Augier's prose is seemingly hurried at times; it shows, besides the effect of its author's poetic experi-

ence, a study of Beaumarchais: one catches at times a faint echo of the "rusé, rasé, blasé" manner of *Figaro.* It is as picturesque, in its nineteenth-century way, as was Beaumarchais's; and it is far more correct and more natural. Indeed, it is the model of dramatic dialogue of our day,—terse, tense, racy, and idiomatic.

Nowhere is M. Augier's style seen to better advantage than in the series of startling comedies of contemporary life, which he brought forth between 1861 and 1869. The avenging pistol-shot was abandoned for the whip-lash of satire. At bottom, both the *Mariage d'Olympe* and the *Lionnes pauvres* were dramas; there can be no doubt that the *Effrontés* and the *Fils de Giboyer* are comedies: they are models of what the modern comedy of manners should be; they show no trace of melodrama, and the interest arises naturally from the clash of character against character. Therefore it is not a little difficult to convey an idea of their high merit; for no rehearsal of the plot fairly represents the play, because the plot is a secondary consideration, and any description of character is pale and weak copying of what in the comedies moves before us with all the myriad hues of life.

In the *Effrontés* an assault was made on discreditable speculation and undue respect for mere money whencesoever derived. In the *Fils de Giboyer,*—in which Giboyer, a Bohemian of the press, and the Marquis d'Auberive, a representative of the old nobility, reappeared from the preceding play,—a plain picture was presented of clerical intriguing in politics. All at once M. Augier found himself in a wasp's nest. Clericalism was in arms, and M. Augier received hot shot in abundance,—accusing him of odious personalities, calling him Aristophanes, and recalling the legend that the death of Socrates was due to the attacks of the great Greek humorist. The likeness to Aristophanes was not altogether inapt; for without the license of the Greek, the Frenchman had the same directness of thrust. He indignantly repelled the accusation of personality, while frankly admitting that one character—and but one—was drawn from the living model. This was Déodat, in which everybody had recognized Veuillot, the ultramontane gladiator and papal-bull fighter. The denial availed little. A disreputable pamphleteer, who called himself De Mirecourt, author of a series of prejudiced and inaccurate contemporary biographies, professed to recognize himself in Giboyer (without warrant, surely, for, in spite of his vice and venality, Giboyer was sound at the core); and this fellow published, in answer to the *Fils de Giboyer,* a stout volume, called the *Petit-fils de Pigault-Lebrun,* in which he tried to hit M. Augier over the shoulder of his grandfather, gathering together stores of apocryphal anecdotes and doubtful jests.

Nothing daunted by this rain of invective, but holding it rather as proof that he had hit the mark, M. Augier returned to the assault. One may guess that he delights in the combat, and is never so happy as when giving battle for the right. In this case he showed that he had what the Yankee calls "grit." He brought out a new pair of plays. In the *Contagion,* as in the *Effrontés,* he attacked a general evil,—the cheap scepticism of the hour, the want of faith in the future, the ribald scoffing at things hitherto held sacred. Then in *Lions et renards,* as in the *Fils de Giboyer,* he used one of the characters, fully developed in the earlier play, as a mainspring of the polemic action of the later. In the *Contagion,* we see the Baron d'Estrigaud, most keen and quick-witted of rascals, carrying off his rascality with an easy grace and taking things with a high hand. In *Lions et renards* clericalism reappears again in the person of a M. de St. Agathe, mentioned already in the *Fils de Giboyer,* and here brought boldly upon the stage; he is one who has sacrificed everything, even his identity, to the order of which he is an unknown instrument, from sheer lust of power wielded in secret. The struggle between these two, D'Estrigaud and St. Agathe, for a fortune which neither of them captures, is exciting. In the end, by a sudden irony, the beaten D'Estrigaud abandons the world, forgives his enemies, and under the eyes of St. Agathe takes to religion, the last resort of rascals,—to paraphrase Dr. Johnson.

While no one of these four comedies, as I have said, is artistically equal to the *Gendre de M. Poirier,* yet taken together they give us a still higher opinion of M. Augier's genius. No other dramatic author of this century can point to four such pieces; no other dramatist of our day has put before us so many distinct individualities and shown them before us in action, each after its kind. There are no longer preachments,—a bit of action and a single line instead,—and the evil is summed up better than by a score of sermons. The dialogue is sharp and short; it has a satiric wit, which cuts like a whip-lash when it does not bite like an acid. The wit is really wit, a diamond of the first water, transparent and clear. There is none of the rough-and-ready repartee only too common in many modern English plays, the rudeness of which recalls Goldsmith's assertion that there was no arguing with Dr. Johnson, for if his pistol missed fire, he knocked you down with the butt. M. Augier's pistol does not miss fire.

The series of comedies of manners, which I have here grouped together, was interrupted in 1865 by *Maître Guérin,* as well as by the poetic drama, *Paul Forestier. Maître Guérin* is analyzed at length in Mr. Lewes' valuable volume on *Actors and the Art of Acting.* Although showing many of M. Augier's ever-admirable qualities, it is lacking in the symmetry of the *Gendre de M. Poirier* and in the sharp savor of the later satires; it pales by the side of either. In the same year (1869) that he brought out *Lions et renards* he gave us also the *Postscriptum,* one of the lightest and brightest little one-act comedies in any language, and to be warmly recommended to American readers. The next year came the war with Prussia and the two sieges of Paris.

The first play which M. Victorien Sardou brought out after France had gone through these terrible trials was the trivial *Roi Carotte,* a fairy spectacle, and the second was the illiberal and reactionary *Rabagas.* M. Augier's first play was the stirring and patriotic *Jean de Thommeray:* love for home and love for the fatherland are rarely separated. *Jean de Thommeray* was a series of energetic pictures of the demoralization which had led to defeat; its fault was that it was only a series of pictures and not a homogeneous drama. M. Augier had borrowed the hero of

M. Sandeau's tale, and Jean de Thommeray himself was almost the only link connecting the succeeding acts. The play thus lacked backbone; its parts were not knit together by the bond of a common life: it is rather a polyp, any one of whose members, when detached, is as capable of separate life as the original whole.

M. Augier's later plays call for little comment. In 1877 was acted the *Prix Martin,* signed by M. Augier and by M. Eugène Labiche. It is not noteworthy; and M. Augier himself tells us that his share of the work was confined to a partnership in the plan and to a slight revision of M. Labiche's dialogue. The year before, M. Augier brought out *Mme. Caverlet,* and the year after, the *Fourchambault.* The latter was very successful, but neither is in M. Augier's best manner. The first is a plea for divorce, and the second a plea for the solidarity of the family, and both are what on the English stage are called "domestic dramas."

In all M. Augier has written twenty-seven plays, great and small. Of these nine are in verse. Eight times he had a literary partner. At least ten out of the twenty-seven are plays of the first order, not to be equalled in the repertory of any contemporary dramatist; and of these ten three—the *Aventurière,* the *Gendre de M. Poirier,* and the *Fils de Giboyer*—are surely classics in the strictest sense of the term.

The first thing which strikes one who surveys M. Augier's literary career is the combination of originality and individuality with great susceptibility to external influence. He is a self-reliant man, but quick to take a hint. He was at first accepted as a disciple of Ponsard; and perhaps the *Ciguë* did owe something to *Lucrèce,* and *La jeunesse* to *L'honneur et l'argent.* But to my mind, even in Augier's comedies of antiquity, there was a greater obligation to De Musset. They wrote together a little piece without consequence; and De Musset's influence may be traced in all M. Augier's earlier plays of fantasy, in which the scene, wherever the poet may declare it to be, in reality is laid in the enchanted forest of Arden, or in that Bohemia which is a desert country by the sea. In the technical construction of *Diane* there was something of the manner of Victor Hugo: that M. Augier's verse was indebted to Hugo for its freedom from the eighteenth-century shackles goes without saying. Neither Scribe nor the elder Dumas tempted him; but with the first work of the younger M. Dumas, M. Augier saw at a glance the prospect it opened. Combining with this suggestion of new worlds to conquer, given by M. Dumas, was a study of Balzac's methods. Without the *Recherche de l'absolu* we should not have had *Maître Guérin,*—just as if there had been no *Dame aux camélias,* there had also been no *Mariage d'Olympe.*

I have ill expressed myself if, from the paragraph above, any one infers that M. Augier has been guilty of any servile imitation. Nothing could be less true. He is a man of marked individuality, and in his works strongly self-assertive. Nothing like imitation is to be discovered in his dramas. Another man's work is to him only an exciting cause, to use a medical phrase. The analogies to Ponsard, De Musset, and Hugo are subtle and probably unconscious; and the indebtedness to M. Dumas is comprised in the assertion that the author of the *Dame aux camélias* turned over a new leaf of the history of French dramatic literature,—a leaf upon which M. Augier wrote his name with his own pen. The obligation to Balzac is no more than that M. Augier studied human nature with Balzac as his master. It is by his knowledge of human nature, and by his skill in turning this knowledge to account, that posterity judges an author. M. Augier is fit to survive; he is a great creator of unforgettable figures, a true poet in the Greek sense, a "maker."

M. Zola—who looks forward to an impossible regeneration of the stage, from which all convention is to be banished, and everything is to be as dull as every-day, in the interest of naturalistic exactness—recognizes in M. Augier a creator of actual characters, and calls him the master of the French stage. "Seraphine," says M. Zola of the heroine of the *Lionnes pauvres,* "is a daring figure, put squarely on her feet, of an absolute truth." And M. Zola praises Guérin who "has a final impenitence of the newest and truest effect." He objects that some of M. Augier's characters are too good to live, and that others change front in an instant before the curtain falls. In M. Zola's eyes any noble character is unnatural,—Colonel Newcome, for instance, is too good to live; but his other criticism has some slight foundation: there are characters of M. Augier's who reform with undue haste,—in *Gabrielle* for example.

M. Augier's women are all admirable. In his devotion to the family, he has drawn woman fit to be the goddess of the fireside. He excels alike in the young girl, clear-headed and warm-hearted, perfectly *jeune fille* according to French ideas, but with a little spark of independence, with a head of her own and a willingness to use it if need be; and in the clever woman of the world, skilled in all the turns and tricks of society, quick-witted and keen-tongued and able to hold her own. His women, good or bad, are thoroughly feminine and human; they are neither men in women's clothes nor dolls; they have hearts and *sex*. He has drawn brilliant portraits of wicked women,—Seraphine and Olympe, and above all Navarette,—and he delights in showing their true womanhood, and, as in the *Aventurière,* redeeming them almost at the last with a few words of simple dignity and pathos. In none of these qualities can any trace of foreign influence be detected; they are purely personal. Purely personal also are his devotion to home, his hatred of hypocrisy, his trust in the future, his belief in progress, his respect for toil. To these last two qualities is due his liking for modern invention and discovery: in the *Beau Mariage* the hero is a chemical experimenter, in the *Lions et renards* he is an African explorer, while in the *Fourchambault* he is a specimen of the highest type of mercantile sagacity. National, rather than personal, is the occasional note of bad taste. In general, the French pay an exaggerated respect to the fifth commandment, to balance perhaps the frequent fracture of the seventh; so the scene in the *Contagion,* where the hero reads one of his mother's love-letters in the midst of a disreputable supper, comes with an unexpected shock. There is another scene in the *Fourchambault,* this time directly between the mother and the son, which no Anglo-Saxon pen could have written. But these taints are rare; for the most part M. Augier's characters live, move, and have their being in a clear, pure atmosphere,—as different as may be

from the moral miasma which hangs over Balzac's landscapes. Mentally and morally M. Augier is a well-balanced writer, and his works are symmetrical. We see in him an intellect in equilibrium, well poised on itself and sure of its stability. A great critic has told us that the grand style is not the so-called classic, with its finish and polish and point, but something larger, freer, ampler; something not incompatible with a homely realism in matters of detail,—if, indeed, a truly grand style does not demand a rigorous calling of the thing by its right name, be it never so humble. As Molière in his day and Beaumarchais in his were in the grand style, so is M. Augier,—each in his degree. The progressive civilization of the nineteenth century is perhaps as hampering as the pseudo-classic formality of the seventeenth. It is high praise to say that the words which describe one of M. Augier's characters, and which Herr Lindau aptly applies to their author, are as fitting to him as they are to his great master, Molière: "Un cœur simple et tendre, un esprit droit et sûr, une loyauté royale." (pp. 353-69)

> *J. Brander Matthews, "Emile Augier," in* The International Review, *Vol. IX, October, 1880, pp. 353-69.*

Adolphe Cohn   (essay date 1890)

[*Cohn was a French-born American educator, journalist, essayist, and critic. In the following excerpt, he assesses Augier's achievement.*]

On the afternoon of May 1, while all the capitals of Europe were anxiously wondering how many of their buildings would still be standing at the close of the day, the French Academy met with the purpose of electing a successor to Emile Augier. The forty, or rather thirty-eight, Immortals took no less than eight ballots and then had to adjourn without a majority of them having been able to agree upon any of the candidates as worthy to occupy the place of the illustrious author of *Le gendre de M. Poirier, L'aventurière, Les effrontés, Le fils de Giboyer, Maître Guérin, Les Fourchambault;* and still there were among the candidates for the honor such men as Brunetière, the critic, Thureau-Dangin, the historian, and, last but not least, the head of the Naturalistic School, Emile Zola. To all who know the life work of Emile Augier this almost unprecedented occurrence must have seemed nothing more than a deserved homage paid to the genius and character of the man who, more than any of the numerous dramatic writers of France, has in our century displayed the qualities of insight and fearlessness which won for the name of Molière its imperishable fame.

It is a rather singular fact that in English-speaking countries, and in the United States more even than in England, the name of Augier, so great in France, is far less known than the names of rivals who are far inferior to him— Dumas the younger, Sardou, Meilhac, etc. How few Americans know of *Les effrontés,* or *Le fils de Giboyer!* But every theatre-goer is sure to have compared with each other many different interpretations of *La dame aux camélias* (Camille), of *Fédora,* of *Froufrou.* The truth is that easy inter-translation between the two languages, French and English, and especially between the two stages, is a sign rather of weakness than of strength. It has taken Shakespeare's masterpieces nearly three centuries to receive worthy treatment on the French stage, while neither the *Misanthrope* nor Beaumarchais's masterpiece, *Le mariage de Figaro,* are ever produced by English or American actors.

Like all the great dramatists of France, Augier wrote his early plays, *Le ciguë* (the Hemlock), *Un homme de bien, L' aventurière, Gabrielle,* in verse. English critics often wonder at the number of verse plays written in the French language. The stiffness of French verse seems to them an insuperable bar to the freedom of dramatic dialogue, and it cannot be contended that there are no strong arguments in favor of such a view. But on the other hand this very stiffness acts upon strong minds as an incentive, compels them to a struggle in which they acquire a mastery of strong speech which is absolutely necessary to strong dramatic writing. But for that schooling there is hardly any defence for the dramatic writer against affectation on one side and the slipshod formlessness of daily conversation on the other.

It is a favorite remark of the celebrated dramatic critic, Francisque Sarcey, that no French actor will ever reach the summit of his art who has not, in the beginning of his career, appeared in the plays of the Classical period. And in the same way it may be said that no truly great French play, great not merely from the standpoint of the playwright, but from the standpoint of the play-writer also, will be written by any man who has not, through his years of apprenticeship, conquered the difficulty of writing a good play in verse. It does not follow, however, that Augier's verse plays are to be counted as his greatest performances, although they include such works as *L'aventurière, Gabrielle* and *Paul Forestier,* the only one of his verse plays that does not belong to his earliest period.

Augier's literary life may be divided into three periods. The first, the period of youth, closes with the production of *Philiberte* in 1853; Augier was then thirty-three years old, having been born in 1820. Nearly every one of the plays of this first period is in verse. The second period may be called the period of collaboration. It extends from the close of the first period to the production of *Les lionnes pauvres* in 1858. Nearly every one of the plays of this second period is the product of joint authorship; the writers whom Augier most often selected as his associates being Jules Sandeau and Edgar Foussier. To this period belongs the celebrated *Gendre de M. Poirier,* written with Jules Sandeau, the most perfect in construction of the French comedies of this century. Then, for the first time, Augier became conscious of his gift of summing up a whole moral or social situation in a few brilliant and terse sentences. Nobody who heard that masterpiece of the French stage will ever forget the lines in which the claims and counterclaims, as well as the prejudices and ridicules of the aristocracy and the rich *bourgeoisie,* are set forth by the light-headed marquis and his hard-hearted and ambitious father-in-law:

GASTON. Come, Hector, come! Do you know

why Jean Gaston de Presles was three times wounded at the battle of Ivry? Do you know why François Gaston de Presles was first to climb over the walls of La Rochelle? Why Louis Gaston de Presles had his ship blown up at la Hogue? Why Philippe Gaston de Presles captured two British standards at Fontenoy? Why my own grandfather met his death at Quiberon? It was in order that Monsieur Poirier might some day become a member of the House of Peers, and a Baron.

POIRIER. Do you know, monsieur le duc, why I worked fourteen hours a day during thirty years? Why I amassed penny after penny a fortune of four million francs, while depriving myself of every comfort? It was in order that Monsieur le marquis de Presles, who thus far died neither at Fontenoy, nor at la Hogue, or anywhere else, might some day die of old age on a feather bed after spending his life in doing nothing!

The third and greatest period opens with the first performance of *Les effrontés* in 1861. With the exception of *Paul Forestier,* all the plays of this period are in prose; with the exception of *Jean de Thommeray,* written with Sandeau, they are written by Augier alone. Their common characteristic is that they deal with the vices of modern society, with the thirst for money more than with any other feature of our times. The importance which this most terrible of all anti-social evils had taken in Augier's mind is most curiously exhibited in the history of the composition of one of his most striking plays, *Maître Guérin.* Augier, when a child, had often seen at his father's house an old gentleman, M. de Lafore, who was the inventor of a mechanical device, the *statilégie,* the object of which was to teach children how to read in an incredibly short time. It need hardly be said that good M. de Lafore squandered his small fortune in his attempt to introduce his invention in all the schools of Europe. Augier had often thought that the struggles and ruin of the hapless inventor and philanthropist would form an interesting subject for a play, and he finally determined to submit the question to a practical test. He set about to write the play, and as he went on he gave greater and greater importance to the man whose victim the inventor finally becomes, so that when finished, the play has for its most important character, not Desroncerets, the dramatic incarnation of good old Monsieur de Lafore, but Maître Guérin, the unscrupulous notary, whose schemes of spoliation finally succeed in impoverishing the inventor and all but driving him out of his old family house to die a beggar in the streets.

As pictures of our money-seeking world, two plays of that period stand out prominently, *Les effrontés* and *La contagion,* the last named of which, however, through some fault of construction, failed to win as much success as the others. While money, as a power to be curbed, is present in all the plays of that period, other themes, however, are also treated; for instance, in *Le fils de Giboyer,* the danger of the introduction of religion into politics; the question of divorce in *Madame Caverlet.* A more delicate subject still is handled in Augier's last play, *Les Fourchambault,* in which the business honor of Monsieur Fourchambault, who has been ruined by his wife's extravagance, is saved by the energy of an illegitimate son whose mother was abandoned by him before his marriage.

When considering Augier as a handler of such social themes as these, it is impossible not to think of another dramatic writer of our times who seems to have adopted them as his chosen specialty, Alexandre Dumas the younger. But, leaving out all that relates to style, Augier's style being beyond and above any comparison, the methods of the two dramatists are absolutely different. In every one of Dumas's plays we have a preacher whose duty it is to inform us of the author's own view of the question. Augier never preaches; the play must tell its own story; without the introduction of any piece of mere oratory (would not rhetoric be perhaps more appropriate?) the impression of horror for what is contemptible, of admiration for the noble deeds and those who perform them, must be, and is produced upon the audience.

A really touching feature of Augier's plays is the treatment given to what we may call the heroine. She is invariably the ennobling force of the play, the star whose mission it is to lead men forward in the path of duty and sacrifice; no weak woman, nothing maudlin in her; she is always a fearless creature, she thinks, she acts when action is needed. Antoinette, Francine Desroncerets, Fernande Maréchal, ideal creations, who sometimes, how rarely, alas! are seen walking through the prosaic and selfish life of the world; let it be Augier's special honor that every young heart, after a hearing of his plays, longs for such a love as yours as the guiding strength and the rewarding blessedness of its life!

What more need be said? That Augier's dialogue is as sparkling as the thousand facets of the most finely cut diamond? That his plays are replete with terse and deep sayings which in a few words give us the substance and marrow of a whole character, of a whole situation? Who does not remember Vernouillet's final ejaculation? "If ever I have a son he will perhaps compel me to pay *his* debts, *mine* never!" or Guérin's answer to his son? "You do not respect the law,—you get around it,"—"I get around it, therefore I respect it" (*Je la tourne, donc je la respecte*), or Madame Fourchambault's unwilling and admiring acknowledgment of the moral superiority of the man whom she has just branded as a brutal monster, because of his ruthless retrenchment of all her favorite expenses? "That's the kind of husband I ought to have had!"

No striving after effect; every one of these sayings, and they are numberless in Augier's works, springs from the very soul of the play, or rather from the soul of the poet himself whose chief inspiration after all is found in

> ces haines vigoureuses
> Que doit donner le vice auxâmes vertueuses.
>
> (pp. 127-31)

Adolphe Cohn, "Emile Augier," in The Harvard Monthly, *Vol. X, No. 4, June, 1890, pp. 127-31.*

Benjamin W. Wells   (essay date 1896)

[*Wells was an American educator and critic. In the following excerpt, he examines the genesis of* Le gendre de Monsieur Poirier *in light of Augier's other works, finding the strength of the play to be Augier's subtle development of character.*]

[*Le gendre de Monsieur Poirier*] bears on its title-page the names of Augier and Sandeau. It is thus an instance of the dramatic collaboration made common in France by the example of Scribe. But Sandeau's share in this, as in other dramas of Augier, hardly goes beyond the general scheme of the dramatic situation, which is the ethical conflict between the old aristocracy and the new democracy, always a favorite subject with Sandeau, though the immediate source of *Poirier* is *Sacs et parchemins* (1851). Yet though the gentle nature of the novelist may have softened the acerbity of the dramatist's satire, the whole work bears the unmistakable stamp of Augier's genius, and is indeed one of his masterpieces, such a masterpiece as only he showed afterward the power to equal. Its place in the evolution of the drama is to be sought therefore in its relation to the other works of Augier, not to those of Sandeau.

Emile Augier came in childhood to Paris, and was carefully trained for the law, his father's profession, in which he began his career; but he inherited rather the tastes of his mother, daughter of that prolific novelist and dramatist Pigault-Lebrun. The law was to him, as he says, *un triste harnais,* hindering the flight of the literary talent that he felt he possessed. He snatched time from it to compose a romantic tragedy, *Charles VII. à Naples,* which met the cold reception from managers that it appears to have deserved. Undiscouraged by this check, he fell in with the neo-classical tendency of Ponsard, and the so-called School of Good Sense, and in the year after the memorable failure of Hugo's *Burgraves* (1843), the knell of Romantic tragedy, his *La ciguë,* as amended by Ponsard's sage counsels, achieved no small success.

This was ostensibly a classical play in regular, if somewhat pedestrian alexandrines. The scene is laid near Athens; and, though both plot and dialogue are fresh and witty, neither suggests the kind of strength that was peculiarly characteristic of his domestic dramas or his social satires. A second Greek drama, the *Joueur de flute,* probably dates from this time, though not produced till 1850. Here, as later in *L'aventurière,* we have the eminently modern thesis of Hugo's *Marion Delorme* sympathetically treated, with a liberality that directly contradicts the teaching of his domestic dramas after his fighting qualities had been roused by the social heresies of Dumas' *Dame aux camélias* (1852). But yet in *L'aventurière* there is a noteworthy progress toward this higher ethical standard; for, though the interest centres still around a frail but rehabilitated heroine, there are noble passages toward the close, where the sanctity of the family is defended and glorified with the eloquent enthusiasm of converted conviction.

The group of Augier's domestic dramas begins with *Gabrielle.* Here, as in all his later work, Augier is essentially a moralist, though he brought over from the former period enough idealization to make the poetic form appropriate; and in his next play, *Diane,* reverted for a moment to the romantic methods of *L'aventurière.* Even *Philiberte,* in spite of the affectionate study of the girl heroine, marks only a technical advance over the youthful *Homme de bien.* But in 1853 Augier began his co-operation with Jules Sandeau. He also abandoned almost entirely verse for prose; and this change in form brought with it a change in character that marks the great turning-point in his dramatic development. He had still many steps to take, but none so long as that which separates *Philiberte* from *Le gendre de M. Poirier.*

Lest the part of Sandeau in this evolution should be exaggerated, *Le pierre de touche* rises as veritable touchstone and barrier. Here we have most of Sandeau, and hence, with wit in plenty, a commonplace plot, and a faulty psychology. *Poirier* was born under the star of Molière. It owed to Sandeau only what *As You Like It* owes to Lodge, or *The Merchant of Venice* to Boccaccio.

This "honest, healthy, and hardy" comedy, "the finest since the *Mariage de Figaro,*" "the model of the modern comedy of manners," "the only one that satisfies the idea formerly held of what a comedy should be," is a satire on that plutocracy which under the bourgeois king, Louis Philippe, first won the social recognition that it had already begun to claim in the days of Le Sage's *Turcaret* (1709). This M. Poirier is a retired cloth merchant, a millionaire who aspires to the peerage. As a stepping-stone to this coveted distinction, he has purchased for his daughter the hand of Gaston de Presles, by agreeing to pay the debts of that spendthrift scion of an ancient family, from whom he hopes for aid in his social and political ambitions. Poirier is too much a believer in the power of money to see that this is not preparing a happy future for his daughter Antoinette, whom he loves as well as he knows how. Gaston naturally is disposed to make the best of his bargain, to live in luxury on the weakness of his father-in-law, and to neglect his wife, whose strength and nobility of character he gives himself no opportunity to learn to appreciate.

Poirier is given a mentor, and Antoinette a sympathetic friend, in Verdelet, more clear-sighted and intellectual than Poirier, and so a connecting link between his narrow commercial philistinism and the middle-class idealism of Antoinette. In the same way the aristocratic narrowness of Gaston is relieved by the patriotic nobility of his friend the duke. Thus the good and bad influences of wealth and of birth are variously illustrated in five characters, none of whom is unsympathetic, while all gain by contact with the others. That these five clearly marked types should be the only characters in the comedy shows a self-restraint in the use of dramatic materials in strong contrast to the then prevailing excess of Scribe, and the present superfluity of Sardou.

The development of the plot is simple. The exposition of situation and characters extends to the fourth scene of the second act. Then the action begins with the introduction of Gaston's creditors. Poirier treats them with commercial shrewdness, and, with the same finesse that had enabled him to accumulate his millions, forces these sharpers to a compromise. This, however, the marquis, with careless hauteur, refuses to accept, and Antoinette sympathizes rather with her husband, whose fine sense of honor touch-

es her romantic idealism, than with the practical probity of her father.

A rapid and dramatic development in the relations of the trio is now inevitable. Poirier is touched in his tenderest point,—his commercial spirit. He is willing to spend money lavishly to attain his end, willing to be, as he says, *coulant en affaires;* but this keen consciousness of the power of money only deepens his indignation at its wanton waste. Gaston's act seems to him unpardonable, and his genuine affection for Antoinette is wounded by what appears to him treason to the family tradition. He determines to reassert himself, naturally in thoroughly bourgeois fashion. He will force his son-in-law into active life, and reform his household radically without consulting him, in accordance with his own rather plebeian tastes.

Meantime Gaston, quite unsuspicious of this thundercloud, has become involved in a duel for a lady in whom he sought a distraction. Poirier discovers this relation by the not very reputable means of opening a sealed letter. He reveals it to the young wife, who, with the same impulsiveness that led her to sacrifice her fortune to Gaston's honor, now conceives him more false to her than the fact or the evidence justifies. And yet she loves him; and when she hears of the impending duel she cannot restrain her emotion. This is skillfully used by the two mediators, the duke and Verdelet, to reconcile husband and wife. Gaston, after a bitter struggle, abandons the duel for her sake, and places the love that she has inspired in him above his aristocratic ideal of honor. But she will equal him in magnanimity, and bids him go from her arms to the combat, placing his honor above her love. What remains is only the rounding out of a happy ending. The adversary withdraws that the chances of a duel may not imperil Gaston's new-found love. Verdelet's generosity enables the marquis to occupy once more the ancestral *château* of his family. He is won to active life and to his wife; she has gained honor and love. Verdelet and the duke unite in mutual esteem; only Poirier is a little puzzled still, not quite converted from his philistinism or his ambitions.

The real strength of this play, however, is not in its plot, but in the unfolding of character. Almost every speech of Poirier throws a new, and often no unsympathetic light, on a nature, many-sided yet simply true, and drawn with a pen not less kindly than keen, while the most delicate irony scintillates through all. But while the hearer is never suffered to forget that Poirier has some right on his side, Gaston, on the other hand, is no Romantic hero. His *blague* in the earlier acts accompanies deeds and sentiments neither righteous nor truly noble, and yet the good in him that won Antoinette's love holds our sympathetic interest from the first. These two figures belong to the highest comedy. The Duke and Verdelet are excellent in a lower kind, and Antoinette, with her simple dignity rising to strength in trial, while never artistically great, is always charming.

The seven years (1854-1861) that separate *M. Poirier* from *Les effrontés* were occupied in the main with what may be called domestic dramas. *Le mariage d'Olympe* and *Les lionnes pauvres* are fearless denunciations of the trifling with family relations that had recently witnessed a belated recrudescence in Dumas' *Dame aux camélias* and its numerous following; in **Ceinture dorée** and **Beau mariage** the domestic enemy is the overmastering desire of wealth. The latter comedy has several points of resemblance to Molière's *George Dandin,* and so stands closest to **Poirer;** but in all these four dramas in prose, and in the verses of **La jeunesse,** one misses the delicate characterization of **Poirier,** and except in **Les lionnes pauvres,** Poor Ladies of Fashion, as we may render the title, the technique of the dramatic execution is less firm, and seems less mature. This last, however, is a wonderful picture of the restless reaching out for material gratification, "that rage for dress and luxury" that during the Second Empire seemed to a thoughtful contemporary, George H. Lewes, likely "rapidly to demoralize the middle classes of Europe."

This wider social satire naturally led Augier to the political field which from 1861 to 1873 drew the chief part of his interest, and produced his strongest, though not his most artistically perfect work. In **Les effrontés** he attacked the mania of unprincipled speculation that had been cynically nursed and fostered by the Second Empire. Here the chief figure is Vernouillet, a bold portrait of the contemporary speculator, de Mirès, and a type that seems likely to endure of the schemer who, in his pursuit of fortune, grazes the utmost bounds of the legal, and occasionally oversteps them while retaining his social position, owing to the easy toleration of our democratic standards. In his schemes he is aided by the cynical noble, d'Auberive, "amusing himself in fomenting the corruption of the bourgeoisie," and by Giboyer, another character that has become typical, the talented but venal journalist whose biting pen is for sale to the highest bidder of whatever party; a natural result, as Augier thinks, of the education of a literary proletariat. In these three the interest centres, while, as in **Poirier,** the plot is of quite subordinate interest.

Le fils de Giboyer is essentially the same subject seen from a new side, a picture, as the German critic Laube has said, "of modern French society in its free struggle between a decaying aristocracy, a vain bourgeoisie, and a gifted but unprincipled body of men of literary training. . . . Yet this struggle is never described abstractly, but always with scenic fulness and a growing dramatic interest, spiced with sparkling dialogue." In short, it is one of the very best plays of the modern stage, never surpassed by its author, though the character of Giboyer is perhaps equalled by the d'Estrigaud of **Contagion** and **Lions et rénards.** His **Contagion** is the desire of wealth without work, personified in the stock-gambler, d'Estrigaud. Here, and in the later play, Augier has shown how pitilessly this spirit saps all idealism, honor, patriotism; and he returned to the subject with emphasis drawn from the disasters of the Franco-German war in **Jean de Thommeray.**

Meantime, at intervals between this sterner work, he had written **Maître Guérin** and **Paul Forestier.** The former is a curious study of the legal mind, of the relation of the moral and the civil law, less sensational than **Giboyer,** but of very profound insight, though with regrettable concessions to the sentimentalism of Scribe. The close of this drama where, though all turn from him, yet Guérin cannot see that his conduct is dishonorable because it is perfectly legal, is a masterpiece of psychologic revelation. A much lower place much be accorded to **Forestier,** a study of the development of love after marriage, "the saint overthrowing the sinner," in the heart of a man too weak to inspire much interest.

Far stronger domestic dramas are the two that conclude the list of Augier's works,—**Madame Caverlet** and **Les Fourchambault.** The former deals with the moral strain imposed by the since reformed divorce laws of France; the latter takes up once more the parable of marriage for money, and shows the author at the close of his dramatic career, but at the height of his genius. It is one of the most compactly built and vigorously executed of all his plays, though the close errs on the side of melodramatic sentimentalism, and the whole lacks the thorough-going realism of **Giboyer** or **La contagion.**

Looking, now, at Augier's work as a whole, we may say that his verse is flowing and plastic, full of the daring metaphors that recall the traditions of Romanticism. His prose abounds in even more vigorous turns, in strong, and sometimes even vulgar comparisons. Where occasion demands or justifies, he does not shrink from the slang of the Boulevard or the boudoir, though he errs in this direction less than Dumas *fils* or Sardou. His picturesque vigor, and the newness of a part of his vocabulary, make him one of the most difficult of contemporary French authors to render satisfactorily into any foreign tongue. One is frequently conscious of a shade of meaning that seems to defy translation save by a paraphrase that would deprive it of its vigor. This is more marked in the dramas of the sixties than in **Poirier,** which for this reason, as for others, is the best drama with which to begin a study of Augier's works. (pp. iii-xii)

No contemporary dramatist has a loftier conception of his vocation than Augier. His aim is to be an educator of the public, and this aim is always before his own eyes, though never obtruded on his readers. He will sacrifice nothing to declamation, as Dumas *fils* is apt to do, nor to show, as is nearly always the case with Sardou. Hence he is sometimes hard and bitter, convinced, as one of his characters says, that "some stings are cured only with hot iron;" though late in life he said playfully that he thought he had used the hot iron too often. But he was always upright and downright, so that he leaves on the mind an impression of serious humor and keen irony that compels respect, together with a robust honesty and sound moral loyalty that inspire love. (p. xii)

Benjamin W. Wells, in an introduction to Le gendre de Monsieur Poirier: Comédie en quatre actes *by Emile Augier and Jules Sandeau, edited by Benjamin W. Wells, D. C. Heath & Co., Publishers, 1896, pp. iii-xii.*

Stuart Symington   (essay date 1899)

[*In the following excerpt, Symington surveys Augier's plays, concluding that Augier has been justifiably compared with Molière.*]

Augier's literary work consists entirely of plays, if we except a volume of poetry written in early youth, and a political pamphlet entitled *La question électorale*. At the age of twenty-four he presented *La ciguë* to the committee of the *Théâtre français*. It was declined. Accepted at the *Odéon*, this half-classic, half-romantic story of a profligate, disenchanted young Greek, who is dissuaded from drinking hemlock by a beloved slave, made the fortune of the theatre and the reputation of the author. But the success of *La ciguë* was due as much to the reaction against romanticism as to its great literary merit. For the failure of Victor Hugo's last play, *Les burgraves* (1843), had been a death-blow to the Romantic Drama, so brilliantly inaugurated by *Hernani* in 1830, and a month later, the public, weary of lyric sentimentality, had applauded with enthusiasm Ponsard's *Lucrèce,* an imitation of the classic tragedies of the seventeenth and eighteenth centuries. Since *La ciguë* was classic in form and setting, at least, its young author was at once hailed as a disciple of Ponsard, and as one of the leaders of the short-lived School of Good Sense. But Augier was not a member of this or of any other school, he was simply 'feeling his way,' as is evident from the fact that his next five plays were alternately classic and romantic. For while *Un homme de bien,* the first of the five, is a comedy of character imitated from Molière, and is therefore, like *La ciguë,* more classic, perhaps, than romantic, the reverse is true in the case of *L'aventurière,* which recounts the almost successful effort of an adventuress, the victim of circumstances, to enter a noble house by marriage, and lead a respectable life. Again, *Gabrielle,* a downright attack on romanticism, in which good sense is carried to the verge of nonsense, and *Le joueur de flûte,* a reworking of the theme of *La ciguë,* were immediately followed by *Diane,* a romantic drama, set, like Hugo's *Marion Delorme,* in the time of Richelieu.

The first period of Augier's literary life closes with two plays betraying the same indecision or eclecticism. For *La pierre de touche* and *Philiberte* are not classic, surely, neither were they acceptable to the neo-classic adherents of the School of Good Sense, and yet they cannot be considered romantic either—in both Augier gives free rein to what J. J. Weiss enthusiastically calls his "divine fancy." The first of these two, *La pierre de touche,* was adapted, in collaboration with Sandeau, from one of the latter's novels (*L'héritage,*) and curiously enough, the "spring" of the piece, an inheritance, and more especially the scene which shows the heirs assembled for the formal reading of the will, forms the basis of a novel by Sandeau's friend and (in a sense) namesake, George Sand. The play begins with a charming picture of artist life under difficulties. Spiegel the painter works that Franz the musician may study, and Franz is to help him in turn when his symphonies shall have brought him fame and money. With them lives an orphan, Frédérique, beloved by both and betrothed to her cousin Franz. The latter inherits a fortune from an eccentric nobleman who had enjoyed his music and who desired him to cultivate it. Under the influence of the disappointed heirs Franz deteriorates rapidly. He forsakes his art, his friend, and even Frédérique—truly an astonishingly unattractive and improbable picture of the power of money—the touchstone—to blast character and happiness. The second of these two fanciful pieces, *Phili-*

berte, has to do with the metamorphosis of a dull, homely girl into a witty, handsome, and attractive woman. It is a dainty picture of the faded gallantry of the last century, recalling vaguely the shadowy guests thronging—in M. Majesté's befuddled vision—the halls of the "Hôtel cidevant de Nesmond."

Now the romanticists had applauded *La ciguë,* refusing to regard its author as an enemy, but they had received with scant favor the two plays which followed it, and *Gabrielle* (1849) was the signal for an explosion. As in *Un homme de bien,* the last line of *Gabrielle* is the key to the piece:

O père de famille! ô poëte! je t'aime.

One can imagine the indignation of the romanticists at this prosaic theme, inspired, as they said, by the "muse du pot-au-feu." Augier opposes to their sentimental ideal of irregular passion the poetry of home and fireside, but the home he describes is so prosaic and stupid, the language of the play is at times so very commonplace—for example, Julien, the 'poet,' speaks of a *machin au fromage!*—that we can attribute its success only to the reaction against romanticism.

All these early plays, except *La pierre de touche,* were in verse; Augier now turns, but under the influence of the younger Dumas, to the realistic prose comedy of manners. For he was in no sense an innovator. Spronck, the sharpest of his critics, deplores this "radical and absolute absence of individuality," but absence of individuality is Augier's creed. In his opinion the theatre should be "the resounding echo of the whisperings of society," should "formulate general sentiment while it is still vague." As an eminent critic [Jules Lemaître] expresses it: "les nouveautés flottent pour ainsi parler, dans l'esprit des contemporains intelligens avant de se réaliser dans un chef-d'œuvre." Now the return of public favor to classicism had been but momentary, since reason, like sentiment, was out of date. By his novels Balzac had long been preparing the reign of observation, but to Dumas the Younger belongs the honor of initiating the realistic comedy of manners which has held undisputed sway on the French stage since the representation of his *Dame aux camélias* in 1852. Just as the success of *Lucrèce* had inspired *La ciguë,* so the success of *La dame aux camélias* inspired *Le gendre de Monsieur Poirier* and all the pieces in Augier's later manner. It is true that in two of his plays, *Un homme de bien* and *Gabrielle,* he had already studied contemporary manners, but of these the first is rather a character sketch, developed later, as Doumic remarks, in Guérin, and the second is an attack on romanticism. So it is really with *Le gendre de M. Poirier* that Augier begins to study the society of his time, a society which he has described as "new, without a past, without traditions, without belief, and even without prejudice; a land of equality in which wealth has become the aim of all ambitions, since it has become the only inequality possible." Holding such views as these, and with his conception of the theatre, it was inevitable that Augier should treat, as he does in most of his plays, the influence of wealth on character and on society. Money has replaced love in the classic conflict with honor.

Le gendre de M. Poirier was adapted by Augier and

Sandeau from a novel by the latter called *Sacs et parchemins* (1851), "money-bags and titles." In *La pierre de touche* Franz gains a title by paying the debts of his adoptive father; M. Poirier's son-in-law reverses the procedure by selling his name and person for a dowry. Represented first at the Gymnase theatre, the play afterwards became (1864), and has since remained, one of the most popular in the repertory of the *Théâtre français*. Some, like Saint-Victor and Saintsbury, regard *L'aventurière* as Augier's masterpiece; many think that he never surpassed *La ciguë,* and yet other plays are selected by those who will not be denied the pleasure of naming the very best, but the weight of critical opinion undoubtedly leans justly towards *Le gendre de M. Poirier.* Émile Montégut, certainly one of the most readable and perhaps not the least acute of the many critics who have studied Augier's work, considers the play to be "not only the best of our time, but the only one which satisfies (qui réponde à) the idea formerly held of a comedy." Among others Brunetière, Lacour, Parigot, Saint-Victor and Doumic regard it as a masterpiece—the latter is inclined to consider it *the* masterpiece of contemporary comedy—and in our own country, Brander Matthews, an authority in matters dramatic, considers it to be "the model modern comedy of manners."

And now as to collaboration. Montégut is sure that the change of *menu* in the play (II, 9) is due to Sandeau, and that certain delicate expressions of sentiment, like "quand j'étais petite fille, je ne comprenais pas que mon père et ma mère ne fussent pas parents" (III, 1), belong to Augier, but precisely because of her delicacy of sentiment Mlle. Poirier resembles Mlle. de la Seiglière more closely than any young girl in Augier's theatre, and it is always difficult, not to say impossible, to tell with any degree of certainty what belongs to one of two collaborators and what to the other. Nevertheless those who have read *Mademoiselle de la Seiglière* (1849) will understand why Sandeau is considered to be the very best delineator of the virtues and foibles of the French nobility of this century, while the one point on which all critics are agreed is that Augier is essentially and typically a bourgeois—surely a rare combination of qualities for the production of a comedy which contrasts the two classes of society! For this reason, doubtless, *Le gendre de M. Poirier* is a far better and more homogeneous play than either *La pierre de touche* or *Jean de Thommeray,* both of which we owe to the same collaboration. And perhaps the best feature of the play is the absolute impartiality with which noble and bourgeois are treated.

Augier also collaborated with De Musset once, with Labiche once, and with Édouard Foussier, whose literary personality is less well known, three times, but in the last instance, at least, the greater part of the work was his, since M. Foussier has declined to accept a share in the parentage of one of the plays which bears his name. Nevertheless it is but fair to recall that in the preface to *Les lionnes pauvres* Augier declares that the authors themselves would find it difficult to say what part of the play belonged to each, "our piece having been written in such perfect harmony—parfaite cohabitation d'esprit." In his address of welcome to Augier, when the latter entered the Academy (1858), M. Le Brun had remarked very justly that one of the chief objections to collaboration was the consequent uncertainty of authorship. In the preface just mentioned Augier admits the justice of the criticism, but defends the practice in a passage worth quoting because it throws light on his private life: "One of my *confrères,* we will suppose, is my intimate friend, no more accustomed to collaboration than I. But neither of us is very worldly and we are apt to pass our evening by the fireside. There we chat of one thing and another, like the Fantasio of our dear De Musset, catching all the cockchafers that flit about the candle; and if among these cockchafers flits the idea of a comedy, to which of us does it belong? To neither and to both."

Augier now continues, without further indecision, the study of contemporary life. In *Le mariage d'Olympe,* a reply to and a refutation of the rehabilitation-of-fallen-angels theory as set forth in Dumas's *Dame aux camélias,* an adventuress (Olympe) marries into a noble family, and unable or unwilling to shake off her former habits, afflicted with "la nostalgie de la boue," she threatens, when her true character is discovered, to publish the letters of a cousin and former playmate of her husband's, and is shot by the girl's father to preserve the honor of his house. Although a strong play, the public received this dénouement with dissatisfaction—"the final pistol-shot killed the play as well as the heroine." [Léo Claretie, *La vie moderne au théâtre*]

But Augier returns immediately to the great central theme of his theatre—money—the cost of it (*Ceinture dorée*), the need of it (*La jeunesse*), the lust for it (*Les lionnes pauvres*), the emptiness of it (*Un beau mariage*), and its power for evil (*Maître Guérin*). In *Ceinture dorée,* which was not very well received, a poor nobleman refuses to marry the daughter of a rich banker until the financial ruin of the latter has atoned in some measure for the shady origin of his wealth—an illustration of the proverb "bonne renommée vaut mieux que ceinture dorée." *La jeunesse,* in verse, shows the increasing difficulty of gaining a livelihood in the big cities, and the consequent tendency not to listen too closely to the voice of conscience in youth. Philip's mother, one of the author's most original creations, and yet cruelly real, has been saddened by hard experience of poverty, and blunts the young man's sensibilities with such maxims as

> Une bonne habitude à prendre est de ne point
> Penser de mal des gens dont nous avons besoin.

Les lionnes pauvres, a study of contemporary married women living beyond their means, is conceded to be one of Augier's strongest dramas. Even Zola, who declares that he is generally considered to have treated contemporary dramatists with "the brutality of a savage gnawed by jealousy," thinks it one of the best of modern plays. Finally, in *Un beau mariage* we see the wretched life of a clever young chemist who, having married the beautiful but disenchanted and cynical daughter of a rich widow of social prominence, finds that he is a convenience, an escort, nothing more, and, having no time to work, is miserable.

With *Les effrontés* Augier enters the field of political comedy, again showing the banker made wealthy by questionable although legal methods. This time, however, he is unrepentant, and when advised by the cynical Marquis d'Aubérive to hold up his head if he will be accepted in society, Vernouillet follows his advice to the letter and buys a newspaper which he wields as a weapon. The strength of his paper lies in Giboyer, the unprincipled bohemian hack-writer, whose redeeming trait is unselfish love for the son whom he has sent to college and kept in ignorance of his birth by representing himself as the young fellow's uncle. Giboyer voices Augier's sentiments. Liberal and democratic at heart, he has written a book upon equality, defining the word: "à chacun selon ses œuvres," but no practical working out of the theory is given. His son, endowed with fine instincts and ability, is the hero of *Le fils de Giboyer,* an attack on the clerical party, and, in general, on the covering of political aims with the cloak of religion.

Money again becomes the dominant theme in *Maître Guérin,* the story of a provincial notary who enriches himself by all questionable means within the law, and cannot see wherein he has done wrong. *La contagion* was directed against *la blague*—the light scoffing at sentiment and things high and noble. The play did not come up to the expectations formed of it and was not well received even after important changes. Some of the scenes are strong, nevertheless, and one character at least, the villainous Baron d'Estrigaud, was successful enough to induce Augier to give him a prominent rôle in *Lions et renards,* a bitter attack upon the Jesuits which was not received with favor. This last play was preceded by *Paul Forestier,* a drama of passion, in verse, and by *Le postscriptum,* in De Musset's manner, a short clever dialogue between landlord and tenant who agree to become husband and wife.

The scene of *Jean de Thommeray,* which Augier and Sandeau adapted from one of the latter's novels, is laid before and during the Franco-Prussian war. Being merely a succession of tableaux, its success was due more to patriotic sentiment and to the stage setting than to its dramatic merit. The last scene is expecially picturesque and strong. Jean, a young Breton of noble birth, is bored at home, and rapidly—too rapidly—deteriorates in Paris. Though fighting has begun he has not joined the army, and, having lost his ill-gotten wealth, is about to leave Paris with his parvenue fiancée and her father, when he hears the bagpipes of the Breton regiment led by his own father and brothers. They halt near him and he hears his father say, in an address to the regiment, that only one man has failed to answer the call to arms.—"Present!" he cries, seized with remorse.—"Who are you?" his father asks, refusing to recognize his degenerate son.—"A man who has lived an evil life and asks to die a worthy death."—"Jean de Thommeray," the old man cries, "entrez dans les rangs."

Augier's literary labors close with two plays "pointing a moral": *Madame Caverlet,* a plea for divorce, and *Les Fourchambault,* in which a natural son raises the fortunes of his father's banking house after it has been brought to the brink of ruin by the latter's wasteful wife. This was Augier's last play. After eleven years of silence he died in 1889.

Lemaître has observed that all those who spoke of Augier during the fortnight after his death rightly compared him to Molière, and it has been well said that he followed the master as closely as talent could follow genius. Each studied the society of his time, exposed its scars and ridiculed its foibles. Augier has created more types than any writer of comedies since Molière, but after reading the seven volumes of his plays one finds it unusually difficult to avoid confusing the characters. The young heiresses, like their fathers, resemble one another closely, and the young heroes, who marry the heiresses in the end, have also many points in common. Here and there, it is true, a character stands out in relief—Guérin the notary, Poirier the rich cloth-merchant, Giboyer the unprincipled journalist—but most of them bear an unmistakable family resemblance.

Augier's prose is clear, direct, and unpretentious— perhaps the best dramatic style of his time. His verse betrays careful study of the classic French writers and especially of Molière. Théophile Gautier said of it: "M. Émile Augier a un style net, large, carré, dans lequel les délicats sentent une appropriation parfaite des tours et des idiotismes de Molière." J. J. Weiss preferred his verse to his prose, and Saint-Victor considered the style of *L'aventurière* to be "du meilleur cru de la langue," but this praise is too high, since Augier was too temperate, too logical, too commonplace, in short, to be a great poet, although very few would agree with Spronck that "he wrote in verse almost as badly as possible." He certainly had the "don du théâtre" to a marked degree, and, all things considered, stands at the head of the French dramatists of the last half-century.

Augier withdrew from the theatre in the heyday of success; not, as Parigot maintains, because the development of his theatre had reached a logical conclusion—indeed *Les Fourchambault* rather marks the beginning of a new period than the close of an old one—nor altogether, as Doumic has said, because, while convinced that the theatre should reflect society, he no longer felt in touch with the society of his time, but rather because he had given his message to the world, he was growing old, he had seen the once successful Scribe ignored by the director of a theatre, and his rare good sense told him what the great Corneille might well have applied to himself:

> Et quand la renommée a passé l'ordinaire,
> Si l'on n'en veut déchoir, il faut ne plus rien faire.
>
> (pp. vi-xviii)

Stuart Symington, "Emile Augier," in Le gendre de M. Poirier: Comédie en quatre actes *by Emile Augier and Jules Sandeau, edited by Stuart Symington, Henry Holt and Company, 1899, pp. v-xviii.*

Edwin Carl Roedder   (essay date 1903)

[*Roedder was an American educator and critic. In the following excerpt, he praises* Le gendre de Monsieur Poirier *as the first indication of Augier's mastery of stagecraft and character development.*]

Le gendre de M. Poirier is by no means a simple dramatization of [Jules Sandeau's *Sacs et parchemins*]. To Sandeau the play owes a fair share of its success; to the novel it owes but the general suggestion of the theme, one of the chief characters, essentially modified, and a few minor matters of detail.

At its first performance, April 8, 1854, at the Théâtre du Gymnase-Dramatique, the play met with a sympathetic reception which toward the close changed to ecstatic applause. Jules Janin, the critic of the *Journal des Débats,* predicted after the first acts that within ten years it would be permanently adopted by the Théâtre-Français; a prophecy fully justified by the events. Among all of Augier's plays, *Le gendre de M. Poirier* to-day stands the greatest favorite of critics, theater-goers, and readers. For it is a serious work of art of lasting import, not merely a good stage-play to while away a few leisure hours; and it stands the strongest test of a classic: it gains with each repeated reading.

The plot is worked out with skill and care, with numerous truly dramatic situations and surprises. The dialogue, bright and lively, full of sparkling wit as well as genuine humor, contains many passages of deep thought and some of striking beauty. But the chief excellences of the play are its marvelously life-like characters and their unfolding under the change of situations. All of them are sharply defined in bearing, sentiment, and speech, so as to retain easily a place in one's memory. Poirier, much manlier and more sympathetic than M. Levrault [in Sandeau's novel], is one of those square and solid bourgeois that only Augier knows how to delineate, and in whose delineation he feels at his ease, knowing them well enough to appreciate fully their homely virtues, and too well to make idols of them. Gaston de Presles, less noble than Gaston de la Rochelandier, is vastly more amusing and brilliant. The bearer of an illustrious name,—a valuable possession even in the most democratic society, much more so in France during the forties,—he is brave, possessed of a truly aristocratic elegance and refinement of manners which cannot be learned but must be inherited from generations, and, despite his faults, which the authors do not endeavor to excuse, good at heart. Nor must all of his faults be charged to him personally; having been brought up in the notion that a nobleman must not work, he is easily started on the wrong path. The duke, who has subordinated his political conviction to the higher demands of patriotism, contrasts favorably with Gaston and illustrates the better side of the nobility; just as Verdelet, more cultured than Poirier, and not blind to the fashionable vices of the nobility or to the narrowness of the bourgeoisie, excellently represents the latter. These two characters, while subordinate, are important as two correctives. Antoinette, the innocent victim of her father's ambitions and her husband's frivolity, equally remote from maudlin sentimentality and from Laure Levrault's worldly-wise lack of sentiment, is the most charming figure of the play. Her husband's aristocratic traits and great name please her womanly idealism rather than the fancy of a little bourgeoise. A woman, she easily adjusts herself to the new sphere; great and lofty sentiments are natural to her, a plebeian's daughter with a patrician soul.

Pontmartin, whose review of the play, written under the fresh impression of the first performance, belongs among the most thoughtful expressions of opinion, thinks the authors originally meant to write *"La revanche de George Dandin,"*—a young nobleman marrying beneath his station, and delivering himself up to a tyrannical father-in-law,—and, deviating therefrom, embodied in the dramatic composition another play,—a prodigal son-in-law, Gaston's relations with Mme. de Montjay, their discovery, the breach between husband and wife, and their final reconciliation. But assuming that Augier's originality would have been satisfied by either of the plays suggested, a *Revanche de George Dandin* was the very thing to be avoided. To quote Pontmartin himself, the theme handled had grown more delicate since the days of Molière, Lesage, and Beaumarchais. Class distinctions had been abolished, but not class feelings. The nobility, now no longer a power, but only a form, a memory, was more sensitive; what in the days of its power had been comedy was now a cruel satire. The bourgeoisie, jealous of its newly-gained political and social equality, was loath to be reminded of distinctions the validity of which it no longer recognized. Pontmartin's objection that true comedy operates with very simple means—partly directed against Scribe's "well-made" plays—would really go against the whole dramatic system of the new *comédie de mœurs,* which Pontmartin seemingly does not fully understand and appreciate. He is also forced to admit that the sources of enjoyment and emotion opened up by the combination indicated enhanced the success of the play.

Le gendre de M. Poirier is often referred to as Augier's, without mention of Sandeau. That is unfair to the author of *Sacs et parchemins.* One critic ascribes to Sandeau a half-paternity in the play. That is crediting him with too much. Which of the two authors first had the happy idea of dramatizing the novel? Most likely it arose in a friendly chat by the fireside, of which Augier was so very fond, and so belonged "to neither and to both." The drama is a much better one than Sandeau alone could have written. "In passing through Augier's brain the ideas which might not have originated there obtain their breadth and value" (Doumic). At the same time the play is much better for Sandeau's collaboration, the chief feature of which is modification and suggestion, rather than dramatic construction and character delineation. Sandeau is for the composition what the duke and Verdelet are for the drama. Augier shows himself in other plays as an opponent of the nobility; Sandeau, "the exquisite Van Dyck of the noble houses in the XIXth century, who alone knows how to paint them without hostile prejudice or servile indulgence, and how to make us love them even in their narrowness and prejudices" (Montégut), shows a strong leaning in the other direction. While both authors separately might have produced the work of a somewhat short-sighted partisan, together they created the work of an impartial, far-sighted statesman. Their literary qualities, too, are blended in harmony, neither over-emphasizing nor weakening but supplementing each other: "The brush was held by two hands at once, one governed by bold vivacity, the other by fond deliberation, each admirably correcting the other's excesses or hesitations; which evidently explains the irreproachably delicate shading of the picture" (Montégut). It also explains the marked absence of the deficiencies of collaboration as stated by Lebrun. *Le gendre de M. Poirier* is the first masterpiece written in collaboration since the days of Beaumont and Fletcher.

And it remained Augier's masterpiece as well. In none of his later dramas, however pronounced their success, did he reach the same serene height of pure art. If Augier had written other plays like *Le gendre de M. Poirier,* or even if he had written but this one comedy, it would be justifiable to call him a master in the same breath with Molière, which now, considering his other work, would be a gross mistake of literary piety and a failure to recognize the laws of historical perspective. For rarely does Augier, outside *Le gendre de M. Poirier,* produce that Molièrean atmosphere in which the spectator good-naturedly laughs at human follies because he feels so far above them. Like all French writers of comedies since Molière, Augier was a pupil of the great master in his youth; like all successful French playwrights since Molière, he was compelled by the new times to shake off the master's yoke. And Augier was indeed a talent empowered to speak forth what the epoch possessed, but not a genius that, the messenger of a new time, could produce what it lacked and clothe in enduring beauteous form great truths after the expression of which humanity was striving. Again, he has put on the stage a number of marked individualities, and his characters easily furnish the composite picture of the French bourgeois; but he has not created any character that is a personality and a type at the same time. Technically he has made no advance beyond Scribe; and the dramatic genre in which his real strength lay had to be pointed out to him by Dumas *fils.*

None the less, Augier's remains the honorable place of the foremost among the French dramatists in the second half of the XIXth century. In his whole intellectual make-up the most striking quality is his good sense and common sense, which characterizes him as a type of the French bourgeois whom only he knew how to portray so faithfully; indeed, Spronck, his sharpest critic, whom undue praise by others has roused to manifest injustice, would concede only that "as documents of a certain social class of a certain historical epoch his plays, being more instructive than any others, will remain valuable." To this good sense he owes his correctness and steadiness of observation, his clear and keen insight, his certainty of mind, his hatred of skepticism and ironical mockery, his successful endeavor to express under a personal form the ideas most generally accepted and fully tested by time (Doumic). To this same good sense—the normal mental attitude of the healthy, well-fed, and well-clad, which has often been the foe of the truly great and individual in French literature—we must attribute Augier's limitations: his aversion to any novel ideas threatening those traditionally received, his undue worship of *"les grands mots,"* his anxiety to have the mass behind him in order to stand his ground firmly. Other characteristic traits are his sanguine temper, his optimistic and robust gayety. "His language, frank, and of manly candor, never makes true virtue blush. He is logical in the construction of his works, which are strong not in single parts, but in their entirety, and all have a beginning, a middle, and an end. He never grows violent like Sardou; his characters walk through the doors rather than through the windows, and on their feet rather than on their hands"

(Montégut). A master of stagecraft, he obtains surprising results with seemingly insignificant means; a true dramatist, he keeps himself invisible in his works, and rather than employing any extra character as his mouthpiece he makes the whole drama voice its idea and its moral. This moral is not patched upon the play in the shape of reward of virtue or punishment of vice, but consists in the impression obtained in the course of the drama; a true artist, he wrote no dramatized sermons. It would be an easy task to point out the workings of poetic justice in all of his plays. Augier's is the good and solid moral of the French bourgeois, a worship and defense of home and family, the foundation of the whole social order. Granting that *"vox populi vox Dei,"* Augier does preach God's word, without, like Dumas *fils,* "enlisting all the tricks of the devil, and presenting a moral possibly good enough to satisfy everybody's conscience, but hardly fit for everybody's ears" (Doumic).

Some of Augier's dramas are losing all but their historical interest; some are almost disappearing even from the literary horizon. But *Le gendre de M. Poirier* to this day remains what Montégut called it, "not only the best comedy of our time, but also answering best the conception formerly held of an ideal comedy." Social conditions have essentially changed since its first performance; the leveling of classes, while not completed, has progressed considerably. But the play will retain its life—a portion of which, let us be mindful, it owes to Jules Sandeau—as long as any of Molière's; for it is purely and delightfully human. (pp. 11-17)

> *Edwin Carl Roedder, in an introduction to* Le gendre de M. Poirier: Comédie en quatre actes *by Emile Augier and Jules Sandeau, edited by Edwin Carl Roedder, American Book Company, 1903, pp. 5-17.*

William Norman Guthrie (essay date 1911)

[*Guthrie was an American clergyman, author, and critic. His literary career included a position as editor of* Dramatic Quarterly *and contributions to numerous periodicals. In the following excerpt, Guthrie discusses the moral content of Augier's works.*]

Roughly speaking, the career of Emile Augier is the record of a bourgeois moralist's development into a national prophet. *Un homme de bien* and *Gabrielle* give us the pro and con for the bourgeois ideal. In the first of these two we are shown M. Feline, the righteous man, distinctly self-righteous, and never without an excellent selfish motive for his righteousness. The pitiless exposure of the *soi disant* moral man's cant must have been wholesome. Why is he righteous? Clearly for safety's sake and ease. "The masque of Don Juan does not seem to fit and become every brow. One must have much wit for that rôle, and in fact it is much less arduous to play the part of the honest man." And what is his spiritual reward? His is the undoubted right to judge, and to condemn! "The right to feel myself and declare myself honest; and I wager nobody will have payed a higher price than I for the precious right of crying 'stop thief' at the heels of the rascal." But the right to judge and condemn is not the only reward, for our hero agrees with some reluctance that it is a matter of extreme pride to him, and promises the ulterior delight of indulging at leisure in cheerful self-admiration. Poor Rose is taken in by M. Feline's display of good nature, and by his parade of magnanimous sentiment: "How could I have despised this honest and good man?" But indeed, it was good for her to be deluded; better than to see too clearly through his disguise.

The other side of this unsympathetic portraiture of the bourgeois was furnished us in *Gabrielle,* in which appeared the much ridiculed line: "O head of the family, O poet, how I love thee!" Yet, laugh as one may at this extraordinary lyrical outburst torn bleeding from its context, the fact remains, as Augier shows, that the poetry of the home is all the poetry possible to the ordinary man. Nor is the poetry of vagabondage truly any commoner. Stephane, who tries to break up his friend Julien's home, is not really a better lover or a more romantic person than her husband; he only occupies the easier rôle from the point of view of immediate theatrical effect. Julien's awakening to his unconscious neglect of his wife (absorbed as he had been in making material provision for her) and his insistence that "they forgive each other all around"—all this, however easily parodied, does not fail to make an impression on the honest spectator's mind and heart.

Augier's next preachment may be said to appear in *L'aventurière* and *Le mariage d'Olympe.* Here he enlarges on the fact that the romantic sympathy is accorded to the sinner. Somehow or other the benefit of the doubt is not granted, as it should be, to those whose position is regular. There is the hypocrisy of morality; but so is there also the hypocrisy of rebellion against society. The doctrine is driven home, perhaps somewhat cruelly, by Augier. Though the adventuress is not incapable of repentance, and though her repentance should be considered sincere until proved otherwise,—nevertheless she cannot be taken back into the bosom of outraged society as though nothing had occurred. She must earn her virtue; acceptance must not come to her as a free gift, for only as an expensive purchase will she prize her virtue at its true worth. The trial as by fire of adversity is what she needs. In an easy prosperity she will but lapse again.

In *Le gendre de M. Poirier* we are given a veritable masterpiece,—Molière's *Bourgeois gentilhomme* brought down to date; and the shafts of wit, hitting the aristocracy quite as often as the bourgeoisie. M. Poirier himself is a delicious personage, and should be known and not read about. His business sense identified with common sense, and claiming for itself a kind of divine sanction,—a sort of mystic mathematic afflatus—is only equaled by his profound contempt for art and artists. His honesty is great, but not as great as his honest fear of being cheated. No honest man will allow a fellow man to be dishonest at his personal expense! His love of abstract honesty is too great to permit his own honesty to stand in the way of imparting to another's virtue! M. Poirier,—why not translate it "Peartree" while one is at it—bears the delicious fruit of unselfishness; but notice that it is unselfishness of so high an order that it succeeds in being selfish also at the same

time. For should one not show good business tact in one's friendship and one's philanthropy, and in the sacred ties and devotions of the family? The nobility come in for wholesome scorn, for their theory of life is gilded idleness, and he for one, M. Poirier, will not regild their idleness where the base metal shows. Again and again he repeats his charges against the nobility, always to be overcome by a sneaking sense of their actual superiority, and speculating in secret as to the money value of it all! Why not invest in a pedigree for one's daughter, if the thing somehow has a market price? His daughter, who loves the ne'er-do-well Gaston, and Gaston himself the impecunious nobleman, who believes in always showing one's nobility by giving more than the law requires, and making up for it by giving very much less on other occasions,—who scorning money, sells himself for money, deems it ridiculous to be in love with one's wife (and yet—and yet . . . Oh, this deceitful heart of ours!) . . . surely this is all excellent matter for delicious laughter!

And the text to the sermon is not lacking in seriousness. Bourgeois and noblemen each affect to despise what they do not themselves have, and they are most graciously convicted by the dramatist of their respective limitations, and of their dire need, therefore, of each other's good qualities possessed at least by friendly proxy.

In *La ceinture dorée* and *Un beau mariage* the economic relations of the French conception of marriage are pointedly discussed, but the plays naturally appeal less to the foreign reader.

Now follows at length that great and terrible series, *Les lionnes pauvres, Les effrontés, Le fils de Giboyer,* in which lust of wealth is shown to be the corrupter of society; and *La contagion* and *Les lions et renards,* in which the hideous cynicism is presented to us, which derives from the plutocratic ideal, such as will, if left to itself, utterly destroy society. Creations like Séraphine, Vermouillet, Giboyer and d'Estrigaud are in themselves sufficient witness to the genius of Augier. We shudder when we think of them, and yet it is rare that we are not made to understand all, and therefore pardon all, before we reach the end of any play.

The situation of *Les effrontés* is simple. M. Charrier is a respectable banker, whose fortune is accumulating to buy a career for his son Henri, and a fine marriage for his daughter Clemence. He failed once, many years back, and there are outstanding outlawed debts, of which nobody knows except Vermouillet, a speculative bankrupt, who scorns all honest folk, and buys a newspaper with which to exploit Charrier's dishonorable secret and, if possible, obtain his daughter in marriage.

We meet two newspaper men—Sergine, the honest editor, and Giboyer, the hired pen, disillusioned, cynical, at bottom hating himself for his venality, but feigning a sinister indifference. When Vermouillet has bought the paper, Sergine resigns his post as editor. "When one cannot drive out from the Temple those who buy and sell in it then—one gets out oneself." To which Giboyer retorts: "Heavens, he is honest! I wonder what he is paid for the pose?" In the end, Charrier acknowledges his outlawed debts, thus destroying the power of the blackmailer, in order to keep the respect of his son, Henri, who will join the army, since, strange to say, poor, unsophisticated youth, he prefers poverty to his father's dishonor.

Such is our introduction into that venal world of the Second Napoleon. Clearly its ideal is "Wealth without Work." Worldly success is the *summum bonum.* "How can one help feeling a certain respect for the owners of so many beautiful things? Riches are a kind of power, whose sacramental sign is luxury" (*La contagion*). "The world does not bow before the people it esteems, but rather before those it envies. Riches or notoriety, these are for the world everything" (*La contagion*). Now, great wealth cannot be had, of course, without work. Therefore the wise man will exploit the workers, or those who are already possessed of wealth and are losing their grip of it; or, last and best of all, exploit the Government, which means has the advantage, besides, of bringing to the exploiter the rewards of patriotism. Now, to work the worker is hard work; therefore the truly wise will exclude that difficult method of "getting on." He will settle down to exploiting the idle wealthy by shameful service, by pandering or flattery; or he will blackmail them, being cognizant of their secret vice. Similarly, the wise man will become a political parasite; malfeasance in office on the the part of the powerful, which is carefully veiled politically and socially, may be delicately looked into, lifting, on the sly, a corner of the snow-white coverlet of respectability. If one's mood be more courageous, one may buy iniquitous special privileges, taxing the public for their good. Or one may wriggle through the loopholes in the laws, carefully provided by hired legal talent of the first order, at the season when the song of the lobbyist is in the land. Of course, one is apt to think; and he who is "to get on" must not think overmuch,—at least not along certain old-fashioned lines. So commercial integrity is a joke, and civic virtue a stuffed specimen of an extinct species at the museum. As for public opinion (which is, of course, the voice of God), it can be manufactured, if one discreetly invests. The majority of the stock of all the principal newspapers can be held by a sort of loose association of rogues (understood, of course, to be successful gentlemen of high standing), who exchange favors (in which, to be sure, money is no consideration), and then the miracle always happens: the voice of God thunders, it "booms" and "boosts," "slams" and "lambasts," coos and purrs, marvelously to order,—nay, rather as if to order,—for of course it is the spontaneous, mystical, esoteric voice of God, which in turn creates that external, exoteric, obvious, irresistible voice of God,—Public Opinion!

But is there no honest remnant by way of public opinion? Certainly. There are those who play the game and understand not the rules; who merely watch the play of the "big fellows," and do likewise. So, also, in the matters of thought and opinion, honest little folk and honest little journals are beyond dispute constitutionally honest; but they somehow catch the infection, and honestly side with the rogues, who are so eminently respectable, and they honestly quote their "great contemporaries," who are so notably competent in the gathering of news and the forming of judicious opinions! Besides, most hitherto honest

men are cautious how they offend the unexposed rogue. Honest men rarely help, and rogues often hinder, the private devices of honest men. Besides, who knows but that we shall have our turn at the swag? Hence, "everybody" is covertly with the exploiters of the public purse, as each expects vaguely that his opportunity may come along soon,—or that of his uncle or his cousin or brother-in-law,—and it's all in the family, don't you know?

In such a society, everything is for sale,—friendship, love, religion,—not to mention glory and social standing! And is there any hope for such a society? Yes, and, what is more, the hopes are two: There is the comic hope, and there is the tragic hope. The comic hope is,—thoroughgoing, excoriating ridicule, tempered with enough good humor and kindliness to conciliate those in whom some little honesty survives. To this kindlier hope Emile Augier makes his brave appeal. But there is another, to which appeal must be made in event of failure. When comedy on the boards cannot preach effectively, then tragedy must stalk the streets and public squares. "Calamity! calamity!" to reënthrone the hero, necessitating courageous action, without a doubt, without discussion. As early as *Le gendre de M. Poirier,* Augier writes these words: "It is rest to the soul, to get one's life ordered ahead without possible discussion, or room for regret." (The speaker alludes to military discipline.) "Only from this tyrannical scheduling of life can you derive a sincerely careless gaiety. You know your duty, you do it, and you are content." Again, "The first cannon ball will shatter all your cynical jests, and the flag will no more be a rag at the top of a pole." . . . When the royalist nobleman is sarcastically rebuked: " 'Enthusiasm for a flag that is not your own?' 'Bah!' retorts he, 'You won't catch the color of the flag through the smoke of the powder.' "

In *La contagion,* four years before the prophecy is fulfilled, Augier makes his honest man cry out: "Good-bye, gentlemen, and farewell! Conscience? Duties? Family? Trample under the hoofs of your herded cattle all that is good and holy! But mark me, a day is coming when the truths that have been jeered at and hooted will be affirmed with a roar of thunder. Good-bye, gentlemen. I am not one of your set."

Clearly it is a case with Augier of kill or cure; cure with comedy, or trust providence to kill, and God—for a resurrection! Augier is a prophet like Hugo. And who is the great utterer of that period? Hugo, who saw things melodramatically from a distance, magnified and out of perspective, and gave us his immortal *Les châtiments,* or Emile Augier with his noble series of satiric plays, silenced by the fulfillment of his prophet's prediction? For after the Franco-Prussian War be it noted the gracious Augier thundered no more.

But to return to our series. If *Les effrontés* introduced us to this decadent world of the Second Empire, *Le fils de Giboyer* makes us understand many things and shows us perhaps for the first time the pathos of corruption. Giboyer has sold his conscience, first to maintain his father; then to rear as an honest man his son, Maximilien Gérard. He has never acknowledged this son, whom he adores, lest his father's example and reputation should injure him. "I

The characters Vernouillet and Giboyer from Augier's Les effrontes.

shall make of Maximilien what I never could be—an honorable and an honored man. It's my fad to serve as manure, enriching the soil, that a certain lily be nourished to perfect beauty. Isn't my fad as good as that of another?" Again Giboyer expresses himself: "I have written a book that contains all my experience—all my own ideas. I think it is good, and what's more—true. I am proud of it. It is a sufficient excuse for my life. But I sha'n't publish it with my name, for fear my name might not unjustly discredit it."

Now this poor Giboyer, this pathetic "game-bagger," serves as the *deus in machina* of **Le fils de Giboyer,** which perhaps is the most charming of the series under discussion. His foil and dupe is Marechal, who can best be described by his own words in pompous soliloquy: "There will soon be nothing sacred on earth; no way of enjoying one's fortune in peace—so that the people *must* have *a* religion" (contemplating himself as the chosen parliamentary tool of the nobility)—"I am born for an orator; see, I have the voice! The personal presence! Gestures! All the gifts a man can't acquire! As for the rest"—(Looking at the speech made by Giboyer and lying on the table)—"that can be learned by heart." After a few bars of the music, Giboyer interrupts himself: "Ha, what a speech! It almost kindles the fire of conviction in myself!"

The plot of our play is ingenious and yet very simple. The speech Giboyer has written for Marechal converts or rather perverts Maximilien. "It distresses me like all reasoning to which you can make no valid answer, but against which nevertheless a deep-seated feeling protests." So Giboyer, to save his son intellectually and politically, confesses to him that he wrote the speech himself. An intrigue robs Marechal before public delivery of the speech, and Giboyer provides another expressing this time his real opinions, which speech he pretends to have been written by Maximilien, and with which Marechal makes a tremendous, unexpected success. Then Giboyer holds over Marechal the secret of the speech, and so obtains his consent

for the marriage of the politician's daughter to Maximilien. It is in vain that Maximilien protests to his father, whom he now knows. "What right can you have to render me dishonorable services?" "Ah, my boy," replies Giboyer, "to keep you, my son, from temptation, to keep you clean and honorable. I began . . . for my father." Maximilien interrupts. "And so now you continue at it for your son?" (Maximilien aside)—"Heaven, I am his virtue." Giboyer returns to the victorious assault. "Grant me this one only boon, my son, to see you happy." Here let the curtain drop. (pp. 12-22)

Granted a society as thoroughly corrupt as that of Napoleon the Third's regime, it is clear there will have to be some sort of cynic philosophy in the mouth of every one for justification at the secret judgment-bar of his neighbor's conscience. However we may acquit ourselves, we know that the spectator—even the friendliest—views our conduct with wholly impartial alien eyes, and penetrates to the core of the mystery—or rather, mystification. For this purpose of throwing dust in the eyes of our interested neighbor, since he is doubtless an indifferent philosopher, no philosophy will serve as such. The antidote to the divine comic is, from the hellish point of view, devilish laughter—in a word the cynic jeer, the jest of unbelief, the vicious caricature of honor and virtue, flippantly light or sardonic—*la blague.* **La contagion** gives us a definition of this devilish laughter in the dialogue of Lucien, the disciple of the villain d'Estrigaud and the tenacious conservative Tenancier:

> LUCIEN. It is a kind of wit—a very modern kind. It is due to a reaction against the emphatic iterations of the commonplace in which our fathers so freely indulged. Yes, they have so used and abused the fine phrases, till these have become a cant, that disgusts us young men of today.

> TENANCIER. So much the worse for you, sir. Fine phrases express fine sentiments. Fatigue with the former soon degenerates into distaste for the latter. What you most delight in covering with ridicule is virtue, enthusiasm, or for the matter of that, any definite convictions. Oh, of course, you don't profess disbelief. Heaven forfend! You don't rise above mere indifference. Anything beyond is in your eyes pedantry. This abominable jesting spirit plays a greater part in lowering the moral level than is generally supposed. Your *blague* is after all nothing more nor less than derision of whatever uplifts the spirit. No school that, for honest men and good citizens. One begins, of course, by being better than one lets on, and then by degrees one is as bad or even worse.

In the course of the play we see Lucien receiving lessons in the art of devilish laughter from the initiate d'Estrigaud. Before the pupil is set up for worship the gilded image of the great king—the traditional Sardanapalus. Lucien holds up his hands in devout astonishment at this masterstroke of genius: "How horribly, how deliciously immoral!" To which d'Estrigaud with a soothing gesture replies: "Oh, no, my boy; just the inevitable logical conclusion, drawn gently from our premises. Of all the sages and worthies of antiquity Sardanapalus is the only one who was endowed with common sense. Compare, for instance, his death with that of Socrates. The one dies pitiably in obedience to the law—the death of a pedantic schoolmaster. The other, like the sublime rebel he was, makes of his palace a funeral pyre, and takes along with him all his delights of which Fate thought to deprive him in the end."

So Augier shows us that the spirit of *la blague* sneering at all unselfishness, all devotion, as callow, silly, absurd, since more or less altruistic, ultimately leads its professors to glorify the vices, pursued and adored as perverse virtues—yes, will even induce on their behalf a devilish enthusiasm, wholly unmindful of self-interest, a devotion to the preposterous, to the criminally magnificent and megalomaniac. Tenancier clearly diagnoses the case: "In order to be caught by fine phrases—by cant as you call it—all that seems to be necessary is that the spirit of the fine phrases prove sufficiently ignoble and dishonorable. Ah, how pitiful! How pitiful!"

In the course of our play the innocent young man, André, is saved by the supervention of a moment's seriousness, as the thought of his mother's supposed shame smote him between the eyes and he awoke to behold the abyss at his very feet.

D'Estrigaud, the incarnation of this evil spirit of detraction and derision, is finally thwarted in *La contagion.* Poetic justice is made to vindicate virtue. This, as a lover of pure comic art, one cannot but regret. Yet no sane critic will over-much blame Augier. If Molière could not trust his audience (including such men as Fenelon), and posterity (with its Rousseaus), to catch the drift of his great satire on the hypocrite done in the cause of sincere piety; if in order to have *Tartuffe* played at all Molière had to resort to the crude device of introducing Louis XIV in the last act as *deus ex machina,* to set all things right by the punishment of the infamous hypocrite; clearly Augier, the less gifted disciple of Molière, having no *Grand Monarque* to side with his masterpiece, to help him out at the last curtain, or to exercise his influence among the hostile *beau monde,* clearly Augier must bow to the will of the Philistine theatre-goer. Really d'Estrigaud should not have been thwarted. He should have been allowed to compass his ruin, by the total extinction of the divine spark in himself. He should have been damned, not punished. His absolute success in depravity would have been a truer damnation ethically, because truer psychologically, and more consistent comically. In plain terms the moral question at issue is so awfully serious to Augier and his audience, that they cannot let the comic Dionysus settle it in his own characteristic and artistic way; the pedagogue and the law-giver must intrude with pointing pole and chastising rod. So there is really no laughter at the expense of d'Estrigaud. He serves like the devils in those Alpine pilgrimages, to which Browning alludes so deliciously, intended to convince the peasant of his righteous devotion by giving an outlet to his energy, in well-aimed mud-slinging—the more mud slung at the depicted devil the holier his soul! It is a pity that human nature has not yet reached that point of development where it can allow the spirit of pure art to draw in sweet equanimity the conclusions from its premises. So Ben Jonson's Fox must meet with condign

legal punishment, and d'Estrigaud must be defeated by the mechanical workings of the plot. The more's the pity, we repeat; because as a consequence the interest of *La contagion* lies chiefly in the logical exposition of the character of d'Estrigaud, while the comedy resides, on the other hand, chiefly in the playwright's intrigue. So the comic spirit and the dramatic interest do not make one common impact, and the work remains from the point of view of the highest art, a *torso*—headless, therefore brainless—provided with artificial limbs of dramaturgic cork!

Looking back over the work of Augier as a whole, we cannot but feel that whatever else he did or did not do, he answered effectively all the calumnies directed by the Puritans of all time against the Stage as an institution. His satiric dramas at least are lofty in spirit, dignified in style, sententious and stern. They exhibit a compact structure—a familiar yet tersely significant dialogue—and a dexterous stage technique. Nothing is lacking to put Augier among the greatest save only enough of that *vis comica,* that vivacious brilliancy, of Aristophanes and Molière, or of that *saeva indignatio* of Juvenal, the Old Testament prophets, of Dante and Swift, and of Hugo at his best. Had either or both of these gifts been granted him, we should not reckon Augier among the great French Comic dramatists, but rather among the score or so of World Geniuses. As it is, all honor to him and all gratitude. (pp. 22-6)

William Norman Guthrie, "Emile Augier," in
The Drama, *Chicago, No. 4, November, 1911,*
pp. 3-26.

Barrett H. Clark   (essay date 1915)

[*Clark was an American drama critic and editor who regularly contributed to various literary magazines including* Drama. *In the following excerpt, he traces the development of Augier's portrayal of social issues from his early harsh judgments in* Gabrielle *and* Le mariage d'Olympe *to the more tolerant stance demonstrated in* Madame Caverlet *and* Les Fourchambault.]

There is so much matter in the dramatic works of Augier which does not properly fall within the scope of the theater, that the casual reader may infer, incorrectly, that Augier was more of a social reformer and champion of the home and fatherland than a man of the theater. True it is that in practically all his plays he attacks some form of social or political corruption, and stands forth to do battle in behalf of the domestic virtues. He condemns political trickery; he aims his shafts at the prostitute honored as a wife and mother, trying to break her way into the homes and families of the respectable; he ruthlessly flays all forms of marital infidelity; and he enters fearlessly the arena in questions of divorce and marriage—but with all this, he is primarily a dramatist. His works are plays, as time has proved. Augier does not, however, take a subject at hazard, as Pinero often does, and then write a play; nor does he, as is usual with his disciple, Brieux, write his play to fit a thesis: his themes evolve naturally out of the fable, with the apparent unconsciousness of art. He is deeply concerned with the vices and virtues of mankind, but rarely does he allow his convictions to warp the dramatic texture of his plays. Rarely, too, is he so fearlessly didactic as his fellow-playwright, Dumas *fils.* Augier has been compared with Molière; it is as a man of the theater and a painter of character that the analogy holds.

Augier's début was made with a graceful comedy in two acts: *Le ciguë.* This is in verse, and recounts the story of a repentant debauchee. His next play, *Un homme de bien,* likewise in verse, in spite of its hesitancy in the development of plot and the delineation of character, indicates the path which Augier was to tread; here [according to Henry Gaillard de Champris in his *Émile Augier et la comédie sociale*] he "manifests his intention for the first time to paint a picture of contemporary life, and attack the customs of the day—in short, to write a social comedy."

But Augier did not at once enter into and develop his new manner. During the next few years, he continued to write verse plays in which the thesis was more or less prominent. *L'aventurière, Gabrielle, Le joueur de flute, Diane, Philiberte,* and *Paul Forestier* are primarily comedies in which the purely dramatic element predominates, although *L'aventurière* and *Gabrielle* are a closer approximation to the later manner than the others.

L'aventurière is a modern play in spite of the fact that the scene is laid in the Italian Renaissance. It tells the story of an adventuress who has managed to get into the good graces of a rich merchant of Padua. He is about to give up friends and family for the woman, when his son, who has been away for ten years, appears upon the scene. Assuming a disguise, he reveals the true character of Clorinde to his father and effects a breaking-off of their relationship. The father and family are saved and the repentant woman goes into a convent.

If in *L'aventurière* Augier was still undecided as to the means of expression best fitted to his temperament, or as to the purpose to which his powers were to be put, in *Le mariage d'Olympe,* six years later, he found his most forceful and realistic manner. Meantime, there is one play, forming a connecting link between the wavering *L'aventurière* and *Olympe. Gabrielle* is, in spite of its poetic form, a realistic play. The husband who labors hard for wife and family, the wife who is bored and seeks a fuller realization of self in the husband's friend—this is a familiar situation. But it should be borne in mind that a serious treatment of such a story was, sixty-five years ago, something of a departure. Scribe's stock in trade was the ménage à trois, but infidelity with him was always a subject for comedy. Augier's play then was a challenge, both to the Romanticists and the "Vaudevillistes." When Julien Chabrière opens the eyes of his wife and her would-be lover to the dangers and miseries of their projected step, the lover goes away and Gabrielle, falling to her knees before her husband, speaks the celebrated line:

> "O père de famille! O poète, je t'aime!"

Leaving the realm of poetic comedy, with its attached "moral" and more or less optimistic dénouement, in 1854 Augier threw the gauntlet in the face of the Romanticists who applauded *La dame aux camélias* of Dumas *fils*—commonly known in English as *Camille.* A curious change in public taste and manners had allowed large numbers of demi-mondaines to assume a place of distinction and honor in the social life of the day. This was due perhaps to the numerous political transformations which France was at the time undergoing, as well as to the spreading of the ideas of the Romantic school of art and literature. When, in 1852, Dumas *fils* made a prostitute the sympathetic heroine of a play, and brought forward the doctrine that "she will be forgiven because she has loved deeply" a feeling of revolt awoke in the breast of Augier, and he wrote *Le mariage d'Olympe.* This is one of the most directly didactic of all his works; it was aimed primarily against the "Reign of the courtesan." He says, in short, that such women as Olympe Taverny do undoubtedly exist, that the men are at fault as much as the women for that fact; possibly he even secretly sympathizes with her, but he denies her the right to marry into good families. When the Marquis de Puygiron shoots Olympe, after endeavoring to force her to give up the family name which she has stolen, declaring that God is his judge, Augier issues his final word on the question.

Le mariage d'Olympe, a play with a purpose, stands apart for that reason from the great mass of Augier's plays. In the three short and well-built acts, the author has merely sketched his characters; every effort has been bent on the idea, the facts, the thesis. Just so much of characterization as is needed to carry the story is given. The admirable and disgusting scene which closes the second act is one of the most trenchant and poignant which ever came from this dramatist's pen. Nowadays, even after Zola and Becque and the Théâtre Libre dramatists, it strikes a note of horror. How it must have shocked an audience of the fifties!

Although the play failed, it aroused considerable discussion and a good deal of adverse criticism. Still, its importance in the dramatic and intellectual development of the dramatist was great. It was his first straightforward declaration of independence. From 1854 on, he followed the path he had himself opened with this early play.

"The Reign of the Courtesan" was not ended by the plays of the day, but Augier did not cease for that reason in his attempts to check its influence. Twelve years after *Le mariage d'Olympe* he wrote *La contagion.* The development of society and its relation to the fallen woman may be clearly traced by a comparative study of *L'aventurière, Le mariage d'Olympe,* and *La contagion.* In the first play, the woman is merely an exception, an adventuress who happened to "break into" society and a good family. In *Le mariage d'Olympe* she is a demimondaine who has carefully planned to obtain for herself, at any cost, a noble name. But she is checked in time—by a pistol-shot. Twelve years later the Olympes and Clorindes are no longer exceptions; the rehabilitated courtesan has triumphed. By skilful manipulation she has insinuated her way into a position of equality with that of the respected mother and wife, and has even begun to corrupt her. "The consequences" [of this triumph of the courtesan], says De Champris,

> were deplorable. As a result of hearing of these 'ladies,' of reading about them in the newspapers, of seeing their gorgeous equipages, of passing their pretty homes, applauding them on the

stage or admiring their silhouettes in the fashion magazines, society women fell a prey to contradictory feelings and ideas: the resentment at being occasionally deserted for these women, the curiosity to know these enemies, so far away yet so near, the wish to rival them, furnished them with weapons, perhaps even a certain desire for forbidden fruit, and gave birth to a regret at being forced to pay for a reputation in society which entailed so rigid a restraint. For these various reasons, many honest women played the part of demi-mondaines.

This was the contagion against which Augier raised his voice. The clever and diabolical Navarette, mistress of a wealthy man of the world, succeeds in ruining her lover and bringing his family to her feet. By subtle scheming she compromises the Baron d'Estrigaud's married sister, is witness of her infidelity, and finally succeeds in holding the entire family at her mercy.

A pistol-shot will do no good here: the evil has gone too far; society itself is corrupted. The woman, successfully rehabilitated, rich, held in high esteem, has at least attained that position for which she has striven.

The war of 1870 and the fall of the Empire put a stop to the particular state of affairs which Augier had fought against. Rarely in his later plays (except in *Jean de Thommeray*) did he again attack the question. To Brieux and Hervieu and François de Curel he left the work of analyzing deeper motives and making a study of the various ramifications, some of which were still invisible in Augier's day—but this is current history.

The three plays which have just been discussed are sufficient to show that Augier is the staunch champion of the family and the home. His hatred of the prostitute is not so much a matter of personal feeling as a social one. Whether or not he believes in what is now known as segregated vice or whether as a man he was occasionally lenient in matters of sex, is beside the question: he saw that the home, of all institutions in France the most important, was threatened by a fearful invasion, and he did his best to put an end to it.

It will be seen that Augier's plays so far considered, are not in chronological order. *L'aventurière, Le mariage d'Olympe,* and *La contagion,* have been grouped together for the purpose of observing a particular trend in the thought of the author. Meantime, such widely different plays as *Philiberte, La pierre de touche, Le gendre de M. Poirier,* and *Les effrontés* made their appearance.

Gabrielle was the first play to treat of a more insidious evil, a greater danger to the home, which Augier was ever so eager to protect: conjugal infidelity. After the comparatively timid *Gabrielle* came *Les lionnes pauvres,* which stands in much the same relation to the earlier play as *Le mariage d'Olympe* did to *L'Aventurière.* Here again is the story of a woman whom the love of luxury, too much idleness, and a natural penchant, lead to take a lover. The honest and industrious husband is long kept in ignorance of the fact, believing that his wife's expensive clothes are paid for out of her savings. Besides being deceived, in the French sense of the word, he is being partly supported in the meantime by his wife's lover. At last he learns the truth, and is even willing to forgive his wife, but when she declares her unwillingness to restore the money given her, on the ground that she is "afraid of poverty," the husband leaves her. He seeks consolation in the home of Thérèse and Léon Lecarmier. Then Thérèse is forced to tell him that her husband, Léon, is Séraphine's lover. Séraphine, then, going the path of least resistance, decides to remain a kept woman. Thenceforth she joins the ranks of Olympe and Navarette.

Augier's sanity, his healthy attitude toward humanity, his belief in the eternal rightness of things, could not long remain obscured by the temporary pessimism incident to the writing of *Les lionnes pauvres.* In 1858, the same year, he turned to light comedy, and in *La jeunesse* produced a genial if somewhat conventional play. In spite of its thesis—that money is an evil, especially in the case where young people are forced into marriages of convenience—it can scarcely be classed among the important social plays. It marks a return to the earlier manner.

The question of money, lightly touched upon in *La jeunesse,* is the second of the important problems which is intimately concerned with the welfare of the family and the home. From this time on, sex and money are to assume a position in the front rank of Augier's work.

Closely allied in spirit with *La jeunesse* is *Un beau mariage.* The question, should a poor man marry a rich wife? is handled with keen insight, and answered in the negative. Pierre Chambaud, a poor young chemist, marries the rich Clémentine Bernier, whose mother, possessing nearly all the money, literally supports the daughter and her husband. Pierre soon becomes a mere figure-head in his own house and, as a result of the social ambitions of his wife and mother-in-law, is forced to give up his scientific pursuits. Soon losing the love and respect of the two women, he complains to them, and is made to feel more keenly than ever the utter degradation of his position. A certain Marquis de la Roche-Pingolley has been over-assiduous in his attentions to Pierre's mother-in-law. When Pierre demands that the Marquis either marry Madame Bernier or cease his visits, he is humiliated once again by being told by his mother-in-law that the Marquis is in *her* home. Receiving no help or sympathy from his wife, he goes to live with his friend, Michel Ducaine, to work out an experiment which, if successful, will revolutionize science and render him celebrated. Fearful of the scandal and inconvenience of a separation, Clémentine sends the Marquis to Pierre in order to effect a reconciliation. Pierre is willing to return to his wife, but only on the condition that the mother-in-law is to have nothing to do with them. Preparatory to making his final experiment, which, we are told, will either kill Pierre or make him a successful man, he sends a letter to his wife. Clémentine arrives at the laboratory just in time to be with her husband in the hour of danger. She has somehow come to see his real worth and is willing to sacrifice comfort and luxury for his sake. She hides during the experiment, and when the seven minutes necessary for its consummation are at an end, she cries "Saved!" and falls into Pierre's arms:

"Oh, Pierre, my love, my life! We might have died together! But you are given to me again! What happiness! God is good! How I love you! Forgive me! I thought you were a coward, I thought you were base, and I hated you! Now I adore you! Oh, courage, oh, genius! Forgive your comrade, your handmaid!"

The last act shows a pretty picture of Pierre and Clémentine at home; she is the incarnation of domesticity, and he, of independence and happiness. The mother-in-law, distracted at not being able to help the couple, ends by purchasing Pierre's discovery. The play's weakness is so flagrant as hardly to call for further comment. With so good a theme the dramatist ought surely to have developed a more credible story, and sought a more logical dénouement. To begin with, his thesis was irretrievably weakened by making Clémentine the sort of woman she was. If, during the entire struggle with his wife and her mother, Pierre had once received some sign of sympathy from Clémentine, we might have hoped and looked for her ultimate change, but when, having stood throughout against him, she finally does go to him and, at the risk of her life, stands at his side during the experiment, and then—*after* his experiment succeeds—falls into his arms, and forever after mends his clothes, we cannot doubt that we have to do with melodrama. Had Clémentine at first been in earnest and made an honest endeavor to understand Pierre, and then gradually been corrupted by her mother and her mother's money, and then eventually been made to see the good qualities in Pierre, we might have believed. As it is, the last two acts spoil the play.

Technically, *Un beau mariage* is important. A man of science as a serious stage-figure, a hero in fact, was a decided novelty in the 'fifties, and, if the play accomplished nothing else, it at least opened the way for the moderns, and broadened the field of the theater. Possibly the doctors and other scientists in the plays of Brieux and Hervieu and Curel owe something to the earnest treatment of the chemist in this early play of Augier.

Ceinture dorée is little more than an expanded fable; it might well be termed Tainted Money. The rich merchant Roussel has an only daughter, Caliste, who seeks among numerous suitors for her hand one who cares nothing for her money. Finally, M. de Tirélan makes his appearance, and Roussel offers to make him his son-in-law. But Tirélan, whose father has been ruined in business by Roussel, and who has scruples against marrying for money, refuses. Roussel swallows the insult, Tirélan decides to go away, and Roussel turns to another suitor. This one Caliste is about to accept when she learns that Tirélan really loves her and will not ask for her hand because of her money. Meantime, Roussel has been particularly sensitive to allusions to the source of his fortune, and this susceptibility finally assumes the form of monomania. Again Roussel makes overtures to Tirélan and offers to restore the money which he took from the young man's father. He is again refused. The knot is cut at last when it is learned that Roussel is ruined by unwise speculation. Tirélan is at last free to declare his love to Caliste; he can marry her now that the barrier of fortune is removed.

The play is so light that it hardly deserves a place among the serious works of Augier. Yet in its own way it constitutes a further document upon the social system in which hard cash plays so large and important a rôle.

To turn from the idealistic and timid *Ceinture dorée* to *Les effrontés* is to realize in the most forceful manner the extreme poles of the genius of Emile Augier. The earlier play appears little other than the work of a dilettante beside the later. *Les effrontés* is a compact yet varied picture of manners, in which the principal portrait is the parvenu Vernouillet, a vulgar, unscrupulous journalist with money and a vast amount of aplomb, or "nerve." Respected by one, he is held in fear by all, for he is influential and rich.

Politically, socially, dramatically, *Les effrontés* is a work of the first importance. It was the first play to treat in a realistic manner the power of the press and to paint a truly modern villain. Says Vernouillet: "I have put my money to the only use to which it has not hitherto been put: making public opinion. I have in my hands the two powers which the Empire has always disrupted: money and the press. Each helps the other. I open up new roads to them; I am in fact making a revolution." Although *Les effrontés* is at the same time a comedy of character and manners, with a complicated intrigue and a love story, it was in its day considered mainly as an attack on the press. But what was not realized so clearly in the many heated discussions aroused by the piece, was that Augier was not so much concerned with the actual state of the press—which was and is bad enough—but with the power which the press, backed by money, may exert. His purpose was larger; it was humanitarian.

Again he had enlarged the scope of the theater, and given the stage a figure which is today one of the most familiar and most often portrayed.

In several of Augier's plays there is a mingling of themes which, while it adds to the atmosphere and interest, often renders any distinct classification of genre, a difficult task. "Money," "Sex," "Politics," and such more or less arbitrary headings are not sufficient to cover more than half of Augier's plays. *Le gendre de M. Poirier,* for example, is a comedy of character, as well as a comedy of sentiment, a picture of the nobility and the bourgeoisie, and a study of the money question. *La pierre de touche,* and *Maître Guérin,* although they are not so unified as *Le mariage d'Olympe,* may still be satisfactorily classified under the heading of "Money." The first is another of the lighter plays with a "moral"; it shows the evil results of the acquisition of large sums of money by those who do not know its proper uses; the second is a study in the character of a bourgeois merchant.

Les éffrontés has been classed among the works of Augier in which money was shown to be at the base of a great part of the evils of the social system. It is likewise one of the three political plays, of which the others are *Le fils de Giboyer* and *Lions et renards.*

Le fils de Giboyer was for the French of the day what was called an anti-clerical play. The Jesuits as politicians were attacked, or believed themselves to be, so that national discussions and conflicts arose, and bitter counter-attacks were made on the author and what was supposed to be his party. Augier denies that his play is political; he declares that it deals with society in a general way. As a story of father and son it indubitably suffers from what now appears as a great deal of topical and contemporaneous discussion, but that is rather the fault of the times and of the subject. The clever but unscrupulous bohemian scribbler, Giboyer—who, together with his protector D'Auberive, was one of the principal characters in *Les effrontés*—has sold himself to the rich Marquis. Through political intrigues, hypocrisy, venality of the basest kind, Giboyer makes his way, until at last through his love for his son, his designated successor, he undergoes a moral rehabilitation. Though the psychology of the transformation may be true enough, and though it would doubtless have been more credible had it been developed at greater length by a novelist like Balzac or George Eliot, somehow we cannot believe in the sudden change, and are prone to ask how it happens that Giboyer can be redeemed by love for his son any more than could Olympe because Henri once loved her?

Lions et renards is valuable and historically interesting as a comedy of manners and character. It is another attack on the Jesuits. But the complicated intrigue, the occasional obscurity of the motivation, were sufficient to account for the failure of the play.

Augier realized, as Balzac did, that money was the root of much evil, and, in the midst of the social readjustments which France was undergoing in the nineteenth century, he made money one of the greatest of his protagonists. In the struggle between the classes, in the personal relationship of the family, the race for money and power was almost always the prime reason for social degradation and disintegration. Social position is mainly a question of money. Olympe Taverny attempted to climb, and the family suffered; Gabrielle's husband was forced to spend the time he should have had with his wife, in earning the money he thought was supporting her; marriages of love, of inclination, are forced to give way before marriages of convenience, which mean ruin for the home and the family; the press and the Church strive for power, political and financial—the very basis and sinew of politics is cash. France, says Augier, is money-mad, and a nation which forgets what is of supreme importance—family and home and the virtues of old—is heading for destruction.

The remaining important plays are all more or less concerned with money, though sometimes it hovers in the background, only apprehended, and sometimes is obscured by other considerations; but it is always present.

Le gendre de M. Poirier, written in collaboration with Jules Sandeau, is without doubt one of the finest comedies of character ever written. The figure of the *bonhomme* Poirier is one of the memorable figures in dramatic literature. In this play Augier was less concerned with social considerations than was his wont, although money again is the basis for the action. The Marquis de Presles, a ruined member of the aristocracy, has in a way entered into a business pact with Poirier, but the business dealings of the two have been utilized by the authors chiefly as a frame in which to depict and contrast the nobleman and the bourgeois. The plot is of necessity rather thin: character is the important consideration.

The last three important plays of Augier, written after the war, might possibly be classified under the general headings which we have so far been using, but each, by reason of a comparative novelty of theme, may well be placed apart in different categories. The plays in question are *Jean de Thommeray, Madame Caverlet,* and *Les Fourchambault.* Besides these, there is, however, *Le prix Martin,* written in collaboration with Eugène Labiche, a conventional and amusing little comedy.

Jean de Thommeray written with Jules Sandeau, whose novel of the same name was used as a basis—is a patriotic piece, in which a young aristocrat, succumbing to the demoralizing influences of the capital, finally redeems himself by fighting for the *Patrie.* The value of the play lies in the separate pictures of the life of the aristocratic De Thommerays, rather than in the story. Jean's redemption is not very satisfactorily explained, while the plot is loose and our interest consequently wavering.

Madame Caverlet is a passionate plea in favor of divorce. Again it points out an evil in the social system which militates against the good of the family. Sir Edward Merson and his wife have been separated for a number of years. She has found consolation in the upright and honorable M. Caverlet, with whom, and her two children, she has been living in what is all but a legal state of marriage. When the daughter, however, is about to marry, Caverlet and "Madame Caverlet" confess to the suitor's father the truth of the case, and the proposed marriage is broken off without delay. Merson then appears, demands his son and daughter, forces Caverlet to go away, and threatens to break up the family until he is offered a large sum of money to go to Switzerland and there become a citizen. This ameliorates the situation, as the wife can then obtain a divorce and become the lawful wife of Caverlet. But Henri, the son, completely disillusioned, joins the army and goes to a foreign country. The marriage then takes place.

We can but feel that Augier's case would have been stronger had he not loaded the dice. If Merson had really cared more for his wife than for her money, and had he insisted on his rights, then the injustice of the law and its bitter consequences would have been more strikingly proved. Had Augier, as Hervieu did in *La loi de l'homme,* pushed his thesis to its logical conclusion, we should have had a more touchingly poignant play, as well as a stronger plea for divorce.

Les Fourchambault is the last play of Emile Augier. In structure, in character analysis, it shows no diminution in the dramatist's powers; it is indeed a proof of his deepening sympathy and broader understanding of human life; it shows a brighter optimism and a more deep-rooted faith in the basic goodness of humanity. Viewed from a strictly logical angle, the play may seem reactionary if not contradictory, yet the young man in the early 'fifties denouncing the fallen Olympes and Clorindes and Navarettes, had with increasing years come to realize that there were exceptions in life, that human nature cannot always be evil. Leaving aside particular questions of the day, wishing to attack no specific institution, law, or social wrong, he bases his play on frailty and human goodness, infusing the whole with a generous portion of good and kindly humor and gentle satire. Madame Fourchambault is after all only silly and weak, not criminally ambitious. Léopold, too, is weak, like his father, not wicked. Madame Bernard, though she once sinned, has redeemed her error by a life of service. Marie and Bernard are almost too good. If a criticism may be urged, it is that the play is too kindly and optimistic. Bernard's and Marie's rhapsody on marriage is a little too much like a sermon. This play is Augier's idealistic swan-song. It seems that, tired of attacking, worn out by the sight of vice and stupidity, he was prompted, in his old age, to raise up an ideal of virtue, and make that ideal triumph over evil.

Augier is the Balzac of the French stage of the last century: his power of observation, his common sense, his straightforward and honest way of speaking the truth, the great extent and variety of his work, bring him into closer relationship with the great novelist than any other dramatist of his time. Considered as a moralist or social reformer, as exponent of the domestic virtues, as champion of the fireside, he is of great importance, but as a painter of the life of his time, of the bourgeoisie as well as of the aristocracy, as a literary artist depicting living men and women, he occupies a position in French literature and drama as sure, though possibly not so exalted, as that of Molière and Balzac. (pp. 440-57)

> *Barrett H. Clark, "Emile Augier," in* The Drama, *Chicago, No. 19, August, 1915, pp. 440-58.*

Benjamin W. Wells   (essay date 1920)

[*In the following summary of Augier's works, Wells contends that* Le fils de Giboyer *represents the pinnacle of Augier's playwriting career.*]

Le fils de Giboyer has been called by the famous critic Laube, "a picture of modern French society in its free struggle between a decaying aristocracy, a vain bourgeoisie, and a gifted but unprincipled body of men of literary training." Yet this struggle, he continues, "is never described abstractly, but always with scenic fulness and a growing dramatic interest, spiced with sparkling dialogue." It is probably the strongest play of its author, but to be fully appreciated it must be judged in connection with **Les effrontés** which preceded, and with **La contagion** and **Lions et renards** which followed it, for several of its characters reappear in them. This group, however, itself presents but one phase of Augier's dramatic development, which may be briefly reviewed before proceeding to a more detailed study of [**Le fils de Giboyer**].

Émile Augier was born in 1820 and died in 1889. He began life as a lawyer, but he says in one of his plays that he found this profession *un triste harnais,* and after some unsuccessful dramatic essays he enrolled himself among the disciples of the then popular Ponsard, and he certainly profited by that dramatist's technical instruction, though it was not till he had emancipated himself from this false classicism that he produced work worthy of remembrance. From **L'aventurière** in 1848 to **Philiberte** in 1853 his dramas, except for the **Flute Player,** which was almost

certainly written earlier, show Augier as the champion "of the average and conventional ethics that knows how to ally the calculation of interest to the language of sentiment," which after all was not such a very bad thing, especially after the literary debauches of romanticism. These plays are essentially domestic comedies, but with **Le gendre de Monsieur Poirier,** which Mr. Brander Matthews does not hesitate to call the finest French comedy since Beaumarchais' *Marriage of Figaro* [see excerpt dated 1880], Augier entered the field of social satire, exposing bourgeois ambition and aristocratic vanity with a genial smile. Then as he turned to the more corroding vices that characterize the society of the Second Empire, and in some measure still characterize that of the Third Republic, his satire grew stronger and more bitter. In **Ceinture dorée** his theme is the Stock Exchange and conventional marriage, in **Le mariage d'Olympe** it is the ill-starred union of a social interloper with a man of noble blood and plebeian instincts. Other phases of French wedded infelicity occupy him in **La jeunesse, Un beau mariage,** and **Les lionnes pauvres.** The last is by far the strongest of the group and contains Augier's greatest female character the "cold, cowardly, and perversely selfish" Séraphine.

In **Les effrontés** Augier turns to wider social questions, to the growth of speculation, the abuses of journalism, and the danger of rearing an educated proletariat who must live by their wits and have not the restraining traditions of social respectability. The central figure of the drama, Vernouillet, has become the type in literature of the scheming speculator and unprincipled journalist. He is helped by Giboyer, a literary pretorian, whose bitter pen is for sale to the highest bidder, and by Marquis d'Auberive, who sees in Vernouillet the most dangerous nightshade blossom of modern democracy, and aristocratically amuses himself, as he says, by fomenting the corruption of the bourgeoisie.

Both Giboyer and the Marquis reappear in **Le fils de Giboyer,** though the former has become more sympathetic, and is indeed the most popular of all Augier's dramatic creations. In him the dramatist has fixed for all time that phase of Rabelais' Panurge and Beaumarchais' Figaro that was naturally evolved from the French Revolution. Beaumarchais' Barber is still unchanged at heart, but he has risen many steps in the social sphere, thanks to democracy and materialism. Our Giboyer is the precocious son of a porter, who has been sent to Paris to secure the imagined benefits of a higher education, and tells his story in **Les effrontés** (iii. 4) in a passage that has become almost as famous as Figaro's own autobiography (*Mariage de Figaro,* v. 3). At any rate, all spectators of **Le fils de Giboyer** knew it, and as it is essential to the understanding of his character I translate it here.

> "As long as school-days lasted I lived in luxury. I carried off all the prizes, and the boarding schools competed for your servant as for a living advertisement; so much so that in the upper class I got by competitive examination a private room and permission to smoke. But I soon had to lower my pretensions. My benefactor offered me a place as school-usher at 600 francs, he suppressed the room, the pipe, and the evening

leaves of absence. I could not stand that, so I dropped teaching and went in for adventures, full of confidence in my powers, and never suspecting that this high road of education in which our fine society lets so many poor devils enter is a no-thoroughfare. . . . Do you know how I lived, I, who could sustain a thesis like Pico of Mirandola, 'on all things knowable'? I was by turns an insurance broker, a stenographer, a book-agent, secretary of a conservative deputy whose speeches I wrote for him, and of a scribbling duke whose books I got into shape, tutor for baccalaureate examinations, editor in chief of the *Weekly Jumping-Jack,* living by my wits, borrowing alms, letting slip some illusion and some prejudice with every five-franc piece; I have reached forty with my vest-pocket empty and my body worn down to the soul."

On the collapse of Vernouillet's journal, Giboyer supports himself and his boy, "le Fils de Giboyer," by various experiments which he recounts in this play (i. 7). He knows that he has been false to honor and probity, a victim to the pathetic belief that half-digested learning will be an "open sesame" to success in life. He has cultivated only his wits, and by them he must live. But he is saved from the extreme consequences of his baseness and rescued to our sympathy by a vein of sentiment, Figaro's *penchant à la sensibilité,* which he shows both in his generous though vague and unpractical socialistic aspirations, and in his intense paternal instinct. In his son he thinks to offer to fate an atoning substitute for his own defection. But, as he pathetically says, "honor costs," and he is obliged to earn his son's respectability by the sacrifice of his own. His devotion goes so far that he is willing wholly to efface himself. The son shall never know as father him for whom he must blush. But at the crisis of our drama filial instinct discovers and rewards paternal love. So the touch of nature that makes the world kin, the tie of blood, redeems the vice of a misguided education.

In the relation of Maximilien and Giboyer there is much that suggests the Fantine and Cosette of Hugo's *Misérables,* and still more Triboulet and his daughter in *Le roi s'amuse.* Giboyer belongs to what Provost-Paradol called "the family of virtuous criminals," the family of Marion de Lorme, of Antony, of the Lady with the Camellias, and their swarming literary progeny. But he is more with them than of them. For while their social tendency had been disintegrating, the central action of this drama is a noble plea for those family bonds that leaven the modern struggle for life. Augier would have us see that it is through the family, through its ties and joys, that the Giboyers of society are to be saved from themselves and society saved from them.

But while this is the central thought of *Le fils de Giboyer,* the framework in which it is set sparkles everywhere with the brightest wit and the keenest satire, which is naturally directed against hypocrisy and cant and their representatives in France, the legitimist and ultramontane reactionaries; for as a rule it is such men who need to buy wit, and who have to buy conscience in order to get it. Literary bravos have always been able to make the best bargains by ministering to such designs and by exploiting such fears. The various types of this once powerful political party are drawn with admirable skill. There is the old aristocrat, Marquis d'Auberive, shrewd and cynical, Baroness Pfeffers a typical Lady Tartufe, Count d'Outreville, mere clay in the hands of political schemers among whom the faintly sketched La Haute-Sarthe reappears as the Fox in *Lions et renards.* But most interesting of all these is Maréchal, the rich bourgeois whom capital has made a timid conservative till wounded vanity reconverts him into a radical again. Less satisfactory are Maréchal's wife and stepdaughter, though it is only just to say that the omission of nine lines, and three verbal changes that seemed called for, have left these essentially minor characters somewhat less significant than Augier made them. By this, however, the drama has suffered no material loss in strength or interest. It still remains a vivid picture of a social struggle that is growing ever fiercer in France, a picture so true to life that this comedy seems likely to be one of the most enduring of our time.

Le fils de Giboyer was followed by *Maître Guérin,* whose central figure is regarded by a French critic as "the most original and clear-cut character that our comedy has given us since Molière's day." But except for this country lawyer, the drama marks a retrogression that was further accentuated in *Paul Forestier.* Then in *La contagion* and in *Lions et renards,* Augier drew a worthy companion to Séraphine, Poirier, and Giboyer: Estrigaud, the stock-gambling *blagueur,* a modern Mephistopheles, mocking duty and virtue and answering every noble aspiration with a sneer, till at last he pays the homage of imitation to his ultramontane adversary's deft unscrupulousness, and so points the author's moral.

With these comedies Augier reached what economists call the stationary state. Neither *Jean de Thommeray* nor *Madame Caverlet* nor *Les Fourchambault* rise to the height of *Giboyer* nor to *Poirier's* serener air. They are too melodramatic, both in subject and treatment. Their author seems to have sacrificed somewhat of his own individuality to the influence of Dumas *fils.* And yet of all the contemporary dramatists of France, Émile Augier is the profoundest student of character, the man who has in him most of the stuff that makes Molière the greatest writer in France. He is not a poet, and of his dramas in verse one need only say that their merit does not lie in their form. At his best, as in the comedy before us, his style is not studied. It abounds in new words and phrases, in the talk of the boulevard and of the boudoir. But even if at times, as Boileau said of Molière, *il fait grimacer ses figures,* yet in a period like ours, bent on substance rather than on form in literature, he takes his natural place among the *classiques populaires* of France, because, as M. Parigot says, "he has the serenity of good sense and reason that is the very basis of classicism," with a perfectly balanced mind and an arch humor that is not pessimistic or destructive, but upbuilding and fortifying. (pp. iii-xi)

Benjamin W. Wells, in an introduction to Le fils de Giboyer *by Emile Augier, Allyn and Bacon, 1920, pp. iii-xi.*

Hugh Allison Smith   (essay date 1925)

[*Smith was an American educator, essayist, and critic who contributed to several periodicals including the* New Republic, Modern Language Journal, *and* France-Amerique. *In the following excerpt, he praises Augier's characters as the richest collection of dramatic depictions in nineteenth-century French drama, and asserts that Augier should be viewed as the finest student of French Realistic social theater.*]

Emile Augier is sometimes given an equal credit and a prior date to those granted to Dumas fils in inaugurating Realistic Social drama. It would be ungrateful to question this claim to honor for a writer who has at least rendered the cause services equally great, if the assumption did not seem to obscure the particular genius of Augier and find contradiction in the dates and real qualities of his plays. Dumas was certainly the pioneer who first explored the realistic field and raised the flag over these new outposts of drama. Not only did Augier lack Dumas's native audacity, but his greater acquaintance with, and affection for, the earlier established forms of the theatre held him back. However, it was he who consolidated most of the positions chosen by Dumas. With his wider experience, his richer training, and especially his breadth, poise and unalterable good sense, he judged and completed the work of his colleague; some of these outposts he rejected as too dangerous, others he reconstructed, and practically all he strengthened, so that if these systems of drama have lasted down to the present day, much of the credit is due to Augier.

It was not until two years after the appearance of *La dame aux camélias*—and five after its composition—that Augier gave his first outright realistic drama, **Le gendre de M. Poirier,** in 1854. Up to that time all his significant plays had been in verse and in the style of the School of Good Sense. No doubt **Gabrielle** is realistic in its details of every-day life, but both its verse form and its adherence to the unities hamper its necessary freedom as a realistic play. Its real significance is its attack on Romantic philosophy; and Augier's verse plays that followed this one during the next four years prove that he might, like Ponsard, have continued longer in this reactionary genre, if it had not been for Dumas's illuminating success in his realistic picture of contemporary society. Augier himself confirms this originality of Dumas both by following his example with **Le gendre de M. Poirier** in 1854, and by attacking his early philosophy with **Le mariage d'Olympe** in 1855.

Our main effort, then, should not be to discover a pioneer of the Realistic Social theatre in Augier, but on the contrary to appreciate in him the finest and most finished product of that school, and at the same time one of the best and most genuine French dramatists of the nineteenth century, whose sincere, virile and solid plays, national in every line, are one of the real assets of French literature and are worthy of appreciation and emulation everywhere.

Augier has been too little known in America and other countries. As has frequently been the case later, we have imported flimsier and more questionable authors and pieces, and then have criticized French morals and literature with these as a basis. Such criticism may be warranted, but before we can use it to set up a superiority of Anglo-Saxon taste or moral standards, we must explain why we pass over the more solid and worthy pieces for the more sensational plays. Augier has had no such public hearing in this country as Dumas, or even as Sardou and Bernstein. Yet among his plays are several of the nearest genuine masterpieces of nineteenth-century realistic French drama, and every one of his twenty-five acknowledged pieces can be read today with pleasure and interest, and often with the maximum profit for their insight into the life and ideals of the French people. Moreover, the moral standards they set are as high, as sincere, and as truly national as any we can predicate as criterions by which to judge other literatures.

Whatever may be our explanation for this and similar neglect on our part—none can fully justify it—it will probably rest on the general principle that the themes and qualities of Augier's dramas are more completely national and less exportable that those of certain other dramatists. His plays are deeply rooted in French soil and life and their subjects deal with the fundamental French virtues. They are defences of the home, the family, the sanctity of marriage and sound morals against the pernicious effects of money, luxury and immorality, and they illustrate the commoner French qualities of labor, economy, sobriety and democracy. Naturally such plays do not offer many startling headlines for the posters of theatrical managers, and their adequate appreciation calls for some knowledge of French life, but they are worth the effort. Moreover, these plays deal with a period of history when French society faced many problems similar to our own today, and the reader of Augier's pieces will constantly be impressed by their contemporary interest.

Augier was born at Valence in the south of France, but at eight years of age came with his family to Paris, where his father bought a notary's practice. He was of good bourgeois stock. At Paris he received a sound education, especially in the classics, and was a solid and even brilliant student. He then entered the law school, and, after his studies there, was placed in a lawyer's office to complete his reading—which he did in the field of literature and the drama.

His contact with gay or Bohemian life, with which Dumas was so familiar, is evidently slight, although one of his biographers relates how the young law student and two of his friends made a figure in these circles about this time, possessed of one dress suit, which they wore by turns, and a single, inalienable gold coin.

From an early age he was drawn to the theatre, and before leaving college had written plays, which he later destroyed. His first published play, **La ciguë,** represented at the Odéon when he was only twenty-four, was quite successful, and from that time he devoted himself entirely to the stage. Nearly all of his plays were well received. It is especially to be noted that his life was a happy and uneventful one. When asked to give his autobiography, he stated that he was born in 1820 and since then nothing had ever happened to him.

Unlike Dumas he had no grudge against society. The key

to his character, however, is his liberal bourgeois spirit. This stands for order and stability and explains his championing of the family as the base of society. The bourgeois is notable for his support of religion and established government, and we note Augier's hostility to the monarchist party. He has some of the restrictions of the bourgeois, but no one of his time saw more clearly the faults and vices of this class. The bourgeois class represents good sense and balance, and Augier avoids extremes; it holds stubbornly to its opinions, is not fond of abstract speculation, and clings to general ideas—those of the majority—and Augier reflects all of this in an enlightened way. In short, he was of the same race as Molière, of the school of good sense and good humor, with conservative leanings, and a liberal spirit.

Augier's dramatic career ran as smoothly as his life, since it was not marked by any startling event or metamorphosis. It is true that his work has been classed in three periods—since all Gaul was divided into three parts few French writers have escaped a similar fate—but to say that he had a verse period, a period of Social drama, and a period of Political-Social satire is very misleading. There is only one real division of his work. His first eight plays are, with one exception, written in verse, and the Classic influence in them is sufficiently marked to include them in the so-called School of Good Sense.

His significant work in the field of realistic prose drama begins with **Le gendre de M. Poirier.** This play, for which a certain credit must also be given to Jules Sandeau, since it is founded on his novel, *Sacs et parchemins,* is Augier's masterpiece, and has often had the honor of being called the model comedy of the nineteenth century.

The theme of the play is the uniting of the two classes, the nobility and the bourgeois, an important problem in France after the Revolution. Augier has treated it with surprising breadth. The Marquis de Presles has the courage, refinement, and liberality of his class, but also the vices—its idleness, its arrogant pride and its contempt for the positive interests of life. The bourgeois in M. Poirier is industrious; he has amassed a fortune by honest diligence. He has common sense and good intentions, a desire for the welfare of himself first, but of society also. But he is vain, and his ambitions make him ridiculous. He is, moreover, too materialistic, and too narrow. The climactic scene of his clash with his son-in-law shows the master hand of Augier.

> GASTON. "Come in then, Hector, come in! Do you know why Jean Gaston de Presles received three crossbow bolts at the battle of Ivry? Do you know why François Gaston de Presles was first in the storming of La Rochelle? Why Louis Gaston de Presles had his ship sunk at La Hogue? Why Philip Gaston de Presles captured two flags at Fontenoy? Why my grandfather was killed at Quiberon? It was so that M. Poirier might some day be knighted and become a baron."
>
> THE DUKE (*aside*). "I understand."
>
> POIRIER. "Do you know why, Sir Duke, I have worked fourteen hours a day for thirty years?

> Why I have earned, sou by sou, four million francs, while depriving myself of everything? It was in order that the Marquis Gaston de Presles, who wasn't killed either at Quiberon, at Fontenoy, at La Hogue, or anywhere else, might die of old age on a feather bed, after having spent his life doing nothing."

Augier has resolved his problem by reforming Gaston and uniting the two classes through the young noble's marriage with Poirier's daughter, Antoinette; in which solution the author has been well inspired and largely justified by recent history. His argument would be that woman is best fitted to unite, in her sympathies, both classes, having less prejudice and less stubbornness, perhaps, and in any case more adaptability, a natural elegance and capacity for rising to any social position. Fortunately, Augier has not tried to reform M. Poirier, who stands as a master portrait in dramatic literature.

Le mariage d'Olympe, in 1855, is a somewhat delayed reply to Dumas's *Dame aux camélias,* and is an indignant protest against the rehabilitation of the courtesan, or her admission into an honorable family, a protest so violent that it ends by killing her on the stage—which also killed the play. It is certain that such acts of violence will always be difficult of acceptance in France, and this accounts for the play's failure. However, despite some strong scenes, it is doubtful if the critics are justified who put this among the best works of Augier. Above all, it lacks his usual balance—owing doubtless to its controversial inspiration—and this in its basic conception of character. Suzanne d'Ange, who is Dumas's own apology for Marguerite Gautier, is a much more reasonable conception. What reason is there to believe that if Olympe were given a respectable position in society she would not have maintained it, at least in appearance? There is really, then, little justification for the *nostalgie de la boue* by which she is supposed by Augier to be affected. The author's thesis in this play was due to his extreme susceptibility when family honor was menaced, and to his strong reaction against the philosophy of the courtesan redeemed by love. But Olympe is as extreme as Marguerite, and Augier has a large enough balance of merit and good sense to assume an occasional mistake of this kind, without his standing being affected.

Augier's **Ceinture dorée,** in 1855, treating marriage and tainted fortunes, is an interesting and worthy play, giving a good picture of the unscrupulous father, but it is not among his finest dramas. The next one, however, **La jeunesse,** in 1858, is both in theme and characters one of the author's most vital plays—and this despite the fact that Augier has again returned to verse, with a realistic subject, and that one can find marked objections to the plot and dénouement. In this piece he not only depicts an unforgettable clash between the idealistic love of youth and the realistic experience of age, but also puts in opposition the simple, contented life of the country with the feverish excitement and luxury of the city. It is, in fact, a strong plea for a return to the soil and to the simple life, and is today, in its motives, one of the most modern of Augier's plays, touching subjects that appeal to youth everywhere.

Les lionnes pauvres, in 1858, written with Edouard Foussier, is similar in tone and characters to *Le mariage d'Olympe,* but it is specifically a protest against the danger to morals found in the luxury of Augier's time. It is a strong play, but not agreeable reading, the depths of depravity being touched. In fact, it is so many shades darker than the author's usual optimism allows, that we naturally suspect the hand of his collaborator, more than is generally the case. Sometimes these collaborators seem to have done little more than sign at the end. *Un beau mariage,* by the same two authors, deals with Augier's most frequent theme, money and marriage, and although clever and interesting, is not the most significant of such pieces.

Beginning with *Les effrontés* in 1861, there is a trilogy of political-social dramas, of which the other two members are *Le fils de Giboyer,* in 1862, and *Lions et renards,* in 1869. Not only are these pieces on the same general themes, but the author dares to repeat the same characters. The three plays read together give an impression of dramatic power that is indubitable—in many ways they are among the strongest of Augier's work. However, it is in these that we see some of the restrictions of the bourgeois in Augier; his prejudice against the Jesuits and the royalists makes it difficult for him to maintain the balance or fairness which in general is his most striking merit. Also, quite naturally, the change in parties and politics has caused some parts of this work to age rapidly. Of these plays the most perfect is doubtless *Le fils de Giboyer,* and in the character, Giboyer, who is found also in *Les effrontés,* the dramatist has again hung an original and strikingly life-like picture in the gallery of drama.

This last merit is also the outstanding one of the *Maître Guérin,* in 1864. As a dramatic character Guérin yields to none of Augier's creations, and, of all, he is drawn with the greatest fullness of line and detail. Because of this, critics have often placed *Maître Guérin* alongside *Le gendre de M. Poirier,* as a masterpiece. As a strong dramatic portrait such evaluation is justified, but in other respects this play not only falls below *Poirier,* but several others of Augier as well. Above all, it lacks unity and simplicity of plot. On the other hand, it rises nearest, both in conception and effect, to the character comedy of Molière, and Guérin, himself, could be acknowledged without loss of prestige by the great master of comedy.

La contagion, in 1866, is an attack on cynicism, and is obviously a play into which the author has put some of his inmost convictions. It is interesting to note the many striking parallels to be found in theme and ideas between this play and Rostand's *Chantecler.* Both dramatists evidently felt most deeply on this matter of skepticism. *Paul Forestier,* in 1868, another relapse into verse, is hardly up to the author's usual standard of this period, and the same might be said of *Jean de Thommeray,* in 1873. The latter play, following the war of 1870, is intensely patriotic and recalls Dumas's *Femme de Claude,* in tone and purpose.

Augier's last two pieces, *Madame Caverlet,* in 1876, which deals with divorce and is one of Augier's rare outright thesis plays, and *Les Fourchambault,* in 1878, a domestic drama, are both interesting and up to a high standard. In fact, Augier, with his usual moderation and good

sense, stopped writing in the full maturity of his dramatic power.

Except in some of his verse plays, where the realistic thought is often not in accord with the verse form, Augier's style is admirable: correct, adapted to his characters, idiomatic and even racy. A special merit is the author's rare power in using the *mot propre* without being vulgar. He is less keenly witty than Dumas, but is more naturally so, and especially is more humorous.

In technique, Augier adopted the *pièce bien faite* as the basis of his plot, but again he differs notably from Dumas. In general, his plots are less breathless and the characters do not seem so driven by the action. This is one of the absolute merits of Augier, that he has, on the whole, been able to defend the independence of his characters both against the narrowness of the well-made play and the encroachments of a social thesis. His action uses suspense as did Scribe's and is perfectly balanced, but it is genuinely motivated in its characters and is less exciting, but more natural, than the plots of Dumas.

Augier's constant themes are money and marriage, or, since he treats marriage largely as affected by money or luxury, we might fairly say that the influence of money is the center of nearly all of his plays. His justification for this theme is not only the great rôle that money plays in modern society, but its particular importance at the time he wrote. In the period of striking industrial expansion of the Second Empire, the sudden wave of commercial prosperity, with its flood of newly acquired riches and luxury, threatened to sweep away or demoralize the racial virtues of honest labor, economy and morality, despite the anchors of home and family. Dumas also defended the family, but against a much more restricted peril, passion and immoral love. This distinction accounts for much in the different character and appeal of the plays of these two writers. The drama of passion of Dumas is undoubtedly of readier appeal—its emotion is in the range of all. Augier's subjects are often soberer, but their import is wider and much more serious.

There is even another distinction that is important between these two authors as moralists. Dumas's morality is that of the converted sinner turned preacher. His language and figures, then, are of the evangelist, colored by the fire and smoke through which he has passed; they are frequently picturesque and sometimes lurid, but are often warped by an overheated imagination. Augier's morality is innate. Its expression is quieter and more natural, and more effective in its unconscious assumption of the cardinal virtues. Above all, it is never merely theoretic; it is the inherent age-long morality of honorable people. This distinction, perhaps a trifle exaggerated, has been keenly expressed by a *bon mot* of Augier, himself, who, when asked what he thought of the moral code of Dumas, replied: *"J'aime mieux l'autre."*

The above distinction suggests the really fundamental difference between these two authors, which affects not only their moral conceptions but their whole work: action, plot, characters and life. Dumas relies continually on logic and formal reasoning; Augier tempers his logic by real experience and good sense. Both of these attitudes are dominated by racial French qualities, only Augier's is much better balanced and is truer to the usual French rationalism.

Dumas was really a one-sided genius. His rigidly logical conclusions are often brilliant, perhaps even irrefutable, but, unfortunately, sometimes existent only in reason and impractical in experience. Many things seem logically most obvious and urgent and are still impossible. The rat orator in La Fontaine's fable demonstrated conclusively the need to bell the cat; what he lacked as a real savior of his race was the reflection of experience. Augier wastes no time belling cats.

The only fundamental principle that has been seriously attacked in Augier's plays is his philosophy of optimism. As for the element of this which is due to the practice of the *pièce bien faite,* it seems just to admit that Augier's dénouements were occasionally given an optimistic twist to fit the Scribe form. But even this is partly inherent in the kind of drama Augier wrote. His theatre deals prevailingly with characters whose principles are sufficiently sound to carry them safely through the tests to which they are put. To believe such characters exist in life is optimism, and it is a philosophy. To see only hopelessly weak, vicious or immoral characters is a philosophy also, pessimism. Augier is frankly an optimist, but he is also a sensible one, and it is hard to see a reproach in this.

The surest test of the higher value of a dramatic author is to be found in his characters, which give the measure of his insight into life and of his philosophy. Augier has without question left the richest gallery of dramatic portraits of any French playwright of the nineteenth century, and this in a form of the theatre which seems, at first thought at least, to lead away from the comedy of character to realistic details and social problems. Obviously this is a supreme accomplishment.

It should be noted that Augier's characters stand up under the double test: they are both types and individuals. They are not mere abstractions, nor are they so exceptional as to be unrepresentative.

The Marquis de Presles and M. Poirier, as representatives respectively of the nobility and of the bourgeoisie, have become classics. Poirier especially is a picture of the bourgeois of which every line is worthy to be engraved and preserved unchangeable. Nowhere else, within so narrow a space, has a more perfect idea been given of one of the strongest elements of the French race: its common sense, its industry and economy, its stubborn force and its stability; and also its exasperating routine. Of course no one would expect a single portrait to depict a whole class, that begins just above the peasant and laborer and rises to include the most cultured and most eminent men of France. Also Augier has given many other representatives of this class, in various stations and situations. But one might say that Poirier is the frame, the chassis, on which he constructs them all: Verdelet, Roussel, Charrier, Vernouillet, Maréchal, Tenancier, Guérin and how many others! Strip them of the coverings requisite for their special model, their trimmings and their color, and you will find the lines of Poirier on which they are built.

Maître Guérin is one of Augier's most completely painted characters, and the result has justified the effort. Guérin is a notary and a rascal, who always manages to cheat his clients and stay within the letter of the law. Why be a lawyer otherwise! In reality he is much more than that; he is a nineteenth century Harpagon. He worships money as much as Molière's miser did and goes as far to have it. Like him, he has lost all feelings, even those most nearly inalienable—family affections. His wife and his son leave him, and he remains impenitent, scarcely touched by this catastrophe. There is but one essential difference between the conceptions of Molière and of Augier, and this is the fundamental one between Character Comedy and Social Comedy. Harpagon is stressed in the universal traits of a miser, his pure love of money, his passion to handle it and gloat over it. Guérin is a product of his age and environment. He wishes money for its power, and he gets it by dishonest speculation rather than by usurious and fraudulent interest. Also, instead of putting it in a strong box and burying it, he buys a château and a title—there are so many opportunities open to the bourgeois of the nineteenth century that were not available in the seventeenth.

What is interesting is to note how much Guérin has in common with Poirier. There is the same strength, the same practical sense, the same cunning in making a deal, and the same vanity and lack of delicacy. The one great difference is that Guérin is an outright scoundrel while Poirier is not consciously dishonest.

But Augier has created a character more original and more a product of his age than Guérin. This is Giboyer, who appears in two plays, ***Les effrontés*** and ***Le fils de Giboyer.*** Giboyer is a porter's son, who by chance has been given a higher education, and who does not have the necessary strength of moral fiber to rise and establish himself firmly against the handicap of poverty and the lack of influential friends. He is one of the problems created by higher education. It is not this education, of course, that is responsible for his lack of principles, but it may increase his power to harm. He sells his pen, his talent, and his convictions to the highest bidder of a venal press. He misleads the public by doctrines that he disbelieves and detests, because he needs money. He even descends to journalistic blackmail.

Giboyer is really a sinister feature of his times, and of our own day. He is found not only in the press but in politics and business. He is the political editor who is hired for his effective sophistry, but he might be the clever lawyer engaged to manage a shady business deal.

The most life-like touch in Giboyer's character is his love and sacrifice for his son. He is not wholly bad, and in reality all this prostitution of his talent and principles is due to the desire to provide for his son, to educate him and to make him an honorable man.

This has raised an interesting question. Critics have often treated Giboyer most kindly and claimed that he was at heart sound. Such views seem purely sentimental and emphasize the warning to be found in this character. If he were more obviously a scoundrel, Giboyer would not be dangerous. But his private virtues do not atone for the harm he does, and are even the cause for it. Parental affection does not justify vice, venality, blackmail, and the moral and political perversion of the people. Giboyer is only a sympathetic rascal—one of the most dangerous sort.

Wholly sympathetic characters, both men and women, are numerous in Augier's plays and are thoroughly well drawn. In his young women and girls, especially, he has an insight and understanding that are rare with French dramatists, and in which he can be compared with Musset. Philiberte, in the play with this title, is a sympathetic and entirely charming example of the young girl, and in such characters as Antoinette, in *Poirier,* he has shown his ability to draw with a few strokes young women who have poise, feeling, idealism and real strength.

A feminine character of a different sort, and which does not seem to have attracted all the attention it deserves, is that of Mme Huguet in *La jeunesse.* The realism, sound psychologic insight and strong lines of this creation are superb, and should put this among Augier's most significant plays. Mme Huguet is the mother of Philip, the young lawyer of ordinary ability, who is in love with his dowerless cousin, Cyprienne. The mother had, herself, married a man of small fortune and mediocre talent, and her life had been the long struggle of an energetic woman to aid her husband to rise and to keep up appearances, in a social circle more ambitious than the one in which she had begun.

Philip has been trained by his mother's precepts, and such is his character that when he is offered the choice between a rich marriage without love and a long struggle in narrow circumstances with Cyprienne, he hesitates. On the one hand he has as example his sister, married to a farmer and content with a simple life, and on the other the worldly experience and arguments of his mother. To persuade him, she lays bare her own life in one of the most masterly realistic scenes of Augier's drama. (pp. 151-67)

A more vivid evocation of all that is hardening for a woman in this struggle with poverty and for petty economy would be difficult to find, as would a more perfect product of such life than Mme Huguet. She is so convincing, indeed, that the author must seriously wrench the logic of events, to give the victory in the end, as he does, to youth, love and idealism. No doubt the questions at stake can not be as poignant to us as to the French, who have no such abundant opportunity to acquire wealth as is found in this country, but our youth also will find, in this play, problems of gripping intensity.

The salient features of Augier's drama have been characterized, but a brief consideration is peculiarly inadequate to give an idea of his full worth. A summary treatment may well suffice with a dramatist whose power lies in some master quality, but in this case the supreme merit is precisely one of ensemble, including numerous factors. It is this broad appeal that offers his greatest excellence and promise of durable worth. A strikingly popular success may be had by a play that exploits a single dramatic virtue; exciting action in *La tour de Nesle;* or passionate emotion in *La dame aux camélias.* But such plays do not entirely satisfy. The spiritual nature has its center of gravity, its

mental and moral poise, quite as much as the physical body, and whatever tends to throw it violently off its balance is disconcerting and is sure to result in quick reaction. A play strikingly exciting in this way brings immediate revulsion, and we leave the theatre after such an experience depressed, perhaps saddened or disgusted, rather than satisfied or inspired. Furthermore, a single dramatic appeal, be it action, passion or any other, is too narrow a foundation for the support of a dramatic system. It is too quickly covered; a broader field is required. This suggests the solid worth of Augier. He appeals to the whole man. With his liberal observation and impartial judgment, his honest and instructive morality and belief in the good, he has given us the most balanced dramatic expression in his century of bourgeois society, and, in fact, one of the most important in French literature. His limitations are those implied in the word bourgeois, taken in its widest acceptation, and of optimist, used in its best sense. But the bourgeois, or great middle class, is the heart of France, and optimism is the philosophy on which the hope and progress of the world are built. (pp. 169-70)

Hugh Allison Smith, "Emile Augier," in his Main Currents of Modern French Drama, *Henry Holt and Company, 1925, pp. 151-70.*

Girdler B. Fitch   (essay date 1948)

[*In the following excerpt, Fitch contends that the subplot of intrusion, which can be found throughout the majority of Augier's plays, demonstrates the dramatist's concern for the preservation of French social structure.*]

Studies of the total work of a dramatic author are likely to be mainly in terms of his subject-matter, ideas, portrayal of character, and literary style. In analyzing and evaluating these, the critic seeks those elements of unity throughout the author's work which will best characterize his art. Less frequently is the same element of unity sought in his plots: sometimes, no doubt, the critic considers them a mere vehicle for the expression of ideas and the presentation of character, although they have certainly had more importance than this to most playwrights; more often the critic assumes that each play has its separate plot, and that while certain comparisons can be made and certain structural tendencies noted there is no reason to seek basic unity in the plots of most dramatists. If by *plot* we mean the total and frequently complex dramatic action, it is of course true that a competent playwright does not repeat it from one play to another. But if we seek the plot beneath the plot, the type of action on which the writer depends to give him the motivation, movement, and climax needed to hold the attention of the spectator, we shall find that he well can, and sometimes does, create an extensive series of plays on a single pattern of dramatic action and that this has revelatory significance for his personality and art.

One could hardly find a better example of this than Emile Augier. No one would classify him among the world's more versatile dramatists, and it is obvious that many of his general ideas and attitudes, the milieux with which he deals, and some of his character-types, are sufficiently repeated to give a considerable degree of unity to his work—a unity which he deliberately furthered more than once by the re-introduction in one play of a character previously used in another. Yet he could not have maintained for three decades the status which the public and most critics accorded him, had his plays not continued to show variety in theme, ideas, treatment, and characterization. That he was able to create this variety is the more to his credit as a craftsman, since the principal plot-mechanism of most of his plays, perhaps of as many as twenty-two of the twenty-five plays from *La ciguë* to *Les Fourchambault,* is provided by the idea of *intrusion.*

To state this theme in its simplest form, suspending qualifications for the moment, the basic action of a typical Augier play is this: *Into a group there comes an intruder whose presence is resisted by one or more persons and accepted by one or more, with resulting conflict, until someone's eyes are opened to the true situation, to the danger, or to a possible solution.* Different outcomes are possible, but the most frequent is the elimination of the intruder.

The term *group* is numerically inappropriate in a few plays, since it may consist of only two persons, but it is usually the family, city, or social class to which the intruder does not belong, or is felt not to belong, this feeling being of sufficient force to produce dramatic action. The term *intruder* is not necessarily invidious: the protagonist of *Un beau mariage* is a fine young man placed by marriage in a false position; Jean de Thommeray is a moderately sympathetic intruder into certain Parisian circles which are unwholesome in themselves and especially so for him. While Pauline and Vernouillet have entered respectable society by fraud, Gaston de Presles has simply made honorable entry into a family circle whose attitudes are apparently irreconcilable with his. The intruder in *Ceinture dorée* is not a person at all: it is ill-gotten money, the explicit barrier to a happy marriage. The elimination of this money, some of which appears on the stage, physically presented as a central character should be, constitutes the same type of problem as the elimination of a personal intruder in the other plays, and the plot is resolved similarly.

In *Diane* the intrusion assumes a very literal form, as the action begins with the sudden entry of a woman seeking refuge, pursued by three men. An even better example of how this *motif* pervades Augier's thought is *Le postscriptum,* where the proposal of marriage by a landlord to his tenant is delicately broached in the form of a notice of eviction: this in addition to the plot in which another man, felt to be an intruder, is eliminated.

But if sometimes very literal, the intrusion can also be symbolic: In *Les effrontés,* Vernouillet is the symbol of a widespread intrusion into respectable society.

In addition to the three plays which are definite exceptions to Augier's typical procedure, there are several in which there are other elements of importance in the plot besides the intrusion-theme, especially *Le fils de Giboyer* and *Maître Guérin.* Yet the main action of the latter is the conflict between two intrusions that seem complementary to the father and irreconcilable to the son: Guérin wishes to take possession of an estate to which he has neither moral nor ancestral right, giving his son entrance to a higher social class; the son sees such action as an absolute obstacle to his marriage.

Usually at least one person is aware of the intrusion as such from the beginning, and at least one other person fails or refuses to see its nature and implications. The essential dramatic action, then, results from the shifting balance when someone becomes aware of the intrusion, changes attitude, and desires expulsion. This then becomes the logical outcome, though there may instead be a solution through reconciliation or compromise.

In *Lions et renards* there is a fundamental weakness in the intrusion-plot itself, in that the key-character is well aware of what is transpiring around her. Catherine is wealthy and as nearly independent as a young woman in her environment could be, and though she is not completely in control of events, we have difficulty in believing that her happiness is seriously menaced. Various reasons have been given for the failure of this play, perhaps all partly valid, but not the least of them is that the author was false to the necessary conditions of his own system of construction: without more blindness on Catherine's part the plot lacks the necessary tension.

It is *Madame Caverlet* which raises most sharply the question of whether Augier was a writer who cast social ideas into dramatic form, or a *playwright* primarily concerned with creating a viable play. To a critic making the first assumption, as many critics do, this play represents an abandonment of, or a relaxation in, Augier's defense of the family: Madame Caverlet is admitted to the temple from which others (Olympe, Séraphine) have been repulsed. Gaillard de Champris quotes the *Constitutionnel* [in his *Emile Augier et la comédie sociale*]: "On a envisagé la pièce du Vaudeville comme une théorie en faveur du divorce . . . Rien dans la pièce ne justifie le point de vue. Le divorce sert à l'action, rien de plus." To this he answers: "Mais c'est s'aveugler volontairement et nier l'évidence. Sans doute, nous le verrons, l'auteur n'a pas institué de discussion, ni de controverse; aux discours d'école il a préféré une action pathétique. Son intention n'en reste pas moins claire. . . ."

But in view of the structural consistency of this play with the others, is it not the *Constitutionnel* which, though rather extreme in denying any social purpose at all, has more nearly the right emphasis? In terms of the dramatic action, it is not Madame Caverlet who corresponds to Olympe, but Merson. Augier had found a variant of his formula in which the husband was the intruder, and could utilize it at least once on condition that he make his social views fit his dramaturgy. To say that he did this is not to accuse him of insincerity; he had every right to claim that some circumstances permitted exceptions to his usual thesis. The fact remains that an author does not readily discard a surprising variation of the plot he can best handle.

The question may well be asked—no doubt the attentive reader has already asked it in his own mind—whether I have not made a forced use of the concept of intrusion to cover situations of marital infidelity, *mésalliance,* and even rivalry for marriage. In any society in which social barriers are fairly rigid, and yet decreasingly so, as in the France of the mid-nineteenth century, the feeling of intrusion will be evoked by each weakening of these barriers, without necessarily having any such significance as I attribute to it in the works of Augier. Moreover, so broad an interpretation of intrusion would seem to offer little basis for distinguishing Augier from the many writers who have used the theme. Balzac's *Le curé de tours* is a masterly study of ejection and persecution; Zola, in *La fortune des Rougon,* deals with the elimination of an entire family group by those who resent their existence and their presence. Mauriac's *Thérèse Desqueyroux* is alternately stifled and rejected by her husband and his community. From Musset's *Histoire d'un merle blanc,* where the bird is expelled from the nest because of his plumage, to Maupassant's *A cheval,* where the utter outsider is triumphantly installed in a resentful household, the forms which such a subject can assume are only less varied than those of life itself. To consider Augier's own medium: Dumas fils uses almost the same plot-mechanism in *Le demi-monde,* and certain elements of it in *La question d'argent* and *La dame aux camélias.*

I can only reply that what distinguishes Augier is his constant use of this one theme as a *ressort,* and his construction of an entire dramaturgic system on it. I know of no other writer who has done this. For him, the feeling of intrusion and the actions resulting from it are not merely an important element of the environment: they are the one on which the action of his plays depends. The environment of constant social self-defense was a reality, and hence he could use the intrusion-plot effectively in combination with a fairly realistic study of moeurs. Marriage, in the society which he portrayed, was entrance into a family, frequently into a new social circle. And Augier constantly emphasizes this aspect of marriage, no doubt because he saw life in such terms, but also because they give the requisite meaning to his plays.

Considering this plot merely as a device, repeated because successful or from lack of inventiveness, we could still find it worth noting, for the plot has certainly conditioned the subject-matter, and probably, as in **Madame Caverlet,** some of the social attitudes. Should we limit its significance to that? The form of a work can serve as well as the explicit ideas to reveal the essential character of the author's thought; if he is a workman of any integrity the form which he most frequently employs will be one in harmony with his deepest feelings and reactions. If Augier finds that his creative thought flows best when he deals with the problem of resistance to the intruder, it is because that problem has deep roots in his being, consciously or subconsciously. No doubt he finds attraction in the stranger, sometimes the most interesting character in his play, sometimes sympathetic. But in total, Augier's resistance to such attraction seems the stronger impulse.

There is no reason to question the fact that he was defending marriage and the legitimate family. But is this not perhaps the surface, and is his defense of marriage not warmest when it is also a defense of *endogamy?* In *Le mariage d'Olympe* the explicit thesis of the play, and the only admissible justification for its outcome, depends on the past and present character of Pauline. At first glance, Geneviève seems to have been used as contrast and as a means of provoking the final pistol-shot. Does she not also exist in order that Pauline, whatever her character, may be marked as an *outsider?* When Geneviève can say of Pauline's husband: *"Il y a de par le monde un homme que j'ai été élevée à regarder comme mon mari,"* Pauline's fate is really sealed; she has violated the laws of endogamy. True, the audience would hardly accept her elimination on this basis alone. She must bring her fate upon herself in more unequivocal fashion, and that she will do so is the explicit thesis of the play, but once this insider-outsider opposition is established in an Augier play we know that the outsider will be removed. A tacit condition of the happy ending of **Le gendre de M. Poirier** is that Antoinette shall never have been in love with a cousin.

To have Augier's fullest approval, marriage would seem to require being within the family, literally or spiritually. Let me quote a few of the clearest examples; there are others.

> CYPRIENNE. Mais je crains d'avoir l'air de me croire sa femme,
> Et mes anciens, mes doux privilèges de sœur
> Ainsi qu'une caresse à présent me font peur.
> *[**La jeunesse**]*

> FORESTIER. Paul?

> CAMILLE. Dans votre pensée
> N'ai-je pas de tout temps été sa fiancée?
> *[**Paul Forestier**]*

> ANTOINETTE. Quand j'ai été petite fille, je ne comprenais pas que mon père et ma mère ne fussent pas parents; et le mariage m'est resté dans l'esprit comme la plus tendre et la plus proche des parentés.
> *[**Le gendre de M. Poirier**]*

> FRANZ. J'aime Frédérique.

> SPIEGEL. Frédérique? Ta cousine? notre enfant?
> *[**Le pierre de touche**]*

> HENRIETTE. . . . Fanny ne l'aime pas . . . ils ont grandi ensemble . . . c'est un frère pour elle . . . (à Fanny) Dis-lui donc que tu ne l'aimes pas!

> FANNY. Pourquoi veux-tu que je mente?
> *[**Madame Caverlet**]*

Making all due allowance for some endogamous tendency in the French bourgeoisie, and for an audience that readily approved these marriages of foster-brothers and sisters and of first cousins, it is still clear that they are much more frequent in Augier than in the society he portrays. His conception of the ideal marriage involves much physical and spiritual inbreeding.

An Augier play, then, is the story of a strongly unified group which is entered by someone who does not really belong. Someone in the group realizes the danger or, at least, the incongruity. Someone in a key position does not realize it, or has some interest in permitting the situation to continue. But at last realization comes, often at the sight of a material object: a letter, a dressmaker's bill, a pearl, a case. A decision results, usually preceded by a silence that marks it as difficult. Finally the intruder agrees to accept in part the standards of the group, or, more often, departs—to his former life, a new life, a marriage, solitude, Uzès, or the next world.

The variations of the formula are many. We may have the intruder entering a family where he does not belong, or leaving his family to enter a society where he does not belong. Either may be with or against parental desires. There is a considerable variety in the milieu and the persons presented. Under all these variations the essential problem of the play remains the same: that of dealing with the person who is where he does not belong. Many social and moral issues may be involved. One could derive from Augier's plays, as from the Spanish *capa y espada* dramas, a whole code of honor. But the real issue is not that Vernouillet is evil or that Pauline is a *courtisane;* it is that they have crossed boundaries that should be defended.

Such plots are the product of a mind to which the resistance to what was alien, even when attractive, was, if not an obsession, at least a matter of profound and constant concern. The society for which he wrote shared this concern sufficiently so that he could base on this one formula, and the artistic expression which he gave it, a successful dramatic career. Inevitably it dates his plays, for though the conflict of the homogeneous with the heterogeneous is an eternal one, its values can be fully felt only with reference to a society with which we are familiar. An audience of a later age, to which the society that Augier portrayed has itself become alien, will inevitably find that the dramatic action, though intellectually comprehensible enough, has lost much of its interest and force. (pp. 274-80)

> *Girdler B. Fitch, "Emile Augier and the Intrusion-Plot," in* PMLA, *Vol. LXIII, No. 1, March, 1948, pp. 274-80.*

Martin Lamm   (essay date 1953)

[*Lamm was a Swedish scholar and critic. In the following excerpt, he examines the origins of the morality themes in Augier's plays, noting the influence of these themes on subsequent playwrights.*]

Emile Augier was born in 1820, and was consequently four years older than Dumas, but his début as a writer of prose plays came much later, and his success, unlike that of Dumas, was not immediate and brilliant. Outside France his plays, which were concerned with politics and class conflicts, had more influence than those of Dumas and from 1860 to 1880 he was received with deeper appreciation in France itself. He was the sober son of middle-class parents, and was brought up to follow his father's profession of the law.

Dumas was an aristocrat even when he fought for social equality, and something of a romantic even when most realistically painting the contemporary scene. Augier, by his whole nature and inclination was a democrat who had no use for romanticism. This is not to say that he was in any way bigoted; no one dealt shrewder blows at philistinism,

the abuses of modern political democracy or a prosaic attitude to life. His fundamental attitude, however, was always bourgeois and unromantic.

This is already apparent in the verse comedies, which were the first works he wrote for the stage. Dumas was a child of the romantic drama; Augier sprang from the reaction against it. The first playwright to give expression to this reaction was Ponsard, who made some not very successful attempts to revive the French classical tragedy. Augier began as his pupil with some short sentimental verse comedies, rather in the vein of Musset's *proverbes*. **Gabrielle,** which appeared in 1849—the same year as *The Lady of the Camellias*—shows Augier's attitude very clearly. The plot is the theme of *L'école des maris (School for Husbands)* in reverse. Julien wins back his wife, Gabrielle, who is on the point of running away with his secretary, by his nobility and his spiritual superiority. Without betraying the fact that he knows whose lover the secretary is, he delivers to him—and to Gabrielle who is listening behind the door—a homily on the unhappy results of free love, and an eloquent hymn of praise about the beauty of home life. Gabrielle, who is left to choose freely, bids the secretary farewell for ever, and praises her husband, whom she now sees in a new light, before an assembled gathering of all the family: "O père de famille, O poëte! je t'aime".

This glorification of the father of the family and of family life is also to be found in the domestic drama of the 18th century. Diderot's *Le père de famille (The Father of the Family)* concludes with a line spoken by the hero: "How sweet and yet how cruel it is to be a father". Since the Romantics had preached free love and the rights of lovers with such zeal, there was need for a new apotheosis of family life. The revolutionary effect of Augier's drama on his age may well be seen in the complaints of one Romantic critic, that he presented passion and poetry as ridiculous fantasies, and pandered to the low taste of the public. The play was, however, very successful in France and even more so in Scandinavia, where the idea of home has a much richer meaning. It contributed something to Björnson's first play, *Mellem Slagene (Between the Battles* (1856)), and his first contemporary play, *De nygifte (The Newly-Married Couple)*. In Ibsen's *Kjaerlighedens Komedie (Love's Comedy)*, the spirit of Augier's play can be discerned, and in Guldstad's final speech there are arguments which had been used by Julien. One can even see traces of *Gabrielle* in *Fruen fra havet (The Lady from the Sea)*.

For his first comedies Augier used a kind of verse, which ran the constant risk of degenerating into rhyming prose. When, following Dumas, he turned to the realist prose drama, he achieved in his very first play the masterpiece of his life, **Le gendre de M. Poirier (*The Son-in-Law of M. Poirier*)**.

Augier found the idea for his play in a novel by Sandeau, *Sacs et parchemins,* and Sandeau collaborated in the writing of the play. The theme to be treated was the relation between the aristocracy of birth and the oligarchy of wealth, and in the conditions of the day it was a topical one. During the July Monarchy and the Second Empire, the Third Estate had steadily increased its powers, while rich upstarts were coming forward in a steady stream to enjoy themselves at the expense of the old nobility. Many of the latter had emigrated, while the influence of the remainder was much diminished owing to the so-called 'inner withdrawal' or retirement of members of noble families who felt constrained by their legitimist principles to refuse public office. One result of this attitude was an irritability, resulting from enforced idleness, which young noblemen in Dumas' plays were always displaying. When they had spent their patrimony, there was nothing else for them to do but marry into the families of the new financial magnates. These plutocrats had a great weakness for such alliances, and the most famous of them—Augier wrote about him in one of his plays—the great financier, Mirès, would not accept as a son-in-law anyone less than a prince of the blood. In Augier's play Poirier, a wealthy merchant, gives his daughter in marriage to a marquis, Gaston de Presles. The conflict between him and his father-in-law is the conflict between the titles of nobility and the moneybags of commerce.

This main conflict is, as always in Augier, closely bound up with a love story. The theme is the same as in *Gabrielle,* but the roles are reversed. Gaston de Presles, newly-married, has deserted his wife for a lady of fashion, but she wins him back by the same means as Julien wins Gabrielle, by native dignity and nobleness of mind. Antoinette, however, acts on impulse, and it is her natural instincts that bring her victory.

The construction of the plot, and the representation of the characters, recall the works of the French classical period by their symmetry. There are two representatives of the nobility, one wise and one foolish, and similarly two business men. Poirier, vain and pompous, has a wise business friend, Verdelet, while his son-in-law, a proud and wanton dandy, has for a friend the Duke of Montmeyran, a man who has overcome prejudice against his noble birth by serving as a common soldier with the Chasseurs d'Afrique. This is an arrangement with which we are familiar in Molière. Each of the chief characters has a confidant who provides a refreshing contrast of good sense, and to some extent plays the part of a raisonneur. The simplicity of the plot is also reminiscent of Molière. It is Poirier's own daughter, the Marquis's deserted wife, who by her understanding of both sides succeeds in reconciling the two parties.

Because of its clear and comprehensible plot, the play became immediately popular not only in France but all over Europe. It was performed in Sweden as early as 1855, and was frequently revived, whereas it was much longer before Dumas' plays were as warmly received. The simple structure of the play had one further advantage, in that it left the playwright plenty of time in which to develop its characterization in greater detail.

The best character is that of Poirier himself. He is the self-made man, so often found in later plays and novels. The type is essentially a product of 19th century industrial progress, but is not unknown in earlier works; Molière's Georges Dandin and Jourdain in *Le bourgeois gentilhomme* (*The Bourgeois Gentleman*) are direct predecessors of Poirier. Augier saw this connexion quite clearly. In the very first scene of the play he makes Gaston say about his

father-in-law, "to describe him in a word, he is Georges Dandin as a father-in-law". Indeed, Augier originally meant to call the play *Georges Dandin's Revenge.*

But Gaston is quite wrong in imagining that he has a mild version of Dandin to deal with, for as the play develops Poirier shows his claws more and more. He is genial or harsh in response to whatever emotion is roused in him, and can be both sympathetic and forbidding at one and the same time.

His counterpart, Gaston de Presles, displays the same subtle mixture of strength and weakness. He is superficial, an idler and a bully, with the exaggerated sense of honour typical of his class. But he shows his breeding in the assurance of his manner, his wit and charm, and his gallant and graceful bearing.

Poirier's daughter, Antoinette, is also an admirable character, a middle-class girl—every inch of her—but sensitive and imaginative enough to rise above her prejudices and read her husband's inmost thoughts.

Gaston has regarded his marriage as a commercial transaction which will enable him to pay his debts, and has devoted no attention to his wife. He continues his bachelor ways, and three months after his wedding is prepared to fight a duel with a rival for a gay countess of fairly easy virtue. He regards it as a point of honour to pay his debts and meet his social obligations, even to the extent of a duel. It has not, however, occurred to him that he has any obligations to the woman he has made his wife; the one act of raising a daughter of the people to the rank of a marquise is enough in itself. Moreover, it was Poirier who had been tempted by the title, and arranged the marriage before Antoinette fell in love with him.

Antoinette is now determined to win his heart, and she succeeds because she can understand, as her father cannot, the aristocratic notions of honour by which Gaston is moved.

The final act brings the climax of the plot. Antoinette commands Gaston, if he wishes to earn her forgiveness, to withdraw from the duel for the countess's good name, and to apologize to his opponent: there follows a bitter struggle in Gaston between his love and his sense of honour. Exhausted, he sinks down at last into a chair and bids his friend convey his apology. Immediately Antoinette goes over to him, kisses him on the forehead and says, "Now, go and fight".

It is a real *scene à faire,* which French literary historians have compared with the finest scenes in the classical tragedies. To secure a happy ending, Augier has recourse to the device of an apology from Gaston's opponent, with the result that the outcome is, if harmonious, also somewhat of an anticlimax.

Augier is happiest when he has numerous characters to manipulate. His technique, unlike that of Dumas, is not based on logic and a conflict of wills, but rather on a kind of internal balance which ensures that every character gets what he deserves. The advantage of this technique is that it affords greater opportunities for introducing a variety of types, and displaying their qualities in all their facets.

This indeed is Augier's chief delight. He often writes a whole episode or whole scene merely to throw light upon some quality in his characters. A good instance in this play is the famous 'picture' scene. Gaston has bought a modern landscape painting, and a whole group of people has gathered round to examine it. The two noblemen express their opinions rather too confidently, but with fine taste and judgment. Antoinette shows the warmth of her feelings, Verdelet his sound common sense. Poirier finds the picture uninteresting, and speaks of an etching of his own, a dog barking at a sailor's hat on the shore: that is something a man can understand, it has a story to tell, it is simple and moving. He is shocked at the price Gaston has paid for this picture—fifty golden louis. "Fifty louis to a poor fool who is starving. By dinner-time you could have had it for twenty-five".

After the production of *The Son-in-Law of M. Poirier* Augier's reputation rose to heights which almost overshadowed that of the younger Dumas. In his social comedies he castigated the moral corruption of his age, and upheld the claims of the family against the tyranny of the courtesan and the speculator in the France of the Second Empire. In his political dramas he branded parliamentary and political corruption.

These political dramas, which had a particularly strong influence on subsequent Scandinavian playwriting, consisted of a series of three plays, *Les éffrontés* (*The Impertinents*), *Le fils de Giboyer* (*Giboyer's Son*), and *Lions et renards* (*Lions and Foxes*). The plays are not connected, but certain characters appear in all three, and they all tell of the struggles in France between the Clerical and Radical parties, a conflict which raged throughout the 19th century, and was not finally resolved until the Dreyfus affair. They have been variously judged by French critics. From a literary point of view they might be said to constitute a novelty, for political issues and personalities had not appeared on the French stage since the days of Beaumarchais. These political issues Augier regarded essentially with the eye of a moralist, and always combined them with a love-story. His example had a stimulating effect on the whole development of European drama, and Björnson and Ibsen were clearly inspired by him when they wrote their political plays.

In *The Impertinents* Augier presents the political decay of his age with some excellently conceived characters, moving through one of his most elaborate and complicated plots. Vernouillet, a speculator on the Bourse, is his chief character. This man has founded a bank, and at its crash has succeeded in enriching himself at the expense of his shareholders by as much as eight hundred thousand francs. At the beginning of the play Vernouillet is a wealthy man but despised and opposed by all. Suddenly he hits on the idea of buying a newspaper; "With my money I can then possess myself of the one instrument of power which money has not conquered—public opinion. The Press is a wonderful instrument whose powers no one yet realizes; so far, journalists have been mere hacks—make way for Paganini".

By allowing his assistants to spread inaccurate reports of foreign affairs, he contrives to direct operations on the Stock Exchange to his own advantage. He declines for his paper the grant which the authorities have been allowing, and transfers its allegiance to the opposition party. Now the Government regards him with a very healthy respect. By using every section of his paper to serve his own ends, he regains his position in society. Friends he secures by printing favourable notices about the dancers and actresses who are their mistresses; his enemies he holds in check by threats of publishing information about scandals in their past. With unparalleled audacity he even turns to his own advantage the awkward situations caused by his libellous articles. In the final act, to be sure, his marriage plans go awry, but he has won complete control over public opinion, and is about to extend his influence and reputation by the purchase of another paper.

For some years before the appearance of *The Impertinents* the Paris press had been in the hands of a number of financial sharks who made use of their newspapers for advertisement and exploitation. The original of Augier's Vernouillet was a financier and newspaper magnate called Mirès. He owned several Paris papers, carried on financial transactions with foreign powers, had a say in all important appointments and consorted with princes of the blood and noblemen of the highest rank. The very year before this play was produced his daughter married the Prince de Polignac. The following year he was charged with fraudulent practices and finally sentenced to a month's imprisonment. Augier needed courage to point him out so plainly.

An even better portrait than that of Vernouillet is that of his assistant in the world of journalism, Giboyer. In *The Impertinents* in particular this character is one of the liveliest and most original ever conceived by Augier. Giboyer is the first instance in the theatre of a type which later became very common, the bohemian journalist. He wears a shabby frock-coat, and carries a pipe which he cannot bear to be parted from, even when entering the elegant ballrooms of the aristocracy. Augier seldom allows his characters to show their individuality by their manner of speaking, but he endows Giboyer with a racy style that is all his own, full of sardonic wit and lively journalese. Politically he is a Socialist at heart, and he loathes the community which has so signally failed to live up the ideals of 1789. Still—one must live—and he is prepared to work for middle-class papers, liberal or conservative, and to write about anything from current political or financial problems to society gossip and fashion notes, using different signatures and pseudonyms, and without any concern for the good or bad effects of his writing—as long as he is paid. One reason for this attitude is that as a Socialist he hates existing society, but a more powerful reason is that this society has treated him so cruelly that he no longer recognizes any obligations towards it. There is one scene in which he describes to Vernouillet and the Marquis de Auberive, who is the raisonneur, the sad story of his life, with his usual sardonic humour. He was the son of the concierge at the Marquis' home. Against the latter's advice his father sent the talented boy to a headmaster who was prepared to teach him as an advertisement for his school. When he left school he got a job as an assistant master with a salary of six hundred francs. He soon became dissatisfied, and cast himself adrift to seek other employment: the path of education he discovered to be a blind alley. After that he lived a very varied life. The Marquis commented that he had also had his vices. Giboyer answered abruptly, "Damn it, of course I had my vices. So have you. Do you think privation spoils a man's appetite? If only I had nothing but my vices, which didn't cost much, to burden me, all would have been well. Unfortunately, there was also a virtue, the only one I never gave up. I was a good son—I wouldn't let my father go to the workhouse—pure childishness of course—but what will you?—Nobody is perfect. He was inconsiderate enough to live to a good old age, and I was simple enough to weep at his death".

Giboyer, like Figaro, comes from the lower class, a man of talent who has been prevented by prejudice and social injustice from rising in the world. Like the unhappy Figaro, he has had to serve counts and barons in their more or less praiseworthy enterprises. Like Figaro he has tried his hand at everything, and has endured many humiliations. But, also like Figaro, he has retained a sense of superiority over his masters and has remained faithful to his ideals, though he has had to betray them in practice. It has often been said that Figaro sounded the reveille for 1789; Giboyer proclaims that the revolution of 1789 has still to be completed. An aristocracy of wealth has replaced one of birth, and a brutal lust for profit rules all. What is needed to resist the power of wealth is a new aristocracy, based this time on personal merit.

A fierce newspaper war followed the production of *The Impertinents.* In their attack on Augier the journalists made Giboyer their chief target, for they considered his character a direct insult to their profession, and were in no way appeased by the amiable character of another journalist whom Augier had been careful to include in the cast as a counter-weight.

When Augier produced his next play, *Giboyer's Son,* in 1862 there was an even greater sensation. Not since Molière's time had there been so much controversy in the theatrical world about a play.

After *The Son-in-Law of M. Poirier, Giboyer's Son* is Augier's finest play. Moreover, it is the play which exercised the greatest influence on the Scandinavian dramatists. Björnson imitated it very closely in *Redaktören* (*The Editor*) and *Det ny system* (*The New System*).

Augier was a fervent supporter of the government, and an opponent of the Clerical opposition. In this play he attacks the leading opposition publicist, Louis Veuillot, under his pseudonym 'Deodat'. In the first act of *Giboyer's Son,* Deodat is supposed to be dead, and a group of Clericals are mourning the loss of this staunch defender of orthodoxy. Fortunately, however, the Marquis of Auberive has found a successor to Deodat in Giboyer, with his cynical, diabolical pen, which spreads filth and poison with every word, a contemptible creature who would fry his own father for a few pence, and eat him with salt for a few more.

It was this unconcealed attack on Veuillot which produced so many angry articles, including one by Veuillot himself. In the preface to the play, Augier defended himself in advance by claiming that his were legitimate reprisals against a scurrilous pamphleteer, who was in any case well able to protect himself. It can scarcely be denied that here Augier has gone too far.

As in most of Augier's plays, there are in *Giboyer's Son* two plots; the political one moves round Maréchal, one of Augier's best bourgeois characters. He is wealthy, pompous, and particularly addicted to the company of marchionesses and countesses. Not much effort has therefore been necessary to lure him over into the Clerical party. On the occasion of the opposition's main attack on the government in the Chamber he is to be the main speaker. He has had a speech written for him by the versatile Giboyer, and he is so pleased that he is constantly repeating phrases from it.

Then comes a party conference in which the speech is taken away from Maréchal and given to someone else to deliver, much to Maréchal's disappointment. Giboyer, who has retained his radical sympathies, manages to rouse Maréchal's irritation to such a pitch that he decides to answer the original speech which Giboyer wrote for him. For this purpose, Giboyer lets Maximilien, Maréchal's secretary, write a new speech which Maréchal delivers with great effect in the Chamber. Maximilien, although he does not know it, is the natural son of Giboyer, but in the end he is united with Maréchal's daughter. The young couple have long cherished each other in secret.

An old-fashioned plot of this kind has its weaknesses. Maréchal has to be a complete simpleton to allow himself to be tossed about by both parties. The two chief plotters are not as diabolically cunning as those of Scribe, nor are the young couple steered through their difficulties as in *The Glass of Water.* But it is the same old plot. The play derives its strength from the scenes between Giboyer and his son.

Maximilien has grown up in the belief that Giboyer is his uncle. By dint of accepting any work, however degrading, and by enduring the most extraordinary privations, Giboyer has succeeded in bringing up Maximilien so well that he is now three times a doctor, and no one has any idea who his father is.

The finest scene in the play comes at the end of the third act, and is played between Giboyer and Maximilien. Maximilien has been so impressed with the first "Clerical" speech, which he had been instructed by Maréchal to copy out, that he has abandoned his liberal convictions. Giboyer is very distressed, and admits that he wrote it for payment. Maximilien in his turn is very distressed that Giboyer should be practising such a trade. When Giboyer asserts that it was for his sake, he replies "For my sake? By what right do you do such dishonourable service? How do you know that I would not prefer poverty?" Giboyer collapses into a chair and Maximilien adds, penitently, "Forgive me, old friend, you didn't know what you were doing".

For the first time Giboyer gives vent to his emotions, and complains about his lot. "I knew I was sacrificing myself for you, and that I had to preserve your youth from the trials that had ruined mine. I have eaten the dust that lay in your path, and it is not for you to reproach me. My pen is not the first thing that I sold for your sake; I had already sold my freedom. I went to prison for two years and was paid a year's salary by a newspaper for so doing, and all to pay your school fees. But what does it matter? I'm just a criminal, and you want no more of me. Oh—God is too hard. I'm not a bad man—only an unfortunate one. My responsibilities have been too heavy; they have ruined me. First I had to labour for my father, and then for my . . ." Here his voice breaks, and Maximilien, who has guessed the secret, throws himself into his arms and interrupts "for your son". It is a *'scène à faire',* but a moving one. Björnson followed it closely in *The New System.*

Augier's later social dramas are also very important. In **The Son-in-Law of M. Poirier** he took up a position of neutrality between the aristocracy and the bourgeoisie. As time passed he became more and more the spokesman of bourgeois morality, *vis-à-vis* the decadent aristocracy of the Second Empire. He was one of the first to observe shrewdly a fact that was commonly acknowledged after the defeat of 1870, namely that the cancer in the body of France was the immorality of the nobility which came to infect the middle classes also. The remedy he preached was moral regeneration. Dumas had said the same thing earlier, but in his eyes the problem was almost entirely one of relation between the sexes. Augier struck not merely at sexual laxity, but also at political corruption, social injustices and above all at the tyranny of wealth.

Money had been the focal point of Balzac's novels, and he was also the first playwright to introduce a modern business setting on to the stage. He did this in *Mercadet,* where a speculator seeks by various shady tricks to avoid the bankruptcy that is threatening him. He is finally saved by a former friend, on condition that he promises never to speculate again.

Augier, on the other hand, appears to have been a typical French 'petit bourgeois', who would never dare to risk any money in speculation. In his plays, however, he delighted in wild and extravagant speculations, which spread all over the world and engulfed whole families and business firms in a welter of destruction. But somehow he never quite succeeded in making clear to his audiences the economic implications of the plays.

Nevertheless, his plays exercised a powerful influence, particularly in Scandinavia. The first great modern play of Björnson, *En Fallit* (*A Bankruptcy*), deals with precisely this sort of topic and presents a bankrupt business man as its hero.

Occasionally Augier allows his financial magnates to meet brilliant inventors and engineers, whose ideas they exploit or suppress with the help of their financial resources. This is a situation which recurs in several plays by Björnson, the earliest instance being *The New System.* The railways of Norway were being constructed at this period, so it was on their affairs that Björnson concentrated his critical attention.

Elsewhere in Europe great interest had been aroused by the construction of the Suez Canal and similar projects. Such a project is the subject of a play to which Augier gave the symbolic name **La contagion** (**The Contagion**) in 1866. The hero is a young engineer called Lagarde, and his epoch-making idea consists of a plan to build a ship-canal across the Algeciras peninsula, thereby ending Gibraltar's domination over the only entrance to the Mediterranean. He comes from the country and looks like a foreman. Like a Dumas hero, he begins by weeping over his mother's death; then he is introduced to the sinful society of Paris, where an English secret agent nearly succeeds in extracting the canal concessions from him for a sum of a million-and-a-half francs. Our young hero from the country is all but succumbing to the lust for gold, when suddenly his eyes are opened. In the final act we see in him a predecessor of Doctor Stockman from *An Enemy of the People*, inexorably advancing to battle against the evils which threaten the community.

Augier has been using a very old-fashioned technique. Unlike the younger Dumas, he soon realized this. His final play was extremely successful in the theatre, but in 1879 he gave up playwriting with the feeling that a new generation, with modern resources, was ready to step into the breach: "Sometimes I feel rather as Bayard's charger might have done if he had been confronted by modern artillery".

It has already been suggested that Augier's conceptions of the moral decadence of the Second Empire had some influence on playwrights in other countries, where social conditions were hardly the same. It is significant that the first contemporary plays of both Björnson and Ibsen depict a fever for speculation and a moral corruption, to such an abhorrent degree that one is driven to ask whether conditions could really have been so bad in the small coastal towns of Norway, where life was still rather simple. Did they not simply, though unconsciously, transfer the atmosphere of the French decadence of the Second Empire straight to Norway? It took a little time before Björnson and Ibsen achieved a genuine Norwegian tone in their plays of contemporary morals and manners. (pp. 29-41)

Martin Lamm, "French Drama of the Second Empire," in his Modern Drama, *translated by Karin Elliott, Philosophical Library, 1953, pp. 16-51.*

FURTHER READING

"Obituary: Emile Augier." *The Academy* n. s. XXXVI, No. 913 (2 November 1889): 294.
    Brief retrospective account of Augier's career.

Brieux, Eugène. "Emile Augier." *The Drama,* No. 19 (August 1915): 353-57.
    Discusses *Le gendre de Monsieur Poirier, Le mariage d'Olympe,* and *Les Fourchambault.*

Harper, George McLean. Introduction to *La pierre de tou-*

che, by Emile Augier, edited by George McLean Harper, pp. iii-xvi. Boston: Ginn & Company, 1897.

Discusses Augier's work in the context of French literature of the late nineteenth century, arguing that Augier produced "vigorous and interesting" plays while communicating a clear moral message.

Hawkins, Richmond Laurin. Introduction to *Le gendre de Monsieur Poirier,* by Emile Augier, edited by Richmond Laurin Hawkins, pp. v-x. New York: Henry Holt and Co., 1921.

Brief overview of the plot and characters in *Le gendre de Monsieur Poirier.*

"Emile Augier." *The Nation* XLIX, No. 1272 (14 November 1889): 388-89.

Retrospective account of the playwright's career which draws strong parallels between Augier and Dumas (fils).

Nicoll, Allardyce. "The Coming of Realism." In his *World Drama from Aeschylus to Anouilh,* pp. 485-523. New York: Harcourt, Brace and Company, 1950.

Surveys Augier's works and classifies the dramatist as a principal founder of a "new style" of playwriting which is characterized by an emphasis on realism, the introduction of social problems into the theater, and the use of the stage to instill values.

Saintsbury, George. "The Modern Drama." In his *A Short History of French Literature,* pp. 546-56. Oxford: Clarendon Press, 1897.

Considers Augier a significant figure in the move toward realism in nineteenth-century French drama.

"French Literature: Emile Augier." *The Saturday Review of Politics, Literature, Science and Art* 68, No. 1775 (2 November 1889): 504-05.

Brief eulogy of Augier in which the critic compares the playwright with his contemporaries and finds him "the best all-around dramatist" of his generation.

Scheifley, William H. "Emile Augier: 1820-1920." *The Drama* II, No. 4 (January 1921): pp. 136-37.

Succinct critical overview of Augier's life and career.

Symington, Stuart. Introduction to *Un beau mariage,* by Emile Augier and Edouard Foussier, edited by Stuart Symington, Louis R. Herrick, and Louis E. Cadieux, pp. v-vii. New York: Henry Holt and Company, 1903.

Summary of Augier's plays in which Symington judges Augier "a sane, solid, talented bourgeois, whose strongest characteristic was common sense."

Van Laan, Thomas F. "The Ending of *A Doll's House* and Augier's *Maître Guérin.*" *Comparative Drama* 17, No. 4 (Winter 1983/1984): 297-317.

Compares Henrik Ibsen's *A Doll's House* with *Maître Guérin,* arguing that while there is no proof that Ibsen was influenced by Augier's play, situations in the two plays strongly suggest a connection.

Weinberg, Bernard. "Contemporary Criticism of Emile Augier, 1845-70." *Modern Philology* XXXVI, No. 2 (November 1938): 179-206.

Examines early criticism of Augier's plays, focusing on considerations of structure, realism, and morality in his works.

Aloysius Bertrand

1807-1841

(Born Louis Jacques Napoleon Bertrand) French poet, dramatist, and journalist.

Bertrand is generally considered the creator of the prose poem as a modern literary form. His major work, *Gaspard de la nuit: fantaisies à la manière de Rembrandt et de Callot,* is a collection of approximately sixty prose poems based on historical and fantastic subjects. These works are especially esteemed for their intense, lyrical style and evocative imagery. Both in their form and subject matter Bertrand's prose poems have been viewed as an influence on authors associated with the literary movements of Symbolism and Surrealism.

Born in the town of Ceva in the Piedmont region of France (now part of Italy), Bertrand was the eldest son of an officer in the French army and his Italian wife. When Bertrand's father retired in 1815, the family settled in Dijon, where Bertrand later attended the Royal College of Dijon, a school which emphasized classical studies. Bertrand began writing poetry when he was sixteen, and, in 1826, became active in the Société d'Etudes, a local literary society. The following year several of his poems and essays were published in *Le provincial,* a Dijon newspaper, where they attracted favorable attention from several important French literary figures, including the novelist Victor Hugo.

After *Le provincial* failed in 1828, Bertrand went to Paris, making several brief but well-received appearances at the literary salons of Charles Nodier and C. A. Sainte-Beuve. During the following year he completed most of *Gaspard de la nuit.* In 1833 Bertrand sold *Gaspard de la nuit* to the publisher Pierre Renduel, who set the manuscript aside, believing that the time was not right for its publication. Throughout the next seven years, Bertrand made several unsuccessful attempts to persuade Renduel to publish *Gaspard.* In 1841, suffering from an advanced case of tuberculosis, Bertrand was admitted to a hospital in Paris, where he died a month later. After Bertrand's death, Sainte-Beuve and the sculptor David D'Angers recovered the manuscript of *Gaspard de la nuit* from Renduel and published it the following year with an introduction by Sainte-Beuve and illustrations by D'Angers.

Bertrand's literary reputation rests exclusively on *Gaspard de la nuit.* The collection begins with two prefaces. In the first, Bertrand reports a fictional encounter with "Gaspard of the Night," who describes his search for "the absolute in Art" and gives Bertrand the manuscript of *Gaspard.* The second preface, signed by "Gaspard," presents Bertrand's vision of art as a two-sided medallion, one side personified by Rembrandt van Rijn, the Dutch painter noted for his skillfully rendered portraits, and the other by Jacques Callot, a French painter who specialized in painting beggars and grotesque dwarves. This second preface, as John Thomas Wright explains, "reveals Bertrand's fundamental concern: the duality of man's personality as personified by the personages of Rembrandt and Callot, the former being the philosopher, that is the ideal of the transcendental self, while Callot is the old soldier representing the ineffable side of man's personality. Art, says Bertrand, is derived from both aspects in his personality." Each of the prose poems opens with a quotation from a song, proverb, or literary work, and consists of four to seven paragraphs or couplets of prose set, according to Bertrand's instructions, "as if they were stanzas in verse." Many of the pieces in the collection were inspired by Bertrand's interest in the architecture and history of fourteenth- and fifteenth-century Dijon and often feature sorcerers, monks, lepers, gnomes, and other characters derived from the fairy tales popular in the early 1800s. Scarbo, the best known of these characters in Bertrand's work, is a deformed dwarf who appears in the middle of the night to torment the narrator of *Gaspard* with threats and tales of impending doom. Frequently likened to miniature paintings in their precise, controlled effects, Bertrand's prose poems have been praised for their imagination and carefully structured rhythms. In addition to the value of *Gaspard de la nuit* as an artistic achievement in its own right, Bertrand's volume has served as a significant influence on such important poets as Charles Baudelaire, Stéphane Mallarmé, and Arthur Rimbaud.

PRINCIPAL WORKS

Le sous lieutenant de Hussards (drama) 1832
Louise (drama) 1833
Gaspard de la nuit: fantaisies à la manière de Rembrandt et de Callot (prose poems) 1842
  [*Gaspard de la nuit: Fantasies in the Manner of Rembrandt and Callot,* 1977]
Le keepsake fantastique (poetry, journalism, essays, drama, and letters) 1923
Oeuvres poétiques: La volupté et pièces diverses (poetry and drama) 1926

Helen Hart Goldsmith (essay date 1959)

[*In the following essay, Goldsmith examines the importance of the page format and typography of* Gaspard de la nuit *and discusses Bertrand's innovations in the prose poem in relation to later writers.*]

Among French symbolists there was a notable preoccupation with the poem as artifact. Rémy de Gourmont once called it *la manie typographique* ["the typographical mania"], defining the phenomenon thus:

La page imprimée prend à la fois une valeur de
tableau pictural et de table de valeurs. Les mots
vivent, les lettres, jusqu'aux blancs et aux
alinéas. Tout dans la page prend une importance
de forme, de position, d'intervalle, de grandeur
comparée.

[The printed page takes all at once a value from
the pictorial tableau and from the table of values. The words live, the letters, up to the spaces
and paragraphs. Everything in the page takes an
importance by its form, position, spacing, and
relative size.]

The critic wrote soon after the appearance of Mallarmé's
complete works, in 1913. But the concern with graphic
presentation of poetry, which he pointed out, had not
begun with Mallarmé; nor, for that matter, was it to end
with symbolism. As early as 1826, Aloysius Bertrand had
conceived of a new kind of prose, wherein typography and
format played an essential rôle. He ultimately embodied
his conception in **Gaspard de la nuit,** a collection which
stands at the beginnings of modern French prose poetry.
In the present article, we shall consider this work as a
manifestation of the "typographical mania" which Rémy
de Gourmont described, and we shall briefly point out
some relationships among Bertrand's use of space and typography and other writers' innovations in poetic design.

Although Bertrand never used the term *"poème en prose,"*
it was as such that he perceived his prose compositions.
In a preface to **Gaspard de la nuit,** he affirmed that he was
a poet "si c'est être poète que d'avoir cherché l'art" ["if
to be a poet is to have searched for art"]. Most of his so-
called *fantaisies* are divided into segments consisting of
not more than one clause or sentence and separated upon
the page by wide spaces. The units are brief and of almost
equal length; they are more like verse stanzas than conventional prose paragraphs. Sometimes the prevailing pattern
of equality among prose stanzas is varied by a pattern of
smooth gradation or of abrupt contrast in length. With
greater latitude than in verse poetry, Bertrand was able to
use graphic arrangement as one means of conveying the
substance and tonality of a prose poem. By varying the relative length of stanzas and the extent of intervening space,
he produced multiple effects of symmetry or asymmetry;
of rapidity or deliberateness; of simultaneity, continuity,
or suspension. The picture compounded of printed word
and blank page gave spatial form to the verbal entity.

Bertrand's instructions for the printer clearly attest his
consciousness of the poem as a pictorial unit. He wrote:

M. le Metteur en pages remarquera que chaque
pièce est divisée en *quatre, cinq, six* et *sept
alinéas ou couplets.* Il jettera de larges blancs
entre ces *couplets* comme si c'étaient des stro-
phes en vers.

[The typesetter will notice that each piece is divided into four, five, six, seven paragraphs or
couplets. He will cast large white spaces between
these couplets as if they were stanzas in verse.
(Translation by John Thomas Wright)]

Clearly, in Bertrand's eyes a poem's merit was closely
linked with its character as artifact. He emphasized this

when he scrupulously distinguished from the rest some
prose poems which were not regularly divided into *couplets* and which contained "des phrases eparpillées, des dialogues, etc" ["scattered phrases, dialogues, etc."]. He
flatly asserted that these pieces were to him "moins impor-
tantes" ["less important"]. For them only, he allowed the
printer to use his own judgment, saying:

M. le Metteur en pages blanchira les pièces
comme il jugera convenable d'après les indications du manuscrit, mais toujours de manière à
étendre et à faire foisonner la matière.—J'ai eu
soin de lui indiquer ces pièces par une x en marge
sur le manuscrit. Elles sont au nombre de neuf.

[The typesetter will leave white spaces about the
pieces if he judges it expedient according to the
manuscript, but always in a way so as to expand
and swell the material.—I have taken care to indicate to him these pieces by an X in the margin
on the manuscript. They are nine in number.
(Translation by John Thomas Wright)]

The remark concerning the manuscript's length taken in
its *proper* context only serves to confirm Bertrand's essentially artistic motives in using space. It underlines the
careful distinction which the poet maintained between the
strophic and the non-strophic form, and it shows the value
he attached to that distinction.

Bertrand was concerned not only with the format of individual poems, but he also paid special attention to the page
as a unit. He desired **Gaspard de la nuit** to be printed with
the title of each poem and book of poems on a preceding
page otherwise blank, bearing the title on its *recto* and the
epigraph or epigraphs on its *verso.* Each book was to be
followed by an additional page having on the *recto* "ici
finit . . . " ["here ends . . . "] and on the *verso,* "ici
commence . . . " ["here begins . . . "]. The poet may
have chosen this arrangement merely to increase the
length of the manuscript. However, in view of his prevailing concern with visual effects, we prefer to assume that
he wished especially to give his compositions a framework
of white space. The author's specifications were followed
by Victor Pavie in printing the post-humous first edition
of **Gaspard.** There one may observe how striking is the
total impression.

In addition to format, Bertrand was concerned with typography. In this matter he took great care but avoided
the ridiculous extremes practiced by some of his contemporaries. He particularly urged the printer not to omit the
asterisks which accompanied double spaces in the manuscript, and he specified that the epigraphs be set in "très
petits caractères" ["very small characters"]. He pointed
out that the numeral references to footnotes should be replaced ultimately by asterisks. Thus, he sought to assure
a particular typographical as well as spatial framework for
the stanzas and the poems.

If we take Bertrand's expressed wishes into account and
examine the prose poems themselves, we notice how nearly these prefigure Gourmont's definition of *la manie typographique.* For, in Bertrand's conception and practice, the
printed page has a pictorial and a proportional value in
which words, spaces, and paragraphs do participate.

One may well inquire why the poet was so preoccupied with the physical presentation of his compositions. We suggest that the reason lies chiefly in his over-all plastic orientation. The latter is implicit in the sub-title of *Gaspard de la Nuit:* "fantaisies à la manière de Rembrandt et de Callot." The Hoffmannesque designation deliberately emphasizes the poetry's pictorial bases. We know that Bertrand was a serious student of art history and of architecture. There is evidence that he preferred the Renaissance artists of the Low Countries and men like Dürer and Callot. This is not surprising, since his verbal art had much in common with their plates and canvases: realism and detail of subject; irony of expression; somber, satanic, or fanciful effects of execution. Placing his volume of prose poetry under the aegis of Rembrandt and of Callot, he pointed to his predilections and also to his desire to suggest another art medium. His insistence that his poems be laid out upon the page with delicate precision and meticulous care, like the engravings of his patrons, is surely an important expression of this latter desire.

While Bertrand's concern with spatial form was perhaps unique in his generation, there had been, long before the nineteenth century, attempts to ally poetry and the visual arts. The influence of the pattern poems of ancient bucolic writers was felt in France as early as the sixteenth century. A familiar instance is Panurge's epileny in the fifth book of *Pantagruel* (Chapter XIV). Since 1565, the song of the bottle has been printed in bottle form.

In Bertrand's own day, too, there was a considerable preoccupation with pictorial effects in literature. Let us remember that in 1831 *Le Figaro* characterized *le jeune-France* with these words: "Le jeune-France est né du jour où la peinture a fait alliance avec la littérature romantique . . . et dès ce jour les peintres ont su écrire, les hommes de lettres ont eu la barbe" ["The jeune-France movement was born on the day when the art of painting joined with romantic literature . . . and since that day painters have known how to write, the literary men have come of age"]. Such an alliance of the arts did not usually depend upon the physical presentation of a literary composition. It was generally manifest in a language rich in color and plastic connotations, often in descriptions of specific canvases and manners. Bertrand went farther than this; he conveyed the plastic media without precisely *imitating* or merely *describing* them. That he succeeded in a more subtle kind of transposition of arts was partly due to his use of space and printing devices.

Bertrand was not entirely alone in making innovations in format and in typography. A poem like "Les Djinns" or a prose tale like "L'Histoire du roi de Bohême et de ses sept châteaux" suffice to remind us that this is so. Hugo's and even Nodier's ideographic experiments should probably be regarded, however, as occasional *tours de force* meant to "épater le bourgeois" ["shock the middle-class"], rather than as consistent procedure.

Particularly interesting are the idiosyncrasies of a lesser poet, Xavier Forneret. He was, like Bertrand, a poet in prose; he wrote about a decade later and was apparently unaware of the other's work. Only since André Breton resurrected him has he enjoyed a certain measure of fame. In his writings he made immoderate use of blank space and peculiar typography. For example, his collection of quasi-prose poems entitled *Pièce de pièces, temps perdu* was printed on one side of the page only. That the author attached considerable importance to this fact is cryptically indicated by his opening sentence: "Le moment *d'alors* est comme cette espèce de livre, il veut du *blanc* dans ses pages" ["That moment *then* is like that kind of book, it wants *white* in its pages"]. Forneret's procedures may have had an import similar to Bertrand's, but they were less consistent. Furthermore, they were undoubtedly in large measure an attention-getting device on the part of a man who cultivated his fame as an eccentric. Unlike Forneret, Bertrand in no sense desired to be conspicuous except as an impeccable artist; he used the blank page and the printed character only in the service of art.

In connection with *Gaspard de la Nuit* and the "typographical mania" we are likely to think of Nodier's *Smarra,* because in it there are some brief, distinctly separated paragraphs of almost equal length, which resemble Bertrand's. Partly on this account, *Smarra* has sometimes been called a prose poem. Yet Nodier's prose stanzas are only an occasional device occurring merely in the *Epilogue.* They are not an essential factor of the tale's existence, since they do not correspond to or help to represent a poetic logic basic to the total composition. They are, however, a graphic imitation of poetry, and they have an affective value because they suggest the disunity of a dream.

These passing remarks should serve to emphasize that there was in the early nineteenth century an emerging tendency to give words a halo of space and a pictorial value apart from their syntactical worth. While this tendency was to some extent demonstrated by the work of several poets, its most fruitful and consistent manifestation was in Bertrand's *Gaspard de la Nuit.* The *Fantaisies à la manière de Rembrandt et de Callot* represent a peculiarly conscious effort to enhance the word's supremacy and to establish the poem as an autonomous reality. The French symbolists whom Gourmont characterized as being possessed by *la manie typographique* of course went farther in this direction.

First, we should notice that Mallarmé and his followers abandoned an element which for Bertrand and his contemporaries had been an important concomitant of verbal plasticity; that is, elaborate pictorial illustration. Mallarmé said of the illustrated book: "Je suis pour . . . aucune illustration, tout ce qu'évoque un livre devant se passer dans l'esprit du lecteur" ["I am for . . . any illustration, all that which evokes a book before passing into the spirit of the reader"]. And we may recall that, before Mallarmé, Baudelaire had banished all "artistic abominations" from the walls of his *"chambre double."*

The symbolists, however, did retain and importantly elaborate the concern with space and typography which activated Bertrand as he composed during the late 20's and the 30's. Mallarmé recognized that it was an integral part of the tendency toward a liberation of language and a mingling of genres, toward the vers libre and the prose poem. And, as Gourmont later pointed out, Mallarmé himself made the most extreme innovations in this direction during the symbolist period. When, like Bertrand, he wrote poems in prose, he demonstrated clearly enough the importance he accorded to space intervening between images, to that *absence* which is itself a presence. However, his prose poems are not so resolutely framed nor so rigorously proportioned as are those of *Gaspard de la nuit.* In his early prose poems brief paragraphs, balanced in length and separated on the basis of poetic logic, often simulate stanzas of verse. Again, there may be such a striking procedure as the italicization and isolation of the key words *le pénultième est mort* [*"the penultimate is dead"*], in "Le démon de l'analogie." The late prose poems of Mallarmé are more fluid than plastic and so convoluted in their movement that any such rigid mold as Bertrand had used would have been inappropriate. Even in the late prose poems, Mallarmé nevertheless made distinct separations and silences with the help of the printed page.

In *Un coup de dés* he most thoroughly demonstrated the symbolist effort to establish a bulwark of space around words and to give them an ideal value. This was Mallarmé's ultimate homage to "le vide papier que la blancheur défend" ["the empty paper that whiteness defends"]. It was the point of departure for Gourmont's remarks on *la manie typographique.* That critic said of Mallarmé's poem: "Mallarmé s'attache à interpréter les espaces et la valeur des caractères" ["Mallarmé is fond of interpreting the spaces and the value of characters"]. The poet himself described his procedure as an essentially *musical* notation. His was a far-reaching effort toward the liberation of idea and spirit; it went beyond Bertrand's primarily *representational* aims. Yet it grew from a like preoccupation with the word, and it depended, after all, upon effects visually conveyed.

"The typographical mania" was carried to an extreme point by Apollinaire and his followers. Apollinaire, like Bertrand, was principally oriented toward the arts of design. The bold consecrator of literary surrealism was closely linked with the painters of his generation and was their most articulate advocate and explicator. Seeking in his writing the element of surprise, which he deemed of first importance, Apollinaire attempted to achieve on the printed page what artists like Picasso were then endeavoring to achieve on canvas; that is, a new dimension brought about by simultaneity of impression. While Bertrand had probably not thought in terms of a new dimension, we notice that one of his chief effects, depending largely upon format, was that pictorial simultaneity which Lessing, in his *Laokoön,* had relegated to the painter's province.

In Apollinaire's poetry, the rôle of space and proportion is important. If we compare definitive versions of his poems with earlier readings, we see that changes are often typographical. Silences replace discursive elements or are interjected between previously unseparated lines of verse. Images are literally carved out of space. Spaces are rearranged to produce greater balance, or they are widened to enhance suspension.

Apollinaire envisaged more boldly than did previous poets a synthesis of the arts. He felt that this end was best served by the ideogram. Specifically, he said:

> Les artifices typographiques poussés très loin avec une grande audace ont l'avantage de faire naître un lyrisme visuel qui était presque inconnu avant notre époque. Ces artifices peuvent aller très loin encore et consommer la synthèse des arts, de la musique, de la peinture et de la littérature.
>
> [Typographical artifices pushed very far with a great audacity have the advantage of giving birth to a visual lyricism that was nearly unknown before our time. These artifices can go even further, and consummate the synthesis of the arts, music, painting, and literature.]

Thus, the poet came to write verse which was so arranged on the page that it imitated for the eye the object evoked. Poems shaped like a tie, a watch, or a fan were nearly autonomous objects. As Bertrand and Mallarmé had done, Apollinaire altered traditional patterns and perspectives in his attempt to establish the poem as a single entity or "artifact."

Finally, we shall mention Saint-John Perse, a present-day poet outstanding among many who make important use of pattern in their poetry. It may seem a far cry from the elaborate and unconventional eccentricities of Apollinaire to the austere restraint of Perse's typical prose stanza. Yet the poet of *Anabase* and *Neiges* has in common with all the artists we have discussed a marked concern for "cette page où plus rien ne s'inscrit" ["this page where nothing more writes itself"]. These words, in their context at the end of *Neiges,* make the unsullied page a symbol, as it was for Mallarmé. Perse casts his poetry in a mold not unlike that which Bertrand first used. It is written in short verses which are often widely separated upon the page, and the sequence and relative proportions have an affective basis. The movement, the construction, and the poetic effect of this prose depend in part upon the graphic picture presented.

So, in French poetry today there persists that kind of alliance between verbal and visual art which Bertrand originally sought early in the last century. Since *Gaspard de la nuit,* format and typography have continued to be intrinsic to poetic expression, serving the renewal of language for which modern poets have labored. *La manie typographique,* variously elaborated or moderated since Mallarmé wrote *Un coup de dés,* has become the norm, increasing in importance as poetry without rhyme or caesura has acquired wide currency. White space is a primary ingredient of much contemporary poetry; thus, we may confirm the continuing significance of Bertrand's general rule: "Blanchir comme si le texte était de la poésie" ["Set as if the text were poetry"]. (pp. 12-18)

Helen Hart Goldsmith, "Aloysius Bertrand and 'The Typographical Mania'," in Kentucky Foreign Language Quarterly, *Vol. 6, No. 1, First Quarter, 1959, pp. 12-19.*

Renee Riese Hubert   (essay date 1964)

[*In the following excerpt, Hubert examines the visual imagery of* Gaspard de la nuit.]

Aloysius Bertrand, generally considered the creator of the modern prose-poem, has received more credit for inspiring Baudelaire, Lautréamont, and Mallarmé than for his own artistic accomplishments. The obvious and apparently conventional romanticism of his "*Fantaisies à la manière de Rembrandt et de Callot*" do not always appeal to modern readers, who may be unwilling to share Bertrand's affection for witches, dwarfs, alchemists, and medieval monks, or for minute, picturesque, and fantastic scenes. These sketches may appear facile, devoid of mysterious proportions or disquieting feelings. The sophisticated reader may refuse to be carried away by such fanciful descriptions. It is not my intention to reveal unexplored depths in the universe of Aloysius Bertrand, but to show that his reliance on surface appearances was intentional.

In her extensive study of the prose-poem [*Le poème en prose de Baudelaire jusqu'à nos jours,* 1959], Suzanne Bernard says:

> C'est presque faire une remarque superflue que de noter l'importance donnée par Bertrand, grand visuel et amateur de peinture, aux effets picturaux, et surtout aux vigoureux contrastes, noir sur blanc: si les "effets de nuit" abondent dans son œuvre (il serait trop long de les citer tous), ce n'est pas seulement par goût du mystère nocturne, de "La Nuit et ses Prestiges" (titre du livre III de *Gaspard*); c'est aussi, par goût d'artiste.

> [It is almost superfluous to note the importance given by Bertrand, great observer and lover of painting, to pictorial effects, and particularly to vigorous contrasts, black on white: if the "effects of night" abound in his works (there are too many to cite them all here) it is not only out of a taste for the mysteries of the night, for "The Night and Its Marvels" (title of book III of *Gaspard*); it is also out of artistic inclination.]

Madame Bernard, in comparing earlier and later versions of Bertrand's poems, notices that repeatedly, "la rêverie immatérielle du poète est remplacée par un tableautin précis ["the insubstantial reverie of the poet is replaced by a small precise painting"]. She gives us the predominantly visual, as well as the pictorial, characteristics of *Gaspard de la nuit,* but she apparently considers it unnecessary to discuss the techniques the poet used to produce these effects. (pp. 76-7)

In order to show the visual impact of the poems, I propose to proceed from the basic contrasts pertaining to sight in terms of the visual arts: light and darkness, details and contours, motion and immobility. Although such contrasts may be found in all the poems, their role and importance vary greatly.

Many texts of *Gaspard de la nuit* evolve from a juxtaposition of day and night, light and darkness. Frequent discoveries of luminous centers in the midst of darkness provide the framework of **"L'heure du sabbat"**: the phosphorescent eye of a cat, hair twinkling with glow worms, white foam surging from obscure rocks, even piercing cries, possess visual force. Not only does the poem give the impression that it consists of bright spots appearing successively upon a dark screen, it also stresses the idea of motion, suggesting a constant search within the obscure world of night. Specks of light may each time create the momentary impression that a goal has been reached, that a discovery has been made, until we find out that all along the poet has been aiming at nothing in particular. Thus we hover from one bewilderment to the next, from illumination to eclipse. Amid this truly romantic Sabbath, we grasp Bertrand's basic procedure, the lightning strokes which impinge themselves upon us without intermediary as gestures rather than as a constituent part of a final tableau. We cannot deny a certain playfulness in this and other poems in which the reader's eye must pursue deceptive sparks without perceiving meaningful constellations.

Bertrand imposes a different kind of visual concentration upon us in **"L'écolier de Leyde"** by demanding that we focus on smaller and smaller objects. Through the eyes of the poor student, we first see the banker and his rich attire, then his impressive bank, then his box of instruments, and finally we peer through a magnifying glass in order to scrutinize a coin. No sooner have we examined the coin than the poem changes its direction with all the details repeated in reverse order: the student steps backwards, distances increase, and, after the characters have taken their final bow, we can no longer focus on anything. Bertrand undoubtedly wishes such scenes to appear colorful. Still, he does not really display a rich, subtle, or varied palette. He draws our attention to objects that sparkle and shine: coins, eyes, collars, and magnifying glass, without bothering to define the specific shades of the velvet coat or the tulips.

Concerning Bertrand's use of shapes, lines, and contours, **"La chambre gothique"** is most significant. It is based on a paradoxical relationship between the container and the contained, a relationship which Baudelaire was to exploit in *Les fleurs du mal.* Night is a flower containing in her calyx the stars and a coat of arms on which devils and dragons are represented; the shape of the window suggests the contours of a halo surrounding a cross; a child lies in a cradle made of knight's armor; the closet contains a skeleton; a frame holds the portrait of an ancestor; the wound contains blood. But Baudelairean transcendence is missing, for the poem offers no more than a series of pictorial analogies which a joke finally disrupts. Bertrand does not often write this kind of poem, based on what one might call a unified design. He aims less at the representation of a complete tableau than at the perception of its elements. His poetic rhythms, derived, according to many critics, from romantic ballads, can nevertheless be considered as the eager and expert pencil strokes of a draftsman whose prime concern is to suggest movement. Thus, in his selection and use of words, Bertrand tries to capture the swift rhythms of these devilish dances and magic conjurations.

"Le fou" consists mainly of a dramatic sequence of playful events or gestures with corresponding visual and even auditory analogies. The tricks of the mischievous Scarbo belong to a twofold universe, for the dwarf has "un œil à la lune et l'autre crevé" ["one eye at the moon and the other gouged out"]. The spectacle takes place simultaneously in the heavens, on the roofs, and in the cellar amid twinkling stars, gold pieces, and the symbolic darkness of false coins.

Bertrand on his deathbed as drawn by David D'Angers.

The action shifts from the sky to the cellar, from lighter to darker regions; this downward movement is intensified by the constant dropping of luminous particles to the ground. The treasures promise to last forever, just like the silver-ringing laughter of the contented dwarf; yet as the moon sinks lower and lower, night etches a luminous image on the window, an emblematic condensation of the events the poet has described. The vitality of **"Le fou"** and its progress depend largely on a downward movement.

"La viole de gamba" may be even more representative of Bertrand's technique, not so much because it takes into account the reader's familiarity with *commedia dell'arte* figures, but because it constitutes primarily a defile, a gay review of characters. As soon as the bow touches the string, an array of well-known characters burst on the scene, linked to one another only by the conjunction *et*. The author thereby suggests not only a succession of new characters, but also succeeds in keeping all of them within range while forcing the reader's attention to shift with each new arrival. Visual suggestiveness is enhanced by recollections of *commedia dell'arte* scenes as represented on Callot prints. The reader has the impression that a pencil is moving rapidly to recapture and recreate the liveliness of the spectacle. Although auditory signals—the touching and the breaking of a chord—indicate the opening and the closing of the performance, visual elements contribute their share too, for the shape of the instrument is outlined, and the final silence coincides with the darkening atmo-

sphere. **"La viole de gamba," "Le fou"**—along with many others—are based on synesthetic effects. This technique, however, merely increases visual and auditory immediacy and, unlike Baudelairean "correspondances," does not lead to some mysterious realm.

Movement occurs in time as well as in space. Suzanne Bernard has discussed Bertrand's literary use of the past: "Si l'artiste qu'est Bertrand utilise de manière extrêment consciente les mœurs et les croyances médiévales, ce n'est pas en archéologue" ["If Bertrand uses in an extremely conscious manner medieval morals and beliefs, it is not that he is an archeologist"]. The spectacles and scenes he evokes often move at such a pace that the reader is bound to feel that time has been eliminated or discounted. The last action of a scene may seem almost simultaneous with the first, even if the hour strikes twelve at the beginning and dawn draws close at the end (**"Les lépreux"**) or if repetition is involved (**"Un rêve"**).

Space with its dimensions, its perspectives, as well as its manifold and deceptive patterns, plays an even more important part in Bertrand's universe than do shapes and colors. **"Le maçon"** may be considered as a gradual extension into space, although Friedrich Banner, in his study on *Gaspard de la nuit,* states that the poem is but a "Folge von Einzelbildern, zusammengehalten durch: Il voit, il distingue. (Blickpunkt des Beschauers.)" Bertrand has indeed achieved an extraordinary tour de force in **"Le maçon."** He chooses words which bring to light the most striking views of a Gothic cathedral, views which finally merge into the surrounding city. His mason is a veritable storehouse of imagery which gradually renders visible the entire town. Distant and vague at first, this city will eventually yield its inexhaustible panorama of castles, fortifications, churches, and soldiers.

In both technique and subject matter, **"Le maçon"** is a verbal equivalent of a Callot engraving. The unwearying eye of the mason brings into focus and coördinates this never-ending wealth of structures without neglecting the slightest detail. But his activity goes beyond the arranging and recording of buildings. He breathes life into the most insignificant foot-soldier in town, into the most grotesque gargoyle on the cathedral buttress. As he focuses at first on extraordinarily shaped stone-figures, they seem, by their very defiance of repetition, to proclaim their own creativity. The increasing sharpness of the focus eventually discloses the laws that bind the architecture of the tower to the pattern of the town. The scene gets brighter until, under the reddening glow of the setting sun, the mason combines the horizon with the cathedral nave into a single construct. His gathering of images appears to be an active process, requiring as much energy as hammering stones into place.

In spite of this gradual extension of the field of vision, however, certain limitations in regard to space are inherent in the structure of the poem. Bertrand's poetic representations do not exceed what might be perceived in a single glance, and the point of view of the spectator or onlooker (from within or without) is normally taken into account. It is not surprising, therefore, that Dutch landscapes, somewhat romanticized, often serve as settings for Bertrand's panoramas. Indeed, he has excluded from his poems daring adventures into vast uncharted lands. However rich in oneiric images they may be, his landscapes are devoid of those endless vistas, those bold color schemes, those aggressive or suggestive lines which surrealist poets usually associate with the world of dreams. In fact, Bertrand, to whom the notion of space was at best synonymous with that of a painter's canvas or an engraver's plate, often imposes arbitrary limitations on his universe; thus, for example, he makes the beginning of a poem coincide with the opening of a volume. In the dedicatory text, **"A M. Victor Hugo,"** he focuses our attention immediately upon a book and thus cleverly transforms the literary work—Victor Hugo's as well as his own—into pure imagery which comes to life at a glance. This evident concreteness, moreover, constitutes the only bridge between the past and the future—between the moment when the poet wrote the work and the moment when it will be read, read by readers paradoxically belonging to a distant past. The physical manifestations of the book can transform time itself and even art, as the author had already suggested in the preface:

> Ce manuscrit, ajouta-t-il, vous dira combien d'instruments ont essayé mes lèvres avant d'arriver à celui qui rend la note pure et expressive, combien de pinceaux j'ai usés sur la toile avant d'y voir naître la vague aurore du clair-obscur. Là sont consignés divers procédés nouveaux peut-être d'harmonie et de couleur, seul

résultat et seule récompense qu'eussent obtenus mes élucubrations.

["This manuscript," he added, "will tell you how many instruments have tried my lips before arriving at the one which renders the note pure and expressive, how many paint brushes I have used on the canvas before seeing born there the shadowy aurora of chiaroscuro. There, are deposited many processes, perhaps new, of harmony and of color, the sole result and sole reward that my laborious study may have achieved." (Translation by John Thomas Wright)]

The image of the book recurs in **"Le bibliophile," "Départ pour le sabbat,"** and especially in **"L'alchimiste,"** where again Bertrand uses the device of having the book and the poem open simultaneously. The impatient alchemist cannot bring to life the mystic symbols of his book, which remain enigmatic, fragmentary, and unreal to him. He is reduced to describing the pranks of a salamander, to which he adds a series of haphazard, dazzling distractions that impress their reality upon us. The presence of the alchemist seems irretrievably linked to a quick-silver atmosphere from which attention cannot be withdrawn.

"Le marchand de tulipes," in which biblical illuminations provide a direct source of images and give the signal for the unfolding of other spectacles, combines the techniques of **"A M. Victor Hugo"** and **"L'alchimiste."** The poet seems to attain concentration through the willful reduction of the tableau to the size of a miniature. For a time the doctor distracts himself from these illuminations merely by gazing at the goldfish in the aquarium. Then, suddenly, through an opening door, he sees a florist bringing a variety of tulips into the house. Illuminations, flowers, and tantalizing sights combine into the suggestive image sequence of sun and passion flowers. The poem ends not when the radiant spectacle is practically inlaid on the casement, but when Doctor Huylten and the Duke of Alba, as represented by Holbein, exchange glances. Characteristically, the doctor had just put away his glasses, thus effacing the barrier between spectacle and spectator, between art and reality. Moreover, this action serves to emphasize the visual analogy between the book and the painting.

In **"Le maçon"** and **"Le bibliophile,"** however, the spectacle, far from being contained in the obvious predetermined outlines of a book or a room, has to be scrutinized and re-created through the eyes of the intermediary himself. In other poems (**"Le fou"** and **"Le falot,"** for example) Bertrand plays the part of an intermediary by using the first person singular, which does not give an emotional overtone to the poems or a meaning to their spatial limitations. Rather, it helps to make the visual contact more obvious and direct, for the narrator serves as an intermediary who filters, channels, or mirrors the scene, and thus is merely instrumental. From a dark room, he peers watchfully or fearfully through a window. His gaze wanders from an enclosed dark world into a lighter, more colorful external realm until, after a series of flashes, the final image crystallizes. When the famed dwarf Scarbo makes his appearance both as a narrator and a creature of "La Nuit et ses prestiges," his multifarious activities become undistinguishable from the flashes of light with which Bertrand heightens the scene.

Bertrand uses still another technique in **"La ronde sous la cloche"** to circumscribe the setting of the spectacle. The poem evokes a dramatic scene created by darkness where moonshine, magicians, church bells, and birds are performers who succeed one another in the limelight. The reader is treated to a concentrated nightmare which takes place, of course, at the witching hour of midnight. He sees a rapid succession of sparks and flashes which dazzle both the dark room and the town. The procession which circumambulates under the threatening thunder and lightning unifies all these elements: the bells, the marching magicians, the number twelve, the frustrated flight of the encaged bird, the slowing down of the weathercock—all are encompassed in the crescendo and diminuendo of the devilish dance of fire and fireflies.

In spite of the circular movement which constitutes the structural basis of the text, it is not so much the accumulation of elements as the continuity of the scene which leads to the final intensified image: a flower falling through the open window onto the poet's pillow. The lightning has ceased, or rather has transformed its identity, for the red fires, threatening magicians, disturbing tintinnabulations, and thunder clouds in motion have all finally fused into the closer image of the jasmine flower. Although the scene does not end in darkness, an eclipse, or a dramatic exit, the gift of the mangled flower to the poet cannot mean a permanent source of illumination. On the contrary, we should regard it only as the last and most precarious image of the entire series.

Several poems describe a sequence of scenes which, unlike the previous ones, do not take place within a set framework. **"La chasse,"** for instance, has no other limitations than the light of day. As long as daylight persists, the hunt will go on. Brightness and color scarcely matter when compared to the creative power of movement. A never-ending cavalcade of hunters, animals, and musical instruments rushes through a landscape so varied that it precludes immobility. This cavalcade only faintly resembles the rhythmic dream patterns encountered in **"La ronde sous la cloche."** The motion, by its swiftness and continuity, does not permit or suggest identification. As swiftness alone gives unity to the spectacle, the poem must end with a sudden arrest of movement. The hunters are attacked, but the arrowlike pattern is not transformed into a battle scene or even a fight. The instant the hunter is killed, all comes to a halt—time and man's identity stand revealed or rather transfixed.

All in all, the presence of visual elements, which are characteristic of the plastic arts, tends to transform the poems into almost palpable spectacles. The texts contain frequent allusions to the various arts and to specific artists, so much so that the kinship between literary creation and the fine arts is central to *Gaspard de la nuit*. Rembrandt and Callot, whose names appear in the subtitle of the volume, are described in the preface as "deux faces antithétiques" of art:

> Rembrandt est le philosophe à barbe blanche qui
> s'encilimaçonne en son réduit, qui absorbe sa

pensée dans la méditation et dans la prière, qui ferme les yeux pour se recueillir, qui s'entretient avec des esprits de beauté, de science, de sagesse et d'amour, et qui se consume à pénétrer les mystérieux symboles de la nature.—Callot, au contraire, est le lansquenet fanfaron et grivois qui se pavane sur la place, qui fait du bruit dans la taverne, qui caresse les filles de Bohémiens, qui ne jure que par sa rapière et par son escopette, et qui n'a d'autre inquiétude que de cirer sa moustache.

[Rembrandt is the white-bearded philosopher, who corkscrews himself into his retreat, who gathers his thoughts in meditation and prayer, who closes his eyes to wrap himself in thought, who communes with the spirits of beauty, science, wisdom, and love and who wastes away delving into the mysterious symbols of nature.— Callot, on the other hand, is the mercenary soldier, braggart, and licentious, who struts about the square, who is noisy in the taverns, who caresses the gypsy girls, who swears only by his sword and his blunderbus, and whose only other care is waxing his moustache. (Translation by John Thomas Wright)]

In other words, Bertrand not only reduces the works of Rembrandt and Callot to two of their most characteristic prints, but also to an antithesis between introvert and extrovert or, in romantic terms, between the sublime and the grotesque. But the impact of these painters is more complex than Bertrand's statement might imply. We have already discussed the transposition into words of Callot's minute etchings, his swift motion, his concern for detail. The Rembrandtesque elements originate more from the impression created by this great artist's etchings than from an awareness of his vision. Poems such as **"La barbe pointue"** and **"L'alchimiste"** echo Rembrandt's mastery of dramatic chiaroscuro. Inspired primarily by the more anecdotal medieval scenes, Bertrand tends to regard the Dutch master as essentially an illustrator.

According to the poet's own statement, other painters also enriched his imagination and contributed to the world of *Gaspard de la nuit*. In the poem **"Harlem,"** he puts the little town within easy reach of the reader. This confrontation is by no means achieved by a descriptive method. The living reality of the town is abstracted from the contemplation of paintings. Striking elements and local color, characteristic of Dutch genre painting, appear in all their vividness. In the description of the town we recognize at one and the same time a landscape, a Dutch interior, and a series of characters. Yet despite these strong pictorial reminiscences, the organization of this and other poems is not conceived according to spatial concepts. It consists of an enumeration in a way analogous to those of **"La viole de gamba"** and **"La ronde sous la cloche."** The poet makes visible, recognizable, even unmistakable, a series of details: canals, bohemians, churches, a stork, and a mayor, each one a self-sufficient entity. They impinge upon the reader's mind, individually and without modifying one another.

One might be tempted to conclude that Bertrand as a poet sought no more than to express the visible. Even a superficial comparison between *Gaspard de la nuit* and *Les illuminations* will show that Rimbaud lets his creations crumble or evaporate, whereas Bertrand holds on desperately to a beautiful flower or a stained glass image as the spectacle nears the end. Bertrand tries to bring within reach what is normally remote, remote not in the unexplored realms of our imagination, but distant in time and far removed from everyday reality: the world of chronicles, legends, etchings, and ballads. He brings this universe so near to us that the present and its demands can no longer interfere. Consequently, its reality becomes so immediate that it does not need to be welded into a coherent tableau.

But are the movements, the metamorphoses, the final crystallization of this imagistic world truly reassuring? Bertrand, in his preface, tries to capture the essence of art, as though he were pursuing an elusive image: "Plût au ciel que l'art ne fût une chimère." Later he states that the pursuit of love and God do not suffice: "Me voilà en quête du diable." The ultimate realization of the artistic endeavor, that is the presentation of a manuscript in which historic sights are transposed from dream to reality and are consequently no longer evanescent, coincides with the declaration that the alleged author of *Gaspard de la nuit* is none other than the devil himself. Bertrand has thus admitted, not without a grain of irony, the diabolic temptation of his cult for the visible. In his "fantaisies" he wanted to preserve and intensify the very concreteness of art, a concreteness which had nothing to do with matter and substance, but only with perception. Inspired by art, though not a student of art, Bertrand hoped to express the immediacy of impressions. He invariably assigned to the reader the part of the spectator. Bertrand, therefore, had no use for that inner vision which Reverdy, Eluard, and Breton presupposed. The initiator of the genre, Bertrand had never really confronted the elusive world of concepts and abstractions. It was thus possible for him to cross blindfolded the many precarious bridges that led to these "fantaisies." (pp. 77-85)

> *Renee Riese Hubert, "The Cult of the Visible in 'Gaspard De La Nuit',"* in *Modern Language Quarterly, Vol. XXV, No. 1, March, 1964, pp. 76-85.*

Paul Zweig (essay date 1964)

[*Zweig was an American critic, poet, and educator who translated a selection of prose poems from* Gaspard de la nuit. *In the following excerpt, he discusses the importance of Bertrand's prose poems in French literature.*]

Gaspard de la nuit has moved in the sub-basement of French literature for more than a century, enjoying an almost clandestine fame. At the time of its publication in 1842, the book was quickly forgotten beneath the verbose grandeur of the French romantics, so different in their manner from Bertrand's careful inspiration; but strangely enough, it has since been equally obscured by the genius of those who eventually recognised in Bertrand a great predecessor.

Bertrand himself already suspected the first of these fates, and in the dedicatory piece of his book abdicated all claims to immortality in favor of his imaginary patron Victor Hugo. But he would surely have been surprised to discover the underground veins by which *Gaspard de la nuit* has since become an obscure classic, and a kind of source book for the formal audacity of men like Baudelaire, Rimbaud, Mallarmé, etc. (pp. 3-4)

The reasons for Bertrand's relative popularity during the second half of the nineteenth century are not hard to discover. After the exhausting rhetoric of the romantics, and their voluminous and often careless inspiration, poets like Baudelaire, Gautier, Banville, etc. felt the need to impose a greater formal mastery in their poetry. It became important to write perfectly, carefully, and not too often. Hugo having exhausted the marvels of quantity, the new generation, inspired by Baudelaire and Poe, tended to envisage *l'art poétique* more in terms of a science, and in fact a metaphysics, of craftsmanship.

The carefully sculpted rhythms of Bertrand's prose, as well as the density and almost visionary precision of his imagination, struck a chord of response in a man like Mallarmé, who could recommend to his daughter: "Prends Bertrand, on y trouve de tout ["Take up Bertrand; there you will find everything"]. But of course the most famous case of direct indebtedness is that of Baudelaire, who wrote, in the dedication of his *Petits poèmes en prose:*

> C'est en feuilletant, pour la vingtième fois au moins, le fameux *Gaspard de la nuit,* d'Aloysius Bertrand [. . .] que l'idée m'est venue de tenter quelque chose d'analogue, et d'appliquer à la description de la vie moderne [. . .] le procédé qu'il avait appliqué à la peinture de la vie ancienne, si étrangement pittoresque.

> [It was while thumbing through Aloysius Bertrand's famous *Gaspard de la nuit,* for the twentieth time at least [. . .] that I got the idea to attempt something similar, and to apply to the description of modern life [. . .] the method he applied in depicting the strangely picturesque life of the ancients.]

The differences between Bertrand's prose poems and those of Baudelaire are of course important. The *Petits poèmes en prose* depend much more on a rigour of analysis which often becomes truly lyrical; in their case it is the argument itself which is poetically dense. To be sure images enter into the poems, but not as the principle of organisation, not as the building-blocks. This is undoubtedly what Baudelaire meant when he complained:

> Sitôt que j'eus commencé le travail, je m'aperçus que non seulement je restais bien loin de mon mystérieux et brillant modèle, mais encore que je faisais quelque chose de singulièrement différent.

> [As soon as I began work, I noticed that not only did I remain quite distant from my mysterious and brilliant model, but that I was doing something singularly different.]

The prose poems of *Gaspard de la nuit* are constructed by a careful juxtaposition of images or tableaux. Each poem is presented as a tale, or as coherent description; but its real force, most often, comes from the addition of evocative images, yoked together by their inter-relatedness, as well as by the narration itself. So that despite the tightness of story-telling, the poems remain essentially paratactic: their method is lyrical rather than analytic. . . . In this sense, *Gaspard* is closer to Rimbaud's *Illuminations,* than to Baudelaire: Rimbaud also builds his poems by reconciling narration and lyrical juxtaposition of images; he also presents a "vision" rather than a dense analysis.

It remains true that *Gaspard* probably did more than any other book to crystallise the later possibilities of the prose poem, and to create the form which has since become familiar in poets as different as Baudelaire, Mallarmé, Rimbaud, Eluard, Char, Michaux, etc. Instead of a diffuse poetic prose, and long, evocative narrations, such as in Chateaubriand or even Nerval, Bertrand worked each poem into a tight, sparse coherence. And this is what the later poets will most remember of his work, along with the visual immediacy which he always managed to convey.

In one sense *Gaspard* resembles some carefully inscribed album brought back by a voyager from his travels. Like Stendhal in Italy, the poet has been delicate and observant. And his writings are meant to evoke, with artful precision, what he has seen. That is to say, what he wants us, his readers, to see. But, unlike Stendhal, Bertrand did not travel. Or he travelled in time rather than in space. The reality that comes so startlingly alive in his poems, belongs to the setting of some inner adventure. So that "seeing," for Bertrand, becomes a truly visionary exercise.

This vision is conditioned by the literary fashion of his time. The "other" reality into which he wished to lead us has much to do with the gothic revival and its medieval atmosphere, as well as with the wilfully subversive terrors of the Jeune-France: the group of "petits romantiques" whose rejection of bourgeois values, and whose cult of literary violence and terror, was the first sign of that disaffection with reality which was to become the keystone of French poetic inspiration.

However European culture has since become openly anti-cultural, and the subversive been crowned as the most legitimate of expressions. It is no wonder then that André Breton, in the *Premier manifeste du surréalisme,* should range Bertrand in his surrealist hall of fame, dubbing him *"surréaliste dans le passé"* ["surrealist in the past"].

But this "passé" that haunted Bertrand's imagination was a very particular one, drenched, as we have said, in the terror-ridden atmosphere of medieval legend. Each poem is consciously designed as a kind of miniature in the manner of any one of a number of painters: Rembrandt, Callot, Brueghel, etc. And most often these condensed visions are organised around a sudden escape into the grotesque, or the mysterious, imparting dramatic tension to the tableau. So that Bertrand, in his prose poems, attempts to appropriate the most intimate qualities of painting, as well as those of literature: sensuous, visual immediacy, as well as the advantages of dramatic sequence. Almost any one of the Scarbo poems could illustrate this combined art. **"The Gothic Room,"** for example, where the reader's expectation mounts through each stanza as it presents and rejects some strange image or scene, until the tension is finally re-

solved in the last sentence, with the grotesque appearance of Scarbo gnawing the poet's neck: here a lyrical accretion of images is modified and justified by the dramatic sequence through which Scarbo comes on the scene.

This poetry of "vision," of which Bertrand gives us such an interesting example, becomes in fact an important mode of lyrical expression during the 19th and 20th centuries. In the case of Rimbaud's *Illuminations,* for instance, the poems attempt to create, for the reader, a sensuous "glimpse" of some strange, and yet very detailed reality. This reality is in every way the contrary of that which determines our "human condition;" it is a realm of the marvelous, where the logic of sensation and experience is not destroyed (as in so much of surrealist literature), but replaced by some other logic. There is certainly nothing incoherent about Rimbaud's poems, although their coherence, just as certainly, is not a familiar one to his readers. One finally comes to the conclusion that if the poems do "mean" anything, they "mean" no more nor less than this insight into some other reality.

A similar, and equally essential, "dépaysement" is conveyed by many of Hölderlin's poems; by passages in Whitman's earlier work (above all in "Song of Myself "); by some poems of Rilke. More recently, we encounter the same strange, one is tempted to say hermetic, coherence in poems of men like René Char, Henri Michaux, some of Wallace Stevens . . .

The attempt to project a marvelous but coherent vision of another "reality," one which, in the mind of the author, is meant to replace the "real" reality of humankind, is in no way new to Western culture. Ever since the secularisation of European thought during the 16th century, the utopian imagination has rarely been dormant. From Thomas More's *Utopia,* to Bacon's *Atlantis,* Campanella's *City of the Sun,* or Fourier's lyrical socialism, a very unmystical attempt to transcend the human condition, or at least to imagine this transcendance, has been everpresent. Even the modern notion of "progress" is perversely based on an idea, albeit a singularly impoverished one, of this material kind of transcendence.

So that it is possible to consider the poetry of vision, which appears in so many different forms during the 19th century, as a new development in the tradition of utopian imagination. Certainly Fourier, with his social-erotic fantasies, can be considered as a bridge between the lyrical vision particular to some modern poetry, and the conventional forms of utopian thought.

But perhaps we are reading too much into Bertrand's sensuous imagination. Especially since *Gaspard* nowhere attempts the accents of utopian lyricism. Yet the intention to broach the logic of "real" experience, by presenting tableaux in which this logic is inoperative, remains clear. One need only consider the everpresent escape into the "insolite" around which each poem is constructed. Bertrand's land of marvelous event is meant to disorient the "reality function," by focusing it onto another, immediately probable reality, which destroys the preconceptions of our own experience.

We must not forget that a similar fascination with the "insolite" in Baudelaire leads him eventually to desire a fantastic land in which: "tout n'est qu'ordre et beauté, luxe, calme et volupté" ["there is only order and beauty, luxury, calm and pleasure"]. And if the utopian impulse here falls to the level of a rather traditional exoticism, this perhaps gives us a clue as to the deeper content of the 19th century's fascination with exotic realities; a fascination which is transcended only by the visionary purity of men such as Hölderlin, Rimbaud, Michaux.

In any case, it is fruitful to situate Bertrand, and *Gaspard de la nuit,* among the pioneers of this new mode of poetic perception. (pp. 5-15)

> *Paul Zweig, in an introduction to* Gaspard de la Nuit: Extraits, *by Aloysius Bertrand, translated by Paul Zweig, M. J. Minard, 1964, pp. 3-15.*

Laurent Lesage   (essay date 1977)

[*In the following excerpt, Lesage discusses artistic and literary influences on Bertrand and the influence of* Gaspard de la nuit *on noted French literary figures.*]

Buried in the histories of French literature is an early nineteenth-century poet who should be summoned back to tingle the sensibilities of another generation as avid of the supernatural and the macabre as his own. He is Aloysius Bertrand, whose epitaph reads inventor of the prose poem, forerunner of the Parnasse school of nineteenth-century poets, the Symbolists, the Decadents, Cubists, and Surrealists. Poets from Baudelaire to Breton have acknowledged their debt to him and expressed their admiration for his *Gaspard de la nuit,* a collection of prose poems which seem often to be direct transpositions of little genre paintings in the Flemish manner. Yet neither historical significance nor intrinsic charm has been powerful enough to revive this poet who has never even been granted a decent translation. Let us attempt a rendering of one of his "gothic" pieces:

> Whether you die absolved or damned, Scarbo mumbled last night in my ear, you will have a spider web for a shroud, and I shall bury the spider with you!
>
> —Oh, at least, I replied, my eyes red for having wept so much, let my shroud be an aspen leaf in which the breath of the lake would rock me.
>
> —No, chuckled the dwarf, you will be food for the beetle that each evening hunts gnats blinded by the setting sun.
>
> Perhaps you might prefer, I replied still weeping, that I be blood-sucked by a tarantula with a trunk the size of an elephant's.
>
> Well, he said, be consoled, you will have for a shroud the gold-spotted bands of a snake skin with which I'll wrap you like a mummy.
>
> And from the shadowy crypt of Saint Benign where I'll place you upright against the wall, you will be able to hear, whenever you like, little children weeping in limbo.

Scarbo is Bertrand's familiar demon. Here he is in another nocturne, one of Bertrand's best:

> The moon was combing her hair with an ebony comb, silvering with a rain of glowworms the hills, meadows and woods.
>
> Scarbo, the gnome with abounding treasures, was on my roof winnowing ducats and florins, that bounced in time to the cry of the weathercock, the counterfeit pieces littering the street.
>
> How he sneered, the half-wit who wanders every night through the deserted city, with one eye on the moon and the other—gouged out!
>
> Moon money, he muttered, picking up the devil's ducats, I'll buy the pillory to warm myself in the sun.
>
> But the moon was still there, the waning moon—and Scarbo was at work in my cellar secretly, silently turning out ducats and florins with his press.
>
> At the same time, with its two horns thrust ahead, a snail led astray by the night, was trying to find its way across my glowing window panes.

Gnomes, dwarfs, and sprites were very popular in French poems and stories around 1830. E. T. A. Hoffmann was challenging the prestige of Sir Walter Scott. For the subtitle of his own book, Aloysius Bertrand borrowed the title of Hoffmann's first: *Gaspard de la nuit: Fantaisies à la manière de Rembrandt et de Callot.* To introduce his poems he invented a sort of "maerchen" in which the author is supposed to have encountered in some garden a stranger with a weasily face and an unkempt beard who strikes up with him a conversation on art. Ultimately he found what seemed to be the secret precisely formulated in the two words *Gott* ["God"] and *Liebe* ["love"], which he noticed on a scroll ornamenting the title of an old book of magic. Henceforth reality turned into fairyland for him—beneath his window he could perceive a mysterious terrace where an old man, on his knees, was praying and a girl (or a wraith) was playing on a harp. He set out to explore nature and ruins—a gargoyle laughed from a nook on the cathedral. God and Love equated in his mind with sentiment. But sentiment is only half of the answer to the question that art poses. The other half is idea. Perhaps this is the devil's half and perhaps the poor devil in the garden is the Devil himself. At any rate, since the Cologne Cathedral was built by the lord of darkness in homage to the lord of light, Bertrand solicits the support of the Devil to compose his poems as an offering to God.

All this medievalism and magic controlled by a certain amount of "romantische Ironie" are surely reminiscent of the German. Yet Bertrand's borrowing was doubtless indirect. The medieval setting had already been used by Victor Hugo. As a matter of fact, Bertrand expressly acknowledges his debt to Hugo: "Vous m'avez communiqué une passion d'architecture gothique . . . " ["You have communicated to me a passion for Gothic architecture"]. It is also Hugo who could have given Bertrand a taste for the grotesque so apparent throughout the poems. Perhaps it was even Hugo who first led Bertrand to Jacques Callot and the Flemish genre painters. In expounding his theory of the grotesque, Hugo mentions Rubens and Callot, the burlesque Michelangelo—as Hugo calls him [in his preface to *Cromwell*]. And there were of course other influences besides Hugo. Scarbo reminds us very strongly of Charles Nodier's Smarra—Scarbo the gnome who gets drunk on the oil from the poet's lamp, who bites him in the neck and, to cauterize the wound, sticks in his iron finger reddened in the fire. Bertrand's sources and inspiration can be found on every hand among the most popular writers of the day. Yet all he found in others he already possessed himself. The malevolent spooks and spirits of which he writes he could find in the ancient quarters of Dijon where he was brought up. Saint Benign, mentioned in our first poem, is a monastery in Dijon which was very powerful in the Middle Ages. Morimont, the old place for executions, figures in another:

> Night had fallen. First there was—I am telling it just as I saw it—an abbey with its walls crevassed by moonlight, a forest cut through with winding paths,—and Morimont swarming with capes and hats.
>
> Then there was—I am telling it just as I heard it—the mournful tolling of a bell to which from a cell were responding mournful sobs—plaintive cries and ferocious laughter at which each leaf shivered along a branch—and the humming prayers of black penitents accompanying a criminal on his way to torture.
>
> Finally there was—I am telling it just how the dream ended—a monk expiring as he lay in the ashes of the dying—a girl struggling as she hung from the branches of an oak tree—and I in wild disorder being tied by the executioner to the spokes of the wheel.

(pp. 101-05)

[Bertrand filled] his days with writing and studying art. He became enamored of painting and drawing, and even did some sketches in the manner of Hugo with which he intended to illustrate *Gaspard de la nuit.* The question of his art studies is interesting because of the graphic inspiration of his poems. *Gaspard* opens with the group called "Ecole Flamande", the first of which is a verbal painting of Harlem:

> Harlem, that admirable bambocciade which sums up the Flemish school, Harlem painted by Jean Breughel, Pieter Neefs, David Teniers and Paul Rembrandt;
>
> And the canal with its trembling blue water, the church with its gold panes gleaming, and the porch with its wash drying in the sun, and the roofs green with hops;
>
> And the storks beating their wings around the town steeple, as they stretch their necks high up in the sky and catch raindrops in their beaks;
>
> And the jovial burgomaster fondling his double chin, and the love-sick florist wasting away with his eyes fixed on a tulip.
>
> And the gypsy in a trance over her mandolin,

Manuscript title page of Gaspard de la nuit.

> and the old man playing on a pipe and the child blowing up a balloon.
>
> And the drinkers smoking in the beer parlor, and the servant girl of the inn hanging in the window a dead pheasant.

The Flemish genre painters of the seventeenth century charmed French Romantic poets for the light of quaint fantasy they cast over the commonplace. Hugo saw in their works illustration of his theory of antithesis and praised Rubens for including the grotesque in his paintings. No one, however, it might seem, found in them greater inspiration than Louis Bertrand who in this poem pays them formal homage. It is as if he had adopted Flanders as a spiritual homeland, seeing his own town Dijon through Flemish art. In his poems the differences between Harlem and Dijon disappear. Of course he did not know Flanders at first hand, yet given his interest, one wonders why in this poem he seems to make such odd mistakes, mistakes which have never been corrected in the subsequent editions of the work. Why he calls Rembrandt, Paul, is hard to say unless it is that he confuses him with Rubens. If so, he does it in his introduction as well as in this poem, a fact which at least rules out a momentary slip. Yet Rubens would have served his purpose just as well as

Rembrandt and surely been more at home with the other painters mentioned than the Dutchman. Another little puzzle involves the Dutch word "stoel", that he uses in the second stanza. A note in the 1842 edition and in several subsequent ones explains this to mean stone balcony. "Stoel", however, means chair. Probably there was confusion with the word "stoep", which is cognate with the English word stoop. We might assume that Bertrand became really knowledgeable in art only after his poems were composed, since we know that he studied painting assiduously during the last years of his life and visited collections in Paris. Incidentally, his studies and visits were recorded in notebooks which exist today in private hands. Perhaps they could lead us to specific prototypes for some of his poems. Now we can only say that they are suggestive of a great many paintings by Jacques Callot and the genre painters to whom he refers here in this poem. Bertrand's own sketches made to illustrate *Gaspard de la nuit* have accompanied several editions. They are not very good. The same might be said of his work in verse, which was collected by Cargill Sprietsma in 1926 (*Oeuvres poétiques*). We find one quite flat satirical piece and numerous sentimental lyrics patently derivative in theme and form from Hugo, Lamartine, and even from the neo-classics. Bertrand must have known where his forte lay, for up to the last he polished away on his prose poems. (pp. 106-08)

Gaspard has had always a strong appeal for a few, a few that include several of the greatest writers of France. Sainte-Beuve esteemed the work, Baudelaire said that at least twenty times he had leafed through it and, in his own *Spleen de Paris,* had tried to do something similar—that is to say, "apply to the description of modern life that technique so strangely picturesque that he had applied to the painting of the past." Mallarmé wrote to his daughter, "Take along with you Bertrand, he has everything!" Among more recent writers, Max Jacob had certain reservations, suspecting that as an artist, Bertrand had "lingered too lovingly over details." Doubtless the form of his ballads is too rigid and his expression too carefully wrought. His poems risk seeming mechanical and arbitrary. A greater artist might have broken the monotony by some bold, spontaneous thrusts and been less mindful of possible incorrections or negligences. But these criticisms, at most, imply the errors of a craftsman rather than an indictment against craft as such; Bertrand's concern for precise technique and form is to a great extent what assures his position as a precursor of modern poets. If we compare his ballads with those that appeared in the Romantic keepsakes, with those of Alphonse Rabbe or with the "translations" of Charles Nodier, we find a far more personal manner. If we compare them with any previous so-called "prose poem" even in Chateaubriand or in Scott where he may have found his models, instead of merely rhythmic prose we find real poems. Eschewing the lyric expansiveness and moralizing that tended to make art subservient to message, Bertrand's poems exemplify the modern ideal of concentrating and distillation, as a comparison of successive versions of a work clearly show. André Breton, as apostle of automatic writing, shared to a point Max Jacob's feeling. But Breton, who felt that Baudelaire also was too formal, was willing to call Bertrand a surrealist.

How could anyone so enthusiastic about Lautréamont fail to respond to the images evoked by **"The Dead Horse"**:

> The refuse dump! and to the left, under a carpet of clover and purple medick, the monuments of a cemetery; to the right, a hanging gallows asking alms of the passers-by like a one-arm man.
>
> The one they killed yesterday, over there, the wolves have ripped up the flesh on the neck in such long ribbons that you could imagine it still festooned for the parade, with a bunch of red streamers.
>
> Every night, as soon as the moon turns the sky wan, this carcass will take off on its flight, straddled by a witch spurring it with the pointed bone of her heel, the breeze blowing into the bellows of its cavernous flanks.
>
> And were there, at this taciturn hour, an eye without sleep, open in some trench in this field of rest, it would suddenly close, for fear of seeing a specter in the stars.
>
> Already the moon herself, shutting one eye, is shining with the other only to light the way, like a waving candle, for this dog, a bone-thin stray, that is lapping water from a pond.

Nightmarish images created by the process of incongruous couplings is an art much savored by the Surrealists, who found a treasure trove in the gothic and ghoulish literature of the Romantic period. Vogues for "diableries" come and go—by the time Sainte-Beuve wrote his preface for *Gaspard* they had become old-fashioned enough to provoke comment. But today the dreadful and the supernatural again captivate. Their popularity may lead us back to a master of the genre and awaken a curiosity for one of France's most exquisite minor poets. (pp. 109-111)

> *Laurent Lesage, "A Gothic Romantic, Aloysius Bertrand," in* The American Society Legion of Honor Magazine, *Vol. 48, 1977, pp. 101-11.*

John Thomas Wright   (essay date 1977)

[*In the following excerpt, Wright praises Bertrand's style and discusses the importance of his two prefaces in interpreting his work.*]

Perhaps the most gratifying aspect of any study of Bertrand's *Gaspard* is that it is totally worthy of the praise that has been given it. In tone and style the individual pieces range from the written counterpart of finely delicate illuminated manuscripts, such as **"Harlem"**, to the subjective, symbolic, and dream-like prose-poems, such as **"A Dream."** Between these extremes lie the "slice of life" pieces, such as **"Tramps of the Night"**; this type often closes with an ironic comment on what has happened. Irony is, in fact, the soul of Bertrand's work. In spite of his stylistic dynamism, Bertrand is often stereotyped as the *poète maudit* of exact, static poems of greater craftsmanship than genius. To limit Bertrand thus is to misunderstand his work; poetic-prose was, however, not new and is sometimes traced back to the Song of Solomon. It was not until the 18th Century, partly under the pressure of rigid neo-classical rules as to what constituted poetry, that the sharp distinctions between poetry and prose broke down in works such as Fénelon's *Télémaque* (1699), Bossuet's sermons, Rousseau's *Nouvelle Héloïse,* and Chateaubriand's *René* and *Atala*. Thus, it was for Bertrand, along with Rabbe, Guerin, Nodier, and Nerval, to make the breakthrough into the true prose-poem. [In his preface to Bertrand's *Oeuvres poétiques*] Cargill Sprietsma contended that Bertrand's poetry was a means of preparation for the writing of the prose-poem, which seems valid enough, although his suggestion that Bertrand turned to the prose-poem because his poetry was inferior is less acceptable since Bertrand's initial fame was due directly to his poems. Bertrand, himself, was fully conscious of what he had done: "*Gaspard de la nuit,* that Book of my tender predilections where I have attempted to create a new genre of prose. . . . "

Bertrand's work is marked by the use of poetic phrases worked to an intense degree of perfection, often with a historical or fantastic theme. The prose-poem as Bertrand developed it is short, compact, intense in effect, and complete in itself. He also asked that his prose-poems be blocked as if they were verse. Bertrand's prose-poem consists, in general, of five to seven couplets, often with a semicolon separating the balanced independent clauses. They also are "without rhyme and without rhythm", to use part of Baudelaire's definition of the prose-poem.

What works and authors influenced Bertrand is difficult to ascertain, but certain influences can be recognized. In pieces such as **"Again a Springtime"** there is, for example, that lyric quality of suffering found in the lieder of Franz Schubert. One can also discern the influence of Scott, Goethe, the Bible, and Chateaubriand, among others.

Perhaps Bertrand's greatest debt, however, is to E. T. A. Hoffmann, for it was about the same time that Loeve-Veimar's translations of Hoffmann's work into French were published (1829-1831) that Bertrand's work took on a strongly bizarre character, deriving even *Gaspard*'s subtitle, "Fantasies in the Manner of Rembrandt and Callot," from Hoffmann's *Phantasiestücke in Callots Manier.*

The structure of *Gaspard*—itself constantly expanded during the years—consisted ultimately of two prefaces, a dedicatory piece, six books of prose-poems, and a closing prose-poem; a selection of poems called "Detached Pieces" was also added by [the publisher of *Gaspard,* Victor] Pavie. The first book, "The Flemish School", is a series of tableaux whose subjects might be taken from Rembrandt or any one of many Dutch painters; "Old Paris" continues in a similar vein but with a more historical emphasis; the third book, "The Night and Its Marvels", is the longest, with eleven prose-poems, and in it the theme of the fantastic and grotesque is most fully developed; "Chronicles" follows and constitutes his earliest work at its most charming and picturesque; "Spain and Italy", the fifth book, presents strikingly, if to the modern reader in somewhat stereotyped terms, these lands of passion and intrigue; and finally "Silves" contains some of Bertrand's most stylistically advanced poems. In the "Detached Pieces" are found some of his earliest and last pieces.

The importance of *Gaspard*'s two prefaces has been largely ignored by the critics in analyzing the work, when, in fact, they provide a philosophical framework by which *Gaspard* can be best understood.

The shorter second preface reveals Bertrand's fundamental concern: the duality of man's personality as personified by the personages of Rembrandt and Callot, the former being the philosopher, that is the ideal of the transcendental self, while Callot is the old soldier representing the ineffable side of man's personality. Art, says Bertrand, is derived from both aspects in his personality. The prose-poems of *Gaspard* explore, therefore, this duality, so evident among transcendental thinkers, and look forward to Baudelaire's "hypocrite lecteur" of the eighteen-fifties, Baudelaire, himself, being one of the first to rediscover Bertrand. Bertrand, moreover, achieved the central goal of all transcendental artists: the creation of the "new", in this case, a "new" art—the prose-poem. "In the manuscript of *Gaspard*," says the old poet of the first "Preface", "are deposited many processes, perhaps new, of color and harmony."

What is most indicative of the literary worth of Bertrand's *Gaspard* is that since its publication . . . it has grown steadily in popularity, thus revealing the need for further widening its renown through translation and scholarship. (pp. xviii-xxi)

> *John Thomas Wright, in an introduction to* Gaspard de la nuit: Fantasies in the Manner of Rembrandt and Callot, *by Aloysius Bertrand, translated by John Thomas Wright, University Press of America, 1977, pp. ix-xxi.*

FURTHER READING

Goldsmith, Helen Hart. "Art and Artifact: Pictorialization in *Gaspard de la nuit*." *The French Review* XLIV, special issue No. 2 (Winter 1971): 129-39.

  Examines Bertrand's techniques for creating visual imagery.

Ransome, Arthur. "Aloysius Bertrand: A Romantic of 1830." *The Fortnightly Review* XCII (2 December 1912): 1153-60.

  A biographical sketch that includes discussion of *Gaspard de la nuit.*

Sieburth, Richard. "*Gaspard de la nuit:* Prefacing Genre." *Studies in Romanticism* 24, No. 2 (Summer 1985): 239-55.

  Discusses the importance of paratextual devices in the works of Bertrand and other writers. Sieburth writes: "I would simply like to explore the ways in which the various paratexts or prefaces of *Gaspard de la nuit* address themselves to the problem of genre, and more specifically, how they dramatize those fundamental paradoxes and perplexities which the prose poem—this misborn, hybrid, 'accidental' genre—proposes both to its author and reader."

Slott, Kathryn. "Bertrand's *Gaspard de la nuit:* The French Prose Poem as a Parody of Romantic Conventions." *Francofonia* V, No. 8 (1985): 69-92.

Examines Bertrand's skillful use of irony in *Gaspard de la nuit* to parody poetic conventions in general and the literary conventions of Romanticism in particular.

Sara Coleridge

1802-1852

English editor, fiction writer, poet, and essayist.

Coleridge is best known as the editor of many works by her father, Samuel Taylor Coleridge. Her edition of his *Biographia Literaria,* considered her most significant contribution to Coleridgean scholarship, is meticulously annotated and includes a lengthy introduction in which she defends her father's philosophy and literary achievement. Although most of her efforts were focused on "setting Coleridge's house in order," Sara was also the author of poetry, fiction, and philosophical essays.

Sara was Samuel Taylor Coleridge's only daughter and the youngest of his four children. Because her father left the family during her infancy, she and her brothers were raised largely under the direction of her uncle, the poet Robert Southey, whose family had moved in with the Coleridges after their father's departure. An insatiable reader, Coleridge profited greatly by her access to Southey's immense library, and listened eagerly to conversations between the poet and his distinguished guests. She later credited her father's friend William Wordsworth, who lived nearby and frequented the Coleridge home, with shaping her intellect and imagination. But her daughter and biographer, Edith Coleridge, noted that "in matters of the heart and conscience, for right views of duty and practical lessons of industry . . . she was [as her mother wrote] 'more, and more importantly, indebted to the daily life and example of her admirable Uncle Southey'." Southey provided a religious home atmosphere, and Coleridge was a pious Christian all her life, devoting much of her personal writing to religious issues and explication of biblical passages. To help pay for the education of one of her brothers, Coleridge, well-versed in six languages, published a translation of Martin Dobrizhoffer's *Geschichte der Abiponer, einer berittenen und Kriegerischen Nation in Paraquay* (*An Account of the Abipones, an Equestrian People of Paraguay*) in 1822. That same year, while visiting her father near London, she met her cousin Henry Coleridge, a Cambridge graduate who was employed as a Chancery barrister. The two became secretly affianced the following year, but endured a protracted engagement because of Henry's meager income. Sara spent the next several years in private study, primarily of theology, and published a translation of the memoirs of the French military captain Chevalier Bayard in 1825. Coleridge and Henry married four years later and moved to London. Her first literary work, *Pretty Lessons in Verse for Good Children,* was published in 1834 and reached its fourth edition within a decade; a fairy-tale romance entitled *Phantasmion,* published three years later, was praised by most reviewers but was not a commercial success. During this time her husband began to edit the works of Samuel Taylor Coleridge, and Sara served as an anonymous co-editor of Henry's publication of *Table Talk* in 1834. Her essay "On Rationalism," an expansion of the ideas con-

tained in Coleridge's *Aids to Reflection,* was appended to Henry's 1843 edition of that work. Following her husband's death that same year, Coleridge began work on her father's *Biographia Literaria,* which was published four years later. She edited three more volumes of his works before her death in 1852.

Coleridge's most important critical work is her introduction to the *Biographia Literaria,* where she defends her father's character and reputation from various charges leveled against him. The lengthy essay is divided into three sections: the first, "Mr. Coleridge's Obligations to Schelling," confronts the accusation that Coleridge plagiarized from the German philosopher, arguing that Coleridge's word for word borrowings from Schelling were simply evidence of carelessness in documentation, as he focused on "the pursuit and enunciation of truth." The second section, entitled "Mr. Coleridge's Religious Opinions," refutes the contention that Coleridge was an ineffectual theologian, asserting that he was no "mere intellectualist" but a reformer who was denigrated by critics solely because of the iconoclasm of his thought. The last section of the introduction, "Mr. Coleridge's 'Remarks on the Present Mode of Conducting Public Journals'," which argues that Coleridge's critical reception suffered unjustly because of the partisan politics of nineteenth-century literary journals, completes what Bradford K. Mudge describes as a "complex apotheosis of a flawed man into an intellectual hero" by "engineer[ing] his martyrdom."

Coleridge's affinity with her father's thought, which enabled her to sympathetically annotate his works, is evident in her essay "On Rationalism," which examines some of the issues raised in the elder Coleridge's *Aids to Reflection* and harmonizes with much of his dissenting theology. While acknowledging the "intellectual power" of the essay, Earl Leslie Griggs concedes that it is unfocused and digressive, noting that Coleridge "seems to have lacked (as her father did) the power of self-discipline in argumentative or philosophical prose." Coleridge's most popular work was her *Pretty Lessons in Verse for Good Children,* a collection of poetry written primarily as an instructional aid for her own children. Morally didactic in nature, *Pretty Lessons* was succeeded by Coleridge's lyric fantasy *Phantasmion,* which critics consider her most accomplished work, revealing her imaginative powers and artistic skill. According to Carl Woodring, *Phantasmion* demonstrates that "the important law for Sara is one reiterated by her father, by Wordsworth, and by [Charles] Lamb. . . . Imagination, not moral precept, brings growth."

PRINCIPAL WORKS

Pretty Lessons in Verse for Good Children (poetry) 1834

Phantasmion (fiction) 1837

"On Rationalism" (essay) 1843; published in S. T. Coleridge's *Aids to Reflection*

Biographia Literaria; or, Biographical Sketches of My Literary Life and Opinions, by Samuel Taylor Coleridge [editor] (prose) 1847

Notes and Lectures upon Shakespeare . . . of S. T. Coleridge [editor] (essays) 1849

Essays on His Own Times . . . by Samuel Taylor Coleridge [editor] (essays) 1850

The Poems of Samuel Taylor Coleridge [editor] (poetry) 1852

Memoir and Letters of Sara Coleridge (reminiscences and letters) 1873

Herbert Wilson (essay date 1874)

[*In the following excerpt from his review of* Phantasmion, *Wilson praises Coleridge's artistry but asserts that the work may be viewed by contemporary readers as monotonous and overwrought.*]

Phantasmion indeed is a beautiful conception of a rarely-gifted mind; but hardly less rare than such minds as that of Sara Coleridge are the minds which, in these fuller and busier times, will be able to appreciate her story. It is no doubt pre-eminently pure and wholesome, reminding us

of no book so much as Philip Sydney's *Arcadia,* which he wrote daintily and euphuistically for the sister of his friend. Like the *Arcadia, Phantasmion* is too refined for the general run of readers. It has barely a plot, barely a distinct character, barely an exciting episode. It grows monotonous before we have read fifty pages, and we are soon painfully aware that its many beautiful passages ought to have been presented to us in a book of elegant extracts, rather than in a connected story. For the connection itself is of the slenderest kind; and, though there is constant change of scene in place of the development of the plot, the changes are never sufficiently marked or contrasted to rouse a large amount of interest. The composition, too, is stiff and unvaried. Three hundred pages of description, enlivened only by such incident as a scientifically trained governess might deem suitable for the "honourable misses" confided to her charge, do gradually pall upon one's taste; and we confess that we have not been able to read *Phantasmion* straight through. The very names of the characters made us shudder to begin with, and no stretch of fancy could render us at home with such drawing-room folks and fairies as Iarine, Karadan, Anthemmina, Feydeleen, Potentilla, Malderyl, Penselimer, and the like. Moreover a fairy tale without allegory, without humour, with meagre fancy and imagery, and still more meagre wonders and excitement, is to our mind unendurably heavy.

There are of course fairy tales and fairy tales, and we incline to the opinion that there ought to be one at least for every year of our allotted threescore and ten. *Phantasmion* would come in suitably enough for the spare moments of, say, our fiftieth year. We certainly should not think of putting it into the hands of an ordinary child. There are old-fashioned children who like old-fashioned books, and here and there perhaps one might be found to like this one; but the stock boy or girl of the present generation would undoubtedly vote it a bore. The precocious child who might be imagined as sitting in a corner to devour *Phantasmion* would be not unlike the boy Hermillian in the story, who, checked in his babble by a lame explanation of the absence of Iarine, mutters, "All a false pretence, I dare be sworn!" The language of the book never gets off the stilts to which its authoress condemns it.

It is, however, more pleasant to praise than to blame, and there is much in *Phantasmion* that is worthy of the highest praise. It is a most unusual thing in these days to meet with a fiction entirely harmless from beginning to end, which not only does not make a mock of sin, or dwell on the pleasures arising from other people's pain, or extol the accidents of birth and wealth at the expense of virtue and honesty, but which does not even depend for its interest upon legitimate satire and ridicule. The writer who discards these and similar modes of allurement naturally cannot tempt his readers with very strong meat, but Sara Coleridge, from her sick bed, provided a fare which is in any case wholesome and innocent, and which to a select few may be delightful and appetising. In spite of all that we have said, we can easily imagine minds to whom this fairy tale will be thoroughly acceptable and satisfying, and who will linger over its serene joys and chaste proprieties with an approbation which we might at first find it difficult to understand. To justify at once both ourselves and such as these we may quote a paragraph which will serve as a fair sample of the whole book, of its description and its action, its depth and its lightness, its beauty and its weakness :—

> But the storm now abated, and Iarine, waving her hand to the fisherman, in token that she needed no help, slowly pursued her way homewards. On the horizon of the plain, beyond the foot of the lake, a border of pale brightness was visible; it seemed to show that there was a silver firmament behind those tumultuous volumes of cloud which had remained unmoved throughout the chaos of the storm. The maid was alone, but for herself she felt no fear; she thought not of Karadan or of Glandreth; of the water witch or of an angry step-dame; she was thinking only of Phantasmion. Her love had hitherto been as a distant strain of music, scarce noted by one that is busily occupied; but now the harmony sounds fuller and more distinct; it will be heard, and the hum of many voices falls into an undersong. With reluctance she recedes from the vessel where she lately saw him taken in, dripping and senseless. That bark was filled with servants of Magnart, who had been despatched from Polyanthida in search of their master's son. Learning from the old fisherman that he had gone upon the lake, they ventured through the storm, guided by the old man, in the direction of the island, whither they supposed he might have taken his course. Phantasmion recovered wholly while Karadan was but just beginning to revive, and, while the men in the boat were still bending around the dark youth, he took flight from the stern, and hastened to rejoin Iarine.

One other feature of the book deserves both notice and quotation. Sara Coleridge came of a poetic stock, and lived in an atmosphere of refined thought and poetic development. It was almost as easy for her to write in verse as to write in prose; a gift of facility which was of course fatal to the production of anything like impassioned poetry. The poetic prose of **Phantasmion** is interspersed with some thirty or thirty-five short lyrical pieces; some of them connected with and almost continuative of the story, others more or less arbitrarily introduced. The following couple of stanzas are perhaps the most beautiful and finished; and they undoubtedly reveal a true poetic instinct:—

> The winds were whispering, the waters glistering,
> A bay-tree shaded a sun-lit stream;
> Blasts came blighting, the bay-tree smiting,
> When leaf and flower, like a morning dream,
>   Vanished suddenly.
>
> The winds yet whisper, the waters glister,
> And softly below the bay-tree glide;
> Vain is their cherishing, for, slowly perishing,
> It doth but cumber the river side,
>   Leafless in summer-time.

(pp. 376-77)

[In] the turbid stream of the literature which daily pours from our prolific authors and publishers such a romance as **Phantasmion** is like a flower, or a flake of foam upon the surface—lovely not only in itself, but by contrast. (p. 377)

> *Herbert Wilson, in a review of "Phantasmion, a Fairy Tale," in* The Examiner, *No. 3454, April 11, 1874, pp. 376-77.*

Mona Wilson   (essay date 1924)

[*In the following excerpt, Wilson favorably reviews* Phantasmion.]

[**Phantasmion** is] the work of a highly cultivated woman. It is written with great charm and ease of style, and breaks naturally into verse when the emotions of her personages seek poetic expression. The story was in some sort a protest against the moral tales of Maria Edgeworth and others. "It is not in such scraps, nor with such a context, however pretty in its way, that I should like to present the sublime truths of Christianity to the youthful mind: 'Florence put the cherry in her mouth, and was going to eat it all up,' etc., just before or after extracts from the Sermon on the Mount, or allusions to the third chapter of St. John's Gospel."

The poor little Prince Phantasmion is not long allowed to enjoy the garden, only a thought more magical than the first garden any child remembers, where the bees are dressed in diamonds, feathered columbines brush the cheek, and the heartsease are tall enough for a child to hide in. He is told brutally of his mother's death, nor is he spared realisation of the nature of death as his little companion drops down poisoned among the flowers. His father too dies and a boy friend, and then, when his lonely youth is shadowed by memories and by the dread of further misfortunes, he suddenly remembers the fairy whom he had met before he had tasted sorrow. He asks of her wings; she waved her wand and:

> . . . soon the air was filled with butterflies, those angel insects pouring from every region of the heavens. Here came a long train arrayed in scarlet, waving up and down altogether like a flag of triumph; there floated a band clad in deep azure, and flanked on either side by troops in golden panoply. Some were like flights of green leaves, others twinkled in robes of softest blue besprent with silver, like young princesses at a festival; and, in front of the whole multitude, a gorgeous crowd, adorned with peacock eyes, flew round and round in a thousand starry wheels, while here and there one butterfly would flit aloof for a few moments, then sink into the circle and revolve indistinguishably with the rest: now the entire wheel flew off into splinters, now reconstructed itself at once, as if but a single life informed its several parts.

The happy boy chooses wings of golden green embroidered with black, and flies away.

Phantasmion's adventures, the various guises he assumed with the help of the Fairy Potentilla, the many personages he met, and the mysterious spirits who aided or thwarted him in his pursuit of the lovely maiden Iarine are too numerous to describe. He has flown out into a world where the relationships between the actors are almost as complex, and their feelings toward one another almost as subtle and changing as in that living world on which the child reader is entering; hence the imaginative child will find this book a better preparation for life than a simpler story with a direct moral purpose. *Phantasmion* is but the history of a mortal company with their loves and hates, ambitions, weakness, variability, and even madness, translated into a fairy land, which is yet the Lake Country in which Sara Coleridge was bred. But the detail is just of the kind which appeals to a child. For instance, what could be more fascinating than the description of Phantasmion receiving from the Fairy the powers of a water-beetle?

> . . . his body was cased in black mail, and he was furnished with ample means of flight. No sooner was this work performed, and his head surmounted with the crest and fiery eyes of a sea-dragon carved on a helmet, than, having expanded his hard black upper wings with a sudden snap, and unfurled the soft silvery pinions that lay beneath, till they stretched far beyond their dark wing-cases, he flew off to the ocean, filling the air with a loud humming and droning, which, when it mingled with the dash of waves below, produced a noise like that of a great water-wheel. But, when the wind sank, and the sea was at perfect rest, he descended and played upon its surface.

and the vision of Seshelma!

> . . . he perceived a strange woman's form rising out of the waves, and gliding towards the beach: a wreath of living moving flowers, like sea-anemones, clung round her head, from which the slimy locks of whitish blue hung down till they met the waters; her skin was thick and glistening; there was a glaze upon it which made Phantasmion shiver; and, trailing her sinuous body beside the place where the youth lay, she cast a glance towards him, with her moony eyes of yellow green, at which his blood ran cold.

The canvas is rather crowded, but the characters are sufficiently defined to prevent confusion between them. The lovely heroine, Princess Iarine, exhibits a noble dignity throughout her adventures, proving that she is cast in a rarer mould than her vivacious cousin, Zelneth. She rebukes the youth, who beseeches her to attempt to love him:

> Dear cousin . . . we have duties enough which nature imposes; for a heart like mine I am sure they are sufficient; never let us make a duty of love.

A useful lesson in the psychology of love is daintily conveyed by the comment on Phantasmion smiling and blushing at the sight of the beautiful maiden while his thoughts are with another:

> Alas for Zelneth! She is deceived by that bright smile, and takes for feelings like her own the glow of youthful fancy, which loves to feed on images of joy, and kindles at the sight of beauty, even while the heart lies still, as a bird beneath its mother's wing.

"Graver thoughts and hallowed musings blent" promised by "L'Envoy" are suggested by the pretty talk between Iarine and the sickly child, Albinet:

> "Dost thou think she wears such a crown as this now?" said Albinet, softly, looking up at the sky. "The flowers she wears," replied the maiden, "are such as will never fade." "Heaven must be very full of flowers," cried he, "if new ones come and yet the old ones never go away. I hope it is not like that picture of a sunny garden which never changes; I hope there are half opened buds in heaven, Iarine, and merry milk-white lambs." "Heaven is happiness," the maid replied; "all that can make us happy we shall meet with there." "I wish," said Albinet, with a sigh, "that we could get thither without going down into the dark grave. Is there no lightsome road to heaven, up in the open air?" "My mother never went into the grave," said Iarine; "she was buried in the waves of the sea." "Oh, from the sea," said Albinet, "it must be easy enough to climb up into the sky, for I myself have marked the very place where it meets the water. When this fog clears away, if I could get to the top of that tree, and look intently, perchance I might descry some very minute trace of the beginnings of heaven."

Many and far are the wanderings of the young Prince and his Princess before they meet—not to be parted again—in the presence of the tragic Queen Anthemmine whose love for Dorimant, Phantasmion's father, has wrought madness in her brain, though she had wedded the father of Iarine:

> "On that dreary coast she roamed . . . till at length every cloud, which hung about the sun's globe and steeped its fleece in splendour, seemed growing into the likeness of Dorimant, every changeful mist that rose from the wave seemed about to take his form. Thus she fared till not a vestige of her former being remained but that one miserable dream." But she recognises her daughter, the sweet Iarine. "Dear child," she said, "thou wast a glimpse of soft blue sky between the clouds of my tempestuous life. Now that it beams forth once again, my day is closed."

Phantasmion appears, another youthful Dorimant, and she dies knowing that her daughter will enjoy the happiness of which she had only had a vision.

One, perhaps the loveliest, of the lyrics which adorn *Phantasmion* shall be wrested from its setting.

> A thousand and a thousand silken leaves
> The tufted beech unfolds in early spring,
>   All clad in tenderest green,
>   All of the self same shape:
>
> A thousand infant faces, soft and sweet,
> Each year sends forth, yet every mother views
>   Her last not least beloved
>   Like its dear self alone.
>
> No musing mind hath ever yet foreshaped
> The face to-morrow's sun shall first reveal,
>   No heart hath e'er conceived
>   What love that face will bring.

May these pages, written by one whom an unkindly fortune deprived of this source of enchantment at the due season, be the means of bringing *Phantasmion* in the way of a few of the many children who might still quench their thirst at it. (p. 367)

Mona Wilson, "A Neglected Fairy Tale and Its Author," in New Statesman, Vol. XXII, No. 559, January 5, 1924, pp. 366-67.

Earl Leslie Griggs   (essay date 1940)

[*Griggs is an American educator and critic specializing in Coleridgean scholarship. In the following excerpt, he discusses* Phantasmion, *praising Coleridge's style and noting the work's superiority to* Pretty Lessons.]

[In composing *Phantasmion,* Coleridge] certainly intended no allegory, but considered it 'no defect in this attempt of mine that it contains neither allegory, nor general moral'. The book was not intended exclusively for mere children. '[Its] likers, if any', she wrote,

> [will be] among the youthful boys and girls in teens or under—those in whom fancy is a more active power than judgment, and whose own state of mind lends a glow and a novelty to that which seems too fantastic, yet not over-original to them who have had more experience in life and literature.

To [her brother] Derwent, who had apparently objected to 'the disproportionateness of the machinery to the events and people of the tale', and who had complained of a want of moral, Sara wrote, acknowledging the justice of his first charge but answering the second:

> Now I fairly admit that the tale in question was written to illustrate no one general truth; I thought it sufficient for the soul and individuality of the piece that there should be upon the whole a unity of conception and feeling throughout. . . . If you ask me, however, what advantage a young person could possibly derive from such a tissue of unrealities, I should say that every work of fancy in its degree, and according to the merit of its execution, feeds and expands the mind; whenever the poetical beauty of things is vividly displayed, truth is exhibited, and thus the imagination of the youthful reader is stimulated to find truth for itself. . . .

> There is no fear of . . . [children] . . . mistaking the people or events of fairy tales for realities, but they may and should perceive the truths and realities both of the human mind and of nature which may be conveyed under such fictions. . . . Tales of daily life, where the ostensible moral is strongly marked, in my opinion, have generally less of this merit, than fictions where the scene lies more out-of-doors, and the materials of which have more to do with the general, than with the petty and particular.

Phantasmion, like *The Ancient Mariner,* has no end but pleasure, and Sara was frankly puzzled by her critics' attempts to discover some allegorical significance in her story. Her tale abounds in supernatural occurrences. Ex-

cept for his devotion to virtue, his unyielding courage, and his love for Iarine, her youthful hero is powerless to act unaided by superhuman beings. Nevertheless, the story of *Phantasmion* keeps up a show of reality. Phantasmion's emotions are human ones. Even the unearthly beings in the tale are but personifications of nature in her many-sided aspects. Natural laws are transcended rather than violated. When Phantasmion flies, it is with the wings of an eagle or of insects. When various persons in the story are miraculously healed of wasting sickness or of deathly wounds, the medicines are made of earthly herbs. It is worth noting, too, that only the living are restored to health; the dead are never reanimated. Sara Coleridge succeeds, then, in winning from her readers 'the willing suspension of disbelief', transporting them for the duration of her story to a region where the ordinary limitations of time and space disappear into nothingness. The world of *Phantasmion* is in many ways the counterpart of the real world. One finds there good as well as evil men; but whereas in the living world right triumphs, if at all, only through the slow process of time, in the kingdom of Phantasmion and the surrounding countries supernatural agencies accomplish at once, or only after a brief period, the achievements of centuries. And that is as children would have it. *Phantasmion* is a more successful work than *Pretty Lessons* because it breaks away from the bonds of didacticism and anticipates, in some measure, such immortal stories as *Alice in Wonderland* and *The Water Babies.*

The style of *Phantasmion* is full of charm and grace, and the descriptions are minute and colourful. The diction is 'pure mother English', as Coleridge had said of Sara's youthful translation from the Latin. There is in the book, as she admitted, 'over-depth of colouring, and prodigality of beauty', but these faults she thought she 'could not afford to lose, being substitutes for better things'. Thoroughly at home in the flowers and trees, the mountains and lakes, she makes her story seem alive by the picturesqueness of the landscape. She wrote feelingly, too, of the animal world, from the roaming tiger and gentle deer to the bees and beetles. London may have deprived her of the rural scenes she loved so well, but the memories of Keswick remained—delicately reproduced through the lenses of her fantastic imagination.

Sprinkled through *Phantasmion* are a series of lovely lyrics. Gone now are the moral lessons of *Pretty Lessons.* In their place we find songs, lyrical poems, and beautiful descriptions, many of them exquisitely wrought. Such lyrics as that which follows bear witness to her poetic ability.

> The winds were whispering, the waters glistering,
>   A bay-tree shaded a sun-lit stream;
> Blasts came blighting, the bay-tree smiting,
> When leaf and flower, like a morning dream,
>   Vanished full suddenly.

> The winds yet whisper, the waters glister,
> And softly below the bay-tree glide;
> Vain is their cherishing, for, slowly perishing,
> It doth but cumber the river side,
>   Leafless in summer-time.

(pp. 117-19)

Earl Leslie Griggs, in his Coleridge Fille: A Biography of Sara Coleridge, *Oxford University Press, London, 1940, 259 p.*

F. J. Harvey Darton   (essay date 1958)

[*In the following excerpt, Darton comments on the merits of* Pretty Lessons *as a collection of moral lessons for children.*]

[An] exceptional imitator of the [popular English children's writers Ann and Jane Taylor] was Sara Coleridge, the poet's charming daughter. She too suffered from lack of humour; but there is no doubt about her being in earnest. She said:

> The [Taylors'] *Original Poems* give too many pictures of mental depravity, bodily torture, and of adult sorrow; and I think the sentiments—the tirades, for instance, against hunting, fishing, shooting—are morbid, and partially false.

That is honestly and plainly expressed, and many would share the opinion. But Sara Coleridge went a very odd way to substitute, in her **Pretty Lessons in Verse for Good Children** (1834), "nothing but what is bright and joyous" for the sentiments she thus deplored. A remarkable moral conclusion is reached in a poem called **"Disappointment"**. A boy named Colin, mountaineering with old and young friends, carried with him an orange, on which he expected, rationally and even greedily, to slake his thirst in due course. He could not help playing with it, dancing about and tossing it up as he leapt over the rocks. Suddenly it jumped out of his hand and rolled far out of reach:

> For some little time he stood still as a stock,
>   His face wore a fixed vacant stare;
> But soon he recover'd this terrible shock,
> And turning away from the edge of the rock
>   Threw off his disconsolate air.
>
> With thoughts of the basket he solaced his heart,
>   From thence real comfort might come;
> For he in the sandwiches still had a part,
> He perhaps might come in for a slice of the tart,
>   And there was the pineapple rum.
>
> Since pleasure is apt through our fingers to slip,
>   And fate we can never withstand;
> Whene'er the full cup is thus dashed from the lip,
> Before we have taken the very first sip,
>   'Tis well to keep temper in hand.

Pickwick did not begin to appear till three years later, so that the author cannot be accused of making Colin an amalgam of the Fat Boy and Mr Stiggins. But none of the didacticists she criticized ever thought of quite such a "pretty lesson" as is afforded by the comfort of a picnic basket and pineapple rum if you carelessly lose an orange.

Her verses were for a time popular: they reached a fourth edition in 1845. But the Taylors, mental depravity and all, have outlived her in fact. She is of some historical importance because she is on the inner fringe of great literature. She proves that the idea of the Moral Tale was at least known to the loftier minds of the day. . . . (pp. 195-96)

F. J. Harvey Darton, "The Moral Tale: (ii) Persuasive; Chiefly in Verse," in his Children's Books in England: Five Centuries of Social Life, *second edition, Cambridge University Press, 1958, pp. 182-204.*

Carl Woodring   (essay date 1979)

[*Woodring is an American educator and critic specializing in nineteenth-century English literature. In the following excerpt, he offers a critical overview of* Phantasmion.]

[**Phantasmion**] is a Victorian *Amadis de Gaul,* a *Thalaba* in prose, a *Don Quixote* without Sancho Panza; or, to find later comparisons, a *Lord of the Rings* with less of Disney's Seven Dwarfs, and a Christian, this-world relation of Ursula Le Guin's *Earthsea.* Battle and single combat are subordinated, as in the nearest Oriental analogues, to illusion, spells, unnatural sleep, and dreams. Of the thirty-five or so inset lyrics, mostly fine, some are Southeyan, some notably Shelleyan. There are touches from *The White Doe of Rylstone.*

The inspiring forces were not all literary. Painting and other arts have their place, most pervasively in the descriptions of landscape, more surprisingly as in the iconographic allusion in Chapter 36 to some version of Henry Fuseli's then most notorious work: "Ulander beheld his own Leucoia lying bound at the feet of Malderyl, and the hideous dwarf crouching like a nightmare on her breast."

Next after literature, however, the book draws on Sara's childhood in the Lake country. There are three slender damsels, often together—the heroine Iarine and the sisters Leucoia and Zelneth. The action is overseen and sometimes redirected by fairies recognized in the vicinity of Greta Woods: the dangerous, fishy, slippery water-spirit, Seshelma; the kindly but usually ineffective Spirit of Flowers, Feydeleen; the spirit of the Blast and of clouds, Oloola; the unattractive Valhorga, male Spirit of the Earth, especially of caverns; the Spirit of the Woods; and Phantasmion's guardian, Potentilla, the fairy artisan of insects. The most memorably exciting passages are not those of combat between Phantasmion and his enemy Glandreth or his rival Karadan, but those descriptive of Potentilla's intervention. Thrust into a dungeon by Glandreth's forces (Ch. 22), "Phantasmion beheld a multitude of saw-flies with yellow bodies and black heads, flitting toward the light of the lamp; along with them came numbers of wasps, and the youth shrank as he beheld the mingled swarm approaching himself." The flies and wasps, alighting on the cords that bound his arms and wings, weakened the threads until he could snap them. Next a swarm of bees deposited above his head "the honey which they had just collected in the gardens of the island." The spirit of insects is exactly the right fairy guardian for any boy who wishes without evil intent for wings.

The story and its topography return us to the legends of a faith exercised and recorded indoors. In antecedent events, narrated in the course of present action, Penselimer of Almaterra dropped the Silver Pitcher awarded by the Spirit of Flowers, whereupon his betrothed, Anthemmina, gave the Pitcher to Dorimant of Palmland, who in turn gave it to Albinian of Rockland, soon coaxed unhappily to marry Anthemmina, who then disappeared. By this first misadventure and a second unfortunate marriage to Maudra of Tigridia, Albinian is reduced to a withered uselessness not greatly different from the moonless insanity (*not* lunacy) of Penselimer. In the older generation, the good want strength. To marry Iarine, Phantasmion must surpass her cousin Karadan (son of Magnart of Polyanthida, and brother of Zelneth and Leucoia) for possession of the Silver Pitcher. The name Polyanthida suggests a land of many flowers, but not entirely floral. Magnart belongs to the literary line of Merlin. His son Karadan morally vacillates. Clearly, then, without expecting help from Polyanthida, Phantasmion must gather allies to overthrow the usurpers of Rockland (Maudra and Glandreth), to restore Albinian and Penselimer to personal health and kingly power, and to afford thrones and brides to worthy claimants. Much of this is what it sounds like, a vastly more sober version of such botanical tales by E. T. A. Hoffmann as "Datura Fastuosa" and his nearer analogue, "The King's Bride," in which the daughter of Herr Dapsul von Zabeltau marries the King of Carrots.

Signs of Zelneth's interest in Phantasmion are accompanied by a lyric concerning the dangers of loving the heights when a "blossomed vale" beckons (Ch. 11), but all three slender maidens are presumed to be appropriately rewarded when Penselimer marries Zelneth, and Ulander, made king of Tigridia, takes Leucoia as Queen. Though unacceptable to later feminists, this pecking order seems in the tale as faithful to the trials of existence as the pointed descriptions of perplexity, anxious dreams, and illness. "Hence," said Mona Wilson of Sara's accounts in **Phantasmion** of death and insanity [see excerpt dated 1924], "the imaginative child will find this book a better preparation for life than a simpler story with a direct moral purpose." Whatever the justice to the damsels, for the male rivals the law later to be expounded by Bronson Howard, that three good hearts cannot beat as one, is put into force. Karadan, not, one supposes, because he woos his cousin, but because his rival is superior in interest to *us,* must and does die. The important law for Sara is one reiterated by her father, by Wordsworth, and by Lamb. She declares it in "L'Envoy of **Phantasmion**": imagination, not moral precept, brings growth. Worldlings can escape the "mickle harm" of worldly toil by avoiding cautionary moral tales and performing the sacred duty of escape into airy dreams. A second stanza goes further: even to the tender spirit who aspires to "blessed works and noblest love," an imaginative flight (of beautiful insects) can do no harm. (pp. 216-19)

> *Carl Woodring, "Sara 'fille': Fairy Child," in* Reading Coleridge: Approaches and Applications, *edited by Walter B. Crawford, Cornell University Press, 1979, pp. 211-22.*

Bradford K. Mudge   (essay date 1988)

[*In the following excerpt, Mudge examines Coleridge's defense of her father's character and literary achievement in her introduction to his* Biographia Literaria.]

The early summer of 1843 saw the publication of the fifth edition of [Samuel Taylor Coleridge's] *Aids to Reflection*, the second volume of which included Sara's lengthy essay **"On Rationalism."** Although she had worked for several years on the project, Sara would not admit to any optimism about its reception. To her cousin, she wrote:

> As to my own production (much as I admire it myself!), I do not expect that it will be admired by any one else. It makes larger demands on the attention of readers than I, with my powers, have perhaps any right to make or can repay. Even if the thinking were sound or important, the arrangement is bad. If bad arrangement in S. T. C. is injurious to readability, in S. C. it will be destructive. Moreover, I have made to myself no friends. A follower out of the principles of S. T. C. myself, withersoever they lead me, because they seem to me the very truth, I can not join hands with any of his half or quarter disciples. I praise and admire and applaud all the combatants on the theological arena, even the hearty opponents of my father, but I can not entirely agree with any one of them. . . . Yet I should never regret the time spent on this little composition, though I should be rather out of pocket and not into reputation by it, as will certainly be the case; for it has sometimes brought one part of my mind into activity, when the other part, if active, could only have been alive to anguish; and it has given me a more animated intercourse with some great minds now passed from our nether sphere than I could have had from merely reading their thoughts, without thinking them over again myself.

Sara's self-effacing judgments fail to hide an understandable anxiety about the essay's reception. But even as she faults her work, as she admits its "bad arrangement," she calls attention to the illustrious tradition of which it is a part. Like her father, Sara cares little for felicitous prose; she is committed instead to the "very truth" of philosophic "principles." Also like her father, she has "no friends"; she stands alone in the "theological arena," contemptuous of the party politics bonding other writers. But unlike his other "disciples," she is brave enough to follow her father's principles "withersoever they lead." Moreover, the quest is therapeutic: "animated intercourse with . . . great minds" forces her own mind "into activity" and prevents a debilitating and solipsistic "anguish."

Many of Sara's readers were impressed. Hartley Coleridge, for example, considered the essay a "wonder": "I say not a wonder of a woman's work—where lives the man that could have written it? None in Great Britain since our Father died. Poor Henry was perfectly right in saying that she inherited more of her father, than either of us [her brothers]; and that not only in the amount but in the quality of her powers" [in E. L. Griggs and G. E. Griggs, eds., *The Letters of Hartley Coleridge*, 1936]. The volumes sold briskly, and John Duke Coleridge claimed to have heard the essay being discussed by William Ward at Oxford. F. D. Maurice, another of her correspondents and avowed "disciple" of Coleridge, began writing her voluminous letters on the fine points of theological doctrine, letters that addressed Sara as an intellectual equal and encouraged her interest in religious philosophy.

Although Maurice's encouragement was important both to Sara's self-confidence and to her increasing theological expertise, it was Thomas Carlyle who intrigued her most in the years following Henry's death. Sara encountered his writings in May and saw immediately his similarity to Coleridge. After preparing a new volume of her father's poetry in August, she began her study: she read *Past and Present* (1843), *History of the French Revolution* (1837), and *On Heroes, Hero-Worship, and the Heroic in History* (1841) in rapid succession. In the middle of *Past and Present,* she wrote her cousin: "Newman, Carlyle, and Tennyson are perhaps the most striking writers, with Dickens in the novel line, . . . now before the public." Six days later, she wrote back: "I am reading Carlyle's 'Fr. Revolution'. . . . The practical sameness of the teaching of Carlyle with that of Pusey and Newman . . . with Coleridge at the bottom of all, is to me very striking." Six days after that, she wrote again:

> Carlyle's "Hero-Worship" trembled in my hand like a culprit before a judge; and as the book is very full of paradoxes, and has some questionable matter in it, this shaking seemed rather symbolical. But, oh! it is a book fit rather to shake (take it all in all) than to be shaken. It is very full of noble sentiments and wise reflections, and throws out many a suggestion which will not waste itself like a blast blown in a wilderness, but will surely rouse many a heart and mind to a right, Christian-like way of acting and of dealing with the gifted and godlike in man and of men.

Normally an exacting judge of literary "culprit[s]," Sara here confesses to having herself been "shaken" by Carlyle's "noble sentiments and wise reflections." Regardless of its "paradoxes" and "questionable matter," *Hero-Worship* was notable, she felt, because it "will not waste itself . . . but will surely rouse many a heart and mind." It would, in other words, encourage the appreciation of previously ignored intellectual "heroes" by demonstrating the "right . . . way . . . of dealing with the gifted and godlike in man and of men."

Sara was gratified by Carlyle's approving references to her father. In "The Hero as Priest," Coleridge is quoted on the subject of religious faith; and in "The Hero as King," he is cited again in support of Carlyle's doctrine of individual fulfillment. Moreover, Sara recognized Carlyle as a prophet in the Coleridgean tradition, a non-partisan philosopher with a pronounced social and religious responsibility unaffected by popular cant. More importantly, Carlyle gave Sara an extended argument supporting precisely the kind of activity in which she was engaged; he explained how she could "deal with the gifted and godlike in man and of men"—in particular, how she could use his theory of "veneration" to excuse her father's personal flaws while arguing for both his philosophical greatness and his political relevance. To clarify her understanding of Carlyle, she composed in October, 1843 a fifteen-page essay, entitled **"Reply to the Strictures of Three Gentlemen upon Carlyle."**

Sara's essay focuses on Carlyle's 1841 collection of lectures, *On Heroes, Hero-Worship, and the Heroic in History,* and defends his concept of "veneration," an idea that justifies intellectual non-partisanship as it celebrates the intellectual as a political and religious hero. Sara rightly insists that Carlyle's dislike of organized religion is counterbalanced by a strong belief in a "living and life-exciting principle" which informs all religions at least in part:

> This principle, which he sets up as the "work of God," against the artefacts of men—vain substitutes for genuine gifts from on high—he maintains to be "Veneration"—the principle of feeling which leads men to bow down before the image of God in the soul of man.

The "image of God," Sara argues, is reproduced "in the soul of man" through a kind of "mental power," which—because it originates with God—is necessarily benevolent and therefore deserving of worship.

Defending Carlyle's approval of the veneration of Voltaire, Sara complicates the notion of hero-worship by insisting that its value depends just as much upon the complex historical situation in which both hero and worshipers take part as it does upon the intellectual power of the hero in question. Voltaire was celebrated by the French because at a particular time in history he answered the needs of his countrymen by exhibiting a power worthy of their respect, thus saving them from "grovelling along in utter worldliness." While his skepticism was objectionable and his character flawed, Voltaire nevertheless evinced an inner strength that communicated itself to his society as "a redeeming spirit." What Carlyle has argued, Sara maintains, is not that the intellectual should be exalted above the moral, but that *"natural gifts"* of individual men exalt God more effectively than "the vain shows and semblances which commonly pass for religion in the world":

> Poor and needy, indeed, must that people be who have no better object of such a feeling than Voltaire. Our author means only to affirm that Frenchmen were better employed in "worshiping" him even for supposititious merits than in . . . pursuing each his own narrow, selfish path, without a thought or care beyond gratification of the senses. Here is no intention to set the intellectual above the moral, or to substitute the one for the other, but to insist on the superiority of *natural gifts,* as means of bettering the souls of men, to the vain shows and semblances which commonly pass for religion in the world. . . .

Even more so than F. D. Maurice, whose "personal religion" restored the "experience of God" to the individual and downplayed the mediating role of the church, Carlyle stressed that God's *"natural gifts"* as embodied in man are divinely bestowed for the greater good of mankind. Thus, the central objection to *Hero-Worship* made by its detractors—"that [Carlyle] sets up mere intellect as the ultimate object of esteem and admiration, and represents a man as truly great and worthy of all honor purely on the score of intellectual gifts"—fails to consider, in Sara's opinion, the author's overriding concern with historical circumstance.

Heroes deserve respect, Sara argues, because they are individuals "whose powers have been employed by God's will and their own, for good and noble purposes on a large scale, chiefly for the purpose of leading men, directly or indirectly, from earth to heaven, from the human to the divine." Like the Christian philosopher she defined and celebrated in her essay on Wordsworth's poem, "Lines Left on a Yew-Tree Seat," and very similar to the elite members of her father's "clerisy," Carlyle's heroes acknowledge their duty as leaders:

> Carlyle's heroes are all men who have striven for truth and justice, and for the emancipation of their fellow-mortals. He represents them as having been misunderstood by the masses of mankind, in the midst of all their effectivity and *ultimate* influence, simply because the masses of mankind are not themselves sufficiently wise and good and perspicacious to understand and sympathize with those who are so in an eminent degree.

Sara is not willing, however, to bestow upon Carlyle her unqualified praise:

> There is *some* originality in Carlyle's opinions; but he seems to me to be more original in manner than in matter: the force and feeling with which he brings out his views are more *remarkable* than the views themselves.

Although never mentioned, Coleridge's presence in both passages is unmistakable. By defining the hero as one "misunderstood by the masses of mankind," Sara places her father squarely in the tradition established by Carlyle, as she confirms the necessity of her own editorial projects. She then immediately undercuts the authority of that tradition by resituating it within an older tradition whose invisibility both provides the basis for and serves as an example of Carlyle's more recent doctrine. From Carlyle's perspective, Coleridge is merely another hero awaiting recognition; but from Sara's point of view, her father is the Ur-hero whose unacknowledged influence generated the tradition of which both Carlyle and his "heroes" are a part. To resurrect Coleridge would be at once to redefine contemporary intellectual history and to stabilize contemporary political unrest.

From Carlyle, Sara learned a healthy disrespect for "systems of belief," but she also learned how to compensate for her new iconoclasm by redefining her understanding of the role of the intellectual in society. Carlyle's concept of veneration originated in a mistrust of worldly institutions and accommodated the irregularities of private life, but it also celebrated public virtues and promised power (of a decidedly orthodox, Christian variety) to both hero and worshiper alike. The hero assumes the immortality of historical influence, living beyond his own time as a benevolent force capable of bringing about spiritual change, while the worshiper recognizes divinity incarnate and is redeemed "from grovelling along in utter worldliness." Both stand to profit from the activity of the other without compromising their Christian values. Thus, if Sara could justify the ways of Coleridge to her contemporaries, then she would participate in and be redeemed by his intellectual and historical influence—all without compromising her selfless, "feminine" ideals.

The three and a half years following Sara's essay on Carlyle were devoted to her edition of the *Biographia Literaria* (1847). A scrupulous researcher, she took painstaking care with the text, investigating her father's sources, checking his notebooks and marginalia, and writing detailed explanatory notes to all potentially troublesome passages. So thorough was her editorial practice that James Engell and W. Jackson Bate, the editors of volume 7 of the *Collected Works* (1983), acknowledge a "particularly heavy" debt. Even so, Norman Fruman, in reviewing Engell and Bate's volume, maintains that "Sara Coleridge's intelligence, energy, learning, and above all her willingness to lay damaging materials clearly before the reader, have . . . never received anything like the praise they deserve." He argues as well that while modern editors have appreciated Sara's detailed commentary, they have failed to recognize that her 1847 text is a more reliable copy-text than that provided by the original 1817 edition. Although quick to acknowledge Sara's achievement, however, modern editors generally, Fruman among them, have consistently ignored her other major contribution to the 1847 *Biographia*—her introduction. The 180-page defense of her father's moral character and literary accomplishments is a carefully orchestrated and convincingly written portrayal of Coleridge as the intellectual "hero" so desperately needed by the Victorian public. It is, as a result, a crucial event in the history of Coleridge scholarship.

Sara began working on the introduction during the fall of 1844. She had recovered from a slight illness that winter and had travelled again to Broadstairs and Eton in late summer. Her "cheerfulness" remained undampened, and her routine was, if anything, socially busier and intellectually more committed than ever before. To her cousin Frank, for instance, she defended the literary *"business of life"*:

> I quite agree with you . . . that no intellectual undertakings are worthy of a wise man that are not directed to a *practical aim,* and that have no bearing on the *business of life.* But what ought our *practical* aims to be?—what is the *business of life?* I think we cannot answer these questions properly without admitting that mental cultivation and the exercise of the powers of thought are indispensable to the formation of sound *practical* aims, and to the doing the *business of life* well. . . . Not only is it necessary . . . that there should be a class who make literature the business of their lives, but that every individual according to his capacity and opportunity should cultivate his intellectual powers. . . . One large part of the *business of life* for my sex is to educate yours. . . .

With her husband dead and her children grown, Sara's "business of life" was very much "directed to a *practical aim*" outside her immediate family. She had committed herself to editing one of her father's most important literary works, and with that project she assumed the responsibility to "educate" her contemporaries about one of their intellectual "heroes." As a representative of a "class who make literature the business of their lives"—a class, in other words, whose responsibility it was to create and maintain a literary "tradition"—she marketed inherited cultural values as much needed social remedies. Her letter makes clear, however, that that responsibility was conceived of as an extension of maternal duty: her own "powers of thought" would be devoted to helping others "cultivate [their] intellectual powers." Thus, as she edited her father's *Biographia Literaria,* literally and figuratively rewriting his literary life and her own patrimony, Sara adopted the guise of the nurturing mother—selfless, committed, and preeminently powerful; for her "children" now were hardly those of the nursery: her father had a sprawling corpus of some twenty volumes, and his readership included the most influential members of the mid-nineteenth-century reading public.

Intellectual responsibility was an issue of extreme importance for Carlyle, and his influence on Sara's preparation of the *Biographia* was no doubt enhanced by their acquaintanceship. They met at a party at St. Mark's College in July, 1844, and Sara was immediately impressed by the famous author:

> He is as like what he writes as flesh and blood can well be in a book. In appearance he is both striking and pleasing, more so than in his pictures, . . . because they do not fully give the brightness and delicacy of his face, nor his light, refined figure, nor the look that overspreads his countenance during his hearty laugh. His refinement, however, is that of thought and intellectual cultivation, not of social aristocratic training: he looks like a Scotch Gardener turned into man of letters by native genius.

However admiring of his works, Sara was not one to give her "Scotch Gardener" an easy time. Months later she wrote to her friend Aubrey de Vere:

> Carlyle, I think, too much depreciates money as an instrument. I battled with him a little on this point when I saw him last. He is always smiling and good-natured when I contradict him, perhaps because he sees that I admire him all the while. I fought in defense of the Mammonites, and brought him at least to own that the laborer is worthy of his hire. Now this contains the pith of the whole matter. The man who devotes himself to gain riches deserves to have riches, . . . and if he strives for riches to spend them nobly or kindly, then he deserves to have the luxury of *that sort* of doing good. . . . But Carlyle seems angry because the Burns or the Johnson or the Milton has not the same honors, . . . as millionaires and fashionists; because the whole world—unphilosophical and unpoetical as the main part of it is—does not fall down and worship them. . . . This is overbearing and unfair. Let him teach the world to be philosophical and poetical as fast as he can; but till it is so, let him not grudge it the rattles and sugar-plums and hobby-horses of its infancy.

Having labored long and hard in the margins of the literary world, Sara had come to realize that there were many ways "of doing good," that intellectual riches were not the only means to an end, and that even the most altruistic of contemporary philosophers could be "overbearing and unfair." Because she considered herself representative of an entire class whose duty it was to "cultivate" the public mind, to market literary culture as an indispensable national commodity, she felt no compunction about "f[ighting] in defense of the Mammonites." Revenues from the sale of her father's works had been, after all, an important motivation behind her ongoing editorial projects. Regardless of their differences, however, it was Carlyle's doctrine of hero-worship, of the intellectual's social, political, and religious power, that provided the model for Sara's most effective tribute to her father. For unlike Carlyle, whose paternalistic predilections only alienated the public he was trying to reform, Sara was comfortable with and could accommodate the world's "infancy": she could teach hero-worship rather than sermonize about it.

Sara's introduction to the 1847 *Biographia Literaria* is divided into three sections. Each section is both a separate, freestanding essay and a fragment of a larger, tripartite argument. The first section, "Mr. Coleridge's Obligations to Schelling," confronts and explains Coleridge's "plagiarisms"; the second section, "Mr. Coleridge's Religious Opinions," maps his relationships to Kant and Luther as it illuminates his difference from J. H. Newman and the Oxford Movement; and the third section, "Mr. Coleridge's 'Remarks on the Present Mode of Conducting Public Journals', " exposes the party politics behind his poor critical reception. Together, the three essays enact a complex apotheosis: they transform an admittedly imperfect human being into an almost perfect intellectual hero. They subordinate unavoidable character flaws and immethodical literary remains to philosophical principles and religious integrity, explaining in the process exactly how one should best approach and profit from the enigmatic eccentricities of the *Biographia Literaria.*

The first essay, on Coleridge's debts to Schelling, is more than a direct and honest answer to J. F. Ferrier's charges of plagiarism; it is a carefully orchestrated exploration of Coleridge as both flawed human being and questing philosopher. The argument begins with the question of intention: do the passages from Schelling *have* to be discussed as "conscious intentional plagiarism"? Ferrier had maintained that her father " 'defrauded' Schelling of his due," first by making "no adequate acknowledgements of obligation," and then by "affirm[ing] that he had in some sort anticipated the system which he proposed to teach." But "defrauding," Sara argues, is clearly a matter of intention: "no man can properly be said to 'defraud' another, nor ought to be so spoken of, who has not a fraudulent 'intention'." Those familiar with her father's "literary habits," she maintains, would recognize that "the passages from Schelling, which he wove into his work, were not transcribed *for the occasion,* but merely transferred from his note-book into the text, some of them, in all likelihood, not even from his note-book immediately, but from recollection of its contents." Extending the position of J. C. Hare, who had defended Coleridge in 1835 from De Quincey's accusations, and anticipating the argument of Thomas McFarland, who has written the most convincing modern defense, Sara explains her father's plagiarisms as the unfortunate result of an eccentric method of composition, of a careless inattention to "fact" that overlooked matters of individual "ownership" in favor of collective enlightenment.

According to Sara, the word for word "borrowings" indicate not that Coleridge stole outright but that he was perfectly oblivious of the debt: he "repeated the *very words* of Schelling, and in so doing made it an easy task for the German to reclaim his own, or for the dullest wight that could read his books to give it back again." Such full-scale appropriation makes it difficult to attribute guile to the perpetrator, for Coleridge never attempted to make the material his own by artfully rewriting it. "It is not easy to see," Sara argues, "how *that which is borrowed* can ever, strictly speaking, become the property of the borrower, so as to cease to be that of the original possessor." In her analysis, Coleridge becomes not a thief but a willful debtor, " 'a divine ventriloquist, not caring from whose mouth the sounds are supposed to proceed, if only the words are audible and intelligible'." He gained no "reputation as a metaphysical discoverer," but instead represented himself as "an introducer of German metaphysics . . . a man of original genius, who had spoiled his own genius by devoting himself to the lucubrations of foreigners." The education of his countrymen, she argues, was more important to Coleridge than his personal "reputation."

Demanding that critics consider his life in conjunction with his ideas, Sara maintains that her father was too "intent upon the pursuit and enunciation of truth" to attend to questions of ownership: "If he was not always sufficiently considerate of other men's property, he was profuse of his own: and, in truth, such was his temper in regard to all *property* . . . he did not enough regard or value it whether for himself or his neighbour." This, she admits, was a fault, a "want of proportion in the faculties of the mind" which precluded the possibility of successful publications. In short, Coleridge was a dedicated metaphysician oblivious to worldly responsibilities: "he loved to go forward, expounding and ennobling the soul of his teaching, and hated the trouble of turning back to look after its body." The victim of a "nerveless languor, which . . . rendered all exercises difficult to him except of thought and imagination," Coleridge reproduced his "illness" textually:

> The *Biographia Literaria* he composed at that period of his life when his health was most deranged, and his mind most subject to the influence of bodily disorder. It bears marks of this throughout, for it is even less methodical in its arrangement than any of his other works. Up to a certain point the author pursues his plan of writing his literary life, but, in no long time his "slack hand" abandons its grasp of the subject, and the book is filled out to a certain size, with such miscellaneous contents of his desk as seem least remote from it. To say, with the writer in *Blackwood* [Ferrier], that he stopped short in the process of unfolding a theory of the imagination, merely because he had come to the end of all that Schelling had taught . . . is to place the matter in a perfectly false light; he broke down in the prosecution of his whole scheme, the regular history of his literary life and opinions, . . . be-

cause his energies for regular composition in any line were deserting him, at least for a time.

"[S]ubject to the influence of bodily disorder," Coleridge's mind composed a work as "[im]methodical" as his health was "deranged." Less plagiarist than invalid, he failed to produce "the regular history of his literary life" not because he had run out of passages from Schelling but because "his energies for regular composition" were depleted. The reader, Sara argues, can effect a mutual cure by "meet[ing] the author half way," for "the chief use and aim of writings of such a character" is therapeutic—"to excite the reader to think,—to draw out of his mind a native flame rather than make it bright for a moment by the reflection of alien fires." Herself in the process of restoring her father's text to a readable health, Sara extends the act of restoration to include her contemporaries, who are to approach Coleridge's work as participants in an ongoing process of educational, and hence social, reform.

Having answered Ferrier's charges of plagiarism, Sara turns to his second accusation—that her father had unlawfully claimed to have anticipated " 'the main and fundamental ideas' of Schelling's system." Her refutation begins by locating both Coleridge and Schelling within the same Kantian tradition and by insisting that their intellectual powers were equivalent. She then argues that given their similar historical conditions they could easily have come to the same conclusions at approximately the same time. More importantly, she maintains that her father was less interested in receiving credit for originality than in having " 'the honour of rendering [German philosophy] intelligible to his countrymen'." Reiterating her belief that Coleridge was always more concerned with truth than with his own popularity, Sara effectively distances him from charges of duplicity by granting him both spiritual vision and worldly altruism.

Sara's strategy is aided considerably by her return at the essay's close to the issue of her father's intellectual and moral flaws. Chief among his intellectual deficiencies, she observes, was a certain inability to retain facts and a corresponding predilection for abstraction: "matter of fact, as such, laid no hold upon his mind; of all he heard and saw, he readily caught and well retained the spirit, but the *letter* escaped him; he seemed incapable of paying due regard to it." Significantly, this weakness was intimately bound to his greatest strength: "his power of abstracting and referring to universal principles often rendered him unconscious of incorrectness of statement." Similarly, Coleridge's moral constitution was flawed by an irresolute will, a mental paralysis that impeded the dutiful exercising of his genius. But here too his deficiency resulted directly from a corresponding virtue, from the greatness of his heart and the depth of his feeling: "his heart was as warm as his intellectual being was lifesome and active, nay it was from warmth of heart and keenness of feeling that his imagination derived its glow and vivacity." Because his feelings operated with such intensity, his mind was frequently overwhelmed and his will paralyzed.

In one sense certainly, the figure who emerges at the conclusion of Sara's essay is, like the text of the *Biographia* itself, deeply humanized. Although his genius is never denied—to the contrary, Coleridge the philosopher is present throughout—that genius functions as a part of a larger personality irreparably flawed by a host of human deficiencies. Making no attempt to obscure her father's faults or the irregularities of his writings, Sara paints a portrait of the artist as an intellectual invalid very much in need of the understanding and compassion of his readers. At the same time, however, this historicized Coleridge is not meant to play the leading role in her argument; he is introduced in all his particularity only to be displaced in favor of his philosophic counterpart—Coleridge the metaphysician devoutly attendant upon distant truths. Just as all his flaws are subservient to greater virtues, so his "humanity" is established in order to be replaced by a metaphysical vision glimmering through his "immethodical" text. Coleridge's readers become active participants in a multiple redemption as Sara remains in the background orchestrating an elaborate redefinition of Carlyle's venerated hero. Whereas Carlyle ignores personal irregularities as irrelevant to intellectual, political, or moral power, Sara traces their interconnections, unafraid of admitting the former as long as she is ultimately assured of establishing the latter.

The second section of Sara's introduction, "Mr. Coleridge's Religious Opinions," continues the process of veneration by defending Coleridge from contemporary critics as it clarifies his position vis-à-vis his theological forefathers. Reacting to a recent article in the *Christian Miscellany,* "Contributions of S. T. Coleridge to the Revival of Catholic Truths," Sara contends that Coleridge has been maligned by critics "far too prone to discredit a man's opinions at second-hand by tracing them to some averred evil source in his character, or perverting influence in the circumstances of his life." After refuting the charge that her father's powers as a theologian were impaired by " 'his profession of literature, his having edited a newspaper, and his having been engaged in a course of heretical and schismatical teaching', " Sara maintains that it was his intellectual independence that caused the misrepresentation: "It was the natural consequence of his having no predilection for any sect or party that parties and party organs have either neglected or striven against him." While he strove "to examine the truth of modes of thought in general," his opponents "assum[ed] the truth of certain modes of thought [as] the ground of their existence as parties." Thus, unlike many of Carlyle's heroes, Coleridge found that his quest for truth offended the beliefs upheld by those who had most to gain from his inquiries.

Coleridge's marginal status in contemporary debates resulted predictably from his originality, and, according to his daughter, he was victimized by party politics of some complexity. Those representing "the dry land of negative Protestantism" saw him as a dangerous innovator halfway to Romanism; those of High Church persuasion saw his unripe Anglo-Catholicism as little more than a helpful beginning along a well-established route. Trapped between warring sects, Coleridge's contributions were fated to be misunderstood by both, for neither party could recognize or appreciate that his real task was to explain "the universal ideas of Christianity . . . according to modern philosophy."

In order to explore the relationship between her father's "modern philosophy" and his Christian beliefs—or, more accurately, the interdependence between his doctrines of reason and faith—Sara presents a genealogical argument. She identifies the two thinkers who most influenced her father—Luther and Kant—and argues that Coleridge's unpopularity stems first from a critical misunderstanding of his intellectual ancestors and then from an inability to grasp how Coleridge succeeded in resolving the doctrines of both men into one system. "My Father's affectionate respect for Luther," Sara writes, "is enough to alienate him from the High Anglican party, and his admiration of Kant enough to bring him into suspicion with the anti-philosophic part of the religious world."

Sara's task, like her father's, becomes one of reconciliation: in order to demonstrate how Coleridge conflated philosophy and religion to the benefit of both, she must uncover the fundamental similarities shared by disparate positions. Thus, she first reconciles the two opposing religious factions—High Church and Low Anglican—by arguing that Luther and Newman are in substantive agreement on the question of justification. She then turns to Kant, whose philosophical system, she explains, provides the means by which her father united faith and reason and so saved the former from descent into dogmatic mysticism. In the same way that Coleridge mediates between the High and Low Anglicans, he unites philosophical speculation to theological doctrine, combining two separate areas of inquiry into one mutually beneficial quest for truth.

Having established and explored the ties that link Coleridge with Luther and Kant, Sara concludes with a predictable but effective discussion of Coleridge as an independent "reformer" within an established tradition. Like both of his German heroes, Coleridge dedicated his efforts to "free[ing] the minds of Christians from the schemes of doctrine, which seemed to him . . . derogatory to God and injurious to man." He was not, then, as his detractors have claimed, an ineffectual thinker "given to contemplation rather than to action." On the contrary, his entire system—like Kant's and Luther's—has a " 'moral origin' " which mandates a "practical" responsibility:

> All the poetry, all the poetical criticism which my Father produced, has a practical end; for poetry is a visible creation the final aim of which is to benefit man by means of delight. As for his moral and religious writings, if practical wisdom is not in them, they are empty indeed, for their whole aim is practical usefulness—the regulation of action, the actions of the heart and mind with their appropriate manifestations—the furtherance of man's well being here and hereafter.

No *"mere intellectualist,"* Coleridge has been victimized, Sara argues, by critics who fail to realize that personal (and stylistic) flaws were counterbalanced by a "practical" concern with the moral betterment of his fellow man. In the same way that in the previous essay she had argued that Coleridge's readers were meant to participate actively in the re-creative process, Sara emphasizes here that that mutually beneficial interaction was conceived as part of a larger socially and spiritually redemptive plan.

By establishing her father's connections to his intellectual forebears, Sara legitimizes his endeavors as she explains his unpopularity. She outlines his lineage to argue first that he had rethought old positions and constructed from them a new system of considerable significance; and second that both the tenor of his works and his position in society are directly analogous to those of his own heroes—men already accepted as intellects of great stature. Engineering an implicit substitution, Sara forges his destiny as the maligned and misunderstood genius, selfless and heroic, who patiently awaits not his own veneration but the redemption of his countrymen.

The last essay from the introduction, "Mr. Coleridge's 'Remarks on the Present Mode of Conducting Public Journals', " completes the redefinition of hero begun by the first two. Ostensibly, the essay seeks to justify Sara's removal of a passage "containing *personal* remarks" about Francis Jeffrey from the new edition. Soon, however, the argument moves from a general discussion of the partisan politics of literary journals, through an account of Coleridge's most misguided reviewers, to a persuasive celebration of Coleridge as an intellectual martyr. From beginning to end, Coleridge's personal shortcomings are carefully balanced by a noble Christian altruism that far surpasses the petty selfishness of his opponents. Thus, Sara transforms the issue of critical reception from a potentially selfish concern with popularity (her father was never worried about his "fame" per se) into a heroic preoccupation with the ways in which religious philosophy can affect "the poetic mind of the community" for its collective betterment.

Sara argues that as "servants of the public in general," both reviewers and journals have a "duty" to do more than "make public taste in literature subservient to their own purposes as members of a party." Unfortunately, such duty was neglected by the early critics of Coleridge, who, like William Hazlitt, "scanned narrowly" in order to "abuse scientifically." For Sara, Hazlitt represents the quintessence of journalistic inequity. His vilifying reviews were focused exclusively on the "attributes of the *man*," while ignoring the substance of his work. Reviewers like Hazlitt "declaim upon virtue and vice, wisdom and folly . . . without any earnest feeling or belief [of their own]"; they are "out of the domain of conscience altogether."

It is "against this system," Sara writes, that "the *Biographia Literaria* . . . protest[s], a protest to which private feeling has given a piquancy, but which in the main it has not corrupted or falsified." Coleridge exposed "what he held to be wrong methods of acting on the mind" and "would not have given way to indignation . . . if he had not believed his cause to be the cause of the public also." He had been reviewed "in a way not to expose his errors but to prevent people from attending to him at all; not to make him understood but to stamp upon him the character of hopeless unintelligibility." If in the *Biographia* Coleridge's writing occasionally seems petulant, extravagant, or overdefensive, readers must recognize, Sara insists, the harsh treatment that fueled his resentment.

After considering Hazlitt's charges and her father's responses, Sara concludes with a quotation from *Aids to Reflection,* a passage " 'on the keen and poisoned shafts of the tongue' " that is, as she puts it, most "applicable to the subject that has been discussed":

> The slanders, perchance, may not be altogether forged or untrue; they may be implements, not the inventions, of malice. But they do not on this account escape the guilt of detraction. Rather it is characteristic of the evil spirit in question to work by the advantage of real faults; but these stretched and aggravated to the utmost. It is not expressible how deep a wound a tongue sharpened to the work will give, with no noise and a very little word. This is the true white gunpowder, which the dreaming projectors of silent mischiefs and insensible poisons sought for in the laboratories of art and nature, in a world of good; but which was to be found in its most destructive form, "in the World of Evil, the Tongue."

Reduced by synecdoche to the malicious "tongue," the "evil spirit" of slander becomes a common human propensity attributable to Coleridge as well as to his detractors, and in that sense the passage assumes a kind of humility. At the same time, however, the voice is, like much of *Aids to Reflection,* more prophetic and Biblical than characteristically Coleridgean or even specifically "human"—it speaks an all-inclusive Truth above and beyond the individual author and his individual readers. This paradoxically aggrandizing self-effacement is reaffirmed by a return to the first paragraph of the aphorism which identifies its intended audience as those who "have attained a self-pleasing pitch of civility or formal religion . . . [and] make their own size the model and rule to examine all by." Coleridge is criticizing those who possess small-minded interpretive certainty while he himself speaks with the assurance of universal vision. Importantly, this vision embraces human fallibility, original sin, and earthly suffering. In other words, Coleridge makes himself a part of the human situation only to stand above it as an authoritative commentator. Thus, his passage enacts precisely the same process being orchestrated by the larger argument in which it appears: Coleridge the man is subsumed by the Truth he speaks. In that last paragraph, father and daughter strike the same note simultaneously.

Taken together, then, Sara's three essays are more than a protracted vindication of Coleridge's life and work; they enact a complex apotheosis of a flawed man into an intellectual hero by first presenting what he was, by then arguing for what he did, and by finally lamenting what he was made into. The first essay establishes Coleridge's humanity, the second maps out his contributions, and the third engineers his martyrdom. In the opening section, Coleridge's humanity transforms plagiarism into an unusual mode of composition. Faults are emphasized only to be subordinated to greater virtues as lack of concern for details is balanced by an obsession with "principles." Thus, the historical self exists to be displaced by the inquiring philosopher. In the second essay, Coleridge's contributions are seen as effecting a reconciliation between religion and philosophy. Like his heroes Luther and Kant (whom he implicitly surpasses), Coleridge is a statesman devoted to no party but speaking for all. His intellectual integrity hinges upon his non-allegiance to worldly sects, but his deep faith in spiritual freedom mandates a "practical" direction for even his most abstruse works: he is unworldly but still a man of action, not just a philosopher but a cleric attempting to use his gifts for the benefit of the people. In the third essay, the process completes itself as the cleric is betrayed by his friends and rejected by his contemporaries; he becomes an unacknowledged hero in a spiteful and inattentive world. The entire introduction then concludes with an apotheosis that is both actual and prophetic: Coleridge's martyrdom has already occurred, but his resurrection is still in progress.

Sara's labors on behalf of her father were both a duty and an exorcism. She labored for Coleridge because he was her father and because his works needed and deserved her assistance. But she also labored for herself, for a "self" not submissive and patronized but only newly "restless," "cheerful," and engaged "in the controversies of the day." Thus, filial duty of the kind required by her father inadvertently encouraged an "egotism" that Sara felt compelled to explain and for which she repeatedly apologized. During the early months of her project, for example, soon after the death of her mother in September, 1845, Sara hesitantly expressed a growing pride in her accomplishments:

> I am not, however, brooding over my grief from want of employment. I am just now, *absurdly* busy. I have to edit my father's fragmentary work, the "Biographia Literaria". . . . The trouble I take is so ridiculously disproportioned to any effect that can be produced, and we so apt to measure our importance by the efforts we make, rather than the good we do, that I am obliged to keep reminding myself of this very truth, in order not to become a mighty person in my own eyes, while I remain as small as ever in the eyes of every one else.

Editing was a selfless activity fully in keeping with early-nineteenth-century strictures against female assertiveness, but the editorial labors necessitated by Coleridge's abstruse and immethodical works were so demanding that Sara was tempted "to become a mighty person in [her] own eyes" even without the public recognition that measured more accurately the social value of her "efforts." As the dissatisfaction in the passage suggests, Sara was in the process of redefining her ideas about female authorship and "feminine" propriety; given the "trouble" taken, she had no real desire to "remain as small as ever in the eyes of every one else." Editing the *Biographia* thus provided the perfect opportunity to test a "restless" intellectual enthusiasm against the restrictive demands of her society.

By the time the *Biographia Literaria* appeared in the spring of 1847, Sara had become accustomed and committed to her "unwomanly" activities. When John Taylor Coleridge criticized her introduction as "arrogant" and "immodest," she retorted:

> If I was justified in attempting to defend my Father's opinions at all, what could have been the use of perpetually interspersing modest *phrases,* which after all mean very little—for the arrogance—if such there be—counts in doing the

thing at all—not in doing it, as I have done it, plainly and straight forwardly.

Several months later, Sara explained herself again to Aubrey de Vere in a remarkable passage that bears quoting in full:

> I had a very interesting talk last night with Mr. H[enry] T[aylor], who is looking remarkably well. He put in a strong light the unattractiveness of intellectual ladies to gentlemen, even those who are themselves on the intellectual side of the world—men of genius, men of learning and letters. I could have said, in reply, that while women are young, where there is a pretty face, it covers a multitude of sins, even intellectuality; where there is not that grand desideratum to young marrying men, a love of books does not make the matter much worse in one way, and does make it decidedly better in the other: that when youth is past, a certain number of persons are bound to us, in the midst of all our plainness and pedantry; these old friends and lovers cleave to us for something underneath *all that,* not only below the region of good looks, skin, lip, and eye, but even far deeper down than intellect, for our individual, moral, personal being, which shall endure when we shall be where all will see as angels ken: that as for the *world of gentlemen at large*—that world which a *young* lady desires, in an indefinite, infinite way, to charm and smite—we that are no longer young pass into a new, old-womanish, tough state of mind; to *please* them is not so much the aim as to set them to rights, lay down the law to them, convict them of their errors, pretenses, superficialities, etc., etc.; in short, tell them a *bit of our mind.* . . . [I]ntellectualism, if it be not wrong in itself, will not be abandoned by us to please the gentlemen.

Sara had indeed adopted "a new, old-womanish, tough state of mind," and no longer, it seemed, would she suffer male "errors, pretensions, superficialities, etc." in silence. Freed from the youthful illusions of the power of female beauty "to charm and smite," she enjoyed a new "intellectualism" that recognized the right of women to "lay down the law" rather than cringe before it. "[P]leasing the gentlemen" with "modest phrases" ran counter to the "plainness and pedantry" of a forty-five-year-old widow who managed her own household, her own finances, and her own publications without assistance from or dependence on male expertise. Begun in filial duty, Sara's labors on the *Biographia* had fostered filial freedom. (pp. 56-64)

> *Bradford K. Mudge, "Sara Coleridge and 'The Business of Life'," in* The Wordsworth Circle, *Vol. XIX, No. 1, Winter, 1988, pp. 55-64.*

Bradford K. Mudge   (essay date 1989)

[*In the following excerpt, Mudge comments on the imagery in Coleridge's poem "Poppies," which is included in her collection* Pretty Lessons in Verse for Good Children.]

Not all of Sara's poems [in ***Pretty Lessons in Verse for***

Small Children] . . . were purely didactic or exclusively for children. In **"Poppies,"** a poem whose inclusion in *Pretty Lessons* she later regretted, Sara juxtaposes Herbert's childish innocence to her own adult "sorrows of the night," producing in the process a complex and revealing lyric in the manner of Blake, the one romantic poet Sara never read:

> The Poppies Blooming all around
> My Herbert loves to see,
> Some pearly white, some dark as night,
> Some red as cramasie;
>
> He loves their colours fresh and fine
> As fair as fair may be,
> But little does my darling know
> How good they are to me.
>
> He views their clustering petals gay
> And shakes their nut-brown seeds.
> But they to him are nothing more
> Than other brilliant weeds;
>
> O how should'st thou with beaming brow
> With eye and cheek so bright
> Know aught of that blossom's pow'r,
> Or sorrows of the night!
>
> When poor mama long restless lies
> She drinks the poppy's juice;
> That liquor soon can close her eyes
> And slumber soft produce.
>
> O' then my sweet my happy boy
> Will thank the poppy flow'r
> Which brings the sleep to dear mama
> At midnight's darksome hour.

Like Blake's *Songs of Innocence and Experience,* Sara's poem explores the tensions between a fragile, naive purity and its fated confrontation with the disillusionment and sorrow of worldly wisdom. The central image, of course, is that of the ambivalent poppy—"Some pearly white, some dark as night." The child sees only "brilliant weeds" and knows nothing of "that blossom's pow'r" or of his mother's "long restless[ness]." But the issue is not simply one of knowledge. The threat of death inscribed within both the poppies and the recurrent images of night and sleep increases the emphasis on maternal self-sacrifice and suggests a causal relationship between Herbert's health and his mother's illness, between his pampered innocence and her misery. When, at the poem's conclusion, the boy is envisioned as thanking "the poppy flow'r," he does so

with an ironic understanding of the parental price paid for the "beaming brow" of his youth. Education, he discovers, is more than a matter of botanical fact. (pp. 65-7)

> *Bradford K. Mudge, in his* Sara Coleridge, A Victorian Daughter: Her Life and Essays, *Yale University Press, 1989, 287 p.*

FURTHER READING

Fields, Beverly. "More than Daddy's Little Editor." *The New York Times Book Review* XCIV, No. 41 (8 October 1989): 42.

> Biographical sketch and review of Bradford Mudge's *Sara Coleridge, A Victorian Daughter.*

Griggs, Earl Leslie. *Coleridge Fille: A Biography of Sara Coleridge.* London: Oxford University Press, 1940, 259 p.

> Study that deals "not only with the facts of Sara Coleridge's life but with her intellectual activities as well." Griggs notes that Coleridge's "wide reading, her ratiocinative gifts, and her theological interests equipped her to become the best of her father's early editors."

Mudge, Bradford K. "On Tennyson's *The Princess*: Sara Coleridge in the *Quarterly Review.*" *The Wordsworth Circle* XV, No. 2 (Spring 1984): 51-54.

> Discusses Coleridge's review of Alfred Tennyson's *The Princess.*

———. *Sara Coleridge, A Victorian Daughter: Her Life and Essays.* New Haven: Yale University Press, 1989, 287 p.

> Important critical biography. Mudge concludes that "to 'know' Sara Coleridge is to glimpse momentarily the complexities of nineteenth-century literary production and reception, to appreciate both the adversities and the accomplishments of nineteenth-century women writers, and . . . to come to a better understanding of the literary and critical traditions of which we are a part."

Woolf, Virginia. "Sara Coleridge." In her *The Death of the Moth and Other Essays,* pp. 111-18. New York: Harcourt, Brace and Company, 1942.

> Presents an overview of Coleridge's life.

Nikolai Gogol

1809-1852

(Born Nikolai Vasilyevich Gogol-Yanovsky; also wrote under the pseudonyms of V. Alov and Rudy Panko) Russian novelist, dramatist, short story writer, essayist, critic, and poet.

The following entry presents criticism of Gogol's *Myortvye dushi* (*Dead Souls;* also published in English as *Tchitchikoff's Journeys; or, Dead Souls*). For additional criticism on *Dead Souls* and Gogol's complete career, see *NCLC,* Vol. 5; for criticism devoted to Gogol's drama *Revizor* (*The Inspector General*), see *NCLC,* Vol. 15.

Dead Souls is an account of the peripatetic adventures of Pavel Ivanovich Chichikov, whose moneymaking scheme involving the purchase of lists of dead serfs from Russian landowners goes awry. The novel is widely regarded as a masterpiece of world literature for its panoramic, satirical portrayal of nineteenth-century Russian character types, manners, and language and its highly original, enigmatic style. A complex combination of realism, lyricism, satire, fantasy, and the grotesque, *Dead Souls* has inspired numerous interpretations of its theme and purpose since its publication, ranging from assessments of the work as a realistic evocation of the social evils of Gogol's age to those that emphasize symbolic, linguistic, and moral aspects of the novel.

Gogol began writing *Dead Souls* in 1835 after Alexander Pushkin suggested that he display his satirical abilities in a major work. In response to Gogol's request that he supply a subject, Pushkin proposed a picaresque novel in which the protagonist would journey throughout Russia on an illegal quest, meeting all segments of the population, including government officials, landowners, tradespeople, and peasants. Gogol originally conceived of the novel as a light satire: "I began to write with no definite plan in mind, without knowing exactly what my hero was to represent. I only thought that this odd project . . . would lead to the creation of diverse personalities and my own inclination toward the comic would bring on amusing situations that I could alternate with pathos." By 1836, however, his intentions for the novel had become more ambitious, and he envisioned the work as a prose poem of comprehensive scope treating universal themes. "The work I am now writing, that I have been thinking about for a long time, and that will continue to absorb my thoughts, is neither a long short story nor a novel. It will be very long, running to several volumes, entitled *Dead Souls.* If God allows me to compose my poem it will be my first decent piece of writing. All Russia will be in it." After opposition by Russian censors, who considered the title blasphemous, the work was published in 1842.

The initial critical reaction to *Dead Souls* was mixed, with commentators disagreeing over the nature and importance of Gogol's work. Some emphasized the novel's universal significance, labeling it an epic poem and Gogol a "Homer

of modern times," a judgment to which Gogol himself subscribed. Others, while finding realistic detail and social relevance in the work, denied the novel epic stature and importance. Still others decried what they perceived to be the novel's indecent realism and the shallowness of Gogol's largely comic approach to important social issues. Stung by the negative assessments of his work, Gogol began to write a second part of *Dead Souls,* which he was confident would unequivocally establish both his artistry and the greatness of his epic vision. Dissatisfied with his results, however, he burned manuscripts of the work in 1843 and again in 1845. During this time, Gogol became increasingly concerned with religion and the state of his soul, attributing his failure to finish *Dead Souls* to his own immorality. Under the influence of Father Matthew Konstantinovsky, a fanatical priest who attempted to convince him to renounce literature and enter a monastery, Gogol burned his third attempt to write Part 2 a few days before his death in 1852. While several chapters from various drafts of the novel survive, most critics dismiss these fragments, in which Gogol begins the reform of Chichikov, as far inferior to Part 1.

Simple in plot, *Dead Souls* begins with Chichikov's arrival in the town of N., where he quickly ingratiates himself with members of the local government. Having determined the status of the major landowners in the area, those with lists of serfs who have died but who are still subject to taxation until the next census, Chichikov sets out to visit these gentry and purchase their lists in order to swindle mortgage money from the bank with this non-existent collateral. Chichikov's encounters with the landowners, in which they are depicted by detailed, often grotesque descriptions of their physical appearance and speech, their estates and possessions, and their reactions to Chichikov's proposal, provide the main action of the novel. As Victor Erlich notes, a Gogolian character is never fully developed psychologically but exists as a type or humor, "an embodiment of a single trait, proclivity, or foible generalized or extended throughout the personality, pushed to the limit of utter rigidity or absurdity." Manilov, for example, a squire defined by his carelessly kept estate, cloying physical familiarity, uncritical acceptance of all acquaintances, and easy acquiescence to Chichikov's plan, is the embodiment of sentimentality and mindless insipidity. Other characters represent such traits as avarice, miserliness, and gluttony. The protagonist of the novel is also delineated by outer appearances, possessions, and actions: his round, well-fed body, of which he is extraordinarily careful, his multi-layered box with its secret drawer and collection of odds and ends, and his chameleon-like responses to the other characters. While Chichikov exhibits positive qualities, and Gogol provides a biographical explanation of his motivations at the end of the novel, commentators agree that he, too, is a type—in the words of Vladimir Nabokov, a slick "traveling salesman from Hades," embodying the same unsavory characteristics that permeate the rest of his world. The phrase "dead souls," as critics note, refers not only to dead serfs but to all the morally corrupt characters exemplifying "poshlust," a Russian word denoting rottenness, banality, and cheapness in human affairs. The end of the novel is marked by the failure of Chichikov's plan and his ignominious departure from N., whose townspeople have begun to suspect and become increasingly hostile over his true intentions in the area.

According to commentators, much of the complexity of *Dead Souls* may be attributed to its multifaceted, exuberant language and style, in which slang, neologisms, technical vocabulary, and Ukrainian dialect are combined in intricately structured sentences. Another aspect of Gogol's verbal inventiveness is his inclusion of comic lists of people, animals, food, and names throughout the narrative that convey additional, often negative, details about his characters. Names are particularly significant in the novel, frequently appearing in repetitive lists or rhyming pairs and serving to satirically delineate such characters as the landowners Nozdrev, "of nostrils," and Korobochka, "little box." In other instances, Gogol's failure to name important charachters, as in the cases of "the lady who was pleasant" and "the lady who was pleasant in every respect," for example, contributes an air of unreality and absurdity to the novel, as does his repetition of bits of non-communicative dialogue. Such stylistic devices as the extended Homeric simile in which characters are often compared to animals, insects, or inanimate objects and hyperbolic descriptions perform a similar function. Gogol's lyri-

cal digressions provide a sharp contrast to such grotesque delineations of character. Critics note that these poetic reflections on the future of Russia, such as a passage at the end of the novel in which Chichikov's troika escapes into a glorious, idealized Russian state, provide glimpses of his more elevated thematic intentions for the multivolume epic he envisioned. Similarly, authorial interpolations on the nature of the artist's task in writing *Dead Souls* also reveal theme and purpose. In his best-known interjection, Gogol wrote: "But for a long while yet am I destined by some wondrous power to go hand in hand with my strange heroes and to contemplate life rushing past in all its enormity, amid laughter perceptible to the world and through tears that are unperceived by and unknown to it!" This statement has been widely discussed by critics, and the relationship between laughter and tears in *Dead Souls* has had various interpretations, including compassionate satire, an artist's grief at the uncomplimentary way in which he must picture his world, and euphoric emotion in anticipation of the advent of an idealized realm.

Due in large part to the disparate narrative and stylistic elements of *Dead Souls,* Gogol's intent and principal themes have been interpreted in a variety of ways throughout the years. Following the lead of Vissarion Belinsky, a prominent nineteenth-century Russian literary and social critic, early Russian commentators emphasized the realistic details of Gogol's work and its portrayal of social corruption under the czars. For these critics, Gogol's purpose was political reform, a view also endorsed by twentieth-century socialist realist critics. At the turn of the century, however, Andrey Bely and other writers influenced by the Russian Symbolist movement focused on the symbolic meaning of the novel's fantastic aspects. To these commentators, Gogol's purpose was not realistic description but a visionary portrayal of an inner, imaginary world peopled by grotesques, of larger human import than a mere reconstruction of social conditions. This emphasis on the hitherto unexplored unreality of *Dead Souls* strongly influenced the direction of subsequent criticism in Russia, and Western criticism of the novel has also developed largely from the work of the Symbolists. While a number of Western critics give some credence to realistic, social interpretations of *Dead Souls,* most advance readings that stress Gogol's creation of an inner world. Vladimir Nabokov, stating that "it is as useless to look in *Dead Souls* for an authentic Russian background as it would be to try and form a conception of Denmark on the basis of that little affair in cloudy Elsinore," finds Gogol's purpose to be the creation of an absurd and irrational universe. Other critics—Victor Erlich, for example—stress a moral reading of the novel in which the author examines the depths of his own soul and that of humankind. Finally, in a reading that focuses on the function of nonexistence or nothingness in *Dead Souls,* Robert Adams finds the novel a "palpitating, pneumatic, fragmented" world enveloped by "void and vacancy." The complex artistry of *Dead Souls* continues to elicit critical response. René Wellek has concluded that its sustained appeal lies in its "rich texture, . . . vivid detail, and its ultimate vision of the world: gloomy but also grotesquely comic."

(See also *Drama Criticism,* Vol. 1.)

Nikolai Gogol   (letter date 1843)

[*In the following letter to an unknown correspondent excerpted from Gogol's* Vybrannye mesta iz perepiski s druzyami *(1847; Selected Passages from Correspondence with My Friends),* Gogol discusses the origin and development of the characters in Dead Souls *and his purpose in writing the novel.*]

You, you who are such an expert and knowledgeable man, you are inclined to set me the same empty questions which others know how to set. Half of them are concerned with things that are still in the future. What is the use of a curiosity like this? One question alone is wise and worthy of you, and I wish that others had set it to me, although I do not know whether I can answer it wisely. Here is the question: Why are the heroes of my last works, and especially those of **Dead Souls**, although far from being portraits of real persons, although their characteristics are so unattractive, close to the soul, without anyone's knowing why, just as though some sort of spiritual circumstance had participated in their composition? A year ago it would have been awkward for me to answer on this point, even to you. Now I say everything directly: my heroes are close to the soul because they come from the soul; all my last works are the story of my own soul. In order to explain all this better, I will define myself to you as a writer.

I have been much interpreted, most of my facets discussed, but no one has defined my principal essence. Only Pushkin perceived it. He always told me that no other writer has the gift of representing the banality of life so clearly, of knowing how to depict the banality of a banal man with such force that all the *petty details* which escape the eyes *gleam large* in the eyes. That is my principal virtue, belonging to me alone, precisely that which is in no other writer. Only afterwards was it deepened in me by its union with some spiritual circumstance. But I was in no condition to reveal it then, even to Pushkin.

This characteristic appeared with greater strength in **Dead Souls. Dead Souls** did not frighten Russia and make such a noise in it because it laid bare some of its wounds or its internal sicknesses, nor even because it presented a shocking picture of evil triumphant and innocence conquered. Not at all. My heroes are not at all villains; if I had only added one good feature to any one of them the reader would have been reconciled with them all. But the banality of all of them frightened my readers. What frightened them is that my heroes follow one after the other, one more banal than the other, that there is not one consoling scene, that there is nowhere for the poor reader to rest and take a breath, and, after having read the whole book, it seems exactly as though he were emerging from some stifling cellar into God's light. I would sooner have been forgiven if I had presented pictures of monsters: but banality I was not forgiven. The Russian is more frightened of his insignificance than of all his vices and shortcomings. A splendid event! A capital fear! Whoever is strongly disgusted at his insignificance probably has everything opposite to insignificance. Thus, this is my principal virtue; but this virtue, I say again, would not have developed in me

with such strength if my own spiritual circumstance and my own spiritual history had not been united with it. None of my readers knew that while laughing at my heroes, he was laughing at me.

There was not one overpowering vice in me which appeared more visibly than all my other vices, just as there was not one picturesque virtue which could have given me a picturesque appearance: but rather, instead of that, in me was a collection of all possible abominations, a little of each, and besides, in such numbers as I have thus far not encountered in any individual. God has given me a many-sided nature. He has also inspired in me, since my birth, some good characteristics; but best of them all, for which I do not know how to thank Him, was *the desire to be better*. I have never loved my bad qualities, and if God's divine love had not commanded that they be revealed to me gradually, a little at a time, instead of being revealed suddenly and immediately before my eyes, at a time when I still had no understanding of His infinite mercy, I would have hanged myself. In proportion to the rate at which they were revealed, the desire to be delivered of them was strengthened in me by a wonderful impulse from on high; by an extraordinary spiritual event, I was driven to transfer them to my heroes. What the nature of that event was you may not know: if I had seen any use in it for anyone, I would already have announced it. From that moment on, I began to provide my heroes with my own rottenness in addition to their abominations. This is how it was done: taking one of my bad qualities, I pursued it under another name and in another field, I tried to represent it as a mortal enemy who had inflicted the worst outrage on me, I pursued it in anger, with sarcasm and anything else that fell to my hand. If anyone had seen the monsters which first issued from my pen, he would promptly have shuddered for me. It is enough for me to tell you that when I began to read the first chapters of **Dead Souls** to Pushkin, in the form in which they formerly were, Pushkin, who always laughed at my readings (he loved laughter), slowly became gloomier and gloomier, and finally he was completely somber. When the reading was finished, he uttered in an anguished voice: "God, how sad is our Russia!" This amazed me. Pushkin, who knew Russia so well, had not noticed that it was all a caricature and my own invention! Then I saw what something whose spring is the soul and is a spiritual truth means, how frightening a sight it can be to a man when he is presented with shadows, and how much more threatening is *the absence of light*. From this time forward I began to think only of how to mitigate the painful impression which **Dead Souls** had produced. I have seen that many abominations are not worth anger; it is better to show all their insignificance, which must be their fate forever. Besides, I wanted to test what a normal Russian would say if he should be regaled with his own banality. Since the plan of **Dead Souls** had been adopted long before, for the first part I needed worthless people. These worthless people, however, are not simply portraits of worthless people; on the contrary, assembled in them are the traits of those who consider themselves better than others, like generals degraded to the ranks. Here, besides my own, are the traits of many of my friends, and yours too. I will prove this to you later in case you find it necessary; until then it is my secret. I had to pick up from all the fine people I know everything banal and nasty that they had caught accidentally and to restore it to its legitimate owners. Do not ask why all the first part had to be *banality* and why every person in it had to be banal: the other volumes will give you the answer—and that is all! The first part, despite all its imperfections, has done the chief thing: in everyone it has inspired a loathing for my heroes and their worthlessness; it has caused me a certain necessary melancholy at the sight of it all. For the moment, this is enough for me; I am after nothing else. Of course, it would all have been more substantial if I had been less in a hurry to publish it and had polished it better. My heroes were still not completely detached from me, and therefore did not receive independence. I had still not lodged them firmly in the land where they were to exist, they had still not entered into the round of our customs, furnished with all the circumstances of real Russian life. The entire book is still no more than a prematurely born child; but its spirit is already invisibly spread abroad, and even its premature appearance may be useful to me in that it will force my readers to point out all my blunders concerning social legislation and particular usages in Russia. So if you, instead of posing empty questions to me (with which half your letter was stuffed, and which had no end other than the satisfaction of an idle curiosity), if you had instead assembled sensible observations on my book, both yours and those of other intelligent people, busy, like you, with experience and a sensible life, if you had been able to adjoin accounts of events and anecdotes such as have occurred either in your immediate neighborhood or throughout the province, in confirmation or denial of what is in my book, so that it would have been possible for me to tidy up tens of them on every page—then you would have done a good deed, and I would have given you hearty thanks. How my horizon would have been enlarged! How my mind would have have been refreshed and how successfully my work would have gone forward! But what I ask no one fulfills; no one considers my questions important but only esteems his own; and some even demand sincerity and frankness of me, not understanding what it is they demand. And why this idle curiosity to know beforehand, and this idle haste without object and without goal which I notice is already beginning to infect you? See how in nature everything is performed decorously and wisely, by harmonious law, and how reasonably everything proceeds, one thing from another! Only we, God knows why, are confounded. Everyone is in a hurry. Everyone is feverish. Well, have you thoroughly weighed your words, "A second volume is now vitally necessary"? Solely because of the general displeasure with me I should hurry the second volume as foolishly as I hurried the first. Have I really gone entirely out of my mind? I need this displeasure; it is in his displeasure that a man will express something to me. And what led you to the conclusion that a second volume is necessary right now? Have you really stolen into my head? Have you sensed the existence of a second volume? For you it is needed now, but for me not for two or three years, because of the rapid movement of circumstances and times. Which of us is right? He who already has the second volume in his head or he who does not even know of what

the second volume will consist? What a strange fashion has now been established in Rus! The very man who is indolent, too lazy for the matter at hand, hurries someone else, exactly as though the someone else should be overjoyed by his friend's indolence. Hardly is a man seriously occupied with something before he is immediately pressed on all sides and given a good rating if he does something foolish; they do not say to him, "Why all the hurry?"

But I have finished my sermon. I have answered your intelligent question and even said more than I have said to anyone else. Do not think, however, after these confessions, that I am just such a monster as my heroes. No, I do not resemble them. I love the good, and I search for it and burn with it; but I do not love my abominations and I do not hold their hands, as my heroes do; I do not love those meannesses of mine which separate me from the good. I struggle, and will struggle, with them, and with the help of God I will expel them. What the foolish, clever men of the world turn out is nonsense, professing that a man may be educated only in school and that afterwards it is not possible for his features to be changed: such a foolish idea could only be formed in a foolish, worldly noddle. I have already got rid of many of my abominations by transmitting them to my heroes, I have turned them to ridicule in them and compelled others to laugh at them as well. I tore myself away from many things because, having deprived them of the fine airs and chivalrous masks under which our loathsomeness struts, I put them beside all the abominations which are apparent to everyone. When I confess myself before He Who commanded me to come into the world and free myself from my faults, I see many vices in myself; but they are already not such as they were but a year ago: a holy power has helped me to tear myself away from them.

I advise you not to ignore these words but, after having read my letter, to remain alone for a few minutes and, far away from everyone, look at yourself thoroughly, passing all your life in review in order to verify the truth of my words. In my answer you will find an answer also to other questions, if you look more intently. It will also explain to you why up to now I have not offered the reader consoling scenes and have not chosen virtuous people for my heroes. They are not invented by the mind. As long as you still somewhat resemble them, as long as you have not acquired constancy and firmly established some good qualities in your soul—all that your pen writes will be a dead thing, as far from truth as earth is from Heaven. As for inventing nightmares, I have not invented any either; these nightmares weigh on my soul: what was in my soul is what issued forth from it. (pp. 102-08)

> *Nikolai Gogol, "Four Letters to Divers Persons Apropos 'Dead Souls',' in his* Selected Passages *from Correspondence with Friends, translated by Jesse Zeldin, Vanderbilt University Press, 1969, pp. 96-110.*

Andrei Bely [pseudonym of Boris Nikolaevich Bugaev] (essay date 1934)

[Bely is recognized as the most original and influential

writer of the Russian Symbolist movement. A brilliant, restless, and undisciplined spirit, Bely consistently sought for spiritual meaning within the social and literary turmoil of pre-Soviet Russia. His enormous body of work, much of it autobiographical, presents a vivid impression of this quest. Bely's explorations of form and language served as a first step toward the modernist revolution in Russian verse, a call-to-arms by many young writers for more individual artistic freedom and the complete overthrow of traditional values and social criticism of the nineteenth century. Though he was hardly a popular writer—his work was too subjective and esoteric for the general public—Bely received great attention and acclaim as the standard-bearer for those Symbolists who felt that Symbolism was more of a worldview than mere literary method. Bely's works are characterized by their verbal artistry, inner rhythm, and keenly developed style. In the following excerpt, he examines fictional technique and theme in Dead Souls.]

The chief technical device in the writing of ***Dead Souls*** is the clearcut, precise development of the "figure of fiction." This figure, of which I shall have more to say in the following pages, may be defined essentially by the following: In the subject matter of the novel—in the particular form that the novel imposes on it—there is nothing besides an indefinite delimitation of two categories: "everything" and "nothing." A given object is characterized by its distance on one side from "everything," and on the other from "nothing." This distance "from" is not a true characterization; rather, it is a parody of a characterization. The subject is an empty, generalized space, within which a fiction is inscribed: The value of the fiction may not be greater than one or less than zero. The particles "not" and "no" generate an entire series of fractions, which is neither "this" nor "that"—"that" being located at a certain distance from "everything," and "this," from "nothing." The subject (person or thing), overgrown with indefinite characteristics, becomes, by means of a system of repulsion from empty categories, the image of a "something" located at the midpoint of the "everything"-to-"nothing" line. This midpoint is itself spontaneous and direct, like $\infty/2$; and from this develops a "fiction of convexity"—a fiction possessing a sort of three-dimensional reality.

If zero is taken to symbolize "nothing," and one, "everything," the figure of fiction then may be represented:

$$\frac{0 + 1}{2} = \frac{1}{2}$$ The universe of half-finished entities depicted in ***Dead Souls*** appears as a positive equilibrium. Yet at the same time the sought-after subject—stand-in for the figure of fiction—may be objectively represented best as $\frac{1}{0}$; that is, as an infinite number of definitions. Thus, raging gales of contradictory concepts underlie this evasive equilibrium. Every minute brings with it a fresh surprise.

Definitions made by means of "some" (how much?), "not a lot, not a little," "to a certain degree" (to what degree?) do not define precisely. A slithering "form" crawls into the "positive" figure of Chichikov, a "form" that is similar to the force that has slipped into the being of the sorcerer

[in Gogol's story **"A Terrible Vengeance"**]. This strange force pokes through all vague, gauzy definitions with its nose, which in profile is reminiscent of the nose of Napoleon. Chichikov is by no means and in no way well-balanced; yet he gives the impression of being so.

It is this that the figure of fiction consists of.

. . . . .

From the standpoint of everyday reality, ***Dead Souls*** presents a somewhat different case: Here delimitation is not carried out by the boundaries of the category "all"; "nothing" is also delimited (in the sorcerer's case, it is not delimited). "Nothing" is bounded in by "something" and by "something to a certain degree." These mutual limitations are defined—but only in principle. Chichikov does not fall away into "nothing." His journeys between "everything" and "nothing" may be schematized as a variety of open figure eights. Indeed, he intrigues us no less than does the sorcerer. The sorcerer is terrifying; Chichikov is pleasantly respectable. Fear of the sorcerer is annulled by the sorcerer's fear, while the decorous Chichikov harbors a strange "something" that causes the sudden death of the public prosecutor (and of how many others?). The sorcerer founders; Chichikov, even in prison, continues to hope for "something": Murazov will rescue him. Spread out before Chichikov is "New Russia," from which, with the help of Gogol, he will worry out his own dead soul; this is something more terrible than all the sorcerer's murders: The sorcerer destroys the body, but Chichikov smothers the soul. It is capitalist Russia, cocooned within Chichikov, that suddenly becomes, in the guise of his own nonexistent troika, a symbol of Russia. Gogol does not respond overtly to the question of what precisely Chichikov's troika is, only approaching the subject sidelong in such phrases as "presented itself dimly" and "we hardly"—phrases that tear ***Dead Souls*** asunder, just as they did Gogol's own life. The figure of fiction ends by casting Gogol out of literature . . . and out of life itself.

Chichikov appears in the first chapter as something impersonal, a round, featureless area concealed in a *brichka* [A light coach; a buggy]. The *brichka* calls attention to itself; it seems to be something of a particular sort (while its owner does not); but the "something," here, is a fiction. It is in *brichkas* such as this that "all those referred to as gentlemen of an average sort" set forth on journeys. Now this "of an average sort" is not a proper definition at all: It has a certain meaning for some people and quite a different meaning for others. A single, concrete meaning cannot be pinned down.

In the *brichka* is sitting something of an ordinary variety, something "neither dashingly handsome nor ugly; neither too stout nor too slender," of whom "it cannot be said that he is old; however, he is no longer young." A something whose "arrival did not make . . . any sort of a stir and was not accompanied by any event of particular interest."

The same "no"s and "not"s are associated with the sorcerer, but there they have a different effect. They serve to set the sorcerer distinctly apart from everyday existence; he exists, as it were, in an abyss in the midst of the ordinary, an abyss whose bounds are set by the mountain Krivan.

Every "not" affixed to the sorcerer serves to estrange him, to place him within that abyss. On the other hand, the owner of the *brichka* in **Dead Souls** merges, with the aid of "not" and "no," with the whole of everyday existence. Chichikov has no distinguishing characteristics; no pit is hollowed out for him. Quite the contrary, in fact: The rough patches separating him from everyday existence are planed away to the point that an affinity, even a close resemblance, may be detected between Chichikov and the governor. Chichikov likewise moves toward merger with the average sort of *brichka.* The quintessential feature of a *brichka,* or any carriage, is the wheel; and all of the wheels exist on the same level, all are round. A couple of peasants take note of a wheel as the *brichka* passes by: "Looky there," says one of the peasants, "What a wheel that is! D'ye think, if it came to that, it would go as far as Moscow, or not?" "It would make it to Moscow," the other peasant replies. "But likely not all the way to Kazan, eh?" "No, not to Kazan."

Here the wheel is defined in terms of the distance of Moscow and of Kazan from some unknown town.

Thus, one is led from traveler to *brichka,* from *brichka* to its wheel: The wheel is not defined in any way. As for the "two *Russian* peasants" standing at the door of a tavern: Why "Russian peasants"? What else but Russian could they possibly be? After all, the action does not take place in Australia!

Nothing has really been said; and yet, it seems that *something* has been said.

The focus now shifts from the "hero" of the poem to someone strolling by, someone who vanishes almost immediately. This person is dressed "in very tight-fitting white duck trousers, a dress coat with pretensions to the fashionable and under which a shirt-front is visible; this latter is held in place by a stickpin of Tula make, which has a head in the form of a bronze pistol."

What is this passerby doing here?

He is here to distract attention from the man in the *brichka.*

"The gentleman was received . . . by a servant, or waiter, as they are called"; "it was impossible to get a good look at his face": An impersonal figure meets another impersonal figure. "The inn was of a well-known type; that is, it was just the way inns usually are." The room assigned to the traveler is, once again, "of that well-known type." The traveler makes his way to the common room: "Everyone knows quite well what these common rooms are like." The pictures on the walls have been brought in "at an unknown time, by persons unknown." The traveler takes off a scarf "of all different colors," of the sort "made by wives for their spouses," and is regaled with "various dishes of the sort one gets in inns." After dinner, the traveler asks the servant some "not entirely pointless questions."

A stream of settled events flows smoothly by: In the wake of the impersonal traveler come *brichka,* wheel, servant, inn, bedroom, common room, dinner—all presented in general, nonindividual terms. This pervasive obscurity of the surroundings stems from a corresponding dullness in the perceptions of the traveler: "The same walls . . . the same . . . ceiling; the same candelabrum . . . ; in short, everything just the same as it is everywhere else."

The sensibilities are bombarded by a sort of active vagueness.

In place of an authorial sketch of Chichikov's personal characteristics, one is provided with a small piece of paper, an information form filled out by travelers for the local police: "Collegiate Advisor Pavel Ivanovich Chichikov, landowner, on private business. . . . " Now "on private business" does not create any sort of picture. A passport is a fiction of an individual; the title **Dead Souls** is a fiction as well, one for which Gogol had to pay a price. The soul either does not exist, or it is immortal: What then can a "dead soul" be?

The next morning, Chichikov makes a round of calls. An enumeration of the people whom he visits is begun, but it is never completed: "It is rather difficult to keep in mind all the mighty ones of the world." Chichikov says something flattering to each host or hostess, speaking somewhat offhandedly. He talks about himself and adds "some sort of general commentary . . . "; he slips in some bookish phrases: For instance, he says that he is "an insignificant worm in this great world." Here the word "worm" *is* significant: "Before one has time to look around, a terrible worm has sprung up inside one . . . and . . . in . . . Chichikov there was a passion, a force from without, which led him on irresistibly; there is something in the essential nature of man that will sooner or later bring him to his knees, and turn him to ashes . . . and the reason that this worm appears is still a mystery."

In view of the future importance of Chichikov—of the fictional figure of Chichikov and his word about himself—and of the generally illusive quality of "photographically realistic" description—a sort of etching on water with a pitchfork, it is evident that Gogol, at the time of the writing of **Dead Souls,** was unfamiliar with the Russian provincial town: nor was he acquainted with the Russian village.

The governor who receives Chichikov is, like Chichikov himself, "neither stout nor thin"; "he had been awarded an order . . . he did embroidery on tulle." Later on he will be pictured with a card in one hand and a lapdog in the other. At first he receives Chichikov; later he refuses to see him. In the words of Manilov, the governor is "most distinguished and extraordinarily amiable"; while, according to Sobakievich, the man is "a thieving rascal of the worst sort" who would "cut your throat for a kopeck." However, the "honorable scoundrel" who emerges here is a fiction.

At the governor's residence, "everything is as it should be." Here, "as everywhere else," there are men "of two sorts": Some are slender; others are stout. Of the slender sort one is informed, much later, that they are "nothing more than something on the order of a bunch of toothpicks." And one learns that the stout men "do not fit into tight corners," and that their wives often refer to them as "dumplings," "piggy-banks," and "pot-bellies." But the governor, that honorable scoundrel, is neither slender nor stout.

A complete and total fiction!

Chichikov, like the governor neither fat nor thin, in the course of the dinner party pays the latter a compliment "suitable for a middle-aged gentleman who holds a rank neither too high nor too low." Chichikov makes his bows "not without a certain agreeableness"; he argues "pleasantly"; he "somehow manages always to be in the middle of things"; and he speaks "neither loudly nor softly, but in just the way he ought" about the glue factory, philanthropists, judicial proceedings, local administrators, and hot claret.

It soon becomes evident that Chichikov is not really interested in these conversations: His essential position in social situations is mirrored by the position of his double, his lackey Petrushka, in regard to reading. It is all one to Petrushka what it is that he is reading: a romantic adventure tale, a primer, or a prayer book; he is enthralled by the way "that, look'ee here, these here letters come together to make up some sort of a word." For Chichikov, then, people are letters; from these letters something will make itself up. People are merely a buzzing cluster of flies: The comparison of the guests at the governor's evening party with flies is not coincidental.

In the second chapter, Chichikov's visit to Manilov's estate is described. Manilov's personality is not one of Gogol's major concerns. Manilov is sketched in vague terms; no sooner has he been presented than smoke begins to billow from his *chibouk* [a Turkish long-stemmed clay pipe]: "The *chibouk* rattled and wheezed, and that was all."

A similar haze of vagueness envelops the environs of the town. "They set out to depict, according to our custom [to what custom?], the assorted odds and ends that lined both sides of the road." The items are enumerated in the text: "a fir grove . . . shrubbery . . . stalks and tree trunks . . . heather; and all that sort of rubbish." The environs of the town are gray; the time of year is unknown. Peasants are sitting around "in . . . sheepskin jackets" as their womenfolk "muck about in the ponds." That same night, Korobochka cries out: "What a blizzard it is." But the fruit trees are covered with nets—to keep the magpies away.

At a certain time of year, Chichikov sets off for a certain place: "manilovka, perhaps, or Zamanilovka." Some place or other, then, is located at some distance or other from this place: "Go on straight ahead . . . a verst or so . . . , then . . . turn right." They went on two versts, "and three, and four": still no sign of Manilovka. In the same vein: "If . . . they tell you . . . it's fifteen versts . . . , that means . . . it's a good thirty."

The distances are unrealistic. Chichikov, after having traveled the thirty versts or so to Manilovka, and having spent the whole day there, dined, and indulged to his heart's content in after-dinner chat, sets out for Korobochka. He loses his way and discovers, at last, that he is some sixty versts from the town. How far did he travel altogether? It appears that he must have covered at least seventy-five versts, and this after spending the day and evening at Manilov's estate: This is unrealistic in terms both of plot consistency and of the realistic capabilities of horses. On the following day, Chichikov drops in on Nozdrev, who lives nearby. On the third day, after spending a rather tempestuous morning with Nozdrev, and then getting mired in the mud on the road, he still manages to eat a hearty supper at Sobakievich's; travel to Plyushkin's, where he transacts some business; and reach town by dusk: The town is a good distance from Plyushkin's estate. The fact of the inordinate length of this third day's journey is unquestionable when one takes into account the locations of the various estates.

Gogol is not concerned with precision; for him, it is sufficient to say: at a certain time, at a certain distance.

The day itself is of just such a fictive nature: "neither clear nor overcast; some sort of shiny-gray."

Some further characteristics of Manilov: "There is a certain type of person . . . the man of a middling sort, neither fish nor fowl, neither the urban Bogdan nor the rustic Selifan." A most precise beginning! Farther on, one learns that Manilov is "the devil known what!": that is, an unknown quantity. "To each his own, but Manilov had nothing that was peculiar to himself." "It cannot be said that he occupied himself " with husbandry and agriculture (although he did draw up agricultural projects, so that it also cannot be said that he did not occupy himself with husbandry and agriculture). Whenever the steward said that it would be a good idea "to do this or that," Manilov would reply: "Yes, that's not a bad idea." The furniture in the room of this not unpleasant person is "not cheap" (it is not stated straight out that it is expensive); but two of the armchairs are not completely covered: "They haven't been finished yet." Manilov's study is "not without a certain pleasing quality," the walls have been painted "some sort of lightish blue, rather grayish." Although everything in the room is dusted over with tobacco ash, there are also small mounds of ash "arranged not without an effort at being attractive." The Manilovs, husband and wife, are "what is spoken of as being happy."

Everything that concerns Manilov is vague, ill-defined; everything is a fiction, a fusion of "not without something" and "not without nothing." This fusion may be expressed as the merging of —0.01 and —0.02, and as zero plus an infinitely small quantity—"nothing; not without something." There are as well the two precise sketch-lines: "He smokes a *chibouk;* his eyes [which he screws up coyly] are like sugar." The screwing up of the eyes diffuses itself throughout the first volume of **Dead Souls** and commingles with the hoarse gurglings of the ash-choked, "not sweet" *chibouk.* Here, again, one finds a fiction rather than a definition: sugar plus ash, divided by two. The gestural repetition discloses nothing of the essential Manilov, of a man who most likely contains a "worm." But Gogol does not fucus on Manilov's inner man, does not disturb this particular "worm." Only take Manilov's estate away and cast him into the midst of St. Petersburg; who, then, could tell what worm would emerge, what sort of "Spanish King" he would turn into?

Every one of Gogol's type characters is, in the author's own words, full of "an elusive individuality": "These gentlemen are terribly difficult to make portraits of "; and, indeed, Gogol gives not a portrait but a sort of expressive sketch, which he sets up like a screen; or, rather, as camouflage.

The fiction creates three-dimension-like portraits, nevertheless; the characters in **Dead Souls** are reductions of a multitude of possibilities. One or two characters are created with the aid of the habitual gesture; for instance, Sobakievich, from his first appearance on, steps on people's toes; then, with head bent, he falls silent, swears under his breath, and finally says, "Pardon me." One seems to recognize the type of rascal; one believes in him: And yet he does not exist. He is like the signboard, "Vasili Fyodorov, Foreigner," like the "honorable scoundrel," like "ashen sugar" and "dead souls."

The stock-in-trade of these fictions is dust and ashes: little mounds of ashes "not without beauty"; Plyushkin's crumbling sheets and his haystacks that are in a state of "rot not without ripe kernels:" The details of the exposition of plot are given in markedly indefinite terms: "It would not be superfluous to make the acquaintance of . . . " (not simply "one ought to"); "although these personages are not so noteworthy" (not simply "not noteworthy"); "the author likes very much . . . to be thorough in everything, despie the fact that he is a Russian. . . . Here, however, such thoroughness does not require a great deal of time [instead of simply 'a little'], because not much need be added to the characterization of Petrushka" (of whom little has yet been said). It appears that the author does *not* have a great liking for thoroughness; he even refuses to bring Petrushka's thoughts to light: "It is difficult to know just what a house serf is thinking . . . when his master is giving him instructions." It is still more difficult to know what the author is thinking as he weaves his subterfuges and circumlocutions into the texture of the work: "In a word, a well-known variety."

But this variety is, in fact, not at all well known.

This, then, is the device that, obliquely and sideways, through "not this" and "not that," carries on the hidden theme. This "oblique, sideways move" of Chichikov is his stereotyped, cliché gesture, as he sits in ambush in a thicket of grayish equilibrium: $\frac{0 + 1}{2} = \frac{1}{2}$ (in fact, $\frac{1}{0} = \infty$).

Chichikov spends his time, "as the saying goes," agreeably (was it really agreeably?) traveling about in "the well-known" *brichka* (which has not been described at all). He says curtly to Petrushka: "What the devil, sir, don't you know . . . "; he does not say straight out "you stink." He even "perceived, not without a certain joy," the crossing-gate, and approaches the swing-arm of the gate "not without satisfaction"; he even becomes a bit muddled from the feeling (which is to be expected). He asserts that: "I have neither a great name nor even an important rank." Manilov corrects him: "All the same, you know, you do have all that, and a bit more besides." Chichikov is a resounding name, and collegiate assessor is a significant rank. This agreeable indefiniteness continues to grow: "Please, if you will, make yourself comfortable in . . . the armchair."—"If you will, I'll just sit on this chair."—"If *you* will, you shall not." Chichikov sits down and reflects: "There is much in nature that even the widely-ranging mind cannot grasp." The demonstration of agreeable indefiniteness referred to above is followed immediately by an unpleasant vagueness: Manilov "became restive and embarrassed," while "Chichikov, for some unknown reason, stared straight ahead" and delivered himself of a speech about the purchase of serfs: "How would you like to buy the peasants? With or without land?"—"It's not exactly just plain peasants that I want. . . . Actually, I'm after dead ones. . . . Could you possibly . . . not actually alive, you see, but alive according to legal form . . . make them over to me, or whatever you think best. . . . "

After which Manilov asks: "Can it be that here . . . in what you just said . . . something completely different is hidden?"

But the function of the figure of fiction is precisely to indicate hidden realities that are obscured by superficial images, to point up the unseen underlying the seen. This is illustrated in Chichikov's proposal to finalize the purchase of the dead souls. The proposal is a fraud: "We'll put down that they are alive. . . . I am accustomed never to step even an inch outside of the law. . . . Duty is something sacred to me. . . . I bow down before the law."

Is the law here a forgery? Or is this forgery a law? What does Manilov make of all this? But "the *chibouk* gurgled hoarsely, and that was all."

Finally Manilov speaks up: "Isn't it true that . . . this transaction might be more, so to speak, as they say . . . more in accordance with the long-range interests of Russia?"

Certainly, forgery is a very bad thing; still, the government will reap tax benefits from it—this is certainly just as good. So, here the juxtaposed values "not very good" and "not very not good" yield "good."

Again, a certain vagueness emerges: This trifling business deal is unrelated to the long-range interests of Russia. Although neither the long-range interests of the country nor the more concrete and localized interests of individuals are brought to the fore, it is clear that the transaction hinges on the latter, as well as on the more immediate interests of Russia itself: "The government will even make a profit, since it gets all the legal taxes. . . . And I think that this is a good thing."

Is Manilov a sincere person? Sincere with himself—no; with the inhabitants of the town—we do not know. It certainly cannot be said that he was deceitful through ignorance, after he had begun to have suspicions; nor can it be supposed that the fiction of lulling-into-calmness had lulled him into calmness. For why then was he "so mixed up and confused," and why did he glance back over his shoulder, and, after Chichikov had left, why did the thought of the little deal just completed somehow "not set right with him"; this despite his warm friendship for Chichikov?

Now Chichikov has disclosed a new side of his nature, something rather antisocial and slimy (the goal toward which this "sliminess" is directed is no longer hidden in the second chapter). Even Chichikov's desire to be agreeable may now be viewed as the superficial offshoot of a deeper desire: to do whatever must be done to reach the ultimate goal. However, "nothing of that sort was visible. . . . His expression was even unusually composed. . . . His eyes . . . were clear; there was no sort of savage fire in them; everything was as it should be, in good order." This shift back to facade lasts up to the time of Chichikov's departure. He says to Manilov's small child, jokingly, "I'll bring you a drum . . . such a drum . . . it will go toorrrooo, tra-ta-ta, ta-ta-ta. . . . Goodbye for now, little darling." Then he "turned to Manilov . . . with a faint smile on his face, the kind of smile with which children are accustomed to greet their parents."

In the second chapter, the fiction is conveyed through details. The fiction establishes a central point in this chapter, from which a long line extends in two opposing directions; such a central point does not exist in the first chapter. This extended line is not the line of the fictive plot; rather, it is the dot on the "i"—as if the author had suddenly whispered to us that everything displayed on the surface is a blind, a decoy.

The author's position is transmitted through the utterance of Manilov: "Perhaps here . . . in the explanation you just gave . . . something else is hidden!"

I shall limit myself to this brief discussion of the technique of the first two chapters in order not to weary the reader. I would only add that the figure of fiction is the hub, the generating core of each of the eleven chapters of **Dead Souls.** (pp. 517-28)

. . . . .

[The] most frequently appearing colors in the first volume of **Dead Souls** are white, black, gray, and yellow, as well as an increasingly significant percentage of light blue. The colors gray, yellow, and light blue are not commonly found in literary works of the first phase. The colors that appear in **Dead Souls** are immanent in that device that generates the fictive "something" in the form of a balanced "everything plus nothing": "Everything" is refracted into a color spectrum just as is a shining, *white* ray of light. "Nothing" here corresponds to darkness (black). The fusion of black and white produces gray—the color that accompanies the fictive equilibrium of the figures in **Dead Souls** (their pseudonaturalism, so to speak): *gray* villages, *gray* wallpaper, abbreviated *gray* days, and so on. Both yellow and light blue have roles in Goethe's theory of colors: Yellow is the opaque medium (darkness) cast upon light, the glimpsed sparkling of "everything" through "nothing"; light blue is light thrown onto darkness, "nothing" glimpsed through a chink in "everything."

Gogol's categories "nothing" and "everything," together with their offshoots ("in a certain way"; "similar to"; "something"; and so forth) may be taken as the subject matter of **Dead Souls,** and the color spectrum is immanent in the book's subject matter: "everything"—white; "nothing"—black; "neither this nor that"—gray. "Something," "in a certain way," "so to speak," and like expressions

generate graduated spectra of yellowish and dark-brownish shades; while expressions such as "not without" give rise to a grayish-light blue shading—the color of Manilov's wallpaper.

The spectrum of the first volume of **Dead Souls** is a powerful means to make the plot concrete. "Everything" and "nothing" are, in the indefiniteness of their counterposed limitations, not only hyperboles; they are also a means of supplying ideas and didactic tendentiousness. That which ruins the second volume of **Dead Souls** is an effective artistic device in the first volume. It is reflected in the style, in the art of depiction and in the action itself. (p. 528)

> *Andrei Bely [pseudonym of Boris Nikolaevich Bugaev], "The Figure of Fiction in 'Dead Souls'," translated by Geoffrey Packer, in "Masterstvo Goglia" by Andrei Bely: Dead Souls: The Reavey Translation; Backgrounds and Sources; Essays in Criticism, edited by George Gibian, W. W. Norton & Company, 1985, pp. 517-31.*

Vladimir Nabokov   (essay date 1944)

[*A Russian-born American man of letters, Nabokov was a prolific contributor to many literary fields, writing in both Russian and English and distinguishing himself in particular as the author of the novels* Lolita *(1955) and* Pale Fire *(1962). Nabokov was fascinated with all aspects of the creative life, and his works frequently explore the origins of creativity, the relationships of artists to their work, and the nature of invented reality. Considered a brilliant prose stylist, Nabokov wrote fiction that entertains and sometimes exasperates readers in its preoccupation with intellectual and verbal games. In the following excerpt, Nabokov explores the meaning of the Russian word* poshlust *and its relationship to* Dead Souls. *He then examines theme, style, and characterization in the novel.*]

The Russian language is able to express by means of one pitiless word the idea of a certain widespread defect for which the other three European languages I happen to know possess no special term. The absence of a particular expression in the vocabulary of a nation does not necessarily coincide with the absence of the corresponding notion but it certainly impairs the fullness and readiness of the latter's perception. Various aspects of the idea which Russians concisely express by the term *poshlost* (the stress-accent is on the puff-ball of the first syllable, and the final "t" has a moist softness that is hardly equaled by the French "t" in such words as "restiez" or "émoustillant") are split among several English words and thus do not form a definite whole. On second thought, I find it preferable to transcribe that fat brute of a word thus: *poshlust*—which renders in a somewhat more adequate manner the dull sound of the second, neutral "o." Inversely the first "o" is as big as the plop of an elephant falling into a muddy pond and as round as the bosom of a bathing beauty on a German picture postcard.

English words expressing several, although by no means all aspects of *poshlust* are for instance: "cheap, sham, common, smutty, pink-and-blue, high falutin', in bad taste."

My little assistant, *Roget's Thesaurus,* (which incidentally lists "rats, mice" under "Insects"—see page 21 of Revised Edition) supplies me moreover with "inferior, sorry, trashy, scurvy, tawdry, gimcrack" and others under "cheapness." All these however suggest merely certain false values for the detection of which no particular shrewdness is required. In fact they tend, these words, to supply an obvious classification of values at a given period of human history; but what Russians call *poshlust* is beautifully timeless and so cleverly painted all over with protective tints that its presence (in a book, in a soul, in an institution, in a thousand other places) often escapes detection.

Ever since Russia began to think, and up to the time that her mind went blank under the influence of the extraordinary regime she has been enduring for these last twenty-five years, educated, sensitive and free-minded Russians were acutely aware of the furtive and clammy touch of *poshlust.* Among the nations with which we came into contact, Germany had always seemed to us a country where *poshlust,* instead of being mocked, was one of the essential parts of the national spirit, habits, traditions and general atmosphere, although at the same time well-meaning Russian intellectuals of a more romantic type readily, too readily, adopted the legend of the greatness of German philosophy and literature; for it takes a super-Russian to admit that there is a dreadful streak of *poshlust* running through Goethe's *Faust.*

To exaggerate the worthlessness of a country at the awkward moment when one is at war with it—and would like to see it destroyed to the last beer-mug and last forget-me-not,—means walking dangerously close to that abyss of *poshlust* which yawns so universally at times of revolution or war. But if what one demurely murmurs is but a mild pre-war truth, even with something old-fashioned about it, the abyss is perhaps avoidable. Thus, a hundred years ago, while civic-minded publicists in St. Petersburg were mixing heady cocktails of Hegel and Schlegel (with a dash of Feuerbach), Gogol, in a chance story he told, expressed the immortal spirit of *poshlust* pervading the German nation and expressed it with all the vigor of his genius.

The conversation around him had turned upon the subject of Germany, and after listening awhile, Gogol said:

> Yes, generally speaking the average German is not too pleasant a creature, but it is impossible to imagine anything more unpleasant than a German Lothario, a German who tries to be winsome. . . . One day in Germany I happened to run across such a gallant. The dwelling place of the maiden whom he had long been courting without success stood on the bank of some lake or other, and there she would be every evening sitting on her balcony and doing two things at once: knitting a stocking and enjoying the view. My German gallant being sick of the futility of his pursuit finally devised an unfailing means whereby to conquer the heart of his cruel Gretchen. Every evening he would take off his clothes, plunge into the lake and, as he swam there, right under the eyes of his beloved, he would keep embracing a couple of swans which had been specially prepared by him for that pur-

Frontispiece to the first edition of Dead Souls.

pose. I do not quite know what those swans were supposed to symbolize, but I do know that for several evenings on end he did nothing but float about and assume pretty postures with his birds under that precious balcony. Perhaps he fancied there was something poetically antique and mythological in such frolics, but whatever notion he had, the result proved favorable to his intentions: the lady's heart was conquered just as he thought it would be, and soon they were happily married.

Here you have *poshlust* in its ideal form, and it is clear that the terms trivial, trashy, smug and so on do not cover the aspect it takes in this epic of the blond swimmer and the two swans he fondled. Neither is it necessary to travel so far both in space and time to obtain good examples. Open the first magazine at hand and you are sure to find something of the following kind: A radio set (or a car, or a refrigerator, or table silver—anything will do) has just come to the family: mother clasps her hands in dazed delight, the children crowd around, all agog, Junior and the dog strain up to the edge of the table where the Idol is enthroned; even Grandma of the beaming wrinkles peeps out somewhere in the background (forgetful, we presume, of the terrific row she has had that very morning with her daughter-in-law); and somewhat apart, his thumbs gleefully inserted in the armpits of his waistcoat, legs a-straddle and eyes a-twinkle, stands triumphant Pop, the Proud Donor.

The rich *poshlust* emanating from advertisements of this kind is due not to their exaggerating (or inventing) the glory of this or that serviceable article but to suggesting that the acme of human happiness is purchasable and that its purchase somehow ennobles the purchaser. Of course, the world they create is pretty harmless in itself because everybody knows that it is made up by the seller with the understanding that the buyer will join in the make-believe. The amusing part is not that it is a world where nothing spiritual remains except the ecstatic smiles of people serving or eating celestial cereals or a world where the game of the senses is played according to bourgeois rules ("bourgeois" in the Flaubertian, *not* in the Marxist sense) but that it is a kind of satellite shadow world in the actual existence of which neither sellers not buyers really believe in their heart of hearts—especially in this wise quiet country.

If a commercial artist wishes to depict a nice little boy he will grace him with freckles (which incidentally assume a horrible rash-like aspect in the humbler funnies). Here *poshlust* is directly connected with a forgotten convention of a faintly racial type. Kind people send our lonely soldiers silk hosed dummy legs modeled on those of Hollywood lovelies and stuffed with candies and safety razor blades—at least I have seen a picture of a person preparing such a leg in a certain periodical which is a world-famous purveyor of *poshlust.* Propaganda (which could not exist without a generous supply of and demand for *poshlust*) fills booklets with lovely Kolkhos maidens and windswept clouds. I select my examples hurriedly and at random— the "Encyclopédie des Idées Reçues" which Flaubert dreamt of writing one day was a more ambitious work.

Literature is one of its best breeding places and by *poshlust*-literature I do not mean the kind of thing which is termed "pulp" or which in England used to go under the name of "penny dreadfuls" and in Russia under that of "yellow literature." Obvious trash, curiously enough, contains sometimes a wholesome ingredient, readily appreciated by children and simple souls. Superman is undoubtable *poshlust,* but it is *poshlust* in such a mild, unpretentious form that it is not worthwhile talking about; and the fairy tales of yore contained, for that matter, as much trivial sentiment and naive vulgarity as these yarns about modern Giant Killers. *Poshlust,* it should be repeated, is especially vigorous and vicious when the sham is *not* obvious and when the values it mimics are considered, rightly or wrongly, to belong to the very highest level of art, thought or emotion. It is those books which are so *poshlustily* reviewed in the literary supplement of daily papers— the best sellers, the "stirring, profound and beautiful" novels; it is these "elevated and powerful" books that contain and distill the very essence of *poshlust.* I happen to have upon my desk a copy of a paper with a whole page advertising a certain novel, which novel is a fake from beginning to end and by its style, its ponderous gambols around elevated ideas, and absolute ignorance of what authentic literature was, is and always will be, strangely reminds one of the swan-fondling swimmer depicted by Gogol. "You lose yourself in it completely,"—says one re-

viewer;—"When the last page is turned you come back to the world of everyday a little thoughtful, as after a great experience" (note the coy "a little" and the perfectly automatic "as after a great"). "A singing book, compact of grace and light and ecstasy, a book of pearly radiance,"— whispers another (that swimmer was also "compact of grace," and the swans had a "pearly radiance," too). "The work of a master psychologist who can skillfully probe the very inner recesses of men's souls." This "inner" (mind you—not "outer"), and the other two or three delightful details already mentioned are in exact conformity to the true value of the book. In fact, this praise is perfectly adequate: the "beautiful" novel is "beautifully" reviewed and the circle of *poshlust* is complete—or would be complete had not words taken a subtle revenge of their own and smuggled the truth in by secretly forming most nonsensical and most damning combinations while the reviewer and publisher are quite sure that they are praising the book, "which the reading public has made a (here follows an enormous figure apparently meaning the quantity of copies sold) triumph." For in the kingdom of *poshlust* it is not the book that "makes a triumph" but the "reading public" which laps it up, blurb and all.

The particular novel referred to here may have been a perfectly honest and sincere (as the saying goes) attempt on the author's part to write something he felt strongly about—and very possibly no commercial aspirations assisted him in that unfortunate process. The trouble is that sincerity, honesty and even true kindness of heart cannot prevent the demon of *poshlust* from possessing himself of an author's typewriter when the man lacks genius and when the "reading public" is what publishers think it is. The dreadful thing about *poshlust* is that one finds it so difficult to explain to people why a particular book which seems chock-full of noble emotion and compassion, and can hold the reader's attention "on a theme far removed from the discordant events of the day" is far, far worse than the kind of literature which *everybody* admits is cheap.

From the various examples collected here it will be I hope clear that *poshlust* is not only the obviously trashy but also the falsely important, the falsely beautiful, the falsely clever, the falsely attractive. A list of literary characters personifying *poshlust* (and thus namable in Russian *poshlyaki* in the case of males and *poshlyáchki* in the case of females—and rhyming with "key" and "latchkey" respectively) will include Polonius and the royal pair in Hamlet, Flaubert's Rodolphe and Homais, Laevsky in Chekhov's *Duel,* Joyce's Marion Bloom, young Bloch in *A la recherche du temps perdu,* Maupassant's "Bel Ami," Anna Karenina's husband, Berg in *War and Peace* and numerous other figures in universal fiction. Socially minded Russian critics saw in **Dead Souls** and in **The Government Inspector** a condemnation of the social *poshlust* emanating from serf-owning bureaucratic provincial Russia and thus missed the true point. Gogol's heroes merely happen to be Russian squires and officials; their imagined surroundings and social conditions are perfectly unimportant factors— just as Monsieur Homais might be a business man in Chicago or Mrs. Bloom the wife of a schoolmaster in Vyshny-Volochok. Moreover, their surroundings and conditions, whatever they might have been in "real life," underwent such a thorough permutation and reconstruction in the laboratory of Gogol's peculiar genius that (as has been observed already in connection with *The Government Inspector*) it is as useless to look in *Dead Souls* for an authentic Russian background as it would be to try and form a conception of Denmark on the basis of that little affair in cloudy Elsinore. And if you want "facts," then let us inquire what experience had Gogol of provincial Russia. Eight hours in a Podolsk inn, a week in Kursk, the rest he had seen from the window of his traveling carriage, and to this he had added the memories of his essentially Ukrainian youth spent in Mirgorod, Nezhin, Poltava—all of which towns lay far outside Chichikov's itinerary. What seems true however is that *Dead Souls* provides an attentive reader with a collection of bloated dead souls belonging to *poshlyaki* and *poshlyáchki* described with that Gogolian gusto and wealth of weird detail which lift the whole thing to the level of a tremendous epic poem; and "poem" is in fact the subtle subtitle appended by Gogol to *Dead Souls.* There is something sleek and plump about *poshlust,* and this gloss, these smooth curves, attracted the artist in Gogol. The immense spherical *poshlyak* (singular of the word) Paul Chichikov eating the fig at the bottom of the milk which he drinks to mellow his throat, or dancing in his nightgown in the middle of the room while things on shelves rock in response to his Lacedaemonian jig (ending in his ecstaticaly hitting his chubby behind—his real face—with the pink heel of his bare foot, thus propelling himself into the true paradise of dead souls) these are visions which transcend the lesser varieties of *poshlust* discernible in humdrum provincial surroundings or in the petty iniquities of petty officials. But a *poshlyak* even of Chichikov's colossal dimensions inevitably has somewhere in him a hole, a chink through which you see the worm, the little shriveled fool that lies all huddled up in the depth of the *poshlust*-painted vacuum. There was something faintly silly from the very start about that idea of buying up dead souls,—souls of serfs who had died since the last census and for whom their owners continued to pay the poll-tax, thus endowing them with a kind of abstract existence which however was quite concretely felt by the squire's pocket and could be just as "concretely" exploited by Chichikov, the buyer of such phantasma. This faint but rather sickening silliness was for a certain time concealed by the maze of complex machinations. *Morally* Chichikov was hardly guilty of any special crime in attempting to buy up dead men in a country where live men were lawfully purchased and pawned. If I paint my face with homemade Prussian Blue instead of applying the Prussian Blue which is sold by the state and cannot be manufactured by private persons, my crime will be hardly worth a passing smile and no writer will make of it a Prussian Tragedy. But if I have surrounded the whole business with a good deal of mystery and flaunted a cleverness that presupposed most intricate difficulties in perpetrating a crime of that kind, and if owing to my letting a garrulous neighbor peep at my pots of home-brewn paint I get arrested and am roughly handled by men with authentic blue faces, then the laugh for what it is worth is on me. In spite of Chichikov's fundamental irreality in a fundamentally unreal world, the fool in him is apparent because

from the very start he commits blunder upon blunder. It was silly to try to buy dead souls from an old woman who was afraid of ghosts; it was an incredible lapse of acumen to suggest such a Queer Street deal to the braggard and bully Nozdryov. I repeat however for the benefit of those who like books to provide them with "real people" and "real crime" and a "message" (that horror of horrors borrowed from the jargon of quack reformers) that *Dead Souls* will get them nowhere. Chichikov's guilt being a purely conventional matter, his destiny can hardly provoke any emotional reaction on our part. This is an additional reason why the view taken by Russian readers and critics, who saw in *Dead Souls* a matter-of-fact description of existing conditions, seems so utterly and ludicrously wrong. But when the legendary *poshlyak* Chichikov is considered as he ought to be, i.e. as a creature of Gogol's special brand moving in a special kind of Gogolian coil, the abstract notion of swindling in this serf-pawning business takes on strange flesh and begins to mean much more than it did when we considered it in the light of social conditions peculiar to Russia a hundred years ago. The dead souls he is buying are not merely names on a slip of paper. They are the dead souls that fill the air of Gogol's world with their leathery flutter, the clumsy animula of Manilov or of Korobochka, of the housewives of the town of N., of countless other little people bobbing throughout the book. Chichikov himself is merely the ill-paid representative of the Devil, a traveling salesman from Hades, "our Mr. Chichikov" as the Satan & Co. firm may be imagined calling their easy-going, healthy-looking but inwardly shivering and rotting agent. The *poshlust* which Chichikov personifies is one of the main attributes of the Devil, in whose existence, let it be added, Gogol believed far more seriously than he did in that of God. The chink in Chichikov's armor, that rusty chink emitting a faint but dreadful smell (a punctured can of conserved lobster tampered with and forgotten by some meddling fool in the pantry) is the organic aperture in the devil's armor. It is the essential stupidity of universal *poshlust.*

Chichikov is doomed from the start and he rolls to that doom with a slight wobble in his gait which only the *poshlyaki* and *postlyáchkis* of the town of N. are capable of finding genteel and pleasant. At important moments when he launches upon one of those sententious speeches (with a slight break in his juicy voice—the tremolo of "dear brethren"), that are meant to drown his real intentions in a treacle of pathos, he applies to himself the words "despicable worm" and, curiously enough, a real worm is gnawing at his vitals and becomes suddenly visible if we squint a little when peering at his rotundity. I am reminded of a certain poster in old Europe that advertised automobile tires and featured something like a human being entirely made of concentric rings of rubber; and likewise, rotund Chichikov may be said to be formed of the tight folds of a huge flesh-colored worm.

If the special gruesome character attending the main theme of the book has been conveyed and if the different aspects of *poshlust* which I have noted at random have become connected in such a way as to form an artistic phenomenon (its Gogolian leitmotiv being the "roundness" of *poshlust*), then *Dead Souls* will cease to mimic a humorous tale or a social indictment and henceforth may be adequately discussed. So let us look at the pattern a little more closely.

> The gates of the hostelry in the governmental town of N. [so the book begins] admitted a smallish fairly elegant *britzka* on springs, of the sort used by bachelors such as retired colonels, staff-captains, country squires who own about a hundred souls of peasants—in short by all those who are dubbed 'gentlemen of medium quality.' Sitting in the *britzka* was a gentleman whose countenance could not be termed handsome, yet neither was he ill-favored: he was not too stout, nor was he too thin; you could not call him old, just as you could not say that he was still youthful. His arrival produced no stir whatever in the town and was not accompanied by anything unusual; alone two Russian *muzhiks* who were standing at the door of a dram-shop opposite the inn made certain remarks which however referred more to the carriage than to the person seated therein. 'Look at that wheel there,' said one. 'Now what do you think—would that wheel hold out as far as Moscow if need be, or would it not?' 'It would,' answered the other. 'And what about Kazan—I think it would not last that far?' 'It would not,'—answered the other. Upon this the conversation came to a close. And moreover, as the carriage drove up to the inn, a young man chanced to pass wearing white twill trousers that were very tight and short and a swallow-tail coat with claims to fashion from under which a shirtfront was visible fastened with a Tula bronze pin in the shape of a pistol. The young man turned his head, looked back at the carriage, caught hold of his cap, which the wind was about to blow off, and then went his way.

The conversation of the two "Russian *muzhiks*" (a typical Gogolian pleonasm) is purely speculative—a point which the abominable Fisher Unwin and Thomas Y. Crowell translations of course miss. It is a kind of to-be-or-not-to-be meditation in a primitive form. The speakers do not know whether the *britzka* is going to Moscow or not, just as Hamlet did not trouble to look whether, perhaps, he had not mislaid his bodkin. The *muzhiks* are not interested in the question of the precise itinerary that the britzka will follow; what fascinates them is solely the ideal problem of fixing the imaginary instability of a wheel in terms of imaginary distances; and this problem is raised to the level of sublime abstraction by their not knowing the exact distance from N. (an imaginary point) to Moscow, Kazan or Timbuctoo—and caring less. They impersonate the remarkable creative faculty of Russians, so beautifully disclosed by Gogol's own inspiration, of working in a void. Fancy is fertile only when it is futile. The speculation of the two *muzhiks* is based on nothing tangible and leads to no material results; but philosophy and poetry are born that way; meddlesome critics looking for a moral might conjecture that the rotundity of Chichikov is bound to come to grief, being symbolized by the rotundity of that doubtful wheel. Andrey Bely, who was a meddler of genius, saw in fact the whole first volume of *Dead Souls* as a closed circle whirling on its axle and blurring the spokes,

with the theme of the wheel cropping up at each new revolution on round Chichikov's part. Another special touch is exemplified by the chance passer-by—that young man portrayed with a sudden and wholly irrelevant wealth of detail: he comes there as if he was going to stay in the book (as so many of Gogol's homunculi seem intent to do—and do not). With any other writer of his day the next paragraph would have been bound to begin: "Ivan, for that was the young man's name" . . . But no: a gust of wind interrupts his stare and he passes, never to be mentioned again. The faceless saloon-walker in the next passage (whose movements are so quick as he welcomes the newcomers that you cannot discern his features) is again seen a minute later coming down from Chichikov's room and spelling out the name on a slip of paper as he walks down the steps. "Pa-vel I-va-no-vich Chi-chi-kov"; and these syllables have a taxonomic value for the identification of that particular staircase.

When speaking of **The Government Inspector** I found pleasure in rounding up those peripheral characters that enliven the texture of its background. Such characters in **Dead Souls** as the inn-servant or Chichikov's valet (who had a special smell of his own which he imparted at once to his variable lodgings) do not quite belong to that class of Little People. With Chichikov himself and the country squires he meets they share the front stage of the book although they speak little and have no visible influence upon the course of Chichikov's adventures. Technically speaking, the creation of peripheral personages in the play was mainly dependent upon this or that character alluding to people who never emerged from the wings. In a novel the lack of action or speech on the part of secondary characters would not have been sufficient to endow them with that kind of backstage existence, there being no footlights to stress their actual absence from the front place. Gogol however had another trick up his sleeve. The peripheral characters of his novel are engendered by the subordinate clauses of its various metaphors, comparisons and lyrical outbursts. We are faced by the remarkable phenomenon of mere forms of speech directly giving rise to live creatures. This is perhaps the most typical example of how this happens.

> Even the weather had obligingly accommodated itself to the setting: the day was neither bright nor gloomy but of a kind of bluey-grey tint such as is found only upon the worn-out uniforms of garrison soldiers, for the rest a peaceful class of warriors except for their being somewhat inebriate on Sundays.

It is not easy to render the curves of this life-generating syntax in plain English so as to bridge the logical, or rather biological, hiatus between a dim landscape under a dull sky and a groggy old soldier accosting the reader with a rich hiccup on the festive outskirts of the very same sentence. Gogol's trick consists in using as a link the word *"vprochem"* ("for the rest," "otherwise," *"d'ailleurs"*) which is a connection only in the grammatical sense but mimics a logical link, the word "soldiers" alone affording a faint pretext for the juxtaposition of "peaceful"; and as soon as this false bridge of *"vprochem"* has accomplished its magical work these mild warriors cross over, staggering and singing themselves into that peripheral existence with which we are already familiar.

When Chichikov comes to a party at the Governor's house, the chance mention of black-coated gentlemen crowding around the powdered ladies in a brilliant light leads to a fairly innocent looking comparison with buzzing flies—and the very next instant another life breaks through:

> The black tailcoats flickered and fluttered, separately and in clusters, this way and that, just as flies flutter over dazzling white chunks of sugar on a hot July day when the old housekeeper [here we are] hacks and divides it into sparkling lumps in front of the open window: all the children [second generation now!] look on as they gather about her, watching with curiosity the movements of her rough hands while the *airy* squadrons of flies that the light *air* [one of those repetitions so innate in Gogol's style that years of work over every passage could not eradicate them] has raised, fly boldly in, complete mistresses of the premises [or literally: 'full mistresses,' *'polnya khozyaiki,'* which Isabel F. Hapgood in the Crowell edition mistranslates as 'fat housewives'] and, taking advantage of the old woman's purblindness and of the sun troubling her eyes, spread all over the dainty morsels, here separately, there in dense clusters.

It will be noticed that whereas the dull weather plus drunken trooper image comes to an end somewhere in the dusty suburban distance (where Ukhovyortov, the Ear-Twister, reigns) here, in the simile of the flies, which is a parody of the Homeric rambling comparison, a complete circle is described, and after his complicated and dangerous somersault, with no net spread under him, as other acrobatic authors have, Gogol manages to twist back to the initial "separately and in clusters." Several years ago during a Rugby game in England I saw the wonderful Obolensky kick the ball away on the run and then changing his mind, plunge forward and catch it back with his hands . . . something of this kind of feat is performed by Nikolai Vassilievich. Needless to say that all these things (in fact whole paragraphs and pages) were left out by Mr. T. Fisher Unwin who to the "considerable joy" of Mr. Stephen Graham (see preface, edition of 1915, London) consented to re-publish **Dead Souls.** Incidentally, Graham thought that "**Dead Souls** is Russia herself" and that Gogol "became a rich man and could winter at Rome and Baden-Baden."

The lusty barking of dogs which met Chichikov as he drove up to Madame Korobochka's house proves equally fertile:

> Meanwhile the dogs were lustily barking in all possible tones: one of them, with his head thrown back, indulged in such conscientious ululations as if he were receiving some prodigious pay for his labors; another hammered it out cursorily like your village sexton; in between rang out, similar to the bell of a mailcoach, the persistent treble of what was probably a young whelp; and all this was capped by a basso voice belonging presumably to some old fellow en-

dowed with a tough canine disposition, for his voice was as hoarse as that of a basso profundo in a church choir, when the concerto is in full swing with the tenors straining on tiptoe in their eagerness to produce a high note and all the rest, too, throwing their heads back and striving upwards—while he alone with his bristly chin thrust into his neckerchief, turns his knees out, sinks down almost to the ground and issues thence that note of his which makes the window-panes quake and rattle.

Thus the bark of a dog breeds a church chorister. In yet another passage (where Paul arrives at Sobakevich's house) a musician is born in a more complicated way remindful of the "dull sky drunken trooper" simile.

> As he drove up to the porch he noticed two faces which almost simultaneously appeared at the window: one belonged to a woman in a ribboned cap and it was as narrow and long as a cucumber; the other was a man's face, and round and broad it was, like those Moldavian pumpkins, called *gorlyanki* from which in our good country *balalaikas* are made, two-stringed light *balalaikas,* the adornment and delight of a nimble young rustic just out of his teens, the cock of his walk and a great one at whistling through his teeth and winking his eye at the white-bosomed and white-necked country-lasses who cluster around in order to listen to the delicate twanging of his strings.

(This young yokel was transformed by Isabel Hapgood in her translation into "the susceptible youth of twenty who walks blinking along in his dandified way.")

The complicated maneuver executed by the sentence in order to have a village musician emerge from burly Sobakevich's head consists of three stages: the comparison of that head to a special kind of pumpkin, the transformation of that pumpkin into a special kind of *balalaika,* and finally the placing of that *balalaika* in the hands of a young villager who forthwith starts softly playing as he sits on a log with crossed legs (in brand new high boots) surrounded by sunset midgets and country girls. Especially remarkable is the fact that this lyrical digression is prompted by the appearance of what may seem to the casual reader to be the most matter-of-fact and stolid character of the book.

Sometimes the comparison-generated character is in such a hurry to join in the life of the book that the metaphor ends in delightful bathos:

> A drowning man, it is said, will catch at the smallest chip of wood because at the moment he has not the presence of mind to reflect that hardly even a fly could hope to ride astride that chip, whereas he weighs almost a hundred and fifty pounds if not a good two hundred.

Who is that unfortunate bather, steadily and uncannily growing, adding weight, fattening himself on the marrow of a metaphor? We never shall know—but he almost managed to gain a footing.

The simplest method such peripheral characters employ to assert their existence is to take advantage of the author's way of stressing this or that circumstance or condition by illustrating it with some striking detail. The picture starts living a life of its own—rather like that leering organ-grinder with whom the artist in H. G. Wells' story *The Portrait* struggled, by means of jabs and splashes of green paint when the portrait he was making became alive and disorderly. Observe for instance the ending of Chapter 7, where the intention is to convey the impressions of night falling upon a peaceful provincial town. Chichikov after successfully clinching his ghostly deal with the landowners has been entertained by the worthies of the town and goes to bed very drunk; his coachman and his valet quietly depart on a private spree of their own, then stumble back to the inn, most courteously propping up each other, and soon go to sleep too.

> . . . emitting snores of incredible density of sound, echoed from the neighboring room by their master's thin nasal wheeze. Soon after this everything quieted down and deep slumber enveloped the hostelry; one light alone remained burning and that was in the small window of a certain lieutenant who had arrived from Ryazan and who was apparently a keen amateur of boots inasmuch as he had already acquired four pairs and was persistently trying on a fifth one. Every now and again he would go up to his bed as though he intended to take them off and lie down; but he simply could not; in truth those boots were well made; and for a long while still he kept on revolving his foot and inspecting the dashing cut of an admirably finished heel.

Thus the chapter ends—and that lieutenant is still trying on his immortal jackboot, and the leather glistens, and the candle burns straight and bright in the only lighted window of a dead town in the depth of a star-dusted night. I know of no more lyrical description of nocturnal quiet than this Rhapsody of the Boots.

The same kind of spontaneous generation occurs in Chapter 9, when the author wishes to convey with special strength the bracing turmoil which the rumors surrounding the acquisition of dead souls provoked throughout the province. Country squires who for years had been lying curled up in their holes like so many dormice all of a sudden blinked and crawled out:

> There appeared a certain Sysoy Paphnutyevich, and a certain Macdonald Carlovich [a singular name to say the least but necessary here to underline utter remoteness from life and the consequent irreality of that person, a dream in a dream, so to speak], about whom nobody had heard before; and a long lean impossibly tall fellow [literally: 'a certain long long one, of such tall stature as had never been even seen'] with a bullet wound in his hand . . .

In the same chapter, after explaining at length that he will name no names because "whatever name be invented there is quite sure to crop up in some corner of our empire—which is big enough for all purposes—some person who bears it, and who is sure to be mortally offended and to declare that the author sneaked in with the express intention of nosing out every detail," Gogol cannot stop the two voluble ladies whom he sets chattering about the Chichikov mystery from divulging their names as if his characters actually escaped his control and blurted out what he wished to conceal. Incidentally, one of those passages which fairly burst with little people tumbling out and scattering all over the page (or straddling Gogol's pen like a witch riding a broomstick) reminds one in a curious anachronistic fashion of a certain intonation and trick of style used by Joyce in *Ulysses* (but then Sterne too used the abrupt question and circumstantial answer method).

> Our hero however was utterly unconscious of this [i.e. that he was boring with his sententious patter a certain young lady in a ballroom] as he went on telling her all kinds of pleasant things which he had happened to utter on similar occasions in various places. [Where?] In the Government of Simbirsk, at the house of Sophron Ivanovich Bezpechnoy, where the latter's daughter, Adelaida Sophronovna, was also present with her three sisters-in-law, Maria Gavrilovna, Alexandra Gavrilovna and Adelheida Gavrilovna; at the house of Frol Vassilyevich Pobedonosnoy, in the Government of Pensa; and at that of the latter's brother, where the following were present: his wife's sister Katherina Mikhailovna and her cousins, Rosa Feodorovna and Emilia Feodorovna; in the Government of Viatka, at the house of Piotr Varsonophyevich, where his daughter-in-law's sister Pelagea Egorovna was present, together with a niece, Sophia Rostislavna and two stepsisters: Sophia Alexandrovna and Maclatura Alexandrovna.

Through some of these names runs that curious foreign strain (quasi-German in this case) which Gogol generally employs to convey a sense of remoteness and optical distortion due to the haze; queer hybrid names fit for difform or not yet quite formed people; and while squire Bespechnoy and squire Pobedonosnoy are, so to speak, only slightly *drunken* names (meaning as they do "Unconcerned" and "Victorious") the last one on the list is an apotheosis of nightmare nonsense faintly echoed by the Russian Scotsman whom we have already admired. It is inconceivable what type of mind one must have to see in Gogol a forerunner of the "naturalistic school" and a "realistic painter of life in Russia."

Not only people, but things too indulge in these nomenclatorial orgies. Notice the pet names that the officials of the town of N. give to their playing cards. *Chervy* means "hearts"; but it also sounds very much like "worms," and with the linguistic inclination of Russians to pull out a word to its utmost length for the sake of emotional emphasis, it becomes *chervotochina,* which means worm-eaten core. *Piki*—"spades"—French *piques*—turn into *pikentia,* that is, assume a jocular dog-Latin ending; or they produce such variations as *pikendras* (false Greek ending) or *pichura* (a faint ornithological shade), sometimes magnified into *pichurishchuk* (the bird turning as it were into an antediluvian lizard, thus reversing the order of natural evolution). The utter vulgarity and automatism of these grotesque nicknames, most of which Gogol invented himself, attracted him as a remarkable means to disclose the mentality of those who used them.

The difference between human vision and the image perceived by the faceted eye of an insect may be compared with the difference between a half-tone block made with the very finest screen and the corresponding picture as represented by the very coarse screening used in common newspaper pictorial reproduction. The same comparison holds good between the way Gogol saw things and the way average readers and average writers see things. Before his and Pushkin's advent Russian literature was purblind. What form it perceived was an outline directed by reason: it did not see color for itself but merely used the hackneyed combinations of blind noun and dog-like adjective that Europe had inherited from the ancients. The sky was blue, the dawn red, the foliage green, the eyes of beauty black, the clouds grey, and so on. It was Gogol (and after him Lermontov and Tolstoy) who first saw yellow and violet at all. That the sky could be pale green at sunrise, or the snow a rich blue on a cloudless day, would have sounded like heretical nonsense to your so-called "classical" writer, accustomed as he was to the rigid conventional color-schemes of the Eighteenth Century French school of literature. Thus the development of the art of description throughout the centuries may be profitably treated in terms of vision, the faceted eye becoming a unified and prodigiously complex organ and the dead dim "accepted colors" (in the sense of "idées reçues") yielding gradually their subtle shades and allowing new wonders of application. I doubt whether any writer, and certainly not in Russia, had ever noticed before, to give the most striking instance, the moving pattern of light and shade on the ground under trees or the tricks of color played by sunlight with leaves. The following description of Plushkin's garden in **Dead Souls** shocked Russian readers in much the same way as Manet did the bewhiskered philistines of his day.

> An extensive old garden which stretched behind the house and beyond the estate to lose itself in the fields, alone seemed, rank and rugged as it was, to lend a certain freshness to these expensive grounds and alone was completely picturesque in its vivid wildness. The united tops of trees that had grown wide in liberty spread above the skyline in masses of green clouds and irregular domes of tremulous leafage. The colossal white trunk of a birchtree deprived of its top, which had been broken off by some gale or thunderbolt, rose out of these dense green masses and disclosed its rotund smoothness in midair, like a well proportioned column of sparkling marble; the oblique, sharply pointed fracture in which, instead of a capital, it terminated above, showed black against its snowy whiteness like some kind of headpiece or a dark bird. Strands of hop, after strangling the bushes of elder, mountain ash and hazel below, had meandered all over the ridge of the fence whence they ran up at last to twist around that truncate birchtree halfway up its length. Having reached its middle, they hung down from there and were already beginning to catch at the tops of other trees, or had suspended in the air their intertwined loops and thin clinging hooks which were gently oscillated by the air. Here and there the green thicket broke asunder in a blaze of sunshine and showed a deep un-

lighted recess in between, similar to dark gaping jaws; this vista was all shrouded in shadow and all one could discern in its black depth was: the course of a narrow footpath, a crumbling balustrade, a toppling summer-house, the hollow trunk of a decrepit willow, a thick growth of hoary sedge bristling out from behind it, an intercrossment and tangle of twigs and leaves that had lost their sap in this impenetrable wildwood, and lastly, a young branch of maple which had projected sideways the green paws of its leaves, under one of which a gleam of sunlight had somehow managed to creep in after all, unexpectedly making of that leaf a translucid and resplendent marvel burning in the dense darkness.

> On the very edge of the garden several great aspens stood apart, lording it over the rest, with the huge nests of crows propped up by their tremulous summits. On some of these trees dislocated boughs that were not quite detached from the trunks hung down together with their shriveled foliage. In a word all was beautiful as neither nature nor art can contrive, beautiful as it only is when these two come together, with nature giving the final touch of her chisel to the work of man (that more often than not he has piled up anyhow), alleviating its bulky agglomeration and suppressing both its crudely obvious regularity and the miserable gaps through which its stark background clearly showed and casting a wonderful warmth over all that had been evolved in the bleakness of measured neatness and propriety.

I do not wish to contend that my translation is especially good or that its clumsiness corresponds to Gogol's disheveled grammar, but at least it is exact in regard to sense. It is entertaining to glance at the mess which my predecessors have made of this wonderful passage. Isabel Hapgood (1885) for instance, who at least attempted to translate it in toto, heaps blunder upon blunder, turning the Russian "birch" into the non-endemic "beech," the "aspen" into an "ashtree," the "elder" into "lilac," the "dark bird" into a "blackbird," the "gaping" (*ziyavshaya*) into "shining" (which would have been *siyavshaya*), etc. etc.

The various attributes of the characters help to expand them in a kind of spherical way to the remotest regions of the book. Chichikov's aura is continued and symbolized by his snuffbox and his traveling case; by that "silver and enamel snuffbox" which he offered generously to everybody and on the bottom of which people could notice a couple of violets delicately placed there for the sake of their additional perfume (just as he would rub on Sunday mornings his sub-human, obscene body, as white and as plump as that of some fat woodboring larva, with eau de cologne—the last sickly sweet whiff of the smuggling business of his hidden past); for Chichikov is a fake and a phantom clothed in a pseudo-Pickwickian rotundity of flesh, and trying to smother the miserable reek of inferno (something far worse than the "natural smell" of his moody valet) permeating him, by means of maudlin perfumes pleasing to the grotesque noses of the inhabitants of that nightmare town. And the traveling chest:

> The author feels sure that among his readers

there are some curious enough to be desirous of knowing the plan and inner arrangement of that chest. Being anxious to please he sees no reason to deny them their satisfaction. Here it is, this inner arrangement.

And without having warned the reader that what follows is not a box at all but a circle in hell and the exact counterpart of Chichikov's horribly rotund soul (and that what he, the author, is about to undertake is the disclosure of Chichikov's innards under a bright lamp in a vivisector's laboratory), he continues thus:

> In the center was a soap-container [Chichikov being a soap bubble blown by the devil]; beyond the soap-container were six or seven narrow little interspaces for razors [Chichikov's chubby cheeks were always silky-smooth: a fake cherub], then two square niches for sandbox and inkstand, with little troughs for pens, sealing wax and all things that were longish in shape [the scribe's instruments for collecting dead souls]; then all sorts of compartments with and without lids, for shortish things; these were full of visiting cards, funeral notices, theatre tickets and such like slips which were stored up as souvenirs [Chichikov's social flutters]. All this upper tray with its various compartments could be taken out, and beneath it was a space occupied by piles of paper in sheets [paper being the devil's main medium of intercourse]; then followed a small secret drawer for money. This could be slipped out inconspicuously from the side of the chest [Chichikov's heart]. It would always be drawn out and pushed back so quickly by its owner [systole and diastole] that it is impossible to say exactly how much money it contained [even the author does not know].

Andrey Bely, following up one of those strange subconscious clues which are discoverable only in the works of authentic genius, noted that this box was the *wife* of Chichikov (who otherwise was as impotent as all Gogol's subhuman heroes) in the same way as the cloak was Akaky's mistress in **"The Overcoat"** or the belfry Shponka's mother-in-law in **"Ivan Shponka and His Aunt."** It may be further observed that the name of the only female landowner in the book, "Squiress" Korobochka means "little box"—in fact, Chichikov's "little box" (reminding one of Harpagon's ejaculation: "Ma cassette!" in Molière's *L'avare*); and Korobochka's arrival in the town at the crucial moment is described in buxological terms, subtly in keeping with those used for the above quoted anatomic preparation of Chichikov's soul. Incidentally the reader ought to be warned that for the true appreciation of these passages he must quite forget any kind of Freudian nonsense that may have been falsely suggested to him by these chance references to connubial relations. Andrey Bely has a grand time making fun of solemn psychoanalysts.

We shall first note that in the beginning of the following remarkable passage (perhaps the greatest one in the whole book) a reference to the night breeds a peripheral character in the same way as it did the Amateur of Boots.

> But in the meantime, while he [Chichikov] sat in his uncomfortable armchair, a prey to troublesome thoughts and insomnia, vigorously cursing Nosdryov [who had been the first to disturb the inhabitants' peace of mind by bragging about Chichikov's strange commerce] and all Nosdryov's relatives [the 'family tree' which grows out spontaneously from our national kind of oath], in the faint glow of a tallow candle which threatened to go out any moment under the black cap that had formed long ago all over its wick, and while the dark night blindly stared into his windows ready to shade into blue as dawn approached, and distant cocks whistled to one another in the distance [note the repetition of 'distant' and the monstrous 'whistled': Chichikov, emitting a thin nasal whistling snore, is dozing off, and the world becomes blurred and strange, the snore mingling with the doubly-distant crowing of cocks, while the sentence itself writhes as it gives birth to a quasi-human being], and somewhere in the sleeping town there stumbled on perchance a freize overcoat— some poor devil wearing that overcoat [here we are], of unknown standing or rank, and who knew only one thing [in the text the verb stands in the feminine gender in accordance with the feminine gender of 'freize overcoat' which, as it were, has usurped the place of man]—that trail [to the pub] which, alas, the devil-may-care Russian nation has burnt so thoroughly,—in the meantime [the "meantime" of the beginning of this sentence] at the other end of town. . . .

Let us pause here for a moment to admire the lone passerby with his blue unshaven chin and red nose, so different in his sorry condition (corresponding to Chichikov's troubled mind) from the passionate dreamer who had delighted in a boot when Chichikov's sleep was so lusty. Gogol continues as follows:

> . . . at the other end of the town there was happening something that was to make our hero's plight even worse. To wit: through remote streets and by-alleys of the town rumbled a most queer vehicle which it is doubtful anybody could have named more exactly. It looked neither like a *tarantas* [simplest kind of traveling carriage], nor like a calash, nor like a *britzka,* being in sooth more like a fat-cheeked very round watermelon set upon wheels [now comes a certain subtle correspondence to the description of round Chichikov's box]. The cheeks of this melon, that is, the carriage doors, that bore remnants of their former yellow varnish, closed very poorly owing to the bad state of the handles and locks which had been perfunctorily fixed up by means of string. The melon was filled with chintz cushions, small ones, long ones, and ordinary ones, and stuffed with bags containing loaves of bread and such eatables as *kalachi* [purse-shaped rolls], *kokoorki* [buns with egg or cheese stuffing], *skorodoomki* [skoro-dumplings] and *krendels* [a sort of magnified *kalach* in the form of a capital B, richly flavored and decorated]. A chicken-pie, and a *rassolnik* [a sophisticated giblet-pie] were visible even on the top of the carriage. The rear board was occupied by an individual that might have been originally a footman, dressed in a short coat of speckled

homespun stuff, with a slightly hoary stubble on his chin, the kind of individual known by the appellation of 'boy' (though he might be over fifty). The rattle and screech of the iron clamps and rusty screws awakened a police sentry at the other end of the town [another character is born here in the best Gogolian manner], who, raising his halberd, shocked himself out of his slumber with a mighty roar of 'Who goes there?', but upon becoming aware that nobody was passing and that only a faint rumble was coming from afar [the dream melon had passed into the dream town], he captured a beast of sorts right upon his collar and walking up to a lantern slew it on his thumbnail [i.e. by squashing it with the nail of the curved index of the same hand, the adopted system of Russians for dealing with hefty national fleas], after which he put his halberd aside and went to sleep again according to the rules of his particular knighthood [here Gogol catches up with the coach which he had let go by while busy with the sentry]. The horses every now and then fell on their foreknees not only because they were not shod but also because they were little used to comfortable town pavements. The rickety coach after turning this way and that down several streets, turned at last into a dark lane leading past the little parish church called Nikola-na-Nedotychkakh and stopped at the gate of the *protopopsha's* [priest's wife or widow] house. A kerchiefed and warmly clothed servant girl climbed out of the *britzka* [typical of Gogol: now that the nondescript vehicle has arrived at its destination, in a comparatively tangible world, it has become one of the definite species of carriages which he had been careful to say it was not] and using both her fists banged upon the gate with a vigor a man might have envied; the 'boy' in the speckled coat was dragged down somewhat later for he was sleeping the sleep of the dead. There was a barking of dogs, and at last the gates, gaping wide, swallowed, although not without difficulty, that clumsy traveling contrivance. The coach rolled into a narrow yard which was crammed with logs of wood, chicken coops and all sorts of cages; out of the carriage a lady emerged; this lady was a collegiate secretary's widow and a landowner herself: Madame Korobochka.

Madame Korobochka is as much like Cinderella as Paul Chichikov is like Pickwick. The melon she emerges from can hardly be said to be related to the fairy pumpkin. It becomes a *britzka* just before her emergence, probably for the same reason that the crowing of the cock became a whistling snore. One may assume that her arrival is seen through Chichikov's dream (as he dozes off in his uncomfortable armchair). She does come, in reality, but the appearance of her coach is slightly distorted by his dream (all his dreams being governed by the memory of the secret drawers of his box) and if this vehicle turns out to be a *britzka* it is merely because Chichikov had arrived in one too. Apart from these transformations the coach is round, because plump Chichikov is himself a sphere and all his dreams revolve round a constant center; and at the same time her coach is also his roundish traveling case. The plan and inner arrangement of the coach is revealed with the

same devilish graduation as those of the box had been. The elongated cushions are the "long things" of the box; the fancy pastries correspond to the frivolous mementoes Paul preserved; the papers for jotting down the dead souls acquired are weirdly symbolized by the drowsy serf in the speckled jacket; and the secret compartment, Chichikov's heart, yields Korobochka herself.

I have already alluded, in discussing comparison-born characters, to the lyrical gust which follows immediately upon the appearance of stolid Sobakevich's huge face, from which face, as from some great ugly cocoon, emerges a bright delicate moth. The fact is that, curiously enough, Sobakevich, in spite of his solemnity and bulk, is the most poetical character in the book, and this may require a certain amount of explanation. First of all here are the emblems and attributes of his being (he is visualized in terms of furniture).

> As he took a seat, Chichikov glanced around at the walls and at the pictures that hung upon them. All the figures in these pictures were those of brawny fellows—full-length lithographic portraits of Greek generals: Mavrocordato resplendent in his red-trousered uniform, with spectacles on his nose, Miaoulis, Kanaris. All these heroes had such stout thighs and such prodigious mustachios that it fairly gave one the creeps. In the midst of these robust Greeks a place had been given, for no earthly reason or purpose, to the portrait of a thin wispy little Bagration [famous Russian general] who stood there above his little banners and cannons in a miserably narrow frame. Thereupon a Greek personage followed again, namely the heroine Bobelina, whose mere leg seemed bigger than the whole body of any of the fops that swarm in our modern drawing rooms. The owner being himself a hardy and hefty man apparently wished his room to be adorned with hardy and hefty people too.

But was this the only reason? Is there not something singular in this leaning towards romantic Greece on Sobakevich's part? Was there not a "thin wispy little" poet concealed in that burly breast? For nothing in those days provoked a greater emotion in poetically inclined Russians than Byron's quest.

> Chichikov glanced again around the room: everything in it was both solid and unwieldy to the utmost degree and bore a kind of resemblance to the owner of the house himself. In one corner a writing desk of walnut wood bulged out on its four most ridiculous legs—a regular bear. Table, chair, armchair—everything was of the most heavy and uncomfortable sort; in a word, every article, every chair seemed to be saying: 'and I also am Sobakevich!' or 'and I also am very much like Sobakevich!'

The food he eats is fare fit for some uncouth giant. If there is pork he must have the whole pig served at table, if it is mutton then the whole sheep must be brought in; if it is goose, then the whole bird must be there. His dealings with food are marked by a kind of primeval poetry and if there can be said to exist a gastronomical rhythm, his prandial meter is the Homeric one. The half of the saddle of mutton that he dispatches in a few crunching and susurrous instants, the dishes that he engulfs next—pastries whose size exceeds that of one's plate and a turkey as big as a calf, stuffed with eggs, rice, liver and other rich ingredients—all these are the emblems, the outer crust and natural ornaments of the man and proclaim his existence with that kind of hoarse eloquence that Flaubert used to put into his pet epithet "Hénorme." Sobakevich works in the food line with great slabs and mighty hacks, and the fancy jams served by his wife after supper are ignored by him as Rodin would not condescend to notice the rococo baubles in a fashionable boudoir.

> No soul whatever seemed to be present in that body, or if he did have a soul it was not where it ought to be, but, as in the case of Kashchey the Deathless [a ghoulish character in Russian folklore] it dwelled somewhere beyond the mountains and was hidden under such a thick crust, that anything that might have stirred in its depths could produce no tremor whatever on the surface.

The "dead souls" are revived twice: first through the medium of Sobakevich (who endows them with his own bulky attributes), then by Chichikov (with the author's lyrical assistance). Here is the first method—Sobakevich is boosting his wares:

> 'You just consider: what about the carriage-maker Mikheyev, for instance? Consider, every single carriage he used to make was complete with springs! And mind you, not the Moscow kind of work that gets undone in an hour, but solid, I tell you, and then he would upholster it, and varnish it too!' Chichikov opened his mouth to observe that however good Mikheyev might have been he had long ceased to exist; but Sobakevich was warming up to his subject, as they say; hence this rush and command of words.

> 'Or take Stepan Probka, the carpenter. I can wager my head that you will not find his like anywhere. Goodness, what strength that man had! Had he served in the Guards he would have got every blessed thing he wanted: the fellow was over seven feet high!'

Again Chichikov was about to remark that Probka too was no more; but Sobakevich seemed to have burst his dam: such torrents of speech followed that all one could do was to listen.

> 'Or Milyushkin, the bricklayer, he that could build a stove in almost any house! Or Maxim Telyatnikov, the shoemaker: with his awl he would prick a thing just once and there was a pair of boots for you; and what boots—they made you feel mighty grateful; and with all that, never swallowing a drop of liquor. Or Yeremey Sorokoplekhin—ah, that man could have stood his own against all the others: went to trade in Moscow and the tax alone he paid me was five hundred roubles every time.'

Chichikov tries to remonstrate with this strange booster of non-existent wares, and the latter cools down some-what, agreeing that the "souls" are dead, but then flares up again.

> 'Sure enough they are dead. . . . But on the other hand, what good are the live peasants of today? What sort of men are *they*? Mere flies—not men!'

> 'Yes, but anyway they can be said to exist, while those others are only figments.'

> 'Figments indeed! If only you had seen Mikheyev. . . . Ah, well, you are not likely to set eyes on anybody of that sort again. A great hulky mass that could hardly have squeezed into this room. In those great big shoulders of his there was more strength than in a horse. I should very much like to know where you could find another such figment!'

Speaking thus Sobakevich turns to the portrait of Bagration as if asking the latter's advice; and some time later when, after a good deal of haggling the two are about to come to terms and there is a solemn pause, "eagle-nosed Bagration from his vantage point on the wall watched very attentively the clinching of the deal." This is the nearest we get to Sobakevich's soul while he is about, but a wonderful echo of the lyrical strain in his boorish nature may be discerned further on when Chichikov peruses the list of dead souls that the burly squire had sold him.

> And presently, when he glanced at these lists of names belonging to peasants who had really been peasants once, had labored and caroused, had been ploughmen and carriers, had cheated their owners, or perhaps had simply been good *muzhiks*, he was seized with a queer feeling which he could not explain to himself. Every list seemed to have a special character of its own, and consequently the peasants themselves seemed to acquire a special character. Almost all those that had belonged to Korobochka possessed various appendages and nicknames. Brevity distinguished Plushkin's list, where many of the peasants were merely defined by the initial syllables of their Christian names and patronymics followed by a couple of dots. Sobakevich's list struck one by its extraordinary completeness and wealth of detail. . . . 'Dear me,' said Chichikov to himself with a sudden gush of emotion peculiar to sentimental scoundrels, 'how many of you have been crowded in here! What sort of lives did you lead, my friends?' [He imagines these lives, and one by one the dead *muzhiks* leap into existence shoving chubby Chichikov aside and asserting themselves.] 'Ah, here he is, Stepan Probka, the giant who would have graced the Guards. I guess you have tramped across many provinces with your axe hanging from your belt and your boots slung over your shoulder [a Russian peasant's way of economizing on footgear], living upon a pennyworth of bread and some dry fish for the double of that, and bringing in every time, I guess, [to your master] at the bottom of your money bag, a hundred silver roubles or so, or perhaps a couple of banknotes sewed up in your canvas trousers or thrust deep into your boot. What manner of death was yours? Had you climbed right up to the domed

roof of a church in trying to make more money [in wages for repairs] or had you perhaps hoisted yourself up to the very cross on that church, and did you slip from a beam thereon to dash your brains out on the ground whereat [some elderly comrade of yours] standing nearby only scratched the back of his head and said with a sigh: 'Well, my lad, you sure did have a fall'— and then tied a rope round his waist and climbed up to take your place. . . . '

'. . . And what about you, Grigory Doyezhaï-ne-doye-desh [Drive-to-where-you-won't-get]? Did you ply a carrier's trade and having acquired a *troïka* [three horses] and a bast-covered *kibitka,* did you forsake forever your home, your native den, in order to trundle merchants to the fair? Did you surrender your soul to God on the road? Were you dispatched by your own comrades in a quarrel for the favors of some plump and ruddy beauty whose soldier husband was away? Or did those leathern gauntlets you wore and your three short-legged but sturdy steeds tempt a robber on some forest road? Or perhaps, after a good bit of desultory thinking as you lay in your bunk, you suddenly made for the pot-house, just like that, and then plunged straight into a hole in the ice of the river, never to be seen again?'

The very name of one "Neoovazhaï-Koryto" (a weird combination of "disrespect" and "pigtrough") suggests by its uncouth straggling length the kind of death that had befallen this man: "A clumsy van drove over you as you were lying asleep in the middle of the road." The mention of a certain Popov, domestic serf in Plushkin's list, engenders a whole dialogue after it has been assumed that the man had probably received some education and so had been guilty (note this superlogical move) not of vulgar murder, but of genteel theft.

'Very soon however some Rural Police Officer comes and arrests you for having no passport. You remain unconcerned during the confrontation. 'Who is your owner?' asks the Rural Police Officer, seasoning his question with a bit of strong language as befits the occasion. 'Squire So-and-so,' you reply briskly. 'Then what are you doing here [miles away],' asks the Rural Police Officer. 'I have been released on *obrok* [meaning that he had been permitted to work on his own or for some other party under the condition that he paid a percentage of his earnings to the squire who owned him], you reply without a moment's hesitation. 'Where is your passport?' 'My present boss, the merchant Pimenov, has it.' 'Let Pimenov be called! . . . You are Pimenov?' 'I am Pimenov.' 'Did he give you his passport?' 'No, he did nothing of the sort.' 'Why have you been lying?' asks the Rural Police Officer with the addition of a bit of strong language. 'That's right,' you answer briskly, 'I did not give it him because I came home late—so I left it with Antip Prokhorov, the bellringer.' 'Let the bellringer be called!' 'Did he give you his passport?' 'No, I did not receive any passport from him.' 'Lying again,' says the Rural Police Officer, spicing his speech with a bit of strong language. 'Come now, where is that passport of yours?' 'I had it,' you

answer promptly, 'but with one thing and another it is very likely I dropped it on the way.' 'And what about that army coat?' says the Rural Police Officer, again treating you to a bit of strong language. 'Why did you steal it? And why did you steal a trunk full of coppers from the priest?'

It goes on like that for some time and then Popov is followed to the various prisons of which our great land has always been so prolific. But although these "dead souls" are brought back to life only to be led to misfortune and death, their resurrection is of course far more satisfactory and complete than the false "moral resurrection" which Gogol intended to stage in the projected second or third volumes for the benefit of pious and law-abiding citizens. His art through a whim of his own revived the dead in these passages. Ethical and religious considerations could only destroy the soft, warm, fat creatures of his fancy.

The emblems of rosy-lipped, blond, sentimental, vapid and slatternly Manilov (there is a suggestion of "mannerism" in his name and of *tuman* which means mist, besides the word *manil,* a verb expressing the idea of dreamy attraction) are: that greasy green scum on the pond among the maudlin charms of an "English garden" with its trimmed shrubs and blue pillared pavilion ("Temple of Solitary Meditation"); the pseudo-classical names which he gives to his children; that book permanently lying in his study, and opened permanently at the fourteenth page (not fifteenth, which might have implied some kind of decimal method in reading and not thirteenth which would

Chichikov's arrival in the town of N.

have been the devil's dozen of pages, but *fourteenth,* an insipid pinkish-blond numeral with as little personality as Manilov himself); those careless gaps in the furniture of his house, where the armchairs had been upholstered with silk of which, however, there had not been enough for all, so that two of them were simply covered with coarse matting; those two candlesticks, one of which was very elegantly wrought of dark bronze with a trio of Grecian Graces and a mother-of-pearl shade, while the other was simply "a brass invalid," lame, crooked and besmeared with tallow; but perhaps the most appropriate emblem is the neat row of hillocks formed by the ashes that Manilov used to shake out of his pipe and arrange in symmetrical piles on the window-sill—the only artistic pleasure he knew.

> Happy is the writer who omits these dull and repulsive characters that disturb one by being so painfully real; who comes close to such that disclose the lofty virtue of man; who from the great turmoil of images that whirl daily around him selects but a few exceptions; who has been always faithful to the sublime harmony of his lyre, has never come down from those heights to visit his poor insignificant kinsmen and remained aloof, out of touch with the earth, wholly immersed in remote magnificent fancies. Ay, doubly enviable is his admirable lot: those visions are a home and a family to him; and at the same time the thunder of his fame rolls far and wide. The delicious mist of the incense he burns dims human eyes; the miracle of his flattery masks all the sorrows of life and depicts only the goodness of man. Applauding crowds come streaming in his wake to rush behind his triumphal chariot. He is called a great universal poet, soaring high above all other geniuses of the world even as an eagle soars above other high flying creatures. The mere sound of his name sends a thrill through ardent young hearts; all eyes greet him with the radiance of responsive tears. He has no equal in might; he is God.
>
> But a different lot and another fate await the writer who has dared to evoke all such things that are constantly before one's eyes but which idle eyes do not see—the shocking morass of trifles that has tied up our lives, and the essence of cold, crumbling, humdrum characters with whom our earthly way, now bitter, now dull, fairly swarms; has dared to make them prominently and brightly visible to the eyes of all men by means of the vigorous strength of his pitiless chisel. Not for him will be the applause, no grateful tears will he see, no souls will he excite with unanimous admiration; not to him will a girl of sixteen come flying, her head all awhirl with heroic fervor. Not for him will be that sweet enchantment when a poet hears nothing but the harmonies he has engendered himself; and finally, he will not escape the judgment of his time, the judgment of hypocritical and unfeeling contemporaries who will accuse the creatures his mind has bred of being base and worthless, will allot a contemptible nook to him in the gallery of those authors who insult mankind, will ascribe to him the morals of his own characters and will deny him everything, heart, soul

and the divine flame of talent. For the judgment of his time does not admit that the lenses through which suns may be surveyed are as marvellous as those that disclose the movement of otherwise imperceptible insects; for the judgment of his time does not admit that a man requires a good deal of spiritual depth in order to be able to throw light upon an image supplied by base life and to turn it into an exquisite masterpiece; nor does the judgment of his time admit that lofty ecstatic laughter is quite worthy of taking its place beside the loftiest lyrical gust and that it has nothing in common with the faces a mountebank makes. The judgment of his time does not admit this and will twist everything into reproof and abuse directed against the unrecognized writer; deprived of assistance, response and sympathy, he will remain, like some homeless traveler alone on the road. Grim will be his career and bitterly will he realize his utter loneliness. . . .

> And for a long time yet, led by some wondrous power, I am fated to journey hand in hand with my strange heroes and to survey the surging immensity of life, to survey it through the laughter that all can see and through unknown invisible tears. And still far away is that time when with a gushing force of a different origin the formidable blizzard of inspiration will rise from my austere and blazing brow and, in a sacred tremor, humans will harken to the sublime thunder of a different speech.

Immediately after this extravagant eloquence, which is like a blaze of light revealing a glimpse of what at the time Gogol expected to be able to do in the second volume of his work, there follows the diabolically grotesque scene of fat Chichikov, half naked, dancing a jig in his bedroom—which is not quite the right kind of example to prove that "ecstatic laughter" and "lyrical gusts" are good companions in Gogol's book. In fact Gogol deceived himself if he thought that he could laugh that way. Nor are the lyrical outbursts really parts of the solid pattern of the book; they are rather those natural interspaces without which the pattern would not be what it is. Gogol indulges in the pleasure of being blown off his feet by the gale that comes from some other clime of his world, (the Alpine-italianate part), just as in **The Government Inspector** the modulated cry of the invisible reinsman ("Heigh, my winged ones!") brought in a whiff of summer night air, a sense of remoteness and romance, an *invitation au voyage.*

The main lyrical note of **Dead Souls** bursts into existence when the idea of Russia as Gogol saw Russia (a peculiar landscape, a special atmosphere, a symbol, a long, long road) looms in all its strange loveliness through the tremendous dream of the book. It is important to note that the following passage is sandwiched between Chichikov's final departure, or rather escape, from the town (which had been set upside down by the rumors of his deal) and the description of his early years.

> Meanwhile the *britzka* had turned into emptier streets; soon, only fences [a Russian fence is a blind grey affair more or less evenly serrated on top and resembling in this the distant line of a

Russian firwood] stretched their wooden lengths and foretold the end of the town [in space, not in time]. See, the pavement comes to an end and here is the town barrier ["Schlagbaum": a movable pole painted with white and black stripes] and the town is left behind, and there is nothing around, and we are again travelers on the road. And again on both sides of the highway there comes an endless succession of mileposts, post station officials, wells, burdened carts, drab hamlets with samovars, peasant women and some bearded innkeeper who briskly pops out with a helping of oats in his hand; a tramp in worn shoes made of bast trudging a distance of eight hundred *versts* [note this constant fooling with figures—not five hundred and not a hundred but eight hundred, for numbers themselves tend toward an individuality of sorts in Gogol's creative atmosphere]; miserable little towns built anyhow with shabby shops knocked together by means of a few boards, selling barrels of flour, bast shoes [for the tramp who has just passed], fancy breads and other trifles; striped barriers, bridges under repair [i.e. *eternally* under repair—one of the features of Gogol's straggling, drowsy, ramshackle Russia]; a limitless expanse of grassland on both sides of the road, the traveling coaches of country squires, a soldier on horseback dragging a green case with its load of leaden peas and the legend: 'Battery such-and-such'; green, yellow and black bands [Gogol finds just the necessary space allowed by Russian syntax to insert "freshly upturned" before "black," meaning stripes of newly plowed earth] variegating the plains; a voice singing afar; crests of pines in the mist; the tolling of church bells dying away in the distance; crows like flies and the limitless horizon. . . . Rus! Rus! [ancient and poetic name for Russia] I see you, from my lovely enchanted remoteness I see you: a country of dinginess and bleakness and dispersal; no arrogant wonders of nature crowned by the arrogant wonders of art appear within you to delight or terrify the eyes: no cities with many-windowed tall palaces that have grown out of cliffs, no showy trees, no ivy that has grown out of walls amid the roar and eternal spray of waterfalls; one does not have to throw back one's head in order to contemplate some heavenly agglomeration of great rocks towering above the land [this is Gogol's private Russia, not the Russia of the Urals, the Altai, the Caucasus]. There are none of those dark archways with that tangle of vine, ivy and incalculable millions of roses, successive vistas through which one can suddenly glimpse afar the immortal outline of radiant mountains that leap into limpid silvery skies; all within you is open wilderness and level ground; your stunted towns that stick up among the plains are no more discernible than dots and signs [i.e. on a map]: nothing in you can charm and seduce the eye. So what is the incomprehensible secret force driving me towards you? Why do I constantly hear the echo of your mournful song as it is carried from sea to sea throughout your entire expanse? Tell me the secret of your song. What is this, calling and sobbing and plucking at my heart? What are these sounds that are both a stab and a kiss, why do they come

rushing into my soul and fluttering about my heart? Rus! Tell me what do you want of me! What is the strange bond secretly uniting us? Why do you look at me thus, and why has everything you contain turned upon me eyes full of expectancy? And while I stand thus, sorely perplexed and quite still, lo, a threatening cloud heavy with future rains comes over my head and my mind is mute before the greatness of your expanse. What does this unlimited space portend? And since you are without end yourself, is it not within you that a boundless thought will be born? And if a giant comes will it not happen there where there is room enough for the mightiest limbs and the mightiest stride? Your gigantic expanse grimly surrounds me and with a dreadful vividness is reflected in my depths; a supernatural power makes my eyes bright. . . . Oh, what a shining, splendid remoteness unknown to the world! Rus! . . .

'Stop, stop, you fool,' Chichikov was shouting at Selifan [which stresses the fact of this lyrical outburst's not being Chichikov's own meditation]. 'Wait till I give you a slap with my scabbard,' shouted a State Courier with yard long moustaches, . . . 'Damn your soul, don't you see that this is a governmental carriage?' And like a phantom the *troika* vanished with a thunder of wheels and a whirl of dust.

The remoteness of the poet from his country is transformed into the remoteness of Russia's future which Gogol somehow identifies with the future of his work, with the Second Part of *Dead Souls,* the book that everybody in Russia was expecting from him and that he was trying to make himself believe he would write. For me *Dead Souls* ends with Chichikov's departure from the town of N. I hardly know what to admire most when considering the following remarkable spurt of eloquence which brings the First Part to its close: the magic of its poetry—or magic of quite a different kind; for Gogol was faced by the double task of somehow having Chichikov escape just retribution by flight and of diverting the reader's attention from the still more uncomfortable fact that no retribution in terms of human law could overtake Satan's home-bound, hell-bound agent.

. . . Selifan added in a special singsong treble key something that sounded like 'Come, boys.' The horses perked up and had the light *britzka* speeding as if it were made of fluff. Selifan contented himself with waving his whip and emitting low guttural cries as he gently bounced up and down on his box while the *troika* either flew up a hillock or skimmed downhill again all along the undulating and slightly sloping highway. Chichikov did nothing but smile every time he was slightly thrown up on his leathern cushion, for he was a great lover of fast driving. And pray, find me the Russian who does not care for fast driving? Inclined as he is to let himself go, to whirl his life away and send it to the devil, his soul cannot but love speed. For is there not a kind of lofty and magic melody in fast driving? You seem to feel some unknown power lifting you up and placing you upon its wing, and then you are flying yourself and everything is flying by: the mileposts fly, merchants fly by on the boxes of their carriages, forests fly on both sides of the road in a dark succession of firs and pines together with the sound of hacking axes and the cries of crows; the entire highway is flying none knows whither away into the dissolving distance; and there is something frightening in this rapid shimmer amid which passing and vanishing things do not have time to have their outlines fixed and only the sky above with fleecy clouds and a prying moon appears motionless. Oh *troika,* winged *troika,* tell me who invented you? Surely, nowhere but among a nimble nation could you have been born: in a country which has taken itself in earnest and has evenly spread far and wide over one half of the globe, so that once you start counting the milestones you may count on till a speckled haze dances before your eyes. And, methinks, there is nothing very tricky about a Russian carriage. No iron screws hold it together; its parts have been fitted and knocked into shape anyhow by means of an axe and a gauge and the acumen of a Yaroslav peasant; its driver does not wear any of your foreign jackboots; he consists of a beard and a pair of mittens, and he sits on a nondescript seat; but as soon as he strains up and throws back his whip-hand, and plunges into a wailing song, ah then—the steeds speed like the summer wind, the blurred wheelspokes form a circular void, the road gives a shiver, a passer-by stops short with an exclamation of fright—and lo, the *troika* has wings, wings, wings. . . . And now all you can see afar is a whirl of dust boring a hole in the air.

Rus, are you not similar in your headlong motion to one of those nimble *troikas* that none can overtake? The flying road turns into smoke under you, bridges thunder and pass, all falls back and is left behind! The witness of your course stops as if struck by some divine miracle: is this not lightning that has dropped from the sky? And what does this awesome motion mean? What is the passing strange force contained in these passing strange steeds? Steeds, steeds—what steeds! Has the whirlwind a home in your manes? Is every sinew in you aglow with a new sense of hearing? For as soon as the song you know reaches you from above, you three, bronze-breasted, strain as one, and then your hoofs hardly touch the ground, and you are drawn out like three taut lines that rip the air, and all is transfigured by the divine inspiration of speed! . . . Rus, whither are you speeding so? Answer me. No answer. The middle bell trills out in a dream its liquid soliloquy; the roaring air is torn to pieces and becomes Wind; all things on earth fly by and other nations and states gaze askance as they step aside and give her the right of way.

Beautiful as all this final crescendo sounds, it is from the stylistic point of view merely a conjuror's patter enabling an object to disappear, the particular object being—Chichikov. (pp. 63-113)

> *Vladimir Nabokov, in his* Nikolai Gogol,
> *1944. Reprint by New Directions Books, 1961,*
> *172 p.*

V. V. Gippius   (essay date 1966)

[*Gippius was a prominent Russian translator and critic best known for his writings on Gogol. He was the first general editor of the fourteen-volume edition of Gogol's collected works, and his* Gogol *(1924) is considered the best critical study of the author in any language. In the following excerpt, Gippius provides an overview of* Dead Souls.]

Gogol defined his conception of **Dead Souls** and its place in the development of his creative work in the following words: "The new social classes will rise up against me" and "All Russia will appear in it." "New social classes" meant primarily landowners; perhaps in the original plan for the sequel, other "social classes" were intended as well. Society in Gogol's consciousness fell precisely into "social classes," not according to any judicial features, nor according to any genuine features of class, but according to those of cultural *milieu* and everyday life. In this sense, the high society of the nobility, the noble officials, and the noble landowners were for him separate social classes. He particularly singles out the "middle class . . . which lives on its salary" (in the article **"The Petersburg Stage"**). But in Gogol's plan "all Russia" meant not simply the sum of various social classes. Gogol strove not only for the variety of everyday life, but first and foremost for generalizations. **Dead Souls** became a poem about "all Russia" first because all the separate depictions are given in their relation to the whole—to Russia—whereby the artistic image of Russia is formed; second, because the poem reflects the basic social contradiction of Gogol's contemporary reality: serfdom. **Dead Souls** is a poem about the Russia of serfdom and its ruling class, the serf-owning landowners. Here the Russia of landowners and peasants is revealed at its foundations; and neither the absence from the poem of sociological questions in the narrow sense of the word (i.e., the questioning of the institution of serfdom) nor the author's primary attention to depicting the landowners in any way contradicts this. By means of his entire artistic method, including both realistic analysis and synthesis, humor and lyricism, Gogol succeeded in unmasking the Russia of serfdom. In **Dead Souls,** as in **The Inspector General,** Gogol did not succeed in reaching the roots of social life; in those years neither as theoretician nor as artist did he pose the question of these roots. But as in **The Inspector General,** in **Dead Souls** the most progressive solutions to the social problems broached in the poem are supported by the entire structure of the poem's artistic means. Gogol had every reason to believe that after **Dead Souls** the "new social classes will rise up" against him.

Gogol constructs his poem according to two plans. The first and most evident is the psychological: the task of "depicting a multitude of the most varied characters." All the major characters are attached to the *milieu* of the landowners. But the significance of Gogol's characters outstrips their original social categorization. Manilovism, Nozdrevism, and Chichikovism (as well as Khlestakovism) acquire significance as broad, typifying generalities. This is not only the result of historical reevaluation; the generalized nature of the types was foreseen in the author's original plan. Gogol mentions this in relation to nearly all of his characters.

The Gogolian method of typifying generalities has nothing in common with that of abstract, psychological schematization. Those human traits first discovered by Gogol (such as Khlestakovism, Manilovism, Chichikovism, etc.) were originally discovered by him in concrete, everyday social conditions. For the characters of *Dead Souls,* these are the conditions of the everyday lives of remotely provincial, serf-owning landowners (while at the same time each character possesses a distinctly individual background). But it was clear to Gogol that reality produces variations of the types he had discovered—in conditions that are not exactly the same, but similar for each variant. This is made particularly clear in the chapter on Sobakievich, where he, with his power over peasants, is compared to a Petersburg bureaucrat who has power over other bureaucrats. All the possible parallels to the main characters, both those directly pointed out and those merely suggested, significantly expand the content of the poem and include in it whole stretches of Russian life.

The second plan according to which the poem is built (which includes the first, psychological plan) is the historical one. Each of Gogol's character types is historical because each is marked with the features of its age. Along with enduring historical phenomena, all of them reflect newly arisen phenomena (Chichikov, for example, is the acquisitive man of the new type). The whole Gogolian image of Russia, composed by combining and interpreting specific images, is placed in the perspective of historical development. Gogol had only the development of Russia in mind; but independent of his intentions, his images acquired an enduring historical significance, not only on a national but on an international scale as well. Chernyshevsky aptly indicated the existence of German Manilovs and English Chichikovs.

The tasks Gogol set himself could not have found full expression in the form of a novel, be it a novel of travel, a novel of picaresque adventures, or a novel of manners. All these elements entered the plot design to varying degrees, but neither separately nor collectively did they exhaust it. The novel, even in the latest broad and encompassing form that had at that time been developed by European literatures (of the kind written by Sir Walter Scott), inevitably remained within the boundaries of a portrayal of persons and events. There was no place in it for a generalized image of a people and a country, nor for an image of the author as a versatile yet deeply subjective poet who pronounces his judgments and his meditations with his evaluation of the present and his dream of the future. Proceeding from these tasks (which did not repudiate but included an intensified portrayal of real life), it was necessary to create a special genre: a large epic form broader than the novel. Gogol did call *Dead Souls* a poem, and by no means in jest, as hostile critics claimed. It is no coincidence that on the cover of *Dead Souls* drawn by Gogol himself the word "poem" is set in especially large letters.

Gogol's intentions are made clearer by the theoretical meditations in his *Textbook of Literature* [*for Russian Youth*]. Here it is directly stated that "the novel does not take in all of life, but a remarkable event in life." In Gogol's understanding the novel approaches drama in its principles of selection and the distribution of its material: In the novel, persons and events are united around the fate of the hero and "that which flies past the scene" finds no place in it.

Different problems are posed by the epic, which "embraces not just certain features, but an entire epoch of time in which there acts a hero with the type of thoughts, beliefs, and even confessions that mankind made at that time." The epic requires a hero of historical significance. There may also arise, on the other hand, "minor epic genres" without this condition. Under this rubric Gogol wrote:

> In modern times there has emerged a type of narrative work that constitutes a sort of middle ground between the novel and the epic, the hero of which is a private and insignificant figure, but one who is nonetheless significant in many respects for the observer of the human soul. The author leads his life through a chain of adventures and changes in order to present, along with a hero, a true-to-life picture of that which is significant in the traits and mores of the time he has chosen: that earthy, almost statistically grasped picture of shortcomings, abuses, faults, and all he has noticed in the chosen epoch and time. . . . Such phenomena have appeared from time to time among many peoples. Many of these incidents, though written in prose, may nonetheless be considered poetic works. It is not the whole world that is portrayed, but there is often a full epic range of remarkable individual phenomena.

There can be no doubt that these lines, written after the completion of the first volume of *Dead Souls* and during work on the second, represent Gogol's own commentary on his poem. He names Ariosto and Cervantes as authors of the "minor epic genres." Both these authors are mentioned in the early versions of *Dead Souls* as Gogol's literary mentors, along with Shakespeare, Fielding, and Pushkin, with a general characterization of all five authors: He speaks of them as having "reflected nature as it is." Thus as early as the first conception of *Dead Souls,* Cervantes' *Don Quixote* was Gogol's model.

A "full epic range" demanded that Gogol draw together diverse material. For Gogol this task of achieving completeness and "faithfulness" was characteristically associated with unmasking: First place among the "traits and mores of the time" is occupied by "shortcomings, abuses, and faults." The author not only depicts but evaluates the depicted as well. His methods of evaluation are multifarious. First among them, as in the earlier tales and comedies, is the method of humor: The vulgar is presented as humorous. But the more substantial the side of life portrayed, the more complex the forms in which the author's humor appears and the more his laughter is "diluted by bitterness" (as Belinsky noted regarding **"The Diary of a Madman"**). While in the objective depictions the author maintains a tone of calm, epic humor and his tears remain, as Gogol expressed it, "unseen," the author reserves the freedom to alternate whenever necessary from the tone of narrator and ironic commentator to the personal tone of a lyrical poet. In doing so he correspondingly varies all the linguistic means, changing from the language of everyday conversation in the variety of its dialects to that of the elevated lyric and the sermon. The form of a "minor epic genre" allows this lyrical-epic variety of tones. The image of the author, who is narrator and poet in one person, is the carrier of this variety.

Character types should naturally occupy the primary (though not the only) place in the design of a poem of "full epic range." That the creation of typical characters was Gogol's conscious task is evident from the structure of the poem. Of its eleven chapters, six represent sketches of particular characters; moreover, beginning with the second chapter, the poem presents what amounts to a "portrait gallery," with accentuated attention given to each portrait individually. It is natural that in a denunciatory poem about the Russia of serfdom, the character types of serf-owning landowners take precedence. This is what Gogol does, presenting, after the first chapter of general exposition, five consecutive chapters on Manilov, Korobochka, Nozdrev, Sobakievich, and Plyushkin.

Gogol steadfastly uses the same method he used in creating the character Khlestakov. He rejects typicality in its usual meaning—in the sense of reproducing "from nature" actually existing persons who are taken as models, if only for their characteristic traits, i.e., for the frequency of those traits' occurrence. Still more decidedly does he reject the method of schematization, of constructing a character from one feature. The great innovative significance of Gogol's method of character portrayal lies precisely in his not portraying the character on the basis of certain "traits," but discovering new human attributes.

The first detailed description in the poem begins with an ironic but declarative introduction on the difficulty of characterizing such "gentlemen" as Manilov, and on the necessity of a special method, a special "science of extraction" in order to catch "all the fine, nearly invisible features." The creation of a large, typical generalization from the depiction of a person who is "neither one thing nor the other," of a person "without any temperament," of a person of the minutest psychological dimension was one of Gogol's most remarkable achievements. This could be accomplished only by a principled refusal to build characters from "traits." Of course, even Manilov has his particular negative attributes: He is a do-nothing, an idle dreamer, a cloying phrasemonger. But these are all traits derived from his general social characterization. Using Gogol's notions and even his expressions, one may define this social basis as "the emptiness and impotent idleness of life," a "stagnant world." Historically, the same notions may be interpreted as a social inertia arising from the parasitism of serfdom. Not only do Manilov's affairs "somehow get along on their own," but even his personal behavior is defined by none other than social inertia. Analyzing the impression produced by Manilov, Gogol with subtlest humor distinguishes three moments: "In the first minute of conversation you cannot but say, 'What a pleasant and kind man!' The next minute you say nothing, and the third you say, 'What the hell is this?' and back away from him; and if you don't back away you'll feel mortal boredom." This scheme is supported by the entire contents of the chapter.

The impression of pleasantness is connected with that form of everyday culture in which the image of Manilov appears. It is a shallow but inoffensive form of sentimental imitation that has passed from literature into everyday life, reaching even the provincial estates. This provincial sentimentalism is expressed not only in the "temples of solitude" and idle daydreaming most frequently associated with Manilovism (of course, this is because this trait has turned out to be the most enduring). Very characteristic is the whole tender "friendship" between Manilov and Chichikov, with its high-flown phrases ("a saint's-day of the heart") and tears "glimmering" in their eyes. All this parodies not so much literary sentimentalism as sentimentalism in everyday life.

The sensitive nature of the character Manilov turns out to be an empty shell. This is revealed in the second minute of acquaintance: "You say nothing," because the essence of this character is emptiness, "neither one thing nor the other." But in the third minute repulsive traits are discovered behind this lack of any personality and at its base: an eagerness to agree with anything at all, to move from any push in any direction—all precisely the result of an inherent lack of content.

One variation of this aspect of Manilovism is the character Mizhnev. Mizhnev's outer wrapping is different—he has the temper of a debator—but behind it one discovers the same essence. It is said of people like Mizhnev that they always "agree to what they had repudiated: The stupid man they will call clever and then go tripping merrily to another man's tune; in short, they will start on the level and end up on the crook."

Of all the typifying generalizations created by Gogol, besides the notion of Khlestakovism, that of Manilovism has entered the general consciousness and the Russian language itself in a particularly lasting way. Manilovism, unmasked by Gogol in its most organic surroundings (amidst the parasitic idleness of the landowners' estates), remains for us to this day a symbol of human attributes that thwart productive labor from within.

Korobochka's character is endowed with less generalizing power. It is a remarkable image of a petty, backwater landlady, in all the concreteness of her everyday life, notions, habits, and of the attributes of a primitive businesslike nature and simpleminded fear of the new and of unclean spirits. Korobochka's image is necessary to the poem not only for its own sake, but also for connections and comparisons. Her simpleminded lack of culture sets off Manilov's pretensions to culturedness, as well as other false glitters of culture, such as the lady aristocrat who awaits behind her unfinished book "the visit of some witty society caller." Korobochka's "blockheaded" obstinacy also turns into an occasion for a brief portrait of "another respectable and official personage." But in drawing all these parallels and having the author pose the question of "whether Korobochka's place in life is really so low in the infinite scale of human perfection," Gogol refrains from accentuating those of Korobochka's qualities and positive traits to which there are hints in one of the drafts. Gogol was particularly inclined to these by the Slavophile Shevyrev. He rejected this idea, limiting Korobochka's "attributes" to purely negative traits and preserving the unity of a denunciatory tone for the images of all his landowners.

In Nozdrev's image Gogol again touched on the theme of Khlestakovism, not only in that both characters lie, but also in that both are capable of acting as if they are unaccountable to anyone. In Nozdrev this Khlestakovian quality is developed to the extreme: not only does he lie "completely without any necessity," but he plays dirty tricks on his closest friends "without any good reason for it." Nozdrevism differs from Khlestakovism in that, in *Dead Souls* as opposed to in *The Inspector General,* the theme of a person's behavior is generally more complex and intensified. *The Inspector General* is constructed around an isolated incident that forces the collective of officials to band together in self-defense; Khlestakov passively submits to this general excitement. In *Dead Souls* the characters are presented in epic manner, and nuances of character may be found in each of them. Manilov and Korobochka differ in the cultural features of their everyday lives, but they absorb equally passively the norms of social life. Nozdrev's social behavior is reflected energetically and with contradictions: The elemental instinct to associate with other people appears in his case in wild, essentially antisocial forms. Nozdrev is humorous in that he embodies in its most superficial and completely debased form the leaven of an old, grand-scale feudal lord, greedy for feasts and even battles. The feasts are replaced by an elementary drunkenness and prodigality; and the battles by "birching the landowner Maximov while he was drunk," by his attempt at beating up Chichikov, and so on. It is characteristic that Nozdrev's "vassals," the houseserfs Porfiry and Pavlushka, take part in his reprisals. Only rarely does the anarchical, feudal element show up in violent outbursts; in the new social conditions Nozdrev easily becomes a "historical person"—a common scoundrel and a cheat.

Nozdrev's character is dependent on his social profile, which is that of a landowner of the transitional era. But the author also indicates the most important of Nozdrev's "anarchical," antisocial features, his ability inexplicably to "play dirty tricks on his closest friends" in the wider sphere of the society of serfowners, mentioning how vile the behavior of a "person of rank . . . with a star on his breast" can be. He also mentions in general that Nozdrev is "everywhere in our midst, though, perhaps, in a different suit; but imperceptive people are thoughtless, and a man in a different suit seems to them a different man." That Nozdrev is prodigal and predatory in his own affairs thus is far from being the most characteristic of his traits; here, as elsewhere, the condition of the nobility's estates is not the basic theme of the poem.

Sobakievich contrasts with Nozdrev, though his character is every bit as monstrous. But Sobakievich's monstrousness does not exceed that which in the everyday life of serfdom passes for "normal." In his "animallike" appearance there is not one human feature, save his practical sense (which is, incidentally, so elementary and utilitarian that it does not affect the nature of his character). Nozdrev's antisocial features are moderated by a sort of vague social instinct; Sobakievich is portrayed as a convinced misanthrope. The exception he makes for Chichikov is motivated in the poem by the attributes of Chichikov himself—his peculiar talent for being "pleasant." Sobakievich's inordinate gluttony is presented, of course, not as a traditional, one-dimensional literary type of mask, but as a feature indicative of his generally animal quality. This impression of something inhumanly soulless is intensified by the comparison made with a piece of wood to which "nature has paid little heed," that is, with an object of the setting, and intensified especially by the comparison with a bear. The comparison of Sobakievich with a bear is widely known; less attention has been paid to one of its particular details: At the moment of his deal with Chichikov, Sobakievich is compared to a bear "who had been trained in the art of turning somersaults and doing various tricks." This qualification refers to Sobakievich's external manners, to a "certain deftness," but this deftness is given a psychological basis: Sobakievich is deft when it comes to profit. And if his basic bearlike qualities correspond to the stagnant everyday life of the feudal estate, then his "deftness," bearlike as it may be, in itself reveals a knack for adapting naturally to the conditions of the new "mercantile" age.

Sobakievich's animalistic, bearlike qualities also have their variations: There are Sobakieviches outside the backwater provincial estates. Chichikov thinks of this after they conclude their bargain. He prefers a bear of a village *kulak* [rich peasant] to that of a clerk in the capital who "snaps his fingers at his inferiors or dips into the public funds." In one of the drafts for the novel, Gogol himself agrees with this, noting that "the scoundrel Sobakievich, who is far from being noble in spirit or emotions, at least did not ruin his peasants or make lazybones or drunkards out of them." However, it was precisely Chichikov whom Gogol convincingly had discover Sobakievich's purely utilitarian motives ("they belong to you, and you would be worse off if you did maltreat them.")

The distortion of human appearance is portrayed statically in Nozdrev and Chichikov. In Plyushkin it is portrayed in its development. Up until his sudden change Plyushkin is "merely . . . a thrifty proprietor" with the qualities of "a mind, experience, a knowledge of the world," "industriousness," and "wise stinginess." These qualities by themselves would not be so far from those of Sobakievich, but in Plyushkin's case it becomes possible for the first time to raise the question of human emotions. Precisely that—only to raise it. Even earlier Plyushkin's feelings were neither weak nor strong ("No great intensity of feeling was observable in his face," and "With every minute the human feelings, of which he had never had a great store, diminished"). The most natural feelings "diminish" in him: With ease he curses first his daughter, then his son, having ceased to have any interest in them. He has wholeheartedly submitted to the inertia of material cares, which have grown up into miserliness and petty predation, to the extent of robbing his peasants of insignificant items. This path is shown as the gradual loss of everything human, as the degradation of a man. Here are given the psychological and even the thematic premises for [Mikhail Saltykov-Shchedrin's] Gogolian chronicle.

Plyushkin's is the most depressing portrait in the Gogolian gallery of ugly landowners; here the comic depiction passes over into the tragicomic grotesque. Here Gogol no longer draws lines to other social variants; on the contrary, he speaks of the "rarity" in Russian life of such a phenomenon as Plyushkin. But, of course, if Plyushkin is an exception, then (to use [Vasily] Kliuchevsky's expression) he is a "typical exception": Plyushkin's degradation, his complete falling away from social ties, and the entire psychology that arises on the basis of that degradation are natural to the life of a serfowner. The image of Plyushkin is especially carefully surrounded with the details of social and everyday life. Not only is he characterized by his talk of the peasants who have died of hunger, not only does he himself speak of his fugitive souls, but in the scenes with Proshka and Mavra he is graphically shown to be an oppressor. These scenes are all the more striking because they are presented as regular scenes of everyday life.

In creating the character of Plyushkin, Gogol followed the path of least resistance by addressing the theme of stinginess. He gave a new, very significant solution to this theme. Plyushkin's stinginess is not a congenital trait, but the result of his personal and social fate; it is not an inherent but a derived characteristic, which is all the more indicative of the process of degradation portrayed in him. The struggle within Plyushkin between his habitual stinginess and the remnants of other feelings is shown with great subtlety. Thus, not even to Plyushkin can one apply a definition of the Gogolian method as one of moral sententiousness, of reducing each character type to one feature.

Chichikov is not simply one portrait in a series of others, but the one conceived as the poem's central image. This complicates an analysis of his character type: in the first place, because he is frequently given the auxiliary role of uniting the poem's elements (though sometimes the role of the author's surrogate seems utterly impossible for him); in the second place, because it is announced in the first volume that his image is not yet complete. But since the first volume is to a certain degree artistically complete, one may discuss Chichikov on the basis of its material. This is all the more true because the material in the second volume does not contradict the image in the first, and the meager information given about the novel's projected sequel contradicts the data of both the first and the second volumes so strikingly as to require special explanation in regard to Gogol's further literary evolution.

Special attention falls, of course, on Chichikov. The basic outline of his portrait is already sketched out in the first chapter; what follows develops and fills it in. Finally, to Chichikov is dedicated a special monographic chapter, the eleventh. In the first chapter Chichikov is revealed more by his generic than by his individual characteristics: For the time being, he is one of Gogol's many inert beings, whose emptiness is covered with an outer gloss. Revealing details of behavior and everyday life portray this emptiness (the day's routine, the torn poster, the contents of the trunk). These are all new variations on the portrayals in the Mirgorod and Petersburg tales. But Chichikov's outer gloss differs significantly from those of Khlestakov and Kovalev, and even of Manilov, who is depicted at the beginning of the same chapter. Here Gogol has not simply applied a veneer of everyday traditions for fashion's sake, but he has expertly constructed a mask. As early as the first chapter, Chichikov appears endowed with the traits of a particularly flexible adaptability and at the same time with a persistence, behind the two of which hides his later revealed "passion." It is these combinations that set Chichikov's portrait apart from the others in Gogol's series.

These qualities are connected with Chichikov's social profile and social behavior. Chichikov's family tree, discovered in the eleventh chapter (his parents were of the nobility, but "God alone knows whether they were so by descent or by personal merit"), is not as important as the entire portrait of him and its whole function in the poem. Chichikov, the owner of two living souls and a few hundred dead ones, is a foreign body in the landowners' milieu, an imposter who does nothing but strive for and dream about the social norm. Gogol used the individual character of Chichikov as a symptom of large social changes that he was diagnosing, as an indication that "all has long ago changed in society," that among the movers of society the "electricity" of monetary capital occupies first place (the article **"After the Theater"**). With great social perspicacity, Gogol made the clash of two social phenomena the basis of his poem: the old foundations of the serf-owning estate and the new "electricity" of capital. This motif of conflict anticipates the comic content of the plot. This is natural, since the conflict is shown in its early stages, in unripe and therefore paradoxical forms. Chichikov's character combines the comic nature of an innovation that has yet to take shape with that of an antiquity that has outlived its time. The Chichikovs of this world bring nothing essentially new into everyday life, nor into psychology, still less into ideology. Each new scene promises only a new variant of the "dark kingdom" of the landowners. Thus through this image of a hero of base gain and in the theme of Chichikov's speculation, Gogol anticipates the character types of Derunov and Razuvaev and the theme of *The Refuge Mon Repos* [by Mikhail Saltykov-Shchedrin].

The social and historical particulars of Chichikov's character determine also his personal traits. As opposed to those characters who either do not act at all or who act "completely . . . without any reason for it," Chichikov acts consciously and with an exact goal. As opposed to those "with no temperament whatsoever" or with a senseless temperament, in Chichikov there is "a passion which draws him on." This passion is a base one, incapable of making Chichikov a positive hero even in part; but taken abstractly, such attributes as "energy" and "activity" appear positive. It is this contradiction that complicates the image of Chichikov in chapter 11, where the author enigmatically hints that "perhaps the passion that impelled Chichikov himself was not derived from within him" and hints at "yet another mystery, that of the reason why this type of hero figures in the poem that is now seeing the light of day." This "mystery" is partly explained by one of Gogol's biographers, who heard from Gogol himself that the poem was to conclude with "Chichikov's first sigh" of longing for a new life. This was written in the last years of Gogol's life, at a time when his religious moralism was becoming more intense; whether or not this finale was in accordance with the original plan for the poem, we do not know. This motif of rebirth does not fit in with the image of Chichikov in the first volume: There is no foreshadowing of it. True, in the same eleventh chapter (in the episode with the sick teacher), the author explains that his hero's nature is not so severe and callous, nor his feelings so dulled, that he should know neither pity nor sympathy. But, as is clear from what follows, this explanation is ironic, its meaning being that "nature" is impotent before the influences of one's environment and the habits of social behavior. Nowhere does Gogol base his hero's behavior on "nature" alone, nor does he do so here. The paternal instruction to "guard" every kopeck and fawn upon the rich; the passion for "life in all its enjoyments," supported by the examples of plebeians who have made it rich (the rich clerk); the experience of having served in positions of varying caliber; and, finally, the general atmosphere of Russian bureaucracy and serfdom: All this turns out to have a greater effect on Chichikov than his "nature," which is furthermore characterized only negatively, as the absence of "severity" and "callousness." In the novel's main plot, Chichikov appears completely "callous," beyond any human sympathies whatsoever. The single, intentional exception is Chichikov's nervousness at the ball upon meeting the governor's daughter; but the subtle analysis made in this episode requires special reservation, even to the point of renaming common human emotions: "It cannot be said with any certainty that our hero was overcome by the feeling of love; it is even doubtful whether gentry of that sort, that is to say, those who are neither too fat nor yet too thin, are capable of love, but taking everything into consideration, there was something strange here, something of a nature he could hardly explain."

Gogol firmly and convincingly binds Chichikov's character to his social biography. But, as in other instances, this does not impoverish the meaning of the character type. Chichikovism is defined by a passion for "life in all its enjoyments" and a readiness to use any means to achieve this goal, from common adaptability to eccentric speculations. In the end Chichikovism is defined by the process of capitalization. The power of money and its psychological results could have been revealed in various social and biographical variants, though they would have been less revealing than Chichikov's biography. Gogol himself underscores the general meaning of Chichikovism: "And who among you . . . will ponder this weighty question in the depths of his soul: 'Is there not a chip of Chichikov in me too?'"

In the chapter on Korobochka a parallel is drawn from typical bureaucratic relations to Chichikov's character and to the motif of his adaptability: "Ivan Petrovich" (also a typifying generalization) is an eagle among his inferiors, but a chicken in the office of his superior. Chichikov himself is also shown as an official wholly typical of bureaucratic Russia: the Chichikov of chapter 11 is a direct variant of the characters in *The Inspector General,* but he is more refined than the simpleminded provincial powers depicted there. In Chichikov the traits of an experienced bribe-taking official are combined with those of an adventurer of the new type, but he dreams of becoming a landowner, at first (in part 1) in name, then (in part 2) in reality. All this makes Chichikov the synthesizing figure in the denunciatory plan of *Dead Souls.*

The six especially emphasized portraits present the concentration of the basic "denunciatory material" and the basic social-psychological problems raised in the novel. This is the foreground, behind which there are several more planes; the poem's genre allows free arrangement of this material.

The characters next on the scale of attention paid them by the author are Chichikov's servants, Selifan and Petrushka. For Gogol to turn immediately from Petrushka to Selifan requires ironic excuses, that special device of authorial "lapsing into silence" ("But knowing as he does by experience how unwilling they are to acquaint themselves with low society, the author hesitates in taking up so much of the reader's time with people of base origin"). Gogol also uses this method later, where he finds it necessary to break abruptly with tradition. Indeed, literature of the nobility traditionally either excluded servants or presented them with the intention of idealizing them morally or, on the contrary, caricaturing them. Not bowing to tradition, Gogol simply made Selifan a good-natured *raisonneur,* and Petrushka a distinctive parallel to Chichikov, both by contrast and similarity: Chichikov's cultural level is not far from that of Petrushka; as "readers" they closely resemble one another, and only in neatness does the collegiate assessor surpass his serf.

Gogol repeats the ironic method of "lapsing into silence" when he proceeds to the provincial ladies. With them it was necessary for him to break with the traditions of the society tale and the novel in still another regard, by deflating and debunking the cliché of the genteel heroine. New apologies preface the remarkable images of the two ladies, Anna Grigorievna, the lady pleasant in all respects, and Sofia Ivanovna, the simply pleasant lady. Despite their episodic roles, these two feminine types have become nominal; their generalized labels, which have stuck to them better than their first names and patronymics, of course, contribute to this. Provincial grande dames and gossips had been satirized a hundred times over in eighteenth-century satire, but didactic satire was unable to lend any lifelike character to these types. Gogol does this, not only by masterfully reproducing their peculiar "dialect," but also by creating complete characters. Sofia Ivanovna, in spreading the news brought by Korobochka, is herself a variant of Korobochka ("She only knew how to be disturbed, but she lacked the wherewithal to form any clear hypothesis"); while Anna Grigorievna, in reaching "with her own mind" the conclusion that upsets "the whole town," is a variation of the know-it-alls and gossips in *The Inspector General.*

The overall picture of the provincial town recedes somewhat into the background. Here, where the theme of "all Russia" appears, it would be inappropriate to lend primary importance to a picture of the town and a characterization of its inhabitants. The collective portrait of society is more vivid than any separate portraits because of the major attention paid to "mores" instead of to separate persons. Relatively greater attention is paid to the chief of police, Aleksei Ivanovich, as to a type indicative of the whole life of the provincial town. A curious parallel to the town's governor, this "wonder-worker" and uniquely "kind bribetaker," beloved of the citizens for being "not proud," makes one recall Gogol's words that "my characters are by no means villains: If I but add one kind feature to any one of them, the reader will make peace with all of them." This experiment (which could hardly be called possible for "any one of them") was realized in this episodic figure.

The postmaster, Ivan Andreich, also occupies a place close to the foreground, not so much because of the way he is characterized (he is a variation on Liapkin-Tiapkin, that lover of "enlightenment," mystic, and author of rash hypotheses), as because it is precisely he who narrates the "Tale of Captain Kopeikin." This tale plays a more significant role than that commonly played by the novellas that, in the tradition of biographical and travel novels, were inserted to lend variety to the narration or to elucidate the author's ideas. The scenes in the capital, such as the torments of the starving invalid as he journeys from one ministry's reception room to the next, the episode with the former soldiers turned robbers, and, finally, the letter from the robber-chief to the Tsar: All this belongs in a poem about Russia and expands its social range. Moreover, Gogol finds a completely organic way to include in the poem this material that seems foreign only at first glance. In the postmaster's comic tale, the reader divines and recreates its genuine, poignantly real content through its paradoxical linguistic and psychological form.

Under the pressure of censorship, however, Gogol was forced to sacrifice the acrimony of his social satire. This acrimony is gradually weakened in the three versions of the tale known to us. The details of the thieves who rob only from public funds are dropped, as well as those of negotiations with the Tsar, and, finally, those of the bureaucracy's soullessness toward a defender of the homeland. In the censored version Kopeikin is made guilty of his own misfortunes. Though he agreed to these compromises, Gogol was not willing to cut out the tale itself. Thus there were artistic reasons for keeping the tale, independent even of the details of the hero's psychology and the degree of denunciatory acrimony. The stylistic completeness of the oral narrative style may have been one of these reasons, but probably not the decisive one. More essential was the compositional role of the tale.

The second part of the first volume represents a parodic and almost comic use of the motifs of adventure. Gogol's contemporaries likened this picture of an "excited town" to the plot of *The Inspector General;* the difference between them, however, is substantial. The mistake of the officials in *The Inspector General* unwittingly discloses their true mores and natures, including those of Khlestakov. In *Dead Souls* false rumors pile up one on top of the other, revealing for the most part stupidity and narrow-mindedness, the lack of culture in provincial society. The chain of hypotheses grows, becoming stronger with every link; but none of the characters can grasp the real Chichikov, although it would seem that each holds the key in his own hands; Chichikov steals away the governor's daughter; he is a robber; and, finally, he is a gang leader,

moreover one who is missing an arm and a leg. Here absurdity reaches such extremes that even the provincial society is aware of it, but this unmasked absurdity only leads them to replace it with an even worse one: that Chichikov is Napoleon in disguise! Had the tale been omitted, this chain of absurdities would have been broken and with it the definitive collective characterization of provincial society.

The awaited arrival of the new governor-general intensifies the town's commotion, and this evokes a direct return to the motifs of *The Inspector General:* the officials' fear and the recollection of "peccadillos" resulting in the accumulation of new material for satire. The whipped noncommissioned officer is paralleled in two concisely alluded-to plots, which are tragicomically told by the author and are more horrifying than humorous: the beating of the merchants and the peasants' mock trial of the assessor Dobriazhkin. The officials themselves speak of bribes with the same faith in their social stability that is exhibited in *The Inspector General.* The scenes in the courthouse in chapter 7 also are close to a "physiological sketch" about the everyday life in government offices. All these episodes and allusions, however, seem mere echoes of and variations on *The Inspector General.* The same themes are developed much more energetically in Chichikov's biography in chapter 2. Here Gogol not only portrays the subtle methods of bribe-taking, but continues, as it were, the very plot of *The Inspector General:* An honest official turns out, unbeknownst to himself, to be deftly ensnared.

Thus, the poem's basic material is the everyday lives of the serf-owners, supplemented by bureaucratic material not new to Gogol's works. The satirical themes of arbitrary rule, lawlessness, and self-interest enter the poem on all levels of the bureaucratic ladder—from the petty clerks to the minister.

By adopting the stance of an epic poet, Gogol found still more opportunities for including diverse material in the poem. In the course of narration, the author is able to introduce images only distantly related to the plot, and sometimes not related at all. Subordinated to the general epic composition of the poem, all these images become commensurate elements of the whole. This is the basis of Gogol's unique method of painting in miniature.

From the first chapter to the last, *Dead Souls* is strewn with such miniature portraits. In some instances, the miniature is based on some detail of plot or even on some secondary plot element that unexpectedly grows to the proportions that suit the author. Chichikov buys up dead and fugitive souls; he has the lists in his hands. The plot should progress farther, to the closing of his deed of purchase. But these dead and fugitive souls have independent meaning in the general design of the poem. Chichikov's adventure is built on the fates of men, both living and dead. Their character types, their exemplary and revealing biographies, become necessary to the internal meaning of the poem. Thus do the remarkable portraits of Stepan Probka, Maxim Telyatnikov, Popov the house serf, and Abakum Fyrov arise. These portraits are attributed in part to Chichikov (in one of the drafts, where, however, certain apologies are made for the intervention of the author himself); in part they are taken over by the author—in those places that require a more profoundly lyrical intonation. The peasant theme of the poem is not only expanded in the miniatures of the seventh chapter, but acquires substantially new emotional nuances.

In other instances the plot provides occasion for generalized portraits of entire social groups and types. The digression on "the thin and the fat" in chapter 1 and the generalization portrait of stewards belong to this type of miniature. The latter is particularly important in that the typifying portrait is followed by a typifying generalization of peasant life: "Having become a steward, he of course conducted himself as do all stewards: He consorted and kept company with the village folk who were better off and augmented the taxes levied on the poorer households. . . ." The miniatures include parallels to the main characters, as mentioned above. Korobochka evokes the image of an obstinate employee of the state and of an aristocratic lady with "rigid ideas." Nozdrev evokes the image of "a person with a medal," who loves to play dirty tricks on his close friends. Sobakievich evokes the image of an official who robs the till. These miniature portraits and their like not only lend overtones to the original characters, but expand the "epic range" as well, indicating the pertinent social variations of the main characters.

A completely special type of miniature is that found in similes. The device of extended similes, a bold variation of Homer's epic similes, fulfills a complex epic function in *Dead Souls.* Their obvious function is to create models of the elevated and beautiful out of the details of everyday, typically comic life. But by this route, which lies completely beyond the plot, vital material also penetrates into the poem. Here is a characteristic example from chapter 5: "As he drove up to the porch, he noticed two faces which were peeping out of the window almost simultaneously: one was a woman's, long and narrow as a cucumber, crowned with a cap; the other a man's, broad and round as the Moldavian pumpkins which go by the name of *gorlyanki* from which Russians make balalaikas—light two-stringed balalaikas, the boast and joy of some smart twenty-year-old lad, saucy-eyed and jaunty, winking an eye and whistling at the white-breasted and white-throated maidens who gather round to listen to his soft-stringed twanging." From the comic comparison of Sobakievich's face with a pumpkin there arises, by capricious association, the lively and charming image of the balalaika player, a merry lad from among the peasants, an image that has no relation whatsoever to the plot, but is included by the author's fiat in the general picture of "all Russia."

There are instances, finally, when the author does not even require external connections with the poem's basic material: The miniatures may arise in the composition of his "broad digressions." Thus, the sixth chapter begins with a lyrical reminiscence of youth, and the author introduces the town and estate scenes, the portraits of the provincial official and the landowner, only to serve as examples of youthful powers of observation and ability to "figure a person out."

Thus the poem is expanded by every means of epic narration. It is filled, even within the bounds of the first volume,

with the broadest possible subject matter, from sentinel and deserter to minister and Tsar, including the provincial capital, the estate, landowners and peasants, officials of all ranks, and—episodically or in miniatures—the aristocracy, the merchant class, the officer class (Kopeikin), and the intelligentsia (in the mocking of the scholarly historian).

But Russia is revealed in *Dead Souls* not only through social types. In the final chapter, which is in many respects a summary, the narration is interrupted by pictures of nature that acquire generalized character: Chichikov's journey is conveyed by a selection of details, whence a shift is made to a generalization of all Russia. This occurs first with regard to Russia's nature: "Russia! Russia! I see you now, from my wondrous, beautiful past I behold you! How wretched, dispersed and uncomfortable everything is about you. . . ." The shift from here to the Russian song, which is presented as an expression of the Russian spirit, and then to Russia's future, returns us to the ideas of the *Arabesques,* in particular to the old idea of the link between geography and history. But what sounds like an abstract thought in the *Arabesques* finds its artistic fulfillment in *Dead Souls:* The ideas of Russia and of history in general influenced the creation of the central image of Gogol's poem—that of Russia.

The image of Russia in her development enters the poem in the so-called lyrical digressions, which first interrupt, then conclude the last chapter of part 1. Russia is a "bird-like troika," flying "in a surge full of terror," Russia, to whom the poet addresses his burning question, "Where are you flying?" This is a romantic generalization, evoked by the writer's deep and long-standing faith in "Russian man in his development," mentioned as early as the article on Pushkin. This image was meant to be indefinite: The roads down which his native land "flies" have no distinct outlines for the poet, and the question "Where are you flying?" is followed by the insignificant words: "There is no answer." The profoundly progressive nature of *Dead Souls* consists precisely of its simultaneous, very concrete, realistic unmasking of the actual Russia and its romantic faith in the possible, future Russia. The poem's pathos, along with its definitive image of Russia, is composed of the contrast between the gloomy present on one hand and the possibilities of the future and a faith in the nation's strengths on the other. While Gogol was still working on *Dead Souls,* Belinsky wrote (in a letter to Botkin, 13 June 1840): "All that is substantial in our people is great and immense, but its definition is vile, filthy, and base." This could be a translation, as it were, of the basic content of *Dead Souls* into the language of philosophical formulas. It is not surprising that Belinsky reacted to Gogol's poem as to the appearance of an ally.

But Gogol's attitude toward the positive possibilities of the Russian people was expressed not only in romantic lyricism and not only in the image of Russia as a troika. He viewed these possibilities in living Russian men, but—very characteristically—not among the characters who are landowners. He found them among the folk characters portrayed in chapter 7, in the miniature portraits that enter the "meditations" on the list of peasants. Here the

Manilov.

author is tolerant and gentle even in humorous scenes; but where he speaks of the barge haulers who trade "the rampages of a boisterous life" for "toil and sweat," his voice is pierced with lyrical animation. It is significant that for none of the characters of part 1, other than the peasants, does Gogol find lyrical intonations similar to those that resound throughout the poem for the generalized image of his native land.

The current expression "lyrical digression" is not accurate in its application to the lyrical passages of *Dead Souls,* because the latter are all necessary links in the whole epic. In particular, the appeals to Russia not only do not "digress" from the poem's basic content, but on the contrary concentrate it within themselves, since it is the image of Russia that organizes and provides a basis for the content.

The second organizing image in the poem is that of the narrating author. In the poem's design, the "author" is not simply a conventional figure who draws together separate elements, but a unified personality. The author openly evaluates all that he himself has narrated, with his own clearly expressed view of things: The whole objective material of the poem, all its images and the image of Russia that unites them, are shown through the author's subjectivity. They are drawn, in Belinsky's words, "through his own *living soul.*" The profound originality of Gogol's poem arises from the combination of an epic method of

narration with an emotionally heightened and lyrical method. Moreover, not only man in general is revealed in the author, but a militant writer as well. The poem's very design represents a literary polemic—its novelty is underscored. This is why neither the separate polemical comments on artistic creation scattered throughout the poem nor the beginning of the seventh chapter, which unites them (the remarkable parallel of the two writers), can be called "digressions."

The beginning of the seventh chapter bears more significance than any other of Gogol's literary declarations. Here Gogol resolutely contrasts the happy and universally recognized writer, who "has never pitched his lyre in a lower key," idealizing reality by composing images "remote from the earth," the writer of Schiller's type, with the Gogolian type, unrecognized, reflecting real life with its "mess of trifling things." In formulas that are accurate despite their metaphoric form, Gogol characterizes the essence and tasks of the realistic method of fiction (but without pronouncing the words themselves). This method is primarily the task of "bringing into the open what is ever before men's eyes, all those things which the indifferent gaze fails to perceive, the whole horrid and shocking slimy mess of trifling things which have clogged our life, the whole depth of those chilly, split-up, everyday characters who swarm upon our bitter and dreary path on earth . . .

" Here Gogol intensifies those theses earlier expressed in his article on Pushkin (the author's justification for selecting common material) and now asserts the predominance in life of "trifling things"; these are not only ineffective but repulsive—but precisely this makes them important to art. Not only is the artist able to include trivial things in the material of art, but his task lies precisely in the unmasking of trivial things, since the mess of trifling things has clogged life. Here, as in *The Inspector General,* the problems of aesthetics are inseparable from those of social morality. Here everyday characters ("chilly, split-up") are contrasted with "characters who embody the highest values of humanity," the "few exceptions," those chosen by the "happy" writer. By "chilly, split-up" everyday characters, of course, Gogol means what in "Four Letters to Divers Persons Apropos *Dead Souls*" is called "the vulgarity of a vulgar man." Thus the "unrecognized writer" is distinguished first of all by the very material he writes about—human vulgarity. But the portrayal of vulgarity requires its own method: Vulgarity must be uncovered and denounced; it requires extensive analysis, the "science of extraction" mentioned in chapter 2, the exposure of the imperceptible and "invisible" ("For . . . the telescope pointed at the sun and the microscope recording the movements of unnoticed insects are equally wonderful"). Then a different task is set before him: ". . . and with the firm power of a relentless chisel to dare and present them roundly and clearly for the benefit of all." The method of analysis is complemented by that of synthesis, the creation of integral images, "round" and "clear" in both their outer and inner aspects, the creation of typifying generalities.

One of Gogol's most important aesthetic formulas is expressed in the words: "Contemporary judgment does not recognize that great spiritual depth is required to illuminate a picture drawn from despised life and to make of it the pearl of creation." The essence of the problem and the indication of a method are important here. The appeal to "despised life" for Gogol meant not the "destruction of aesthetics," but the widening of aesthetic content. The beautiful coincides neither with the elevated nor with the comely. From this thesis, adopted by the majority of the Romantics and by whole Romantic schools of art, Gogol made the logical, realistic conclusions that "despised life" must give the artist his material. In the revised version of **"The Portrait,"** written simultaneously with *Dead Souls,* this is expressed in the words "for him [i.e., the artist] nature contains no base objects." The parallels between *Dead Souls* and **"The Portrait"** also help to explain the expression "illuminate . . . and make of it the pearl of creation." Reality must be "illuminated" by the author's subjectivity; the "soulless" imitation of nature alone cannot be called the creation of art. These words about "illumination" and "being made the pearl of creation" are connected with the subsequent aesthetic formula, "for contemporary judgment does not allow the high laughter of delight a worthy place side by side with lofty lyrical emotion." In **"After the Play"** and other articles on the theater, Gogol finds the "illuminating" sources precisely in laughter. But the laughter of comedy is none other than the author's subjective point of view. "Laughter" is one of the possibilities of "illumination," the comprehension of reality. It is not the only possibility, but in Gogol's aesthetics it is the most essential, since the unmasking of vulgarity comes about primarily through the methods of humor and satire.

The "microscopic" analysis of vulgarity, the synthetic creation of generalized images, the "illumination" of those images with laughter and, in general, with the author's subjectivity—these were Gogol's guiding principles as he opened the way for critical realism in Russian literature. (pp. 493-517)

> *V. V. Gippius, "An Introduction to 'Dead Souls'," translated by Thomas Seifrid, in "From Pushkin to Blok" by V. V. Gippius: Dead Souls: The Reavey Translation; Backgrounds and Sources; Essays in Criticism, edited by George Gibian, W. W. Norton & Company, 1985, pp. 489-517.*

Robert Martin Adams [pseudonym of R.M. Krapp] (essay date 1966)

[*An American educator and critic, Adams is the author of works on religion, opera, and a variety of literary topics, including the highly regarded* Stendhal: Notes on a Novelist *(1959). In the following excerpt, he analyzes the structural significance of "nonexperience" in* Dead Souls.]

On every score, Gogol is no doubt a greater artist than Poe; but in both may be felt the same special dualism, which is easy to schematize: a violent subsurface energy distorts or destroys the surface arrangements, rational and limited, of the social narrative. This undercurrent is felt from the beginning in *Dead Souls* (1842); it moves and works even on seemingly inanimate things, which provide, perhaps, the best evidence of its intermittent, unpredictable working. For the universe of *Dead Souls* has a com-

position not very easy to describe with assurance; it can be, at moments, thick and fleshy, almost disgusting, while at other times it is airy, genteel, and a little bit evasive. On occasion it has no quality at all, it is perfectly blank and featureless, as if a hot iron had passed over a wax figure, obliterating its wrinkles and features; very often pieces get arbitrarily detached from the continuum and sail off into orbits of their own. There are all sorts of gaps and interstices, which are filled in a random, inconsistent way—frequently with Nothing, so that they are just inconclusively there. And it is Nothing which haunts the author's vision, Nothing which inspires his most agonizing vertigo.

The opening pages of the novel are justly famous. They describe the arrival of a gentleman with no characteristics in a town which has no name other than N:

> The gentleman in the carriage was not handsome but neither was he particularly bad-looking; he was neither too fat nor too thin; he could not be said to be old, but he was not too young either.

Two peasants, watching him arrive, detach for purposes of conversation a single wheel from his carriage; idly, vacantly they set arbitrary limits to the powers of the wheel. It would get to Moscow, all right, but not to Kazan; and the conversation, having served its only purpose, to relieve the two peasants of their inner emptiness by making them for a moment critics of the world, lapses and is never resumed. A young man walks by, wearing specific canvas trousers, a swallow-tail coat, and a very individual pin indeed. The wind almost blows off his cap, but instead blows him out of the story forever.

Thus specific bits and vivid meaningless fragments of cosmos fly between the reader and that featureless, indeterminate gentleman who happens to be the hero of the story; what wind blows them we do not yet know. But the wall of represented substance which forms the backdrop for Gogol's characters has oddities of its own. It is unexpectedly neutral; it bulges and clots to a thickness in unanticipated places. Chichikov is ushered almost immediately into a familiar, ordinary Russian room at an inn—"where for a couple of roubles a day travellers are given a quiet room with cockroaches peering out from every corner like prunes." And these cockroaches, scuttling behind the woodwork, transform themselves imaginatively into that quiet, inquisitive man next door, who is all the more present in his silent curiosity as his presence is remarked just once and then left vacant. Chichikov now makes his way to the inn's public room, which is just like every public room everywhere else, exactly the same in every detail—"the only difference being that a nymph in one of the pictures had such enormous breasts that the reader cannot possibly have seen anything like it before." It is the essence of Gogol's grotesque that one feature of a drab landscape can suddenly swell to such obscene proportions; just so, in the story **"The Nose,"** his nose separates itself from Kovalev, swells to human dimensions, dresses itself up in a fine uniform, and goes off to pay house-calls.

Amid this palpitating, pneumatic, fragmented universe wander the characters of Gogol—among them, no less bemused than the others, the story's narrator. This is not a very steady-gaited narrator to begin with, and amid the perils and pitfalls of this peculiar cosmos, he reels, staggers, and teeters from difficulty to disaster. Right away he gets tangled up in Chichikov's scarf, which for an ordinarily competent narrator would be no obstacle at all:

> The gentleman took off his cap and unwrapped from his neck a woollen rainbow-colored scarf, such as wives are in the habit of knitting with their own hands for their husbands, furnishing them with suitable instructions on how they should wrap themselves up; who provides them for bachelors I'm afraid I cannot tell—goodness only knows—I have never worn such scarves myself.

His narration is particularly apt to bog down on a worldly generalization (like those of Poe) such as a categorical distinction between fat and lean civil servants, which has nothing to do with his fable; for the moment, wrenching himself away from the scarf problem, he gives Chichikov dinner, allows him a short nap, and takes him on a tour of the town. It is a dreary little town; the depths of its dreariness are measured in the thoroughness with which Chichikov inspects some spindly trees and reads the playbill through from beginning to end, both sides, including the printer's label. And its officials are perfectly commonplace, including the governor who, like Chichikov, was neither fat nor thin. We do learn about him that "he wore the order of St. Anne round his neck and it was even rumored that he had been recommended for the order of St. Stanislav; he was, however, a good fellow and sometimes even did embroidery on tulle." Thus, agile and insecure as a clown on skates, our narrator slides from skewed *non sequitur* to vapid irrelevance; words are used in what the second part of the book will call the "haemorrhoidal" sense; and in tripping over his own verbal feet, the narrator announces the hollowness not only of his characters but of his whole narration.

He explains very seriously that he will introduce Selifan and Petrushka, the servants of Chichikov; for he is a methodical narrator, and even though these are only secondary, or even tertiary characters, still he will introduce them. So he tells us that Petrushka was always reading books and had a very distinctive disagreeable odor; while, as for Selifan—but this is going *too* far, nobody wants to meet such a low-class person. And so we are never introduced to Selifan. Similarly when Chichikov meets Manilov—who has no character at all, no interests, and isn't even middle-aged—we are told at length of the disorder of the ménage. The chairs are not all covered, one of the candelabras is splendid, the other grubby, the house is messy, and Manilov in fact a sloven. "His wife. . . . Still, they were perfectly happy with one another." Or again, a page or two later: "One might perhaps make the further observation that Mrs. Manilov. . . . But I must confess I'm very much afraid of talking about ladies, and, besides, it is time I returned to our heroes."

As the narrator tumbles into and climbs laboriously out of little holes and pockets of void, so the personages of the novel are haunted almost tragically by void and vacancy. Manilov is well-mannered inane emptiness in a cellophane wrapper; his life is composed entirely of yawns, good in-

tentions, and great, goggling, watery daydreams. He is so meager mentally, he does not even know he is bored; and he sees the whole world in his own insipid image. Nozdryov is a contrasting character, frantic with emptiness; he rushes about, kicking at reality or provoking it to kick him, in order at least to escape momentarily the frightful emptiness of his existence. His mania is for betting, cheating, quarreling; he bets to lose, makes wild assertions to be contradicted, cheats to be caught, and quarrels in order to feel, beating on his face, the fists of inescapable, undeniable reality. One of the saddest and funniest scenes in the book is that in which Nozdryov takes his brother-in-law and Chichikov on a tour of his property. They see two mares and a stallion, for which Nozdryov says he paid ten thousand roubles. The brother-in-law has doubts about this improbable price, and Nozdryov wants to bet on it, but nobody will bet with him. Then they look at some stalls in which there were once good horses. They inspect the fishpond and hear of fish so enormous that two men were hardly able to pull one out. They look at some dogs with excellent haunches.

> Then they went to have a look at a Crimean bitch which was blind and, according to Nozdryov, would soon be dead, but which two years ago had been a very good bitch. They inspected the bitch too, and, to be sure, the bitch was blind. Then they went to have a look at a watermill, which had lost its 'flutterer' or iron ring on which the upper stone rests as it turns rapidly on its axle or 'flutters,' as the Russian peasants so wonderfully express it.
>
> 'We shall soon come to the smithy,' said Nozdryov.
>
> And, to be sure, on going a little farther they saw the smithy; they inspected the smithy too.

The vacancy of those terrible open empty fields, the gentlemen plodding bored through the mud, the landowner fretting and exploding in his vain rage for something worthy of notice—it is a remarkable episode in a remarkable book. Plyushkin the miser lives in an even more squalid and sinister wilderness; we are not surprised to find his character defined specifically in terms of void. Peasant revenues, paid to him in the form of goods, were "put away in the storehouses and got mouldy and full of gaping holes and in the end he himself became a kind of gaping hole in humankind."

Vapid, suspicious, blockish, frantic, grasping—the landowners encountered by Chichikov are at the roots of their characters so many responses to the void that surrounds, invades, and threatens to supplant them. Chichikov himself is, socially speaking, a perambulating hollow; his enterprise, the purchasing of dead souls, is the shell of a substantial enterprise. When he finally opens a mysterious box which has been teasing us for some time, we are given an elaborate account, not of its contents, but of the partitions which divide it. And, like other empty characters whom he meets, Chichikov is avid to fill himself up in the most direct way possible; he is a frantic eater. Gentlemen of the middling sort, it seems, are all fond of sucking pig with horseradish and sour cream, roast veal, sturgeon cheeks, fish and cabbage pie, sterlet soup, mushrooms, curd tarts, and a thousand other delicate dishes with which they try, on every opportunity, to give themselves some substance. **Dead Souls** is a romance overflowing with food; the author misses no opportunity to specify in loving detail all the dishes in the enormous meals which his characters devour. Petukh, talking to Platon in the second part of the novel, tries to tell him that life is never boring; and indeed, as he lives it, ennui is quite impossible:

> I wake up in the morning and there's the cook to see, dinner has to be ordered, then I have breakfast, and then I have to see my estate agent and then I go fishing and then it's dinner time. You have hardly time to take a nap after dinner when it's time to see the cook again and order supper. When is there time to be bored?

This monologue has a clear satiric point to make against Petukh (whose name means "cock" or "rooster"); but it leaves little room for complacency on the part of handsome, empty Platon, whose boredom admits of no relief at all. If Platon with his philosophical name "stands" in some sense for the life of the mind and Petukh for that of the gut, a point is reinforced here which can be traced, like a scarlet thread, throughout the mesh of **Dead Souls;** it is a deep suspicion and hatred of thought.

Chichikov returns late and tired from his adventures in the countryside, goes to his room at the inn, is greeted by the waiter, and lied to by Petrushka—all accepted routines:

> Ordering a very light supper, consisting only of sucking pig, he undressed immediately after it, and getting under the bedclothes fell fast asleep, fell into a sound sleep, into that wonderful sleep which only happy mortals enjoy who know nothing of haemorrhoids, or fleas, or strongly developed intellectual faculties.

This is one sort of Gogolian by-blow at the philosophic mind. Or again, when he approaches Plyushkin's house, Chichikov passes through a grotesque and gaping forest, full of unlit chasms,

> yawning like the open mouth of some huge wild animal; it was plunged in shadow and in its dark depths could be dimly discerned: a narrow path disappearing in the distance, broken-down railings, a tumbledown summer-house, a decaying willow trunk, full of holes, and from behind the willow-tree a dense gray caragana thrust out its thick stubble of twigs and leaves, tangled and intertwined and withered from growing in this terrible thicket; and, finally, the young branch of a maple-tree, stretching sideways its green claw-like leaves, under one of which a shaft of sunlight suddenly transformed it, goodness only knows how, into a transparent, fiery leaf, gleaming wonderfully in that dense darkness.

The wilderness as described is scarcely charming; on the contrary, everything about it suggests distortion, violence, savagery. Yet its effect, in juxtaposition with the miser's house, is unexpectedly beautiful, beyond the reach of either nature or art by itself,

as only happens when they unite together, when nature's chisel puts its final touch to the often unintelligently heaped up labor of man, relieves the heavy masses, destroys the all too crudely palpable symmetry and the clumsily conceived gaps through which the unconcealed plan reveals itself so nakedly, and imparts a wonderful warmth to everything that has been created by the cold and carefully measured neatness and accuracy of human reason.

Upon these principles, a bramble-patch would add beauty to the Parthenon. But evidently Gogol is not talking simply about forests and residences. . . .

Though by no means subtle indications of attitude, passages like these are marginal; the book's real impatience with conscious mind explodes in the author's recurrent, intermittent outbursts against his own story. Chichikov is a traveler, a bachelor, a rootless, insubstantial man on a kind of pilgrimage; he drives into the book from nowhere, going only vaguely anywhere; and the author expresses or implies frequent impatience to get him through with the masquerade. As early as the opening of Chapter 2, the reader is being assured that he will learn about Chichikov's project "gradually and in good time, if only he has the patience to read through this very long story, which will assume greater and much vaster dimensions as it nears its end, which crowns all." The digression at the end of Chapter 5, on the peculiar, rushing, restless power of the Russian word calls one's attention to an energy which is not finding, and cannot find, expression in the human comedy. Indeed, the occasion for the digression is precisely a word that cannot be repeated, that is represented in the text of **Dead Souls** only by a discreet nineteenth-century dash. But this screened and latent energy erupts again at the opening of Chapter 7, in an apostrophe to the happy traveler. He is the one who has a family to come home to. "Happy the family man who has a home of his own, but woe to the bachelor!" The happy traveler, the married man, is identified with the idealistic poet, the writer who "without touching the earth has immersed himself completely in his own exalted images that are so far removed from it." All mankind is his loving family, they welcome him home and bathe him in love and affection. But the writer who picks a low topic from real life, the outsider, the bachelor, gets no such reward:

> without fellow feeling, without response, without sympathy, he is left standing alone in the middle of the road like a homeless wayfarer. Hard is his calling in life and bitterly he feels his solitude.

> And [the passage continues, modulating into unabashed first person singular] for a long time to come am I destined by the mysterious powers to walk hand in hand with my strange heroes, viewing life in all its immensity as it rushes past me, viewing it through laughter seen by the world and tears unseen and unknown by it. And the time is still far off when the terrible storm of inspiration will rise up in another stream out of a head encircled with a halo, inspiring sacred terror and, abashed and in trepidation, men will hear the majestic thunder of other words. . . .

This passage, like similar outbursts in the last two chapters, is stirred by an image of the story itself as a journey, an adventure. Behind its pathos and rhetoric, intruding upon the artifice of the novel and whirling its paper-cutout characters into wild spirals, is the breath of a passion for the infinite and the limitless which finally translates itself into the mad gallop of those mythical horses, the wild careering of that supernatural troika beyond time, space, artifice, convention—out of this world. The novel simply goes out of control at the end, as it was threatening to do all along, peels off into a long climbing turn, and disappears among the thunderous stars.

Looking back, one senses how telling was that reversal, managed by Gogol's feeling at the start of Chapter 7, where the idealist was described as a domestic figure, the disagreeable realist as a bachelor. This exactly reverses the conventional posture of things as represented, for example, by Marchbanks and Morrell, in Shaw's *Candida.* For Gogol, the lofty and inspirational writer winds up taking what amounts to the short view of experience (ideals unify, comfort, soften life; they bring people together), while the embittered bachelor, who forces people to see what is directly under their noses, takes an ultimate perspective on it. He can perhaps do so because the Nothing of things offers him easy passage through them; but if he had a married man's confidence in the surface tension of life, the void might not be there at all. Perhaps in the storm of inspiration both ways—the way above and the way through—will be made one. But for the moment they are terribly opposite; and in their opposition the old heroic mode is irremediably fractured. The old-fashioned hero, like his own statue, imposes himself as a monumental shape or shell; the new ultimate is reached by a collapse of the ordinary, which collapses more radically, and enables us to see more deeply into the hollowness of things, as it is emptier. Such a psychic action accomplishes neither the cruel distancing of comedy nor the sympathetic release of tragedy but a wry and violent tension beyond which, for the moment, we need not look. (pp. 50-60)

> *Robert Martin Adams [pseudonym of R. M. Krapp], "Mirrors and Windows: Poe, Gogol,"* in his *NIL: Episodes in the Literary Conquest of Void During the Nineteenth Century, Oxford University Press, Inc., 1966, pp. 41-60.*

Carl R. Proffer   (essay date 1967)

[*Proffer was one of the founders of Ardis Publishers, the largest publisher of Russian literature outside the Soviet Union. This venture has been responsible for the publication of works by dissident and exiled Russian authors who otherwise would have remained unknown. In addition, he is recognized as an important critic and translator of Russian literature. In the following excerpt, Proffer analyzes Gogol's use of the extended simile in* Dead Souls.]

The publication of *Dead Souls* in 1842 occasioned one of Russian literature's most violent journalistic free-for-alls. There were no neutrals in this battle. O. I. Senkovskij, a shrill-voiced, contemptuous foe of Gogol since the days of *Mirgorod* and *The Inspector-General,* took one look at

Dead Souls and was certain he had discovered donkey dung in the house of Russian literature. In the opposite corner was Belinskij, a famous but often rather dull fellow, whose prolix essays in defense of *Dead Souls* were as much the result of his social ideology and political beliefs as an understanding of Gogol's art. Much to the amusement and anger of both Senkovskij and Belinskij, Konstantin Aksakov maintained that *Dead Souls* was a modern version of the Homeric epic. One of Aksakov's specific points was that in his similes Gogol was a worthy pupil of Homer. In subsequent criticism and scholarship this aspect of the polemic has been almost entirely ignored. I propose . . . to examine the peculiarities of Gogol's extended similes and their multiple functions in *Dead Souls.* (pp. 67-8)

Why did Gogol decide to use Homeric similes so frequently in *Dead Souls?* Why should he consider this device especially suited for extensive use in this particular work, in his prose poem? Part of the answer lies in the very fact that Gogol did consider it a sweeping poem about Russian life. It is precisely in this type of work that the Homeric simile had been used most fruitfully in the past. Gogol may also have been cognizant of the fact that the device was commonly used in French mock epics; Scarron was particularly well-known. The Homeric simile had been used in a comic manner by Ariosto, whom . . . Gogol mentions in the *Textbook of Literature* and in *Dead Souls* itself, *Orlando Furioso* being given as an early example of the genre of *Dead Souls.*

In a preliminary draft of his *Textbook of Literature* Gogol had also mentioned Fielding's novels as examples of the smaller kind of epos. For some reason, perhaps because he feared someone would draw a parallel between Fielding's novels and *Dead Souls,* Gogol deleted this reference. It is interesting to note that Fielding frequently uses and parodies the Homeric simile in *Joseph Andrews* and *Tom Jones.* One chapter of *Tom Jones* is even entitled "In which a Simile of Mr. Pope's Period of a Mile Introduces as Bloody a Battle as Can be Fought . . . " In some cases Fielding discusses the similes with the reader, speculating on how successful they might be, or giving the reasons for employing a certain image. Gogol must have read these passages attentively. In an early draft of *Dead Souls* he reveals that the pictures he always keeps on the wall before his writing desk are those of Shakespeare, Ariosto, Fielding, Cervantes, and Puškin. In the final version Fielding's name is omitted.

The humorous application of the Homeric similes in *Orlando Furioso,* burlesques, and Fielding's comic novels provides part of the answer to the question of why Gogol used the device. The very fact that the original object of comparison is lost from view can be a source of humor. The reader feels that something strange is happening, that he is being led astray by the author, that he is being played with—that the author, tongue-in-cheek, is using his illustration in a most illogical manner. Gogol suddenly turns the world upside down, diverts our attention, and leads us into what is, or seems to be, a completely unrelated setting: . . . .

> There wasn't a face that did not express pleasure

or, at least, a reflection of the general pleasure. Thus do the faces of all the bureaucrats light up when some high official arrives for an inspection of the departments entrusted to them, after their first fright has subsided and they perceive that not a few things are to the liking of the great man; he himself has at last condescended to jest a little—that is, to drop a few words with a pleasant smile—whereupon those bureaucrats who are around him, and somewhat nearer him in rank, laugh in response to his sally twice as hard as need be; those who, truth to tell, had heard but poorly the words he has let drop, make up for that by laughing with all their heart; and, finally, some policeman or other, stationed far off near the door, at the very exit, who has never laughed in all his born days and who just before had shaken his fist at the people outside— why, even he, in accordance with the immutable laws of reflection, expresses on his face some sort of smile, although this smile resembles rather the grimace of someone getting set to sneeze after a pinch of rappee.

We are led away from the Governor's ball in two jolting steps: from the smiling faces of the guests at the ball to the smiling faces of *činovniki* drawn up in ranks for inspection, and then, in a typically Gogolian shift of focus and simile within a simile, to a bullypoliceman—and even to his birth (he had never laughed in all his born days) and what he was doing immediately before the inspection. What was for the epic poets basically a serious device has been used for humor, for satirical purposes. Most similes are also value judgments—the author reveals his opinion by the kind of things to which he compares his characters. Here it is the smiles which give rise to the similes; but, inevitably, the reader juxtaposes more than just the smiles of the guests at the ball, *činovniki* at inspection, and the policeman. The obsequiousness and servility of those standing inspection is carried over to those who surround Čičikov. The brutishness of the policeman is also associated with Čičikov's hosts: recall the murder of a local policeman mentioned in Chapter Nine and the politely rapacious character of the police-chief. Gogol makes us laugh by the actual description of the various character types in the vehicle of the simile, the ironic tone he uses to describe them, and by a tacit awareness of the fact that he is digressing. But the value judgment he is making becomes clearer when we see that the digressive part of the simile is actually relevant to the tenor. This is a point to which I will return.

Gogol uses the developed simile as more than just a humor device or a value judgment. This figure of speech has a compositional function, a function described by Belyj in a comparison of his own:

> It is necessary to note a series of extended similes, expanding as if to divert attention; but these are pauses which give our attention a rest so that it can be concentrated again with new strength—they are like the sudden, stormy development of the accompaniment during which the voice is silent, so that it can begin again. . . .

If we do not understand that the device is being con-

sciously we will not be able to take this "rest" as Belyj suggests; we will make the same objections that Senkovskij and Masal'skij made and complain of being diverted from the action. Of course, the whole point is that Gogol wanted us to be diverted momentarily.

The purpose of this diversion is not just to make us laugh. These "rests" have still another function. What is the "accompaniment" in these digressive similes? We see bedraggled soldiers in a wretched barracks in the provinces, an amorous youth strumming on a balalaika as girls stand listening, a group of bewildered peasants gathered around a pond impotently watching a drowning man, an old peasant woman cutting cubes of sugar on a hot summer day, the bustling Chip Market in Moscow, a church choir, a lieutenant charging across a battlefield, amazed peasants watching a golden carriage roll through their poor village, slim-waisted dandies on the streets of St. Petersburg, the mischievous occupations of students, a young man returning from a play by Schiller in St. Petersburg, and the glib heroes of society tales, servile civil servants during inspection, shrieking young girls meeting for the first time since leaving school, an avid huntsman pursuing a frightened rabbit, scientists and historians pursuing their hypotheses, and so on and on. It would seem that none of these things has anything to do with Gogol's fanciful tale of Čičikov's adventures. But it is important that these are all part of the Russia that Gogol wanted to portray in his poem, his prose epic. As he said: "In this novel I want to show, at least from one side, all of Russia". And elsewhere: "All of Russia will appear in it". "All Russia will be reflected in it". By using the Homeric similes Gogol was able to present a far broader picture of Russia. In these similes brief life is breathed into dozens of new characters and scenes.

It is true that there are many digressions in ***Dead Souls*** which are not in similes. We may look at the Homeric simile as one important variation in the technique of digression. Certainly it would have been difficult for Gogol to have intercalated over forty more digressions with no transition, and it is this point of transition which the similes provide. The simile is at least partially pertinent to the subject matter at hand; it begins as a more or less logical explanation or illustration of something, and only then does it pursue other ends. Its intrusion into the narrative is gradual, at times almost imperceptible; this contrasts to the knife-like incisiveness of the usual straightforward authorial digression.

Briefly summarizing, the Homeric similes in ***Dead Souls*** have the following basic functions (apart from that of nearly every simile—as an illustration or clarification). They serve: (1) as a humor device, (2) as a value judgment, (3) to broaden the scope of the material presented, allowing a more detailed and variegated picture of Russia, (4) to give the reader's attention a rest after which it can be refocused with new strength, (5) to vary and enliven the technique of digression. As I will show below some of the Homeric similes also serve as "lyric relief".

Now I wish to proceed . . . to an examination of particular similes, their external characteristics, the question of the inappositeness of details given in digressions, and

Gogol's use of "interlocking detail", that is of related images in widely separated similes.

Frequently (in some twenty cases) the Homeric simile in **Dead Souls** is complicated by other shorter similes, by metaphor, or by hyperbole within the original long simile. For example: . . . .

> "Beat him up!" Nozdrev kept yelling, all ablaze and sweating, straining forward with his cherrywood chibouk, as though he were storming an impregnable fortress. "Beat him up!" He kept yelling in the same sort of voice that some desperate lieutenant, whose harebrained bravery has already gained such a reputation that a specific order is issued to hold him back by his arms during the heat of battle, uses to yell "Forward, lads!" to his platoon during a great assault. But the lieutenant has already felt the martial fervor, everything has begun going 'round and 'round in his head: Suvorov, that great general, soars in a vision before him; the lieutenant strains forward to perform a great deed. "Forward, lads!" he yells, dashing ahead, without reflecting that he is jeopardizing the plan of attack already decided upon, that countless gun muzzles are thrust out of the embrasures of the fortress, the impregnable walls of which reach up beyond the clouds, that his impotent platoon will be blown up into the air like so much swan's-down, and that the bullet with his name on it is already whizzing through the air, just about to shut off his vociferous throat. But if Nozdrev was portraying in his person the lieutenant attacking the fortress, desperate and at a loss, the fortress he was storming did not in any way resemble an impregnable one. On the contrary, the fortress was experiencing such fright that its heart was in its very heels.

The simile gives way to hyperbole, then a short simile ("like so much swan's-down") is injected; then the original comparison is picked up again—and finally it is transformed into a metaphor. A series of metamorphoses such as this is typical for Gogol. This example also illustrates a device which Čiževskij calls "realizing" a simile. It could also be called "metaphorizing" a simile. Initially the relationship between two things is pointed out by "like" or "as"; then, in an unexpected transformation, the two things are no longer simply *like* each other; they are not presented in juxtaposition—instead the vehicle is used in place of the tenor. What began as a simile ends as a metaphor. Nozdrev is first compared to a fortress; but then the "pointing word" is omitted; Nozdrev becomes in fact a lieutenant, and Čičikov a fortress. The humor which often results from this tropological trickery is apparent. Gogol used the device as early as **"Ivan Fedorovič Špon'ka"**, but never very frequently, and only seven times in **Dead Souls,** always in Homeric similes. Perhaps the most memorable example in **Dead Souls** is the comparison of Korobočka's carriage to a watermelon:. . . .

> It resembled neither a tarantass, nor a calash, nor a light covered carriage, but rather a round-cheeked, bulging watermelon placed on wheels. The cheeks of this watermelon—i.e., its small doors—which still bore traces of yellow paint,

closed but poorly, owing to the sad state of the handles and catches, which were haphazardly tied together with bits of rope. The watermelon was filled to bursting with calico pillows shaped like tobacco pouches, like bolsters, or simply like pillows; it was stuffed with bags of bread loaves (plain and braided), rusks, biscuits, and pretzels of biscuit dough. There was even a chicken pie, and another of salted beef, both peeping coyly out of one of the bags.

This begins as would any simile ("resembled . . . a round-cheeked, bulging watermelon"). Then, when the simile is metaphorized, Gogol has to explain the first part ("The cheeks . . . i.e., its small doors); but then what was simply a carriage like a watermelon, becomes in fact a watermelon ("The watermelon was filled . . . "), which is not only itself a kind of food, but which is filled with other kinds of food. And then: "Dogs began barking, and the *gates, gaping open* at last, *swallowed,* though with difficulty, this cumbersome conveyance". Thus the "watermelon" is consumed. It is interesting that Herzen uses virtually the same simile in *Who is Guilty,* borrowing even the device of realization.

Gogol exploits the device of the developed simile in another way which Homer did not; he often includes a number of points at which the tenor and vehicle can be compared. Referring to the *Iliad* and the *Odyssey,* Cedric Whitman says the epic simile is "like a prismatic inverted pyramid" which rises "upon its one point of contact with the action". And in his discussion of the Homeric simile C. M. Bowra concludes:

> Their aim is not to provide a series of points in which one thing can be compared to another, but to stress a single common characteristic. This done, the poet follows his fancy and develops the picture without much care for his reason for using it.

However, the copious detail given in the vehicle of many of Gogol's developed similes is not superfluous. The fact that there is digression does not always mean that the tenor has been abandoned and forgotten entirely, either by the author or the attentive reader. The *tertium comparationis* may be broader than is immediately apparent. For example, in the comparison of frock-coats to flies the basic *tertium comparationis* is the black color in motion. Then, as the narrator expatiates, we are placed in what seems to be a completely unrelated setting. But further on in the vehicle there are new grounds for comparison—and the comparison creeps in almost unnoticed: "They have flown in not at all in order to eat but merely to show themselves, to promenade to and fro over the mound of sugar . . . " As M. G. Kačurin recently pointed out, this is characteristic not so much of flies as of dandies at a ball. But he does not, as one should, extend the observation to still other parts of the comparison. For example:

> They have flown in . . . to rub either their hind- or their forelegs against each other, or scratch with them under their gossamer wings or, having stretched out their forelegs, to rub them over their heads, and then once more to turn around

and fly away, and once more come flying back with new harassing squadrons.

Isn't there a parallel here with the dandies clicking their heels, rubbing their hands together, touching their foppishly-combed hair to keep it in place, brushing pieces of fluff from their black frock-coats, flipping the tails of the coats up in the air, hopping around nimbly to please their superiors and the ladies, rushing in and out of the main ballroom? Note also that the brightness of the ladies' dresses is comparable to the whiteness of the gleaming sugar:. . . .

Then too women are often referred to metaphorically as "sugar". For example, later in the novel the little blonde is called a "sweet little piece" (*lakomyj kusoček*), the sugar cubes are called *lakomye kuski.* The similarity of the men to the flies and women to the sugar is really very close. So it is manifest that, in this case at least, the details in the "digressive" part of the simile are more pertinent than it would seem at first glance. There is much less irrelevancy than Gogol's critics (from Masal'skij to Mandel'štam) claimed.

Now it must be asked if this is true of all of Gogol's developed similes. A few more examples will be instructive. The comparison of Pljuškin's eyes to mice is one case:. . . .

> The fire in his little eyes had not died out and they darted about under his high, bushy eyebrows very much as mice do when, thrusting out of their dark holes their sharp little snouts, their ears perked and their whiskers twitching, they are spying out whether the cat is lurking about in ambush somewhere or whether some mischievous boy is about, and sniff the very air with suspicion.

Again the details are all carefully selected and are related to other details in the novel. In fact Pljuškin *is* like a mouse who has stuck his head *iz temnyx nor* ("out of dark holes"), that is, from his dark, dank, death-infested house. The mice in the simile have *ostren'kie mordy* ("sharp snouts"). This is much like Pljuškin who is described in this way: *odin podborodok tol'ko vystupal očen' daleko vpered* ("just his chin jutted very far forward"). The mice "sniff the air suspiciously" which is precisely what the cautious Pljuškin is doing at this point. The mice fear a cat; Pljuškin fears Čičikov. What does Čičikov have in common with a cat? The answer is in the final chapter where Gogol applies this simile to Čičikov: . . . "And there the future beginner of a dynasty, like a cautious cat, shifting one eye only to the side to see whether the master is looking from somewhere, hurriedly grabs everything that is closest to him . . . ". Thus the sharp-nosed mouse, Pljuškin, is suspicious of the cat, Čičikov, who grabs everything he can. (pp. 77-86)

A further example is the comparison of the confused townspeople to the sleeping schoolboy who has been the subject of a practical joke by his comrades. . . .

> The town was positively stirred up; everything was in a ferment—and if there were but one body that could make out anything! The ladies were so successful in beclouding the eyes of everybody that all, and especially the officials and

clerks, were left stunned for some time. During the first moment their state was like that of a schoolboy up whose nose, while he's asleep, his mates, who have risen before him, have thrust a *hussar,* a small twist of paper filled with snuff. Having in his half-sleep drawn in all that snuff with all the heartiness of a sleeper, he awakens, jumps up, stares about him like a fool, his eyes popping in all directions, and can't grasp where he is or what has happened to him, and only later does he make out the walls lit by the indirect rays of the rising sun, the laughter of his mates, who have hidden themselves in corners, and the arrival of morning as it peeps in through a window, to the accompaniment of the awakened forest, resounding with thousands of bird voices, and a glimpse of a shining river, disappearing here and there in glittering eddies between slender reeds and with clusters of naked urchins everywhere, egging on one another to dive in—and only after he has taken all this in does the victim become aware that there's a hussar stuck up his nose.

. . . [The sections of the simile dealing with the schoolboys] are paralleled in the description of the inhabitants of N. which follows the simile:. . . .

> Each one stopped like a ram with his eyes bulging. The dead souls . . . got mixed up in their minds . . . and later . . . they seemed to begin to distinguish one from the other . . . how can one buy dead souls. Where would such a fool be dug up?

But what is particularly important is that the *hussar* is not chosen at random. If we look back one chapter, we find that when Čičikov first catches sight of the young blonde daughter of the Governor he is greatly agitated, his eyes go dim as everything seems to be covered with fog, but:. . . . He felt himself something completely like a young man, almost a hussar. Thus an important link in the comparison of the townspeople and the schoolboy is found in an earlier passage" the *gusar* (hussar) is Čičikov himself. Recall that Čičikov's name itself is from *čixat'* (to sneeze); he is the *gusar* who makes the townspeople-schoolboy sneeze. Again every detail, each word is chosen with great care. The novel is a maze of these interrelated details and repetitions.

As we have seen already, Nozdrev's chibouk-waving attack on Čičikov is likened to an impetuous lieutenant's dash towards a fortress. In this simile we find this detail:

> "Beat him up!" He kept yelling in the same sort of voice that some desperate lieutenant, whose harebrained bravery has already gained such a reputation that a specific order is issued to hold him back by the arms during the heat of battle, uses to yell "Forward, lads!" to his platoon during a great assault.

Reading closely we see that the parallel between the lieutenant and Nozdrev is *not only* in the fact that they are both attacking and shouting, but also in that those around know very well that they are highly excitable, irresponsible, and unreliable. Unless one reads carefully, keeping

Nozdrev's character in mind, this extension of the basic *tertium comparationis* may be lost.

When Sobakevič and Čičikov are arguing about the value of dead serfs, Sobakevič makes a strong point, but:. . . .

> The last words he uttered with his face already turned to the portraits of Bagration and Kolokotronis, as usually happens during a conversation when one of the speakers will suddenly, for some unknown reason, turn not to the person to whom his words are directed, but to some third person who chances to come in, even a total stranger, from whom he knows he will receive neither an answer nor an opinion, nor any confirmation, but upon whom, nevertheless, he will fix his gaze as though he were calling him in as a mediator; and, somewhat confused during the first minute, the stranger does not know whether he should make any answer in a matter which he has heard nothing of, or simply to stand there a while, as an appropriate observance of the civilities, and only then take his leave.

In this instance, in spite of the length of the comparison, a close parallel extends almost from beginning to end. Of course, the taciturn Sobakevič "knows he will receive neither an answer nor an opinion, nor any confirmation", but still he fixes his determined eyes on the portraits. Also interesting is the fact that, instead of turning to living people, Sobakevič turns to *inanimate* people (the portraits). This is entirely appropriate, because at the moment he is arguing about *dead souls,* not living people as he apparently believes.

Perhaps the best example of a comparison which appears to be filled with pointless details (because the tenor is forgotten by the reader before he finishes reading the vehicle), but which actually remains a close parallel throughout, is the remarkable comparison of the two wildly gossiping women to learned historians and other sober scholars (Chapter Nine). The gossips as well as historians begin with timid questions and moderate suppositions; but they are emboldened and soon hints of answers are transformed into incontrovertible facts; and in the end the conclusions are proclaimed *ex cathedra* and "the newly discovered truth is sent travelling all over the world, gathering followers and disciples". This is what happens in **Dead Souls;** the truths (so-called) discovered by the ladies are disseminated through the town, but simultaneously various alternative conjectures about Čičikov's affairs are made, and various parties form. The historians in the simile wonder, "Are we sure that such a people does not mean quite another people?" And the townspeople imagine that Čičikov is someone else—Napoleon, a counterfeiter and brigand, or a government inspector.

In once case there is a variant kind of parallelism in a digressive simile. Here the parallel is antithetical. This serves to emphasize the insipidity of Čičikov's dreams. He returns to the town after making his purchases and:. . . .

> At rare intervals there would come floating to Čičikov's ears such exclamations, apparently feminine, as "You lie, you drunk, I never let him take no such liberties as that with me!" or: "Don't you be fighting, you ignoramus, but

come along to the station house and I'll show what's what!" In brief, such words as will suddenly scald, like so much boiling water, some youth of twenty as, lost in reveries, he is on his way home from the theater, his head filled with visions of a Spanish street, night, a wondrous feminine image with a guitar and ringlets. What doesn't he have in that head of his and what dreams do not come to him? He is soaring in the clouds, and he may just have dropped in on Schiller for a chat, when suddenly, like thunder, the fatal words peal out over his head, and he perceives that he has come back to earth once more, and not only to earth, but actually to Hay Square, and right by a pot-house, at that. . . .

Although Čičikov and the youth are in similar euphoric states, the euphoria is caused by dissimilar circumstances. The young man has been to the theater, he has been Schiller's guest; Čičikov has just returned from Pljuškin's estate, he has been the guest of a miser who is surrounded by death and decay. The youth has in his mind visions of a sultry Spanish night, *čudnyj ženskij obraz s giraroj i čudnymi kudrjami.* Contrasting to this is the kind of street and night Čičikov has before him as he dreams about his riches:

> The striped toll-gate had taken on some indeterminate hue; the mustachios of the soldier on sentry duty seemed to be up on his forehead and considerably above his eyes, and as for his nose, why, he seemed to have none at all.

And Čičikov, instead of a wondrous feminine image, is dreaming about his dead souls; and, as we learn elsewhere in the novel, when he reaches points where he seems to have success in his hands he begins to think it wouldn't be a bad idea to have a plump *babenka* who could provide him with descendants. These contrasts between Čičikov and the youth increase both the humor and the pathos of the simile, a simile which is itself based on the sad contrast between the youth's poetic dreams and the vulgar life which "has begun strutting its stuff before him in its workaday fashion". So in this instance Gogol reverses his usual practice and chooses details which establish an antithetical parallel.

These examples show how seemingly inapposite detail may actually be important and germane to a given simile. Gogol's critics did not recognize this fact. Baffled by the labyrinth of detail, they closed their eyes and were unwilling or unable to perceive and interpret the double applications of many passages, the subtle mastery with which motifs are interwoven and interconnected.

Rapidly shifting moods and tones are found in many of Gogol's works. The sometimes weird transitions from comedy to pathos that occur in early works such as **"The Fair at Soročincy"**, **"The Tale of Two Ivans"**, and **"Notes of a Madman"** also occur in **Dead Souls.** Thus, in several of the Homeric similes Gogol suddenly and unexpectedly proceeds from coarse or humorous images to lyric images presented in a poetic style. In these cases the elaborate detail of the vehicle is not involved in the basic *tertium comparationis.* As the author digresses the tenor of the simile is forgotten. (pp. 87-91)

In other similes Gogol digresses, interpolating brief scenes from Russian life, life of a different kind than that lived by the Pljuškins or Sobakevičes. These lyric digressions loom up in the most unlikely places; they extend from the most insultingly grotesque of similes. For example:. . . .

> As Čičikov drove up to the front entrance he noticed two faces that had peered almost simultaneously through the window—one feminine in a house-cap, and elongated like a cucumber, and a masculine one, round, broad, like those Moldavian pumpkins called *gorliankas* or calabashes, out of which they make, in Russia, balalaikas, two-stringed light balalaikas, the pride and joy of some frolicsome, twenty-year-old country lad, a fellow who knows how to wink and is a dandy, and who not only winks at but whistles after the snowy-breasted and snowy-necked maidens who gather around to listen to his soft-stringed strumming. Having peered out, both faces hid at the same moment.

Thus Gogol suddenly transforms a fat face which looks like a Moldavian pumpkin into a lyrical scene.. . . . [The] change in vocabulary and rhythm clearly indicates the poetic nature of the digression: *krasa, na Rusi, belo-grudye i belošejnye devicy, tixostrunnoe tren'kan'e.* There are several parallelisms and repetitions: *migača i ščegolja; i podmigivajuščego, i posvistyvajuščego; belogrudyx i belošejnyx; balalajki, dvuxstrunnye, legkie balalajki.* These, including the polysyndeton, tend to make the passage more rhythmical and help create the lyric tone. We are almost in the world of folk song with its parallelisms and *belogrudye devicy.*

Why should this simile digress just at this point in this lyric manner? Examination of earlier variants and Gogol's own comments helps answer the question. This is how the passage appears in two of the latest variants:. . . .

> He noted two faces that peered out through the window simultaneously: one feminine in a house-cap, narrow and long like a cucumber, the other masculine, round and broad, rather reddish, like good Moldavian pumpkins. Having peered out, they immediately disappeared.

This shows that the digressive and lyric part of the simile was added at a later stage in the writing of the novel. I would suggest that Gogol's purpose in interpolating the digression later was to relieve momentarily the rather depressing picture for his Russian readers. As evidenced by Gogol's letters and by polemical comments within the novel itself, he knew that many would be critical of *Dead Souls,* even more violently than they had been critical of *The Inspector-General,* that it would be called dirty, insulting, and grotesque—and with some reason. In *Selected Passages* [see excerpt dated 1843] Gogol wrote: "If anyone had seen those monsters which came out from under my pen in the beginning, for me alone, they would have shuddered". Gogol then notes that when he read the early draft to Puškin, the poet surprised him by remarking, "God, how sad our Russia is!" Whether or not this story is entirely true is not important. What is important is Gogol's avowal that in subsequent stages of his work on *Dead Souls* he took steps to lessen the darkness:

Here I saw what a matter taken from the soul means, what spiritual truth in general is—and in what terrifying strength darkness and the frightening *absence of light* can be presented to man. From that time I began to think only about how to lighten that painful impression which *Dead Souls* could produce. (Gogol's emphasis.)

The lyrical interpolations in several of the Homeric similes may be part of Gogol's effort to throw some light into the dark world of *Dead Souls* (thus the lyric expansion of the face-pumpkin simile). A tragedian often uses comic relief; in his comedy Gogol uses "lyrical relief". Lyrical passages are especially numerous in the last five chapters of the novel—both in the similes and in authorial digressions. This culminates in the famous comparison of Russia to a speeding troika. In this Homeric simile, as in several others, we rise momentarily above the sunless world of dead souls. (pp. 92-4)

> *Carl R. Proffer, "The Homeric Simile in 'Dead Souls'," in his* The Simile and Gogol's "Dead Souls", *Mouton, 1967, pp. 67-94.*

Victor Erlich   (essay date 1969)

[*Erlich is a Russian émigré educator and critic who has written extensively on Russian literature. In the following excerpt, he demonstrates how the idiosyncratic unreality of plot, characterization, and style in* Dead Souls *reveals Gogol's theme and purpose.*]

[Congruence between texture and structure] is conspicuously absent from Gogol's middle and late works. What we confront here, it seems to me, is not so much a sustained illusion of reality as an intermittent illusion of realism induced by the accumulation of homely trivia, and by that lack of squeamishness in the choice of language and subject which was part of Realism's challenge to the early nineteenth-century literary and social taboos. Yet when matter as well as manner are properly attended to, it becomes clear that this "realistic" detail serves here not as the subsoil of an autonomous yet reality-like world, but as a factor of contrapuntal tension between the ultra-realistic mode of presentation and a narrative framework which brazenly disclaims credibility.

This is clearly the case with **"The Nose,"** a story whose effect . . . rests on a grotesque discrepancy between the matter-of-fact narrative tone and an utterly incredible central event. **"The Nose,"** which calls into question the basic realistic criterion of "plausibility," admittedly is an extreme case. In such "post-Romantic" works of Gogol's as **"Two Ivans,"** *The Inspector General,* and *Dead Souls,* credibility is not altogether eliminated, but it is strained to the breaking point. As Dmitry Cizevsky persuasively argued [in his "The Unknown Gogol," *Slavonic and East European Review* 30 (1952)], Gogol's most "realistic" plots are remarkably farfetched. The tedium and inanity of the Ukrainian backwater epitomized by the preposterous quarrel between the Ivans was all too real. But it was *not* customary for brown pigs to break into county court buildings and steal complaints lodged against their owners. By the same token, the stupidity and venality of provincial officialdom satirized in Gogol's greatest comedy were altogether plausible themes. Yet it does not necessarily follow that silly chatterboxes such as Bobchinskij and Dobchinskij were likely to jump to the conclusion that a young man who did not pay his hotel bill and refused to move out could be no one else but the Inspector General. Even if one pays parochial obtuseness its full due, one may have trouble imagining a tightwad old landlady such as Korobochka in *Dead Souls* haggling in all seriousness about the market prices of dead serfs. Nor was it usual for small-town gossips to proclaim a shoddy character whose whereabouts was shrouded in mystery no less a figure than Napoleon who had just escaped from his internment on the isle of St. Helena. (This bizarre notion of Chichikov's real identity makes rapid headway among the befuddled inhabitants of the town of N.) More centrally, Chichikov's bizarre financial scheme—that of buying up serfs who have died since the last population census at appropriately low prices—is neither plausible nor typical. It is a morbidly extravagant parody of actual frauds committed in the Russia of Nicholas I, rather than a reliable example. And need I insist on the ambiguity of that title, *Dead Souls,* which means both "dead serfs" and "dead souls"? Need I point out that Chichikov's traffic in corpses is symbolic, as it epitomizes the soulless vulgarity, the moral deadness of Gogol's uncanny world?

Korobochka and Chichikov.

Is it not true, a champion of Gogol's "realism" may remonstrate at this point, that the plot of *Dead Souls* was based on an actual happening? So it seems. Yet this would argue for a *sui generis* authenticity of the plot rather than for its typicality. Friedrich Engels' dictum that realistic literature portrays "typical characters under typical circumstances," mercilessly abused though it has been by Soviet literary hacks, does have some validity. "Realism" is geared not to what somehow managed to happen, but to what was likely to happen. Its realm is the plausible, the recurrent, the representative, rather than the barely conceivable, the freakish anecdote, the stranger-than-fiction actuality.

In his . . . 1842 postscript to *The Inspector General,* "After the Play," one of the many displeased spectators, an "experienced" official, loudly berates the author: "What does he know? He doesn't know a damn thing! That is not the way bribes are taken! The "expert" clearly refers to that brilliantly hilarious sequence in Act IV where quivering officials pop into the alleged Inspector's room one by one, engaging Khlestakov in an utterly inane conversation that leads to a clumsily timid offer of a "loan," or, as Khlestakov increasingly catches on, to his own abrupt request for such "assistance." Technically, the irate bureaucrat has a point. Moreover, it is one which, mutatis mutandis, is applicable to many other Gogolian plots or incidents. With equal justice, and equal irrelevance, a literal-minded reader of *Dead Souls* could argue, "That is not the way frauds were committed." Clearly, verisimilitude was not Gogol's forte, nor was it, most of the time, his avowed goal. "I never had the desire to reflect reality as it is around us," he declared in a moment of candor.

This relative lack of concern with the way things actually happen, this whimsical or cavalier attitude toward reality, permeates much of Gogol's world. In his idiosyncratic universe where the actual is incessantly intruded upon, distorted and magnified by a disheveled imagination, there are few consistent "realists." Not only exuberant liars such as Khlestakov and Nozdryov, but also, as Nabokov shrewdly notes [see excerpt dated 1944], stolid, earthbound characters like Sobakevich, are susceptible to wacky flights of fancy. In a memorable scene in which Sobakevich is haggling with Chichikov over the prices of his dead serfs, a rather important ontological distinction becomes obliterated as Sobakevich waxes lyrical over the late Mikheev, the carriage-maker. To be sure, Sobakevich is a man who drives a hard bargain, and this strenuous boosting of nonexistent wares can be construed in part as a morbid travesty of his tightfistedness. Yet somewhere along the line his enthusiasm seems to acquire a disinterested, nearly poetic quality. "Why, of course, they are dead," he admits reluctantly when Chichikov confronts him with the reality. "Moreover, it may also be said, what good are the people of today that are numbered among the living? What sort of people are *they?* They're so many flies—not people." As Chichikov timidly observes that "the others" are "but a dream," Sobakevich replies with genuine indignation, "Well, no, they're no dream! You'll never find such men as Mikheev was. I'd like to know what other place you'd find such a dream in! It may not be altogether facetious to echo Cizevsky's observation that the only reality-oriented person among Gogolian protagonists is Welfare Commissioner A. F. Zemljanika in **The Inspector General,** who, when confronted with a somewhat surrealistic description of himself in Khlestakov's notorious letter to his friend, addresses a plaintive query to the audience: "Who has ever seen a pig in a skullcap?"

The same principle of exuberant tampering with the actual through exaggeration and intensification that shapes Gogol's later plots is discernible at the level of character-drawing. A typical Gogol protagonist is an embodiment of a single trait, proclivity, or foible generalized or extended throughout the personality, pushed to the limit of utter rigidity or absurdity. Stolid Sobakevich; insipid Manilov; the seedy martyr of greed, Pljushkin; the brazen bully and braggart, Nozdrjov; the foppish nincompoop Khlestakov; and last, that faceless "acquirer," that slick peddler of non-existent goods, Chichikov—all these are types, or "humors," to use Ben Jonson's term, "psychic automatons," role-players in a masterfully contrived puppet show rather than full-fledged human beings. Frozen in their characteristic poses, incapable of movement, development, or growth, they are vivid rather than alive; their faces Goya-like masks.

Although in some of Gogol's earlier works man's pathetic inadequacy was often conveyed by an orgy of synecdoches, by reducing a man to his whiskers or moustache, in **Dead Souls** the characters's subhumanity is often driven home through the medium of an animal simile. Sobakevich is likened to a bear, Pljushkin to a spider. In fact, "is likened" is an understatement; it would be more accurate to say that Sobakevich becomes a bear. The fluidity of the existential boundaries is not confined to Gogol's early openly Romantic works. If in his goblin tales, metamorphosis is negotiated through black magic, in **Dead Souls** it is the novel's magnificently exuberant, disheveled style that serves as an agency of transformation, however short-lived. Time and again, the similes and metaphors are "realized," projected into the plot. Figures of speech taken literally become events. "After beginning a simile," said Cizevsky [in his "Gogol: Artist and Thinker"; see Gibian's edition of *Dead Souls* in Further Reading], "Gogol seems to forget about it [or rather about it being a mere figure of speech] and a strange process takes place: A vendor of hot mead who was likened to a samovar, turns into a samovar; Chichikov, into a fortress and Pëtr Petrovich Petukh, into a watermelon." Chichikov's likeness to a fortress appears at the time he is being threatened by Nozdrëv and his servants. Promptly "fortress" becomes the subject of a sentence: "The fortress was experiencing such fright that its heart was in its very heels." A similar shift occurs in the description of Korobochka's carriage entering the town of N.: "It resembled neither a tarantass, nor a calash, nor a light covered carriage, but rather a round-cheeked, bulging watermelon placed on wheels. *The cheeks of this watermelon* [my italics]—i.e. its small doors—closed but poorly owing to the sad state of the handles and catches." No wonder that in this topsy-turvy world Sobakevich seems to be not so much a bear-like individual as a medium-sized bear who does his best to look like a stolid landowner.

As the boundary between the human and the animal becomes fluid, so does the distinction between the animate and the inanimate. "Every object, every chair in Sobakevich's house seemed to proclaim: 'I, too, am Sobakevich!' " The statement could be reversed. In line with the dehumanizing quality of Gogol's imagery, it might be equally proper to proclaim Sobakevich as the central object, the most strategic piece of furniture in his uncannily homogenous surroundings. Gogol's compulsion to extend the characteristics and mannerisms of the protagonist into the physical environment which he dominates is matched by the characteristically downgrading strategy of reducing him to an integral part of that environment.

With notions such as the downward similes and the "realization of the metaphor," our argument has almost imperceptibly veered from the problems of plot and characterization to those of style. This is not surprising. Imaginative literature, as a German critic has put it, is "the world transformed into language." This is doubly true of Gogol's "poem," where language is a demiurge of reality in the most literal sense imaginable, where—as I shall indicate in a moment—subordinate clauses give birth to peripheral characters and potential subplots. Thus it is singularly appropriate that in **Dead Souls** a characteristic urge to grotesquely distort the natural dimensions and the relative size of objects, persons, and events, which we have already seen operate in the realms of plot and characterization should assert itself so powerfully at the level of language through Gogol's favorite stylistic device, the hyperbole.

Gogol's addiction to this figure of speech has been commented upon by a host of astute and knowledgeable critics from the Russian Symbolists down to Dmitry Cizevsky. Andrej Belyj spoke of Gogol's hyperbole-ridden vision of life which "resolves earth into ether and dung and humanity into giants and dwarfs." Whether dithyrambic or debunking, satirical or rhetorical, his prose is always bent on overstating the actual, on magnifying it beyond recognition. In Gogol's earlier writings, the hyperbolic mode seemed of a piece with the rhapsodic drift of so many rhetorically "swollen" sequences, be they eulogies of the Dnieper or the Ukrainian night, or celebrations of Cossack supermen. The language of Gogol's later satirical or ironic works is less rapturous but no less exuberant. To convey the notion that someone's laughter was loud, Gogol or his narrator says: "like the bellowing of two bulls as they stand facing each other." Ivan Nikiforovich's trousers, we may recall, had such ample folds that, "if they were blown out, you could put the whole courtyard with the barns and the outhouses into them." In **Dead Souls** the hyperbolic impulse asserts itself time and again. Pljushkin shaves so rarely that "his chin and jaws resembled a wire-bristled currycomb." In the scene in which Chichikov and Manilov visit the administrative offices of the town of N., the cumulative effect of the scratching of copying clerks' pens is described thus: "the sound thereof was as if several carts loaded with brushweed were being driven through a forest piled with dead leaves a yard deep." Finally, when Chichikov enters the Governor's Ball, the provincial fool who suddenly takes over the narration starts raving about the ineffable refinement attained by the attire of the ladies: "There was no end of tastefulness about their attire: the muslins, satins and tulles were of such fashionable pastel shades that one could not even give their names, to such a degree has the refinement of taste attained!" This latter passage is a good example of a hyperbole which one might call "negative." The adjective fits both the formal structure of this mode of overstatement—the protestation of one's inability to do justice to the subject—and, more importantly, its essentially ironic or parodistic function. For the import of the "negative hyperbole" is to diminish rather than to magnify; more specifically, to point up the pathetic inadequacy of the point of view, the embarrassing smallness of the observer. This was already the case in **"Two Ivans"** where the parochial narrator raves about things that clearly are not worth raving about and where the misplaced hyperbole, instead of lifting the subject, serves only to reveal its essential triviality.

Ironic incongruity of this kind is an essential part of the texture of **Dead Souls.** So is the larger-scale contrast between the stagnant, petrified world of the "poem" and its magnificently disheveled, irrepressible style. It is not necessary to labor this point since it was brilliantly made and amply documented by Nabokov. His essay is at its whimsical best in showing how digressive paragraphs injected into the narrative with supreme lack of concern for relevance or coherence beget such compellingly vivid "fleeting characters" as a lieutenant trying on his shiny new jackboots while Chichikov is asleep, the forgotten people of the town of N. re-emerging amid the turmoil of the Chichikov affair, or Sobakevich's dead serfs brought to life twice, first by their owner's extravagant eulogy, then by Chichikov's uncharacteristically lyrical musings. Nabokov is singularly effective in describing and exhibiting Gogol's "life-generating" syntax so fully exemplified by the remarkable account of Chichikov's first impressions of the Sobakevich household where a round face glimpsed by a traveler begets a Moldavian pumpkin which, in turn, gives birth to a balalaika, only to conjure up the vivid image of a nimble balalaika player and the "wide bosomed" country lasses who constitute his eager audience. In this dizzyingly centrifugal orgy of subordinate clauses, language is on a rampage.

Passages such as this have been called "Homeric." It is not necessary to share Konstantin Aksakov's rhapsodic estimate of **Dead Souls** in order to grant this parallel some validity. For in Homer too, most notably in *The Iliad,* a comparison often acquires a momentum of its own. After a battlefield has been likened to a sea-tossed ship, the latter realm becomes for a number of lines the sole focus of the poet's attention, displacing temporarily the scene or event which occasioned the analogy. One might go one step further. It is at least arguable that Gogol's descriptive "digressions" perform a function not altogether dissimilar from that of the extended similes in *The Iliad.* In both works, these interpolations seem to offer a respite from the stringency or the oppressiveness of the agon. In Homer, a glimpse of the life beyond seems to provide a wider prospective on the grim proceedings, a salutary reminder that, whatever happens on the crowded battlefield, life will go on. A somewhat similar mechanism may well be at work in **Dead Souls,** where the foreground is stifling rather than tragic, where the stage is filled not by the clangor

of armies, but by seedy bric-a-brac, or, in Gogol's own words, by "the slimy morass of minutiae that has bogged down our lives." It is as if Gogol's erratic, freewheeling imagination, unwilling or unable to stay put within the limits of the appalling world it has conjured up, kept overflowing these boundaries, teasing out shadowy appearances and thus calling into question the seriousness, indeed the reality of Chichikov's ghastly enterprise.

The centrifugal impulse in **Dead Souls** partakes of the duality built into the structure of the novel. Thus one might distinguish between two types of digressions—the lateral darts and the upward flights. The passages mentioned or alluded to thus far clearly belong in the former category. The relief offered by these picturesque detours rests entirely on their bracing irrelevance, their utter fortuitousness and, to be sure, on the verbal dynamism which calls them into existence. No spiritual uplift, no substantive transcendence can be derived from the spectacle of a smug lieutenant in love with his boots or of the fatuous village dandy. These vignettes are part and parcel of the novel's moral universe. Their protagonists dwell, however precariously or fleetingly, on the same plane of grossness and triviality that harbors the Korobochkas and the Sobakeviches.

This emphatically is not the case with the rhetorical or lyrical digressions which both in their tone and their overall thrust point far beyond the hermetic staleness of Pljushkin's overgrown garden, toward another world, a higher reality. Once again we are presented with a stylistic and tonal polarity, an alternation of pathos and bathos, of low-grade comedy and high-pitched rhetoric.

The most famous and most widely quoted example of the latter is, of course, the troika passage:

> And art not thou, my Russia, soaring along even like a spirited, never-to-be-outdistanced troika? The road actually smokes under thee, the bridges thunder, everything falls back and is left behind thee! The witness of thy passing comes to a dead stop, dumbfounded by this God's wonder! Is it not a streak of lightning cast down from heaven? What signifies this onrush that inspires terror? And what unknown power is contained in these steeds whose like is not known in this world? Ah, these steeds, these steeds, what steeds they are! Are there whirlwinds perched upon your manes? Is there a sensitive ear, alert as the flame, in your every fibre? Ye have caught the familiar song coming to you from above and all as one, and all at the same instant, ye have strained your brazen chests and, almost without touching earth with your hoofs, ye have become all transformed into straight lines cleaving the air, and the troika tears along, all-inspired by God! . . . Whither art thou soaring away to, then, Russia? Give me thy answer. But Russia gives none. With a wondrous ringing does the jingle bell trill; the air, rent to shreds, thunders and turns to wind; all things on earth fly past and, eyeing it askance all the other peoples and nations stand aside and give it the right of way.

"Beautiful as this final crescendo sounds," comments Nabokov, "from the stylistic point of view it is merely a conjuror's patter enabling an object to disappear, the particular object being Chichikov." This structural observation is a welcome antidote to the portentously ideological interpretations of the thunderous finale of Part One, a lyrical paean rather than a coherent credo. This is not to say, however, that the frenzied flight of patriotic rhetoric was merely a musical accompaniment to Chichikov's abrupt disappearance. It was also a grandiloquent expression of Gogol's emotional nationalism, exacerbated, no doubt, by his mounting uneasiness over having become a virtual expatriate.

Yet what gave the troika passage so wide a cultural resonance was the fact that Gogol's headlong eloquence happened to articulate the growing preoccupation with the destiny and essence of Russia which was to characterize Russian intellectual life in the 1840s. More importantly, it fell to Gogol's imagery to embody and anticipate the themes that were to reverberate through a near century of Russian cultural history, the notions of Russia's "manifest destiny"—a glorious future vouchsafed by her boundless expanse—of her distinctive mission, of her turbulent, unfathomable essence.

Viewed within its context, the much-anthologized set-piece appears to give a resounding lie to the main body of Gogol's narrative. In this unexpected ending the subject of the novel is not merely transcended or displaced; it is emphatically denied. So glaring is the discontinuity between the bleak and trivial surfaces of Russian life as reflected or burlesqued by the novel and the awe-inspiring prophecy that an inordinately literal-minded reader might be provoked into a spurious query: "How will a Russia of petty crooks, grafters and half-morons ever astound the world? How will she manage to compel universal awe and admiration?"

A partial attempt at bridging the gap between the visible shabbiness and the yet-to-be-revealed greatness, is provided by another apostrophe to Russia, a guilt-ridden declaration of love for the distant, indeed temporarily forsaken motherland.

> Russia, Russia, I behold thee—from my alien, beautiful far-off place do I behold thee. Everything about thee is poor, scattered, bleak; thou wilt not gladden, wilt not affright my eyes with arrogant wonders of nature, crowned by arrogant wonders of art, cities with many-windowed towering palaces that have become part of the crags they are perched on, picturesque trees and ivies that have become part of the houses, situated amid the roar and eternal spray of waterfalls . . . All is exposed, desolate, and flat about thee; like specks, like dots are thy low-lying towns scattered imperceptibly over thy plains; there is nothing to entice, nothing to enchant the eye. But just what is the incomprehensible, mysterious power that draws one to thee? . . . What is there in it, in this song of thine? What is it about that song which calls one, and sobs, and clutches at one's very heart? What sounds are these that poignantly caress my soul and strive to win their way within it, and twine about my heart? Russia! What wouldst thou of me, then? What incomprehensible bond is there between us? . . . What does that unencompass-

able expanse portend? Is it not here, within thee and of thee, that there is to be born a boundless idea, when thou thyself art without mete or end? . . . Ah, what a refulgent, wondrous horizon that the world knows naught of! Russia!

In the stark contrast it urges between the dinginess of the writer's native land and the showy, spectacular beauty of his captivating exile, in its anguished insistence on the "incomprehensible bond" between Russia and her far-flung bard, the above passage is not only more revealing than the finale of Part One, but ideologically more resonant as well. As the guilt-ridden expatriate blames the glamorous seductress, Italy, for his own susceptibility to her "arrogant" charms and goes out of his way to give the abandoned motherland the benefit of every doubt by turning its very weaknesses into potential virtues, Gogol's imagery once again turns personal anguish into an archetype. The notion of the bleakness and "underdevelopment" of rural Russia as a sign of grace, a testimony to her moral superiority vis-à-vis the proud West, an outward sign of Christian humility, was to become by the middle of the nineteenth century an important tenet of the Slavophile faith. Fëdor Tjutchev, one of the finest Russian poets of the era, whose political verse shows a distinct affinity for the Russian brand of romantic nationalism, was to echo Gogol's sentiment: "The proud foreigner's gaze will neither comprehend nor discern what . . . shines through your [Russia's] humble beauty."

Once again the reverberations of Gogol's eloquence have led us beyond its immediate framework. For within it the conflict between Russia as actuality and Russia as dream remains unbridged, indeed unbridgeable. Even if physical shabbiness could be parlayed into Christian virtue, the moral tawdriness of the Chichikovs and the Sobakeviches—as the failure of Part Two of **Dead Souls** was to show—would remain unredeemed. Nor should this surprise a close reader of Gogol. The yawning chasm between reality and vision had been a major theme ever since **"Hanz Kuechelgarten."** Within the Gogolian scheme of things the tangible, the given is nauseating and oppressive. Conversely, anything that is worthy of admiration belongs perforce to the realm of the mythical, the imagined or the fervently wished for. To speak, with Cizevsky, of romantic utopianism is almost to understate the matter. For all its apparent discontinuity with the present, a utopian image of the future is presumably an extrapolation, however bold and extravagant, from incipient realities, from dimly perceptible trends. Gogol's prophecy is a spectacular escape from his sense of the human predicament, a panicky flight out of this world, so that, to quote Poprishchin's desperate plea, "nothing is seen of it—nothing."

The digressions, especially those of the lofty variety, are an integral part of the overall pattern of **Dead Souls,** a strategic dimension of its elusive genre. Gogol chose to label this, his only full-length novel, a "poem." He seems to have meant by it a "small-scale epic," something like Fielding's definition of the novel as a "comic epic poem in prose." Yet to at least one reader this subtitle suggests the unwieldy image of a mock-epic blown intermittently by the gales of what Vasilij Rozanov strikingly called "upward-bound and disembodied lyricism" into the interstellar spaces of romantic myth-making. Thus, the tortuous movement of Gogol's "poem" reenacts on a larger scale than any of his previous works the fundamental split in his world view as it shuttles precariously between savage satire and eulogy, between close-range nausea and long-range euphoria.

It is at least arguable that Gogol was hinting at some such duality in his much-quoted, and, to my mind, widely misrepresented, aside to the reader: "But for a long while yet am I destined by some wondrous power to go hand in hand with my strange heroes and to contemplate life rushing past in all its enormity, amid *laughter perceptible* to the world and through tears that are unperceived by and unknown to it!" (my italics). The italicized part of the sentence, often reduced simply to "laughter through tears," has had an inglorious career in Gogol criticism. In line with the influential notion of Gogol as a champion of the underdog, it was often interpreted as satire tempered by compassion or pity. Now this cliché, I submit, may have some applicability to a truly humanitarian and at times downright sentimental "humorist" such as Charles Dickens, but it is profoundly misleading with reference to Gogol. Compassion, sympathy, empathy, as distinguished from mere pity, presuppose the basic humanity of those who might evoke them and thus, some opportunity on the reader's part to identify. Yet this is precisely the opportunity which Gogol's reader is steadfastly denied. His satire demeans its targets by reducing them to psychic automatons dominated by an *idée fixe,* forever distorted by a physical or moral deformity, scarcely worthy of our tears.

Rozanov offers a significantly different interpretation of Gogol's "tears." One of the first Russian men of letters to call attention to the willfully misshapen and truncated nature of Gogol's moral universe, he argued that the writer's "unperceived tears" were not so much those of pity or compassion for the victims of his laughter but of anguish, if not guilt, over the limitations of one's own vision, over one's accursed inability to see and portray goodness: "It is the great pity for man thus portrayed, an artist's grief over the law of his creation, his cry over the remarkable picture which he cannot draw in any other way, an artist's sobbing over his own soul."

Rozanov's reading clearly has something to recommend it. . . . However, I am even more strongly drawn to Cizevsky's view that in *Dead Souls* "laughter" and "tears" have two entirely different destinations, that they are addressed respectively to two disparate realms of existence between which the novel is precariously poised. "Laughter" derides, castigates, debunks the spiritual vacuity, the unbearable triviality of this world. "Tears" are addressed to the beauty and magnificence of the never-never land, of a lyrically projected millenium. To put it differently, they are tears not of compassion shed over one's unfortunate brethren, but of transcendent rapture, of anticipatory bliss. Cizevsky's observation strikes me as a plausible one; nearly every time the narrator's voice starts to quiver, the author or the persona seems to be moved to tears by his own words and daydreams rather than by any predicament of the thoroughly disreputable protagonists.

Whatever the precise destination of Gogol's tears, they remain, admittedly, the emotional undertow of the novel rather than its principal tenor. It is "laughter perceptible to the world" that dominates the scene. Perhaps it is time to inquire about the precise nature and target of this laughter and thus to revert to the problem of Gogol's later satire.

Are Belinskij's view of *Dead Souls* as primarily an exposure of the regime and Nabokov's flat denial of the novel's social relevance the only serious options open to us? I don't think so. Yet I may as well confess that I consider the latter emphasis somewhat more congenial. To a modern reader of Gogol, not encumbered by the message-mindedness of the nineteenth-century Russian critic, the sociopolitical interpretation can easily appear a piece of high-minded wishful thinking. For one thing, from what is known about Gogol's own views and intentions, it is safer, though perhaps less satisfying, to see *The Inspector General* as an attack on bad officials rather than on Tsarist bureaucracy, and *Dead Souls* as an exposure of grasping squires who took unfair advantage of the loopholes in the system rather than a challenge to the system itself. More importantly and more broadly, as Cizevsky and some others have persuasively argued, the basic tenor and the ultimate thrust of Gogol's satire, the core of his ideological concern such as it was, was not social but ethical and metaphysical. Not unlike the bulk of the greatest western satirists, Swift, Molière, and Pope, Gogol aimed his laughter at foibles or follies which cut across national boundaries, at dullness, grossness, and cupidity, rather than at any recognizable set of social conditions. Thus it is fair to assume that his reported astonishment at Pushkin's famous sigh, "Oh Lord, how sad is our Russia!" [see excerpt dated 1843], was not the self-protective, pious fraud many intelligentsia spokesmen assumed it to be. The great poet's alleged exclamation may have been, at least in part, beside the point. For *Dead Souls* is not primarily about decaying Russian squires and dead Russian serfs, but about the moral stupor, deadness, and tawdriness of it all. Heine's melancholy sigh: "Gott, wie gross ist dein Tiergarten!" (*"Lord, how large is your zoo!"*) would have been more apposite. To paraphrase Edgar Allan Poe, the horrors depicted or burlesqued in *Dead Souls* are not of Russia but of the soul—the soul of man, and more specifically, of Nikolaj Gogol.

Clearly what Cizevsky calls Gogol's "cosmic satire" and the introspective dimension of his laughter are inexplicably intertwined. If the protagonists of *Dead Souls* are the objectification or projection of the writer's private nightmares, the reverse is also true. The deformities of Gogol's "zoo" are introjected; they become part of the author's self. For a writer so morbidly self-centered, so vulnerable to moral hypochondria, so plagued by the sense of his own unworthiness, the weaknesses and vices that he detected in himself were bound to appear as a major case in point, a salient symptom, a proof positive of man's corruptibility.

In Gogol's "poem," where the wealth of personal digressions offers ample scope for self-reference, laughter at the expense of the Chichikovs and the Sobakeviches periodically turns inward as it becomes soul-searching, if not breast-beating, in one's own behalf as well as that of the reader—*mon semblable, mon frère.* The query "Come now, isn't there a bit of Chichikov in me, too?" echoes in a somewhat different key the mayor's memorable outburst: "What are you laughing at, you fools? you are laughing at yourselves!" *De te fabula narratur* is Gogol's pervasive leitmotif.

Yet to say all this is not necessarily to contend with Nabokov that Gogol's masterpiece bears no discernible relation to the Russia of his day. If the venality and parochialism of the Russian small-town officials in *The Inspector General,* the sloth, the greed, the stupidity of the freakish squires in *Dead Souls* are not *the* point, these are graphic illustrations of the point, a telling mode of symbolization. The social institutions which were part of Gogol's immediate environment provided here the appropriate set of images, or to use T. S. Eliot's phrase, the "objective correlative" for an idiosyncratic moral vision of reality shuttling precariously between the personal and the universal, between private nightmares and cosmic demonology. Gogol had known at first hand, however briefly, the desiccating impact, the wastefulness and tedium of the St. Petersburg office routine. Moreover, as a subject of Nicholas I— timidly loyal and wary of subversive generalizations, but endowed with an uncannily keen eye for the inane and the preposterous—he found in the world around him all too many striking instances of what, as a writer and a self-styled moralist, he endeavored to exemplify and castigate. To be sure, there is nothing uniquely Russian about waste, corruption, inefficiency, and double-talk. Yet it is at least arguable that some of these qualities, endemic in any vast bureaucratic and arbitrary system, tended to acquire a special dimension in Russia. In a culture where the gap between "State" and "Society" or, as a French political scientist would put it, between *"le pays légal"* and *"le pays réel,"* between stated goals and actual performance, is as glaring as it was in the Russia of Nicholas I, brazen manipulation of facts becomes a built-in feature of the System, shamming becomes institutionalized. After all, it was Tsarist Russia, though the Russia of Catherine the Great rather than that of Nicholas I, that is credited with having produced that archetypal instance of window dressing known as the "Potemkin villages"—hamlets frantically cleaned up on the eve of the Tsarina's visits to the region administered by her powerful protegé, Grigorij Potemkin: (Whether or not these alleged last-minute attempts to conceal mismanagement and squalor were actually what they rumored to be—a number of historians are inclined to doubt this—the story has been a persistent strand in Russian bureaucratic folklore.) Eyewitness testimony bearing on the Gogol era abounds in instances of quite ludicrous and self-defeating bureaucratic procedures. In his remarkable memoir, *My Past and Thoughts,* Alexander Herzen, a brilliant liberal writer and publicist, tells a characteristic story: It seems that having been banned from the capital for his political activities and placed under police surveillance in Novgorod, he was assigned as a clerk to the district court headquarters. Because of the illiteracy and laziness of the local officials, the subversive was increasingly entrusted with various responsible assignments including that of writing elaborate reports on his own behavior! All in all, it is difficult to escape the conclusion that there was something intrinsically "grotesque" about the institutional patterns to which Gogol and his contemporaries were occasionally subjected.

It would be a gross simplification and a methodological fallacy to conclude that the texture of Gogol's writings is grotesque because such was the nature of the social practices which were the immediate foil for his satire. The drift of an artist's vision, especially if, like Gogol, he is a wacky poet of genius, is never simply or primarily a by-product of his social environment. It might be more meaningful to suggest that the thrust of Gogol's imagination which included special alertness to the trivial, the preposterous, and the automatic, while not conducive to a reliable or accurate portrayal of any realities, however freakish, enabled him to dramatize the grotesque, incongruous, absurd, "as if" elements of his society more compellingly, more vividly or hauntingly than a true realist ever could. In doing so, he proved conclusively, if proof indeed were needed, that "realism" has no monopoly on social or moral relevance.

What remains is to pin down the mode of relevance congruent with Gogol's art, to identify more specifically the principal target of his laughter. The point has been made before but it is worth restating: the bureaucratic, manorial imagery serves here as a dismally fitting local vehicle for Gogol's *idée fixe,* his persistent obsession with the demeaning impact of the base passions gnawing at the heart of man, the insidious prevalence of *poshlost.*

It is high time that this absolutely indispensable Russian noun whose untranslatability is celebrated by Nabokov on seven gloating pages be injected into our discussion. For poshlost', a disreputable and slimy syndrome which, to simplify the matter, is compounded of such notions as shoddiness, vulgarity, grossness, self-satisfied mediocrity, has been with us for quite a while now—ever since **"Two Ivans"** and **"The Nose,"** and most emphatically, since *The Inspector General.* It is singularly appropriate that this cluster of traits, which Pushkin had allegedly recognized as the field of Gogol's special competence, should have become the prime subject of his largest work, and that this, the author's *bête noire,* should have been embodied in the "scoundrel harnessed" for the unlikely role of the "poem's" hero, Pavel Ivanovich Chichikov.

Clearly, Chichikov, the driving force of the loose-jointed agon, is here the chief focus of Gogol's erratic yet deadly serious moral concern. The other denizens of the vividly differentiated gallery serve primarily as foils for Chichikov's sinister and futile acquisitive frenzy, as well as a cumulative documentation of the ineradicable and unredeemable moral stupor of the world in which Chichikov operates. (In *Gogol's Craftsmanship,* Andrej Belyj aptly calls Chichikov's successive visits with various landowners a "crescendo of deadness." Each new landowner is more dead than the previous one. Pljushkin, the last to be approached, is the deadest of them all, "the corpse's corpse.") The limelight throughout is on that canny schemer whose existence ever since his childhood was dominated by a craving for status, wealth, and comforts to the complete exclusion of any moral scruple, any genuine human feeling.

Yet as Belyj pointed out, the most striking thing about Chichikov is not a lack of morals but a lack of personality. A Nozdrëv, a Pljushkin, a Sobakevich represents a grotesque exaggeration, a reductio ad absurdum of a single character trait or proclivity. The rotund, smoothly-shaven Chichikov is a bouncy vacuum, or as Robert Martin Adams puts it, "a perambulating hollow" propelled by a tawdry daydream, down the "long, long" Russian road [see excerpt dated 1966]. Most readers will recall that in the opening paragraph of the novel the hero is introduced in entirely negative terms: "The gentleman seated in this carriage was no Adonis, but he wasn't bad to look at, either; he was neither too stout nor too thin; you couldn't say he was old, but still he wasn't what you might call any too young either." (The utter spuriousness of this pseudo-description is pointed up by the opaqueness of irrelevant detail featured on the first pages of the novel, such as Chichikov's many-hued neckerchief and, to be sure, the enormous breasts of a nymph represented in an oil painting in the local inn.) On the face of it, the absence of any distinctive traits, any rough edges urges the image which Chichikov is only too eager to convey—one of *comme il faut* respectability, moderation, devotion to the golden rule. Yet at a more significant level, this array of vaporous negatives epitomizes an utter lack of human substance, in a word, a void.

Gogol's obsessive concern, *poshlost*, stands unveiled in this, his last major fictional statement, as nothingness. To quote again Adams' wide-ranging exploration, "it is Nothing which haunts the author's [Gogol's] vision, Nothing which inspires his most agonizing vertigo." It is the fear of the void, I would add, that underlies Gogol's already-noted desperate urge to get away from it all, so that "nothing be seen of it—nothing."

Poshlost as vacuity had already been dramatized in **The Inspector General.** Compared to Chichikov's slimy, relentless drive, Khlestakov's infantile exuberance seems almost appealing. What in the self-indulgent babbler was excruciatingly funny becomes sinister, if not frightening in the calculating, smug, self-promoting "acquirer." Nabokov's notion of Chichikov as "the ill-paid representative of the Devil, a traveling salesman from Hades" is not entirely fanciful. For this unheroic hero is truly evil. Indeed, he is a chief agent of moral decay and corruption in **Dead Souls.** No ablutions, however strenuous, could ever obliterate his moral stench, which is uncomfortably externalized [in] the smell exuded by his seedy servant Petrushka. It is an ultimate testimony to that domestication and trivialization of evil which had begun in **Mirgorod.**

As the sinister becomes commonplace, the commonplace is increasingly revealed as sinister. Once again on his uneasy journey, Gogol stumbles upon an important and influential notion: to use a recent phrase, "the banality of evil." The Devil is a sneaky customer, boring from within or from below, rather than the dark yet commanding figure Milton's Satan or Byron's Lucifer calls up. Here was a new brand of literary demonology which was to encompass the unbearably repulsive Smerdjakov in *The Brothers Karamazov* and the loathsome Peredonov in Fëdor Sologub's *A Petty Demon*. The threat becomes more insidi-

ous for being internalized, more ubiquitous for becoming ordinary, but the underlying moral is still the same: There is no place to hide. The Devil, Gogol wrote to his friend, the Slavophile poet, Jazykov, in 1845, "seeks various means of sticking his nose in. If he cannot manage to do so when we are healthy, he will squeak in through the door of sickness." His best opportunity, highlighted by poshlost' is man's susceptibility to "petty" passions, to low-grade temptations. (pp. 119-41)

Victor Erlich, in his Gogol, *Yale University Press, 1969, 230 p.*

Simon Karlinsky   (essay date 1970)

[*In the following essay, Karlinsky explores Gogol's use of language in* Dead Souls, *comparing it to that of François Rabelais, Laurence Sterne, and Gertrude Stein.*]

The literary style seemingly most admired by present-day critics or teachers of literature can be described in such terms as "precise," "concise," "succinct," or "terse." In this ideal prose style individual words, as it were, dissolve and become invisible. Models of this precise and transparent prose are usually sought in Stendhal and in the prose of Pushkin. Twentieth-century examples are provided by the sparse, hard-hitting prose of Ernest Hemingway or the laconic compression of Mayakovsky's prose. Admiration for this style is understandable and justified.

Yet, if we praise and admire only this tradition of prose writing, we risk overlooking the tradition that is its very opposite—the tradition of the dense and ornamental prose in which the words, far from dissolving step boldly forward and remind us that the individual word and the arrangement of words in groups are not only a means of conveying ideas, but are also the basic building blocks of the art of literature. This opposing tradition was represented by some of the most important writers in various periods and literatures. Such writers, while dealing with the human, social, or psychological predicaments that are the subject of imaginative literature, never cease to be concerned with the way the language as such works, to be fascinated with individual words and their respective arrangements and, to be quite frank, to play games with words.

Examples occur even in antiquity: a case can plausibly be made for Lucretius as a typically word-conscious writer because of his free use of neologisms, his liberties with grammar and his fondness for developed and extended comparisons. François Rabelais in the sixteenth century, Laurence Sterne in the eighteenth, and Nikolay Gogol in the nineteenth are other obvious examples. Twentieth-century writers "guilty" of purely verbal preoccupations are Gertrude Stein, Aleksey Remizov, Dylan Thomas in his prose, and many of the Soviet prose writers of the 1920's.

Now, obviously, Lucretius, Rabelais, Gogol, and Gertrude Stein are writers who differ from each other in many important and basic respects. Yet all of them share to a remarkable degree the stylistic peculiarity of verbal exuberance—an appetite for words that can only be described as verbal gluttony. Despite the differences of languages and epochs, we find in the writers of this type certain stylistic traits that are close to the very core of their respective styles: predilection for repetition and tautology used for artistic effect; tendency to list and enumerate things at great length; extraordinary proper names given to humans, animals, and objects (thus, in Gogol there is a horse named *Zasedatel'* and a deck of cards called Adelaida Ivanovna); and the tendency toward inventing words and devising macaronic verbal coinages involving several languages. All of these traits can and do occur in the work of many writers of many periods, but it is the sheer concentration of them that sets the work of the verbal gluttons apart, that make a Rabelais, a Gogol, or a Gertrude Stein stylistically the very opposite of Stendhal, or Tolstoy, or Hemingway.

Among the Russian critics who have written on Gogol only Andrey Bely has really given the verbal and phonetic aspects of Gogol's art the attention they deserve. One might also mention a few perceptive observations of Yury Tynyanov in his study of Gogol and Dostoevsky about the frequent precedence of sound effects and phonetic considerations over meaning and over semantics in Gogol. Yet, no one who reads *Dead Souls* attentively should fail to notice Gogol's overwhelming interest in language in general, in its phonetic aspects and in various other linguistic phenomena and problems. This interest is so general and all-embracing that it begins even before the stage where actual verbalization is reached on that pre-verbal level where tone or pitch alone can convey the meaning, that is the vocal rather than the verbal kind of communication which animals also use.

Thus, at one point Plyushkin, the miser, mutters something unintelligible to Chichikov, and Gogol tells us that the tone of this muttering conveyed the message decipherable as: "May the devil take you and your respects." Similarly, the gobbling of the tom turkey in Mme Korobochka's barnyard is interpreted by Gogol to mean "Bless you, sir!" The entire novel *Dead Souls* is permeated with remarks or formulae that call our attention to the verbal side of things—such qualifying expressions as: "spending his time, as they say, very pleasantly," or "as these are called in Russian inns," or "as the French say," or "according to a wonderful expression used by Russian peasants."

Throughout the book, Gogol never quite recovers from his fascination with the way language works. He examines the problems of tone and diction in his commentary on the conversation between Chichikov and Mme Korobochka on the morning after he had spent the night at her estate. Gogol points out that the tone used by Chichikov on that occasion was far less respectful than the tone he used when speaking to Manilov and this observation is followed by a detailed discussion of various degrees of respect or servility that it is possible to express in Russian in various social situations. At the end of part one, chapter 5, there is the commentary on the comparative virtues of the English, French, German, and Russian languages and on their suitability to express the respective national character of each nation. And when Chichikov, in his meditations at the governor's ball, uses one single word that may be consid-

ered substandard or sub-literary (*galantërnyj*), Gogol seizes this pretext to launch on a page-long examination of various lexical usages in the literary Russian of his day and of the various current attitudes to literary and sub-literary strata existing in the language.

Although he has no term to describe it, Gogol is clearly aware of what we today call the phonemic systems peculiar to various languages. For instance, while preparing to go to the ball, Chichikov emits various sounds which we are told sounded like French even though he did not know any French. Elsewhere in the novel, Gogol says that in order to pronounce English correctly one has to make a birdlike face. If we discount the humor of this statement, what remains is evidence of Gogol's understanding of the type of articulation required by the phonemic system of a language which uses sounds that do not exist in Russian. . . . Similarly in the ***Inspector General*** the doctor, Christian Ivanovich Hübner, identifies himself as a German merely by uttering several times a sound that Gogol describes as being halfway between *i* and *je,* which could be either a stressed *schwa* or the German *ö*. Both of these are nonexistent in Russian and pronouncing either one would produce an overwhelmingly Germanic effect on an untrained Russian ear.

When we come to individual separate words, we note that a particular word may play a key role in Gogol's plots, which goes far beyond its inherent meaning. In **"The Quarrel of the Two Ivans"** the entire plot revolves around the supposedly insulting meaning of a single key word *gusak.* As that story develops, the word acquires a weight and a momentum that go far beyond anything this word could convey outside of the context of that particular story. In ***Dead Souls,*** we see Chichikov toppled from his earlier position of wealth and power because on one single occasion he called his partner in crime *popovič.* In the unfinished second part of the novel, the love affair between Tentetnikov and the ideal girl Ulenka collapses because of the brief word *ty* used by Ulenka's father General Betrishchev when addressing his daughter's suitor. Gogol points out such ability of a word to acquire a significance and a momentum beyond its original meaning when he comments on the sudden popularity of Chichikov with the ladies after his purchase of the serfs becomes known: "The word 'millionaire' was to blame—not the millionaire himself but just the word alone."

Here we see what is usually taken to be Gogol's social criticism operating as it always does on two levels: while seemingly investigating a social phenomenon, Gogol is also investigating how words work and how he can play with them. In the same way, the verdict of the divine Bottle in Book Five of *Gargantua and Pantagruel* which consists of the single word *Trinch!* can be taken as an epicurean philosophical message, while being at the same time a good imitation of the sort of sound any glass bottle would make when plunged into boiling water. It would be very difficult to find a plot in Pushkin or Tolstoy in which an individual word is so much an internal part of the mechanism as Gogol's *gusak* or the *Trinch!* of Rabelais.

From this preoccupation with verbal power there is only a step to the concept of the word as a magical spell or incantation. This concept is very much present both in Gogol's work and in his general mentality. In **"Viy,"** Khoma Brut protects himself from the witch during their ride and later during the first two nights in the haunted church by reciting magic spells taught him by a certain holy hermit. Incantations play an important part in other Gogol tales, **"The Terrible Vengeance"** and **"The Enchanted Spot,"** for example. Even in the supposedly realistic *Dead Souls,* part two, after describing Tentetnikov's inactivity and his need to be awakened by someone who will come and say "forward" to him, Gogol extends Tentetnikov's predicament to the whole of Russia and says that all his country needs is a statesman who will command the whole of Russia to arise by uttering this all-powerful single word "forward!" Lest we take this for an allegory, we should remember that Gogol seriously expected the whole of Russia to experience a profound moral regeneration the moment Zhukovsky's translation of *The Odyssey* was published and read by all social classes; that he expected deep-going social reactions to result from publication of some new poems by Yazykov; that in his *Selected Passages from Correspondence with Friends* he recommends the landowners to use certain designated swearwords on their serfs that should immediately change these serfs' character and outlook; and, finally, we may recall the passages in his private letters where he warns people that his own words are divinely inspired and that misfortune awaits those who would not heed his prophetic words.

Gogol does not have as great an interest in the graphic side of language as does Laurence Sterne, with his typographical tricks, lines full of asterisks, and blank pages. But even this aspect of language does not escape Gogol's attention entirely and in *Dead Souls* we get the charming vignette of the valet Petrushka who reads any sort of book whatsoever because his main interest is the reading process itself and the curious fact that the separate letters on the printed page are always sure to form some word or other.

Gogol shares with Rabelais, Sterne, and Stein an interest in an aspect of the speech act of which most other writers are not even aware. When Chichikov, immersed in his checkers game, absent-mindedly reiterates the same sentence three times, and Nozdrev, equally absorbed in his cheating, repeats his answer twice, we are given a sample of speech that has nothing to communicate beyond asserting the presence of the speaker. Chichikov's horses, we are told, also require such communication for its own sake. The thing that pleases these animals most about Tentetnikov's stables is that any horse can neigh at any other horse there and receive a reply. Anton Chekhov was later to develop such non-communicating verbalization to the level of a full-fledged dramatic device in his plays.

In the work of writers who are word-gluttons, non-communicating dialogue is often assigned to choruses of episodic minor characters in the background. The conversations between the unidentified soldiers in Tolstoy's *War and Peace,* on the other hand, may not push the plot forward, but they are about definite subjects and they convey to us something of the common soldier's attitude to the historical events as well as Tolstoy's own attitude to both soldiers and events. The six young Princesses Tu-

goukhovsky in Griboedov's comedy *Woe from Wit* are as episodic as dramatic characters can be, yet of their two brief chattering choruses the first helps to establish the atmosphere of the salon and the second is significant in the development of the plot. In both these scenes definite issues are discussed: the scarf given to one of the princesses by her cousin and fashions in general in the first scene and Chatsky's insanity in the second.

But the chorus with which Chichikov is greeted upon his arrival at the ball in part one, chapter 8, or the description of how the kindly officials of the town would address each other earlier in the same chapter are webs of generalized exclamations, containing as much concrete information as the chirping of sparrows at sunset. Such passages can be compared to the remarkable tour de force of Rabelais in Book One, chapter 5, a brilliant display of verbal fireworks and invention, where a group of unidentified people talk about drinking without saying anything more concrete than a few memorable puns.

Gertrude Stein, of course, has built a considerable portion of her literary output on setting down conversations that convey no concrete or paraphrasable information. Her little plays (in the collection *Geography and Plays*) are about people talking of nothing in particular, and the little prose piece "Johnny Grey" in the same collection, which may be interpreted as being about the experiences of two American soldiers on leave in Paris during the First World War, consists for the most part of disjointed fragments from their streams-of-consciousness, which the reader can interpret only instinctively and intuitively, if at all.

Persons who study Russian complain frequently that they find Gogol impossible to read in the original. Indeed, the prose of Gogol presents to a foreign reader difficulties that he would never encounter in Pushkin, Tolstoy, or Chekhov. I have not seen any statistics on the subject, but it seems likely that Gogol used one of the largest and most varied vocabularies among nineteenth-century Russian writers. He made use of almost the entire lexical range of spoken and written Russian of his time, from the most elevated philosophical and theological vocabulary rooted in Old Church Slavic to the most vulgar and crude slang he could find, not to mention the rich admixture of Ukrainian in his early stories.

In matters of vocabulary, the position of Gogol in Russian literature is exactly analogous to that of Rabelais in French literature. Like Rabelais three hundred years before him, Gogol found the standard literary vocabulary insufficient and resorted to dialectal forms, to special vocabularies, and took to inventing his own words. Andrey Bely's masterful study of Gogol's style demonstrates the wide use of regional, colloquial, rare, and invented verbs in *Dead Souls.* The special and professional vocabularies used in *Dead Souls,* such as agricultural terminology, the slang of hunters and dog-breeders, bureaucratic language, military slang that Nozdrev had picked up from his officer friends, and special culinary terminology are described in detail by Bely and by V. V. Vinogradov. The lists of Nozdrev's dogs (part one, chapter 4) and Korobochka's cakes (part one, chapter 3) show that Gogol revels in difficult and rare words, many of which could not be easily understood by the Russian reader of his time and are even less accessible today.

The character in **Dead Souls** whose vocabulary shows the greatest verbal invention and variety is Nozdrev. L. A. Bulakhovsky sees in his speech a sort of compendium of bad speech habits of his age (*splošnye frazeologizmy durnogo tona*). Here we get a mixture of slangy expressions of varied derivation, and it is curious to note that the verbal imagination of his character seems to stimulate Gogol to a verbal inventiveness of his own, even in the descriptive passages. In the next chapter, devoted to the miser Plyushkin, the method is visual rather than verbal, in keeping with the verbal paucity of Plyushkin himself, and the descriptive passages are accordingly toned down.

The postmaster, who tells the story of Captain Kopeykin, shares with Nozdrev the predilection for the macaronic mixture of French and Russian. In this, Gogol is not unique in the Russian literature of his time. We know from other writers the important role of the French language in Russian society of the first half of the nineteenth century. Griboedov objected to the mixing of French "with the dialect of Nizhny-Novgorod" and Pushkin obtained humorous effects by having a character in *Dubrovskij* conjugate a Russian verb in accordance with French grammar. In 1840, there appeared a long satirical macaronic poem *Sensacii i zamečanija gospoži Kurdjukovoj za granicej dan l'ètranže* by Ivan Myatlev which had a considerable popular success. The method of Myatlev is that of Gogol's two ladies, the simply pleasant one and the one pleasant in every respect: the Russian is sprinkled with French words and phrases, but without doing any actual violence to either language. What Nozdrev and the postmaster do to French on the other hand is similar to what Rabelais often does with Latin, especially in the speech of the Limousin scholar whom Pantagruel meets (book two, Chapter 6). French words are russified with Slavic prefixes and suffixes: *bezeška* from *baiser, razsupè-delicatesse, burdaška* for *Bordeaux*.

The macaronic neologisms of the postmaster represent only a small portion of the coined and invented words Gogol uses in **Dead Souls.** Eighteenth-century Russian writers invented words because there was a practical need for new words. Dostoevsky introduced new words to convey new shades of meaning and some of his coinages have entered the language permanently. Gogol, like Rabelais and like Sterne in the tale of the abbess and Margarita, invents words that he needs only for one particular occasion. At the simplest level, he follows the earlier tradition much used by Tredyakovsky, the quasi-Homeric double adjective: *umno-khudoščavoe slovo, vsespasajuščaja ruka*. These are easily intelligible and so are many of the strange new verbs Gogol coins from existing nouns (*omedvedit'*, "to make someone like a bear"; *oščelivat'*, "to cover with cracks or slits"), or nouns from unexpected verbs (*vospoitel'nica*, "female nourisher, who gave drink"). The reader has to make contextual guesses when Nozdrev coins a verb from a nonexistent noun (*poddeljulit'*) or when Gogol himself comes up with a verbal noun like *vzbutetenivanie* in a descriptive passage. Vinogradov, in line with the Soviet view of Gogol as critical realist and ethnographer, treats Gogol's coinages as genuine regional or slangy terms which Gogol had overheard and faithfully recorded. He cites the cardplayers' slang as an example. Vladimir Nabokov is probably nearer the truth when he conjectures that the odd coinages in the passage quoted by Vinogradov are actually Gogol's own invention.

The proper names of his characters constitute the area in which Gogol gives his extraordinary verbal inventiveness a completely free rein. As Andrey Bely puts it: "Family names are Gogol's delirium;" or, even more imaginatively: "His need to gush forth in whistling sounds runs amok in a squadron of names." In **Dead Souls,** this applies less to the names of the principals than to minor and episodic characters. There have been attempts to explain such names as Chichikov and Plyushkin as having specific significance, but their semantic suggestivity is too vague and indefinite for any precise identification. Gogol's method has nothing to do with the eighteenth-century Russian comedy of Fonvizin and Kapnist where the name was used to designate the type of character. As far as concrete significance goes, Bely makes a convincing case for Korobochka being the double of Chichikov's cassette (*škatulka*): the fact that she catches him with the cassette open, the similarity of the description of the insides of the cassette and the insides of her coach, the danger that her arrival in town constitutes to his most precious possession. As Bely puts it, she is the very opposite of the fairy-godmother even if she does travel in a pumpkin-like conveyance. In fact, Korobochka is not only the double but also the nemesis of the cassette. One might also venture to suggest that there is a strange reversal of names between Sobakevich ("dog's son") and Nozdrev ("of nostrils"). It is Nozdrev who is constantly surrounded by dogs, while *his* name suggests the ring through the nostrils by which the trained Russian bears, to whom Sobakevich is compared, are led about.

Once we move away from the principals, the names of Gogolian characters seem to have but one purpose: to be as subtly unusual and unexpected as possible. There is a broad humor in the names of the dead serfs that Chichikov buys, all those Korovy-Kirpich ("Cow's brick"), Elizaveta Vorobey ("Elizabeth the sparrow"), Neuvazhay-Koryto (nicely rendered by Mrs. Garnett as "Never mind the trough!"). Episodic characters are invented merely in order to bring in absolutely impossible, unlikely names, such as that strange Russian Scot Macdonald Karlovich. The urge for name-giving extends to objects and animals.

The publication of Gogol's complete notebooks for **Dead Souls** in the 1951 Soviet Academy of Sciences edition of his Collected Works provides us with a number of new insights into Gogol's verbal preoccupations. In his researches into the rural life of central Russia (with which he had had little first-hand contact), Gogol was aided by P. M. Yazykov, the brother of the poet Nikolay Yazykov (for whom Gogol conceived a passionate emotional attachment when he was writing **Dead Souls**). Of the long lists of local Simbirsk proper names, professions, household utensils, birds, bird-calls, etc., provided by P. M. Yazykov (an amateur ethnographer of sorts), Gogol inevitably selected the most bizarre and outlandish items, many of which found their way into the first or the second part of his novel. Much of the dog-lore displayed in the description of Nozdrev's kennel, Korobochka's pastries, the waterfowl in the second part, are all traceable to Yazykov's lists. In every case, Gogol, the supposed realist, chooses the more whimsical items and then adds some particular verbal invention of his own that is not found in the notebooks.

Thus, of the six names of rural saloons listed by Yazykov, Gogol selects the rather unexpected name Agashka (the pejorative diminutive of Agafya or Agatha). By the time this name found its way into the second part of **Dead Souls,** Gogol had transformed it in a way that provides a one-word illustration of the difference between raw ethnography and artistic creation. The name of the tavern that appears in the novel is Akulka, the derogatory form of Akulina.

The noble Roman name of Aquiline had undergone a strange degeneration in Russia and became the symbol of everything low and common. In the household of Sobakevich, Akulka is the name of the kitchen maid who takes out the slops. To show the prosaic turn Tatyana's mother took after a long residence in the country, Pushkin (in *Eugene Onegin*) tells us that she took to calling a servant she had formerly addressed as Celina by her real name of Akulka, the two names presumably representing the greatest possible contrast in terms of elegance and vulgarity. A hundred years later, Vladimir Nabokov, in translating *Alice in Wonderland,* rendered Lewis Carroll's "will speak in contemptuous tones of the shark" as "he addresses the shark (*akula*) as Akulka." Agashka as a tavern name was bizarre, but Akulka is so outlandish as to merit the twentieth-century term "surrealistic."

In contrast to the riot of strange names of episodic figures is the odd fact of namelessness of some of the important characters. The lack of names of the two gossipy ladies in chapter nine is just an amusing game, for although Gogol refuses to reveal their names, they themselves do so in the course of their conversation. Wolfgang Kasack in his study of Gogol's characters points out the interesting and possibly significant fact that the characters in Gogol who have no names are the young and beautiful women: the two heroines in **"Nevsky Prospect,"** the Polish girl in **"Taras bulba,"** the beautiful witch in **"Viy."** We can add to Kasack's list the character who can be dubbed the antiheroine of **Dead Souls,** the governor's daughter. She plays an important role in the plot, appears and is discussed in a number of scenes but she has nothing whatsoever to say, is a total blank as a character, and has no name. This strange anonymity of young and desirable women fits very well with those studies of Gogol which try to explain his work in psychoanalytic terms, such as those of [I. D.] Ermakov or Hugh McLean.

The names in **Dead Souls,** have been examined by Bely, who lists the strangest ones; by Kasack, who explains their etymologies, occasionally in rather farfetched ways; by Ermakov, who tried to treat these names in Freudian terms; and by Vladimir Nabokov, who commented on the humorous use to which these names are put by Gogol.

Nozdrev.

None of these investigators seems to have noticed that Gogol amuses himself by arranging his strange names into definite patterns. In this respect, the practice of Gogol again has close parallels in Rabelais and in Gertrude Stein.

The simplest arrangement in Gogol involves two closely similar names usually with a rhyming effect: Uncle Mityay and Uncle Minyay; Foma the Elder and Foma the Younger; Father Carp and Father Polycarp; Moky Kifovich and Kifa Mokievich. The rhyming pair can also be hidden inside a longer list: among the landowners enumerated for Chichikov by Korobochka, the pair Kharpakin and Trepakin are surrounded by four other names. The next morning the innkeeper located only a few versts from Korobochka's estate comes up with an entirely different set of neighbors and this time the point of the joke is the squire with the sudsy name of Myl'noy ("soapy"), inoffensively hidden among four other comparatively reasonable names.

The most usual form taken by the longer listings of names in **Dead Souls** is a sort of musical composition, with several minor climaxes and the final culmination in a blast of absurdity at the very end. The pattern can be seen in its basic form when some of the serfs that Plyushkin sold to Chichikov are enumerated (part one, chapter 6): "Paramonov and Pimenov and Panteleymonov, and even a certain Grigory Doezzhay-ne-doedesh." The reader is at first lulled by the alliterative series of names derived from

Greek Orthodox saints, only to be suddenly jolted by the completely impossible name which contains two mutually contradictory statements: "go right up to it" and "you will not get there."

This is also the essential pattern of the extended list of young ladies of whom Chichikov happens to think when he runs out of conversation with the governor's daughter at the ball (part one, chapter 8). This is the passage which most English translators of Gogol either delete or abbreviate and simplify beyond recognition. Vladimir Nabokov quotes it in its entirety, comments on it and explains some of the names [see excerpt dated 1944]. In terms of a musical crescendo, we might note that the first minor climax in this list occurs when we learn that a name very rare in Russia is represented in the same family in both its French and German versions (Adelaide and Adelheid); the second and lesser one is connected with sisters Roza Feodorovna and Emilia Feodorovna. The final cymbal crash of absurdity occurs at the very end of the list with the appearance of Maklatura Aleksandrovna, "maklatura" (more usually spelled *"makulatura"*) being no name at all, but a technical term meaning "paper pulp" or "worthless paper."

Still more sophisticated is the list of Nozdrev's dogs (part one, chapter 4). In the first part of the list Gogol merely embroiders on the technical kennel terms he obtained from P. M. Yazykov. The dog names listed by Yazykov were often imperative forms of verbs—a widespread nineteenth-century Russian custom (dogs with names in the imperative also figure in the hunting scenes of Tolstoy's *War and Peace* and in Chekhov's farce *The Marriage Proposal*). Gogol uses some very rare Simbirsk area regional terms in this list. (His translators should have consulted an etymological dictionary to learn that *skosyr'*, which looks like an imperative of some obscure verb, is really a northern Russian word meaning "fop" or "insolent one," and that *severga* is a dialectal term meaning "impatient one" and not "northerner," as Mr. Guerney has wrongly guessed.) The effect of the list is one of crudity and vigor, but the last item comes from an entirely different lexical stratum, an elegant word that suggests a stately and aristocratic dowager (*popečitel' nica*, i.e., "a patroness of charitable activities"). Here again, the whole point seems to be the careful preparation of the final surprise. By placing his own invention against the ethnographic background provided by his informant, Gogol again achieves an effect of surreal fantasy.

The lists of Gertrude Stein have a similar way of wavering between the believable and the impossible, as for example her enumeration of the saints in the opera *Four Saints in Three Acts:* Saint Therese, Saint Ignatius, Saint Matyr (*sic*), Saint Paul, Saint Settlement, Saint William, Saint Thomasine . . . Saint Electra, Saint Paul Seize, etc. In Rabelais, as in Gogol, the listings and the descriptions usually move on several levels at once. During the visit to the Satin Island Zoo (Book Five, chapter 30), we are shown both real rare animals known in Rabelais' day and the fantastic creatures that were usually depicted on tapestries. In the middle of this long enumeration we get "Shrove-Tuesday on horseback, mid-August and mid-March held

his stirrups." The list goes on with werewolves, centaurs, leopards, hyenas, etc., and then ends with a final flourish of surrealistic whimsy by describing some milch crawfish who march in fine order. The method is of course strikingly similar to that of Gogol.

Names are the most frequent item that Gogol arranges into lists, but there are many others. When Tolstoy lists objects, as he does in the first of the Sebastopol stories, he does so to convey the impression of the scene and the verbal side of the list is of no interest to him: "you go to the wharf—a peculiar odor of coal, manure, dampness and of beef strikes you; thousands of objects of all sorts—wood, meat, gabions, flour, iron, and so forth lie in heaps about the wharf." Tolstoy lists only five objects out of the thousand and then breaks the list off with "and so forth," knowing that he had created the impression he needed. Gogol, however, at the very idea of the things Nozdrev *could have* bought at the fair if he had the money, lists nineteen hypothetical purchases, most of them with a modifying adjective. The lists of foodstuffs in **Dead Souls** can compete with anything in Rabelais, including the list of delicacies that make up the anatomy of the King Caremeprenant. Bely counts eighty-six various dishes mentioned in **Dead Souls,** the comedies and the Petersburg tales and comments "Not an Iliad but a Gobble-iad (*Žratv-iada*)." Wolfgang Kasack points out that many of these food lists constitute an important means of characterization. And indeed, the foods served by Nozdrev, Korobochka, and Sobakevich definitely contribute to their general characterization. A very interesting proof of this can be seen in the case of Korobochka. She offers Chichikov mostly baked things and meat pies during his visit in chapter 3. Five chapters later we recognize her before her name is ever mentioned as the mysterious traveller in the watermelon carriage by the baked items in her luggage. The identification is made even though only one item is repeated from the earlier list: *skorodumki* (translated by Nabokov as "Skoro-dumplings"). Gogol had some more bakery goods to enumerate and he was not going to miss his chance.

Once we realize Gogol's love for words, his need to play with them in every imaginable way, we can see the origin of some of his stylistic extravagances and understand their odd resemblance to similar aspects in the style of writers seemingly so different from Gogol. In Gertrude Stein or Rabelais, as in **Dead Souls,** we encounter the wide use of tautology, of repetition of all sorts, of recapitulation and parallel syntactic constructions. Dostoevsky, using an effect of this sort in the very beginning of *Notes from the Underground,* aims at a psychological characterization of his hero (none of the English translations conveys the whining effect produced by the forward movement of the adjective in the Russian original: Ja čelovek *bol'noj* . . . Ja *zloj* čelovek. *Neprivlekatel'nyj* ja čelovek). There is no decorative effect in this subtle arrangement of words, only a psychological one. But when Gogol writes: "he started again trying to find out whether it was possible to find out from the expression in the face or in the eyes which one was the lady who wrote the letter, but it was utterly impossible to find out from the expression in the face or from the expression in the eyes which one was the lady who wrote the letter" (part one, chapter 8), there is a definite decorative effect produced by the arrangement of the words which is quite independent of the meaning conveyed. We can profitably compare this with the battle scene in *Gargantua and Pantagruel,* Book One, chapter 27: "Some died without speaking, others spoke without dying, some died while speaking, others spoke while dying. Still others cried loudly: 'Confession! Confession! Confiteor, miserere, in manus.' " This may be taken as a realistic depiction of the disorderly conditions of the battlefield, but it must be admitted that the verbal means used are so striking as to claim all our attention. This method of verbal arrangement reaches its ultimate development in such stories of Gertrude Stein as "Miss Furr and Miss Skeene," which for all its verbal complexity has also been described as a social satire which amusingly conveys the uselessness of the life of American expatriates in Paris.

Gogol's powerful visual imagination joins his verbal exuberance to produce his famous developed comparisons, such as the likening of the men at the ball to flies or Korobochka's dogs to a church choir. A very striking one occurs at the end of chapter 4, when Nozdrev, who is attacking Chichikov, is likened to a desperate young lieutenant about to take a fortress. After developing this comparison, Gogol withdraws the visual props but keeps the verbal ones by referring to Chichikov as the fortress. for a few more sentences. A comically unexpected effect is produced at this point because due to the gender of the word "fortress" (*krepost'*) Chichikov is suddenly spoken of in the feminine.

There are other verbally exuberant qualities in Gogol's style: his elaborate sentence structure, analyzed in detail by Bely, who speaks of Gogol's "exploded sentence, scattered about in splinters of subordinate clauses" and the devices which Pereverzev in his chapter on Gogol's style calls amplification and self-interruption. The best example of the use of amplification is the "Tale of Captain Kopeykin," a good early illustration of what later came to be called *skaz.* The narrative manner of the postmaster who tells this story is announced in chapter 8; the auxiliary expressions he uses to stretch out and amplify the tale occupy roughly half of the text, and if we were to bluepencil the extraneous matter and the repetitions, the story could probably be cut down to about one-third of its length.

The suspended logic of the "Tale of Captain Kopeykin" (the man who is suspected of being Chichikov, we are told at the very beginning, is without an arm and a leg) has a close parallel in Rabelais, when Master Janotus de Bragmardo is made to plead with Gargantua at great length for the return of the church bells which had been returned earlier (Book One, chapters 18, 19, 20). In such passages, the humor is in the explicitly absurd situation and the verbal humor plays an auxiliary role.

A related technique, peculiarly Gogol's, depends on the tacit assumption of an absurd proposition that is never verbalized. In the parable of Kifa Mokievich and Moky Kifovich, the really absurd idea is not that elephants hatch from an egg, but the tacit assumption that people go hunting bird eggs with rifles. Here we might again use the word

surrealism. Another prime example of verbal surrealism in **Dead Souls** is the direct quotation from the dapple horse, a member of Chichikov's *troika* (all three horses are developed as very individual human characters). The odd thing is not that the horse thinks or speaks, but that it uses the language of an uneducated Russian peasant. This social and educational characteristic of the horse is what we may term Gogol's realism squared, super-realism, with the typical telescoped logic which is now called surrealism.

The stylistic peculiarities of Gogol stand in a paradoxical relation to those of other verbally exuberant writers discussed in the present study. The closest in time to Gogol is Laurence Sterne, who was also undoubtedly a direct influence. There are not only stylistic affinities between these two writers, but also deep-going psychological ones. When James Aiken Work points out that "the suspicion . . . [of sexual impotence] . . . hovers like a dubious halo over the head of every Shandy male, including the bull," we realize how well this statement applies to the majority of Gogol's males (not excluding the horses of Chichikov's *troika*). Yet in verbal gluttony, Gogol seems closer to Rabelais (whose work he probably did not know) and to Gertrude Stein.

Like Gogol, Gertrude Stein spent a great portion of her creative years abroad, while exercising a powerful influence on the literature of her native country. Both she and Gogol can be seen as pivotal writers who introduced new literary styles that were taken up and developed by successors not given to verbal excess or exuberance. Thus, a comparison of Gogol's impact on the young Dostoevsky with Stein's impact on Hemingway should reveal a number of unexpected and significant parallels.

Rabelais, the logophage closest to Gogol verbally, was also the one who psychologically and temperamentally was least like him. In his chapter on Gogol's style, Pereverzev states that study of style is only interesting when it reveals the environment which had brought about the given style. He accordingly derives Gogol's enumerations and pleonasms from the stagnant state of Russian provincial life in Gogol's time. Marxist scholars always know exactly what they should find in literature. It is amusing therefore to read the remarks on Rabelais' style by another Marxist commentator, E. M. Evnina. She attributes the very same features in Rabelais (which in Gogol Pereverzev blamed on provincial drowsiness) to the explosive and militant mentality of the Renaissance. The two equally plausible explanations cancel each other out and make it clear that there is no satisfactory sociological or literary explanation for the stylistic similarities between the writings of the joyous French doctor and the tortured Ukrainian, who was one of the most pessimistic humorists in world literature.

Buffon's usually valid maxim that "the style is the entire man" is obviously no help here. All we can postulate is that a simple physiological appetite seems to be at work in these so similar and so dissimilar writers, like a shared appetite for oysters or for collecting postage stamps. Or for striking words arranged in an interesting and satisfying pattern. (pp. 169-86)

Simon Karlinsky, "Portrait of Gogol as a Word Glutton," in California Slavic Studies, Vol. V, 1970, pp. 169-86.

Richard Freeborn   (essay date 1973)

[*Freeborn is a Welsh critic, educator, and translator who has written and edited numerous studies of Russian history, literature, and literary figures. In the following excerpt, he considers how narrative structure, characterization, and setting determine the form of* Dead Souls.]

There can be no doubt that *Dead Souls* is 'subjective'—it is stamped, permeated, enlivened and enriched by the unique personality of Gogol. Belinsky was the first to note this and his explanation of the author's 'subjectivity' contains an important insight into Gogol's art:

> We consider it a very great success and step forward on the author's part that in *Dead Souls* his subjectivity is everywhere consciously and palpably apparent. Here we do not mean a subjectivity which, by its restrictedness and onesidedness, distorts the objective reality of what the poet depicts, but that profound, all-embracing and humane subjectivity which reveals in the artist a man with a warm heart, a sympathetic soul and personal spiritual integrity—the kind of subjectivity which does not allow him, out of apathetic indifference, to be foreign to the world which he depicts, but forces him to pass the phenomena of the external world through his *living soul* and by this means to breathe a *living soul* into them.

The *living soul* of Gogol in its relationship to the external world is thus both activated and activating. More than this—to carry Belinsky's insight further—the *living soul* of Gogol is creative as well as receptive, inspirational as well as representational in its transmutational alchemy, in, as Gogol himself puts it, the need for 'much spiritual depth so as to illuminate a picture taken from despised life and raise it into a pearl of creation'. And more still—it is resurrectional, perhaps also redemptive, for Gogol's *living soul* is what breathes life into the dead souls of the external world, envelops them in a multitude of life-giving words, scrutinises them with a compassionate and fearful wonderment, protects and nurtures them with an apprehensive solicitude that is at once both critical and loving. No work in Russian literature cries out to be treated as a work of love with such anguish of spirit as does *Dead Souls.*

Gogol called it 'a poem'. In the subjectivity of its lyricism and the looseness of its structure it bears some resemblance to a poem, even though written in prose. But far more apposite to any discussion of the poetic nature of the work than the attempt to squeeze it into the categories of epic or lesser forms of that genre is the impression of inspired, carefully wrought, endlessly pondered, sinuously intricate workmanship which the prose language of this masterpiece conveys. There are moments in it when nature and art seem to meet, when literary art ceases to have any of the lineaments of artifice and assumes an appearance so like nature that it is as if the words grew on the page with the same prolific, natural abundance as do the trees and shrubbery in Plyushkin's overgrown garden. In this very context Gogol offers a key, summarising the appearance of the garden (*Dead Souls,* Ch. 6) in the following sentence which, in the seeming three-dimensional depths of its meaning, eludes reproduction in another language as surely as photographic reproduction misses the hollows and surface eminences in an oil painting:

> In a word, everything was somehow desolate and beautiful as neither nature nor art can make it but as can only happen when they come together, when over the amassed, often senseless, labour of man nature will pass its final cutting edge and lighten the heavy masses, obliterate the crudely palpable rectitude and torn beggar's rags, through which the uncovered, naked plan is to be glimpsed, and will give a wondrous warmth to everything that has been created in the cool of a measured purity and neatness.

The poetic nature of Gogol's prose art, at least as an ideal to which Gogol aspired, seems to possess the meaning of this sentence and suggest the source of that novelty and experimentation, that exuberant verbal richness, which distinguishes his prose from the felicitous simplicity of Pushkin's or the racy elasticity of Lermontov's. Gogol aspired to 'write solidly', but his is a prose solidity always lightened by a natural comic cutting edge which does 'obliterate the crudely palpable rectitude' of the prosaic, the naked plan of the language, and gives the warmth of poetic feeling to everything created 'in the cool of a measured purity and neatness'.

Though he liked to call it 'a poem', *Dead Souls* is recognisable as a novel even in Gogol's own definition of the genre. In his unfinished *Schoolbook of Literature for Russian Youth,* which he probably wrote at some time in the first half of the 1840s, perhaps partly under the influence of Belinsky's dispute with Aksakov over the genre of *Dead Souls,* he gave the following definition:

> A novel, despite being in prose, can be a highly poetic work. A novel is not an epic. It can be called rather a drama. Like a drama, it is an excessively formal work. It also has a strictly and cleverly thought-out plot. All the characters who have to take part or, better, between whom the action should happen, must be chosen beforehand by the author; the author is concerned with the fate of each of them and cannot move them about hurriedly and en masse, like things that go flying by. Each appearance of a character, initially apparently insignificant, heralds his participation later. Everything that happens happens only because it is connected with the fate of the hero himself. Here, as in a drama, an only too close unity between the characters is allowed; any distant relations between them, or encounters of a kind which can be done without, are a vice in a novel and make it long-winded and boring. It flies along like a drama, unified by the vital interest of the characters of the chief plot in which they have been entangled and which in its bubbling way makes them evolve and reveal ever more strongly and quickly their personalities, thereby increasing the entertainment. For this reason each character must have

a complete role to play. A novel does not cover the whole life but a notable happening in life, of a kind which has made life reveal itself in a brilliant form, despite the formal spatial limits.

One has the strong impression from this not only that Gogol was not entirely sure about the formal characteristics of the novel—judging from his correspondence and other sources, he does not seem to have read many works that could really be called novels—but also that in defining the genre he was drawing very largely from his own experience in writing *Dead Souls.* The initial reference to the possibility that a novel can be a highly poetic work is a pointer. Equally interesting is the way in which he insists on the resemblance between the novel and the drama and the similarity between a novel's characters and the *dramatis personae* of a play (he uses the Russian expression *deystvuyushchiye litsa,* the equivalent of *dramatis personae*). The stipulation that 'all the characters . . . must be chosen beforehand by the author; the author is concerned with the fate of each of them and cannot move them about . . . ' suggests that Gogol is talking quite as much to himself as to the schoolchildren for whom he was ostensibly writing. Also, the importance which he attaches to the central and unifying role of the hero, the dramatic expeditiousness of the plotting and the 'notable happening' (*zamechatel'noye proisshestviye*) on which the action of the novel should hinge gives good reason for supposing that he was not thinking about the leisurely, spacious form of the Walter Scott type of novel, the complex interaction of plot and sub-plot characteristic of the Dickensian novel or the love-story form upon which the majority of European novels were based. But everything he says can be seen to be applicable to *Dead Souls,* although the lyricism of the work—that is to say, what Gogol in the first person brought to his narrative—can be regarded as additional to his definition of a novel and the possible cause of his entitling it 'a poem'.

Dead Souls, as it was published in 1842, consists of eleven chapters. Of these, Ch. 1 is introductory, depicting the arrival of Chichikov in the town of N; Chs 2-6 are largely dramatised episodes devoted to Chichikov's visits to the five landowners from whom he purchases the 'dead souls'. These five chapters are the central moments in the novel's action, while the remaining chapters serve as a *dénouement.* The plot is simple, but of central importance, like the hero; and in this respect, *Dead Souls* may be compared with *Eugene Onegin.* Like Pushkin, Gogol constructs his novel about the central theme of the hero and presents his theme in the threefold pattern of dramatised episode, narrative and commentary. But the affinity cannot really be taken much further than this. There is no love story in *Dead Souls* and there is a looseness or fluidity about the internal structure which, taken at its comic face value, seems almost to parody the classical discipline of Pushkin.

Such looseness or fluidity is to be seen in the way in which the central action of the novel is composed. Each of the dramatised episodes in Chs 2-6 is so designed as to create a situation which is essentially comic. The only common factor uniting these episodes is the theme of Chichikov himself and his desire to buy 'dead souls'; the 'misunderstandings' arising from his desire are what promote and

sustain the comic element. The situations are not strictly speaking related one to another by a developing plot or intrigue; they are intended simply as a means of presenting the two participants, Chichikov and whichever it is of the landowners, in a statis, in a separate portrait or a kind of one-act playlet with all the necessary trappings of scenery and atmosphere that can 'illustrate' the character of the landowner in question. Gogol's insistence, in his definition of the novel, that it should resemble a drama, is well illustrated by his method of presenting the characters in *Dead Souls.* The novel 'flies along like a drama, unified by the vital interest of the characters of the chief plot [or "happening", *proisshestviye*] in which they have been entangled' and which thereby makes them reveal their characters. Although Gogol states that a novel has 'a strictly and cleverly thought-out plot', this 'plot', it seems, is apparent chiefly through what happens to the hero, whereas the novel as a drama is unified in its forward flight by the vital interest of the characters who become involved in the hero's 'happening'. A sequential plot based on a logical concatenation of happenings seems to be unimportant to Gogol; it is certainly unimportant in *Dead Souls* where the meetings between Chichikov and the landowners occur without logical order, with the possible exception of the final visit to Plyushkin. They could be rearranged with no detriment to one's enjoyment of the novel.

A similar looseness is to be seen in the numerous narrative digressions that erupt in the shape of asides, elaborations or gossip from the main current of narration. There is never any doubt about the source of this narration: Gogol as narrator is ubiquitous, but he is dressed up in a clownish costume of coyness, feigned astonishment, throwaway remonstrances and arch patter in order to play the role. In the majority of cases such narrative asides are no more than slightly more obviously garrulous items in a prolix narrative and to bestow upon them so formal a title as 'digression' is to suggest that the main current of narration is not digressive. On the contrary, for Gogol the business of narration involves digression. To quote Sterne about his own work (though it is doubtful whether Gogol ever read *Tristram Shandy*): 'Digressions, incontestably, are the sunshine . . . take them out of this book for instance—you might as well take the book along with them.' The digressions, indeed, are what illuminate the narrative of *Dead Souls,* providing comic relief, flippant and mildly satirical comments on questions of language, narrative method, characterisation and so on, touching on and lightly implicating matters of great social and human import. In many ways, and in most cases, they have the appearance of being travesties of the type of topical, social commentary with which Pushkin embellished his narrative in *Eugene Onegin.*

A further digressive or deviant element in Gogol's narration is provided by his use of the simile, especially the extended or Homeric simile. These are so famous—the dancers at the governor's ball swarming like flies over a loaf of sugar, Nozdryov threatening Chichikov like a lieutenant storming an unassailable fortress, the town of N gripped by unease at the news of Chichikov's purchases like a schoolboy awaking to find a roll of paper stuck up his nose—that they require no detailed enumeration here.

Their essence is exaggeration, often to the point of grotesqueness. They resemble deeps in the narrative, momentary vistas of another consciousness and time upon which to base an archaeological understanding of the nursery-world Atlantis beneath *Dead Souls.* Or there are delightful, often paradoxical, shifts of focus in the narrative itself, which digress into glimpses of some lieutenant from Ryazan trying on boots (end of Ch. 7) or some Kifa Mokiyevich wondering what might happen if elephants were to be born in egg-shells (peeping out of a little window at the end of the poem). The effect of these digressions is primarily comic; their tone is usually subjective, deriving, that is to say, from the narrator himself and often giving expression to associations that are of greater significance to the narrator than to the reader. In this sense they have a poetic quality analogous to the type of simile or personal reference which may be found in a lyric poem rather than in a Homeric epic.

A further digressive tendency is more easily identifiable, for in this case Gogol is present in his novel more as first-person commentator than as narrator. The first of such commentaries occurs half-way through the novel, at the beginning of Ch. 6, when Chichikov is travelling towards Plyushkin's estate. Here Gogol clearly emerges in his own guise as a man regretful of his vanished youth, a solemn and gloomy companion of his delightedly chuckling hero:

> Now I drive up indifferently to every unfamiliar village and gaze indifferently at its commonplace exterior; to my chilled gaze all is unwelcoming, nothing is funny, and what in former years would have aroused animation in the face, laughter and unceasing talk now slips by and my motionless lips preserve an apathetic silence. O my youth! O my freshness!

Or at the opening of Ch. 7 when he contemplates the difficulty of his own lot as a bachelor and a writer who attempts to depict 'what is ever before one's eyes . . . all the terrible, insufferable slime of trivia that has encased our lives' by comparison with the good fortune of the family man and the writer who chooses to depict characters that evoke the lofty nobility of man. Here the comic, almost forced, jollity of the narrative is replaced by a tone of serious, even embittered, self-justification, which is not very different from the tone of his *Selected Passages.* In Ch. 11 the tone of the lyrical commentary which occurs before the author's final remarks about Chichikov and the revelation of the 'truth' about him is prophetic, exultant and oddly moving:

> Russia! Russia! I look at you, from my wondrous, beautiful distance I look at you . . . Russia! what do you want from me? what incomprehensible, secret link is there between us? Why do you look at me like that, and why is it that everything in you has turned to me eyes full of expectancy? . . . And still, full of doubts, I stand motionless, while my head's in the shadow of an ominous cloud heavy with imminent rain and my thoughts have grown numb before your vast empty spaces. What does this unencompassable vastness prophesy? Is it not here, is it not in you that some limitless idea will be born, when you are yourself without limit? Is it not

here that a *bogatyr* will arise, where there is space to spread himself and make his way in the world? And ominously the power of the vast spaces enfolds me, reflecting with fearful strength in the depths of my soul; and my eyes are alight with unnatural power: Oh, what glittering, wondrous distances unlike anything on earth! Russia!'

These, for all their naive rhetoric, are the 'serious' passages in *Dead Souls,* evidence—as Gogol put in his **"Author's Confession"**—of 'the lyrical power which I had at my disposal' and would use to depict the positive qualities in the Russian man. Perhaps this is the only serious element in the novel and all that really can be said to form a counterpoise to the essentially comic bias of the narrative and the narrative digressions.

Naturally these first-person commentaries are not isolated sections within fiction. They are like surges of inspiration in the current of the narrative and are in each case accompanied by passages that reveal Gogol in full descriptive spate. In Ch. 6, for instance, Gogol's cry for his lost youth is instantly followed by the brilliant description of the approach to Plyushkin's estate. The same thing is true of the commentary at the beginning of Ch. 7, which is accompanied by probably the most moving section in the whole novel (Chichikov's scrutiny of his dead souls). It is also true of the final, lyrical commentary in Ch. 11, which develops from the description of the countryside through which Chichikov is travelling and announces the last, revelatory section devoted to Chichikov's biography and his rushing troika. These are the supreme moments in the novel in the sense that they are supremely inspired, moments when the alchemy works and a picture taken from despised life becomes pure gold. But the terms of reference are Gogol's own, profoundly personal and subjective, inseparable from the chemistry of the fiction as a whole.

In *Eugene Onegin* Pushkin always attempted to separate his first-person commentary from the action of the novel, but in *Dead Souls* Gogol tends to intrude into his fiction with his first-person commentaries, to make it quite plain that the existence of his fiction is conditional upon his presence as its author. Yet Pushkin not only withheld himself from his fiction but, as a feature of this objectivity, used a technique of documentation by facts as a means of establishing his characters in a valid, historical context. The same technique is observable in *Dead Souls,* but so exaggerated as to be a parody of itself.

Before introducing the reader to Manilov, Gogol states his case in the following way:

> It is far easier to portray characters of great size: simply fling colours in gay abandon at the canvas—black blazing eyes here, jutting eyebrows there, a forehead furrowed with wrinkles, a black cloak, or one crimson as fire, thrown over the shoulders—and the portrait is ready; but as for all those gentlemen, of whom there are many in the world, who look so like each other, and yet when you peer closer you'll see many of the most elusive particularities—these gentlemen are frightfully hard to portray.

Manilov's 'elusive particularities' are not given anything

faintly resembling a biographical or historical setting; they are apparent only in the context of Manilovka itself, in the sugariness of his appearance, his turn of speech, his smile, in the total absence of any kind of enthusiastic hobby (*zador*), however impractical, and in such inconsequent facts as the book in his study forever open at page 14, the two uncovered chairs of the dining-room suite, the entirely unfurnished room, the magnificent candlestick, made of dark bronze and its ludicrous copper partner lopsidedly draped in wax. Here is the depiction of minutiae brought to the point of idiosyncrasy at which it ceases, practically speaking, to have any relevance as documentation.

Dead Souls is a mausoleum of such trivia, like the things relating to Korobochka, Sobakevich, Plyushkin and to Chichikov himself, especially his dead souls. It is tempting to assume that all the characters are little more than constructs of so many inconsequent eccentric facets, embedded deep within the layers of words which constitute *Dead Souls* as a novel, that they are, as it were, digressions from their settings in much the same way as the similes are digressions from the narrative or the narrator digresses from his purpose, that they are themselves chatterboxes forever losing their train of argument in their digressive fascination with words, and that this characteristic tendency to digress is best exemplified in the story of Captain Kopeykin as narrated by the post-master. But clearly, even though none of the characters is documented in the sense that Eugene Onegin can be said to be documented, none of them is such a mulch of words, so inhumanly fluid in characterisation, so moribundly composed of spiritless things.

In his **"Author's Confession"** Gogol has interesting things to say on the question of characterisation, confused though they may be through a characteristic vagueness and contradictoriness in the terminology. He insists that he has never created in the imagination:

> I have never created anything in the imagination and never had this ability. My results have only been successful when they have been taken from reality, from data known to me. I could only divine what a man was like when I had a picture of the most minute details of his external appearance. I have never *painted* a portrait, in the sense of making a simple copy. I have *created* a portrait, but I have created it as a consequence of consideration, not of imagination (*vsledstviye soobrazhen'ya, a ne voobrazhen'ya*). The more things I took into consideration, the more truthful was my creation. I had to know far more than any other writer, since I had only to overlook, or not take into consideration, certain details for the falsehood to stand out much more clearly in my case than in the case of any other writer.

The distinction between 'consideration' and 'imagination' is a major possible source of confusion here. That Gogol took from life, that he did not 'invent' characters, that he based his characters on contemporary reality as he understood it—such assertions can be accepted at their face value and are not really incompatible with the statement that: 'I have never *painted* a portrait, in the sense of making a simple copy.' He stresses that he *created* his por-

traits, but through consideration and not imagination, by which he presumably means that the creative process was not a question of simply flinging colours at the canvas but one of conscious accretion through considered observation of external appearance, of the things capable of making the portrait truthful. Yet the most essential, and, by any standards, most easily comprehensible, condition of this creative process was that the nucleus of the character, its embryo, should exist initially in Gogol's mind:

> This full embodiment in flesh, this full rounding of a character was achieved by me only when I gathered in my mind all the prosaic inherent pettiness of life, when, holding in my head all the principal features of the character, I would simultaneously collect round it all the old rags down to the smallest pin which daily surround a man—in a word, when I mentally considered everything from the greatest to the least, omitting nothing.

From this it seems possible to deduce that Gogol took from life, or from life at least as he understood it, certain principal features of a character which could only achieve full embodiment or roundness through Gogol's own accretion to it of all the prosaic inherent pettinesses of life, all the rags which surround a man in his daily life. At what point the 'external' appearance became the 'Gogolian' appearance it is impossible to say, but that Gogol's portrayal of character involved a 'Gogolianisation' of character seems to be beyond doubt. His claim that his characters are from his soul is by no means so difficult to understand as it may appear at first sight. His primary concern as a writer—spiritual causes and justifications apart—was the creation of character. No doubt it is a truism to say that all his characters emanated from him, but the point is that, in a work so full of digressive tendencies, the only real centres or constancies in *Dead Souls* are the characters. 'My heroes,' said Gogol, 'have still to become entirely separate from me, and therefore have not achieved real independence.' They can be said to have their source in his soul, in his creation of them, yet even if they can never be regarded as wholly independent of him they have a dominant role in his fiction, none more so than Chichikov. By Ch. 11, almost at the novel's conclusion, Gogol proclaims, albeit not too seriously: 'And readers mustn't be indignant at the author if the characters which have so far appeared have not suited his taste; that's Chichikov's fault, here he is completely in charge, and wherever he resolves to go we must follow in his wake.' Yet Gogol is only stating the obvious: the whole of *Dead Souls* is dominated by Chichikov and his 'undertaking'. There is no other causal factor in the work. Wherever Chichikov has gone the reader has to follow. And if Chichikov dominates the work as a whole, no less dominant in their several settings and episodes are the characters of those landowners whom it has suited Chichikov's taste to meet. Those sections upon which Gogol seems to have lavished the greatest care and spent the greatest time in writing are precisely those in which he was concerned with portrayal of character—that is to say, the first half of his novel, approximately to the end of Ch. 6. Knowing his work better than anyone else could, he had good reason to claim in the second of his letters about **Dead Souls** in the **Selected Passages,** referring to his first critics:

> No one even noticed that the last half of the book is less finished than the first half, that it has great gaps in it, that major and important issues are compressed and diminished, unimportant and secondary ones dwelt on at length, that it is not so much the inner spirit of the whole work that emerges clearly but the eye is distracted by the motley raggedness of its parts. Briefly, it would have been possible to make many attacks on me incomparably more to the point and to scold me for more than they do now, and to scold me roundly for not doing my job.

Gogol knew that his task as a writer was the creation of character and nowhere is this seen to greater effect than in the first half of **Dead Souls.**

The hero enters the novel anonymously, out of nowhere, amorphously, 'neither handsome, but neither of ugly appearance, neither too stout, nor too thin; it could not be said that he was old, and yet again it could not be said that he was too young', and it is not therefore this shadowy gentleman who attracts the attention of the two Russian peasants and the young man with the Tula tie-pin in the shape of a pistol, but the carriage in which he travels and the doubtful wheel, just as it is the problem of Chichikov's motive or purpose which forms the central theme of the novel. The dramatic character of his entry into the town of NN and equally the total absence of any information about NN itself (supposedly north of Moscow) conform both to Gogol's idea that a novel should fly along like a drama and to that lack of concern for setting save in relation to character which is so important a principle of Gogol's technique. Like a chameleon, the hero seems to blend with the town, to exhibit, throughout the first chapter, a congruity in keeping with the stoutness and thinness of the town itself, spacious in some parts and cramped in others, with the Governor, who resembled him in being neither too stout nor too thin, with the fat and thin groups of men at the Governor's ball. Before the reader even knows his name, he knows more about the average character of the inn with its prune-size cockroaches peering out of the corners or its waiter hurrying by with his tray piled with as many tea cups as there are birds on the sea-shore. For the inn is the hero's only true setting, and only a transient one at that. The transience of his character is evident throughout the novel in the sense that he is the only source of movement, judged almost invariably by the other characters (and the reader) on the basis of appearances but little else. More is known about his two servants, his luggage, and very significantly, his trumpeting nose—insinuating itself like a snake, as Andrey Bely suggests, among the chiaroscuro of lunatic facts—than is known about him before his name revealed. And even when the name is revealed, it is not Chichikov who reveals it, but the waiter who spells out its extraordinary syllables as he comes down the stairs. Chichikov never reveals himself: others reveal, or unearth, details about him—the waiter his rank and name, the landowners his nefarious plan, the narrator (obligingly in conclusion) his former life. Chichikov's pre-eminent characteristic is his air of familiarity; he is presumed to be known to everyone, he is the eminently familiar stranger whom everyone knows, respects, befriends, even loves—tubby, laughable, lovable Chichikov.

To the officials and dignitaries of the town he is an immediate source of flattery and respectful interest, but they are little more than ciphers—Governor, Vice-Governor, Public Prosecutor and so on—who have no more specific identity than the town. To them, if he said anything at all, he addressed only commonplaces, with noticeable modesty and in a bookish turn of phrase—suited, it may be supposed, to their official tastes and no doubt to their fatuously self-important notions of service. Coupled with his chameleon-like ability to accommodate himself to any situation, so that he was always able to speak on any (never very exacting) topic with a certain acumen and novelty 'neither too loudly nor too softly, but exactly right', such accoutrements, such bland suavity of dress, quickly earned him the reputation of being 'a very decent chap'—a reputation multiplied into successive grades of excellence by all officials from the Governor downwards. To put it briefly, Chichikov takes the town by storm. The situation is one of comic opera founded on the author's artful concealment of real motives. But there are no real motives ascribable to the town's officials; throughout the novel they are figures of comedy for all their grotesqueness. The only figures of moment are those so casually named and introduced—Manilov, Sobakevich, Nozdryov—who fit Gogol's remark in his definition of a novel: 'Each appearance of a character, initially apparently insignificant, heralds his participation later.' These are the figures whom it suits Chichikov's taste to meet later. On the way he meets two more by accident, but it is worth remarking that this novel, apparently so filled with people, really has no more than six characters.

Equally noteworthy, though perhaps not immediately apparent, is that the time occupied by the events in the novel is remarkably short. Chichikov spends just over a week in the unsuspecting town of NN before starting on his visits in Ch. 2. Having started on his visits, he stays overnight only with Korobochka, by accident, and with Nozdryov, equally accidentally. Presumably it was his original intention to use the town as a base from which he would sally forth on his visits by day and return to at night, but a comic fate intervenes to destroy this plan. Such fate is actually no more comic an agent than the weather, that 'light-gray coloured' weather which characterises the day of his visit to Manilov and resembles the colour of the old uniforms of garrison soldiers ('those peaceful troops, but always a little tipsy on Sundays'); and yet this bland, seemingly innocuous weather has become ominously thundery by the beginning of Ch. 3 and obliges him to seek refuge at Korobochka's house after Selifan has overturned him into the mud. The second agent of fate is Nozdryov—and Nozdryov is indeed a fateful figure in Chichikov's story, as later events show. But the fact remains that Chichikov spends only two nights away from town, the amorphous town which never provides a setting for him and endlessly fails to make up its mind about him. Altogether, we know Chichikov for less than a month: his story is no more than Gogol believed a novel's should be—'a notable happening in life, of a kind which has made life reveal itself in a brilliant form'.

The visit to Manilov in Ch. 2 is prefaced by a question-and-answer routine between Chichikov and a peasant with a wedge-shaped beard that establishes the comic tone of the whole Manilovka episode. There never has been a Zamanilovka, the peasant assures Chichikov (and save for Chichikov's playful inventiveness there is no reason why it was ever mentioned at all), but of course Manilovka exists, with its English garden and Temple of Solitary Thought set above a pond covered with green duckweed, suggesting in its combination of genteel pretentiousness and disorderly squalor the character of its owner. Yet such details do no more than suggest Manilov's character. He is a question mark and he expresses himself in terms of questions which are designed to elicit an invariably unquestioning and affirmative response. Manilov's polite but meaningless interrogation of Chichikov about the respective virtues of the town's officials is followed by Chichikov's equally polite but meaningless interrogation of Femistoklyus, the elder Manilov son, and finally by the scene in which Manilov's expectation of an affirmative response to his inquiry about Chichikov's intended purchases is rudely shattered. Here, for the first time in the novel, Chichikov divulges his purpose:

> "But for what reasons do you need this?" asked Manilov after the steward's departure.
>
> This question, it seemed, embarrassed his guest and there appeared on his face a kind of tense expression from which he even reddened, a tenseness of feature connected with expressing something that was not entirely amenable to words. And in fact Manilov finally heard such strange and unusual things as no man's ears had ever heard before.
>
> "You ask for what reasons? The reasons are these: I would like to buy peasants . . . " said Chichikov, stumbled and did not finish what he was saying.
>
> "But allow me to ask you," said Manilov, "how you would like to buy the peasants—with land or simply for transfer, that is without land?"
>
> "No, I didn't have in mind peasants as such," said Chichikov: "I want to have dead ones . . . "
>
> "What was that? Forgive me . . . I'm a little hard of hearing, but I seemed to hear a very odd word . . . "
>
> "I am proposing to acquire dead ones, who, however, would be designated as alive in the last census," said Chichikov.
>
> Here Manilov let his pipe fall to the floor, and no sooner had he opened his mouth than he remained for several minutes with his mouth wide open.

Manilov's shock at this revelation is obviously farcical, but it is farcical in a theatrical sense. The scene leaves the impression of being staged, as though it had been composed originally for the stage but with the stage directions baldly revamped to suit the purposes of a novel. There is a deliberate comic distancing of the characters and their reactions with the clear aim of suggesting not an intimate understanding of how they will behave (any author's prerogative), but a wonderment at the "strangeness" of Chichikov's undertaking, at the misunderstandings which form the basis of the confrontation and the comic shattering of Manilov's composure. The scene is played in the manner of farce or burlesque.

Manilov's reaction to Chichikov's request is true to his questionable character: he asks a refined question about whether or not their 'negotiation' will be out of keeping with the civil regulations and the future prospects of Russia. No one in *Dead Souls* is more cerebral than Manilov. And this trait, for all its comic ineptness, is infectious not only within the confines of his own Manilovka and the whole of Ch. 2, but beyond, in the following chapter and Selifan's admonitions. If Manilov's daydreaming comes to an abrupt end with Chichikov's incomprehensible desire for dead souls, then Selifan's equally meandering outpourings to the horses are just as unceremoniously curtailed by the thunderclap, which forewarns of the accidental visit to Korobochka.

It forewarns of Korobochka because everything associated with Korobochka's twin appearances in the novel involves thunderous noise and darkness. The chorus of barking dogs which greets Chichikov's arrival at Korobochka's estate is only one of the variety of remarkable noises which he finds there: the clock and farm animals later enliven night and morning. The second appearance of Korobochka, at the end of Ch. 9, is just as noisy, but this time it is her watermelon-shaped carriage which makes such a din and attracts such attention as it rattles through the dawn streets. What epitomises Korobochka, and so obviously distinguishes her from Manilov, is the abject materialism of her character, her total involvement with things for their own sake. Her most solicitous gesture of hospitality is an offer to scratch her guest's heels and her reaction to his offer to buy her dead souls is eminently practical: 'You wouldn't be wanting to dig them out of the earth, would you?' She incarnates a domesticity so total that no abstract notion has a place in it, least of all an abstraction so utterly unworldly as dead souls. Chichikov, we note, suits himself at once to her tastes. Gogol remarks that he spoke to her with much greater freedom than with Manilov—a remark which provokes a digression on the shades and refinements of Russian social intercourse. But the digression ends, significantly enough, with the author addressing himself directly to the reader: 'But let us, however, turn to our *dramatis personae*. Chichikov, as we have already seen, had resolved not to stand on ceremony at all and therefore, picking up the cup of tea and adding the fruit liqueur to it, spoke as follows.' Gogol is obviously emphasising the 'theatricality' of the episode. The reader is placed in the position of an audience at a play, and Gogol for the most part gives the illusion of witnessing the confrontation of his characters on the same terms. He is a playwright, as it were, sitting in his audience. Rather fussily, quirkily and ambiguously, in a manner teetering between the ponderous and the ludicrous, he is perpetually agitated over the way in which the roles of his characters are acted and the way his audience should react. Korobochka is projected to us as a comic or grotesque character through a conscious exaggeration of her domesticated and obtuse manner. Her role is dependent for success on the props of her setting; without them her character would consist of a number of amusing lines which would require careful overplaying to achieve the requisite effect (her over-serious concern with the price of dead souls, her superstitious terror at Chichikov's mention of the devil).

In conformity with the ambience of the episode, Chichikov also needs his props. For the first time in the novel he is no longer presented as a mask. His inner reactions to the old woman's obstinacy are described in some detail, as is the most important of his props, his box. Both are built on two layers. In outward appearance Chichikov is suave, urbane, well-dressed, with all the required social accomplishments, but beneath this facade is the acquisitive desire to possess dead souls. The upper part of his box therefore contains all the materials necessary for maintaining Chichikov's man-of-the-world urbanity and elegance: the soap, razors, ink, quills, sealing wax and other social mementoes such as visiting cards and funeral notices. All this might be lifted out to reveal the sheaves of paper beneath it (as useless as the 'dust' of his lists of dead souls) and the secret money drawer which he invariably opened and shut so quickly that it was impossible to judge how much money it contained. The visit to Korobochka is the first glimpse of that second—acquisitive—layer of Chichikov's character. Yet the two are inseparable: if he gorges his acquisitive ambition on Korobochka's dead souls, he also gorges his plump urbanity on her pancakes dipped in butter.

Chichikov leaves Korobochka, but Korobochka's domestically feminine ambience follows him into Ch. 4 and into the scene at the hostelry when he once more gorges himself and chats with the resident old maidservant about the local landowners (whom she appears to know a great deal better than Korobochka), mentioning by name both Manilov and Sobakevich. In an instant, though, up drives Nozdryov and the rest of the chapter is pervaded by his tipsy, repetitive loquacity which revels in bombast and grotesquely hearty camaraderie. Nozdryov is the only landowner from whom Chichikov makes no purchases, and it is his careless immaturity which, in divulging Chichikov's desire to buy *dead* souls, causes Chichikov's eventual downfall. Gogol emphasises Nozdryov's callowness: 'Nozdryov at thirty-five was completely as he had been at eighteen and at twenty: a great fellow at having a good time.'

This characteristic is the source of his lack of caution and his bombast, and is the feature which 'infects' Chichikov in his encounter with him:

> Chichikov remained after Nozdryov's departure in a most unpleasant state of spirits. He was inwardly vexed with himself and blamed himself for having visited him and lost time to no purpose. But he blamed himself even more for having started talking about his business [i.e. about dead souls] and having behaved incautiously, like a child, like a fool.

In other words, for having behaved exactly like Nozdryov. The exchanges between the two are of an outrageously farcical character without parallel in the other episodes; and it is virtually impossible to distinguish between them in degree of comic invective, exclamation and riposte. The point is that, appearances to the contrary, Chichikov and Nozdryov are the characters most nearly similar to each other in the whole novel; or, to put it another way, Nozdryov is, of all the landowners, the one least firmly related to a particular setting. His 'world' is not distinguishable in the terms of a Manilovka or such a domestic ambience as characterised Korobochka; his is a world of bits and pieces, of hostelry, fair-ground and town, of wifeless, partly whitewashed home which he cannot abide for more than a day at a time and where, if he relates to anyone at all, it is to his pack of dogs with such verbally imperative names as Shoot, Curse, Jump, and Fire. His world is that of a bivouac, rather martial in character, filled with showy, second-hand trash which neither works properly (like his hurdy-gurdy) nor is exactly what he claims it is (like his Turkish daggers and collection of pipes). The bombastic exaggeration of Nozdryov has its repeated martial grace notes, of which the most effective is the description he gives to the taste in his mouth after the abominable wine of the previous night's dinner: 'and my mouth feels just as if a troop of horse had spent the night in it!' The martial aspect of his character is finally epitomised in the Homeric simile of a desperate lieutenant storming an unassailable fortress; and the scene ends on a note of exaggeration which typically represents the frightened Chichikov as being 'in the most pitiful state in which mortal man ever found himself'. Rescued from Nozdryov's wrath in the nick of time by the intervention of the captain of police, Chichikov jumps into his carriage and sets off for Sobakevich's estate.

Yet the issue of Chichikov as 'mortal man' slips over from the end of Ch. 4 into the first paragraphs of Ch. 5. One might legitimately wonder whether Chichikov is mortal at all, but he clearly has no doubts on that score; his apprehensions have another basis:

> "Say what you like," he said to himself: "If the captain of police hadn't arrived in time, I might never've had the chance of glimpsing God's world again! I'd've vanished like a bubble on water without a trace, leaving no descendants, leaving my future children neither property nor an honest name!" Our hero was very much concerned about his descendants.

With this thought dominant in his mind, he is greeted shortly afterwards by a vision of his Dulcinea in the shape of a girl of sixteen, who later proves to be the Governor's daughter; but the resemblance of the pretty oval of her face to a newly-laid egg lends the requisite air of farce to the incident. The symbolism of this momentary debacle is apt. Chichikov's carriage, interlocked with the carriage carrying the mother and daughter, is slowly unhitched by the clumsy efforts of peasants upon whose deaths Chichikov is intending to build his future, while his eyes are fixed on the fertility-symbol which can provide him with all his descendants or—as Merezhkovsky describes it—'the millions of happy little Chichikovs, in which are repeated, as the sun in the waters of the Pacific Ocean, the single *begetter* of this kingdom, the deathless *hero* of dead souls, the noumenal Chichikov'. But Chichikov is already middle-aged and of cautious temperament. The vision understandably stirs him from his customary habit of thought for a while, but on coming to his senses he is content to regard the whole matter in terms of profit and loss and to endow the girl with a dowry of two hundred thousand roubles. The Homeric simile accompanying the incident hints at that pursuit of inessentials, of the glamorous trivia of life, which characterises both Nozdryov and Chichikov, especially the former, and is perhaps at the source of Chichikov's downfall:

> Everywhere, across whatever sorrows from which our life is woven, gaily there will dash a glittering joy, just as sometimes a glittering carriage with golden harnessings, picturesque horses and a flashing brilliance of glass will suddenly dash unexpectedly past some stagnant impoverished village which has seen nothing save a country cart, and the peasants stand for a long while gaping at it with open mouths, their caps in their hands, although the wondrous carriage has long since driven away and passed from sight.

After two failures, Chichikov finally succeeds in reaching Sobakevich. The dog-like, or bearish, clumsiness and obstinacy in his character are amply illustrated by the stoutness of his house, the portraits on the wall and his furniture. His is a world of obtuse, lumbering practicality which eschews the subtleties and pretentions of the town and is contemptuous of the fanciful cuisine of the Governor's house or the gentry in general (for Sobakevich is self-made, a kulak). Sobakevich knows his own mind. His eating habits demonstrate as much:

> "They've invented dieting, the starvation cure! What with their thin-boned German nature, they imagine they can do the same thing with our Russian stomach! No, it's not the thing, it's all their invention, it's all . . . " At this point Sobakevich even shook his head angrily. "They talk about enlightenment, enlightenment, but this enlightenment—I say fook to it! I'd've said something else, only it's impolite to use such a word at table. That's not how I do things. When I have pork, I say serve the whole pig, mutton—bring in the whole sheep, goose—the whole goose! I'd rather eat only two dishes, but eat enough of each, as the soul demands." Sobakevich affirmed this by doing so: he overturned half the side of mutton on to his plate, ate it all, gnawing and sucking it clean down to the last little bone.

It is hardly surprising that at the end of the gargantuan meal at Sobakevich's house Chichikov (who had by no means starved himself the day before) should feel that he had put on a whole pood, or thirty-six pounds, in weight.

Sobakevich's world, though it resembles Korobochka's, has a solidity which is oddly leavened by sensitivity. In his bear-like fashion he has a habit of stepping on people's feet, but his first words to Chichikov are a recognition of this 'sin' of his: 'I haven't inconvenienced you, have I?' (*ne*

pobespokoil li ya vas?). Later, at the height of the negotiations, he does stand on Chichikov's foot, but is instantly overcome by a bruinish solicitude for the hurt done to his guest. He has a soul in the quite superficial sense that he eats as much as 'the soul demands' and in the funnier, more humane sense, that he, of all the landowners, is the one best able to conjure life into his dead serfs, even if only for purposes of profit. The divide between Chichikov and his host is neatly summarised by Chichikov's pragmatic, whimsical and even faintly animating description of all that remains of the dead souls as 'only a sound imperceptible to the feelings' (*odin ne osyazaemy chuvstvami zvuk*) and Sobakevich's heated insistence that what remained of them was their skill, strength and size, far more animate to him than the puffs of sound of their several names—Stepan the Cork, carpenter; Milushkin, bricklayer; Maxim Telyatnikov, shoemaker—and worth every copeck of a hundred roubles.

In his approach to Sobakevich Chichikov uses the circuitous manner beloved of Manilov and the town's officials—a misjudgment on his part due perhaps to his having first encountered Sobakevich in the town, perhaps also to the shock of his recent escape from Nozdryov, but chiefly because by this stage in the novel he is no longer a chameleon. His style and manner are now his own, and he pre-empts in the scene of the exchanges with Sobakevich the role of narrator in his asides and the comments which he passes finally on his host. He was of course cheated by Sobakevich, who turned out to be cleverer than he was at hard dealing. It is hardly surprising at this departure that 'He was dissatisfied with Sobakevich's behaviour. Regardless, no matter how you look at it, he was an acquaintance, they'd met at both the Governor's and the police chief 's, but he'd behaved exactly like a stranger, he'd taken money for a lot of old rubbish!' He had behaved like Sobakevich, for Sobakevich manifestly *is* in a more absolute or incontrovertible sense than any of the other landowners: no matter where he was he would always remain the same bear-like Sobakevich with the canine nature. Chichikov acknowledges as much to himself during his musings on his host's appearance, and Gogol, entering the novel as author/commentator at the chapter's conclusion, fixes the idea for ever by underlining the power of a Russian nickname to characterise a person from head to foot. In other words, Sobakevich is more dog-like than Nozdryov is snoutish, Korobochka is boxy, Manilov is unctuous. Even so, in terms of characterisation, he exists primarily as a figure whose role is enacted within the confines of his setting, dependent upon the props of his world.

With Chichikov's final visit, to the miserly Plyushkin, the elegiac tone already discernible in the Sobakevich episode, if only like the remnant of a sound which Chichikov uses to describe his purchases, begins to make itself felt not only in Gogol's own lament on his vanished youth but in the whole lamentable condition of Plyushkin's world. Ironically Gogol lavishes more of his precious gift of verbal alchemy on Plyushkin than on any other landowner in ***Dead Souls.*** For baroque exuberance of detail, for suggestion of light upon dark, foreground and distance, heights and depths, the description of the broad expanse of old garden behind Plyushkin's house is justly celebrat-

Chichikov visiting Plyushkin.

ed. But it is scarcely more than an overture to the symphonic evocation of junk, dilapidation and decades of dust which fill Plyushkin's house and make of ***Dead Souls*** an elegiac poem to uselessness, to every form of human detritus and, above all, to that 'gap in humanity' through which the unredeemed dead souls peer momentarily in their hundreds and thousands. Plyushkin is prophetic of ends, not means, for means are pointless in his profitless junkyard—prophetic, that is, of the end of Chichikov's labours, just as the commentary in Ch. 7 is prophetic of the author's labours, but equally prophetic of the decay of all human endeavour, of all human acquisitiveness, of what may indeed come to pass in the destinies of all the other landowners and not least in Chichikov's own. Of all the characters in the novel significantly enough only the hero and Plyushkin, who embodies the likely gruesome culmination of the hero's ambitions, are given beginnings; they alone have biographies; and it is conceivable that Chichikov's dream bubble of respectability, a wife, a home and children, ludicrously unrealised in the novel as we know it, may be anticipated and forever pricked by the eminently moral, not to say conventional, tale of Plyushkin's decay into miserliness. The asexual, curmudgeonly Plyushkin is nevertheless superbly animated through dialogue as packed with bric-à-brac expressions as his setting. His speech rummages in the Russian language and raises

a veritable dust storm of pleonasms. But the staginess of his characterisation, creature of his own world though he is, gains depth and substance through the poeticised squalor of his setting and the elaborate description of his own person, particularly in the horrific reality of the Homeric simile describing his smile.

Plyushkin is the only landowner so totally related to his setting in the novel that it would be impossible to conceive of him in any other circumstances. Yet his miserliness has universal connotations: it is no more Russian or particularised than Scrooge's. Whether or not Gogol hoped to elicit the reader's sympathy for this 'fallen' Plyushkin by introducing his biography is not really clear, but such treatment can hardly be said to sentimentalise the portrait. Plyushkin emerges, especially through the grotesque abundance of his dialogue, as a miser of singular robustness; and it is the comic, rather than the pathetic, aspects of his condition which seem paramount. To Chichikov, of course, the visit is a source of acute pleasure. Some lively negotiation and even more lively mental arithmetic net him more than two hundred of Plyushkin's dead souls, and he returns to a town curiously metamorphosed by dusk—sentries wearing moustaches on their foreheads, women flitting bat-like over street crossings, a metaphorical young man with his head full of Schiller—and to the inn, his only home, while Gogol, at the opening of Ch. 7, muses on his own homelessness as a writer.

The musings are an obvious prolongation of that elegiac mood associated with the crabbed senility of Plyushkin, but magnified into a plaint about the contrast between the ideal and the real which repeats the comic contrast between the young man's dreams of Schiller and the day-to-day spectacle of life. How seriously should one take Gogol's lyrical argumentation, which totters so flamboyantly along its tightrope of poetic prose and only just avoids teetering into the bathos of his ***Selected Passages?*** For the temptation is clearly there. Diamond-like though some passages are, others are a florid paste. Eventually Gogol shakes himself free of his own rhetoric and returns to the life of his fiction: 'Let's be off! Let's be off! Begone the wrinkle alighting on the brow and gloomy severity of feature! Let us plunge all at once into life, with all its noiseless nitter-natter and tinkling bells, and see what Chichikov is doing.' And practically all the rest of the novel is concerned either with Chichikov's doings or with the doings of the town in response to Chichikov's strange enterprise. And practically all is narrated with that inimitable serio-comic gossipiness at which Gogol excels, which, however surreal in some of its arabesques, contrives to suggest unremitting mental sobriety, surpassing respectability of tone and even an almost unfeigned disapproval of our levity.

Chichikov returns to the town as a proprietor in his own right. The object of his three-day journeyings has been accomplished, much to his satisfaction—and he signifies the fact with his two spirited uncharacteristic leaps about the room, dressed in a short kilt-like nightshirt and whacking the heel of his foot against his bare behind. His future happiness is now almost ensured. It is such dedication to ends at the expense of means, such determination to make an honest, or honoured, man of himself which tends to raise Chichikov in the esteem of the reader and even, paradoxically enough, endows him with a certain moral superiority over the other characters. He is at least given a purpose and a certain competence in attaining it. He has, what is more, buoyancy as a character and an inherent propensity for surprising one by suggesting unsuspected aspects of himself. The hint is of course his hallmark. But by comparison with Manilov and Sobakevich, who now reappear in the novel, Chichikov exudes a remarkable vivacity and versatility of character, and one almost suspects that he has hidden depths.

At the height of his happiness the interest of the novel shifts (Ch. 8) from him to the townspeople and their diverse conjectures about Chichikov's identity and the nature of his wealth. The pattern here faintly echoes Pushkin's shift of emphasis in Ch. 7 of *Eugene Onegin* from Onegin himself to Tatyana, whose commentary upon him serves to highlight the enigmatic and contrary characteristics of this 'Moscovite in Harold's cloak'. To all appearances, Chichikov is as novel a phenomenon in the town of N as was Onegin in the society of the Larins. Like Onegin, he becomes an object of doting admiration for the womenfolk, a millionaire of the provinces and the recipient of a love-letter from some appalling rural Tatyana with most distressing lines of verse appended to it. Quite unlike Onegin, he pays the letter and its author the supreme compliment of setting it alongside a theatre bill and a wedding invitation in his box. His reaction is appropriately 'bourgeois': the letter contained a 'beautiful' thought, he would wish therefore to have it for himself. Sentimentality and acquisitiveness are dominant features of his character.

At the Governor's ball, which is the last complete scene in the novel, the two people who are instrumental in causing Chichikov's downfall reflect these twin aspects of his character. Though anxious to discover the author of the love-letter, he is quickly attracted to the Governor's daughter, about whom his sentimental dreams of marriage had recently hovered, and in paying her undue attention he naturally offends all the other ladies. Similarly, it is Nozdryov, the most ludicrously acquisitive of all the landowners, who broadcasts the fact of Chichikov's desire to purchase *dead* souls. This causes irreparable harm to his reputation. But his fate is sealed finally by the arrival of Korobochka's strange vehicle, clattering noisily through the streets after his return from the ball, which is as stolid and decrepit as his own troika-drawn *brichka* is swift and birdlike, and which sets off the mechanism of retribution.

The question which vexes the townspeople of N is not what Chichikov may have intended in his enterprise—dead souls, after all, can mean so many things—but who this Chichikov is; and the question could equally well exercise the reader at this stage in the novel. That he is not likely to abduct the Governor's daughter, or be mistaken for Captain Kopeykin, or Napoleon, or a forger of banknotes, or an inspector general may strike the reader as obvious enough, even though it is not so obvious to the townspeople. That the object of all such comic speculation in Chs 9 and 10 is simply to excite interest in the 'truth' about Chichikov before Gogol reveals his past in Ch. 11

must strike the reader as equally obvious. By the same token, the 'story' of *Dead Souls* as a novel is that of Chichikov's gradual maturation from anonymity to the point where he assumes an overwhelmingly dominant role in the fiction, so that the fiction itself begins to appear in retrospect as no more than a vehicle for his characterisation. Then, at the point when all eyes are on him, when all disbelief is suspended, Gogol divulges the 'truth'—and it appears that everyone, reader included, has been duped: Chichikov is quite simply a rogue, there is not a scrap of virtue in him.

Who is Chichikov? He is, Gogol seems to be saying, the acquisitive urge in all of us; and such an urge grows out of the impoverished state of our being, manifests an impoverishment of spirit which we seek to overlook and yet remains a universally comic aspect of the human condition. But the pathos of Chichikov's characterisation resides less in the special pleading which Gogol makes for his hero towards the close of his novel than in the pathetic detail of the portrait itself. The reader, scorning that which is least noble in himself, will laugh at Chichikov, unaware that he is laughing either at Gogol himself, Chichikov's only begetter, or at that very boyishness which Chichikov himself has turned into the impulse to acquire the trappings of social status or what might perhaps be called 'poshness'. It began with half a rouble given him by his father; it grew by way of a coloured bullfinch made of wax, some judicious profiting from his classmates' hunger and a mouse which he trained to do tricks, into five roubles; and from five roubles into Holland shirts, fragrant French soap, a carriage, two servants and a yearning for social status, obtainable by fair means or foul. The sheer bourgeois ordinariness of this boyish ambition invites amusement, compassion and abhorrence in almost equal measure. The universality of Chichikov's acquisitive urge is particularised in the semi-feudal circumstances of pre-reform Russia into a buying of 'dead souls', but he seeks no more than this, so far as one can tell. He does not seek salvation for his own soul, as his creator did, even though Gogol is ready to impute to him a soul ('Had not the author peered deeper into his soul, had he not stirred up at the bottom of it . . .') which is presumably capable of salvation or at least of repentance (the final surviving episode of Pt 2 suggests as much). For Chichikov, no matter how much is revealed about his past and his motives, never leaves the impression of having a private existence, an essentially private realm of experience.

Such an impression springs naturally from Gogol's theatricalisation of his hero. Mock-humorous though his exaggerated solicitude for his hero may be, it produces the effect of setting Chichikov at some removes from the reader's intimate scrutiny, as though he were on public exhibition in a theatre with Gogol, his manager, always protectively at hand. The artifice is obvious towards the novel's close:

> But we have begun to talk rather loudly, forgetting that our hero, who was asleep throughout the story of his life, has already awakened and could easily hear his own name being repeated so often. He is, after all, a man quick to take offence and dissatisfied if people pass disrespectful

remarks about him. The reader couldn't care less whether Chichikov is angry at him or not, but as for the author, he must on no account quarrel with his hero.

Chichikov is projected in terms of a stage character, complete with all the props needed for his act; but the least effective of such props is precisely the one which violates his theatricality—the story of his life—for it aspires to give him a private existence when his effectiveness as a character lies exclusively in his public image. All the most effective episodes in this 'poem' of a novel are conceived and presented in theatrical terms. The basis of such episodes is naturally dialogue; and there can be little doubt that, in writing **Dead Souls,** Gogol drew on his experience as a playwright of comedy in the writing of **Revizor.** The separate episodes of the visits to the five landowners, the town's reactions to the news of Chichikov's purchases (at the beginning of Ch. 8), the exchanges between 'the lady who was pleasant' and 'the lady who was pleasant in every respect' (at the beginning of Ch. 9), the postmaster's story of Captain Kopeykin (at the beginning of Ch. 10) suggest that Gogol's primary impulse, in creating character and situation, was to 'dramatise'. The characterisation of Chichikov is dependent upon this same 'dramatising' process, until, by the novel's end, he has emerged as a character whose public image is projected so skillfully that considerations of privacy become irrelevant.

Dead Souls can clearly be seen to fit Gogol's own definition of a novel as a highly poetic work which resembles not an epic so much as a drama. The relation of character to setting, the central significance of the hero, the brevity of the time-span in which the events occur, not to mention the singular importance of dialogue, are factors which contribute very strongly to this impression about the novel. The dramatic form is undeniably obscured in part by the numerous narrative interpolations, lyrical digressions, first-person commentaries and other digressive tendencies, but these may also be seen as exuberant embellishments—as exuberant as Gogol's language—of what in essentials is a story conceived as 'flying along like a drama'. The decrease in the dramatic form from the end of Ch. 6 onwards reflects Gogol's increasing preoccupation with the serious ends of his work, couched though it is in a mock-serious narrative manner which resembles gossip rather than the sermonising of his **Selected Passages.** It is very probable that the last character Gogol ever created was Plyushkin; at least, he is the last character to have been created in **Dead Souls,** and all that follows, though it tells the story of Chichikov's discomfiture, is thinner, less splendidly detailed and less inventive than the marvellous first half-dozen chapters of the novel. The shades, one feels, of Gogol's religious manner are already beginning to fall across his work, inhibiting that ebulliently unselfconscious talent for depicting the *poshlost' poshlogo cheloveka* and turning the theatre of his literary art, where laughter could resound so easily, into the church of his spiritual fears, where little could be heard save unending lamentation. (pp. 87-114)

> *Richard Freeborn, " 'Dead Souls'," in his* The Rise of the Russian Novel: Studies in the Russian Novel from "Eugene Onegin" to "War and Peace," *Cambridge at the University Press, 1973, pp. 74-114.*

Jesse Zeldin   (essay date 1978)

[*An American critic specializing in Russian literature, Zeldin is the editor and translator of Gogol's* Selected Passages from Correspondence with My Friends. *He is also the author of* Nikolai Gogol's Quest for Beauty: An Exploration into His Works, *in which he argues that "Gogol was primarily interested in the nature of reality, which he identified with beauty." In the following excerpt from that work, Zeldin considers the nature and purpose of Part 2 of* Dead Souls.]

What we have of **Dead Souls,** Part 2, is more a group of fragments than it is a connected whole, giving rise to the suspicion, which we have already expressed, that, no matter what the author's intentions may have been originally, he was finding it next to impossible to fulfill them. Certainly, continuity from Part I (assuming that we do have the beginning of Part 2) is lacking, as though Chichikov's troika had either stalled or broken down entirely. Perhaps Gogol discovered himself caught between what he wanted to do and what his public wanted. His own desires . . . were hard enough to accomplish without the pressure to produce a sequel in the same vein as Part 1. Compromise was equally difficult, although that seems to be the path he chose, so far as we can judge from the fragments that we have. Unfortunately, compromise was but a way to ensure failure, as Gogol quickly realized. Whether or not the burnings were a result of the failure of compromise, whether he finally gave it up and attempted to follow his own vision, we do not know. All that we do know for certain is that, if he was not totally frustrated, he was at least convinced finally that success was beyond his grasp.

A glance at the history of Part 2 (Part 3 was probably never even begun) illustrates Gogol's problems. We know that he was at least thinking of Part 2 even before the final revisions of Part 1 had been completed. By August 1842, under pressure from both friends and critics to continue and troubled by this pressure because of the questions posed by the new path that he wished to take, Gogol wrote to S. T. Aksakov that "the full meaning of the lyrical hints can only be elucidated when the last part is published." That very elucidation was the difficulty, even though he was fully persuaded of the value of his position. Beauty and truth, perfection indeed, was his ultimate subject, but, he says in the first paragraph of Part 2, "What is to be done if the writer's character is such that he has fallen ill of his own imperfection?" I would suggest that it is not only moral imperfection that Gogol had in mind here; of equal import, if not of greater import, was what he perceived as his own *artistic* imperfection, as a person and as a writer. Actualization of beauty had, to him, both aspects, and neither could be accomplished without the other. It was not that his artistic powers were failing, that he had "burned himself out," but that the goal was of a different order from those powers—means and ends could not meet. As the latter portions of Part 1 indicate, he was identifying himself with his work. Several times in Part 1 he had spoken of lyricism, and he spoke of it again in his letter to Aksakov. In *A Textbook of Literature for Russian Youth* he defined the lyric, or rather lyrical poetry, as follows:

> Lyrical poetry is a portrait, a reflection and a mirror of the loftiest movements of the poet's soul, notes necessary to him, the biography of his ecstasies. It is, from the loftiest to the lowest of its kinds, nothing other than an account of the poet's own sensations. Whether he thunders in an ode, sings in a song, plains in an elegy, or narrates in a ballad, everywhere the poet is expressing the personal secrets of his own soul. In short, it is the pure personality of the poet himself and pure truth [*pravda*]. A lie in lyrical poetry is perilous, for the inflation will expose it: the moment someone who has the flair of a poet hears it, he will call him a liar wearing the mask of a poet. It is vast and comprises the entire internal biography of a man.

The lyric, self-expression, had been Gogol's ambition at the very beginning of his career, and we know that he returned to it in some of the digressions at the end of Part 1 and at the time of his first attempts at Part 2. Even before beginning Part 2 he had evidently realized that Gofreddo was impossible, and he had resolved upon a shift to the lyrical mode, which meant—as both the first paragraph of Part 2 and *A Textbook* indicate—a shift to himself. The epic went the way of compromise. Rather than write a totally new work, Gogol went backwards, abandoning the line of development that had been followed from Virgil to Dante to Milton (and including Ariosto himself), a line that James Joyce was later to make much of; he proposed to replace the objective by the subjective. This shift in form was even more drastic than Gogol's first impulse to change from the comic style to the epic itself, and just as doomed, as he discovered. The task was not only beyond his powers; I suggest that it would be beyond anyone's powers. Perhaps the proper course would have been to turn away from *Dead Souls* entirely—this he later also tried to do. Unfortunately, he used the wrong form again, at least so far as the public was concerned—namely, *Selected Passages.*

In any event, Gogol did try to go on, but was decidedly dissatisfied, for in November 1843, eighteen months after the publication of Part 1, he burned just about all he had thus far written of Part 2, deciding to start anew. This he did, although the work proceeded slowly. By April 1845 he had reversed himself, and the following July he again burned everything that he had written of the second version of Part 2. This was not a total abandonment, however; he meant, rather, to redo the work, and probably thoroughly to revise Part 1 at the same time, so that an overall wholeness could be achieved. By the end of 1847, after the almost totally negative reception of *Selected Passages,* he put the continuation aside entirely in favor of accomplishing his long-felt desire to visit the Holy Land. He returned to Russia in the spring of 1848, never to leave it again. During the last four years of his life, Gogol continued to work on *Dead Souls,* and he worked fairly regularly through 1849. By August of 1849, two chapters were finished and given to Shevyryov; in January 1850 he showed the same chapters, revised, to Aksakov. Work was dropped, then taken up again in the winter of 1850/51. It seems to have gone rather slowly, then increased in tempo during the spring and summer, during which time he frequently read finished or almost finished chapters to various friends. In July 1851 he asked Pletnyov to get ready for the publication of the whole of Part 2. By the fall it seems fairly certain that he had eleven chapters—a perfect match to Part 1, and thus probably the whole—ready. By November he was thinking of a complete revision. Then, on the night of 11/12 February 1852, he burned the entire manuscript, for the third time, and died ten days later.

Whatever was written of *Dead Souls* between 1846 and 1851, thus, was known only to some friends to whom Gogol had read what he wrote in these years. What we now have are either fragments written before the first burning of 1845 or later first drafts found by Shevyryov among Gogol's papers. The first four chapters are usually dated as being of 1841 or 1842; the other fragment, sometimes called chapter 5, is probably earlier; some think it belongs to 1840 or 1841. Indeed, some even think that the so-called chapter 5 belongs to Part 3 rather than to Part 2.

What has come down to us is interesting, not for its intrinsic merit (since we do not have the whole, judgment of merit is next to impossible for us; the only person who knew the entire work and could judge it was Gogol himself, and he decided against it), but for its clarification of matters raised in one way or another by Part 1. In other words, it serves largely the same function as *Selected Passages,* in this sense.

Most immediately obvious in Part 2 is that Gogol has moved his story out of town and into the countryside. Furthermore, approximately two-thirds of chapter 1 will pass before Chichikov enters on scene. We start instead with a description of the life and character of the landowner Andrei Ivanovich Tyentyetnikov, "a young thirty-three-year-old master, a collegiate secretary, an unmarried man." In many ways Tyentyetnikov is anticipatory of Ivan Goncharov's character Oblomov in the novel of that name, which was begun in the late 1840s, about the time that Gogol and Goncharov met in 1848. There is no reason to believe, however, that Goncharov took his character directly from Gogol, although that the latter had some influence on the former seems a reasonable proposition. "Andrei Ivanovich's existence was neither good nor bad—it was simply a waste. Since there are not a few people in the world who waste their lives away, why should not Tyentyetnikov waste his away?" (7:9). The account of his day is the story of nothing done; like Oblomov, he can barely get out of bed. But as he did with Plyushkin and Chichikov, Gogol tells us how Tyentyetnikov got that way: intelligence and education made superfluous by a world that had no place for them. There is nothing at all amusing in his story, nothing to make the reader laugh as he did in Part 1. It is, rather, the story of a serious man who wishes to do serious things and is constantly hindered by formalities, by rigid artificial relationships. The city, where Tyentyetnikov had spent some time in the service, was the alien environment that did much to destroy his ambitions to use his talent and brains.

One is immediately sent back to the essay that Gogol had written not too many years before, **"St. Petersburg Notes of 1836,"** which amounts to an excoriation of St. Petersburg as a foreign city, an artificial construction divorced from the real Russian character, a city built for and inhabited by aliens to Russia. Indeed, all through his life the only city Gogol seems to have found congenial was Rome. He appears to have felt that the urban environment—even the small-town urban environment—was destructive of the soul, for the city was the habitat of officials and merchants, those who reduce people to paper and those who deal in material things. St. Petersburg was the worst of all, the most completely false; the point is made not only in **"Petersburg Notes of 1836"** but in every one of the Petersburg tales as well. Here the lie has become a mode of life (or death), and reality is utterly lost, for Petersburg is the very exemplar of foreign intrusion into Russia. In contrast was the land (Gogol's happiest descriptions, his most lyrical evocations, are of the Russian landscape), where the real, the true, and the beautiful were to be found, where God's work was to be done.

So Tyentyetnikov concluded when he decided to give up the service and return to his estates. A "sophisticate" who had learned much of theory, Tyentyetnikov aimed to put his estates in order and to direct his peasants in a humanitarian way so that his land would become a model of owner-peasant cooperation and efficiency, all in accordance with the principles of political economy that he had studied. But despite all his efforts, his schemes based on abstract considerations go awry: somehow Tyentyetnikov's land does not produce, while the land that the peasants cultivate for themselves flourishes. As Gogol puts it, the peasants "soon understood that, although the master was a lively sort of chap and desirous of undertaking much, he did not yet know how, he somehow talked too correctly and intricately, so that peasant learning could not grasp it. The result was that, while master and peasant did not completely misunderstand each other, they simply did not sing together, were not adapted to raise one and the same note. The point is a familiar one to readers of romantic literature in general and of nineteenth-century Russian literature in particular. Tyentyetnikov, because of his artificial education and because of the time that he has spent in the artificial capital, has lost contact with his country; communication has been cut, and harmony has been destroyed; the problem now is how to reestablish that harmony. But Tyentyetnikov was so frustrated that "finally he entirely stopped going to see to work being done, completely threw up administering justice, stayed indoors and even ceased to accept reports from his steward." He is now totally apathetic, incapable of making a decision and acting upon it—a complete Oblomov.

Tyentyetnikov was almost roused from his lethargy by his love for a young lady who was visiting a neighbor, but an insult by the girl's father sent him back to his dressing gown. This is the sort of man Tyentyetnikov is, and this is the situation that he finds himself in when a visitor arrives at his house—Pavel Ivanovich Chichikov.

Chichikov is older, we are told, than he was when last we saw him, and somewhat shabbier. He still travels in his troika, but evidently his road has not been an easy one, and his destination is as unsettled as ever. His ability to make himself agreeable, however, is greater, and he makes a fine impression upon Tyentyetnikov, into whose home he soon moves, and he immediately seems to be the bringer of life, searcher after dead souls though he may have been: "A transformation occurred in the house. Half of it, hitherto in a state of blindness, . . . suddenly recovered its sight and was lit up." Instead of the mere catalyst that we found in much of Part 1, Chichikov is now active, and positively active at that; instead of simply adapting himself to situations and people as he finds them, he now sets things in motion, at least so far as Tyentyetnikov is concerned. He makes a positive contribution in that he does much to arrange a reconciliation between Tyentyetnikov and his beloved, a young lady who is reminiscent of the governor's daughter of Part 1: "If a transparent picture, illuminated by a lamp from behind, had suddenly blazed in a dark room, it would not have been so startling as this statuette, radiant with life, that had appeared as though expressly to light up the room. It seemed that a ray of sunlight flew into the room with her, suddenly illuminating the ceiling, the cornice, and the room's dark corners." It is as though Annunziata had once again appeared. This is at least the fourth time that Gogol has used this symbol: the essay **"Woman,"** the fragment **"Rome,"** and Part 1 of *Dead Souls* are the previous three. . . . I would suggest that this symbol—whose ultimate derivation is Platonic, which developed through Venus cults and the courts of love, which culminated in the *dolce stil nuovo* of Dante and his circle, and which was passed on through Petrarch and Platonists like Ficino of the fifteenth century to the poets of the Renaissance in Italy, France, and England (Ariosto is only one such poet in sixteenth-century Italy—one could also mention Michelangelo; France had its Heroët, Scève, Bellay, and Ronsard; England had its Sidney, Spenser, and Donne, not to mention Shakespeare; Spain had its Cervantes)—was the one that Gogol, attempting to give himself an artistic tradition as well as a Russian one, had in mind. It was a symbol that encompassed the Virgin Mary; Venus; Astraea; Helen of Troy; Queen Elizabeth, for Donne (the *Anniversary Poems*) and Spenser (Gloriana of *The Faerie Queene*); for the successors of Dante, Beatrice; as for the successors of Petrarch, a successor himself, it was Laura. She was also, of course, employed by Renaissance painters—Botticelli, for example. At the same time she could be used as a symbol of pure art, an ultimate revelation, an Annunziata, sent to the poet by God in order to bring the poet—and through his inspiration, all mankind—to beauty, to truth, to goodness—to perfection, to divinity itself. Translated into Russian terms, she becomes an icon.

It stretches credulity to ask one to believe that Gogol—with his interest in medieval history and with his knowledge of both Dante and at least some of the writers and painters of the High Renaissance, much of it probably gained during his sojourns in Rome—was unaware of this tradition. It was not, I would suggest, a mere romantic idealization of woman which arose because of Gogol's own sexual difficulties; it was, rather, a genuine attempt to use, for purposes of his own quest for beauty as well as for purposes of Russian nationalism, a well-recognized and long-hallowed symbol. As Beatrice did for Dante, so "woman," the governor's daughter, Annunziata, and Tyentyetnikov's lady show, for Gogol, the possibility of salvation, not in themselves, but because through love they lead to ultimate harmony and reconciliation. They are conduits, so to speak, through which man may rise to ultimate reality. Now we find that it is Chichikov who pours oil on troubled waters; it is he who arranges a reconciliation between Tyentyetnikov and the girl, Ulinka, who is pictured, in all her attitudes as well as in her appearance (although she is not quite plump enough for Chichikov's taste), as just about perfect in virtue, as all her predecessors were, because, given their function, they had to be. Gogol, who is constantly aware of the role of this feminine figure, over and over again uses tricks of light to describe Ulinka—not because she is deceptive but because reality transcends the material. He wishes to indicate the truth that supersedes physical sight, the beauty that is to be seen by the inner eye, rather than the appearance that is available to the outer one.

Like the road and the three-horse carriage, this feminine image has been repeated throughout Gogol's work. It differs from the road and the troika, however, in that it is the image of a goal to be attained; a reality that depends at least partially upon us for actualization; something to be quested after, as Spenser's knights quest, rather than an object passively to be received. After all, Beatrice did not come to Dante until canto 30 of *Purgatorio,* after Dante had been purified. So, for Gogol, "Rome" remains unfinished, Chichikov does not get the governor's daughter, and although Chichikov arranges a reconciliation between Tyentyetnikov and Ulinka, they are never brought together before our eyes, and that part of the story, at least so far as the fragments are concerned, is uncompleted. Also, Chichikov himself continues to yearn for happiness with "a good woman": "a fresh, white-faced wench, perhaps even of the merchant class, while at the same time formed and educated like a noblewoman—so that she would understand music, although music was not the chief thing, but why, if it is so accepted, why go against social opinion?" This is coupled in his mind with the idea of settling down and running an estate as it ought to be run, finding the beauty and peace of a harmonious life on the land. If he can accomplish this, then "he would not have passed through the land like a kind of shadow or specter, he would not be ashamed before the fatherland." Chichikov's quest, like Gogol's, is still not finished, nor does he yet, despite his impulses, fully understand it.

The concentration upon the land, the peasantry, and the landowner, and the proper relationships among them, continues through the remainder of these four chapters, which read really more like an essay on how harmony is to be attained than they do like a piece of fiction. It is, perhaps, an interlude of rest for Chichikov on his travels, a period of evaluation. This soon changes, however, as Gogol attempts to "accentuate the positive." Tyentyetnikov is left with hope, and truth is shown to Chichikov. The comic epic begins to take on aspects of the classical epic journey, although Gogol remains ambivalent in his handling of the material. Chichikov is even supplied with

a companion for his travels, one with whom he may leave the cave, Platon Mikhailovich Platonov, who "was an Achilles and Paris at once: a shapely build, picturesque stature, freshness—it was all brought together in him. A pleasant smile with a light expression of irony, as it were, strengthened his beauty. But, despite all this, there was a certain lack of liveliness and a somnolence in him. Neither passions nor sorrows nor shocks had put any wrinkles on his virginal, fresh face to enliven it."

It is this innocent classical figure whom Chichikov invites to travel with him, thinking that, if he is lucky, he will be able to stick Platonov with all their expenses. This indicates a curious kind of uncertainty in Chichikov's character in Part 2: on the one hand, he brings light to Tyentyetnikov's house and attempts to improve Tyentyetnikov's relationship with Ulinka—both praiseworthy activities; on the other hand, he plans to cheat Platonov. It is as though Gogol could not quite manage to fit Chichikov in with what he wanted to do. Chichikov apparently realizes his ambitions and undergoes a reformation when he legitimately buys land, under the influence of Platonov's brother-in-law, Skudronzhoglo, a representative of the really proper Russian landowner who is devoted to his estates and to those who work them. Skudronzhoglo describes Chichikov's new position to him and defines the values that he should adopt:

> You have peasants so that you may protect them in their peasant way of life. What is that way of life? What is the peasant's occupation? Tilling the soil. So you do your best for him to be a good tiller of the soil. Is that clear? There are clever people who say, "He must be raised from this state. He leads too simple and gross a life: he must become acquainted with objects of luxury." It's not enough that, thanks to this luxury, they have themselves become milksops and not people, and have picked up the devil knows what diseases, and that there is not an eighteen-year-old boy who has not tried out everything, so that he's toothless and bald—they now want to infect the peasants. Thank God one healthy estate is still left that is unacquainted with these fancies! For this we should simply thank God. Yes, for me, tillers of the soil are the most honorable of all. God grant that all be tillers of the soil!

> . . . Experience has shown that the purest morals are those of a man of the agricultural calling. Where tilling the soil is the basis of social life, there is abundance and prosperity; there is neither poverty nor luxury, but there is prosperity. . . . First think of making every one of your peasants wealthy. Then you yourself will be wealthy, without factories, without mills, without foolish ventures.

This statement of Skudronzhoglo's comes close to an enunciation of Gogol's creed, to be even more specifically declared in **"To a Russian Landowner."** The ideas of Western civilization are the infections; they are at fault, and Russia must return to its roots, while exorcizing the demons from abroad. Although Skudronzhoglo's remarks on the subject may be regarded as the clearest made in Part 2, all of the first four fragments add up to a tract on estate management, an exhortation on the subjects of peace, harmony, and the establishment of a Garden of Eden, a garden that existed in the old Russia—in Rus—and that has, among some, been lost because of the new, false ideas of Western commercialism and libertarianism. Gogol's medieval studies have not been lost, for his view of the social structure is very close to the concept of mutual obligation that supposedly existed in the West before the rise of the bourgeoisie. In the literal meaning of the term, Gogol is a reactionary, as opposed to liberalism as were his potential opponents of the far Left, in the name, like them, of harmonious relationships that assure the well-being of all. For both sides the guilty party is the bourgeois liberal; it is he who brings chaos and fosters false values. For Gogol, what is needed is a return to the Russian way of life, which involves a reawakening of the old spirit. The point is made threetimes by Platonov's brother Vasily. The first occurs when Vasily tells Platon that Platon is the victim of a "spiritual lethargy." The other two occur in remarks to Chichikov: "Fashion is not a decree for us, and Petersburg is not a church"; and "custom for me is a sacred thing." These observations come very close to the end of chapter 4 as we have it: they are followed by a hiatus after a few more lines and a short fragment that constitutes a complete change of scene as Chichikov meets Lyenitsyn, a rogue, with the implication that Chichikov is going to take up a swindling career in a much more serious way.

There has already been a serious break in Part 2, however, in that, while Chichikov has become acquainted with—and has even cultivated—good things, while he has acquired genuine land and live serfs, while he has considered proper management and peace, his character seems to have shifted in the opposite direction. While in Part 1 the governor's daughter was Chichikov's vision, now Ulinka is Tyentyetnikov's love, and Chichikov finds her a little too plump for his taste anyhow. In addition, he actively and consciously lies as he pursues his affairs, telling General Betrishchev, for example, an involved tale about a nonexistent uncle in order to get the general to give him some dead souls. This kind of deliberate, elaborate falsification for a calculated purpose was not indulged in by Chichikov in Part 1. If he is our "old friend" when he finally appears in the first fragment, he at best bears a resemblance to the Chichikov of the beginning of Part 1, certainly not to the Chichikov at the close of Part 1. He seems to have developed—or rather degenerated—in contrast to his surroundings rather than in accordance with them. The influence that they should have upon him—and for which Part 1 prepared us—simply does not take place. In addition, the symbol that seemed to be growing in the latter portions of Part 1 new reverses direction, so that Chichikov is no longer even an attractive rogue, capable of being saved, much less the germ of an epic hero. Instead, he has become simply nasty.

It is possible, of course, that Gogol was thinking of a change of heroes, that Patonov, perhaps, was to take over and become the Gofreddo who would conquer the infidel. Certainly he has the potential. But if Gogol allowed such a development, what would happen to the unity of the work as a whole? On the other hand, if he went back to the style and tone of Part 1, what more was there to be said, why should there be a continuation at all? In either case, the problem of Chichikov's regeneration remained before Gogol, and it was insoluble without a complete change of form, which in itself would have meant (and, I suggest, did mean) an artistic failure.

At the same time, Gogol was faced with other problems: he was convinced that, much as Part I had been praised (Gogol was always highly sensitive to criticism), it had also been misunderstood; it now, therefore, had to be clarified (the four fragments appear to be aimed largely in this direction). Also of importance was the constant pressure to produce a continuation that, to Gogol at least, would be largely repetitious. To give in to this pressure would be only to compound the misunderstanding. How could these difficulties be resolved so that he could fulfill the grand design—or rather, conception—of a work in three parts which would form a harmonious whole, a proportioned, balanced poem that in its very form would indicate that beauty which he thought the goal of every genuine artist? To Gogol, **Dead Souls** was unfinished. Part 1 in his mind was only Part 1, much as *Inferno* is only a part of the whole that is *The Divine Comedy*. If the first four chapters we have were really intended to be the beginning of Part 2, then they seem to me to constitute a false start, and Gogol's dissatisfaction with his work was probably well grounded. The comic epic was turning counterproductive; transition to the epic was doomed to artistic disunity; the lyric—as Gogol understood the lyric—was equally, now, out of place. The only solution available was the nonfiction of **Selected Passages,** whose public failure sent Gogol back to try once more, and burn once more.

Whether what we have said applies equally to the second and third versions of Part 2 we cannot, of course, know; but I, for one, am inclined to go along with Gogol's judgment. I do not think that the burnings were wanton, fanatic destructions committed in moments of aberration; more probably, they were considered critical judgments which were made on the basis of the work in hand (we do have evidence that Gogol retained his critical abilities to the end). The tragedy is that Gogol did not leave—or was not allowed to leave—Part 1 as it was and that he did not go on to write a completely new work of fiction to embody his vision. For some reason, however—perhaps the very strength of his convictions coupled with his unease with the critical reception of his poem—he forced himself to continue. (We may also recall Gogol's problems when **The Inspector General** was produced.) Finally, in February 1852, he resigned himself to what he regarded as his failure and destroyed not only his work, but himself. (pp. 133-44)

Jesse Zeldin, in his Nikolai Gogol's Quest for Beauty: An Exploration into His Works, *The Regents Press of Kansas, 1978, 244 p.*

Robert A. Maguire   (essay date 1987)

[*Maguire is an American critic and educator specializing in Slavic and East European literature. In the fol-*

lowing essay, he provides an analysis of the structure, theme, and techniques of Dead Souls.]

Nikolai Gogol enjoyed enormous popularity in his lifetime; by common consent, he was the greatest Russian writer after Pushkin. And he has remained popular, never suffering any of the diminution of reputation that often besets celebrities after their demise, including Pushkin for a time. In fact, it would be possible to write virtually the entire history of Russian literary criticism, from the mid-nineteenth century on, around responses to his works. *Dead Souls* is of course the best known of them. It has been read and admired by generations of Russians, who first encounter it as a staple of the school curriculum even today, and it has often been translated into English. Yet many readers have real problems with it. They find few of the kinds of social and political conflicts that are the staple of other nineteenth-century fictions. They find a story line sometimes so subdued as to suggest what a well-known critic has called "the tendency of the Russian novel to do without all narrative interest." They find a large and varied cast of characters, but little concern with psychological complexity and subtlety; even the protagonist is introduced as "neither dashingly handsome nor yet unbearably ugly, neither too stout nor yet too thin; it could not be claimed that he was old, but he was no stripling either." They find a welter of styles, dictions and voices that if not calculated to disorient, certainly do not provide the kinds of reassuring guidelines that we customarily find in nineteenth-century novels. Indeed, the book is not even called a novel but a "long poem" (*poema*), which if nothing else seems anachronistic. The structure of this "poem" is problematic too. We have to wait until the last chapter to find out anything about the chief protagonist's background, family, education, and crucial life-experiences—matters that most nineteenth-century writers normally take care of toward the beginning. The critics have not been of much help to us either. Of all the great books I know, *Dead Souls* has probably received the least sustained critical attention. Various aspects have been treated, to be sure, but I do not know of a single first-rate monograph, in any language, that shows the non-specialist how to approach the book as an entity. What, then, can we as teachers do to make it more accessible, enjoyable and meaningful to ourselves and to our students? In the remarks that follow, I assume that we are presenting *Dead Souls* to English-bound readers in survey courses in the humanities or Russian literature, and that we are confining ourselves to Part I.

Gogol is a master of the tease, nowhere more effectively and exasperatingly so than in *Dead Souls.* The title itself is a tease: "souls," in both Russian and English, refers to living human beings, or, more specifically, to their immaterial animating essence; how then can they be "dead"? (Gogol's censor was troubled enough to make him rename the book *The Adventures of Chichikov,* relegating "dead souls" to the subtitle.) And the opening paragraph is a series of teases. Who are these "gentlemen," these "Russian peasants," and above all this "young man" with the bronze pin, and why is such a fuss being made over an ordinary carriage? These are questions which cannot begin to be answered until we have moved well into the book.

And it is really only when we are done that we see how skillfully Gogol encapsulates the entire work into the opening paragraph. (We will look at it in greater detail later on.) Reading Gogol is really a matter of re-reading. That is why I advocate a fast first reading of the entire novel (by Russian standards it is not long) before a detailed discussion is undertaken.

It is the larger structure of the book that causes students the most trouble. After the opening chapter, where Chichikov is introduced to the town and to the reader, come five chapters, each devoted to one of the landowners whom Chichikov visits in hopes of persuading him or her to turn over "dead souls," those serfs who have died since the last census and whom Chichikov can use as collateral for an estate he hopes to acquire. With Chapter VII we are back in the town, where Chichikov's strange purchases become the subject of more and more talk. The narrative flow is interrupted, in Chapter X, by the apparently whimsical tale of Captain Kopeykin. Chapter XI presents a biography of Chichikov that purports to explain his actions. The "poem" ends with Chichikov once more on the open road, and the narrator invoking a picture of Russia as a troika speeding through the air with such force that "other people and states move aside and make way." From a shabby provincial town to all of Russia, from an ordinary carriage to an airborne troika, from a man who is "neither this nor that" to a well-rounded character, from a narrator who seems intent on recording the trivia of a drastically foreshortened provincial world to the narrator who concludes the work with a ringing paean to Russia, the entire world as his audience—such is the movement of this extraordinary "poem." In attempting to see how Gogol gets from Point A to Point B, the reader discovers much of this intriguing yet difficult story opening up to him.

Let us begin with Chichikov, the most striking presence in the book, and ostensibly the "hero." He does not so much undergo growth and development as progressively reveal sides of his character that are present from the beginning but hidden. Crucial to this process are his encounters with the landowners. Each of them is of course a type: Manilov the impractical dreamer; Korobochka the obsessively thrifty housewife; Nozdrev the bully; Sobakevich the tough-minded practical man; Plyushkin the miser. One of Chichikov's functions—and here he resembles a picaresque hero—is to give us entree into the self-sufficient, tightly circumscribed world that each inhabits. But he also interacts strongly with them, and in the process shows, all unwittingly, sides of his character that he would have preferred to keep concealed.

The order of the encounters is important. Manilov comes first, I think, because he offers no resistance to Chichikov's proposal. Chichikov can therefore continue to wear the same kind of featureless mask that in Chapter I he has presented to the town as well as to the narrator and the reader. Manilov is a peaceable man who not only does not wish to offend Chichikov, but, as a throwback to Sentimentalism, hopes to find in him a true friend, and has no trouble in creating a Chichikov that almost lives up to his ideal. We notice how he and his wife feed Chichikov his lines:

> "And what do you think of our governor?" asked Madame Manilova.
>
> "A *most estimable and obliging person,* isn't he?" interjected Manilov.
>
> "Absolutely true," exclaimed Chichikov, "a *most estimable man*"(. . .).
>
> "And how well he knows how to receive people and how *considerate* he is," added Manilov (. . .).
>
> "A most *considerate and agreeable person,*" continued Chichikov (. . .).
>
> "And what a *nice man* the vice-governor is, isn't he?" said Manilov (. . .).
>
> "Really, a *most worthy* man," replied Chichikov.
>
> "And, pray, how does the chief of police impress you? A *most agreeable man,* is he not?"
>
> "*Extremely agreeable*" (. . .).
>
> "Well, and what do you think of the wife of the chief of police?" asked Madame Manilova. "A *most charming woman,* isn't she?"
>
> "Oh, I think she is one of the *most delightful women* I know," replied Chichikov (emphases supplied).

Besides establishing Chichikov as the creation of the Manilovs—and here Gogol borrows a technique he used for characterizing Khlestakov in Act III of *The Inspector General*—the dialogue is replete with the terminology of Sentimentalism, where the "pleasant" (here "agreeable," "charming," "delightful") and the "good" (here "estimable," "worthy") are synonymous and therefore interchangeable. This point is crucial for understanding how Chichikov, toward the end of the chapter, easily overcomes Manilov's momentary misgivings about the legality of transacting in dead souls. He simply says: " 'I think it would be a *good* [or 'pleasant'] proposition,' " and Manilov, true to his Sentimentalist ethos, replies: " 'Ah, if it is a *good* thing, then I have nothing against it'." Chichikov even gets the souls free: Manilov would not dream of charging a friend. We learn a great deal about Manilov from this scene, about the ways in which language can be manipulated, and about the perils of trying to operate in the modern world with an outmoded ideology like Sentimentalism. But we learn little more about Chichikov beyond that he is clever, smooth and ruthless. We also expect that the encounters to follow will be equally painless and successful.

One of the reasons why Korobochka comes next is that she is a woman, and as such ought to be no match for the wily and hard-hearted Chichikov. To our surprise, and his, she offers real resistance. The effect is comic because it undoes our expectations. But there is a serious side to it too, as is always the case in Gogol. Chichikov gets the souls, but only after he is driven to exasperation by the stubborn old woman and begins to abuse her. This shows

quite another side of him and also helps motivate the appearance of Nozdrev, the next landowner, who not only refuses outright to sell his souls on Chichikov's terms but makes clear that he sees through the scheme, abuses him verbally, and summons his servants to administer a thrashing. Nozdrev's aggressive protestations of friendship are a comic magnification and parody of Manilov's Sentimentalism; his abuse of Chichikov not only magnifies but reverses the Korobochka scene. (Magnification and reversal are well-established Gogolian techniques). The issue of the dead souls has now turned serious indeed. The encounter with Sobakevich, the next landowner, begins with what seems to be a recapitulation of the Manilov chapter, only reversed: here it is Chichikov who gets matters underway with Sentimentalist banter, and Sobakevich who echoes but then reverses it:

> (Chichikov): "(. . .) take the governor, for example, he's a *delightful person!*"
>
> (Sobakevich): "The governor a *delightful person?*"
>
> (Chichikov): "Yes, isn't he?"
>
> (Sobakevich): "He's the biggest bandit of them all!" (emphases supplied)

Chichikov suspects that he is in for trouble. At first he finds Sobakevich acquiescent, even more (in another comic hyperbolization) than Manilov: " 'This fellow is ready to sell before I have even hinted at the idea'." But it soon becomes apparent that Sobakevich is a formidable adversary: he begins with an asking price so exorbitant that in effect he seizes control of the entire negotiation, in a reversal of the Chichikov/Manilov situation. Still another reversal, hinted at in the Korobochka chapter and fully realized here, is Sobakevich's habit of treating the dead souls as if they were still alive: " 'A rogue would cheat you, sell you some worthless rubbish instead of souls, but mine are as juicy as ripe nuts, all picked—they are all either craftsmen or sturdy peasants'." This is more than just a bargaining tactic: it raises the whole question of the "value" of human beings in ways that Chichikov has never imagined and now refuses to accept. As a bear-like man, Sobakevich embodies and elevates another motif that has been planted in the Korobochka and Nozdrev chapters: dogs who are all but human (his last name is derived from *sobaka,* the Russian word for dog: his nickname, Misha, is what Russians fondly call bears). This too is more than merely comic. It reminds us that the successive landowners represent a descending scale of values, from more to less human. A knowledge of Russian reinforces the point, but is not essential. Manilov's name comes from the verb *manit'*, "beckon," "lure," a sensuous and for Gogol rather "human" quality. Korobochka literally means "little box," an object, to be sure, but one made by human hands. Nozdrev derives from *nozdrya,* "nostril," and is therefore a part masquerading as a whole. Sobakevich, as I have said, leads us into the animal realm. Plyushkin, the last of the landowners, probably takes his name from *plyushch,* "ivy," and therefore exemplifies the vegetable world.

Plyushkin seems highly susceptible to manipulation by Chichikov. This in itself is a comic reversal of our expectation: we have been conditioned to a pattern of growing resistance to Chichikov's schemes; we therefore expect the greatest resistance here; instead we find the least. The echo of the Manilov scene is of course deliberate. But echoes in Gogol are never mere repetitions. By now the souls are no longer simply a means to Chichikov's personal end; they have taken on larger moral, ethical, even religious meanings. And Chichikov himself is no longer the smooth, bland character who has conned Manilov. His encounters have forced him to reveal more and more of himself. To be sure, he shows only one side of that self to Plyushkin, but we are now aware that there are other sides as well. Among them are anger, frustration, bewilderment, and increasingly complex emotions such as love and compassion, which reveal Chichikov as more than a mere schemer. The encounter with the young girl in the carriage (Chapter VI) is the first instance of this capacity for deeper feelings: "the alarm imprinted on her parted lips, the tears in her eyes, were so captivating that our hero stared at her for some minutes without paying any attention to the mess in which the coachmen and horses were involved." After she drives off, he meditates on the fate of such well-bred girls: though now fresh and unspoiled, " 'only wait until the mammas and aunties take her in hand. Within a year they will fill her with so many feminine wiles that her own father would not recognize her'." Although commonplace, this is a more articulate and developed judgment than the Chichikov of earlier chapters could have generated; but by now enough "sides" of him have emerged from his encounters with the landowners that we expect more and are therefore not surprised to find intimations of a man of substance, breeding and intellect. This same technique of gradually peeling away the facade makes it possible, in Chapter VI, for Chichikov plausibly to experience compassion, a far greater quality in Gogol's world than the kind of good judgment that deplores the bad upbringing of young girls. Chichikov is so taken aback by the appearance of Plyushkin that if he "had met him so attired at the entrance of a church, he would in all likelihood have given him a copper coin. For be it said in our hero's favour that his heart was compassionate and that he could not resist giving a farthing to a beggar." To be sure, such feelings are immediately translated into the more common coinage of calculation, as Chichikov wonders how rich the girl's father is, and reminds himself that Plyushkin "owned more than a thousand souls." Still, those other sides have been established, and in the ensuing chapters, they continue to unfold. For instance, in Chapter VIII, there is an extended reflection on the harmfulness of balls, in the best manner of a sententiously moralizing narrator. In fact, we notice that as the "poem" progresses, there is a tendency to confuse, commingle and even interchange the realms of "hero" and "narrator."

A hint of this comes as early as the Manilov chapter. It begins with a generalization, by way of scene-setting, on the part of the narrator—"The situation of Manilovka was anything but alluring"—and it then proceeds to what this narrator sees at a "long distance." Suddenly Chichikov's "eyes" are introduced: "for reasons known only to himself, our hero instantly began to count them [the peasant huts] and made them add up to over two hundred." Then comes a description of two peasant women, but it is no longer clear whether the scene is being observed by Chichikov, by the narrator, or by both. A far more developed instance comes in Chapter VI. Chichikov wakes up refreshed from a good night's sleep and addresses himself to the list of the serfs he now owns:

> . . . when he looked over these lists—at the names of peasants who had once really been peasants, who had toiled, ploughed, got drunk, driven their carts, cheated their masters, or had simply been good peasants—he was overcome by a strange and to him incomprehensible emotion. Each of the scrawls seemed to have a special character of its own and in this way the peasants themselves acquired a character of their own (. . .) it seemed as if the peasants were alive but yesterday.

He then proceeds, for nearly four pages, to invent lives for these peasants, much as any narrator could. Toward the end, the "real" narrator takes over almost imperceptibly:

> "Abakum Fyrov! What about you? Where are you knocking about? Have you taken to the Volga? And have you grown fond of a free life among the barge-haulers? . . . " At this point Chichikov paused and reflected. What was he thinking about? Was he pondering on the lot of Abakum Fyrov? (. . .) And indeed, where is Fyrov now? He leads a carefree and boisterous life on a corn wharf, bargaining with the merchants (. . .).

An almost complete reversal of narrator and hero occurs in Chapter XI, where we are told how the scheme of the dead souls occurred to Chichikov: "In this fashion, this strange *theme* matured in our hero's head. I do not know if the readers will be grateful for it, but the author's gratitude is more difficult to express. For, say what you will, had this *idea* not occurred to Chichikov, this *poem* would not have seen the light of day" (emphases supplied). The Russian word rendered here as "theme" is *syuzhet,* which means specifically a literary theme, or a plot. "Idea" (*mysl'*) and "poem" (*poema*), or course, reinforce the notion of literariness, of the scheme as an invention for literary purposes. Presently the "real" narrator goes even further and makes Chichikov responsible for the characters who appear in the book: "(. . .) the reader must not be indignant at the author for introducing him to characters who might not be to his taste; that is Chichikov's fault, he is the master here, and we must follow him as his fancy dictates." Two pages later, however, the "real" narrator seems to be firmly back in control: "It does not worry me if readers are dissatisfied with my hero."

In many ways this interrelationship of narrator and hero reminds us of Pushkin's *Eugene Onegin.* Yet the similarities cannot be pressed. Onegin remains essentially the same character throughout the poem, with the narrator unmistakably in control. Chichikov is a far more developed or revealed character, with a much greater share in narrative functions than Onegin. Paradoxically, however, as he takes on weight and solidity he understands less and less of the world around him. Ultimately he can no more manage his situation than can Onegin. We have noted some signs of progressive powerlessness in his encounters with the landowners, with the easiest success—Plyushkin—being achieved in a world he finds repellent yet cannot alter. And with his return to the town, in Chapter VII, the motif of non-control and non-understanding begins to develop apace. The themes which have been stated if not developed in the earlier chapters reappear here, imported, as it were, by the narrator, by Chichikov, and by the landowners themselves, all of whom turn up in the town in Chapters VII and VIII, except Plyushkin (and he is in a sense present as well, since he is talked about).

The most important of these themes is of course the souls. At first it would seem that Chichikov has accomplished his mission, despite all the frustrations. He hopes to register his purchases and take his leave. But he soon discovers that matters are not so simple. The townsfolk refuse to let him depart: " 'No, Pavel Ivanovich (. . .) you must spend a little time with us! (. . .) No, once you are here, you must not complain. We don't like trifling'." On the one hand, these are the sentiments of bored provincials who thirst for the excitement that a visitor can bring to their otherwise familiar and predictable daily round, particularly when that person is unattached and promises to be rich. On the other, the note of menace ("We don't like trifling") signals that the town is a collective character which can thwart Chichikov at least as effectively as any of the individual landowners he has encountered. And like the landowners, it can create new realities. For instance, in Chapter VII, Chichikov, back in town, has the following conversation with the president of the court:

> "But may I ask, Pavel Ivanovich," enquired the president, "how is it that you are buying peasants without the land? Or is it for transplantation?"
>
> "Yes, for transplantation."
>
> "Well, that is a different matter. And where?"
>
> "Oh . . . . In the Kherson province."
>
> "Ah, there is fine land there!" said the president, and he spoke very favourably of the luxuriant vegetation in that region.
>
> "And have you plenty of land there?"
>
> "Quite enough. As much as the peasants I have purchased will be able to look after."
>
> "Is there a river or pond on your estate?"
>
> "A river. However, there is also a pond."

For the president, as well as for those who witness the legal proceedings, the souls have now become a social entity, and as such are presumed to be attached to an estate. And before the celebrating is done, these new realities have become utterly convincing to Chichikov as well: "he already saw himself as a real Kherson landowner, talked about various improvements he was going to introduce"; in the carriage on the way home "he babbled a great deal of nonsense about a comely bride, Kherson villages, and capital funds"; and once he is in bed, "he drowsed off like a real Kherson landowner."

As in any small town, the word spreads quickly:

Profile of Gogol in 1852.

"Chichikov's affairs became a topic of conversation. The town was full of rumours, opinions and arguments as to whether it was a profitable thing to buy up peasants for transplanting elsewhere." Once in the larger social arena, the peasants are no longer Chichikov's. They quickly become identified with and then identical to Russian peasants generally. This process of expansion is established, in the following passages, by a constant shifting back and forth between the specific and the general:

> "But how will [*Chichikov's*] peasants manage without water? (. . .) Lack of water is not the worst (. . .) but transplantation itself is not a very reliable proposition. You know *what peasants* [generally] *are:* if you plant them on strange land (. . .) they will simply run away (. . .). I disagree with what you say, that *Chichikov's peasants* would run away. *A Russian* can adapt himself to anything (. . .) you haven't asked what *Chichikov's peasants* are like. You have quite overlooked the fact that *a landowner would not sell off his best peasants;* you can chop my head off if *Chichikov's peasants* are not thieves and drunkards, wastrels and rowdies (. . .). It's quite true; *no one would sell their best folk and so Chichikov's lot must be drunkards.*" (emphases supplied)

The inexorable process of expansion then moves beyond the town and the present day into Russian history, which has always been marked by peasant violence: "Many were seriously concerned with Chichikov's dilemma and much perturbed at the difficulties of transplanting such a multitude of peasants; they even began to worry lest a revolt might break out among such unruly folk as Chichikov had bought (. . .). Many suggestions were offered as to how to extirpate the spirit of rebellion which was rife among Chichikov's peasantry." Possibility becomes actuality. The effect is to create a world removed in time and space from that of the town (and thus twice removed from Chichikov), a world that can no longer be controlled by those who have helped create it.

In the eyes of the town, Chichikov himself is no longer the pleasant nonentity of Chapter I, but is now a rich landowner, even a "millionaire," and a very eligible bachelor. The power of public opinion traps him into confirming the misapprehension. But once this misapprehension comes into being, it too develops a life and a dynamic all its own. When Chichikov does not act according to the image fashioned for him, he ends up ostracized, and becomes the subject of fresh speculation. One identity does not fit, and the town creates others, each more removed from the original Chichikov than the next: a putative abductor of the governor's daughter, a forger "hiding under various aliases," even "Napoleon in disguise." To put it another way (and to pick up another important theme of the book), we see a series of reflections, each very different, no one "truer" than any other, and all of them when taken together failing to create a full picture. It is something like an amplification of the technique of Picasso's famous picture of the woman standing in front of a mirror where we cannot tell which is the original and which the reflection. The result, in **Dead Souls,** is total confusion—"a whirlwind swept through this once apparently drowsy town"—which evokes the appearance of characters never before seen, and even affects the public prosecutor "to such an extent that, on returning home, he began to think and think, and all of a sudden, as they say, he died for no reason at all."

Chichikov himself does not understand why he has suddenly fallen from hero to outcast; and as for the speculation rife in the town, he "had not the slightest idea about what was going on." It is only when Nozdrev visits him in his hotel room that he becomes aware of some of the more spectacular particulars of the gossip that is circulating: "The charge of forgery, that of eloping with the governor's daughter, the prosecutor's death of which he was supposed to be the cause, the arrival of a [new] governor-general—all this gave him quite a fright." He decides that " 'if things have gone as far as this (. . .) there is no point in staying on. I must get out of here quick'." And so he does, setting out once more on the open road.

Chichikov has not understood much about his experiences, and seems to have learned nothing from those that he does understand. In this sense he represents a type of character that persists throughout Gogol's work, as exemplified, for instance, by Major Kovalev (**"The Nose"**) and Khlestakov (*The Inspector General*). Kovalev and Khlestakov, however, remain nonentities, never more than caricatures. Chichikov becomes a full-blown character, who is capable of sensitivity and acuity. The townsfolk understand even less about him, and cannot even come up

with a plausible explanation of the dead souls. Can we not then look to the narrator? In some ways, as I have said, he is reminiscent of the narrator in *Eugene Onegin*. He dips in and out of the story, now as Chichikov's friend, now as an intimate of the reader, now as a kind of stage-manager, now as an independent agent with his own story to tell. But Pushkin's narrator is a well-articulated, palpable presence who rules with a firm hand from beginning to end: *Onegin* is "his" story. Gogol's narrator is elusive, unreliable, and often incompetent; he has no consistent voice, and his various voices and viewpoints suggest several different characters, rather than, as in Pushkin, one character who is versatile. Though often interesting, he rarely enables us to find our feet.

The "Tale of Captain Kopeykin," in Chapter X, provides an excellent example of the ways in which Gogol plays upon the incompetence and impotence of the narrator, the townsfolk, and Chichikov. Generations of readers have been intrigued by this tale. When the censor refused to pass the first version, Gogol, in despair, wrote to a friend as follows: "The elimination of Kopeykin has disturbed me deeply. This is one of the best passages in the poem, *without which there is a hole that I am absolutely unable to patch and sew*. I have made up my mind to recast it rather than be deprived of it altogether" (emphases supplied). Why did Gogol attach so much importance to what might seem merely an amusing anecdote? And why did he want it placed precisely here, in Chapter X? There is no doubt that the story displays yet another style, the oral narrative, or *skaz,* as uttered by a man of the lower classes (Kopeykin) with cultural pretensions; but Gogol could presumably have inserted that elsewhere in the work with equal effect. There is no doubt too that it foreshadows the biography of Chichikov that is to come in the next chapter. More important, however, it is the most highly developed and in some ways the most absurd of all the public speculations about Chichikov's identity, yet it is completely credible in its own terms. As such, it once again demonstrates the powerlessness of the town, and certainly of Chichikov, to "control" the course of events once they are set in motion. And because the narrator of this story, the postmaster, refers to it as a fiction—" 'this absorbing subject for a writer, a whole poem in its way (. . .) here, as we may say, begins the thread, the plot of the story' "—we are prepared for the "real" narrator's account of Chichikov's life in the very next chapter. That account is presented in a tone that suggests objectivity and factualness. We are inclined to "believe" it, and to feel a sense of relief that we are at last on solid ground. But the postmaster's listeners also "believe" him, long enough at least for him to tell his tale. And we must then ask why this presumably "real" account is any more credible than the Kopeykin story, or any of the other stories put forth by the other characters, including Chichikov himself ? Is not the narrator equally "powerless?"

In **Dead Souls,** then, we see at least four different viewpoints: the narrator's, Chichikov's, the townspeople's, and the reader's. (There are perhaps nine if we include each of the landowners, but unlike the others, they do not operate throughout the story.) In effect, these provide four different stories, or one story told in four different ways, all operative simultaneously. None of them by itself is definitive, and all of them taken together do not really add up to a satisfactory version of what has occurred. As readers, we find that we have been made characters in the story too. We "see" more than any one of our fellow-characters, perhaps, but we are hard-pressed to gratify our readerly inclination to say what the book has been all about.

In these ways, Gogol underscores what I take to be his main point: events, once set in motion, move beyond the comprehension and control of any one character or point of view. Intelligence, sensitivity and perceptiveness are ultimately no more effective than the obtuseness of characters like Korobochka or the townsfolk in grappling with the elusive, baffling world that an apparently simple idea—the purchase of dead souls—has called into being.

Returning now to the opening paragraph, we see how much it contains embryonically of the structures, themes and techniques of the work as a whole.

The first sentence—"A fairly smart, medium-sized chaise on springs rolled through the gates of an inn of the provincial town of N."—establishes a theme that is common throughout Gogol's works: the violation of self-contained places by a force from outside. Specifically, it foreshadows the visits of this same chaise to the isolated estates of the landowners, its movement back to the same town and inn, and its departure—in a good Gogolian reversal of the action—from the inn, the town and even the earth's surface, at the end of the poem. Though destined to play a vitally important role in the story, the carriage is described in only the most general detail. The qualifiers surrounding the noun do lend it a certain weight; but it really acquires a presence by being mentioned eight times in this relatively short paragraph and viewed from several angles. First it is seen by the narrator. Then it is said to be the locus of "bachelors," who are duly enumerated, and of the "gentleman" who is sitting in it. Then it attracts the attention of "two Russian peasants." Finally, it is seen by "a young man" who "swung around," and "inspected the turn-out." In the process it acquires three different names: "chaise" (four times), "wheel" (twice) and "turn-out" (twice), each carrying a slightly different meaning, suggesting a slightly different angle of vision, and implicitly involving a value-judgment. By naming the object variously, and viewing it from several angles, Gogol establishes it as a solid and unforgettable presence, without ever actually describing it. The technique is familiar to readers of Gogol's other works. We are hereby alerted to the possibility that this particular detail may play an important part in the story to come. We are also conditioned, as it were, to assume that any detail, however small, is potentially important. In other words, Gogol here, as elsewhere, uses detail to alert us to the problem of detail.

The human characters enumerated in this paragraph mark a progression from the general to the specific. The "bachelors" are a class, and are identified, taxonomically, by labels: "retired lieutenant-colonels, staff-captains and landowners with no more than about a hundred serfs to their name." With the "gentleman" in the carriage we move from plural to singular, that is, to a specific instance, and to a semblance of characterization: "*neither* dashingly

handsome *nor* yet unbearably ugly, *neither* too stout *nor* yet too thin; it could *not* be claimed that he was old, but he was *no* stripling either. His arrival in the town created *no* stir and was *not* marked by anything [literally '*nothing*'] out of the ordinary." The technique is apophatic, that is, it characterizes through negation and is typical of Gogol's style in all periods. In one sense, it tells us little about this "gentleman." Yet the mere fact of enumeration does lend him a certain weight, and prepares us for the question that is raised ever more insistently as the work progresses: who is Chichikov? What is he up to? If he is neither this nor that, then he can be both this and that—and that—and that. Then come the "two Russian peasants." They are not described in any way; but they are given solidity by the fact that they mark an abrupt shift in diction, providing the only instance in this paragraph of direct speech, which is further emphasized by being framed ("ventured on a few remarks . . . the conversation ended").

Finally comes the "young man," who does not speak but is instead described in the kind of detail denied all the other characters: "attired in white dimity trousers, very narrow and very short, and a swallow-tailed coat with some pretensions to fashion which disclosed a shirt-front fastened with a bronze pin of Tula design in the shape of a pistol." The earlier characterizations are built on generalizations, or appeal to the ear (as in the dialogue of the peasants). Now the eye is involved, with a whole little portrait that is focused on the striking detail of the bronze pin, and grounded by the very length and syntactic complexity of the sentence. Something of the medley of styles in the "poem" is hereby suggested too. Furthermore, there is a kinetic factor now at work: the young man is not merely riding like the bachelors, "lolling" like the gentleman, or "loitering" like the peasants, but is endowed or associated with a series of gestures: "The young man *swung round, inspected* the turn-out, *clutched* his cap as a gust of wind was threatening to *blow it away,* and *strolled* on his way." Compared to the others, he is virtually a fully-developed personage. But he completely disappears from the story. As Vladimir Nabokov has observed: "With any other writer of his day the next paragraph would have been bound to begin: 'Ivan, for that was the young man's name' . . . But no: a gust of wind interrupts his stare and he passes never to be mentioned again." Nabokov has no explanation for the appearance of this character, beyond seeing him as another instance of the kind of "spontaneous generation" which creates such a wealth of secondary personages in the work. While agreeing, we can suggest other factors. For one thing, Gogol is surely teasing us, as is his wont, and in doing so, raising questions to which there may be no answers, but which compel us to read closely. Who is this young man? What part does he play in the story? What is the significance, in particular, of that striking pin he is wearing? We do not yet know whether these are important questions, but we do know that we must sharpen our eyes lest we miss important cues. The bronze pin, like the "Russian peasants," is one of those details which ensure that a well-disposed reader will treat the text with sufficient attentiveness. Then again, the young man, like the other characters in this paragraph, is also an observer, who at the same time is himself being observed, certainly by the implied narrator, perhaps too by the gentleman in the carriage. In these ways, the young man provides further evidence of the presence of several observers within the text, and thus looks ahead to the operation of multiple points of view in the work as a whole. Finally, this young man is the culmination of a paragraph that increases in specific density, from general to particular, sketch to portrait; and at the end, he simply takes his leave, never to be seen again, like the narrator in Chapter XI. This too is the long line of *Dead Souls.*

The entire first paragraph, then, is organized around the carriage, just as the entire book is organized around dead souls. It provides the same kind of answer to the question "what is this carriage" as the book does to the question implicit in the title: "what are these dead souls?" We see that the paragraph is really more about the carriage than about the people in it, just as the book ultimately is more about dead souls than about Chichikov, the narrator, the townsfolk or the landowners. Yet the characters perform the essential function of demonstrating how an ordinary object can be viewed in several different ways, each of which has a certain validity—conferred if only by the fact of being observed and judged—but none of which is complete in itself. These are conclusions, however, which suggest themselves only after a reading of the entire book; and I hope in this paper to have outlined some approaches to reading that may help students make their way more pleasurably and profitably through this most difficult yet most intriguing of all Russian novels. (pp. 10-23)

> Robert A. Maguire, "Reading 'Dead Souls'," in Teaching Language through Literature, Vol. XXVI, No. 2, April, 1987, pp. 10-23.

FURTHER READING

Annenkov, P. V. *The Extraordinary Decade: Literary Memoirs.* Edited by Arthur P. Mendel, translated by Irwin R. Titunik. Ann Arbor: The University of Michigan Press, 1968, 281 p.

Account of the Russian literary milieu from 1839 to 1849 that includes discussions of Gogol's career and the critical reception of his works.

Annenskij, Innokentij. "The Aesthetics of Gogol's *Dead Souls* and Its Legacy." In *Twentieth-Century Russian Literary Criticism,* edited by Victor Erlich, pp. 51-60. New Haven, Conn.: Yale University Press, 1975.

Describes the themes and techniques of *Dead Souls* and underscores the importance of the novel in Russian literature.

Bowra, Sir Maurice. Introduction to *Dead Souls,* by Nikolai Gogol, p. v-ix. London: Oxford University Press, 1961.

Overview of *Dead Souls* in which Bowra emphasizes the comic aspects of the novel.

Davies, Ruth. "Gogol and the Dead Souls." In her *The Great Books of Russia,* pp. 26-49. Norman: University of Oklahoma Press, 1968.

Examines three of Gogol's "landmark" works: "The Cloak," *The Government Inspector,* and *Dead Souls.* Acknowledging the enigmatic nature of Gogol's artistic intentions and the debate over the social significance of the novel, Davies states: "*Dead Souls* is a black record of an anachronistic feudal system based on the assumption that human life has no meaning and no value, that the human being has neither dignity nor rights."

Debreczeny, Paul. "*Dead Souls.*" In his *Nikolai Gogol and His Contemporary Critics,* pp. 29-50. Philadelphia: The American Philosophical Society, 1966.

Summaries of contemporary critical reactions to *Dead Souls* and Gogol's response.

Franklin, Simon. "Novels without End: Notes on *Eugene Onegin* and *Dead Souls.*" *The Modern Language Review* 79, No. 2 (April 1984): 372-83.

Views Alexander Pushkin's *Eugene Onegin* and *Dead Souls* as "experiments in form and genre." Franklin asserts: "A sense of transition, of potential, of passionate and often somewhat perplexed exploration, permeates both the critical responses to the novels as they appeared and . . . the very fabric of the novels themselves."

Frantz, Philip E., ed. *Gogol: A Bibliography.* Ann Arbor, Mich.: Ardis, 1989, 360 p.

List of works by and about Gogol. The bibliography includes secondary sources in Russian, Ukrainian, English, German, French, and other languages.

Gibian, George. Introduction to *Dead Souls,* by Nikolai Gogol, translated by George Reavey, pp. v-x. New York: W. W. Norton and Co., 1971.

Overview of *Dead Souls* that stresses its complexity.

———, ed. *Dead Souls: The Reavey Translation, Backgrounds and Sources, Essays in Criticism.* New York: W. W. Norton and Co., 1985, 583 p.

Contains the text of *Dead Souls,* Gogol's letters concerning the novel, and representative critical essays, including English translations of works by Soviet critics Yuri Mann, Viktor Shklovsky, M. M. Bakhtin, and Yuri M. Lotman as well as excerpts from "Gogol: Artist and Thinker" by Dmitry Čiževsky.

Gifford, Henry. "Gogol's *Dead Souls.*" In *The Novel in Russia: From Pushkin to Pasternak,* pp. 42-52. London: Hutchinson University Library, 1964.

Introduction to the novel that concludes: "With Gogol, whether he understood it or not, the sensibility of urban Russia, the mood of protest and denial, forced its way into prose fiction. Half the achievements to come in the great age of the Russian novel may be traced back to Pushkin. For the other half, strained and urgent and declamatory, Gogol was the prime mover."

Gippius, V. V. "The Poem," "An Assemblage of Freaks," and "The Final Course." In his *Gogol,* edited and translated by Robert A. Maguire, pp. 113-26, pp. 127-37, pp. 163-75. Ann Arbor, Mich.: Ardis, 1981.

Highly respected 1924 study often cited as the best book written on Gogol. Gippius provides a history of the composition of *Dead Souls,* discusses its critical reception, and examines its characterization and theme.

Heldt, Barbara. "*Dead Souls:* Without Naming Names." In *Nikolay Gogol: Text and Context,* edited by Jane Grayson and Faith Wigzell, pp. 83-91. London: Macmillan Press / School of Slavonic and East European Studies, 1989.

Analyzes "unnamed names," or common nouns used to designate characters, in *Dead Souls.* Heldt states: "Such unnamed names provide a key to the peculiar tension between the general/harmonious and the specific/negative in the Gogolian textual universe. The different effects of not naming names highlight questions of gender, of violent abuse or coercion, of identity and of the narrator-reader-text triangle."

Karlinsky, Simon. "The Sexes in *Dead Souls.*" In his *The Sexual Labyrinth of Nikolai Gogol,* pp. 225-39. Cambridge, Mass.: Harvard University Press, 1976.

Examination of the novel's "view of sexuality . . . and its treatment of the relationship between the sexes."

Lavrin, Janko. "*Dead Souls.*" In his *Nikolai Gogol (1809-1852): A Centenary Survey,* pp. 95-119. London: Sylvan Press, 1951.

Critical introduction to *Dead Souls.* Lavrin states: "What [Gogol] presents in *Dead Souls* is an artistic image of life in its everyday tedium, vulgarity and drabness, but condensed and intensified as only Gogol knew how. If taken on the surface only, the method is realistic. Yet, as in *The Greatcoat,* Gogol disintegrates as it were the reality he deals with into its innumerable details and *petits faits,* after which he modifies, retouches and changes all the proportions according to his own subjective vision of human existence."

LeBlanc, Ronald D. "Dinner with Chichikov: The Fictional Meal as Narrative Device in Gogol's *Dead Souls.*" *Modern Language Studies* XVIII, No. 4 (Fall 1988): 68-80.

Examines the structural function of food and eating in *Dead Souls.* LeBlanc asserts: "The fictional meal . . . serves as a particularly useful device which allows the author to comment at length both upon the psychology of his characters and upon the nature of the fictional world they inhabit. At the same time, it remains central to the hero's scheme for acquiring dead souls, since it enables him not only to discover the personality of his victims, but also to manipulate their weaknesses."

Lindstrom, Thaïs S. "*Dead Souls.*" In her *Nikolay Gogol,* pp. 135-78. New York: Twayne Publishers, 1974.

Discussion of plot, character, theme, language, style, and major critical interpretations of *Dead Souls.*

Little, T. E. "*Dead Souls.*" In *Knaves and Swindlers: Essays on the Picaresque Novel in Europe,* edited by Christine J. Whitbourn, pp. 112-38. London: Oxford University Press, 1974.

An analysis of picaresque elements in *Dead Souls* that concludes: "Chichikov is a picaresque hero, on the move and on the make, journeying through a moral, not a social hell. One can finally call *Dead Souls* a picaresque Odyssey through the inferno. . . . "

Magarshack, David. "Part Five: *Dead Souls.*" In his *Gogol: A Life,* pp. 150-215. New York: Grove Press, 1957.

Describes the writing of *Dead Souls* and its critical reception.

Peace, Richard. "*Dead Souls.*" In his *The Enigma of Gogol: An Examination of the Writings of N. V. Gogol and Their*

Place in the Russian Literary Tradition, pp. 213-81. Cambridge, England: Cambridge University Press, 1981.

Examines characterization, satire, and comic and narrative devices in *Dead Souls.*

Reeve, F. D. "*Dead Souls* (Gogol)." In his *The Russian Novel,* pp. 64-102. London: Frederick Muller, 1966.

Studies the background, genre, and structural elements of *Dead Souls.*

Rowe, William Woodin. "*Dead Souls:* Part One" and "*Dead Souls:* Part Two." In his *Through Gogol's Looking Glass: Reverse Vision, False Focus, and Precarious Logic,* pp. 155-74, pp. 175-83. New York: New York University Press, 1976.

An analysis of narrative technique and structure in Parts 1 and 2 of *Dead Souls.*

Setchkarev, Vsevolod. "*Dead Souls*" and "The Second Part of *Dead Souls.*" In his *Gogol: His Life and Works,* translated by Robert Kramer, pp. 182-215, pp. 247-56. New York: New York University Press, 1965.

Provides plot analyses of Parts 1 and 2 of *Dead Souls,* and discusses literary influences on the works.

Simmons, Ernest J. "Gogol: Live or Dead Souls." In his *Introduction to Russian Realism,* pp. 44-90. Bloomington: Indiana University Press, 1965.

Biographical and critical introduction to Gogol's works that includes an analysis of Parts 1 and 2 of *Dead Souls.*

Shevyrev, Stepan. "The Adventures of Chichikov; or, Dead Souls: A Narrative Poem by N. Gogol." In *Literature and National Identity: Nineteenth-Century Russian Critical Essays,* translated and edited by Paul Debreczeny and Jesse Zeldin, pp. 17-64. Lincoln: University of Nebraska Press, 1970.

Contemporary review of *Dead Souls* first published in the periodical *Moskvitianin* in 1842. Shevyrev discusses the novel's realistic elements and the nature of its artistry.

Todd, William Mills, III. "*Dead Souls:* 'Charmed by a Phrase'." In his *Fiction and Society in the Age of Pushkin: Ideology, Institutions, and Narrative,* pp. 164-200. Cambridge, Mass.: Harvard University Press, 1986.

Proposes to examine the novel's "interaction with the literary institutions of its time, then pursue its elusively devastating reproduction of the ideology which had shaped those and other institutions of early nineteenth-century Russia, crystallizing, playing with, travestying, and ultimately fragmenting that cluster of values, social patterns, and styles."

Troyat, Henri. "The Fight over *Dead Souls,*" "*Dead Souls,*" and "The End of *Dead Souls.*" In his *Divided Soul: The Life of Gogol,* translated by Nancy Amphoux, pp. 245-66, pp. 267-92, pp. 407-38. Garden City, N.Y.: Doubleday & Co., 1973.

Biography of Gogol. Sections on *Dead Souls* detail his battles with censors over the novel, its critical reception, and the burning of Part 2.

Weathers, Winston. "Gogol's *Dead Souls:* The Degrees of Reality." *College English* 17, No. 3 (December 1955): 159-64.

Labels *Dead Souls* an epic study of reality characterized by comedy, illusion, and paradox.

Wellek, René. Introduction to *Dead Souls,* by Nikolai Gogol, translated by Bernard Guilbert Guerney, pp. v-x. New York: Rinehart & Co., 1948.

Overview of *Dead Souls* that concludes: "The artistic value of *Dead Souls* surely is not in the plot, the psychology, or even the ideas, but in the rich texture, the vivid detail, and its ultimate vision of the world: gloomy but also grotesquely comic."

Woodward, James B. Gogol's *Dead Souls*. Princeton, N.J.: Princeton University Press, 1978, 276 p.

Contends that "the central theme of the novel ('dead souls') is developed . . . primarily with the aid of inter-related symbolic themes conveyed by elusive patterns of details which in combination with one another comprise the most complex and aesthetically compelling moral allegory in the Russian language—an allegory that is related to no Russian literary tradition, but rather harks back to the tradition of the medieval moral allegory and, beyond that, to the tradition of the allegorical journey through the underworld, which was a staple ingredient of the classical epic."

Yarmolinsky, Avrahm. Introduction to *Chichikov's Journeys; or, Home Life in Old Russia,* by Nikolai Gogol, translated by Bernard Guilbert Guerney, pp. vii-xvi. New York: Heritage Press, 1942.

Overview of *Dead Souls*. Yarmolinsky states: "The book's chief claim to attention . . . lies in the comedy at the heart of it and in the various men and women who people it."

Yelistratova, Anna. *Nikolai Gogol and the West European Novel.* Translated by Christopher English. Moscow: Raduga Publishers, 1984, 262 p.

Comparative analysis of *Dead Souls* and several eighteenth- and nineteenth-century West European novels.

Henry Mayhew

1812-1887

English journalist, dramatist, novelist, and poet.

Mayhew is best known as the author of *London Labour and the London Poor,* an encyclopedic work of journalism in which he documented the lives of the urban poor of London during the mid-nineteenth century. Combining exhaustive social and economic statistics with personal interviews, Mayhew introduced middle- and upper-class readers to a stratum of society of which they were largely ignorant, and his prose accounts of street life have been favorably compared to those in Charles Dickens's novels. Recognized as a significant influence on the Victorian social novel, *London Labour and the London Poor* is equally praised as a valuable record of social conditions among the lower classes during the Industrial Revolution and as a precursor of the modern social survey.

Mayhew was born in 1812, one of seventeen children of a successful solicitor whose penurious, domineering, and abusive nature Mayhew later satirized in his poem, "A Highly Respectable Man." Mayhew's father pressed his sons to follow him into the practice of law, but Mayhew showed little inclination toward that profession. He dropped out of school at age fifteen to sail to India as a midshipman, and later attempted to make his fortune by manufacturing artificial diamonds and fabric dyes in a home laboratory, before finally becoming a free-lance writer. Mayhew devoted most of his early literary efforts to comic farces and humorous journalism intended for a mass audience and designed to earn money. He also edited several undistinguished journals and associated with a circle of political writers and humorists including Douglas Jerrold, William Makepeace Thackeray, and Dickens. In the 1830s Mayhew edited the humorous journal *Figaro in London,* and in 1841 he helped found the satirical periodical *Punch,* which became hugely successful. However, Mayhew's involvement with *Punch* was brief and limited, and in the 1840s he turned to more scholarly writings. He initiated two instructive serials on education, both of which he abandoned after the first installment, and in 1847 he began collaborating with his brother Augustus on a series of comic novels and moral fables.

Mayhew was named metropolitan correspondent for the London newspaper the *Morning Chronicle* in 1849, and began the most productive and famed stage of his career. In a series of articles on the working class of London, Mayhew interviewed laborers in various trades with the intent of exposing their poverty and prompting remedies for their often unhealthy living conditions. Because of an upsurge in English philanthropic movements, the audience for such investigations was great, and Mayhew wrote a prodigious number of articles. In 1850 he resigned from the *Morning Chronicle* over an editorial dispute, but continued publishing his reports in the form of the weekly serial *London Labour and the London Poor.* Mayhew turned

his attentions increasingly from trade workers to "street-folk," the poorest Londoners, driven to street vending or scavenging. In 1852 he forsook the project after a legal dispute over his publishing contract and returned to it for only a brief period in 1856; critics doubt, however, that the suit forced the end of the series, and some suspect that Mayhew simply grew frustrated with and tired of the monumental project. He never worked as enthusiastically or productively again after *London Labour,* although in 1856 he attempted a similar project, *The Great World of London,* intended as a survey of twenty-one facets of life in London. He abandoned this project in the middle of its first section. Mayhew spent his later years struggling with debts and writing children's books and several caustic travel books on Germany, none of which was successful. He died in 1887.

Mayhew's writings on the poor provide almost the entire basis for his literary reputation, and critics generally dismiss his drama and fiction as hack work. Many commentators believe Mayhew's work exhibits a conflict between his desire to write works with wide popular appeal and his intellectual and scientific inclinations, a conflict which he resolved successfully only in his writings on the poor. In these works Mayhew sought to "deal with human nature as a natural philosopher or chemist deals with any material object," hoping that, by juxtaposing interviews with statistics on the poor, he would discover patterns revealing the causes of poverty in English society. His further commitment "to publish the history of a people, from the lips of the people themselves" is considered among his most important contributions to social reporting, and the monologues he transcribed are valued for their faithful rendering of his subjects' language as well as their vivid descriptions of London slum life.

Mayhew envisioned *London Labour* as both a social study and a comprehensive catalog of working-class life. He devised a complex taxonomy of workers in English society and originally intended the series to encompass all of these groups, but in its final form the study focused exclusively on the desperate poor of the streets, those driven by poverty into such degrading forms of work as rag-selling or dung-collecting. Whereas in the *Morning Chronicle* he had limited his commentary to occasional bursts of moral outrage, Mayhew devoted a section of each *London Labour* installment to the interpretation of his findings. As the series developed, his views became increasingly radical, and he attacked the popular *laissez-faire* economics of his day, which held that an unregulated market will best provide for the needs of all. He also dismissed the popular belief, influenced by the population theories of Thomas Malthus, that low wages were the result of an overabundant work force. According to Mayhew, wages had been driven down over the years by employers who instituted low-paid piecework in place of salaried labor. This forced employees to produce more for the same pay, in turn making work scarcer for others, resulting in a spiral of shrinking wages. Mayhew never proposed concrete political or legal solutions to this situation, but he did consolidate his economic theories in the essays *Low Wages: Their Causes, Consequences, and Remedies.*

By the time *London Labour and the London Poor* was published in its entirety in 1861, the English philanthropic movement had subsided, and interest in studies of the poor had declined as well. Mayhew's studies remained of value to social scientists, but were of little literary interest until the 1950s, when his essays were issued in selected editions. Contemporary critics primarily focused on Mayhew's achievements as a reporter, but more recent commentators have noted parallels between descriptions of London in Mayhew's works and those in novels by Dickens and Charles Kingsley. Mayhew's detractors have charged that his analyses were based in part on intuitive theories unsupported by evidence (for example, his claim that the street poor derived from a race of nomadic humans), and historian Gertrude Himmelfarb has argued that Mayhew exacerbated middle-class contempt for the poor by portraying a minority of degraded individuals as representative of the lower class. However, *London Labour and the London Poor* is generally regarded as a pioneering and masterful literary work, and critics consider Mayhew among the first Victorian writers to portray the poor unpatronizingly. As a work of social science, *London Labour* is considered all the more remarkable given its almost complete lack of precedents and the limited time Mayhew spent compiling

it; in the words of critic E. P. Thompson, Mayhew's writings on the poor represent a "brief burst of illumination, when Mayhew's prodigious but undisciplined talents and his bohemian irreverence combined in a unique human investigation."

(See also *Dictionary of Literary Biography,* Vols. 18 and 55.)

PRINCIPAL WORKS

The Wandering Minstrel (drama) 1834

"*But, However—*" [with Henry Baylis] (drama) 1837

What to Teach and How to Teach It: So That the Child May Become a Wise and Good Man (nonfiction) 1842

The Prince of Wales's Library: No. 1—The Primer (nonfiction) 1844

The Greatest Plague of Life; or, The Adventures of a Lady in Search of a Good Servant [with Augustus Mayhew] (novel) 1847

Whom to Marry and How to Get Married! or, The Adventures of a Lady in Search of a Good Husband [with Augustus Mayhew] (novel) 1848

1851; or, The Adventures of Mr. and Mrs. Sandboys and Family, Who Came up to London to 'Enjoy Themselves,' and to See the Great Exhibition [with George Cruikshank] (novel) 1851

*London Labour and the London Poor (journalism) 1851

Low Wages: Their Causes, Consequences, and Remedies (essays) 1851

†The Great World of London, Parts 1-9 (journalism) 1856; also published as *The Criminal Prisons of London and Scenes of London Life* [enlarged edition], 1862

The Rhine and Its Picturesque Scenery (travel essay) 1856

The Upper Rhine: The Scenery of Its Banks and the Manners of Its People (travel essay) 1858

German Life and Manners as Seen in Saxony at the Present Day. 2 vols. (travel essays) 1864

Mont Blanc [with Athol Mayhew] (drama) 1874

The Unknown Mayhew (journalism) 1971

---

*This work was published in four volumes under the same title. The first volume and parts of the second and third volumes were published in 1851; all four volumes were published in 1861.

†The enlarged edition was completed by John Binny.

The British Quarterly Review   (essay date 1850)

[*In the following excerpt, the critic discusses Mayhew's* Morning Chronicle *letters in relation to English socialism.*]

Mr. Mayhew's primary object [in his *Morning Chronicle* articles] was simply to bring facts to light; to furnish, piece by piece, to the English public and the English legislature, a more thorough and minute report than had ever before been attempted, of the state of the working classes and of the poor in London. When finished, and thrown into the form of an encyclopædia, alphabetically arranged [the pieces were not, in fact, alphabetically arranged], his *Morning Chronicle* Letters will form a work unique in literature. But, brought, as he has been, by his investigations, into contact with such varied forms of misery, and invested, as he has been, by the popular appreciation of his services, with a kind of unofficial authority or chiefship in the metropolis, he has not been able to confine himself to the mere task of procuring information, but has been induced, nay, almost compelled, to bring his own energy and resources to bear in the meantime, and, as it were, provisionally, on certain parts of the general problem presented for solution. All that have read Mr. Mayhew's letters must know, that among the horrors they revealed, none were more fearful than those ascertained to exist among the operative tailors and the needle-women of the metropolis. In these two occupations, competition and *laissez-faire,* those demons incarnate of the socialist theory, had produced their most ruthless results. The condition especially of the operative tailors of London, a body of men numbering about 23,000 in all, was shown to be perfectly hideous. While a small proportion of them were employed in what are called in the trade 'honourable' shops, and were in the receipt of sufficient wages, the immense majority, it was shown, were living in a state of incessant toil and starvation, under the slavery of a class of middle men, or *sweaters,* who, receiving work in large quantities, and at a reduced rate of contract, from the 'cheap' or 'dishonourable' shops, kept chiefly by Jew clothiers, let out this work again, at a still lower rate of wages, either directly to the operatives, or again to other sweaters intervening between them and the operatives. In consequence, too, of the increasing patronage that the public, and even some of the richest and noblest families in the land, were bestowing, from very natural motives of economy, on the cheap in preference to the dear shops, it was shown that the 'honourable' part of the trade was rapidly declining, (at the rate, it was calculated of 150 journeymen every year, thrown out of fair work, and irrevocably kidnapped for the Jew shops by the sweaters,) and in a sure way to die entirely out. Now it is as a partial remedy for this state of things, (fully to appreciate the miseries of which, the reader must be familiar with the details as published in the *Morning Chronicle,*) that Mr. Mayhew has proposed the establishment of what he calls 'the Tailors' Guild,'—a proposal, the essence of which is, that refraining from any organic innovation, or any use of the specifically socialist methods of amelioration, it seeks to concentrate, as it were, within one spot, and for the benefit of one class of men, all the recognised principles and devices of the best existing English practice of commercial insurance. The following extract from Mr. Mayhew's prospectus will give the best idea of his scheme:

> All that is needed is association. The suffering, the squalor, and the abasement of the single victim are to be met and overcome by union. And by such union, be it distinctly understood, no combination is meant or intended that shall in any way interfere with either the social or the commercial freedom of the individual. Every man is to stand upon his own feet, single in the use and enjoyment of his powers of skill and industry—united only to obtain the fair reward of his labour, and the enjoyment of his self-respect as a free citizen. The object of THE TAILORS' GUILD is, then, unequivocally, neither political nor communistic. Its aim, like that of the ancient fraternities from which it borrows its title, is principally commercial. . . . The vital principles of the contemplated institution are:—I. That the institution shall be known as THE TAILORS' GUILD. II. That the benefits of the guild shall be operative alike for working tailors of both sexes. III. That on the books of the guild shall be kept a registration of the names and earnings of the members, so that the statistics of the past and present condition of the trade may at once be known. IV. That an office for the insurance of an uniform rate of income to the workman throughout the 'brisk' and 'slack' seasons of the year be a part of the institution. V. That a savings' bank and loan office be another part. VI. That a poor fund, by which the aged and disabled may be duly relieved, be also instituted; the fund to be supplied by general subscription. VII. That the unemployed be found employment, at a less rate than the ordinary wages of the trade, upon making the clothes of the members of the institution and their families. . . . It is, moreover, intended that the guild, combining with its general aim some of the principles of a club-house, shall offer, at cost price, the means of refreshment, together with the occasional advantage of assemblies for the recreation of *all* its members. It is further intended that a library be founded, and that lectures and evening classes be instituted for the instruction of all desirous of participating in their obvious utility.

From the socialist point of view, and perhaps even from a more ordinary point of view, some of the parts of this scheme, (as, for example, Art. VII., on the means of employing the unemployed,) might appear open to criticism. The essential features of the scheme, however, particularly as seen in its provisions for insurance of uniform wages and for loans, are such as, while recommending it to economic practice and to ordinary commercial good sense, cause it to be regarded, even by socialists, as a step to be encouraged rather than resisted. At present, the scheme is but in embryo; but Mr. Mayhew, we believe, has received assurances in its favour not only from influential men in society generally, but also, which is more important, from the trade itself; from 'honourable' master tailors, on the one hand, and from operatives, in great numbers, on the other. (pp. 491-93)

> *"Recent Aspects of Socialism,"* in The British Quarterly Review, *Vol. II, May 1, 1850, pp. 467-99.*

The Eclectic Review (essay date 1851)

[*In the following excerpt, the critic discusses Mayhew's revelations concerning English society in* London Labour and the London Poor.]

The revelations of this work should give a new tone and colour to the contemporary history of these times. A picture of England in the middle of the nineteenth century is usually drawn in vivid tints to flatter the vanity of our civilization. Political supremacy in Europe; the enjoyment of true liberty; the glories of extended empire; a commerce which visits the remotest shores, and colonies which make a chain round the globe—these, with inferior sources of congratulation, form the invariable substance of our complacent hymns in praise of our own achievements. We forget, or we have hitherto neglected to notice, the existence of a large class, in our metropolis, more degraded than the savages of New Zealand, than the blacks of the Great Karroo, or the insular communities of the Pacific. It is not a petty tribe, composed of outcasts and vagrants, incident to every social system; but a nation, numbered by thousands, which daily wanders through our streets, and carries on perpetual warfare against society. Such a fact should be remembered by us when we indulge in grandiloquent panegyrics upon the refined and polished state of manners, the general happiness, the public riches, and the universal freedom, under the discipline of just laws, which render England the Corinthian capital—the moral Acropolis—of Europe. We despise other times and other systems; we look on this as the illuminated age, whose lustre radiates from our own central city; but Athens had no such class, nor had Rome. North America has no such class, nor have the Swiss cantons.

Henry Mayhew has dug up the foundations of society, and exposed them to light. He has travelled through the unknown regions of our metropolis, and returned with full reports concerning the strange tribes of men which he may be said to have discovered. For, until his researches had taken place, who knew of the nomade race which daily carries on its predatory operations in our streets, and nightly disappears in quarters wholly unvisited as well by the portly citizens of the East as by perfumed whiskerandoes of the West End? An important and valuable addition has thus been made to our knowledge. In a volume replete with curious facts, authenticated by absolute proof, as well as by the high character of the author, we have a description of a class of the population perfectly marvellous to contemplate. We shall lay before our readers the leading facts which our author has brought to light, but refer them to the book itself for the wonderful details, for the innumerable anecdotes, for the episodes of romance, for the philosophic reflections, and the infinite variety of pictures, which render it the most remarkable work of the age.

The population of the globe is divided into two distinct and broadly-marked races—'the wanderers and the settlers—the vagabond and the citizen'—'the nomadic and the civilized tribes.' The nomadic exist, more or less, in most regions. Such are the Bushmen and Sonquas of the Hottentot race; such are the Fingoes; such are the savages of New Holland. Such, also, are the street folk of London; and these are distinguished from the other classes of the community precisely as nomades in all parts of the world are distinguished—by a greater development of the animal than of the intellectual or moral nature; by their high cheek bones and protruding jaws; by their use of a slang language; by their lax ideas of property; by their general improvidence; by their repugnance to continuous labour; by their disregard of female honour; by their love of cruelty; by their pugnacity; and by their utter want of religion. They form several orders, and we shall now notice the street sellers, buyers, finders, performers, artists, showmen, artificers and labourers; but the traders will occupy our chief attention, for Mr. Mayhew promises another volume to complete the subject.

It is first important to ascertain the numbers of this strange race, which increases faster than any other class of the population—a portentous fact, when we remember that in the United States the contrary is true. There the prosperous multiply; here, the poor. From the most strict and moderate calculation, there are upwards of fifty thousand individuals, or about a fortieth of the inhabitants of London, gaining a livelihood in the streets—the most precarious of all means of livelihood. Their yearly 'takings' amount to 2,500,000*l.* They are intellectually, morally, and religiously degraded. They are in an unchanging atmosphere of ignorance, vice, and want. 'The public,' says Mr. Mayhew, 'have but to read the following plain, unvarnished account of the habits, amusements, dealings, education, politics, and religion of the London costermongers in the nineteenth century; and then to say whether they think it safe—even if it be thought fit—to allow men, women, and children, to continue in such a state.'

These costermongers form a distinct, and, to a great extent, an isolated class of the street folk. Under the term is included those who deal in fish, fruit, and vegetables, bought at the markets, which they sell at their stalls, or on their 'rounds,' varying from two to three miles. Saturday night and Sunday morning are their great opportunities for business, and then the street-marts are held with mighty clamour and excitement. There are ten of these street-markets on the Surrey, and twenty-seven on the Middlesex, side of the Thames; attended by 3,801 hucksters, with an average of 102 to each.

The amusements of this class are characteristic of their condition. Four hundred beershops, consecrated to their use, supply them with places of resort. Gambling, skittles, sparring, boxing, and other practices, enliven their leisure hours; and we learn the truth of the remark, that 'there is a close resemblance between many of the characteristics of a very high class, socially, and a very low class.' 'Two-penny hops,' or cheap dances, with the galleries of the inferior theatres, supply them also with entertainment. Three times a week is the usual dramatic allowance of a prosperous 'coster.' They cannot, as they say, make end or side out of *Hamlet. Macbeth* would be better liked if it contained nothing but the witches' scenes, and the fighting. Music is popular. Nigger songs once pleased, but are now out of date. Translations of 'Mourir pour la patrie' and the 'Marseillaise' are much in vogue. A good chorus is necessary. 'They like something, sir,' said one informant, 'that is worth hearing—such as 'The Soldier's Dream,' 'The Dream of Napoleon,' or 'I 'ad a Dream, an 'appy Dream.' Those in ridicule of Marshal Haynau, and in praise of Paul Jones, are especial favourites; but the chorus of 'Rule Britannia'—'Britons never shall be slaves,' is often rendered, in bitter allusion to the monopoly of political privileges, 'Britons always shall be slaves.'

The sports of the 'coster' are peculiar. Rat-killing, dog-fighting, pigeon-shooting, and boxing, are in high estimation. No amusement, however, is so popular as annoying or harassing the police; and many a boy has willingly gone to prison for the satisfaction of inflicting a brick-bat wound upon some particular enemy in the force. In connexion with this subject, the politics of the costermonger should be noticed. They are all Chartists; but often with the most vague ideas of the principles they profess to adopt. Free trade is frequently supported, because it brings a cheap loaf; but, with this exception, their ideas seldom go beyond the tyrants in blue coats and shining hats, who overlook their proceedings, and whom they regard as their natural enemies. 'I am assured,' says Mr. Mayhew, 'that in case of a political riot, every 'coster' would seize his policeman.' Nor can they at all understand why their leaders exhort them to peace and quietness, 'when they might as well fight it out at once.' This proves that the statesman should regard them as a dangerous class. There is a sleeping volcano in the bosom of the State.

Formidable as they are in a political point of view, the members of this class should be dreaded for the moral disease which they perpetuate and spread. The social law with them is little binding. Not more than one-tenth of the couples living together are married; but in Clerkenwell, where the incumbent performs the ceremony without a fee, a fifth of the whole are lawfully wedded—a fact for the consideration of the ministers of religion. The fee thus exacted is proved to be a tax upon morality. Few, however, attach much significance to the tie which unites them at the altar, except as a legal link which they cannot break at pleasure—for, as a class, they have no religion at all, little idea of a future state, and scarcely any respect for the missionaries, who descend, as it were, from an upper world to teach them. Nor is this a wonderful circumstance, since true religion is incompatible with total ignorance. No more than one in ten is able to read; but they are eager to learn, and grateful to those who come among them in a philanthropic spirit, mingling care for their present welfare with solicitude for their moral elevation. At this moment, a large order of men remains, as Mr. Mayhew phrases it, in brutish ignorance; and he truly adds, that it is a national disgrace.

But the costermongers are aliens, not only from our amusements, from our tastes, from our customs, from our education, but also from our language. They have a dialect of their own, of which the volume supplies many curious specimens. Their original names are laid aside for slang appellations, and their children are taught in this tongue, as well as by example, that the duties of their future life consist in earning a livelihood, little matter by what means. Yet there is a literature among these barbarians, and there are those who can read it to the others. Tales of vice, with pretended revelations and real accounts of courts, with other loathsome subjects, they greedily devour. Cruickshank's 'Bottle' was highly admired, but men who pronounced it 'prime,' became drunk three hours afterwards. Altogether, the kind of writing relished among them is of a low order, and the most contemptible scrawlers, for the most part, fill the high places in their literary Pantheon.

Among men so removed in sentiment and practice from all that appears virtuous or pure, it seems remarkable to find honesty a characteristic. That is to say—they will defraud their customers to any extent, but they never rob each other, nor do regular thieves often assail them. It is computed that property worth ten thousand pounds, belonging to costers, is daily left exposed in the streets or markets, yet instances of theft are extremely rare. They never give a culprit into charge, but punish him by Lynch law.

The means of livelihood adopted by the costermongers are generally uniform. With pony or donkey-carts, hand-barrows, baskets, cans, trays, boxes, or slings, they patrol the town, or station themselves in various places, vending their humble commodities. Their beasts of draught are purchased at Smithfield, and are almost universally well treated—as much from good-feeling as from prudence. The costermonger, though a trader, is not often a capitalist. Three-fourths of them traffic upon borrowed property—paying no less than an average interest of twenty per cent. per week, or at the rate of 1,040*l*. a-year for every 100*l*. advanced. The people who buy from them suffer by this iniquitous system of usury, for, of course, the amount is added to the real value of the article, and thus a cruel robbery is perpetrated upon the humble and the poor; for fraud is resorted to, not from choice, but from necessity. The indigent are by nature honest. 'Mrs. Chisholm has lent out, at different times, as much as 160,000*l*. that has been entrusted to her for the use of "the lower orders," and the whole of this large amount has been returned with the exception of 12*l*.! I myself have often given a sovereign to professed thieves to get changed, and never knew one to make off with the money.'

False weights and measures are in general use; but it is not so much from inclination as from necessity that this fraud is resorted to. A man starts to sell cherries fairly at fourpence a pound. A boy starts after him, and cries them at twopence, giving half the just quantity. The man, therefore, in order to do any business, lowers his charge. 'The coster makes it a rule never to refuse an offer, and if people *will* give him less than what he considers his proper price, why he gives them less than their proper quantity.' An association, however, has been formed among them, pledged to deal fairly, and any member of it infringing the rule is liable to be expelled. There is a strong disposition, indeed, to trade honestly if all would consent alike. 'There's plenty among us,' said one, 'would pay for an inspector of weights. I would.' (pp. 424-28)

One of the most original and interesting chapters in Mr. Mayhew's extraordinary work is that on the publishers, authors, and salesmen of street literature in London. One printer made 10,000*l*. in this way. Songs are sold by the yard, and they must be of a peculiar quality. The topic must suit the day, and be one of present interest. A ballad on Jane Wilbred was very successful. It was not written in language so choice as Haynes Bailey would have used, but it struck the taste of the nomade tribe:—

> Jane Wilbred we did starve, and beat her very
>   hard,
> I confess we used her very cruel,
> But now in a jail two long years we must bewail,
> We don't fancy mustard in the gruel.

Of the standard songs, 'The Pope He Leads a Happy Life,' 'There's a Good Time Coming,' 'Kate Kearney,' 'I Dreamt That I Dwelt in Marble Halls,' 'I've Been Roaming,' and others, are great favourites. Invented murders, and other tragedies, especially if accompanied with romantic and startling details, or revelations of crimes among the upper classes, circulate wonderfully. The real achievements of the assassin also, such as Rush, the Mannings, and others, were taken advantage of. The Papal aggression was a great boon. For the first time in his life, a 'patterer' declared he had been patronized by clergymen for singing songs against the Pope. One gave half-a-crown, another a fourpenny-piece, another was liberal in contributing to the pleasures of the fifth of November. If there is nothing really startling, somebody is killed for the occasion. One man told Mr. Mayhew that he had put the Duke of Wellington to death twice: once by a fall from his horse, the other time by a 'sudden and mysterious fate.' He had performed the same mortal office on two occasions for Louis Philippe: once by stabbing, and then by shooting. He would have poisoned the Pope, but was afraid of the Irish Catholics. He had broken Prince Albert's leg, and made the Queen bear three children at a time. He had apprehended Feargus O'Connor on a charge of high treason. He had assassinated that wretched pretender Louis Napoleon 'from a *fourth* edition of the *Times,*' which 'did well,' and was probably as true as many of 'our own correspondent's' announcements. Marshall Haynau had died under his hands after the assault by the draymen. Rush had hung himself in prison. Jane Wilbred had perished from the ill-usage she experienced; and Mrs. Sloane was dead of remorse.

Famous buildings also are burned down by these imaginative wanderers. Canterbury Cathedral, Dover Castle, Edinburgh Castle, the Brighton Pavilion, or Holyrood House, succeed; but it is no use attempting Windsor Castle or Hampton Court, 'for unless people *saw* the reflection of a great fire, they wouldn't buy.' They also parade the squares with second editions of the evening papers—the brilliant leaders and abundant intelligence of the *Sun,* and the news of the *Globe.*

Political litanies, catechisms, satirical dialogues, are vended in considerable abundance. There is a class of street literature so incendiary, libellous, irreligious, or indecent, that no one dares to *vend* it. The patterer, therefore, escapes the enactment by *selling* to each customer a *straw,* and *giving* him the publication. Before the press was so free as at present, this system was very extensively practised, even with publications of admirable spirit. The *Republican,* about twenty-six years ago, was circulated in this manner. Remarks on the trial of Queen Caroline were also thus distributed; and at the time of the old Reform Bill, when the Tory party sought to defend their feudal tyranny, they were assailed by flying squadrons of light tracts, dispersed over the town by the *straw* system. Men could not be prosecuted for *giving,* but only for *selling*

such writings. Next spring there will be less need for such devices. The liberty of unlicensed printing is almost complete, and when the fiscal burdens are removed, will be perfectly so. About fifty sellers of religious tracts perambulate the streets; more than half of them are Hindus, Negroes, or Malays from the Indian Archipelago. We have full accounts of all these classes, their places of habitation, modes of life, and characteristics of the low lodging-houses they frequent; of the filth, dishonesty, and immorality there prevalent; and of all the phases of existence displayed among them. (pp. 431-32)

We have, we believe, justified our assertion that there is a nation of men, women, and children in London, overwhelmed by ignorance, vice, and poverty—a dangerous leaven in our society, a slumbering fire which may one day break out and devastate the higher regions of the commonwealth. As long as they continue as they actually are, our civilization will be but a partial scheme, excluding the poor from its advantages. We have made laws for hundreds of years; we have achieved great social triumphs; we have become the first nation; we have piled up, in various stores, the accumulated trophies of our art, our industry, and our versatile skill; we have acquired naval and military fame; and the benignant influences of order, peace, and happiness, have sprung from our bosom to bless whole millions in distant parts of the world. In India we have substituted a wise and beneficent government for a desolating tyranny; in Australia we are reclaiming the desert; in New Zealand we are redeeming the savage; but in our own metropolis vast tribes of barbarians remain unvisited by religion, unrefined in manners, unenlightened by education. Are these debased, immoral, irreligious, fraudulent, and reckless classes civilized? If they are, then we have no right to call the Fingoes barbarians; but if they are not, we have no right to boast of our social institutions. We should rather blush that fifty thousand human beings are thus abandoned in the capital of our empire to the most degrading and dangerous influences. It is not for charity to help them. It is not for private enterprise to elevate them—it is for the Legislature, and until a new spirit is infused into the Legislature, reform among the poor is hopeless. Can the reader imagine what men and women must grow from children who never knew what play was; never enjoyed a gambol in the fields; never breathed one breeze of country air; children that pass at one step from the helplessness of infancy to the self-dependence of maturity, and are taught to labour almost as soon as they leave the mother's breast! In illustration of this let us quote a passage from the account of a little creature, whose whole existence was occupied in supplying the breakfast-tables of the poor with the refreshing but simple luxury of water-cresses.

> The little girl who gave me the following statement, although only eight years of age, had entirely lost all childish ways, and was, indeed, in thoughts and manner, a woman. There was something cruelly pathetic in hearing this infant, so young that her features had scarcely formed themselves, talking of the bitterest struggles of life with the calm earnestness of one who had endured them all. I did not know how to talk with her. At first I treated her as a child, speaking on

childish subjects; so that I might, by being familiar with her, remove all shyness, and get her to narrate her life freely. I asked her about her toys and her games with her companions; but the look of amazement, that answered me, soon put an end to any attempt at fun on my part. I then talked to her about the parks, and whether she ever went to them. 'The parks,' she replied, in wonder, 'where are they?' I explained to her, telling her that they were large open places with green grass and tall trees, where beautiful carriages drove about, and people walked for pleasure, and children played. Her eyes brightened up a little as I spoke; and she asked, half doubtingly, 'Would they let such as me go there just to look?' All her knowledge seemed to begin and end with watercresses, and what they fetched. She knew no more of London than that part she had seen on her rounds, and believed that no quarter of the town was handsomer or pleasanter than it was at Farringdon-market or Clerkenwell, where she lived. Her little face, pale and thin with privation, *was wrinkled where the dimples ought to have been,* and she would sigh frequently. When some hot dinner was offered to her, she would not touch it, because if she ate too much 'it made her sick,' she said; 'and she wasn't used to meat only on a Sunday.'

The work contains many anecdotes illustrative of the truth that the more precious sentiments of human nature are often plants of hardy growth, which bloom in the coldest winter of poverty. Girls have worked themselves blind to support their parents; paralyzed old men have dragged themselves through the streets to maintain their bedridden wives; orphan sisters have laboured day and night providing food for their younger brothers, and many of them preserve themselves in virtue and modesty, notwithstanding all temptations. There are hearts so rich in feeling that the longest trials will not exhaust them. We know of one poor widow, accustomed to much sorrow, who planted a cypress on the spot where her son was killed by accident, and yearly went to view the tree, until its foliage flowed in full beauty above the place. Henry Mayhew supplies numerous similar anecdotes, which will entertain all readers.

We entreat public attention to Mr. Mayhew's revelations of London. If ignorance could, up to this time, be pleaded in defence of our neglect, there is no longer any such retreat for the consciences of indolent politicians. It is idle to reiterate the hollow remark that legislation cannot deal with such classes, that law cannot elevate them, purify their morals, or refine their manners. Parliament can and must effect a change, or we may be awakened from an indifference by a catastrophe not the less portentous because

Illustration of London needlewomen, which accompanied one of Mayhew's reports reprinted in London's Penny Illustrated News.

it should have been foreseen. This is by no means mere speculation. It is impossible to deny that a large class of men, such as we have shown the street-wanderers to be, must form a dangerous element in society. That element is continually increasing its power, because it is perpetually multiplied. The process will not go on for ever. Combustible materials will not for ever accumulate, without an explosion one day taking place. It is, consequently, imperative on the Legislature to direct an inquiry into the means of reforming these people. We cannot here suggest a plan, but Henry Mayhew has, doubtless, matured one, and his opinion will be very valuable. (pp. 433-36)

> *"Mayhew's Revelations of London," in* The Eclectic Review, *n.s. Vol. II, October, 1851, p. 424-36.*

Peter Quennell   (essay date 1951)

[*Quennell is an English biographer and critic who has written extensively on the literature of the eighteenth and nineteenth centuries. He has served as editor of two important journals,* History Today *and* Cornhill Magazine. *In the following excerpt, he discusses Mayhew's approach to his subject and outlines his methods of presentation in* London Labour and the London Poor.]

During the first thirty years of the [nineteenth] century the population of the Greater London area rose from 865,000 to 1,500,000; and in the next twenty years another million inhabitants were somehow piled in. They were housed (writes a contributor to that valuable compilation, *Early Victorian England*) "by overcrowding, and by lateral expansion in houses, mainly two-storied, built on estates it was desired to develop, and ribboned along roads. That is why, in the *Pickwick Papers,* Mr. Wicks, of Dodson and Fogg's, found it was 'half past four before he got to Somers Town' after a convivial evening . . . and Mr. Jaggers cultivated the family affections behind a ditch in Walworth." As the population thickened, so did its occupations grow more and more miscellaneous, its character more amorphous. Parasites fastened on parasites; the refuse and leavings of one class helped, literally as well as figuratively, to provide a means of livelihood for the class immediately beneath it; and, while the poor but "respectable" members of commercial society, the clerks and small employees, tended to gravitate towards pretentious gimcrack suburbs pullulating uncontrolled upon London's shabby outer edge, the lowest and weakest of its citizens, the scavengers, rag-pickers and pedlars, drifted into its noisome central slums, into one or other of the many "rookeries", clusters of dilapidated ancient houses—such as "Tom All Alone's," under the shadow of Westminster Abbey, scathingly described as *Bleak House.*

The first chapters of that novel—together with *Our Mutual Friend,* probably Dickens' most ambitious attempt to delineate the London landscape—were published in periodical form during the Spring of 1852. But the public conscience was already aroused, for the Victorian Age, in spite of its numerous detractors, was neither self-complacent nor insensitive; and throughout the 'thirties and 'forties repeated plans had been made for the delivery of at least a preliminary attack on the gigantic Augean stable that London, at its then rate of development, was in danger of becoming. There were sanitary commissions, inquests on water-supply, while a vast and compendious *Report on the Sanitary Condition of the City of London* for the years 1848-49 provoked the indignation and excited the alarm of every thoughtful Londoner. Though "rookeries" still bred disease, their existence was threatened, if not by the moral scruples of the English upper classes, at all events by the practical necessity of opening up new thoroughfares; and, to clear the approaches to New London Bridge, a million and a half pounds' worth of old property had been purchased and demolished. The spirit of reform and philanthropy was omnipresent; and by a singular stroke of good fortune an enterprising philanthropist of the period happened at the same time to be an extremely able journalist. Two volumes of articles, which had originally appeared in the London daily press, were collected by their author, Henry Mayhew, and published under the title *London Labour and the London Poor* in 1851.

Considering the scope of his works on London and the remarkable quality of their content, it seems odd that Mayhew's name should be so little known to the ordinary modern reader. On the career of this gifted and industrious man the *Dictionary of National Biography* is concise and informative but somewhat unenthusiastic. Born in 1812, the son of a London attorney, he survived till 1887, dying at a house in Charlotte Street, to which, so far as the present writer is aware, the London County Council has not yet contemplated attaching its commemorative blue tab. His activities during that time were numerous and varied. He began his working-life as a dramatist, his first production being a one-act play entitled *The Wandering Minstrel* in which he introduced the celebrated Cockney song, "Villikins and His Dinah", and was the author of many other successful comedies and farces. As a middle-aged journalist, he attended at the birth of *Punch,* of which for a while he acted as joint-editor; and, in addition to his dramatic, journalistic and philanthropic efforts, he found time to turn out travel-books, biographies, novels and stories and treatises on popular science. The bulk of his work was ephemeral; but there can be no doubt that *London Labour and the London Poor,* reissued in 1861, 1862, 1864 and 1865 with copious additions and supplementary volumes, is an achievement that deserves the respectful attention of posterity. Not only was Mayhew a pioneer in this particular type of sociological record but, thanks to the original cast of his mind and to his extraordinary gifts both as an observer and as a reporter, he left behind him a book that one need not be a student of history or a sociologist to find immensely entertaining.

The plan is ambitious. Disregarding the strongholds of wealth and privilege, Mayhew's intention was to plumb to its depths the dark ocean of poverty or semi-poverty by which they were encircled, to discover how the poor lived—the hopelessly poor, as well as the depressed and struggling—and to examine the means, ignoble and commendable, furtive and above-board, by which the majority of London's unorganized millions precariously scraped a livelihood. Had he been exclusively concerned with economics, Mayhew's *magnum opus* might make useful but tedious reading. In fact, his interests were many-sided; and no less than three persons appear and reappear as we turn the pages of his survey. First, there is the impassioned *Statistician;* but in this guise, it must be admitted, Mayhew with the best intentions in the world is often slightly ludicrous. He loved figures for their own sake, and welcomed every opportunity of drawing up vast ingenious tables. . . . (pp. 16-19)

Luckily, another aspect of Mayhew's personality is very soon in evidence. As the philanthropic *Social Investigator,* he feels a deep concern with the material needs and financial vicissitudes of his fellow human beings. He is intensely preoccupied with the lives of others; and no detail is so trifling that it can slip through the meshes of his inquisitorial drag-net. We are informed, for example, that a working scavenger of the 'fifties, having earned fifteen shillings by his week's labour, had spent, in the instance selected, the sum of exactly thirteen shillings and twopence-farthing—one-and-ninepence being the rent of an unfurnished room, sevenpence going on tobacco, two-and-fourpence on beer, one-and-a-penny on gin, a penny-three-farthings on pickles or onions, and two-and-fourpence on boiled salt beef. A journeyman sweeper was maintained by his master at the cost of approximately sixpence-half-penny. His week-day diet was as follows:

	s. d.
Bread and butter and coffee for breakfast	0 2
A saveloy and potatoes, or cabbage; or a "fagot", with the same vegetables; or fried fish (but not often); or pudding, from a pudding-shop; or soup (a two-penny plate) from a cheap eating-house; average from 2d. to 3d.	0 2½
Tea, same as breakfast	0 2

But we learn, with relief, that "on Sundays the fare was better. They then sometimes had a bit of 'prime fat mutton taken to the oven, with 'taturs to bake along with it'; or a 'fry of liver, if the old 'oman was in a good humour', and always a pint of beer apiece." But Londoners had not only to be fed; they must also be clothed; and in certain callings a decent appearance must be carefully kept up:

> A prosperous and respectable master green-grocer (writes Mayhew), who was what may be called "particular" in his dress, as he had been a gentleman's servant, and was now in the habit of waiting upon the wealthy persons in his neighbourhood, told me that the following was the average of his washing bill. He was a bachelor; all his washing was put out, and he considered his expenditure far *above* the average of his class, as many used no nightshirt, but slept in the shirt they wore during the day, and paid only 3d., and even less, per shirt to their washer-woman, and per-

haps, and more especially in winter, made one shirt last the week.

	s. d.
Two shirts (per week)	0 7
Stockings	0 1
Night-shirt (worn two weeks generally, average per week)	0 ¾
Sheets, blankets, and other household linens or woollens	0 2
Handkerchiefs	0 0¼
	0 11

These extracts . . . have been chosen more or less at random, but may serve to illustrate the meticulous humanity with which Mayhew pursued his subject. And now a further facet of his character emerges. It would be presumptuous, no doubt, to call him the nineteenth-century Defoe; but, if he had none of Defoe's imaginative genius, he had the same devotion to the literal fact, the same grasp of detail and the same observant eye, that makes Defoe the most poetic of the great European realists. Mayhew's notes on economic conditions were accompanied by brilliant portraits of individual men and women. One would like to know what were his methods of work. This Victorian Mass-Observer would appear to have spent long hours of conversation in attics, pubs and back-streets, asking innumerable questions and patiently noting down the answers. Here he reveals his third facet—perhaps the most important—the dispassionate *Literary Portraitist,* who bore some resemblance both to Daniel Defoe and to Restif de la Bretonne. Like them he browsed and botanised; but he had a knack of recording living speech which was peculiarly characteristic of the period he lived in. Take, for instance, this speech by an old soldier:

> "I'm 42 now (he said), and when I was a boy and a young man I was employed in the *Times* machine office, but got into a bit of a row—a bit of a street quarrel and frolic, and was called on to pay £3, something about a street-lamp; that was out of the question; and as I was taking a walk in the park, not just knowing what I'd best do, I met a recruiting sergeant, and enlisted on a sudden—all on a sudden—in the 16th Lancers. . . . Well, I was rather frolicsome in those days, I confess, and perhaps *had rather a turn for a roving life,* so when the sergeant said he'd take me to the East India Company's recruiting sergeant, I consented, and was accepted at once. I was taken to Calcutta, and served under General Nott all through the Affghan war. The first real warm work I was in was at Candahar. I've heard young soldiers say that they've gone into action the first time as merry as they would go to a play. Don't believe them, Sir. Old soldiers will tell you quite different. You *must* feel queer and serious the first time you're in action; it's not fear—it's nervousness. The crack of the muskets at the first fire you hear in real hard earnest is uncommon startling; you see the flash of the fire from the enemy's line, but very little else. Indeed, oft enough you see nothing but smoke, and hear nothing but balls whis-

tling every side of you. And then you get excited, just as if you were at a hunt; but after a little service—I can speak for myself, at any rate—you go into action as you go to your dinner."

"Something about a street-lamp"—how admirable the phrase is! Mayhew's pages are illuminated, again and again, by these sudden vivid flashes in which the essentials of a situation or character—here the headstrong young man on a spree; the tinkle of broken glass; the mood of exhilaration passing into the mood of angry desperation during which he meets the sergeant—seem concisely summed up. As memorable are his impressions of interiors; for his omnivorous curiosity was not confined to street-life; and, bound on a visit to an impoverished costermonger, he had climbed a flight of tottering and broken stairs, and entered a room thick with smoke that was pouring from the chimney:

> The place was filled with it, curling in the light, and making everything so indistinct that I could with difficulty see the white mugs ranged in the corner-cupboard. . . . On a mattress, on the floor, lay a pale-faced girl—"eighteen years old last twelfth-cake day"—her drawn-up form showing in the patch-work counterpane that covered her. She had just been confined, and the child had died! . . . To shield her from the light of the window, a cloak had been fastened up slantingly across the panes; and on a string that ran along the wall was tied, amongst the bonnets, a clean nightcap—"against the doctor came", as the mother, curtsying, informed me. . . . The room was about nine feet square, and furnished a home for three women. The ceiling slanted like that of a garret, and was the colour of old leather, excepting a few rough white patches, where the tenants had rudely mended it. The white light was easily seen through the laths, and in one corner a large patch of the paper looped down from the wall. . . . They had made a carpet out of three or four old mats. They were "obligated to it for fear of dropping anything through the boards into the donkey stables in the parlour underneath. But we only pay ninepence a week rent", said the old woman, "and musn't grumble".

Mayhew's impressions, however, are not of gloom unmitigated or poverty unrelieved; and many have the cheerfulness and distinction of a Dutch or Flemish *genre* picture. He describes, for example, his visit to the home of a thriving costermonger, where "the floor was as white as if it had been newly planed", and "the wall over the fire-place was patched up to the ceiling with little square pictures of saints. . . . On the mantel-piece, between a row of bright tumblers and wine glasses filled with odds and ends, stood glazed crockeryware images of Prince Albert and M. Jullien. . . . In the band-box, which stood on the stained chest of drawers, you could tell that the Sunday bonnet was stowed away safely from the dust." Even the room occupied by a family of struggling costers was not entirely squalid:

> The man, a tall, thick-built, almost good-looking fellow, with a large fur cap on his head, lived with his family in a front kitchen, and as there

were, with his mother-in-law, five persons, and only one bed, I was somewhat puzzled to know where they could *all* sleep. The barrow standing on the railings over the window, half shut out the light, and when any one passed there was a momentary shadow thrown over the room, and a loud rattling of the iron gratings above that completely prevented all conversation. When I entered, the mother-in-law was reading aloud one of the threepenny papers to her son, who lolled on the bed, that with its curtains nearly filled the room. There was the usual attempt to make the fireside comfortable. The stone sides had been well whitened, and the mantel-piece decorated with its small tin trays, tumblers, and a piece of looking-glass. A cat with her kittens were seated on the hearth-rug in front. . . . By the drawers were piled up four bushel baskets, and in a dark corner near the bed stood a tall measure full of apples that scented the room. . . . On a string dangled a couple of newly washed shirts, and by the window were two stone barrels, for lemonade, when the coster visited the fairs and races.

Still more vivid, in its extremely Dickensian way, is Mayhew's account of his meeting with Jack Black, "Rat and mole destroyer to Her Majesty", whom he discovered at his house in Battersea, and whose expression radiated a kindliness that did not "exactly agree with one's preconceived notions of rat-catchers. His face had a strange appearance, from his rough, uncombed hair being nearly grey, and his eyebrows and whiskers black, so that he looked as if he wore powder". He, too, lived surrounded by the apparatus of his daily work—he was, incidentally, taxidermist and bird-fancier as well as rat-catcher; his parlour was "more like a shop than a family apartment. In a box . . . like a rabbit-hutch, was a white ferret, twisting its long thin body with a snake-like motion up and down the length of its prison, as restlessly as if it were a miniature polar bear. When Mr. Black called 'Polly' to the ferret, it came to the bars and fixed its pink eyes on him. A child lying on the floor poked its fingers into the cage, but Polly only smelt at them. . . ." (pp. 20-4)

> *Peter Quennell, in an introduction to* Mayhew's London *by Henry Mayhew, edited by Peter Quennell, William Kimber, 1951, pp. 15-25.*

John L. Bradley   (essay date 1965)

[*Bradley is an English critic who edited* Selections from Mayhew's London Labour and the London Poor. *In the following excerpt, he traces the development of Mayhew's fiction and nonfiction, and assesses his influence on the authors of his era.*]

Mayhew's three farces—*The Wandering Minstrel* (1834), *But However* (1838), and *A Troublesome Lodger* (1839)—share the ingredients of their genre as mixed to appeal to a crassly ignorant and raucous audience. Writing at a time when the theatre was in aesthetic darkness, when quantity rather than quality determined the success or failure of the evening, when extravaganza, bizarre colour, and noisy declamation triumphed over good taste, dramatic construction, and perceptive consideration of fundamental problems and verities, Mayhew fashioned his little plays to meet the lowest of dramatic demands. Thus his farces turn upon such exhausted devices as mistaken identity, the trickster tricked, and noisy confusion modulating to sentimental calm by the final curtain. In addition, they are plays of bumbling exposition laced with bathos and replete with stock figures whose speech is almost wholly pun-ridden. And, while characterized by surprisingly little vulgarity, they contrive to be coarse, loud, and clumsy. But one of them, *The Wandering Minstrel,* written alone rather than in collaboration, possesses a curious duality that distinguishes it from the run-of-the-mill farcical fare of the thirties. In fact, it is a Janus-like play; for, though broadly comic and thus representative of its genre, it is also, because of Mayhew's treatment of the sub-plot involving Mr. and Mrs. Crincum, anticipatory of the realistic plays of Robertson and others which were to shape Victorian drama in subsequent decades.

The Crincum relationship concerns an elderly, dignified husband and a young, flighty wife. Early in *The Wandering Minstrel* Crincum reveals his worldly self-knowledge as he comments on his marriage:

> Well! Thus it is when an old man forgets himself and marries a young wife; it's ten to one but she follows his example and forgets him, too. . . .

There is also about him a poignant regret and mature awareness not wholly consistent with the world of unrestrained farce. And his lines are free from nonsense; when reading the paper, for instance, he passes over the fashion news, criminal activities, and amusements to consult Parliamentary reports—and when he comments upon them he does so with critical astringency.

Furthermore, Mr. Crincum's point of view throughout is anti-Romantic. He early debunks his wife's absurd notion of the wandering minstrel with 'Romance, fiddlesticks'. Neither is he deceived by the minstrel when that worthy arrives. And, though henpecked by a vulgar wife, he does not respond as the conventionally harassed husband of farce by becoming a foil for the harridan. Instead, he retains his self-respect, thereby exposing her fully and removing himself more and more from the world of the play. His scenes with Mrs. Crincum are suggestive of a deeper current of domestic drama, faint but perceptible here, that is to reinvigorate the British theatre about a quarter of a century later. For Mr. Crincum, in his domestic relationship, displays a critical attitude, an experienced awareness of human foibles, a set of rational values and adult responses common not so much to the passing works of the eighteen-thirties as to the plays of the fifties and sixties which were to supersede them. Thus it would seem that Mayhew, in this play, while yielding to contemporary tastes by giving his audiences the simple entertainment they expectetd, looked ahead to those realistic years when dramas of domestic life grappled with basic problems. In this way, then, *The Wandering Minstrel,* while essentially of its time, is also the forerunner of the urbane and socially discerning dramas given with such deserved success by the Bancrofts at the Prince of Wales's Theatre in the fifties—

the theatre, that is, of such men as Robertson, Taylor, and Boucicault.

Less significant than his farces are Mayhew's two burlettas which, nevertheless, are strikingly representative of that genre which no theatrical historian through the years seems wholly comfortable in trying to delineate. Suffice to say, with the passage of the nineteenth century the components of the burletta shift and change so that by the thirties—when Mayhew contributed *The Barbers at Court* (1835) and *The Young Sculptor* (1839) to this proliferating form—he would seem to be writing a short, romantic, historical piece with musical and humorous interpolations. For both plays look to the past for their settings—the first to the England of Charles II and the second to the Italy of Michelangelo. Both have extravagant, far-fetched plots, high-flown, bombastic dialogue, and sentimental music in the ballad tradition. Where *The Young Sculptor* leans to melodrama, *The Barbers at Court* stresses the farcical, presumably because the important role of Maximus Hogsflesh was played by the great comedian, Liston. But they share more similarities than differences. In sentimental appeal, in bustling action, and, above all, in looking to the remote figure of an amorous monarch or to the artistic genius of a Michelangelo, the two plays (like thousands of their time) lifted the noisy, ignorant audiences of early Victorian England out of the drabness and monotony of their squalid daily lives.

Yet even as he served trivia to the escapist, through the theatre and through minor writings for the *Comic Almanac* (which he later edited in 1850-1), *Cosmorama,* the *Comic Magazine,* and dozens of other transient jest-books, Mayhew, with his friend, Gilbert A'Beckett, was also conducting *Figaro in London,* a journal of no little substance. The young men began the paper in 1831, with A'Beckett in the editor's chair; but Mayhew was sole editor from January 1835 until the demise of the journal in August 1839. (pp. x-xiv)

During the A'Beckett years, the main news article was generally given to a subject politically topical and frequently dealing with the Reform Bill. This was followed by mildly satirical passes at such set targets as the Duke of Gloucester, the Duke of Wellington, and others among the politically conservative. Officialdom, the cruel magistrate for instance, came in regularly for its drubbing with the editor invariably siding with the victims of injustice and bumbledom. And, finally, the theatrical personalities of the day—Bunn, Kean, Mme Vestris—were closely considered. But to the end of 1834 *Figaro in London* shows a good-humoured critical attitude toward established institutions and keeps within acceptable journalistic limits. There is an almost total absence of coarseness, and public figures are never viciously pilloried. It is the relative mildness of approach, a quizzical, even-tempered scrutiny, that gives the paper a civilized individuality and makes it stand out in contrast to the journalistic outrages perpetrated by rogues like Renton Nicholson, Barnard Gregory, and Charles Molloy Westmacott.

From the beginning of Mayhew's editorship in January 1835 *Figaro in London* took considerably less interest than heretofore in theatrical activity and a good deal more in public affairs. In September 1835, for instance, the Whig budget is flayed; on another occasion the House of Lords is severely censured; and even the social activities of the Queen herself do not escape *Figaro's* sharp tongue. More significant, however, is that where the paper tended, under A'Beckett, to be essentially Whiggish, it now rises above party, as the leading article of 5 September 1835 suggests:

> The body of poor John Bull, it is well known, has for a length of time been full of disease, which, from want of proper treatment at the hands of the physicians to whom he has been entrusted has, in some cases, become so extremely dangerous to his constitution that his friends have often been fearful of his total dissolution.

Furthermore, the 'squibs' which leavened some of the political weightiness now become more critical, more sardonic in tone; where they once dealt with inconsequential social customs or petty human weaknesses, they now discuss, with grim prescience, the corruption of cemetery companies, election bribery, court sycophancy, and the problems of a standing army. Certainly, until the end of 1838 *Figaro* pursues sterner policies than in its youth, thus becoming more incisive, more sententious, than in the A'Beckett years.

But by the autumn of 1838 the paper encountered difficulties, as the 29 September number indicates when announcing that *Figaro* will double its size while remaining at the same price. It is also noted that the paper will enlarge its theatrical intelligence and make other concessions to facile popularity. And there is no question but that, in the last months of its life which terminated in August 1839, *Figaro* diminishes in satirical force, grows more colloquial, and sinks distressingly close to the level of the lesser journals which, throughout the thirties and forties, came and went with unregretted regularity.

To reflect upon Mayhew's writing in the thirties is to recognize the clear dichotomy it represents. On the one hand, a critical investigator of man's institutions stamps his impression of them upon column after column of *Figaro;* on the other, a casual writer of farces, burlettas, and jestbooks seems remote from all but entertaining at a miserably low level of intelligence. Yet one senses a resilient, fertile mind playing over the human dilemma, a mind which if ordered and disciplined could make salient contributions in a variety of literary forms. But Mayhew rarely focused upon anything for long; indifference, torpor, thoughtlessness, invariably conquered other more significant inclinations. Indeed, Spielmann seems close to the truth about the man in noting "There can be no doubt that Henry Mayhew was a genius, a fascinating companion, and a man of inexhaustible resource and humour—although humour was but one side of his brilliant mind. Indolence was his besetting sin; and his will was untutored.' Vizetelly, Hodder, and other writers of memoirs attest to the same qualities in Mayhew; and to the end he appears to have developed no sense of responsibility; neither did he, in the face of indifferent literary success, become in the least embittered. He seems, from first to last, to have remained charming, amusing, consistently entertaining, intermittently enthusiastic, and utterly irresponsible. (pp. xv-xviii)

[With] the experience of editing *Figaro* behind him and encouraged by his literary companions, he became one of the four original proprietors of *Punch* and co-editor with Mark Lemon from the initial number of 17 July 1841 until December of that year when, under not wholly happy circumstances, Lemon assumed full editorship. Eased out of the editorial chair, Mayhew remained, but tenuously, with the magazine until early 1846; during that awkward four-year period he contributed small articles and squibs, wrote almost single-handed one Almanac, and not infrequently offered an idea to one of the artists for a political cartoon. But although brief, Mayhew's association with the magazine in its fledgling period was of outstanding importance.

A measure of this importance might be ascertained by considering the remarks of Charles L. Graves in *Mr. Punch's History of Modern England* about the tone of the magazine at its outset:

> For *Punch* began as a radical and democratic paper, a resolute champion of the poor, and desolate and the oppressed, and the early volumes abound in evidences of the miseries of the 'Hungry Forties' and in burning pleas for their removal. The strange mixture of jocularity with intense earnestness which confronts us on every page was due to the characters and antecedents of the men who founded and wrote for the paper at its outset.

Graves then sketches Mayhew, A'Beckett, and Jerrold as 'humanitarians first and humorists afterwards'. And while the two last named were among those who discussed with Mayhew the possibility of such a magazine long before it came into being, it was Mayhew alone who conceived the idea of *Punch* and who wrote for it from its first issue. The others contributed later—only a little later, it is true—but their relationship with the magazine in its early stages is not as consistent and as close as Mayhew's. And when they came to write for *Punch* they did not so much determine its tenor as give impetus to policies already established. Thus as the attacks came forth on the Poor Law, Protection, and other social and political machinations, it was primarily because of Mayhew's influence that the work of A'Beckett, Jerrold, Leech, Brooks, and others took the sharply satirical direction it did. Looking through the early volumes of *Punch* one notes the preponderance of items concerning the 'condition of England'. Even more striking is the treatment afforded those subjects; for humour, unless satirically barbed, is quite plainly subservient to the intention to reveal and amend. In the fifties and sixties *Punch* tends to seek a truer balance between satirical and non-satirical humour. But its earliest pages burn with social zeal and its humour is constantly directed towards corrective ends. (pp. xix-xx)

During the forties Henry Mayhew, in collaboration with his brother Augustus, published several works of fiction. Two of these, ***The Greatest Plague of Life*** (1847) and ***Whom to Marry*** (1848), were illustrated by George Cruickshank. They are brief, humorous books designed for easy reading yet directed toward problems of concern to the middle classes. For ***The Greatest Plague*** is about the difficulties of getting a servant and ***Whom to Marry*** records the adventures of a young woman in search of a good husband. Such subjects offered humorists a wealth of mildly satirical material, and the Mayhew brothers took advantage of this to indulge their corrective propensities. But they do so with a temperate touch. And while facile craftsmanship and sustained lightness of tone inform both writings there lies, beneath the banter, a tolerant awareness of some of the social foibles and pretensions constantly manifested by the acquisitive middle classes. In their genial condescension and amused surveillance of the trivialities which, to the parvenu, meant so much, the Mayhews, though not among the noted satirists, recall, momentarily, the well-intentioned Gulliver in Lilliput as their wit plays gracefully over the embarrassments, social gaffes, and absurdities so common in Victorian England regarding 'the servant problem' and the painfully genteel search for an eligible young man.

Both works were well received and, over the years, went into sundry cheap editions. Critics, while noting their humour, frequently emphasized the social awareness of the two books preferring, quite plainly, not to dismiss them as mere ephemera. One reviewer, in fact, delivered a homily on the relationship between masters and servants, ending with the admonition that 'The lower classes must be better instructed before we can have a race of really good servants, contented with the true respectability and importance of their position. . . .' And it is clear, to judge from the two books and from reaction to them, that *The Greatest Plague* and *Whom to Marry* (as representative of hundreds upon hundreds of their genre) had an appeal both in terms of amusement and instruction.

Two further works, written once more in collaboration with his brother Augustus, came from Mayhew's pen in 1846(7) and 1849 respectively. These were *The Good Genius That Turned Everything into Gold* and *The Magic of Kindness,* two fairy tales of particular interest for the social and moral currents running so potently through them. Both possess a duality of tone: on the one hand, they share a gaiety and lightness common to the world of magic and wonder; on the other hand, those characteristics are often overshadowed by a sombre quality emphasizing the deeper objectives of the two books. For while *The Good Genius* is termed a 'Christmas Fairy Tale' and *The Magic of Kindness* found its way into a children's library, both books are plainly designed to bring certain moral and social matters to the awareness of the adult reader. In them satirical intention is put aside and equilibrium between disparate elements discarded in favour of laying stress upon the importance of social amelioration, necessity for concord and benevolence among men, and steady adherence to the moral virtues. Both are written with more incisiveness than *The Greatest Plague* and *Whom to Marry;* both are informed with a seriousness, a grimness even, characteristic of numerous books of the eighteen-forties centring upon the 'condition of England' question.

It is not an exaggeration to remark that the presence of Carlyle looms over *The Magic of Kindness* and *The Good Genius.* The past juxtaposed to the present, the chasm between rich and poor, the yearning for benevolence in human intercourse, are all echoes of Carlylean concepts—concepts which severally find their ways into both books.

And while, in *The Magic of Kindness,* confidence is expressed in the laws of kindness as operating in the interests of man's moral well-being, contemporary problems involving the workings of the penal law, the treatment of insanity, and vigilance in the face of tyranny resound throughout the book. And in *The Good Genius* the analyses of starvation and avarice carry the purport of the tale far beyond the circumscribed objectives of the fairy story. In a review, probably by Douglas Jerrold, the volume is hailed for exposing 'dusty fallacies' and for brushing down 'the cobwebs of time and prejudice that too often film the minds of our serious writers'. Certainly, *The Magic of Kindness* and *The Good Genius,* whatever their appeal to children and to readers of Christmas stories, bear intentions in social and moral terms that transcend the bounds of simple entertainment for an idle hour.

In general, Mayhew's work in the forties, while sometimes merely of a transient nature, assumes a more significant tone than heretofore. In much of his casual journalism, in the direction taken by *Punch,* as well as in his four novels, a wider knowledge of the evils of *laissez-faire,* a critical awareness of middle-class absurdities and, above all, a profound concern for the human condition, become increasingly noticeable. And it is now that Mayhew, surrounded by friends strongly desirous of reform and spurred by the spirit of the times, moved into the salient phase of his career. For in these years he laid the foundation for his major work, *London Labour and the London Poor,* by initiating in the *Morning Chronicle* a series of articles devoted to the atrocious condition of London's underprivileged. It is on these writings, no less powerful now than in their own time, that his reputation will rest. Sociologically, they are of primary significance as precise and compassionate delineations of the lives of the flotsam and jetsam of a great city, as poignant evocations of human misery, and as mathematically exact records of daily drudgery supported by those statistics to which Mayhew was so strongly addicted. Again, from a literary point of view, their style and influence have yet to be considered; unquestionably they stimulated others to inquire into London low life, and the outcome is evident in the plethora of studies by journalists and parsons in the fifties and sixties. Furthermore, their influence upon some of the sociological fiction of the time has to be marked; only Cazamian, in a brilliant work now a half century old, hints at this. And in the case of Charles Kingsley it is undeniable that Mayhew's work played an important role. In various ways, then, the articles, both in original and expanded form, have their place in the literary and sociological canon of mid-Victorian England. (pp. xxiv-xxvii)

Regarding his work on the poor, Mayhew makes three significant claims. Asserting that it is 'curious', he comments upon it 'as being the first attempt to publish the history of a people, from the lips of the people themselves—giving a literal description of their labour, their earnings, their trials, and their sufferings, in their own "unvarnished" language. . . . ' Second, he notes the work 'as being the first commission of inquiry into the state of the people, undertaken by a private individual, and the first "blue book" ever published in twopenny numbers'. And, finally, he sees his work 'as supplying information concerning a large body of persons of whom the public has less knowledge than of the most distant tribes of the earth. . . .' To judge from the critical response over the years, it is clear that these claims, while large, were most seriously entertained. In fact, from its inception in 1849 Mayhew's examination of the metropolitan poor drew comment from one end of the kingdom to the other. Initially, it was the practice of the provincial newspapers to quote from his articles, allowing the excerpts to speak for themselves; at that time, too, the *Chronicle* set aside an office to receive donations for alleviation. Later, when part publication commenced, it became Mayhew's habit to reply—on wrappers of the individual parts—to the hundreds of questions that poured in about the destitute. And, through the gestatory years of this immense work, one finds Mayhew addressing slop-tailors, wives of coal-whippers, and similar groups formed in response to the stark conditions of which he wrote. In such ways did **London Labour** rouse individuals to examine the plight of the impoverished.

Mayhew's writings worked for the poor in still another way—one yet to be fully evaluated. For it is evident, when reading the sociological novelists of the forties and fifties, that his writings made a profound mark upon them. This is especially apparent in two works by Charles Kingsley:

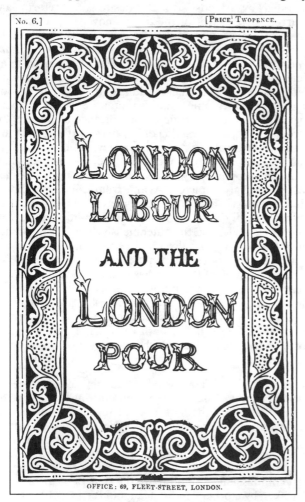

No. 6.]   [PRICE] TWOPENCE.

LONDON LABOUR AND THE LONDON POOR

OFFICE: 69, FLEET-STREET, LONDON.

Cover of one of the weekly issues of London Labour and the London Poor.

his pamphlet 'Cheap Clothes and Nasty' and his novel *Alton Locke*. While the former is little more than a series of acknowledged excerpts from Mayhew's *Chronicle* articles, the latter looks to them for urban descriptions, for means of advancing the narrative, and for certain specific incidents.

How closely Kingsley must have read Mayhew's articles is seen in the similarity between the following passages. In his letter to the *Chronicle* of 24 September 1849 Mayhew describes that notorious lazar spot, Jacob's Island:

> On entering the precincts of the pest island the air had literally the smell of a graveyard, and a feeling of nausea and heaviness came over any one unaccustomed to imbibe the moist atmosphere. Not only the nose, but the stomach told how heavily the air was loaded with sulphuretted hydrogen; and as soon as you crossed one of the crazy and rotten bridges over the reeking ditch, you knew, as surely as if you had chemically tested it, by the black colour of what was once white lead paint upon the door posts and window sills, that the air was thickly charged with this deadly gas. The heavy bubbles which now and then rose up in the water showed you whence at least a portion of the mephitic compound issued, while the open doorless privies that hung over the water-side, and the dark streaks of filth down the walls, where the drains from each house discharged themselves in to the ditch, were proofs indisputable as to how the pollution of the ditch occurred.
>
> The water was covered with scum almost like a cobweb, and prismatic with grease. In it floated large masses of rotting weed, and against the posts of the bridges were swollen carcases of dead animals, ready to burst with the gases of putrefaction. Along its shores were heaps of indescribable filth, the phosphoretted smell from which told you of the rotting fish there, while the oyster-shells were like pieces of slate from their coating of filth and mud. In some parts the fluid was as red as blood from the colouring matter that poured into it from the reeking leather dressers' close by.

In the thirty-fifth chapter of *Alton Locke* Kingsley describes the slum where the drink-sodden Jemmy Downs lives (the parallels in diction and phraseology are too obvious to escape notice):

> And what a room! A low lean-to with wooden walls, without a single article of furniture; and through the broad chinks of the floor shone up as it were ugly glaring eyes, staring at us. They were the reflexions of the rushlight in the sewer below. The stench was frightful—the air heavy with pestilence. The first breath I drew made my heart sink and my stomach turn.

And then, as the crazed, alcoholic wretch hurls himself into the ditch:

> We rushed out on the balcony. The light of the policeman's lantern glared over the ghastly scene—along the double row of miserable housebacks, which lined the sides of the open tidal

ditch—over strange rambling jetties, and balconies, and sleeping-sheds, which hung on rotting piles over the black waters, with phosphorescent scraps of rotten fish gleaming and twinkling out of the dark hollows, like devilish grave-lights—over bubbles of poisonous gas, and bloated carcases of dogs, and lumps of offal, floating on the stagnant olive-green hell-broth—over the slow sullen rows of oil ripple which were dying away into the darkness far beyond, sending up, as they stirred, hot breaths of miasma—the only sign that a spark of humanity, after years of foul life, had quenched itself at last in that foul death.

Not only does Kingsley build on the descriptions but he puts to use Mayhew's recordings of humble lives to advance the narrative of *Alton Locke.* In a letter of 18 December 1849 Mayhew describes how unknowing, inexperienced Irishmen coming to London were trapped and put to work in sweaters' dens. In the twenty-first chapter of his novel Kingsley dramatizes Mayhew's letter as the Irish wife of Downs, the tailor, accosts the hero and entices him to the sweatshop. Similarly, the dastardly custom, noted by Mayhew in his letter of 18 December, of appropriating the clothing of the sweated victim, thus compelling him to stay indoors, is used by Kingsley in connexion with the finding of the long-lost Mike Kelly. In such a manner does recognition of Mayhew mount in *Alton Locke.* Significant relationships may also be seen between the indigent daughter of an army officer, of whom Mayhew writes so compassionately, and the genteel old lady who dies poverty-stricken in the eighth chapter of the novel; further, Mayhew's letter of 13 November 1849, about the illegal profiteering of army officers through the purchase of uniforms, takes dramatic form in *Alton Locke* in Crossthwaite's bitter outburst against governmental complacency in the face of such dishonesty. Even the moral corruption of the lowest type of Victorian theatrical entertainment, written of so vividly by Mayhew, does not escape Kingsley. And, finally, Mayhew's moving account of the needlewoman forced into prostitution is strongly imprinted upon the shocking events of the eighth chapter of *Alton Locke.* The association between the materials used by the two men is made the stronger when one recalls that 'Cheap Clothes and Nasty' was published in January 1850 and *Alton Locke* in August of the same year. Well before those dates, in fact by mid-December 1849, Mayhew's articles which most interested Kingsley had appeared in the *Chronicle.*

Although London has compelled the attention of writers through the centuries, Mayhew's work plainly gave rise to many books devoted to the themes he had so assiduously sounded. In the eighteen-fifties, especially, studies of the poor and needy, as noted above, mainly by journalists and parsons, made frequent appearances. Often, for example in Beames's *Rookeries of London* (1851) and J. Ewing Ritchie's *Night Side of London* (1857), Mayhew's work is respectfully commended and their authors indicate that their own interests had been stimulated by his pioneering efforts. But while Beames, Ritchie, and a number of others examined Mayhew's subjects, none did so as effectively as he. Even so experienced a journalist as James Greenwood in his *Seven Curses of London* (1869), covering much of

Mayhew's ground, reduces squalid, teeming slums to no more than sociologically significant areas. Of the hundreds of books, articles, and pamphlets about the London poor none records the miseries of their lives with the insight and humanity of Henry Mayhew. (pp. xxxiv-xxxix)

> *John L. Bradley, in an introduction to* Selections from "London Labour and the London Poor" *by Henry Mayhew, edited by John L. Bradley, Oxford University Press, London, 1965, pp. vii-xl.*

V. S. Pritchett (essay date 1966)

[*Pritchett is a highly esteemed British novelist, short story writer, and critic. Considered one of the modern masters of the short story, he is also one of the world's most respected and well-read literary critics. Pritchett writes in the conversational tone of the familiar essay, approaching literature from the viewpoint of a lettered, but not overly scholarly, reader. In his criticism Pritchett stresses his own experience, judgment, and sense of literary art, rather than following a codified critical doctrine derived from a school of psychological or philosophical speculation. In the following excerpt, Pritchett praises Mayhew's undramatized portrayal of his subjects in* London Labour and the London Poor.]

Mayhew is the unique "short and simple" analyst of the lives of the London poor in the nineteenth century. The historians still consult him; the novelists and the journalists of his own time helped themselves to the strange material he collected from the mouths of dismal or cheerful wretches between 1849 and 1862. Interest in him was revived in the Thirties of this century when the documentary movement in journalism and cinema was tormented by the difficulty of being both earnest and true to life. How did this Victorian philanthropist escape sentimentality? How did the verbatim disentangle itself from the verbose? Why was Mayhew so alive and real, and documentary so worthy and yet so dead?

One answer is that the writers and camera men of the Thirties were overweighted with political faith. They were respectable men. The poor were not and are not respectable: They have to live. The best books about the lives of the poor in Great Britain—the account of builders' laborers, for example, in *The Ragged Trousered Philanthropists* (circa 1906)—note the ambiguities, the silly delinquency, the half-cracked behavior, even the willingness of the victims to be victims. Mayhew's success owes a lot to his lack of respectability, his Bohemianism, his instability as a person. He is a bit of a rogue; he has more than a touch of the unscrupulous hack. Englishmen of his type—and he was very English—are insubordinate, devious, plausible, and always fall on their feet. They can get on with anybody. Mr. Bradley, who introduces the present selection of Mayhew's writings, says that Mayhew is in the tradition of Chaucer and Fielding; that is far too elegant. Mayhew belongs to the Grub Street that was founded by Defoe; he has something in common with Cobbett, or with the first, clumsy, vulgar minor Elizabethan playwrights. It is interesting to remember, here, that in his early years (he was born in 1812) he was one of the large number of crude hacks who turned out bad plays, by the ton and for very low pay, for the popular Victorian theater; like the stuff put on by television now, it had to appeal to the lowest taste. (p. 5)

Like Defoe, Mayhew would turn to anything in journalism and exploit any situation. He certainly did not confine his attentions to the appalling social problems of his time, even when he became famous for this side of his writing. Here we can put our finger on the nature of his talent: He combined earnestness with jocularity; the satire could be fierce but the humor must not be too humorous. That is to say, it must not be so humorous that you laugh your way out of a serious consideration of the facts. In some of its aspects, London humor depends on its explanatoriness; it is deliberately unwitty. It relies—and a large part of the English novel relies—on a regard for nature and human nature just as they shapelessly are; it was this regard that Taine so strongly criticized. Mayhew's sense of nature— when he was writing about the poor—led him not only to describe the human being and his work, but to do so in the man or woman's own words. That, for 1850, was revolutionary.

Take this passage from the life of a coster lad:

> On a Sunday I goes out selling, and all I yarns I keeps. As for going to church, why, I cant afford it—beside to tell the truth, I dont like it well enough. Plays, too, aint in my line much. I'd sooner go to a dance—its more livelier. The "penny gaffs" is rather more in my style; the songs are out and out and makes our gals laugh. The smuttier the better, I thinks; bless you! the gals likes it as much as we do. If we lads ever has a quarrel, why, we fights for it. If I was to let a cove off once, he'd do it again; but I never give a lad a chance, so long as I can get anigh him. I never heard about Christianity; but if a cove was to fetch me a lick of the head, I'd give it him again, whether he was a big 'un or a little 'un. I'd precious soon see a henemy of mine shot afore I'd forgive him,—what's the use? Do I understand what behaving to your neighbor is?— In coorse I do. If a feller as lives next me wanted a basket of mine as I wasn't using, why, he might have it; if I was working it though, I'd see him further! I can understand that all as lives in a court is neighbors; but as for policemen, they're nothing to me, and I should like to pay 'em all off well. No; I never heerd about this here creation you speaks about. In coorse God Almighty made the world, and the poor bricklayers' laborers built the houses arterwards—that's *my* opinion; but I cant say, for I've never been in no schools, only always hard at work, and knows nothing about it. I have heerd a little about our Saviour—they seem to say he were a goodish kind of man, but if he says as how a cove's to forgive a feller as hits you, I should say he know'd nothing about it. In coorse the gals, the lads goes and lives with thinks our walloping 'em wery cruel of us, but we dont. Why dont we?—why, because we dont.

Mayhew collected back-slang. The lads begged a "yennep" to get a "tib of occabot"; you occasionally hear it still

in London, but rhyming slang is commoner, like "titfer" for hat—tit for tat; or "Barnet" for hair—Barnet Fair. He knew the "penny gaffs," the noisy theaters where the teenagers danced, rioted, and sang obscene songs; in fact, teenager rioting was a Victorian specialty, for the kids started work young, skipped school, and were soon living promiscuously eight to a bed in rooming houses. Sexual intercourse began at the age of eleven or so among the coster boys and they fought for their girls. This used to shock the Irish immigrants whose modesty was appalled by the London boys and girls larking about naked. The coster boys

> are as sharp as terriers and learn every dodge of business in less than half no time. There's one I knows about three feet high, that's up to the business as clever as a man of thirty. Though he's only twelve years old he'll chaff down a peeler so uncommon severe, that the only way to stop him is to take him in charge.

The boys started work at the age of seven, leading the father's donkey and shouting what they were selling; father by this time having lost his voice. At thirteen they had a sort of ritual quarrel with the father and would start off with a barrow of their own, undercut the old man, and drive their mothers to the workhouse.

An idle man himself, Mayhew was pertinacious in his interest in other people's work. He investigated the flower girls, the sellers of pig's trotters and ham sandwiches, prostitutes, all the street traders, dog fanciers, rat catchers, bird-duffers—they painted the birds—the dredgers and mud-larks of the Thames, street clowns, bus conductors, "regular scavengers." They were all of strictly separated trades, ruled by their own customs. One of the oddest were the "running patterers." They screamed old and new broadsheets about murders as a sort of Stop Press item, in the streets, and were particularly proud to get to an execution and beat the newspapers with a lurid account of the crime. Mayhew found a fine Dickensian humorist who could run off a litany of murderers:

> Greenacre didn't sell so well as might have been expected, for such a diabolical out-and-out crime as he committed, but you see he came close after Pegsworth and that took the beauty off him. Two murderers together is never no good to nobody. Why there was Wilson Gleeson, as great a villain as ever lived—went and murdered a whole family at noon-day—but Rush coopered him—and likewise that girl at Bristol—made it no draw to any one. Daniel Good, though, was a first-rater; and would have been much better if it hadn't been for that there Madam Toosow. You see, she went down to Roehampton and guv 12 for the wery clogs as he used to wash his master's carriage in; so, in coorse, when the harristocracy could go and see the real things—the wery identical clogs—in the Chamber of 'Orrors, why the people wouldn't look at our authentic portraits of the fiend in human form. Hocker wasn't any particular great shakes. There was a deal expected from him, but he didn't turn out well. Courvoisier was much better; he sold wery well, but nothing to Blakesley. Why I worked him for six weeks. The wife of the murdered man kept the

King's Head, that he was landlord on, open in the morning of the execution and the place was like a fair. I even went and sold papers outside the door myself. I thought if she warn't ashamed, why should I be?

There were disappointments for this sensationalist. He was trying to get a Mrs. Manning to "clear her conscious afore she left this here whale of tears" but she failed to react properly as a "monster in human form." A forerunner of the mimsy generation of television interviewees, she said "I have nothing to say to you, Mr. Rowe, but to thank you for your kindness." Mr. Rowe was disgusted with this gentility: He "guv her up entirely."

A self-made outsider but in no sense a slummer or a high-class bum, Mayhew had the gift of making people talk. He had knocked about the world, he responded to "tricks of the trade," but he was firmly serious. He noted—as Mrs. Gaskell had done in the slums of Manchester—that the poor were irreligious, but not anti-religious. They just didn't care about religion or politics; yet a scavenger who said politics meant nothing to him also said in the same breath that he was a Chartist! One reason for Mayhew's success in getting on the right side of people was his interest in their work. Everyone enjoys talking about that. But he was lucky in his Cockneys; they are still incurable talkers but are not fact fetichists. They were conscious, even in misery, of their role. They were interested in themselves and this gave them—and still gives them, now they are well off—their vitality. Some of Mayhew's trades survive. There are still one or two old-fashioned rat catchers about, who, with the meditative sadism of their trade, pick a handful of live rats from their sacks when they get home in the evenings and study the "form" of their terriers, as they set them loose on the vermin for the pleasure of a few privileged friends.

The merit of Mayhew was fully recognized during his lifetime, but by the time he was old—he lived to the age of seventy-five—he was neglected and poor. This is sad, but one can see why it fell out this way. He was unorthodox and undisciplined; better and more prosperous times had come in. Mid- and late-Victorian melodrama became far more sophisticated than it had been in the early days of Mayhew's apprenticeship. To a later generation, Mayhew's work appeared unshaped. To us it seems all the better for that, but the Victorian taste was for pious and posh self-dramatization on the grand scale whereas the best of Mayhew comes from a quiet compassion and an undramatized curiosity. There *was* a dramatist in him and it was a bad dramatist; fortunately his personality as a writer was split and *London Labour and the London Poor* is good because no drama falsifies it. (p. 6)

> *V. S. Pritchett, in a review of "True to Life: Selections from 'London Labour and the London Poor',"* in The New York Review of Books, *Vol. VI, No. 4, March 17, 1966, pp. 5-6.*

W. H. Auden   (essay date 1968)

[*Often considered the poetic successor of W. B. Yeats and T. S. Eliot, Auden is also highly regarded for his literary criticism. As a member of a generation of English writers strongly influenced by the ideas of Karl Marx and Sigmund Freud, Auden considered social and psychological commentary important functions of literary criticism. As a committed follower of Christianity, he considered it necessary to view art in the context of moral and theological absolutes. Thus, he regarded art as a "secondary world" which should serve a definite purpose within the "primary world" of human history. This purpose is the creation of an aesthetic beauty and moral order, qualities that exist only in imperfect form in the primary world but are intrinsic to the secondary world of art. While he has been criticized for significant inconsistencies in his thought throughout his career, Auden is generally regarded as a fair and perceptive critic. In the following excerpt, Auden comments on Mayhew's methods of information gathering and presentation in* London Labour and the London Poor.]

After a random sampling of ***London Labour and the London Poor,*** I am inclined to think that, if I had to write down the names of the ten greatest Victorian Englishmen, Henry Mayhew would head the list. I say "random sampling" because I can no more imagine a man reading straight through it from beginning to end than I can imagine him so reading the Encyclopædia Britannica. The new reprint . . . appears to be a photo-offset of the 1865 edition. The four volumes contain nearly two thousand pages in double columns and a print so small that even a myopic like myself finds it a strain on the eyes. (p. 121)

Mayhew was a compulsive classifier. Grouped under four main headings—"Those Who Will Work," "Those Who Cannot Work," "Those Who Will Not Work," "Those Who Need Not Work"—his list of human occupations takes up sixteen pages. "Authors" are classed not as "Benefactors," like teachers and clergy, but appear under Sub-Group D, "Makers or Artificers," sub-sub-group 3:

> Workers connected with the Superlative Arts, that is to say, with those arts which have no products of their own, and are engaged either in adding to the beauty or usefulness of the products of other arts, or in inventing or designing the work appertaining to them.

Among those with whom he ranks us are "Desiccators, Anti-dry-rot Preservers, Scourers, Calenderers and French Polishers."

On the function of "Employers," Mayhew disagrees violently with J. S. Mill:

> Mr. Mill's mistake in ranking the Employers and Distributors among the Enrichers, or those who increase the exchangeable commodities of the country, arose from a desire to place the dealers and capitalists among the productive labourers, than which nothing could be more idle, for surely they do not add, *directly,* one brass farthing, as the saying is, to the national stock of wealth. A little reflection would have shown that gentleman that the true function of employers and dealers was that of the *indirect aiders* of production rather than the direct producers.

A metropolis like London is seldom, if ever, the center of

a heavy industry like mining or steelworking or cotton-spinning. In Mayhew's London, the largest class of employed worker was the domestic servant. Consequently, unlike Engels, Mayhew is not concerned with the lot of factory hands. He does deal with the problems of small craft industry, but devotes most of his attention to those who earned their living, honestly or dishonestly, on the streets—a class which in his day, he reckoned, comprised one in forty of the population of London. His first two volumes are concerned with street sellers, street collectors, and street cleaners; his third with vermin exterminators, street entertainers, small artisans, and casual laborers like dockhands; his fourth with prostitutes, thieves, swindlers, and beggars.

Among social anthropologists Mayhew is unique, so far as I know, in his combination of a Fabian Society passion for statistics, a Ripley passion for believe-it-or-not facts as sheer oddities, and a passion for the idiosyncrasies of character and speech such as only the very greatest novelists have exhibited. Lovers of statistics can learn from him, for example, that the rate of alcoholics among button-molders was 1 in 7.2, among clergymen 1 in 417, and among domestic servants 1 in 585.7, and that a horse excretes 38 lbs. 2 oz. of dung every twenty-four hours. Lovers of odd facts will learn that the first modern water closet was patented by Bramah in 1808, that the poets who sold best in the street were Shakespeare, Pope, Thomson, Goldsmith, Burns, Byron, and Scott, but there was little demand for Milton, Dryden, Shelley, or Wordsworth, that rape was commonest in Monmouthshire, bigamy in Cheshire, and that Herefordshire came second only to London in the number of its female criminals. I myself was particularly enchanted by the results of his enquiry among a group of boys as to the first article they ever stole. His list runs thus:

> Six rabbits, silk shawl from home, a pair of shoes, a Dutch cheese, a few shillings from home, a coat and trousers, a bullock's heart, four "tiles" of copper, fifteen and sixpence from master, two handkerchiefs, half a quartern loaf, a set of tools worth 3 £, clothes from a warehouse, worth 22 £, a Cheshire cheese, a pair of carriage lamps, some handkerchiefs, five shillings, some turnips, watchchain and seals, a sheep, three and sixpence, and an invalid's chair.
>
> (pp. 121-22)

I would recommend the reader to sample his interviews with Jack Black, Rat-Killer to Her Majesty, with Billy the whistling and dancing boy, and with a young pickpocket. These have led me to revise my critical notions of Dickens, whom I had always thought of as a fantastic creator of over-life-size characters; it is evident that he was much more of a "realist" than he is generally taken for. (p. 122)

Since Mayhew's primary purpose is to present the objective facts about the life of the poor and let the reader draw his own conclusions, he is generally as reticent about his political opinions as he is about his religious convictions, but now and again he has an outburst of rage:

> The only effectual mode of preventing this system of jobbing being persevered in, *at the expense of the workmen,* is by the insertion of a clause in each parish contract similar to that in-

troduced by the Commissioners of Sewers—that at least a fair living rate of wages shall be paid by each contractor to the men employed by him. This may be an interference with the freedom of labour, according to the economists' "cant" language, but at least it is a restriction of the tyranny of capital, for free labour means, when literally translated, *the unrestricted use of capital,* which is (especially when the moral standard of trade is not of the highest character) perhaps the greatest evil with which a State can be afflicted.

Of the average Victorian equivalent of a welfare worker he takes a dim view. If, he is never tired of insisting, you wish to do anything to raise the cultural and moral level of the poor, then you must stop thinking in terms of your own middle-class experiences and values, and learn to think in terms of theirs. Employment, to someone of the middle classes, means a regular job with a regular salary, however modest, paid at regular and foreseeable intervals; to him, therefore, thrift is an obvious virtue and its practice possible. But to a casual laborer who lives from one day to the next, the idea of saving is unimaginable. The discipline of regular hours, natural to the middle class, becomes a tyranny when, as in model lodging houses, it is imposed on the poor:

> It is thought by the managers of these establishments, and with some share of propriety, that persons who get their living by any honest means may get home and go to bed, according to strict rule, at a certain prescribed hour—in one house it is ten o'clock, in the others eleven. But many of the best conducted of these poor people, if they be street-folk, are at those very hours in the height of their business, and have therefore to pack up their goods, and carry homeward their cumbersome and perhaps heavy load a distance usually varying from two or three to six or seven miles. If they are a minute beyond time, they are shut out, and have to seek lodgings in a strange place. On their return next morning, they are charged for the bed they were prevented from occupying, and if they demur they are at once expelled!

Again, it is very difficult for the average middle-class person to believe that some people are by temperament rovers. (Reading Mayhew, I have been astonished at the number of young persons in nineteenth-century England who ran away from home, many of them from good homes.) Addressing a group of ticket-of-leave men, Mayhew told them:

> I know that as a class you are distinguished mainly by your love of a roving life, and that at the bottom of all your criminal practices lies your indisposition to follow any settled occupation. Continuous employment of a monotonous nature is so irksome to you that immediately you engage in it you long to break away from it. . . . Society, however, expects that, if you wish to better yourselves, you will at once settle down as steadily as it does, and immediately conform to all its notions; but I am satisfied that if anything effectual is to be done in the way of reforming you, Society must work in consonance and not in antagonism with your nature. In this connec-

tion it appears to me that the great outlet for you is street-trading, where you are allowed to roam at will unchafed by restraints not congenial to your habits and feelings.

Social-history textbooks taught me in my youth that the living conditions of the poor in 1850, though still grim, were an improvement upon the horrors they had suffered at the beginning of the century. So far as conditions in mills and mines are concerned, this may have been true, but Mayhew demonstrates beyond all possible doubt that the position of craft artisans, like carpenters and tailors, and of casual laborers was much worse than it had been twenty years before. The wages of cabinetmakers, for example, had been no less than three hundred per cent greater in 1830 than they were in 1850. Between 1840 and 1848, although the increase in production and the national wealth had been much greater than the increase in population, the annual increase in paupers on relief had been seven per cent. Mayhew attributes this deterioration to a change in the methods of hiring labor and of distributing work to be done. In agriculture and, it would seem, in some trades as well, the traditional method had been to hire laborers by the year, during which time the employer was bound to pay them an agreed wage, whether he had work for them or not. Increasingly, this method had been replaced by hiring them by the day and turning them off whenever work was slack. The change in working methods had been the adoption of piecework and the contract system. In 1830, for example, the cabinet trade had been mainly in the hands of "trade-working masters":

> They worked not on speculation, but to order, and were themselves employers. Some employed, at a busy time, from twenty to forty hands, all working on their premises, to whom they supplied the materials.

By 1850, the trade-working master had been largely replaced by the "garret-master":

> [The garret-masters] are in manufacture what the peasant-proprietors are in agriculture, their own employers and their own workmen. There is, however, this one marked distinction between the two classes—the garret-master cannot, like the peasant proprietor, eat what he produces: the consequence is, that he is obliged to convert each article into food immediately he manufactures it, no matter what the state of the market may be. . . . If the market is at all slack, he has to force a sale by offering his goods at the lowest possible price. What wonder, then, that the necessities of such a class of individuals should have created a special race of employers, known by the significant name of "slaughter-house men;" or that these, being aware of the inability of the garret-masters to hold out against any offer, no matter how slight a remuneration it affords for their labour, should continually lower and lower their prices until the entire body of the competitive portion of the cabinet trade is sunk in utter destitution and misery?

Yet, for all its harrowing descriptions of squalor, crime, injustice, and suffering, the final impression of Mayhew's great book is not depressing. From his many transcripts of conversations it is clear that Mayhew was that rare creature, a natural democrat; his first thought, that is to say, was never "This is an unfortunate wretch whom it is my duty, if possible, to help" but always "This is a fellow-human being whom it is fun to talk to." The reader's final impression of the London poor is not of their misery but of their self-respect, courage, and gaiety in conditions under which it seems incredible that such virtues could survive.

Today, urban poverty is very much on all our minds. The percentage of the population that is really poor is, I suppose, less than it was in Mayhew's time. I am not at all sure, however, that for those today who are really poor the situation is any better; I suspect that it may be worse—at least psychologically. It is astonishing, reading Mayhew, to learn how many of the poor were self-employed and the extraordinary diversity of the ways by which they managed to earn a living, however meagre. Even when I was a child, the streets were still full of vendors, musicians, Punch-and-Judy men, and such. Today they have vanished. In all modern societies, the public authorities, however at odds politically, are at one in their fear and hatred of private enterprise in the strict sense; that is to say, self-employment. The fiscal authorities hate the self-employed man because he keeps no books to audit, the health authorities hate him because it is easy for him to avoid their inspectors, etc. Aside from crime and prostitution, the only contemporary alternative for the poor is either to be the employee of a firm, a factory, or the municipality, or to be on relief. Perhaps this is inevitable, perhaps it is better, but I have yet to be convinced that it is.

Though, as I said at the beginning, ***London Labour and the London Poor*** is not a book that can be read through from cover to cover, it is a book in which one can browse for a lifetime without exhausting its treasures. (pp. 128-33)

> *W. H. Auden, "A Very Inquisitive Old Party,"* in The New Yorker, *Vol. XLIV, No. 1, February 24, 1968, pp. 121-24, 128-33.*

John D. Rosenberg   (essay date 1968)

[*An American educator and critic, Rosenberg is the author of the highly regarded study* The Darkening Glass: A Portrait of Ruskin's Genius *(1961). In the following excerpt, he discusses the image of London presented in Mayhew's journalism.*]

The image of London that emerges from Mayhew's pages is that of a vast, ingeniously balanced mechanism in which each class subsists on the drippings and droppings of the stratum above, all the way from the rich, whom we scarcely glimpse, down to the deformed and starving, whom we see groping for bits of salvageable bone or decaying vegetables in the markets. Such extreme conditions bred weird extremities of adaptation, a remarkably diverse yet cohesive subculture of poverty. Ragged, fantastic armies, each with its distinctive jargon and implements, roamed the streets: "pure-finders" with bucket and glove, picking up dog dung and selling it to tanners; rag-gatherers, themselves dressed in the rotted cloth they salvage, armed with pointed sticks; bent, slime-soiled "mud-larks," groping at low tide in the ooze of the Thames for bits of coal, chips of wood, or copper nails dropped from the sheathing of barges, a regiment of three hundred who subsisted on average earnings of *threepence a day*. Describing the life of a boy who began mud-larking at the age of eleven, Mayhew writes:

> He worked every day, with 20 or 30 boys, who might all be seen at daybreak with their trowsers tucked up, groping about, and picking out the pieces of coal from the mud on the banks of the Thames. He went into the river up to his knees, and in searching the mud he often ran pieces of glass and long nails into his feet. When this was the case, he went home and dressed the wounds, but returned to the river-side directly, "for should the tide come up," he added, "without my having found something, why I must starve till next low tide." In the very cold weather he and his other shoeless companions used to stand in the hot water that ran down the river side from some of the steam-factories, to warm their frozen feet.

The remarkable first-person narrative that follows this excerpt, like hundreds of others in *London Labour and the London Poor,* recalls Mayhew's claim in his Preface that his is the first book "to publish the history of a people, from the lips of the people themselves—giving a literal description of their labour, their earnings, their trials, and their sufferings, in their own 'unvarnished' language." Mayhew invented "oral history" a century before the term was coined. He is also the explorer, as he puts it, of a class of whom "the public had less knowledge than of the most distant tribes." The rapid, wrenching industrialization of England (London's population trebled between 1800 and 1850) was breeding a new species of humanity, a rootless generation entirely environed by brick, smoke, work, and want. Mayhew devised new techniques for penetrating the uncharted regions of the disaffected and for recording their experience. With the incredible energy of the Victorians, this "indolent" journalist uncovered and codified data on the modern proletariat that whole municipal and federal agencies are only now beginning to assemble. Michael Harrington's *The Other America,* Danilo Dolci's *Inquest at Palermo,* Kenneth B. Clark's *Dark Ghetto,* Oscar Lewis' *La Vida: A Puerto Rican Family in the Culture of Poverty* are all in one way or another the offspring of *London Labour and the London Poor.*

The very virtues which make Mayhew's achievement so original have impeded its proper recognition. It is difficult to praise a book which fits into no established category. More than any other work I know, *London Labour and the London Poor* strains that flimsy boundary separating fact from art, life from literature. As Thackeray wrote, Mayhew provides us with "a picture of human life so wonderful, so awful, so piteous and pathetic, so exciting and terrible, that readers of romances own they never read anything like to it."

Consider, for example, this excerpt from the narrative of a "running-patterer," a man who hawks and at times invents accounts of murders, disasters, and the like:

> There's nothing beats a stunning good murder,

after all. Why there was Rush [a homicidal farmer]—I lived on him for a month or more. When I commenced with Rush, I was 14*s.* in debt for rent, and in less than fourteen days I astonished the wise men in the east by paying my landlord all I owed him. . . . Why I went down to Norwich expressly to work the execution. I worked my way down there with "*a sorrowful lamentation*" of his own composing, which I'd got written by the blind man expressly for the occasion. On the morning of the execution we beat all the regular newspapers out of the field; for we had the full, true, and particular account down, you see, by our own express, and that can beat anything that ever they can publish; for we gets it printed several days afore it comes off, and goes and stands with it right under the drop; and many's the penny I've turned away when I've been asked for an account of the whole business *before* it happened.

The patterer is indistinguishable from a character out of Dickens. Although he is a bonafide "case-history," he belongs as much to literature as to journalism, criminology, or sociology. Reading *London Labour and the London Poor,* with its brave abundance of life, its vast scope yet minuteness of detail, its celebration of the intricate, dense, eccentric texture of Victorian London, its moral outrage and grotesque wit, brings one closer to the feel of Dickens than to anything else in our literature. To pass from Mayhew's case-histories to Dickens' inventions is merely to cross sides of the same street; only the point of view shifts, not the landscape. Knowledge of Mayhew persuades us that Dickens the comic-caricaturist is in essence a great

Illustration titled "The Lucifer Match Girl," from London Labour and the London Poor.

realist, just as reading Dickens persuades us that Mayhew was not merely a fine reporter but also a superb artist.

Mayhew's artistry manifests itself above all in the shaping of his characters' monologues. As a dramatizer of character through speech, Mayhew is as superior to the tape recorder as Hamlet is to the ordinary run of Danish princes. He does not distort, but he edits, shapes, and intensifies, until we are stunned by the slang beauty and inventiveness of the spoken voices he recreates. His years of editorial experience, his nose for animal effluvia, his ear for quirks of speech, his novelist's eye for significant detail ("the girl with her basket of walnuts lifts her *brown-stained fingers* [italics mine] to her mouth, as she screams, 'Fine warnuts!' sixteen a penny, fine war-r-nuts.")—all found the richest possible field for exercise in the inventively vociferous streets of London. The bardic speech of much Victorian verse is further from true poetry than the idiom of Mayhew's costermongers and peep-showmen.

The analogy with poetry suggests that Mayhew should be credited with evolving a new art form, a kind of dramatic monologue in prose. Just as the speaker in a Browning monologue is always talking *to* someone, the silent auditor actually functioning as a second character, so the speaker in a Mayhew interview is never merely a disembodied voice talking into a recording machine. Mayhew is always there, a pleasantly neutral, transparent presence into which we gradually fit our own image, until we feel uncannily that we have ourselves gained entry into some bare hovel and are overhearing the life-story of a street vendor. The monologues are not interrupted by the formality of direct questions, but the *implied* questioner is always present, as in these sentences spoken by a woefully ignorant seller of crabs:

> I don't know what the Pope is. Is he [in] any trade? It's nothing to me, when he's no customer of mine. I have nothing to say about nobody that ain't no customers. My crabs is caught in the sea, in course. I gets them at Billingsgate. I never saw the sea, but it's salt-water, I know. I can't say whereabouts it lays. I believe it's in the hands of Billingsgate salesmen—all of it? I've heard of shipwrecks at sea, caused by drownding, in course. . . .

The few selections from *London Labour and the London Poor* which have appeared in recent years reproduce a fair sampling of such monologues but drastically alter the quality of the book. They provide the reader with a gallery of picturesque portraits but tear from the fabric of the work the larger social background that gives it coherence and authority. Mayhew, for example, was obsessed with statistics, and in his innumerable tables he portrays the workings of London as a macro-organism, ingesting so many tons of solid or liquid matter and passing it out, so many tons or gallons per borough, onto the streets and into the sewers, the very drains providing the subject of an elaborate chart analyzing "The Soluble Matter in Different Specimens of Street Drainage Water."

Despite the monstrous suffering it depicts, *London Labour and the London Poor* also possesses the minute and circumstantial gaiety of a Dutch painting. To savor this curiously mixed quality, the reader might compare Mayhew's account of five hundred vagrants, their bare limbs blue from the snow, seeking entrance to the Asylum for the Houseless Poor, with the narrative of the "Exhibitor of Birds and Mice," whose canaries ride in a chariot drawn by a goldfinch and whose mice "dance the tight-rope on their hind legs, with balance-poles in their mouths." Whether reporting the careers of mice or of men, Mayhew is always exhaustive, conveying that superabundance of detail we associate with actual life. The massive intricacy of *London Labour and the London Poor* mirrors unerringly the labyrinthine vitality of London itself. (pp. v-viii)

> *John D. Rosenberg, in an introduction to* London Labour and the London Poor: The London Street-Folk, Vol. I *by Henry Mayhew, Dover Publications, Inc., 1968, pp. v-ix.*

Eileen Yeo (essay date 1971)

[*In the following excerpt from* The Unknown Mayhew, *a collection of Mayhew's* Morning Chronicle *letters which Yeo edited with E. P. Thompson, Yeo argues for consideration of Mayhew as a serious social investigator and theorist.*]

Henry Mayhew has never received serious consideration as a systematic empirical investigator. Historians and sociologists, who appreciate the rich social evidence in his work, see him as no more than a gifted journalist, with an undisciplined zest for collecting facts about the poor and picturesque characters among the poor. This image derives from a reading of *London Labour and the London Poor* in the 1861 edition which contained only a part of the London investigations and a puzzling sample of interpretive writing. To assess Mayhew as an investigator, it is more useful to follow him chronologically, examining the London survey as it developed. His starting point, the letters to the *Morning Chronicle* between 1849 and 1850 . . . and the "Answers to Correspondents" column, a feature of the weekly parts of *London Labour* in 1851, reveal his anxiety about the methods of social investigation and an eagerness to analyze his findings. These were the years, as E. P. Thompson has shown, when Mayhew was capable of his best work. Freed temporarily from financial worries and able to stretch his mind in ways not immediately designed to make quick money, his intense commitment to the project was continually sharpened by public interest and controversy. On the basis of this earlier and largely unstudied material, Mayhew emerges as a self-conscious investigator whose survey of industrial conditions in London and attempts at economic and sociological analysis entitle him to an important place in the history of social investigation.

The *Morning Chronicle* project appeared at the end of two decades which had produced a rich crop of investigations into the condition of the working class. In the face of dramatic industrial and urban change, frightening developments like cholera and radical protest movements, middle class investigators saw systematic fact collecting at once as true scientific empiricism and as the necessary first step to formulating social policy and programmes of action.

The increasing use of government investigatory bodies was a feature of these years; the Royal Commissions and Select Committees which took evidence on the administration of the Poor Laws, on the Health of Towns and on conditions in selected industries are well known. Not surprisingly the prejudices of the investigators coloured the scope and terms of the inquiries as well as the conclusions. Few of these inquiries were centrally concerned with the extent and causes of poverty or with the relation between employment conditions and poverty. Blinkered by the political economy maxim that the adult male worker must be left free from legislative "interference" to the mercies of the free market and disturbed that the factory system might tend to destroy the family, the major industrial studies of factories (1833), mines (1842) and agriculture (1843) focused on the physical and moral condition of children (and women) at work. The outstanding exception, the inquiry into the condition of the hand-loom weavers (1838-41), did consider the economic position of the whole family. Its sensitive questionnaire gave clear instructions to calculate net wages, taking into account expenses necessary to work and the amount of unemployment during the year, and to find the economic causes of hardship—albeit with a built-in bias against trade unions and strikes which were automatically assumed to be causes of low wages. But the Commission's brief was not imitated during this period.

Less familiar, though directly helping to create the climate for government survey work, voluntary statistical societies existed in nearly every major city and carried out rigorous and systematic investigations into the condition of the local poor in places like Manchester, Bristol and London. The members of the provincial societies were mainly prosperous, powerful and philanthropic local businessmen while London's largest contingent was professional and academic. The Manchester Statistical Society, with a membership limit of fifty, was the most remarkably close-knit; its leading members, often related by marriage, were either owners of spinning mills or bankers, who worshipped together at the Cross Street and Moseley Street Unitarian chapels and underwrote philanthropic agencies like the Manchester and Salford District Provident Society. Although basically satisfied with the new manufacturing system and the rapid expansion of port cities, the statisticians were deeply worried by the concentration of the poor in the centre of large towns away from contact with the upper classes, who had been the traditional force for social guidance and control. They regarded their societies not only as the pioneers of "statistical science" but as the most relevant agencies in the new urban setting to collect information which would serve as the preliminary to effective philanthropic action. (pp. 51-3)

Their inquiries into the "condition of the working classes" examined the extent to which social *discipline* prevailed among the poor. It was "moral and intellectual condition" they were concerned with, to be measured by a stock questionnaire about overcrowding, domestic management, religious affiliation, church going, literacy and school attendance. Making pioneer use of the door-to-door survey, they visited all working class families (those below the rank of shopkeeper plus small shopkeepers selling to the

poor in a designated area (usually a parish or police district) and published their findings in statistical tables preceded by a brief report. But innovations in the technique of making an inquiry should not obscure the fact that these were social discipline surveys not poverty surveys. Indeed the early inquiries seemed to be based on the assumption that the broader social and economic environment had little bearing on respectable behavior. No questions were asked about wages, hours or regularity of employment, although occupations were listed. After the depression of 1841 more attention was paid to wages and the London society's survey of St. George's in the East (Stepney) even tried to correlate wages with the usual moral indices concluding that "the excess of inferior habits in the inferior occupations will be traced generally". But the report gave no indication of how the average weekly wage was arrived at, whether expenses necessary to the job had been deducted or seasonal unemployment had been allowed for. And no deeper questions were asked about why certain occupations provided only low wages.

It was Henry Mayhew, as metropolitan commission for the *Morning Chronicle,* who set out to conduct the first empirical survey into poverty *as such.* A comparison between Mayhew's opening letter and those of the industrial and rural commissioners highlights what a new and, for a journalist, what a remarkable role he set himself. They poured out highly emotive paragraphs about the late revolutions in Europe and the startling social contrasts between rich and poor in England before announcing their intention vaguely to explore the condition of the working classes. Mayhew, by contrast, tried for the first time in the history of English social investigation to define a poverty line:

> Under the term "poor" I shall include all those persons whose incomings are insufficient for the satisfaction of their wants—a want being, according to my idea, contra-distinguished from a mere desire by a positive physical pain, instead of mental uneasiness, accompanying it. The large and comparatively unknown body of people included in this definition I shall contemplate in two distinct classes, viz., the *honest* and *dishonest* poor; and the first of these I purpose subdividing into the striving and the disabled—or, in other words, I shall consider the whole of the metropolitan poor under three separate phases, according as they *will* work, they *can't* work, and they *won't* work.

(pp. 53-4)

The survey began with an exploration of "those who *will* work". At no point . . . did he intend to take a door-to-door poverty census or count the heads of the poor. Rather, to "methodize" the work, he posited a relationship between poverty and low wages, which quickly proved a promising line of inquiry after pilot visits to the Spitalfields weavers, casual labourers at the docks and the many kinds of needlewomen. He was not content to do quick impressionistic sketches of industry like the peripatetic provincial commissioners. Nor was he satisfied to follow in the footsteps of the earlier statisticians and calculate wages for workers from a miscellany of occupations located by means of a door-to-door survey. He wished systematically to establish conditions of employment, especially wage levels, in the metropolitan trades, relate these to the life style of the poor and, at the same time, explore the industrial causes of low wages and poverty. Later questionnaires reflect his continued and maturing pre-occupation with the task of documenting conditions of employment while seeking for their causes. For example, replying to a keen draper's assistant who wanted to send evidence, Mayhew wrote,

> The information required upon this and, indeed every other trade is, (1) The division of labour in the trade, citing the nature of the work performed by the different classes of workmen; (2) the hours of labour; (3) the labour market, or the mode of obtaining employment; (4) the tools employed and who finds them; (5) the rate and mode of pay to each different class of workmen, dividing the wages or salaries into two classes, the "fair" and the "unfair"; (6) the deductions from the pay in the form of fines, "rents", or stoppages of any kind; (7) the additions to wages in the shape of perquisites, premiums, allowances, etc.; (8) a history of the wages of the trade, with the dates of increase or decrease in the pay, and the causes thereof; (9) the brisk and slack season of the trade, with statement of the causes on which they depend, as well as the number of extra hands required in the brisk season as compared with the slack; (10) the rate of pay to those who are "taken on" only during the brisk season; (11) the amount of surplus labour in the trade and the cause of it, whether from (*a*) overwork, (*b*) undue increase of the people in the trade, (*c*) change from yearly to weekly hirings, (*d*) excessive economy of labour, as "large system" of business, (*e*) introduction of women; (12) the badly-paid trade—(*a*) the history and causes of it, (*b*) what is the cheap labour employed, or how do the cheap workers differ from those who are better paid: are they less skilful, less trustworthy, or can they *afford* to take less, deriving their subsistence from other sources? (*c*) is the badly-paid trade maintained chiefly by the labour of apprentices, women, etc, etc.? (*d*) it upheld by middlemen, "sweaters", or the like? (*e*) are the men injured by *driving* (that is, by being made to do more work for the same money) or by *grinding* (that is, by being made to do the same or more work for less money), or are they injured from a combination of both systems? (*f*) who are the employers paying the worse wages?—are they "cutting men", that is to say, men who are reducing the men's wages as a means of selling cheap; or are they "grasping men", who do it merely to increase their profits; or small capitalists, who do it in order to live? Proofs should be given of all stated. Accounts of earnings and expenditure are of the greatest importance; also descriptions of modes of life and habits, politics, religion, literature, and amusements of the trade. . . .

An industrial survey had another advantage. "I am unable to generalize", he apologized in letter III, "not being acquainted with the particulars, for each day's investigation brings me into contact with a means of living utterly unknown among the well-fed portion of society". Astounded

at his own ignorance, a subsidiary aim of the survey became to compile a "cyclopaedia of industry", to make the working life of the poor known to the rich. The study of the London poor in an industrial context, first occupation by occupation and then trade by trade, became the large organizing principle of the first part of the survey. He "digressed" only occasionally, to make immediate use of contacts who would otherwise be lost to him, and so began a study of other groups like vagrants (a section of those who *won't* work). Or he personally examined what conventional philanthropic wisdom called causes of poverty, like low lodging houses or remedies, like ragged schools. The study of employment conditions was the continuous thread giving coherence of purpose to the majority of the *Morning Chronicle* letters.

But how to study employment conditions and poverty was problematic, especially as the legacy of technique bequeathed by earlier investigators like the statisticians was not very useful. Moreover Mayhew was an anthropologist, though not a relativist. With a sensitivity and tolerance almost unique among his contemporary investigators, or later "social scientists", he had a sure sense that the opinions of the poor, their aspirations and expectations, their evaluation of their lot and life in general were as important to the inquiry as facts about wages. "My vocation", he announced, "is to collect facts and register opinions". Of course, Mayhew was also a journalist who had to supply copy that was good to read but, as the reader can judge, this was secondary. The metropolitan letters were packed with a surprisingly large amount of statistics and very laborious wage calculations. Besides, the other commissioners did not automatically feel that the opinions of the poor would make a lively text for they made only sparing use of them. Mayhew the anthropologist and journalist complemented and strengthened each other. For both, an entirely statistical method of presenting fact was not appropriate, just as a door-to-door inquiry was not adequate to explore a trade.

The early *Morning Chronicle* letters show how Mayhew painstakingly evolved a method of investigation, which may not have been totally successful, but was relevant to the kinds of factors he wished to explore. To determine the history, structure and wages of any trade, Mayhew had hoped to compose a counterpoint between the testimony of employers and working men, accompanied by information from government reports. But government statistics for wages were unavailable and Mayhew attributed this to the secretiveness of employers, another stumbling block in his investigations:

> The chief difficulty which besets an undertaking of this character lies in the indisposition of the tradesmen—and especially those who are notorious for selling cheap, and consequently giving a less price to their workpeople—to make known the sums that they pay for the labour employed upon the different arts of manufacture in which they deal. I believe, this, is the main reason why such information remains to be acquired. To obtain it, the workpeople themselves must be sought out, and seen privately in their own homes. Another obstacle to the attainment of the information, is that the workpeople are in

general but poor accountants. They are unused to keep any account, either of their income or expenditure. Hence they have generally to trust to their memories for a statement of their earnings; and it is only with considerable difficulty and cross-questioning that one is able to obtain from them an account of the expenses necessarily attendant upon their labour, and so, by deducting these from the prices paid to them, to arrive at the amount of their clear earnings. Moreover, though I must confess I have met with far more truthfulness on the part of the operative than on that of the employer, still, I believe the workpeople are naturally disposed to imagine that they get less than they really do, even as the employer is inclined to fancy his workmen make more than their real gains.

In most cases, Mayhew had to rely almost entirely upon workpeople for evidence, which led to constant concern about his sample and the credibility of the information that was offered. He finally settled on a technique of interviews with a representative cross-section of workers in a trade about their conditions of employment and life style. The selection of informants was always made in consultation with a "gentleman" acquainted with the trade, workpeople well known by other workpeople to have a comprehensive view of the trade and, increasingly and preferably, with trade societies where they existed. The letters on the tailors give a clear picture of how, in the best of the industrial profiles, he sliced through a trade in several ways to get representative types. Quite explicitly readers were informed,

> I consulted several of the most experienced and intelligent workmen, as to the best means of arriving at a correct opinion respecting the state of the trade. It was agreed among us that, first, with regard to an estimate as to the amount of wages, I should see a hand employed at each of the different branches of the trade. After this I was to be taken to a person who was the captain or leading man of a shop; then to one who, in the technicality of the trade, had a "good chance" of work and finally to one who was only casually employed. It was considered that these classes taken in connection with others, would give the public a correct view of the condition, earnings and opinions of the trade.

As with every trade, the division of labour was one crucial cutting edge and a representative worker doing each job was contacted, in this case, trousers, coat and waistcoat hands. But great care was always taken to establish the wage range and different terms of hire within particular jobs. Supplementary interviews were conducted with the highest paid "captain" of a shop, with a fully employed tailor and with a hand who worked only during the "brisk season". Moving from the unionized to the cheap branch of the trade, the interviews continued with men who worked on the premises of a slop-shop, men who took work direct from the slop-house to make up at home and finally those who received their outwork through the hands of middlemen. Constantly on the lookout for the *causes* of low wages, whenever Mayhew found systems or practices which maintained the cheap trade, extra inter-

views were collected to probe them. The sweating system was subjected to multiple scrutiny, through interviews with an actual sweater, a journeyman lodging with a sweater and an outdoor worker for a show-shop (this was Nicoll of Regent Street) which had discharged all its tailors to carry on working through sweaters. The same was done with the "kidnapping system" to recruit Irish and country lads and with the immigration of foreign labour.

Yet Mayhew still worried lest this technique of locating representative individuals be confused with an attempt to tell extreme sob stories. "I seek for no extreme cases", he assured his readers, "if anything is to come of this hereafter, I am well aware that the end can be gained only by laying bare the sufferings of a *class,* and not of any particular individuals belonging thereto". He worked out a system of multiple and usually statistical checks on individual testimonies. In keeping with his original intention, he presented any information from government reports or standard statistical manuals which might test allegations about the causes of economic change. But he also went to great trouble to pursue original inquiries—which yielded information available nowhere else—collecting facts from employers, increasingly from tradesmen and merchants, from local authorities and voluntary societies and even from the metropolitan and provincial police. He kept inventing new ways to use working class informants for cross-checking purposes. He solicited account books for written evidence of wages especially over a "series" of years. He called meetings of operatives in order to get a larger number of informants and "arrive at a correct average as to the earnings of the class". He availed himself eagerly of any trade union surveys about wages and conditions, covering a large sample of members.

Apart from invaluable evidence in the letters themselves, it is hard to catch a glimpse of Mayhew actually at work in the field or composing the articles since none of the original notebooks seem to have survived. There is only one breezy account written by a catty acquaintance, Sutherland Edwards, fifty years later:

> He was in his glory at the time. He was largely paid, and the greatest joy of all, had an army of assistant writers, stenographers, and hansom cabmen constantly at his call. London labourers . . . were brought to the *Chronicle* office, where they told their tales to Mayhew, who redictated them, with an added colour of his own, to the shorthand writer . . . Augustus helped him in his vivid descriptions, and an authority on political economy controlled his gay statistics.

This club-man's view, though misleading, does contain some significant half-truths. The investigations were the work of a team, several of whose members can be identified. "Gus" Mayhew, Henry's younger brother who had collaborated with him on several novels and pot-boilers, probably helped fairly often both in collecting material and in writing it up. Two other important assistants came to light during the controversy with the Ragged School Union, when they leapt to Mayhew's defence after his whole method had been impugned by the Union Secretary. Both Richard "late of the City Mission" Knight and

Henry Wood stayed with Mayhew when he left the *Chronicle* and Mayhew paid Wood the compliment of having contributed so much material to **London Labour and the London Poor** that he might be "fairly considered as one of its authors". We have not been able to find out anything more about Wood. He may possibly have been the backroom boy who worked through and prepared the standard national and metropolitan statistics which Mayhew drew upon so lavishly. But Knight had impeccable credentials. In the two years before he joined Mayhew, he had been a salaried missionary of the London City Mission, serving the district of New Court in the City. His work there included routine visits to the poor in their own homes and would have given him valuable contacts and experience. The selection process for agents was stiff; a candidate had to produce testimonials from his pastor and "two or three other approved Christian persons" and outlast a series of interviews and a three month probation period.

The team had been working together for "several months" before the ragged schools inquiry, and had probably established a fairly constant division of labour. It would seem that Mayhew defined the framework of the investigation and then gave to Knight the job of finding some of the addresses of credible and representative informants. "I beg to be permitted to state", Knight wrote of Mayhew,

> that, having been engaged for these several months past, it never has been his practice either to select his cases or to publish the statements of individuals without previously obtaining some voucher for their credibility. I can conscientiously declare that I have never received instruction from him to furnish him with the addresses of such parties as might not be justly considered fair types of the class into whose condition he has been inquiring at the time.

From Henry Wood's testimonial, it is clear that some of the less important interviews were farmed out to him, and his notes were then passed on to Mayhew. The more important interviews were conducted jointly, with Mayhew interrogating the witness and Wood performing the role of stenographer. Wood also insisted that Mayhew did not "lead" the witnesses with any bias, or suppress evidence which he disliked, and confirmed that "your Correspondent's instructions to me have invariably been, to take average cases and to test their truthfulness by all possible means".

It is not, in these latter days of sociology, surprising that Mayhew employed interviewers; what is surprising is the care with which he supervised the work, and his own personal presence in the work at every stage, with a scrupulousness which might well put some incomparably better financed and equipped investigators of the present day to shame. Throughout the first twelve months of the inquiry the columns of the *Morning Chronicle* were open to critics who wished to challenge his evidence in any form, and thereafter he made the wrappers of the parts available for critical correspondence. What is remarkable is that he came under searching attack, on grounds of selection and misrepresentation of evidence, on only one occasion (the Ragged Schools case), and, in our view, the honours of this contest were emphatically his. Other critics who challenged the statements of some of his informants were usually willing to give credit to the general authenticity of his reports. Thus the managers of a Sailors' Home, defending themselves against criticism, added that "your Correspondent, with his companion, had during the last two or three weeks paid several visits" to the Home, consulted its cashbooks, ledgers and accounts, and conversed with the boarders privately, and acknowledged that all had been done in "a spirit of truth and justice".

Mayhew was clearly in control of the operation and beyond devising the ways to get information, his remarkable gifts as an interviewer, his rare ability to inspire confidence and establish quick rapport, made these techniques produce their best results. Far from causing embarrassment, in Mayhew's hands, the meetings of operatives helped to create a strong sense of shared experience which encouraged rather than inhibited the most intimate personal statements. The needlewomen, who had turned to prostitution to supplement their meagre earnings, laughed together and cried together and one by one gave very frank accounts of their life stories. His visits to working men and women in their homes, where he must have appeared a most unusual upper-class caller, treating them with obvious respect and actually eager to hear their opinions, were not considered intrusions. If it wasn't for his sympathetic presence, tricks like fingering a utensil or looking pointedly at an object in the room to force a comment on it would not have been sufficient to draw out people like the proud upholsteress who insisted, "I don't tell my affairs to everybody. It's quite enough for me to struggle by myself. I may feel a great many privations that I do not wish to be known", or the distressed gentlewoman who refused to say anything which might reveal her identity but ended up by giving such a detailed life history that her friends could not help but recognize her.

By means of the interviews with representative operatives, the core of his method, Mayhew was able to elicit the range of information he wanted. When possible, the informants were seen in their own homes where they could talk most freely. Of course, Mayhew led his witnesses, as any interviewer must, but it is easy to reconstruct the more-or-less standard questionnaire which was evidently rehearsed. The interviews nearly always began with questions about wages and conditions of employment—job held, length of time in the trade, payment for quantity of work performed, expenses necessarily attached to the job, hours of work, regularity of employment throughout the year, net weekly wage in the "brisk" and "slack" seasons, average weekly wage over the year. Then the informant was usually asked to contrast wages and conditions at present with the past (most workmen had at least twenty years of experience to draw on) and to account for changes which had taken place in the trade or to discuss features of the work situation which particularly pleased or disturbed him. Frequently, though less consistently, consumption patterns were assessed by questions about household expenditure and pawning. Mayhew did not paraphrase the interviews but compressed (and no doubt edited) the informant's own words into a continuous monologue which enabled readers to see the world through the eyes of the poor and were often very revealing about language and values. However, this should not be confused with a journalistic desire to create picturesque and colourful "characters" for their own sake. The largest part of the testimony was always devoted to the often tedious business of calculating wage figures and to the informants' views on economic change.

One way to test the truth of the assertion that "Mayhew's work was essentially a form of higher journalism, not of social analysis", is to compare his *Morning Chronicle* letters with the various genres of social reporting which burgeoned between 1840 and 1860. While the statisticians were boasting that "the spirit of the present age has an evident tendency to confront the figures of speech with the figures of arithmetic", their claims were being undercut by the fashion among newspapers and periodicals for sponsoring investigations of the working class, often out of a grandiose sense of professional mission. "The extraordinary influence of the Newspaper Press in this country", the *Newcastle Chronicle* editorialized,

> has been exercised in a manner alike remarkable and praiseworthy. In addition to the formation and guidance of public opinion, some of its more influential organs have taken upon themselves an important function, rightly belonging to the Government; they have ascertained, by minute investigation, the real condition of the masses, and have thus revealed to the astonished public, facts . . . imperatively needful to be known and pondered, not only by the legislature, but by all who feel an interest in the mitigation of evil, and the elevation of humanity.

The higher journalism can be divided into area studies and industrial studies. Where the correspondent was itinerant, whether the Eyewitness (ex-Chartist Thomas Cooper) or the *Morning Chronicle* provincial commissioners and could stay in each place for only a short time, the area studies tended to give only a quick sketch of the economic situation, usually focussing on the major industry in the locality, and then moved on to the moral and intellectual condition of the operatives much in the tradition of the statistical investigators, though working through word pictures instead of numbers; the *Newcastle Chronicle* inquiry hardly touched on employment at all. The industrial studies, superficially closer to Mayhew's format, suffer from being more concerned to describe than to collect material for analytical purposes. George Dodd's work for the *Penny Magazine* was a species of industrial tourism, which gave clear pictures of how the workshop looked and how the product was made, but said little about social relationships of production or wages and hours of work, while James Devlin's articles on the "Industrial Interests" quickly abandoned the present to explore the remote history of trades "till the time of the conquest". Only the survey of "The Condition of the Working Classes of Edinburgh and Leith", appearing in the *Edinburgh News* approached Mayhew's standard, but then it was directly modelled on Mayhew's work, and yet while more tidy and compact, it lacked much of Mayhew's sociological fascination. In all these journalistic studies, there was little of Mayhew's scrupulous attention to making clear what methods of investigation were to be followed or how the credibility of evidence was to be established. Nor were the working people allowed to speak for themselves. (pp. 55-66)

[The journalists'] main concern was to create dramatic word pictures; C. M. Smith assured his readers that though he never knowingly overstepped the limits of fact, he had "endeavoured, however trivial the topics to clothe each one in something resembling at least a literary garb". Favourite themes were fairs, pubs or markets which lent themselves to description in language like "the bustle and variety of the spectacle" and "the nature of each particular scene and the character of the actors therein". Individuals were inflated into theatrical characters so that a beggar became "a *tableau vivant* of unmerited poverty", a coal heaver "the next who figures upon our picturesque stage—the knight of the fan-tail and shovel". In his industrial studies, Mayhew kept such purple passages and theatricalizing of work people down to the minimum. Although Mayhew's idea of taking testimonies from the poor is seen as a journalistic device, it is interesting how little direct quotation figured in this characters and scenes genre. If the author used speech at all, he invented dialogue for his characters for literary purposes; C. M. Smith wrote in the first person as a bus conductor, using his working class character only as a literary vehicle to tell a story about the affairs of a family who used the bus.

Artisans or labourers did not often appear among the London characters, the street folk were more "picturesque", but when occasionally they were dealt with, the treatment was so inferior to Mayhew's that comparison almost becomes a nonsense. Thus C. M. Smith managed to cover the ethnic character of more occupational groups in a piece called "Genesis of the Workers", than Mayhew studied in the whole of the *Morning Chronicle,* linking his piece in a casual stream of consciousness way. Why his subjects should have come to London or what effect they have on the trades they enter was not of much interest to him—though of consuming concern to Mayhew. In C. M. Smith's voluminous output there was also a profile of the "Garret Master" which ended with a visit to a garret master at home, and turned into a nasty little drama about the wages of gin, with no dialogue at all:

> I heard a light foot on the stairs; and the door opening, a little girl of about six, almost decently clad in comparison with the others, entered the room, clasping a black bottle carefully in both hands. The mother, apparently unwilling that a stranger should be aware of the nature of the burden brought by the child, was about concealing it in a cupboard; but the father, who I now for the first time perceived, was on the high road to intoxication, swore at her angrily for pretending to be ashamed of what he proclaimed she liked as well as anybody, and loudly demanded the gin-bottle. With a sigh and a look of shame she complied with his desire, when he immediately applied himself to the contents with an air of dogged satisfaction . . . here want was not the destroyer; a fiend of more hideous aspect and deadlier purpose held undisputed sway in this wretched abode of perverted industry and precocious intemperance . . . the hateful vice of intoxication. . . .

Illustration for a Mayhew article on "slop workers," who did tailoring piece-work for minimal wages.

Although Mayhew sometimes, and with scrupulous brevity, set the scene of the interior where he was to do an interview, the primary job was the interview establishing wages and employment conditions. In matters like his task and methods of social investigation, Mayhew completely transcended the London low life genre.

Of course, Mayhew could not be as systematic in the presentation of material as he wished. The relentless schedule of weekly or more frequent deadlines virtually forced him to publish his notebooks as he went. In these circumstances, his various techniques of investigation (interviews and multiple checks) became the contents of the letters, introduced by a general picture of the division of labour, work-processes, history and union organization of each trade. No one was more aware than Mayhew of how unsystematically he moved from trade to trade and he continually apologized that,

> this unsystematic mode of treating the subject is almost a necessary evil attendant upon the nature of the investigation. In the course of my inquiries into the earnings and condition of one class of people, sources of information respecting the habits and incomings of another are opened up to me, of which, for several reasons,

I am glad to avail myself at the immediate moment, rather than defer making use of them at a more fitting and orderly occasion.

But lack of system of this kind should not obscure the more basic consistency and continuity of the major questions he asked and techniques of investigation he used. (pp. 66-9)

> *Eileen Yeo, "Mayhew as a Social Investigator," in* The Unknown Mayhew *by Eileen Yeo and E. P. Thompson, Pantheon Books, 1971, pp. 51-95.*

Graham Parry   (essay date 1972)

[In the following excerpt, Parry assesses Mayhew's writing style and his claims toward scientific authority.]

[Eileen Yeo, see excerpt dated 1971] is . . . concerned with Mayhew's methodology, and is particularly anxious to make us see him as a systematic empirical sociologist, a claim that Mayhew himself would have been sympathetic to, for he liked to think that his enquiries were quickened by a scientific spirit:

> I made up my mind to deal with human nature as a natural philosopher or chemist deals with any material object; and . . . I did most heartily rejoice that it should have been left to me to apply the laws of the inductive philosophy for the first time, I believe, in the world to the abstract question of political economy.

Indeed, his work is clothed in the trappings of a superficial scientism that was fashionable in the 'forties and 'fifties; for example, in order to organise his subject, he attempted to classify the various occupations generically in an almost Linnaean system, establishing first the principal classes of labour and then the categories and subdivisions that lay within them. The heavy emphasis on statistical information also helped to reinforce the air of impartial scientific enquiry, the principal object of which was to identify the causes of poverty and low wages across the whole spectrum of the urban poor. Observation and investigation he hoped would give rise to hypotheses about the origin and progress of poverty in a capitalist society, and in turn suggest means for its alleviation.

But can one in fact say that Mayhew's work conformed to the rigorous standards that he claimed for it, and did the enormous mass of information that he gathered enable him to construct a coherent critique of the prevailing theories of political economy? Miss Yeo builds up a picture of Mayhew as a proficient social and economic theorist, compiling her argument from the many brief comments and hypotheses scattered through his work, and drawing particularly on the polemical series of "Answers to Correspondents" that he conducted on the wrappers of the weekly numbers of *London Labour* in 1851, and on the four pamphlets *Low Wages, Their Causes, Consequences and Remedies* of the same year. However, the sporadic manner in which these pieces were issued, their incompleteness, and the absence of sustained argument indicate how difficult it is to regard Mayhew seriously as a systematic sociologist or economic critic. The very conditions under which he worked impeded the development of an extensive considered critique of the problems of Victorian society: constant interviewings, rapid reporting and frequent publication, and the rather hasty use of statistics caused by these pressures did not favour the growth of a coordinated study. Mayhew's own increasing interest in the street folk also drew him further away from the central issues of poverty in the regular trades. He certainly had more detailed information on the urban poor than any of his contemporaries, but it would be overstating the case to suggest that he managed to construct any substantial critical structure from his material. One has only to think what Engels did with considerably less information but with very acute selectivity in his *Condition of the Working Class in England* to see how Mayhew in comparison is simply suffocated by the abundance of his own material and the relative weakness of his conceptual faculties.

There can be no doubt, however, that these new papers show Mayhew writing with considerable power, and behind the objective tone one constantly feels the suppressed waves of shock and anger. He is dealing here not with the eccentric occupations of the street folk, but mainly with the regular well-established trades, and is therefore forc-

ing his readers to confront a radical poverty which could not be evaded or ignored. He vigorously dismisses some of the standard mid-Victorian assumptions about the causes of poverty and the measures for its relief. Overpopulation, the favourite explanation of the Malthus-inspired political economists and the censorious leader-writers of the respectable press, is shown to be an evasion of the real reasons; the apparently inflexible laws of the labour market are seen to be the contrivance of opportunist employers, while charity and emigration, the recommended panaceas, are exposed respectively as a near-futile half-measure and a callous form of deportation.

Beginning his survey with an enquiry into the condition of the most completely depressed section of the London labour market, the weavers, needlewomen and tailors, Mayhew reveals behind the starvation wages the inhuman operation of unregulated competition. The glossy West End merchants try desperately to undersell their rivals, and grind their East End workers in order to do so. A mania for cheap prices infects the country. The same story comes out time and again in the interviews: how ten or fifteen years ago wages were higher and life was tolerable, but wages have since been ground down by price wars and by the growth of the real parasites of the capitalist system, the middlemen. Hood may have briefly twisted Victorian consciences with his "Song of the Shirt", but week after week Mayhew appalled his newspaper audience with his dispassionate, factual accounts of an economic system that was driving its crowds of victims to destitution and death. The pictures of Ministers of the Crown having their Court dress assembled by starving tailors, of the British Army being clothed by a system that enriched the contractors and beggared the operatives, of distressed needlewomen turning *en masse* to prostitution because an eighty-hour sewing week would not produce enough to exist on, all bring out the social barbarism and the degradation that was the price of middle-class prosperity.

These investigations sharpen our understanding of the mid-Victorian scene in a number of ways. We are constantly being reminded of the raw power that an individual in authority could exercise over others. The petty tyrants who figure so noticeably in Dickens' novels, usually as schoolmasters, head clerks, small-time employers who make life miserable for their underlings in a world where there is no redress, no appeal, make their appearance in many of these sad narratives of the poor. Here they are the sweat-shop operators who work their employees in conditions that amount to slavery, or the relentless landlords, or middlemen who refuse to pay for goods delivered a minute late, or small ship-owners who contrive to fine a sailor almost the whole of his wages earned on a voyage. All show inhumanity activated by the profit motive; a society of predators and prey, the world of Dombey, Dorrit, Podsnap and Bounderby, where the commercial middle classes contain the real enemies of the people.

Conversely, in a setting where a man can so easily mutilate his economic dependents, and where a worker has no rights or protection, the good-hearted man stands out as the main hope for a better way of life. Mayhew refers several times in his account of the state of the seamen to one benevolent ship-owner noted for his fair dealing, who runs a home for his employees and cares for the well-being and education of their families; such a man enables some addition to be made to the sum of human happiness, and he enjoys moreover the goodwill of his workers. The change-of-heart syndrome often found in Victorian fiction, exemplified by Gradgrind or Scrooge, and often condemned by modern readers as ineffectual sentimentalism, appears in Mayhew as one possible way of combating unregulated capitalism: in the absence of organised labour or legal restraint, the responsible employer has to make a stand and endeavour to improve the condition of his men. Certainly Mayhew saw little enough evidence of this happening, and recognised that only the unionisation of labour could combat the system, but he tends to feel that the introduction of humane relationships into the economic circuit is a first and necessary corrective.

So much probing into the depths of society revealed many oddities. Extreme poverty turns people into grotesques, and there are numerous figures in these papers who behave like fantastic characters from a novel of social condemnation, such as the destitute needlewoman who sleeps in the finery of a half-made-up lady's gown because she has been forced to pawn her own bedclothes, or the tailor who cannot get married because his coat is always in pawn. A reading of Mayhew reminds us that many of the incidents in Dickens' novels that seem like grotesque fantasy may simply be the result of acute social observation.

One feature of the current economic situation that Mayhew is particularly concerned over is the way in which low wages and intolerable hours forced women into prostitution. The many interviews with women who turned reluctantly yet deliberately to the streets show Mayhew at his most compassionate, and they confront his audience with the fallen fruit of the tree of Victorian prosperity in a way that irrefutably demonstrates the hypocrisy of "respectable" opinion. A chain of economic circumstances links cheap clothes for the middle class with the prostitution of needlewomen, and the clergyman buying his cut-price cassock is unreflectingly participating in the process that sends some young woman on to the streets. One realises why there were 80,000 prostitutes in mid-Victorian London, and why their plight is one of the frequent minor subjects in Victorian fiction and painting. They were a major social problem, but the morality of the time preferred to ignore its existence whenever possible.

With so much intimate knowledge of the details of people's lives, Mayhew has an almost Darwinian sense of the struggle for existence on the tangled banks of Victorian society. As his ***London Labour and the London Poor*** showed, people can scrape a living from virtually anything: the rehabilitation of used tea-leaves, the recycling of the excrement of dogs, the sale of rats, and dozens of other bizarre occupations vividly indicate how precarious yet how tenacious was the existence of the poor on the inhospitable soil of Victorian England. Mayhew is wonderfully aware of the complex interconnections of all things in the world of the poor, and the cost in human misery when some factor in the system is adjusted. (pp. 78-81)

Graham Parry, "Letters from the Under-

world," in Encounter, *Vol. XXXVIII, No. 5, May, 1972, pp. 78-81.*

Jonathan Raban   (essay date 1973)

[*Raban is a British dramatist, novelist, critic, and travel writer who has written extensively on Mark Twain's* Huckleberry Finn *(1884). In the following essay, he examines the narrative personae adopted by Mayhew in his fiction and journalism.*]

There is something very odd about Henry Mayhew. In ***London Labour and the London Poor*** he gave faces, voices and characters to people who had hitherto only existed as figures of rumour and nightmare. He made the invisible visible, lifted the metropolitan fog to reveal a sector of English society—the men and women who had fallen clean through the industrial system—which his contemporaries had been keeping deliberately dark. But Mayhew himself has disappeared; and his invisibility is not so much the tactful withdrawal of the reporter who leaves his reports to speak for themselves as a case of abduction—he has been spirited away into the same fog which he did so much to clear. Dickens and Mayhew knew each other, probably well; certainly they acted together at least twice in an amateur production of *Every Man in His Humour,* and Mayhew's younger brother Horace wrote for *Household Words.* But nowhere in Dickens's papers is there a mention of Mayhew. Douglas Jerrold, the editor, socialite and man of letters, was Mayhew's father-in-law and he and Mayhew were among the contested founders of *Punch;* there are two biographies of Jerrold, and in both Mayhew is just an occasional name, more shadowy than the servant-girl. He knew George Augustus Sala, but Sala's copious memoirs leave no record of Mayhew. In that chronically gossippy milieu of Victorian literary bohemia, Mayhew, who was as keen a drunken clubman as anyone, is an Enoch Soames in search of a Beerbohm.

He clearly didn't think of himself as anonymous and peripheral. He had his portrait engraved for ***London Labour and the London Poor,*** and it has a preternatural solidity, all girth, weight, and heavy black cross-hatching. It shows a great, flattened-oval slab of a head—tufty, balding, symmetrical—with the fleshy nose, sunken eyes and querulous mouth of a butler who has been too long at the port. It is a portrait of the author as Victorian busybody. All Mayhew's interviewees insistently call him "Sir"; and here, in waistcoat and wing-collar, is the substantial personage they were addressing. (It was a device with a double point. Mayhew's readers knew his characters only as a lewd-mouthed rabble with no respect for person or station. Mayhew makes his dog-dung collectors and mudlarks exaggeratedly genteel, simultaneously enhancing their status and his own.) Indeed, his anecdotal prose is studiedly stodgy, much given to elaborate circumlocutions and judicial parentheses; as a literary manner it is almost comically self-important. He presents himself as the ambassador of the genteel world, and the "I" of ***London Labour*** embodies the stuffiness, the pedantic curiosity, the moralism, and the crackpot theorising of the Victorian gentleman at large. It is an artfully stage-managed posture.

For, until 1849 when the cholera epidemic broke loose in Bermondsey and Mayhew contributed his first piece on the wretched of London to the *Morning Chronicle,* Mayhew had kept steadily on the run from gentility. He was 37 when he began the London project; and for nearly twenty years he had lived in the nether world of the Victorian freelance, editing short-lived satirical magazines, writing squibs and articles, dashing off dreadful farces, and collaborating with his brother Augustus on a series of novels. In 1846, he went bankrupt, owing £2000, with an income of around £400. From his own memoirs, quoted—with a parsimonious note on their authorship—in Walter Jerrold's biography of his father Douglas, Mayhew seems to have spent an inordinate amount of time in the Garrick Tavern in Bow Street, where he and his friends got up a drinking club called The Rationalists. Writing afforded a congenially dissipated way of life; it took Mayhew out on to the rim of society, displaced him from the shabby bourgeoisie into which he had been born. But he had neither a subject nor a style of his own. He flirted with fashionable radicalism and educational theory, and attempted—in the novels, the plays and the pieces for *Punch*—to write brittle satiric comedies of manners. His one sure quality lay in his position as a professional outsider of society, and he became a railer, sniggering entertainingly at the mannerisms of both the wealthy, from whom he was cut off, and of the poor, whom he was precariously avoiding joining.

The novels he wrote with Augustus are displays of winking ventriloquism. The brothers' great party-piece was female impersonation, and in *The Greatest Plague of Life; or, The Adventures of a Lady in Search of a Good Servant* and *Whom to Marry and How to Get Married! or, The Adventures of a Lady in Search of a Good Husband* they went cackling in drag, doing proficiently vulgar travesties of the Victorian nice young lady. They are sharp on genteel hypocrisy, religiosity and the rapacious greed with which their heroines treat money, but the real energy of the books springs from their naughtiness as they trespass on the secrets of the toilet, and creep, clad in heavy double-entendres, between the sheets of the marital bed.

> Charles and I thought that our happiness was never to end. Scarcely a pleasure but what we could join in it, and enjoy it together. We hunted, and shot, and fished together; and scarcely a sport that he indulged in that I didn't participate in the pleasure with equal joy. . . .

Both novels are crammed with domestic details—prices, materials, bits of kitchenware, meals, lessons in etiquette, brand names, and London topography. They are bewitched, and clearly revolted, by the bric-à-brac of Victorian family life. They burst sporadically into a hopeless ironic savagery at the twittering awfulness of the mistress of the suburban villa, mixing her sentimental whimsies with her contemptuous treatment of her social inferiors in a style of shrill mockery. It is customary to detect at least a hint of serious social concern for the conditions in which servants worked in *The Greatest Plague of Life,* but the Mayhews are much more interested in ridiculing the mistress than in sympathising with the servants; that she flings them one after another into the street is supposed to tell us more about her than about them.

The novels are shot through with an aimless, insouciant talent for observation. They are inexhaustibly curious, and they delight in simple mimicry—getting a voice down on paper, writing exaggeratedly "in character". But they stand in a complacent, cock-a-snook attitude to the society whose manners they catalogue; their satire is without control or direction and they fizzle out in bumptious foolery. Yet, between 1847, when *The Greatest Plague of Life* was published, and 1849, Henry Mayhew was able, somehow, to transform himself from the facetious bohemian outsider of the novels into the solemn, stolid enquirer represented in his portrait in *London Labour.*

His first *Morning Chronicle* assignment took, him, in September 1849, to Jacob's Island, an unsavoury, overcrowded patch of land around St Saviour's Dock below Tower Bridge at the wrong end of Tooley Street, where the cholera epidemic was at its worst. Eleven years before, Dickens had used Jacob's Island as the setting for the death of Sikes in *Oliver Twist;* and in 1850, Charles Kingsley used it for the grotesque climax of *Alton Locke.* The place hardly needed writers to make it a crucial symbol of the state of the Victorian city: it was a line of mean cottages and broken-down warehouses perched over an open sewer. The Thames, still the main artery of London commercial life, pushed sluggishly past it. It was from near here that Gaffer Hexham practised his profession of fishing bodies out of the river; and even now—Jacob Street, Dockhead and Mill Lane stand, although Mr Seifert has posted notices of demolition on the warehouses—it is an eerie, empty, half-ruined quarter, smelling of turmeric and Thames sludge. There are tramp-fires on the floors of deserted buildings, and the dock water is gurgling and opaque. For Dickens, Mayhew and Kingsley, Jacob's Island was natural raw material; they each imprinted on it their vision of the city, and the three passages, so close in subject yet so different in details of execution, are exact measures of their authors' individual styles. Set beside his contemporaries, Mayhew's peculiar qualities of mind become immediately and dramatically apparent. I quote parallel paragraphs from each passage.

> It is a creek or inlet from the Thames, and can always be filled at high water by opening the sluices at the Lead Mills from which it took its old name. At such times, a stranger, looking from one of the wooden bridges thrown across it at Mill Lane, will see the inhabitants of the houses on either side lowering from their back doors and windows, buckets, pails, domestic utensils of all kinds, in which to haul the water up; and when the eye is turned from these operations to the houses themselves, his utmost astonishment will be excited by the scene before him. Crazy wooden galleries common to the backs of half-a-dozen houses, with holes from which to look upon the slime beneath; windows, broken and patched, with poles thrust out, on which to dry the linen that is never there; rooms so small, so filthy, so confined, that the air would seem too tainted even for the dirt and squalor in which they shelter; wooden chambers thrusting themselves out above the mud, and threatening to fall into it—as some have done; dirt-besmeared walls and decaying foundations; every repulsive

lineament of poverty, every loathsome indication of filth, rot, and garbage; all these ornament the banks of Folly Ditch.

(Dickens, Oliver Twist)

The striking peculiarity of Jacob's Island consisted in the wooden galleries and sleeping rooms at the back of the houses overhanging the turbid flood. These were built upon piles, so that the place had positively the air of a Flemish street, flanking a sewer instead of a canal; while the little rickety bridges that spanned the ditches, and connected court with court, gave it the appearance of the Venice of drains. At some parts of the stream whole rooms had been built out, so that the houses on opposite sides nearly touched one another; and there, with the very stench of death arising through the boards, human beings slept night after night, until the last sleep of all came upon them years before its time. Scarce a house but yellow linen was hanging to dry over its rude balustrade of staves, or else they were run out on a long oar where the sulphur-coloured clothes fluttered flag-fashion over the waters, and you were startled not to see their form and colour reflected in the putrid ditch beneath.

(Mayhew, "Pest-Nests")

The light of the policeman's lantern glared over the ghastly scene—along the double row of miserable house-backs, which lined the sides of the open tidal ditch—over strange rambling jetties, and balconies, and sleeping sheds, which hung on rotting piles over the black waters, with phosphorescent scraps of rotten fish gleaming and twinkling out of the dark hollows, like devilish grave-lights—over bubbles of poisonous gas, and bloated carcases of dogs, and lumps of offal, floating on the stagnant olive-green hell-broth—over the slow sullen rows of oily ripple which were dying away into the darkness far beyond, sending up, as they stirred, hot breaths of miasma—the only sign that a spark of humanity, after years of foul life, had quenched itself at last in that foul death. I almost fancied that I could see the haggard face staring up at me through the slimy water; but no—it was as opaque as stone.

(Kingsley, Alton Locke)

One needs to add, perhaps, that in Kingsley a man has fallen into the ditch; which may account for the hectic stew of dashes, hyphenations and lurid adjectives. By contrast with both Dickens and Kingsley, Mayhew is oddly detached and leisurely. He is not insensitive to the poverty and suffering of the cholera victims, but, even as he describes their deaths, he can afford to be playful, curious, exact. He notices that some washing is hung out on oars, some on staves; another writer might have been content with the bizarre echo of Venice, but Mayhew carefully qualifies the image by referring to the Flemish street as well; along with the oars, he introduces "flags", and manages to suggest a quaint, picturesque armada. While Kingsley diverts himself in an orgy of theatrical moral feeling, and Dickens cunningly depopulates and recreates the place for his private fictional purposes, Mayhew keeps his eyes open and keeps cool. He is wonderfully faithful

to the irreverence and irrelevance of the eye as it enjoys itself when it ought to be shocked and sees things from which it ought to have averted its gaze. This spectator's lack of natural morality—the habitual outsider's essential trick of the mind—paradoxically enables Mayhew to be more, not less morally forceful. Later on, Kingsley observes with horror how the inhabitants of Jacob's Island draw buckets of polluted water from the sewer and make tea with them. He is so shocked that he cannot bear to look further. Mayhew does, and notices that the buckets are left to stand for a day or two on the windowsills, then the fluid is skimmed "from the solid particles of filth and pollution which constitute the sediment." Such details of ordinary, commonsense practicality, like the single red dahlia which Mayhew notices sprouting at the foot of the benighted Providence Buildings, are totally submerged in the writing of conventional moralists. But Mayhew is liberated from a concern with his own finer feelings; he is, among Victorian writers, uniquely unsententious.

He understood very well what he was doing and cultivated this innate oddity of vision. In a piece on **"Getting Up a Pantomime"**, he remarks on how the decline of the theatrical spectacular has led to the mass unemployment of "supers":

> There was a goodly show of fine old regulation "supers" at Astley's while "Mazeppa" was being played some time ago; and I confess that the sight of the curious old banner-bearers in that extraordinary drama had more interest for me than the developed charms of the "beauteous Menken".

The dreariest bohemian prides himself on standing outside the conventions of the middle class, but Mayhew was able to translate that commonplace affectation into a deliberate blindness to all conventions. At the theatre, he didn't notice the star; in society at large, he failed to observe any of the rules of the morality of perception. He followed his eye, and it told quite a different story from the one which the educated Victorian was supposed to listen to. Mayhew's imagination was astonishingly and fruitfully uncontrolled: it carelessly and casually broke every law it encountered, and in 1874, explaining why he had attended a public execution, Mayhew was able to boast that he had "been everywhere—seen everything, which maybe a gentleman should not."

Ungentlemanliness was his style. It started out as naughtiness and thumb-nose satire, and developed into the magnificent disregard for convention which enabled him to write his masterpiece. Yet when he came to portray himself in **London Labour,** it was as *Sir,* Mr Mayhew doubling as Mr Bumble, a travesty-gentleman. The phrasing of the preface is interesting here. Mayhew proposed to investigate London life as if the East End was a jungle of savages and he a venturing anthropologist setting forth with canoe and native guides. The tactic was a subtle one: it enabled him to see the poor not as a class but as a caste. His street folk are outside the class-system, they are not members of the industrial proletariat; their status is determined, as in a real Indian caste, less by their relationships with each other than by their relationships with objects—the things they can touch, or, in the case of London, the things they buy and sell, from fresh eatables down to dog-dung. From anthropology Mayhew borrowed the distinction between "settlers" and "wanderers." Settlers had big heads; wanderers big jawbones. Civilised people (including the industrialised working class) settled, uncivilised people wandered. The street folk of London were uncivilised wanderers with large jawbones. It was an alarmingly plausible statement of the sense of profound difference and alienation which the metropolitan middle class felt when they confronted their impoverished brethren. But Mayhew took pains to underline it even further.

> The nomad is distinguished from the civilised man by his repugnance to regular and continuous labour—by his want of providence in laying up a store for the future—by his inability to perceive consequences ever so slightly removed from immediate apprehension—by his passion for stupefying herbs and roots, and, when possible, for intoxicating fermented liquors—by his extraordinary powers of enduring privation—by his comparative insensibility to pain—by an immoderate love of gaming, frequently risking his own personal liberty upon a single cast—by his love of libidinous dances—by the pleasure he experiences in witnessing the suffering of sentient creatures—by his delight in warfare and all perilous sports—by his desire for vengeance—by the looseness of all his notions as to property— by the absence of chastity among his women, and his disregard of female honour—and lastly, by his vague sense of religion—his rude idea of a Creator, and utter absence of all appreciation of the mercy of the Divine Spirit.

This is Casaubon, or the gentleman in the engraving, speaking; not Mayhew. Yet the impersonation, as shrill in its way as the drag-acts of the novels, is deeply mixed up with what is most serious and necessary in Mayhew's method. Henry Mayhew, ex-bankrupt, lover of fermented liquor, devoutly satiric, anti-clerical, reputedly bad husband, is dressing up in frock coat and gaiters for a dangerous expedition into the territory of the depraved. Disraeli's Two Nations are about to meet between the covers of the book.

Yet the people Mayhew finds, or creates (and in *London Labour* it is impossible to draw the line accurately between the two), turn out to be nature's gentlemen. The language they use, as they recite their lives of extreme poverty, illness and degradation, has a consistent poetic dignity. It is, undoubtedly, a literary language; highly-organised, poised, often syntactically elaborate. Mayhew's most fully developed single character, Jack Black the Queen's Ratcatcher, illustrates this with a resonant, labyrinthine story:

> One night in August—the night of a very heavy storm, which, maybe, you may remember, sir—I was sent for by a medical gent as lived opposite the Load of Hay, Hampstead, whose two children had been attacked by rats while they was sleeping in their little cots. I traced the blood, which had left lines from their tails, through the openings in the lath and plaster, which I follered to where my ferruts come out of, and they must have come up from the bottom of the house to the attics. The rats gnawed the hands and feet

of the little children. The lady heard them crying, and got out of her bed and called to the servant to know what the child was making such a noise for, when they struck a light, and then they see the rats running away to the holes; their little night-gownds was kivered with blood, as if their throats had been cut. I asked the lady to give me one of the night-gownds to keep as a cur'osity, for I considered it a *phee*nomenon, and she gave it to me, but I never was so vexed in all my life as when I was told the next day that a maid had washed it. I went down the next morning and sterminated them rats. I found they were of the specie of rat which we term the blood-rat, which is a dreadful spiteful feller—a snake-headed rat, and infests the dwellings. There may have been some dozens of 'em altogether, but it's so long ago I a'most forget how many I took in that house. The gent behaved uncommon handsome, and said, "Mr Black, I can never pay you for this"; and ever arterwards, when I used to pass by that there house, the little dears when they see me used to call out to their mamma, "O, here's Mr Ratty, ma!"

It is a condensed, highly-coloured allegory of the English class system, and it has the promiscuously suggestive symbolism of a dream. The stormy night, the violation, the stained night-gown, the "snake-headed" rat, and the saving presence of the proletarian in the Hampstead house, a ratlike creature himself who turns by day into the children's favourite, "Mr Ratty"—these are exactly the same ingredients which we meet with in the most delirious and secret passages of Kingsley's fiction. Sex and class are inextricably mixed up, and the story is full of the illicit excitement of trespass and invasion as a man from one class goes, literally, with all the trappings of a gothic phantasmagoria, to the bed of the children of another. Jack Black, of course, was real, and no doubt he did tell Mayhew about a night-call to the house of a Hampstead medical gent; but the actual telling belongs to fiction not sociology. Pulsing just beneath the surface of the language, one can feel Mayhew's own thrill at tasting the forbidden fruit of class-transvestism as he speaks in the voice of the rat-man.

In *London Labour,* Mayhew was able to let loose, at full power, the passion for going about in the clothes of another sex, another class, which he and Augustus had toyed with in the novels. But in the street life of the London poor, he hit on a rich seam of mythic gold—the great underground power source of the Victorian imagination. *London Labour,* is Mayhew's *My Secret Life.* It is an infinitely greater book than that shoddy, ponderous sexual fantasy, because Mayhew's private imaginative drive was being constantly held in check by his remorselessly truthful eye. He buttressed himself by statistics (his love of figures verged on the self-parodic, as when he solemnly quantified, in grammes and pounds, the daily input and output of a horse), by prodigious and untiring research, and by a genuine sense of concern and outrage at the living conditions he found himself exposing. Yet the heart of the book is a personal drama. Mayhew was playing out a fantastic, guilt-ridden romance between the gentleman and the proletarian, and he lets us in, as no other Victorian writer dares, on its secrecy, its darkest, most sequestered pleasures.

It was, in fact, the secrecy of the city which aroused Mayhew most. He loved what was hidden, the foggy places, the areas into which he could go incognito, in disguise. He grasped the central paradox that a great city is one of the most truly private places on earth, where a single man by playing many parts may become invisible—one moment a gentleman, the next a coster-girl, the next a rat-catcher, the next an unclouded eye floating free over the urban profusion of detail. Looking over London from the gallery around the dome of St Paul's, Mayhew noticed that:

> The haze which hung like a curtain of shadow before and over everything, increased rather than diminished the giant sublimity of the city that lay stretched out beneath. It was utterly unlike London as seen every day below, in all its bricken and hard-featured reality; it was rather the phantasm—the spectral illusion, as it were, of the great metropolis—such as one might see in a dream, with here and there stately churches and palatial hospitals, shimmering like white marble, their windows glittering in the sunshine like plates of burnished gold—while the rest of the scene was all hazy and indefinite. . . . It was impossible to tell where the sky ended and the city began. . . . But as the vast city lay there beneath me, half hid in mist and with only glimpses of its greatness visible, it had a much more sublime and ideal effect from the very inability to grasp the whole of its literal reality.

This intrinsic illegibility and hiddenness of the city acted as a powerful liberating force on Mayhew's imagination. He set out, a professional nomad, to lose himself in the fog. He gave himself over to a sustained, wildly diverse, career of impersonation. Nowhere in his work can one put a finger on a style and say that *that* is Mayhew. Everything, except his extraordinary accuracy of observation which is so devastatingly truthful as to be impersonal, is disguise, imposture, dramatic monologue. He wanted, in a lifetime of what he modestly called "knocking about London", to be *the* man of the city, embodying in one frame all its classes, sexes, contradictions, secrets. No wonder his contemporaries seem to have conspired to exclude him from their memoirs. His whole work and existence mock at the conventions of order, degree and category by which society is customarily kept going. He was a dangerous figure whose Protean character reflected everything that the Victorians most feared in the Protean nature of the industrial megapolis. The bitchy remarks which were made about him by several of his fellows while he was working on *London Labour*—he was accused of indulgent invention and grotesque embroidery, and it was said that he was simply living it up on *Morning Chronicle* money, taking cabs everywhere and eating out lavishly—pinpoint the nagging mistrust which attended his progress through the city. People didn't quite believe in Mayhew. They sensed in him a basic lack of continuity, as if he had carried bad faith to the point of moral principle. So, in a sense, he had. He had been inside the £600-a-year mansion in Hyde Park Gardens, and the sempstress's garret at half-a-crown a week

which the mansion concealed, and he could talk in the language of each with equal conviction.

But the passion for crossing class boundaries, for extreme impersonation coloured by guilt and sexual excitement—the side of Mayhew which inspired Gissing and Orwell—fizzled out as Mayhew grew older. He wrote a puzzling, under-read, late book called **London Characters,** which was published in 1874. The first part, a facetious charivari, with "thumb-nail sketches" of London legal, theatrical, and social life, can be skipped; and the final chapters are rejigged versions of his early *Morning Chronicle* articles. But three substantial essays, **"Outsiders of Society and Their Homes in London", "Life in London",** and **"Housekeeping in Belgravia",** form the aborted beginnings of a study of genteel society which might have been comparable in scope and detail to **London Labour.** **"Outsiders of Society"** is a sad, exact and funny dissection of the personal columns of Victorian newspapers, and of the people who masquerade behind such titles as "respectable elderly lady" and "City gentleman of convivial disposition". Mayhew's eye is still sharp and scathing, and he allows himself a style of full-blown satire, a sarcastic orotundity which is new in his work. On the lady housekeepers of Belgravia, he meticulously documents their accounts, tells one exactly how to set about getting a cut-price ostentatious carriage, goes fascinatingly into the details of mistress-servant ritual relationships. The subject should have been perfect for Mayhew, but something is drastically wrong. A quotation from the general introductory section of **"Housekeeping in Belgravia"** shows the shift in his tone:

> Oh railroads! much have ye to answer for. Twenty years hence we may look in vain for the social, kindly, hospitable country life now only to be met with in remote counties, in Cornwall, in Scotland. Already have you made the "Great Houses" independent of their neighbors. Their fish and their friends come down from town together. And the squire, the small proprietor despairing of husbands for his girls or his rubber for himself, where the doors around are closed nine months in the year, leaves his acres in the care of his bailiff and takes refuge in the nearest watering-place, or yields to his wife's solicitations, and launches also into the cares and troubles of HOUSEKEEPING IN BELGRAVIA. . . .

The trouble is that Mayhew here has no one to impersonate. He aspires to the most dangerous of all satirist's tones, that of patrician irony, the lordly aristocrat condescending to the lesser life beneath him. Accuracy turns into mere knowingness; the alert eye, though it still sees, is bored with the view. Mayhew made a good travesty-gentleman because, in 1851, he had a thorough-going contempt for gentility. But the new, quasi-aristocratic Mayhew has a plaintive earnestness; one feels him straining for the right to condescend.

Perhaps the effort of holding all of London in his head had told on him; perhaps he was searching for a secure identity—a dignity commensurate with his sense of the importance of what he had already achieved. It is a pity that such an intensely productive bohemianism should have

Mayhew's portrait for the frontispiece of A Jorum of Punch *by his son, Athol Mayhew.*

turned so easily—as it turns so often—into snobbery. And there is a deep irony—which Mayhew himself might have appreciated—in the fact that the invisible man, crossing and recrossing the city in borrowed clothes, striving to become the soul of London, should have finally revealed himself as a parvenu. (pp. 64-70)

> Jonathan Raban, "The Invisible Mayhew," in
> Encounter, *Vol. XLI, No. 2, August, 1973, pp.
> 64-70.*

Gertrude Himmelfarb   (essay date 1973)

The 'Condition of the People' was as much a set topic for Victorians as it has since become for historians. It was the subject of Royal Commission reports and parliamentary debates, statistical analyses and sensationalist exposés, sermons, articles, novels, even poems. The historian would seem to be well served by this abundance of material. Yet he would be wise to approach it warily. And not only for the usual reasons—doubts about its accuracy, consistency, and bias—but also because it is not always clear what all of this evidence is about, what subject it is that is being elucidated.

The variety of titles under which the subject was discussed is itself suspect; in place of 'the People' one may read 'the Labouring Population,' or 'the Labouring Poor,' or 'the Poorer Classes,' or 'the Working Classes,' or, more grand-

ly, 'England.' Contemplating these alternatives, the historian may find himself attending less to the question of the Condition of the People than to the question of the identity of the People who were so variously and, as it appeared, synonymously described. And the question of identity, in turn, raises that of image. Was there a common image that would account for the assumption of a common identity? The questions are of some importance, not only in defining and clarifying the subject of the Condition of the People— what condition and which people—but also in understanding what was or was not being done about that Condition and those People. For there is no doubt that the way the People were perceived played a large part in the way they were treated, in the kinds of legislation, the modes of administration, the types of philanthropy, the forms of public policy and private behavior which so materially affected their Condition.

Questions of identity and image persist even when the subject appears to be more carefully delineated, more precisely located in time, place, and rank. Henry Mayhew's *London Labour and the London Poor,* published in the middle of the century, would seem to be sufficiently well-defined. Referring explicitly and exclusively to the metropolis, it has only a partial relevance to the larger body of urban labor and poor, and no necessary relevance to the much more considerable body of rural labor and poor. And certainly in comparison with studies purporting to deal with 'the People' or 'England,' it suggests a commendable clarity and specificity. It also has the virtue of being eminently readable, indeed one of the most fascinating social documents of the century. Mayhew's work, therefore, may well serve as a case study of the ambiguities both of the historical situation and of the historical enterprise.

The most obvious ambiguity lies in the title itself. Were the two categories, 'Labour' and the 'Poor,' meant to be conjunctive or disjunctive? And how do the subtitles of the several volumes relate to the overall title? The first three volumes were subtitled: 'The London Street Folk; comprising Street Sellers, Street Buyers, Street Finders, Street Performers, Street Artisans, Street Labourers'; and the fourth, 'Those That Will Not Work, comprising Prostitutes, Thieves, Swindlers, Beggars.' These subtitles obviously do not add up to the title either in its conjunctive or disjunctive sense. And it is the subtitles rather than the title which accurately describe the plan of the work and the bulk of its contents.

Unfortunately this difficulty cannot be resolved, as one might think it could be, by simply ignoring the title and concentrating on the substance of the work. For in fact the ambiguity is of the substance of the work. It is not just a question of setting the record straight, of putting aright those contemporaries and historians who used the work as a source of information about London Labour and the London Poor, even Labour and The Poor, instead of about the London Street Folk. One would also have to put Mayhew aright; for he too seems on occasion to have been a victim of the same confusion. What is important is not so much the confusion itself as its significance, the reasons why so many people found it possible to identify the Street Folk with the Labouring Poor, why even those who were aware of the distinction tended to ignore it at crucial moments. (pp. 707-08)

About the same time that Mayhew's first volume was being published, there also appeared, as it happened, the results of the census of 1851. This census is of particular importance in English social history, since it was the first to treat in some detail such subjects as religious affiliations and practices, the first to single London out for separate consideration, and because it was altogether more satisfactory than any previous one. It is also instructive as a contrast or corrective to Mayhew's work. For it gave as the largest occupational groups in the metropolis: domestic workers (200,000, or one-tenth of the total population of London), building workers (60,000), tailors, dressmakers, and milliners (60,000), shoemakers (40,000), etc.—none of whom figured in Mayhew's work. Included in the census figures were the self-employed and better-paid artisans; but these—the 'labour aristocracy,' as recent historians have designated them—constituted no more, according to Mayhew himself, than one-tenth of the laboring population. The rest, and surely the vast bulk of domestic workers, indubitably belonged to Labour and the Poor, however that category may be understood.

But it did not take the census to reveal just how limited was the population with which Mayhew dealt. Mayhew himself was explicit enough—and not only in subtitles and chapter titles but in numbers and ratios. Repeatedly in the first two volumes he gave the total of street-folk as approximately 50,000, this figure including men, women, and children. And, lest there be any doubt about their relative numbers, he specified, in the opening pages of Volume I and again of Volume II, that these 50,000 represented 'a fortieth part' of the population of the metropolis. Volumes III and IV added other groups of street-laborers (dockworkers, transport workers, etc.) and non-laboring street-folk (prostitutes, beggars, criminals, paupers). But even assuming that the addition of these groups doubled the original number, Mayhew's population still constituted only about one-twentieth of the population—which is far short of anything that could reasonably come under the category of Labour and the Poor. Mayhew protested, and quite rightly, that most of his street-folk were missing from the census. But if the census had its non-persons, Mayhew as assuredly had his—and in even larger numbers.

More important, however, than the question of numbers is that of characterization. For Mayhew's street-folk were not only quantitatively distinct from the population of laboring poor; they were qualitatively distinctive, indeed a race apart. And here too Mayhew could not have been more explicit. The very first pamphlet, which was also the opening chapter of the first volume, was entitled, 'Of Wandering Tribes in General.' And the opening sentences set the theme: Mankind had always consisted of 'two distinct and broadly marked races, viz., the wanderers and the settlers—the vagabond and the citizen—the nomadic and the civilized tribes.' Each of these tribes, or races, had its 'peculiar and distinctive physical as well as moral characteristics.' Physically the nomadic race was distinguished by

'a greater relative development of the jaws and cheek bones.' Morally the differences were no less conspicuous:

> The nomad then is distinguished from the civilized man by his repugnance to regular and continuous labour—by his want of providence in laying up a store for the future—by his inability to perceive consequences ever so slightly removed from immediate apprehension—by his passion for stupefying herbs and roots, and, when possible, for intoxicating fermented liquors—by his extraordinary powers of enduring privation—by his comparative insensibility to pain—by an immoderate love of gaming, frequently risking his own personal liberty upon a single cast—by his love of libidinous dances—by the pleasure he experiences in witnessing the suffering of sentient creatures—by his delight in warfare and all perilous sports—by his desire for vengeance—by the looseness of his notion as to property—by the absence of chastity among his women, and his disregard of female honour—and lastly, by his vague sense of religion—his rude idea of a Creator, and utter absence of all appreciation of the mercy of the Divine Spirit.

It was curious, Mayhew remarked, that no one had thought to use this universal distinction to explain 'certain anomalies in the present state of society among ourselves.' Yet the distinction, he insisted, did apply as much to the English metropolis as to the interior of Africa or Arabia. Like the Bushmen and Bedouins, the London street-folk were noted for the 'greater development of the animal than of the intellectual or moral nature of man . . . for their high cheek-bones and protruding jaws—for their use of a slang language—for their lax ideas of property—for their general improvidence—their repugnance to continuous labour—their disregard of female honour—their love of cruelty—their pugnacity—and their utter want of religion.' And lest there be any doubt of which Londoners he was talking about, he specified that they included pickpockets, beggars, prostitutes, street-sellers, street-performers, cabmen, coachmen, watermen, sailors, 'and suchlike.'

If Mayhew found it curious that no one before him had thought to study the London street-folk from this point of view, we may find it still more curious that Mayhew himself has been studied to so little effect. For in spite of subtitles and chapter titles, of figures on the number of street-folk and graphic descriptions of their nature, Mayhew's work continues to be interpreted as an enquiry on the subject of London Labour and the London Poor. E. P. Thompson has described Mayhew's book as 'the fullest and most vivid documentation of the economic and social problems, the customs, habits, grievances, and individual life experiences of the labouring people of the world's greatest city of the nineteenth century.' And the introduction to an American reprint of the work praises him for having 'uncovered and codified data on the modern proletariat that whole municipal and federal agencies are only now beginning to assemble.'

In view of Mayhew's own description of the street-folk, it is surely bizarre to identify them with 'the modern proletariat'; Marx himself would have been more likely to characterize them, with all the contempt reserved for that term, as 'lumpen-proletariat.' (In fact, as Mayhew presented them, they seem to have been less a class in the Marxist sense than a species in the Darwinian sense.) And it is only a little less bizarre to find one-fortieth (or even one-twentieth) of London's population equated with the 'labouring people of the world's greatest city,' and to find the problems, customs, life-experiences, etc. of Mayhew's 'nomadic race' equated with the problems, customs, life-experiences, etc. of the 'labouring people.' Yet such statements, from reputable and ordinarily authoritative sources, cannot easily be dismissed—not only because they are apt to influence future commentators and historians, nor because they are typical of the judgments of lesser commentators and historians, but also because they reflect something in the work itself which is conducive to this kind of interpretation; and, more important, because the work itself reflects something in the times, something in the subject, which permits the confusion of street-folk with the laboring poor. For even more curious and significant than this confusion on the part of historians is a similar not uncommon confusion on the part of contemporaries.

On the simplest level, part of the confusion, as has been suggested, can be explained in terms of the peculiar publication history of the work. Those contemporaries who had read or heard of the *Morning Chronicle* articles may have carried over into their reading (or non-reading, as was often the case) of the later pamphlets and volumes the impressions and expectations derived from those early articles. Much the same process of assimilation may have occurred in the case of those few historians familiar with the early articles. Mayhew himself encouraged this confusion by opening his first volume with the announcement that the completed work would constitute 'a cyclopaedia of the industry, the want, and the vice of the great Metropolis.' It was all too easy for the reader to take the promise for the fact. (One reviewer was so dazzled by the idea of a 'cyclopaedia' that he assumed it would be 'alphabetically arranged,' as if this would be an added warrant of its comprehensiveness and definitiveness.)

Another source of confusion—more excusable on the part of the contemporary reader than of the professional historian—is the massiveness of the book, with its profusion of facts, figures, tables, charts, life-histories, interviews, and the like, all of which seem to add up to something like the promise of the title and preface. The ordinary reader, assaulted by so many numbers and impressive charts, was apt to overlook the occasional reference to 'one-fortieth' buried in the text (which lacked even the visual distinctiveness of arabic numerals). Nor was he likely to perform the arithmetical calculations which would put those figures in proper proportion to the whole. Moreover, the very profusion of statistics had the illusory effect of suggesting a profusion of people. Somehow the number of tons of shipping handled annually in the London docks, the pounds of refuse collected annually from the London streets, the miles of streets yielding that refuse, were insensibly fused with the numbers of people engaged in loading those ships, collecting that refuse, cleaning those streets. Mayhew was, as his editor justly remarked, 'obsessed with statistics'—although those statistics were not always such as to give his work the 'coherence and authority' claimed for it. What the statistics did do, however, was to give his subject a weightiness it might not otherwise have had, to create an impression of magnitude which facilitated the identification of the street-folk with the laboring people as a whole.

This inflation of subject was compounded by faulty statistics and faulty logical deductions from the statistics. The first volume, of 1851, contained two pages of errata with about eighty items. Both the mistakes in the text and the appended errata (to say nothing of a host of unacknowledged mistakes) were reproduced in every subsequent edition, including the most recent. The other volumes contained no such lists of errata but quite as many mistakes. Typical was one table enumerating the hackney-drivers, stage-drivers, etc., licensed in each year from 1843 to 1850, including a column designated 'total,' in which the figures for all the years were added together to produce a grand total that was most impressive but completely meaningless. (It is as if one were to add together the census figures for each of eight years to arrive at the total population.) Similarly, tables on poor relief and the incidence of crime were presented as evidence of the pauper or criminal population, without any indication of the amount of recidivism—the same person receiving relief or committing crimes more than once during a given period. One of Mayhew's most dramatic figures—that 14 percent of the population of England 'continue their existence either by pauperism, mendicancy, or crime'—contains half a dozen fallacies, starting with a simple arithmetic miscalculation, and including the use of questionable sources, the collation of data pertaining to different periods and otherwise not comparable, and the adding together of several categories to produce the 14 percent as if each were distinct and mutually exclusive—as if paupers did not also, on occasion, figure among the crime statistics, or beggars on the pauper rolls.

When the reader was not being overwhelmed by statistics of this sort, he was being overwhelmed by images, descriptions, case studies, and life histories. The last were presented either in the neutral tones of a commentator or in the dialect—the 'unvarnished' language, as Mayhew put it—of the subject; in either case the emotional impact was all the greater for the apparent objectivity of the narration. One need not suppose that this was the result of any conscious strategy on Mayhew's part—although one of his friends, describing Mayhew's procedure, said that the 'picturesque specimens' brought to the *Morning Chronicle* office told their stories not to the stenographer who was present, but to Mayhew, who then redictated them to the stenographer, 'with an added colour of his own.' But, consciously or not, he could hardly have helped adding such color. He was, after all, a skilful, professional writer trying to reach the largest popular audience. Each article or pamphlet had to make its point and create its effect quickly and dramatically. However scrupulous he may have been in handling his material, however much he may have resisted making a good story better, he could not have helped but make the most of his material, choosing true stories that made good reading rather than true ones that were dull, interspersing dramatic episodes with pedestrian ones so as to give authenticity to the one and drama to the other. Even if every detail had been true (and from the nature of the sources and of the medium this is unlikely), the whole would have added up to something more than the truth—as Mayhew's street-folk seemed to add up to rather more than one-fortieth of the population. (pp. 710-14)

The paradox of Mayhew's work—that the image derived from a relatively small, highly distinctive group of moral and social 'aliens' should get superimposed on the entire class of London Labour and the Poor—has so far been accounted for in terms of the work itself: the history of its publication, the expectations aroused by its title, the encyclopedic-like massiveness of the work, the inflationary effect of its statistics and style, and the blank check of credibility normally extended to the traveler in unknown lands. But the paradox is so great that it could hardly have been generated, still less sustained, by this work alone. And indeed, the work, whether in the earlier series or in the complete edition, was not nearly so often referred to as might be thought. There is, for example, no mention of Mayhew in the letters, memoirs, or biographies of many of his contemporaries who might be expected to have spoken of him: Dickens, George Eliot, Mrs Gaskell, Disraeli, Gladstone, Bright, Mill, Marx, Engels. And there were prominent journals and newspapers that never reviewed or even alluded to his work. To be sure, books do not have to be read or reviewed to be influential. But the paucity of references and reviews does suggest a more limited influence than might be supposed.

Mayhew was, in fact, less influential than symptomatic. If he did not create a novel image of the poor, he did reflect, disseminate, and perpetuate a not uncommon image. The impressionable reader may have been taken in by Mayhew's claim to originality, but one reason why he was taken in was precisely because Mayhew was not all that original, because enough of his 'unknown' world was familiar from other sources to make it credible.

One might plausibly suppose that a major source of this image was the actual condition of the poor at the time, the extreme impoverishment and debasement of the 'Hungry Forties.' Yet it is now generally accepted that the forties were not nearly so hungry as they were once made out to be, and that the late forties were less hungry still. But if the time was not one of acute hunger, it was one of anxiety and crisis: the Irish famine, the financial crisis, revolutions on the Continent and the fear of revolution at home, and, climactically and most disastrously (for London slum-dwellers at any rate), the cholera epidemic.

This atmosphere of anxiety and crisis, a sense of psychic and social dislocation, pervades all of Mayhew's work. The 'miasma' of noxious vapors which contemporaries held responsible for the epidemic seems to have infected the very pages of his book. Although his article on Jacob's Island was not reprinted in the pamphlet series or in the later volumes, the memory and impressions of that visit to the most wretched of all slums at the worst of all times may well have affected his vision of the slum-world in general—and not only his vision but also his expectation, so that he later looked for similar cases of desperation and

degradation. Or perhaps he simply felt impelled to sustain the dramatic pace of that initial article. For whatever reason, the life of the street-folk, as Mayhew described it, had all the symptoms of an epidemic situation—feverish, frenetic, anxiety-ridden, demoralized, and dehumanized. The society he depicted was in a visible state of dissolution, the people in a morbid, pathological condition, a condition that was permanently critical, imminently fatal.

But the forties were not only a decade of crisis. They were also a decade of reform—actual reforms, proposals for reform, and most important in this connection, revelations of the need for reform. Paradoxically, this movement for reform intensified the sense of crisis and reenforced the most extreme image of pathological poverty. The famous Blue Books—Royal Commission and Select Committee reports on sanitation, housing, health, interment, and the like—presented the Condition of the People in terms not very different from Mayhew's; indeed Mayhew himself drew upon the Blue Books for his own work. The reports were ostensibly intended to elicit the condition of the laboring classes as a whole. But inevitably the tendency was to emphasize the worst conditions of the lowliest poor. In part this was the result of an obvious strategy—to attract attention and promote the desired reforms; in part the result of an entirely natural and unconscious disposition towards the dramatic. Even the actual reforms provoked by the reports, reforms intended to ameliorate the worst of those conditions and to some degree at least having that effect, had also the unwitting side-effect of focusing attention on those conditions, thus perpetuating the image of unredeemed and unredeemable poverty.

The most influential of these reports was *The Sanitary Condition of the Labouring Population of Great Britain*, published in 1842 and extensively discussed in parliament, the press, and the journals. In view of the astonishment later expressed by Thackeray and other readers of Mayhew's work over the existence of an unknown world in their very backyards, it is interesting to find the report, a decade earlier, making the same claim to the discovery of the same unknown world:

> The statements of the condition of considerable proportions of the labouring population of the towns into which the present inquiries have been carried have been received with surprise by persons of the wealthier classes living in the immediate vicinity, to whom the facts were as strange as if they related to foreigners or the natives of an unknown country . . . The inhabitants of the front houses . . . have never entered the adjoining courts, or seen the interior of any of the tenements, situated [sic] at the backs of their own houses, in which their own workpeople or dependents reside.

Edwin Chadwick, author of the Sanitary Report, invoked the metaphor of the unknown country for much the same reason as Mayhew later did: to account for the public's ignorance of the shocking conditions described in that report—the foul odors of open cesspools; the garbage, excrement, and dead rats rotting in the streets; the filth and scum floating in the river; the sewage that passed as drinking water. If it was not an entirely successful metaphor (surely the smells at least must have reached the front houses and given the rich a whiff of the world behind them), it did serve to distract attention from the question of the actual extent and pervasiveness of those conditions. How considerable, in fact, were the 'considerable proportions of the labouring population' who were subjected to these noisome conditions? The report did not say. But it did have the effect of irrevocably associating the 'labouring population' of the title with the most vivid, the most dramatic, and the most disagreeable scenes depicted there. And because those scenes were so much worse than anything the reader could be presumed to have witnessed— hence the metaphor of the unknown country—the report also had the effect of making 'foreigners,' aliens, out of the 'labouring population' who lived in such unnatural and repulsive circumstances.

Mayhew's work was, in a sense, a dramatic rendition of the Sanitary Report. Where the report merely had the laboring classes living in the midst of rubbish, filth, offal, and excrement, Mayhew's street-folk, or at least the more memorable of them, lived *off,* actually made their livelihood out of that rubbish and filth. In grisly and fascinating detail, Mayhew described the several varieties of 'streetfinders': bone-grubbers, rag-gatherers, rat-catchers, sweeps, scavengers, dredgermen, and, most unforgettably, the 'pure-finders' ('pure' being the euphemism for dog's dung, which was used in the tanning of leather).

There is a curious and disturbing correspondence between the 'sanitary condition' described by Chadwick and the human condition described by Mayhew. And there is the equally disturbing habit of contemporaries of using the same word to describe both: 'residuum' referred to the offal, excrement, and other waste that constituted the sanitary problem, and was also the name applied to the lowest layer of society that constituted the social and political problem. In Mayhew's work, the two usages of the word dramatically, tragically merge. (pp. 717-18)

> *Gertrude Himmelfarb, "The Culture of Poverty," in* The Victorian City: Images and Realities, *edited by H. J. Dyos and Michael Wolff, Routledge & Kegan Paul, 1973, pp. 707-36.*

Anne Humpherys   (essay date 1977)

[*In the following excerpt, Humpherys discusses* The Criminal Prisons of London, *focusing on Mayhew's presentation of the London penal system and his treatment of women in his writing.*]

Six years before **London Labour and the London Poor** achieved its final four-volume form, Mayhew tried another version of his investigations in **The Great World of London.** It was not to fare much better than his earlier work, and in later years he referred to **The Criminal Prisons of London,** as the new project was then known, as a "wretched fragment of a well-meant scheme." (p. 111)

Mayhew proposed to survey twenty-one different types of life in London, such as Legal London, Criminal London, Fashionable and Serving London. Though this design was abortive, he did manage to survey with some thoroughness London penal institutions and the controversies over prison discipline.

To his modern readers this work does not have the interest of his earlier investigations, although it does provide a fitting conclusion to them for in it Mayhew finally achieved the form of reporting at which he had aimed from the very beginning. . . . [In] both his contributions to the *Morning Chronicle* and in **London Labour,** he wanted to investigate the condition of labor and the poor "scientifically" or inductively and then to present the results of his observations in the deductive mode. In both his earlier works this plan was essentially destroyed by his increasing use of the long interview. Mayhew's loss of control over his projected form of investigations certainly contributed to his failure to complete the two previous works, although external events precipitated the end of each.

The Criminal Prisons of London was another effort on Mayhew's part to follow the "scientific" mode of reporting in his generalizations and observations. This time he was fairly successful in that goal but not because his obsession with detail had lessened. Had the author been given a chance, **The Criminal Prisons** would soon have become inundated by life histories of criminals; but Mayhew was not given the opportunity. Authorities sharply limited what he experienced in each prison. He could report what prison officials allowed him to see and what he felt about what he saw; he could also recount what the authorities told him. But he could not tell his readers what the inmates felt because he was not permitted to talk to them. Only in the juvenile section of Tothill Fields prison did he ask the prisoners a few simple questions in the presence of the guards.

The absence of the interviews, while it eliminated the elements of Mayhew's talent which were most productive, enabled him for once to be organized in his procedures and conclusive about his material. He wrote up the first numbers on each prison after he had collected his information, both official and personal. He might have made several visits to each prison before he sat down to write. He had also collected official documents from the prison officials, read books on the subject (Hepworth Dixon's *The London Prisons* [1850], which originally appeared in the *Daily News,* and George Chesterton's *Revelations of Prison Life* [1856] were the most frequently mentioned), and absorbed information from the prison commissioners and government committees. In addition the various arguments over prison discipline were long established. Mayhew knew in advance what to look for in his prison visits and what points to begin with in his reports. (pp. 111-13)

When the actual survey of the prisons began, he was once again back in form, detailing how things looked at a particular time and place and juggling his data with skill. Here as elsewhere in his work he combined his statistics and the disinterested descriptions of his empirical survey with journalistic liveliness. This led, as it had in the earlier works, to an informative survey. Obviously the form of his reports on the prisons had to differ considerably from his other investigations of the lower classes because much of his data was secondhand. He handled this statistical and documentary burden much more effectively in **The Crimi-**

nal Prisons than in *London Labour* by relegating many of his charts, prison documents, and other such material to footnotes, and allowing the reader, if he wished, to follow the narrative without the interruption of the specific proofs.

Mayhew also tried to maintain journalistic immediacy in his reports. After one or two sections on the history or special characteristics of a prison, he distilled his personal experiences from the several visits that he had made; and he built the survey on a single day at whatever prison was involved. The journalist put his account in the present tense, and he engrossed the reader with a step-by-step account of a typical but seemingly unique day in prison, which began as he walked out his own door. In the trip out to the prison he took in as much of "The Great World of London" as possible.

The advantages of the "day at" structure were mainly literary. In the first place it helped him overcome the repetitiveness of his experiences. The ingrained monotony of prison life appeared novel at every prison because Mayhew's immediate experience, distilled from a larger body of information, was itself different each time. More important, by writing of his experience of each prison as it happened to him, Mayhew gave some sense of what it was like to be a prisoner, a sense lacking in Hepworth Dixon's account of London prisons, the source for much of the popular knowledge on the subject in the 1850s. Each "day at" a prison was severely limited because Mayhew had to see it essentially as the warders did, but the degree to which the prisoners' experience of the regime finally emerges from *The Criminal Prisons of London* is the measure of Mayhew's success as a reporter.

Mayhew looked insistently for different ways of increasing his and his readers' understanding of the prisoners. For instance he tried to project himself into the lives of the inmates as much as he could. He did a stint on the treadmill, and spent an hour in a dark punishment cell. He also developed the glimpses of individual life which he was permitted to see.

> One youth, with closely cut hair, and protruding ears, when asked whether he had ever been in prison before, without the least hesitation replied, "Never, s'elp me!" "I know better," replied the warder, looking earnestly at him. "I'm sure I haven't," continued the lad, with an innocent expression of face. "We'll see whether some of the officers will recognize you," said the examiner. "But it wasn't for felony, sir," muttered the lad, who plainly saw that further concealment was of no avail.

Other means of giving the reader a sense of the individual personalities of the prisoners were less successful. Mayhew relied heavily on descriptive passages, and though his eye for physical detail was as sharp as ever in these passages, his range of vision had been reduced. The drabness of the setting and the identical dress of all the inmates robbed him of his usual source of differentiating material. The only thing that distinguished prisoners was their faces, and the masks the men wore at Pentonville made even this distinction impossible. In prison scenes, then, Mayhew had to project individuality only through analysing facial features.

Physiognomy was considered a fairly exact science by the Victorians, and reliance on it was especially evident in comments on the lower classes. Carlyle saw the criminal character of a Chartist prisoner in "his thick oily skin, his heavy dull-burning eyes, his greedy mouth, the dusky potent insatiable *animalism* that looked out of every feature of him." In the same year as Mayhew wrote *The Criminal Prisons of London* Dickens argued in *Household Words* that you could always tell a man's character from his face.

Mayhew seesawed back and forth between this assumption and what he knew from experience was closer to the truth: "If one were to assemble a like number of individuals from the same ranks of society as those from which most of our criminals come . . . we should find that their cast of countenances differed so little from those seen at the Model Prison, that even the keenest eye for character would be unable to distinguish a photograph of the criminal from the non-criminal congregation." In a footnote to this remark he both denied that "brutal-violence" men "in general" had their characters "stamped on their faces" and asserted that "the generality" of this class were characterized by a "peculiar lascivious look . . . [and] that short and thick kind of neck which is termed 'bull,' and which is generally characteristic of strong passion."

Mayhew's uncertainty about the realibility of physiognomy suggests the uneven responses that he had to other broad questions about prison discipline and the causes of crime. Public debate over the organization of prison life and the ideal balance of punishment and rehabilitation in society's response to its lawbreakers is a perennial phenomenon. The nineteenth century was a good period for the ventilation of some of the different positions as well as for actual prison reform because there were numerous opportunities to try new schemes. Some old prisons were closed—in 1842, the two ancient debtors prisons, the Fleet and the Marshalsea, and in 1855, the City of London House of Correction, Giltspur Compter—and between 1842 and 1852 three new prisons were built. At each stage there was much discussion of the different regimes.

Though there was steady and slow progress toward uniform and decent prisons throughout the nineteenth century, at midcentury there were still many inequalities. Sentences for the same crime differed widely, as did discipline in individual prisons. Not until 1865 was there a fairly uniform standard of treatment, and not until 1877 did the country achieve a nationally administered penal system.

The ideas of the first great prison reformer, John Howard (1726?-1790), who exposed the brutal conditions of English prisons in the late eighteenth century, had a strong influence on public policy in the nineteenth century. Howard had been eager to prevent hardened criminals from corrupting the inexperienced ones while in prison, and this was one of the main goals of the two principal forms of prison discipline in Victorian England: the separate system, in which prisoners lived and usually worked alone in their cells; and the silent system, in which they slept and worked in groups but were prohibited from speaking to one another. To prevent the idleness condemned by Howard and others, all versions of these two systems featured some form of hard labor. This "labor" included the grueling ordeal of the treadmill and the shot drill (moving a pile of cannon balls from one place to another, usually for seventy-five minutes at a time). This latter torture was so physically exhausting that men over forty-five years of age were usually excused.

As far as rehabilitation went, the Victorian prisons were woefully inadequate. Since conventional pieties generally prevented those responsible from really examining the psychology of crime, nearly all efforts at rehabilitation were directed toward religious conversion. A common justification for the separate system was that it induced a self-examination which would lead to a religious conversion sufficient to enable a prisoner to resist a life of crime in the future. Mayhew himself was obsessed with self-communion in prisoners although he was uneasy about its effectiveness as a deterrent for future crime. (pp. 116-19)

The prison inspectors, created by an act of 1835, had consistently favored separation. The 1865 prison act said that all local prisons should have separate cells. In the 1860s, penal regimes seemed at their harshest, as did public opinion on these matters, perhaps in response to an outbreak of violent crimes in London. Carlyle and Dickens again reflect public sentiment. Both advocated flogging and life imprisonment for repeated offenders. Mayhew's attitude at that point was almost as stern. He argued in 1865 that first offenders should get light sentences and occupational training and that then the government should "insure" them to their future employers. Afterward any repeated offenders should get *penal servitude for life.*"

When Mayhew began his survey of prisons in 1856, however, he had not made up his mind about the issue. He at first denied that the evidence irresistibly pointed to any conclusion. Invoking his usual excuse when uncertain about a social question, he hid behind the role of "collector of facts": "it forms no part of our present object to weigh the advantages and disadvantages of the altered mode of dealing with our convicts." He soon abandoned this position under the weight of his direct experience.

In the beginning Mayhew relegated his judgment on the merits of four different forms of prison discipline to a long appendix to the general descriptive section entitled "The London Convict Prisons and the Convict Population." There he devoted the least attention to the classification and the "mark" systems. In the classification mode of prison organization, designed to prevent corruption of new prisoners by old, criminals were incarcerated in cells and buildings according to their offenses. Mayhew was horrified by the looseness of this system, for habitual criminals were not always arrested for the same crime. In any case the expense of separate prisons for different crimes was prohibitive.

In the mark system, praised by Dixon and by Dickens, a man was "sentenced to perform a certain quantity of labour [which] . . . the convict would be bound to perform before he could regain his freedom, whether he chose to occupy one year or twenty about it." Mayhew was also fa-

vorably disposed to this system of work sentences rather than time sentences because it seemed to induce a sense of personal responsibility and the proper attitude toward work. Since the process was not operating at any of the London prisons, however, he did not linger over its advantages.

That left the separate and silent systems. Mayhew's first judgment was unqualified: they were "as much *in extremis* as was the old plan of allowing indiscriminate intercourse to take place among all classes of prisoners." In addition, he said (though he later seemed to change his mind), both systems failed in rehabilitating the criminal because "they one and all make labour a *punishment.*" At this point he appeared to recognize some conflict between the punitive and rehabilitative processes, but the idea later slipped away from him. Mayhew had no suggestions as to what to substitute for the unproductive labor of the treadmill and the shot drill. For example, he was against women prisoners sewing for tailors because such unfair competition drove down the wages of the women seamstresses outside the prison.

At this point in his discussion Mayhew was equally contemptuous about the only overt effort at rehabilitation in prison—religious conversion. "Can it be said that the merchant in the city honours his bills for the love of God? . . . It is worse than foolish to strive to give any such canting motives to criminals, and certainly *not* true, when it is asserted that people cannot be made honest by any other means than by special interpositions of Providence." Usually such an insistence simply forced the convict to add hypocrisy to his other sins, Mayhew concluded.

In this first evaluation of prison organization, Mayhew saw weaknesses in all the systems; but after he had investigated Pentonville and Coldbath Fields prisons he was in a position to make more specific criticisms. In Coldbath Fields most of the inmates slept alone in their cells but worked together in groups. At Pentonville most prisoners were on the separate system. Mayhew noted that the high rate of madness and suicide attempts indicated that both systems could exact a heavy psychological toll from the inmates. Nonetheless he felt the separate system was the best because it both punished and reformed. Still he could not ignore the fact that "the ratio of lunacy at Pentonville [is] still almost as high again as the normal rate deduced from the average of all other prisons."

Reformation under the separate system might occur, he said, because this system "seeks not only [to put an end to the contamination of prisoners by stopping all *inter*-communion among them], but at the same time to bring about the reformation of the prisoners by inducing *self*-communion," a contention Mayhew had earlier seemed to reject. Now he felt that solitude would lead the convict to see the error of his ways. He also believed that the system made labor "so agreeable a relief to the monotony of solitude, that it positively becomes a punishment to withhold it, and thus, by rendering idleness absolutely irksome to the prisoner, causes him to find a pleasure in industry."

He also thought the silent system was more inhumane. Mayhew came to this conclusion by projecting himself into the lives of the prisoners whom he saw at Coldbath Fields, but he offered a statistical "proof " of it. By bringing men together but preventing them from speaking, the silent system imposed a far greater strain on the convicts than did isolation. This was demonstrated by the very high number of extra punishments the officials at Coldbath Fields had to inflict in order to ensure silence. This actually proved nothing, of course, since the lack of opportunity at Pentonville to do anything to be punished for would naturally result in lower numbers. To help alleviate the strain of the silent system, Mayhew suggested the men be read to while they worked.

He remained uncertain enough about the value of any of these prison regimes to offer a completely different one. His suggestion was not very original, and he may have taken it from Dixon, who argued that prisons should surround "the offender in his state of expiation" with conditions "as near as is possible consistent with strict discipline, to those in which the new-made man will be placed on liberation."

Mayhew was probably attracted to this idea because it brought together a number of aspects of his thought. Coupling his theory of man's natural reluctance to work with the definition of a good citizen implicit in the categories of those who will, can't, and won't work, he concluded that only by changing a criminal's attitude toward work could he be reformed. Instead of having food, clothing, and security given outright to him when he first arrived, Mayhew suggested:

> We would have every man placed, on his entering a jail, upon the punishment diet, *i.e.* his eleemosynary allowance of food should be only a pound of bread and water *per diem.* We would *begin* at this point, and make all creature comforts beyond it purchasable, as it were, by the amount of labour done, instead of first leading the prisoner, as now, to believe that he is entitled to receive such creature comforts without work, and being *afterwards* obliged to resort to the punishment diet as a means of enforcing a certain amount of work from him."

Yet Mayhew was not convinced of the value of even this system, for when in August 1856, the same period that he was posing this new system in *The Criminal Prisons of London,* he addressed the committee working to abolish capital punishment, he never mentioned the idea of convicts working for their board in prison. Instead he simply advocated that a modified separate system be used in place of capital punishment.

In this connection let us look at Mayhew's position on capital punishment. Basically he argued against the sentence on the ground that it failed as a deterrent. He believed that it hardened criminals rather than deterred them because it did not appeal to their better selves. More significant Mayhew advanced an important moral objection to capital punishment: the very act of the State taking a life seems to justify an individual's taking one. In the midst of other irrelevant or unsubstantiated objections, this challenge of Mayhew's is still unanswered. That he could see that state or official violence can breed citizen violence is a tribute to his insight into the individual mind and to his recognition of society's share in the causes of crime. It would perhaps be too much to expect him also to see that this argument was far more significant than the necessity of punishment "rendering [the criminal] penitent" and "purifying his nature." Mayhew's paper on capital punishment was another example of his ability to expound popular sentiments and profound insights in the same breath.

Other uncertainties of opinion found voice in *The Criminal Prisons of London.* Mayhew's remarks on juvenile offenders were intelligent and sensitive if not original, but those on women criminals were plain silly. Both discussions grew out of a general survey of the causes of crime which in turn was part of a discussion of rehabilitation and crime prevention. Referring obliquely to the ragged-school controversy in the *Morning Chronicle,* Mayhew showed he was still unrepentant for his attacks on education as a deterrent to crime: "Some years back . . . we took the trouble of testing the greater number of the popular reasons for crime, by collating the statistics in connection with each theory, and thus found that none of the *received* explanations [i.e. ignorance, overcrowding, poverty, drunkenness, original sin, etc.] would bear the searching test of figures." Although earlier in his career he had been unwilling to give his explanations for men and women becoming criminals, in 1856 he was ready to do so. Hints of his position had appeared early in *The Criminal Prisons of London,* as well as in *London Labour and the London Poor;* but the experiences of Tothill Fields prison for boy and female offenders gave him the opportunity to formulate his thoughts on the issues of rehabilitation as they were linked to the causes of crime.

Mayhew had first visited Tothill Fields prison in the course of his investigations of the ragged schools in 1850, and perhaps his many years of thinking about the problem of juvenile crime enabled him to open the section on Tothill Fields prison with some ideas about the causes of it, a topic which itself immediately led him to a larger subject—the general nature of crime and of the criminal. The ambivalences of *London Labour* reappeared in this section. Mayhew reiterated the idea expressed in the first number of *London Labour:* the criminal and vagrant population of England were an inevitable subclass of the population, a kind of "wandering tribe" who were parasitic and lived off the industrious part of society. In this definition Mayhew reflected the Victorian belief in the existence of a criminal class "which lived a life of its own separate from the rest of the community." Most Victorians believed that elimination of this class would eliminate crime.

Mayhew accepted the idea of a criminal class, but his passion for classification led him to recognize that the "professional" criminals were only a part of the problem. He had noted in the introductory section on "nonworkers" in the extra volume of *London Labour and the London Poor* that most current theorists about crime erred because they did not distinguish between "habitual" criminals, who broke the law no matter what, and "casual" criminals, who were driven to break the law by reduced circumstances or economic conditions. In his view only the first constituted the criminal class.

Mayhew rightly saw that the crucial element as far as the state was concerned were the members of the criminal classes who were forced into crime. The prison system should direct its efforts toward preventing these "casual" criminals from repeating and becoming "habitual." Since most boys started as casual offenders, by rehabilitating them the "professional" criminal class could best be reduced.

The question was how. This subject had sparked a long discussion which culminated two years before Mayhew's survey in an act of Parliament establishing reformatories for juvenile offenders. This had been preceded by the Select Committee on Juvenile Offenders in 1852 which in turn was the result of public pressure, much of it generated by Mary Carpenter and Matthew Davenport Hill. Mary Carpenter's influential book *Juvenile Delinquents—Their Condition and Treatment* appeared in 1853, and it is peculiar that Mayhew did not mention it in his discussion. She classified juvenile offenders even more narrowly than he did and made a number of similar remarks. Her main thrust was to substitute reformatories for prisons, and perhaps Mayhew did not mention her work because he had chosen to limit his subject to prisons and their relation to boy offenders.

Mayhew shared with Mary Carpenter the belief that little could be done toward changing a boy's way of life in prisons as they were then organized. The cursory instruction in reading and writing could not do it, Mayhew asserted, reverting to his familiar sentiments: reading and writing "are but the means of obtaining either *good* or *bad* knowledge, according to the cultivation and tendencies of the mind which uses them." Nor did he think much of the job training available because it was too limited in scope and uncertain in prospect.

If neither education nor job training by itself could rehabilitate boy offenders, what could? Mayhew felt that the solution had to lie in steps taken both before the boys reached prison and after they left it. The crimes committed by children were due, he said in several places and in several ways, "mainly to a want of proper parental control," a common reason given for juvenile crime throughout the century.

Mayhew knew from personal experience that parents could not be forced to accept their responsibilities, but this difficulty did not doom the effort to eliminate juvenile offenders. Although he was not an advocate of state intervention in general, here, as in the regulation of low wages, it seemed the only hope. If natural parents would not, then the state must accept responsibility for its citizens, particularly for juvenile delinquents. The state must become a foster parent, he said, a sentiment Dickens would echo in "The Short-Timers" in *All the Year Round*. Once again Mayhew's expression of this common idea was more trenchant in its vision of social accountability when he repeated it in his essay on capital punishment, perhaps because of the more identifiably sympathetic audience. "Society is only beginning to understand that it owes a duty even to its criminals, and that the moral pestilence of crime is due almost to the same guilty neglect of those laws for the social health of a State, as the physical pestilence of cholera is due to the violation of sanitary principles among the people." What "those laws" for social health were Mayhew did not say. He did not make any practical suggestions as to how the state could take over children from bad parents, nor did he note any of the difficulties of doing so. As in his remarks on the causes of low wages, he was wary of any concrete suggestions.

In one case, however—his attacks on magistrate courts and on the inequities of the law practiced there—his simply pointing out the problem was challenging. As with his feelings about religious conversion as a means of rehabilitation, Mayhew seemed to hold two different opinions about judges in the early and later parts of his work. Very early in "The Great World of London" part of the volume, in a general look at "Legal London," Mayhew gave fulsome praise to judges: "If there be one class in whose iron integrity every Englishman has the most steadfast faith—of whose Pilate-like righteousness he has the profoundest respect, and in the immaculateness of whose honour he feels a national pride—it is the class to whom the high privilege of dispensing justice among us has been intrusted, and who constitute at once the chiefs and the ornaments of the profession of which we are about to treat." This sounds like what his father might have said to him when he expounded the glories of the law to his young son.

Mayhew's iteration of these sentiments sounds the more strange because the only judges we catch a glimpse of in *The Criminal Prisons* turn out to be among the causes of juvenile crime. After the establishment of reformatories in England, fewer children found their way into prison, but there were still felons under ten years of age in some prisons. If the threat of prison was to be a deterrent to juvenile crime, boys should be kept out of jail as long as possible, since its threat lay in its unknown quality, Mayhew said. "The rule with the Middlesex magistrates, though, appears to be the very reverse, viz., to thrust a lad into prison on the most trifling occasion, and to familiarize him, even in his childhood, with scenes that he should be made acquainted with the very last of all in his manhood."

At this point he had even more devastating charges to make about justice in England. As he extended his attacks on the magistrates he came to the very brink of a recognition of class discrimination in justice. As far as trifling actions such as stealing a peach or breaking a window were concerned, there was definitely one law for the rich and one for the poor. In Tothill Fields, he said with barely concealed anger, "we find little creatures of six years of age branded with a felon's badge—boys, not even in their teens, clad in the prison dress, for the heinous offense of throwing stones, or obstructing highways, or unlawfully knocking at doors—crimes which the very magistrates themselves, who committed the youths, must have assuredly perpetrated in their boyhood, and which, if equally visited, would consign almost every child in the kingdom to a jail."

Mayhew was equally disturbed by the number of people he found in prison because they had defaulted on a debt

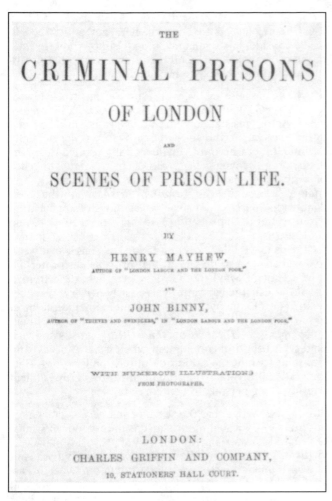

Title page for The Criminal Prisons of London.

or could not pay a fine levied by the magistrate. He was particularly moved when he learned that in Tothill Fields the women prisoners who were not prostitutes had nearly all been imprisoned for their inability to pay a fine. The use of jail as an alternative to paying a fine was another way in which the law discriminated against the poor. Some men "are incarcerated for their poverty, rather than their transgression." In his suggestion for an alternative way of meting out justice in matters of fines, he recognized class differences. The law should not always set the same fine for the same crime but should moderate it according to the means of the offender: "Assuredly the well-to-do and, therefore, the well-educated, have not one tithe of the excuse for their transgressions that can be fairly pleaded by those who have seldom been schooled by any kinder master than want and ignorance."

Mayhew at this point in his life's work was as close as he ever came to a significant social analysis which would break unreservedly with received opinion. It had taken him some seven years of erratic social investigation to reach a position where his antagonism to the Victorian attitudes endorsed by his father might become conscious. Though his past history did not indicate much chance that he could reconcile his uncertainties now at the age of

forty-four, the uncompromising attack on the way class could determine justice in England, and his shrewd views on social accountability in his essay on capital punishment at least suggest that if he had had the chance to continue *The Great World of London* he might finally have achieved a new social vision. The abandonment of the subject of labor and the poor when *The Great World of London* failed—an event just weeks away when he wrote his remarks on justice—destroyed such a chance. Without that topic Mayhew never again rose above the commonplace.

His banality is painfully evident in the discussion on women criminals which followed that on boys. Victorian attitudes toward women are notorious and have been the subject of an increasing number of studies. Woman was idolized both as the source of the moral standards of society and as the bulwark of peace and security. She was at the same time considered inferior to man. Though her main role was as mother, she was taught to reject her body, and to lace her thoughts as tightly as she did her stays, hiding all "lower" notions as thoroughly as her voluminous undergarments hid her shape. Though he certainly did not subscribe to these notions, as intelligent a man as John Stuart Mill idolized his wife in a manner that to us seems incredible; one should not be dismayed perhaps that Mayhew, a man of far less intellectual powers, maintained the most thoroughly conventional ideas about women.

In the novel *Whom to Marry* (1848), the kind of simple satire on the foibles of the ladies which *Punch* published frequently, Henry and Augustus Mayhew had implicitly defined their ideal woman. Though Mayhew's wife was certainly neither as silly nor as avaricious as the "bad" woman in this novel, nor as sweetly empty-headed as the "good" sister, the moral was clear: the way to a happy marriage if one were a woman, was to be passive and docile, weak and weak-headed, soft, and sweet-tempered—and, if a man, to find such a creature.

That Mayhew himself believed this is clear from his other remarks on women. Explaining the devotion of some prostitutes to their fancy men, he said "the admirable with woman would thus appear to be the powerful rather than the sensuously beautiful; they seem to prefer bravery to symmetry." Mayhew did remark that in this if in nothing else the prostitute was like all women.

In *The Criminal Prisons of London*, Mayhew expressed his attitudes on women in their grossest form. His surrender to the conventions here as elsewhere weakened his prose style, which became exaggerated in its metaphors:

> In a natural state of things, it has clearly been intended by the Great Architect of the universe that the labour of the man should be sufficient for the maintenance of the family—the frame of the woman being in itself evidence that she was never meant to do the hard work of society, whilst the fountains of life that she carries in her bosom, as well as the kindlier and more affectionate qualities of her nature, all show that her duty was designed to be that of a mother and a

nurse to the children, rather than a fellow-labourer with the man.

On such assumptions as this Mayhew based his analysis of female crime, which to him simply meant prostitution. (pp. 120-30)

Mayhew did not intend to survey prostitution at this point, but he used the sections on women prisoners to make some points about it. Earlier he had recognized some difficulty in insisting that prostitution was a criminal act. As we have seen, he was trying to answer the question of whether or not there was an innate revulsion against prostitution. A few years later, in *The Upper Rhine,* he seemed to admit that the oldest profession might be inevitable. Society had only three choices, he said: illegitimate children, "public women," or that anathema "early marriages." He offered no judgment as to the best choice, although his society frowned on both illegitimate children and early and financially insecure marriages. By the time he wrote *The Criminal Prisons* this disinterested response had disappeared.

Mayhew's attempts to account for prostitution in *The Criminal Prisons of London* had little consistency except his abhorrence of the practice. Sometimes he inferred social causes, sometimes biological, sometimes psychological, both innate and learned. In this multiplicity of explanations he reflected his age. Ignoring his early attempt to deal with it historically, Mayhew turned to psychological explanations. Prostitution was a substitute for honest work; like thieving for males it was "an easy mode of living" and so was resorted to by those women who "are born to labour for their bread, but who find work inordinately irksome to their natures, and pleasure as inordinately agreeable to them." They were the female members of the roving tribes who "have only to trade upon their personal charms in order to secure the apparent luxury of an idle life."

Although Mayhew first introduced his explanation of prostitution as the avoidance of work in the extra volume, he did qualify it there by developing a four-part classification to distinguish types according to their motivations. As he saw it at that point, each social class had a different motive for turning to prostitution. "The prostitutes who proceed from the *poorer* classes of society become depraved because they perceive that greater creature-comforts can be obtained in our community by immoral practices than by regular industry; whereas those prostitutes who proceed from the *middle* classes are led to adopt a vicious life principally from the craving for admiration," he said, echoing one of the most common Victorian explanations of prostitution, namely the inordinate love of vanity.

In addition to these two types who took to it were those who were "*driven* to prostitution, either through want or seduction" or "those who are *bred* to a vicious course of life, being early depraved or allowed by their parents to associate with whomsoever and go whithersoever they please." Despite the important distinctions in this classification, Mayhew gave the name *prostitute* to all women with any sort of irregular arrangement. This inflexibility itself resulted in higher numbers of professional "public women," though Mayhew did not see it that way. As Kellow Chesney has pointed out, the tendency of the Victorians to consider any woman who had "slipped" on the level of the professional harlot all too often assured that prostitution did indeed become her actual fate.

Mayhew nowhere in his work showed an awareness of what Mrs. Gaskell hinted cautiously in *Ruth* (1853), and what Acton insisted on strenuously: the middle- and upper-class men who used the prostitutes were equally "criminal." For his part Mayhew finally seemed to lay the blame on a psychological weakness in women. The mark of a civilized man or woman was the capacity to feel shame, he said in *The Criminal Prisons,* for the main counter to anarchy in a society was "love of approbation and dread of disapprobation." If this were true, a woman could turn prostitute only if she had no sense of shame, for then she was "left without any moral sense, as it were, to govern and restrain the animal propensities of her nature." Though Mayhew did not specify what the woman should be ashamed about, it was clearly her body and her sexuality. Like many people he thought shame the most important curb to licentiousness, stating the sentiment quite openly in *The Upper Rhine:* "Love, in its spiritual quality, is beautiful enough; but when it has the least animal taint with it, the exhibition of passion becomes—like the gratification of any inordinate appetite—grossly offensive for other persons to contemplate."

Still he did realize that the sense of shame was not innate but must be educated in girls just as industriousness must be taught to boys. This explanation of prostitution had the virtue of implying that the "crime" was largely the result of environmental factors. Mayhew could not leave this assertion alone, however; on the very page after he said that shame must be taught in order to curb prostitution, he posited a deterministic cause for the shamelessness which lay behind female crime. Female criminals, he said, were frequently given over to violent outbursts of temper, which were "perhaps referable to the same derangement of functions Esquirol, in his work on madness, has shown to be intimately connected with insanity among women."

These mixed responses toward women in general and women criminals in particular led Mayhew down some curious paths. While visiting the prison nursery in Tothill Fields, he remarked how the mothers there did not have "the brazen looks and the apparent glorying in their shame that prevails among the more debased of the female prisoners." Indeed, he said, warming to the subject, "the very fact of their being mothers is sufficient to prove that these prisoners do not belong to the class of 'public women,' since it is a wonderous ordination of Benevolence that such creatures as are absolutely shameless and affectionless should be childless as well; so that the sight of these baby prisoners was at once a proof to us that the hearts of the women that bore them were not utterly withered and corrupt."

Despite the sentimentality in these remarks, they do demonstrate some enlightenment on Mayhew's part. Like Mrs. Gaskell, Mayhew here repudiated the time-honored notion that the child of a "fallen" woman was a badge of shame. To Mrs. Gaskell, in *Ruth,* a child could be the means of moral reformation of the mother; to Mayhew, in *The Criminal Prisons,* a child was the sign of a basically good heart. In a later recounting of his prison trip, moreover, Mayhew further modified the sentimentality of this remark by touching on social realities. In *Young Benjamin Franklin* the matron of the prison stated that even if the children touched their mothers' hearts, when the women left prison there was little for them to do, however good their intentions, but to return to their old ways. As a result the children of these mothers would grow up into "young devils."

In Mayhew's attitude toward women prisoners we witness forcefully the important role his interviews played in his earlier works and the weakness their absence exposed in *The Criminal Prisons.* In the previous surveys Mayhew's long interviews controlled his own triteness and gave to the whole an air of sympathy, balance, and realism. Though in direct statements he seemed to have little charity for women forced into prostitution, in his report of the meeting of needlewomen who were also prostitutes, he seemed to be on their side because he gave each woman a chance to explain fully the details of her life. In addition, side by side with his own rigid moralizing about prostitutes, he faithfully repeated the opinions of the lower classes, who were invariably sympathetic toward the "women of the town." Much of Mayhew's own censoriousness was undermined by the tolerance expressed by his informants:

> "Now, those poor things that walk down there," [a street seller tells Mayhew] (intimating, by a motion of the head, a thoroughfare frequented by girls of the town), "they're often customers, but not near so good as they was ten year ago; no, indeed, nor six or eight year. *They* like something that bites in the mouth, such as peppermint-rock, or ginger drops. . . . I've trusted them ha'pennies and pennies, sometimes. They always paid me. Some that held their head high like, might say: 'I really have no change; I'll pay you to-morrow.' She hadn't no change, poor lass, sure enough, and she hadn't nothing to change either, I'll go bail."

By publishing nearly everything his informants said and by equating their opinions with his own in terms of the space and emphasis he gave them, Mayhew ensured a balance in his earlier works wherever the author's prejudices might distort the picture.

Mayhew wrote only ten more pages following his observations on women and boy prisoners. John Binny finished the survey with dispatch five years later. He kept the statistical data to a minimum and limited himself to describing the regime of each remaining prison with few comments or interpolations. His part in *The Criminal Prisons of London* was very minor, and it is unfortunate for Mayhew's reputation that Binny is consistently listed as a co-author. In its summary of prevailing controversies about the penal system and its evocation of prison life, *The Criminal Prisons of London* forms a solid part of Mayhew's achievement. It also sadly marks the end of his survey of London's poor and of London's workers. (pp. 130-34)

Anne Humpherys, in her Travels into The

Poor Man's Country: The Work of Henry Mayhew, *The University of Georgia Press, 1977, 240 p.*

Richard Maxwell   (essay date 1978)

[*In the following excerpt, Maxwell discusses Mayhew's perceptions and presentation of the street people of London.*]

[Mayhew's] choice of subject matter—for it was a conscious choice and not a whim or an accident—has worked to both the advantage and disadvantage of Mayhew's reputation. The advantage has been that the street-folk were an extraordinarily diverse and verbal population; Mayhew's talent for getting them to talk has often been praised, as has his instinct for communicating the variety of street life. He had, observes W. H. Auden [see excerpt dated 1968], "a passion for the idiosyncrasies of character and speech such as only the very greatest novelists have exhibited. . . . It is astonishing, reading Mayhew, to learn how many of the poor were self-employed and the extraordinary diversity of the ways by which they managed to earn a living, however meager." Raymond Williams [in *The Country and the City*] also praises "Mayhew's incomparable records of conversations," and then adds: "It is not only the convincing talk. It is Mayhew's range and care, about the details of so many kinds of work. . . . "

Auden and Williams are careful to praise *London Labour* both as literature and as a sociological study. Those who have concentrated on the second aspect have not always been so kind. In 1955, when the Mayhew boom was just beginning, Ruth Glass duly noted the vividness and scope of *London Labour,* and then continued:

> Despite his apt use of various methods of investigation and presentation, he did not produce a social survey but social reportage of a high order of sympathy and versatility. There is no theme; by and large there is description without selection and analysis. . . . And though his volumes describe a large variety of occupations and types, their scope is rather narrow: they deal only with one nomadic heterogeneous section of the London working classes—those who traded, morally or immorally, in the streets and those who worked in the streets.
>
> ["Urban Sociology (Great Britain)," *Current Sociology,* IV (1955)]

These complaints have been repeated and amplified in subsequent studies. Gertrude Himmelfarb's formidable criticisms . . . [see excerpt dated 1973] develop Glass's main points. For Himmelfarb, the reader of *London Labour* is "overwhelmed by images, descriptions, case studies, and life histories. The last were presented either in the neutral tones of a commentator or in the dialect—the 'unvarnished' language, as Mayhew put it—of the subject; in either case the emotional impact was all the greater for the apparent objectivity of the narration." The variety and liveliness of the book are by this account positive disadvantages: at best distractions, at worst rhetorically and factually misleading. The heart of this deception is Mayhew's obsessive concern with the street-folk. "Then, as now, what passed as 'the culture of poverty' was the culture of a small subgroup of the poor." No one, as yet, has really answered this charge. So sympathetic a student of Mayhew as Anne Humpherys is inclined to accept Himmelfarb's charge, albeit with qualifications. The fine essays in *The Unknown Mayhew* tactfully circumvent *London Labour,* the better to concentrate on the *Morning Chronicle* letters which preceded it. These letters, where the street-folk are only one of many groups studied, become Mayhew's masterpiece, his genuine—and historically relevant—accomplishment. Even Auden and Williams note regretfully that Mayhew's manner of thinking seems to belong to another age; comparing Mayhew to Charles Booth, Williams says that "Booth's deliberate impersonality—mapping and grading before visiting; systematic tabulation—is less readable and less attractive, but it belongs to a way of seeing which the new society itself was producing." Thus the most enthusiastic readers of *London Labour* have had their doubts; the book starts to seem like a wonderful indulgence, a sort of holiday after the *Morning Chronicle* letters.

London Labour, then, is not to be trusted. That this is so, however, may say more about scholarly ways of reading the book than about its intrinsic merits. What is needed, perhaps, is a fresh understanding of how Mayhew's obsession with the streets allowed him to move towards a distinctive vision of city life—a vision which asks for the serious consideration of literary and historical students alike. This essay investigates two types of evidence illuminating Mayhew's intentions: first, the page-by-page logic or illogic of his classifications, his breakdown of the street-people into species and sub-species; and second, continuities between minor work, mostly journalistic, and the huge monument of *London Labour.* This accumulation of small facts yields some conclusions about the aesthetic and political implications of Mayhew's great compendium. (pp. 88-90)

One attraction of the street-people was that they were an undiscovered population; a second attraction was that they were in a state of economic crisis. The crisis was partly inherent in the trades themselves, which tended to be last resorts. One needed, as a rule, little capital and no permission to start in a business like sandwich-vending, so people began and either got on or failed. In the latter case, there was the workhouse or the possibility of moving on to another street trade; even if success did come, "of all modes of obtaining subsistence, that of street-selling is the most precarious," dependent on tolerable weather and subject to seasonal fluctuation. Finally, social and economic pressures of a new intensity were threatening the street-folk. The people Mayhew interviewed often mention that they had made more money ten or twenty years previously. Furthermore, many of the principal occupations seemed to be disappearing by mid-century. This pattern, not obvious at first, becomes clear as one reads:

> Of all the great capitals, London has least the appearance of antiquity, and the Thames has a peculiarly modern aspect. It is no longer the "silent highway," for its silence is continually broken by the clatter of steamboats. This change has mate-

rially affected the position and diminished the number of the London watermen. . . . A few years ago the street pie-trade was very profitable, but it has been almost destroyed by the "pie-shops". . . . The sale of books by auction, in the streets, is now inconsiderable and irregular. From this historical sketch it appears evident that the ballad-singer and seller of to-day . . . is, indeed, the minstrel having lost caste and being driven to play cheap. The number of Vermin-Destroyers and Rat-Catchers who ply their avocation in London has of late years become greatly diminished. One cause which I heard assigned for this was that many ruinous old buildings and old streets had been removed, and whole colonies of rats had been thereby extirpated. The street-sweeping machine, therefore, assumes an importance as another instance of the displacement, or attempted displacement, of the labour of man by the mechanism of an engine. After the excavation of the various docks, and after the larger shipping had departed from the river, the finders were obliged to content themselves with the chances of mere dredging. . . . The railway communication supplies the local-dealer with fish, vegetables, or any perishable article, with such rapidity and cheapness that the London itinerant's occupation in the towns and villages about the metropolis is now half gone.

The point is not that all the street trades declined in this way. By Mayhew's account, however, a large number of them did, and in the long run most of them were to contract or disappear entirely. Even in the forties and fifties, many of the street-people were put out of work by specifically modern trends. Discounting competition from the shops, which had been going on for centuries, the street trades were threatened by urban renewal, the building of docks, the growth of transportation, mechanization and marketing, even the decline of aristocratic patronage. These developments, illustrated in the passages above, mesh with each other in terms of what was happening to London. The city had grown too large to operate as it had in the past; new kinds of services were becoming necessary and these services (drainage for instance) had to be developed systematically, through government or large business concerns and with comprehensive planning. The free lancer may have survived for a time—his numbers may even have increased in the short run—but his ultimate fate grew even clearer. (pp. 91-3)

[Does] the free-form street-collecting which *London Labour* describes hold out real possibilities for an improvement in the quality of poor people's lives? There are two possible answers to this question, both of them embodied in a conflict which took place before Mayhew's eyes: "The pure-finder [Pure is dog dung] is often found in the open streets, as dogs wander where they like . . . they may be seen pursuing their avocation in almost every street in and about London, excepting such streets as are now cleansed by the 'street orderlies,' of whom the pure-finders grievously complain, as being an unwarrantable interference with the privileges of their class." The pure-finder is the old, self-employed kind of street-collector. The street-orderly, on the other hand, is a new phenomenon, described in detail a few pages later: "That the street-orderly system is the only rational and efficacious mode of street cleansing both theory and practice assure us. . . . Mr. Cochrane . . . has introduced, in connection with this body, a system of scavaging which, while it employs a greater number of hands, produces such additional benefits as cannot but be considered an equivalent for the increased expenditure."

Cochrane is one of the few philanthropists Mayhew admired. His idea was that thousands of those without regular employment could be hired to clean the streets, each man to clean continuously and within a limited area. Through financing from local government, the men would be paid relatively good wages and would, Mayhew estimates, save millions of pounds' damage caused annually by urban pollution. This system is attactive. Not even the street culture is dispossessed, for many belonging to it would have a chance to engage in roughly the same kind of work and yet make regular wages instead of depending on chance and weather. If anything is lost in the implementation of such plans, it is an element in London life rather difficult to describe. Mayhew tries:

> In London, where many, in order to live, struggle to extract a meal from the possession of an article which seems utterly worthless, nothing must be wasted. Many a thing which in a country town is kicked by the penniless out of their path even, or examined and left as meet only for the scavenger's cart, will in London be snatched up as a prize; it is money's worth. A crushed and torn bonnet, for instance, or, better still, an old hat, napless, shapeless, crownless, and brimless, will be picked up in the street, and carefully placed in a bag by one class of street-folk—the STREET-FINDERS. And to tempt the well-to-do to *sell* their second-hand goods, the street-trader offers the barter of shapely china . . . for "the rubbish."

Mayhew hovers in this passage on the borderline between two types of description. He is describing an economic condition and also a state of consciousness. These categories are not completely separable. When a bone-grubber says, "The greatest prize I ever found was the brass cap of the nave of a coach-wheel," he implies that he counts on trifles, on junk, to make a living. However, economic necessity does not subsume another level of motivation. The street-people, like London itself, could be defined through their relationship to junk. The class was itself a form of waste, individuals thrown out by the economic machine of the city as superfluous beings. This economic irrelevance became a source of identity, pointing such people towards the universe of excrement or cast-off things—a universe they were specially equipped to transform, since only they could feel towards it that combination of empathy and miserly delight which *London Labour* describes.

This point might seem a little on the frivolous side. Were the street-people's desperation to have been eliminated from London surely no one would have missed it. Suffering is suffering, and should be striven against even if certain appropriate emotions are rendered impossible. At the same time, the street state of mind is important to Mayhew. He would never argue against something like the system of street-orderlies, yet there is a strong undercurrent in *London Labour* which pulls him in just that direction. Images of suffering in the book are balanced by images of freedom; visions of the good life can slip into visions of dullness.

One way of explaining this ambivalence is suggested by an article Mayhew published in *Douglas Jerrold's Shilling Magazine* a few years before *London Labour.* The article owes much to a philosophy of education which its author had outlined in a previous book, and which is now used to the purpose of speculation within a framework of associational psychology. "What," Mayhew asks, "is the cause of surprise?" Out of this question develops a thesis, that "there are certain emotions which arise in the mind, invariably on the stoppage or alteration of the natural current of our thoughts." Mayhew proposes to study these emotions, chief among them surprise: "The term *Surprise* stands for that emotion which arises in the mind immediately upon the occurrence of an event which is wholly disconnected with our previous thoughts, and, consequently, for which we were totally unprepared. . . . Imprimis of the first state of mind—the antecedent train of thoughts. This is either a state of deep attention or dreamy reverie." Surprise, then, is defined in contrast to attention or reverie. It is "the abrupt introduction into the mind of some *sensation* which is wholly disconnected with our previous conceptions . . . the intensity of the Surprise depends, among other things upon the degree of disconnection. . . . 'The discontinuous in our sensations . . . produces a correspondent jar and discord in our frame.' " These comments repeat rather than amplify each other but they do emphasize a key term in Mayhew's vocabulary. The opposition between surprise and attention-reverie is shadowed by a more general conflict between *continuity* and *discontinuity.*

Mayhew gives common examples of situations which produce discontinuous sensations; for instance, a person absorbed in thought is interrupted by someone sneaking up behind him. This is an individual case; in *London Labour* discontinuity becomes a mass emotion, characterizing the street-folk especially. As in the essay on surprise, an educational philosophy underlies Mayhew's terminology: "A vagrant, therefore, is an individual applying himself continuously to no one thing . . . the cause of the vagrant's wandering through the country—and indeed through life—purposeless, objectless, and *unprincipled,* in the literal and strict meaning of the term, lies mainly in the defective state of our educational institutions." Here the concern is with vagrants generally; for the most part Mayhew focuses on vagrants who grew up in London: "The education of these children is such only as the streets afford; and the streets teach them, for the most part—and in greater or lesser degrees,—acuteness—a precocious acuteness—in all that concerns their immediate wants, business, or gratifications." Like the passion for junk, immediacy is connected with urgent need, for if the street-folk are not concerned about the here-and-now they will perish. An initial, practical stance develops into a general habit of mind; a taste for the immediate becomes one principle of the costermonger's humor: "O, yes, I've heard of God; he made heaven and earth; I never heard of his making the sea; that's another thing, and you can best learn about that at Billingsgate. (He seemed to think that the sea was an appurtenance of Billingsgate.) Jesus Christ? Yes, I've heard of him. Our Redeemer? Well, I only wish I could redeem my Sunday togs from my uncle's." Mayhew's attempt to gauge the man's ignorance becomes the occasion for repartee which affirms a local, immediate situation.

In the context of **London Labour** immediacy means sticking closely to the life of the streets. Since the streets are a constantly changing environment, this obsession with the concrete further implies a desire for discontinuity, that is, for constant change: "These boys hate any continuous work. So strong is this objection to continuity that they cannot even remain selling the same article for more than a week together." The street-people, Mayhew tells us repeatedly, want to keep moving. This is not to say that they all lead exciting lives or lives unfounded on habit; still, they are easily bored without the stimulant of variety. "The muscular irritability begotten by continued wandering" makes the hawker who has settled down "sigh after the perfect liberty of the coster's 'roving life.' " So Mayhew insists; and on this basis he builds his broadest characterization of the London itinerants, who thrive on a permanent elusiveness, an inability to be pinned down. Seen in these terms, the street-people are an embodiment of the city.

At certain points in **London Labour** Mayhew's theory of the streets begins to open out under the pressure of built-in ambivalences, so that it becomes a theory of London. He is, therefore, forced to grapple with some large social and moral questions. Most important, he must decide whether discontinuity works for good or evil in the society of the metropolis. At times he has a bias towards the latter view, for how could it be laudable to wander through life "purposeless, objectless, and *unprincipled*," or have as one's motivating desire "a precocious acuteness—in all that concerns . . . immediate wants?" On the other hand, street-life also suggests "a perfect liberty" which Mayhew comes to find attractive. Thus, although he sometimes tells stories about the degrading effects of a roving life, he more often admits discontinuity to be an acceptable mode of existence. Mayhew told a meeting of ticket-of-leave men:

> I know that as a class you are distinguished mainly by your love of a roving life. . . . Continuous employment of a monotonous nature is so irksome to you, that immediately you engage in it you long to break away from it. . . . Society, however, expects, that if you wish to better yourselves, you will at once settle down as steadily as it does, and immediately conform to all its notions; but I am satisfied that if anything effectual is to be done in the way of reforming you, Society must work in consonance and not in antagonism with your nature. In this connexion it appears to me that the great outlet for you is street trading, where you are allowed to roam at will unchafed by restraints not congenial to your habits and feelings.

This speech skirts condescension, perhaps; but Mayhew's attempt to reconcile middle-class morality with the ethic of the street-folk is striking for its effort. Not only are his sympathies at a distance from those of Society; he is able to recognize alternative ways of life. Broadly speaking, his attitude is cosmopolitan, even though the cosmopolitanism exists side-by-side with a bias towards "respectability."

London Labour does not resolve this dialectic; one can, however, get a sense of the direction in which Mayhew was working. At first, he defines the street-folk in a remarkably unswerving way: "Each civilized or settled tribe has generally some wandering horde intermingled with, and in a measure preying upon, it . . . in each of the [nomadic] classes above-mentioned, there is a greater development of the animal than of the intellectual or moral nature of man . . . they are all more or less distinguished for their high cheek-bones and protruding jaws." This early exercise in ethnology asserts that the street-people, by virtue of their taste for wandering, are set absolutely apart from other city dwellers; they are another race with distinguishing physiological and psychological characteristics. Throughout **London Labour** this theory is influential and, with some justice, it has been taken as a guiding principle of the work.

However, Mayhew's notion of a nomadic race has at once more limited and more general applicability than a definition can afford to have. It is too limited because not all the street-folk have an active desire for the wandering life they lead: "those who are *bred* to the streets" and "those who are *driven* to the streets" are capable of adapting to a settled existence, unlike "those who *take* to the streets" by choice. Only the latter are drawn to a discontinuous existence and thus permanently committed to street-life. The others have no definite psychological make-up to set them apart from other Londoners. So, at least Mayhew hopes, for the philanthropic strain in his existence urges him to reclaim as many lost souls as he can: "If it be their lot [those who are bred and driven to the streets] to be flung on the wide waste of waters without a 'guiding star' above, or a rudder or a compass within, how can *we* (the well-fed) *dare* to blame them because, wanting bread, they prey and live upon their fellow creatures?" That sounds like a final word on the subject. It is nothing of the sort. Shortly after this division of the street-folk into the damned and the redeemable, Mayhew initiates another train of thought: "Might not 'the finest gentleman in Europe' have been the greatest blackguard in Billingsgate, had he been born to carry a fish-basket on his head instead of a crown? and by a parity of reasoning let the roughest 'rough' outside the London fish-market have had his lot in life cast, 'by the Grace of God, King, Defender of the Faith,' and surely his shoulders would have glittered with diamond epaulettes instead of fish scales." The comment seems to be another philanthropic gesture, a plea to the rich to give the deserving poor a chance. Yet more goes on here than is apparent. Besides asserting that environment influences character, Mayhew wonders whether all Londoners might not make good street-folk. Further on in **London Labour,** this notion is explicit: "We are taught to regard all those who object to work as appertaining to the class of natural vagabonds; but where is the man among us that loves labour? for work or labour is merely that which is irksome to perform, and which every man requires a certain amount of remuneration to induce him to perform." At this point, the urge to wander is perceived not as a basis for ethnological classification so much as a characteristic of the human race generally, including, of course, Londoners from all walks of life. A startling metamorphosis may occur at any moment. One of Mayhew's interviewees tells the story of Mr. Children, "a bootmaker of Bethnal-green-road," who "went to hear a lecture on astronomy by Dr. Bird":

> When he came home he was so delighted with what he had seen, that he began telling his wife all about it. He said, 'I cannot better explain to you the solar system, than with a mop,' and he took the mop and dipped it into a pail of water, and began to twirl it round in the air, till the wet flew off it. Then he said, 'This mop is the sun, and the spiral motion of the water gives the revolutions of the planets in their orbits.' Then, after a time, he cried out, 'If this Dr. Bird can do this, why shouldn't I?'

A perfectly respectable man decides to take to the streets; to become an itinerant lecturer on astronomy. The story is comic but it embodies an exhilaration above the level of farce. Bootmakers may not often act this way; on the other hand, all of us feel like Mr. Children at times, expecially, Mayhew would say, when we walk through the streets of London:

> Then the sights, as you elbow your way through the crowd, are equally multifarious. Here is a stall glittering with new tin saucepans; there another, bright with its blue and yellow crockery, and sparkling with white glass. Now you come to a row of old shoes arranged along the pavement; now to a stand of gaudy tea-trays; then to a shop with red handkerchiefs and blue checked shirts, fluttering backwards and forwards, and a counter built up outside on the kerb, behind which are boys beseeching custom. . . . One minute you pass a man with an umbrella turned inside up and full of prints; the next, you hear one with a peepshow of Mazeppa, and Paul Jones the pirate, describing the pictures to the boys looking in at the little round windows.

At the end of this passage (typical of many market scenes described in **London Labour**) Mayhew attempts to emphasize the sadness of the spectacle; he comments that "the confusion and uproar of the New-cut on Saturday night have a bewildering and saddening effect upon the thoughtful mind." The discontinuity of the markets and of the street-seller's life imply the existence of a Malthusian struggle, a "scramble that is going on throughout London for a living." So the passage stands in the *Morning Chronicle* version. In **London Labour,** on the other hand, a post-script describes how police regulations virtually destroyed the market, and here the tone is different. "The New Cut has lost much of its noisy and brilliant glory," Mayhew writes. What at the time he had interpreted as an image of suffering seems in retrospect to have been equally an image of freedom. Nor is this merely nostalgia. The virtues

of discontinuity are reasserted, both for the street-folk and for city dwellers in general. A complicity emerges between all Londoners. Anyone who enjoys the market scene—and by the nature of the actual description, it is hard not to enjoy it—must admit the virtues of discontinuity, its role as a redeeming grace. Whether it is an overall pattern of life or the moment-to-moment experience of a random pedestrian, the discontinuous nature of city life has turned into a rallying point, not a means of setting the poor apart from everyone else.

This complicity may seem a limited and a poor thing but it helps give Mayhew's work an imaginative base that it sometimes appears to lack. He is engaged in the study not of one minor class among the urban poor but of a representative group, whose styles of life—however wretched—suggest what it should be to live in London. Even when the suggestion remains implicit, it is a presence in the book. Street life comes to embody dreams and desires that London brings out generally: dreams of freedom, reconciling an environment that "assassinates you with reality" and an individual sensibility that wants alertness and mobility. The problem is that this reconciliation can be achieved only by means of systems, of a kind of efficiency that would destroy the street-people as well as other aspects of a lively, multifarious metropolis.

Mayhew's strategy is to study the street-people and by this means to establish their imaginative as well as their historical place in London. The systematizer, by contrast, cannot even *see* such people; they are beyond his ken, as Mayhew points out in the *Comic Almanack* for 1851:

> The earnest care of the Government to know the exact number of people that the parish of Clumpley-cum-Boggles-mere contained on an especial night—how many folks slept in 43, Parson's Court, Upper Bloater Street, Chandler's Market, on the same occasion: who populated the police-cells; who put up at hotels; who dozed the night away in cabs and coffee-shops—on billiard-tables and heaps of cabbages—anywhere, everywhere, and nowhere—this great investigation of those who cannot believe their Census any longer is about to come off again, and again to furnish its utterly false returns.
>
> We say utterly false, for the means taken to insure correctness, as to the number of persons who slept in a particular place on a particular night, are contemptibly inefficient. . . . The people unnumbered in the Census compose waiters, tramps, stokers, carriers, gamblers, piemen, breakfast-stall keepers, steamboat stewards, mail-train passengers, moon-shooters, show-folks, Vauxhall lamp-men, and renowned individuals of all sorts, whose night's repose is doubtful; such as Mr. Braidwood; the toll-keepers at the bridges, the beadles of the arcades, Mr. Green, if on a night ascent; the editor of the *Times;* and, on certain debates, Mr. Chisholm Anstey.

This catalogue is notable for its variety. Many of the "people unnumbered in the Census" are studied in **London Labour** as street-folk; others, such as the editor of the *Times,* fall into a different class. Yet by trade or temperament, each of those mentioned possesses an elusiveness, a desire to avoid the regulated courses of life, which suggests above all the discontinuity of the streets. Playing with the faulty definitions of the census takers, Mayhew asserts his preoccupations with restlessness and the irregularities of freedom. Beyond this preoccupation is a vision of London centering on street-life: "These same London thoroughfares *are,* simply, the finest of all sights—in the world, we may say—on account of the never-ending and infinite variety of life to be seen in them. . . . Is there any other sight in the metropolis, moreover, so thoroughly *Londonesque* as this [the streets] in its character?" By participating in the life of discontinuity which the streets embody, one lives at the heart of London. (pp. 95-104)

> *Richard Maxwell, "Henry Mayhew and the Life of the Streets," in* The Journal of British Studies, *Vol. XVII, No. 2, Spring, 1978, pp. 87-105.*

Nancy Aycock Metz   (essay date 1982)

[*In the following excerpt, Metz focuses on Mayhew's descriptions of material goods in* London Labour and the London Poor *and analyzes his use of objects to characterize people and society.*]

Though Henry Mayhew's importance was recognized in his own day and has been emphatically reaffirmed in ours (W. H. Auden called him "one of the ten greatest Victorian Englishmen" [see excerpt dated 1968]), the nature of his achievement has never been easy to define. **London Labour and the London Poor,** which began in a series of articles Mayhew wrote for the *Morning Chronicle* in 1849-50 and was expanded and reissued in four volumes in 1861-62, is a vast sourcebook on the customs, clothing, diet, and entertainment of an important segment of the London poor; it is also an ambitious attempt "to publish the history of a people from the lips of the people themselves." Its usefulness in illuminating Dickens' sources and subjects has kept Mayhew under the scrutiny of twentieth-century critics, and indeed whenever the terms "social realism" or "fiction with a purpose" appear in discussions of nineteenth-century literature Mayhew is almost certain to be mentioned, quoted, and compared—often in parallel columns—with the novels and bluebooks that first awakened the Victorian social conscience. Nevertheless, to evaluate **London Labour and the London Poor** on its own terms remains difficult, for as fascinating as this vast catalog still is—as full of whimsy and horror and serendipity—it is also overwhelming in its formal disarray. Mayhew's study tries to do too many things, with the paradoxical result that its implied objectives clash and subvert one another. It is easier to say what **London Labour** is *not* than what it *is.* But though it lacks the informing intellectual framework of the classic sociological studies, though Mayhew's interviewing technique regularly calls into question the book's status as oral history, though it consistently blurs the distinction between journalism and fiction, the book is held together, finally, by the same kind of consistency of tone, philosophy, and point of view one might encounter in an eccentric novel. At the heart of this "philosophy" is a hobby-horsical fascination for the material furnishings

of the world and for their power to illuminate its values and structure.

Mayhew's London is crowded with things—things bought, sold, and bartered; things seen, heard, and felt; things ingested and excreted; things piled together obsessively or surveyed with a social scientist's arch and remote curiosity. Open the book anywhere and the materiality of the world asserts itself in the magic lanterns, Dutch clocks, barometers, Jenny Lind hats, teetotums, umbrellas, fishing rods, boot jacks, cribbage boards, and stuffed birds that spill out. "My vocation is to collect facts, and to register opinions," Mayhew had said in the second of his *Morning Chronicle* articles. Had he been more self-conscious about the sources of his professional energies, he might have added that for him a fact always began in an artifact—that an opinion acquired interest only insofar as it expressed a relationship to the substantial realities of everyday life.

In Mayhew's world, the identity of persons is always indissolubly tied up in the identity of the things with which they traffic. He tells us in volume one that "I found it common enough among the street-sellers to describe themselves and their fraternity not by their names or callings, but by the article in which they deal. . . . 'Is the man you're asking for a pickled whelk, sir?' was said to me. In answer to another inquiry I was told, 'Oh, yes, I know him—he's a sweet stuff'." Mayhew laughs at the tradesmen's identification of one another with their commodities, but a simple look at his table of contents and chapter headings will show that he has done the same thing. There the classification scheme implies—what the individual monologues emphatically contradict—that the essential, characterizing difference between one man and another is that one sells oysters and one sells sprats.

Some organizing scheme was necessary, of course, in so ambitious a survey, and classification, by its very nature, will always abstract and reduce its objects to manageable types. But in choosing this particular basis of classification over all others, Mayhew precludes a fully elaborated sociology, or at least a conventional sociology of the London costermongers. Having failed to draw his taxonomy from some overarching First Principle, he will find it difficult to tell us why the street people are powerless, where they get their values, how they raise their children. In an important sense he has already atomized them. Yet at the same time, Mayhew's habit of seeing people in relationship to things gives the study a graphic immediacy and concreteness it would otherwise lack. People connect, and the pattern of their connection throws intermittently into relief the working principles of a culture we glimpse tantalizingly in fragments, catalogs, and editorial asides.

From Mayhew's wonderful but bewildering stockpiles of details, three implicit premises emerge as continuous threads of his discussion—that everything is useful to some person or trade; that commerce is analogous to language; and that a culture may be judged by its artifacts. The first of these axioms is the most basic. Against a human backdrop, sometimes horrifyingly frozen in poverty, *matter* goes through an endlessly energetic and intricate series of transformations. Sometimes the changes are

Mayhew interviewed several "long-song sellers," who sold lyric sheets to popular and topical songs on the streets of London.

mechanical; second-hand linen reappears in the form of shirt collars and waistcoats; cigar-ends are swept up and repackaged as "the best Havannas" ("worked up again to be again cast away, and again collected by the finders and so on perhaps, till the millenium comes.") Often the change involves a chemical breakdown, as when the by-products of the gas-works are recycled as coke. In the service of these changes, whole professions of buyers and finders and collectors spring up, whose business is with the waste-paper, hare and rabbit skins, old umbrellas, bottles and glass, broken metal, rags, drippings, grease, tea-leaves, and old clothes cast off by others as worthless.

Mayhew does not try to disguise his admiration for the ingenuity and desperate creativity of those who turn refuse into new articles with new uses. To Mayhew the measure of usefulness is production, and the cause of economic depression is that "our operatives are continually ceasing to be producers, and passing from the creators of wealth to the exchangers or distributors of it, becoming mere tradesmen, subsisting on the labour of other people rather than their own . . . ." If the mark of usefulness is production, clearly nothing could be more useful than to transform what has become economically "no thing" to something which has some value to someone.

Mayhew's expanding inventory of things and their trans-

formations helped to reinforce from a different perspective a theme that the oral histories made dramatically clear—that even the commonplace physical properties of the world look different—are different—depending upon where one stands. The possibility of seeing through another's eyes revealed wonderful anomalies and paradoxes. Not only is waste not waste to the mudlark or pure-finder who makes his living from it, but all external reality becomes a function of usefulness and point of view. Nothing has intrinsic, objective value. Rather, value is invested in things by the powers of the subjective, sympathetic imagination. Thus, the rat-killer has long since lost any revulsion towards the beasts he routinely strangles and bites. And the exhibitor of microscopes makes a handsome profit, not from the scientific utility of his instruments, but from the sense of awe and wonder they bring to those who pay a penny for a glimpse of a new and unimagined dimension of life. Mayhew found, of all things, Acts of Parliament—foot-deep shelves of them—used to wrap up rock candy in a confectionery shop, and he listened as a running patterer explained how a fire or a popular murder might be converted into valuable raw material for trade.

The ingenuity and resourcefulness of his subjects in adapting themselves to marketable commodities clearly fascinated Mayhew. Necessity drove them to incredible feats of metamorphosis. "I've been a costermonger, a lot-seller, a nut-seller, a secret paper-seller. . . . , a cap-seller, a street-printer, a cakeman, a clown, an umbrella-maker, a toasting-fork-maker, a sovereign-seller, and a ginger-beer-seller," he quotes one man as saying. "I hardly know what I haven't been." Moreover, since the leavings of one trade were the raw materials for another, the cycle of barter and exchange put the costermonger in touch with a larger ecological process, then being widely discussed by reformers and sanitarians. As professional converters of "waste" into "value," Mayhew's street people became themselves the medium through which decaying refuse passed, on its way to new life in new forms. In an elaborate table at the end of volume two, Mayhew charts in pounds, shillings, and pence, the second-hand worth of everything from carriage wheels, to pickling pots, to dogs' dung. Fixed firmly in imposing rows of objects and columns of figures, the table raises the image of a world of inanimate objects in a perpetual round of motion, of human beings merely standing by as guides and functionaries to the conversion process. In an important sense, of course, the profitable disposal and use of human "leavings" was *the* critical problem of the urban culture Mayhew described; it was literally poisoning itself with its own sewage. Any Mayhew consciously played on the double meanings of the term "waste," when he talked about the underworld's keen eye for the value of repulsive or cast-off matter. Theoretically, at least, the principle that everything has value, the doctrine of "universal compensation" articulated in volume two, was as benign as it was natural, "making each mutually dependent on the other, and so contributing each to the other's support."

In practice, the system of interdependencies that worked itself out on the London streets was far from consoling—and this for several reasons. Mayhew saw and presented with considerable clarity that the labor of the poor tended to degrade individuals to the levels of the objects they worked. The tradesmen's shorthand way of referring to each other as "pickled whelks" or "sweet stuff" revealed a sad sort of insight, after all. Years of sifting through dust and mud worked a horrifying kind of biological adaptation. Mudlarks became indistinguishable from what they sought; one sewer hunter, legend had it, grew webbed fingers and toes. Paradoxically, while objects moved up and down the social scale by a kind of natural alchemy, fine linen decomposing to rags and being reconstituted into expensive stationery, people were locked into a class structure that made them invisible, alien, vaguely terrifying.

The desperate dependence of the street classes on the wealthy class produced a final and unpassable barrier, both of man from man and of man from object. The very livelihood of many a costermonger depended entirely upon the most promiscuous caprice of taste and fashion. Mayhew points out that when gentlemen stopped wearing swords, periwigs, and large shoe buckles, many artisans were reduced to poverty. And because the upper classes invested their own articles with a subjective value the street classes could not always share, the costermongers often suffered the ultimate degradation of trafficking in goods they did not understand. "I've been asked by women if dates was good in dumplings? I've sometimes said, 'yes,' though I knew nothing at all about them. They're foreign." Here is a personal testimony to a degree of alienation not exceeded for its pathetic meaninglessness in all of Marx. Anne Humpherys [in her *Travels into the Poor Man's Country*] has pointed to the way Mayhew's long series of life histories, following each other without overlap or connection, testifies movingly to the isolation and fragmentation of the culture he surveys. In the face of poverty, ignorance, and an eroded family life, his characters define themselves and connect with one another often through things alone.

That they do so through a complex and highly inventive system of equivalencies suggested a relationship—implicit in Mayhew's discussion—between trade and language. On a direct level, Mayhew observed that the mechanics of trading produced language—or at least a specialized vocabulary capable of differentiating commodities and the customers who purchased them. Slang terms and coinages were among the "curiosities" of street life, and Mayhew collected them with the same self-conscious regard for the picturesque that led him to catalog the "cries of London" and the costumes of gypsies and itinerant foreigners.

The life-histories of the people Mayhew interviewed suggested a far more disturbing connection between words and things. Trade, for many of the costermongers, became itself a kind of bastard language, with its own set of symbols and its own kind of rough grammar—a reduced and spiritless version of a much larger and richer form of human interchange. The tradesmen who described themselves as "translators" of second-hand shoes were aware on some level of the metaphoric connection between the principles of conversion and exchange they acted out on the streets and the logic of semantics. Like language, trade was a systematized network of communication. What the outsider perceived as a chaos of donkeys and carts and

street-cries revealed, on closer examination, an inner structure elaborately regulated by convention. Mayhew's interviewing techniques emphasized that the lowliest trade had its methods of inventory and sale, its special requirements and prescribed rules of behavior. Sales of everything from sprats and chickweed to nutmeg-graters and last dying speeches followed intricate codes that the costers tacitly understood and patiently outlined for Mayhew. The very mistletoe that trimmed the holiday homes of the wealthy arrived there through a dangerous and complicated system of procurement, utterly unknown to the purchaser.

Knowing the rules of his trade, Mayhew made clear, was what gave the coster his identity and place; participating in a formal exchange of goods gave him often his only fleeting opportunity to be a part of a coherent group. Mayhew's descriptions of the Old Clothes Exchange in Petticoat Lane, the cattle exchange at Smithfield, the fish exchange at Billingsgate, and the fruit, vegetable, and flower exchange in Covent Garden are among the great set-pieces of *London Labour and the London Poor.* The "wonderful restlessness" of these places, scenes apparently of "riot, rags, and filth," gave Mayhew a chance to underscore the paradox that functionally they were small societies, efficient and purposeful in their operations, however they might appear to the casual observer. Rightly seen, their efficiency—and not their disorder—made them terrifying: for these moving panoramas dramatized more concretely than any formal social criticism could, the extent to which the costers' relationships had become attenuated into an endless series of transactions, connections made on the basis of currency or barter alone. Their entire commerce with the world had become, in the narrow sense, commercial. "Our Redeemer?" one of Mayhew's subjects responded, "Well, I only wish I could redeem my Sunday togs from my uncle's."

Showing that the street people comprise a sophisticated, internally ordered society—that they are in many ways "just like us" (perhaps but for fortune), natively good, driven to help their families, and to take care of their own, is one of Mayhew's goals. Yet he cannot risk offending his middle class readers by suggesting that they are *too much* like us. And, indeed, for all his empathy with the sufferings of his subjects, Mayhew is never willing himself to assert their equality with his own kind. They are "poor creatures" or, less charitably, "this vast dung-heap of ignorance and vice"; he is—always and respectfully—"Sir," the concerned, occasionally bemused or touched, often condescending listener. Though he throws himself ventriloquist-fashion into an astonishing variety of characters, Mayhew manages to keep separate and secure the assumptions that define his own allegiance to the middle class. He could be, as Jonathon Raban has astutely pointed out, "one moment a gentleman, and next a coster-girl, the next a rat-catcher, the next an unclouded eye floating free over the urban profusion of detail." But this very "Protean character" prevented him from bridging the gap between gentleman and beggar in any intellectually coherent way. Mayhew was always one *or* the other. Listening to the monologues reveals a Mayhew perfectly merged in coster values; listening to the explicit social commentary calls up an embarrassing gap between interviewer and subject. One imagines him, a faintly ridiculous figure of middle class respectability, vainly trying to melt into the crowd of rowdy urchins at the Old Vic, or solemnly asking an incredulous crab-vendor if he knows how far it is to the moon.

By couching the difference between street people and their social betters in terms of a difference in language, Mayhew showed his own half-conscious understanding of the ways in which trade had supplanted the normal resources of communication in the costers' lives. He illustrated the existence of a subcultural, specialized ethic among them, more meaningful than the values of the larger society, and he catalogued the curious argot that allowed them to maintain their defensive separateness from officials and policemen. By showing his readers how the costers' language worked, Mayhew offered them an appreciative insight that made them see the street classes—heretofore voiceless—as a fellow people (like the French, or at least the Chinese). But there remained a hint of Dickens's Podsnap in Mayhew. Making dramatically real a whole submerged population—giving life and psychological complexity to their special way of seeing the world—Mayhew harbored a small, vague suspicion that his creations were, after all, something less, a race apart, and therefore by definition—"not English." (pp. 41-6)

Mayhew accepts the terms of the material universe he surveys. He is at his best and most characteristic, as many critics have pointed out, when he is counting up and charting, listing and enumerating. But he never renders the relationship of people and things fully comprehensible, as he had set out to do, because he is seduced by the pleasures of cataloging. The book as a whole finally outgrows the assumption that "the story of one coster girl's life may be taken as the type of the many." Behind the shifting classification scheme is the half-conscious realization that none will do; none will contain the variety; just as, ultimately the theoretical framework of the book—the theory of wandering tribes with huge jaw bones and tiny intellects—gives way to the canny sagacity of the individual voices.

The urge endlessly to classify does *not* result in a broadening of the focus, though Mayhew's claim that he is writing a "cyclopaedia" suggests that he thinks this is what he is about. Rather, the infinitely complex overlapping of categories suggests a compulsion to see his subjects in their several aspects, from multiple points of view. We see the subject by *what* she sells; by *when* and *where* she gets her goods; we see her as a *female* seller; we see her as a *stationary* figure against the movement of city life. And we see her, finally, as uniquely herself. The real movement of the book is always downward and around the subject, and this is the book's weakness and its strength. However impressive the illusion of lateral movement may be, the fact is that the classification scheme tempts Mayhew to subdivide further and further until the particularity of the world asserts itself again. Seduced by every particular which he would have preferred to subsume into some universal, Mayhew is unable to fulfill whatever didactic goals he may have had for his study. And yet if we listen not to what he has told us he will tell us, but to what he is telling

us, if we appreciate that his meaning lies in his means of telling, we attain an altogether uncommon appreciation for the value and the power of things in the world, and a new way of attending to them for what they tell us about ourselves and our society.

So we have lists—wonderful lists, sometimes—whose arrangement of detail suggests a psychological insight stopping just short of self-consciousness. And we have things—flannel waistcoats and japanned boxes—real in themselves and in the quality of life they suggest. And finally the book itself—four volumes of its double-columned pages—becomes what it so lovingly accepts and reports. It is itself the longest and most comprehensive of Mayhew's lists, doomed to incompleteness from its very obsession to cover it all. And it is itself the most insistent object of all—so many twopenny numbers absorbed into the street trade in stationery during the very process of the book's composition—destined like the Shakespeare's and the Moliére's and the Bibles; the music books, histories, stories, and tracts; the children's copybooks and the lover's effusions, to fill "the insatiate bag of the waste collector" who, Mayhew tells us, "of late has been worried because he could not supply enough." (pp. 47-8)

Nancy Aycock Metz, "Mayhew's Book of Lists," in University of Hartford Studies in Literature, *Vol. 14, No. 2, 1982, pp. 41-9.*

George Woodcock (essay date 1984)

[*Woodcock is a Canadian educator, editor, and critic best known for his biographies of George Orwell and Thomas Merton. He also founded Canada's most important literary journal,* Canadian Literature, *and has written extensively on the literature of Canada. In the following excerpt, Woodcock describes Mayhew's narrative technique and notes his anticipation of such twentieth-century social writers as Orwell.*]

[In *London Labour and the London Poor*] we find impersonality and personality inextricably mingled and constantly inspiring each other. The impersonality appears in the self-consciously scientific goals that Mayhew set himself when he embarked on his task, which he expressed in a letter during the period when he was still working on his reports for the *Morning Chronicle*.

> The labour question was to be investigated without reference to any particular prejudice, theory, party, or policy, and it was with this spirit that I set out upon my mission. I made up my mind to deal with human nature as a natural philosopher or a chemist deals with any material object; and, as a man who had devoted some little of his time to physical and metaphysical science, I must say I did most heartily rejoice that it should have been left to me to apply the laws of the inductive philosophy for the first time, I believe, in the world to the abstract questions of political economy.

Engels and others might have disputed Mayhew's claims to priority, early as they were made; but even if they were unjustified, such claims do illuminate his pioneering urge to go to the very source of information that is expressed in Mayhew's description of his ***London Labour:*** "It surely may be considered curious as being the first attempt to publish the history of a people, from the lips of the people themselves—giving a literal description of their labour, their earnings, their trials, and their sufferings, in their own 'unvarnished' language; and to portray the condition of their homes and their families by personal observation of the places, and direct communion with the individuals."

The desire to be impersonal, to be scientific and objective, led Mayhew to interrupt his accounts of the lives of the poor with statistics that remind you of those calculations of the cost of feeding poor families with which Orwell punctuated *The Road to Wigan Pier.* What was a scavenger's weekly budget? What did it cost a master chimney sweep to feed his apprentices? But Mayhew went beyond Orwell's task of calculating how the poor made do with next to nothing. He was also concerned to show the contribution to the economy that even the poorest people made, and so to defend the street sellers and other marginal classes from the respectable shopkeepers who sought to remove them from the pavements and gutters. In one massive calculation he showed that 41,040 street sellers in London generated a total trade of £2,634,350 sterling, which provided them with an average yearly yield of £60 and an average weekly gain of eight shillings. Elsewhere he calculated the total capital involved in the street selling of coal

There are about 30 two-horse vans continually engaged in this trade, the price of each van being £70. This gives	£2100
100 horses at £20 each	1200
160 carts at £10 each	1600
160 horses at £10 each	1600
20 donkey or pony carts, value £1 each	20
20 donkeys or ponies at £1. 10s. each	30
Making a total of 210 vehicles continually employed, which, with the horses &c., may be valued at	
	6550
This sum, with the price of 210 sets of weights and scales, at £1.10s. per set	315
Makes a total of	
	£6865

Following Mayhew's example, we may perhaps finally dispose of the mathematics of ***London Labour*** by remarking that the four volumes of the 1861-62 edition consist (another strange Orwellian anticipation) of 1984 double-columned pages, each containing approximately 860 words, which makes a total of almost 1,700,000 words; Quennell's three volumes of selections consist of just over a third of this encyclopedic mass. In gathering this material, Mayhew claimed to have conducted more than two thousand interviews, apart from those attributable to his assistants. It is an impressive record of industry for a man reputed to be indolent, but neither that effort nor Mayhew's attempt to be scientifically impersonal is what makes ***London Labour*** memorable. Its power derives from the elements that lie outside the impersonal and scientific approach—from Mayhew's extraordinary power of empathizing with people from backgrounds entirely different

from his own, and from his sheer artistry as a descriptive writer.

The skill and tact with which Mayhew made his way into the poorest parts of London and created the trust that induced their inhabitants to speak to him so frankly are all the more remarkable when one remembers that, unlike Orwell, he never tried to share their lives or to disguise himself as one of them. Whether he was sitting in his office in Fleet Street or entering a crowded Houndsditch sweatshop or talking to a ragged little mudlark beside the Thames, he must always have looked much as he does in the engraving drawn from a daguerreotype that serves as frontispiece for the 1861 edition of his great book. He wears the frockcoat and waistcoat, the winged collar and bowtie, that one would expect of a mid-Victorian man of letters; but the cut of the clothes suggests an inexpensive tailor, the tie is carelessly tied, and the longish hair on each side of the high balding brow looks uncombed and greasy: this is certainly not the figure of a dandy or a prosperous burgess. The face is arresting, however, for between the heavy jowls and the domed brow his black-ringed eyes look out with a kind of bloodhound's gaze, sad and powerful at the same time; and the mouth has a similar mixture of firmness and sensitivity. You can imagine him the melancholy detective in an early crime novel, and this indeed was the kind of role in which he saw himself, as an investigator of the great collective crime that was responsible for "the condition of a class of people whose misery, ignorance, and vice, amidst all the immense wealth and great knowledge of 'the first city in the world,' is, to say the least,`a national disgrace to us."

On the way the sheer joy of narration led Mayhew, who was as determined as Orwell to make an art out of didactic writing, into his remarkable descriptions of popular life in Victorian London, that teeming heartless realm of laisserfaire. He was a master at setting a scene, with all its appeals to the senses of sight and smell, and in all the minutiae of evocative and significant detail. In his account of the costermongers and their way of life he begins by discussing the numbers of costers in London, the origins of their class, the economics of their tiny businesses; but, having got these "scientific" matters out of the way, he is eager to tell us what kind of human beings the costers are, and before proceeding to the interviews that poignantly bring out individual circumstances and predicaments, he sets the scene with the description of an evening street market in which his zest for the life of London's thoroughfares and back lanes is vigorously evident.

He begins with light, the most striking aspect of the scene.

> There are hundreds of stalls, and every stall has its one or two lights; either it is illuminated by the intense white light of the new self-generating gas-lamp, or else it is brightened up by the red smoky flame of the old-fashioned grease lamp. One man shows off his yellow haddock with a candle stuck in a bundle of firewood; his neighbour makes a candlestick of a huge turnip, and the tallow gutters over its sides; whilst the boy shouting "Eight a penny, stunning pears!" has

rolled his dip in a thick coat of brown paper, that flares away with the candle. Some stalls are crimson with the fire shining through the holes beneath the baked chestnut stove; others have handsome octohedral lamps, while a few have a candle shining through a sieve: these, with the sparkling ground-glass globes of the tea-dealers' shops, and the butchers' gas-lights streaming and fluttering in the wind, like flags of flame, pour forth such a flood of light, that at a distance the atmosphere immediately above the spot is as lurid as if the street were on fire.

Having taken us into the light and among the people of the market, Mayhew proceeds to deafen us with the bedlam of the "eager dealers, all shouting at the tops of their voices, at one and the same time."

"So-old again," roars one. "Chestnuts all 'ot, a penny a score," bawls another. "An 'aypenny a skin, blacking," squeaks a boy. "Buy, buy, buy, buy, buy—bu-u-uy!" cries the butcher. "Half-quire of paper for a penny," bellows the street stationer. . . . "Twopence a pound grapes." "Three a penny Yarmouth bloaters." "Who'll buy a bonnet for fourpence?" "Pick 'em out cheap here! three pair for a halfpenny, boot-laces." "Now's your time! beautiful whelks, a penny a lot." "Here's ha'p'orths," shouts the perambulating confectioner. "Come and look at 'em! here's toasters!" bellows one with a Yarmouth bloater stuck on a toasting-fork. "Penny a lot, fine russets," calls the apple woman: and so the Babel goes on.

Now he takes us around the stalls, pointing out with his sharp visual sense the colors and the special characters of each display and the way in which a hundred different ways of scraping a poor living go on beside one another.

Here is a stall glittering with new tin saucepans; there another, bright with its blue and yellow crockery, and sparkling with white glass. . . . Here, alongside the road, are some half-dozen headless tailors' dummies, dressed in Chester-fields and fustian jackets, each labelled, "Look at the prices," or "Observe the quality." After this is a butcher's shop, crimson and white with meat piled up to the first-floor, in front of which the butcher himself, in his blue coat, walks up and down, sharpening his knife on the steel that hangs to his waist. A little further on stands the clean family, begging; the father with his head down as if in shame, and a box of lucifers held forth in his hand—the boys in newly-washed pinafores, and the tidily got-up mother with a child at her breast. This stall is green and white with bunches of turnips—that red with apples, the next yellow with onions, and another purple with pickling cabbages. One minute you pass a man with an umbrella turned inside up and full of prints; the next, you hear one with a peepshow of Mazeppa, and Paul Jones the pirate, describing the pictures to the boys looking in at the little round windows.

So it goes on, and in two of his long columns Mayhew has presented a sense of the variety and vitality of London street life, has communicated his own fascination with it,

and has introduced a good variety of the merchants and mongers, the mendicants and mummers, who will fill the four volumes to come. *London Labour* is punctuated with such vigorous scenes, ranging from the clamorous cheap theaters known as "penny gaffs" that entertained the cos-termongers to the noisome lodging houses of East London (which had changed surprisingly little by the 1930s when George Orwell first stepped into Lew Levy's Kip) and the shoddily sparkling nighthouses of Haymarket where the prostitutes met their clients.

All these are fine genre pieces, typically Victorian in their anecdotal interest and their local color and strongly remi-niscent of those enormous canvases, crowded with people and anecdotal action, that attracted attention in the Royal Academy exhibitions of the time, like William Frith's *Derby Day* (1858) and *Railway Station* (1862).

In the character sketches he developed out of his inter-views Mayhew is still more successful. He quickly learned the wisdom of the questioner's making himself appear si-lent, and of his relying on his power of visual description to set a scene in which the interviewee would appear main-ly as a monologuist, though his theatrical endeavors had also taught him the value of dramatic interventions by third parties. (pp. 564-70)

Mayhew did not openly support either Chartism or Kings-ley's Christian Socialism, but it is clear that his natural radicalism drew him toward such views. In some of the most striking passages in *London Labour* he reveals the tragic decay of the craft tradition in London and its re-placement by the sweatshop and slop systems that were turning the formerly independent handworkers into a starving proletariat. The lament recurs again and again: "It was not always like this."

London Labour and the London Poor not only stands as a valuable social document and a witness to the varieties of human patience and ingenuity in adversity, but also em-bodies an elegiac vision, very similar to that which a cen-tury later haunted Orwell, of a better past when men lived more proudly and more decently. (p. 573)

> *George Woodcock, "Henry Mayhew and the Undiscovered Country of the Poor," in* The Se-wanee Review, *Vol. XCII, No. 4, Fall, 1984, pp. 556-73.*

FURTHER READING

Annan, Noel. "How the Poor Live." *The New York Review of Books* 17, No. 1 (22 July 1971): 32-3.
　　Reviews *The Unknown Mayhew*, providing an overview of Mayhew's writings on the poor and summarizing scholarly debate over the validity of his research.

"Mr. Henry Mayhew." *The Athenæum* 2, No. 3119 (6 Au-gust 1887): 181-82.

Obituary of Mayhew, crediting him with extraordinary versatility as a writer.

Bradley, John L. "Henry Mayhew and Father William." *English Language Notes* 1, No. 1 (September 1963): 40-2.
Comments on Mayhew's adaptation of Robert Southey's poem "The Old Man's Comforts" for a children's primer, comparing Mayhew's version with Lewis Carroll's adaptation of the poem into "Father William" in *Alice's Adventures in Wonderland* (1865).

Clayton, Herbert B. "The Henry Mayhew Centenary." *Notes and Queries* 5 (24 February 1912): 145-46.
Commemorates the centenary of Mayhew's birth by providing an anecdotal account of his life.

Dunn, Richard J. "Dickens and Mayhew Once More." *Nineteenth-Century Fiction* 25, No. 3 (December 1970): 348-53.
Examines parallels between Mayhew's *London Labour and the London Poor* and Dickens's *Bleak House* (1853).

Hibbert, Christopher. "Henry Mayhew's Other London." *Horizon* 17, No. 2 (Spring 1975): 48-57.
Offers a summary of *London Labour and the London Poor* and a biography of Mayhew.

Hodder, George. "Chapter III." In his *Memories of My Time Including Personal Reminiscences of Eminent Men,* pp. 39-66. London: Tinsley Brothers, 1870.
Recounts the founding of *Punch,* crediting Mayhew with conceiving the idea for the magazine, and recollects Hodder's acquaintance with Mayhew and his brothers.

Humpherys, Anne. Review of *The Unknown Mayhew,* edited by Eileen Yeo and E. P. Thompson. *Victorian Studies* 15, No. 2 (December 1971): 243-45.
Deems *The Unknown Mayhew* "a welcome contribution to the Mayhew revival" and addresses questions about the value of Mayhew's scholarship.

Nelson, Harland S. "Dickens's *Our Mutual Friend* and Henry Mayhew's *London Labour and the London Poor.*" *Nineteenth-Century Fiction* 20, No. 3 (December 1965): 207-22.
Suggests that Dickens may have used *London Labour and the London Poor* as a source of information and characters for *Our Mutual Friend* (1865).

Price, R. G. G. *A History of Punch.* London: Collins, 1957, 384 p.
Describes the evolution of the satirical periodical *Punch,* which Mayhew helped to found.

"Henry Mayhew." *Punch* 93, No. 2404 (6 August 1887): 53.
Elegiac poem marking Mayhew's death.

Roberts, F. David. "More Early Victorian Newspaper Editors." *Victorian Periodicals Newsletter,* No. 16 (June 1972): 15-28.
Surveys the bohemian circle of London periodical editors to which Mayhew belonged.

Smith, F. B. "Mayhew's Convict." *Victorian Studies* 22, No. 4 (Summer 1979): 431-48.
Researches the background of a convict interviewed by Mayhew for *London Labour and the London Poor,* finding discrepancies in Mayhew's published interview which Smith argues cast doubt on the accuracy of Mayhew's scholarship.

Smith, Sheila M. "Problems, Not People." In her *The Other Nation: The Poor in English Novels of the 1840s and 1850s,* pp. 135-205. Oxford: Clarendon Press, 1980.
Discusses Augustus Mayhew's incorporation of information from *London Labour and the London Poor* into his novel *Paved with Gold; or, The Romance and Reality of the London Streets* (1858).

Stevenson, David. "Mayhew and the London Poor: A Mediocre Genius and His Book." *The Denver Quarterly* 12, No. 1 (Spring 1977): 332-46.
Summary of *London Labour and the London Poor* that includes extensive excerpts and a biography of Mayhew.

"A Founder of *Punch.*" *The Times Literary Supplement,* No. 2399 (24 January 1948): 48.
Reviews *The Street Trader's Lot: London, 1851,* a collection of Mayhew's articles edited by Stanley Rubenstein, praising Mayhew's talent for description.

Jules Michelet

1798-1874

French historian and nonfiction writer.

A historian, social critic, and nature writer, Michelet is considered one of the greatest prose stylists in the French language. Best known for his historical studies, particularly the seventeen-volume *Histoire de France,* Michelet imbued these works with meticulous attention to facts, yet was often criticized for lack of objectivity because he freely interpreted the significance of the events he presented. The fervent imagination and passionate sentiment that characterize his writings have led to his identification with the Romantic movement.

Michelet was born in Paris and worked from a very early age in his father's printing shop. Napoleon's restrictions of the press forced Michelet's father to close his shop in 1810, and the family endured dire poverty throughout Michelet's youth. Biographers speculate that these circumstances, which contributed to the illness and death of his mother in 1815, fostered Michelet's sympathy for the working class and the egalitarian ideals of the French Revolution. Despite the family's financial hardship, Michelet, regarded as a prodigy by his parents and teachers, received an education at the Collège Charlemagne and graduated at the top of his class.

After completing his doctoral dissertation, he accepted a position teaching history at the Collège Sainte-Barbe in 1822. He married two years later and became professor of history and philosophy at the École Normale Supérieure in 1827, the year he published a translation of Italian philosopher Giovanni Battista Vico's *Scienza nuova* (1730; *Principes de la philosophie de l'histoire, traduits de la Scienza nuova de J. B. Vico*). Michelet's translation introduced Vico's work to French readers and was favorably received. His subsequent appointment as keeper of the National Archives allowed Michelet to avail himself of a wealth of original historical documents, greatly enhancing both the depth and stylistic quality of his histories.

Introduction à l'histoire universelle, completed in 1831, was Michelet's first significant contribution to historical scholarship, and later that year he published *Histoire de la République Romaine* (*History of the Roman Republic*). Publication of the first volume of his *Histoire de France* in 1833 marked the beginning of several decades of effort culminating in the completion of the set in 1867. Michelet received an appointment as professor at the Collège de France in 1838, where he lectured vigorously on liberal ideologies and the need for democratic reforms in France. His *Des Jésuites* (*The Jesuits*), published in 1843, and *Du prêtre, de la femme, de la famille* (*Priests, Women, and Families*), published two years later, attacked the Catholic church as a divisive influence in French society; these two works marked the beginning of a series of confrontations with religious and political authorities that would eventually result in Michelet's dismissal from the Collège. Mi-

chelet voiced his sympathy for the working class with his publication of *Le peuple* (*The People*) in 1846; a best-seller in his time, the work was simultaneously translated into English, and is presently considered among Michelet's greatest achievements. He spent the next several years completing his seven-volume history of the French Revolution.

Critics view the succeeding years of Michelet's life as a second phase in his career. He was dismissed from his position at the Collège de France in 1851; the following year, he lost his position as keeper of the Archives because of his refusal to offer allegiance to the Second Empire. Thus, for the remainder of his life Michelet and his wife were financially dependent on income generated from the sale of his works. As a result, Michelet turned to writing books on more popular subjects, including a series of nature books and works on the role of women in society. Michelet also continued work on his *Histoire de France* during these years, and after its completion began work on his *Histoire du XIXème siècle,* publishing three volumes before his death in 1874.

Michelet had concluded that previous histories were too superficial, omitting consideration of ideas, customs, and socioeconomic and geographical factors which he considered essential in discerning the "great progressive movement of the national soul." Michelet's method of historical analysis, which he termed a "resurrection of the integral life of the past," reflects his self-designation as an "artist-historian." His love of nature, passionate defense of human rights, and sentimentality have led critics to label him a "Romantic" historian. Highly subjective, his histories are characterized by an emotion that G. P. Gooch has described as Michelet's "sympathetic imagination." Gooch writes: "[Michelet's volume on the Renaissance] abounds in striking ideas and in brilliant pictures. Many of its pages are beautiful and precious, and the sympathy for the poor and suffering is deep and real. The chapters on the revocation of the Edict of Nantes ring with noble indignation. He is incomparable on the corruption of the Valois, the pride of the Grand Monarque, the madness of law. . . . He feels something of the greatness of Henry IV and Sully, and weeps over the grave of the Duc de Bourgogne." Incorporating such diverse materials as the personal recollections and diaries of various historical figures, interviews with surviving personages, and popular accounts, Michelet's histories are unified by a network of interpretive symbol and metaphor. Lionel Gossman writes that Michelet was "convinced that every product of human culture, humble or grand, is historically significant if the historian knows how to interpret it. Interpretation is thus from the outset, along with 'facts,' at the heart of the historian's activity. His task is not merely to relate the facts of the past but also to discover and interpret them for the future." Michelet's perception and interpretation of history, by his own admission, were greatly influenced by the writings of Vico. Vico's assertion that history had progressed from a world of gods, through one of heroes, to one of men, was paralleled in political terms by Michelet, whose history depicted an evolution from theocracy, through aristocracy, to democracy. But whereas Vico had described the historical process in terms of a repetitive cycle, Michelet viewed it in terms of a progressive spiral; thus Michelet's sympathy for the French Revolution, and his contempt for any individual, organization, or institution that opposed or hindered the advancement of its ideals.

Michelet's earliest popular works, such as *The Jesuits* and *Priests, Women, and Families,* warned of the divisive influence of the church, which Michelet saw as a reactionary wedge aimed at undermining the achievements of the revolution and effecting social discord. *The People,* which John McKay has called "the classic portrait of French society," examined social conditions in France during the transformation from agrarian to industrial society, cautioning against suspicions and class hatreds while promoting nationalism as a unifying and constructive force for human progress. Each of Michelet's popular works, including *La femme* (*Woman*) and *L'amour* (*Love*), helped influence the democratization and secularization of French thought and institutions in the nineteenth century, and continue to be valued by modern critics as aids in understanding French culture at that time. His essays on nature, entitled *L'oiseau* (*The Bird*), *L'insecte* (*The Insect*), *La mer* (*The Sea*), and *La montagne* (*The Mountain*), address human concerns allegorically through an anthropomorphic depiction of the natural world. Intended to impart moral lessons, these works, according to Edward Kaplan, "use[d] nature to civilize and nurture humanity," and were commercially successful because they "spoke at once to individual needs and to those of European society at large."

In discussing Michelet's histories, Pieter Geyl summarizes a common criticism of Michelet's style, noting that "when it came to expressing a judgment, [Michelet] always subjected reality, even where he had properly discerned it, to the abstractions of [his] doctrine." Similarly, Michelet's contemporaries, notably Hippolyte Taine and Charles Augustin Sainte-Beuve, denounced many of his works as excessively sentimental and moralistic. Modern critical consensus, however, sides with Kaplan's assertion that, "because of his style's emotional intensity and pictorial concreteness," Michelet is considered by many "the greatest lyrical prose writer of the French language."

PRINCIPAL WORKS

De percipienda infinitate secundum Lockium (essay) 1819
Tableau chronologique de l'histoire moderne (history) 1825
Tableaux synchroniques de l'histoire moderne (history) 1826
Précis de l'histoire moderne (history) 1827
Principes de la philosophie de l'histoire, traduits de la Scienza nuova de J. B. Vico [translator] (nonfiction) 1827
Histoire de la République Romaine. 2 vols. (history) 1831
  [*History of the Roman Republic,* 1947]
Introduction à l'histoire universelle (history) 1831
Précis de l'histoire de France jusqu'à la Révolution française (history) 1833
Histoire de France. 17 vols. (history) 1833-67
Mémoires de Luther, écrits par lui-même (biography) 1835
  [*The Life of Luther, Gathered from His Own Writings, by M. Michelet,* 1846]
Origines du droit français (nonfiction) 1837
Des Jésuites (nonfiction) 1843
  [*The Jesuits,* 1845]
Du prêtre, de la femme, de la famille (nonfiction) 1845
  [*Priests, Women, and Families,* 1846]
Le peuple (nonfiction) 1846
  [*The People,* 1846]
Cours professé au Collège de France (nonfiction) 1847-48; also published as *L'étudiant,* 1877
Histoire de la Révolution Française. 7 vols. (history) 1847-53; [*History of the French Revolution,* 1967]
Les Femmes de la Révolution (nonfiction) 1854
  [*The Women of the French Revolution,* 1855]
Légendes démocratiques du Nord (nonfiction) 1854
L'oiseau (nonfiction) 1856
  [*The Bird,* 1869]
L'insecte (nonfiction) 1857
  [*The Insect,* 1875]
L'amour (nonfiction) 1858

A. Potter   (essay date 1843)

[*In the following excerpt, Potter praises Michelet's style, but warns the reader of Michelet's nationalistic bias.*]

[Michelet] is one of the most learned, laborious, and elegant of that remarkable school, who have been engaged during the last twenty years, in France, in illustrating ancient and modern history. . . . With great philosophical sagacity, he combines what is so apt to be wanting in the German historians—a brilliant imagination, a clear and picturesque style, and great felicity of illustration. *Universal histories,* especially if in the form of abridgments, are usually meager and spiritless. The reader will find that Michelet, like his great predecessor Bossuet, is an exception. His summary is constantly relieved by reflections full of weight and vivacity, and his generalities are made significant and interesting by examples as vivid as they are novel.

Another circumstance which gives interest to the work, while it calls, at the same time, for some caution in accepting its conclusions, is, that the author has been accustomed to survey history from a point very different from that occupied by English and American historians. He is a Frenchman, a monarchist, and a Roman Catholic; and, though more than usually free from prejudices, it is not to be expected that he should escape them entirely. To those who are sincerely desirous to take an enlarged and philosophical view of events, it must sometimes be grateful to neutralize the force of their own prepossessions by the aid of tolerant and enlightened minds, who have been formed under different systems of religion and law. It is due to the author to add that he is no bigot. A Roman Catholic, he still acknowledges with gratitude the inestimable blessings conferred on the world by the Protestant Reformation; a monarchist, his sympathies are still with the people; a Frenchman, and therefore bound, as he supposes, in common with all Frenchmen, to regard "his glorious country as the pilot of the great vessel of humanity," he has yet a heart and an understanding large enough to do justice, with few exceptions, to virtue and greatness, wherever he finds them. (pp. ix-xi)

> *A. Potter, in an introduction to* Modern History: From the French of M. Michelet, *Harper & Brothers, 1843, pp. vii-xiii.*

Jules Michelet   (essay date 1846)

[*In the following excerpt, Michelet explains his research methodology and his purpose in writing* The People.]

I have made [***The People***] out of myself, out of my life, and out of my heart. It is the product of my experience rather than of my studies. I have derived it from my observation and my conversations with friends and neighbors; I have picked it up along the highways, for fortune loves to favor the man who is always following the same line of thought. I have found it above all in the recollections of my youth. To know the life of the people and their toils and sufferings, I had only to question my memory. (pp. 3-4)

No one should be surprised that after knowing the past condition of [the] people as well as anyone, and after sharing their life myself, I feel a burning desire that the truth be spoken about them. When the progress of my *History of France* led me to study the questions of the day and I cast my eyes upon the books where they are discussed, I must confess that I was surprised to find almost all of them contradicting my recollections. So I closed my books and went among the people again as much as I could; the solitary writer plunged again into the crowd and listened to the noise and noted the words. It was indeed the same people; only the outward appearances had changed, and my memory had not tricked me. So I went about consulting men, listening to their account of their own condition, and gathering from their lips what is not always found in the most brilliant writers—words of common sense.

I began this inquiry at Lyons about ten years ago. I have continued it in other towns, studying urban problems with practical men of the most positive minds, as well as the true situation of the rural areas, which is so neglected by our economists. It is hard to believe what a mass of new information I have thus acquired, and which is not in any book. Next to the conversation of men of genius and of the most outstanding scholars, that of the people is certainly the most instructive. If you cannot talk with Béranger, Lamennais, or Lamartine, go into the fields and chat with a peasant. What is to be learned from the middle class? As for the salons, I never left them without finding my heart shrunken and chilled.

My wide-ranging studies of history had revealed facts of the greatest interest about which historians are silent—the different phases and the changes in the pattern of small landholding before the Revolution, for example. In the same way, my on-the-spot investigation taught me many things that are not in the statistics. (pp. 4-5)

The Romantics believed that art is found especially in the ugly. They thought that art finds its most powerful effects in moral ugliness. Fickle love seemed more poetic to them than family ties, theft more than labor, or the galleys more than the workshop. If they had gone down into the profound realities of life today through their own personal sufferings, they would have seen that the family, the work, and the humblest life of the people have themselves a sacred poetry. To feel and show this is not a mechanical affair; there is no need to accumulate theatrical devices here. It requires only that we have eyes formed for that gentle light, eyes to look into the dark, into the petty and the humble; and the heart helps, too, to see into those corners of the home and those shadows of Rembrandt.

Whenever our great writers have looked there, they have been admirable. But generally they have turned their eyes toward the fantastic, the violent, the whimsical, the unusual. Nor have they deigned to warn us that they were sketching the exception. Their readers, and especially their foreign readers, thought they were describing the rule. So they said, "That is the way those people are."

And I—who have sprung from them, who have lived and toiled and suffered with them, who more than any other has earned the right to say that I know them—I am coming forward now against all these views to establish the personality of the people.

I have not taken this personality from the surface, in its picturesque or dramatic aspects. I have not seen it from the outside, but experienced it from within. And in this very experience I have understood more than one deep quality of the people which they have but do not understand. Why? Because I was able to trace it in its historical development and see it come from the depths of time. He who limits himself to the present will not understand the present. He who is satisfied with seeing the exterior and painting the form will not even be able to see it. To see that personality accurately and translate it faithfully, he must know what it covers. There is no painting without anatomy. (pp. 8-9)

> *Jules Michelet, "Preface: To Edgar Quinet,"* in his The People, *translated by John P. McKay, University of Illinois Press, 1973, pp. 3-24.*

L. J. Trotter   (essay date 1863)

[*In the following excerpt from the preface to his translation of Michelet's* La sorcière, *Trotter comments on the salient features of the work.*]

In this translation of a work [*La sorcière*] rich in the raciest beauties and defects of an author long since made known to the British public, the present writer has striven to recast the trenchant humour, the scornful eloquence, the epigrammatic dash of Mr. Michelet, in language not all unworthy of such a word-master. . . . In one point only is he aware of having been less true to his original than in theory he was bound to be. He has slurred or slightly altered a few of those passages which French readers take as a thing of course, but English ones, because of their different training, are supposed to eschew. A Frenchman, in short, writes for men, an Englishman rather for drawing-room ladies, who tolerate grossness only in the theatres and the columns of the newspapers. Mr. Michelet's subject, and his late researches, lead him into details,

moral and physical, which among ourselves are seldom mixed up with themes of general talk. The coarsest of these have been pruned away, but enough perhaps remain to startle readers of especial prudery. The translator, however, felt that he had no choice between shocking these and sinning against his original. Readers of a larger culture will make allowance for such a strait, will not be so very frightened at an amount of plain-speaking, neither in itself immoral, nor, on the whole, impertinent. Had he docked his work of everything condemned by prudish theories, he might have made it more conventionally decent; but Michelet would have been puzzled to recognize himself in the poor maimed cripple that would then have borne his name.

Nor will a reader of average shrewdness mistake the religious drift of a book suppressed by the Imperial underlings in the interests neither of religion nor of morals, but merely of Popery in its most outrageous form. If its attacks on Rome seem, now and then, to involve Christianity itself, we must allow something for excess of warmth, and something for the nature of inquiries which laid bare the rotten outgrowths of a religion in itself the purest known among men. In studying the so-called Ages of Faith, the author has only found them worthy of their truer and older title, the Ages of Darkness. It is against the tyranny, feudal and priestly, of those days, that he raises an outcry, warranted almost always by facts which a more mawkish philosophy refuses to see. If he is sometimes hasty and onesided; if the Church and the Feudal System of those days had their uses for the time being; it is still a gain to have the other side of the subject kept before us by way of counterpoise to the doctrines now in vogue. We need not be intolerant; but Rome is yet alive.

Taken as a whole, Mr. Michelet's book cannot be called unchristian. Like most thoughtful minds of the day, he yearns for some nobler and larger creed than that of the theologians; for a creed which, understanding Nature, shall reconcile it with Nature's God. Nor may he fairly be called irreverent for talking, Frenchman like, of things spiritual with the same freedom as he would of things temporal. . . . At any rate, no translator who should cut or file away so special a feature of French feeling would be doing justice to so marked an original.

For English readers . . . , the present work will offer mainly an interesting study of the author himself. It is a curious compound of rhapsody and sound reason, of history and romance, of coarse realism and touching poetry, such as, even in France, few save Mr. Michelet could have produced. Founded on truth and close inquiry, it still reads more like a poem than a sober history. As a beautiful speculation, which has nearly, but not quite, grasped the physical causes underlying the whole history of magic and illusion in all ages, it may be read with profit as well as pleasure in this age of vulgar spirit-rapping. But the true history of Witchcraft has yet to be written by some cooler hand. (pp. v-viii)

> *L. J. Trotter, in a preface to* La Sorcière: The Witch of the Middle Ages *by Jules Michelet, translated by L. J. Trotter, Simpkin, Marshall, and Co., 1863, pp. v-viii.*

The Quarterly Review (essay date 1901)

[*In the following excerpt, the critic assesses the strengths and weaknesses of Michelet's analyses of French history.*]

The great source of Michelet's strength lies in the clearness with which he conceives his end. He does not care a fig for mere erudition, he eschews footnotes, he rarely affords the readers a glimpse of his scaffoldings. He may be tediously emphatic in his rhetoric, but he is a man with a gospel, and the power to hold his audience. The gospel according to Michelet can be packed into two words, *Nature* and *Patrie*. He tells us himself how, when he began to think and study, he found his country utterly demoralised by the cruel legend of military idolatry, the monarchic superstition, and the cult of force; how the memory of the historical continuity of France, of her mission among the nations, had been effaced by a series of political convulsions; how the solidarity of the family was broken up by the confessional, by loose morals; how humiliating was the image of French life reflected in the mirror of her current literature. The thing needed was to teach France to Frenchmen, to arouse them to a deep patriotic interest in the past of their fatherland, to give them a faith in its destinies that should supply the place of Christianity, which, being essentially monarchical and feminine, was unsuited to the manly gravity of republican manners. Men talk of cosmopolitanism and the family of nations. For Michelet the European concert was a harmony composed of distinctive national notes; and the notes became more distinctive as time went on. It was true that geography was most influential in the springtide of nations, but then other discriminating agents took its place; and 'the more a man advances the more he enters into the genius of his country.'

We will not here stop to enquire how far patriotism is an all-sufficient *credo,* or what kind of European concert would be the result of an artificial intensification of national traits all round. It is, however, only fair to Michelet to point out that, like his friend Quinet, he has no sympathy with the view that all has been for the best in the best possible of worlds. He believed, indeed, that the history of France had special properties of a religious nature. In somewhat vague language he sums up thus: 'This nation has two very strong things, which I see nowhere else. She has the principle and the legend, the most large and human idea, and at the same time the most continuous tradition. The idea Fraternity, the tradition, the Moral Idea of the world.' By the latter phrase he seems to mean that France has participated more fully and continuously in the Romano-Christian and democratic tradition than the other nations of Europe, and that in her the development of civilisation is, as Guizot too thought, most clearly exhibited. But, at the same time, the pathway is strewn with gigantic blocks of error. The scholasticism which obscured the dawning light of the twelfth century, the Inquisition which crushed the Albigenses, the reception of the Jesuit Order, the wild and unpatriotic follies of the politicians of the sixteenth century, the Spanish influence at the Court of Lewis XIII, the expulsion of the Huguenots, diverted France from her true course of democratic and colonial development, and gave the primacy of industry and the rule of the seas to Holland and Great Britain. The Terrorists again diverted the Revolution from the paths of democracy, and Robespierre paved the way for Bonaparte.

It is well to recognise these things, and it is also well to be patriotic, but we confess that Michelet's national vanity seems, notwithstanding his admissions, to be somewhat fantastic and overdone. France supplies 'the sympathetic tie of the world.' It is the source of all illumination. The French language penetrates everywhere, and chases mystery from the dark sanctuaries of the earth. 'Une telle langue est la guerre aux dieux.' Conversely, England, which is Anti-France, comes in for even more than her proper share of castigation. Ireland, of course, has been shamefully maltreated by the brutal Saxons. We will not quarrel with Michelet over his estimate of the Celts, although perhaps it is excessive to say that 'it is the glory of the Celts to have founded in the West the law of equality,' upon the double ground that an early Welsh philosopher believed in the freedom of the will, and that Celtic tribal property was subdivided by 'a law of precocious equity.' It is, however, surprising to learn that Cornwall has been the Peru of England, only valued for her mines; that in Norman England serfdom approached in horror to ancient slavery; that the comedies of Shakespeare are mournful and betray signs of national degeneration; that the sea is English by inclination, and does not love France, but breaks her vessels and fills her ports with sand. We feel here that however much Michelet may have gained by the lowliness of his origin, he has certainly lost something by sharing the vulgar prejudices of the man in the street.

In palliation it may be said that the Frenchmen of his time were nurtured upon the Pitt-Coburg legend; that the boy was sixteen years of age when the battle of Waterloo was fought; that he saw the allied armies occupy Paris, and that Thierry had set him a bad example in his history of the Norman conquest of England. Michelet also would probably have replied to his critics that it was not the function of the historian to correct national traditions, but to justify them.

> This is what France demands of us historians, not to make history—it is made for the essential facts morally, the great results are inscribed in the conscience of the people—but to reestablish the chain of facts and ideas from which these results have issued. "I do not ask of you," she says, "that you should make my creeds, and dictate my judgments; it is for you to receive them and conform yourself to them. The problem which I propose to you is to tell me how I came to act as I have acted, and to judge as I have judged."

This was sound enough doctrine as against Hamel, who wrote three volumes to deify Robespierre, and the numerous apologists of the Emigration. The massive popular tradition, which reported the *émigrés* to have been unpatriotic and selfish, the King to have been incompetent, and the Terror to have been a gigantic crime as well as a blunder, was very much more trustworthy than the elaborate sophistries of the partisan historians. But it is one thing to trust the national memory upon facts within the range of recent national experience, and another thing to trust its report upon facts about which, from the necessity of the case, it was imperfectly informed. The Parisian who, in 1794, was in hourly terror of the guillotine, had every right to express and record an opinion of the ways of the Mountain; but of European diplomacy he knew nothing, and of England he was, despite Montesquieu and Voltaire, almost as ignorant as of Tartary or Timbuctoo.

There is another somewhat serious deduction from the value of Michelet's historical work, which may equally be traced to the character of the intellectual influences in France at the time of his youth. For all his emotional and poetic nature, he had inherited the one-sided Revolutionary view of Christianity. In an eloquent little book, the *Bible de l'humanité,* published in 1864, that is to say, after Strauss and Renan had respectively abolished and evaporated Christ, he reviewed the leading creeds of the world, indicating his own marked preference for the ancient religion of the Persians. The creeds fall into two classes, those of the Peoples of the Light, and those of the Peoples of the Twilight, the Night, and the *Clair-Obscur.* In the first division we have India, Persia, and Greece: in the second division Egypt, the religion of death; Syria and Phrygia, the religion of enervation; the worship of Bacchus-Sabbas, typifying tyranny and military orgies; Judaism, the religion of the slave; Christianity, the religion of the woman. Of the last religion he writes:—

> Three women begin the whole thing. Anne, mother of the Virgin; Elizabeth, her cousin, mother of St John, and another Anne, prophetess, and wife of the high priest. . . . The Messianic condition (to be elderly and so far childless) was found precisely in the cousins Anne and Elizabeth.

The 'Protoevangelium Jacobi,' 'innocent and amusing,' is the book which throws the clearest light upon this feminine aspect of Christianity. It is unnecessary to say more of Michelet's treatment of Christian origins, for it is confessedly slight, and indeed little more than a repetition of Renan's sentimental and unsatisfactory idyll. The curious fact is that Michelet seems never to have recognised that Christianity has anything to say to grown men. The whole history of Christian development is explained upon the hypothesis of a secular conspiracy between the priest and the woman, culminating in the domination of the Jesuits, the organisation of the confessional, the break-up of family life, the Vendée, and the counter-Revolution. The antidote to this emasculating influence was to be found in the study of national history, in a closer and more refined union between man and wife, and in a sense of the solidarity of man with nature.

It is well that an historian should offer prescriptions, and Michelet's prescriptions are admirable. No one, excerpt perhaps Georges Sand in 'Mdlle la Quintinie,' has described the evils of the confessional so eloquently, or has studied with such delicate insight and sympathy the influence of priest upon woman through history. But while there are clearly many elements of truth in Michelet's view, it is nothing short of astounding that an historian, a poet, and a moralist, steeped in the literature of the Middle Ages, should have been dead to the rational and practical side of Church teaching, should have ignored the extent to which it fortified mind and character in barbarous

ages, and should have attributed the ultimate victory of a great institution and scheme of thought to the insidious influence of priest upon woman and woman upon man. Fortunately this unsympathetic attitude had not been adopted until after the completion of the first six volumes of the *History of France,* which carry the reader down to the end of the Middle Ages.

For diplomatic correspondence he had little taste, and in this was the opposite of Ranke, 'notre aimable savant ingénieux, Ranke, qui nous a tant appris,' who seems to find nothing but state papers entirely interesting. It was necessary, of course, to read Granvelle and similar authorities for the period of Charles V; and Michelet is careful to explain that if his treatment of the reign of Louis XIII seems to be a tissue of Court intrigue, it is because (as Cardinal Mazarin explained to the Queen) the capture of the King for two days meant a revolution in policy. But having chosen the people for his hero, he despises cabinet intrigues, deeming that they have been accorded an excessive importance in historical works. Thus Cato introduces him to the 'rudeness of the old Latin genius,' revealing 'a people patient and tenacious, disciplined and regular, avaricious and avid.' Germany is made manifest in Grimm's *Weisthümer,* that splendid collection of old legal custom and ritual, and in the writings and table-talk of Luther, from which Michelet published two volumes of extracts. So, too, Haxthausen's agrarian studies first discover for him the true Russia.

Michelet always looks behind the courtly records for clues to the real popular life, and thus shows the way to Mr. J. R. Green and the later group of social historians. He claims to have discovered 'the great, the sombre, the terrible fourteenth century,' by discarding Froissart, who, spinning like a gaudy dragon-fly over a dank and turbid pool, has attracted all eyes by his iridescence. The life of the Flemish Communes and of Jacques Bonhomme is for him more fundamental and more attractive than the feudal society depicted by Olivier de la Marche and Chastellain. He fell in with fifteen folio volumes of street ballads and fashion plates when working at French life under Louis XIV; and it was a great windfall, for he loved the work of the microscope, and claimed it as one of his greatest merits that he was able to extract significance from 'le menu détail.' Not that he was destitute of general ideas. He may be said to have rediscovered Vico, the father of philosophical history, and he learnt from the Italian writer the doctrine that 'humanity creates itself,' changing its character by continuous mutual interaction as time goes on. Thus Thierry's conception of Race as a constant struck him as unscientific; and it was one of his objects to show how 'France had made France,' how in the course of the multitudinous intercourse of men the national character had undergone numerous changes. But to exhibit the national psychology in all its delicate manners and varieties, it was not sufficient merely to narrate a string of battles and negotiations and treaties. The physical basis of life, climate, geography, food, must be studied, so that the story should not be 'like a Japanese picture,' the figures resting on air. A whole society should be, so to speak, surprised in its intimate moods, when it is off guard, and its pose is natural.

The task requires delicate sensibility and a wide conspectus of life, for the indications are often trivial, and very heterogeneous. A picture, a medallion, a coin, the sentiment of a Burgundian hill-side, a fragment of old building, a scrap of song or of painted glass, a rustic proverb or the joke of a chronicler—what marvels may they not be made to perform by the magician of history? Sometimes he divines a truth; often his fancy floats him away into some painted cloud. And so, with the best intentions to be real, his works are full of symbolism and of the 'pathetic fallacy'—the malady which afflicts those who search too zealously for sentiment and significance among common things. The 'fresh rosy mask' of Francis II of Austria, 'in its terrible fixity,' as it hangs in the gallery of Versailles, appals him. 'Such a being visibly will never feel remorse; it commits crime conscientiously. Pitiless bigotry is necessarily written in this bigoted face.' A drawing of Danton gives rise to the following reflections: 'The most terrifying thing is that there are no eyes. At least, one scarcely sees them. What? This terrible blind man shall be the guide of nations? Obscurity, vertigo, fatality, absolute ignorance of the future—this is what one reads here.' It is characteristic of him to seize upon some little scrap of personal evidence and hold it up to the spectators as typical and decisive of a man or even of a period. In the hands of a great imaginative writer such a method is always effective, often convincing, sometimes very misleading.

It is generally agreed that the finest portions of Michelet's historical work are the first six volumes of the ***History of France.*** They were written between 1833 and 1843, when he was Professor at the École Normale and the Collège de France, and also chief of the historical division of the Archives Nationales. The ***History of the French Revolution*** was written between 1845 and 1853, the ***Renaissance and the New Monarchy*** from 1855 to 1867, the ***History of the Nineteenth Century*** in 1869. It will thus be seen that the histories of the sixteenth, seventeenth, and eighteenth centuries were composed after the author had steeped himself in the passions of the Revolution. They are less complete, less sure, less massive than the earlier work. They are defaced by the introduction of pathological explanations which are often repellent and seldom convincing, and by an uncontrolled hatred of monarchy and religion. Besides this, the literature of these later centuries was too vast to be mastered in its entirety; and Michelet selected and used his fragments with caprice. Melody, eloquence, divination are there: the voice is no longer that of the poet-savant but that of the poet-politician.

It has been truly said by a distinguished scholar that we are apt to overrate the morals and to underrate the brains of the Middle Ages. Michelet certainly underrated the value and originality of mediæval thought; and, despite the work of Hauréau and other writers, his estimate of scholasticism is no fairer than that of Voltaire. He was not unacquainted with philosophy, and had even taught it at the Collège Charlemagne and at Ste-Barbe; but the strength of his anti-ecclesiastical bias prevented him from doing justice to any thinker save Abélard and Arnold of Brescia. (pp. 134-42)

On the other hand, the sanctity of mediæval morals was certainly overrated in the first six volumes [of the ***History of France***], although Michelet's opinion of them changed decidedly for the worse after working at the second volume of the *Procès des Templiers,* and reading the striking evidence contained in the *Cartulaire de St Bertin* and the *Journal des visites épiscopales d'Eudes Rigaud.*

The first six volumes were eloquent and poetical and learned; and they were an attempt to tell the history of the French people rather than that of the monarchy. But the ***French Revolution*** is more than eloquent, learned, and poetical: it marks a new departure.

> Every history of the Revolution up till now has been essentially monarchical. This has been the first republican history, the first which has broken the idols and the gods. From the first page to the last it has only had one hero, the people. . . . All the glory of the Mountain has been monopolised by the Committee, that of the Committee by Robespierre; that is to say, republican history has constantly been written in a monarchical sense.

The supreme merit of Michelet's history lies just in the fact that it is the attempt of a powerful genius to evoke the spirit of a whole people from the tomb. Of all the histories of the French Revolution this is the greatest, and yet it is written by a man without a scrap of true political judgment. It is as poetical as Carlyle's, but fuller, closer to the complex and passionate reality. It does not deal out frigid judgments like Taine, but tells the story with the clear fervour of a disciple recounting the origins of his creed. It rings with sounding epigrams and noble eloquence and absurd rhapsody. It is prefaced and inspired by the ridiculous belief that the Revolution was in essence and origin antagonistic to Christianity, that 'to the genius of Christianity one thing only could be opposed—the genius of St Bartholomew.' It is disgracefully lenient in its estimate of the men of the Convention, who acquiesced in the most monstrous cruelties which a civilised city has ever witnessed.

> They were all, we swear it, excellent citizens, ardent lovers of their country. It was in general the jealous and terrible love which they had for the republic which threw them into these ways of unjust accusation and extermination.

The truth is, they suffered from abject cowardice and hysterical suspicion; and Michelet quotes only to forget the fine phrase of Fabre d'Eglantine, 'Rien de grand sans la pitié.' [Nothing great without pity.] Nevertheless, making all allowances for exuberant perversion, it is a wonderful book, for it reveals the raptures and the passions of a whole nation, enabling the reader to understand the truth of the statement with which it is prefaced, that 'never since the Crusades has there been such a convulsion of the masses, so general and so profound.' (pp. 142-43)

[Michelet's] task is to describe the enthusiasm of '89, the Federations of '90, the spontaneous organisation of France in '91, the growth of republican feeling and the popular movements in '92. With the ascendency of Robespierre and the Committee of Public Safety the wine for him has lost its flavour. The *élan* has gone; the spirit of

Fraternity has evaporated; and the Revolution is checked by the gloomy repression of the Terror. Though he consulted the manuscript register of the Committee of Public Safety, the material in which he delights to revel is not administrative but popular—the letters of the provincial federations to the National Assembly which he found 'entire, burning as of yesterday after sixty years,' and full of the naïve and unreserved confidences of the child to its mother; the *procès-verbaux* of the Commune under Chaumette, which illustrate the miscellaneous philanthropy that went on together with the guillotine; the manuscript reports of the debates in the Assembly; the Archives de Police. He travels to Toulon to get a sight of the registers which record the names of the galley-slaves; he ransacks the judicial registers of Nantes for light upon the Vendée and the Noyades; he picks up lessons and valuable crumbs of oral information from his father, from one of the combatants of August 10th, from a Nantes merchant, from the family of the artist who painted Charlotte Corday; and he is actually acquainted with a lady who took the part of Goddess of Reason in a provincial festival, 'une femme sérieuse et d'une vie irréprochable.' No other history written so long after the events gives such an impression of being contemporary.

The drawback of trying to be contemporary is that you lose the advantages of being subsequent. Michelet's book is vitiated by a certain superficiality of judgment. He loves the Revolution, which was 'gloriously spiritualistic, daughter of philosophy, not of the deficit'; but, on the other hand, he hates the Terror, and has arrived at a very just estimate of Robespierre. He is therefore forced to explain how it was that so glorious a movement, 'which demanded that a whole people should elevate itself above its material habits,' should decline upon so miserable an issue. His answer is that certain assignable mistakes were committed. In the first place, the Constituent lacked *le sens éducatif.* It was prolific in laws, but it did not supply the means of education by which those laws could be made intelligible. Its work was merely political and superficial, fruitful in laws, sterile in dogmas; whereas it ought to have been social, profound, positive. Then the Constituent, tempted by the virtues of Rabaut, Grégoire, and Camus, made the mistake of compromising with the Church; while, lastly, war should have been declared a year earlier, before the air had become thick with suspicion, and when France could have taken the offensive against unready foes, for it was the defensive war which produced the September massacres.

These explanations neglect the facts that the Reign of Terror and spontaneous anarchy had really begun in 1789; that the process of political education cannot be accomplished by a stroke of the pen; and that France was wholly unready for a breach with Catholicism. The one remedy which to Mirabeau and Malouet seemed possible—the establishment of a constitutional monarchy after the English pattern—is by Michelet rejected with scorn.

> The Middle Ages . . . only possessed one hypocrisy; we possess two: the hypocrisy of authority, the hypocrisy of liberty; in a word the priest, the Englishman—the two forms of Tartuffe. The priest acts principally on women or the peasant; the Englishman on the *classes bourgeoises.*

Perhaps after all Michelet was right, and the experiment of parliamentary government is alien to the genius of French republicanism. Yet the hypocritical side of English liberty was not so apparent in 1789 as it was thirty years later; and Montesquieu's ideal picture of us had not yet been torn to shreds by the inconoclasts of constitutional history.

Anacharsis Clootz once said on a famous occasion, 'France, guéris-toi des individus' [France, cure yourself of individuals]. Michelet, who individualises everything, who paints character so boldly and brilliantly, gives this to his country by way of crowning precept after issuing from the fiery furnace of '94. The great things of the Revolution were, in his view, done, not by a few men, but by the masses; he disbelieved in the artificial mechanism of the revolutionary day. The growth of France was not, as so many had written, the result of the fostering care of the monarchy; and it was Michelet's aim to prove the fact in his concluding volumes. Germany and Italy had lived by the light of a few bright stars; France 'by the common soul': 'sans la France le Français n'est plus' [without France, French is no more]. All the more difficult was the task of the historian, called upon to evoke this varied and multitudinous life. (pp. 144-46)

'The Renaissance did not regard antiquity as a varied world of mingled ages and infinitely different colours, but as Eternal Venus.' Michelet, who sweeps the field of history with a microscope, was not in danger of falling into the error which he attributes to the Italians of the sixteenth century, and which certainly vitiates the æsthetic criticism of Winckelmann and Goethe. His antiquity is living and concrete, and coloured with all the hues of the spectrum. He paints the movement and the passion of crowds with the power of Tintoret, overhears the chatter of the peasant's cottage and the wineshops, listens to the *curé* and his housekeeper, to the priest and his *pénitente,* watches the fingers of the machinist tending his tyrant of steel, follows the plough as it shears through the loam, catches the malevolent gossip from the backstairs of the palace, and throws his ardent nature into every aspect of human toil and every manifestation of human character. The great spectacle of historic France, with its varying climes and tempers and manners of living, emerges for the first time into clear light with the advent of the Capetian dynasty. There is a character which persists, discerned equally by Polybius and Strabo and by the intelligent English traveller of the eighteenth century, a buoyancy, an *insouciance,* a brilliant courage, a nimble wit, a sensual appetite. Multiply coarseness and power and it gives you Rabelais or Danton; add the nervousness which comes from crowds, and you get the furies of 1358 and 1792. Some large spirits, a Fénelon or a Renan, seem to contain all the intellectual nuances in their Protean variety; but, large as that variety is, there is no trait of national thought or feeling which has escaped Michelet's piercing vision. He has written, says Taine, 'the lyrical epic' of French history, lyrical in the intensity of its personal feeling, and yet an epic in that it recreates poetically the story of a nation.

Von Ranke thought that the historian's mission was merely to relate what had actually happened, 'was eigentlich geschehen ist.' Michelet, however, was constitutionally incapable of seeing anything through plain glass. In his best period he felt passionately with every movement and every phase, breathing life and love whithersoever he passed. 'Let it be,' he writes, 'my part in the future not to have attained but to have marked the goal of history, to have given it a name which no one as yet has uttered. Thierry called it narrative and M. Guizot analysis. I have named it resurrection, and this name will remain to it.' In view of the historical methods at present practised in France, the prophecy will seem a little sanguine, but it contains the explanation and the aim of Michelet's work. The term 'resurrection' applies to the work of the best period, to the first six volumes, and to the *History of the Revolution.* The later books are prophetic, critical, onesided, the work of the Professor who used his chair for political propaganda, 'transforming his lectures,' according to the words of a pupil, 'into pieces of oratory addressed, not to a select body of students, but to the crowd.'

The *History of the Nineteenth Century* must indeed be judged leniently, for it was written with the hand of extreme old age; and it could not be expected that a teacher who had been deprived of his chair under the Second Empire should appreciate the merits of the First. He could measure the evils, but not the necessity or the services of Cæsarism, nor yet was his mind rid of the brilliant phantasmagoria of the revolutionary dreamers. He thinks that during the Directorate Europe was longing to be free; he says that Napoleon did not know Italy, or he would have confiscated the Church lands and freed the peninsula from sea to sea. Napoleon knew Italy better than Michelet, and saw that the Italian was superstitious through and through, and that the revolutionary movement was superficial, confined to a handful of merchants, doctors, and lawyers in the big towns. Michelet scolds the Corsican for making peace with Austria, that is to say, with the counter-revolution, at Campo-Formio, whereas most historians would say that it was one of Napoleon's wisest acts. The Concordat is condemned, as it is by Lanfrey, and the civil work of the Emperor passed by with a mere statement that it was a revival of the *régime* of Louis Quatorze. The military genius of the man is belittled, and wherever possible the credit of a victory is transferred to some one else. Too much is made of the fear of socialism as an element in determining Napoleon's rise to power. Too little is said of the incompetence, the profligacy, the crimes of the Directorate. We are invited to admire La Reveillière Lepaux as a model of all the civic virtues. We are expected to believe that it would have been statesmanlike for France to maintain the Girondin propaganda against crowned heads. We are told that the financial ruin of the Directorate was due to the milliards of false assignats forged by Pitt. We are asked to lament 'the deplorable philanthropy' of Fructidor, which preferred to send its victims to rot away in Cayenne rather than to expiate their royalism on the block. M. Houssaye, working from the police reports in the Paris archives, shows how much popularity still remained to Napoleon even in the Hundred Days. Michelet, who remembered how the Dames des Halles stood under their umbrellas in the Marché des Innocents and cursed the man who had robbed them of their coffee, will have none of this. The misfortune is that in order to blacken Napoleon he must needs gild the last moments of the Directorate.

But when all is said, Michelet remains a force in historical literature which no subsequent generation can afford to neglect. His reflection is often childish, his analysis deficient, his passion strained; there are pages of inaccuracy, pages of hallucination, pages of prurience. Whole nations are sometimes travestied, and the wilfulness of an overstrung genius often flings its fantastic colours upon the page. But we are brought face to face with men and women who think, feel, and act. All things, indeed, which pass through the furnace of that glowing mind come out human. Nations and rivers, birds and storms, mountains and insects are endowed with living personality. Every province has its special character and $\eta\theta o\varsigma$. The Ardennes is 'dry, critical, serious'; Flanders is 'a prosaic Lombardy, lacking the vine and the sun'; we read of 'the spiritual lightness' of Guyenne, the pompous and 'solemn eloquence' of Burgundy, the 'contradictory genius' of Poitou, the 'violent petulance' of Provence. Upon such passages the foe of subjective history might write a sufficiently crushing dissertation.

Many histories may be more methodical and judicious, but is there another historian endowed with Michelet's poetic vision, with his broad grasp of human motives, his immortal velocity of style? Texts do not say everything; often they do not say the important things. Like the moon at night, they reveal the dim silhouette of the forest, leaving it for the inner eye to figure the various wealth of foliage, the fresh dewy lawns, the glancing colours of the birds and butterflies, the green bracken rustling with living things. Yet it must not be supposed that Michelet neglected his texts. He had read enormously, especially in manuscript material; and the *History of the French Revolution* derives a special importance from the fact that the author had access to documents which were burnt in 1871. It must be confessed that few men have learnt so little wisdom from so vast a study of human transactions; and we question whether such amazing knowledge has ever before been united with such a vivacious stock of empty childishness. But then, on the other hand, what historian of equal knowledge has felt so deeply the pathos of common life? There was no rumour of heroism or tenderness or love so faint or so distant but that it sent a melodious quiver through that sensitive spirit as it travelled through the halls of time.

Frenchmen will always continue to read Michelet for his style. He is the one writer of French prose who, albeit widely departing from the classic tradition, holds an audience by sheer force of native melody. Like Carlyle he has no predecessors, and will have no successors. (pp. 146-50)

"Michelet as an Historian," in The Quarterly Review, *Vol. 193, No. 385, January, 1901, pp. 130-50.*

Albert Leon Guérard   (essay date 1913)

[*In the following excerpt, Guérard examines Michelet's*

attitude toward religion in some of his non-historical works.]

No school, no Church can claim the mobile, ardent, and tender soul of Michelet. He ignored or despised abstractions, formulæ, dogmas: he was all life and love. "Other [historians]," he said, "were more brilliant, more judicious, more profound: I loved more." Individuals, nations, nature, were alike alive to him. They lived again in him; his soul would thrill at the recital of their sufferings or of their happiness; he lived again in them: he lent them his passions, his aspirations. Every one of his books was a "resurrection," or an interpretation, of life. Of every one could be said what he wrote on the front page of **The People:** "This is myself."

Thus Michelet, perhaps the most subjective of all Romanticists, was at the same time the least egotistic. His personality was ever present, but ever in the form of unselfish sympathy. He was not infected with Chateaubriand's melancholy, because he knew neither the gloom of moral isolation nor, like Vigny, "the burden of greatness." Fully conscious of his own powers, free from shrinking self-diffidence, he was yet, like George Sand, without pretence and without vanity. This simplicity of heart . . . saved him from the first danger that menaces whoever bases his philosophy on love: sentimentalism. So sincere was he, so true of soul, that in his thousand pages of lyric effusions there are many which are bizarre, excessive, disconcerting, even ridiculous; there is not one that is downright mawkish and unmanly.

The second danger which threatens too loving a soul is *quietism,* repose in God, a kind of mystic optimism that kills energy. Michelet was born in poverty, and rose in life through superhuman efforts on his parents' part and on his own. He was a son of the Revolution and saw the Great Empire. Thus his own experience and that of his country taught him to believe in the necessity and the virtue of effort. The first characteristic of religion, in his mind, was that faith which prompts to action. "Will and Power are one. Whoever *wills,* strongly, continuously, and in spite of everything, conquers every obstacle." His religion was not contemplative, beatific, but militant.

Love has a third danger: its arbitrariness. Love is bound by no law; it effaces the distinction between good and evil; it ruins justice. Romanticism, at a certain period of its development, seemed disposed to sacrifice everything to the rights of passion: now, for Michelet, the ideals of justice and love were inseparable. Justice was the supreme crown of love, and love the flower of justice. In this puzzling, incomplete world of ours, apparent conflicts between the two are not impossible: in such a case, Michelet would unhesitatingly take the side of justice. If he admired the Revolution it was for its "profoundly pacific, kindly, humane spirit," no doubt, but chiefly because it was the "advent of law, the resurrection of Right, the reaction of Justice." The same criterion will be applied to Christianity: "[The question is] to know whether the dogma of Grace and Salvation through Christ, the only basis of Christianity, can be reconciled with *Justice;* to know whether this dogma is *just,* and will stand." And as Reason is but the way to Truth, and Justice but Truth in action, Michelet worshipped "at the altar of Right and Truth and eternal Reason, which has . . . not lost one stone." "Identical in all ages, on the firm foundation of Nature and history, Eternal Justice shines."

The religion, not of love alone, but of justice and truth in the spirit of love, and of activity for the sake of justice, such was Michelet's faith. The centre, the foundation of it was *le foyer,* the hearth, a sacred and tender word which "home" does not fully render. "The hearth is the stone upon which the City is builded." It must be pure, austere, united: war to any system or individual that would attempt to divide or weaken it! There the first lessons of work and sacrifice must be learnt; there must reign harmoniously the two principles, justice and love, embodied in the father and the mother. Michelet was a man of the people, like Veuillot and Proudhon: it is significant that all three, so radically different in many other respects, had the same uncompromising devotion to the family altar. This devotion is evident everywhere in Michelet's life and writings. It was the origin, it remains the saving grace, of his strange books **L'amour** (Love), **La femme** (Woman), so often condemned equally by Gallic levity and Saxon prudishness. It was the basis of his treatise on education, **Nos fils** (Our Sons). On the sanctity of marriage, the integrity of the home, the Catholic journalist, the socialist polemist, the Romantic historian were as intractable as any old Roman or any Puritan.

The city is but a larger family, whose service requires the same virtues. First of all it must be united, not by outward compulsion, but in the bonds of love. And France in the nineteenth century was not united. "Our boasted unity," said Michelet, "is superficial. The cultured few and the illiterate populace have little in common." To bridge the chasm between the classes and the masses was Michelet's constant preoccupation. Himself born among the poor, he knew them well, and loved them, for their patience under hardships which he had shared to the full, and for their pure ideal of brotherly assistance. To his students, sons of the bourgeoisie, he preached the duty of going to the people, simply, fraternally. He felt that even the best intentioned writers—himself as well as the rest—had left the people spiritually unfed and unclothed. As the highest function of the "foyer" is to educate the child, the highest function of the State is to educate the people. "What is the first part of politics? Education. And the second? Education. And the third? Education." Just because he was himself of humble origin, his aspirations for the social betterment of the lower classes were sane, moderate, and at the same time idealistic: it is bourgeois politicians, not the working men themselves, who formulate in the name of the people Utopian demands. Michelet was not blind to the present limitations of the poor, and he knew that it was not bread alone they were craving for, but truth, justice, and love.

The home of this immense family is France: patriotism is with Michelet as with the Ancients an essential part of religion. He loved France passionately, in the harmonious diversity of her provinces, in her tragic and glorious past, in her generous aspirations, in her living personality. In him the historian, the patriot, and the prophet were inseparable. On the question of patriotism, as on that of the family, he accepted no compromise. "Another religion," he said, "the humanitarian dream of philosophy, which believes that it can save the individual by destroying the citizen, by denying the right of the Nation, by denouncing the Fatherland, that other religion, too, I have sacrificed. The Fatherland, my Fatherland, alone can save the world."

Yet, ardent patriot though he was, and opposed to internationalism, Michelet was not indifferent to other countries. He hailed, in 1848, "the eagle of Poland, which has so often bled for us, the tricolour of Italy—Italia mater—the red, black, and gold of Germany, my beloved Germany." All nations are persons, like France, sisters to be respected, and helped, and loved. All will sit some day at the universal banquet of peace. It is true he hated England as much as he loved Germany: he shared the popular prejudices of the men of his generation, who could not forget Waterloo and St. Helena; England represented in his eyes materialistic strength and national selfishness. On the whole he was, like Hugo, Quinet, Lamartine, a humanitarian patriot.

"My country alone can save the world." Michelet believed in the mission of France. "For the last two centuries, one may say that the true Pope was France; authority lies here, under one form or another; here is the centre of Europe, through Louis XIV, Montesquieu, Voltaire, and Rousseau, through the Constituent Assembly, the Code and Napoleon; all other nations are eccentric." France in the eighteenth century formulated the creed of the modern world, and the Revolution undertook its practical application.

In the worship of the Revolution, all the tendencies of Michelet's thought united—love and justice, patriotism and humanitarianism. The Revolution was for him the incarnation of the French spirit: "France and Revolution are henceforth synonymous." It was truly a religion: it had all the characters of one. "The Revolution, some one said [Quinet?] ought to have placed itself under the banner of Luther or Calvin. I answer: this would have been an abdication. The Revolution adopted no Church. Why? Because it was itself a church." "It created the faith that accomplishes miracles, or rather for which there are no miracles, so simple do the most superhuman tasks appear. As agape, as communion, nothing in this world was ever comparable to the enthusiasm of the federations in 1790. Sacrifice in its absolute, its infinite grandeur, the surrender of self without holding back anything, was seen in its most sublime form in the enthusiasm of 1792: a sacred war on behalf of peace, and for the freedom of the world." Whenever Michelet spoke of the Revolution, it was in tones of fervour and awe: "What am I," he said, with the mystic self-abasement of a monk before the Cross, "what am I that I should be allowed to relate these scenes?" The Revolution is divine, nay, it is God: " . . . Justice, the new God, whose war-name here below is the Revolution." [*Nos fils*] appeared in 1869, after twenty years of materialistic and sceptical reaction had taught France to jeer at her own past; Michelet had spent seven years in a close study of his idol, yet his faith was unshaken.

The family; the people; the nation, France; mankind, as the great family of families; the Revolution, as the highest expression of France and mankind in the service of justice and truth: such were the objects of Michelet's adoration. To this list, should we add Nature? During the Second Empire, the great historian ventured into a new field, and wrote his delightful medleys of science, poetry, sentiment, fantasy, *The Bird* (1856), *The Insect* (1857), *The Sea* (1861), *The Mountain* (1868). Sick, body and soul, after the triumph of reaction; deprived of his professorship, of that contact with young men which had always been such an inspiration to him; exhausted by his great effort in writing the history of the Revolution, he sought peace, oblivion, and fresh courage in the heart of nature. He was no doubt influenced also by the immense progress of natural sciences in the middle of the century. But Michelet was not strictly a nature-worshipper, a naturalistic pantheist. What strikes him most in nature is neither the spectacle of its beauty, as in the case of the other Romanticists, nor the idea of inflexible law, as with the Positivists. Natural history, like human history, was for him a "psychomachy," a drama of souls. His anthropomorphic imagination saw the love, the struggles, the sufferings of animals, and perhaps even of the elements. He insisted on the relations of nature to man—the possibility of a state of harmony rather than of war between the higher and the lower creation, the usefulness of our humble friends and fellow-workers, birds and insects, of our great doctors, mountain and sea. These books of the new St. Francis, full of delicate observations and accurate descriptions, are yet, first of all, sermons and lyrical poems. Michelet remained even in his nature studies the apostle of effort and love.

Beyond and within nature and mankind, God; God, as the supreme realisation of justice and love, "the universal soul of the worlds, who is but Truth and Justice, impartial and immutable Love." Michelet was no metaphysician and no theologian. Philosophers are not certain whether his conception of God as both immanent and transcendent should be called spiritualism or pantheism. Let them dispute: his God was the living God, and a loving Father.

Justice and love—righteousness and charity: is not that the whole of Christianity? Michelet, when a child, read with emotion the *Imitation of Christ;* he was the reverse of a cold rationalist, of an iconoclast; he had the true historical spirit of respectful sympathy for the past; he had "faith in faith and the love of love." He should have been an excellent Christian. Yet from 1843 to his death he was an irreducible adversary of historical and organised Christianity. Not only, at a time when State education was attacked with unscrupulous violence, did he deliver and publish, in self-defence, denunciatory curses against the priests and the Jesuits, but in March, 1848, when all was still hope and trust, when Catholics and socialists fraternised, he, the apostle of national reconciliation, was almost alone in sounding a note of diffidence and warning.

There are three things in a religion: the Church, the doctrine, the spirit. The Church, in France, was the Roman Catholic. Now, this Church, in Michelet's mind, was opposed to his dearest objects of worship—the hearth, the Revolution. The hearth: the priest, bound to celibacy, to an unnatural ideal of absolute chastity, scorned family life, if not as unholy, at least as inferior, and was a stranger to the most legitimate and ennobling affections. The father should be a priest at the altar of his own fireside, and be united with his family in truest soul-communion; but the Catholic intruder, through confession, robbed him of his wife's spiritual allegiance, turned her against him, divided that which God had united. The Revolution: the Church had unequivocally sided with autocracy; since the condemnation of Lamennais, no doubt was possible: the Church was the centre of all reaction, of the counter-revolution. And in the very spirit of love the Church was deficient: rich, powerful, ambitious, rebellious wherever it could not be tyrannical, it had become hard, materialistic. It was in the name of religion, of charity, of the ideal that Michelet, like Quinet, George Sand, Victor Hugo, revolted against Rome.

Michelet drew splendid portraits of Luther and Calvin. Luther, especially, so natural, so popular, active, sincere, merry, and tender, won his heart. But, different in this respect from Quinet, he never was in active sympathy with Protestantism. The rival influences of Catholicism and eighteenth-century philosophy, which fought for dominion in his soul, were so strong that he could not escape from one without falling under the other. The Protestants were in close touch with England, which he hated; he could not bear the stiffness, the coldness, the reactionary spirit of their best-known representative, Guizot. An orthodox reformation, possible in the sixteenth century, was out of the question in the nineteenth. Therefore Catholicism stood as the sole representative of Christianity, and Michelet's hostility was extended from clericalism to theology. Monarchical and Christian idolatry, injustice, arbitrariness, favour, grace, all, he thought, were linked together; he detested them all equally.

Christianity and the Revolution agreed on the sentiment of human brotherhood, but the Revolution founded this sentiment "on mutual duty, on right, and justice," Christianity on "a doubtful historical conception, the common fall through Adam, the salvation of all through Christ." Grace, original sin, the small number of the elect, eternal punishment, shocked Michelet's sense of justice and love. In his eyes, Christian theology was irreligious. On all points he had a substitute for its doctrines. To the creation in seven days he opposed continuous creation, which excluded miracles, but not evolution; to the Fall, his faith in moral progress, in the slow ascent of man through unending efforts; to the condemnation of nature by the mediæval Church (Rabelais's *Antiphysis*), the rehabilitation of all legitimate joy, the Greek ideal of life, "a heroic smile"; to the exclusive Judeo-Christian revelation, the universal revelation, of which each people writes a chapter, each great poet a verse, "the Bible of Mankind."

Michelet, in his earlier writings, had paid full tribute to the Christian ideal. Under the Second Empire, his radical antipathy to the Church made him more sensitive to the excesses, the contradictions, the obscurities, which, in his eyes, dimmed or marred the Divine character of the Bible. The aspiration to more justice and love, the glorification of sacrifice, were not specifically Christian, but eternal and universal. The Hebrew revelation, "beautiful and unsafe, even as Night," should not be deemed unique and exclusive. "Mankind pours incessantly its soul into a common Bible. Every great people wrote its verse therein." Primitive India gave us the family in its natural purity, in its incomparable grandeur, which no later age could surpass; Persia, a lesson of heroic labour; Greece, the greatest of all arts, the art of making men. The hearth, work, education: these we owe to the three great civilisations, "a trinity of light and life, the main current of human thought." The Egyptians, the Phœnicians, the Jews were "the lesser half of mankind, the peoples of darkness and death"; when Rome was conquered by the East, Syrians and Jews, she declined, and her decay made possible "the centuries of terror and gloom," which Michelet now hated as much as he once loved them, the Christian Middle Ages.

"Jerusalem can not for ever remain the centre of the world," such is the first conclusion of this survey. "Let mankind, free in its immensity, go everywhere. Let men drink where their earliest ancestors drank. With its enormous work, its tasks extending in every direction, its titanic needs, mankind must have much air, much water, much sky—the whole sky!—space and light, infinite horizons, the whole earth as promised land, and the world for its Jerusalem."

Such universal worship cannot be narrowed down to the limits of a local and historical organisation; yet collective adoration, a ceremonial, are necessary. Michelet's ideal was the Greek festival: games, processions, the drama; in modern times, the "Federation" in 1790 and 1791. On the 4th of March, 1848, took place a celebration in honour of the dead of February. With deep joy Michelet witnessed the admirable spectacle; a whole nation, pure, enthusiastic, fraternal; the flags of other nations side by side with the French tricolour. But the Government had the unfortunate inspiration of holding the ceremony at La Madeleine (St. Magdalen's Church): "I did not go up. I had my church there, the great church of heaven. I held my celebration alone, under the sky, within my heart, saddened, however, at the spectacle of France shrinking in order to enter the little tomb." "We must turn about quickly, frankly turn our back on the Middle Ages, on that morbid past, which, even when it does not act, has a terrible influence, through the contagion of death. We must neither combat nor criticise, but forget. Let us forget and progress."

But this conclusion is negative, and negation is not Michelet's normal attitude of mind. ***The Bible of Mankind*** ends with a positive confession of faith, the best summary of Michelet's religion.

> The hearth is the stone on which the City is builded. . . . It must become again what it used to be—an altar. . . . In the circle by the fireside should be admitted all the heroes of mankind, the great Church of justice. . . . It is illumined by a reflection from the universal soul of the worlds—Truth and Justice, impartial and immutable Love.
>
> It is this strong hearth that this book would help you build, or at least begin. It hopes to give you

what it so often gave me, in the course of this long task, which absorbed me by day and woke me in the night: a heart at rest from all earthly trial, grave and holy joy, the profound peace of light.

Michelet's religious philosophy is not systematic; it can neither be classified, discussed, nor refuted. The only original and positive point about it, the worship of the Revolution, cannot be fully appreciated by our generation. France was recovering from the shock of 1848 when the worse disasters of 1870-71 befell her; sixty years of diffidence and discouragement have been weighing upon her; she is no longer in tune with Michelet's heroic optimism. She honours him, not as a prophet, but as a poet.

Michelet was too spontaneous, too individual a thinker and a writer to have any real disciples. Yet his influence was great. "Those of us whose childhood and early youth were spent during the first twelve years of the Second Empire," wrote Gabriel Monod [in his *Taine, Renan, Michelet*], "will ever remember the chill and weary gloom which oppressed their souls during that sad epoch. Youth, enthusiasm, hope, which had filled all hearts before and after 1830, seemed to have gone out for ever. . . . For many, and I was among them, the books of Michelet were then a comfort and a cordial. . . . With him one gained faith in the future of the country, in spite of the sadness of the times. One could not escape the contagion of his enthusiasm, of his hopes, of his ever youthful heart." If ever France dares once more to believe in her own destiny, Michelet's books, which now irritate or sadden her like a sarcasm or a dirge, will be again a source of inspiration. (pp. 131-41)

> *Albert Leon Guérard, "Romantic Humanitarianism," in his* French Prophets of Yesterday: A Study of Religious Thought under the Second Empire, *D. Appleton and Company, 1913, pp. 118-41.*

Edmund Wilson   (essay date 1940)

[*Wilson, considered America's foremost man of letters in the twentieth century, wrote widely on cultural, historical, and literary matters. He is often credited with bringing an international perspective to American letters through his widely read discussions of European literature. Wilson was allied to no critical school; however, several dominant concerns serve as guiding motifs throughout his work. He invariably examined the social and historical implications of a work of literature, particularly literature's significance as "an attempt to give meaning to our experience" and its value for the improvement of humanity. Although he was not a moralist, his criticism displays a deep concern with moral values. Another constant was his discussion of a work of literature as a revelation of its author's personality. Though Wilson examined the historical and psychological implications of a work, he rarely did so at the expense of a discussion of its literary qualities. In the following excerpt, he presents an overview of Michelet's political philosophy.*]

What were Michelet's conclusions from the crises which seemed continually, during his lifetime, to be reviving the revolutionary issues and in which the revolutionary tradition seemed always to be defeated? In what direction did he believe that human progress had manifested and was to manifest itself?

Not long before 1848, and just before beginning the *History of the Revolution,* Michelet wrote a little book called *The People.*

The first half, "Of Slavery and Hate", contains an analysis of modern industrial society. Taking the classes up one by one, the author shows how all are tied into the social-economic web—each, exploiting or being exploited, and usually both extortionist and victim, generating by the very activities which are necessary to win its survival irreconcilable antagonisms with its neighbors, yet unable by climbing higher in the scale to escape the general degradation. The peasant, eternally in debt to the professional moneylender or the lawyer and in continual fear of being dispossessed, envies the industrial worker. The factory worker, virtually imprisoned and broken in will by submission to his machines, demoralizing himself still further by dissipation during the few moments of freedom he is allowed, envies the worker at a trade. But the apprentice to a trade belongs to his master, is servant as well as workman, and he is troubled by bourgeois aspirations. Among the bourgeoisie, on the other hand, the manufacturer, borrowing from the capitalist and always in danger of being wrecked on the shoal of overproduction, drives his employees as if the devil were driving him. He gets to hate them as the only uncertain element that impairs the perfect functioning of the mechanism; the workers take it out in hating the foreman. The merchant, under pressure of his customers, who are eager to get something for nothing, brings pressure on the manufacturer to supply him with shoddy goods; he leads perhaps the most miserable existence of all, compelled to be servile to his customers, hated by and hating his competitors, making nothing, organizing nothing. The civil servant, underpaid and struggling to keep up his respectability, always being shifted from place to place, has not merely to be polite like the tradesman, but to make sure that his political and religious views do not displease the administration. And, finally, the bourgeoisie of the leisure class have tied up their interests with the capitalists, the least public-spirited members of the nation; and they live in continual terror of communism. They have now wholly lost touch with the people. They have shut themselves up in their class; and inside their doors, locked so tightly, there is nothing but emptiness and chill.

What then? The second half of *The People* seems as ridiculous to us today as the first half seems acute. Michelet, like many nineteenth-century writers, is at his worst when he is preaching a gospel. We know them well in English, these nineteenth-century gospels: Ruskin's Beauty, Meredith's Nature, Matthew Arnold's Culture—large and abstract capitalized words, appearing in cloudy apocalypses, as remedies for practical evils. Once Michelet leaves history proper, once he gets outside his complex of events, he shows the liberal nineteenth century at its worst. Great displays of colored fire are set off, which daze the eye with crude lurid colors and hide everything they are supposed to illuminate. The bourgeois has lost touch with the people, Michelet tells us; he has betrayed his revolutionary tradition. All the classes hate one another. What is to be done about it, then? We must have love. We must become as little children; for truth, we must go to the simpleton, even to the patient animal. And Education!—the rich and the poor must go to school together: the poor must forget their envy; the rich must forget their pride. And there they must be taught Faith in the Fatherland. "Here," Michelet is forced to confess, "a serious objection arises: 'How shall I be able to give people faith when I have so little myself ?' " "Look into yourself," he answers, "consider your children—there you will find France!"

With all this, he says some very searching things, of which he does not perceive the full implications. "Man has come to form his soul according to his material situation. What an amazing thing! Now there is a poor man's soul, a rich man's soul, a tradesman's soul. . . . Man seems to be only an accessory to his position." And his conception of the people, which at moments sounds mystical, comes down at the end to something that seems to be synonymous with humanity: "The people, in its highest idea, is difficult to find in the people. When I observe it here or there, it is not the people itself, but some class, some partial form of the people, ephemeral and deformed. In its authentic form, at its highest power, it is seen only in the man of genius; in him the great soul resides."

Socialism he rejects: property in France, he believes, has

An early portrait of Michelet.

been too far subdivided, and the French have too strong a sense of property. And he is appalled by a nightmare of the national resources administered by French public officials. No: the bourgeoisie and the people must learn to know and love one another.

The Revolution of '48 followed. The Paris proletariat, led by Socialists and demanding the municipal workshops they had been promised, were shot down by the bourgeoisie. "Let the day be stricken out," he wrote in his journal; and "I should never write *The People* now," he said.

Yet he was to remain a man of his age, a man of a generation who had seen many political systems fail, who had been exposed to the Romantic idealism, and who had been played upon by a confusion of social forces. "Young and old, we are tired," he had written already in *The People.* "Why should we not confess it, almost at the end of that laborious day which now makes half a century? . . . Even with those who, like me, have passed through several classes and who have preserved through all sorts of trials the fecund instinct of the people, that has not saved them from losing on the way, in the conflicts they have waged within themselves, a considerable part of their forces." Michelet continued to elaborate a typical nineteenth-century moral gospel in a series of social studies which he alternated with the volumes of his history. *Love* and *Woman,* evidently inspired by his late second marriage after a series of unhappy or uncomfortable liaisons, were an attempt to hold the French family together by recalling the casual French to the sacredness of domestic relations; and Michelet was naïvely delighted when some mischievous person assured him that his book was driving the brothels out of business. *Our Sons* returned to education, the last hope of the liberal in all periods; and *The Bible of Humanity* was an effort—of a kind all too familiar in our own day—to provide a new substitute religion by combining all the best features of the old ones.

It was the positive pole of his nature keeping him steady against the pull of the negative, toward which his history in its later phases was gravitating; and we cannot grudge him a little well-meant nonsense in compensation for those terrible volumes written under the oppression of Napoleon III and dealing with the last days of the old regime. Here Michelet's chief literary vice, a kind of romantic verbiage, has entirely faded away; the influence of Tacitus, from his earliest reading one of Michelet's great admirations, seems to assert itself. Here he anatomizes politics and intrigue in a style which grows more and more incisive and terse and with a caustic coldness like Stendhal's; and, by an incomparable power of tragic horror, he weights this chronicle with the burden, ever more heavily dragging, of the lives of political prisoners and inconvenient nuns stifled in blind prisons and *in pace's,* the slaughter and eviction of whole Protestant communities by Louis XIV's *dragonnades,* the long tortures under the whips of the galleys of those whom thought or conscience had brought there— filling up the abysses of history with those millions of human beings who had been dropped out of life and forgotten, till we ourselves are almost ready to shut the book and hear no more about the past of humanity. Even Michelet's interest in natural history—inspired, also, by his new wife: it was one of her enthusiasms—which stimulated him during the same period to publish a succession of books, *The Insect, The Bird,* etc., that celebrate lyrically the marvels of nature, has a more sinister side in his history, where the doings of human beings begin to seem to have more and more in common with the doings of insects and birds. It was the moment of *The Origin of Species,* and Naturalism was already in the air.

The events of 1870-71 had a shattering effect on Michelet. He had been away from Paris at the time of the invasion; and at the news of the first French defeats, he returned in the belief that he was needed, that he could somehow be of use. In the course of the siege of Paris, the house in which he was living was burned; his apartment miraculously escaped, though the chair in which he had worked got scorched. Michelet was then in his seventies, and he retreated before the attack.

Before the declaration of war, he had signed, with Marx and Engels and others, an international pacifist manifesto; and he now brought out a pamphlet called *France before Europe,* in which as "a worker to the workers of the world," he summoned them to create "an armed peace league." But his confusion between the cause of France and the cause of the workers of the world is very evident here. "The great labor party, the laboring, the industrious, the productive nations" are to arm against "the party of death," which is simply "Prusso-Russian militarism." He praises the moderation with which the revolution has thus far been carried on; only one man, he notes, has been killed. The Socialists have shown admirable restraint; and Socialism is largely a local matter: there are still only ten million industrial workers to twenty-six million peasants, and the peasants, who have made possible the Second Empire, are still strong on the side of property. All the classes are coöperating fraternally; France need not fear "the social question."

Not long afterwards, in his exile at Pisa, the news of the Paris Commune reached Michelet, following the news of the surrender of Paris; and he had an apoplectic stroke. It was the third workers' revolt during his lifetime; and this time a Communist government was to hold Paris for two and a half months. The bourgeois government at Versailles shot its prisoners; the Commune slaughtered bourgeois hostages, including the Archbishop of Paris. The bourgeoisie bombarded the city; and the Commune burned public buildings. The population of Paris fought the Versailles troops for eight days and were finally defeated by the massacre of from twenty to thirty thousand men and women. When the reports of this civil war reached Michelet, he had a second and more serious stroke, which paralyzed his right arm and his organs of speech.

Yet he recovered to continue his task. He had brought his notes with him, and he returned with furious industry to his history, taking it up where he had dropped it, at the fall of Robespierre. The final volumes of Michelet are not merely somber, but bitter. Though his organic conception of history enabled him to see humanity as a whole, he was in the habit of thinking of it and dealing with it in terms of its components: nations. He had, however, a special version of nationalism which enabled him, in the case of

France, to identify the *"patrie"* exclusively with the revolutionary tradition. In the name of the Revolution she had been chosen to lead and enlighten the world. But the old nationalism, the growing inspiration of common interest and purpose, of which Michelet had been following the development—the nationalism of which Jeanne d'Arc had been the prophet and the Federations of 1789 the explicit realization—was now turning into something which had nothing to do with the principles of '89: it was turning into modern imperialism. Napoleon, a foreigner among the French and a traitor to the Revolution—and how much more, Napoleon III—is for Michelet the mockery of the national ideal. Michelet's history, in its latest volumes, is bursting out of its old conception. "I was born," he writes in one of his prefaces, "in the midst of the great territorial revolution and I shall have lived to see the dawning of the great industrial revolution. Born under the terror of Babeuf, I have lived to see the terror of the International." The history of the nineteenth century may be summed up, he says, in three words: industrialism, militarism, socialism.

But he was too old to go far with that story: he breaks off with the banishment of Napoleon. The last words of his last volume are like an epitaph: "But by a singular blunder," he writes, "they situated him on St. Helena—so that of this high and conspicuous stage the scoundrel could make a Caucasus, exploiting the pity of the public and preparing, by force of his lies, a bloody second repetition of all the disasters of the Empire." They were to be Michelet's epitaph, too: not long after writing them, his heart failed, and he died (February 9, 1874); his last volumes came out after his death. He had intended to continue his history further; but, characteristically, he dropped it and died with it, at precisely the right moment, both of the story he was telling and of contemporary events. A new point of view, as we shall see, was needed to deal with what followed. Who can imagine Michelet confronted with the Third Republic?

But his work was complete in itself; and when we look back on it, we can see that the breaking-off leaves it as an artistic whole admirably proportioned and rounded. The early centuries of comparative barbarism succeed one another fast; they lead up to modern nationalism, Jeanne d'Arc; a brief lapse, then a great international movement of enlightenment and independence—the Renaissance, the Reformation—causes the story to overflow its frame (or, more accurately, Italy and Germany to overflow into the frame); then the Renaissance lapses, the pace slows up, the scale of presentation expands, we see the unification of France, the intensification of French nationalism, and, with them, the development of a new Renaissance, which has its climax in the Revolution; the scale becomes enormous, we trace the motives in every heart, a day may now sometimes last longer than a century of the Middle Ages; then, the great drama done, the pace accelerates and the scope opens out again; the interest of the revolutionary drama and of the national epic are both finished. I am not here interpreting history, nor even quite faithfully interpreting Michelet, if we follow all his statements and indications: I am describing the impression which he actually, by his proportioning and his emphasis, conveys. This was the story which he had to tell and which, through all the shifts of his contemporary world, the vicissitudes of his personal career, kept its consistency and reached its completion. We can study in it how far it is possible to reconcile the nationalistic ideal with a concern for the life of mankind.

The *History of France* stands unique, a great work of imagination and research of a kind perhaps never to occur again—the supreme effort in its time of a human being to enter into, to understand, to comprehend, the development of a modern nation. There is no book that makes us feel when we have finished it that we have lived through and known with such intimacy so many generations of men. And it makes us feel something more: that we ourselves are the last chapter of the story and that the next chapter is for us to create.

But what and how? Michelet cannot tell us. The fierce light of his intellect flickered out in a rhetoric smoky and acrid. (pp. 28-35)

> Edmund Wilson, "Michelet between National-
> ism and Socialism," in his To the Finland Sta-
> tion: A Study in the Writing and Acting of
> History, *Harcourt Brace Jovanovich, Inc.,*
> *1940, pp. 28-35.*

Roland Barthes   (essay date 1959)

[*Barthes was among the most influential and revolutionary writers in modern critical thought. His importance
derives less from persuasive illumination of his themes
or from his introduction of certain nonliterary perspectives into his writing (he has at various times employed
viewpoints adopted from Marxism, psychoanalysis, and
structuralism), than it does from a dominant method of
critical analysis which Barthes applied to both literary
and worldly subjects. This method is based on the insight
that language—or any other medium of communication—is a "system of signs." The aim of Barthes's method is to expose the "myths" of a specific sign system, revealing their origins in custom and convention, in order
to practice what Barthes views as the only valid purpose
of criticism: to observe the inner workings and interrelationships governing a sign system. In the following excerpt, Barthes assesses the merits of Michelet's treatment
of witchcraft in* La sorcière, *noting that his method is
both historical and novelistic.*]

Probably *La sorcière* is the favorite book of Michelet lovers. Why? Perhaps because it has a special boldness, expresses all of Michelet's temptations in an extravagant mode, deliberately establishes itself in ambiguity, which is to say, in totality. Is *La sorcière* a work of history? Yes, since its movement is diachronic, since it follows the thread of time from the death of paganism to the dawn of the Revolution. No, since this thread is novelistic, attached to a figure and not to an institution. But it is just this duplicity which is fruitful; at once history and novel, *La sorcière* generates a new insight into reality, initiates what we might call a historical ethnology, or a historical mythology. As novel, the work solidifies time, keeps historical perception from being dispersed or sublimated in the vision of distinct ideas: a whole connection becomes

evident which is precisely the tension of a history made by men themselves. As history, it immediately exorcises the ghost of psychological explanation: witchcraft is no longer a lapse of the soul, but the result of a social alienation. The witch is thus both product and object, apprehended in the double movement of a causality and a creation: born of the poverty of the serfs, she is nonetheless a force which acts upon this poverty: history perpetually tangles cause and effect. At their intersection, a new reality, which is the very object of the book: myth. Michelet keeps correcting psychology by history, then history by psychology: it is this instability which generates *La sorcière.*

For Michelet, as we know, history is oriented: it proceeds toward an illumination. Not that its movement is purely progressive; the rise of liberty encounters obstacles, setbacks: according to the metaphor Michelet borrowed from Vico, history is a spiral: time restores anterior states, but these circles are wider and wider, no state exactly reproduces its homologue; history is thus a kind of polyphony of splendors and eclipses which ceaselessly correspond, though swept on toward a still point where time must fulfill itself: the French Revolution.

Michelet starts with the institution of serfdom: here the notion of the witch is formed; isolated in her hovel, the serf's young wife listens to those petty demons of the hearth, vestiges of the old pagan gods the Church has routed: she makes them her confidants, while her husband is away at his work. In the serf's wife, the witch is still merely potential; there is no more than an imagined communication between woman and the supernatural: Satan is not yet conceived. Then times grow hard, poverty and abjection intensify; something appears in history which changes men's relations with each other, transforms property into exploitation, drains all humanity from the link between serf and lord: gold. Itself an abstraction of material goods, gold abstracts the human relation; the lord no longer knows his peasants, but only the impersonal gold in which they must pay their tribute. It is here that Michelet, anticipating all subsequent study of alienation, accurately locates the birth of the witch: when the fundamental human relation is destroyed, the serf's wife turns from the hearth to the heath, makes a pact with Satan, and collects in her wilderness, as a precious trust, the nature excluded from the world; the Church faltering, alienated from the great and cut off from the people, it is the witch who then undertakes the magistracies of consolation, the communication with the dead, the fraternity of the great collective sabbaths, the cure of physical diseases for the three centuries in which she triumphs: the leprous (fourteenth), the epileptic (fifteenth), the syphilitic (sixteenth). In other words, with the world condemned to inhumanity by the terrible collusion of gold and serfdom, it is the witch who, by withdrawing from it, recovers and preserves humanity. Thus, throughout the waning Middle Ages, the witch is a function: virtually useless when social relations involve a certain solidarity in and of themselves, she develops to the degree that these relations become impoverished: when they are null and void, the witch triumphs.

Up to this point, it is clear that as a mythic figure, the witch is identified with the progressive forces of history;

just as alchemy was the matrix of chemistry, witchcraft is merely the first medicine. In contrast to the Church's sterility, symbolized by the darkness of its *in-pace,* the witch represents light, the beneficent exploitation of Nature, the bold use of poisons as remedies, magical rites being the one way a technique of liberation could be acknowledged by an entire alienated collectivity. What happens in the sixteenth century (a period all the more significant in that we owe to Michelet the very notion of "Renaissance")? The obscurantist crust splits open: as ideologies, the Church and feudalism recede, the exploration of nature passes into the hands of laymen, scholars, and physicians. Thus the witch is no longer necessary, she enters her decadence; not that she disappears (the numerous witchcraft trials sufficiently attest to her vitality); but, as Michelet says, she becomes a professional; deprived of most of her curative vocation, she now participates only in affairs of pure magic (charms, spells), as the suspect confidante of the lady. And Michelet loses interest in her.

Yet his book does not end here. Because the witch is in eclipse does not mean that nature has triumphed. Disclosed by the subsidence of sorcery, the physician becomes the progressive figure of the next two centuries (seventeenth and eighteenth), but the Church is still there; the conflict continues between darkness and day, between priest and physician. By a series of bold transformations, Michelet reverses the functions: beneficent because he was himself a physician during the Middle Ages, Satan now becomes the physician's enemy, becomes the priest; and woman, at first Satan's bride, becomes, in the monarchical period, his victim. This is the meaning of the four great witchcraft trials Michelet fictionalizes at length in the second half of his book (Gauffridi, Loudun, Louviers, Cadière). On one side, the wretched victims, trusting and delicate, the possessed nuns; on the other, the frivolous or Machiavellian seducer-priest; behind these figures, the Church, which pulls the strings, hands them over to the stake, to the *in-pace,* either for obscurantist motives or because of the internecine war between its clans, monks, and priests; in the background, the physician, the layman, impotent judge of these crimes, whose voice alone, unfortunately stifled, could have restored this demonomania to its physical nature (the sanguineous or nervous plethora of girls doomed to spinsterhood and boredom).

Such is the sequence of forms, or to introduce a more ethnological term, of hypostases taken by the double figure of good and evil. Evil is serfdom and gold, the slave's poverty and abjection, in a word, the alienation which causes man to be excluded from nature, which means, for Michelet, from humanity. Good is the very countercurrent of this alienation, Satan, the witch, the figures which focus the light of a dying world, plunged into the dungeons of the Church. Man's exclusion from nature is set in opposition to the witch's exile from the inhabited world. For the witch is essentially labor, humanity's effort to create the world in spite of the world: it is in order to act more effectively that the witch goes into exile. Faced with the drought of medieval history (from the thirteenth century), defined by Michelet under the rubrics of two great themes of sterility, imitation and boredom, the witch, in her triumphant period, typifies all human *praxis:* she is at one

and the same time the consciousness of alienation, the movement to destroy it, the ferment of a frozen history, in short, fecundity of time. *Satan,* Michelet says, *is one of the aspects of God.*

This movement of liberation is a general form of history. But the specific point of Satan, Michelet insists, is that in relation to the original servitude, he effects an exact and indeed proportionate subversion: witchcraft is a *reversal.* We all know that the demoniac rites reverse the Christian liturgy, Satan is the obverse of God. But Michelet has taken this inversion much further, construing it poetically, making it a total form of the medieval world: for example, the alienated serf lives by night, not by day, poisonous plants become remedies, etc. This leads to the heart of the Micheletist vision: every substance is double, to live is to choose one of two contraries, to endow the great duality of forms with signification. The separation of substances sets up an internal hierarchy for each. For example, drought, which is the mark of the waning Middle Ages, is merely a state of sterility; sterility itself is the divided-up, the portioned-out, the disjunct, annihilation of human communication; Michelet will therefore contrast to the dry, all undivided substances as the substances of life: the moist and the warm define nature because nature is homogeneous. Such chemistry obviously assumes a historical signification: as the mythic form of nature, the witch represents an undivided state of human labor—the (more or less ideal) moment when man is happy because he has not yet specialized his tasks and his techniques. It is this communism of functions that the witch expresses: transcending history, she attests the happiness of primitive society and prefigures that of future society; passing through time in the manner of a more or less occult essence, she shines forth only in the theophanic moments of history: in Joan of Arc (sublimated figure of the witch), in the Revolution.

Such are the great historical states of the witch: latent (the serf's wife), triumphant (the priestess), decadent (the professional). After which, Michelet turns to the figure of Satan-as-priest. At this level of analysis, what we have are actually phases of one and the same institution, that is, of history. The novel appears when Michelet "thickens" the historical thread, resolutely transforms it into a biographical warp: Function is incarnated in an actual person, organic maturation is substituted for historical evolution, so that the witch unites in herself the general and the particular, the model and the creature: she is at once *a* witch and *the* witch. This novelistic accommodation is very audacious because it is not in the least metaphorical: Michelet keeps his promise to the letter, he discusses the witches, for three hundred years of their history, as one and the same woman.

Novelistic existence is established the moment the witch is provided with a body, scrupulously situated, abundantly described. Take the witch at her first appearance, when she is merely the serf's wife: she is then a slender, weak, timid creature, assigned the physical quality which most touched Michelet, diminutiveness, i.e., he supposed, fragility: her mode of corporeal existence is a minor slither, a kind of household quarantine which makes her lend an ear to the spirits of the hearth, those exiled pagan gods who have taken refuge in the serf's hovel: she exists only by a certain passivity of the ear: such is her body and her atmosphere. The second witch, nourished on the misery of the times and this misery being enormous, is a full-fledged woman; she has exchanged a humiliated body for a triumphant, expansive one. Even the erotic sites have changed: first came the slender waist, the pale flesh, a passive nervousness, a body reduced to utter vulnerability; now we are arrested by the wicked yellow eyes and their offensive glances, what Michelet calls their *gleam,* always a sinister value for him; above all, there is the hair, snaky and black as some Medea's; in short, everything too immaterial or too elusive to be defeated. The third witch is a combined state of the two previous bodies; the delicacy of the first is corrected by the combativeness of the second: the professional witch is a diminutive but malicious woman, slender and oblique, delicate and cunning; her totem is no longer the frightened doe but the cat, graceful and mischievous (also the totem animal of the sinister Robespierre). With regard to Michelet's general thematics, the third witch derives from the knowing little girl (doll, perverse toy), pernicious in that she is double, divided, contradictory, uniting in equivocation the innocence of her age and the knowledge of an adult. Moreover, the witch's transformation through her three ages is itself contradictory: it is an aging process, yet the witch is always young (see in particular the whole passage concerning the young Basque witches, Murgui and Lisalda, whom Michelet condemns though he is obviously attracted to them).

Thereafter, and this is an important novelistic sign, the witch is always located, she participates substantially in a physical site, interior (objects) or landscape. This site is first of all the hearth, spatial substitute for intimacy; the hearth is an eminently beneficent site insofar as it is the terminal point of rape, the place where man is weak woman's absolute owner, thereby regaining the natural state par excellence, the undivided nature of the couple (Michelet specifies that the hearth constitutes a great advance over the erotic communism of the primitive *villa*). Further, this hearth, defined by contiguous objects, bed, chest, table, stool, is the architectural expression of a privileged value (already noted apropos of the pre-witch's body): diminutiveness. Altogether different is the habitat of the adult sorceress: a forest of briars, bristling moors, overgrown circles of dolmens, the theme here is the ragged, the tangled, a state of nature which has absorbed the witch, closed over her. The dreadful partitioning of medieval society (in its corrupt phases) has this corresponding paradox: the witch is imprisoned in the open place par excellence: nature. Nature thereby becomes an impossible site: the human takes refuge in the inhuman. As for the third witch, of whom, moreover, Michelet speaks much less—the suspect confidante of the great lady—her mythical surround (as we know from other books) is the cabinet, the alcove, the professional locus of the chambermaid (a personage abhorred by Michelet as the husband's insidious rival), in short the disgraced category of the intimate, the stifled (which is to be linked with the malefic theme of monarchic intrigue).

This general witch is therefore an entirely real woman, and Michelet sustains relations with her which we are obliged to call erotic. Michelet's eroticism, naïvely exhibited in his so-called nature books, appears piecemeal in all his history books, especially those written in the second half of his life, after his second marriage (to Athénaïs Mialaret). Its central figure is precisely this Athénaïs, who greatly resembled Michelet's portrait of the first witch. The general quality of an erotic object is, for Michelet, fragility (here, diminutiveness), which permits man both to ravish and to protect, to possess and to respect: here we have a sublimated eroticism, but whose very sublimation, by a kind of strictly Micheletist return, becomes erotic all over again. The witch, especially in her first state, is indeed Michelet's bride, frail and sensitive, nervous and abandoned, the *pâle rose* who provokes a double erotic impulse of concupiscence and elevation. But this is not all. We know (from *La femme,* from *L'amour*) that Michelet embellishes this fragile creature with a very particular photogenics: blood. What arouses Michelet, in woman, is what she conceals: not nakedness (which would be a banal theme) but the menstrual function which makes woman rhythmic, like Nature, like the ocean, also subject to the lunar rhythm. The husband's right and joy is to accede to this secret of nature, to possess in woman, by this unheard-of confidence, a mediatrix between man and the universe. Michelet exalted this marital privilege in his books on woman, defending it against the rival who is not the lover but the chambermaid, confidante of the natural secret. This whole theme is present in *La sorcière:* constitutively, one might say, since the witch is a sibyl, in harmony with nature by her lunar rhythm; then when the witch is replaced by the priest, the theme reappears indiscreetly: the relation between the seducer-priest and the chosen nun is entirely erotic, in Michelet's style, only when it involves the essential confidence, the communication of *those shameful and ridiculous things whose avowal is so cruel for a young girl.*

For what Michelet condemns in the sacerdotal or satanic seduction is also what he has always delighted in describing: insidious possession, gradual habitation within woman's secret. The images, in this very book, are countless: sometimes the elfin spirit *slithers* into the serf's wife, sometimes the spirits enter her *like a tapeworm,* sometimes Satan *impales* the witch with a fiery dart. What prevails throughout is the image, not of a penetration—banal metaphor of ordinary eroticism—but of a passing-through and of an installation. The Micheletist utopia is evidently that man be woman's parasite, it is the oceanic marriage of sharks which for months drift in the sea coupled to one another: idyllic adventure in which the motionless penetration of bodies is doubled by the external slither of waters (Michelet has described these ichthyic nuptials in *La mer*). Beyond woman, we are obviously concerned here with a whole coenesthesia of man in nature, and we understand why the witch is a major figure of the Micheletist pantheon: everything about her prepares her for a great mediating function: installing himself in her, it is in all of nature that man bathes as in a substantial and vital medium.

We see that Michelet's presence in *La sorcière* is anything but a simple romantic expansion of subjectivity. What Michelet must do, in fact, is to participate magically in the myth without ceasing to describe it: his text is both narration and experience, its function is to compromise the historian, to keep him on the verge of the magical substance, in the state of a spectator who is on the point of falling into a trance; whence the ambiguity of rational judgment, Michelet both believing and not believing, according to the formula he himself used about the Greeks' religious attitude toward their fables. One very remarkable thing about *La sorcière,* in fact, is that Michelet never contests the effectiveness of the magical act: he speaks of the witch's rites as successful techniques, rationally performed though irrationally conceived. This contradiction, which has embarrassed so many positivist historians, never troubles Michelet: he speaks of magical effects as real: causality is precisely what his narrative permits him to omit, since in fiction the temporal link is always substituted for the logical link. Consider how he deals, for example, with the transformation of the lady into the she-wolf: in the evening, the witch gives her a potion to drink. A rationalist historian would here present a file of documents, a study of the evidence, an explanation of the illusion. This is not Michelet's method. *The potion was taken,* he says, *and in the morning the lady awakened exhausted, bruised . . . she had hunted, killed, etc.* It is just this disjunction between the real and the rational, this primacy of the event over its material cause (*the potion was taken*) which it is the narrative's function to display; thus nothing could come closer to mythic narrative than the Micheletist novel, the legend (i.e., the continuum of narrative) establishing, in both cases, in and of itself, a new rationality.

Instead of intervening between him and the truth, the novel helped Michelet to understand witchcraft in its objective structure. With regard to magic, it is not the positivist historians that Michelet suggests; it is scholars quite as rigorous but whose work is infinitely better adapted to its object: I am thinking of ethnologists like Mauss (notably in his essay on magic). For example, in writing the history of the witch (and not of witchcraft), Michelet anticipates the fundamental choice of modern ethnology: to start from functions, not from institutions; Mauss takes magic back to the magician, that is, to any person who works magic. This is what Michelet does: he describes the rites very summarily, he never analyzes the content of the beliefs (of the representations): what interests him in witchcraft is a personalized function.

The benefit of this method is very great, and gives *La sorcière,* despite some outmoded dialogues, a very modern accent. First of all, what Michelet declares of the sibyl, in his maniacal feminism, is what the soberest ethnologist would also say: that there is an affinity between woman and magic. For Michelet, this affinity is physical, woman being in harmony with nature by the rhythm of the blood; for Mauss, it is social, their physical particularity establishing women as a veritable class. Nonetheless, the postulate is the same: this erotic theme, far from being a prurient mania of the lovesick old historian, is an ethnological truth illuminating the status of woman in magical societies.

Another truth: I said that Michelet is not concerned to describe the rites themselves; he deals rather with their destination, their effect (summoning the dead, curing the sick). This suggests that he makes little differentiation between rite and technique, a correspondence ethnology has adopted in its assertion that magical gestures are always sketches of a technology. Michelet never distinguishes the witch from her activity: she exists only insofar as she participates in a *praxis,* which is precisely what makes her a progressive figure, according to Michelet: as opposed to the Church, established in the world as a motionless, eternal essence, she is the world making itself. The paradoxical (but correct) result of this intuition is that Michelet's witch has virtually nothing of the sacred about her. Of course there is a close relation between magic and religion, which Mauss has carefully analyzed and which Michelet himself defines as a *reversal;* but it is precisely a complementary and therefore exclusive relation; magic is marginal to religion; it gives over the being of things for the sake of their transformation: this makes the Micheletist witch much more of a worker than a priestess.

Finally, anticipating the principle of all sociology, Michelet does not treat the witch as "other," does not make her the sacred figure of the singular, as romanticism conceived the poet or the magus. His witch is physically solitary (in the woods, out on the heath), not socially alone: a whole collectivity joins her, expresses itself in her, makes use of her. Far from setting herself in noble opposition to society (as the pure rebel does), the Micheletist witch fundamentally participates in her economy. Michelet takes the paradox which sentimentally opposes the individual to society and resolves it in an altogether modern manner; he has clearly understood that between the witch's singularity and the society from which she is detached, there is a relation not of opposition but of complementarity: it is the entire group which establishes the particularity of the magical function; if men expel the witch, it is because they acknowledge her, project a part of themselves into her, a part which is at once legitimate and intolerable; by means of the witch, they legalize a complex economy, a tension that is useful since, in certain disinherited moments of history, it permits them to live. Carried away by the role's positivity, Michelet doubtless scanted the behavior of "normal" society with regard to the witch; he never says, for instance, that in terms of total structure, the Inquisition had a function, not positive of course but significant—in a word, that it exploited the great witchcraft trials with a view to the society's general economy. At least he indicates that between "normal" society and the witch excluded from it there was a relation of sadism, not just of eviction, and that consequently this society consumed the witch, so to speak, much more than it sought to annul her. Does he not say this surprising thing somewhere, *that witches were put to death because of their beauty?* In a sense this makes all of society participate in that complementary structure Lévi-Strauss has analyzed apropos of shamanic societies, the aberration here being merely a means by which a society works out its contradictions. And in our present society, what best resumes this complementary role of the Micheletist witch is probably the mythic figure of the intellectual, "the traitor," sufficiently detached from society to discern its alienation, seeking a correction of reality yet impotent to effect it: excluded from the world and necessary to the world, directed toward *praxis* but participating in it only by the motionless mediation of a language, just as the medieval witch comforted human misery only through a rite and at the price of an illusion.

If we thus glimpse in **La sorcière** a thoroughly modern description of the magical myth, it is because Michelet has had the audacity to venture himself altogether, to preserve that redoubtable ambiguity which makes him at once the narrator (in the mythical sense) and the analyst (in the rational sense) of history. His sympathy for the witch is not at all that of a liberal author striving for comprehension of what is alien to him: Michelet has participated in the myth of the witch exactly as the witch herself participated, in his own view, in the myth of magical *praxis:* both voluntarily and involuntarily. What he has undertaken once again, in writing **La sorcière,** is neither a profession (the historian's) nor a priesthood (the poet's), it is, as he has said elsewhere, a *magistracy.* He felt obliged by society to administer its intelligence, to narrate all its functions, even and especially its aberrant ones, which he has here anticipated were vital. Seeing his own society torn between two postulations, Christian and materialist, which Michelet considered equally impossible, he sketched out a magical compromise, he made himself a sorceror, a gatherer of bones, a reviver of the dead; he took it upon himself to say *no* to the Church and *no* to science, to replace dogma or brute fact by myth.

That is why today, when mythological history is much more important than at the time Michelet published **La sorcière** (1862), his book recovers its actuality, once again becomes serious. Michelet's many enemies, from Sainte-Beuve to Mathiez, supposed they could be rid of him by confining him in a poetics of pure intuition; but his subjectivity, as we have seen, was only the earliest form of that insistence on totality, of that truth of comparisons, of that attention to the most insignificant detail of the concrete, which today mark the very method of our human sciences. What was disdainfully labeled poetry in his work we are beginning to recognize as the exact outline of a new science of the social: it is because Michelet was a discredited historian (in the scientistic sense of the term) that he turns out to have been at once a sociologist, an ethnologist, a psychoanalyst, a social historian; although his thought and even his form include vast wastelands (a whole part of himself he could not wrest free of his *petit-bourgeois* background), we can say that he truly anticipated the foundation of a general science of man. (pp. 103-15)

> *Roland Barthes, "La sorcière," in his* Critical Essays, *translated by Richard Howard, Northwestern University Press, 1972, pp. 103-15.*

G. P. Gooch (essay date 1960)

[*Gooch was an English historian, educator, and critic who wrote extensively on European history. In the following excerpt, he examines Michelet's ideas on the role of women in achieving and maintaining social order.*]

Two books, **L'amour** and **La femme, la famille et le prêtre,** may be regarded as the first and second volumes of a single enterprise. In his sympathy with suffering in body and mind Michelet had always ranked woman above man, sa-luting her not merely as the creator of life but as the guardian angel of the family. Though generally regarded as a man of the Left, he was unashamedly conservative in his estimate of the vocation of women. Unlike Mill, who was pleading for a wider and richer life in *The Subjection of Women,* he never ceased to proclaim that her place was in the home and that only as wife and mother could she fulfil her destiny. With his first wife, who gave him three children, there was no intellectual comradeship. The second was interested in his work, but he had little contact and little desire for contact with the clever ladies who presided over the salons of the capital. Yet no troubadour has paid higher tribute to the matchless virtues and spiritual worth of the other sex.

Every woman, he declared, was an altar because it was a holy task to rear a family. That her effort was often a tragic failure was due in most cases to the husband. The perfect marriage of his dreams rarely gladdened his eyes. Was he too severe to the male element and did he underestimate the proportion of successful unions? He could call as witnesses contemporary novelists, for Balzac, George Sand, Flaubert, Zola and Maupassant painted much the same dark picture of disenchantment and loveless homes, though in their lurid pages the responsibility for disaster is more evenly distributed.

L'amour opens with the declaration that love precedes the family, for it is as old as woman. The family rests on love and society on the family, so love is the starting point of everything. George Sand herself had not sounded all its depths in her novels. Material and intellectual progress was superficial in comparison, and Europe was confronting the industrial age with an impoverished soul. It was the task of France to change the world by changing herself. Part of the decline was due to the increasing use of alcohol and narcotics. Polygamy was growing, legal marriage decreasing. Their era would be called the century of diseases of the womb. Woman was a sacred creature, the holy of holies, all pity, all tenderness, all faith. Infinitely less sensual than man, her thoughts centred on motherhood, giving pleasure and happiness to her husband, more than on her own enjoyment. Nowhere is there to be found a purer, more tender or more reverent picture of a young wife. With the arrival of the first child the family becomes the Kingdom of God in miniature, the strong serving the weak, the smallest member of the group in full command. The celestial vision often fades with advancing years, but the elderly woman can always employ her leisure in works of mercy. With her heart full of love age is not an enemy but a friend.

La femme, la famille et le prêtre opens on a sombre note. Woman was being left behind by man, and the gulf was widening. How often was the hearth cold, the table silent, the bed a block of ice! **L'amour** had been sharply attacked, but it had been read and wept over by women who turned to it in their spare hours. Since its purpose had been to restore woman to the hearth it could hardly please a man of the Middle Ages or a woman who preferred the cloister or the street. Adultery had almost become an institution, and in the big cities marriage was avoided unless property was concerned. Poverty drove young women to sell themselves and men preferred to change partners any day, if they wished. The bachelor was afraid to marry a rich girl who was conscious of her social status and who often divided her affections between her children and her old home, leaving her husband to feel himself unwanted. Some men with modest incomes could not give their wife the smart clothes they craved, and in some cases religion was a barrier. The *ouvrière* was miserably paid and underfed, and tuberculosis was rife. The educated woman who had to earn her living had no fewer difficulties. The governess from the country who appeared alone in the evening in a street or a restaurant was taken for a prostitute, and she was liable to be molested by the father or son in the household of her employers. The actress who received a paltry wage was advised to take a lover. No wonder that a girl, hungry and lonely, should be led astray, but a woman's soul was never so deeply corrupted as that of a man.

With decades of teaching experience behind him, Michelet offers advice on education at every stage. Children, like flowers, needed sunlight, books on natural history, a garden, preferably in the country. Interest them in the growth of flowers and in the way birds build their nests. Fruit and vegetables were much better for them than meat. Writing at a time of terrifying child-mortality which kept the mother in a state of perpetual anxiety, he urged that everything should be done to ensure the rearing of a healthy family. The crown of education was the training of every young child to love and serve its country.

Michelet adored France to such an extent that he frowned on any mixture of European races. Profound differences, he declared, existed between French and English, even in their skeletons, and offspring of mixed marriages were often sub-normal. While the German wife was a gentle creature, French, Polish and Magyar women possessed much more personality and often dominated their husbands. Frenchwomen, indeed, were the most many-sided in Europe and the most difficult to know, each of them differing enormously from all the others. When she gave herself forever the bond was stronger than anywhere else. The Englishwoman, who made an excellent wife, obeyed in material things but was averse to change. The German woman, so good and gentle, wanted to belong to someone. With the pronounced personality of the Frenchwoman great care in the choice of partners was essential. And now for once the ardent patriot finds a large spot on the sun. The great fault of the French nation was impatience, always in a hurry about everything. Michelet gets out of his depth in the pronouncements on the women of other countries, of whom he had little knowledge. Of French marriages he could speak with more authority, and here, despite his flaming patriotism, he finds little to give him joy.

The author paints a touching picture of the young bride leaving the family circle and feeling at times rather lonely in her new sphere. Would she be happy? He knew of few really happy marriages. Some required a high temperature, some a medium, others zero. So we had to ask how much are they married? Everything depended on the start, and it was usually the husband's fault if things went wrong. The wife should interest herself in her partner's work. She should play to him and they should read books together and enjoy the arts. A cultivated woman enriched by a man's comradeship would become his superior. She leaned on his arm, but she had wings. The book closes on the same note of something approaching adoration of woman. "If she does not continually sanctify and ennoble the family, she has missed her vocation. Her vocation is love, her salvation making man happy. To love and have children is her sacred duty."

La femme, la famille et le prêtre may be described as a voluminous appendix to *L'amour*. It devotes hundreds of pages to the shrill complaint of priestly influence over woman as an offence against her spiritual independence and a threat to the harmony between husband and wife. The most dangerous of such interlopers in Michelet's eyes were the Jesuits, because they were the most powerful of the Orders, the most zealous, and the most unscrupulous. He had witnessed the Catholic revival, and the more he saw of it the less he liked it. He had been brought up without religious influences, had never felt the need of a faith. Like his parents, he regarded the Church as the champion of the rich, a tragic degeneration of primitive Christianity. *The History of France* had saluted St. Louis, the Maid, and the *Imitation of Christ,* but in the middle age his attitude to ecclesiastical influence hardened, and in 1843 he and Quinet thundered against the Jesuits from their chairs in the Collège de France. The précis of his addresses, which had aroused nation-wide controversy, appeared in a little volume entitled *Les Jésuites,* which ran through six editions in eight months and was translated into several languages. Though there were only about one thousand Jesuits in France their influence was enormous and increasing. They were growing into a national danger, for they were the police of the Pope, a worse tyranny than any secular autocracy. They carried treachery into the house, the wife spying on her husband, the children on their mother. Without allegiance to the local Bishop, they obeyed their Superior—*perinde cadaver*—in order to reign themselves. With their soft wheedling voices they wormed their way into the impressionable hearts of women. They were the counter-revolution, an instrument of war, and their aim was the death of liberty. Never before or after did the most popular of French historians write a book so one-sided, so emotional, and so unworthy of his fame.

La femme, la famille et le prêtre was a more dignified performance. In a preface added many years later, the author declared that the book, however severe, had been written without hate, and that he should have pronounced a still harsher verdict in view of the records of clerical sexual offences. The 40,000 confessional boxes were the strongholds of the Church, and the head of the family felt lonely under his own roof since his wife and daughter told an outsider secrets of which he was unaware.

The original Preface of 1845 declared that he had been violently denounced and insulted in the Catholic press, which showed that priests had been wounded in their most vulnerable spot, namely, taking the woman's side in family quarrels. Would it not be better if the clergy were free to marry? Would not a married man understand the problems of domestic life better than a celibate? Women needed other champions than the priest, and laymen should take up their cause.

The most instructive section of the book is the survey of spiritual direction in the "Grand Siècle." Here the publicist gives place to the scholar, who supplies vivid portraits of outstanding ecclesiastics. The story opens with François de Sales and Madame de Chantal, who stand out in shining contrast to the Jesuits. They were the tempters of Kings and Popes, of the former through their lusts, of the latter by exalting their office. The quietism which Mme. Guyon had learned from Molinos had its dangers, since the theology of repose weakened the sense of individual responsibility. Far worse was the sensualism of the cult of the Sacré Coeur and Maria Alacoque. The saintly Fénelon is admired as much as Francois de Sales and is saluted as *le grand et bel esprit.* Bossuet, the Eagle of Meaux, an even more commanding figure, is greeted as the wisest of Directors, since he never surrendered to the fashionable quietism. After surveying the illustrious figures of the seventeenth century, Michelet reiterates his detestation of "the abdication of the soul".

Passing to the nineteenth century the author notes the disappearance of quietism and the survival of the system of confession in undiminished rigour. The Enlightenment had bequeathed a far less credulous France, and popular education had deprived the priests of their cultural superiority. The curé, often the son of a peasant, knew nothing of society and could do little for members of an unfamiliar superior class. On the other hand he retained influence and the old evils persisted; the husband possessed the body of his wife, the priest her soul. The plight of women in convents, cut off from all contact with the life of the community, seemed to Michelet a living death. Some inmates had been immured without their consent and some were mentally subnormal. It was a world of boredom and trembling obedience. Many girls received their education exclusively from *réligieuses.* Prisons and asylums were open to official inspection, but no secular authority was entitled to cross the threshold of a convent. It was a dark picture and it never occurred to the artist that many women found peace, fulfilment and happiness behind convent walls.

The fifth and last of Michelet's sociological works, written at the age of 70, appeared on the eve of the Franco-Prussian war. *Nos fils* is a treatise on education based, as the author explains, on 30 years of teaching experience. Many themes discussed in his earlier books are treated at greater length, such as the need for the study of animate and inanimate nature. Next to natural history in the curriculum comes the literature of travel, beginning with *Robinson Crusoe.* Thirdly comes history, the story of *la Patrie,* "the mother of us all". Here, as everywhere, Michelet is a preacher no less than a teacher. His message is the goodness of human nature. The world is a good place full of sunlight and creative energies. The Middle Ages were a vale of tears, the modern centuries the age of liberation. Far from needing the services of the Church, the child requires to be saved from its false and degrading doctrine of the Fall of Man. The Church, moreover, hated liberty, the life-blood of humanity. *"Elargissez Dieu,"* Dide-

rot had exclaimed, and Michelet proceeds to interpret the injunction in the spirit of his beloved Spinoza. "Enough of temples. The Milky Way is our temple. Enough of dogmas: God suffocates in these little prisons. Liberate the divine essence fermenting in us longing to pour forth in torrents and to express itself in creative work. The soil awaits our aid, yearning to enrich us with its beauty. *La terre, c'est la liberté, la dignité, la moralité."*

Michelet proclaimed the blessings of country life from the cradle to the grave. The most critical phase in education begins with school life in a big city, especially for French youth, the most precocious, impressionable and highly strung of types. The best defence against its temptations is to interest the boy in the marvels of science. Training for life must start in the home, and the mother's milk is the earliest lesson. Some German doctors had declared that a child deprived of this birthright rarely laughed. In this latest treatise the author speaks of the father with more appreciation than ever before. As a rule, he declares, the French father was admirable. Both parents should be careful in their language, for a child is very observant. Himself an abstainer, he advises them to bring up their family without wine. The mother must strive against her instinct to bestow more of her love on a son than on her daughter. The range of studies in universities had broadened during the nineteenth century, and the classics had been supplemented by history and science. Geological and botanical excursions should be arranged and the student should never be overstrained. Two hours without a break were too long. The teacher needed an alert class as much as the class required a stimulating instructor.

A quarter of the volume is dedicated to the educational pundits of the modern centuries with Rabelais at the top of the list. Ever since his declaration of war on the medieval doctrine and practice of asceticism there had been a running fight between believers that human nature deserved the privilege of liberty and those who taught that all men were born sinful and need to be kept in the straight path by threat of hell and hopes of heaven. The healthy tradition of the creator of Gargantua was carried on by Rousseau, Pestalozzi and Froebel. All these pioneers were inspired by a new faith no less ardent than that of the Christian theologians, namely the faith in man. Michelet's final message to his generation was: be yourself and work with others in creative activity. He lived long enough to welcome the Third Republic in which Church and priest were to count for less in the life of the people than at any period of the turbulent history of France. (pp. 685-89)

> G. P. Gooch, "Michelet on French Society—II," in Contemporary Review, Vol. 198, December, 1960, pp. 685-89.

Charles Rearick   (essay date 1971)

[*Rearick is an American historian, educator, and critic specializing in French history. In the following excerpt, he discusses Michelet's use of folklore and popular accounts in his histories.*]

[As] a historian [Michelet] brought to his subject a poetic mentality that Vico had considered characteristic of primitive man and the child, giving "sense and passion to insensate things," animating the inanimate and personifying the nonpersonal—France, the Revolution, cities, armies, even buildings such as the Bastille. When he looked over his life upon completion of his history of France (1869), he distinguished his own work by saying that he was the first historian to treat France "as a soul and a person." Perhaps as much as anything else this fundamental bent of Michelet's mind disposed him to be sympathetic to folklore.

His philosophical education, which was inseparable from his historical education, provided a reasoned basis for such a sympathy. The philosophies of history by Vico, de Condorcet, Kant, Lessing, Herder, and others that Michelet read in the decisive year 1824 all offered speculations on the development of the world of men in contrast to the world of nature. But it was Vico who fully revealed to Michelet the important rôle of folklore in the early stages of civilization. Eager to contemplate the wisdom of the past Michelet welcomed Vico's protest against the arrogance of Cartesian philosophers who scorned the changing world of history, language, and poetry and valued only the timeless truths attainable through individual reason. Imbued with democratic sentiments Michelet readily received the demonstration that the people had made themselves through their institutions, founded by a spontaneous "common sense" in ages prior to reflective, analytical thought. In Vico he found elaborated the idea that the wisdom of the past was embodied in religion, poetry, and institutions created by "humanity" rather than a few great men or divine intervention: he learned that "vulgar wisdom" was the mother of philosophic wisdom, that the "true Homer" was the Greek people themselves, and that other founding fathers were also poetic characters representing an entire society. Vico's symbolic interpretations of the founding fathers and his rehabilitation of "vulgar wisdom" thus transformed all early ideas and traditions into a kind of folklore, a creation of the popular mind. Michelet adopted this view and carried it further, attaching great importance to "vulgar wisdom" and popular accounts of history even in periods far beyond the early times treated by Vico.

For his detailed historical studies, Michelet looked to folklore for evidence of popular *moeurs* and character. At first he considered the use of popular vocabulary and general literature for this purpose. Then in 1828, the year when Edgar Quinet's first work on Herder appeared, he read the *Nibelungenlied* and other works of folk literature in preparation for a study of the "old German nationality" and made his first German trip to gather other materials of this kind. To Vico's ideas that primitive literature was a collective creation and that it was spontaneous rather than reflective Michelet added the idea—more German than Vichian—that a distinct national character was reflected in popular traditions. He concluded that folklore was therefore a true history even though erroneous in historical minutiae:

> The myths and the poetry of barbarian peoples present the traditions of this [barbaric] time; they are ordinarily the true national history of a people, such as its genius has made it. The story of William Tell has for centuries aroused the enthusiasm of the Swiss. . . . This narrative may well not be real, but it is eminently true, that is to say, perfectly conformable to the character of the people which has given it for history. The history of Roland, nephew of Charlemagne, is false in its details. Einhard says only one word; he reports that at Roncevaux *Rolandus praefectus Britannici limitis* perished. People have built on so light a foundation a true history, that is to say conformable to the genius and to the situation of those who have invented it.

Interest in national "genius," common in that era of increasing national consciousness, naturally had appeal for the passionately patriotic Michelet.

But he looked for regional as well as national character in folklore, as one would expect of a man intent upon resurrecting the French past in all its diversity. Besides familiarizing himself with the literary legends of France— Roland, Mélusine, Renard, Merlin, the Four Sons Aymon—he was careful to note local folklore in the course of his travels and to record his observations in his journal. As he went through Dauphiné in 1830, for example, he noted the satiric songs popular with young villagers, copied down several titles of popular poems sold at Grenoble, and recorded such local customs as the practice of planting a weeping willow at the door of a forsaken lover. A few years later he studied Breton songs at Morlaix. Traveling through Wales in 1834, he was eager to question a fellow passenger—a peasant—on popular songs of the region, and in Aquitaine the next year he noted the motifs of a Poitevin song he had heard in the original dialect. In no other section of his history did he concentrate more of this local folklore than in his famous "Tableau de la France." There he noted such expressions of popular character as the violent wild dances of Provence and the ironic, witty fabliaux of Champagne. There, too, he introduced folklore into his geographical descriptions: Breton lore on the nearby islands and rough coast of Brittany, the popular belief that the Rhône was a living and often angry monster, stories of the miraculous stage and Saint-Hubert in the Ardennes forest. As he made observations on social structure, popular beliefs came to mind; for example, in discussing the small social distance between the Breton nobleman and the peasant he noted not only the poverty of the Breton nobles but also the belief of many peasants that they were descended from Arthur or the fairy Morgan.

First, then, Michelet acquired a philosophical understanding of folklore—folklore regarded as a spontaneous, instinctive wisdom and an expression of character—and then looked for specific examples to be included in his historical writing. In his ***Introduction à l'histoire universelle*** (1831) for the first time he set forth his own philosophy of history and attempted to elucidate the personality or genius of France by contrasting it with that of the surrounding states. His conviction, like Augustin Thierry's and others' in that time of sharp social and political conflict, was that the nation needed to cut through the fog of contemporary confusion and to sight once more its historical character and mission.

For Michelet national character was generally expressed in popular traditions, language, heroic figures such as Joan of Arc, and particular historical events. In his universal history of 1831, however, he neglected French folklore and devoted most of his remarks on France to the other expressions of national character. He commented on examples of German and Italian folklore but pointedly dissociated the French genius from this kind of thought. Caught up in the enthusiasm of the Revolution of 1830 and eager for the French to lead Europe into the future, Michelet urged his compatriots to arm themselves with reason and to assert their will for liberty, casting off such encumbrances of the past as poetry, symbol, material and concrete images. In developing his theme of the age-old struggle between liberty and fatalism Michelet restated the Vichian progression of human history from mute symbol through poetry to prose, but he omitted any *ricorsi,* relegating symbol and poetry exclusively to the distant past and hailing prose as the way of progress. Freedom's vanguard, France, was the land of prose, he insisted, and prose was the most advanced form of language. For prose was the least materialized form, the least concrete and figurative, the most abstract and therefore the freest of matter and nature, the form that was most common to all men, and therefore the most egalitarian. In the progression of language it was the last form, the one beyond which there was only action, and therefore it was the one befitting a people who by acting led Europe to freedom. In glorifying the "Three Glorious Days" of 1830, Michelet thus revived the spirit of the Enlightenment, praising the dissolvent power of reason and revolution. "March, then, child of Providence," he cried, meaning march in the course that he believed natural to the French: analysis, the dialectic, criticism, action. In the present and future life of France Michelet in 1831 saw no place for folklore.

But subsequently, as he wrote his Roman history and the first volumes of the history of France, his desire to "resurrect" the integral life of the past led him to include folklore in his purview. He was willing to do justice to folklore, as to the Church, in the past even though he considered it retrogressive in the present. The Michelet of the thirties was after all a scholar, bold in his interpretations yet energetic in his researches, chief of the historical section of the Archives nationales, professor of history at the Ecole normale supérieure, and prolific writer of history.

It was in these years that he offered one of his outstanding contributions to the study of popular traditions, his ***Origines du droit français cherchées dans les symboles et formules du droit universel*** (1837). As he proudly acknowledged, the work was inspired by Jacob Grimm's study of early German law, *Deutsche Rechtsalterthümer* (1828), which Quinet had sent from Germany to his friend in 1829. When Michelet was planning to translate Grimm's *Meistergesang* in 1829, he entered into correspondence with the author and continued it in the thirties on the subject of early German law. Grimm offered him encouragement and helped him to translate some of the more obscure texts.

Michelet's subject was French law in its early poetic forms, which according to Vico's scheme were first mate-

rial rather than verbal symbols, and then spoken formulae. Law in this stage was popular, a kind of folklore living among the people. In a book like Grimm's, Michelet declared, one could hear "not the hypotheses of a man, but the living voice of antiquity itself." To Michelet such a law revealed the people's most intimate beliefs and morals. These he arranged and presented in the form of a "juridical biography" of man in the poetic age, beginning with the laws relating to birth and then moving to those concerning childhood, manhood, marriage, property, and so on through death. For Michelet this law was "an enchanted forest" that held him spellbound regardless of his will. "I wandered there in all directions; every instant I found new scenes there, clearings, shadows, half-light, full of mystery. . . ." It was a "kingdom of dreams" that he left only with great reluctance. "Men and peoples, we have difficulty detaching our eyes from it. We leave this fairyland of youth only with regret. We resume our march, but we turn our heads away; we sigh, old children." In no other work did he reveal so clearly his fascination for popular symbol, in this case the symbols of German law.

Michelet also revealed great delight in discovering the similarity of symbols in the laws of many peoples. Never an exclusive nationalist, he welcomed the support that the new comparative studies of law, language, mythology, and religion were lending to the idea of the common origin and brotherhood of all mankind. He felt a kind of religious awe in contemplating the "fraternity of peoples, fraternity of ideas, in ancient law." "It filled me with great emotion when I heard this universal choir for the first time. . . . From my little existence of a moment, I saw, I touched, unworthy, the eternal communion of mankind."

But he sensed that many others would not be so moved by ancient law. Those accustomed to the austerity of modern French law could only smile and scorn "the gravely puerile forms of ancient jurisprudence." As a historian he defended its symbols and formulae from such prideful moderns. He knew well the power of symbol to imprint itself firmly on the memory of man in a nascent civilization, a power that he ascribed to an elegant simplicity and a close association of moral law with nature. Solemnly preserved over generations, such legal forms were strong safeguards against setbacks to civilization: law so fixed in traditional form often necessitated lengthy interpretation, but it was in little danger of being lost or destroyed.

At the same time, however, such cumbersome and equivocal poetic forms eventually hampered the progress of the critical mind. Though enchanted by popular symbols, Michelet was as certain now as in 1831 that they were childish things which should be given up in maturity. He hailed the advance of the human mind beyond symbol and formula as a liberation from the "tyranny of forms." The mind became freer when it broke with the mute symbol and expressed itself in the spoken symbol, the formula; it further freed itself when it cast off the bonds of rhyme and rhythm. For Michelet, again, prose was the form of the wholly free intellect; only with prose could the mind dispel the ambiguity of symbol, make distinctions, define, and thereby create the world of man. And once more he affirmed that prose was the form most congenial to the

French genius. To "ultrasymbolic" Germany he opposed "antisymbolic" France.

In strictly French law Michelet could find little remaining evidence of poetic symbols. Over half the texts in his book actually came from German sources, even though Michelet had not limited his research to law books but had searched through chronicles, tales, and fabliaux as well. The problem was not simply that the evidence had disappeared, he concluded, but that France had had but a brief period of symbolic law. The French genius was antipathetic to symbol: "France is the true continuer of Rome. It pursues the work of interpretation. Logical, prosaic, antisymbolic work." French history to the Michelet of 1837 appeared, appropriately, a work of reason: "To generalize, to centralize is to suppress originality of detail, to strip it of its individuality in order to dissolve it in a great unity. In all forms France has rigorously followed this procedure of reasoning in its history. Its history is a living logic, a syllogism of which royalty was the middle term." Thus characterizing the French genius as antisymbolic and rational, and French history as a "living logic," Michelet dissociated the French identity from symbolic folklore.

Michelet himself, of course, was not entirely antisymbolic. In his Roman history and his history of France not only mythical figures like Hercules, or men like Charles VI and Martin Luther but even buildings like the contrasting Parisian churches of Saint-Jacques-de-la-Boucherie and Saint-Jean served to symbolize ideas or the people. As a method of historical interpretation Michelet obviously approved of symbol, though with reservations. It was useful for generalizing, he thought, but an antisymbolic exposition was equally useful and indeed necessary for bringing out details and distinctions. Michelet's point was that in order to progress a people had to move beyond the stage in which there was only symbolic and poetic thought. Once thought had freed itself of the concrete, material form, it could be master of what before had been its prison; moderns writing in prose and capable of critical reason did well to exploit occasionally the literary advantages of symbol. When Michelet denigrated symbol, then, he did so out of a belief that it had served its purpose and served it well but that criticism and prose in the present situation promised the greatest progress for the human mind.

In the decade after he published the ***Origines du droit*** Michelet significantly altered his views of the primitive mind, history, and folklore. The change was apparent in his intensely personal book, *Le peuple,* published in 1846 and often viewed in retrospect as a harbinger of the revolution two years later. Having thrown himself into vigorous opposition to the July Monarchy and the Jesuits, Michelet now believed more strongly than ever that troubled France needed to know itself through its history: "In order to regain faith in France, to hope in its future, it is necessary to go back to its past, to study thoroughly its natural genius." While the governments and conservatives had blackened the memory of the Revolutionary years, the devotees of the Revolutionary faith had blackened the memory of the centuries before 1789. As a result the common people were ignorant of themselves, and cultivated Frenchmen were ignorant of the people.

To correct what he considered a profound misunderstanding dividing the educated from the *peuple* Michelet devoted considerable attention in *Le peuple* to expounding the nature of the popular mind. In the interval since the ***Origines du droit*** Michelet had clearly had second thoughts about the primitive poetic mentality. He now exalted it, not only as a worthy part of the past, but as a valuable force for the present and the future. Whereas before he had seen progress in the movement away from instinct toward reflection, from the concrete to the abstract, and from the synthesis of symbol to analysis and criticism, now he sang the praises of the less advanced form of thought, and now he lamented that his own thought had become excessively abstract. Finally, he now depreciated scholarly writing about the primitive mind and heartily commended direct observation of the child and the peasant:

> Your son, like the peasant of Brittany and the Pyrenees, continually speaks the language of the Bible or of the *Iliad.* The boldest criticism of the Vicos, of the Wolfs, of the Niebuhrs, is nothing in comparison with the luminous and profound flashes of light that certain words of the child will suddenly cast for you into the night of antiquity. While observing the historic and *narrative* form that he gives even to abstract ideas, how often will you feel how the infant people have had to *narrate* their dogmas in legends and to make a story [*histoire*] of each moral truth.

But Michelet was now interested in the mind of those whom he called the *simples* for much more than an understanding of history. Tired of the self-satisfaction and immobility of the government of Guizot and Louis-Philippe, he longed for an assertion of heroic will, a renewal of the Revolutionary tradition. The abstract prose that he once had thought bordered on action seemed to lead only to endless, sterile discussion and writing, while the young mind of the *simple* seemed to divine the truth at once and to act by instinct.

Yet Michelet was not a thoroughgoing primitivist. His ideal was the genius who combined both instinct and reflection. One cannot help thinking that he was painting a self-portrait as he described this ideal. Certainly he made it clear that he combined both kinds of mentality within himself and that he personally faced the same problem of reconciling the two that society faced: "The general battle of the world [between instinct and reflection] is less discordant still than the one that I carry in me, the dispute of me with myself, the combat of the *homo-duplex.*" Michelet as conciliator tried to explain to the *simples* the value of reflection, and to the educated he tried to impart an appreciation of the *simples.* Yet it is clear that he labored more to defend the *simples,* not only because he now favored them, but also because this type of mind seemed to him the one in greatest need of an apology: increasing mechanization and the dry abstract education forced upon children were stifling the instincts and imagination, while the widespread failure to appreciate the primitive genius, along with the Church's doctrine of original sin, was resulting in the slaughter of the "infant peoples" around the world. The book *Le peuple,* Michelet hoped, would help protect the "infant peoples" which remained by convincing men of the goodness of the people and the blessings of the primitive mind.

A threat to these doctrines of *Le peuple* lay in the dark history of superstitions, popular beliefs in demons and witchcraft. Unlike many folklorists who brought to light only the happier traditions of the people, Michelet faced the challenge squarely. In the early volumes of his history of France he had discussed the medieval practice of sorcery, but it was in *La sorcière* of 1862 that he fully developed the story and his conclusions. More than ever alienated from the Church and the government, now the Second Empire, Michelet in the village of Hyères reaffirmed his faith in the people.

Michelet's *Sorcière,* one of the most penetrating studies of witchcraft written in nineteenth-century France, "resurrected" a part of the past long condemned to ignominious death—the thousand-year life of the sorceress in western Europe. Telling the story from the point of view of the popular mind, recreating its ideas and emotions, he sought to show that the folklore about Satan and the sorceress was a consequence of popular despair, and not simply of "human flightiness," the "inconstancy of fallen nature," or the "fortuitous temptations of concupiscence."

Never doubting the good heart of the people, Michelet easily found support for his faith in medieval folklore other than witchcraft: the legends of saints, in which he found the dreams and values of the people, and popular tales, in which he saw the pitiable wishes of the abject peasants, their desire for a treasure to end poverty or for a sleeping beauty to love. It was especially the woman who poured into such tales her compassion, compassion for the child beaten by the stepmother, for the scorned and abused younger sons, and for the beasts which she endowed with souls and feelings. But it was also the woman who took up the practice of sorcery. Not without help, however. Michelet savored the irony of the Church's rôle in arming its enemy. By preaching against demons and a corporeal Satan the Church testified to their existence and power. By fearfully trying to stop the popular creation of legends about miracles and saints, the Church helped turn the popular imagination back to the local pagan spirits, fairies, elves, and deities who had always lived on in the shadow of Christianity.

Still, something more was necessary. For the people to accept hell as they did in the company of Satan and the sorceress, Michelet maintained, they had to be fleeing another hell on earth—a feudal society in which the common people suffered from economic deprivation, social tyrannies, and a harsh, repressive Church doctrine that held man and nature to be evil. In the beliefs and practices of sorcery the people found relief from their toilsome life and release for natural appetites and emotions denied by the Church. Instead of docilely accepting the sexual abstinence or monogamy dictated by economic necessity and the Church, the people found fulfillment in the nocturnal *sabbat,* using the sorceress' art of birth control and abortion; instead of fasting, they feasted; instead of resigning themselves to death and accepting all the ills of life as trivia and preparation for the hereafter, they came to the sorceress and received medicine, treatment, sympathy, and

the consolation of contact with deceased loved ones. Michelet thus explained the folklore of the sorceress by recreating medieval popular life, a life in which the imagination was heightened by desperate circumstances, irrepressible hopes, and the sorceress' drugs. The folklore of the sorceress, he contended, was not the product of malevolence, simple fantasy, or the design of evil men. It was a popular dream of liberty and joy on earth and a surreptitious effort to realize them.

Michelet did not hide the worst of witchcraft. His story unfolded as a tragedy which ended in the cruel persecution of pitiful, half-mad, old women. But out of the tradition of sorcery, he argued, came the natural sciences which the Church had condemned. Michelet's Satan was "this dangerous magician who, while some argued over the sex of angels and other sublime questions, worked unceasingly with realities, created chemistry, physics, mathematics. . . . Medicine, especially, is the true satanism, a revolt against illness, the deserved scourge of God. [It was] manifest sin to stop the soul on its way toward heaven, to plunge it again into life." Michelet here executed an extraordinary coup for folklore. To credit the people with epic poems such as the Homeric masterpieces had been a bold move. But to proclaim folklore the mother of science, the idol of the age, was to bestow on it the most prized laurel. While not regretting the ultimate destruction of sorcery by the sciences, Michelet wanted the victorious new spirit, science, to know its humble, barbaric beginnings among the people.

Though Michelet now added his voice to the chorus of those who exalted science, he did not by the same token relegate folklore to the past. From at least as early as the 1840's he believed that there was a future for folklore, and he even wanted to make a contribution to that future himself. Michelet came to reconsider the potential rôle of folklore in the present, because he became eager to mold popular opinion and to win it for his cause. As a youth he had written in his journal of an ambition to write popular books: "If I have the talent for it, I would love to write for the people books that would be sold at a very low price." In the latter half of his life his ambition bore fruit—not only in the fifties, when he wrote popular books for his meager living, but also in the forties, when he wanted more than ever to exert an influence on the course of national life. Having resigned from the Ecole normale supérieure in 1837, he now lectured at the Collège de France to a more popular audience and began to reflect at length on the question of popular education, particularly as he became more politically engaged in the early 1840's. This question became most urgent perhaps during the Second Republic, but over the decades his books and journals reflected his continuing concern for the education of the people.

His basic conviction was that such an education should be simple and direct so that it could reach even the most untutored of Frenchmen. Specifically he proposed schools for adults, newspapers, circulating libraries, and short bulletins for the literate; an illustrated press, songs sung in different dialects across France, posters, clubs for public readings, popular dramas, and concerts for the illiterate.

But in the end he devoted his energies to writing books. Reexamining his style of writing during the 1840's he found it wanting and yearned to satisfy more popular tastes. In *Le peuple* he lamented that his thought and language were too abstract, too far removed from the mentality of the *simples;* he had not attained the ideal of "grandiose simplicity" he had once envisioned. There was too much art in his writing, he observed several years later, sighing "O santa simplicitas." In 1854, again: "How I would like to speak in *prose!* The oratorical rhythm pursues me and makes of me a kind of aborted poet. I escape it only at times, in rare moments of passionate simplicity."

Michelet had already looked for new models; he had searched for the characteristics of books that had exerted a strong influence over the people. In his journal (December 3, 1847), he summarized his investigation, grouping popular books into three categories:

1. Examination of great popular books, for and by the people: their formation, their influence. Here Vico [has put it aptly]: *The people has made the people.*

2. Examination of semipopular books which, although aristocratic, have been adopted by peoples. Example: Virgil, Dante, Tasso.

3. Examination of books made for a class, at first didactic, then popularized. Example: the manuals that prepared for the *Imitation.*

Michelet hoped to write books like those in the first category, popular creations. Of the various forms legend seemed the most promising to him. As he pondered the problem of educating the people in the religion of *la patrie,* the efficacy of medieval legend came to mind: "See, in the Middle Ages, how the popular or pacific legend of the saints, the popular and noble legend of the gallant knights led to the noble and chivalric ideal. Reciprocal education which redescended and ennobled all the people." He now hoped and believed that the legend of France could have the same civilizing, educating effects. He wanted to be more than a historian of such folklore; he wanted to be the propagator of legend, a legend that would educate the French people in the present.

Michelet pinned his hopes on legend because he believed that it could reach the largest audience and have the greatest appeal, conveying ideas as it did in a simple, imaginative form. The bases of his belief were Vico's theories of understanding and of folklore. According to the first, one understood not by rational analysis or external observation but by *making,* proceeding anew mentally through the steps in the formation of man's intellectual or institutional world. And since—according to the folklore theory—the people made legend, they could therefore best understand legend.

In the 1840's one legend above all occupied Michelet's mind: the legend of France. The history he once called "living logic" was now legend: the story of the people, made by the people, and much of it still told by the people. The ambition of an individual to write folklore apparently contradicted the current theory that held folklore to be collective, spontaneous, and oral, but for Michelet there

was no contradiction. The people had made the legend and still cherished it, though they now knew it only inadequately; *he* merely recorded it. For that matter, he was one with the people—no intellectual was ever more convinced of that—and so he was merely continuing the work of popular creation. Moreover, in writing the legend of France, particularly the recent part, he relied directly on oral tradition, as he proudly announced. On the subject of small property before the Revolution, for example, he reported having learned much from conversation with peasants and deplored the infrequency of such research *sur le vif.* It was for his *Histoire de la Révolution,* more than for any other work, that he practiced this method. While not neglecting books and manuscripts, he supplemented them with oral tradition, which he recommended to future historians with the highest praise: "The base which deceives the least, we are happy to say to those who will come after us, is that which young scholars distrust the most, and which a persevering science ends by finding as true as it is strong, indestructible: it is popular belief."

Though in details it was often mistaken, he conceded, on the whole it was true. Michelet meant first that legend was true as the "history of the heart of the people and of its imagination." But he also maintained that it was a reliable guide to the history of observable events. When historical "science" conflicted with popular belief, he had found that additional research proved the people to be correct. He noted, for example, that the newspapers had presented the Revolutionary Federations simply as popular fêtes; finding these accounts in conflict with the effusive reminiscences of the people, Michelet investigated further into minutes and reports and found that the Federations were large armed gatherings in towns and villages throughout France, comprising all elements of the population and thus capable of demonstrating the immense strength of the revolutionary nation to a quickly dispirited aristocracy.

Oral tradition he found particularly reliable in its moral judgment, which appeared to him almost unanimous. Regarding things, he conceded, the people were sometimes mistaken, though most often silent; but regarding men the people were rarely mistaken. The popular acclaim accorded the two Napoleons was obviously evidence to the contrary. Michelet explained this mistake on the part of the people by simply remarking that "gloire" and misfortune, Austerlitz and Saint-Helena, had led popular judgment astray, and apparently unperturbed, he continued his apologia for the popular mind. Using arguments that resembled Prosper de Barante's ideas on tradition and Rousseau's concept of the general will, he maintained that oral tradition was the best moral guide because it carried the judgment of the entire population rather than the special pleading of parties which one found in newspapers. His supreme argument, however, was inspired by Vico: the people knew history best because they had made it. Therefore the conscientious historian must begin by noting the traditions preserved in the hearts and mouths of the people.

Michelet wanted not only to teach French history as legend but also to convince the people that the legend of France was as complete, as uplifting as any legend ever conceived by man. One of the chief rivals of the legend and religion of France was, of course, Christianity. To counter its attractions Michelet felt obliged to show that none of them was lacking in the legend of France, and he did so in *Le peuple.* For saints France had Saint-Louis, the Virgin of Orléans, and the efficacious young generals of the Revolution. Miracles? What else was the military victory of 1792? Redemptions? There were two: one by Saint-Joan, the other by the Revolution. "Finally," he concluded, "for the supreme lesson, the immense faculty of devotion, of sacrifice, that our fathers have shown, and how so many times France has given its life for the world."

But there were rivals besides Christianity: namely, other national legends. So Michelet felt obliged to show the French legend superior to them too. Declaring the French tradition the most universal, he asserted that it best continued the "great human movement" from India through Greece to Rome; that it carried forward the ideals of all humanity through such Frenchmen as Charlemagne, Saint-Louis, Louis XIV, and Napoleon; and that it was also the one that had captured the imagination of all peoples and had become the "talk of the world." In contrast the German legends of Siegfried, Frederick Barbarossa, Goetz with the iron hand, and others were "poetic dreams which turn life toward the past, toward the impossible and vain regrets." The historic legends of England—the victories of Edward III and Elizabeth—were not moral models, and in any case their tradition was broken and incomplete: "The ballads of Robin Hood and others which the Middle Ages cherished ended with Shakespeare; Shakespeare was killed by the Bible, by Cromwell and by Milton, who were effaced by industrialism and the half-great men of recent times." Michelet's arguments for the superiority of the French legend (now in his mind indistinguishable from history) contained something of the familiar idea that France is a microcosm of Europe or of mankind, but they were less arguments than scattered illustrations of his assertions. A faith like Michelet's did not admit of closely reasoned demonstrations.

In the 1850's, with France firmly under the control of Napoleon III, Michelet concentrated on one episode in the legend: the Revolution and its heroes—the people, women, and soldiers. But he also took a growing interest in the current legends of other nations, particularly the small oppressed nationalities. By writing their legends he hoped to encourage the democratic sentiments not only of the people of France but also of other European nationalities not yet enjoying national autonomy. Soon after his dismissal from the Collège de France following the coup d'état of Napoleon III, Michelet began planning a *Légende d'or de la démocratie.* In 1854 he realized his plan, in part at least, by publishing the *Légendes démocratiques du Nord,* stories of the heroic efforts of democratic leaders in Poland, Russia, and Rumania. Indeed, all the elements of legend were there: martyrs, heroes, saints—the new saints of democracy—even an "homme-fée" in the person of the astonishing Polish general Benn. These stories were legends, like the legend of France, because they were on the lips of the people across Europe, and because the people were making the stories through their actions and through their representatives, the heroic leaders. Michelet

gave such peoples their own legend in written, literary form, and he also encouraged them to treasure other forms of their folklore such as Rumanian popular songs and Polish popular poems. His hope was that folklore in his time would have the same effects that his contemporaries Augustin Thierry and Claude Fauriel had described in their histories: it would hearten the defeated, unite them, and steel them for the struggle for independence.

Michelet's last effort to educate by folklore was his *Bible de l'humanité,* published in 1864. Again he considered himself merely the recorder of traditions created by the masses of men: "All was so well prepared that the weakest hand has sufficed to write it, but the author is mankind itself." What mankind had created was nothing less than its own Bible. Through the centuries from ancient India on, Michelet showed, the people had created the finest religious traditions, the highest ideals known to man. From humanity itself came all the values that Michelet held most dear: love, justice, liberty, reverence for nature, family, and work. Repeating his summary of Vico of some thirty years earlier, and the conclusion of Renan one year before in the *Vie de Jésus,* he asserted that there were no divine men. Nor was there a great primitive revelation or a priesthood that had preserved truth and educated the people, contrary to the beliefs of Creuzer and the orientalists. A precept such as "Love thy neighbor as thyself" could be found in Confucius, the Stoic philosophers, and Leviticus, as well as in the New Testament, but in each case the popular master echoed the thought of the people. The people made themselves. Hence their Bible contained nothing miraculous or supernatural. The gods were "sons of the human soul," "effects" of a particular national genius, and in turn they were "causes" shaping the history of that national genius.

In this final survey of traditions Michelet set forth his vision of the reconciliation of all men, holding that the traditions of humanity were harmonious. Despite such retrogressive religions as the Near Eastern cults of Grace and medieval Catholicism, man's traditions had on balance progressed from oldest India through the French Revolution. One brilliant light streamed through the corridor of time illuminating a procession of men joined together in a common fraternity and in common hope. These men constituted one humanity creating one continuous tradition. Michelet, among the most nationalist of French historians, ended by writing one of the most cosmopolitan essays on folklore in his century. (pp. 75-91)

In [Michelet's] view, all folklore—including the legend of France—welled up from the people in a ceaseless, free act of creation; it was not a set doctrine imposed from above once and for all, but a continuing process of self-definition; not indoctrination, but self-creation. To combat the readiness of the French masses to submit to kings, priests, and Napoleons, it was perhaps useful to emphasize, even to overemphasize, the people's capability to decide their own fortunes, to formulate and to realize their own ideals. And to convey a sense of its newly emerging historical identity to this divided people not yet cut off from folklore of centuries past, it was fitting that the historian should look to a traditional folkloric form—legend—for a model to guide his own efforts. It was, in any case, consciously and purposefully as folklorist-historian that Michelet worked to present to the people their legends, their Bible, and their history. (pp. 91-2)

Charles Rearick, "Symbol, Legend, and History: Michelet as Folklorist-Historian," in French Historical Studies, *Vol. VII, No. 1, Spring, 1971, pp. 72-92.*

Hayden White (essay date 1973)

[*White is known for his books and essays analyzing the narratives of nineteenth- and twentieth-century historians and philosophers. In several of these he suggests that historical discourse is a form of fiction that can be classified and studied on the basis of its structure and its use of language. White ultimately attacks the notion that modern history texts present objective, accurate explanations of the past. Furthermore, as he postulates in his* Metahistory: The Historical Imagination in Nineteenth-Century Europe *(1973), historical discourse can be classified into the literary patterns of tragedy, comedy, romance, and irony. In the following excerpt from that work, White examines Michelet's use of metaphor and romance in his histories.*]

Constant, Novalis, and Carlyle were all manifestly "Romantic" thinkers, and their reflections on history turned upon their apprehension of the historical field as a "Chaos of Being" which they then proceeded to comprehend respectively as simply a chaos, a plenum of creative force, and a field of struggle between heroic men and history itself. These comprehensions, however, were not so much earned as merely asserted as truths, to be accepted on faith in the poetic sensibilities of their different advocates. The French historian and philosopher of history Jules Michelet represented a different position *within* the Romantic movement apropos of its conception of the historical process. In the first place, Michelet purported to have discovered the means by which to raise the Romantic apprehension of the world to the status of a scientific insight. For him, a poetic sensibility, critically self-conscious, provided the accesses to a specifically "realistic" apprehension of the world.

Michelet specifically denied that he was a Romantic. The "Romantic movement," he said in his letters, had passed him by; while it had flourished, he had been busy in the archives, fusing his knowledge and his thought together into a new historical method, of which Vico's *The New Science* could be regarded as a prototype. He characterized this new "method" as that of "concentration and reverberation." In his view, it provided him with "a flame sufficiently intense to melt down all the apparent diversities, to restore to them in history the unity they had in life." As will be seen, however, this new method was nothing but a working out of the implications of the mode of Metaphor, conceived as a way of permitting the historian actually to identify with, resurrect, and relive the life of the past *in its totality.*

Michelet began the effort to escape Irony by abandoning the tactics of Metonymy and Synecdoche alike, and by taking a stand immediately on a faith in the adequacy of Metaphorical characterization of the historical field and its processes. Michelet denied all worth to Mechanistic (causal) reductions and to Formalist (typological) integrations of the historical field. The Metaphorical apprehension of the essential *sameness* of things overrides every other consideration in his writing and distinguishes him absolutely from Carlyle and other Romantic devotees of individualism. It was this apprehension of sameness which permitted him to claim for his perfervid characterizations of history the status of scientific truths, in the same way that Vico had claimed scientific status for his essentially "poetic" conception of history. Michelet strove for a *symbolic fusion* of the different entities occupying the historical field, rather than for a means for characterizing them as individual symbols. Whatever uniqueness there is in history was conceived by Michelet to be the uniqueness of the whole, not of the parts that comprise the whole. The individuality of the parts is only apparent. Their significance derives from their status as symbols of the *unity* that everything—in history as in nature—is *striving to become.*

But the mere fact that there is *striving* in the world suggests that this unity is a goal to be reached, rather than a condition to be described. And this has two implications

HISTORY

OF

THE ROMAN REPUBLIC.

BY J. MICHELET,

MEMBER OF THE INSTITUTE, AUTHOR OF "LIFE OF LUTHER," ETC.

TRANSLATED BY WILLIAM HAZLITT, ESQ.

OF THE MIDDLE TEMPLE, BARRISTER-AT-LAW.

LONDON:

DAVID BOGUE, FLEET STREET.

MDCCCXLVII.

Title page of Hazlitt's English translation of Michelet's Histoire de la République romaine.

for Michelet. One of them is that the historian must write his histories in such a way as to promote the realization of the unity that everything is striving to become. And the other is that everything appearing in history must be assessed finally in terms of the contribution it makes to the realization of the goal or the extent to which it impedes its realization. Michelet therefore fell back upon the mode of emplotment of the Romance as the narrative form to be used to make sense out of the historical process conceived as a struggle of essential virtue against a virulent, but ultimately transitory, vice.

As a narrator, Michelet used the tactics of the dualist. For him, there were really only two categories into which the individual entities inhabiting the historical field could be put. And, as in all dualistic systems of thought, there was no way in his historiographical theory for conceiving of the historical process as a dialectical or even incremental progress toward the desired goal. There was merely an interchange between the forces of vice and those of virtue—between tyranny and justice, hate and love, with occasional moments of conjunction, such as the first year of the French Revolution—to sustain his faith that a final unity of man with man, with nature, and with God is possible. At the extreme limits of human aspiration, Michelet envisioned the discovery of the ultimate symbol, the Metaphor of Metaphors, which may be precritically apprehended as Nature, God, History, the Individual, or Mankind in general.

How the mode of Metaphor and the myth of Romance function in Michelet's historiography can be seen in his *History of the French Revolution.* His description of the spirit of France in the first year of the Revolution is a sequence of Metaphorical identifications that moves from its characterization as the emergence of light from darkness, to description of it as the triumph of the "natural" impulse toward fraternity over the "artificial" forces which had long opposed it, and ends, finally, in the contemplation of it as a symbol of pure symbolization. France, he wrote, "advances courageously through that dark winter [of 1789-90], towards the wished-for spring which promises a new light to the world." But, Michelet asked, what is this "light"? It is no longer, he answered, that of "the vague love of liberty," but rather that of "the unity of the native land." The people, "like children gone astray, . . . have at length found a mother." With the breakup of the provincial estates in November, 1789, he averred, all *divisions* between man and man, man and woman, parent and child, rich and poor, aristocrat and commoner, are broken down. And what remains? "Fraternity has removed every obstacle, all the federations are about to confederate together, and union tends to unity.—No more federations! They are useless, only one now is necessary,—France; and it appears transfigured in the glory of July."

Michelet then asked: "Is all this a miracle?" And his answer, of course, was "Yes, and the greatest and most simple of miracles, a return [of man] to nature." For, since "the fundamental basis of human nature is sociability," it had "required a whole world of inventions against nature to prevent men from living together." The whole *Ancien Régime* was seen as an *artificial barrier* to the *natural impulse* of men to *unite* with one another. The whole burdensome structure of customs, duties, tolls, laws, regulations, weights, measures, and money, the whole rotten system of "carefully encouraged and maintained" rivalries between "cities, countries, and corporations—all these obstacles, these old ramparts, crumble and fall in a day." And, when they crumble, "Men then behold one another, perceive they are alike, are astonished to have been able to remain so long ignorant of one another, regret the senseless animosity which had separated them for so many centuries, and expiate it by advancing to meet and embrace one another with a mutual effusion of the heart." There is nothing, Michelet said,

> but what breathes the pure love of unity. . . . *geography* itself is *annihilated.* There are no longer any mountains, rivers, or barriers between men. . . . Such is the power of love. . . . *Time and space,* those material conditions to which life is subject, *are no more.* A strange *vita nuova,* one eminently spiritual, and making her whole Revolution a sort of dream, at one time delightful, at another terrible, is now beginning for France. *It knew neither time nor space.* . . . All the old emblems grow pale, and the new ones that are tried have little significance. Whether people swear on the old altar, before the Holy Sacrament, or take the oath before the cold image of abstract liberty, the true symbol is elsewhere.

> The beauty, the grandeur, the eternal charm of those festivals, is that the symbol is a living one.

> This symbol for man is man.

And then, switching to a voice which was at once his own and that of the people who believed in the Revolution on that day, Michelet wrote:

> We, worshippers of the future, who put our faith in hope, and look towards the east; we, whom the disfigured and perverted past, daily becoming more impossible, has banished from every temple; we who, by its monopoly, are deprived of temple and altar, and often feel sad in the isolated communion of our thoughts, we had a temple on that day—such a temple as had never existed before! No artificial church, but the universal church; from the Vosges to the Cévennes, and from the Alps to the Pyrenees.

> No conventional symbol! All nature, all mind, all truth!

It was all, he said, "the greatest diversity . . . in the most perfect unity."

Michelet *emplotted* his histories as dramas of disclosure, of the liberation of a spiritual power fighting to free itself from the forces of darkness, a redemption. And his conception of his task as a historian was to serve as the preserver of what is redeemed. In his book *The People,* written in 1846, he said of his conception of historical representation: "Let it be my part in the future to have not attained, but marked, the aim of history, to have called it by a name that nobody had given it. Thierry called it *narration,* and M. Guizot *analysis.* I have named it *resurrec-*

tion, and this name will remain." This conception of history as "resurrection" applies both to the plot structure which the various histories that Michelet wrote were intended to figure and to the explanatory strategies used in them. It determines both the contents of Michelet's histories and their form. It is their "meaning" as both explanation and representation. But because Michelet located the macrohistorical point of resolution at the moment when, during the Revolution, perfect freedom and perfect unity are attained by "the people," through the dissolution of all the inhibiting forces ranged against it, the *tone* of his historical work was bound to grow more melancholic, more elegiac, as the ideals of the Revolution in its heroic phase receded into the background among the social classes and political elites which had originally fostered them.

Michelet dominated the field of historiography in France during the July Monarchy; his **Précis d'histoire modern** (1827) was the standard survey of European history in the French schools until 1850, when a new wave of Reaction swept Liberalism into its own Conservative phase and destroyed Michelet's career in the university in its wake. His **History of the French Revolution** (in seven volumes, published in the heat of passions which the years 1847-53 generated among Frenchmen of all parties) is prefaced by a note in which the elegiac tone is associated with Michelet's memories of the death of his father, which occurred while he was painfully watching the slow death of the ideals of the Revolution. His historical reflections, he wrote, had been carried out in "the most awful circumstances, that can attend human life, between death and the grave,—when the survivor, himself partly dead, has been sitting in judgment between two worlds." Michelet's Romantic emplotment of the history of France up to the Revolution was thus set within a larger Tragic awareness of its subsequent dissipation. This realization of the Tragic nature of his own time gave to Michelet another reason to claim the title of a realist. He conceived this condition to be precisely the same as that which had existed in France in the 1780s.

The **Précis** ends on the eve of the Revolution, with a characterization of the fractured condition into which the whole of French society had fallen by that time. As Michelet described it:

> All the world was interested in the people, loved the people, wrote for the people; *la Bienfaisance était de bon ton, on faisait de petites aumones et de grandes fêtes.*

But, while "high society" sincerely played out a *"comédie sentimentale,"* the "great movement of the world" continued in a direction that would shortly transform everything.

> The true confidante of the public, the Figaro of Beaumarchais became more bitter each day; it turned from comedy to satire, from satire to tragic drama. Royalty, Parlement, nobility, all staggered from weakness; the world was drunken [*comme ivre*].

Philosophy itself had become ill from the "sting" of Rousseau and Gilbert. "No one believed any longer in either religion or irreligion; everyone, however, would have liked to believe; the hardier spirits went incognito to seek belief in the illusions of Cagliostro and the tub of Mesmer." However, France, like the rest of Europe, was caught up in "the endless dialogue of rational skepticism: against the nihilism of Hume arose the apparent dogmatism of Kant; and everywhere one heard the great poetic voice of Goethe, harmonious, immoral and indifferent. France, distracted and anxiety-ridden, understood nothing of this. Germany played out the epic of science; France produced the social drama." The comic sadness (*le triste comique*) of these last days of the old society was a result of the contrast between great promises and the complete impotency of those who made them: "L'impuissance est le trait commun de tous les ministères d'alors. Tous promettent, et ne peuvent rien."

The Comic resolution which succeeded this severed condition was the Revolution itself. The contest which precipitated the Revolution is laid out as a struggle "between two principles, two spirits—the old and the new." And the "new" spirit, the spirit of justice, comes "to fulfill, not to abolish." The old spirit, the spirit of injustice, existed merely to oppose the fulfillment of the new. And this principle of radical opposition gave to Michelet the basis for his characterization of the Revolution in a single phrase: "The Revolution is nothing but the tardy reaction of justice against the government of favor and the religion of grace." The Revolution was a reversal, a substitution of perfect justice for absolute tyranny. But this reversal was not so much accounted for as simply characterized as such. It was the "redemption" of the people in whose history Michelet had been vicariously participating all along.

Another image used by Michelet to characterize the Revolution was that of a birth process. But the birth envisaged was more Caesarean than natural. During his travels, he wrote, he went for a walk in the mountains. Reflecting on a mountain peak that had thrust itself up "from the deep bowels of the earth," Michelet said, he was driven to muse:

> What were then the subterraneous revolutions of the earth, what incalculable powers combated in its bosom, for that mass, disturbing mountains, piercing through rocks, shattering beds of marble, to bust forth to the surface? What convulsions, what agony forced from the entrails of the globe that prodigious groan!

These musings, he said, produced a desperate anguish in his heart, for "Nature had but too well reminded me of history." And "history" in turn had reminded him of "justice" and its burial for years in the prisons of darkness:

> That justice should have borne for a thousand years that mountain of [Christian] dogma upon her heart, and, crushed beneath its weight, have counted the hours, the days, the years, so many losing years—is, for him who knows it, a source of eternal tears. He who through the medium of history has participated in that long torture, will never entirely recover from it; whatever may happen he will be sad; the sun, the joy of the world, will never more afford him comfort; he has lived too long in sorrow and in darkness; and my very heart bled in contemplating the long resignation, the meekness, the patience, and the

efforts of humanity to love that world of hate and malediction under which it was crushed.

An essential difference between Herder's and Michelet's approach to history should be noted here. On the one hand, Michelet certainly did not refuse to judge the various figures which he discerned in the historical landscape. Moreover, he did not perceive the historical process as an essential harmony which manifests its goodness and beneficence to mankind in all its operations. Like Ranke, Michelet took struggle and conflict seriously, as ineluctable aspects of historical existence. This is another earnest of his "realism." But, since he located the resolution of that drama in a period and a set of events which were progressively being shorn of their status as ideal incarnations of human community—that is to say, in the Revolution in its popular (and, to him, Anarchist) phase—Michelet's essentially Romantic apprehension of the historical process was progressively colored by a doleful apprehension of its growing meaninglessness as a principle around which history-in-general can be organized. He continued to assert his belief in the ideals of the Revolution and in the social vision which justified both the belief and the ideal, but his tone became increasingly desperate as the events of 1789 receded in time.

The historical situation from which he looked back upon the period of the Revolution, a situation in which the forces of tyranny had once more gained control of the national and international life, forced upon him an increasingly Ironic apprehension of the historical process, a sense of the eternal return of evil and division in human life. But he resolutely interpreted this eternal return of evil and division as a temporary condition for mankind over the long run. The doubt which the recognition of his own condition inspired within him was transformed by an act of will into the precondition for hope—in fact, was *identified with hope*. He could say to himself, as he said of "the people" on the eve of the Revolution, when life must have looked darkest to them:

> Be not alarmed by thy doubt. That doubt is already faith. Believe, hope! Right, though postponed, will have its advent; it will come to sit in judgment, on the dogma and on the world. And *that day* of Judgment will be called the Revolution.

Thus, the Romantic plot structure of the *whole* historical process remained intact. The conditions of Tragedy and Irony could be set within it as *phases* of the total process, to be annulled in the fire of Revolution which his own histories were meant to keep alive.

Unlike Herder, who conceived history as a *gradual* transformation of humanity from one unique set of particulars to another, Michelet conceived it as a series of cataclysmic reversals caused by long-growing tensions which force humanity into *opposed* camps. In these reversals, false justice is replaced by true justice, inconstant love replaced by true love, and the false religion of love, Christianity, the tyrant which "covered the world with [a] sea of blood," by its true antithesis, the spirit of the Revolution. And his purpose, Michelet said, was to bear true witness against the flatterers of kings and priests, "to drown false history and the hired flatterers of murder, to fill their lying mouths."

The emblem of the old monarchy was, in Michelet's account, the Bastille; it was the symbol of the Ironic condition in which a "government of grace" showed its "good nature" by granting *lettres de cachet* to favorites on a whim and to the enemies of justice for money. The most horrible crime of the old regime was to condemn men to an existence that was neither life nor death, but "a middle term between life and death: a lifeless, buried life," a world organized "expressly for oblivion," the Bastille. It was this "buried" life which the Revolution exhumed and called to sit in judgment. The Revolution was the political and moral *resurrection* of everything good and human "buried" by the old regime.

As thus envisaged, the Revolution represented the revenge which memory—that is to say, "history"—takes on the selective immolation of living men and the annullment of the rights of the dead. In the Bastille, men were not simply killed, Michelet wrote; instead, they were—more horribly in Michelet's mind—simply "forgotten."

> Forgotten! O terrible word! That a soul should perish among souls! Had not he whom God created for life the right to live at least in the mind? What mortal shall dare inflict, even on the most guilty, this worst of deaths—to be eternally forgotten?

But, in a passage which reveals his own conception of the sanctity of the historian's task, Michelet insisted:

> No, do not believe it. Nothing is forgotten—neither man nor thing. What once has been, cannot be thus annihilated. The very walls do not forget, the pavement will become accomplice, and convey signs and noises; the air will not forget.

Rather than fall into the Ironic contemplation of life itself as a prison, Michelet took it upon himself to "remember" the living dead and the ideals of the Revolution, which had aimed to restore the living dead to their rightful place among the living.

On the eve of the Revolution—as in the world which Michelet was forced to inhabit after the renewed immolation of the Revolutionary ideal by Napoleon III—"The world [was] covered with prisons, from Spielberg to Siberia, from Spandau to Mont-St.-Michel. The world [was] a prison!" And, writing the history of the Revolution's advent, Michelet sympathetically entered into and relived the popular movement that would soon explode in violence against this offense to memory and life alike:

> From the priest to the king, from the Inquisition to the Bastille, the road is straight, but long. Holy, holy Revolution, how slowly dost thou come!—I, who have been waiting for thee for a thousand years in the furrows of the Middle Ages,—what! must I wait still longer?—Oh! how slowly time passes! Oh! how I have counted the hours! Wilt thou never arrive?

And when the women and children descended upon the Bastille to liberate their husbands, sons, lovers, and brothers imprisoned there, Michelet broke out in a cry of joy: "O France, you are saved! O world, you are saved!"

This salvation resulted in a dissolution of all differences among men, between men and women, young and old, rich and poor, which finally transformed the nation into a people. This condition of perfect integration was symbolized by the image of Joan of Arc: "Again do I behold in the heavens my youthful star in which so long I placed my hope—Joan of Arc." But then, in another of those lyrical effusions, in which he offended both reason and science, but not Metaphor, Michelet remarked: "What matter, if the maid, changing her sex, has become a youth, Hoche, Marceau, Joubert, or Kleber."

In his enthusiasm for the events he was depicting, Michelet dissolved all sense of difference among men, institutions, and values. His Metaphorical *identification of things* that appear to be different utterly overrode any sense of the *differences among things,* which is the occasion for Metaphorical usage to begin with. All difference was dissolved in his apprehension of the unity of the whole. Thus, Michelet wrote, "the most warlike of men" become the "harbingers of peace"; and "Grace, in whose name Tyranny has crushed us, is found to be consonant, identical with Justice." Conceived as a process, the Revolution, he said, is nothing but the "reaction of equity, the tardy advent of Eternal Justice"; in its essence it is "truly Love, and identical with Grace."

These conflations of one abstraction with another were not dialectically earned; they were merely asserted. But they were experienced neither as abstractions nor as conflations by Michelet, but as *identifications* of the one essence which is both the substance of history and the cause in whose name Michelet worked as a historian. "Love" and "Grace" were for him "Justice," which he called his "mother," and "Right," which he called his "father." But even justice and right were too distinct for him, and so he finally identified both with God ("ye who are but one with God!").

Thus, finally, God sustained Michelet in his service to history, and insured his objectivity, which was but another form of "Justice" and "Grace." At the close of the Introduction to his ***History of the French Revolution,*** Michelet addressed God directly, as he had earlier addressed the "Revolution":

> And as thou art Justice, thou wilt support me in this book, where my path has been marked out by the emotions of my heart and not by private interest, nor by any thought of this sublunar world. Thou wilt be just towards me, and I will be so towards all. For whom then have I written this, but for thee, Eternal Justice?

Now, there is no denying that the tone and point of view of Michelet's work stand in the starkest of contrasts to those of his more "realistic" counterpart in Germany, the judicious Ranke, who steadfastly insisted on his unwillingness either to "judge" the past or to legislate for the future. But, on the matter of "objectivity," the principal differences between Michelet and Ranke are more superficial than real. They reside in the fact that the principles of love, grace, and justice, which informed Michelet's approach to the study of history, were worn on his sleeve and explicitly incarnated in the principles of "the nation, the people, and the Revolution" rather than implicitly honored and identified with "the state, the church, and established society" as in Ranke. Michelet was no less interested in the truthful representation of the past, in all its particularity and unity, than was Ranke; but he believed one could write history, not out of any "private interest" nor governed "by any thought of this sublunar world," but simply by following the "path marked out by the emotions of [his] heart." That Ranke professed to be governed by the desire to rise above such "emotions" should not obscure the fact that his own histories are no less marked by evidences of personal preference and party biases than are Michelet's. The important point is that both historians acted as custodians of the memory of the race, against any tyranny which might have offended that memory by systematic suppression of the truth.

Michelet conceived the historian's task to be precisely similar to that of those women who descended upon the Bastille to restore the claims of its "forgotten" prisoners. The historian, Michelet said in one of his most self-critical moments, is "neither Caesar nor Claudius, but often in his dreams he sees a crowd which weeps and laments its condition, the crowd of those who have not yet died, who would like to live again. . . ." These dead do not ask only for an "urn and tears," and it is not enough merely to repeat their "sighs." What they require, Michelet said, is:

> an Oedipus who will solve for them their own riddle, which made no sense to them, one who will explain to them the meaning of their words, their own actions which they did not understand.

This seems to suggest that the historian, writing on behalf of the dead, is also writing *for* the dead, not to some living audience in the present or the future.

But then Michelet changed the image once more, and substituted the figure of Prometheus for that of Oedipus. As Prometheus the historian will bring to the dead a fire sufficiently intense to melt the ice in which their "voices" have been "frozen," so that the dead will be able "to speak once more" for themselves.

But even this is not enough. The historian must be able to hear and to understand "words that were never spoken, words which remained in the abysses of [the dead's] hearts." The task of the historian, finally, is "to make the silences of history speak, those terrible organ notes [*points d'orgue*] which will never sound again, and which are exactly its most tragic tones." Only when the voices of the dead, and their silences, have been restored to life will

> the dead rest easily in their graves. [Then] they begin to comprehend their fate, modulate their dissonances into a softer harmony, to say to themselves and very softly the last words of Oedipus: "Be fortunate for all the time to come." The shades are saluted and are appeased. They permit their urns to be closed. . . . Precious urn of forgotten times, the priests of history carry it and transmit it with what piety, what tender

care! . . . as they might carry the ashes of their father or their son. Their son? But is it not themselves?

Again, in 1872, at the end of his life, in the preface to his *Histoire du XIXe siècle* Michelet spoke of the historian's role as essentially a custodian of the "memory" of the dead.

> Yes, each dead person leaves a little goods, his memory, and demands that someone take care of it. For him who has no friends, a magistrate must care for it. For the law, justice is more certain than all our forgetful tendernesses, our tears so quickly dried.
>
> This magistrate is History. . . . Never have I in my whole career lost sight of this, the Historian's duty. I have given to many of the dead too soon forgotten the aid of which I myself will have need.
>
> I have exhumed them for a second life.

This conception of the historian's duty in no way conflicted with Michelet's notion of the necessity of the historian's "frank and vigorous partiality for the right and the truth." False partiality entered into history only when historians wrote in fear, or in the hope of currying the favor of established authority. The most honorable historian, Michelet insisted in 1856, at the conclusion of his *History of France,* had to lose all "respect" for certain things and certain men in order to serve as the judge and redeemer of the world. But this loss of respect would permit the historian to see the extent to which, *"dans l'ensemble des siècles et l'harmonie totale de la vie de l'humanité," "fact and the right coincide* over the long run, and never contradict one another." But, he warned,

> to locate in the details, in the conflict, this fatal opium of the philosophy of history, these *ménagements* of a false peace, is to insert death into life, to kill history and morality, to have to say, in the manner of the indifferent soul: "What is evil? what is good?"

Michelet frankly admitted the "moral" orientation of his work, but his research, he insisted, had permitted him to see the true "physiognomy" of the centuries he had studied; and he had at least given *"une impression vraie"* of it.

Michelet cited Vico as the thinker who had provided the theory of the interaction of consciousness with society by which the fact of mere succession of social forms could be entertained as a providential process of a purely secular nature. Vico's theory permitted Michelet to dissolve all apparent formal collectivities into particularities and, after that, to characterize in purely Metaphorical terms the essential natures of both the particularities and the larger process in which they have a place. Ranke's suspicion of large-scale theories of any kind inclined him to halt his search for meaning and order in history with the apprehension of the finished forms of society and culture that had taken shape in his own time and to use these forms as the standard for whatever meaning history in the large might have. Thus, these two historians, who had so much in common in the way they prefigured the historical

field and its processes, tended toward alternative modes of characterization which gave them escape from the threat of Irony.

Michelet came to rest in the mode of Metaphor, and emplotted history as Romance, because his sense of the coherence of the whole process was sustained by a belief in the unitary nature of the parts. Michelet grasped the essential point that Vico had made about any specifically historical conception of human reality—namely, that the forces which are overcome in any advance in society or consciousness themselves serve as the materials out of which the new society and consciousness will be fashioned. As Michelet commented in the introduction to his translation of *The New Science,* "Principes de la philosophie de l'histoire," faith in the providential nature of the historical process is secured, not by belief alone, but by society itself:

> The miracle of [society's] constitution lies in the fact that in each of its revolutions, it finds in the very corruption of the preceding state the elements of the new form which is able to redeem it. It is thus eminently necessary that there be ascribed to it a wisdom greater than man . . . [*au-dessus de l'homme*].

This "wisdom" does not govern us by "positive laws," he continued, but serves itself by regulating those "usages which we freely follow." Thus, Michelet concluded, the central principle of historical understanding lies in the ideas which Vico set forth in *The New Science:*

> men themselves have made the social world what it is [*tel qu'il est*]; but this world is not less the product of an intelligence, often contrary and always superior, to the particular ends which men have set for themselves.

He then repeated the list of public goods (issuing from privately projected interests) that mark the course of human advancement from savagery to civilization and concluded with the remark that, "even when nations try to destroy themselves, they are dispersed into solitude . . . and the phoenix of society is reborn from the ashes."

This phoenix image is important because its suggestion of an eternal return points to the inherently antiprogressivist tendency contained in any system of tropological characterization not informed by a firm dialectical sense. The Metaphorical mode promotes the degeneration of the conception of the historical process into a "chaos of forms" when a presumption of history's Metaphorical integrity begins to fade. Once Michelet's faith in the triumph of right and justice began to dissipate, as the antirevolutionary forces gained the ascendancy, there was nothing left but a fall into melancholic reflection on the defeat of the ideal whose original triumph he had chronicled in his early histories.

The principal differences between Michelet's conception of history and that of Herder may now be specified. Herder characterized the objects occupying the historical field in the mode of Metaphor, and then proceeded to a Synecdochic integration of the field by the explanatory strategies of Organicism and the emplotting strategies of Comedy. Michelet began in the same way, but the patterns of integration which he discerned in that field were represented from a perspective given to him by his Ironic awareness of their evanescent and transitory nature. The "Romance" of the French people's struggle against tyranny and division and their attainment of a perfect unity during the first year of the Revolution is progressively distanced by the growing awareness in Michelet of the resurgence and (at least temporary) victory of the blocking forces. Michelet continued to write history as the defender of the innocent and just, but his devotion to them was progressively hardened, rendered more "realistic," by his awareness of the fact that the desired outcome was still yet to be attained. Unlike Herder, who was capable of believing that every resolution of a historical conflict was desirable simply because it was a resolution, Michelet recognized that the historian must take up a position pro or contra the forces at play in different acts of the historical drama. His own perspective on the agents and agencies in the historical process was Ironic; he distinguished between those that were good and those that were evil, even though he was governed by the hope that the conflict between their representatives would have the kind of triumphant outcome for the forces of good which he thought had been achieved in France in 1789. The supposed "realism" of his method consisted in his willingness to characterize in a language heavily freighted with Metaphor the representatives of both types of forces in the historical process. Unlike his eighteenth-century predecessors, Michelet conceived his task as a historian to be that of the custodian of the dead, whether they be conceived as good or evil by him, though in the interest finally of serving that justice in which the good are finally liberated from the "prison" of human forgetfulness by the historian himself.

Although Michelet thought of himself as a Liberal, and wrote history in such a way as to serve the Liberal cause as he understood it, in reality the ideological implications of his conception of history are Anarchist. As can be seen in the way he characterized the condition to which the French people attained in 1789 in his *History of the French Revolution,* he conceived the ideal condition to be one in which all men are naturally and spontaneously united in communities of shared emotion and activities that require no formal (or artificial) direction. In the ideal condition of mankind distinctions between things, and between things and their significations, are dissolved—in pure symbol, as he puts it, in unity, perfect grace. Any division of man from man is viewed as a condition of oppression, which the just and virtuous will strive to dissolve. The various intermediary unities represented by states, nations, churches, and the like, regarded by Herder as manifestations of essential human community and viewed by Ranke as the means to unification, were regarded by Michelet as impediments to the desired state of anarchy, which, for him, would alone signal the achievement of a true humanity.

Given Michelet's conception of the sole possible ideal form of human community, it seems unlikely that he would have been able to accredit any specific form of social organization actually met with in history as even a remote approximation to the ideal. Whereas Herder was

compelled, by the logic of his conception of history, to accept everything, to criticize nothing, and to praise anything simply for having come to be, Michelet was unable, by the logic of his conception of history, to find virtue in anything except the one moment of pure conjunction that he thought he had seen in the history of France during a single year, 1789. In the end, he could praise those individuals he identified as soldiers in the service of the ideal, and he could dedicate his life to telling *their* story in a tone and mood that would promote the ideal in the future. But the ideal itself could never be realized in time, in history, for it was an evanescent as the condition of anarchy which it presupposed for its realization. (pp. 149-62)

> *Hayden White, "Michelet: Historical Realism as Romance," in his* Metahistory: The Historical Imagination in Nineteenth-Century Europe, *The Johns Hopkins University Press, 1973, pp. 135-62.*

John P. McKay   (essay date 1973)

[*McKay is an American historian, educator, and critic who has written extensively on the social and economic history of Europe. In the following excerpt, he presents an overview of* The People.]

I first came across **The People** as the unjustly neglected classic study of French society in the first part of the nineteenth century. **The People** is indeed that, and the insight from this point of view alone is enough to warrant consideration. Almost half of the book is a portrait of the social change and social dislocation peasants, workers, factory owners, officials, and all other groups of France experienced in the difficult transformation from agrarian to industrial society. This portrait of France is certainly unsurpassed, and it is also representative of general European problems in this time of rapid social and economic change.

Particularly noteworthy is Michelet's feeling for how the condition of each group is evolving over time. One is not a great historian, or even a serious student of history for that matter, without bringing to current problems an understanding that will often elude his contemporaries. Clearly **The People** is excellent testimony to Michelet's dictum that "he who limits himself to the present will not understand the present."

In addition to this general understanding of the complexity and dynamic character of the social process, Michelet has a flair for penetrating details and sympathetic description in very human terms. His examination of the effects of industrialization on the new factory workers, for example, could almost stand as a compassionate, honest, somewhat "pessimistic" summary of the most discerning scholarly discussions and studies on the subject. Thus he emphasizes the factory worker's psychological problems—boredom, dependence, dehumanization—in his new circumstances, while recognizing the attempt to show any alleged decline in living standards from earlier times as the quicksand it is. Michelet understood the hard life of pre-industrial labor better than many other historians have, and certainly well enough to avoid idealizing that condition. Another example is his analysis of established capitalists who are unimaginative and timid, in contrast with the "new" men constantly rising from below, particularly in the textile industry. Here is a suggestive commentary on the problem of the French business class and the paradox of an apparently immobile upper middle class and a rate of economic growth that was quite rapid in the 1830s and 1840s. The treatment of other groups is often equally enlightening.

While some of Michelet's insights will no doubt escape readers who are unfamiliar with such questions, no one will miss the main thrust of his analysis. As the parts suffer, so is the whole dangerously ill. France, according to Michelet, is on the verge of tearing herself apart, as modernization and industrialization exacerbate the political and ideological dissensions of the restoration era. Michelet felt a tremendous concern and terrible anguish before this prospect of social disintegration and civil war, and perhaps recurring civil war. Nor was Michelet exaggerating the danger. France did engage in bloody class war in June 1848; she repeated the tragedy in the Commune of 1871; she did wander for almost fifty years before reconstituting some fundamental unity. Michelet knew what he was talking about.

Here is a second contribution of *The People.* A contemporary reader will feel on many a page a flash of recognition. Michelet understood the general problem of social division and hatred as well as the particular one. Those hates and dissensions of the fragmented society that Michelet speaks of with such anguish are problems that plague us today. We, too, fear that some of the basic bonds holding us together are weakening. When Michelet speaks of politicians who exploit our fears and drive us further apart, of critics who cannot or will not see our good qualities, of the lack of knowledge and understanding of separated groups, or of how each class tries to isolate its children in the educational process as soon as possible, one is forced to examine his own country and conscience.

Is there not a certain ambiguity, however, about the nature of the social problem and the division between classes as presented by Michelet? This question deserves special attention, for it has perplexed and mystified not only France but the world as well.

On one hand, Michelet says that the division in society is between the bourgeoisie and the people: "Ancient France was divided into three classes; new France has only two—the people and the bourgeoisie." Here is an early formulation of the socialist position, which in its dominant Marxian variety would emerge as the doctrine of irreconcilable class struggle, the struggle between the haves and the have-nots, the struggle between the bourgeoisie and the ever-enlarging proletariat. Here is the essence of that latter-day Manicheism that would divide society between two opposing principles, one good and one bad.

On the other hand, Michelet is quite critical of the early socialists. He consistently speaks of the people in such a way as to include almost the entire society. Only the aristocracy and the clergy are constantly ignored as in no way forming part of the people. The bourgeoisie is referred to as the people corrupted, but by no means as implacable

class enemies. The tragedy would be precisely to create such class hatred and strict division. Everyone is capable of being part of the people and therefore uniting the society in this way. There is only a difference of degree, only a difference in the extent to which the potential values and qualities of the people are actually realized in individuals.

This ambiguity on the nature of class relations is one of the work's strengths. . . . Michelet shared in the romanticism of his age, and this no doubt contributed to his sometimes unrestrained lyricism. But he was a historian first and a romantic poet second. As he put it with his usual incisiveness, "I would not live by my pen. I wanted a real craft."

Therefore when Michelet's concern and commitment compelled him to focus on the dynamics of society in an attempt to chart a course that would avoid disaster, he spoke from his heart, but he still proceeded like a scrupulous historian who respects and presents those hard-to-fit facts uncovered by keen observation. He did not romanticize or fictionalize or, still worse, merely theorize. Rather, he looked at the data before him and tried to interpret them honestly. To do so, he used not only statistics and personal experience, but above all the investigation of the "living documents"—those countless discussions with people from all ranks of society. It is this precise observation, the product of the historian's craft, that does so much to make this the classic portrait of French society.

So he presented puzzling contradictions born of careful investigation rather than the strictly logical formulas of rigorous theorizing. The problems of private property and the ownership of what Marx would shortly call the means of production—a source of irreconcilable division? On one hand, there was the reality of the new factory production of the industrial revolution; on the other, the fact of widespread peasant ownership and the attachment to peasant property. The low wages and difficult conditions of mechanized industry—a source of division? Yes, but what of the reality of the higher standards of living as the machine-produced textiles were diffused, and the corresponding moral progress of all?

In short, here are the contradictions—the improvements and the hardships—of the early stages of industrialism, when the lines of thought and analysis were quite fluid and had not yet hardened into dogma. Ultimately this is tribute to the truth and importance of Michelet's insights. Working class or working classes, middle class or middle classes, many divided groups or two unifying enemies on different sides of the barrier? Michelet recognized conditions in 1845 that supported both positions. Only then could the honest man conclude that on balance the barriers were many but reducible, not unique and insurmountable.

No doubt Michelet's own experience was important here. As he said, he was a man who had many classes within himself and lacked that complete unity he would have wished. He was candid enough to admit that to remain simple and among the people required a continuous effort. But just as he contained different classes and contradictions, so did society. And in both cases a generous heart and an act of will could impose a harmony. This may be seen in the dedicatory preface, which was written not first but last. There one sees a serenity and a certainty concerning his own position among the people that many an earlier page lacks. In writing **The People** and in reexamining himself, Michelet had developed himself and strengthened his humanity and ties to the masses. Others could do the same.

In the second and third parts of the book, Michelet seeks the cause of France's social dislocation and division, and pleads for the cure of common bonds in the love of one's country. This is his answer to the earthquake of industrialization and modernization. The reader must be careful not to skip over these sections. I remember in my own case how certain ideas of the increasingly didactic and moralistic Michelet left me rather cold on my first reading, particularly those in certain sections of Part Two. Later investigation showed that others who have enthusiastically praised Michelet's analysis of the people's ills have questioned sharply the cures he prescribed.

The reasons for such a feeling are not hard to find. We live in an age where shallow cynicism all too often passes for wisdom, and where pure idealism is often pure fanaticism. Thus Michelet's faith in instinct and the innate goodness

Michelet in later years.

of the masses, his call to Love as the solution for the problems he had so acutely described, and the attacks on the church and traditional religion in the baroque pseudo-Christian language of the mid-nineteenth century may at first appear as little more than worn-out prejudices of another time. As for Michelet's nationalism in general, and his deification of France in particular, that is a credo many will be quick to label retrograde and atavistic.

Yet upon further reflection, it seems to me that in spite of unquestionable shortcomings and excesses, Michelet the prophetic moralist is as profound as Michelet the social analyst. It is all too easy to read Michelet's message as pious pronouncements of what things should be—impractical Sunday school maxims divorced from the harsh realities of our mundane existence. It is easy, but it is superficial and inadequate. Much of Michelet's message is not simply preaching about what should be—within the family, between those who love, among the members of a nation, and so on—but contains an inspired vision of some of these ultimate realities and most basic human truths. "Listen, my young friends," he is saying. "Here are the grains I have winnowed. They are the fruits of my life; may they be seeds of knowledge and fulfillment for yours."

Michelet's discussion of the family and the loving ties that hold it together is no vain abstraction, for example. It reflects the double reality of the tight, intimate circle he created and recreated all his life, which was absolutely essential for his happiness and equilibrium. He is also telling us that this is the natural and instinctive pattern. Of course patterns and styles of familial and conjugal relationships are themselves subject to historical change. Some women may now uncover inequality where Michelet saw cooperation and a reasonable division of labor. Yet they will want to consider to what extent they still seek a similar fulfillment, though by means of a more equitable partnership.

Similarly, Michelet's conception of creativity and development is based on his own experiences, which observation led him to generalize. The discussions on the nature of genius, and the union of simplicity and mental development that genius nurtures, make sense when one understands that Michelet is speaking of himself and his own enormously creative process. This helps explain the power of his insights on education—insights not into what education should be in some ideal world but simply into what it is when it works—and the picture of the destructive consequences of an education that is based on the ceaseless negativism of the purely critical intellect. Michelet had seen firsthand that endless negative criticism leads to a terrible destruction: the destruction not only of the fabric of society, which is horrible enough, but also of the "educated" youth himself, who loses contact with his society and destroys himself.

It follows for Michelet that education must be positive. (Did Michelet in his heart regret what he termed "those purely negative polemics" against the clergy that he had just written—**The Jesuits** in 1843 and **The Priest** in 1845?) It must lift up and not push down. This could be done by teaching Frenchmen love of France and devotion to her. With such treatment Frenchmen would find an antidote to unchecked social dislocation and psychological tension.

For them and for other peoples as well, the unity of the all-embracing nation would refashion a sense of community and interdependence to replace old values being eaten away by the acids of individualism, competition, and industrialization. Here is a positive program that rises above hand-wringing and pious lamentations and leads to a new social unity.

Many today will question whether the road to the good society passes primarily by way of the nation-state, as others will wonder if personal happiness is so closely tied to the family. Americans in particular may be quick to see nationalism more as a curse than a blessing, a foreign affliction they have generally escaped. Part of the reason for this may be that throughout most of our history we never faced a real external threat of our own dimensions. Therefore we were never forced to establish systematically a "we-they" spirit. Yet nationalism is certainly one of the world's strongest ongoing forces. No doubt one of the reasons is that, as Michelet says, it corresponds to deep and profound realities that will not be wished away. Another is that nationalism is a more positive and constructive force than we often believe.

Of the many things Michelet has to teach us [in *The People*], notice first the generous character of his conception of the nation. Of course there is the much-abused rival, the English, against whom in part the French defined themselves historically. There is also a certain chauvinism and florid rhetorical militarism that may be explained by the relative isolation of France, especially of French liberals, in Metternich's Europe. Yet basically there is early nationalism at its best, and in the form in which it is most beneficially revived and diffused. Every people, like every citizen, has a natural right to exist in freedom and to develop its character and genius. The independence and freedom of other nations, as for other citizens within a nation, does not lessen the freedom of the first nation, but promotes the unity of the world through diversity on the common theme.

In Michelet's pages one sees how love of nation can be a force for human progress. Even the "infant" peoples are entitled to a collective personality and their own destiny. Here is certainly one of the first and most prophetic views of nationalism as the liberating force that would break the old empires and is still shaking the new ones. When this vision of the liberating force of nationalism is coupled with that of the rise of the common people, then Michelet, the soaring poetic prophet, appears once again as a great and profound realist as well. (pp. xxiv-xxxi)

> *John P. McKay, in an introduction to* The People, *by Jules Michelet, translated by John P. McKay, University of Illinois Press, 1973, pp. xiii-xxxi.*

Edward K. Kaplan   (essay date 1977)

[*In the following excerpt, Kaplan surveys Michelet's writings on nature, discussing their relevance to his depiction of nineteenth-century society.*]

Like Pierre-Simon Ballanche (1776-1847), the modern prophet, Michelet sought to mediate between past and present in order to transform the future. The nature books effect the characteristically Romantic synthesis of politics and inward inspiration. This mission was symbolized at the time by the myth of Orpheus, the poet-teacher. Maurice Z. Shroder summarizes it as he describes the career of Victor Hugo in terms of Ballanche's *Orphée* (1829):

> "The complete poet," [Hugo] wrote later in his life, "consists of these three visions: Humanity, Nature, and the Supernatural." These correspond exactly to the three functions of Orpheus: to civilize men by establishing political and educational institutions; to reveal nature to them, nature considered in its two aspects—as the material world and as a collection of symbols pointing to a meaning beyond matter; to reveal to them the mysteries by "reading" the symbols of nature, by attending to the supernatural forces of the universe and thus to indicate the routes ordained for man by God, and, finally, to make possible the perception of God Himself.

Michelet the naturalist joins the first two Orphic tasks: he uses nature to civilize and nurture humanity.

Michelet's educational and historical works all challenge the decadence of his century. The historian of the Revolution believed that universal progress had stopped by 1790. The Second Empire was the nadir in a continuum of cultural ups and downs. Sadness and pessimism were not foreign to Michelet. He wrote in his preface to *The People* that the Napoleonic Empire was a period of poverty and gloom for his family. In the "Preface" of 1869 to the completed *History of France* he quotes Jouffroy's famous pronouncement that dogmas had come to an end. Traditional religious faith was no longer possible. "In July 1830," he wrote, "the Church found itself deserted." The Saint-Simonians failed to invent a religion of humanity to replace reactionary Christianity. Michelet deplored the "moral cholera" which flourished during the bourgeois monarchy of Louis-Philippe. The failure of the 1848 Revolution, and the historian's subsequent rejection of Napoleon III, solidified his increasing distance from the Romantic generation's deepest hopes. He dealt with their realistic anxiety in a personal manner. Michelet's production was a protest against despair.

The historian's nature books—*The Bird, The Insect, The Sea,* and *The Mountain*—directly answer the severe moral depression of the Second Empire. It is true, as Pierre Barbéris points out, that this period of expanding capitalist individualism and competition exacerbated the *mal du siècle,* the aimlessness and isolation expressed by alienated writers from the century's beginning. The Restoration made it impossible to believe in the government's moral authority and killed the system of sacred values upon which France traditionally rested. Those dread realities explain Michelet's optimism, but not, as Barbéris explains, because of the historian's escapist bourgeois ideology. Michelet's faith did not deny his era's anxiety; he understood the material realities which excited his compassion and sadness. Michelet was simply compelled to counter fatalism and meaninglessness with hope. His readers craved evidence of humanity's self-affirmation: against the threat of fate and death, against the Second Empire's emptiness and meaninglessness. That is why Michelet, like many contemporaries, combines democratic idealism and the belief in human immortality.

Michelet's nature books present a revitalization program which harmonizes science and faith. He exemplifies the struggle to reconcile idealist Romanticism and Positivism in a transitional age. This struggle is reflected by Michelet's mixture of poetic and rational discourse. He puts the scientific studies upon which the nature books are based into the framework of didactic poems which follow Boileau's injunction to "please while educating." Michelet usually expresses his inspirational and practical messages by a traditionally allegorical method, interpreting the animate world as symbolic of human concerns. However, this conventional pedagogic device did not suffice. He completes these abstract lessons in esthetically seductive passages in which he exercises his gift for poetic lyricism or dramatically evokes personal experiences. Readers of his day were touched by the author's incandescent style while their minds were convinced by his obvious analogies to humanity. The nature books' immense success was due to the fact that they spoke at once to individual needs and to those of European society at large.

Michelet begins his naturalist series with a book whose main theme is religious. The epigraph which graces the cover of *The Bird*—"Wings! wings!"—expresses the metaphysical aspiration at the heart of the author's study of nature. He cites the expression from the German poet, philosopher, and Orientalist Friedrich Rückert (1798-1866) and completes it later in the book:

> Wings above life!
> Wings beyond death!

Michelet's initial presentation of the "divine tribe" of birds is strikingly anthropomorphic. Birds symbolize humanity's wish to dominate the present and the future.

Was Michelet's second wife solely responsible for this extension of the historian's religious ideas? It is true that *The Bird* originated in Athénaïs' research and writing. Its inspirational motto became the trademark of the Michelets and they would often seal their letters with the phrase "Des ailes!" imprinted in the wax. But the historian's diary reveals that the book's theme existed well before his second marriage. That theme emerged from Rückert's poem on wings. Michelet first encountered the poet's work on a trip to Germany which followed the death of Madame Dumesnil. He left France on 19 June 1842 with his son and daughter, Charles and Adèle, and his son-in-law to be, Alfred Dumesnil. His goal was not mere distraction, but the conquest of his despair. His contact with the Rückert poem was colored by this severe emotional stress, in his absorption with thoughts of death and immortality, as he noted in his diary on 2 July:

> [Rückert] is so German that it is no longer just German; it is, beyond Germany, the higher region in which Germany joins with the Orient: the dying flower (*"Wings! wings! O sea, o sun, o rose!"*) and the admirable piece about the swallow. . . . Philosophy, poetry, oriental eru-

dition, all harmonies melded into a powerful melody, a concentrate of the world itself.

Michelet found in Rückert's images a profusion of mystical yearnings he had always associated with mysterious Germany, that Orient of Europe. The historian's secret past becomes alive again fourteen years later as he celebrates, in *The Bird,* his new love and the renewal of his faith in life.

The personal significance of the book, however, does not prevent the author from utilizing a rigorous rhetorical technique. Part I of *The Bird* elaborates a single allegory: Michelet first introduces the flight of birds as a symbol of mankind's desire to be released from its bodily limits. He then traces the natural history of wing development while interpreting flight as symbolic of increasing spiritual freedom. Finally he applies to humanity the lesson he learns from animals.

Michelet characterizes the human condition as a play between aspirations for the ultimate and a sense of limits. *The Bird* symbolizes this view through the flight of Icarus, a dominant myth of Romanticism. Mankind, like all nature, yearns for a condition of absolute freedom of will. Only birds dominate the world physically and by sight; they realize what Michelet and many others believed was the goal of historical progress:

> It is in his best age, his first and richest existence, in his youthful dreams, that man has sometimes the good fortune to forget that he is man, a serf of weight and chained to the earth. Behold, yonder, him who takes flight, who hovers, who dominates over the world, who swims in a sunbeam; he enjoys the ineffable felicity of embracing in one glance an infinity of things which yesterday he could only see one by one. Obscure enigma of detail, suddenly made luminous to him who perceives its unity! To see the world beneath oneself, to embrace, to love it! How divine, how sublime a dream! . . .

A deep conviction rings through the artist-historian's cry for full mental freedom. But only flying birds appear to be released from gravity and from the partiality of normal sight. Birds indeed appear to attain an ideal vision which reflects an almost divine knowledge. Michelet, a faithful disciple of Vico, interprets the winged gods of mythology as a projection of the human desire to become an angel. He too wishes to become an angel, a person existing as a pure mind entirely freed from its material prison, the body.

Here we encounter the paradox of Michelet's spiritualism. On the one hand, he is the national historian of France, toiling to capture and to recount worldly events of utmost significance, while another side of Michelet desires to escape from earthly reality and enjoy a pure, atemporal existence. He boldly asserts this otherworldly wish in the sentence that closes the chapter under discussion, explicitly stating its lesson: "Something tells us that these dreams are not all dreams, but glimpses of the true world, momentary flashes revealed behind our foggy world below, certain promises to be hereafter fulfilled, while our so-called reality would be but a bad dream." How did Michelet reconcile these contradictory attitudes toward the mundane?

He symbolizes his attempt by the fall of Icarus. Michelet's fleeting glimpse of absolute freedom becomes restricted, as was that of Icarus, by physical necessity. Like other artists of mystical temperament, he must postpone his dreams of ultimate transcendence and embrace the workaday world:

> Do not wake me, I pray you, never wake me! . . . But what is this? Here again are the day, the uproar and labor; the harsh iron hammer, the ear-piercing bell with its voice of steel, dethrone me and dash me down headlong; my wings have melted. Heavy earth, I fall back to the earth; bruised and bent, I return to the plow.

The negative lesson is that complete spiritual freedom in this life is impossible. Michelet affirms social responsibility: "I return to the plow." His "harsh iron hammer" even expresses a willingness to deal with the industrialism from which he seeks repose. Humanity's contrary desires give a dimension of religious hope to an otherwise flatly materialistic view of existence.

He then translates the allegory of wing evolution to teach a similar combination of activism and resignation. The frigate bird, which is all wing, like Baudelaire's albatross, cannot maneuver while grounded. Michelet's history of the evolution of wings concludes that "no existence is really free here below . . . no wing can suffice. The most powerful one is a bondage. The soul must await, ask and hope for others." Nature's eternal desire reinforces its powerful aspirations although progress remains implacably limited.

Part 2 of *The Bird* describes the evolution of moral and artistic qualities within the animal world. The allegorical technique of subordinating nature to mankind is reversed: qualities usually associated with human beings now serve to illuminate the natural world. Michelet's anthropomorphism expresses literally the spiritual equality of nature and humanity. His argument relates matter to spirit: the smaller the physical size of the bird, the fuller its creative and moral capacities. Michelet's treatment of little birds is democratic in its social ideology; yet he is mainly interested in their artistic genius. For him artistic creativity and love are nature's fullest spiritual attainments.

The book's last two chapters return to the bird as an image of the human soul and creative imagination. Their very title, "The Nightingale, Art and the Infinite," stresses the religious orientation of Michelet's account of birds' mating songs. The Conclusion of *The Bird* states its underlying theme of wildlife conservation, that civilized people should preserve nature. Michelet's natural history of birds aims to reconcile humanity with these misunderstood creatures. We should respect the avian race as spiritual equals who aspire as we do to conquer physical necessity. The religious yearnings which propel mankind's Icarian quest should enrich daily life with a faith in the transcendent, while if we imitate the artistic imagination of birds, human civilization would be pushed forward.

The coexistence of the earthly and the heavenly in Michelet's vision is elaborated more deeply in *The Insect* (1857).

This second naturalist book both defends the doctrine of metempsychosis and expresses the author's absolute commitment to social justice. The book's introduction stresses nature's moral dimension. The insect "loves most truly"; "that maternal genius extends so far, that, surpassing and eclipsing the rare gropings of birds and quadrupeds, it has enabled the insect to create republics and establish cities!" The moralist-historian discovers in insect collectivities his fundamental political and social values; as he says at the very end of the book: "The noblest work of the world, the most elevated goal to which its inhabitants tend, is without any contradiction the city." Michelet's ideal of natural moral perfection is thus a democratic society. It also conquers time. "How shall we elude death? . . . Let us create society." The historian's dream of a utopian community reveals the spiritualistic basis of his passionate dedication to social transformation.

Book I, with the loaded title "Metamorphosis," defines *The Insect's* properly religious view of human possibilities. The author supports his allegorical demonstration with scientific rationalizations of ancient beliefs in personal immortality. His entomology is guided by the Egyptian mythology of insects. Metamorphosis refers to the transformation of an egg into a larva, cocoon (or mummy), and finally an adult insect. Michelet interprets this natural process in such a way as to call into question the usual categories of life and death. Insect metamorphosis represents for him "the identity of three beings. It seems as if there could be no intermediary deaths; one single life is continuously carried on." He then translates this "miracle" of the insect world into human terms. He cites a passage from an unnamed "ingenious philosopher"—directly after the text describing his own "metamorphoses"—in which the author associates the process of foetal development with an adult's aspiration for a life after death:

> If the human embryo, while imprisoned in the maternal womb, might reason, it would say: "I see myself endowed with organs of which here I can make no use, —limbs which do not move, a stomach and teeth which do not eat. Patience! These organs convince me that nature calls me elsewhere; a time will come when I shall have another residence, a life in which all these implements will find employment. . . . They are standing still, they are waiting . . . I am but a chrysalis of a man."

Michelet's citation of the word *chrysalis* to describe the prenatal stage of human existence is the final link in his equation of the insect with the human life cycle. This passage reasons exclusively by analogy and suggests that beyond this world lies another, more advanced realm of being. Like the insect, earthbound people may be called to fly in the beyond.

Michelet's attempt to defend his belief in personal immortality was so crucial that in *Woman* (1859), in which he proposes, among other things, a non-Christian religious faith, he takes pains to elucidate the inspirational intent of *The Insect.* He quotes the same passage and explains its references: "The eloquent words of today's religious men, the *migrations* of J. Reynaud and the *consolations* of Dumesnil, sustain [the innocent woman], and give her hope. In the book of metamorphoses (*The Insect*) did she not read . . . [here he quotes]. A Scotsman (Ferguson) spoke these grave, ingenious words, of striking truth. . . ." The latter example is the philosopher and historian of the Roman Empire, Adam Ferguson (1723-1816), though Michelet does not elaborate. More familiar is Michelet's friend, the mystical socialist Jean Reynaud, who defended the doctrines of metempsychosis and the afterlife in his articles "Ciel" (1837) and "Terre" (1840) which Michelet had read in the *Encyclopédie nouvelle* by January 1841. Michelet cites Reynaud's complete religious and philosophical statement, *Terre et Ciel* (1854) in *The Witch* (1862), along with the name of a disciple of Reynaud, Michelet's friend and fellow historian, Henri Martin, and *La foi nouvelle* (1850) and *L'immortalité* (1861) by his son-in-law, Alfred Dumesnil. The immortality of the soul was very much a live issue in France well into the 1860s, and our author—in a variety of books—takes a firm, unequivocal stand in its favor.

Michelet completes his discussion of immortality in the four chapters on bees which terminate *The Insect.* In "The Bees of Virgil," he interprets the fable of Aristaeus (*Georgics,* 4) which tells of bees generated spontaneously from the entrails of sacrificed bulls; the Virgilian poem is "a song full of immortality, which, in the mystery of nature's transformations, embodies our highest hope: that death is not a death, but the beginning of a new life." The historian then uses this literary reference to give symbolic meaning to a visit he actually made (dated in the text) to the grave of his son, Yves-Jean-Lazare, the only child of his second marriage who had died three months after birth (1850): "I had named him Lazarus in my religious hope of the awakening of the nations . . . Oh vanity of our hopes!" Michelet considered his life and his works as one and the same; in the present episode, the presence of some "Virgilian bees" on his son's tomb excited promises of his power as an artist-historian to bestow immortality; the insects reminded him of his capacity to resurrect the integral life of the past. Michelet's visit to the tomb of Lazarus suggests that the historian, like Christ, could quicken the dead and that his writing could produce some sort of messianic redemption.

Michelet defines the theoretical bases of his apostolic mission in book 3, "Societies of Insects." His democratic ideology implies a precise political morality. His allegorical lesson now elaborates the traditional image of ant colonies as the ideal republic. The author is particularly concerned with the problem of slavery and with the relation of individual to collective values in society. His entomological inquiry begins and ends with an ethical perspective:

> What! I turn aside from the history of men in search of innocence; I hope at least to discover among beasts the evenhanded justice of nature, the primitive rectitude of the plan of creation. I seek in this people [that is, ants], whom I had previously loved and esteemed for their laboriousness and temperateness, the severe and touching image of republican virtues . . . and I find this indescribable horror!

He goes on to describe (following Pierre Huber), in very dramatic fashion, how an army of red ants abducted the young of a black ant colony: "It was an exact replica of a descent of slave-dealers on the coast of Africa."

The parallels between this natural history and problems of international ethics are obvious. The historian's analysis of this ant colony's social structure is more subtle. The little black ants are enslaved and toil for the victors; though they held no governmental power, they nevertheless retained their creative autonomy, for they controlled the *culture* of the red tyrants: "And who knows but that the pride of governing the strong, and of mastering the masters, may be for those little blacks an inner liberty—an exquisite and sovereign freedom—far superior to any they could have derived from the equality of their native land?" Michelet's ultimate value is mental autonomy. Political freedom is a lesser virtue than intellectual independence in his primarily spiritual system. His interpretation of ant slavery recalls the cultural domination of Greece over her Roman conquerors: "the class of the little ants, who build the city and by education build the people, is truly the city's essential part, its life, its genius, its soul; the one which of itself could, if need be, constitute the motherland." At the end of the chapter Michelet reiterates that political values are ultimately derived from spiritual ones: "Singular triumph of intelligence! Invincible power of the soul!"

His model of a perfect democracy appears in *The Insect*'s penultimate chapter, "Architect Bees. The City." His moral ideal of political union seems to be realized by this apian collectivity:

> If the wasp's nest resembles Sparta, the beehive is the veritable Athens of the insect world. There, all is art. The people—the artist elite of the people—incessantly create two things: on the one hand the City, the motherland,—on the other, the universal Mother whose task it is not only to perpetuate the people, but moreover to become its idol, its fetish, the living god of the City.

The queen bee is a constitutional monarch who is fed and sustained by her people; yet her authority depends upon *their* will, in the way that Rousseau describes the people's "general will" as the removable basis of a social contract. The final sentence of the book's last substantive chapter in fact describes the beehive according to principles which sustained the Revolution of 1789: "[The people] guard her, and wait upon her, but with the pride worthy of a people who adore only their own handiwork, chosen by them, nourished by them, created by them, *able to be undone by them* [my italics]. It is their pride that when necessary they know how to create their God." Michelet considers the personal freedom and creativity of insect citizens in this social system as another vehicle of "the tenderness of the universal Love in the universality of the soul." This last sentence of the book's summary asserts once and for all that natural morality springs from a divine power available to all.

After *The Insect* Michelet wrote two books on marriage and femininity; he completed his *History of the Renaissance* and returned to the natural world in his study of *The Sea.* He develops in that book one basic metaphor: the sea as the earth's womb. His theory of creation was one result of his desire to demonstrate that intuition scientifically. This organic imagery finds another important application. Michelet uses it to justify his proposal that bathing in the ocean could renew his exhausted nation. His idea that the sea is a single organism adds essential philosophical consequences to this social mission.

The author leads us into his way of thinking with a calculated strategy. He introduces his book by systematically leading us from *comparisons* of the sea to an animal to the *literalization* of those comparisons. Volcanoes, for example, produce the two life-giving currents of warm water "which *might be called* the two aortas of the globe." (All italics in this paragraph are mine.) The Indian and American oceans "*seem* to be the deep womb, the tender and warm cradle, of a world of living organisms." "Such is the sea. She *seems* to be a huge animal arrested in the first stage of organization." Michelet's transition from comparisons based on his speculative animism to their literalization is authorized by the American "poet of the sea," Lieutenant Matthew Fontaine Maury. Michelet gives a penetrating analysis of Maury's masterwork, *Physical Geography of the Sea* (1855)—French selections of which were published in the *Revue Britannique* in 1858—and discovers support for his own cause in the scientist's style: "He endows the sea with a pulse, arteries, even with a heart. Are these mere figures of style, mere poetical comparisons? Not at all. He cherishes (and it is the secret of his genius) an overruling and invincible feeling for the personality of the sea." The sea emerges for Michelet, literally, as a complex organism. He adds to the "soul" or "personality" of birds, insects, and jellyfish the *person-ness* of the earth's womb.

Michelet's "scientific" defense of this organicist thinking produces the rich description of evolution of book 2, "Genesis of the Sea". . . . *The Sea's* philosophical agenda is equally essential. The prodigious fertility of sea creatures demonstrates Michelet's vitalism. He characterizes animal reproduction as a continuing genesis independent of divine intervention. He views the sea as "the great female of the globe, whose indefatigable desire, permanent conception, and prolific birth never cease." We know that these doctrines are fundamental to his theory of evolution, for nature's inherent spirituality hinges upon the power of matter to form living organisms. Michelet boldly asserts his panvitalism as he cites Lamarck as his authority (incorrectly, for Lamarck, a product of eighteenth-century materialism, was thoroughly mechanistic): " 'Everything,' he said, 'is alive or has lived. All is life, past or present.' This was a great revolutionary effort against inert matter, which will continue until the inorganic is suppressed." The sea and its self-forming power of life, like the mental liberty of black ant educators, testify to the action of an immanent spiritual process.

Michelet concludes this passage from *The Sea* with an echo of the profession of faith in progress which underlies his historian's manifesto of 1831:

> The word [life] has swollen with a mighty breath the sails of the nineteenth century. . . . We are now launched on the voyage of inquiry, asking

of each thing, in history or natural history: "Who are you?"—"I am life."—Death has taken flight before the gaze of the sciences. The spirit [or mind: *l'esprit*], continuing its triumphal advance, ever forces it to retreat.

Michelet's vision of infinite advance unifies his historical and "scientific" works. Had he not affirmed in his *Introduction to Universal History* that the world was the theater of liberation? What more could humanity seek than the conquest of death itself?

Michelet's spiritualistic interpretations of science show him to be a Romantic son of the French Revolution. He adds to the Enlightenment doctrine of progress a religious dimension it did not originally possess. For example, he termed Lamarck's putative vitalism a "great revolutionary effort." His manner of enlisting materialists to preach his gospel of the spirit appears in his presentation of Condorcet's *Tableau des progrès de l'esprit humain* (1794). This epitome of atheistic optimism was written during the Terror while the author was hiding from the Jacobins. Michelet interprets it using his own century's categories in a passage originally published in his *History of the French Revolution.* Condorcet, for him, symbolizes the mission of modern history:

> By the end of March [1794, Condorcet] had relived, saved, and consecrated every century and age; the vitality of the sciences, their power to bestow eternity, seemed to be manifest in his book and in himself. What is history and science? The struggle against death. The vehement aspirations of a great immortal soul to communicate immortality carried away the sage to the point of expressing his wish in this prophetic form: "Science will have conquered death. And then, no one will die any more."

Michelet descends from eternity to current events in book 3, "Conquest of the Sea." There he is concerned with the protection of certain marine species threatened with extinction. He anticipates the desire of today's ecologists to preserve nature and stresses the importance of humanity's moral balance. Michelet recounts gruesome stories of animal slaughter by thoughtless and sadistic men. He then gives many examples of love in rabbits, bats, even crustaceans while emphasizing the insensitivity of human beings to the moral superiority of aquatic mammals, such as whales and sea cows: "How much more do love, the family, and marriage in its literal sense, exist among the tender amphibians!" The nineteenth century was especially avid for seal pelts. It is brutally ironic, states Michelet, that people butcher those creatures which have perfected qualities not yet realized in human society. His practical suggestion is to establish an international code to regulate exploitation of the marine world.

Michelet then focuses pragmatically on the decline of *human* civilization in the final book 4, "Renaissance through the Sea." This title expresses the author's hope for the physical and intellectual rebirth of his nation. The term *renaissance* refers to reincarnation, physical and spiritual rebirth, as well as to the enormous intellectual energy of the French sixteenth century. The nature books, in effect, complete Michelet's *Renaissance,* published in 1855 one year before *The Bird.* In *The Sea,* Michelet turns to the Second Empire's decadence of spirit and body in the terms of nineteenth-century materialists who explained mental activity in terms of physiology. Our naturalist acts as a physician. He first describes the sea's pervasive vitality and then explains how it can heal mankind. The deteriorating fishing industry of Dieppe and Etretat symbolizes his society's immense fatigue. He then attributes this exhaustion to the prodigious advances of science and technology made available to large masses through a plethora of newspapers and popular books. The century's principal malady is thus a "dispersion of mind" which, according to Michelet, consumes his fellow citizens:

> We pour forth from our brains a wonderful flood of sciences, arts, inventions, ideas, products, with which we deluge the globe, the present, even the future. But at what cost is all this achieved! At the cost of frightful expenditure of vital strength, of cerebral force which proportionately enervates the entire generation. Our works are prodigious and our children miserable.

Michelet proposes that the government establish public health spas on the ocean, available at no cost to all social classes. Vacations at the seashore should cure the strains suffered by his rapidly industrialized nation. Overworked parents would no longer weaken their progeny through the inheritance of their acquired degeneration.

The final chapter of *The Sea* expands the Dantesque symbolism of its title, *"Vita nuova* of the Nations," into a vision of the sea as a fountain of human regeneration. Since the ocean is the original and eternal source of earthly life and the cradle of the universal vital mucus (its water!), bathing in the sea could restore the body of humanity, and consequently its mind. Michelet stresses the social utility of his book in a confidence published in its final chapter: "While I was finishing this book, in December 1860, the resuscitated Italy, the glorious mother of us all, sends me some beautiful New-Year's gifts. A brochure, a bit of news, reaches me from Florence . . . [which] contains a seed of incalculable consequence, and which might change the world." He had received a medical pamphlet telling how the lives of two sick children were saved by sending them to the seashore. He again underlines the pragmatic seriousness of *The Sea* in two notes he added to its second edition (also 1861); there he confirms through a message from his friend Dr. Lortet of Lyon the medical virtues of sea bathing. The author's final note, anticipating success, starts thus: "I learn with great satisfaction that the Parisian Board of Public Welfare is now founding an establishment of this kind [health spas on the sea]. May I be permitted to express some suggestions . . ." Michelet's didactic poem on *The Sea* combines fantasy, science, and realistic social criticism in a sincere attempt to restore his overworked nation.

Michelet had completed his *History of France* by the time his final nature study was published in 1868. After a period of intense introspection he wrote a new preface to his *History of the French Revolution* and drafted an examination of his entire career as an historian. At the age of seventy the author of *The Mountain* could thus trace the

inspirational message of his nature series with confidence. He did so in the section of the book in which he describes his physical and emotional renewal through mud bathing at Acqui, Italy. His rebirth revealed the theme his *History* shared with his social and naturalist works: "[Nature] had increased me with life and power. May I be worthy of her (I told myself), may I draw from her sources, and with a more prolific heart enter into her sacred unity! Such was the origin of *The Bird, The Sea, The Insect,* as well as of *The Renaissance,* and of that which created them, and which creates all: *Love.*"

Michelet's naturalist, social, and historical writings all attack the pessimism of early Romanticism which persisted in his day. It was a sacred duty to refute those literary masterpieces which lent authenticity to the discouragement of his contemporaries:

> Cries of despair have been uttered from century to century. Grainville, around 1800, wrote *Le Dernier Homme* [*The Last Man*]. Senancour and Byron, and so many others believed in the end of the world. I believe it to be immortal. By many unforeseeable aspects and still youthful but unsuspected fibers, it always revives.

The obscure Jean-Baptiste Cousin de Grainville (1746-1805), constitutional priest and protégé of Bernardin de Saint-Pierre (1737-1814), drowned himself in the Somme River after the failure of his ambitious epic poem. The poem then became popular with the Romantics. Michelet gives great importance to this forgotten piece, and in an appendix to his *History of the Nineteenth Century* (volume 2, 1873) he summarizes its story of human annihilation while affirming that mankind can be redeemed through love. Etienne Pivert de Senancour (1770-1846) created the memoirs of the disenchanted *Obermann* (1804) which describe a young man adrift in the world who surrenders to reverie and neurotic melancholy. The satanism of Lord Byron (1788-1824) also nourished the Romantic generation, whose rootlessness is typified in Alfred de Musset's quasi-autobiographical *Confession d'un enfant du siècle* (1836). In mid-century, the disgust with life which Michelet resolutely opposed achieved its finest literary expression in *Les Fleurs du mal* (1857) of Charles Baudelaire and his posthumous prose poems (1869) which express his ennui, or metaphysical boredom, and his ferocious anguish at the poverty and degradation of city-dwellers.

A comparison of how Baudelaire and Michelet handle their gloom could focus a valuable theology of culture. Both writers suffer from acute sensitivity to social affliction and are obsessed with the absence, or injustice, of God. They agree that mankind's yearning for the infinite can strengthen civilization. Yet they grew up in different periods and formed opposing views of human nature. Baudelaire sees humanity as enslaved; his compassion alternates with anger at displays of original sin and God's indifference. Michelet's pity and resentment are excited by mankind's corruption of its essential goodness and he is exalted by human freedom. Michelet was nurtured on the dreams of the Revolution and grew to full intellectual maturity before 1848. While Baudelaire, born in 1821, disgusted by Louis-Philippe and the Empire of Napoleon III, could not sustain such idealism. Baudelaire plunged into his era's anxiety; Michelet revolted against it. The historian's last nature book defines that struggle. *The Mountain* was written within the three years preceding the disastrous Franco-Prussian War. It resists the moral lassitude of the crumbling Second Empire and seeks once and for all to counteract this literature of despair.

Part I of *The Mountain* attempts to establish a modern faith on science, while part 2 defines Michelet's prophetic conception of history. The book begins with a trip around and then within the earth. This geological journey is meant to demonstrate scientifically the earth's powers of creation. He then interprets this geology allegorically and presents the mountain as a symbol of human aspirations. Michelet draws his lesson in the chapter, "The Upward Progress of the Earth—Its Aspiration," as he interprets philosophically the rise of liquid rock toward the sun. It becomes another incarnation of nature's Icarian quest:

> With the force of her [earth's] restrained impulse toward him [the sun], her bosom seems, at times, to heave and expand . . . Regret? Aspiration? ever vain, incomplete, and powerless, like all things in this world. The aspiration falls back to earth as if after reflection it had overcome its yearnings, though not without a sigh.

Physical reality limits the freedom of all creation, humanity included. Yet this vision does not preclude an essential hope. For the "sigh" of aspiration which nourishes desire and progress is as eternal as Mother Earth.

Michelet defines his career as an historian in book 2. The allegory takes the form of a journey on the earth's surface. He studies plants and trees and then translates the meaning of this odyssey in the chapter, "Forests—The Tree of Life—The Golden Bough." Four years before, Michelet had published a sweeping history of world religions, *The Bible of Humanity* (1864). In *The Mountain* he borrows from it various religious interpretations of the tree (Persian, Egyptian, Celtic, Virgilian, and so forth) and relates the tree as a symbol of inspiration to his own mission:

> Vast forest! sea of leaves and dreams . . . How long have I wandered in its glades! How was my youth spent, if not in gloomy seeking? up to the day when at last I found and seized that golden bough, with which I summoned departed nations from the world of shadows.

Michelet translates these symbols autobiographically. He equates the forest with the underworld of *The Aeneid,* his Orphic power as artist with that of the golden bough, and his *History of France* with a resurrection of the dead. In *The Insect* he described the "Virgilian bees" on his son's tomb which symbolized his ability to resuscitate the Lazarus of nations. Now he uses the Virgilian branch of mountain trees to portray the talisman which allows him to enter the past and return from darkness with lost souls. That "golden bough" is his empathy with the dead and his artistic gift of reliving their events through sympathetic imagination. Michelet's powerful compassion explains his almost magical conception of himself as a writer.

Michelet reappears as the moral judge of his nation in the chapter on "The Pass of the Grisons—The Death of the Mountain." These notations are based on a trip the Michelets made to the Engadine region of Switzerland. The stark landscape provided images of both geological and moral erosion: "How closely does nature resemble man! While writing this, my soul was horror-stricken with the thought of the moral *lapiaz* which I have witnessed in these days." Michelet then explicates his condensed metaphor, "moral *lapiaz*" (*lapiaz* is a technical term referring to cracks made in rock by water):

> But what will happen if this devastation, from the lower grades and the vulgar *lapiaz* of egotism and moral sterility, should extend further, and if the process of erosion gain upon the immense masses [of the people], indifferent to all things, and deficient both in the desire and the capability of good?

The term "vulgar *lapiaz* of egotism" combines natural and social ecology as it describes the self-seeking, morally corrupt and indifferent middle classes portrayed throughout the century by Balzac, Stendhal, Flaubert, and Zola, among many others. Egotism is Michelet's term for amoral individualism, unfeeling self-interest. He fears that the natural goodness he believes the common people to possess will be contaminated by the social putrescence of the Second Empire. Michelet literalizes the geological metaphor he used in *The People* to describe the simple classes: that the vital heat comes from below. Twenty-three years later the author of *The Mountain* trusts that a morally committed science (exemplified by his own approach) will reveal to middle-class France "the wellsprings of the spirit and the moral flame."

He recapitulates this message in his long final chapter, "Will Our Era Succeed in Ascending?" There he defines conclusively the educational purpose of his career. *The Mountain* attempts to establish the study of nature as the basis of a new moral order. The following year, in 1869, Michelet particularized his methods in the masterful treatise on education, ***Our Sons.*** The final paragraph of *The Mountain* suggests how the author's experience of writing can change his reader's life:

> This is the whole secret of this book. If it has again renovated me, if it has blotted twenty centuries from my memory, may you, young traveler, who come with strength and all the day before you, may you find herein a starting point! May it be for you one of those midway summits where we halt at dawn, to examine oneself a brief moment, to mark the goal with a sure eye, and then to ascend, to thrust oneself even higher upward.

The historian shares his homeopathic cure by the study of nature. This book and Michelet's entire corpus should show the path to self-knowledge. Readers would then be liberated by the understanding that nature is a source of eternal power; they could then, like birds and mountain climbers, "thrust [themselves] even higher upward." Michelet encourages us to view the world as a reflection of our own creative genius. (pp. 79-96)

Edward K. Kaplan, in his Michelet's Poetic

Vision: A Romantic Philosophy of Nature, Man, & Woman, *University of Massachusetts Press, 1977, 211 p.*

Stephen A. Kippur   (essay date 1981)

[*In the following excerpt, Kippur examines Michelet's* History of the French Revolution, *discussing his treatment of principal revolutionary figures.*]

The unfolding of Michelet's dramatic version of the French Revolution had all of the trappings, including the pretentious bombast, of a great romantic play. The dominant imagery throughout the *Histoire de la Révolution Française,* perhaps reflecting his current ideas on a new culture, was visual. Michelet filled his historical stage with vividly colored representations of the dramatis personae, despite his continual emphasis on "the people" as his only hero. Fortunately, his not wanting to personify the Revolution in men, as Lamartine had done, did not prevent Michelet from drawing portraits of innumerable individuals, groups, and clubs. "The people" were but one actor—and Michelet used that word frequently—in the initial rise, fulfillment, then slow, painful collapse of the loving spirit of the Revolution. Mirabeau, the Constituent Assembly, and Louis XVI; the Jacobins, Girondins, and Cordeliers; Marat, Danton, and Robespierre—each of them made their entrance and exit; enlivening the stage with the passion and drama of the Revolution. Each character went through his own development, ending, in most cases, in death. "The most tragic subject that history offers us, is certainly Robespierre. But it is also the most comic. Shakespeare offers us nothing comparable." As with his depiction of Robespierre, Michelet often spoke of the Shakespearean quality of the Revolution, fully aware that this five-year upheaval, this tragedy in five acts, had outlived its prime participants. The chorus or "people" swayed with the rhythm of the Revolution, while the players moved forward to center stage when it was their turn to be at the forefront of history. Assemblies, clubs, and individuals may not have personified the Revolution, but, at the very least, they personified the varying moods of the Revolution. Without all of these richly woven characters, alternately dominating the action then receding to the background, Michelet's French Revolution would only have been a pale replica of its original self, but his imaginative and complex fashioning of this cast was probably the crowning achievement of this work.

Michelet's personal involvement with his characters was total. Statements such as, "I hope to kill Mirabeau tomorrow," were common in his diary and letters, as he concurrently composed the text. In a posthumously published conclusion to the *Histoire de la Révolution Française* Michelet passionately indicated his close attachment to the major individuals in his work:

> Throughout this work, which was my life and internal world for ten years, I made, on my way, among these re-created and reborn deaths, some very dear friendships which affected my heart. Then, when they were mine, when I had already lived with their genius and in exhilarating familiarity with them, I had to break them, to wrench

them from myself. Can one believe that it didn't cost me anything to immolate Mirabeau? How much more I loved the Gironde, its glorious crusade for the liberties of the earth! . . . But my greatest heartbreak was to leave Danton. Who will ever know what it cost me to admit, towards the end, his moral fall, his equivocations, his fears, his duplicity?

Danton was particularly difficult for Michelet to criticize. But, in varying degrees, Michelet felt that he had respect and compassion for all of the actors of the Revolution. "None of the great actors of the Revolution left me cold. Did I not live with them, did I not follow each of them as a faithful companion, to the core of their thought, and through their transformations?"

By admitting Danton's "moral fall" and by following each individual "through their transformations," Michelet was adhering to his methodological ideas on describing men. From time to time in his *Histoire de la Révolution Française,* Michelet stated that he always characterized individuals in a complex manner by illuminating both attributes and defects. His portraits of the leaders of the French Revolution were not static representations dependent upon religious, political, or social bias. Instead, Michelet consciously attempted to present the intricate, multi-leveled, and often contradictory, nature of each man. Michelet psychologized individuals, groups, and clubs. His individuals might mature, alter roles, or degenerate, and in each event or situation, a different aspect of their personality would emerge. Michelet captured the essence of his method in a passage comparing his historical portraiture to the style of Rembrandt:

> We have judged actions as they have occurred day by day, and hour by hour. We have noted our prejudices; and these have permitted us to frequently praise some men while blaming them harshly later. The forgetful and stern reviewer often condemns praiseworthy beginnings because he knows the ending ahead of time. But we don't want to consider this end in advance; whatever this man could do tomorrow, we will still mark to his advantage the good that he has done today; the bad will come soon enough: let him have his day of innocence . . .
>
> . . . It would be unfair for such a changeable creature as man to be stereotyped by one definitive portrait: Rembrandt made thirty portraits of himself, I believe, all resembling each other, all different. I have followed this method; art and justice counseled me equally. If one takes the trouble to follow in these two volumes each of the great historic actors, one will see that each of them has a whole gallery full of sketches, each one made at a particular time, according to the physical and moral modifications the individual had undergone. The Queen and Mirabeau appear and reappear, five or six times, looking distinctly different on each occasion. Marat appears in the same manner, under different aspects, all of them accurate, though dissimilar. The timid and sickly Robespierre, scarcely seen in '89, is drawn in November '90, in profile, at the rostrum of the Jacobins: we [have] drawn him frontally (in May '91) in the National Assembly,

> with a rather masterful air, dogmatic, already threatening.

> We have then dated carefully and minutely, the men and the subjects, and the moments of each man.

> We have already stated and repeated a word which has remained prominent in our mind and which has dominated this book: *History is time.*

Frequently, Michelet studied paintings of revolutionary leaders, hoping to sense their various internal forces and moral dimensions. Through these pictures, writings, and actions, Michelet tried to describe the "moral modifications" and variety of poses of each individual, thereby unraveling and evincing the maze-like threads of "the inner man."

One result, Michelet often surmised, from his method of carefully dissecting the many parts of individuals, was the dilution of their supposed greatness. At the end of his work, Michelet wondered whether he had "reduced, because of the extraordinarily thorough anatomy of people, the grandeur of heroic men who, in '93 and '94, sustained the faltering Revolution through their indomitable personalities?" In his questioning Michelet seemed to fear that his psychological studies of the attributes, weaknesses, and mistakes of the leaders, automatically lowered their stature for himself and for his readers. Since Michelet, in all of his writings, preferred units of wholeness as a goal or final value, his assumptions of individual reduction were, at least, personally valid. Individuals united with France, the ultimate amalgamation of unity and fullness, only in their highest and most selfless moments. Michelet realized that inner divisiveness and inability to merge totally with France became apparent when he revealed the faults and contradictions within a man. Individuals were "secondary" in relation to France in Michelet's philosophy, and the further evidence of a man's lack of unity could only diminish his importance.

"The people," the hero of the *Histoire de la Révolution Française,* were the large, amorphous unit of wholeness. A thorough description of them unearthed neither divisions, duplicity, nor disharmony. Who were "the people," Michelet's hero, who apparently communicated rather than received the ideas of the Revolution? How did they act? As in *Le peuple* Michelet did not define "the people" precisely. Most often, they seemed to be the illiterate. When speaking of some workers, for example, Michelet added: "Several are already literate rather than people." While the composition of "the people" was not analyzed by Michelet, he did scorn those historians who attempted to categorize "the people" or separate them from the rest of society. France simply could not be divided into "property-holders and non-property-holders, or between the rich and the poor" as "the authors of *Histoire parlementaire*" had done. Contemporary social interpretations, Michelet felt, while perhaps relevant to the France of 1848, were not at all applicable to the Revolution. Buchez, Roux, and other socialists had confounded grievously the nineteenth-century concept, "the working class," with "the people." "The big cities, the working class, absorb all of the attention of the authors of the *Histoire parle-*

mentaire. They forget one essential factor. This class was not yet born."

Another type of mistaken assumption, this one advanced by Blanc, was the dualism of French society. In positing two revolutions, the individualistic-bourgeois and then the fraternal-people phase, Blanc had tried to separate revolutionary France into two hostile groups. Michelet noted, however, as he had in *Le peuple* for the France of the 1840s, that "the people" and the bourgeoisie could not be distinguished distinctly for the French Revolution. France was only one; at least that was her aim, and any interpretation, like Blanc's, which prevented this goal *ab initio* was incorrect and anathema to Michelet.

"The people" in the *Histoire de la Révolution Française,* as in *Le peuple,* represented, in the highest sense, France. They were a unit of wholeness which could not be divided, because their major moments of participation in the French Revolution were only during the culminating events reflecting French unity. When "the people" symbolized France, they could not, as in Rousseau's idea of the general will, err. In fact, during the Festival of the Federation, there were no people, only Frenchmen. (pp. 160-64)

Since "the people" were Michelet's symbol of France, no negative aspects could be ascribed to them. They were all present during the majestic attainments of the Revolution, but were *never* involved in the nadirs. Both quantitatively, in numbers, and qualitatively, in actions, Michelet was emphatic in showing "the people" unrelated to the horrors of the Revolution:

> A thing to be told to everybody, and which it is but too easy to prove, is that the humane and benevolent period of our Revolution had for its actors the very people, the whole people,—everybody. And the period of violence, the period of sanguinary deeds, into which danger afterwards thrust it, had for actors but an inconsiderable, an extremely small number of men.

> That is what I have found established and verified, either by written testimony, or by such as I have gathered from the lips of old men.

> The remarkable exclamation of a man who belonged to the Faubourg Saint-Antoine will never die: "We were all of us at the 10th of August, and not one at the 2nd of September."

All of Paris was aroused on July 14, 1789; all of France on July 14, 1790; August 10 was an act of all Frenchmen; but during the September massacres, "the people" stayed away while "three or four hundred" misfits bloodied the good name of France. Only the great events had a large number of actors, while the violent, harmful events had not only a small amount of individuals, but also none of them even belonged to "the people." For one Michelet summit, the 1792 élan for war, he described the dramatic, tearful meeting of Frenchmen, embracing each other as brothers and expressing their immense faith in fighting together for France—a meeting, according to [Gérard] Walter, which did not exist except in "the unquenchable imagination of Michelet."

Although Michelet glorified "the people" he did not think they aspired to equality during the Revolution. Lamartine had written of the desire for equality among "the people"; an interpretation Michelet opposed. Liberty, far more than equality, appeared to Michelet as the fundamental aim of the French people during the revolutionary period. Occasionally during 1789 and 1790 debates on equality, Michelet would interject his own opinion to show disfavor with the propagators of equality. In his judgments Michelet would reveal not only a realistic hesitancy towards permitting "the people" to vote, especially after having witnessed the election results of December 1848, but also an attitude, unlike his formal, methodological statements, in which "the people" apparently did not know what they were doing or how to act. In a passage written in 1847, or before the peasantry all voted for Louis-Napoleon, Michelet questioned the wisdom of allowing the majority of "the people" to vote:

> On the 22nd of October, the Assembly decreed that nobody could be an elector unless he paid in direct taxes, as proprietor or tenant, the value of three days' labor.
>
> With that one line, they swept away from the hands of the aristocracy, a million rural electors.
>
> Of the five or six hundred electors produced by universal suffrage, there remained four millions four hundred thousand proprietors or tenants.
>
> Grégoire, Duport, Robespierre, and other worshipers of the ideal, objected, but in vain, that men were equal and ought therefore all to vote according to the dictates of natural law. Two days previously, Montlosier, the royalist, had likewise proved that all men are equal.
>
> In the crisis in which they then were, nothing could have been more futile and fatal than this thesis of natural law. These Utopists thus bestowed a million electors on the enemies of equality in the name of equality.

Rejecting the thesis of the drive for equality among "the people" and even manifesting a personal disapproval of this desire was only one instance when Michelet showed his distrust of "the people." Another area of discord appeared during the trial of Louis XVI when he questioned the wisdom of "the people" as a moral judge. In this broad, reflective passage Michelet's ambivalence towards "the people" and their instinctive, anti-intellectual qualities, again emerged:

> Yes, throughout the centuries, the voice of the people, on the whole, is undoubtedly the voice of God; but for one occasion, for one place, for one particular affair, who would dare claim that the people are infallible?
>
> In judicial proceedings especially, the judgment of the great crowds is singularly fallible. Take some juries with a few men of the people and quickly isolate them from the passion of the day; they naively follow good sense and reason. But the people as a whole, are the least certain, perhaps the most dangerous of judges. A great risk, foreign to all reasoning, rides on these violent

and uncertain decisions; no one knows what will come from this immense urn in which storms lie buried. Civil war will come from them sooner than justice.

Despite the frequent admission that "the people" were his principal hero and his leading actor for the Revolution, a strange contradiction surfaced in this section on the sagacity of "the people." Although "the people" generated the high points of the Revolution, usually through their instinctive wisdom, Michelet did not want them to acquire equality nor did he trust them to take part in the judicial process during the Revolution. In these cases, reflection and intelligence, not spontaneity and immediacy, were the superior attributes.

Aside from "the people" there were numerous other players of the revolutionary period. Although Michelet denied it, did he have any other heroes? Despite his methodological statements, did certain privileged leaders speak for "the people"? As in *Le peuple* there was a continual tension in the interaction between the men of instinct and the men of reflection, where only the genius approached a synthesis of the two, thereby merging with France. Were there any geniuses during Michelet's French Revolution who combined the wisdom of the educated and the spontaneity of the illiterate and who spoke not only for "the people" but also for the new religion and France? Only a genius could escape from the divided and secondary nature of individuals and achieve fullness through representing France, undivided. The true genius, in a Hegelian sense, would have to appear continually in the forefront of history, and for Michelet, this was no mean task.

The question of heroes, a perennial focus of debate, was paramount among the historians of Michelet's generation. Blanc's apology for Robespierre and Michelet's for Danton began the major historical controversy over the great men and visionaries of the Revolution. Michelet praised Danton as well as Desmoulins, Chalier, and the Paris Commune. Was Danton, as Blanc suggested, Michelet's real hero, instead of "the people"? Did Danton fulfill the criteria Michelet established for a hero of France?

A Michelet hero had to symbolize the new religion of the Revolution. Therefore, men or groups could not have divided loyalties, nor represent an external force or internal antagonist. Moreover, even if committed to the new religion, a hero could not be a partial representative of France, namely, by speaking only for some Frenchmen or by espousing such causes as decentralization theories. Mirabeau, the National Assembly, the Jesuits, England, the Vendée, Louis XVI, the Girondins, and Robespierre were the best examples of these mistaken or incomplete visions. Danton, the greatest individual of Michelet's *Histoire de la Révolution Française,* possessed none of these defects. Internal threats and external obstacles were the foci for many of Michelet's chapters, as the omnipresent heretics attempted to extinguish the fresh flames of the new religion.

During the 1920s Mirabeau was seen as the premier hero of the French Revolution. Thiers and Mignet portrayed him as the epitome of Enlightenment thought. Even Carlyle stopped his tirade against the Revolution long enough to praise Mirabeau as "the chosen man of France . . . who shook old France from its basis; and, as if with his single hand, has held it toppling there, still unfallen. What things depended on that one man!" With Mirabeau's death "the French Monarchy may now therefore be considered as, in all human probability, lost; as struggling henceforth in blindness and will as weakness, the last light of reasonable guidance having gone out." By the 1840s, however, the exalted position of Mirabeau was no longer accepted, and he began to lose forever, to new heroes, the prestige that once was his alone. Blanc could not resist emphasizing Mirabeau's sudden accumulation of wealth during the Revolution. In attacking Mirabeau, Blanc facetiously noted: "He was a man to give heroic proportions even to baseness."

In theoretical terms conforming to his philosophy of the Revolution, Michelet deflated the exaggerated greatness of Mirabeau. Mirabeau, according to Michelet, was tragically caught between the two religions. "He wanted to save two things—royalty and liberty; believing royalty itself to be a guarantee of liberty." Unfortunately, Mirabeau was not far-sighted enough to realize the fundamental incompatibility of the old and new faiths. A Michelet hero must have a unitary vision, for individual genius was worthless if "in that man ideas are warring together, if principles and doctrines carry on a furious struggle in his bosom." Mirabeau was this type of genius. He was "contradiction personified. What was he in reality? A royalist, a noble in the most absolute sense. And what was his action? Exactly the contrary; he shattered royalty with the thunders of his eloquence." Mirabeau's attempt to straddle two differing world views was doomed to failure. Initially, he led the National Assembly into the bright, but unknown sunshine of the future, but uncertainty and doubt cast him "back upon what was called the old order—true anarchy and a real chaos. From that fruitless struggle he was saved by death."

If Mirabeau, one of the great representatives to the National Assembly, or what was later called the Constituent Assembly, was divided between two competing world views, then the other members certainly had to have comparable or even more serious theoretical misunderstandings. The National Assembly was not a homogeneous body, committed to the principles of the new religion. All types of views and ideas were present. "Created before the great Revolution which had just taken place, it was profoundly heterogeneous and confused, like the chaos of the *ancien régime,* whence it sprang." This form of heterogeneity was distasteful to Michelet, who wanted all of the legislators to represent the new principles of France. Because of this harmful conflict of viewpoints, Michelet often described the Assembly as "floating," "divided," or "wavering." Other groups, most notably "the people," through their feelings and actions, forced the Assembly to make new laws. Followers rather than leaders, the National Assembly representatives, nevertheless, served the useful function of "the recorder of France." Often, in their debates, the legislators were unable to come to a consensus or to make a decision. Michelet's methodological device for arousing the Assembly from their torpor was to have a member dramatically stand up and set forth what Michelet considered to be the desired course of action. Suddenly, the Assembly would become quiet. Realizing that he was expressing the opinion of "the people", of "all" Frenchmen, the legislators would accept his position immediately. In this manner, the ideas and emotions of "the people" were made known, then accepted, and recorded as the law of the new France.

Mirabeau and the National Assembly were caught between the two faiths, but the Jesuits, priests, Vendée, England, Europe, and Louis XVI were the persisting tentacles of the old religion, trying to hold onto a vestige of the past. These internal and external threats to the new religion continually attempted to thwart the progress and success of the Revolution. The Jesuits and England were long-time enemies of France, who merely continued their antagonistic methods. Europe was a new opponent. In the first years of the Revolution, France had opened up her arms to the world in love and brotherhood, but had been rejected by, what Michelet perceived to be, the anachronistic monarchical regimes of Europe. England, the great power of Europe, actively and successfully convinced her fellow nations of the evil and corruption that had befallen France. Therefore, France, despite the loving nature of her new faith, was forced to go to war with Europe.

Fear and hatred continued to be widespread in the new France of 1789 and 1790. One principal cause of this unwarranted fear was the false propaganda circulated by the Jesuits and their blind spokesmen, French priests. The bourgeoisie, meanwhile, copied the English in their individualistic, egotistical ways, devoid of self-sacrifice. "To the simple, credulous crowd, to the woman and the peasant, the priest has given the opium of the Middle Ages, troubling the mind with wicked dreams. The bourgeois had drunk English opium with all its ingredients of egotism . . . and liberty without sacrifice." In Avignon in 1791, the major battle was between France and the priests. Throughout the country confrontations ensued, pitting the advocates of the new religion against the remnants of the old.

The best example of priest infiltration and control was afforded by the famous counterrevolution in the Vendée. For Michelet, Vendéen peasant attacks against the Revolution were the result of a "cruel misunderstanding" as well as "unbelievable ingratitude, injustice, and absurdity." Much like his pamphlet on the Jesuits, Michelet described the manipulation of peasants and women by the evil priests. This harmful control of thoughts and emotions led these naive peasants and women to become, unknowingly, agents of the counterrevolution. These misled "people" had not been informed that the Revolution was the new and true religion. Moreover, this lack of communication, Michelet explained, between the center of the Revolution in Paris and the Vendée enabled the counterrevolution to succeed. Isolation from the Revolution had kept the Vendéens unaware of its loving nature. If "the people" had known of the new faith, they would have embraced it immediately, rather than tragically attacking "France":

> The Vendée, whatever one may think, was an artificial creation, cunningly prepared by a skillful

worker. In this obscure and remote corner of the world, without roads, the priests found a strong element of resistance in a people naturally opposed to all centralized authority. With the aid of women, the priest could slowly, at his leisure, create a bizarre and unique work of art: a revolution against the Revolution, a republic against the Republic.

> . . . The Vendéen, enclosed, blinded, in his own savage thicket, could not see the movement flowing around him. A momentary glimpse would have discouraged him and he would not have fought. Someone should have taken him to a mountain peak, where he could have surveyed and seen the momentous events taking place in the distance. He would have made the sign of the cross, believing himself at the Last Judgment and said: This is the work of God.

In the person of Louis XVI the internal and external threats coalesced. Michelet believed, as did his fellow historians, that Louis XVI was guilty, but probably should have been exiled rather than guillotined in order to show the humanity and mercy of the Revolution. In his last years, Louis XVI had kept in contact with the enemies of France, the European monarchs, in the hope that they would help restore him to his throne. This continual plotting of Louis XVI against France, and therefore, against the Revolution and the new faith, was a criminal act of the first magnitude. By fostering intrigues against the France of love, justice, and law, Michelet's Louis XVI was guilty of the heinous moral crime of attempting to kill a nation. "A person is a holy thing. But as a nation takes on the attributes of a person and becomes a soul, its inviolability increases in proportion. The crime of transgressing against the national personality becomes the greatest of crimes."

Aside from all of the poisonous arms of the old religion, individuals and groups attempting to unite with the new religion unknowingly infected the Revolution with deadly viruses. The Girondins in 1793 went counter to Michelet's whole philosophical views of France by supporting decentralization theories. Michelet had always fervently believed in the necessity of French centralization. In his ***Histoire de France*** each monarchical act leading to further centralization was unquestionably recognized as beneficial to the country. No Proudhonian concepts of small, separate, and autonomous regions of France pierced Michelet's consciousness. Centralization had given France the unique ability to harmonize totally. Administrative centralization of the Middle Ages, now seen as insufficient by Michelet, was enhanced during the Revolution by fraternal and moral centralization. The Festival of the Federation was the momentary realization of this multi-leveled centralization—administrative, social, political, emotional, and moral—which Michelet felt would be repeated in the nineteenth century. Without this vision of the future, the Girondins, although "united in heart," were drawn into an "involuntary federalism." The Girondins had forgotten that France could never "accept the weak federative unity of the United States or Switzerland, which were only systems of voluntary dissension."

Decentralization theories, if accepted during the Revolution, could only have led to further disunity and decay.

Forgetting that "unity is the eternal dream of humanity," the Girondins hastened their own downfall by following the opinions of their new, rightist members—advice contrary to the true nature of France and of the Revolution.

> The regional directors, the local nobles, the rich, all the lukewarm part of the republican party including disguised royalists, called themselves Girondins. Their common attitude, infinitely dangerous, was to loosen the nerve of the Revolution, to diminish central influence, and to increase local influence in themselves. Basically, these men were the enemies of unity.

The heroic Girondin leaders, many of them men of letters, who had founded the Republic, had led the war preparations against Europe, and had started the tenth of August, had now evolved to the unenviable position of defending a motley group of supporters opposed to "the unity of *la patrie*." Their only other alternative, at the time, was to have reconciled themselves with the Mountain and "vote for the revolutionary Tribunal and the Terror . . . They preferred to perish."

The greatest internal dividers on the side of the Revolution were the Jacobins, personified in Robespierre. Michelet's rancor towards Robespierre was chided in an unremitting sally of charges in Blanc's *Histoire de la Révolution française*. Blanc's incessant and vituperative responses to Michelet's interpretation of Robespierre, Danton, and the French Revolution, were scattered throughout his twelve-volume work. A total of over one hundred pages in his text and footnotes were devoted to correcting Michelet's errors of fact and of explanation. Blanc's most common method was to write a six or eight-page appendix after each major subject, listing Michelet's textual errors, his unsubstantiated forays against Robespierre, and his self-deceptive praises of Danton.

Blanc's thesis was monotonously the same. Michelet had singled out Danton during the high points of the Revolution and had accused or implied Robespierre to be responsible for the most hideous aspects of the Revolution. Blanc's own interpretation was precisely the reverse. For example, with the September massacres, Robespierre was implicated by Michelet as an instigator, whereas Danton was absolved completely of preparation or participation. For Blanc, the facts proved just the opposite. Although agreeing with Michelet's basic analysis of August 10, Blanc showed Danton's role to be minimal not central, and stated that Michelet's hatred for Robespierre had prevented him from seeing the pivotal position he had had during this period.

Blanc's unparalleled obsession with proving the incorrectness of Michelet's work, reflected, in part, the fundamental differences of interpretation between these two men. For Blanc, Robespierre, as leader of the second revolution, spoke for "the people," and represented the highest attributes of *patrie* and brotherhood. Michelet's Robespierre, although occasionally aiding the Revolution, did not speak for "the people" and did not further the principles of the new religion—love, justice, and law. Instead, Robespierre reverted in the last months of his life to the ideas of the *ancien régime,* by becoming a "priest" and by artibrarily condemning to death his fellow Frenchmen. Blanc's Robespierre was at the forefront of the Revolution, a shining visionary of the future, while Michelet's Robespierre blocked the progress of the new religion and its principles by turning into an agent of the counterrevolution, and reviving the discredited and injurious principles of the old religion.

Blanc described Robespierre and the Jacobins as the incarnation of Rousseau's ideas on unity and brotherhood, but Michelet began his version less propitiously. The Jacobin headquarters were indicative of the closed and conspiratorial nature of this club:

> I prefer—by the yellow glare of the lamps glimmering through the fog on rue Saint-Honoré,— to follow the dark, dense crowd all wending in the same direction to that small door of the convent of the Jacobins. It is there that the agents of the insurrection come every morning to receive orders from Lameth or the money of the Duc of Orleans from Laclos. At this hour the club is open. Let us enter cautiously, for the place is poorly lit.

As the Revolution progressed, Michelet's imagery of this dark meeting place become more Nietzschesque. At the entrance "one's mind was disturbed and one's heart became ill at ease"; then members descended "a somber stairway"; "everything was narrow and shabby . . . There was no air down there; it was difficult to breathe." In the Jacobin clubs there were no men of "the people." While Michelet agreed with Blanc and Lamartine that Robespierre became, perhaps, the most popular man among "the people," he felt, unlike his contemporaries, that Robespierre did not understand nor speak for "the people." Out of touch with the heartbeat of the Revolution, the Jacobins increasingly assumed the character of a priesthood, while Robespierre "gradually became the head of this clergy."

The Jacobins represented diverse opinions in the beginning of the Revolution, but, more and more, they lost their individual independence while one man, alone, thought and reasoned for them. "I perceive at the summit of this prodigious edifice of one thousand associations the pale head of Robespierre." What kind of man had come to speak for the mental and emotional frame of mind of the Jacobins? "Boring" and "monotonous" were Michelet's common images of the personality of the "Incorruptible." He was a sickly, dull, and lifeless man who kept secret his outrageous plots against the person of France. No man of feeling could get close to this austere individual; only colder, more heartless people such as St. Just could enter into this chilly world. This frequent seclusion in an emotionless world isolated Robespierre from the "popular instinct." Nevertheless, in trying to maintain his policy of giving all sides of a man, Michelet admitted that Robespierre exerted "great moral authority."

In 1792, before their support of decentralization theories, the Girondins, in Michelet's opinion, were the primary advocates of war against all external enemies. The Jacobins, on the contrary, feebly acceded to the war effort, because they preferred to begin an internal war against all of their enemies within France. "The Gironde wanted external war . . . the Jacobins, internal purification, the punishment of evil citizens, and the crushing of all resistance by means of terror and inquisition." On this issue, Blanc blasted Michelet for "mutilating and falsifying history," because the facts proved that Robespierre was not against the policy of foreign war. However, for Michelet, the Girondins in 1792 understood the spirit of the Revolution, of unity and transcendence of internal conflicts through mutual love of France. The Jacobins, though, did not grasp the higher unity of *patrie* and proceeded as if they, alone, represented the brotherhood of France. In Michelet's world view, schemes of internal purification, as well as decentralization theories, were divisive, retrogressive, and contrary to the principles of the new religion. All Frenchmen, after coming into contact with the Revolution, would eventually accept it with open arms; there was no need to punish dissenters through violent internal purges, the Jacobin and Robespierre position of internal rather than external war, further manifested, for Michelet, their foreignness to the "popular instinct."

Fortunately, the Girondin position prevailed temporarily, while the Jacobins continued to support the Revolution. However, as the unity of the Revolution began to fade and decompose, the artificial associations of Jacobins increasingly gained control of the country and of the Revolution. "For lack of a natural association which gave to the Revolution living unity, it was necessary to have an artificial association, a league, a conjuration, which gave it at least a kind of mechanical unity." The "positive force" of the Jacobins was their support of the Revolution, but their "negative force" of "political and moral censure" overrode their previous contributions. By 1793 the inquisitorial spirit of the Jacobins had gained the upper hand, proliferating fear, hatred, and terror throughout the country. Under the evil rule of Robespierre and the Jacobins, all of the principles of the Revolution were abrogated; "all Frenchmen," who in July 1790 had embraced in love and brotherhood, were now, "after fifteen months of Jacobin reign, . . . suspects."

As Michelet's Robespierre unleashed his bloodthirsty horde against other supporters of the Revolution (Blanc and Lamartine, who opposed this thesis, suggested, as do most modern commentators, that Robespierre tried to be a moderating force during the Terror), he also reinstituted the forms and customs of the old religion. Under the title "Supreme Being," Robespierre brought back the corrupt doctrines of the Middle Ages. During, what Michelet called, his "papacy," Robespierre filled the Jacobin clubs with priests and tried to forge for himself the image of the new "messiah." This ostentatious mimesis of the past did not convert "the people," who were in tune with the true Revolution. Robespierre's elaborate Festival of the Supreme Being on June 8, 1794, was a failure; his appearance before "the people" was "met by a silence of death." As Thermidor approached, Robespierre sank more and more into a self-made quagmire. Unwittingly, this "great moral authority" had led the Revolution into the avaricious arms of the ancient faith; the priestly religion maintained by internal repression and violence. The cyclical nature of the revolutionary years became apparent for Michelet in retracing January 1794 when "the mass, the vespers" returned and was heard on "rue Saint-André-des-Arts . . . which is near the Pont-Neuf, that is to say, the center of Paris."

In one of his many derogatory footnotes, Blanc accused Michelet of deluding himself by thinking he had written the first republican history, when, in reality, Danton had been his only "idol." Michelet, replying to this attack in an 1869 preface, denied having "taken Danton for a hero." For evidence, Michelet assumed his typical methodological pose, recalling his juxtaposition of the varieties of Danton's behavior, which had included Danton's disastrous equivocation before Robespierre. "It is especially his fatal softness in November '93 that I have never been able to pardon. I looked unfavorably upon his cowardice." After this example Michelet dismissed Blanc's criticism, and he reiterated that "the people" were his only hero. But Blanc's charge had stung, for it questioned Michelet's central premise. Reading the **Histoire de la Révolution Française,** without accepting literally the methodological statements, perhaps as Blanc did, makes one wonder whether Danton was in fact Michelet's idea of a hero?

The atmosphere of the Cordeliers emitted all of the freedom and openness that had been lacking in the headquarters of the Jacobins. Honesty, passion, and emotional intensity characterized their discussions. "Their genius, entirely instinctive and spontaneous . . . distinguishes them profoundly from the calculating enthusiasm and the moody cold fanaticism which characterizes the Jacobins." The instinctive quality of the Cordeliers allied them naturally with "the people." Unlike Robespierre, who albeit was popular among "the people," the Cordeliers associated with, listened to, and understood "the people." "It was the originality of the Cordeliers to be and ever remain mixed with the people. . . . They believed in the people and had faith in the instinct of the people." Marat and Desmoulins were two of the most potent forces behind the Cordeliers, but as far as contact with "the people," intellect, or emotional strength were concerned, neither of them could equal the power of Georges Jacques Danton.

For an image of Danton, Michelet studied a portrait begun by David and completed by disciples:

> What is most frightening, is that he has no eyes; at least, they are scarcely perceptible. What! is this terrible blindman to be the guide of nations? . . . What we read here is obscurity, dizziness, fatality, and absolute ignorance of the future.
>
> And yet this monster is sublime. This face, almost without eyes, seems like a volcano without a crater,—a volcano of fire,—which, in its closed furnace, turns over and over the conflicts of nature . . . How awful will be the eruption.
>
> In that hour, an enemy, frightened at his language, but doing justice, even in death, to the genius that has blasted him will describe him with these everlasting words: the Pluto of eloquence.

Later, Michelet described Danton's appearance as "half bull and half man," who "in all his majestic hideousness was a tragic mask to trouble any heart." This monster

with overflowing passion, knew no hatred; he only loved. He was "the greatest genius and probably the most penetrating intellect of the Revolution." Through Danton, the instinct of "the people" combined with the wisdom of the educated in love, harmony, and brotherhood. (pp. 165-77)

Michelet's Danton was the most creative thinker of his times and the greatest mediator between political parties. During the debate on going to war, for example, "Danton, as always, was the most original." In the controversy over decentralization theories, Danton, as he had often done in the past, arbitrated between the Girondins and Jacobins. For the high points of the Revolution, such as August 10, Danton managed to be at center stage, frequently speaking for "the people," although Michelet insisted in a footnote that no one, not even Danton, was the author of that event. (p. 178)

Danton was able to fill this dual role of creative intellect and successful mediator, because, for Michelet, he, alone of the revolutionary figures, was capable of understanding all men and feeling all passions. "Danton, in whom life was so powerful, through whom vibrated all life, always had under his hand a vast keyboard of men whom he could play; men of letters, servants of execution, fanatics, intriguers, sometimes heroes even; the whole immense and varied scale of good and bad passions." Danton was the consummate actor of the Revolution, filling any role the script required. But there was method in Danton's uncanny ability; all of his skill was devoted to the principles of the Revolution—love, justice, right, and brotherhood. This former minister of justice was "the great artist of the Revolution who took all of the parts of the pure and impure elements, good and evil, virtues and vices, and threw them together into meaningful matrices, he made surge from them the statue of liberty." Because of Danton's genius for penetrating into, understanding, and expressing all passions and feelings, "all history was in him." It was Danton "who made the supreme effort for the unity of *la patrie.*" His lofty qualities and commitment to the principles of the new religion made him, during the crowning moments of the Revolution, as had been the case with "the people," synonymous with France. "Danton was . . . the voice even of the Revolution and of France."

Michelet balanced this worship of Danton, he felt, with a blistering assault upon Danton's cowardice in 1793 and gradual turn into the arms of his betrayer, the Jacobins. Beginning in April 1793, Danton's attitude was "deplorable." He was probably the only person "who could have saved the Republic but instead the parties each did their best to destroy him." The Girondins had initially forced Danton to retreat, because of their calumnious accusations that he had connived in traitorous activities with Dumouriez. With his mediating position threatened, where he had stood above all parties and all internal power struggles, Danton foolishly sought support with the Jacobins. On April 13 Danton went against his basic principles, an unpardonable crime in the eyes of Michelet, by agreeing with Robespierre to abandon the war in Europe and thereby tacitly sanctioning the shifting of the battle to the inner confines of France. By the summer of 1793, the Jacobins, through the voice of Robespierre, wanted to destroy the

Girondins, who were increasingly allying themselves with royalists. Danton, whose position was always the pacification and reconciliation of the internal divisions of France, was theoretically against stringent measures, but, having already compromised himself with the Jacobins, his strength to resist and his power to block large-scale massacres, had lost their former force. The hate-filled side of the Revolution personified in Robespierre now prevailed over the loving side, personified in Danton. By the fall of 1793 Danton, whose power had been eroded through indecision and equivocation, blindly followed the dictates of the "Incorruptible." It was pathetic "to see Danton speaking against Dantonists," while "begging the favor of his" Jacobin enemies.

On April 5, 1794 (16 Germinal year 1), the "voice of the Republic" was guillotined. In recounting the trial and Danton's last moments, Michelet poured forth all of his sympathies for this giant of the Revolution. Michelet again reiterated that Danton had been totally blameless and uninvolved in the conspiratorial actions of the Orleanists and Dumouriez. In the spring of 1794, not only Danton and the Dantonists, but also Chaumette and the Paris Commune perished. Michelet had lavishly praised the Commune while neglecting the atrocities committed in its name. The end of the Republic and Revolution "dates for us, not from Thermidor, when it lost its formula, but from March and April," when the bearers of the principles of the new religion were fatally silenced; "when the genius of Paris disappeared with the Commune, when the Mountain collapsed under the terror of the right, when the speaker's platform, the press, and the theater were razed in the same blow." (pp. 179-80)

For Michelet, "the great dream of Danton was an immense table where reconciled France would sit together in order to break the bread of brotherhood, without distinction of class or party." Danton and his colleagues had overthrown the throne and created the Republic, had saved the Revolution by organizing it around justice, and had exhibited model behavior as citizens of the new faith by "hating no one and loving each other until death." Such was the last scene of all, that summarizes and ends this strange eventful history. As mediator of the new religion, Danton spoke for "the people" and approached an internal synthesis of the instinct and reflection duality. He had had his moments on stage as the pure embodiment of la patrie, but his moral fall of 1793 showed that, as an individual and not an abstract group, he was still susceptible to weakness and divisiveness. Not completely harmonized nor full, Danton was unable to resolve the tension between the educated and the illiterate or between classes, except on occasions. Danton was a genius, but only a near hero for Michelet. After Joan of Arc he had come closest to resolving in himself the dichotomies of man's nature and the varieties of classes in order to become forever one with France. Having been able to play all the parts of the new religion and having represented all of its principles, Danton made his lasting mark on France. At his guillotining Michelet quoted a "patriot," who exclaimed: "They have decapitated France!" (pp. 181-82)

Stephen A. Kippur, in his Jules Michelet: A

Study of Mind and Sensibility, *State University of New York Press, 1981, 269 p.*

Oscar A. Haac   (essay date 1982)

[*Haac is an American historian, educator, and critic who has written extensively on French history and literature in general and on Michelet in particular. In the following excerpt, he presents an overview of Michelet's style and of the primary themes of his works.*]

The historian's principal task is to organize the multitude of data from the past into historical knowledge, to organize the facts into meaningful trends to be conveyed to an audience. This ability was one of Michelet's great accomplishments. By observing his mind and sensibility at work, we can derive the following model for his process of interpretation.

From omnivorous reading and the study of original documents, he has the genius to reconstruct the past, identifying each country or period with an idea which lends its logic to the chain of events. With often uncanny insight he will marshall actions and movements into a meaningful order, described in striking images which the reader can understand and retain. This task for the historian was complex, for he would distinguish himself from his predecessors by writing a "democratic" history, a record of the people and not one of battles and kings. The *History of the French Revolution* may be the best illustration of such an enterprise, picturing, as it does, innumerable simultaneous actions, drawing a multiple canvas which the individual actors of history enter in turn. It will include not merely political and diplomatic events, but literature and the arts, philosophy and religious concerns, all viewed through the essential perspective, constantly kept in mind and used to illuminate every aspect.

Michelet puts mind and soul into this task; in other words, he manifests sympathy and compassion for the aspirations of those he describes, with distinct appraisals of victors and victims in the ongoing struggle of men and issues. At times he will approve and come close to sanctifying forces of progress, like Joan of Arc; at other times he will apply bitter irony and black humor to the proponents of intolerance, or despotism, such as those who set out to rid France of its Protestant minority. He will, however, not simply praise or condemn, as his predecessors had done, but visualize what each was trying to accomplish, with unending human concern and empathy. In the Revolution, even Louis XVI and Robespierre have his ear. None shall be judged without a full hearing, an attempt to portray their background, the circumstances which dictated their action. Still, the historian is increasingly aware of the moral dimension of the past and asserts that there must be no weak compromise with the facts, with victories and power, for the forces which triumph are not necessarily those of progress.

This partiality shapes his understanding of forces and events. It implies an invincible faith in the future which will not capitulate before defeats, and these are many, not only in the past but in the present; the constant disappointments of successive governments and regimes, from the

Restoration to Napoleon III and defeat in the Franco-Prussian war. There are moments when Michelet is tempted to give in. The last volume of his history contains, in an appendix, his comment on Grainville and his poem, *The Last Man,* a vision of despair, but in the face of such gloom he will resist and return to his task; he would have carried on even then, had life given him time. A final act of faith remains his essential conclusion to every issue and every contest he portrays.

In many ways, Michelet's popular books on science and society follow a similar pattern. He is open to scientific discovery; he depicts the life force, the "soul," even in microorganisms; but he will reconcile it with the forces of determinism, just as he will at times describe the actors of the past as men caught in the inevitable mesh of fate, but still view them as human beings worthy of their hopes. His picture of woman in modern society shows many parallels with this view. Ultimately and in spite of all obstacles, he will add his word of encouragement and reaffirm his hope in life, and in the future.

Here we touch on the haunting theme of his entire work, best expressed in terms of death and resurrection. *The Mountain,* which contains some of his most intimate confessions, speaks of the death wish of the child. Material

Michelet's grave at Père-Lachaise.

distress, awkward unpreparedness at the Collège Charlemagne which called forth the mocking ridicule of his classmates and sent the boy hurrying to the cemetery of Père Lachaise, to seek consolation in his studies and the classics he was reading with passion; all this sets the stage for a lasting orientation, reinforced by the death of Paul Poinsot (1821) and of his wife, Pauline (1839), then of Mme. Dumesnil (1842), not to mention the less traumatic experiences. The historian comes to feel that men and women of the past are claiming his attention, asking him to speak for them, to translate their actions in a perspective they did not possess. History becomes a living, personal experience, the interpretation of the past so as to inspire present and future generations. In *The People* (1846), Michelet finds his definition, resurrection, on which he will elaborate in the great "Preface" to the *History of France* (1869).

Death must lead to life. From the start, the eschatology of the Christian church, fears in anticipation of the end of the world, first illustrated in his picture of the year 1000, but repeated in all of his accounts of Christian unworldliness, are not to his liking. Michelet prefers the rationalism of an Abelard, or else the mysticism of heretics like Joachim of Flores who seems to announce a revolutionary end of the world, an "eternal gospel" transcending the established church, for such independence of thought is preferable to an acceptance of what seemed to be thought-control and superstition perpetrated by a powerful hierarchy. From the start, in 1833, but increasingly so, Michelet's attacks may sound sacrilegious. . . . His assault, first on scholasticism, later on the Jesuits and priests who are directors of conscience, is indeed an ever more strident call for action, the kind of action and advocacy of reform in which he tries to drown his personal sorrow, as he comes to consider himself, more and more, a "modern monk," a priest of the new faith, using his chair at the Collège de France to convert as much as to inform. This explains why his academic life, resolutely apart from the political scene, seems ever more offensive to successive conservative governments which will suspend his teaching, first in 1848, and definitely in 1851.

Surely then, his form of "resurrection of the past" is no colorful literary attempt to recreate scenes from history, the way Chateaubriand practiced it, but a reawakening of the revolutionary fervor, of the spirit of 1789-1790 which united France from the taking of the Bastille to the feast of the General Federation on the Champ de Mars. In a way, the spirit of the Renaissance, defined in the introduction to volume 7 of the *History of France,* and the "Creed of the Eighteenth Century," evoked in volume 16, are transpositions of the same spirit. The "uses of the past" are to be understood essentially in terms of the inspiration Michelet could pass on to his contemporaries. Of course this implies a commitment to principles which arouse enthusiasm in readers just as they sustain his own sensitivities. Such are the themes of his inspiration. . . . They involve ideals to be shared with his public, but they do not constitute a "philosophical system," for he consistently opposes systems which, like straitjackets, might fetter the free mind.

His passion for biology, especially in the field of reproduction, his books on natural science and on women, lead much to the same conclusion. Here the analogy to the resurrection of the past is found in the regeneration of the family and in constant rebirth, in the life cycle of birds and insects or sea life, even in the geological transformations viewed in *The Mountain.* Ultimately there is a great unity in Michelet's world view, called forth by the experience of death, and in response to it. His image of revolutions which failed have led critics (e.g., Hayden White) [see excerpt dated 1973] to speak of his "cataclysmic" view of history, but while failure and death seem omnipresent, the life force appears always new. Science supports our hope for a better future, as does history! There are moments when Michelet hesitates, as when he views the unparalleled devastation of modern war, the abuse of the machine and man's creativity, but soon he conceives a ray of hope. Even *France before the Eyes of Europe* has a positive conclusion.

We have found our historian resisting the appelation "romantic," because he was far more concerned with his message than with descriptive technique. Still he remains the romantic historian par excellence. Without the dramatic detail and his empathy, for the battles of history as for those of ants and spiders, he would not be the great author he is. Besides, there are other qualities which have fascinated his readers. He appears as a voyeur not only in the *Journal,* when he observes Athénaïs, but in picturing the cruelty of man to man, the intolerance of the Inquisition, witch trials, the quartering of a regicide, or the atrocities of the Russian police in repressing the serfs. He often seeks out the abnormal, the satanic, the destruction of the individual by thought control. His realistic illustrations from the past outstrip literary fantasy, and so it is amusing to find his objection to novelists like Balzac who depict decadence: his own scenes of exploitation and injustice break through the conservative, bourgeois framework of a moral society which he wants to uphold. We have made it a point to cite some of the scenes which bear the distinction of great literature. His style is never wordy, but nervous, appropriate to the variety of subjects described, the very opposite of the swell of sentimental platitude in which Athénaïs buried his prose when she began "editing" some of his manuscripts after he died. True, she inspired him; she transformed his image of woman and marriage. We can be thankful that he let her collaborate in the nature books, but also that he reserved his right to modify and revise.

Even more remarkable is the framework he imposes on what he observes. He seeks out the "silences of history." He subordinates man's battles to his long struggle with nature, to the conquest of matter by the spirit, of fate by freedom. This is how we are to understand the progress of religion and civilization from the earliest days of India to the manifestation of brotherhood on 14 July 1790. Michelet conceives of it as a long voyage from *terra mater* ("mother earth") to the victory of the spirit, such as he finds it in history or in his own life, magically restored at Acqui. It is not an easy road as we are so often reminded, for instance in *The Witch:* the chthonic forces of the underworld must be tamed if culture is to triumph over nature,

and if man with his science is to be "his own Prometheus," to create a better world for his fellowmen out of compassion. These concepts are never far from his mind: they provide the "structure" and the myths of his "text," as Lionel Gossman put it in his masterful summary of fundamental themes [in *Modern Language Notes* 89 (1974)].

Implied here is a commitment to progress—Michelet's idealistic transfiguration of the past; but fortunately, for all his insistence on the triumphant spirit, on his faith in the future, he never hides the truth: he describes the ugly reality, the dangers of the single girl in Paris, the inadequacies of well-intentioned ministers and kings at Versailles, and the brutality of the masses, a topic particularly painful to the historian who set out to write *their* story, even though, from Hannibal and Caesar to Napoleon and his generals, he all too often concentrates on individuals. Still, the noble intent is there, the desire to place the people squarely in the center of the historical action as a testimony to his own humble origins and to his democratic ideology.

As Michelet advances in his career, he becomes ever more aware of the distance which separates him from "the people" among whom he was born, with whom he wants to communicate, who must be reached if France as a whole is to be propelled to action. His courses, his appeals to students to become missionaries among the people, are attempts to reach out, as are the "popular" books addressed to as wide an audience as possible, whether they deal with political action in the past or present (like the *Democratic Legends of the North*), with scientific or social observation.

His commitment to popular education became part of his "method," as he understood the term. Moral and religious themes permeate his work. The progress of civilization, the movement of the torch of freedom he follows in the *Introduction to Universal History* and again in the *Bible of Humanity,* is after all the progress of the people. He would never have attacked the inadequate (i.e., unworldly) faith of the early church, or of the Middle Ages, if the affirmation of a new religious faith and solidarity had not been so essential. His call on Christianity to be reborn is the echo of a profound concern, a way of reaching out to the people. Here Vico's message, summed up in the formula, "man is his own Prometheus," becomes part of his "method" and fundamental purpose, and is not unrelated to the belief that the divine voice of conscience (proposed in Rousseau's *Emile* and basic in spite of Michelet's late rebuttal that Rousseau capitulated to the Christian church) enables us to create a moral and humane society. The historian perceives a call to act, a categorical imperative, which is the essence of his message, of what Michelet calls his "method."

Of course, we can also define his "method" in more habitual terms and refer to his subordinating historical detail to dominant themes—though in discursive style—and so distinguish him as much from chroniclers like Barante or even Sismondi, as from philosophical analysts like Guizot, Mignet, and Thiers, but less so than Michelet thought from the admittedly more limited scope of an Augustin Thierry. Michelet was proud of having combined the emphasis on the spirit and meaning of history, with "material" considerations, such as race, geography, and economics; he dwelled on this for many pages in his "Preface" of 1869. Even so, his is an epic view compared to the factual, "scientific" history of other contemporaries or successors, of Ranke and Renan in particular. Michelet subordinates facts to a vision of the past which Ranke's ideal of writing history "just as it was" cannot recapture with its emphasis on objectivity. Michelet might well have listed other "material" factors which distinguish his "method," the introduction of scientific theories—some, like telegony, seem fanciful since they have long been discarded—to explain actions and influences of the past, such as the power of women behind the throne. This is especially noticeable after his marriage to Athénaïs. We read of seduction at Versailles, of the "Austrian" pressure (through Marie-Antoinette) on Louis XVI. We may wonder why the "Preface" of 1869 analyzes only the "methods" of the early volumes; possibly it is because Michelet hesitates to reveal his later self in such a public statement. (pp. 163-69)

[His] later works may not be monuments of historiography like his **History of the Middle Ages** and the **Revolution,** but they are remarkable applications of his method. If the reader becomes interested in the way Michelet's mind works, in his use of "material" factors to explain the spiritual unity of France and its eternal mission, he will find as much of interest after 1853 as before that year, when the historian completed his **Revolution.**

Michelet's resurrection of the past expresses his commitment to the democratic ideal. Michelet may be biased, but he will always be biased in a noble, selfless way. That is why even today readers are moved by his work. (p. 169)

> *Oscar A. Haac, in his* Jules Michelet, *Twayne Publishers, 1982, 199 p.*

Roger Huss   (essay date 1986)

[*In the following excerpt, Huss examines Michelet's depiction of nature as both an escape from and a metaphor for human society.*]

In the autobiographical essay 'How the Author Was Led to the Study of Nature', which opens his first nature book, **The Bird** (1856), Michelet describes nature as a retreat and source of consolation. Adopting his favourite pose of historian-martyr he recalls himself working, a sick man, amidst the ruins of the Republican hopes of 1848, on his account of the conflicts of 1793 ('the sadness of the past merged with the sadness of the present'), and seeking solace after a day's suffering, in the 'innocent peace' of the accounts of naturalists read to him by his young wife Athénaïs. He claims that **The Bird** avoids 'human analogy' and provides 'an escape (*alibi*) from the world of men, the deep solitude and wilderness of the distant past'. There is certainly a sense in which Michelet's nature books represent a withdrawal to another place, a form of absenteeism (the term *alibi* used by Michelet simply means an elsewhere: modern connotations of bad faith are not intended) and it will be argued below that one function of the books is to constitute nature as refuge by associating nature study with the protected private world of the conjugal

home which figures prominently as an ideal in Michelet's propagandist writing. What initially strikes the reader of the nature books, however, is the fact that, while they appear to present nature as a retreat from the 'world of men', far from avoiding human analogy and taking nature on its own terms, they are shot through with anthropomorphism. Nature is constantly presented in human terms and at the same time perceived as containing models and lessons for humanity.

It will be seen that this assimilation of natural and human realms functions in a way that, ambiguities notwithstanding, is fundamentally confirmatory of the social *status quo*. This is consistent with the natural theological framework which gives the nature books their overt structure: although Michelet's concept of nature, inspired in part by his reading of Lamarck, is a dynamic and transformationist one based on the evolution of species, it is still informed by a providential teleology and presents the features of harmony and equilibrium to be found in the classical French natural theologies of Fénelon (*Treatise on the Existence of God,* 1712), Bernardin de Saint-Pierre (*Studies of Nature,* 1784) and Chateaubriand (*Genius of Christianity,* 1802), or of the more vigorous Anglo-Saxon tradition reflected in Paley's *Natural Theology* (1802) and in the *Bridgewater Treatises* (Chalmers *et al.,* 1833-6). As such Michelet's view of nature attempts to minimize conflict and inequality: a reference to Darwin and the 'struggle for life' is followed by the remark that the struggle is innocent, creates the harmony and balance of nature, and is in fact not a struggle at all but rather peace, exchange, rotation. Michelet implicitly recommends respect for the larger order in which particular species or groups have their proper function and utility. Just as society needs its garbage collectors and undertakers so in nature 'the essential task of public sanitation' is discharged by gulls and crustacea, while minute crabs sweep the beaches clean of dead jelly fish like agile undertakers. Like his contemporary Charles Kingsley, who in *The Wonders of the Shore* (1855) remarks of the madrepore, 'by profession a scavenger, and a feeder on carrion', that 'he' is 'as useful as he is beautiful', Michelet emphasizes the noble or beautiful appearance of creatures who exercise such base functions: vultures resemble Turkish pashas 'draped in a noble cloak of grey', carrion-beetles carry out their 'sinister trade' in the most beautiful dress, while the dung-beetle 'which disposes of droppings is dressed in sapphire in payment for this service'. What such ennoblement implies for the organization of human society is in no sense a disturbance of a rather paternalistic hierarchy: rather it seeks to authorize a more generous attitude towards deserving subordinates. Michelet's pervasive theme of raising the lowly (whether animals, women, children or the people) remains largely an affair of the sympathetic heart.

It would nevertheless be inaccurate to describe Michelet's writing merely as complacently paternalistic. Much of the nature books' interest lies precisely in the anxieties that they attempt to exorcise through language which constantly implies but evades its disturbing subject: writing becomes an unstable mixture of alibi (in the modern sense of the term) and confession. One prominent anxiety concerns Michelet's relation to what he describes as 'the people', an ambiguous relation which appears figuratively in his uneasy attitude to the masses of the insect and marine worlds. Michelet likes to assert that in spite of his success he has been true to his popular origins, remaining a man of the people, sharing its vitality, instinctiveness and simplicity. He sees his role as that of intermediary, both explaining the people in its true dignity to his readers and using a language which will be accessible to the people itself. The dream of a language which is an act, breaking down the barriers between men, is not, however, realized: 'I was born of the people, I carried the people in my heart. . . . But its language, its language was closed to me. I have failed to make the people speak'. This failure of communication is dramatized metaphorically in *The Insect.* Michelet had already (in *The People*) established equivalences between the people, the child, woman and nature itself and it is such equivalences which make for much of the metaphorical density of the nature books. Although an overview of Michelet's production suggests that each equivalent term provides the subject of a separate work or number of works (nature in *The Bird, The Insect, The Sea* and *The Mountain,* woman in *Love* (1858) and *Woman* (1859), the child in *Our Sons,* and the people in *The People*), in fact Michelet's totalizing tendency, his aspiration to write about all subjects at once, makes such a classification inadequate: the nature books are also metaphorical (and sometimes literal) reflections on the people, woman and the child as well. The identification of the people with nature which concerns us here is most evident in *The Insect* and *The Sea,* and the analyses which follow will be drawn from the first of these books.

In the light of Michelet's anxiety to communicate with the people there is a certain logic in the contrast he establishes between the bird, with whom imaginative communication was easy—'we exchanged our languages. I spoke for him, he sang for me'—and who was readily characterized by Michelet as a fellow artist (Michelet as nightingale), and the insect (or people), alien, hidden behind warlike armour, inaccessible to communication. This distance represents a challenge to the writer's empathy, a gulf which he tries to overcome by presenting the insect as a creature which is sensitive and industrious:

> If you work and if you love, insect, whatever your appearance, I cannot shun you. We are in a sense related. And what am I myself, if not a worker.

In *The People* Michelet had sought to correct an ill-conceived and negative view of the people, to rehabilitate them in the eyes of their critics. In the course of this process, however, Michelet expresses preferences for certain groups within the people (a term never adequately defined) at the expense of others: he shows particular tenderness for the small proprietor and the peasant while evoking with distaste 'the rabble of the factories', the industrial proletariat which, he hastens to remind the reader, is untypical of French society at the time. One senses Michelet making an *effort* of sympathy: 'this crowd (of factory workers) is not inherently bad'.

Similarly, a somewhat uneasy rehabilitation of the teeming insect world is the theme of the opening chapter of *The Insect,* entitled 'Terrors and Aversions of a Child'. Here Michelet uses a fragment of his wife's autobiography (a longer section of which is also used to introduce *The Bird*) in which she describes her family's empty country house invaded by spiders, centipedes and woodlice, while the garden's fruits are destroyed by wasps. The immediate interest of the passage lies in Michelet's assertion that we are all, like the young Athénaïs, vulnerable to such fears and repulsion, and his use of the following analogy to support his point:

> How would we react to our workers if they always went around bristling with the steel and metal implements they use in their labours? They would strike us as strange and monstrous; they would frighten us.

The comparison is preceded by a self-contradictory attempt to explain away the insect's weapons: the insect lives in a world of conflict so his panoply of weapons which seems so threatening to man is only to be expected and, in any case, most of them are not weapons at all, just 'the peaceful implements they use to earn their living, the tools of their trade'.

In the rehabilitation of the insect its social characteristics play a significant role (the social insects, bees, ants and termites, are the subject of a large part of the book). Considered simply in terms of numbers the insects are terrifying: Michelet writes of them demanding a hearing, addressing to the higher species, man, a 'claim terrifying because of the number of the claimants', but once they are organized in a 'city' the spectator's terror is exorcized and gives way to admiration. The shift, metaphorically, is from the people as disturbing mass to the people as a republic of citizens. Michelet's first description of an ant colony accordingly develops in an elevated manner. Furthermore, as will be seen, it has a temporal dimension which invites the reader to historicize the political analogy contained in the term 'city', and interpret the passage in terms of republican history.

The description is, typically for Michelet, given the authority of personal experience: in a wood near Lucerne, Athénaïs Michelet, prodding at a rotten treestump, whose previous inhabitants, scolytids, had been overthrown by a colony of ants, breaks down the walls of the city to reveal the galleries within. While his young wife empathizes excitedly with the sudden agitation of the colony (an empathy which reinforces the equivalence between woman, child, nature and, by implication, the people), Michelet reflects that the occupation of the scolytids was ancient history: they had been eliminated by some 'great chemical transformation' (the reference is to formic acid) which had enabled the ants, over a period of generations, to burn out and 'cleanse' (the French uses the verb *assainir,* a term evoking the domain of public health) their edifice, the equal, in its way, of Babylon and Babel (Thebes and Nineveh are also mentioned), but now, like them, a ruin. Michelet does not develop his reflection into an explicit allegory of recent French history; instead, after referring to his familiarity as an historian with the fall of republics and empires, he quotes a line from Homer on the fall of Troy, but the pathos attending the fall of the ant republic nevertheless encourages the reader to identify it with the short-lived Second Republic, just as the earlier 'great chemical transformation' which evicted the scolytids may be read as standing for the Revolution of 1789. Homeric pathos does not simply distance it also lends a recent defeat the dignity of myth.

In a series of rhetorical questions which closes this episode, Michelet presents himself as powerless to reconstruct 'this devastated world', incapable of helping 'this great insect people, industrious and deserving, persecuted, devoured or scorned by all the tribes of animate nature, and which nevertheless provides all of us with the most vivid examples of disinterested love, of civic duty and of sociability'. This melancholy resignation implicitly expresses the limits of Michelet's practical activity as a republican, and his acceptance of the *fait accompli* of the Second Empire which had sent his fellow republicans Quinet and Victor Hugo into exile. What Michelet offers is simply an oblique and figurative service to republicanism: 'What can I do for this great people of insects? . . . one thing. Understand it, explain it and, if I can, cast upon it the light of a benevolent interpretation'.

While the virtues attributed to the ants can be read as exemplary for human society (Michelet celebrates their altruism, industry and sense of posterity), the imprecision of the analogies implied between the two realms allows the text to legitimize certain assumptions. For example, the idea of the ants constructing their 'city' (the French term *cité* is itself usefully ambiguous indicating both a place to live and a political system, a republic) implies an idealized conflation of the worlds of work and politics. In fact, human workers could not be said to contribute to the construction of the republic simply by continuing their 'persevering work', although such an illusion would appeal to a writer who, like Michelet, excluded violent change as a prelude to a new political system. Furthermore, the ants' struggle to construct their republic is basically a struggle against an environment (Michelet sees this colony finally succumbing to the autumn rains) and thus provides an insufficient analogy for the obstacles which threaten human organization from within. Finally, the distinction between private and public realms is also interestingly obscured by the fact that the ants, while building dwellings for themselves (the terms *demeure* and *appartement* refer to private dwellings), are also constructing a collective habitat. Thus although Michelet finds a metaphor for political disillusion in the natural world, the natural also provides him with a reassuring simplification of the human world.

The simplification is most evident in passages which bring together humans and insects on a literal level. In the forest of Fontainebleau ants and quarrymen (together with woodpeckers) are associated in an edifyingly industrious concert which Michelet contrasts with 'the great sickness of the day, restlessness and pointless agitation'. Rhetorically it is all the easier for Michelet to assimilate men and ants to each other since the contiguous space they occupy justifies a metonymous transference: 'the ants work the sand, the quarrymen work the sandstone. They share the same spirit' (Michelet uses the word *génie,* which has the appropriate secondary meaning of 'engineering'), 'ant-

men above the ground, ants which are almost men beneath'. This symmetry of work, described by Michelet in moral terms ('their industrious patience', 'their admirable perseverance') distracts the reader from the distinctions it would be possible to draw between the activity of the quarrymen and that of the ants: the product of the quarrymen's work is not directly enjoyed by the quarrymen themselves but goes to pave the streets of Paris, and their occupation not only brings them into contact with a natural resistance (like that encountered by the ants) but also subjects them to the constraints of a market. These distinctions are evaded and Michelet simply foregrounds the active but modestly contained and unambitious life (*'vie active et recueillie'*) of the ants as exemplary for human workers. The suppression of difference is further evidenced in Michelet's assimilation of the work of ants and quarrymen to his own 'tireless labour' as an historian. The paradox is worth noting that in this text Michelet finally uses social insects as a way of focusing on individual effort—the contradiction is an important one to which we shall return later in this essay when discussing the public and private functions of the nature books and their individualistic petty-bourgeois ideology.

Significantly, the most sustained evocation of work in *The Insect* occurs in connection with the solitary spider (included in the book in spite of the zoological distinction between arachnida and insects). Michelet's celebration of the republican virtues of the social insects (bees are republicans too, in spite of appearances) might have suggested a negative appraisal of the reclusive spider. Instead Michelet particularly values the withdrawn self-reliance of the spider, which he assimilates first to a self-employed artisan and next to the small manufacturer: his body is his spinning-mill and the substance he draws from himself to make the web and thus live is described as a personal capital investment (*'une mise de fonds'*). Michelet shows the same sympathy for the vulnerable spider caught up in a vicious circle—'to spin you must eat, to eat you must spin'—as he had for the small businessman in the chapter of *The People* entitled 'Servitudes of the Manufacturer': but once again the analogy has obvious shortcomings since it identifies owner, factory and worker in the individual person of the spider and thus simplifies the implications of the term *chômage* (unemployment) which Michelet uses merely to describe an inactivity which would be fatal to the spider. Here unemployment is simply related to individual effort and the analogy contains no term equivalent to the wage-earners who would also suffer unemployment if the mill closed.

Thus far our discussion of the nature books has concentrated on Michelet's exploitation of the natural to exemplify and present as unproblematic certain social and political ideals. The area of human experience referred to has been, ostensibly at least, public ('la cité'). The ideals which will be examined below can be described as domestic or private. Here, as above, the unproblematic surface presented by the nature books is often belied by the content of Michelet's examples.

The nature books and the didactic works, *Love* and *Woman,* which contain Michelet's most literal evocations of the joys of domestic life, are closely interconnected. While *Love* and *Woman* use natural examples to support the values of conjugal harmony and the home, the nature books in their turn provide metaphorical celebrations of these values, as well as introducing the conjugal dimension literally in the persons of the Michelet couple, united in nature study.

The ideal home is the 'small detached house' which the wife adorns (she does not work outside the home) and in which she is safe, like a bird in a nest. This 'delicate, impressionable and penetrable person' must be protected from the miasmas and moral dangers of the outside world, 'the disturbing mixture of a hundred corrupt and corrupting things which rise up to her from the street'. In an exemplary passage of *The Mountain* the home appears as a fortress, under assault from without: with their thick walls the old houses of the Engadine give protection against the harshest winter and even contain a refuge within a refuge in the shape of a small chamber hidden above the stove, a 'paradise' reached by a discreet staircase, a 'happy nest' where husband and wife 'take refuge, huddle together and live like marmots'. This retreat Michelet sees both in terms of the cultivation of conjugal harmony and, quoting the sixteenth-century Huguenot naturalist Bernard Palissy, as a contrast to the conflicts of politics and public life: 'How to wrap oneself up, to enclose oneself in a deep repose? Is not the model of a secure shelter the carapace or the shell whose thick whorls are a guarantee of safety?' The symbolic value of the house closed against the hostile elements is also evident in a section of *The Sea* entitled 'The Storm of October 1859' in which the sounds of the raging sea heard from within a beleaguered cliff-top house are compared to the howling of 'a ghastly mob' and a 'horrible rabble'. Also in *The Sea,* the sea urchin provides a model of defence, although it is less admirable than forms which are not only enclosed but are also double, made up of 'two associated halves': the example of certain shellfish implicitly poeticizes the private delights of the protected conjugal home:

> Each shell is double, containing both lover and beloved. Just as the palaces of the Orient hide their marvels behind gloomy walls, so here the outside is rough and the interior dazzling. The marriage takes place by the glow of a small sea of mother of pearl which, multiplying its mirrors, gives the house, even though it is closed, the charm of a mysterious enchanted twilight.

Yet although Michelet asserts that nature provides authority for the state of marriage—'In natural history, the higher animals tend to married life and attain it at least for a time. And this is, to a great extent, what makes them the higher animals'—and waxes lyrical over animals as homemakers and selfless mothers, educators of their young and loving couples, the sexual relationships which he presents in the nature books are in fact most frequently fraught with difficulty. Mating whales (described as 'lovers') present a pathetic and grotesque spectacle, slipping against each other in a union which looks more like a combat. The spider may evoke agreeable images of domestic seclusion—one has a 'back-room' hidden behind the end of a funnel, while another constructs a nest with a door—

but the male must approach the female with great care lest he be devoured: the human connotations are reinforced here by a reference to cannibalism on the notorious raft of the *Medusa*. When she acknowledges him, even responding ardently, he sometimes panics and flees. The fact that Michelet imagines such sombre courtship taking place on the domestic ceiling introduces a lugubrious note of sexual conflict into the idealized home.

The union of male and female is hardly less problematic in the world of plants, but in this case the theme is that of difficulty overcome and the dominant tone in a highly anthropomorphic text is that of the erotic novel. Michelet attacks the standard botanic nomenclature because French uses feminine nouns to designate the male parts ('stamen' and 'anthera' are feminine in French) and masculine nouns (*'le* pistil' and *'le* stigmate') for the female. Instead he prefers terms like 'lover,' 'husband', 'lady', which transform his account into a figurative representation of human sexual intercourse. In the blue gentian, observed by Michelet in the peace of his room, the pistil towers above the stamens and makes fertilization seem a hopeless task: 'It is she who totally dominates. Sovereign and colossal in comparison with her tiny lovers, she seems to confront them with an everlasting difficulty'. The scene is 'half tragic'. Michelet sympathizes with the lovers ('I felt pity for these unfortunates') confronted by the virginal whiteness of 'the lady'. A style characterized by exclamation and rhetorical questions strives to generate erotic suspense and empathy as one airborne 'atom', one 'husband' among a thousand candidates, miraculously scales the peak: will she receive him, 'will she, proud, still closed, not relent towards him?' A drop of honey, 'the flower's yes', appears on her threshold and signals his victory. He encounters no further resistance, it is as if she replies, 'I surrender, you are my master!' Now Michelet is surprised to see, with the help of his microscope, the male swelling prodigiously. For a moment he is alarmed and, in a phrase which naively reveals the vicarious nature of the writer's involvement, imagines an exchange of roles between spectator and actor: 'If he had continued thus with his prodigious impetus, our roles would have been reversed and I would have become the atom'.

It can be seen from the above examples that in its implications for the private sphere as for the public, nature is not merely an exemplary realm. It also provides the writer with a language in which he can express sexual frustration and, on occasion, obtain imaginary relief for this frustration.

The frustration or displacement of desire is particularly relevant to the view of marriage expressed in *Woman* and *Love.* In these works it is made clear that male desire has to be tempered to the vulnerable, innocent creature that is woman. At the same time a woman's own desire is presented as dangerous to her. For example, in a complex passage in *Woman,* flowers are seen as usefully calming the excitability of the girl child—'woman, particularly as a child, is totally subject to her nerves'—and are said to possess a 'relative innocence'. Yet the 'organ of love' of certain species, seen under the microscope, is surprisingly similar to the sexual organs of the higher life-forms (the style is euphemistic in its indirectness); the flower thus ceases to be innocent. Indeed, its heady perfume might 'penetrate' the child were she not busily engaged in tending the flower like a mother. Thus 'maternal feelings counterbalance and cure love'. The flower ceases to be a 'lover' and is safely transformed into a daughter (not just a child but a female child, to be doubly safe). The 'pernicious and dangerous rapture' is held at bay. A similar pattern of repression is reflected in *The Mountain* in a sustained symbolic representation of female desire. Here the earth is presented as a woman, with cyclical movements, yearning in vain for the sun, her 'adored lover'. Her aspiration subsides 'as if she had reflected and was holding herself back, though not without a sigh'.

Turning now to the function which Michelet claims for nature study and the somewhat different function which, we shall argue, it principally fulfils, we encounter again the divergence between public and private realms which has been referred to above. Although Michelet refers to nature as an *alibi,* a means of escape, he just as often claims a public function for nature. The nature books were conceived as popular books, as is evident from their style, and indeed reached a wide audience. In them Michelet sees himself as contributing to the moralization of his audience (the theme of regeneration being particularly important in *The Sea* and *The Mountain*). He even makes certain practical recommendations relating to public health and recreation: the sea and the mountains provide a hygiene which is both physical and moral. Nevertheless, much of the thrust of nature study as Michelet presents it remains directed away from the public realm. By placing his own idyll with Athénaïs in the foreground of each of the nature books he explicitly presents nature study as an intimate conjugal pursuit, and by the association of woman with nature, he makes nature study an annex of the private world of the home with which woman is exclusively identified.

In each of the nature books the domestic context of nature study is given great prominence. The introductory chapter of *The Bird* incorporates Athénaïs's autobiographical account of the country house and garden, with its harmonious community of men and animals, in which she spent her childhood, a paradise lost on her father's death. Michelet resumes with a detailed description of the house and garden near Nantes to which the couple withdrew in 1852 (after Michelet had refused to sign the oath of allegiance to the Empire) and which reconstituted the childhood paradise (Athénaïs refers to Michelet as a second father). In *The Insect* their house and garden again figure prominently. Even where nature is experienced away from home (as in *The Sea* and *The Mountain*) a domestic context is carefully re-established. For the ailing young wife sent by her husband to spend a restorative summer by the sea, Michelet prescribes with an architect's detail the house she should take: in particular it should have a small garden protected from the wind, and its own sea-water pool 'in which she can place the day's discoveries and small curiosities given her by the fishermen'. The process by which nature is thus domesticated can be clearly traced in *The Sea,* where the ocean appears first as a threatening desert and later as 'God's great swimming-pool'. Its life can be ob-

served with impunity in the sheltered confines of rock pools, 'those miniature oceans' which can finally be reproduced more privately at home. In *The Mountain* interiors are frequently evoked as are the gardens of Athénaïs's childhood and marriage; at Bex, in the Alps, nature is enjoyed from a balcony and flowers are brought by a willing local girl to be studied by the Michelets under the microscope in their room. The microscope can indeed be regarded as taking the process of domestication or privatization a stage further, as it provides a still more intimate frame for nature than do either the garden or the room which contains the instrument. An ideal representation of nature concentrated on a narrow private space within the larger private space is provided by an earlier visit to the Alps: Michelet stays at an inn near Lucerne and takes as his study 'an exceedingly spacious room which, with its seven windows opening onto the mountains, the lake and the town, and its triple aspect, provided me with a marvellous light at all hours of the day. From morning till evening the sun was my faithful companion and turned around my microscope, placed in the middle of the room'. Here the seven windows and triple aspect give the scene the mythical quality of fairy tale as if to emphasize its exemplary character.

Another connotation, that of femininity, reinforces Michelet's use of the microscope to symbolize withdrawal from the world. For Michelet the qualities demanded by microscopic study are specifically feminine: 'one must become something of a woman in order to succeed with it'. The instrument requires patience, dexterity and, above all, time, the freedom to repeat over and over again the same observation. In short, to use the microscope one must be 'out of the world, outside time'. This, for Michelet, feminine connotation supports the other recurrent themes of woman as mediator of nature and woman as nature herself.

The microscope, then, evokes a composed world in which the hours pass with no sense of urgency and external reality is not allowed to intrude. Such is the tender familiarity the instrument inspires that it is even personified as 'my little copper man'. Of course, the peaceful context in which the observer scrutinizes the object beneath the lens might conceivably be troubled by the character of the observer's discoveries. Indeed, when Michelet introduces the microscope by means of a vivid, hagiographical excursus on the Dutch naturalist Swammerdam he stresses the horror of 'the living infinite' and imagines the inventor recoiling from 'the abyss of nature in conflict, devouring itself '. He goes on to compare the effect on Swammerdam of his discoveries to the reactions of a man in a boat being carried calmly but inexorably towards the Niagara falls. Yet Michelet modulates from this starting point in a typically reassuring fashion: above all the microscope offers wonderful transformations of reality, revealing the unexpected beauty of humble objects. This theme is a commonplace of popular scientific writing in the nineteenth century and similar passages can be found in, for example, the *Household Words* of Charles Dickens.

The attractions of home nature study as it is presented by Michelet do not, however, depend merely on the beauty of the objects examined (nor even on the morally edifying lessons which, as has been seen, Michelet attempts to draw from the scrutiny of nature). There is in the control and manipulation of living things, in the spectacle of their conflicts, of their sexual activity and even of their death, a satisfaction which overrides the disturbing effect of what is observed. Contained by the Michelets within their garden or on the table in their study, nature, in its smaller representatives the insects, can provide a miniature theatre of human affect in disguise. Even when anthropomorphism is most rampant in Michelet's description of such performances the result for the spectator is still a diverting one, just as literary fictions may give pleasure and reassurance even when calling upon the reader to identify with human suffering. Recurrent terms from the world of spectacle— 'prodigious drama', 'phantasmagoria', 'mime', 'coup de theatre'—show nature functioning as entertainment. To conclude this section two passages from *The Insect* in which the 'spectacular' element is prominent will be discussed in some detail, since they demonstrate the way in which potentially disturbing material can be dramatized, contained and distanced. In both cases Michelet presents his wife and himself as experimenters and spectators, witnessing and to some extent provoking spectacles of violence, sex and death.

The first scene takes place during a stay in Switzerland where Michelet and Athénaïs begin to study insects seriously. No longer satisfied with the external view offered by entomological collections, they decide to 'penetrate the internal organs with scalpel and microscope' and are thus forced to 'commit our first crimes' (the conjugal harmony which is one desired effect of nature study is given a lugubrious yet comic twist by this picture of two accomplices). Michelet stresses the intensity of their feeling in a way which unwittingly points up its literary component: 'this preoccupation, this emotion, more *dramatic* than might be imagined, spoilt our trip'. The spectacle of 'suffering life (and life on which we had to inflict suffering)' is presented as spoiling their enjoyment of the mountains: 'the eternal epic of the infinitely great hardly competed with the *drama* of our infinitely small'. Yet there is in the following elaboration of this antithesis between the vast and the diminutive an aestheticizing elegance which devalues the emotion it seeks to reinforce: 'A fly concealed the Alps from us. The agonies of a coleopter which took ten days to die cast a veil over Mont Blanc; the anatomy of an ant caused us to forget the Jungfrau'. The victim whose sufferings Michelet chooses to relate in detail is a stag-beetle discovered by Athénaïs during a solitary walk and brought back by her to be etherized. The insect is presented in her first-person account as a horrifying apparition: locked in combat with a smaller beetle, it destroys the harmony of the peaceful landscape Athénaïs had been enjoying. The anthropomorphism of her account is negative and stigmatizes the beetles as feudal lords used to devouring their vassals and thus not deserving of pity. Nevertheless, with the tip of her parasol she instinctively interrupts the struggle without harming either beetle. In the rest of the account, continued by Michelet, the couple's sympathy is shown shifting to the stag-bettle. Although the observations, and worse, to which the beetle is subjected are at first presented as a punishment for its 'fratricidal vora-

ciousness' the suffering of the insect when etherized becomes an occasion for the Michelets to empathize with it. Ether usually provides 'a faster and seemingly sweeter death' but the 'prisoner' after an hour or two revives, attempts to walk, and falls as if drunk. A further dose is no more effective. The Michelets are surprised to see that although the beetle's powers of locomotion are impaired the ether has excited 'what one might call its amorous faculties' (the formulation conveys coy reticence and perhaps also the awareness that the interpretation is questionable). The beetle painfully approaches a dead female of its own species (which *happens* to be lying on the same table), groping at her in an apparent attempt to resuscitate her (the theme of resuscitation is, it may be recalled, at the centre of Michelet's picture of his relationship, as historian, to the dead past). We are directed to interpret this 'strange, funereal spectacle' in human terms, as 'touching for anyone who knows (with the knowledge of the heart) that all nature is identical'. Michelet and Athénaïs try to separate 'this Juliet from this Romeo' but he still refuses to succumb to the ether: 'the indomitable male mocked all poisons'. Eventually they shut the beetle in a box (shades of premature burial) where it is subjected to further massive doses of ether and takes a fortnight to 'consummate its torture' and die. Michelet claims that its tender-hearted executioners shared this ordeal, reflecting all the while on the strange persistence of love and comparing their own role to that of the Fates cutting the thread just before the victim's moment of fulfilment.

In this sombre tale the distancing and aestheticizing of the themes of sex and death is achieved by a variety of means: there is the intrinsic distance of the experimental context—the protagonist is manipulated, his reactions observed; there are the aestheticizing analogies from the world of dramatic fiction (Romeo and Juliet) and of mythology (the Fates); and there is reflection and comment from the experimenters in their somewhat disingenuous role as epic witnesses. This distancing framework contains and domesticates the sometimes disturbing elements which work in the opposite direction to establish identity not distance: nature is one, therefore the indomitable urge of the stag-beetle is that of the human male; the beetles are Romeo and Juliet, admittedly characters in fiction but still a *human* couple, like the only other couple present, Michelet and Athénaïs who, it is claimed, experience the beetle's torture themselves. Like the stag-beetle, Michelet, the historian, was concerned to resuscitate the dead. A further identity, supported by the autobiographical evidence of Michelet's *Journal,* published posthumously between 1959 and 1976, as well as by the symbolic content of much of his other writing, involves an implied assimilation of Athénaïs to the dead Juliet: If Michelet = Romeo = the stag-beetle = the persistent male, Athénaïs is the frigid female, the corpse he tries unsuccessfully to resuscitate. Similarly, if Michelet and Athénaïs execute the stag-beetle before it can achieve sexual fulfillment this can be read as an attempt to present censorship of male sexuality as a joint decision taken by the story-book Michelet couple, perfectly united in their murderous work ('our crimes').

A second example of nature's home theatre is provided by Michelet's account of conflict between two species of ant witnessed in his garden at Fontainebleau. The main difference displayed by this episode, entitled 'Civil War', is that its implications, albeit undeveloped, are political as well as private. As before, the events observed are provoked by the fascinated spectators themselves for it is they who bring one species of ant (carpenter ants) from the forest into the garden and onto the territory of the other species, the smaller mason ants. In effect, the Michelets stage-manage the destruction of the carpenter ant republic, for the ant society introduced into the garden has already been diminished by the process of transplantation and is now overwhelmed by the more enterprising smaller ants. The Michelets' initial sympathy for the mason ants (who have been invaded) gives way to indignation as they watch them tear the nymphs (pupae) of the interloper ants out of their protective covering in a scene graphically described as a collective rape. Typically, Michelet exploits the episode's dramatic possibilities, adopting an epic style to trace the peripeteia of the conflict, and leaving the implications of the title, with its potential reference to the civil conflict of 1848, unworked out. The most specific of his anthropomorphic analogies, which assimilates the virulent mason ants to savage Iroquois or Hurons, is remarkably distancing and defuses any implied reference to the civil conflicts which preceded the fall of the Second Republic. The destruction of the ant republic certainly generates pathos as Michelet pictures a sole survivor bearing a cradle away into the shadows, but the pathos remains unfocused. In spite of the episode's title, sexual implications emerge more strongly than do political ones. The brutal scene of the rape of the nymphs is linked with Michelet's account of his own painful extraction of a nymph from its casing. Thus once more the analogy between the observer (Michelet) and the actors (the violent mason ants) in the drama observed indicates a displacement of desire (censorship by diversion) and foregrounds the vicarious use to which the scrutiny of nature is so often put in the works we have been discussing.

This essay has attempted to show that in Michelet's work nature supports a discourse which is both euphoric and problematic. An exemplary nature, figuring as the second or principal term of analogies with humanity, is used by Michelet to legitimize certain values, but the analogies lack rigour and imply simplifications of national, social, economic and conjugal reality. Even when the euphoric surface of Michelet's writing is troubled by the apprehension of conflict, death and sexuality in nature, this disturbance, presented through the eyes of the amateur naturalist and his wife, takes on a spectacular and aesthetic quality. Nature is thus not only a source of value and a vehicle of ideology but also a theatre in which realities at odds with this ideology can still be contemplated, even enjoyed, at a distance. The hesitation between ideological and diversionary uses of nature combines with the tension between public and private values, which has been another theme of this essay, to make the nature books unresolved and challenging texts, in spite of the gestures of resolution they contain. (pp. 301-21)

> *Roger Huss, "Michelet and the Uses of Natural Reference," in* Languages of Nature: Critical Essays on Science and Literature, *edited by L. J. Jordanova, Rutgers University Press, 1986, pp. 289-321.*

FURTHER READING

Allen, James Smith. " 'A Distant Echo': Reading Jules Michelet's *L'amour* and *La femme* in 1859-1860." *Nineteenth-Century French Studies* 16, Nos. 1-2 (Fall/Winter 1987-88): 30-46.
> Examines the negative reception of Michelet's *L'amour* and *La femme* in terms of what it implies about nineteenth-century French society.

Atherton, John. "Michelet: Three Conceptions of Historical Becoming." *Studies in Romanticism* IV, No. 4 (Summer 1965): 220-39.
> Analyzes the "convergence in Michelet's writing" of "three separate ways of viewing the past: history as progress, as natural growth, and as fulfillment."

Barthes, Roland. *Michelet.* New York: Hill and Wang, 1987, 226 p.
> Searches for unity in Michelet's thought. Barthes refers to this work as "pre-criticism" which seeks merely to "recover the structure of . . . an organized network of obsessions."

Besançon, Alain. "Michelet and Dostoyevskism in History." *Clio* 6, No. 2 (Winter 1977): 131-47.
> Compares Michelet with Dostoyevsky for the "subjectivism" of their artistry. Besançon focuses on each author's fostering of the imagination as "the mistress of truth and accuracy" who "invokes, summons, provokes reality."

Burrows, Toby. " 'Their Patron Saint and Eponymous Hero': Jules Michelet and the *Annales* School." *Clio* 12, No. 1 (Fall 1982): 67-81.
> Assesses Michelet's influence on the ideas and methods of historians associated with the journal *Annales: économies, sociétés, civilisations.*

Duclaux, Madame Mary. "Michelet in '48." In her *The French Procession: A Pageant of Great Writers,* pp. 198-206. New York: Duffield & Company, 1955.
> Examination of events that took place in 1848 which, according to Duclaux, greatly influenced Michelet's life and writings.

Geffen, Arthur. "Walt Whitman and Jules Michelet—One More Time." *American Literature* 45, No. 1 (March 1973): 107-14.
> Comparative study of Michelet and Whitman. Geffen concludes that "the full treatment of the close and curious correspondences between the two classic messianic democrats of the nineteenth century still remains unperformed."

Geyl, Pieter. "Michelet and the History of the French Revolution." In his *Debates with Historians,* pp. 71-111. Glasgow: William Collins Sons, 1955.
> Critical overview discussing Michelet's treatment of the

French Revolution. Geyl concludes that Michelet was "great by the passion of his devotion, by his life-creating imagination, by his love" but "suffered conspicuously from the defect with which the popular saying charges love: that it is blind."

Gooch, G. P. "The Romantic School in France." In his *History and Historians in the Nineteenth Century,* pp. 151-77. London: Longmans, Green, and Co., 1952.
Praises Michelet's "sympathetic imagination." Gooch considers Michelet "the greatest literary artist who has ever devoted himself to history in France."

———. "Michelet on French Society." *Contemporary Review* 198 (October 1960): 555-59.
Examines Michelet's treatment of the society of his time, noting that his works "retain their importance both as realistic pictures of mid-nineteenth century France and as powerful agents in the democratization of her institutions and the secularization of her thought."

Gossman, Lionel. "Jules Michelet and Romantic Historiography." In his *European Writers: The Romantic Century,* Vol. 5, edited by Jacques Barzun, pp. 571-606. New York: Charles Scribner's Sons, 1985.
Examines influences on Michelet's thought and artistry.

Guérard, Albert. Introduction to *Joan of Arc,* by Jules Michelet, pp. v-xiv. Ann Arbor: University of Michigan Press, 1957.
Overview of Michelet's life and literary career.

Kohn, Hans. "France: Michelet." In his *Prophets and Peoples: Studies in Nineteenth Century Nationalism,* pp. 43-76. New York: The Macmillan Company, 1946.
Examines Michelet's influence on and reaction to nationalist sentiment in nineteenth-century France.

Lanson, Gustave. "Historic Method of Jules Michelet." *The International Quarterly* XI, No. 1 (April 1905): 71-101.
Discussion of the development of Michelet's ideas and technique.

Le Goff, Jacques. "The Several Middle Ages of Jules Michelet." In his *Time, Work, & Culture in the Middle Ages,* pp.3-28. Chicago: University of Chicago Press, 1980.
Traces the evolution of Michelet's views on and treatment of the Middle Ages in his *Histoire de France.*

McCallum, Pamela. "Michelet's Narrative Practice: Naturality, Populism, and the Intellectual." *Cultural Critique* 1 (Fall 1985): 141-58.
Detailed analysis of the style and structure of Michelet's histories. McCallum concludes that "Michelet's formidable creative achievement gains much of its subversive impulse from his representational techniques that endeavour to give figural expression to the field of force which is history."

Mitzman, Arthur. "Michelet, Danton, and the Corruption of Revolutionary Virtue." *Journal of the History of Ideas* XLVIII, No. 3 (July-September 1987): 453-66.
Examines influences on Michelet's histories. Mitzman focuses "on those personal experiences which, in interaction with mentalities and socio-political conditions, established the modes of fear or hope in which a historian used the materials around him to construct visions of the past."

Moreau, Thérèse. "Revolting Women: History and Modernity in Jules Michelet." *Clio* VI, No. 2 (Winter 1977): 167-79.
Examines Michelet's treatment of women and his use of the female body as "a determining structure in [his] view of history."

Neff, Emery. "Resurrection of the Past: Michelet." In his *The Poetry of History: The Contribution of Literature and Literary Scholarship to the Writing of History Since Voltaire,* pp. 129-49. New York: Columbia University Press, 1947.
Overview of Michelet's life and historical works.

O'Brien, Conor Cruise. "Michelet Today." In his *Writers and Politics,* pp. 45-60. New York: Pantheon Books, 1965.
Argues that Michelet, through his subjective treatment of French history, was "in some ways more honest and therefore more scientific than most modern scientific historians."

Orr, Linda. *Jules Michelet: Nature, History, and Language.* Ithaca: Cornell University Press, 1976, 215 p.
Examines Michelet's use of language and his perception of nature as it relates to his histories and other works.

Pugh, Anne R. *Michelet and His Ideas on Social Reform.* New York: Columbia University Press, 1923, 243 p.
Discusses the role of Michelet's personality and temperament in shaping his social criticism. Pugh describes Michelet's "emotion of pity," writing of its significance: "An examination of some of its sources and of some of its manifestations cannot but have a real interest, for it helped to model all of Michelet's conceptions of God and nature, it played a paramount role in determining his ideas in regard to woman, and determined the form of his humanitarian idealism."

Williams, John R. "Jules Michelet and the Notion of Literary Commitment." *The French Review* XLVI, No. 3 (February 1973): 543-50.
Discusses Michelet's "belief in the moral responsibility of the writer to commit his art fully to social progress."

Edward Pinkney

1802-1828

(Full name Edward Coote Pinkney) American poet.

Pinkney is considered by many critics to be one of the finest American poets of the early nineteenth century. In his poetry, he expressed ardent sentiment in technically polished verse. He is best known for his graceful, passionate love poems, including "Serenade," in which he expressed his admiration for feminine charm, "Lines from the Port-Folio of H—," a poem about unrequited love, and most prominently "A Health," which Edgar Allan Poe described as "full of brilliancy and spirit."

Pinkney was born in London to American parents. His father was a lawyer and statesman serving as a diplomatic representative of the United States in England. Pinkney's formal education, which began in London and continued in Baltimore, came to an early end when he joined the United States Navy in 1815. He served primarily in the Mediterranean, an experience that inspired his poems "Italy" and "The Voyager's Song." Resigning his commission in 1824, Pinkney married Georgiana McCausland, to whom several of his poems are addressed. He practiced law in Baltimore until 1826, when he was offered a professorship in rhetoric and belles lettres at the University of Maryland. The following year Pinkney left the university to become editor of the biweekly *The Marylander,* which was founded to promote the reelection of John Quincy Adams, but he soon left that position because of declining health. He died in 1828.

Pinkney's single published volume, *Poems,* comprises twenty-one poems, more than half of which address love in some manner. Pinkney's work has been compared to that of the seventeenth-century Cavalier poets as an amoral, intellectual celebration of amorous experience and the physical pleasures of an aristocratic lifestyle. Described as musical and lively, Pinkney's poems are praised for expression of deep emotion and masterful display of metaphor. In form, his poetry is often imitative of the English Romantic poets, especially Lord Byron. Critics agree that while there are passages of great beauty in Pinkney's poetry, often too much meaning is awkwardly compressed into a line, and his use of archaic verbs, unconventional language, and remote allusions sometimes results in obscurity. Nevertheless, Pinkney was an eminent figure in the nascent period of American poetry and, as noted in the English magazine *The Athenæum,* author of "one or two of the prettiest things in American poetry."

PRINCIPAL WORKS

Poems (poetry) 1825
The Life and Works of Edward Coote Pinkney (poetry, prose, and memoir) 1926

F. W. P. Greenwood (essay date 1825)

[*In the following review of* Poems, *Greenwood analyzes Pinkney's faults and strengths as a poet.*]

Of the last piece but one in [*Poems*], entitled **'Rodolph,'** we have heretofore given a short notice. It was first published separately and anonymously; but is now accompanied by several shorter poems, and by the author's name, which there is certainly no reason for concealing. With all its faults, **'Rodolph'** abounds with beauties, which any of our poets might be glad to claim. The promise, which it held forth on its first appearance, that there was more gold in the same mine, has not been broken. Some of the small pieces in this very small volume are really exquisite. At least they appear so to us; and we are quite willing to submit our opinion to the judgment of our readers, by making two or three extracts for their perusal.

Let us take **'Italy,'** which stands first in the book, as one of our specimens. It is an imitation of Goethe's celebrated *Kennst du das Land.* To imitate excellence successfully, one must be something more than a mere imitator. Dulness, or mediocrity, can do nothing but repeat with servility the ideas of its model, 'and regularly weaken all it re-

267

peats.' Genius catches the thought and spirit of kindred genius, and gives them a fair and well proportioned body of its own. In short, when what is borrowed is good, what is altered or added must be good too, or we shall perceive the vast disparity, and be displeased at it, and be moved to tell the imitator that he had no business with such beautiful things, if he knew not how to make a better use of them. We think our readers, however, will feel no disposition to say so to the author of the following lines.

> Know'st thou the land which lovers ought to
>   choose?
> Like blessings there descend the sparkling dews;
> In gleaming streams the crystal rivers run,
> The purple vintage clusters in the sun;
> Odors of flowers haunt the balmy breeze,
> Rich fruits hang high upon the veruant trees;
> And vivid blossoms gem the shady groves,
> Where bright plum'd birds discourse their care-
>   less loves.
> Beloved!—speed we from this sullen strand
> Until thy light feet press that green shore's yel-
>   low sand.
>
> Look seaward thence, and nought shall meet
>   thine eye
> But fairy isles like paintings on the sky;
> And, flying fast and free before the gale,
> The gaudy vessel with its glancing sail;
> And waters glittering in the glare of noon,
> Or touched with silver by the stars and moon,
> Or flecked with broken lines of crimson light
> When the far fisher's fire affronts the night.
> Lovely as loved! towards that smiling shore
> Bear we our household gods, to fix for evermore.
>
> It looks a dimple on the face of earth,
> The seal of beauty, and the shrine of mirth;
> Nature is delicate and graceful there,
> The place's genius, feminine and fair;
> The winds are awed, nor dare to breathe aloud;
> The air seems never to have borne a cloud,
> Save where volcanoes send to heav'n their curled
> And solemn smokes, like altars of the world.
> Thrice beautiful!—to that delightful spot
> Carry our married hearts, and be all pain forgot.
>
> There Art too shows, when Nature's beauty
>   palls,
> Her sculptured marbles, and her pictured walls;
> And there are forms in which they both conspire
> To whisper themes that know not how to tire;
> The speaking ruins in that gentle clime
> Have but been hallowed by the hand of Time,
> And each can mutely prompt some thought of
>   flame—
> The meanest stone is not without a name.
> Then come, beloved!—hasten o'er the sea
> To build our happy hearth in blooming Italy.

Are not the two lines, beginning 'Save where volcanoes,' sufficient to give a more than ordinary character to this piece? Are they not poetry, and grand poetry? The similitude contained in them is one, which the memory cannot refuse to keep and cherish, because it is rich in those sublime associations which the memory loves, and loves to hoard among its treasures. And it is one of the peculiarities of the volume before us, that it is replete with compari-

sons of a highly poetical nature. We have an instance in the second piece, called **'The Indian Bride.'**

> Their sun declines not in the sky,
>   Nor are their wishes cast,
> Like shadows of the afternoon,
>   Repining toward the past.

No less than three of these figures are contained in the two last verses of the **'Picture Song.'**

> The sportive hopes, that used to chase their
>   shifting shadows on,
> Like children playing in the sun, are gone—
>   forever gone;
> And on a careless, sullen peace, my double-
>   fronted mind,
> Like Janus when his gates were shut, looks for-
>   ward and behind.
>
> Apollo placed his harp, of old, awhile upon a
>   stone,
> Which has resounded since, when struck, a
>   breaking harp string's tone;
> And thus my heart, though wholly now from
>   early softness free,
> If touched, will yield the music yet, it first re-
>   ceived of thee.

There is much richness in the following evening scene. Enough has already been said about the loves of the angels, but we will pardon those four lines, for the sake of the rest.

> 'Twas eve; the broadly shining sun
> Its long, celestial course had run;
> The twilight heaven, so soft and blue,
> Met earth in tender interview,
> Ev'n as the angel met of yore
> His gifted mortal paramour,
> Woman, a child of morning then,—
> A spirit still,—compared with men.
> Like happy islands of the sky,
> The gleaming clouds reposed on high,
> Each fixed sublime, deprived of motion,
> A Delos to the airy ocean.
> Upon the stirless shore no breeze
> Shook the green drapery of the trees,
> Or, rebel to tranquility,
> Awoke a ripple on the sea.
> Nor, in a more tumultuous sound,
> Were the world's audible breathings drowned;
> The low strange hum of herbage growing,
> The voice of hidden waters flowing,
> Made songs of nature, which the ear
> Could scarcely be pronounced to hear;
> But noise had furled its subtle wings,
> And moved not through material things,
> All which lay calm as they had been
> Parts of the painter's mimic scene.

And now we will pass to an effusion, which is in the true antique spirit of gallantry and hyperbole. If the name of Harrington or Carew had been subscribed to it, we should, in all probability, like other antiquaries, have been completely taken in.

SERENADE.

> Look out upon the stars, my love,
>   And shame them with thine eyes,

On which, than on the lights above,
There hang more destinies.
Night's beauty is the harmony
Of blending shades and light;
Then, Lady, up,—look out, and be
A sister to the night!—

Sleep not!—thine image wakes for aye,
Within my watching breast;
Sleep not!—from her soft sleep should fly,
Who robs all hearts of rest.
Nay, Lady, from thy slumbers break,
And make this darkness gay,
With looks, whose brightness well might make
Of darker nights a day.

Our next specimen is in a much higher strain. If he who reads it is a lover already, it will make him love the more, and if he is not, he will determine to become one forthwith. There is a devotion and delicacy about it, an ardent and at the same time respectful and spiritual passion breathed out in it, which must insure for it a ready admiration.

A HEALTH.

I fill this cup to one made up of loveliness alone,
A woman, of her gentle sex the seeming paragon;
To whom the better elements and kindly stars
have given,
A form so fair, that, like the air, 'tis less of earth
than heaven.

Her every tone is music's own, like those of
morning birds,
And something more than melody dwells ever in
her words;
The coinage of her heart are they, and from her
lips each flows
As one may see the burthened bee forth issue
from the rose.

Affections are as thoughts to her, the measures
of her hours;
Her feelings have the fragrancy, the freshness of
young flowers;
And lovely passions, changing oft, so fill her, she
appears
The image of themselves by turns,—the idol of
past years!

Of her bright face one glance will trace a picture
on the brain,
And of her voice in echoing hearts a sound must
long remain;
But memory such as mine of her so very much
endears,
When death is nigh, my latest sigh will not be
life's but hers.

I filled this cup to one made up of loveliness
alone,
A woman, of her gentle sex the seeming paragon—
Her health! and would on earth there stood some
more of such a frame,
That life might be all poetry, and weariness a
name.

We will now pass on to a more particular consideration, than we before gave, of **'Rodolph,'** which is the only poem of much length in the volume. It is divided into two parts. The first begins in a fine style.

The Summer's heir on land and sea
Had thrown his parting glance,
And Winter taken angrily
His waste inheritance.
The winds in stormy revelry
Sported beneath a frowning sky;
The chafing waves with hollow roar
Tumbled upon the shaken shore,
And sent their spray in upward showers
To Rodolph's proud ancestral towers,
Whose station from its mural crown
A regal look cast sternly down.

For the story, we cannot pretend the least affection. This Rodolph arrives, at the season so poetically described above, and after a long absence, at his own domain. He is a changed man, 'grown old in heart, infirm of frame;' and the causes of this change are stated. He had loved, and loved successfully, the wife of another. The husband comes upon them 'at an untimely tide,' and is slain. The lady retires to a convent, and there dies. Rodolph, in despair and bitterness of heart, wanders into distant climes. Here the first part leaves him. The second opens thus;

How feels the guiltless dreamer, who
With idly curious gaze
Has let his mind's glance wander through
The relics of past days?—
As feels the pilgrim that has scanned,
Within their skirting wall,
The moon-lit marbles of some grand
Disburied capital;
Masses of whiteness and of gloom,
The darkly bright remains
Of desolate palace, empty tomb,
And desecrated fanes;—
For in the ruins of old hours,
Remembrance haply sees
Temples, and tombs, and palaces,
Not different from these.

But these 'mere musings,' we are told, are not for Rodolph to indulge, who is now at home. He feels some sad and disturbing presentiment; backs his steed, and takes his way to a cemetery. He does not return, and in the morning his vassals find him in a senseless state, 'beside his lady's urn.' A raging fever attacks him, and in its delirium he raves of many crimes, which he had committed abroad, but dwells particularly on 'one dark deed.'

He spoke of one too dearly loved,
And one unwisely slain,
Of an affection hardly proved
By murder done in vain.

Pretty soft terms, we think, to apply to adultery and murder. He basely and incurably wrongs a man, murders him, and then reproaches himself for having done an *unwise thing*—and chiefly, because he had done it in vain.

Some of his ravings are recorded. They commence with the following original figure.

The evil hour in which you traced
Your name upon my heart, is passed,
And hidden fires or lightning-flashes

Have since reduced it into ashes;
Yet oft will busy thought unrol
That fragile, scorched, and blackened scroll,
And shrink to find the spell, your name,
A legend uneffaced by flame.

All will agree that this is what we have called it, original, highly so; in our opinion, it is also, notwithstanding its boldness, in thus bringing into poetry the mechanical operation of unrolling Herculanean manuscripts, beautiful. The figure is remarkably well sustained throughout. But to return to Rodolph; he dies in his madness, and the poem closes abruptly and coldly.

In this piece are displayed most of the predominant faults of the writer; for he has faults, and it is our duty to point them out with the same candor and sincerity, with which we have praised his excellencies. He is often obscure. This is in many cases the consequence of his compressing a great deal of meaning in a single line, or hinting a remote allusion, which obliges the reader to stop and ponder; who in such cases will be rewarded for his trouble. But in others there is obscurity without cause, and involving no important meaning, and then it is a mere stumbling block. As a general rule, it is no doubt better that a reader should be induced to stop from admiration of an apparent and palpable beauty, than be obliged to stop to investigate the signification of what he has read, let it turn out beautiful or otherwise.

Our author is fond of classical allusions and comparisons, and is not fond of explaining them, though they are often drawn from the least known events of ancient history or mythology. If the reader, therefore, is not pretty thoroughly versed in this kind of lore, he is constantly obliged to resort to a Lempriere, if he has one, when a short note would have answered the purpose in a much more convenient, and we doubt not, pleasant way.

It is easy to see, that Mr. Pinkney is well acquainted with the best old English poetry, and perhaps he suffers his own to be tinged somewhat too deeply by some peculiarities of its phraseology. In the **'Widow's Song,'** for instance, which is a sweet composition, we have for the last line, 'And *falls* these heavy tears.' To many this use of the verb in an active sense will appear unwarranted and unwarrantable. But there is Shakspearian authority for it.

If that the earth could teem with woman's tears,
Each drop she *falls* would prove a crocodile.

The word is also thus used in Dryden's prose. As another instance, we may notice, that he gives to the verb *arrive,* without a preposition, the active sense of *to reach.* Thus in **'Rodolph'** he says,

At such a season, his domain
The lord at last *arrived* again.

The reader would not here be resolved of his doubts, as in the former instance, by resorting to Johnson's large dictionary, for Johnson gives no such use of the word. In the second book of *Paradise Lost,* however, he will find Beelzebub inquiring of the assembled demons, which of them will

Spread his airy flight,

Upborne with indefatigable wings
Over the vast abrupt, ere he *arrive*
The happy isle?

There is an instance to the same purpose also, in the third part of Shakespeare's *Henry Sixth.* Notwithstanding these authorities, it still is a question of criticism and taste, whether a writer of the present day is justifiable in such obsolete usages. We are inclined to think that he is not.

These are small objections. But we have more serious faults to find. We do not like the moral tone of this poetry. It is too close and too loud an echo to that of Byron. There is that abstracted and selfish gloom and moodiness about it, that solitary want of kindly human sympathies, that stiff and hard casing of pride that sullen dissatisfaction with the present state, and that reckless doubt or disbelief of a future one, which seem to have been caught from Byron, and of which we have already had too much in Byron. We are sorry to be obliged to speak in this manner of poetry, and American poetry, in which there is so much that is elevated and captivating. But if there is anything valuable in character, in life, in the world, it is a firm principle and habit of virtue, benevolence and piety; and we can never afford our entire approbation to any production, which shows an indifference to these. (pp. 369-76)

F. W. P. Greenwood, in an originally unsigned review of "Poems," in The North American Review, *Vol. XXI, No. 49, October, 1825, pp. 369-76.*

The United States Literary Gazette   (essay date 1826)

[*In the following review, the critic acknowledges Pinkney's poetic genius but unfavorably compares his work to the poetry of Lord Byron and finds the value of Pinkney's poems diminished by their obscurity.*]

There is an anecdote told of a Spanish author, of Lope de Vega, we believe, that a friend came to him one day, and complained that he could not understand one of his sonnets, and requested an explanation of it. The author read it carefully, and returned it, with the frank confession, that he could not himself tell what it meant. We do not know that Mr Pinkney would be willing to confess so much; but we have carefully read his book [**Poems**] several times over, and borne with patience more than one severe headach, which the efforts to comprehend his meaning have cost us, but still the greater number of his lines remain to us a mystery. We laboured the more, because we did admire many lines whose meaning was obvious; so many, indeed, that had we met with any one poem composed of an equal number of such lines, we should have promptly pronounced the author one of high poetical promise. Having given up, in despair, the task of discovering his meaning, we next set ourselves to find out, if we could, the reason of his general obscurity; but here again we were baffled. We will own, that at first, we admitted the uncharitable surmise, that Mr Pinkney was an imitator of Byron, and had caught his obscurity of language, without having his vigour of conception; but upon comparing these poems with those of Byron's which we suspected might be their prototypes, we found, that, though Byron was indeed occasionally obscure, his darkest passages were lucid in comparison with those of his supposed imitator. At length our attention fell upon four lines in one of these poems, which furnished the most probable solution of the difficulty.

> The mind is capable to show
> Thoughts of so dim a feature,
> That consciousness can only know
> *Their presence, not their nature.*

Mr Pinkney has put such thoughts as these into rhyme, and no wonder, if the author does not himself know their nature, that his readers should be at fault. Almost all the poems in this volume are of this kind. Now a man must be possessed of very strong powers who can hope, with any prospect of success, to interest the public by detailing in verse the workings of his own mind upon itself. The great poets have generally gone out of themselves for subjects;—have, if we may use the expression, infused their souls into other objects, animate or inanimate, and returned fraught with their essence; as a bee gathers honey from flowers, they have converted into their nature what they had thus acquired, and then poured it forth as their own. Byron is almost the only poet of any note who has written much from his own musings on his own proper nature; and we believe that when all interest has ceased in him as a living individual, those parts of his writings will be the least popular. Every man, however dull, has some thoughts, if they may not rather be called "moods of mind," which are peculiar to himself alone, and which are for that very reason incommunicable; there is no language in which to utter them, and if by forced analogies, any one could succeed in giving to others an idea of them, it must always be a misty and doubtful idea, and none could be interested to receive it, besides those who were interested in the individual who attempted to embody it. This is, we believe, the great difficulty in Mr Pinkney's poems; they are not imitations of Byron, but their author has done ill what Byron has not done well; he has attempted to give to others an idea of his own peculiar feelings, and he has not, like Byron, selected those which most resemble the feelings common to all men. Nor is this the whole difficulty; either from the nature of the subject on which he has chosen to write, or from want of practice in rhythmical composition, Mr Pinkney has used so many inversions of language as would tend somewhat to confuse the plainest subject. We suspect, that the former is the true cause, because in his descriptions of natural scenery the inversions are far less numerous.

The following extract will give our readers some notion of the faults which we have mentioned.

> By woods and groves the oracles
>   Of the old age were nursed;
> To Brutus came in solitude
>   The spectral warning first,
> When murdered Cæsar's mighty shade
> The sanguine homicide dismayed,
>   And fantasy rehearsed
> The ides of March, and, not in vain,
> Showed forth Philippi's penal plain.
>
> In loneliness I heard my hopes
>   Pronounce, "Let us depart!"

And saw my mind—a Marius—
    Desponding o'er my heart:
The evil genius, long concealed,
To thought's keen eye itself revealed,
    Unfolding like a chart,—
But rolled away, and left me free
As Stoics once aspired to be.

It brought, thou spirit of my breast,
    And Naiad of the tears,
Which have been welling coldly there,
    Although unshed, for years!
It brought, in kindness, or in hate,
The final menaces of fate,
    But prompted no base fears—
Ah, could I with ill feelings see
Aught, love, so near allied to thee?

The drowsy harbinger of death,
    That slumbered dull and deep,
Is welcome, and I would not wake
    Till thou dost join my sleep.
Life's conscious calm,—the flapping sail,—
The stagnant sea nor tide nor gale
    In pleasing motion keep,—
Oppress me; and I wish release
From this to more substantial peace.

Star of that sea!—the cynosure
    Of magnet-passions, long!—
A ceaseless apparition, and
    A very ocular song!—
My skies have changed their hemisphere,
And forfeited thy radiant cheer:
    Thy shadow still is strong;
And, beaming darkness, follows me,
Far duskier than obscurity.

To what straits is the author here evidently put, to portray his feelings; what can we, what can any reader, what can the author himself understand, by representing a man beholding his own mind desponding over his own heart? and what possible aid towards understanding this is to be derived from comparing this mind to Marius among the ruins of Carthage? Then, again, what was the concealed "evil genius?" and what more do we know of him and his properties from his unfolding like a chart? then, in the last quoted stanza, what are we to make of "*beaming* darkness?" Surely such writing as this can add nothing to the stock of poetical ideas. We may give a faint guess,—but after all it can be nothing but a guess,—that the "spirit of the breast and Naiad of the tears" is some lost object of the writer's affection; but the affection of common men or women would not be so expressed. On the contrary, it is the nature of the human mind to brood over external objects connected or associated with scenes of past joys, to recall the outward semblance of that which was loved; not to dwell upon the emotions which were excited in the mind itself by the joy of the presence, or grief for the absence of that which was loved. The state of mind, therefore, which we suppose the author here meant to describe, is unnatural, and being so, the description could not be pleasing, if it could be understood. In endeavouring to make himself more intelligible, Mr Pinkney uses many images and comparisons, few of which tend to elucidate his meaning; but they are poured forth with wonderful profusion, and seem to have cost him no little labour to collect.

How feels the guiltless dreamer, who
With idly curious gaze
Has let his mind's glance wander through
The relics of past days?—
As feels the pilgrim that has scanned,
Within their skirting wall,
The moon-lit marbles of some grand
Disburied capital;
Masses of whiteness and of gloom,
The darkly bright remains
Of desolate palace, empty tomb,
And desecrated fanes:—
For in the ruins of old hours,
Remembrance haply sees
Temples, and tombs, and palaces,
Not different from these.

Now we have heard of tracing out such images among the
expiring embers of a coal-fire; but we cannot conceive any
the better of a man's past feelings because he says they resemble ancient ruins.

Perhaps, presentiment of ill
Might shake him—hearts are prophets still.
What though the fount of Castaly
Not now stains leaves with prophecy?—
What though are of another age
Omens, and Sibyl's boding page?—
Augurs and oracles resign
Their voices—fear can still divine:
Dreams and hand-writings on the wall
Need not foretell our fortune's fall;
Domitian in his galleries,
The soul all hostile advents sees,
As in the mirror-stone;
Like shadows by a brilliant day
Cast down from falcons on their prey;
Or watery demons, in strong light,
By haunted waves of fountains old,
Shown indistinctly to the sight
Of the inquisitive and bold.

Here is an instance of the conglomeration of comparisons
which we mentioned above, and perhaps the most successful in the volume; but they tend to confuse the reader from
their very multitude; and the mood of mind *here* described
is so common as not to need illustration;—all have felt depression of spirits, and the superstition that it presages evil
is a very common one. We do not mean, however, to deny
that some of these images are very beautiful, and we believe they are all original; but one of them alone would
have been sufficient to give beauty and spirit to the whole
subject. The simile of the falcon's shadow is such as could
have occurred only to a genuine poet.

Mr Pinkney appears to have read Wordsworth, and we
would recommend him to study this great poet's style, and
observe how much effect is added even to the harmony of
his lines as well as to the force of his expression, by the
order in which he arranges his words, how rarely he uses
any inversion of language, and how transparent he thus
makes his meaning. Wordsworth, too, rarely inverts the
order of nature; he does not often attempt to illustrate the
workings of his mind by comparing them to outward objects; but he describes outward things, and tells us the
train of thought which they excited, and this is the natural
order.

We should not have bestowed so much time and pains
upon Mr Pinkney's poems, if, amid all his mist and obscurity, we had not discovered gleams of unquestionable genius, not so much "words that breathe" as "thoughts
that" might "burn," if they were not enveloped in smoke.
As a general illustration of our meaning we would notice
the difference between the last twelve lines of the last
poem, and those which precede them. It is too long to be
extracted here; but we would call the author's attention to
it. The first part of the poem is a pretty clear and a pleasing
account of the thoughts excited by the removal of an old
tree familiar to infancy, and the last twelve lines have, for
aught we can see, no possible connexion with the preceding; but are a rhapsody exactly like the first of our extracts.
The use which we would draw from this, is an encouragement to Mr Pinkney to write more in the style of the first
part of the poem; to "look abroad through nature," and
give us the result of such meditations, and their operations
on his mind;—not the result of his solitary, self-
observation. By pursuing this course,—as we understand
he is still a young man,—we believe he will gain for himself no inconsiderable name among the Anglo-American
poets, whose number we would gladly see increased; and
to men of true genius,—and of them Mr Pinkney clearly
is,—the field is ample, and promises a rich harvest of fame.
(pp. 328-33)

> *A review of "Poems," in* The United States Lit-
> erary Gazette, *Vol. III, No. 9, February 1,
> 1826, pp. 328-33.*

Charles Hunter Ross   (essay date 1896)

[*In the following excerpt, Ross offers a favorable retrospective view of Pinkney's poetry.*]

It is not the purpose of this article to enter into a discussion of the comparative merits and demerits of poetry at
the South, but simply to call attention anew to an almost
forgotten poet, one who lives barely in the memory of a
single song. Future historians of Southern literary conditions will have to note among others, one important fact:
there is hardly a Southern poet who is not a "one-poem
poet." Why all else has been buried and only one song remains cannot easily be explained. Music has fettered the
fleeting character of some; patriotism has enshrined others
in people's hearts; and elocution, that bane of all good
verse, has drawn the life out of still others as a price for
making them famous. Pinkney lives in **"A Health,"** Key
in "The Star-Spangled Banner," Wilde in "My Life is Like
a Summer Rose," Cooke in "Florence Vane," O'Hara in
"The Bivouac of the Dead," Ticknor in "The Virginians
of the Valley," and Father Ryan in "The Conquered Banner." Another curious fact is that the popularity of these
poems is almost without exception in inverse ratio to their
quality. Key and Pinkney were both Marylanders, and
one would not think for a moment of comparing as to literary worth the latter's exquisite lyric with Key's bombastic
effusion; yet they are building a monument to Key, and
Pinkney is not even a name to many of the reading public.
(p. 287)

Pinkney seems not to have tried to make a living by litera-

ture, and he must have had some means, for he was married in 1824 to Miss Georgie McCausland, a beautiful
young lady of Baltimore. The same year he was admitted
to the bar. The following year he published a collective
edition of his poems under the title of *Poems.* This little
volume, mean and insignificant to the eye, and a wretched
specimen of book-making, contains within its seventy-six
pages his entire poetical output. And yet, though the
greater portion of its contents is not worth preserving, it
holds enough to make it precious in the eyes of all lovers
of true poetry. The longest poem, **"Rodolph,"** is a fragment, somewhat Byronic in story and treatment, full of
obscurity, misanthropy, and despair. Its verse is extremely
wooden at times, and there is nothing in the poem that is
inviting to the reader. It is amazing that Duyckinck [*Cy-
clopedia of American Literature*] should have thus praised
it so highly: "It is a powerful sketch of a broken life of passion and remorse, of a husband slain by the lover of his
wife, of her early death in a convent, and of the paramour's wanderings and wild mental anticipations.
Though a fragment, wanting in fullness of design and the
last polish of execution, it is a poem of power and mark.
There is an occasional inner music in the lines, demonstrative of the true poet. The imagery is happy and original."
Griswold [*Poets and Poetry of America*], it seems to me,
has really expressed the right criticism on it when he says:
"There is no novelty in the story, and not much can be said
for its morality. . . . It has more faults than Pinkney's
other works." Though, as will be seen later, it was
Pinkney's ill fate "to fall into the hands of the Reverend
Mr. Griswold," yet the latter can hardly be blamed for cri-
ticising **"Rodolph"** as he did.

Pinkney is seen in a much better light in certain of the
short poems of this volume. His lines on **"Italy,"** in evident imitation of Goethe's famous song of Mignon in *Wilhelm Meister,* are strikingly expressed:

> Know'st thou the land which lovers ought to
>   choose?
> Like blessings there descend the sparkling dews;
> In gleaming streams the crystal rivers run,
> The purple vintage clusters in the sun;
> Odors of flowers haunt the balmy breeze,
> Rich fruits hang high upon the verdant trees;
> And vivid blossoms gem the shady groves,
> Where bright-plumed birds discourse their care-
>   less loves.
> Beloved!—speed we from this sullen strand,
> Until thy light feet press that green shore's yel-
>   low sand.
>
> Look seaward thence, and naught shall meet
>   thine eye
> But fairy isles, like paintings on the sky;
> And flying fast and free before the gale,
> The gaudy vessel with its glancing sail;
> And waters glittering in the glare of noon,
> Or touch'd with silver by the stars and moon,
> Or fleck'd with broken lines of crimson light,
> When the far fisher's fire affronts the night.
> Lovely as loved! toward that smiling shore
> Bear we our household gods, to fix forever more.
>
> It looks a dimple on the face of earth,
> The seal of beauty, and the shrine of mirth;

> Nature is delicate and graceful there,
> The place's genius, feminine and fair;
> The winds are awed, nor dare to breathe aloud,
> The air seems never to have borne a cloud,
> Save where volcanoes send to heaven their curl'd
> And solemn smokes, like altars of the world.
> Thrice beautiful!—to that delightful spot
> Carry our married hearts, and be all pain forgot.
>
> There Art, too, shows, when nature's beauty
>   palls,
> Her sculptured marbles, and her pictured walls;
> And there are forms in which they both conspire
> To whisper themes that know not how to tire;
> The speaking ruins in that gentle clime
> Have but been hallow'd by the hand of Time,
> And each can mutely prompt some thought of
>   flame:
> The meanest stone is not without a name.
> Then come, beloved!—hasten o'er the sea,
> To build our happy hearth in blooming Italy.

These vigorous verses clearly show the influence of
Pinkney's life on the Mediterranean, and we do not wonder at the spell the "land of poetry and of song" threw over
him just as it had done over the impassionable German
poet thirty years before. Another poem, **"The Voyager's
Song,"** is full of the breath of the sea:

> Sound trumpets, ho!—weigh anchor—loosen
>   sail—
> The seaward flying banners chide delay;
> As it 'twere heaven that breathes this kindly
>   gale,
> Our life-like bark beneath it speeds away.

The poems, however, in which Pinkney is seen at his best
and by which posterity remembers him, are his love songs:
"Serenade," "A Picture-Song," "A Health," and one or
two untitled **"Songs."** It is said that the inspiration and
subject of these poems was a young lady of Baltimore,
Miss Mary Hawkins, a noted belle and beauty of the time.
Pinkney, it seems, was deeply in love with her, but his
wooing and beautiful verses were without avail. Like
"Annie of Tharaw," she married another. It is an easy feat
to imagine with what fervor the unfortunate poet sang to
her his **"Serenade,"** and drank to her that incomparable
"Health." History but repeats itself in these unhappy
loves of men of genius, and Pinkney is by no means the
only poet that has embalmed in glowing verse one that left
his love unrequited.

These little songs give Mr. Stedman [in his *Poets of America,* 1885] occasion to speak of Pinkney as singing his
"Lovelace lyrics," and if we make allowance for environment, the remark is not inappropriate, though I would not
say that Pinkney wrote anything that approaches the perfection of "To Althea in Prison." It seems to me that the
"Serenade" has something of the Caroline lyrical flavor:

> Look out upon the stars, my love,
>   And shame them with thine eyes,
> On which, than on the lights above,
>   There hang more destinies.
> Night's beauty is the harmony
>   Of blending shades and light;
> Then, lady, up,—look out and be
>   A sister to the night!

Sleep not!—thine image wakes for aye
    Within my watching breast:
Sleep not!—from her soft sleep should fly,
    Who robs all hearts of rest.
Nay, lady, from thy slumbers break
    And make this darkness gay
With looks, whose brightness well might make
    Of darker nights a day.

Another little **"Song"** is more lively:

Day departs this upper air,
    My lovely, lovely lady;
And the eve-star sparkles fair,
    And our good steeds are ready.
Leave, leave these loveless halls,
    So lordly though they be;—
Come, come—affection calls—
    Away at once with me.

Sweet thy words in sense as sound,
    And gladly do I hear them;
Though thy kinsmen are around,
    And tamer bosoms fear them.
Mount, mount,—I'll keep thee, dear,
    In safety as we ride;—
On, on,—my heart is here,
    My sword is at my side!

A poem of another kind and lacking the indefinable charm of the **"Serenade,"** is **"A Picture-Song:"**

How may this little tablet feign
    The features of a face,
Which o'er informs with loveliness,
    Its proper share of space;
Or human hands on ivory,
    Enable us to see
The charms, that all must wonder at,
    Thou work of gods in thee!

But yet, methinks, that sunny smile
    Familiar stories tells,
And I should know those placid eyes,
    Two crystal shaded wells;
Nor can my soul, the limner's art
    Attesting with a sigh,
Forget the blood that deck'd thy cheek,
    As rosy clouds the sky.

They could not semble what thou art,
    More excellent than fair,
As soft as sleep or pity is,
    And pure as mountain-air;
But here are common, earthly hues,
    To such an aspect wrought,
That none, save thine, can seem so like
    The beautiful in thought.

The song I sing, thy likeness like,
    Is painful mimicry
Of something better, which is now
    A memory to me,
Who have upon life's frozen sea
    Arrived the icy spot,
Where man's magnetic feelings show
    Their guiding task forgot.

The sportive hopes, that used to chase
    Their shifting shadows on,
Like children playing in the sun,

Are gone—forever gone;
And on a careless, sullen peace,
    My double-fronted mind,
Like Janus when his gates were shut,
    Looks forward and behind.

Apollo placed his harp, of old,
    Awhile upon a stone,
Which has resounded since, when struck,
    A breaking harp-string's tone;
And thus my heart, though wholly now,
    From early softness free,
If touch'd, will yield the music yet,
    It first received of thee.

The finest song, however, of Pinkney's collection is the famous **"Health,"** which Poe spoke of as "a poem of so much brilliancy and power." It is a trite remark to say that if Pinkney is to be kept in lasting remembrance, it is by this one poem. By its side all the rest of his slight productions pale into insignificance. All the anthologies contain it, but one may be pardoned for reproducing it here:

I fill this cup to one made up
    Of loveliness alone,
A woman, of her gentle sex
    The seeming paragon;
To whom the better elements
    And kindly stars have given
A form so fair, that, like the air,
    'Tis less of earth than heaven.

Her every tone is music's own,
    Like those of morning birds,
And something more than melody
    Dwells ever in her words;
The coinage of her heart are they,
    And from her lips each flows
As one may see the burden'd bee
    Forth issue from the rose.

Affections are as thoughts to her,
    The measures of her hours;
Her feelings have the fragrancy,
    The freshness of young flowers;
And lovely passions, changing oft,
    So fill her, she appears
The image of themselves by turns,—
    The idol of past years!

Of her bright face one glance will trace
    A picture on the brain,
And of her voice in echoing hearts
    A sound must long remain;
But memory, such as mine of her,
    So very much endears,
When death is nigh my latest sigh
    Will not be life's, but hers.

I fill'd this cup to one made up
    Of loveliness alone,
A woman, of her gentle sex
    The seeming paragon—
Her health! and would on earth there stood
    Some more of such a frame,
That life might be all poetry,
    And weariness a name.

                    (pp. 289-95)

In December, 1827, a paper in the interest of John Quincy

Adams, entitled *The Marylander,* appeared in Baltimore, and Pinkney was chosen editor. He soon made a reputation in this new sphere, his style being noted for its grace and vigor, though marred by extreme party-spirit and merciless invective. But this good fortune did not long continue. His health, which had been feeble for some time, began rapidly to decline, and on April 11, 1828 he died, aged only twenty-five years and six months. He was buried in Greenmount Cemetery, Baltimore.

In his admirable life of Poe Professor Woodberry gives it as his opinion that Pinkney died "from the effects of poverty and discouragement suffered just as his genius was breaking forth." It seems to me that this statement must be taken with a grain of salt. Pinkney was certainly not entirely neglected before his death, and besides he had practically published all his existing poems before he was twenty-three. With the exception of his editorial work we have no record that he wrote anything after the publication of his little volume in 1825. Whether this was due to the indifference of the public cannot be known, but I doubt if we shall be far wrong in supposing that such was the case. Still one cannot but think that Pinkney, like Poe, brought much of his trouble on himself. We are told that he was dissipated, and from the meagre facts of his life we can gather that his nature was such as to get him constantly into trouble. He was doubtless rash, impulsive, and headstrong, warm in his friendships and violent in his dislikes,—in fact, a typical young Southerner of the olden time. Yet he must have had all the fine qualities of that class, for it is said that he was generous to a fault, having even been known to pawn valuable jewelry in order to help those in want.

Poe put himself on record about Pinkney in a way that seems to us extraordinary. In his essay on "The Poetic Principle," after commenting on **"A Health,"** he says: "It was the misfortune of Mr. Pinkney to have been born too far south. Had he been born a New Englander, it is probable that he would have been ranked as the first of American lyrists, by that magnanimous cabal which so long controlled the destinies of American Letters in conducting the thing called the *North American Review.*" The only excuse for reprinting this utterly uncalled for criticism rests on the plea of its being a curiosity, and an example what a sane critic, and Poe undoubtedly wrote a great deal of sane criticism, can sometimes say in moments of provocation and imagined injury. Did not Poe remember that in that very *North American Review* he had contemptuously called a "thing," there appeared in 1825, an appreciative review of Pinkney's poetry by Mr. F. W. P. Greenwood [see excerpt dated 1825]? Besides, the poet William Leggett contributed in 1827 an article on Pinkney to the New York *Mirror,* a journal of which, I believe, Poe was afterwards assistant editor. We are also told that when it was determined to publish biographical sketches of the few greatest poets of the country, with their portraits, Pinkney was requested to sit for his miniature to be used in the proposed volume. After his death his poems were thrice republished: in Baltimore in 1838—a second edition of the little volume of 1825; in 1844, with a brief introduction, in the series of the "Mirror Library," entitled *The Rococo;* in 1850 in Morris and Willis's *Prose and Poetry of Europe*

and America. His work was even favorably noticed in the London *Athenæum* for 1835. In the face of these facts a Southern critic [Colonel J. L. Peyton] is abundantly justified in saying that no one "but a man of diseased mind and imagination, like Poe, would have uttered such sentiments as he did as to Edward Coate Pinkney."

Pinkney's life is a sad story, but its pathos should not cloud his real excellence as a poet. In a time when Sydney Smith's sneering remark, that "literature the Americans have none," was almost too true, Pinkney piped a few simple numbers that had in them the promise of better things. He was the forerunner of Poe, Pendleton Cooke, Timrod, Hayne, Meek, and the other songbirds of the Southern choir, and he shared the common fate of forerunners. Nothing could be more scant and limited than his poetical output, yet it is informed with some of the best qualities that belong to true poetry—a haunting music, a peculiar grace of expression, and a remarkable sureness of touch. Even in the crudest portions of his poetry there are, as the Editor of [*The Sewanee Review*] says, "traces of a virility of thought and expression not usually perceptible in the work of American poets."

Yet the Reverend Mr. Griswold had to come forward in order to destroy even this meed of praise. Only hear his remarkable effusion: "Pinkney's is the first instance in this country in which we have to lament the prostitution of true poetical genius to unworthy purposes. Pervading much that he wrote there is a selfish melancholy and sullen pride; dissatisfaction with the present, and doubts in regard to the future life. The great distinguishing characteristic of American poetry is its pure and high morality. May it ever be so!" What did the worthy divine wish Pinkney to write? Sunday-school stories, forsooth? It is true that in **"Rodolph"** we see plenty of misanthropy *à la* Byron, and in some of the shorter poems we find such expressions as "my sacrifice of sullen years," "my misused and blighted powers," "my waste of miserable hours;" but who ever cared for **"Rodolph"** and these particular poems? Surely the reverend gentleman did not find "selfish melancholy and sullen pride" in the lyrics quoted above. Doubtless his mind was too narrow to appreciate any song, however beautiful, that touched on "love and wine and sunny skies," and he seemed to lack utterly that love for the beautiful which, if wanting in the heart, Heine tells us, finds that "the sun is simply so many miles in circumference, and the trees are good for firewood, and the flowers are classified according to their stamens, and the water is wet." We cannot be too thankful that our poet had no such Mentor at his elbow and that, in spite of poverty, discouragement, and the frailty of human nature, he left us a little legacy of song which, we trust, "the flight of years" cannot destory. (pp. 295-98)

> *Charles Hunter Ross, "Edward Coate Pinkney," in* The Sewanee Review, *Vol. IV, No. 3, May, 1896, pp. 287-98.*

Wightman F. Melton   (essay date 1912)

[Melton was an American educator and critic. In the fol-

lowing excerpt, he examines influences on Pinkney's poetry and the influence of the poetry on other writers.]

With all Pinkney's Romanticism, his verse abounds in classical touches. In his own footnotes he refers to Herodotus, Suetonius, and Horace. Prof. W. L. Weber [in *Selections from the Southern Poets*] calls attention to a thought from Ovid (VIII., 13) in line 22 of **"A Picture Song."** The **"Prologue—Delivered at a Greek Benefit, in Baltimore,—1823,"** reveals Pinkney's attitude toward

> The place of gods whom yet our hearts adore.

Some portion of the six years spent by Pinkney in the United States Navy, he was cruising in the Mediterranean Sea, and saw and learned to love Italy. In **"A Health,"** **"The Indian Bride,"** and some of the shorter pieces, there are striking similarities to Petrarch. Pinkney may not have been able to read Italian, but he could have become familiar with Petrarch's poem through "Totel's Miscellany," or other translations. The Italian spirit and the Petrarch-touch are unmistakable. Lines in evidence of this might readily be cited for comparison.

Pinkney's indebtedness to Shakespeare is slight. In **"Lines from the Port-Folio of H—,"** No. I., 15-17:

> A strange and ominous belief,
> That in the spring-time the yellow leaf
>   Had fallen on my hours,

is suggested by *Macbeth,* V., iii, 22, 23:

> My way of life
> Is fall'n into the sear, the yellow leaf.

In Pinkney's **"Lines from the Port-Folio of H—,"** No. II., 46-48, there is the following echo of Hamlet's soliloquy:

> Star of that sea—its current bear
>   My vessel to that bourne,
> Whence neither busy voyager
>   Nor pilgrim may return.

The opening line of *Macbeth,* and line 268 of Pinkney's Rodolph, Part II., are enough alike:

> Macbeth,—When shall we three meet again?
> Rodolph,—When shall we two meet again?

In the following there is a strong trace of the influence either of Marlowe or of one of his several imitators:

> Marlowe,—Come live with me and be my love,
>   And we will all the pleasures prove.

> Pinkney,—Come thou . . .
>   Where we may through all pleasures rove
>   And live like votaries of love.
>   —**"Rodolph,"** II., 215-220.

It is generally understood that Pinkney's **"Italy"** is in imitation of Mignon's song in Goethe's *Wilhelm Meister.* It would be interesting to know the exact date of the writing of **"Italy,"** for the *North American Review* (vol. XIX—October, 1824) contains some twenty-one pages (303-325) on the "Life and Genius of Goethe." A number of his poems are translated,—among them "Mignon." Pages 337-389 are devoted to "Italian Narrative Poetry." It was

the January number of the *Review,* the same year, that contained a review of Pinkney's **"Rodolph."**

Pinkney quotes Fletcher and Byron, introductory to **"Rodolph,"** and his **"Italy"** contains at least one line (8) which has a prototype in Byron's "Bride of Abydos," and none in "Mignon"; furthermore, the spirit of **"Rodolph"** is quite suggestive of Byron-influence.

Pinkney quotes Wordsworth: "She was a phantom of delight, etc.," introductory to the poem **"To——,"** beginning, "Accept this portraiture of thee." **"The Indian Bride,"** aside from being a subject dear to the mind of Wordsworth, contains an expression (lines 67-68) distinctly Wordsworthian:

> The world, or all they know of it,
> Is theirs.

A Wordsworth padding-note is to be found in **"Rodolph,"** Part II., lines 86, 87:

> What boots it to protract the verse
> In which his story I rehearse?

Wordsworth's "Peter Bell," line 285,

> The grass you almost hear it growing,

may have suggested to Pinkney,

> The low strange hum of herbage growing,

which is line nineteen of the poem, **"To ——,"** beginning: " 'Twas eve; the broadly shining sun."

To work out Pinkney's influence upon others would be almost impossible, and possibly not worth while. The following observations are offered for the interest they deserve.

Compare the movement of Pinkney's **"Evergreens,"** and Tennyson's "Brook." Pinkney,

> When Summer's sunny hues adorn
>   Sky, forest, hill and meadow,
> The foliage of the evergreens,
>   In contrast casts a shadow.

Tennyson,

> With many a curve my banks I fret
>   By many a field and fallow,
> And many a fairy foreland set
>   With willow-weed and mallow.

It may be folly to suggest that robust, old English, Browning was at all influenced by the frail, young American, Pinkney, but there is haunting similarity between three of their thoughts. Let it be remembered, however, that Pinkney's verse was read and appreciated in England. *The Atheneum,* vol. 8 (1835), p. 149, says, "One or two of the prettiest things in American poetry were written by Edward C. Pinkney."

Pinkney,

> Exchanging lustre with the sun,
>   A part of day she strays—
> A glancing, living, human smile,
>   On nature's face she plays.
>   —**"The Indian Bride,"** lines 15-18.

Browning,

> Sky—what a scowl of cloud
>   Till, near and far,
> Ray on ray split the shroud:
>   Splendid, a star!

>   . . . . .

> Till God's own smile came out:
>   That was thy face!
>   —"Apparitions," lines 4-7, 11, 12.

Again compare:

Pinkney,

> A music visible, a light
> Like lamps unto an infant's sight—
> A temple of celestial soul,
> Too lovely for aught ill to mar,
> Which love from beauty's planet stole,
> The morn and evening star.
>   —"Rodolph," Part II., lines 209-214.

Browning,

> But here is the finger of God, a flash of the will
>   that can,
>   Existent behind all laws, that made them, and,
>   lo, they are!
> And I know not, save in this, such gift be al-
>   lowed to man,
>   That out of three sounds he frame, not a
>   fourth sound, but a star.
>   —"Abt Vogler," lines 49-52.

And again:

Pinkney,

>   Let
> My thoughtful clay all thought forget.
> Suffer no sparkles of hot pain
> Among mine ashes to remain.
>   —"Rodolph," Part II., lines 325-329.

Browning,

> Finished and finite clods, untroubled by a spark.
>   —"Rabbi Ben Ezra," line 18.

Lowell's "The Vision of Sir Launfal," lines 250, 252:

> Sir Launfal turns from his own hard gate

>   . . . . .

> An old, bent man, worn out and frail,

suggests the possibility of the author's familiarity with Pinkney's **"Rodolph,"** Part I., lines 35, 36, 38:

> At such a season, his domain
> The lord at last arrived again,

>   . . . . .

> Grown old in heart, infirm in frame.

Professor W. L. Weber calls attention [in *The Southern Poets*], to the similarity in thought between Pinkney's "two shaded crystal wells" **("A Picture Song")**, and Lanier's "shining depths" of "my two springs" ("My Springs").

As editor of *The Marylander,* Pinkney gave himself up, almost entirely, to the writing of prose, and prose of a political rather than of a purely literary nature. He boldly exposed falsehood, and in a dignified manner defended the truth. (pp. 331-35)

The Marylander, Vol. I., Nos. 1, 8, and 29, contains three poems, at least two of which are by Pinkney. The first, an unsigned, mediocre **"Song,"** of three stanzas, tells of the smile, the frown, and the blush of some fair face. The second, signed "Editor," is a very pretty song, of two stanzas, sixteen lines, inspired by the "cheerful, auspicious eyes" of some "maiden fair." The third, by "Edw. C. Pinkney," contains forty-eight lines, of which the last two are blank. The title of the poem is **"The Beauty—a Fragment."**

The brief and brilliant poetical career of Edward Coote Pinkney began with **"Rodolph—a Fragment,"** and ended with **"The Beauty—a Fragment."** The latter poem, printed one month, less one day, before the death of the author, concludes with the lines:

> Enough;—on graver subjects I have mused
>   Too much, as was my pleasure, pain, or
>   duty—
> My heart and harp have been too long disused,
>   To celebrate aright this perfect beauty.

Pinkney's verse, though light and airy, will live because of its pure beauty and the universality of its appeal. He is our Petrarch and our Carew, standing at, or near, the head of the limited list of American cavalier lyrists. What a pity his last year was spent in grinding out, in "pain, or duty," political prose, when like Sidney Lanier, he might have been singing himself into the very heavens, beside some "crystal star." (pp. 335-36)

> *Wightman F. Melton, "Edward Coote Pinkney," in* South Atlantic Quarterly, *Vol. XI, No. 4, October, 1912, pp. 328-36.*

J. P. Simmons   (essay date 1929)

[*In the following essay, Simmons likens Pinkney's poetry to that of the Cavalier poets.*]

Almost alone among American poets of whatever rank, Edward Coote Pinkney wrote his exquisite lyrics without reference to Puritanism. Other American writers, almost to a man, have written with the American Puritan ethical and moral tradition definitely in mind, either by way of its support or in reaction of one degree or another from it. Bryant, Longfellow, Lowell, and most of the others were upholders of either the current or traditional Puritanism in one form or another. Holmes greatly disliked it but was satirical just enough not to injure it greatly. Our own contemporaries, like Dreiser, Anderson, and Mencken, have gone to lengths of vituperation and hate that have branded them in method at least as Puritan as the most violent of the crusading zealots of Puritanism. Even Emerson, Poe, and Whitman, working with a more detached attitude and presenting a more nearly cosmic, or in the case of Poe, a more completely differentiated individual viewpoint, were not unmindful of the conscious opposition of their works to the prevailing points of view.

Pinkney was born in London in 1802, where his father was residing on a diplomatic mission. The boy was educated in England largely and entered the navy as midshipman at the age of fifteen. Only at widely remote intervals did he spend time in the Baltimore home of the family until his resignation from the navy on the death of his father in 1823. Marriage a short time after to Miss Georgiana Mc-Causland confirmed his residence in Baltimore and Charleston, which, however, was to last for not much over two years because of his early death in 1828. He therefore escaped the miseries of spending his best years, as did Herman Melville, in serious, eager literary endeavor, only to be spurned and repudiated by a public that would not accept him because he did not conform to its traditions. His long residence abroad, his service at sea, and a career terminated by an early death served to give him a point of view dissociating him from Puritanism.

Poe, whose additional fourteen years of existence were merely heaped up miseries resulting from the tragedy of trying to make a materialistic populace understand the poetic expression of his exotic ideas, in addition to praising Pinkney as the greatest American lyrist [see Further Reading], could certainly have felicitated him on his early release from certain increasing miseries. For his gift, while not so intensely individualized as was Poe's, was assuredly not of the nature to satisfy either the adherents of the traditional viewpoints or the calm opponents of a Puritanism, which after all they found much in to love, like Emerson, Hawthorne, and Holmes. Rather was his gift a quite exotic one, foreign to most American culture and tradition.

Pinkney's gift undoubtedly admitted the influence of the English Romantics, Byron, Scott, Moore, Wordsworth, and Keats. The influence of Bryant is not undiscernable. But such diverse influences argue little in showing the dominant trend of his thought and attitude. Numerous parallels to each of the above named poets may be cited from his works; but they are parallels rather of phrase than of profound attitude of mind, and reveal only a young and inexperienced writer grasping for felicities of expression of which he is not yet master. In the things which are distinctly Pinkney's, those exquisite lyrics that show the true bent of his genius, there is little or no echo of any of the Romantics, either in thought or in phrase. Rather does he hark back to the Caroline period of the Cavalier English poets and show the spirit of Lovelace, Suckling, and Carewe, without, indeed, showing the specific influence of any one or of all of them. His gift is his own, one that grew out of his own inner consciousness, out of his personal predilections, and out of the traditions of his family.

It is unusual to find a poet apparently so completely disassociated from the spirit of his times. Yet the dissociation is only apparent. Of the spirit of rebellion that characterized the Romantic movement of the first part of last century against the civilization of a preceding age, there is nothing in Pinkney. Even of the spirit that is conscious of rebellion against an established order and desires to maintain the status of that order in the face of change, there is nothing in Pinkney. He is not the champion of the existing Revolutionary civilization that flourished so exquisitely along the sea-coast of America, from the Carolinas to New York, and which was not entirely destroyed until the Civil War, nor indeed is he the champion of anything else. He is rather the expression of that civilization, its perfect flower, flourishing unconscious that it flourishes at all, simply enjoying itself in the abundance and assurance of its existence, questioning nothing, either itself or the forces that rise against it. He is in this particular comparable to Frances Hopkinson in his earlier work, before the burdens of a political career and the necessity of thinking in terms of changing social and political conditions caused him to lose the early grace and assured beauty of trifles like "My Gen'rous Heart Disdains."

Pinkney's birth into a Maryland family of distinction undoubtedly furnished the background for his Cavalier attitude. His long dissociation from the rapidly changing points of view in American life, which, indeed, during his lifetime were fairly well stabilized by the succession of Virginia and Massachusetts aristocratic-republican Presidents, only intensified the traditions of that birth and did nothing to indicate to his mind that change was pending or that indeed it could impend. Until a few years ago there existed, and perhaps still exist, in parts of Maryland not far from Baltimore, charming relics of an old civilization that has withstood the changes and vicissitudes of time, with little alteration in points of view and general attitude toward a system of living that reverts to the days of good King Charles. It is in essence a pure aristocracy. It is urbane, gracious, assured; ready to make love impetuously or to fight equally impetuously and whole-heartedly; it looks at life not as a problem to be solved nor as a game to be beat, but as a privilege bestowed by God upon his favored ones. It is religious, though it says very little about religion, which it takes as a matter of course. It is kind and humanitarian, treating its servants with justice and a large degree of kindliness that amounts almost to a sort of apparent equality. It has little arrogance of position and advantage, which it feels, if it thinks about the matter at all, have been bestowed, like all earth's blessings and curses, upon righteous and unrighteous alike. With the Roman Horace, it recognizes Death, as well as Life, knocking with equal foot at the door of palace and hovel, and with Horace, also, it is not concerned with the vagaries of either life or death and never feels that it is its business or its opportunity to meddle with what the gods have ordained. In a word, its satisfaction and assurance with life are as medieval as the system of theology on which it was founded, which believed in a somewhat remote imitation of Plato's, "As it is in heaven, so it is on earth"; and its practical assurance of itself is as medieval as is the system of groundrents in Baltimore which has so long given the city a financial foundation and continuance.

It has its codes of honor, its rigorous disciplines, which are joyously undertaken because of the satisfactions they inevitably bring. It prefers the balance and poise of the Greek to the repression of the Puritan. Because it believes in the Golden Mean, it finds codes of honor rather than systems of morality, the first of which bind the individual, whereas the latter bind the group, the most inviting system of discipline. Its discipline, therefore, is one of the individual imposed by the personal acceptance of its code, promising personal satisfaction in its performance, and more attractive than the discipline of public will, imposed by a majority in the name of God. What Vernon Parrington has mistakenly named its Puritanism in his discussion of the writers of the Charleston group has only the disciplinary appearance of Puritanism, not its foundational urge. All the good things of life it approves of. It is healthily fond of its things to eat and drink, its horses, its hounds, its pleasures of material existence. All the gifts of life are abundantly used, nothing is eschewed, if in the using it can prove the strength of its power to master them and use them to its own advantage.

Here is the cultural heritage of Pinkney, as it is of the Cavalier wherever found. The Cavalier as a rule writes little, because he has no problems to write about. It takes a problem to form the basis of a discussion. If he does write, as he sometimes does, it is either because the full expression of his existence has been dammed back somewhere, or because he happens to have some spark of that divine afflatus of genius which kindles where it listeth and has no respect for systems of civilization. For the Cavalier the most potent source of damming is in love matters. The old system of courtly love, which bourgeois Jean de Meun so broadly satirized in the latter part of "The Romance of the Rose," was a part of the heritage of the original Cavalier and held almost without change through the vicissitudes of Cavalier existence in America. Hence Cavalier poetry is almost always love poetry. The repressions of the emotion imposed by the system cause the poet to give written expression to his dammed-up passions. Troilus, restraining his love for Cressida, falls into uncontrollable fits of fainting and profuse prostration because he has no way of expressing his passion. In a later age, when middle class women, accustomed for centuries to free expression of their passions, come by reason of financial elevation into the higher class which was under the imposition of the restraints of the courtly system of love applied so long through the ages to courtly dwellers in towered Camelots, they fall into the faints depicted in the novels of Miss Burney and Miss Austen. They had no means of freeing themselves through the gentle art of poesy. Pinkney had the gift of this method of release. Therefore most of his poetry consists of exquisite love lyrics addressed to the lady who became his wife.

Of the forty poems and fragments of items which make up the total collection of Pinkney's poetic output, very much more than half deal with the subject of love. Thus, eleven are addressed, or claimed by the lady herself to have been addressed, to Miss Georgiana McCausland, who became his wife. Six are addressed to Miss Mary Hawkins, an early sweetheart. Five are addressed to various ladies, and two, including his long poem, **"Rodolph,"** are on the general subject of love. Three poems celebrate contemporary events, three depend upon history for their inspiration, with the immortality of love as the central theme of the magnificent ode, **"The Voyager's Song."** One deals with his own personal attitude toward the world, and one, **"Invitation and Reply,"** is a splendid drinking song in the pure Cavalier manner. Of the remainder, including fragments, there is one each on the subject of his mother's reverence for his father, one that grew out of an incident in his navy career, and one on the general subject of death.

It will be seen, however, that the great preponderance of subject favors the theme of love, and for the most part the subject is treated from the Cavalier viewpoint of personal experience.

Of the poems addressed to Mary Hawkins there is the beautiful lyric, **"We Break the Glass,"** one of the best known of Pinkney's poems. It is characteristic of Pinkney's, and of Cavalier poetry in general, that it considers love as an exquisite emotion of life, calling, not for sighs and groans or for philosophizing concerning its evanescence or its grief, but for a beautiful gesture of well-trained men and women expressing itself in symbols devised after the courtly tradition to make life and love a part of the delightful business of living.

> We break the glass, whose sacred wine
> 　　To some beloved health we drain,
> Lest future pledges, less divine,
> 　　Should e'er the hallowed toy profane;
> And thus I broke a heart, that poured
> 　　Its tide of feeling out to thee,
> In draughts, by after-times deplored,
> 　　Yet dear to memory.
>
> But still the old empassioned ways
> 　　And habits of my mind remain,
> And still unhappy light displays
> 　　Thine image chambered in my brain,
> And still it looks as when the hours
> 　　Went by like flights of singing birds,
> Or that soft chain of spoken flowers,
> 　　And airy gems, thy words.

The characteristic note sounded in this poem, that love is a matter of exquisite intellectual apprehension rather than the deep longing of the heart, which characterizes the courtly rather than the romantic gesture toward love, is struck again in the beautiful, but somewhat uneven **"Picture Song,"** also addressed to Miss Hawkins, especially in this exquisite figure in the last stanza:

> Apollo placed his harp, of old, awhile upon a
> 　　stone,
> Which has resounded since, when struck, a
> 　　breaking harpstring's tone;
> And thus my heart, though wholly now from
> 　　early softness free,
> If touched, will yield the music yet, it first received of thee.

The same (to the true Romantic) somewhat hard and intellectual apprehension of love, is seen in **"Lines from the Portfolio of (Miss Hawkins)."** We have here the heartbroken lover who can nevertheless contemplate metaphysically the results of the ravage to his emotions. The exquisite music that Pinkney put into beautiful conceits of love is evident no less in **"Serenade"** than it is in those exquisite trifles from Provençe, France and the England of the Cavaliers. The clear sweet loveliness of these lines has scarcely been surpassed.

> Look out upon the stars, my love,
> 　　And shame them with thine eyes,
> On which, than on the lights above,
> 　　There hang more destinies.
> Night's beauty is the harmony
> 　　Of blending shades and light:

> Then, Lady, up,—look out, and be
>   A sister of the night!—
>
> Sleep not! thine image wakes for aye,
>   Within my watching breast:
> Sleep not!—from her soft sleep should fly,
>   Who robs all hearts of rest.
> Nay, Lady, from thy slumbers break,
>   And make this darkness gay,
> With looks, whose brightness well might make
>   Of darker nights a day.

One naturally does not find any more pure passion in the poems addressed to Georgiana McCausland. The Cavalier measure of passion, however, is there, namely; the music and the depth of exquisiteness in the labored conceit. The successful Cavalier lover was ever the man of achievement, achievement either of war or of intellectual brilliance. Simplicity and genuineness of emotional expression were sought for by Wordsworth and his Romantic followers in the primitiveness and directness of simple rural life; were found by Moore in the passionate directness and energy of the Celtic life and imagination; and by Byron in the sensuous passionateness of his own nature and of the Orient. They were mistakenly sought for among the intellectual artifices of medieval courtly life by Walter Scott, and so mistakenly imposed upon middle-class Englishmen and American Southerners as the genuine expression of emotional honesty and righteousness. This is a vastly different thing from the intention of true early nineteenth-century romanticism, although in our South, due to the influence of Scott, it has long passed for such. Pinkney was of the medieval courtly tradition without owing any allegiance to Scott or without needing any inspiration from him. The sole poem of Pinkney's that shows decidedly any of Scott's influence is the **"Song,"** which is quoted entire for comparison with the strictly Cavalier **"A Health,"** which follows. . . .

> Day departs this upper air,
>   My lively, lovely lady;
> And the eve-star sparkles fair,
>   And our good steeds are ready.
> Leave, leave these loveless halls,
>   So lordly though they be;—
> Come, come—affection calls—
>   Away at once with me!
>
> Sweet thy words in sense as sound,
>   And gladly do I hear them;
> Though thy kinsmen are around,
>   And tamer bosoms fear them.
> Mount, mount,—I'll keep thee, dear,
>   In safety as we ride;—
> On, on—my heart is here,
>   My sword is at my side.

The naïve braggadocio and bravado of this sort of thing is foreign to the true Cavalier, although it is the essence of the Scott tradition. Pinkney rarely let himself be betrayed into the sham and pinchbeck bravado that a middle-class following in England and America mistook in Scott for the genuine. The most characteristic of Pinkney's Cavalier lyrics, next to **"We Break the Glass,"** is **"A Health,"** addressed to Georgiana. The dashing brilliance, the gay assurance of power and ability to charm and win, the lilt of exquisite music, which in its rhythms reflects the assured and harmonious rhythms of the life of the courtly aristocrat, smooth and elegant as court life at Versailles or at the court of Queen Anne, that rather successful middle-class imitation—a music without either the monotony of ordinary life or the deeps of tragedy and heights of inspired passion of the true Romantics.

> I fill this cup to one made up of loveliness alone,
> A woman, of her gentle sex the seeming paragon;
> To whom the better elements and kindly stars have given,
> A form so fair, that like the air, 'tis less of earth than heaven.
>
> Her every tone is music's own, like those of morning birds,
> And something more than melody dwells ever in her words;
> The coinage of her heart are they, and from her lips each flows
> As one may see the burthened bee forth issue from the rose.
>
> Affections are as thoughts to her, the measures of her hours;
> Her feelings have the fragrancy, the freshness, of young flowers;
> And lovely passions, changing oft, so fill her, she appears
> The image of themselves by turns,—the idol of past years!
>
> Of her bright face one glance will trace a picture on the brain,
> And of her voice in echoing hearts a sound must long remain,
> But memory such as mine of her so very much endears,
> When death is nigh my latest sigh will not be life's but hers.
>
> I filled this cup to one made up of loveliness alone,
> A woman, of her gentle sex the seeming paragon—
> Her health! and would on earth there stood some more of such a frame,
> That life might be all poetry, and weariness a name.

The same mental passion is seen in the poem **"To (Georgiana),"** suggested by Wordsworth's "She Was a Phantom of Delight."

> Accept this portraiture of,
> Revealed to Wordsworth in a dream—
> One less immortal stays with me,
> Whose airy hues thine own may seem:
> Mental reflections of thy light,
> A rainbow beautiful and bright;
> A shining lamp of constant ray,
> To which my fancy shall be slave;
> A shaping that cannot decay,
> Until it moulder in my grave.

This is the passion of the courtly lover that is

> All breathing human passion far above
> That leaves a heart high sorrowful and cloyed,
> A burning forehead and a parching tongue.

There is one somewhat decided departure from the true Cavalier tone. **"The Indian's Bride,"** a poem celebrating the marriage at Cornwall, Connecticut, of John Ridge, a Cherokee Indian, and Miss Sarah Northrup, Pinkney makes the means of a praise of true love in quite the manner of the romantic French conception of Indian life. The incident appealed to Pinkney, who is said to have remarked concerning the romance, "Ah, this, indeed, is love." The appeal of this romantic conception of love, however, may have been due in part to Pinkney's own situation at the time of the composition of the poem, for he was about to marry a lady who could hardly have appealed greatly to his family. However beautiful she may have been and however charming, there is always to be remembered that she was the daughter of an Irish brewer, not long in Baltimore. Pinkney was about to defy conventions, and the defiance was further complicated by the marriage by a Baptist minister. In the Baltimore of that elder day and in families of the Pinkney type, neither defiance was one that could be lightly passed over. That there was little comment in the family annals was only a part of the genteel tradition that would say very little but feel much. After this there is no evidence other than that the poet mines anew the former vein of courtly love.

But even courtly love does not always run smooth, and there is in it a convention to fit its grief as well as to fit its triumph. It is in **"Rodolph,"** by far Pinkney's longest poem and his most ambitious, that he recounts the story of disappointed and thwarted love. It is noteworthy, however, that this is not a lyric expression, but is conceived in more nearly the manner of the Gothic romance of a somewhat earlier period. Pinkney was apparently but lightly personally acquainted with his theme, for although he had had one unsuccessful love affair, that with Mary Hawkins, he dismissed it in airy Cavalier fashion, not without a sigh, to be sure, but certainly with little of the grief of thwarted passion.

Rodolph loves a married woman. He kills her husband. The lady seeks a convent cell,

> Thrice blest, that she the waves among
> Of ebbing pleasure staid not long,
> To watch the sullen tide, and find
> The hideous shapings left behind.

Then the lady also dies. Rodolph seeks far and wide for pleasure, but cannot find it. He becomes insane, and in his last imaginings fancies he sees her in the beauties of life about him. At last he, too, dies.

> None wept o'er his bier,
> Although above such things we weep,
> And rest obtains the useless tear,
> Due rather to the state of sleep;—
> For why?—because the common faith
> Of passion is averse from death.

The courtly tradition is broken, however, mainly in the incidents of the story only. In these last somewhat awkward lines, imperfectly carrying the burden of their thought, is still the courtly attitude toward love: "None wept . . . because the common faith of passion is averse from death." In spite of his Cavalier heritage, Pinkney lived too far away from Chaucer's "Man of Law's Tale," with its story of perfect courtly love and its naïvely sincere concluding question, "Now which of the two loved her best?" for him to repeat unadorned that courtly tale. Through the centuries religious morality had too profoundly entered into and modified the courtly tradition even among the Cavaliers; but inherently Pinkney reflects the medieval courtly exultation of passion. Death must ensue for all, but there is no blaming of Rodolph, and passion lives on immortal, even in death. The great story of Paolo and Francesca da Rimini, with its dire and potent punishment of a too hot love, had set the fashion of a modified tradition. To those, therefore, who in the name of morality would have demanded the death of Rodolph for his crime, Pinkney grants satisfaction. The lady is needlessly sacrificed from the viewpoint even of the moralist. Pinkney's intention, however, is made clear in his assertion of the deathlessness of passion in the last lines of his poem.

There remains not much else in the small output of this poet of charming lyrics to note. But wherever we may turn, there is always the insouciant Cavalier charm. Even the single moralistic piece to be found in Pinkney's poetry, the much quoted **"Evergreens,"** is turned with a bright little compliment to a lady. A delightful little drinking song, composed impromptu, carries to the end the gay carelessness of the Cavalier life. It is good enough to be in every anthology of convivial verse, for it carries through so joyously the best traditions of gentlemanly imbibing.

INVITATION AND REPLY

> Come, fill, my friend, the bumper bright,
>   And give a parting pledge to sorrow,
> Let's very merry be tonight,
>   And what the Gods decree to-morrow.
>
> If I must fill more bumpers bright,
>   I give indeed a pledge to sorrow,
> For I shall be dead drunk to-night.
>   And sick as death itself to-morrow.

It is a mistake, then, to class Pinkney with the Romantics without qualification. What they assumed as part of an attitude was with him an inborn tradition. There is in his poetry no preoccupation with nature, nor with individualism, nor with the rights and wrongs of the down-trodden. He is wholly medieval, not a reversion, but in the sense that the civilization of which he was a part was in essence a medieval civilization. Pinkney belonged to its best tradition, a rare example of the courtly aristocrat who broke into song. (pp. 406-18)

J. P. Simmons, "Edward Coote Pinkney— American Cavalier Poet," in South Atlantic Quarterly, *Vol. XXVIII, No. 4, October, 1929, pp. 406-18.*

FURTHER READING

French, John C. Review of *The Life and Works of Edward*

Coote Pinkney. Modern Language Notes XLII, No. 1 (January 1927): 62-3.

Describes Pinkney's poetry as "narrow in range but mature and finished in workmanship, and notably free from the common faults of youth and provincialism."

Hubbell, Jay B. "Edward Coote Pinkney." In his *The South in American Literature,* pp. 301-04. Durham, N.C.: Duke University Press, 1954.

Considers Pinkney's best poetry to have a "lyric fire that suggests sometimes Shelley and sometimes Lovelace or Herrick."

Hubner, Charles W. "Edward Coate Pinkney." In his *Representative Southern Poets,* pp. 166-76. New York and Washington: The Neale Publishing Company, 1906.

Declares that "as a painter of female loveliness, as a writer of love-lyrics, as an interpreter of the language and dreams of Love, Pinkney stands in the front rank of our singers."

Leggett, William. "Biographical Notice of Edward Coate Pinkney." In *The Rococo: Number Two,* edited by N. P. Willis, pp. 15-16. New York: Morris, Willis and Co., 1844.

Admiring portrait of Pinkney in which the poem "Italy" is called a work of "uncommon sweetness and spirit."

Mabbott, Thomas, and Pleadwell, Frank, eds. "Life of Edward Coote Pinkney." *The Life and Works of Edward Coote Pinkney: A Memoir and Complete Text of His Poems and Literary Prose. Including Much Never Before Published,* pp. 1-92. New York: The MacMillan Company, 1926.

Biographical sketch in which Pinkney is complimented for his "rich and fervid imagination, his command of rhythmic music, and classical elegance of diction."

"The Late Edward C. Pinkney." *New York Mirror, and Ladies' Literary Gazette* V, No. 42 (26 April 1828): 332-34.

Obituary encomium which mourns the loss of "one so high-minded, so honourable, so brave, so lovely, so wise, so accomplished, so unfortunate."

Poe, Edgar Allan. "The Poetic Principle." In *Edgar Allan Poe: Essays and Reviews,* pp. 71-94. New York: The Library of America, 1984.

Passing mention of Pinkney, of whom Poe said it was his "misfortune to have been born too far south. Had he been a New Englander, it is probable that he would have been ranked as the first of American lyrists, by that magnanimous cabal which has so long controlled the destinies of American letters, in conducting the thing called 'The North American Review'."

Review of *The Life and Works of Edward Coote Pinkney. The Saturday Review of Literature* III, No. 19 (4 December 1926): 393-94.

Observes that "with the possible exception of Bryant and Whittier, Edward Coote Pinkney may be accorded the place of the most important poet in America prior to Edgar Allan Poe."

Leopold von Sacher-Masoch

1836?-1895

(Full name Leopold Ritter von Sacher-Masoch) Austrian novelist, short story writer, essayist, historian, and critic.

Sacher-Masoch was a prominent author of novels and short stories espousing liberal social and political ideals; today he is chiefly identified with masochism, the psychosexual condition named for him. The term was introduced in 1893 by the German neurologist Richard von Krafft-Ebing after he learned of Sacher-Masoch's penchant for subjecting himself to domination and abuse by beautiful, imperious women. Krafft-Ebing defined masochism as a sexual perversion characterized by pleasure at being cruelly treated, particularly by a love object. Such relationships recur throughout Sacher-Masoch's work, most notably in the novel *Venus im Pelz* (*Venus in Furs*), which is perhaps the most famous depiction in literature of a masochistic alliance.

Sacher-Masoch was born to the family of a police official in Lemberg, the capitol of Galicia, then a province of the Austro-Hungarian Empire. Although interested in literature and the theater, he complied with his father's wish that he study law, and graduated with a law degree from the University of Prague in 1855. The following year Sacher-Masoch became a history teacher at Karl Franz University in Graz, Austria. In 1857 he published *Der Aufstand in Gent unter Kaiser Karl V,* a historical account of the 1539-42 revolt against Emperor Charles V, but the success in 1858 of his first novel, *Eine Galizische Geschichte,* based on an episode from Galician history, encouraged him to concentrate on writing fiction. In 1860, after two more novels had been favorably received, Sacher-Masoch gave up his university post to pursue a literary career. The next year he met Anna von Kottowitz and with her commenced his first serious masochistic relationship.

Biographers consider an autobiographical essay that Sacher-Masoch published in 1888 to be significant with respect to his sexual preferences. In it he wrote that at the age of ten he witnessed a beautiful relative whom he adored betraying and later flagellating her husband. These events, Sacher-Masoch wrote, made him "aware first of the mysterious affinity between cruelty and lust, and then of the natural enmity and hatred between the sexes which is temporarily overcome by love, only to reappear subsequently with elemental force, turning one of the partners into a hammer and the other into an anvil." Although Sacher-Masoch may have embellished or wholly invented the episode, it is nonetheless revealing, establishing the principal elements of his obsession: psychological and physical abuse of a man by a fur-clad woman in luxurious surroundings. Throughout his life he encountered women who were amenable to his inclinations, and several times he entered into contracts specifying the terms of his subjection. By the age of thirty-five Sacher-Masoch was a

popular author of histories, journalistic essays, and dozens of volumes of fiction. He traveled extensively, living and working abroad, and married twice. Toward the end of his life he underwent periods of mental illness; in a fit of madness he killed a pet kitten and subsequently suffered the delusion that he was being torn to pieces by cats. He had largely recovered his mental equilibrium and was living in Lindheim, Germany, when he died in 1895.

Sacher-Masoch's fiction often draws on the history and folklore of his native region, and almost invariably depicts relationships between subservient men and authoritative women. Most of his fictional works were intended for inclusion in *Das Vermächtnis Kains,* a cycle of novels, novellas, and short stories in which he intended to address prevailing political, economic, social, and moral issues. The series was to be published under the headings *Love, Property, The State, War, Work,* and *Death.* Sacher-Masoch considered corrupt and ineffective governments, rampant militarism, faltering economic systems, and exploitative business and personal relationships some of the chief failings of modern times. His recommendations for reform included a proposed United States of Europe, with a government based on altruism, the abolition of private property, equal rights for women, strong support for the rights of Jews, and tolerance for a wide variety of sexual relationships. Sacher-Masoch's fervently idealistic political philosophy and convictions have been assessed as sincere but naïve. Only the first two volumes of *Das Vermächtnis Kains* were completed, although Sacher-Masoch published numerous works individually that were intended to be grouped later under the remaining four headings. *Venus in Furs*, his most famous work, was first published as part of *Love*, and is considered to be largely a transcription from personal experience. The bulk of the text purports to be the "Memoirs of a Super-Sensualist," in which the protagonist establishes a masochistic contract with a beautiful young woman. Although reluctant at first, she comes to enjoy dispensing the punishment importuned by her lover, whom she ultimately abandons. He concludes that "the treatment was cruel but radical, and the main thing is that I am cured." The formerly abject masochist then announces that woman can be man's slave or his mistress but cannot be his companion as long as the sexes remain unequal in education, employment, and rights.

Contemporaries of Sacher-Masoch did not focus on the pathological or clinical elements of his work, perhaps because, as an anonymous reviewer speculated in 1967, Sacher-Masoch's "splendid viragos and their self-sacrificing worshippers fitted into the folk traditions of the Austro-Hungarian Empire"; further, the themes of will and power featured in these works were in accord with the Nietzschean and Darwinian thought current in much of nineteenth-century European culture. Twentieth-century commentators are primarily concerned with whether Sacher-Masoch's works deserve consideration as literature or as clinical documents of a pathological obsession. While some maintain that his novels are of high literary quality, others argue that they are stylistically unremarkable expressions of his personal pathology, and issues of aberrant sexuality remain central to most discussions of Sacher-Masoch and his works.

PRINCIPAL WORKS

Der Aufstand in Gent unter Kaiser Karl V (history) 1857
Eine Galizische Geschichte (novel) 1858
Graf Donski (novel) 1859
Der Emissar (novel) 1860
Ungarns Untergang und Maria von Österreich (history) 1862
Falscher Hermelin (short stories) 1863
Don Juan von Kolomea (novel) 1864
Der letzte König der Magyaren (history) 1867
Die Geschiedene Frau (Passionsgeschichte eines Idealisten) (novel) 1870
* *Der Wanderer* (preface) 1870
* *Der Kapitulant* (novel) 1870
* *Mondnacht* (novel) 1870
† *Die Liebe des Plato* (novel) 1870
† *Venus im Pelz* (novel) 1870
   [*Venus in Furs*, 1921]
† *Marzella* (novel) 1870
Über den wert der Kritik (criticism) 1873
‡ *Volksgericht* (novel) 1874

‡ *Der Hajdamak* (novel) 1874
‡ *Hasara Raba* (novel) 1874
‡ *Das Testament* (novel) 1874
‡ *Basil Hymen* (novel) 1874
‡ *Das Paradies am Dniester* (novel) 1874
Der neue Hiob (novel) 1876
   [*The New Job*, 1891]
Falscher Hermelin (short stories) 1879
Die Aesthetik des Hässlichen (essay) 1880
Basyl der Schatzgräber und andere seltsame geschichten (short stories) 1880
Der Ilau (novel) 1882
Das Schwartze Kabinett (novel) 1882
Zwei Soireen der Eremitage und Diderot in Petersburg (novellas) 1886
Die Schlange im Paradiese (novel) 1890
Jüdischen Leben in Wort und Bild (short stories) 1891
   [*Jewish Tales*, 1894]
Grausame Frauen (short stories) 1901
Contes et romans. 3 vols. (short stories and novels) 1968

*These works were published as *Das Vermächtnis Kains. Erster Teil. Die Liebe, Band I* in 1870.

†These works were published as *Das Vermächtnis Kains. Erster Teil. Der Liebe, Band II* in 1870.

‡These works were published as *Das Vermächtnis Kains. Zweiter Teil. Das Eigentum* in 1874.

Leopold von Sacher-Masoch   (essay date 1888)

[*In the following essay, Sacher-Masoch recounts the childhood episode that established for him the ideal of the beautiful, imperious woman that dominated his fiction and his life.*]

Whether she is a princess or a peasant girl, whether she is clad in ermine or sheepskin, she is always the same woman: she wears furs, she wields a whip, she treats men as slaves and she is both my creation and the true Sarmatian woman.

I believe that every artistic creation develops in the same way that this Sarmatian woman took shape in my imagination. First there is the innate tendency common to all of us to capture a subject that has eluded most other artists; then the author's own experience intervenes and provides him with the living being whose prototype already exists in his imagination. This figure preoccupies him, seduces him, captivates him, because it corresponds to his innate tendencies and mirrors his particular nature; he then transforms it and gives it body and soul. Finally, in the reality which he has transformed into a work of art, he encounters the problem that is the source of all subsequent images. The inverse path that leads from the problem back to the configuration is not an artistic one.

When I was still a child I showed a predilection for the 'cruel' in fiction; reading this type of story would send shivers through me and produce lustful feelings. And yet I was a compassionate soul who would not have hurt a fly. I would sit in a dark secluded corner of my great-aunt's house, devouring the legends of the Saints; I was plunged into a state of feverish excitement on reading about the torments suffered by the martyrs.

At the age of ten I already had an ideal woman. I yearned for a distant relative of my father's—let us call her Countess Zenobia—the most beautiful and also the most promiscuous woman in the country.

It happened on a Sunday afternoon; I shall never forget it. I had come to play with the children of my aunt-in-law—as we called her—and we were left alone with the maid. Suddenly the countess, proud and resplendent in her great sable cloak, entered the room, greeted us, kissed me (which always sent me into raptures) and then exclaimed: 'Come, Leopold, I want you to help me off with my furs.' She did not have to ask me twice. I followed her into her bedroom, took off the heavy furs that I could barely lift, and helped her into the magnificent green velvet jacket trimmed with squirrel that she wore about the house. I then knelt to put on her gold-embroidered slippers. On feeling her tiny feet in my hands I forgot myself and kissed them passionately. At first my aunt stared at me in surprise, then she burst out laughing and gave me a little kick.

While she was preparing our tea we played hide-and-seek; I do not know what devil prompted me to hide in my aunt's bedroom. As I stood concealed behind a clothes-rack, I heard the doorbell and a few moments later my aunt entered the bedroom followed by a handsome young man. She closed the door without locking it and drew her lover into her arms.

I did not understand what they were saying, still less what they were doing, but my heart began to pound, for I was acutely aware of my situation: if they discovered me I would be taken for a spy. Overcome by dread, I closed my eyes and blocked my ears. I was about to betray my presence by sneezing, when suddenly the door was flung open and my aunt's husband rushed into the room accompanied by two friends. His face was crimson and his eyes flashed with anger. But as he hesitated for a moment, wondering no doubt which of the two lovers to strike first, Zenobia anticipated him.

Without a word, she rose, strode up to her husband and gave him an energetic punch on the nose. He staggered; blood was pouring from his nose and mouth. But my aunt was still not satisfied; she picked up a whip and, brandishing it, showed my uncle and his friends the door. The gentlemen were only too glad to slip away, and not last, among them, the young admirer. At that moment the wretched clothes-rack fell to the ground and all the fury of Madame Zenobia was poured out on me: 'So you were hiding, were you? I shall teach you to play at spying.'

I tried in vain to explain my presence, but in a trice she had seized me by the hair and thrown me on the carpet; she then placed her knee on my shoulder and began to whip me vigorously. I clenched my teeth but could not prevent the tears from springing to my eyes. And yet I must admit that while I writhed under my aunt's cruel blows, I experienced acute pleasure. No doubt her husband had more than once enjoyed a similar sensation, for

soon he returned to her room, not as an avenger but as a humble slave; it was he who fell down at the feet of the treacherous woman and begged her pardon, while she pushed him away with her foot. Then they locked the door. This time I was not ashamed, and did not block my ears, but listened attentively at the door—either from spite or childish jealousy—and again I heard the crack of the whip that I had tasted only a moment before.

This event became engraved on my soul as with a red-hot iron; I did not understand at the time how this woman in voluptuous furs could betray her husband and maltreat him afterwards, but I both hated and loved the creature who seemed destined, by virtue of her strength and diabolical beauty, to place her foot insolently on the neck of humanity.

Subsequently other strange scenes, other figures, in regal ermine, in bourgeois rabbit fur, or in rustic lamb's fleece, produced new impressions on me; until one day this particular type of woman became crystallized in my mind, and took definite shape for the first time in the heroine of *The Emissary*.

Much later I isolated the problem that inspired the novel *Venus in Furs.* I became aware first of the mysterious affinity between cruelty and lust, and then of the natural enmity and hatred between the sexes which is temporarily overcome by love, only to reappear subsequently with elemental force, turning one of the partners into a hammer and the other into an anvil. (pp. 231-33)

> *Leopold von Sacher-Masoch, "A Childhood Memory and Reflections on the Novel," in* Masochism *by Gilles Deleuze and Leopold von Sacher-Masoch, translated by Jean McNeil, Zone Books, 1989, pp. 273-76.*

Harriet Lieber Cohen   (essay date 1894)

[*In the following excerpt from her introduction to* Jewish Tales, *Cohen commends Sacher-Masoch's literary artistry and the moral standpoint exhibited in the stories.*]

Owing to the fact that the Israelite has become a citizen of the nation in which he is born, he has insensibly fallen under its influence, adopted its customs, conformed to its manners, and though some of his racial peculiarities still resist the onslaught of time and circumstance, the old Jewish family life and the curious life of the Ghetto is now nothing more than a poetic remembrance.

To find again the old-time Israelite with his Biblical characteristics, his naïve superstitions, romantic legends, and strong attachment to the ancient patriarchal life, we must seek him in the villages and very small towns of the East, in Alsace, Germany, Austria, Poland, even in England and Spain; in other words, we would seek him in vain in the cities.

In these quiet, out-of-the-way villages has Sacher-Masoch, united to the Jew by no tie of creed, found material for his *Jewish Tales.* It is here he has discovered the types which inspired these little prose poems. Racy, piquant, spirited, crowded with striking contrasts, replete with dialogue, now bright and comic, now grave and serious, they follow rigorously the lines of truth.

Sacher-Masoch excels in warmth and movement. He traces his pictures as though with the point of a needle; and yet sensation crowds upon sensation, there is always room on the canvas for more figures, and the unexpected is forever happening. These tales are marked from first to last with the author's vigorous, brilliant style; they are evidence of his intellectual humor, his poetic penetration, his nervous strength, his personal mode, his striking originality, and his gentle philosophy with its gay, generous qualities, its fleeting shade of pessimism.

The work imposes itself upon us from its moral as well as its literary standpoint, and must unquestionably take high rank as one of the most original and artistic productions of the day. (pp. vi-viii)

> Harriet Lieber Cohen, in a preface to Jewish Tales *by Leopold von Sacher-Masoch, translated by Harriet Lieber Cohen, A. C. McClurg and Company, 1894, pp. v-viii.*

The Bookman, New York   (essay date 1896)

[*In the following excerpt, the reviewer surveys Sacher-Masoch's works, focusing on the uncompleted Legacy of Cain novel series.*]

Although he wrote verse and several dramas that were successfully produced in Austria and Germany, Sacher-Masoch's best work was done as a novelist, but even more especially as a writer of short stories. No recent writer, however, has produced work so unequal in quality. Much of it is not only relatively good, but it is full of purpose, fresh, vigorous and virile. Some of it, on the other hand, is but the ill-turned-out product of a literary slop-shop, unworthy of any serious attention at all, and this apparently not because there were material reasons for desiring to turn poor literature into good money, for Sacher-Masoch seems to have had enough of the goods of the world to keep the pot boiling without it.

His material Sacher-Masoch has chosen from various places. He has written dubious historical novels of the Court of Maria Theresa, and several of his works are collections of short stories of low phases of high life in Vienna, French in intention, but in the German, in which they are written, plump and utterly devoid of the *espièglerie* ["mischievousness"] that in the case of this sort of writing is the only excuse for its being. Fortunately for him, the author had a better source of supply nearer at home in the Little-Russian life that was his own by birth and education. It is here that he has done by all odds his best and most distinctive work. He has, in fact, opened up a new world to us, and one thus far almost wholly his own; a world, to be sure, seen in some of its aspects in Turgénieff and Tolstoy, but yet here under different lights and with different colours. It is the same "melancholy Slavonic world," the gloomy landscape of steppe and forest, but it is here a people whose blood surges with Oriental heat; a world of men and women as untamed in their passions as wild animals, and as eager to gratify them; who neither spare nor are spared, nor expect to be spared. If, as Sacher-Masoch says, these are the Slavs "to whom the near future as unquestionably belongs as does to the Germanic race the present," then may Heaven have mercy upon the future, for here is a folk that knows not forbearance in its faintest promptings. As to the inherent truth of his pictures, they do not leave one in doubt. There is in his evolution of plot often an unmistakable romanticism, but it is carried out in detail with a realism not seldom offensive. In his mental attitude toward his material the same pessimism so characteristic of Turgénieff is even more apparent in Sacher-Masoch. It is the Slavonic birthright of the one as well as the other, and not a matter of individual temperament. Both of these men are faithful disciples of Schopenhauer, our author assertively so; but they are that primarily not because of the philosopher, but because of themselves. His German critics, with sweetness and light, have called him a pessimist, a cynic, a Panslavist, and a nihilist, and I have no doubt but that confirmation may be found in his books for all these several indictments.

What has generally been regarded as Sacher-Masoch's best work is in the cycle of stories called by the common name of The Legacy of Cain, the first part of which was written in 1870. This first part was received in Germany with a storm of critical abuse, which the subsequent parts, however, mollified, and the whole, as far as it was ever completed, even received at the end from many quarters an extravagant praise. The author himself had no mean opinion of it. In a little work on the **Value of Criticism** (1873), which shows pretty conclusively, among other things, the valuelessness of his own, he modestly says that the first story of the cycle, **Don Juan of Kolomea,** "caused a sensation such as no literary work has caused in Germany since *Werther* . . . . The overwhelming originality of the entire composition and the manner of its presentation took the whole reading public at once by storm." And this of his own work, too!

The Legacy of Cain (Das Vermächtniss Kains), according to the author's own characterisation of its purpose, is intended to illustrate the universal struggle for existence in the whole field of human activity. Its entire conception is robust and original. The beginning is in the form of an epilogue. A sportsman, who has brought down an eagle with a shot of his rifle, is suddenly greeted with the cry of "Cain, Cain," and a "Wanderer," the member of a Russian sect whose members flee the world to lead an ascetic life in the forest, confronts him with the dead bird. "What have you gained by this?" he asks sternly. "You, too, are of the race of Cain." "Break loose," he warns him, "from the legacy of Cain; learn to know truth; learn to renounce; learn to despise life and love death." "These six, Love, Property, the State, War, Work, and Death are the legacy of Cain, who slew his brother; and his brother's blood cried unto Heaven, and the Lord spoke to Cain: Thou shalt be cursed upon the earth, a fugitive and a vagabond." The words of the "Wanderer" in the prologue thus present the great problems of humanity which it is the purpose of the whole cycle of this "novelistic theodicy," as it has been characterised both by the author and by his critics, to solve. Each problem, furthermore, was, according to the plan, to consist of a series of six stories. The first five of these were intended to illustrate the rule, to exhibit, in other words, the reality as it is in life. The last, on the contrary, was to contain the exception, and to present the ideal to be striven for. The completed whole was thus to furnish an harmonious solution of the manifold dissonances of human life, whatever their kind. It is a matter for regret, for The Legacy of Cain, with all its idiosyncrasies, has always the unquestioned element of strength, that it remained but a torso. *Love* and *Property* were the only parts ever completed, although opportunity was found in superabundance for work that is not worth reading, and assuredly was not worth writing.

Sacher-Masoch's whole problem, as he presents it in The Legacy of Cain, is a union of Schopenhauer and Darwin, as he himself, in the tract on criticism, already mentioned, carefully points out. Its fundamental ideas are as follows: This world in which we live is not the best possible, but rather the worst possible. Nature and man alike are inherently bad. In the air, in the water, and on the earth all animate and inanimate nature is continuing uninterruptedly the struggle for existence. Man, in particular, wages an unceasing warfare with his surroundings. Every member of this unhappy race, too, seeks to live at the expense of the other, ceaselessly striving, like Cain, to murder his brother, to rob him, to make him his slave. Man, however, does not remain in his original bestial condition. By the development of his soul and his intellect he lifts himself gradually above it, conquers it, and in the struggles of centuries makes himself more and more its master. Neither does he rest here. Not only does he make nature serviceable to him, but under his influence nature itself changes and becomes less and less his enemy. In the first part, *Love,* the author seeks to solve the problem of the sexes. The first five stories—*Don Juan of Kolomea, The Capitulant, A Moonlight Night, Plato, Venus in Furs*—represent the various phases, healthy and morbid, of what is, from his point of view, the natural hostile opposition of the sexes, the struggle of man and woman for existence. He has filled out the details of the picture with a terrible reality, more terrible because it bears the evident stamp of truth. Love may be joined, upon the one hand, with true affection, with poetic fancy, with spiritual sympathy, or it may be accompanied, on the other, with malevolent lust. The heartless "Venus" of the last story in this way knouts the man who madly loves her as he cringes like a dog at her feet, and he feels a physical enjoyment in the smart of her blows! It is, in fact, because of the physico-psychological motive of this curious book that specialists in neurology have given the name "masochism" to one of the recognised forms of sexual perversity. The last story of the cycle, *Marzella; or, The Fairy Tale of Love,* the ideal as an offset to the real, is, from the nature of the case, the weakest, in its execution, of all. Woman, the daughter of Cain, is by man raised spiritually to his own level. She hurls from her the ointment with which she has anointed his feet and the knout with which she has scourged his back. Man has here lifted himself above nature, and with him woman. He still serves nature, but nature also serves him. He perpetuates the race and continues the great work of civilisation in that he not merely brings up his children, but gives them the impress of his own spirit. Like a new

Prometheus, says the author, he sits at the sacred hearthstone of his family and forms men.

The second part of Sacher-Masoch's theodicy continues on the same lines an investigation of the problem of *Property.* The story of the eternal warfare between the rich and the poor is told, as before, in five tales—*The Folk Tribunal, The Hajdamak, Hasara Raba, A Will, Basil Hymen.* An ideal solution is contained in the sixth, *The Paradise on the Dniester,* where a better Tolstoy deserts his home to live among the people and found an ideal state whose basis is labour. It is here that the author's Panslavistic tendencies come most distinctly into the foreground. It is the Slav who is to bring about this regeneration of the human race. Here his prose epic ends, unfortunately, for however we may agree with the fundamental statement of his problem, or his manner of solving it, his evident seriousness of purpose must, at the outset, command respect. There is no question of its value as a series of pictures of the lights and shadows of the life of a little-known corner of the world, and there can scarcely be but a single opinion as to the graphic power of the painter who has made them. If the fancy is at times too glowing, the depicted passions too unrestrained in their appeal to a Western imagination, it is the environment at fault that has produced them.

Sacher-Masoch has done in some ways even better work in *Der neue Hiob* (*The Modern Job,* 1874), in which his field is, as before, his own Little-Russia. This story, particularly, shows undeveloped possibilities. The author's earlier impetuosity has been brought under a restraint that cannot but be felt to be more salutary, and his point of view of life and society has been bettered by a maturer experience. If his touch is truer, it is not, however, the less brilliant. *The Modern Job* seems to prove that Sacher-Masoch's best book was never written. (pp. 402-04)

> *W. H. C., "Leopold Sacher-Masoch," in* The Bookman, *New York, Vol. II, No. 5, January, 1896, pp. 401-04.*

The Times Literary Supplement   (essay date 1967)

[*In the following excerpt, the critic maintains that Sacher-Masoch's fiction contains insufficient literary value to be of more than pathological interest.*]

It will come as a surprise to many readers to learn that Sacher-Masoch enjoyed quite a respectable reputation during the second half of the nineteenth century and that the equivocal nature of his subject-matter passed unnoticed, or at least uncommented upon, until Krafft-Ebing used his name to designate a sexual perversion. The explanation is, apparently, that the Gothic quality of his fictions about splendid viragos and their self-sacrificing worshippers fitted into the folk traditions of the Austro-Hungarian Empire, of which Sacher-Masoch was a very cosmopolitan subject. He was born of mixed Spanish, Polish and Bohemian ancestry in Lemberg (Lvov), was brought up by a Ruthenian nurse, educated in German in Prague from the age of twelve and eventually became a professor of history in Gratz before devoting himself to literature. After a very chequered sentimental career, he spent his last years in a state of relative calm in or near Berlin, having—

according to M. Georges-Paul Villa [the editor and translator of Sacher-Masoch's *L'esthétique de la laideur suivi de Diderot à Pétersbourg*]—found emotional equilibrium in his marriage to Hilda Meister, his children's nurse.

M. Villa's thesis is that the satisfactions of Sacher-Masoch's last sexual relationship, like the imaginary situations in his work, contain a general message for the men of today, or at least for some of them. The old dominance of man over women has been upset; let men willingly accept this reversal and they may find peace and contentment under the imperious governance of some splendid female. This situation may not be quite as new as M. Villa implies. The submission of the man to the woman is a still unexplained aspect of courtly love, the characters of Elizabeth I and Catherine the Great have an undying fascination and, in *Alice in Wonderland,* it is the Queen who snaps: "Off with his head!" However, some henpecked husband in the suburbs, mowing the lawn with a delicious sense of obedience, may reflect that he is no figure of fun but a noble archetype. Let him look tremulously on while his Junoesque wife copulates with a muscular paramour; let the gleeful adulterers tie him to the bedstead and whip him between orgasms, and all will be for the best; he will be fulfilled and so will they, and Sacher-Masoch will not have written in vain.

Actually, the message is only as clear as this in *La Vénus à la fourrure* (*Venus im Pelz*), in which the slave-like hero binds himself by contract to a capricious mistress (as Sacher-Masoch did, or tried to do, in real life) and is thankful to be thrashed by her active lover, a vigorous, although somewhat hermaphroditic, Greek. To some extent, the hero arranges this *mise-en-scène* himself and, as with so much writing about sexual fantasy, one wonders if it is not an imaginative, theatrical performance that would not be so enjoyable, were it suddenly translated into genuine, concrete experience. It is not so much the reality of torture that is wanted as a fairly convincing simulation, which will produce the required sexual reaction by allowing the hero to play the various parts simultaneously himself, in his mind more than in actual experience. It follows that the henpecked suburban husband referred to above should have actively encouraged his wife to bully him and should have himself invited in some burly labourer from the nearest building-site; if the humiliation is imposed upon him without his having any say in its arranging, the pleasure will not be the same.

This seems to be the implication of *Diderot à Pétersbourg,* a fantasy about the writer's genuine sojourn at the court of Catherine the Great. According to legend, Diderot was so much at ease with the Empress that he tapped her familiarly on the knee as he made points in discussion. Masoch reverses this situation and presents Diderot as being sexually excited by the terrifying power of Catherine and her closest woman adviser; but when another, strong-armed lover of Catherine tries to murder him, he does not enjoy the danger and is very glad to escape with his life, as any traditional hero would have been. In *L'esthétique de la laideur,* a hunchback painter of genius becomes the happy husband of a dazzlingly beautiful girl, having ousted his strong, handsome, cruel and aristocratic rival. Ob-

viously, the treatment of the erotic triangle varies from story to story, and one would have to read the complete works in chronological sequence to see if there is any intelligible progression from the acceptance of suffering to its conquest. The constants are the triangle itself (handicapped, physically inferior lover; strong, beautiful mistress; cruel second male of great beauty), the presence of suffering (which may, or may not, be joyfully apprehended) and the fetishism of fur on naked flesh, which neither M. Villa nor M. Deleuze [in *Présentation de Sacher-Masoch* (translated in 1971 as *Sacher-Masoch: An Interpretation* and excerpted below)] make much effort to explain, perhaps because they feel that the average, sensual reader will easily think up his own explanations.

On first contact, Masoch is not unlike de Sade, except that he is never explicitly obscene. There is the same sensation of a man writing compulsively out of his obsessions, and the same occasional intrusion of unelaborated philosophical or social ideas. Just as de Sade develops a crazy theory of nature, which is a kind of parody of Rousseauism, so Masoch is sometimes liberal and anti-aristocratic and at other times a feverish admirer of aristocratic haughtiness and beauty. If anything, he has a rather better narrative gift than de Sade and his stories make easy reading as slightly sinister, Germanic folk-tales of moderate literary interest.

Such, it must be admitted, is not the view of M. Deleuze, who sets Masoch alongside de Sade, not only as a "great anthropologist" but also as a "great artist." His long *Présentation* is much more technical than M. Villa's introduction and his main interest is to prove that masochism is not a simple concomitant of sadism, as has so often been assumed, but a complex structure with its own laws. A masochist is not necessarily a sadist as well, nor does he want to be whipped by a sadist; he requires his own kind of torturer. In fact, M. Deleuze rejects the term *sado-masochism* as a "semiological monstrosity" and lists no fewer than eleven ways in which masochism differs fundamentally from sadism. The argument is not always easy for the layman to follow, and it is developed with a wealth of references, not only to Freud but also to Plato, Kant, Klossowski, Lacan and others. Suffice it to say that M. Deleuze reads into Masoch's stories a complex mythology involving Cain and Christ, and a triple series of ritual actions: hunting rites, agricultural rites and rites of regeneration and rebirth. He takes the stories as archetypal dreams, so that, for instance, one short passage in *La Vénus à la fourrure* can be made the basis of an immensely learned commentary about parthenogenesis, the absorption of the uterine mother and the oedipal mother into the glorious oral mother, and so on.

While it is clear that Masoch is clinically interesting, since his unconscious is expressing itself more or less freely, [*La Vénus à la fourrure, Diderot à Pétersbourg,* and *L'esthétique de la laideur*] seem hardly coherent or substantial enough to bear the weight of such an enormous interpretation. In any case, if de Sade and Masoch are to be termed "geniuses"—and M. Deleuze does not hesitate to use the word—it is time their admirers explained in what sense their works are not merely pathological documents but deserve to be considered on the same level, aesthetically, as those of the more traditional literary geniuses. Until this is done. M. Deleuze's encomiums of Masoch must sound as eccentric as M. Gilbert Lély's high claims for de Sade.

"Apologia for the Whipping Boy," in The Times Literary Supplement, *No. 3424, October 12, 1967, p. 962.*

James Cleugh   (essay date 1967)

[*In the following excerpt, Cleugh presents an overview of Sacher-Masoch's principal works.*]

In 1857 the first printed work by Dr Leopold Ritter von Sacher-Masoch, Lecturer in History at the Karl Franz University of Graz, was published by the firm of Schaffhausen. This quite substantial volume was entitled *The Rebellion in Ghent under the Emperor Charles V.* The author, armed with fresh data, had challenged current ideas about this revolt (1539-42) and wrote in a brilliant, antithetical style more suited, perhaps, to fiction than to scholarship. Amateur critics compared him with Macaulay. But his academic colleagues were either grimly silent or briefly contemptuous.

It was known that Leopold was only twenty-one, had a passion for the stage and some wild notions about universal freedom for everyone, such as all youngsters with brains have entertained at one time or another. Nor did the experts, few of whom ever condescended to read novels, approve of the way in which their junior used the German language. This manner repelled them by its fondness for bold generalisation, its lack of ambiguity and qualification and in general its zealous optimism. All these puerile affirmations, the learned declared, derived from Schiller, who was now going out of fashion.

But to modern readers Leopold's narrative, with its short paragraphs and clear touches of realism, seems sober enough. There is no concentration, as might have been expected, on bloody details. But inevitably, though discreetly, the portrait of a beautiful termagant emerges in one passage:

> Kathelyne van Haverbecke, the wife of Wilhelm van der Nampt, a cobbler, made her way to the guildhall of his trade and there gave utterance to provocative and seditious sentiments. She abused certain Government officials, declaring that they should be seized and forced to turn out their moneybags, exclaiming, 'Now the rat's in the trap!' She proceeded to do her best to persuade those present, especially the younger men, to join the revolt. Those whom her sharp tongue could not convince she ensnared in the shining meshes of her luxuriant hair and went so far as to alternate her invectives and face-slappings with affectionately smiling and admiring glances, fondly caressing handclasps and kisses. Those who declined to acknowledge the imperious power of the Flemish spirit in Kathelyne were subdued by the glory of the Flemish physique.

This kind of thing annoyed the literary authorities of 1857. But the acclamation of less exalted circles was encouraging. Nevertheless, Leopold came to the conclusion, for the time being, that he had better give up the ungrateful task of trying to put life into the dry bones of history. His colleagues seemed to like it dry. For one of their complaints was that in his work the apparatus of erudition did not extend to more than a few notes of French and Latin sources. The impatience of the budding scholar with this pettifogging pedantry led him to devote his talents for a while to more purely imaginative efforts.

He looked back, for the setting, first to the days of his childhood in Lemberg . . . and to the strange inhabitants, Jews, Slavs or mixtures of the two, of the Galician countryside. (pp. 20-2)

His study of [Galician history and folklore] was prolonged. But he began to exploit his researches in 1858 with the publication, at first anonymous, of *A Galician Tale,* dealing with the revolt of 1846. This was his first experiment in mingling history with fiction. It sold very much better than *The Rebellion in Ghent.* The hero, a Jew named Isaac Mendel, is represented as the prime mover of the insurrection, after he had been forced to give up his beautiful wife Malke to an old Austrian cavalry officer. The Jew, as is usual in Sacher-Masoch's stories, is a sympathetic character. But both the Polish rebels and the Polish peasants who support the Austrian Government are brutal. The realism in this respect, unsurpassed in German literature of the day, and the objectivity of the author is not playing down the bestiality of the Polish tenant farmers and labourers who attacked their landlords and thus assisted the imperial forces, shocked the more conventional critics. But ordinary Austrian readers eagerly absorbed accounts of atrocities related on a much higher literary level than that of the novelettes on the same subject which had been on the market for the last ten years. Leopold did not reach, with this book, the heights he was afterwards to attain. But it assured him a certain reputation as a novelist to be watched.

In 1859 he issued a further work of this kind, *Count Donski,* concerned with the same theme. This effort was a technical advance on *A Galician Tale* and is on the whole more readable today, though still not much above the local fashion of its period in historical romance. The heroine, a boisterous amazon who inspires the rebellious Polish nobles, is called Wanda. This was Leopold's favourite feminine Christian name for a Slav. He uses it again for the 'Venus in furs' of his key novel bearing that title and first issued in 1870. He also insisted on applying the name Wanda to his first wife, though she wasn't a Slav at all and the very reverse, in fact, of a hard-riding, authoritarian aristocrat.

The Emissary of 1860, however, is rather more ambitious than the first two stories. It is largely a study of a character resembling his aunt Zenobia in the setting of the Viennese insurrection of 1848. An Austrian named Burg and a Pole named Roman are rivals for the hand of a lady named Karola. (pp. 23-4)

[The] underlying theme of the novel [is] the feasibility of

coexistence for Pole and Austrian. . . . The contrast between them is rather like that between Cavalier and Puritan in the English civil war. The gallant, reckless and romantic sportsman confronts the inflexible moralist for whom public law and order, abstract justice, take precedence over private sentiment and self-indulgence. (p. 25)

This intricately plotted and dexterously developed novel, full of vivid scenes and striking phrases, puts the reader on terms at once with the author's chief interests, intellectual, emotional and physical. Sacher-Masoch judges the Polish-Austrian dispute quite impartially, recognising both the virtues and the faults on each side. Roman and Waleska are as sympathetically treated as Burg and Karola. Leopold's awe of sinister but voluptuous females, especially if Polish, and his respect for male chivalry and courage wherever he finds them are also conspicuous. (p. 26)

Hungary's Decline and Maria of Austria, a purely historical study, had been published [in 1862] and caused some stir in literary circles. The style remained new at the period for this sort of work, consisting again of short, pungent paragraphs resembling the notes of a lecturer, but this time one whose imaginative realism far outstripped the average don's. The content, too, was exciting, being in the first place an account of the regeneration of a lazy and precociously debauched child, Ludwig II, who had succeeded to the throne of Hungary in 1516, into the tragic figure of a national hero left by the rest of Europe and traitors in his own country to face alone the formidable power of the Sultan of Turkey, Suleiman the Magnificent, leader of an Islam then intent upon the conquest of Europe.

Leopold's basic obsession appears in his reading of the character of Maria, Ludwig's wife, whom he married in 1522, when they were both still teenagers. A younger sister of Charles V, she is here represented as an expert in history, politics, science and art, a beauty of strong character who entirely dominated Ludwig. She crushed the plans of rebellious Hungarian magnates, executed a *coup d'état* and could only be dissuaded with great difficulty from joining her husband on the fatal field of Mohacs (1526) where the small, ill-equipped Hungarian army was utterly annihilated by the Turks and the king himself perished. Nor does the author forget to mention the subordination of the mighty Suleiman himself to his favourite female slave, Kasseki Kourem. Leopold was the very man to call the attention of conventional historians of the day to the still grossly underestimated influence of women in sixteenth century politics and administration.

But the chief importance of this book for its author in the eighteen-sixties was to accord him the respect of editors and publishers as something more than a purveyor of daringly vivid fiction. They suddenly became accessible to almost anything he cared to write. They were delighted with the twenty-five short stories of theatrical life which appeared as a collection in 1863 under the highly significant title of *Imitation Ermine.* This volume . . . was still being reprinted ten years later. (pp. 33-4)

Apart from ephemeral journalism which, as usual, paid best, [during the years 1862-66 Sacher-Masoch wrote] a number of tales in which the characters struggled not only against others and their environment, as had been the rule in European fiction of the previous generation, but also with their more or less secret selves. This was particularly the case with the sovereigns and courtiers depicted in *Hungary's Decline.* But in *Imitation Ermine* and many other stories he knew both the settings and the inner conflicts at first hand. So they had an especially vivid realism. In the Galician narratives particularly a strangeness was presented that differentiated them altogether from novels and short stories by other hands.

Readers were astonished by the fierce energy of Sacher-Masoch's Slav heroines. Those of Dostoievsky were still little known in Central Europe. In any case Leopold's 'female demons' were placed, not in any familiar urban environment, but most often in the wild and melancholy landscape of the Carpathian foothills, inhabited by an exotic race, half barbarous, half unexpectedly sophisticated, by turns dreamy and shockingly eruptive. They were experts in and even constantly concerned with the dark side of life. They could be imagined as furious egotists roaming the nightmare kingdoms of folly, passion and vice.

The younger set in Graz discussed these works excitedly. The older people, apart from editors, publishers, agents and booksellers, who detected their appeal to the unsophisticated masses, were less interested. They could see no depth, little but sensation-mongering, in these accounts—written, to be sure, from the Austrian standpoint—of the extravagantly crude behaviour of semi-savages. The author, however, was even then engaged upon compositions which were to compel the attention of professed intellectuals.

The novel *Don Juan of Kolomea* (Kolomea was a village not far to the south-east of Lemberg) strikes a modern reader, allowing for the idiom of the day, as greatly superior to the contemporary literary provender for maidservants and footmen. The tale, first published separately in 1864, . . . has a gripping atmosphere and memorable characters. The dialogue is natural and the social indignation discreetly muted. (pp. 42-3)

Leopold followed *Don Juan of Kolomea* with *The Separated Wife,* a novel which appeared in 1865 and concerned the relations of a super-woman, Frau von Kossov, who closely resembles [Sacher-Masoch's mistress] Anna von Kottowitz, with a man, who closely resembles the author himself, whom she dominated physically, though he was her intellectual and spiritual superior. Here Leopold develops his views of the sexual problem even more elaborately than in *Don Juan of Kolomea.* For the protagonists are no longer regional 'semi-savages' but highly sophisticated urban people. The heroine grows from a delightful and mysterious plaything, who would have pleased 'Don Juan', into a purely cerebral force of destruction.

Although the fully mature woman, according to Sacher-Masoch, is an egotist of so unadulterated a type that she can practically do without a mind, the primitive will in her to psychological aggression and tyranny acts only too effectively in the place of planned calculation. As a poet, he was attracted by a certain barbaric splendour, 'beyond good and evil', in this behaviour. A few years later the more truly philosophic mentality of Nietzsche was to perceive that subversion, wrath and denial, though he regarded them as specifically male characteristics, might be accompanied by beneficence, creation and affirmation. Leopold personally, in his most engrossing sexual experience, had already come to the same conclusion. To put it crudely, when Anna von Kottowitz turned him upside down and inside out, he felt all the better for it.

The Separated Wife, nevertheless, proves that in spite of his deep appreciation of feminine power, equated in his judgment with typical feminine beauty, he would never for a moment admit that any woman could be his intellectual equal. Conqueror in the fields of volition and physical energy, she cannot even be a competitor, he insists, in the terrains of imagination and logic. She can release them to perform their functions, like a princess smashing a bottle of champagne over the stern of a battleship, which then slides away, in all its glory, to seas she will never know. But once she has performed her symbolic gesture it is an impertinence for her to pretend any further interest in the launched career. (pp. 49-50)

The Separated Wife, though much longer and more elaborate than *Don Juan of Kolomea* and generally regarded as the author's first major work, is on the whole inferior as literature to *Don Juan.* Individual scenes are vivid and exciting, being so often direct transcriptions from personal experience. But in spite of some fine, even noble, passages of social criticism, the general tone repeatedly descends to shrill melodrama and the indulgent humour of *Don Juan* is almost entirely absent. The overall impression is therefore uneven. The author was not yet mature enough and the events which inspired the book were still too near to him to be recollected without a peevish and self-righteous manipulation. The difference between *The Separated Wife* and the masterpiece which he was then already beginning, *Venus in Furs,* though both novels were closely based on personal adventures, is strikingly in favour of the latter.

The unusual combination in the former work of genuine chastity with intense sensuality was highly praised by professional critics. But they were not slow to point out inconsistencies and exaggerations. The Austrian poet Robert Hamerling (1830-1889) wrote in a private letter to Leopold dated the 14th February 1870, by which time *The Separated Wife* was being read all over Central Europe:

> I'm afraid people are going to say that your attempt to delineate an admirable male character hasn't quite succeeded. Your heroine says to your hero: 'When I've had enough of you, and I shall soon get bored with you as I do with everyone else, I'll literally kick you out. I've sent more than one man to his death. I've contravened every earthly and divine law. I'm a devil who sees nothing in this world but a hunting-ground!' The hero nevertheless affirms: 'I beheld my ideal stand before me in the flesh!'
>
> That such a female should always have been the allegedly noble and morally exalted hero's ideal is necessarily prejudicial to his character. Why can't you ever write a love-scene without referring to the lady kicking her suitor, any more

than you can imagine a beautiful woman without a fur jacket?

Hamerling goes on to suggest that there is a happy medium between all-too-masculine Teutonic husbands and all-too-feminine Slav ones (like Julian and Sacher-Masoch, he implies). And actually, says Hamerling, the 'devilish' Anna von Kossov is often found, even by Julian himself, not to live up to his infernal ideal. She is repeatedly shown as feeble and relenting. The judgment in his letter seems reasonable enough. Leopold was mixing up what he had observed in Anna von Kottowitz, a real and very typical woman, with what he wanted to present in his fictional character of a female demon incarnate. He couldn't make up his mind between the two and the result in the book is to render Anna von Kossov incredible as either.

He could indeed give a lighter turn to these ideas. For he delighted in farcical situations, though, like most East Europeans, he lacked the kind of humour specifically associated with the West. About the year 1860 he had written a short historical novel called *Kaunitz,* eventually published in 1865. It is hardly one of his best, if by no means negligible. He afterwards based one of his comedies, *The Verses of Frederick the Great* (1864) on the plot of *Kaunitz,* which is the name of a real person, a former Austrian ambassador in Paris, Prince Wenzel Anton von Kaunitz-Rietburg (1771-1794), who once tried to get Louis XV to combine with Austria against Prussia. The French king, in the story and in the play, is ruled by his autocratic mistress, Madame de Pompadour. Frederick had permitted himself to be satirical in verse about this typical 'masochistic' liaison. Kaunitz, by applying to the lady, was therefore enabled to reverse traditional French policy and arrange the alliance against the indiscreet royal poet. In the novel the tale is told by Leopold almost wholly through lively dialogue, with fine appreciation of the ironic features of the situation. But his sympathy with the supine Louis is also very evident.

Yet the four years with Anna von Kottowitz, mentally abject as she was, with all her superb carnality, had stimulated her lover to embark on more ambitious projects than accounts of vindictive mistresses, temperamental actresses, despotic queens and Slav viragos, to more, even, than comedies and an exposition in fiction of the view of women to which his name afterwards became attached. It was towards the end of the period of Anna's influence that he came to conceive his *magnum opus,* at which, like Goethe, he was to work, on and off, for most of his life, but which, unlike Goethe, he was never to finish.

The Legacy of Cain was planned as a vast work, in six parts, to be nothing less than a complete diagnosis of what the author felt to be the contemporary sickness of society and a statement of the only possible remedy for it. Part One was eventually published, complete, in 1870 under the title *Love.* All the other parts remained fragmentary for the time being. But Part Two, called *Property,* was finished three years later and issued in 1874. The remaining four Parts were to have been named respectively *The State, War, Work* and *Death.*

Love contains six stories, of which the first, *The Wanderer,* forms a sort of prologue, to prepare the reader's mind for a new attitude to sex relations. The rest expounded this standpoint under various aspects, including homosexuality and monogamy. . . . [The] best of them, the almost world-famous *Venus in Furs,* though begun under the aegis of Anna, owed more to the inspiration of a subsequent mistress, who didn't last so long but had a stronger character and a more acute intelligence. She therefore understood the author better. (pp. 53-5)

[*Venus in Furs* was published in 1870] as one of the six narratives in Part One, entitled *Love,* of The Legacy of Cain. The other five, which came out with it, were called respectively *The Wanderer, The Man of Surrenders, Moonlight Night, Plato's Love* and *Marzella.* The volume, issued by the firm of Cotta at Stuttgart, also contained a reprint of the earlier *Don Juan of Kolomea* (1864).

Meanwhile the house of Paul Kormann at Leipzig had brought out *The Diary of a Cosmopolitan,* a collection of mainly humorous anecdotes, thirty-four in all. None exceeded an average of two thousand words. One, however, was entitled **'Platonic Love'** and reappeared at greater length, with certain additions and changes of development, in The Legacy of Cain, Part One, as *Plato's Love.* The shorter tale relates how Henryk, a young homosexual, receives a letter from a person claiming to share his tastes, naming himself as Anatol and inviting the other to meet him in a darkened room. But Anatol then turns out to be a woman in male dress. At a second meeting the girl receives the youthful invert in feminine clothing and they agree to differ and part.

The Wanderer constitutes a sombrely eloquent prologue to the grand design of The Legacy. The style is modelled consciously on that of Turgenev (1818-1883), whom Sacher-Masoch afterwards came to dislike, feeling that the Russian master was being unfairly regarded by contemporaries as superior to himself. The chief character is a saintly hermit belonging to a Russian mystical sect, who censures the narrator's companion for shooting an eagle and compares him with Cain. For men and women, says the hermit, are worse than brutes and implacably opposed to each other in their so-called loves. Their institutions of property, the nation-state and war are all bad. Only work and the peace of death are good. The sole proper object of worship by humanity is Darwinian 'Nature', which eventually produced the human wolves or lambs—there are no others—by whom we are now surrounded.

This exposition of pessimistic pantheism is followed by the reprinted *Don Juan of Kolomea,* which glorifies the frank common sense, especially about marriage, of the Russian peasant at the expense of the tortuously minded, romantic Pole. The hero, neglected by his wife after the birth of their first child—a perfectly natural reaction, he maintains—turns elsewhere for sexual satisfaction, but continues to love his wife, so much so that when he catches her with a lover he magnanimously shoots in the air at the subsequent duel. He goes on living with his wife for the sake of the children but spends most of his time with other women, making no secret of it to anybody.

The Man of Surrenders is a veteran who has voluntarily done far more military service than he is obliged to. He too, like the 'Wanderer', is a pessimistic atheist, and like 'Don Juan' had been betrayed by his wife and done nothing about it, though she had gone to live with the local squire, a Pole, and is behaving there like a sultana. Yet during the revolt of 1846 the hero saves the squire from being lynched by his tenants. The story ends with 'The Man of Surrenders' allowing his former wife, who is now married to the squire, to cross the frontier into Austrian territory, though she has no passport. The moral of this tale is throughout a passionate affirmation of the right to absolute personal freedom.

Moonlight Night is more sentimental and melodramatic. A strayed hunter seeks hospitality for the night at a country house. His bedroom is invaded by his hostess, who is apparently sleepwalking. She tells him the tragic story of her life, how her shy, awkward tutor loved her and died of consumption, how she married a tough little squire, to whom she was cruel, then began to love him when she had already antagonised him by her behaviour. He didn't respond, so she took an intellectual lover, who shot himself on being challenged by the husband. The merits of this piece lie less in the somewhat banal plot than in the treatment, which is wonderfully poetic in the evocation of the weird atmosphere of the interview between the traveller and his ghostlike hostess in the moonlit bedroom. The whole story is much more readable than any brief summary can indicate.

In *Plato's Love,* the weighty elaboration and recasting of the previous sketch (**'Platonic Love'**) in *The Diary of a Cosmopolitan,* an ironical turn is given to the theme by emphasising the contrast between the masquerading 'Anatol', at bottom a cheery cynic of a girl, rather like some of Shaw's heroines, and the priggish Henryk, the intense, high-minded young invert, who eventually tells 'Anatol' when she receives him in her true character as a woman, that she has 'ruined his ideal'. But all the same he marries her six years later when she has become a widow, only to desert her once more in favour of a solemn German homosexual named Schuster who had once rescued him from a brothel. Sacher-Masoch's ingrained heterosexuality, which he carried, indeed, to excess, always made him in the end pitiless to inverts, though he could not help being fascinated by their frequently exalted sensitivity. Henryk is the victim of subtle ridicule throughout this mainly humorous if often tenderly sympathetic account of his misadventures.

Marzella describes how a sophisticated Count decides to train a peasant girl of that name to develop the qualities he considers ideal in a wife. But she proves not too easy to deal with, being still in love with a dead suitor. There are long arguments between the Count and Leopold himself—in his own person—about what wives should and should not be allowed to do and also discussions of 'progress' and atheism with the girl's father. Then Marzella comes round and marries the Count. Many years later she has grown into an energetic pro-Austrian Countess who tussles with the rebellious Polish peasants of 1863, flogs a servant for being cruel to a caged vulture, writes frantically passionate letters to her husband and comments learnedly on Turgenev, Darwin and the English historian Henry Thomas Buckle (1821-1862). This 'idyll of happiness', as the author calls it, must be pronounced a failure. It is much too smug and pretentious to be convincing, nor could Leopold resist dragging in his fetish of feminine ferocity in the last few pages of this too artificially contrived vision of what education imparted by the masculine partner can do for matrimony.

Of all this literary activity *Venus in Furs* was destined to live longest. . . . The keynote of the book is struck in a dialogue between Severin and Wanda on an early page. 'In love,' he tells her, 'There is always the hammer and the anvil'. 'Aha,' retorts the lady. 'And you're the anvil, eh?' When he swears eternal fidelity, she comments: 'Oh, I could never love a man longer than a month unless I could try him out for a year first.' It may be observed that the hammer and anvil metaphor had already been used by the author in *Don Juan of Kolomea.* Leopold was never afraid of repeating the same verbal motifs in different books, just as Wagner did, musically, in different parts of his operas.

Venus starts, like a famous story by Pierre Louÿs, with a dream in which the author interviews a statue. In the French tale she turns out to be an ancient Athenian courtesan. In the German one she is Aphrodite herself. 'I'm cruel,' she says. 'And I have a perfect right to be. Man covets, woman is coveted. That is the decisive advantage he receives from Nature, through his passions, but any woman who doesn't see how to make him her subject, her slave, her plaything and betray him in the end with a laugh, can't be described as intelligent.'

The narrator's friend, Severin von Kusiemski, when he hears about the dream, remarks that he knows very well what the goddess meant. 'I've been thoroughly thrashed in my time,' he says. 'But now I'm cured. Like to read all about it?' And he hands over his *Memoirs of a Super-Sensualist.* It is these *Memoirs* which constitute the bulk of the novel. (pp. 64-8)

Severin signs, at Wanda's request, the following statement, recalling rather pathetically the author's own disillusion with Anna von Kottowitz. 'Having had enough, for years now, of life and its deceptions, I hereby voluntarily put an end to my existence, in which I take no further interest.' Wanda, in other words, can go so far as to kill him if it amuses her to do so.

Venus in Furs, naturally enough, relates much more exuberant episodes than actually took place in [Sacher-Masoch's life]. These passages of kaleidoscopic action are preceded, however, by Severin's exposition of the development of his character, which is important for the assessment of that of Sacher-Masoch himself.

> As a little boy I puzzled people with my shyness in the presence of women. But this behaviour only veiled the disturbing curiosity I felt about them. The grey arches and dim light of a church terrified me. I experienced positive anguish at the sight of the glittering altars and sacred pictures. But I would creep secretly, as to forbidden delights, to contemplate a plaster cast of Venus which stood in my father's little study. I used to kneel to it and recite the prayers I had been

taught, such as the Paternoster, the Ave Maria and the Creed.

> Once I got out of bed to visit the figure in the middle of the night. The goddess shimmered in the pale blue light of the crescent moon. I bent to kiss her cold feet, as I had seen our local peasants kiss the feet of the crucified Saviour.

> I was seized by an irresistible fit of longing.

> I sprang up, flung my arms round the beautiful cold body and kissed its cold lips. Then I shuddered, ran back to my room and fell asleep, to dream that the goddess stood at my bedside, threatening me with upraised arm . . .

> I came early to maturity and was immensely stimulated, I remember, when at the age of about ten I started reading the legends of the Christian martyrs with a horror that was really delight, how they pined away in prison, were grilled, pierced by arrows, boiled in pitch, thrown to wild beasts, crucified and underwent the most atrocious tortures with a kind of enjoyment. To suffer, to endure cruel torments, thenceforth seemed pleasurable to me, above all if such pain were inflicted by a beautiful woman, for I always considered that all poetry, like all fiendishness, came to a head in the opposite sex. I made a regular cult of this sentiment.

> I held sensuality to be sacred. In fact nothing else appeared sacred to me. There was something divine, I believed, about a beautiful woman, since the most important preoccupation of nature, the propagation of the species, is primarily her affair. I regarded the female as the personification of nature, the goddess Isis, and the male as her priest and slave. I recognised in her the same cruelty as that of nature, which rejects all that serves it as soon as the service provided is no longer needed. As for the man, ill-treatment and even death at the hands of a woman are experienced by him as voluptuous bliss.

> I envied King Gunther, whom the mighty Brünnhilde tied up on their bridal night. I envied the poor troubadour whom his capricious mistress ordered to be sewn up in a wolf's hide and then hunted like a wild beast. I envied the knight Ctirad, whom the bold amazon Sharka seized by cunning in a wood near Prague, carried off to her castle and after diverting herself with him for a while had him broken on the wheel . . . I read with the greatest eagerness stories in which the most fearful cruelties were described. I took a special pleasure in examining pictures and engravings that illustrated them. All the bloodthirsty tyrants who ever occupied a throne, all the inquisitors who racked, burned and slaughtered heretics, all the women characterised in the pages of global history as lascivious, beautiful and prone to violence, such as Libussa, Lucrezia Borgia, Agnes of Hungary, Queen Margot, Isabeau, the sultana Roxolana and the Russian czarinas of the eighteenth century, all were imagined by me as wearing furs or robes edged with ermine.

He adds to this list Delilah, to whom Samson returned after being once betrayed by her. When she betrayed him again and the Philistines bound him to put out his eyes, they 'remained to the last moment, intoxicated with rage and love, riveted to her fair and faithless countenance'. He remembers that Judith beheaded Holofernes and that Circe changed the companions of Odysseus into swine. (pp. 68-70)

[*For the Honour of God* (1872)] continued the attack on religious orthodoxy begun in The Legacy of Cain, Part One. The later tale, subtitled 'A Historical Sketch', castigates the cruelties of the Jesuits of former centuries and contains, as might have been expected, dialogues about torture between a tyrannical mistress and her 'slave' which closely resemble those in *Venus in Furs.* The volume issued in 1872 in fact does little more than paraphrase themes better illustrated elsewhere in the author's production to date. . . .

The strong childish element in his complex disposition enabled him to turn easily from ambitious literary work to lurid popular narrative. The consequence was that throughout 1873 he was turning out a series of unedifying 'revelations' under such titles as *Tales of the Court of Vienna, The Messalinas of Vienna, Tales of the Russian Court, Shadows of Society*—these were detective stories involving the Austrian secret police—and *A Female Sultan.* (p. 105)

The second Part, *Property,* published in 1874, of The Legacy of Cain contained six stories, of which the best are *Peasant Justice, The Hajdamak* and *Hasara Raba.* The basic idea of the whole of this Part is the moral iniquity of private property on any large scale. Sacher-Masoch can hardly be said to have cherished any practical political theories. But his bent, like that of most thoughtful artists, was essentially anarchical. He did not of course consider that bombs should be thrown in order to destroy the existing constitution of society. But he felt strongly that moral if not formally political liberty must be the birthright of any adult individual above the mental age of ten.

He therefore admired such men and women as managed to work out and defend a private system of ethics while refraining from legally punishable activities. All the heroes and heroines of his most effective tales, accordingly, exemplify in various ways more or less discreet rebellion against generally accepted rules of conduct under an autocracy, in this case that of the contemporary Austro-Hungarian empire.

In *Peasant Justice,* for instance, the villagers of a remote community, who frame and execute their own laws, are dominated by a certain Theodosia, widow of a miller. She is also much respected by their natural enemies, the local brigands, who are in the habit of disguising themselves as wolves in order to steal the farmers' horses. (p. 122)

The uncompromising realism of *Peasant Justice* is by no means always [grim]. . . . Sacher-Masoch sees the rural scene whole, with its humours and virtues as well as its horrors. His main point is that if most estate owners, themselves the descendants of bandits, treat their tenants like brutes, the tenants will behave like brutes on occasion,

if not all the time. The author's sympathy with this oppressed class comes out in his affectionate recording of their equally noticeable unselfishness and industry. His amused contempt for certain members of the aristocracy, one of whom is generally the narrator of his stories of the Galician countryside, when it is not himself in person and by name, also appears in such anecdotes as that of the elderly rake said to be so decrepit that he literally fell at the feet of any pretty woman he was courting.

In *The Hajdamak*—a generic term for brigands in the locality—a party of ladies and gentlemen on a hunting expedition is regaled by their huge, black-haired and swarthy guide, himself once a Robin Hood of the forests and mountains, with some horrific accounts of the rough justice he used to administer. In general, he said, the peasants themselves were too cowed and spiritless to attempt such acts of vengeance for their miseries. They left it, he added with a savage grin, to professional criminals such as he had been in his younger days, when he could well remember having sawed certain noble scoundrels in half, after nailing them between a couple of planks. Another time he and his gang had besieged the castle of a squire who had carried off a village girl. They stormed the courtyard, caught the steward and crucified him on the door of a barn. They hanged all the feudal retainers they did not slaughter on the spot. Then it was the turn of the squire himself. He was tied to the tail of a horse, which one of the brigands then rode at full gallop to an anthill, situated at the foot of a tree. The whimpering lecher was strung up by the heels to one of the branches and his face smeared with honey, for the disturbed insects to devour.

Apart from the retired Haidamak's ferocity, however, he turns out to be readily and jovially informative about the remarkable habits and superstitions of the bandits among themselves. They were continually reinforced by members of the dissatisfied peasantry and while cheerfully robbing the latter regularly treated them as an athletic and adventurous elder brother would deal with the junior members of his family. The field-workers, in their turn, regarded these daring and picturesque highlanders, often their own blood-relations, with alternate respect and fury.

Hasara Raba is a tale of rural Jewish life, the title being the name given to the seventh night of the Feast of Tabernacles, when oracular answers can be expected to puzzling questions. The tone, as is regularly the case with Sacher-Masoch's frequent references to the bewildering various practices and superstitions of Jewish sects, which so often strike the Gentile as utterly absurd, is humorously tender throughout, almost like the idiom of a fairy-tale. It is clear that he delighted in this sort of material and never passed the usual outsider's scornful judgment on it. (pp. 125-26)

The folklore upon which the author has based his ingenious comic fable . . . runs away with him, becoming too extravagant for disbelief to be suspended. . . . But two-thirds of the book has all the charm and unexpectedness of the best of its models and is as elegantly written as any of the literary masterpieces of this kind. Not only Leopold's personal brand of gently teasing humour but also certain of his intellectual convictions, such as the folly of racialism and the superiority of natural phenomena to the arguments of philosophers as a guide through life, are effectively evident in this brilliantly entertaining example of replies to those searching questions which one feels inclined to ask on *Hasara Raba* night.

Property, published at Bern in 1874, contained in addition to the three tales referred to above, *A Testament, Basil Hymen* and *Paradise on the Dniester.* In contrast to the first three tales, *A Testament* displays a wealthy man driven by ambition to become a slave such as the author in his own life was to cruel women. In *Basil Hymen* another 'man of property' finds himself incapable of maintaining it, runs away from it and yet never finds happiness even then. *Paradise on the Dniester* reveals the other side of the picture, offering proof that only those who have earned property by useful work can ever enjoy it. The ideal young Adam and Eve in their Eden by the river Dniester are so lovingly presented as almost to take the step from a dream to reality. But these last three stories are on the whole less forcible than the first three.

Other publications of the year 1874 included a collection of six tales entitled *Love Stories from Several Centuries,* another called *Good People and Their Adventures,* comprising three separate narratives, and a slight but diverting essay, *The Polish Faust,* translated into French for the *Revue des deux mondes.* This last piece dealt with a sixteenth century charlatan from Cracow, named Twardowski, who embarks on a long series of indecisive conflicts with the Devil and is eventually killed by the Polish king.

None of these productions is of much importance for the understanding of the author's genius. Except for a few characteristic touches they simply illustrate his versatility and readability as an excavator of the byways of history and folklore, while continuing to prove his moral idealism. On the whole Sacher-Masoch set his sights lower here than he did in The Legacy of Cain.

But the first two parts of the Legacy were all that he ever completed. Tales belonging to the subsequent four, *The State, War, Work and Death,* came out separately during the next few years. But most remained in fragmentary manuscript jottings. The sexual frustrations to which the author was simultaneously to be subjected did not ruin his creativity. Nevertheless, it declined. By 1875 he had done nearly all his best work, in its general trend an attack on the platform from which sexual questions were regarded in his time. He considered this pattern of thought, with its hopeless attempt—in his view—to confine physical passion within the bounds of Christian monogamy and poetic fantasy, quite inadequate for the arrest of a moral rottenness in society, which every thoughtful European in the second half of the nineteenth century had been deploring for years. His own solution was the modern theory of equality between the sexes in every activity, both mental and bodily, open to the human race. (pp. 127-28)

[Sacher-Masoch's] new volumes, as distinct from reprints, issued between 1888 and the end of the century, merely repeat the old themes, whether taken from past or contemporary social history, of dominant female and submissive male. The treatment is competent enough, readable in its

own day. But nearly seventy years later German novelists of Sacher-Masoch's own generation, such as Theodor Fontane (d. 1898) and Hermann Sudermann (1857-1928), are more digestible. The Chevalier's significance as an all-round man of letters depends mainly upon his earlier work.

The Legacy of Cain remained an ambitious but barely identifiable torso. Part One, *Love,* and Part Two, *Property,* had been published in 1870 and 1874 respectively. Since the latter year isolated tales, really belonging to subsequent parts, had been printed at various times and places. *The Black Cabinet* (1882), concerned with the Austrian secret police, and *The Ilau* (Jewish name for an expert on the Talmud), also of the year 1882 and dealing with the effects upon scholars and scientists of political absolutism, had originally been designed as components of Part Three, *The State.* 1882 also saw the publication of *The Old Castellan,* first conceived as a section of Part Five, *Work,* and describing the conquest of suffering by industry and self-denial, and *The Mother of God* from the projected Part Six, *Death,* set among the woman-worshipping, anarchical and suicidally-given Doukhobor fanatics of Russia. The heroine of this last narrative, styled 'God's Mother' by her co-religionists, . . . uses her unlimited power with appalling results, ultimately crucifying her lover with every circumstance of dramatically sombre horror.

But the ideas which Sacher-Masoch noted as forming the basis of this gigantic life-work never took detailed and complete shape on paper. In 1869 he had begun like other social reformers, with an indictment of the ruin of hopes for mankind perpetrated, generation after generation, by those whom power corrupts, 'great princes, great generals and great diplomats'. These people, he held, as Pietro Aretino and the Marquis de Sade had held before him—to mention only writers who got a bad reputation in other ways—deserved the gallows or gaol far more richly than most common murderers, thieves, forgers, coiners, brigands, conspirators against Church or State, persons convicted of illegal violence or fraudulent traders.

In *The State,* Sacher-Masoch had intended to prove that the only remedy for the eternal deceptions of even constitutional governments would be a United States of Europe, with the same legal code valid in all parts of the continent. The principle of militarism, disguised by national administrations as self-defence, was to be attacked from every angle, including the patriotic. *Work* was to lay bare the ignoble roots of the contemporary economic system, to show how it sapped the normal delight of the average man in his mental and physical energy and encouraged his opposite tendency to idleness, greed and the cruel exploitation of poverty. The cure of such abuses by an organisation which would abolish both wage-servitude and the parasite would then be explained.

Finally, a vision of true Christianity would close the sequence, proposing altruism as its basic motive, involving the disappearance of personal ambition and selfishness, of all desire for exclusive possession in the fields of both sex and property, of all insular flag-waving and sabre-rattling.

Whatever one may think of the naivety of such idealism, coincident in a surprising number of particulars with the utopian notions of Leopold's opposite number in the domain of erotics, Donatien de Sade, but leaving room, as de Sade did not, for specifically Christian feeling, there is no denying the generosity or the moral fervour of the much abused and ridiculed Sacher-Masoch's vision. Nor can the general truth of its intellectual diagnosis, its logic, be set aside as wholly irrelevant.

His philo-semitism, in which he stood almost alone among prominent authors of the period, derived in part from the preoccupation with politics, economics and morals that had led him to plan The Legacy of Cain. He had been born in Galicia, where Jews of every sort were extremely numerous. He was attracted by their humour, their conspicuous mysticism and the strange forms it took in Western society, both the romanticism and the materialism of which differed so fundamentally from the Eastern varieties. But it was mainly the Jew as the typical underdog of Central Europe that the Chevalier felt to be an essential starting-point for his projects of political, economic and moral reform.

He once wrote in a newspaper article:

> I know I have made many enemies, especially in Germany, where I am abused as favouring French and Jewish opinions. But that doesn't worry me. I got to know the Jews where they are poorest, in Galicia. I saw them providing services to society in the most industrious manner and yet persecuted by their Slav masters simply and solely because they were Jews. I was deeply touched by the constancy of this helpless people to the customs and ethics of their forefathers. When I came, later on, to acquire some position and influence in the world I used both to the best of my ability in the interests of the weak. It was never the rich and powerful who attracted me. I have always thought it my duty to take the side of the dispossessed and the injured. When I am confronted by a victim of misfortune I do not first ask, Are you Jewish or Gentile?

Such were Sacher-Masoch's most edifying characteristics in his prime, both as writer and as human being. Something must be allowed for the discretion required in approaching a public so largely hostile or contemptuous. Much of his work, especially as the peculiarities of his purely sexual behaviour, which he never took much trouble to conceal, became better known to his critics, bears a slightly smug and self-righteous air. He was somewhat unheroically concerned to defend and justify himself. He always preferred, on principle, persuasion to aggression. He was no Nietzsche. He stands much lower, therefore, intellectually and morally, than the stormier prophets. His character was undoubtedly flawed, rendered disproportionately apologetic, by his erotic obsessions. Yet they were ultimately responsible for most of his originality in abstract thought and literary impact. The idea of the terrible power of Aphrodite or Ashtaroth descended to Christian Europeans from the ancient civilisations of Greece and Asia. But it was this half Slav, half Austrian author who gave it the logical, the symbolic, the eventually physical twist, so prolific of poetry in the last quarter of the

nineteenth century, till the insidiously intoxicating goddess became as towering a demon as any Attila or Genghis Khan.

The subordination of the male to this destructive female deity had been more uncompromising in oriental than in Western mythologies. Consequently this notion was more comprehensible to the Slav than to the Latin or Teutonic mind. There is a high probability that it suggested to Leopold the subjection of Jew to Gentile, of the mass of mankind to a few powerful individuals, of decency and reason, love and generosity, to tyranny, lust and selfishness. This analogy may well have been the spur that drove him to the heights he reached as artist and thinker. They were not the Alps of a Goethe or even of a Thomas Mann. But they were solid eminences in the landscape of German letters, not merely mirages. (pp. 195-98)

It must be acknowledged that much of [Sacher-Masoch's] writing does not reach a very high literary standard. Even in **Venus in Furs** such stylistic lapses as his specific sexual obsession and sometimes careless fluency imposed on thought and expression are liable to irritate purists. His strong points were those of a dramatist, the immediate, vivid effect rather than narrative refinement or the virtues associated with restraint in an artist, except of course in his sedulous avoidance of coarse phrasing, which in any case no editor of that time would have passed. His inferior works resemble garish posters, not pictures of any impressive subtlety or significance. In that sense they are comparable with bestsellers of the mid-twentieth century. At the same time he can be as coy as any aged spinster of his day in hinting at his erotic prepossessions. His plots can be mechanical and laboured.

But the best work of Sacher-Masoch has been strangely neglected by historians of literature. This has probably been due partly to the tabu still in force up to about 1930 on overt references to sexual pathology in fiction. Themes involving masochism, like those involving sadism, homosexuality and incest, could not then expect to be taken seriously by professional critics.

Such censors are more liberal today. But fashions in love have swung in a direction contrary to the romanticism of a century ago. Amorous adventures in fiction are painted in the plainest of earth-colours, with every imaginable physiological detail presented in words of one or at most two syllables, such as had not been written down in English books in the period between Chaucer and D. H. Lawrence. Consequently the heroes and heroines of modern popular novelists, in order to get into histories of literature, must live up to this sort of poster-art, at the same time more primitive and less melodramatic than Leopold's gaudier novelettes, by being as commonplace in their debaucheries as possible. Anything like Sacher-Masoch's acutely framed analysis of sexual relations, a study conceived even more uncompromisingly than Shaw's in its balance between ruthlessly pursuant female and timidly adoring male, to say nothing of his intensity of passion and evasion of linguistic brutality, seems likely to bore the contemporary reader and therefore the contemporary critic.

Fortunately the pendulum of the mode in this field cannot

remain long at so extreme a point. A more scientific and imaginative attitude to the eternal sexual preoccupations of mankind must sooner or later transform the vulgarity, sentimental or scabrous, of the bulk of present-day fiction. When that change occurs it will necessarily be accompanied by a better informed and more sympathetic view of social history. Then Leopold von Sacher-Masoch, nothing if not a mirror of every level of society in his time, will again be read with pleasure and even excitement. (pp. 207-08)

James Cleugh, in his The First Masochist: A Biography of Leopold von Sacher-Masoch, *Stein and Day, Publishers, 1967, 220 p.*

Gilles Deleuze   (essay date 1967)

[*Deleuze is a French critic and the author of* Sacher-Masoch: An Interpretation, *in which he argues that masochism is not the complementary opposite of sadism, but a separate and necessarily unrelated condition. The volume includes extensive comparison of the thought and literature of Sacher-Masoch with that of the Marquis de Sade, an English translation of* Venus in Furs, *and appendices including a reprinted essay by Sacher-Masoch (see excerpt dated 1888), the texts of his masochistic contracts, and an excerpt from the memoirs of his first wife. In the following excerpt, Deleuze examines the roles of description, female characters, and suspense in Sacher-Masoch's fiction, as well as his intent in writing fiction, concluding with an assertion of the essential differences between Sacher-Masoch and Sade.*]

What is known as pornographic literature is a literature reduced to a few imperatives (do this, do that) followed by obscene descriptions. Violence and eroticism do meet, but in a rudimentary fashion. Imperatives abound in the work of Sade and Masoch; they are issued by the cruel libertine or by despotic woman. Descriptions also abound (although the function of the descriptions as well as the nature of their obscenity are strikingly different in the two authors). It would appear that both for Sade and for Masoch language reaches its full significance when it acts directly on the senses. Sade's *The One Hundred and Twenty Days of Sodom* hinges on tales told to the libertines by 'women chroniclers', and in principle the heroes may not take any initiative in anticipation of these tales. Words are at their most powerful when they compel the body to repeat the movements they suggest, and 'the sensations communicated by the ear are the most enjoyable and have the keenest impact.' In Masoch's life as well as in his fiction, love affairs are always set in motion by anonymous letters, by the use of pseudonyms or by advertisements in newspapers. They must be regulated by contracts that formalize and verbalize the behaviour of the partners. Everything must be stated, promised, announced and carefully described before being accomplished. However the work of Sade and Masoch cannot be regarded as pornography; it merits the more exalted title of 'pornology' because its erotic language cannot be reduced to the elementary functions of ordering and describing. (p. 17)

In the work of Masoch there is a . . . transcendence of the imperative and the descriptive towards a higher function.

But . . . it is all persuasion and education. We are no longer in the presence of a torturer seizing upon a victim and enjoying her all the more because she is unconsenting and unpersuaded [as in Sade]. We are dealing instead with a victim in search of a torturer and who needs to educate, persuade and conclude an alliance with the torturer in order to realize the strangest of schemes. This is why advertisements are part of the language of masochism while they have no place in true sadism, and why the masochist draws up contracts while the sadist abominates and destroys them. The sadist is in need of institutions, the masochist of contractual relations. The Middle Ages distinguished with considerable insight between two types of commerce with the devil: the first resulted from possession, the second from a pact of alliance. The sadist thinks in terms of institutionalized possession, the masochist in terms of contracted alliance. Possession is the sadist's particular form of madness just as the pact is the masochist's. It is essential to the masochist that he should fashion the woman into a despot, that he should persuade her to cooperate and get her to 'sign'. He is essentially an educator and thus runs the risk inherent in educational undertakings. In all Masoch's novels, the woman, although persuaded, is still basically doubting, as though she were afraid: she is forced to commit herself to a role to which she may prove inadequate, either by overplaying or by falling short of expectations. In *The Divorced Woman,* the heroine complains: 'Julian's ideal was a cruel woman, a woman like Catherine the Great, but alas, I was cowardly and weak. . . . ' In *Venus,* Wanda says: 'I am afraid of not being capable of it, but for you, my beloved, I am willing to try.' Or again: 'Beware, I might grow to enjoy it.'

The educational undertaking of Masoch's heroes, their submission to a woman, the torments they undergo, are so many steps in their climb towards the Ideal. *The Divorced Woman* is sub-titled *The Calvary of an Idealist.* Severin, the hero of *Venus,* takes as a motto for his doctrine of 'supersensualism' the words of Mephistopheles to Faust: 'Thou sensual, supersensual libertine, a little girl can lead thee by the nose.' (Ubersinnlich in Goethe's text does not mean 'supersensitive' but 'supersensual', 'supercarnal', in conformity with theological tradition, where Sinnlichkeit denotes the *flesh, sensualitas.*) It is therefore not surprising that masochism should seek historical and cultural confirmation in mystical or idealistic initiation rites. The naked body of a woman can only be contemplated in a mystical frame of mind, as is the case in *Venus.* This fact is illustrated more clearly still in *The Divorced Woman,* where the hero, Julian, under the disturbing influence of a friend, desires for the first time to see his mistress naked. He begins by invoking a 'need' to 'observe', but finds that he is overcome by a religious feeling 'without anything sensual about it' (we have here the two basic stages of fetishism). The ascent from the human body to the work of art and from the work of art to the Idea must take place under the shadow of the whip. Masoch is animated by a dialectical spirit. In *Venus* the story is set in motion by a dream that occurs during an interrupted reading of Hegel. But the primary influence is that of Plato. While Sade is spinozistic and employs demonstrative reason, Masoch is platonic and proceeds by dialectical imagination. One of Masoch's stories is entitled **"The Love of**

Plato" and was at the origin of his adventure with Ludwig II. Masoch's relation to Plato is evidenced not only by the ascent to the realm of the intelligible, but by the whole technique of dialectical reversal, disguise and reduplication. In the adventure with Ludwig II Masoch does not know at first whether his correspondent is a man or a woman; he is not sure at the end whether he is one or two people, nor does he know during the episode what part his wife will play, but he is prepared for anything, a true dialectitian who knows the opportune moment and seizes it. Plato showed that Socrates appeared to be the lover but that fundamentally he was the loved one. Likewise the masochistic hero appears to be educated and fashioned by the authoritarian woman whereas basically it is he who forms her, dresses her for the part and prompts the harsh words she addresses to him. It is the victim who speaks through the mouth of his torturer, without sparing himself. Dialectic does not simply mean the free interchange of discourse, but implies transpositions or displacements of this kind, resulting in a scene being enacted simultaneously on several levels with reversals and reduplications in the allocation of roles and discourse.

Pornological literature is aimed above at confronting language with its own limits, with what is in a sense a 'nonlanguage' (violence that does not speak, eroticism that remains unspoken). However this task can only be accomplished by an internal splitting of language: the imperative and descriptive function must transcend itself towards a higher function, the personal element turning by reflection upon itself into the impersonal. When Sade invokes a universal analytical Reason to explain that which is most particular in desire, we must not merely take this as evidence that he is a man of the eighteenth century; particularity and the corresponding delusion must also represent an Idea of pure reason. Similarly when Masoch invokes the dialectical spirit, the spirit of Mephistopheles and that of Plato in one, this must not merely be taken as proof of his romanticism; here too particularity is seen reflectively in the impersonal Ideal of the dialectical spirit. In Sade the imperative and descriptive function of language transcends itself towards a pure demonstrative, instituting function, and in Masoch towards a dialectical, mythical and persuasive function. These two transcendent functions essentially characterize the two perversions, they are twin ways in which the monstrous exhibits itself in reflection. (pp. 19-22)

Since the transcendent function in Sade is demonstrative and in Masoch dialectical, the role and the significance of descriptions are very different in each case. Although Sade's descriptions are basically related to the function of demonstration, they are nevertheless relatively independent creations; they are obscene in themselves. Sade cannot do without this provocative element. The same cannot be said of Masoch, for while the greatest obscenity may undoubtedly be present in threats, advertisements or contracts, it is not a necessary condition. Indeed, the work of Masoch is on the whole commendable for its unusual decency. The most vigilant censor could hardly take exception to *Venus,* unless he were to question a certain atmosphere of suffocation and suspense which is a feature of all Masoch's novels. In many of his stories he has no difficul-

ty in presenting masochistic phantasies as though they were instances of national custom and folklore, or the innocent games of children, or the frolics of a loving woman, or even the demands of morality and patriotism. Thus in the excitement of a banquet, the men, following an ancient custom, drink out of the women's shoes (*Sappho's Slipper*); young maidens ask their sweethearts to play at being bears or dogs, and harness them to little carts (*The Fisher of Souls*); a woman in love teasingly pretends to use a document signed in blank by her lover (*The Blank Paper*). In a more serious vein, a woman patriot, in order to save her town, asks to be brought before the Turks, surrenders her husband to them as a slave and gives herself to the Pasha (*The Judith of Bialopol*). Undoubtedly in all these cases the man derives from his humiliation a 'secondary gain' which is specifically masochistic. Nevertheless, Masoch succeeds in presenting a great part of his work on a 'reassuring' note and finds justification for masochistic behaviour in the most varied motivations or in the demands of fateful and agonizing situations. (Sade, on the other hand, could fool nobody when he tried this method.) Consequently Masoch was not a condemned author but a fêted and honoured one. Even the blatantly masochistic elements in his work gained acceptance as the expression of Slavonic folk-lore or of the spirit of Little Russia. He was known as the Turgeniev of Little Russia: he could equally well have been compared to the Comtesse de Ségur! Masoch did of course produce a sombre counterpart to these works: *Venus, The Mother of God, The Fountain of Youth, The Hyena of the Poussta,* restore the original rigour and purity of the masochistic motivation. But whether the descriptions are rosy or sombre, they always bear the stamp of decency. We never see the naked body of the woman torturer; it is always wrapped in furs. The body of the victim remains in a strange state of indeterminacy except where it receives the blows.

How can we account for these two kinds of 'displacement' in Masoch's descriptions? We are led back to the question: why does the demonstrative function of language in Sade imply obscene descriptions, while Masoch's dialectical function seems to exclude them or at least not to treat them as essential elements? (pp. 23-4)

[There] can be no masochism without fetishism in the primary sense. The way in which Masoch defines his idealism or 'Super-sensualism' seems at first sight rather trivial. Why believe in the idea of a perfect world? asks Masoch in *The Divorced Woman.* What we need to do is to 'put on wings' and escape into the world of dreams. He does not believe in negating or destroying the world nor in idealizing it: what he does is to disavow and thus to suspend it, in order to secure an ideal which is itself suspended in phantasy. He questions the validity of existing reality in order to create a pure ideal reality, an operation which is perfectly in line with the judicial spirit of masochism. It is not surprising that this process should lead straight into fetishism. The main objects of fetishism in Masoch's life and work are furs, shoes, the whip, the strange helmets that he liked to adorn women with, or the various disguises such as we find in *Venus.* The scene mentioned earlier from *The Divorced Woman* illustrates the split that occurs in fetishism and the corresponding double 'suspension': on the one hand the subject is aware of reality but suspends this awareness; on the other the subject clings to his ideal. There is a desire for scientific observation, and subsequently a state of mystical contemplation. The masochistic process of disavowal is so extensive that it affects sexual pleasure itself; pleasure is postponed for as long as possible and is thus disavowed. The masochist is therefore able to deny the reality of pleasure at the very point of experiencing it, in order to identify with the 'new sexless man'.

In Masoch's novels, it is the moments of suspense that are the climactic moments. It is no exaggeration to say that Masoch was the first novelist to make use of suspense as an essential ingredient of romantic fiction. This is partly because the masochistic rites of torture and suffering imply actual physical suspension (the hero is hung up, crucified or suspended), but also because the woman torturer freezes into postures that identify her with a statue, a painting or a photograph. She suspends her gestures in the act of bringing down the whip or removing her furs; her movement is arrested as she turns to look at herself in a mirror. . . . [These] 'photographic' scenes, these reflected and arrested images are of the greatest significance both from the general point of view of masochism and from the particular point of view of the art of Masoch. They are one of his creative contributions to the novel. The same scenes are re-enacted at various levels in a sort of frozen progression. Thus in *Venus* the key scene of the woman torturer is imagined, staged and enacted in earnest, the roles shifting from one character to another. The aesthetic and dramatic suspense of Masoch contrasts with the mechanical, cumulative repetition of Sade. We should note here that the art of suspense always places us on the side of the victim and forces us to identify with him, whereas the gathering momentum of repetition tends to force us on to the side of the torturer and make us identify with the sadistic hero. Repetition does occur in masochism, but it is totally different from sadistic repetition: in Sade it is a function of acceleration and condensation and in Masoch it is characterized by the 'frozen' quality and the suspense.

We are now in a position to account for the absence of obscene descriptions in the work of Masoch. The function of the descriptions subsists, but any potential obscenity is disavowed or suspended, by displacing the descriptions either from the object itself to the fetish, or from one part of the object to another part, or again from one aspect of the subject to another. What remains is a strange and oppressive atmosphere, like a sickly perfume permeating the suspense and resisting all displacements. Of Masoch it can be said, as it cannot be of Sade, that no one has ever been so far with so little offence to decency. This leads us to another aspect of Masoch's art: he is a master of the atmospheric novel and the art of suggestion. The settings in Sade, the castles inhabited by his heroes are subject to the brutal laws of darkness and light that accelerate the gestures of their cruel occupants. The settings in Masoch, with their heavy tapestries, their cluttered intimacy, their boudoirs and closets, create a chiaroscuro where the only things that emerge are suspended gestures and suspended suffering. Both in their art and in their language Masoch and Sade are totally different. Let us try to summarize the

differences . . . : in the work of Sade, imperatives and descriptions transcend themselves towards the higher function of demonstration: the demonstrative function is based on universal negativity as an active process, and on universal negation as an Idea of pure reason; it operates by conserving and accelerating the descriptions, which are overlaid with obscenity. In the work of Masoch, imperatives and descriptions also achieve a transcendent function, but it is of a mythical and dialectical order. It rests on universal disavowal as a reactive process and on universal suspension as an Ideal of pure imagination; the descriptions remain, but they are displaced or frozen, suggestive but free from obscenity. The fundamental distinction between sadism and masochism can be summarized *in the contrasting processes of the negative and negation on the one hand, and of disavowal and suspense on the other*. The first represents a speculative and analytical manner of apprehending the Death Instinct—which, as we have seen, can never be given—while the second pursues the same object in a totally different way, mythically, dialectically and in the imaginary. (pp. 30-2)

With Sade and Masoch the function of literature is not to describe the world, since this has already been done, but to define a counterpart of the world capable of containing its violence and excesses. It has been said that an excess of stimulation is in a sense erotic. Thus eroticism is able to act as a mirror to the world by reflecting its excesses, drawing out its violence and even conferring a 'spiritual' quality on these phenomena by the very fact that it puts them at the service of the senses. (Sade, in *Philosophy in the Bedroom*, distinguishes between two kinds of wickedness, the one dull-witted and commonplace, the other purified, self-conscious and because it is sensualized, 'intelligent'.) Similarly the words of this literature create a counter-language which has a direct impact on the senses. It is as though Sade were holding up a perverse mirror in which the whole course of nature and history were reflected, from the beginning of time to the Revolution of 1789. In the isolation of their remote chateaux, Sade's heroes claim to reconstruct the world and rewrite the 'history of the heart'. They muster the forces of nature and tradition, from everywhere—Africa, Asia, the ancient world—to arrive at their tangible reality and the pure sensual principle underlying them. Ironically, they even strive towards a 'republicanism' of which the French are not yet capable.

In Masoch we find the same ambition, to hold up a perverse mirror to all nature and all mankind, from the origins of history to the 1848 revolutions of the Austrian Empire—'The history of cruelty in love'. For Masoch, the minorities of the Austrian Empire are an inexhaustible source of stories and customs (hence the Galician, Hungarian, Polish, Jewish and Prussian tales that form the main part of his work). Under the general title The Legacy of Cain, Masoch conceived of a 'universal' work, the natural history of humanity in a cycle of stories with six main themes: love, property, money, the State, war and death. Each of these forces was to be restored to its cruel physical immediacy; under the sign of Cain, in the mirror of Cain, he was to show how monarchs, generals and diplomats deserved to be thrown in jail and executed along with murderers. Masoch liked to imagine that the Slavs were in need of a beautiful female despot, a terrible Tsarina, to ensure the triumph of the revolutions of 1848 and to strengthen the Panslavic movement. 'A further effort, Slavs, if you would become Republicans.'

To what extent can we regard Sade and Masoch as accomplices or complementary forces? The sado-masochistic entity was not invented by Freud; we find it in the work of Krafft-Ebing, Havelock Ellis and Féré. The strange relationship between pleasure in doing and pleasure in suffering evil has always been sensed by doctors and writers who have recorded man's intimate life. The 'meeting' of sadism and masochism, the affinity that exists between them, is apparent in the work of both Sade and Masoch. There is a certain masochism in Sade's characters: in *The One Hundred and Twenty Days of Sodom* we are told of the tortures and humiliations which the libertines deliberately undergo. The sadist enjoys being whipped as much as he enjoys whipping others. Saint-Fond in *Juliette* arranges for a gang of men to assail him with whips. La Borghèse cries: 'I would wish that my aberrations lead me like the lowest of creatures to the fate which befits their wantonness: for me the scaffold would be a throne of exquisite bliss.' Conversely, there is a certain sadism in masochism: at the end of his ordeals, Severin, the hero of **Venus in Furs,** declares himself cured and turns to whipping and torturing women. He sees himself no longer as the 'anvil' but as the 'hammer'.

However, it is remarkable that in both instances the reversal should only occur at the end of the enterprise. Severin's sadism is a culmination; it is as though expiation and the satisfaction of the need to expiate were at last to permit the hero what his punishments were previously intended to deny him. Once they have been undergone, punishments and suffering allow the exercise of the evil they once prohibited. Likewise the 'masochism' of the sadistic hero makes its appearance at the outcome of his sadistic exercises; it is their climax, the crowning sanction of their glorious infamy. The libertine is not afraid of being treated in the way he treats others. The pain he suffers is an ultimate pleasure, not because it satisfies a need to expiate or a feeling of guilt, but because it confirms him in his inalienable power and gives him a supreme certitude. Through insults and humiliations, in the throes of pain, the libertine is not expiating, but in Sade's words, 'he rejoices in his inner heart that he has gone far enough to deserve such treatment'. This kind of paroxysm in Sade's heroes is highly significant, for it means, as Maurice Blanchot points out [in *Lautreamont et Sade,* 1963] that 'in spite of the similarity of the descriptions, it seems fair to grant the paternity of masochism to Sacher-Masoch and that of sadism to Sade. Pleasure in humiliation never detracts from the mastery of Sade's heroes; debasement exalts them; emotions such as shame, remorse or the desire for punishment are quite unknown to them.'

It would therefore be difficult to say that sadism turns into masochism and vice versa; what we have in each case is a paradoxical by-product, a kind of sadism being the humorous outcome of masochism, and a kind of masochism the ironical outcome of sadism. But it is very doubtful whether the masochist's sadism is the same as Sade's, or the sadist's masochism the same as Masoch's. The masochist is able to change into a sadist by expiating, the sadist into a masochist on condition that he does not expiate. If its existence is too hastily taken for granted the sado-masochistic entity is liable to become a crude syndrome that fails to satisfy the demands of genuine symptomatology. It rather falls into the category of disturbances . . . which are coherent in appearance only and which must be broken down into discrete clinical entities. (pp. 33-5)

The woman torturer of masochism cannot be sadistic precisely because she is *in* the masochistic situation, she is an integral part of it, a realization of the masochistic phantasy. She belongs in the masochistic world, not in the sense that she has the same tastes as her victim, but because her 'sadism' is of a kind never found in the sadist; it is as it were the double or the reflection of masochism. The same is true of sadism. The victim cannot be masochistic, not merely because the libertine would be irked if she were to experience pleasure, but because the victim of the sadist belongs entirely in the world of sadism and is an integral part of the sadistic situation. In some strange way she is the counterpart of the sadistic torturer (in Sade's two great novels which are like the reflections of each other, Juliette and Justine, the depraved and the virtuous girl, are sisters). Sadism and masochism are confused when they are treated like abstract entities each in isolation from its specific universe. Once they have been cut off from their *Umwelt* and stripped of their flesh and blood, it seems natural that they should fit in with each other.

This is not to say that the victim of the sadist is herself sadistic, nor that the torturer of masochism is masochistic. But equally unacceptable is Krafft-Ebing's view according to which the torturer of Masoch is either a true sadist or else pretends to be one. In our opinion the woman torturer belongs entirely to masochism; admittedly she is not a masochistic character, but she is a pure element of masochism. By distinguishing in a perversion between the subject (the person) and the element (the essence), we are able to understand how a person can elude his subjective destiny, but only with partial success, by playing the role of an element in the situation of his choice. The torturess escapes from her own masochism by assuming the active role in the masochistic situation. It is a mistake to think that she is sadistic or even pretending to be so. We must not imagine that it is a matter of the masochist encountering a sadist by a stroke of luck. Each subject in the perversion only needs the 'element' of the same perversion and not a subject of the other perversion. Whenever the type of the woman torturer is observed in the masochistic setting, it becomes obvious that she is neither a genuine sadist nor a pseudo-sadist but something quite different. She does indeed belong essentially to masochism, but without realizing it as a subject; she incarnates instead the element of 'inflicting pain' in an exclusively masochistic situation. Masoch and his heroes are constantly in search of a peculiar and extremely rare feminine 'nature'. The subject in masochism needs a certain 'essence' of masochism embodied in the nature of a woman who renounces her own subjective masochism; he definitely has no need of another subject, i.e. the sadistic subject. (pp. 37-8)

The heroines of Masoch have in common a well-developed and muscular figure, a proud nature, an imperious will, and a cruel disposition even in their moments of tenderness and naivety. The oriental courtesan, the awe-inspiring Tsarina, the Hungarian or the Polish revolutionary, the servant-mistress, the Sarmatian peasant girl, the cold mystic, the genteel girl, all share these basic traits: 'Whether she is a princess or a peasant girl, whether she is clad in ermine or sheepskin, she is always the same woman: she wears furs, she wields a whip, she treats men as slaves and she is both my creation and the true Sarmatian Woman.' But beneath this apparent uniformity we may distinguish three very different types of women.

The first type is that of the Grecian woman, the pagan, hetaera or Aphrodite, the generator of disorder. Her life, in her own words, is dedicated to love and beauty; she lives for the moment. She is sensual; she loves whoever attracts her and gives herself accordingly. She believes in the independence of woman and in the fleeting nature of love; for her the sexes are equal: she is hermaphrodite. But it is Aphrodite, the female principal, that triumphs—as Omphale unmans Hercules with woman's attire. She conceives equality merely as the critical moment at which she gains dominance over man, for 'man trembles as soon as woman becomes his equal'. She is modern, and denounces marriage, morality, the Church and the State as the inventions of man, which must be destroyed. She is the dream character who appears in the opening chapter of *Venus;* we meet her again at the beginning of *The Divorced Woman,* where she makes a lengthy profession of faith; in *The Siren* she is the 'imperious and coquettish' Zenobia who creates havoc in the patriarchal family, inspires the women of the household with the desire to dominate, subjugates the father, cuts the hair of the son in a curious ritual of baptism and causes everyone to dress in clothes of the opposite sex.

At the other extreme we find the sadistic woman. She enjoys hurting and torturing others, but it is significant that her actions are prompted by a man or otherwise performed in concert with a man, whose victim she is always liable to become. It is as though the primitive Grecian woman had found her Grecian man or Apollonian element, her virile sadistic impulse. Masoch often introduces a character which he calls the Greek, or indeed Apollo, who intervenes as a third party to incite the woman to sadistic behaviour. In *The Fountain of Youth,* Countess Elizabeth Nadasdy tortures young men in collaboration with her lover, the fearful Ipolkar; to this end they invent one of the rare machines to be found in Masoch's writing (a steel woman in whose arms the victim is held fast: 'The lovely inanimate creature began her work; thousands of blades shot out of her chest, her arms, her legs and her feet'). In *The Hyena of the Poussta,* Anna Klauer performs her sadistic acts in league with a brigand chief. Even the heroine of *The Fisher of Souls,* Dragomira, in charge of the chastisement of the sadistic Boguslav Soltyk, is swayed by his argument that they are both 'of the same race' and concludes an alliance with him.

In *Venus* the heroine, Wanda, sees herself at first as a Grecian woman and ends up believing she is a sadist. At the

beginning she identifies with the woman in the dream, the Hermaphrodite. In a fine speech, she declares:

> I admire the serene sensuality of the Greeks—pleasure without pain; it is the ideal I strive to realize. I do not believe in the love preached by Christianity and our modern knights of the spirit. Take a look at me: I am worse than a heretic, I am a pagan. . . . Despite holy ceremonies, oaths and contracts, no permanence can ever be imposed on love; it is the most changeable element in our transient lives. Can you deny that our Christian world is falling into decay?

But at the end of the novel she behaves like a sadist; under the influence of the Greek she has Severin whipped by him:

> I was dying of shame and despair. What was most humiliating was that I felt a wild and supersensual pleasure in my pitiful situation, lashed by Apollo's whip and mocked by the cruel laughter of my Venus. But Apollo whipped all poetry from me as one blow followed the next, until finally, clenching my teeth in impotent rage, I cursed myself and my voluptuous imagination, and above all woman and love.

Thus the novel culminates in sadism: Wanda goes off with the cruel Greek towards new cruelties, while Severin himself turns sadist or, as he puts it, becomes the 'hammer'.

It is clear, however, that neither the hermaphroditic nor the sadistic type represents Masoch's ideal. In *The Divorced Woman* the egalitarian pagan woman is not the heroine but the friend of the heroine, the two friends being like 'two extremes'. In *The Siren* the imperious Zenobia, the hetaera who spreads havoc everywhere, is finally defeated by the young Natalie who is just as domineering but in an altogether different way. The opposite pole, the sadistic woman, is equally unsatisfactory. Dragomira, in *The Fisher of Souls,* is not truly sadistic in the first place; moreover, in forming an alliance with Soltyk, she degrades herself and loses all significance; she is finally defeated and killed by the young Anitta, whose type is more truly in keeping with Masoch's idea. In *Venus* the adventure begins with the theme of the hetaera and ends with the sadistic theme; yet the essential part of the story is enacted in between these two extremes, in another element. The two themes do not represent the masochistic ideal but rather the end-points between which this ideal swings, like the span of the pendulum. At one extreme masochism has yet to come into operation, and at the other it has already lost its *raison d'être.* The character of the woman torturer regards these outer limits with a mixture of fear, revulsion and attraction, since she never quite knows whether she will be able to maintain her prescribed role, and fears that she might at any moment fall back into primitive hetaerism or forward into the other extreme of sadism. Anna, in *The Divorced Woman,* declares that she is too weak, too capricious—the capriciousness of the hetaera—to incarnate Julian's ideal. In *Venus,* Wanda only becomes sadistic because she can no longer maintain the role that Severin has imposed on her ('It was you who stifled my feelings with your romantic devotion and insane passion').

What is the essential masochistic element, the scene between the two boundaries where the crucial action takes place? What is the intermediate feminine type between the hetaera and the sadist? Only by piecing together the various descriptions of her in Masoch's writings can we hope to arrive at this fantastic character, this phantasy. In a *'conte rose', The Aesthetics of Ugliness,* he describes the mother of the family: 'an imposing woman, with an air of severity, pronounced features and cold eyes, who nevertheless cherishes her little brood'. Martscha is described as being 'like an Indian woman or a Tartar from the Mongolian desert'; she has 'the tender heart of a dove together with the cruel instincts of the feline race'. Lola likes to torture animals and dreams of witnessing or even taking part in executions, but 'in spite of her peculiar tastes, the girl was neither brutal nor eccentric; on the contrary, she was reasonable and kind, and showed all the tenderness and delicacy of a sentimental nature'. In *The Mother of God,* Mardona is gentle and gay, and yet she is stern, cold and a master torturer: 'Her lovely face was flushed with anger, but her large blue eyes shone with a gentle light.' *Niera Baranoff* is a haughty nurse with a heart of stone, but she becomes the tender fiancée of a dying man, and eventually meets her own death in the snow. In *Moonlight* we finally come upon the secret of Nature: Nature herself is cold, maternal and severe. The trinity of the masochistic dream is summed up in the words: cold—maternal—severe, icy—sentimental—cruel. These qualities point to the difference between the woman torturer and her 'counterparts', the hetaera and the sadist; their sensuality is replaced by her supersensuous sentimentality, their warmth and their fire by her icy coldness, their confusion by her rigorous order.

The sadistic hero, just as much as the feminine ideal of Masoch, professes an essential coldness which Sade calls 'apathy'. But one of our main problems is precisely to ascertain whether, with respect to cruelty, the apathy of the sadist is not completely different from the coldness of the ideal masochistic type. There is once more a danger of merely reinforcing the sado-masochistic abstraction by equating what are in fact two very different kinds of coldness. The 'apathy' of the sadist is essentially directed against feeling: all feelings, even and especially that of doing evil, are condemned on the grounds that they bring about a dangerous dissipation which prevents the condensation of energy and its precipitation into the pure element of impersonal and demonstrative sensuality. 'Try to turn into pleasure all things that alarm your heart.' All enthusiasm, even and especially the enthusiasm for evil, is condemned because it enchains us to secondary nature and is still a residue of goodness within us. In the novels of Sade, the true libertines mistrust those characters who are still subject to emotional outbursts, and who show that, even in the midst of evil and for evil's sake, they are liable to be 'converted to the first misfortune'. The coldness of the masochistic ideal has a quite different meaning: it is not the negation of feeling but rather the disavowal of sensuality. It is as if sentimentality assumed in this instance the superior role of the impersonal element, while sensuality held us prisoner of the particularities and imperfections of secondary nature. The function of the masochistic ideal is to ensure the triumph of ice-cold sentimentality by dint of coldness; the coldness is used here, as it were, to suppress

pagan sensuality and keep sadistic sensuality at bay. Sensuality is disavowed, and no longer exists in its own right; thus Masoch can announce the birth of the new man 'devoid of sexual love'. Masochistic coldness represents the freezing point, the point of dialectical transmutation, a divine latency corresponding to the catastrophe of the Ice Age. But under the cold remains a supersensual sentimentality buried under the ice and protected by fur; this sentimentality radiates in turn through the ice as the generative principle of new order, a specific wrath and a specific cruelty. The coldness is both protective milieu and medium, cocoon and vehicle: it protects supersensual sentimentality as inner life, and expresses it as external order, as wrath and severity.

Masoch was acquainted with the work of his contemporary Bachofen, an eminent ethnologist and Hegelian jurist. Is not Bachofen, as much as Hegel, the inspiration behind the dream at the beginning of *Venus?* [In *Das Mutterrecht,* 1861] Bachofen distinguished three eras in the evolution of humanity. The first is the hetaeric or Aphroditic era, born in the lustful chaos of primeval swamps: woman's relations with man were many and fickle, the feminine principle was dominant and the father was 'Nobody' (this phase, typified by the ruling courtesans of Asia, has survived in such institutions as temple prostitution). The second, or Demetrian era, dawned among the Amazons and established a strict gynocratic and agricultural order; the swamps were drained; the father or husband now acquired a certain status but he still remained under the domination of the woman. Finally the patriarchal or Apollonian system established itself, matriarchy surviving in degenerate Amazonian or even Dionysian forms. Masoch's three feminine types can easily be recognized in these three stages, the first and third eras being the limits between which the second oscillates in its precarious splendour and perfection. Here the phantasy finds what it needs, namely a theoretical and ideological structure which transforms it into a general conception of human nature and of the world. Talking about the art of the novel, Masoch remarked that we must proceed from the 'schema' to the 'problem'; from our starting point in the obsessive phantasy we must progress to the theoretical framework where the problem arises.

How does the Greek ideal become transformed into the masochistic ideal, the chaotic sensuality of the hetaeric era into the new order of gynocratic sentimentality? Obviously through the catastrophe of the glacial epoch, which accounts for both the repression of sensuality and the triumphant rise of severity.

In the masochistic phantasy, fur retains its utilitarian function; it is worn less for the sake of modesty than from fear of catching cold. 'Venus must hide herself in a vast fur lest she catch cold in our abstract northern clime, in the icy realm of Christianity.' Masoch's heroines frequently sneeze. Everything is suggestive of coldness: marble body, women of stone, Venus of ice, are favourite expressions of Masoch; his characters often serve their amorous apprenticeship with a cold statue, by the light of the moon. The woman in the dream, at the beginning of *Venus,* expresses in her speech a romantic nostalgia for the lost world of the Greeks: 'You cannot begin to appreciate love as pure bliss and divine serenity . . . you modern men, you children of reason . . . as soon as you try to be natural you become vulgar. . . . Stay in your northern mists and Christian incense. . . . You do not need the gods—they would freeze to death in your climate.' That is indeed the essence of the matter: the catastrophe of the Ice Age having engulfed the world of the Greeks and with it the type of the Grecian woman, both sexes found themselves impoverished. Man became coarse and sought a new dignity in the development of consciousness and thought; as a reaction to man's heightened consciousness woman developed sentimentality, and towards his coarseness, severity. The glacial cold was wholly responsible for the transformation: sentimentality became the object of man's thought, and cruelty the punishment for his coarseness. In the cold-hearted alliance between man and woman, it is this cruelty and sentimentality in woman that compel man to thought and properly constitute the masochistic ideal.

Like Sade, Masoch distinguishes two natures, but he characterizes them differently. Coarse nature is ruled by individual arbitrariness: cunning and violence, hatred and destruction, disorder and sensuality are everywhere at work. Beyond this lies the great primary nature, which is impersonal and self-conscious, sentimental and supersensual. In the prologue to Masoch's *Galician Tales* a character known as 'the wanderer' indicts Nature for being evil. Nature replies in her own defence that she is not hostile and does not hate us, even when she deals death, but always turns to us a threefold face: cold, maternal, severe. . . . Nature is the steppe. Masoch's descriptions of the steppe are of great beauty, especially the one that appears at the beginning of *Frinko Balaban;* the representation of nature by the identical images of the steppe, the sea and the mother aims to convey the idea that the steppe buries the Greek world of sensuality and rejects at the same time the modern world of sadism. It is like a cooling force which transforms desire and transmutes cruelty. This is the Messianic idealism of the steppe. It does not follow that the cruelty of the masochistic ideal is any the lesser than primitive or sadistic cruelty, than the cruelty of whims or that of wickedness. Although masochism always has a theatrical quality that is not to be found in sadism, the sufferings it depicts are not, for all that, simulated or slight, neither is the ambiant cruelty less great (the stories of Masoch record excruciating tortures). What characterizes masochism and its theatricality is a peculiar form of cruelty in the woman torturer: the cruelty of the Ideal, the specific freezing point, the point at which idealism is realized.

Masoch's three women correspond to three fundamental mother images: the first is the primitive, uterine, hetaeric mother, mother of the cloaca and the swamps; the second is the Oedipal mother, the image of the beloved, who becomes linked with the sadistic father as victim or as accomplice; and in between these two, the oral mother, mother of the steppe, who nurtures and brings death. We call her intermediate, but she may also come last of all, for she is both oral and silent and therefore has the last word. Freud saw her thus in *The Theme of the Three Caskets,* in agreement with many themes from mythology and folklore. 'The mother herself, the beloved who is chosen after

her pattern, and finally the Mother Earth who receives him again . . . the third of the Fates alone, the silent goddess of Death, will take him into her arms.' Her true place, however, is between the two others, although she is displaced by an inevitable illusion of perspective. In this connection we feel that Bergler's general thesis is entirely sound: the specific element of masochism is the oral mother, the ideal of coldness, solicitude and death, between the uterine mother and the Oedipal mother [the critic cites E. Bergler, *The Basic Neurosis,* 1949]. We must wonder all the more why so many psychoanalysts insist on discovering a disguised father image in the masochistic ideal, and on detecting the presence of the father behind the woman torturer. (pp. 42-9)

There is a fundamental aesthetic or plastic element in the art of Masoch. It has been said that the senses become 'theoreticians' and that the eye, for example, becomes a human eye when its object itself has been transformed into a human or cultural object, fashioned by and intended solely for man. Animal nature is profoundly hurt when this transmutation of its organs from the animal to the human takes place, and it is the experience of this painful process that the art of Masoch aims to represent. He calls his doctrine 'supersensualism' to indicate this cultural state of transmuted sensuality; this explains why he finds in works of art the source and the inspiration of his loves. The lover embraces a marble woman by way of initiation; women become exciting when they are indistinguishable from cold statues in the moonlight or paintings in darkened rooms. *Venus* is set under the sign of Titian, with its mystical play of flesh, fur and mirror, and the conjunction of cold, cruelty and sentiment. The scenes in Masoch have of necessity a frozen quality, like statues or portraits; they are replicas of works of art, or else they duplicate themselves in mirrors (as when Severin catches sight of his own reflection in the mirror).

Sade's heroes, by contrast, are not art lovers, still less collectors. In *Juliette,* Sade explains why: 'Ah, if only an engraver could record for posterity this divine and voluptuous scene! But lust, which all too quickly crowns our actors, might not have allowed the artist time to portray them. It is not easy for art, which is motionless, to depict an activity the essence of which is movement.' Sensuality is movement. In order to convey the immediacy of this action of one soul against another, Sade chooses to rely on the quantitative techniques of accumulation and acceleration, mechanically grounded in a materialistic theory: reiteration and internal multiplication of the scenes, precipitation, over-determination. (The subject is at once parricide, incestuous, murderer, prostituter and sodomite.) We have seen why number, quantity and quantitative precipitation were the specific obsessions of sadism. Masoch, on the contrary, has every reason to rely on art and the immobile and reflective quality of culture. In his view the plastic arts confer an eternal character on their subject because they suspend gestures and attitudes. The whip or the sword that never strike, the fur that never discloses the flesh, the heel that is for ever descending on the victim, are the expression, beyond all movement, of a profound state of waiting closer to the sources of life and death. The novels of Masoch display the most intense preoccupation with arrested movement; his scenes are frozen, as though photographed, stereotyped or painted. In *Venus* it is a painter who says: 'Woman, goddess . . . do you not know what it is to love, to be consumed by longing and passion?' And Wanda looms with her furs and her whip, adopting a suspended posture, like a *tableau vivant:* 'I want to show you another portrait of me, one that I painted myself. You shall copy it.' 'You shall copy it' suggests both the sternness of the order and the reflection in the mirror.

Waiting and suspense are essential characteristics of the masochistic experience. Hence the ritual scenes of hanging, crucifixion and other forms of physical suspension in Masoch's novels. The masochist is morose: but his moroseness should be related to the experience of waiting and delay. It has often been pointed out that the pleasure-pain complex is insufficient to define masochism; but humiliation, expiation, punishment and guilt are not sufficient either. It is argued, justifiably, that the masochist is not a strange being who finds pleasure in pain, but that he is like everyone else, and finds pleasure where others do, the simple difference being that for him pain, punishment or humiliation are necessary prerequisites to obtaining gratification. However, this mechanism remains incomprehensible if it is not related to the form and in particular to the temporal form that makes it possible. Thus it is a mistake to treat the pleasure-pain complex as a raw material able intrinsically to lend itself to any transformation, beginning with the alleged transformation of sadism into masochism. Formally speaking, masochism is a state of waiting; the masochist experiences waiting in its pure form. Pure waiting divides naturally into two simultaneous currents, the first representing what is awaited, something essentially tardy, always late and always postponed, the second representing something that is expected and on which depends the speeding up of the awaited object. It is inevitable that such a form, such a rhythmic division of time into two streams, should be 'filled' by the particular combination of pleasure and pain. For at the same time as pain fulfils what is expected, it becomes possible for pleasure to fulfil what is awaited. The masochist waits for pleasure as something that is bound to be late, and expects pain as the condition that will finally ensure (both physically and morally) the advent of pleasure. He therefore postpones pleasure in expectation of the pain which will make gratification possible. The anxiety of the masochist divides therefore into an indefinite awaiting of pleasure and an intense expectation of pain.

Disavowal, suspense, waiting, fetishism and phantasy together make up the specific constellation of masochism. Reality, as we have seen, is affected not by negation but by a disavowal that transposes it into phantasy. Suspense performs the same function in relation to the ideal, which is also relegated to phantasy. Waiting represents the unity of the ideal and the real, the form or temporality of the phantasy. The fetish is the object of the phantasy, the phantasized object *par excellence.* Consider the following masochistic phantasy: a woman in shorts is pedalling energetically on a stationary bicycle; the subject is lying under the bicycle, the whirring pedals almost brushing him, his palms pressed against the woman's calves. All the elements are conjoined in this image, from the fetishism of the woman's calf to the twofold waiting represented by the motion of the pedals and the immobility of the bicycle. We should say, however, that there is no such thing as a specifically masochistic kind of waiting, but rather that the masochist is morose, by which we mean that he experiences waiting in its pure form. For example, Masoch arranged to have a healthy tooth pulled out while his wife, dressed in furs, stood before him with a threatening air. What is true of masochistic writing is equally true of masochistic phantasy: there is no specifically masochistic phantasy, but rather a masochistic art of phantasy. (pp. 61-4)

The belief in a sado-masochistic entity is not really grounded in genuine psychoanalytic thinking but in pre-Freudian thinking which relied on hasty assimilations and faulty etiological interpretations that psychoanalysis merely helped to make more convincing instead of questioning their reality.

This is why it is necessary to read Masoch. His work has suffered from unfair neglect, when we consider that Sade has been the object of such penetrating studies both in the field of literary criticism and in that of psychoanalytic interpretation, to the benefit of both. But it would be equally unfair to read Masoch with Sade in mind, and with the intention of finding in his work a proof or verification that sadism effectively reverses into masochism, even if masochism in turn evolves towards a form of sadism. The genius of Sade and that of Masoch are poles apart; their worlds do not communicate, and as novelists their techniques are totally different. Sade expresses himself in a form which combines obscenity in description with rigour and apathy in demonstration, while the art of Masoch consists in multiplying the disavowals in order to create the coldness of aesthetic suspense. There is no reason to suppose that Masoch would suffer from such a confrontation. Influenced by his Slavic background and by German Romanticism, Masoch makes use of all the resources of phantasy and suspense rather than of the romantic dream. By his techniques alone he is a great writer; by his use of folk-lore he manages to tap the forces of the myth, just as Sade was able to achieve the full power of demonstration by his use of descriptions. The fact that their names have been linked with two basic perversions should remind us that diseases are named after their symptoms rather than after their causes. Etiology, which is the scientific or experimental side of medicine, must be subordinated to symptomatology, which is its literary, artistic aspect. Only on this condition can we avoid splitting the semiological unity of a disturbance, or uniting very different disturbances under a misbegotten name, in a whole arbitrarily defined by non-specific causes.

Sado-masochism is one of these misbegotten names, a semiological howler. . . . (1) Sadism is speculative-demonstrative, masochism dialectical-imaginative; (2) sadism operates with the negative and pure negation, masochism with disavowal and suspension; (3) sadism operates by means of quantitative reiteration, masochism by means of qualitative suspense; (4) there is a masochism specific to the sadist and equally a sadism specific to the masochist, the one never combining with the other; (5) sadism negates the mother and inflates the father; masochism disavows the mother and abolishes the father; (6) the role and significance of the fetish, and the function of the phantasy are totally different in each case; (7) there is an aestheticism in masochism, while sadism is hostile to the aesthetic attitude; (8) sadism is institutional, masochism contractual; (9) in sadism the superego and the process of identification play the primary role; masochism gives primacy to the ego and to the process of idealization; (10) sadism and masochism exhibit totally different forms of desexualization and resexualization; (11) finally, summing up all these differences, there is the most radical difference between sadistic *apathy* and masochistic *coldness*.

These eleven propositions taken together should account not only for the differences between sadism and masochism, but equally for the differences in the literary techniques and in the art of Sade and Masoch. (pp. 114-16)

> *Gilles Deleuze, in* Masochism, *by Gilles Deleuze and Leopold von Sacher-Masoch, translated by Jean McNeil, Zone Books, 1989, 293 p.*

Raymond Durgnat   (essay date 1972)

[*In the following excerpt, Durgnat examines Gilles Deleuze's contention that the text of* Venus in Furs *exemplifies the condition of masochism, finding it incomplete but insightful and valuable to an appreciation of Sacher-Masoch's novel.*]

[Peter Weiss's play *Marat-Sade*] ensures that our sympathy goes to a Marquis de Sade who is quite devoid of sadism in the usual sense. Instead, he's a rebel, a loser, a prophet and sage, and a masochist. So it's obviously time for the Chevalier von Sacher-Masoch to emerge from the demi-limbo of ludicrous obscenity to which his speciality has consigned him. Obligingly, the Velvet Underground's first LP devoted a track to his best-known novel, *Venus in Furs,* while the Procol Harum's first LP offers another such pop classic, *She Wandered through the Garden Fence.* In 1967 James Cleugh's biography *The First Masochist* (odd title, since the first autobiographical recognition of erotic masochism is Rousseau's) redirected attention to him as a personality of some ideological consequence [see excerpt dated 1967]. Gilles Deleuze . . . attempts an even more intimate and sympathetic approach [see excerpt dated 1967].

Young Leopold's father was a Chief of Police in the old Austro-Hungarian Empire. He was active in repressing determined revolutions in 1846 and 1848, when the boy was 10 and 12. After a brief spell as Professor of History the youth turned to writing the novels which made him a literary and social lion in Paris and indeed throughout Europe. His literary expressions of his obsession earned him his recognition as a profound writer, and a more innocent age compared his work to Goethe, Dostoevsky and Gogol. His preoccupation with strength of will, power and punishment relates well enough to a powerful current in European thought of the time (Nietzsche, Schopenhauer, Dostoevsky, Strindberg, and 'carnivorous' Darwinism). He anticipates modern radical attitudes: notably a certain

combination of idealism and amorality, a mixture of anarchism and social activism, anti-authoritarianism, anti-militarism, anti-racialism (his sympathy for Jewish minorities was conspicuous), Women's Lib and the immorality of private property. His notion of a new type of man, the 'supersensualist', who has 'transcended' specifically sexual desire, could overlap with modern exaltations of 'whole-body eroticism' as compared to 'genital imperialism'. Masoch himself was gentle and considerate to women, physically and socially courageous whenever necessary. He was not so much a charmer as a bewitcher, and no less dashing for a certain feminine grace which added to his seductive intensity. One of his mistresses (in the normal sense of the word), Kathrin Strebinger, blandly outdazzles even the least neurotic of Warhol's Superstars, and Masoch's skill at getting posses of pretty girls to play at robbers and tie him up makes the edgy, nervy chit-chat of *The Chelsea Girls* look like ultra-bourgeois inhibition. His career had innumerable ups and downs, as normal for a writer of his time, and his sanity resisted the neurosis behind his obsession until his late 50's, when he suffered paranoid hallucinations about cats, strangled one and suffered fits of almost homicidal fury. His second wife devotedly nursed him through his crisis, and he seems to have enjoyed a brief peace of mind, or at least an exhaustion-engendered serenity, before dying at the age of 60, of heart failure. The French film director, Jacques Baratier, dreams of a musical comedy to be called *Mister Masoch,* based on a life which might equally be filmed in the style of *Performance.*

In his invaluable biographical study, James Cleugh is concerned with persuading us to respect Masoch the man, and restricts himself to biographical detail. He balances his 'sympathy for the devil' by a scathing tone about his subject's female accomplices, as if worried about seeming too uncritical of the syndrome. Deleuze, less apprehensive, wants to help us understand, not only the man and the philosophy, but the masochistic wavelength as well. And in a sense it's easier for us to respect Sade, as a man of action, than a victim. Ever since Christianity and martyrdom lost their grip on the imagination of Western man, Europeans, and Americans in particular, have found passivity more of a threat to their self-respect and more embarrassing than activity. In addition, Sade's impersonal style lends itself to a safely detached philosophical approach. But Masoch's best remembered novel requires the same sympathetic involvement which we grant romantic poetry.

Deleuze concurs with Georges Bataille's point that Sade's style is abstract, raging, totalitarian. Its aim is to obliterate every rival consciousness, including the reader's. But Masoch's hero, Severin, has to coax his Wanda into willing to play the part he has assigned her. His speech is educative and persuasive. Deleuze's book begins with a long (120-page) introduction to the full text of *Venus in Furs,* which constitutes the volume's second part. And his introduction brings out the full richness of the novel's sinewy logic and lucid amorality.

For underlying Masoch's romantic atmosphere there was a game far more subtle than Sade's. Masoch, winning to lose, must embark on a strange contradiction between the instinct of self-preservation (*ie,* power) and an erotic self-giving, which slyly parodies love. The complications in Sade's game only become evident when one compares his diverse texts with one another and with his life. But Masoch's work and life are quite consistent. Indeed, his first wife seduced him by posing as a soul-sister of his novel's heroine, and he walked a resourceful yet tragic line between fantasy made reality and his internal contradictions. He lived some of his dream, and though his life was probably internally tragic he wasn't in the usual sense a loser. Sade's gift for getting himself incarcerated suggests a masochism which was by no means absent from his erotic experiments. Indeed, Sade can no more keep masochism out of his philosophy than Masoch can keep sadism out of his. Sade wanted freedom, not for its own sake, but so that a free-for-all would maximise men's natural pleasure in destructive domination. But if we're all sadists, what happens to all those sadists who are losers? The usual answer is to renounce sadism for some form of social contract, of which one might have expected Sade to counsel a relentless defiance. Instead, he suggests a kind of philosophical detachment. If one becomes a victim, one should be filled with joy at one's fate being in conformity with nature. Thus sadism concludes in masochistic acceptance. Conversely, Masoch's Severin clearly pulls the strings of Wanda, as his puppet, until she, finally, becomes what he wants, in earnest. But then he renounces her and adopts a 'sensibly' sadistic attitude towards women. Here Masoch switches to sadism. And the underdogs whom Masoch champions possess an amoral, quasi-sadistic power through which their author seems to gratify a vicarious sadism. Revenge interests him more than justice. On the other hand, Sade is quite uninterested in power as an expression of life-force, of potency. The tyrants whom Sade champions in *The 120 Days of Sodom* lack even such brute qualities as courage and energy. They are as despicable as Sade can make them, for even pride is a concession to the opinions of others. (pp. 26-8)

Deleuze takes Masoch as an example of a type whom he calls 'the masochist'. But it doesn't take a particularly wide experience of literature or life to convince one that there are as many varieties of masochist as of sadist, homosexual or heterosexual. Thus, some sadists delight in mastery (of which actual pain is only a symbol) and preserve above all an aloof impassivity. Others abandon themselves to orgasmic frenzy—while others again seem to study the victim's pain as if fascinated by an inner masochism which they deny themselves (through fear, or sadism, or masochism?). Deleuze suggests that 'the sadist' has too little ego and 'the masochist' too much, so that the former needs to overwhelm, the latter to be overwhelmed. Yet this formulation hardly seems complete for those masochists who are visibly a bundle of nerves, on every social occasion and indeed when on their own, or to necessary distinctions between apparently depressed masochists, stiff and prickly (paranoid) masochists, snaky, joky masochists, calm, manly masochists, kind and sensitive masochists, and seraphically serene (schizoid) masochists. In the same way there are stiff, pseudo-paternal sadists, narcissistic sadists, nervous giggling sadists, transvestite sadists, (like Myra Breckinridge, or 'Auntie' Grabow in Stephen Schneck's *The Night Clerk*) and some with a partic-

ularly edgy and nasty oscillation between their active homosexuality and their sadism (*ie,* their rage at the male partner who has seduced them away from the female, at the female for being absent, and at both the failed male and the female in that male—whom they hysterically beat up). A heterosexual erotic sadist may be a homosexual moral masochist (*ie,* contemptuously dismissive of feminine weakness, yet profoundly subservient to male authority). And there is always that enigmatic character, the kind-hearted sadist, whom Sade the man may, in the end, have become. For sadism can be only a philosophical attitude, a nihilist irony. And, however pervasive in that mental sector, it makes no appearance in his personal relationships, which may rather be marked by a dynamic, if sometimes subtly impersonal, tenderness. (p. 29)

There is often enough an association in men between heterosexual masochism and transvestism, with passive homosexuality as a crisis point. Deleuze, by restricting himself to Masoch, can skate over it, but it's prominent in American pornography, and once one has seen it there, it's possible to sense its presence under the defences which Masoch successfully put up against it. Nonetheless, any one of these attitudes may function as a defence against either or both of the others, and then their sufficiently emphatic appearance immediately breaks the erotic spell (being whipped by his wife's lover is Severin's turning point, though not Masoch's). But it's obvious that Severin and Masoch are both fascinated by their idea of the triumphant male, whose victim, their spouse, is to be. All of which undermines Deleuze's insistence on masochism as being fixated on the mother, without involving the appearance of a father-figure as climax and crisis.

There are other subtle distinctions. In the technical language of paid sexuality, *correction* (flagellation), *bondage* (tying-up) and *humiliation* ('lick my feet') aren't simple tautologies. Certainly, some enthusiastic punters relish all three. But some are only interested in whipping (and take it as a challenge to show as little feeling as possible—nearer *If* . . . than Isherwood's Mr Norris). The devotee of ritual humiliation may chicken out at the slightest actual pain and be bored by enforced passivity. The bondage fan may want to be kept trussed up for hours or even days. With him, as with transvestites, a principal aim seems to be to postpone his post-orgasmic anti-climax as long as possible, before it returns him to his tormenting ambivalence. The paternal emotional masochist may choose the fickle, kittenish vamp (as in the films of Jean Renoir), while the childlike emotional masochist prefers the big, marmoreal woman (*à la* Theda Bara).

And so on and so on. Most masochists are mixed types, within as well as beside their masochism, and the word, as a label, is misleadingly crude. After all, the essential of any erotic relationship seems to be its resolution of the desired and the forbidden, *eg,* the man who wants a girl just like the girl that married dear old dad couldn't have an erection for his dear old mum to save both their lives. And so we can all feel the force of arguments from the affinity of heroism and masochism, or the role of moral masochism in making society possible, or love's involvement of a radical generosity, *ie,* a giving-away of oneself, *ie,* a constructive masochism, however assertive and demanding the same love in counterbalancing respects. Maybe all that distinguishes masochism and love is the introverted and destructive yielding of masochism and the extroverted, generous and parental yielding of love; and love without masochism is emotional imperialism.

In the end, it becomes important to distinguish between aggression as wanting and therefore needing, and a destructive aggression born of frustration and fear. In sado-masochism the latter deforms or subsumes the former, although the object (the opposite sex) is retained. In homosexual passion, the former resists the latter, but the object is changed. The destructive aggression may be directed outwards against other people, giving us sadism, or it may be directed inwards, against certain mental impulses, giving us masochism. The two are inseparable insofar as the sadist must be repressing his aggression of desire, and behaving, in that respect, masochistically. At the same time, orthodox analysis tends to underplay the secondary differences which arise as a consequence of whether the destination of the destructive aggression is other people or another part of the same mind. In this latter case, the self-preservative instinct will be more fully engaged; hence our assumption that the masochist tends to 'softer' punishments than those which delight the sadist (although cases of really gruesome masochism aren't absent from psycho-medical textbooks).

In acknowledging and emphasising the differences, the Deleuze book has a merit of which the clinical approach is conspicuously devoid. He listens to what a masochist has to say. He attempts an imaginative involvement with the symptoms of masochism. He neither dismisses its subjective realities as 'mere fantasies' nor states them only to convert them into their underlying opposite. Whether or not he reads all that is written between the lines . . . , he certainly helps one to read the lines. Freud had an often awkward, often unfortunate, predilection for what in art was peripheral. Deleuze, in the style of Bachelard and Mauron, picks on literary points which, while quite obvious, yet only yield their full meaning by being seen as part of a structure which isn't obvious. Thus he spots the connections between Masoch's fur fetish, a touch of comic relief in which his Venus keeps sneezing, and his conception of woman as something between a cat and a galvanic battery. Confronted with Masoch's almost enigmatic style such a morally neutral yet imaginatively generous interpretation is as precious as it's rare. I'd made several attempts to read *Venus in Furs* (admittedly, in earlier, bad translations), but had soon given up, seeing only the rather monotonous lyricism of a minor decadent. After Deleuze, every detail of description, every line of dialogue, every move in the complex interpersonal game, takes on a new meaning, a new life, and acquires its own 'fearful joy', its 'terrible beauty'. (p. 30)

Raymond Durgnat, "Towards Eros: The Machinery of Masochism," in Books and Bookmen, Vol. 17, No. 10, July, 1972, pp. 26-31.

Walter Benn Michaels   (essay date 1984)

[*In the following excerpt, Michaels discusses the characteristics and conditions of the masochistic contract in* Venus in Furs.]

[If] the masochist's desire to be owned is perverse, it is nevertheless a perversion made possible only by the bourgeois identification of the self as property. Without that, no truly modern slavery is possible, since only if you identify freedom with self-ownership can being owned by someone else seem an intrinsic abridgment of that freedom. Hence, an increased investment in the values of autonomy will naturally be accompanied by an increased insecurity about the status of that autonomy; a self that can be owned can also be sold or stolen or gambled away. [The] founding text of masochism, Sacher-Masoch's *Venus in Furs* (1870) marks . . . clearly the erotic potential of the self in a market economy.

"The ancient world's freedom of pleasure," observes Wanda, the cruel mistress of *Venus in Furs,* "would have been unthinkable without slavery," and she grows "melancholy" contemplating the apparent impossibility of ever really making Severin, Sacher-Masoch's hero, her slave. Even more eager to be enslaved than Wanda is to enslave him, Severin immediately proposes that they travel to Turkey where slavery is still legal, but Wanda soon has a better idea. After all, anyone can have a slave in Constantinople, she says; she wants her slave here, in the "civilized, reasonable and philistine" world of Europe. And she proposes to Severin that they draw up a contract, making him "completely her property," giving her the right to "mistreat" him and even kill him if she pleases, and requiring her, in consideration, to "appear as often as possible in furs, particularly when she is being cruel to her slave."

The erotic advantages of such a contract are considerable. For one thing, it is, with its narrative of promised duties and punishments, itself something of a pornographic text. Indeed, Sacher-Masoch was so enamored of the genre that, in addition to the contract in *Venus in Furs,* he drafted two real-life contracts, one committing him to six months of servitude with Fanny von Pistor and one for life with Aurore Rumelin, who called herself Wanda and whom he married in 1873. But more important than the contract's pornographic possibilities is its recasting of slavery and of the "ancient world's freedom of pleasure."

Slavery in the West had ended, at least nominally, with the American Civil War, but Progressives like Richard T. Ely worried that it had really only changed its form and was now reappearing in the guise of the "peonage contract" employed in the South and increasingly in the world at large. In his massive *Property and Contract in Their Relations to the Distribution of Wealth,* Ely offers the example of a contract that came before a South Carolina judge in 1901 in which, having acknowledged the "right" of his employer "to use such force as . . . he may deem necessary to compel me to . . . perform good and necessary services," the contracting laborer goes on to specify that his employer "shall have the right to lock me up for safekeeping, work me under the rules and regulations of his farm, and if I should leave his farm or run away he shall have the right to offer and pay a reward of not exceeding $25 for my capture and return together with the expenses of same, which amount so advanced, together with any other indebtedness, I may owe . . . I agree to work out under all rules and regulations of this contract." The only thing missing is the right to murder the laborer, but, as Ely points out, "in some cases they have been shot for attempting to escape." Citing the one-sided contracts laborers sign in Angola, Ely quotes Henry Nevinson's *Modern Slavery:* "In what sense does such a man enter into a free contract for his labour? In what sense, except according to law, does his position differ from a slave? . . . The difference between the 'contract labour' of Angola and the old-fashioned slavery of our grandfather's time is only a difference of legal terms. In life there is no difference at all." Such contracts epitomized to Progressives like Ely the unfortunate tendency of contract "to preserve advantages once secured," "to keep the existing condition of things." Thus the elimination of "old-fashioned" slavery in the West had not really brought an end to slavery after all. And Wanda is right to think that she needn't go to Constantinople to obtain the freedom of pleasure that slavery makes possible; the contract makes pleasure possible even in "philistine" Europe.

But at the same time, it is impossible to understand the masochistic contract as a straightforward transformation of "old-fashioned" or "feudal" slavery. Apologists for American slavery had praised its familial and paternalist character, contrasting the security of a society modeled on the natural order of the family to the insecurity of an industrial society indifferent to natural modes of organization, and preferring the sentimental relations of the South to the market relations of the North. Sacher-Masoch, however, repudiates these feudal attractions. The offer of contract made him by Wanda stipulates that he be "neither a son, nor a brother, nor a friend" to her, and the contract with Fanny von Pistor explicitly deprives him of any "pretention to her love, or right to be her lover." If slavery in the "ancient world" invoked, however disingenuously, the ties of family and affection, modern slavery, as depicted in the masochistic contract, prohibits any noncontractual relation between owner and owned and seems to derive part of its erotic power from the very absence of any such relation.

Furthermore, at the same time that the contract proclaims its hostility to traditional social forms, it declares its indifference to the values that accompany those forms. For a long time, Ely notes, there was no idea of contract, no idea, that is, of "binding agreements to be enforced by public authority"; "our English ancestors had no notion of the state's duty to enforce private agreements." Sometimes the Church might exert a certain moral pressure on the parties to an agreement, but not until the eighteenth century did the "secular courts" begin to play a role. And even then, "the theory under which a creditor could collect debts due him was . . . that he was getting back his due and it was not looked upon as the result of contract;" parties to an agreement might thus be held accountable, but the source of this accountability was a certain religious morality or a social sense of what was fair. In the modern understanding of contract, however, the source of accountability is the contract itself, and what Ely calls the "police power" of the state serves only to guarantee the contract, not to enforce some external morality. The state appears here in collaboration with the individual, recognizing and enforcing the desires of its subjects, holding them accountable neither to religious nor to civic morality but only to the wants they have themselves expressed.

The character of these wants and their value relative to one another are thus imagined as a purely private matter. Ely points out that, although in contract "there must be some consideration," there is "no inquiry into the adequacy of the consideration. . . . We can have a consideration which is merely nominal." A radical inequality of exchange—Severin's "body" and "soul," say, for Wanda's appearance in furs—will thus be permitted and enforced by contract with no attention to the moral or social equity of the exchange. Or perhaps one should say, with no attention to the equity of the exchange as perceived by anyone other than the contracting parties—for the institution of the contract assumes that any voluntary exchange is equitable, that the match between what the contracting parties want supersedes any external judgment about the relative worth of what they exchange. In this respect, the contract may be said to legitimate every desire, if only by enacting a legal form in which to imagine its satisfaction. And, in the same gesture, the contract provides a mechanism for determining the value of those goods or services offered in exchange. How else, in what Ely calls "the struggle between buyers and sellers," could Wanda's occasional appearance in furs be thought a suitable compensation for Severin's enslavement? It is suitable because it is what he wants, and so, although even the contract laborer in South Carolina is, in some sense, better paid than Severin, Severin, whose very subjectivity bears the inscription of the free market, has struck a better bargain.

For what does the contract laborer want, and what must he give up to get it? According to Ely, the laborer is unlike the "seller of goods" insofar as in the "labour contract he binds himself and must render his service with his person." He thus gives himself over to his employer for eight, ten, or twelve hours a day, performing the required service and receiving in payment the wherewithal to sustain himself on his own for the remaining hours of the day. He gives up his labor, and hence something of his "person," in order to retain something of his "person." The masochist, by contrast, is on the job twenty-four hours a day, receiving in payment only an occasional beating or a glimpse of Wanda in furs. But it would be wrong to think of this as an unequal exchange of services; in fact, it would be wrong to think of it as primarily an exchange of services at all. Severin values Wanda's appearing in furs not as payment for his enslavement but as the mark of that enslavement. He offers her the opportunity to have a slave; she repays him with the opportunity to be a slave: his work is, literally, its own reward—not merely labor but the very commodity labor is designed to buy. Where the contract laborer enslaves himself, as it were, temporarily, in order to buy a little freedom, the masochist enslaves himself permanently and buys his own enslavement.

To put this more strictly in Ely's terms, we might say that

the contract laborer sells his labor and only incidentally his person, whereas the masochist sells his person and only incidentally his labor. The masochistic contract thus bespeaks the indifference of both parties to the conveniences or inconveniences of ownership, to the services a slave's labor might provide or the attentions that might be provided him. The masochist is, in this sense, more truly a slave than the wage slave of South Carolina. But, imagining the slave as a buyer and seller, the contract at the same time defeudalizes slavery, replacing a social fact that exists independent of the desires of master or slave with a market agreement that insists on and enacts the priority of those desires. Stowe's and Hawthorne's fear of slavery as a modern invention rather than a feudal relic is thus ecstatically borne out in the masochistic contract, where all things are made alienable and the thrill is in the act of alienation itself. Here the ancient world's freedom of pleasure made possible only by slavery has been transmogrified into a pleasure available to no one in that ancient world, the pleasure of buying and selling in a free market.

Hence, the "new feudalism" that Progressives like Ely feared and that Wanda briefly flirts with when she contemplates taking Severin off to Constantinople can never quite come into being, not because conditions as bad as and even worse than those obtaining under "old-fashioned" slavery cease to exist but because the intervention of the market, even when it leaves these conditions intact, alters their meaning. In other words, the apologists for "modern slavery" defended it not by appealing to the usual paternalist ideals but by appealing to freedom, in particular freedom of contract. (pp. 124-29)

But in justifying the restraints that will keep the strong from enslaving the weak, Ely has also suggested that the strong, insisting on their natural right to unregulated freedom of contract, are already slaves themselves. Transforming "freedom of contract" into "freedom of savagery" and "natural right" into "slavery to nature," Ely imagines the strong as already enslaved. In this, he extends—by inverting—the argument the Illinois court used to strike down the sweatshop laws. The court had outrageously interpreted regulation in that case not as an effort to protect the weak against the strong but as an attempt to limit the rights of the weak. Now, imagining the strong as slaves to their own conception of natural right, Ely invokes the restraints of "true freedom" in an unwitting but inevitable attempt to protect the strong against themselves. What the Illinois court had refused to do for the sweatshop workers, Ely rushes to do for the sweatshop owners—they all need to be protected against their perverse love of freedom.

What makes that love perverse is that it's indistinguishable from the masochistic love of slavery. Loving freedom of contract for its own sake, Ely thinks, you will end by destroying what you love and will find yourself enslaved. But the masochist cannot love a freedom that does not lead to slavery; indeed, what the masochist loves is only the freedom to be a slave, a freedom, in other words, that is confirmed, not betrayed, by enslavement. To put this another way, the masochist loves what the capitalist loves:

the freedom to buy and sell, the inalienable right to alienate.

In this respect, the masochist embodies the purest of commitments to laissez-faire while at the same time somewhat altering our usual sense of what those commitments were. "The strong want unregulated contract," Ely writes; the "economic conservatives" want their freedom. They want it, he tries to think, because they know that without regulation there will be no limit to their accumulation of property; eventually, they will own everything and everyone. But what the masochist understands (and what Ely's own text begins to show) is that the desire to own cannot be separated from the desire to be owned. The masochist wants to be owned—which is to say really that he wants to be sold, to sell himself, to own the right to sell himself. The masochist wants, in other words, to own. If, according to Ely, "voluntary contract must . . . sometimes be forbidden in order to avoid slavery," then according to the masochist, slavery must be allowed in order to guarantee freedom. The right of the individual to own himself must not be infringed, and so the right of the individual to sell himself and to be owned by someone else must not be denied. Insisting on these rights—loving property, loving freedom—the capitalist and the masochist are one and the same.

At the end of *Venus in Furs,* having returned to his father's estate and, on his father's death, taken his place as proprietor of that estate, Severin receives a letter from Wanda. She describes her life during the three years since she abandoned him in Florence, and more important, explains her reasons for leaving. From the moment he wanted to be her slave, she writes, she knew he could never be her husband. She had agreed to act out his "ideal" partly to amuse herself and partly in the hope that her cruelty might "cure" him—as indeed, Severin notes, it has. When Wanda ran off with her Greek, the "strong man" she "needed," Severin himself began to turn into a version of that strong man. With women, he says, you can be either a "slave" or a "tyrant"; now he beats his serving girls (they love it), and when asked for the "moral" of his story, he replies, in the accents of a certain social Darwinism, "anyone who lets himself be whipped, deserves to be whipped."

This ending enacts a double effort of normalization. Most obviously, the sexes are returned to their appropriate roles: Wanda finds a real man and Severin becomes one. More important, however, than the reordering of the sexes is the simple fact of reordering itself. With women, you can be only a tyrant or a slave; this makes it seem as if Severin, having made the wrong choice before, now makes the right one. But the either/or logic of this choice means more than the particular role you might choose. It definitively separates the tyrant from the slave, the strong from the weak, and it leaves the individual free to find his place according to his preference, ability, or nature. "Anyone who lets himself be whipped, deserves to be whipped." *Venus in Furs* ends with a gesture toward the free market as meritocracy and with a vision of the masochistic contract as an instrument of social and natural selection.

But the text itself, the actual masochistic contract, does

not allow such a separation and does not authorize the appeal to a natural law, a set of natural distinctions between strong and weak, owner and owned. Indeed, the whole point of contract, as I have described it, is to exhibit these distinctions as aspects of identity rather than identity itself. In contract no one is simply a tyrant or a slave; everyone is a buyer *and* a seller. This is why the contract, in making slavery modern, makes it, in a certain sense, no longer slavery at all, or at least no longer the feudalism that writers like Stowe and Ely imagined they feared. What Ely really feared was contract, and what he really wanted was the feudalism he thought he feared, a feudalism in which the restraints on alienation that once derived from "custom" would derive instead from the state. Ultimately, then, for Ely and Severin both, the strong are the strong and the weak are the weak; the difference is just that Ely wants to regulate the tyrant whereas Severin wants to be one. (pp. 132-34)

> *Walter Benn Michaels, "The Phenomenology of Contract," in his* The Gold Standard and the Logic of Naturalism: American Literature at the Turn of the Century, *University of California Press, 1987, pp. 113-36.*

John Ash   (essay date 1988)

[*In the following excerpt, Ash discusses Sacher-Masoch's career, focusing on* Venus in Furs.]

To call Masoch "the first masochist" is misleading. There are many elements in the works of his precursors and contemporaries—notably Gautier, Flaubert, Swinburne, and Baudelaire—which we would now define as "masochistic." There are also elements in Masoch's books not encompassed by the popular understanding of that term. It was only after the publication of *Psychopathia Sexualis* in 1892, three years before Masoch's death, that he began to be regarded chiefly as a pervert and pornographer. This deeply distressed Masoch, who considered himself a serious artist and thinker. He was of the opinion that "imaginative writing ought to be an illustrated natural history of mankind": its purpose was to "describe the moral situation and demand reform." This is exactly what he set out to do in *Venus in Furs.* He would have been appalled by the idea that he was writing pornography.

Venus in Furs is only one volume of a huge cycle of novels called The Legacy of Cain, in which Masoch intended to treat *all* the outstanding ethical and political problems of his day, under six headings: love, private property, money, the state, war, and death. Only the first two parts of this wildly overambitious project were completed, though by 1874 it already amounted to 13 novels—including *Paradise on the Dniester,* a tale of agrarian communism, and *Plato's Love,* which contains a sympathetic treatment of male homosexuality. In this context, no one was likely to mistake Masoch for a pornographer. Nor do the predilections revealed in *Venus in Furs* seem to have been considered shocking or unusual at the time of its publication in 1869. There was a widespread popular response to the novel, and Masoch carried on a vast and enthusiastic correspondence with respectable female admirers, one of whom became his wife.

While it may be unjust, the exclusive identification of Masoch with a sexual perversion does not, in itself, account for the neglect. It may be that readers approaching *Venus in Furs* expecting pornography feel cheated; the language is decorous, there are no explicit descriptions of sexual intercourse, and there are confusing references to Plato, Hegel, Schopenhauer, and the emancipation of women. This is definitely a book to be read with both hands. Disappointed readers may have expected Masoch to write from the position of a Sadean victim. Nothing could be further from the truth, and Deleuze is right to dismiss the term *sadomasochism* as a semiological howler [see excerpt dated 1967]. It certainly confuses the issue by suggesting that sadism and masochism are always in communication, whereas in their classic forms they constitute completely separate worlds; it implies the primacy of sadism, that masochism depends on the presence of a sadist. As a consequence, masochism is always seen as subsidiary and secondary—Masoch's 90 novels as a footnote to Sade's. But the presence of a sadist destroys the masochistic ritual, as the climactic scene of *Venus in Furs* makes clear. When a man bursts in upon the ritual and brutally beats the hero, the latter is filled only with disillusionment and disgust.

Classic masochism, as it appears in *Venus in Furs,* is not simply a matter of deriving pleasure from pain, but a complex of specialized tastes that center on symbolic acts. The most important is flagellation; the lover/slave is tied up and beaten or whipped by his mistress. The mistress is elaborately dressed—rarely without furs. She must appear magnificent (a little à la Catherine the Great). Her breasts may sometimes be exposed to imitate Titian's *Venus with a Mirror,* a painting also much admired by Swinburne. The flagellation scenes take place in sumptuous settings—a room whose ceiling is painted with a fresco of Samson and Delilah, a bathhouse roofed by a dome of red glass. In public, the lover may assume the role of servant—walking behind his mistress in the street, carrying her belongings, serving at dinner.

There is nothing titillating about these scenes; the atmosphere is claustrophobic, intense, and oddly desexualized. Masoch's lovers, Wanda and Severin, are not the two-dimensional constructs of pornography. They are capable of laughter. Severin acknowledges the absurdity of his situation, while Wanda sometimes finds their play-acting tiresome and silly. Between scenes of flagellation and ritual humiliation, they engage in Platonic dialogues, exchange conventional expressions of tenderness, and read poetry together (Lermontov or Goethe's *Roman Elegies*). They travel to Italy, and Severin composes Swinburnian apostrophes to his "tender demon," whose "marble body" reclines "among the myrtles and the aloes."

Despite the attempts of psychoanalysts to turn her into a man (the vengeful father *en travestie*) in the interest of furthering their tidy Oedipal schemes, Masoch's Venus is obviously a version of that favorite 19th century figure, the Fatal Woman. She is not a sadist, however. Her cruelty and disdain are roles, assumed with some difficulty. Wanda does this because it amuses her to satisfy the eccentric preferences of her lover. In the process, she is transformed from a spirited modern woman of independent means into an archetype. She becomes Woman reclaiming her legitimate rights. These are the rights of Johann Jakob Bachofen's *Das Mutterrecht,* the historical rights of matriarchy.

First published in 1861, Bachofen's book proposed the revolutionary idea that civilization had its origins in matriarchy. According to his scheme, the development of culture can be divided into four phases: Aphrodisian, Artemisian, Demeterian, and Apollonian. *Venus in Furs* adheres strictly to this scheme, without which it is difficult to make sense of some of the most important episodes in the novel. For example, the nearly surreal scene in which Severin is harnessed to a plow and forced to till a field while being driven on by negresses with whips is (among other things) a fertility rite related to the cult of Demeter; it therefore corresponds to Bachofen's third phase of culture. Similarly, the man who destroys the masochistic idyll is referred to as "the Greek," and his appearance marks the beginning of Bachofen's Apollonian phase—the patriarchal takeover, the end of Severin's dreams of a new sexual order.

The masochistic male is not merely the passive victim of his imperious mistress; he is her active collaborator, even her instructor. The purpose of the ritual they enact is the symbolic abolition of patriarchy. The relationship between Severin and Wanda is governed by a series of written contracts of increasing stringency that invert and parody the conventional marriage contract. Severin's voluntary surrender of male privilege is the model for the overthrow of all entrenched male authority in the world at large—something borne out by the more overtly political volumes of The Legacy of Cain.

These matters cannot be understood on the basis of the primacy of sadism—indeed, the idea subjects much of later 19th century literature to gross misinterpretation. This is what happens in Mario Praz's study of 19th century erotic literature, *The Romantic Agony,* in which Masoch merits only one mention in a footnote. Here is part of Praz's comment on Flaubert's delirious novel of ancient Carthage, *Salammbô:* "with Flaubert we have entered the dominion of the Fatal Woman, and sadism appears under the passive aspect which is usually called masochism (as though the active and passive aspects were not usually present in sadism, and a mere change of proportions really justified a change in name)." In fact, the conflict in *Salammbô* between the barbarian Matho (the representative of militant, solar potency) and the fanatically moon-worshiping heroine dramatizes the shift from a predominantly sadistic ethos before 1848 to a predominately masochistic ethos after 1870. Praz's "mere change of proportions" is more in the nature of a revolution—a fact that writers as diverse as Laforgue, Mallarmé, and Wilde recognized. Swinburne, whom Sade's *Justine* had reduced to helpless laughter, found *Salammbô* "stunning." There are female libertines in Sade, but their participation in the Sadean world cannot be compared to the absolute rule of the Fatal Woman or her challenge to male authority.

At once sumptuous and cruel, *Salammbô* still retains sa-

distic elements—children are sacrificed, lions and lepers crucified, apes burned alive. Baudelaire's *Les fleurs du mal* is transitional in the same way. Sadistic elements (blasphemy, mutilation of the sexual object) coexist with a masochistic aestheticism centered on the figure of a severe and dominant woman. By its very nature, sadism is hostile to aestheticism. There are elaborate settings in Sade, but they are purely functional. They are elaborate because they must accommodate the continuous and diverse activities of sadism—its perpetual motion. By contrast, masochism is characterized by immobility, coldness, and suspension, and it is inseparable from aestheticism: lush textures, gorgeous interiors, objects d'art, opulent reds and purples, and always *hair* and *furs.*

This brings us to the question—why is Venus in furs? Baudelaire notes in his *Fusées:* "The early taste for women. I confused the smell of fur with the aroma of women." In *Venus in Furs,* Severin claims to have been born with a taste for fur: "it is a natural law that fur has a stimulating effect on highly-strung people." This law has to do with the electricity of fur; we might almost say that the masochistic ritual is statically charged. Quite naturally in these circumstances, both Masoch and Baudelaire loved cats. For Baudelaire, they were "fervent lovers" and "austere scholars" which resembled sphinxes when asleep. According to Masoch, "cats have always had . . . a beneficial and magical effect on spiritual and impressionable people: the movement of their long, graceful tails, their magneticism, their fur crackling with electricity. . . . No wonder they were the favorite pets of men such as Mohammed, Richelieu, Crebillon, Rousseau and Wieland." When his mental stability collapsed in his last years, Masoch strangled his favorite angora cat. Thereafter he dreamed repeatedly that he was being eaten alive by cats. Since the cat is the symbol of the imperious, sphinxlike women clothed in furs, Masoch murdered his ideal. It is a tale worthy of Poe.

Closely allied to the taste for fur is a fascination with female hair and clothing. Masoch's Venus has brilliant red hair and can afford to dress magnificently: "A heavy sea-green silk plastically encloses her divine form leaving the bust and arms bare. In her hair, which is done into a single flaming knot, a white water-lily blossoms, from it the leaves of reeds interwoven with a few loose strands fall down toward her neck." (pp. 49-50)

Venus must also resemble as much as possible a statue. Baudelaire's "Beauty" describes herself as "a dream of stone": she is cold and white as snow and swans; she hates movement. In this respect, Baudelaire was following the example of Théophile Gautier (to whom *Les fleurs du mal* is dedicated), who declared in an autobiographical essay: "I always preferred a statue to a real woman and marble to flesh." In *Venus in Furs,* Severin confesses that his first real love was a plaster statue of Venus in his father's library:

> One night I left my bed to pay her a visit: the light from the crescent moon fell upon me and bathed the Goddess in a cold, blue light. I prostrated myself and kissed her foot. . . . An insuperable desire took hold of me; I stood up and threw my arms around her beautiful body and kissed her ice-cold lips.

From this early experience springs his "excessively developed aestheticism" and his "supersensual sentimentalism." The experience is reinforced when Severin first meets Wanda. They are staying in the same hotel at a spa. In the gardens is a statue of Venus which Masoch's lyrical prose halos with gorgeous atmospheric effects—moonlight, storm clouds, shafts of sunlight, and clouds of butterflies. As he pays court to the real woman, Severin secretly worships the statue. Wanda signals her acceptance of his suit by draping her fur-trimmed jacket over it. In *Venus in Furs,* we find the same tendency that Victor Brombert discerned in *Salammbô:* the tendency toward the "immobilisation of life and the animation of the inanimate." The living woman becomes a statue; the statue comes to life. The masochist is a Pygmalion in search of his Galathea.

To read *Venus in Furs* as a revelation of one man's psychosexual problems is to misread it. In the first place, Masoch was a highly self-conscious literary artist of considerable skill. The novel is also a landmark in the history of sexuality. With exemplary self-awareness, Masoch determined to isolate the symptoms of his condition and build them into a coherent imaginative structure—a paradigm, an absolute standard by which we may judge the masochistic in others. At the same time, Masoch's ideas on sexuality should not be divorced from his historical and political theories or from the larger context of 19th century literature. It follows that while the term *sadomasochism* may be useful to describe conflicting impulses in individuals and relationships, it is a barrier to understanding Masoch's work. Aware that misunderstanding was likely to be his fate, Masoch took steps to prevent it; on the last page of the novel we find this blunt statement:

> woman, as Nature has created her and as man up to now has found her attractive, is man's enemy: she can be his slave or his mistress *but never his companion.* This she can only be when she has the same rights as he and is equal in education and work. For the time being there is only one alternative: to be the hammer or the anvil.

Masochism exposes the hypocrisy of civilized manners. Severin's final reversion to male domination ("I was an ass. . . . If only I had whipped her!") is not presented as a solution to the problem of relations between sexes, but as a defeat. All he can do is lapse into the sterile misogyny of Schopenhauer. Severin can no longer hope to become the ideal "new man" who, through his submission and suffering, has earned the right to be the companion of the "new woman." The masochistic ritual finally appears as an intuitive response to an unjust and unsatisfactory status quo, and as a tactic in the arena of sexual politics. (p. 50)

John Ash, "Bound for Glory," in The Village Voice, *Vol. XXXIII, No. 8, February 23, 1988, pp. 49-50.*

FURTHER READING

Anderson, Mark M. "Kafka and Sacher-Masoch." *Journal of the Kafka Society of America* 7, No. 2 (December 1983): 4-19.

> Suggests that *Venus in Furs* influenced Kafka's *The Metamorphosis* and assesses Kafka's novella in the light of this presumed influence. Excerpts from both works appear in German without English translations.

Solomon, Charles. Review of *Venus in Furs,* by Leopold von Sacher-Masoch. *The Los Angeles Times Book Review* (3 September 1989): 11.

> Attributes a feminist point of view to *Venus in Furs* and evaluates "this infamous novel" as dreary and boring.

"Cross of Delight." *The Times Literary Supplement,* No. 3,472 (12 September 1968): 1000.

> Review of *Contes et romans* noting the inherent interest of Sacher-Masoch's Galician settings but maintaining that his fiction merits consideration primarily as a clinical examination of obsession.

Catharine Parr Traill

1802-1899

(Born Catharine Parr Strickland) English-born Canadian novelist, essayist, and short story writer.

Among the first Canadian women to gain literary recognition, Traill is the author of *The Backwoods of Canada,* a domestic manual and chronicle of her experiences as a British settler in southeast Ontario during the 1830s. While the practical value of *Backwoods* has declined in the twentieth century, it remains of historical interest, and critics have praised the rich detail with which Traill portrayed the domestic demands on the nineteenth-century frontier wife.

Traill was the seventh of nine children born to the Stricklands, an affluent English couple descended from royalty. Raised in Suffolk county at Reydon Hall, the family's country estate, Traill spent much of her childhood reading and exploring the woods surrounding her home, activities strongly promoted by her parents as the basis for a well-balanced education. During this time, Traill and her brothers and sisters began writing stories. Most of Traill's siblings went on to attain literary recognition in adulthood, the most famous perhaps being Susanna Strickland Moodie, a prolific contributor to Canadian literary journals and the author of the popular autobiography *Roughing It in the Bush; or, Life in Canada.* In 1826, after publishing several stories for children, Traill published *The Young Emigrants; or, Pictures of Canada, Calculated to Amuse and Instruct the Minds of Youth,* a novel based on the experiences of a British family in Canada with whom Traill corresponded.

In 1832 Traill married an officer in the English army, and shortly afterward the couple emigrated to Canada, at the time a largely unsettled country offering opportunities for adventure and financial success. Traill's brother, Samuel Strickland, had already established a home and business near Peterborough, Ontario, and Traill and her husband obtained four hundred acres adjacent to Strickland's property through a grant available to English officers. On their arrival, the Traills cleared the land, built a house, and began farming. During the next several years, Traill wrote essays and kept journals describing the hardships she and her husband encountered as pioneers and detailing the natural surroundings, particularly the plant life of Canada. These writings, combined with her letters to her mother, provided the basis of *The Backwoods of Canada,* which was published in England in 1836. An immediate popular success as a handbook for English gentry considering emigration to Canada, the work was translated into German and French the following year.

Traill and her husband left the backwoods in 1838 when they moved to a nearby village, and in 1846 they settled on the south shore of Rice Lake. During this time and throughout the next several decades, Traill published essays and books on natural history, botany, and domestic concerns while raising ten children. Her essays on wildflowers and other plant life are contained in such collections as *Rambles in the Canadian Forest* and *Pearls and Pebbles; or, The Notes of an Old Naturalist.* Recognized for her contributions to Canadian studies as a writer and naturalist, Traill received a stipend from the Royal Bounty Fund of Canada and was presented by the Dominion Government the title to island property on the Otonabee River. She died in 1899 at the age of ninety-seven.

Critical examination of Traill's works focuses on *The Backwoods of Canada,* which has been praised for both its documentary and literary value. Offering advice on such various aspects of pioneer life as procuring and preparing food, treating illnesses, and interacting with frontier servants, as well as providing observations on Native American culture and skillful descriptions of the plants, birds, and animals common to the region, *Backwoods* has been called "the dictionary of pioneer economy." Among its most important features is its presentation of one of the first literary images of the British settler in Canada, a figure later popular in Canadian fiction. In addition, the narrative voice of the pioneer woman in the book is considered of particular literary and historical significance. Carl

P. A. Ballstadt has called Traill's accomplishment in *Backwoods* a "rhetoric of balance," in which she portrayed both the hardships and the splendor of frontier life in Canada and employed a combination of subjective and objective points of view. Recent commentary stresses the historical value of *Backwoods* as a record of the daily life of a British frontier settler in Ontario and as an individual portrait of Traill, noting her vitality and her sense of fulfillment in her new surroundings. As Desmond Pacey has concluded, the rich detail of *Backwoods* allows modern readers to "experience vicariously the life of the pioneers."

PRINCIPAL WORKS

Little Downy; or, The History of a Field Mouse: A Moral Tale (short story) 1822

The Young Emigrants; or, Pictures of Canada, Calculated to Amuse and Instruct the Minds of Youth (novel) 1826

The Backwoods of Canada; Being Letters from the Wife of an Emigrant Officer; Illustrative of the Domestic Economy of British America (nonfiction) 1836

The Canadian Crusoes: A Tale of the Rice Lake Plains (novel) 1852; also published as *Lost in the Backwoods: A Tale of the Canadian Forest,* 1882

The Female Emigrant's Guide, and Hints on Canadian Housekeeping (nonfiction) 1854; also published as *The Canadian Settler's Guide,* 1855

Rambles in the Canadian Forest (essays) 1859

Canadian Wild Flowers (nonfiction) 1869

Studies of Plant Life in Canada; or, Gleanings from Forest, Lake, and Plain (nonfiction) 1885

Pearls and Pebbles; or, The Notes of an Old Naturalist (essays) 1894

Hampden Burnham   (essay date 1895)

[*In the following review of* Pearls and Pebbles, *Burnham praises Traill's descriptions of the Canadian wilderness and comments on her works of fiction.*]

We are accustomed to judge of a writer by what that writer has put on paper, but in the case of the author of *Pearls and Pebbles* that would be quite an unsatisfactory text. Neither is it an easy thing to focus the characteristics of a personality that has not been fully revealed in her writings—as it would be difficult to describe a country from a few specimens of its *flora,* or from the music of its songbirds.

Though the writer of this sketch is no more than an acquaintance of the famous author, yet, perhaps, he is not simply on that account the less fitted to comply with the editor's request.

Mrs. Traill's latest book has again aroused the interest of the public in one who has devoted the greater part of her ninety-three years to the building up of the natural history of Canada. My first thought, on meeting her some years ago, was that if I had been the father of a family of girls I should bring them to see her without delay, so large a share does she possess of that gentleness and dignity of mind and heart, which is at once the charm and pre-eminence of womankind.

Though one admires her writings, the best of her is unwritten. Her extensive and important researches in Canadian wild-flowers are not literary but botanical, and her descriptions of life in the forest are entertaining but not intended to be more. With the exception of these latest "leaves from the journal of an old naturalist," which are literary in the tenderest sense, her work has been useful more than ornamental. Hence, if we would know the worker we must see her—see her in her happy moods, when the lustre of her eyes makes easy the reading of her thoughts, and the undisturbed flow of her conversation holds the interest of the listener.

Her earlier writings, published in England, brought her recompense both in pocket and reputation. There she has a reputation like that of A.L.O.E. in this country.

She is not valued in Canada as she should be. Her ideal is too high and her work too consistent for that. The two-and-two-are-four fashion of the day has driven out the ideal, and in two generations more, young Canada will have learned to smile at a world that could have stood in awe of Agamemnon for three thousand years. Her contributions to English magazines began at a very early age, but the novelty of Canadian life and the wild beauty of Canadian scenes caused her to turn to the natural rather than to the intellectual.

In her works of fiction Mrs. Traill cannot be acquitted of faults. **Lost in the Backwoods,** the most typical of these, is both dramatic and descriptive to a degree, but the dialogue is stilted, and the wisdom that of the old rather than of the young. The story opens in Lower Canada at the time of the "famous battle of Quebec," when the wounded Scottish soldier, Duncan Maxwell, meets for the first time the widow's daughter, the *petite habitante,* Catherine Perron. A few years elapse. They marry. Catherine has a brother, Pierre, who is a hunter, and who, in his hunting expeditions, had gone up as far as the Plains of the Rice Lake. He suggests that Duncan and he, with their wives, should found on the shores of the Rice Lake their future homes. Thither they go and establish themselves amid the loneliness and isolation of the forest. We wonder at their courage, but, as the author tells us, "there was in those days a spirit of resistance among the first settlers on the soil, a spirit to do and bear that is less commonly met with now." Hector, a boy of fourteen, is the eldest child of Duncan. Louis, of the same age, is the only son of Pierre. Catherine, the sister of Hector, is two years younger. All three set out one lovely morning in May to find the cattle. They lose themselves in the forest, and their wanderings furnish the materials of the narrative. As the warlike Mohawks and the Chippewas still "held their councils and their hunting-parties on the hills about the Rice Lake," the fear of capture and of torture add horror to the anguish of the parents. The author avails herself of every occasion to inculcate practical Christian teaching and to describe the manner of life in the forest and among the Indians. One would suspect, however, a different conclusion from the children when "they beheld a savage enemy in every mass of leafy shade, and every rustling bough struck fresh terror into their excited minds." "They might have exclaimed," says the author, "with the patriarch Jacob, 'How awful is this place!' "

Yet no more accurate and entertaining description of the woods, flowers, forest-animals and Indians could be wished. Nor dramatic, as it is, is it one particle overdrawn.

Even the old frequenter will know the Rice Lake country the better for having read this book. Who can resist the flowers' appeal, when Mrs. Traill interprets; still, the botanical names, hidden though they be in parentheses, give one a sort of chill. The naturalist has clearly overborne the romancist. The minuteness of detail is extraordinary, but it sometimes lengthens into a catalogue. Her imagination, too, is restrained by an intensely religious spirit, and her candour is such that she does not forbear to acknowledge the legend which she has made use of to develop the story. This is as it may be, but it is not literature in the strictly literary sense. When the weirdness of the tale has secured the reader the reading will do much more than entertain, and the reprinting of the tale by the publishers speaks for itself. It would indeed be a great pity if no record of the fortitude of these pioneers had not been kept. The chronicles are few, and the tale of patient courage is such as will never again be told in Canada. Unlike Cooper, Mrs. Traill tells of the white man rather than of the Indian, excelling him in her descriptions of nature, though his greater field admits a greater plot and a more elaborate treatment.

In *Pearls and Pebbles* one will find a book of poems in prose. There is nothing more difficult to describe, perhaps, than the Canadian seasons. They have been done almost to death. But I know of nothing more exquisite than some of her shadow-dreams of Autumn. (pp. 388-90)

> *Hampden Burnham, "Gable Ends," in* The Canadian Magazine of Politics, Science, Art and Literature, *Vol. IV, No. 4, February, 1895, pp. 388-90.*

Clara Thomas (essay date 1966)

[*In the following excerpt, Thomas discusses Traill's works in the context of her experiences as an immigrant in Canada.*]

The Backwoods of Canada records only the first three years of the Traills' Canadian experience, though for later editions Catharine added a supplement describing their reaction to the Rebellion of 1837. The 1836 edition, however, is exactly what it announces itself to be: a compendium of commentary on conditions and useful advice, given form by its narrative of personal experience. More than a third of the text deals with the experiences of their long journey to their land; the rest is weighted toward description of the flora and fauna, of the Indians, and of general customs and conditions that all settlers must meet. Success, given good sense and hard work, is taken for granted. Had Elizabeth Bennet and Mr. Darcy, well refined of their "Pride" and their "Prejudice," decided to emigrate for the future of their family, we would expect to find in them a capability, an adaptability, and a cheerful common sense similar to Catharine and Thomas Traill's.

Catharine was frankly delighted to be rid of the social pretentiousness that she deplored in England and as a ridiculous import to Canadian towns and villages: "we are totally without the fear of any Mr. or Mrs. Grundy; and having shaken off the trammels of Grundyism, we laugh at the absurdity of those who voluntarily forge afresh and hug their chains." Her mind was scientific, rational, and inquiring in its bent, accumulating and assimilating the facts and conditions of her new existence and organizing these to be passed on usefully to others. She saw their situation as a "Robinson Crusoe sort of life" and her naturally empiric mind accepted and welcomed the challenge.

Her love of nature, which went far beyond emotional enthusiasm to a scientist's patience and particularity, was, from the first, an absorbing hobby and must have been a major sustaining factor in the years of pioneer hardships. In an early letter she promises to collect a *hortus siccus* for her sister Eliza—"I now deeply regret I did not benefit by the frequent offers Eliza made me of prosecuting a study which I once thought dry, but now regard as highly interesting." She commenced a programme of self-tuition which led her beyond the status of amateur and which made her, finally, an international authority on Canada's plants and flowers. The beginnings of this future reputation are strongly marked in *The Backwoods:* she devotes two paragraphs only to her attack of cholera, but requires more than forty pages of her text to describe the birds, small animals, and particularly the flowers that she has observed around her home.

She is concerned that a truthful picture be given of the problems of emigration and is particularly anxious to instruct prospective emigrant women, both on the attitudes they should wisely develop and the skills they must anticipate acquiring. On the first she says, "we bush-ladies have a wholesome disregard of what Mr. or Mrs. So-and-so thinks or says. We pride ourselves on conforming to circumstances." Toward the latter purpose she reports at length on all the facets of housekeeping in the bush, and finally appends thirty-five pages of useful information of all kinds, including a collection of recipes for making maple-sugar, soft soap, candles, vinegar—processes which might well be unfamiliar to an Englishwoman but which were a necessary part of the knowledge of a Canadian housewife.

Catharine found Canadian society no rude shock to her understanding of class distinctions: "As a British officer must needs be a gentleman and his wife a lady, perhaps we repose quietly on that incontestable proof of our gentility, and can afford to be useful without injuring it." She considers that it is the quality of the Peterborough settlement that the "lower or working classes are well-disposed," perhaps underestimating her own and her husband's abilities to command both affection and respect. In any case, the Traills have no personnel problems:

> Our servants are as respectful, or nearly so, as those at home; nor are they admitted to our tables, or placed on an equality with us except at "bees," and such kind of public meetings; when

they usually conduct themselves with a propriety that would afford an example to some that call themselves gentlemen, viz., young men who voluntarily throw aside those restraints that society expects from persons filling a respectable situation.

(*Backwoods,* Letter xv)

The final letter in the *Backwoods of Canada* carries a dominant note of satisfaction and optimism: "On the whole we have been fortunate, especially in the situation of our land, which has increased in value very considerably; our chief difficulties are now over, at least we hope so, and we trust soon to enjoy the comforts of a cleared farm" (*Backwoods,* Letter XVIII). The book ends with no peroration, no recapitulating, but simply as a letter ends, and particularly a letter from Catharine Traill. She has been describing a strange light she observed in the winter sky which seemed like and yet strangely different from the *aurora borealis.* And then, suddenly, "I must now close this epistle; I have many letters to prepare for friends, to whom I can only write when I have the opportunity of free conveyance, the inland postage being very high. . . . Adieu, my kindest and best of friends."

Its several editions attest the book's success, both in terms of its declared purpose, as a manual for emigrants, and as "entertaining knowledge" for a wider reading public who were attracted by its low-keyed charm and air of authenticity. (pp. 52-4)

The Traills lived in the village of Ashburnham [from 1838] until 1846 when they moved again to the country, this time to a partially cleared farm on the south shore of Rice Lake, near the village of Harwood. They named their home "Oaklands" and the rise on which it stood, Mount Ararat. For ten years they lived here with their family, which finally numbered nine, four sons and five daughters. Catharine, like [her sister, Susanna Moodie, who was also an immigrant in the region] implemented their always meagre income by writing sketches and short tales, but unlike Susanna, she wrote fiction largely as a means of earning and not in any similar degree as an end in itself, a pleasure and a necessity of her personality. She was glad to move to "Oaklands" from Ashburnham, partly because of the increased scope the country gave to her botanical investigations. Here she wrote *The Canadian Crusoes* and *Lady Mary and Her Nurse,* the children's books for which she is best remembered, and *The Female Emigrant's Guide,* a dictionary of useful knowledge for the pioneer woman and a useful companion-piece to *The Backwoods of Canada.*

Lady Mary and Her Nurse, also published as *Afar in the Forest* and *Stories of the Canadian Forest,* is a collection of animal stories, sentimentally told, but with evident keen observation of the kinds and habits of Canadian animals. *Canadian Crusoes* is a minor classic among Canadian children's books. It is the story of two Scottish Canadians, Hector Maxwell and his sister Catharine, and their French-Canadian friend, Louis Perron. The three young people are lost on the Rice Lake plains, and in the course of their wanderings they learn the arts and crafts of survival in the wilderness. They are joined by a young Mohawk

girl, Indiana, whom they have rescued from exposure and death at the hands of her tribe's enemies, the Ojibways. The story ends on a high note of romance: the French, Scottish, and Indian strains are united in the marriages of Louis and Catharine and Hector and Indiana.

Such a plot no more strains the bounds of credulity than does, for instance, *The Last of the Mohicans.* In fact, Catharine Traill was probably influenced by Cooper and almost certainly by Scott, in her own impulse toward the making of romantic Canadian legend. She was entirely herself, however, in the weight she gave to practical natural lore—the plot does not obscure the book's assembling of instructions for survival in the wilderness. It is in this aspect that *Canadian Crusoes* attracts curiosity and then admiration today; it was reprinted in 1923. The book carries heavy strains of sentimental melodrama and evangelical moralizing which are now outdated, but its voice of an expert telling plainly and clearly how to make, how to find, how to live in the Canadian woods is still clear and compelling. The title, *Canadian Crusoes,* is of course, a particularly happy choice, true to Catharine Traill's outstanding rational and empiric nature and to her own experience. Like the events of her own life, her characters' adventures are informed and directed by intelligence, common sense, and adaptability; a potentially hostile environment is dominated and put in its proper perspective, to be respected for its strengths and enjoyed for its beauties. In 1852, the book was published in London, given the prestige of her sister's name by the addition of "edited by Agnes Strickland," and in 1853 an American edition was published in New York. There were several later editions of both *Canadian Crusoes* and *Lady Mary and Her Nurse,* but Catharine Traill received for them nothing more than the $50 that Thomas Nelson & Sons paid when they bought the copyright.

The Backwoods of Canada had been designed and had been successful as a basic text for emigrating gentlewomen. In 1854 Catharine Traill published *The Female Emigrant's Guide,* a more specific instruction manual, combining all sorts of useful information, and particularly stressing the food and medicinal possibilities of native Canadian plants and the various ways of preparing and cooking both plants and animals. From the lore of Indians, from observation of the habits of birds and animals, and from her own keen and constant observations and experiments, she had, after twenty years in Canada, assembled a complete dictionary of pioneer economy. The usefulness of the book in her own day is obvious—she even includes a calendar summary, instructing her readers on what they may expect of the weather and of plant and animal life, month by month, through the Canadian year. Its charm today, when we do not need its instruction, is in its harking back to things past, with all the simplicity, clarity, and expert knowledge that Catharine Traill commanded when she reported what she found and what she saw, what she knew and what she used. (pp. 63-5)

In the introduction to *Studies of Plant Life,* Catharine Traill described the progress of her self-education in botany during her years in Canada, and her ambition that her work might become a "household book, as Gilbert

White's Natural History of Selborne is to this day among English readers." The text reflects Catharine herself; it has a candid, diary quality, an expectation that the reader's pleasure will match the writer's, and a literary flavour from the many poetic epigraphs chosen to complement her descriptions. She ranges from Chaucer to Longfellow, from Milton to William Cullen Bryant to find fitting tributes to her flowers, and on one occasion she composes her own verses to the violet, "after the manner of Herrick."

Her work, though not scientifically botanical by the standards of the twentieth century, is remarkably precise and encyclopaedic to the lay reader. Usually, her method is to name a plant, by popular and Latin names, to categorize it, and then to go into its special properties. For example, we find that the Marsh marigold, vividly recalled by its description, has leaves which are edible as "pot-herbs," while the Mayapple, which she links to the Mandrake of age-old notoriety, has leaves of deadly poison. The fruit, however, is pleasant to eat, "sub-acid," and "is a fine preserve with white sugar and when flavoured with lemon peel and ginger." Goldenrod makes yellow or green dye, the milkweed fibre would give a long strong thread, a possible valuable addition to the manufacture of Canadian fabrics, mullein leaves have great healing properties and are also supposed to drive away rats and mice; "but this virtue may be only a fond illusion. Commend me rather to Miss Pussy." The combination of meticulously observed detail, of practical suggestion, and of affectionate familiarity with all the range of plant life gives a timeless attraction to her work.

She was eighty-two when her *Studies of Plant Life in Canada* was published; ten years later, she gathered together her final work, *Pearls and Pebbles,* a compendium of her personal recollections and her naturalist's observations. Meanwhile, she had received various tokens of the recognition she had earned, both as a Canadian pioneer and as a devoted naturalist. In 1883 she had been officially fêted in Ottawa; a fern which she had found growing near Lakefield had been named for her, "A. marginale (Swz.) var: Traillae"; finally, the government had granted her an island in Stoney Lake, a grant which Mr. Sandford Fleming described to her as "the smallest acknowledgment which is due to you for your life-long devotion to Canada."

She took possession of her new summer home in 1893, and enjoyed her summers in it until her death, in her 98th year, in 1899. She retained her enthusiasms and the faculties for enjoying them, living graciously with age as she had adapted gracefully to life. Her faith had always been sustaining to her, but in the works of her old age she voices more than orthodoxy, a conviction of the spirituality of all matter. The essay on her island closes with these lines:

Nor think though men were none
That heaven would want spectators, God want
   praise:
Millions of spiritual creatures walk the earth
Unseen, both when we wake and when we sleep.

The final essay in *Pearls and Pebbles* is at once a statement of her belief in the unity of all matter and the final affirmation of a benign life—"Something gathers up the fragments, and nothing is lost." (pp. 66-7)

Clara Thomas, "The Strickland Sisters," in The Clear Spirit: Twenty Canadian Women and Their Times, *edited by Mary Quayle Innis, University of Toronto Press, 1966, pp. 42-73.*

William D. Gairdner   (essay date 1972)

[*Gairdner is a Canadian critic and educator. In the following excerpt, he contends that the structure of* The Backwoods of Canada *is informed by Traill's religious views.*]

In talking with a number of people who have read *The Backwoods of Canada,* I have been endlessly discouraged by a certain unwillingness to consider it as anything more than a collection of letters written ostensibly as "a handbook for emigrating gentlewomen" by a dowdy pioneer to her mother. While the average reader knows approximately between what years the letters were written, what hardships Mrs. Traill and her family had to endure, how disillusioning was the Canadian experience, and how difficult for anyone with imagination to write novels in early Canada—and therefore how little good literature we really have, they hastily mention—they all seem to refer to this collection of letters as though it should be placed in brackets, critical thinking to be directed only to the more serious modern novelists in whose works they can recognize the traditional elements of plot, character, symbol, and so on, or whose writing seems more "relevant" to their lives. In the essay which follows, I shall treat aspects of the book which seem to me quite germane to modern Canadian life, for this collection of letters is not merely the "recording" of her daily activities, but the end result of a certain way one individual at a particular point in history embodied her experiences in language.

The first structural feature to be noticed is that the book begins and ends with two essentially religious "views", or visions, which frame the matter of her experiences, while between them appear and drop from sight various themes having to do with the author's basic relation to the universe and God, to human life and morality, and to the physical realities of her particular environment. This basic structural feature tends to colour the whole work and give rise to speculations of an epistemological nature. Consider the following passage:

> So rapid are the changes that take place on this fogbank that perhaps the next time I raise my eyes I behold the scene changed *as if by magic. The misty curtain is slowly drawn up, as if by invisible hands,* and the wild, wooded mountains *partially revealed,* with their bold, rocky shores and sweeping bays. At other times the vapoury volume, *dividing,* moves along the valleys and deep ravines *like lofty pillars* of smoke, or *hangs in snowy draperies* among the dark forest pines. (italics mine)
>
> (p. 75)

[If] it is true that Man is driven by a search for truth in nature, it seems also true that he has a thirst for God, for a sense of justification of what his mind discovers; and these two desires are rarely compatible, in fact, seem diametrically opposed. Looking back at our little paragraph, we can see this state of opposition in the very style of the passage. The ordinary, factual world of nature is "revealed" by "invisible hands". The fog is a series of "pillars", as in a cathedral. The final passage . . . produces an even more vivid effect, thus enclosing the book between two visions which in themselves speak of a tension Mrs. Traill never fully resolves.

In addition to this, and despite the predominantly scientific nature of all her observations, the book is also a religious allegory of the flight from Egypt to the promised land, of the flooding of the world and man's ultimate salvation through suffering. While we often sense that Mrs. Traill takes these allegorical allusions lightly, they occur too often to be trivial. For example, in the entry for August 7th, she has seen a little bird, and likens it to the dove carrying the olive branch in the story of Noah. Anyone who has read the Bible cannot overlook this allusion. But this little scene is also a conventional marker, or sign, referring us to the nature of the Christian "instant", and the idea of revelation it purveys. For to someone whose God is not immanent, and yet exists, his presence, since he is not continually *in* the world, must be a *revealed* presence. That is, the Christian prepares himself for God and, if he is fortunate, He will be revealed through signs—such as this little bird. A Hindu could expect no such thing, I think, because his God is never absent. God *is* the world, and consequently never hidden from view. Later, she compares her disappointment in Montreal to "the fruits of the Dead Sea". And upon her first occasion of worship in the New World, bows on her knees in thankfulness "to that merciful God who had brought us through the perils of the great deep and the horrors of the pestilence", the Flood and the flight from Egypt, respectively.

But one of the disturbing results of this belief in a transcendent God who is "hidden" from us, is that all nature thereby falls prey to the will of man; he can now do what he wants—chop it, burn it, bury it—he has no fear he is injuring God himself or any part of God's body. This is a very curious fact, and in the very early pages of this book we can see its effects aptly commented upon.

At first she simply notices that man is engaged in the "taming" of nature, and she watches "the progress of cultivation among these rugged and inhospitable regions with positive pleasure"; but later she begins to suspect that this cultivation of the wilds, in addition to its practical dimension, disguised other hidden significances. Indeed, in the entry entitled "Clearing the Land," she writes most powerfully of the fire which sweeps over the forest, and of the desolation wrought by the axe of the settler. I think this entry is particularly significant, both in the energy and beauty of her description and in its revelation of her ambiguous attitude toward nature. For although she later refers to the study of botany, flowers, and so on, as "a ladder to Heaven," and in keeping with her rationalist's mind extends His goodness into nature itself (that is, since God is good, He is incapable of creating anything bad, therefore nature is good, therefore the study of nature will reveal God's goodness and, perhaps, at certain moments, even God himself), nevertheless, her feelings are absolutely

ambivalent; she loves nature because God made it, but she derives pleasure from seeing it "tamed" because, like the other settlers, she is afraid of it. Thus, at one and the same time, the fire is destructive, but beautiful; the axe of civilization is satisfying, but also disturbing; for, as she so aptly observes,

> On first coming to this country nothing surprised me more than the total absence of trees about the dwelling-houses and cleared lands; the axe of the chopper relentlessly levels all before him. Man appears to contend with the trees of the forest as though they were his most obnoxious enemies; for he spares neither the young sapling in its greenness nor the ancient trunk in its lofty pride; he wages war against the forest with fire and steel.

In itself, the perspicacity of observation is welcomed, but even more surprising because of its superficiality is the immediately following paragraph which gives the "analysis" of her observation. We cannot remain insensible to the fact that here, as elsewhere, her explanations for everything remain on the rational level. Although she often hints at the irrational, she immediately retreats from interpretation because she obviously regards it as non factual, and therefore fanciful. For my own part, I regard these searchings for botanical justification a result of her own wish to evade the more basic underlying motivations for the actions she has just observed, for she never once suggests that these men wage war against nature because, having been transplanted from an ancient, vertical class culture in which all immediate surroundings bore the imprint of human life, they quite naturally reacted against the overwhelming emptiness of the Canadian wilds. Imagine their first confrontations with such immense solitude! Men who had been used to seeing fences, a pathway, a clearing, now saw only solid virgin forest. The associations are easy, for the forest hid within it wild, dangerous animals—bear, rattler, moose, wolf; and even worse, from its depths came the silent arrow of "the savage." Thus, the backwoods came to equal not only resistance to cultivation because of its stumps, weeds, and the beasts which ate the crops, but more importantly, because of resistance to peace of mind, silence, darkness, and the threat of death. The axe of the chopper was indeed waging war against an enemy, one ever present at that, for death always comes robed in darkness, and his shadow stirs men to action even now. While modern Canadians bury themselves in material trivia in order to escape this uncomfortable reality, our pioneer forefathers removed the threat in admirably pragmatic fashion—they simply chopped away until it was gone. "Practicality is everything here," Mrs. Traill reminds us, and Canadians of her day looked to their fears before they looked to their need for beauty, and they still do. But the difficulty for we who have inherited the fruits and thorns of their labours, is that although the real dangers of the forest are gone, its psychological dangers remain, for it seems we cannot prevent ourselves from digging and chopping at the invisible enemy, while instead of botanical excuses, we find other "practical" reasons such as the need for toilet paper, or newsprint, or telephone poles.

But it was not only the fact that Mrs. Traill lived in a pre-

Freudian era that militated against her divining psychological reasons for what she observed; it was rather because both from temperament and from education, she belonged to a rationalist tradition the weight of which lay behind her, whereas her sister, Susannah Moodie profited from that other major movement so important to us now, called Romanticism, whose greatest impact extends forward to our own time. . . . [Mrs. Traill] couldn't bear to divine psychological motives for human behaviour because of her intellectual-theological beliefs. In short, to her mind, anything not amenable to rational explanation had therefore to be irrational, and anyone believing as she did in a good rational God, was forced, logically, to believe in a good rational world. It is for this reason she is so manifestly disturbed by the incident with the yoke of oxen. They were borrowed for the purposes of houseraising, but wandered off one day and were presumed lost, until, one month later, they were discovered back at their former master's house some twenty miles away. Mrs. Traill expresses her bewilderment in no uncertain terms: ". . . but how is this conduct of the oxen to be accounted for? They returned home through the mazes of interminable forest, where man, *with all his reason and knowledge,* would have been bewildered and lost" (italics mine).

It is obvious from these comments that she partook of an opinion concerning man and his relations to other forms of life which has it that he is situated above the beasts, yet below the higher forms of life such as Saints, Angels, and finally God himself; that by living a "good" life he may rise slightly from his fallen condition—by studying botany, for example, which is a "ladder to heaven"—but through lack of surveillance may sink to deplorable depths, and here the catalogue of Christian sins supplied a convenient measure of his fall. Situated between God and the beasts, Mrs. Traill is rightly bewildered by the behaviour of her oxen, for what she suspects is that perhaps, underneath the rational level of behaviour, there exists another level which we might call instinctual. But although she raises the possibility, she never attempts an answer. Part of the reason must be because any suggestion there existed in beasts powers which in certain circumstances made them superior to rational man would completely inverse the implied world view in terms of which she conceived reality, and leave her open to fundamental uncertainty. Instead, she withdraws from speculation. (pp. 36-7)

Looking back a hundred years or more, it is easy to forget that Mrs. Traill did not have the presumed advantage of studying Darwin, Freud, or Einstein, nor it appears, was she of basically subjectivist or relativist temperament, so that in any case, for the sake of equilibrium, the world *had* to appear rational and ordered. That is understandable. It was only the generations which immediately followed her which so defiantly rebelled against all the precepts she seems to have held, and plunged themselves into that revolution against the conception of an ordered rational world whose results were to so shake man's confidence in himself and in the God who purportedly created him. For it is precisely the revolt against reason whose Canadian beginnings we can detect in her sister, which eventually led to the loss of faith in everything once held sacred by our predecessors. Once we begin to believe that those oxen are superior to us in certain ways, we seem to sink a little in our own estimation, and the whole plan of the universe which seemed previously acceptable, is upset. Mrs. Traill didn't want to destroy that universe, and so, throughout her entire book, retreats from speculation on the irrational. "How infinite," she asserts in her closing pages, "is that wisdom that rules the natural world!"

But one is tempted to ask just how, for a woman as dependent on reason, the paradoxes so apparent to others who followed her were resolved. The answer seems to be that the contradictions which resulted from the exercise of reason were resolved in faith, absorbed into a system of beliefs so that they "made sense." And what made sense to her mind was that those who indulged in intemperance and all manner of other vices should be struck down with cholera! In fact, she seems to take pleasure in the association between vice and disease, for it trusses up both scientific and religious beliefs at once. Fantastically enough, when she herself succumbs to cholera, she is not at all unhappy. She suppresses her suffering and says, "suffice to say, they were intense; but God, in His mercy, though He chastened and afflicted me, yet gave me not over unto death". In fact, in keeping with entirely banal Puritan concepts, the suffering endured by the faithful is entirely justified by the belief that this is God's method for testing faith . . . that it is atonement for sin, however slight. In this way, the rational belief in an ordered world and the Puritan resolutions of its paradox dovetail neatly. The remarkable differences between she and her sister in regard to the expression of feeling are witness to this. Once more, their particularities attest to the generalities of their times. Mrs. Traill's sense of order, buttressed by her religious beliefs, forbade the expression of feeling of any kind. Thus, she describes flowers endlessly, but never the feelings she has in their presence, even for those given by her husband. All emotional life is contained, and must be controlled and mastered by reason. Again, this dovetails with religion. The general Puritan belief that human suffering must be borne silently in atonement for human sin was simply generalized to all emotional expression and all concern for the physical. Bumping over an intolerably bad road one day, she writes, "Sometimes I laughed because I would not cry". Emotional expression, it seems, was contradictory to the epistemology she basically depended upon. In fact, crying, for her, would have been an act of philosophical treason, an admission of the inadmissible. If the book gives us the overwhelming impression of coldness and factualness, this does not mean she herself felt no emotion, but speaks of the entirely conventional tactics she employed to act out her beliefs. We see, then, that for Mrs. Traill the world is simply a testing ground, a place created for man by God and therefore amenable reason, where scientific investigation and Puritan belief go hand in hand. For such as she, the world had no "natural" mystery, and rational man stood on firm ground, never subject to the fears so common in a modern world rife with the irrational and atheistic on whose borders she stood.

In reading this book for the first time, however, the confusion in Mrs. Traill's mind upon emigration to Canada is indeed a matter of interest, and it is only after many pages that we see how the apparent difficulties she experiences with the people around her are in part a result of social attitudes themselves simply a reflection of her worldview. Just as man is situated in a vertical chain of being, so is the entire social structure she left behind vertical in nature. I mean by that, all information, standards, and authority passed from top to bottom, from upper to lower classes, from older to younger people. In a class society where the privileged spent their time creating more privilege, it was only natural to presume this was preordained—especially if one belonged to the upper classes. In this way, the social order itself became a measure of that climb toward the angels, and snobbism a natural offshoot of success. It also happens that such a vertical society blended perfectly with a Puritan conception of the prophet. Jesus, of course, was a perfect existential prophet, in that he lived his example instead of merely preaching about it. In a very unsubtle manner, the upper class English, having arrived with a footing of some altitude in the vertical axis, and a firm belief in Christianity, naturally tended to consider themselves "examples" to the heathen of Canada, and since for Mrs. Traill this was a necessary reality, she was in great distress upon remarking that in Canada the sons of gentlemen were often worse debauchers than the poor. For how can the heathen learn good manners, if we cannot show them? This is an attitude which has not entirely vanished, even after a hundred years of radical social change. Coming as she did from a vertical, class-structured society in the throes of industrialization in which money and values were increasingly those of exchange, to a basically classless, horizontal society in which economy was basically of the barter type, and men who were not yet organized into groups for the purposes of industrial or manufacturing production exhibited no class tendencies particularly Canadian, she could only maintain her system of values by a renewed dependence on a set of extraordinarily flimsy upper class English values which were basically tautological and supremacist in origin. It is not difficult to see that Mrs. Traill and others like her maintained their "standing" by affirming a certain set of daily social precepts all based on "the laws that good taste, good sense, and good feelings have established among persons of our class". In other words, her criteria circumscribe the physical, the rational, and the emotional realms of human life, and as long as anything in Canadian experience fails to answer to these reference points, especially early in her adventures, Mrs. Traill is helpless as to solutions. By the way, her comprehension of social process is quite inferior to that revealed in the many perspicacious comments made on the problems of class societies by her sister. In any case, Traill's transplantation to Canada was bound to be a shock, for here she discovered that verticality in the social order held no immediate sway; that success based on privilege was transformed into success based on the pragmatic; and that belief in an inherited sense of traditions was swept away by a dependence on physical strength and endurance. The first effect on her was a sense of her loss of importance and authority. Low class chore-girls rebuked her without the slightest fear. The result of this was a certain leaning toward the most basic human resources of trust and dependence which, in fact, were precisely those purveyed by Puritan Christianity, but lost

through institutionalization within a class culture. In this manner she was led through physical suffering to an understanding of herself and the life she chose more surely, perhaps, than she would have been had she remained in England. By the time the end of the book is reached, we feel she has been indeed chastened by her experiences here, and is, if anything, much mellower than at the beginning.

In the same way that the sudden revelation of Christ's being is a reward for the bearing of suffering by the faithful, so, in this book, after the chastening of suffering, after the proud heart has been softened and the inhuman haughtiness driven out, the humbled body of the penitent becomes like a receptacle, ready to receive its reward. While the progression of this series—pride, chastening, revelation—is subdued here, and leavened with a lot of hearty, scientific skepticism, it nevertheless exists. That is, the structure of the book is that of a conversion experience enclosed between two visions; the first, the reader should note, is an announcement concerning only the nature of the world in which the experience will take place, a natural world revealed by an impersonal hand. But in the last vision, borne to us in one paragraph, Christ himself is "cheated into fancy." Mrs. Traill, albeit enduringly rational, sees a vision which is akin to a sign from heaven, a revelation signifying that the Holy Land is attained at last. In its exterior manifestation, this progression structures the entire book, in its interior, it resolves the conflict outlined between the Scientific worldview and the Puritan by affirming a God momentarily immanent in Nature, and is thus a unifying vision, for just as it signals this brief resolution of alienation between God and the world, so it signals her final humbling through suffering which places her in a state of grace, that is, of acceptance. (pp. 75-8)

> *William D. Gairdner, "Traill and Moodie: The Two Realities," in* Journal of Canadian Fiction, *Vol. 2, No. 3, Summer 1973, pp. 75-81.*

Carl P. A. Ballstadt   (essay date 1983)

[*In the following excerpt, Ballstadt discusses the development of themes and styles in Traill's writings about Canada.*]

[Traill's] Canadian career may be said to begin with *The Young Emigrants; or, Pictures of Canada, Calculated to Amuse and Instruct the Minds of Youth* (1826) because it so obviously reveals the interest she had developed in Canada following the emigration of a Suffolk family of her acquaintance in 1821 and of her brother, Samuel, in 1825. Her book is based on letters received from these people and on her own reading of John Howison and Lieutenant Hall. Descriptions of the country are often directly quoted from the latter sources, and, presumably, information on the emigration process and the settlement on a cleared farm come from letters received. Indeed, the principal technique of the book is a series of letters written by two members of the emigrant family to a sister who remains in England because of illness; the letters provide her with accounts of Canadian customs, crafts, and people, the natural features of the country, and the advantages of diligence, prudence, and humility in the management of affairs. The book is Traill's most original early work, anticipating Captain Frederick Marryat's *The Settlers in Canada* (1844) by almost twenty years and showing Catharine's awareness both of the exigencies of emigration and the suitability of letters as a device for settlement narrative, the device she was to use for her book of "entertaining knowledge," *The Backwoods of Canada: Being Letters from the Wife of an Emigrant Officer* (1836). (p. 163)

The Backwoods has rarely been examined as a literary construction; rather, it has been seen largely as an historical text depicting life in a certain phase of Canadian development. And yet, that it has been so often referred to by historians, literary and social, indicates that it is a work of quality: it survives by its stylistic character and, perhaps by implication, its structural elements, as well.

With *The Backwoods of Canada,* Traill was addressing a fertile subject in Canadian literature; the subject of emigration had already been given form in statistical accounts, handbooks, journals, and letters and was to find expression in numerous poems and novels. Her choice of form is probably derived from her familiarity with Crèvecoeur's *Letters from an American Farmer,* her own experiment with *The Young Emigrants,* and possibly from a knowledge of other settlement accounts.

A volume of letters as a medium for reporting to the homeland what transpires and what is found in the New World has the advantage of combining a sense of immediacy with judicious observation and reflection on general issues. In Traill's *The Backwoods,* we find such a balancing of subjectivity and objectivity: that is, we discover what happens to the Traills on the journey and during settlement, personal illness, and unforeseen difficulties; but we also find the author distancing herself by choosing or creating other voices for the expression of opinions on the advantages of emigration, or desirable attitudes in the emigrant, or for reporting success stories and raising questions on emigration issues.

Balance is, in fact, the chief structural and thematic principle of *The Backwoods,* and it is explicitly stated by Traill in Letter xv, one of the letters addressed to the idea of Canada as a land of opportunity:

> Let the *pro* and *con* be fairly stated, and let the reader use his best judgment, unbiassed by prejudice or interest in a matter of such vital importance not only as regards himself, but the happiness and welfare of those over whose destinies Nature has made him the guardian.

Here Traill's intent and personality are succinctly reflected; she writes not to lure the prospective emigrant to a false paradise, as some emigrant writers had done, but to delineate advantages and disadvantages. To do this, she chooses a rhetoric of balance. One significant manifestation of balance is the emulation of biblical phraseology and the frequent use of biblical quotations to convey advice to the emigrant, as in the following example from Letter XI:

> Like that pattern of all good housewives de-

scribed by the prudent mother of King Lemuel, it should be said of the emigrant's wife, "She layeth her hands to the spindle, and her hands hold the distaff." "She seeketh wool, and flax, and worketh willingly with her hands." "She looketh well to the ways of her household, and eateth not the bread of idleness."

Such biblical parallelism provides a model for Traill's own prose, which is characterized by compound and compound-complex sentences with many parallel constructions, as in the following typical passage:

> For my part, I see no reason or wisdom in carping at the good we do possess, because it lacks something of that which we formerly enjoyed. I am aware it is the fashion for travellers to assert that our feathered tribes are either mute or give utterance to discordant cries that pierce the ear, and disgust rather than please. It would be untrue were I to assert that our singing birds were as numerous or as melodious on the whole as those of Europe; but I must not suffer prejudice to rob my adopted country of her rights without one word being spoken in behalf of her feathered vocalists. Nay, I consider her very frogs have been belied: if it were not for the monotony of their notes, I really consider they are not quite unmusical. . . . Their note resembles that of a bird, and has nothing of the creek in it.

Since she is stating *pro* and *con,* the first half of *The Backwoods,* especially, is marked by antithesis as the reader is given details concerning Old World/New World, wilderness/cultivation, picturesque scenery/cholera-infested city, present evils/future good, comfortable shanties/disgusting shanties, economic progress/destruction of natural scenery. A complete list of contrasting observations would be very long, indeed. Even in the detailing of the antithetical elements, we are given parallelism: a bird's note is "sweet and thrilling"; flowers expand in "woods and clearings"; Canada is a land of "vast lakes and mighty rivers"; the emigrant's wife is "pining . . . and lamenting"; and the Yankees are "industrious and ingenious." The book is replete with such balanced expression and antithesis as Traill strives consciously to be honest and just in her assessment of Canada.

In its overall structure, the book evidences this rhetorical balance, as well, having four basic parts, the first two predominantly negative and the last two positive: the journey, the settlement, the naming, and the expectation.

The first seven letters are devoted to the emigration journey from the Old World to the site of the new home, and although we find the characteristic balance of expression and fairness of attitude in these letters, their focus is on the difficulties of the journey, "the perils of the great deep and the horrors of the pestilence." The inland journey, particularly, is marked by a succession of *trials:* people with bad manners, a "surly Charon," night in a forest maze, a hazardous bridge, corduroy roads, untracked woods, evidences of bad taste, inferior trees, and a wearying "immensity" of landscape. The following brief paragraph presents an image of the new immigrant's bewildered condition, a condition Traill alludes to and plays upon later in the book:

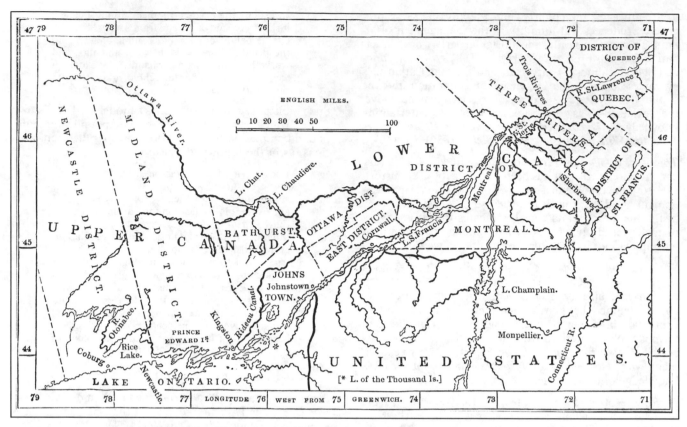

Frontispiece from The Backwoods of Canada *depicting areas in Ontario in which Traill lived.*

Imagine our situation, at ten o'clock at night, without knowing a single step of our road, put on shore to find the way to the distant town as we best could, or pass the night in the dark forest.

Letters VIII to XII, the settlement, do contain Traill's wish to be a namer of new things, but the emphasis is upon present evils, the forces of expediency and necessity, the battle by fire and steel against the wilderness, trials by the elements of wind and fire, the afflictions of bad roads and insects, and the loss of Old World historic lore and mystery.

Letters XIII to XVII reveal the emergence of the author as namer and discoverer, for in this section, more than in any of the others, we find catalogues of the wonders of the new surroundings together with an accounting of Canadian advancement and success. At the beginning of Letter XIII, the author virtually rejects expressions of regret for her exile and proceeds to dwell on the splendours of the Canadian winter, a visit to the winter camp of the Indians, and the attractiveness of Canadian birds. Letter XIV is exclusively devoted to descriptions of the botanical life of Upper Canada, which Traill finds "flung carelessly from Nature's lavish hand among our woods and wilds." The most notable rhetorical feature of these sketches is the emphasis on the plentitude and superlative nature of the plant life. In observing that particular plants are "very handsome," "exceedingly large," "extensive," "beautiful," "very elegant and numerous," and even "strong scented," Traill is both showing the excitement of discov-

ery and refuting the common charge of English immigrants that there are no beautiful birds or charming flowers in Canada.

By this stage of the book, the author is sufficiently adapted to her surroundings that she can playfully threaten to lead her reader into "the pathless mazes of our wild woods, without a clue to guide you, or even a *blaze* to light you on your way," as she had been led and abandoned on the journey to Peterborough. What she does in Letter XV, however, is to celebrate the progress of settlement and testify to Canada as "the land of hope," newness, and excitement. She declares her own happiness with the simplicity of her life in an extended passage contrasting European etiquette and fashion with the Canadian primals of liberty, prudence, economy, and industry, and, to prove the effect of these virtues, she recounts a Canadian success story of movement from trials, such as her own early letters reflect, to the achievement of the blessings of flourishing settlement. The effect of the story on Traill herself is to give an "additional stock of contentment, and some useful and practical knowledge." Letters XVI and XVII continue the evidence of progress and add to the catalogue of wonders in Indian life and flora and fauna, even though the narrative aspect of the letters necessitates the account of the ague which afflicts the family in the autumn of 1834 and which she notes "few persons escape" in the second year.

The final letter, XVIII, clearly embodies several features which make it an appropriate resolution to the whole work, first because it contains a restatement of the author's contentment:

> . . . yet I must say, for all its roughness, I love Canada, and am as happy in my humble log-house as if it were courtly hall or bower; habit reconciles us to many things that at first were distasteful. It has ever been my way to extract the sweet rather than the bitter in the cup of life, and surely it is best and wisest so to do. . . . My husband is becoming more reconciled to the country, and I daily feel my attachment to it strengthening.

In part, this attachment stems from the achievement of a comfortable and friendly society. One of Traill's persistent themes is to transform the wild "by the hand of taste" and to create a human proportion in the bush setting; to this end, she repeatedly endeavours to cultivate the wild plants and make them part of her garden. In the final letter, she extends the accomplishment of this task by envisioning a future in which

> . . . all will be different; our present rude dwellings will have given place to others of a more elegant style of architecture, and comfort and grace will rule the scene which is now a forest wild.

I think it is not extreme to interpret the aurora borealis and "a splendid pillar of pale greenish light in the west," which she describes on the last page of her text, as emblems of the promise she anticipates. Characteristically, she gives the pillar of light a scientific explanation as part of her balanced perception of things, but her treatment of it as "a vision" associated with "another and a better world," perhaps both temporal and spiritual, accords with her expectation of mature settlement.

As has been noted above, the structure of *The Backwoods of Canada* derives not only from chronological elements but from differences in tone, subject, and authorial attitude. In part, deviations from dominant aspects of each section are accounted for by the rhetoric of balance which issues from Traill's personality, but some deviations also result from the retrospective character of portions of the letters. For example, Letter IX, concerning the early trials in the construction of a log house during the winter, also contains a catalogue of wild fruits and their uses, but much of the information, including descriptions of blossoms and summer conditions for a walk along the lakeshore, could only have come from later observation by Traill. By April 1833, she had not spent a summer in the backwoods. Such additions to early letters of information and analysis, which Traill must have gained later and recorded in her journals, serve to maintain the balanced view of the whole pioneer process and to show the author as a person with curiosity, an open mind, and a determination to be a namer of New World phenomena, even in the midst of the hardships of first settlement.

By the time of the publication of *The Backwoods,* Traill was a devoted writer of daily journals, and she was to continue the practice, although not with absolute regularity, for most of her life in Canada. Early letters indicate that she was planning a sequel to *The Backwoods* based on her journals, but the sequel was not published as a book in the early years; rather, it took the forms of stories, essays, novels, and botanical studies, the journals forming the raw data for her writing, even for *Pearls and Pebbles* and *Cot and Cradle Stories.* The journals, therefore, deserve some attention in a consideration of her literary career.

Since they encompass so many years and are rich in detail concerning domestic life, nature, excursions, and the lives of other settlers, they cannot be fully dealt with in this essay, but a few observations are worth making. One is that they show Traill developing a more poetic style immediately subsequent to the publication of *The Backwoods,* the journals possessing a greater volume of imagery than the book. The image of the "splendid pillar of pale greenish light in the west" on the last page of *The Backwoods* is, indeed, a prelude to a frequently recurring motif in Traill's journals, a motif which helps to counter the usual conception of her as a cool rationalist interested only in the scientific description and utility of objects. In numerous passages, she reveals herself as one enchanted with the transforming power of mist, frost, and snow, three phenomena which she associates with the power of fancy because they have the capacity to "veil" or alter the otherwise harsh and displeasing aspects of bush scenery. The following passage from her journal entry for 11 December 1837 is typical in its poetic imagery and the expressed enthusiasm for the magic:

> Nothing can surpass the loveliness of the woods after a still heavy snow shower has loaded every bough and spray with its feathery deposit. The face of the ground so rough and tangled choked with a strange mass of uptorn trees broken boughs and timbers in every stage of unsightly decay seems as by the touch of some powerful magician's wand to have changed its character; unrivaled purity softness and brilliancy has taken the place of confusion and vegetable corruption. It is one of the greatest treats this country affords me to journey through the thick forest after a heavy snow whether it be by the brilliant light of the noonday sun shining in cloudless azure and giving a gemlike brightness to every particle that clothes the surface of the ground—and in heavy masses on the evergreens converting their dark fan shaped boughs into foliage of glittering whiteness and most fantastic form—or by the softer light of the full moon and frosty stars looking down through the snowy tops of the forest trees sometimes shining through a veil of silvery haze which the frost converts into a sparkling rime that encases every spray and twig with crystal.

It is primarily such transformations and the ensuing enchantment that make winter Traill's favourite Canadian season, and she writes at length upon it, both from the vigour and time which the season gives her to expend upon her journal entries.

In entries for all seasons, however, she reveals her curiosity and her openness to all aspects of her surroundings and restates her favourite themes: that everything in nature, no matter how small, is significant and wonderfully adapted; that God's goodness and power are proclaimed in all things; and that she prefers "nature's volume" to the crowded drawing room or ballroom. It is in the journals, also, that she first gives form to the most significant theme in her fiction, child lost—child found.

The theme first appears in an advertisement copied from *The Cobourg Star* for 2 August 1837 which notes the loss of a child near the Rice Lake plains and offers a reward for her discovery. Traill gives further details in her entry and then adds to it the notice in the same issue of *The Cobourg Star* that the child had been found near Cold Springs, "having wandered in the woods five days and nights." She proceeds to give accounts of other children lost and found, both in her own district and in others, including one concerning the loss of three children who entered the forest in search of cows. The piece is fascinating because it reveals Traill turning fact into fiction in one spontaneous, uninterrupted movement. The passage begins, "It must now be three or four years ago since the sympathies of the inhabitants in the township of ——— in one of the Western Districts of the Province were excited to a high degree of most painful interest by the sudden disappearance of three young persons, the eldest a girl about thirteen years of age. . . . " Before long, Traill gives names to the mothers of the children, gives an account of a consoling friendship which develops between them during the months and years of the children's absence, creates conversations between them on earthly affliction and heavenly hope, and brings the story to a climax with the implied return of the children at a time when Thirza Hill, the mother whose cows were being sought, is near death by consumption. This is, of course, the prototype story for *The Canadian Crusoes,* Traill's most extended piece of fiction.

Before finding its form as a novel, however, the story of children lost in the woods underwent several changes and appearances. In 1843 Traill had a story published in *Chambers' Edinburgh Journal,* "A Canadian Scene," about the loss of, and search for, a neighbour's child. Traill and her husband took part in the search, so that much of the story is about the techniques of searching and the progressive loss of energy for the search as hope wanes and the attention of the searchers is distracted by the profusion of berries and the pleasantness of the weather. The resolution, sudden and brief, is the discovery of the child near an abandoned house. The style here is very concrete and restrained, giving a vivid sense of the actions of the searchers and the irony of their exciting encounters with life in the forest. There is little sentiment here.

Another appearance of the motif, in **"The Mill of the Rapids: A Canadian Sketch,"** is also restrained, the incident of children lost forming only a portion of the sketch, being an account by the daughter of the miller about an occasion when she and a brother were lost not more than a mile from their home. The chief interest of the sketch is that it contains the following statement by Traill:

> Now, I have almost as great a love for a story about being lost in the woods, as I had when a child on the knee for the pitiful story of the Babes in the Wood. I eagerly besought Miss Betty to favour me with the history of her own and her brother's wanderings.

The comment helps to confirm what the frequency of Traill's attention suggests, that she was a fascinated collector of stories of children lost.

In 1849 **"The Two Widows of Hunter's Creek"** appeared in *The Home Circle.* It is reportedly part of a letter addressed to Agnes Strickland, as are some of the other pieces which found publication in Britain; it is also a rewrite of the journal entry discussed above. In the published story, however, the narrator is an old American major, although the setting is the Canadian woods near the Credit River. The two families are American settlers, the Hartley family being of New England Puritan stock, and the Bridges family staunch United Empire Loyalists. The names of the widows are the same as in the journal entry, Thirza and Mary, but the roles are reversed. Mary becomes the consumptive and dweller in hope, while Thirza is the nurse and comforter. The body of the story is about the mutual support of Mary and Thirza in their loss of Thirza's one child, Rachel, and Mary's two, Anne and Michael. On the day of Mary's death, five years after the disappearance of the children, she experiences a resurgence of hope, and the children return out of the bush in Indian dress, Rachel leading by the hand a child whom she had by her Indian husband. Missionaries near the Lake Huron shores have directed the children towards the homes they had never forgotten. The emphasis in this story is, of course, on the sufferings of the widowed mothers and the tension between Mary's earthly hope for her children and her longing for heavenly release; the dialogue, therefore, is sentimental, formal, and marked by biblical archaisms.

At the end of the story, the major rises saying, "I only am left of all whom they once knew as friends in this place," and he walks away, "his head bent down, and his thoughts evidently busy with scenes and friends of past days." The significance of this ending for us is that the words apply to Catharine Parr Traill, concerning both the treatment of the lost-child motif and the general character of her literary career. The Englishwoman who reports in *The Backwoods* that there is nothing of historic lore and supernatural mystery to stimulate the imagination becomes the voice of the Canadian pioneer, an apostle of his suffering, endurance, accomplishments, and the milieu in which he lived.

Certainly this is one of her major accomplishments in *The Canadian Crusoes: A Tale of the Rice Lake Plains,* the culmination of her lost-child entries and sketches. The story is set in the Rice Lake district immediately following the Seven Years' War, when the Indian in Upper Canada could still be thought of as enemy and the woods a few miles from major waterways were unknown or travelled only by the trapper. In choosing such a period and a setting, Traill intensifies the problems of pioneer life, creates her own story of the maze and enigma of the forest, and depicts the qualities of character necessary to confront it and survive in it.

As in its earlier versions, the story involves three children, Catharine and Hector Maxwell and their cousin Louis Perron, who enter the forest on a June day in search of the cows. They become lost, wander north to Rice Lake, and effect their own survival by their Crusoe-like resourcefulness over a two-year period. They also rescue an Indian girl from death by exposure; she becomes one of the party, and a mutual exchange of knowledge takes place. The climax of the story involves captivity by the Indians and a second rescue of Indiana; the resolution includes the return home of the young people by the guidance of the old trapper, Jacob Morelle, and the marriages of Hector and Indiana, Louis and Catharine.

The novel has two main levels of meaning: it is a fable about the creation of a civilized society, and it is a manual of elemental pioneering and survival. On both levels the story is interesting, and the considerable success which the book enjoyed may be attributed to both the timeless quality of this fable and the authoritative and detailed nature of its guidance. Its weaknesses are the rather stiff, formal dialogue and the excessiveness, for the modern reader, at least, of its religious sentiment and proselytizing.

As fable, *The Canadian Crusoes* has a wealth of association with all the lost-children stories of fairy tale, legend, and poetry. It also has specifically Canadian associations, for, as the evolution of Traill's book indicates, the incidence of children and hunters lost in the woods was, and still is, a common occurrence. Traill even extends its meaning by including in Appendix A a reference to the "Wild Man of the far West," indirectly connecting her tale with stories of the "Wild Man" and suggestions that he was a lost child. In that it is a story of survival and self-realization celebrating the strengths of an earlier age, one may be tempted to see *The Canadian Crusoes* as related to Margaret Atwood's *Surfacing* with its four wanderers, even though the circumstances of challenge and survival are extremely different.

In any case, for its own time Traill's *Crusoes* expresses the myth of Canadian virtue deriving from contact with the immense wilderness. Her children are not brutalized by the experience, but made whole. Given the evidence of Traill's fascination with the lost child, her story may indeed be motivated by her own success in meeting the challenge of pioneer life, so different from what she had known in England.

In its political rather than psychological character, *The Canadian Crusoes* offers a microcosm of the society Traill envisions. The cooperation of her characters with one another, Scots, French, and Indian, each contributing his or her strength to a common enterprise, suggests a model for Canada. Such an interpretation is warranted not only by the mutual instruction of the four young people but by the events, language, and vision of the concluding chapters.

The most significant event is that "Beam of the Morning," daughter of the Ojibwa chief and enemy to the Mohawk, Indiana, releases the latter from torture and execution, having been counselled to do so by Catharine. Thus, the violence of Indian law is replaced by Christian forgiveness and a "covenant of peace and good-will [is] entered upon by old Jacob and the chief." Following her release, Indiana decides to rejoin her white friends and accompanies Jacob and Catharine down the Otonabee River towards Rice Lake. In the account of their journey, the author gives a vision of a new order:

> The sun is now rising high above the pine trees, the morning mist is also rising and rolling off like a golden veil as it catches those glorious rays— the whole earth seems awakening into new life— the dew has brightened every leaf and washed each tiny flower-cup. . . .

The sense of newness in nature accords with the emotional state of the two girls, but the author takes the reader beyond this to a vision of the future: of Gore's Landing, the village church, the plank road, the tasteful garden, and the pretty farms. The Crusoes are the forerunners of this transformation, seeing in Mount Ararat and the Rice Lake shore a good place to settle. In the manner of romance, however, they return to their parents and follow their adventures with marriages and movement to a new settlement area.

In her preface to the book, Agnes Strickland dwells on its capacity as a manual to Canadian geography and natural history. The richness of its detail does, in fact, contribute a sense of authenticity to the book as well as help to display the practicality and resourcefulness of these Canadian children. In considerable degree, it is also a book of wisdom literature containing maxims on conduct and expressions of Christian faith. Many of the latter are directed to the savage, although physically superior, Indiana, as the white children, with a conviction of moral and intellectual superiority, seek to enlighten her. Their proselytizing zeal is an expression of Traill's own belief, but it is also an essential preparation for the Christian acts of the resolution: Indiana's willingness to give her life for Catharine's and Catharine's counselling of Beam of the Morning to forgive her enemy. Along with their missionary zeal, however, Traill's characters show their openness and tolerance, most fully expressed in the marriage of Hector to Indiana at the end.

In much of her fugitive prose, Traill continues to perform the role of chronicler of pioneer life. The writing falls into two divisions, the informal, discursive essay and the story, which she often characterizes as "Forest Gleanings" both in specific pieces of writing and in the title she gives to a major series published in *The Anglo-American Magazine*. Most of the stories are less interesting to the modern reader than the essays. The former are not distinguished by any novelty of form or structure; their chief interest is thematic, and the theme is emigration and settlement. **"The Blockhouse"** is the tale which is least successful and which is also least devoted to the settlement process. Although the setting is backwoods, the plot is a melodramatic unfolding of the secret of the English birth and history of the hero, Philip Harding, and his beloved neighbour, Alice. Not surprisingly, Philip returns to the Old World when he gains his inheritance. **"The Lodge in the Wilderness"** displays more irony and humour. It is an incomplete fictionalized treatment of the arrival of an English gentleman and his lady at a prepared backwoods farm, the rude realities of the farm dispelling the dream in which they had journeyed. The Traills' own experience seems to be reflected in this tale.

A scene from Traill's Canadian Crusoes: A Tale of the Rice Lake Plains.

The longest and most interesting treatment of the pioneer process is **"The Settlers Settled; or, Pat Connor and His Two Masters."** It is a humorous story in four parts, "The Outset," "The Purchase," "The Progress," and "The Settlement," the humour being derived from ironic techniques and the lively dialect of the servant, Pat Connor. Arthur and Charles Windham, youngest sons in a disinherited family, adopt emigration as a means to maintain an appropriate station in life. With the blessing and financial support of their Uncle Philopson, they buy a cleared farm near Cobourg from a disillusioned Englishman, Tom Walker, who is very similar to Tom Wilson of Susanna Moodie's *Roughing It in the Bush* and like him is returning to England with his pet bear. The story is advanced both by third-person narration and by the exchange of letters between Charles Windham and his uncle; it is by means of these two devices that the ironic treatment of the settlement process is rendered. While Uncle Philopson dispenses in his letters from afar impractical advice on farming, the engagement and management of servants, and the maintenance of social position, the narrative reveals Charles and Arthur facing the exigencies of settlement, including the problems created by a poor choice of

land, the dishonesty of their hired domestic help, the borrowing propensities of their Yankee neighbours, and the harsh realities of Canadian agriculture. Contrary to their uncle's observations about Irish servants, Pat Connor turns out to be the boys' salvation, indeed, the true master. His industriousness and reliability, his homely and practical wisdom are balanced against the uncle's maxims based on English farming practice and aristocratic conduct. Under Pat's tutelage, Charles, whose tastes run to the simple and natural, acquires the humility, practicality, and habits of hard work necessary for success as a Canadian farmer, while Arthur, who is less suited to the hardness of pioneer life, finds a position in Toronto. The only exception to the following of Pat's advice is that Charles, instead of taking a Yankee girl as wife, chooses a neighbouring, recent English emigrant who is discovered to be a second cousin, a member of an estranged branch of his mother's family. The resolution of all is that the family is reunited; Uncle Philopson finds pleasure in Charles's progress and marriage, provides him with a more suitable farm, and even approves of Pat Connor.

The style of **"The Settlers Settled"** varies with the techniques employed, from the judicious, unpretentious observations of Charles on his affairs, to the more formal, imperative tone of Uncle Philopson and the lively, humorous brogue of Pat Connor, sprinkled as it is with Americanisms that remind one of Sam Slick's language in T. C. Haliburton's sketches. The following excerpt is a good example of the latter type:

> "If them praties arn't illigantly boiled, and dried too with the pickle (i.e. pinch) of salt just dusted over their jackets by way of sauce! There's a pretty go now—if the handle arn't clean comed off the tea-pot! That tin-man's ware arn't worth the snuff of a rush candle."

> "That was your setting the tea-pot on the hot coals," said Charles, somewhat tartly; "you know, Connor, I warned you of that a week ago, and told you, besides, I detested boiled tea. You Irish can never make tea without setting the tea-pot on the embers."

> "Well, thin, if it isn't the raal Yankee fashion, your honour. Why bless you, their tea-pot stands it like anything."

> The Windhams could hardly help laughing at the adroit way in which Pat turned the question from the tea to the tea-pot.

> "But what is to be done? this is one of the miseries of this horrid place," broke forth Arthur, with a sigh, almost deep enough for a groan, "how is the tea to be poured out?"

> "Why, Master Arter, the spout isn't gone yet, and worse things will happen in this country than the handle coming unsoldered of a tin tea-pot," said Pat, seizing the dilapidated vessel in his huge fist; and, pouring out the tea, set the cups reeking on the table, with an air of infinite satisfaction, remarking upon its superior strength and high colour from the mode of cooking it.

In sketches and informal essays, such as **"The Rice Lake Plains," "Female Trials in the Bush," "Society in the Bush,"** and **"A Walk to Railway Point,"** Traill finds another medium for the celebration of the accomplishments of the pioneer. Essentially she is showing that the promise of *The Backwoods of Canada* has been fulfilled, indeed, so successfully that by mid-century Canadians need to be reminded of the steps by which the "desert" has been transformed, with God's blessing, into a "fruitful garden." She reminds her readers of the disillusionment and suffering of British gentlemen and gentlewomen, and of the endurance, industry, and self-sufficiency by which they survived and flourished. Together with the poor Irish and Scots immigrants, they are proclaimed as the heroes of Canadian development and mid-century prosperity.

Yet other essays are contradictory to her chronicles of the pioneer, revealing a degree of ambivalence about the impact of settlement and cultivation on the Canadian forest. In **"A Glance within the Forest," "Voices from the Canadian Woods: The White Cedar,"** and **"Love of Flowers,"** she is a natural-history essayist and ecologist developing her role as namer of Canadian life, showing the pleasure of examining and appreciating all natural phenomena, preserving a record of what was, and lamenting the disappearance of the flora and fauna that settlement destroys. The lament is implicit in, and one motivation for, her studies of plant life, but it is frequently stated explicitly in the resolutions of essays, as in the concluding paragraph of **"A Glance within the Forest"**:

> To those who love the forest and its productions, the continual destruction of the native trees will ever be a source of regret, even while acknowledging its necessity, for with the removal of the sheltering woods must also disappear most of the rare plants, indigenous to the soil, that derive their nurture from them, some indeed so entirely dependent on the decaying vegetation of the trees beneath which they grow that they perish directly they are deprived of it. Exposed to the effects of drying winds and hot sunshine they wither away and are seen no more. Soon may we say, in the words of the old Scotch song—
>
> "The flowers of the forest are a'wede away."

The reference to many of Traill's essays and stories as "Forest Gleanings" suggests that they were to form part of a book on life in the colony, and such an intention is confirmed by her unpublished manuscripts. She worked on several pieces of very large design. "The Pioneers" and "The United Empire Loyalists" are both drafts of novels meant to perform the same function as the essays, and "Under the Pines" was to be her autobiography and sequel to *The Backwoods,* including large-scale treatment of the Strickland family in England and the chronicle of her own trials as a backwoods settler who becomes a successful author devoted to the articulation of Canadian life.

Of course, another of Traill's books on the accomplishments of the pioneer was published two years after *The Canadian Crusoes. The Female Emigrant's Guide, and Hints on Canadian Housekeeping* (1854), also known as *The Canadian Settler's Guide* (1855), was, to judge by the frequency of its publication, a very popular work. As the original title indicates, this book is a further development of that facet of *The Backwoods of Canada* which is derived from the English manuals for women. In contrast to the English books, Traill's *Guide* is concerned with the useful arts rather than elegant manners, and doing for oneself rather than managing others.

Although *The Female Emigrant's Guide* has elements similar to *The Backwoods,* it exhibits differences in both content and tone. After more than twenty years as a resident of Upper Canada, Traill wished to remedy the earlier book's deficiencies in instruction by providing more essential information on horticultural and domestic resources and procedures, and less personal narrative, but a comparison of the two books shows a marked advance in the degree of Traill's Canadianization, as well. The promise of the earlier book has been realized and is conveyed in a very affirmative attitude towards the new country:

> Here all is new; time has not yet laid its mellowing touch upon the land. We are but in our infancy; but it is a vigorous and healthy one, full of promise for future greatness and strength.
>
> . . . . .
>
> It is delightful this consciousness of perfect security: your hand is against no man, and no man's hand is against you. We dwell in peace among our own people. What a contrast to my home, in England, where by sunset every door was secured with locks and heavy bars and bolts; every window carefully barricaded, and every room and corner in and around the dwelling duly searched, before we ventured to lie down to rest, lest our sleep should be broken in upon by the midnight thief.

Throughout there is a sense of well-being and delight, dignity and independence to be found in the new land.

Another difference in the later book is that the emigrant is cautioned against having a too negative attitude to the forest. Its resources are celebrated, and this is nowhere more apparent than in the most "literary" section of the book, the series of appreciations of the months of the year and the extracts from "Letters from Canada" which form its conclusion. In these, as in all of her writing, Traill is affirmative: "there is good at all seasons, and in everything."

Throughout her long literary career, she sustained her positive attitude towards Canada, and towards life generally. In additional books for children, *Lady Mary and Her Nurse; or, A Peep into the Canadian Forest* (1856) and *Cot and Cradle Stories* (1895), she expresses her love of nature and her close observation, chiefly in stories of small animals. In the latter book, she draws heavily upon her own childhood years and some of her early literary work. *Lady Mary,* in contrast, depicts Canadian customs, Indians, and natural phenomena, mostly of the Rice Lake plains, and celebrates Canadian virtues of liberty and independence. The form is the dialogue between the wise teacher and the curious child, and the style successfully reflects the manners and enthusiasm of each. The distinctions are particularly apparent when the child tells a story; she is easily distracted from her main topic by associated ideas and by her own impetuosity. The nurse, as a persona for Traill, is rich with information, is aware of what appeals to children, and is constant in her praise of Canada.

Although Traill continued to write in many modes, including drafts of an autobiography following the publication of Jane Margaret Strickland's *Life of Agnes Strickland* (1887), her principal publications were on natural history. *Studies of Plant Life in Canada; or, Gleanings from Forest, Lake and Plain* was apparently prepared as early as the mid-1860s, but a publisher could not be found for the rather large work, and a selection was made to accompany lithographed illustrations of flowers by Agnes Fitzgibbon, Susanna Moodie's daughter, and issued as *Canadian Wild Flowers* (1868). The complete *Studies* was eventually published in 1885, with twenty plates of illustration by her niece.

In some degree, these are scientific works containing necessary technical, botanical information, but Traill conceived of them as literature, as "forest gleanings" which she hoped would be a Canadian version of Gilbert White's *Natural History and Antiquities of Selborne.* She was a self-taught botanist in whose philosophy the study of flowers is a civilizer and a medium for the development of love of country. It was the medium of her own attachment to Canada, and she seeks to promote it in others by the charming informality of botanical essays replete with anecdote, folklore, analogy, and historical, ethical, and religious observations. The lives of the old settlers and Indians are touched in her reminiscences, and poets, major and minor, are quoted to demonstrate the universality of the love of flowers. Often her own imagination is called into play to reflect the character of species, as in this description of the water lily with its imagery of courtship and its sense of the design in nature:

> On the approach of night our lovely water-nymph gradually closes her petals, and slowly retires to rest on her watery bed, to rise again the following day, to court the warmth and light so necessary for the perfection of the embryo seeds, and this continues till the fertilization of the germ has been completed, when the petals shrink and wither, and the seed-vessel sinks down to the bottom of the water, where the seeds ripen in its secret chambers. Thus silently and mysteriously does Nature perform her wonderful work, "sought out only by those who have pleasure therein."

The shape of each piece is determined by the special character of the species and by the wide range of information which Traill has acquired, often from others, but mostly from her own observation. Thus it is that the essays contain many recollections of her first settlement and her life on the Rice Lake plains, and even a retelling of her favourite motif, the lost child, in her essay on the swamp blueberry. Clearly, the botanical works are the culmination of the urge to explore and to name Canadian phenomena which Traill first declared in *The Backwoods of Canada.*

Pearls and Pebbles; or, Notes of an Old Naturalist (1894), Traill's last published work for adults, is an appropriate summation of her career, for it includes reflections of her life, both early and late, and a restatement of all her major themes: that all of nature is wonderfully ordered and adapted; that small things lead to great; that man will develop humility and awe, and find rules for his own conduct in the study of nature; that nothing is lost. Once again the reader is impressed with the balanced perception evidenced in style and structural elements, for these essays are organized about such concepts as yesterday and today, illusion and reality, great and small, life and death.

Even though the book is a collection of essays, like *The Backwoods of Canada* and *The Canadian Crusoes,* it has a discernible, artistic shape based upon the Bible. All three books begin with an exile or departure and end with the attainment of a new home. Such a pattern is obviously derived from Traill's religious convictions that man's earthly home, although fascinating, is not his true home. The first essay in *Pearls and Pebbles,* "Pleasant Days of My Childhood," is a reminiscence of May Day at the childhood home on the banks of the Waveney, "our Eden" where the children gathered flowers and "the garden was laid out right daintily." But the reminiscence ends with a "Lament for the May Queen":

> The cowslip bends her golden head,
> And daisies deck the lea;
> But ah! no more in grove or bower
> The Queen of May we'll see.

All that remains are memories which "come back to my wearied soul to cheer and soothe the exile in her far distant forest home."

The second essay, "Sunset and Sunrise on Lake Ontario: A Reminiscence," is similar in shape. It is about the beauty of the voyage up the Saint Lawrence, including "visions of pleasant rustic homes," "childish delight," the magic landscape of the Thousand Islands, and Lake Ontario, which "like a sea of gold" with "clouds of mist . . . broke into all sorts of fanciful forms." But "in a moment all was changed." The mist lifts and the fanciful illusion is gone leaving "but a dream of beauty on the gazer's mind—a memory to be recalled in after years when musing over past scenes of a life where lights and shadows form a mingled pattern of trials and blessings."

The essays which follow, for example, "The First Death in the Clearing" and "Alone in the Forest," give some sense of those trials and the unpleasantness of the pioneer landscape, but the emphasis is upon the blessings to be discovered in the place of exile. Even here there are ordered sequences. The essays on birds are followed by those on the forest in general and the people who dwell in it. The last segment of essays is on relatively obscure subjects, vegetable instinct, pollen, grasses, mosses, and lichens, as Traill endeavours to show that nothing is without significance.

Her investigation of the minute and the obscure prepares the reader for the insights and affirmations of her finest and concluding essay, "Something Gathers Up the Fragments." It is about natural processes and the interrelatedness of all things, themes which are rendered in lucid and concrete prose:

> As the lichens decay they give place to the mosses, and these, as they increase, send down their

wedge-like roots between the fissures of the bark, penetrating into the tissue of the wood, already softened by the decomposition of the former occupants. The dew, the showers, the frosts and snows of winter, falling upon the sponge-like mosses, fill them with moisture, invigorate them and increase them till they form thick mats that hide the surface of the wood. . . .

The very heart of the wood has yielded up its strength and hardness under the influences of the agencies brought to bear upon it. A few more years and that fallen tree will be no more seen. The once mighty tree, with the mosses and lichens alike, will have returned their substance to Mother Earth. "Ashes to ashes, dust to dust."

The whole essay has a quality of consolation about it. Tragedy and death are not the end; nothing is lost. The fallen forest becomes "the rich black vegetable mould" in which "a stranger and an emigrant from a far-off land" may sow the grain "for the life-sustaining bread for himself and his children" in his new homeland. In Traill's outlook, as in that of the early American Puritans, the white man's transformation of North America is part of God's design. Although, as we have seen, she laments the disappearance of specific forms, for her the ideal landscape is one reflecting human taste and order.

The structure of the book is reinforced by the longest essay in it, **"In the Canadian Woods,"** a four-part piece on the seasons beginning with spring with its wild flowers, like the Indians "fast passing away," and ending with winter, which Traill makes the analogue of the change from wilderness to civilization:

The Frost King is abroad, and as by the magic touch of an enchanter's wand has wrought a wondrous change within the forest as well as on lake and stream.

What has become of the unsightly heaps of brushwood, the *débris* of fallen rotting leaves, of stalks of withered flowers and rank herbage, the blackened stumps, the old prostrate wind-blown trees? Where are they now? Here is purity without a sign of decay. All that offended the sight in our forest walks has vanished.

As the snow transforms the stumps and fallen trees to "purity without a sign of decay," so "fair dwellings, tasteful gardens, fruitful orchards, . . . the steamboat, the railroad, the telegraph" replace "the primeval settlement house," "the disfiguring stump," and "the ugly snake-like rail fences"—"all are gone—things that *were,* not things that *are.*"

Each of Traill's major works, therefore, *The Backwoods of Canada, The Canadian Crusoes, The Female Emigrant's Guide,* and *Pearls and Pebbles,* is ultimately ironic. While celebrating the achievement of a new home, each draws its energy from her own fascination with the primeval forest and its resources. She laments its passing and expresses her own ambivalence in a poem which concludes the essay **"In the Canadian Woods"**:

Oh! wail for the forest! the green shady forest!
No longer its depths may the hunter explore;

For the bright golden grain
Shall wave o'er the plain.
Oh, wail for the forest, its glories are o'er!

Such fascination and ambivalence she shares with many other Canadian writers. (pp. 163-84)

> *Carl P. A. Ballstadt, "Catharine Parr Traill,"*
> *in* Canadian Writers and Their Works, Vol.
> I, *Robert Lecker, Jack David, and Ellen Quig-*
> *ley, eds. ECW Press, 1983, pp. 149-193.*

FURTHER READING

Boutelle, Ann Edwards. "Sisters and Survivors: Catharine Parr Traill and Susanna Moodie." In *Nineteenth-Century Women Writers of the English-Speaking World,* edited by Rhoda B. Nathan, pp. 13-18. New York: Hofstra University, 1986.
  Compares characterization and style in the writings of Traill and her sister Susanna Moodie.

———. "Margaret Atwood, Margaret Laurence, and Their Nineteenth-Century Forerunners." In *Faith of a (Woman) Writer,* edited by Alice Kessler-Harris and William McBrien, pp. 41-7. New York: Hofstra University, 1988.
  Depicts Traill as one of the "forerunners who broke the silence, making it possible for the single voices now to be heard," in an examination of literary models for the fiction of Margaret Atwood and Margaret Laurence.

Burpee, Lawrence J. "The Last of the Stricklands." *The Sewanee Review* VIII, No. 2 (April 1900): 207-17.
  Reflects on the life and career of Traill, noting that "her literary work, even where most weak, was always sincere and its tone always elevating."

Klinck, Carl F. "Literary Activity in the Canadas (1812-1841)." In *Literary History of Canada: Canadian Literature in English,* Vol. I, 2nd ed., edited by Carl F. Klinck, pp. 139-58. Toronto: University of Toronto Press, 1972.
  Includes an appreciation of Traill's contribution to Canadian literature.

Kroller, Eva-Marie. "Resurrections: Susanna Moodie, Catharine Parr Traill, and Emily Carr in Contemporary Canadian Literature." *Journal of Popular Culture* 15, No. 3 (Winter 1981): 39-46.
  Comments on the use of Traill as a model for the protagonist in Margaret Laurence's novel *The Diviners* (1974).

MacLulich, T. D. "Crusoe in the Backwoods: A Canadian Fable?" *Mosaic* IX, No. 2 (Winter 1976): 15-26.
  Examines the ways in which Daniel Defoe's *Robinson Crusoe* offers a paradigm of human exile in fiction on which Traill and Susanna Moodie drew in their writings.

Pacey, Desmond. "The Colonial Period (1750-1867): The Beginnings in Upper and Lower Canada." In his *Creative Writing in Canada: A Short History of English-Canadian Literature,* pp. 21-34. Toronto: The Ryerson Press, 1961.
  Notes the literary contributions of Traill and Susanna Moodie as immigrants in Canada.

Rouslin, Virginia Watson. "The Intelligent Woman's Guide to Pioneering in Canada." *Dalhousie Review* 56, No. 2 (Summer 1976): 319-35.

> Emphasizes the importance of education for Traill and other Canadian women writers in adapting to life in the Canadian wilderness.

Weaver, Emily P. "Pioneer Canadian Women." *The Canadian Magazine* XLVIII, No. 5 (March 1917): 473-76.

> Documents the personal and literary achievements of Traill and Susanna Moodie.

Susan Warner

1819-1885

(Full name Susan Bogert Warner; also wrote under the pseudonym Elizabeth Wetherell) American novelist.

Warner is best known for her novel *The Wide, Wide World*, which was one of the best-selling American novels of the nineteenth century. Noted for its accurate portrayal of the social limitations imposed upon nineteenth-century women, *The Wide, Wide World* traces the development of a young girl from childhood to adolescence. This work is often valued less for its literary merit than for its historical significance as one of the earliest examples of the sentimental or domestic novel—a genre that focused on the lives of women and became extremely popular after 1850.

Born in New York City, Warner was the daughter of a prominent and ambitious lawyer. Educated by private tutors, she studied literature, music, and Italian. In 1828 her mother died, and her paternal aunt moved into the household to care for Warner and her younger sister Anna. Her father's successful investments in real estate enabled the family to move several times into successively more affluent neighborhoods, and Warner frequently attended fashionable social gatherings. However, an economic downturn in 1837 forced the family to move from their mansion at St. Mark's Place to an old farmhouse on Constitution Island near the United States Military Academy at West Point. During the next ten years, her father's failing law practice and his involvement in several lawsuits over his property created additional financial difficulties. In 1848 Warner began working on *The Wide, Wide World* with the hope that the novel would serve as a source of income.

After being rejected or ignored by several publishers, *The Wide, Wide World* was issued in a limited edition under the pseudonym Elizabeth Wetherell in 1850. Demand for the book far exceeded the initial expectations of the publisher; reissued through fourteen editions in the next two years, *The Wide, Wide World* established an unprecedented record for sales. Encouraged by the success of her first novel, Warner wrote *Queechy,* another novel portraying the development of a young girl. Throughout the next three and a half decades Warner remained on Constitution Island and continued writing, producing more than thirty works of her own and writing six in collaboration with her sister Anna. None of Warner's subsequent works, however, achieved the same level of popular success as *The Wide, Wide World*. During the last decade of her life, she held weekly Bible study lessons for West Point cadets. Susan died in 1885, and Anna completed a biography of her sister several years before her own death in 1915.

Warner's literary reputation rests primarily on *The Wide, Wide World,* which traces the emotional and spiritual development of Ellen Montgomery from childhood to adolescence. At the beginning of the novel, Ellen's father has lost a lawsuit, and the family doctor has prescribed a vacation for Ellen's severely ill mother. Because of the family's

limited resources, her father decides to leave Ellen with her aunt in a small, rural village while taking his wife on a business trip to Europe. Mistreated by her aunt, who denies her requests for a formal education and withholds her mother's letters, Ellen obtains support and spiritual guidance from Alice and John Humphreys, the children of a local minister. While in Europe Ellen's parents die, and she is sent to live with her relatives in Scotland, who often treat her as little more than property. Ellen is, however, permitted to write to John Humphreys, and the final paragraph of the book suggests that the two will eventually marry. In a concluding chapter left out by the original publisher but restored in the 1987 edition, Ellen and John are presented as a married couple.

Early criticism of Warner's novels frequently focused on the excessive weeping of her heroines and occasionally criticized her verbose style and fervid religiosity. Often emphasizing the difficulty of interpreting the nineteenth-century religious and moral values expressed in Warner's works from a twentieth-century perspective, commentators have disputed whether religion in *The Wide, Wide World* functions as an evasion of or a submission to patriarchal authority. Nevertheless, modern critics often note that the control exercised over Ellen by her father, husband, and other relatives represents an accurate portrayal of the restrictions imposed upon nineteenth-century women in making decisions governing their own lives.

(See also *Dictionary of Literary Biography*, Vols. 3 and 42.)

PRINCIPAL WORKS

The Wide, Wide World [as Elizabeth Wetherell]   (novel) 1850; also published as *The Wide, Wide World* [expanded edition], 1987
Queechy   [as Elizabeth Wetherell]   (novel)   1852
The Hills of the Shatemuc   (novel)   1856
Say and Seal [with Anna Warner]   (novel)   1860
The Old Helmet   (novel)   1863
Melbourne House   (novel)   1864
Daisy   (novel)   1868
The Gold of Chickaree [with Anna Warner]   (novel) 1876
Wych Hazel [with Anna Warner]   (novel)   1876
Diana   (novel)   1877
My Desire   (novel)   1879
The End of a Coil   (novel)   1880
The Letter of Credit   (novel)   1881
Nobody   (novel)   1882
Stephen, M. D.   (novel)   1883
A Red Wallflower   (novel)   1884
*Daisy Plains   (unfinished novel)   1885

*This work was completed by Anna Warner.

The Literary World   (essay date 1850)

[*In the following excerpt, the critic discusses* The Wide, Wide World.]

[*The Wide, Wide World*] is a very excellent example of the now common class of religious novels. The heroine is a little girl, whose mother is forced to leave, for the healing influences of a foreign clime, her native land, while her child is placed by her father in the care of Miss Fortune, a New England spinster of most vinegar composition. There is no let up to her severity. She is, however, sketched with considerable humor, and several scenes of rude country life are presented in a very agreeable style. (p. 524)

Without laying claims to an elaborately planned plot, the story is not devoid of interest, and its religious teachings are worthy of all praise for their gentleness and earnestness, and the happy manner in which they are introduced. The author's chief fault is diffuseness. She tells a story or describes a scene with a woman's indiscriminate minuteness. The consequence is, that the reviewer, hardened to novel reading, gets over her two sizable volumes at a rate which she would hardly think complimentary. The book would stand a great deal of compression—a fact the author would do well to bear in mind, if disposed for another experiment on the public. But this is a common and characteristic trait of the novel literature of the day, particular-

ly of English literature; and, we may add, of this especial class of religious fictions. So that the *Wide, Wide World,* in taking a canvas proportional to the text, is by no means unique. (p. 525)

> *A review of "The Wide, Wide World," in* The Literary World, *Vol. VII, No. 204, December 28, 1850, pp. 524-25.*

Holden's Dollar Magazine   (essay date 1851)

[*In the following review, the critic offers an unfavorable assessment of* The Wide, Wide World.]

It seems to savor somewhat of the sacrilegious to parade the literary defects of a book which is so excellent in its design, and so wholly and unmistakably good in the moral and religious instruction as is the one before us. And yet when the frame-work of a story is badly constructed, when it is disjointed and rickety, when its style is artificial and forced, when its embellishments are bad English, and its adornments poor rhetoric, one cannot but allude to such facts, although the orthodoxy of the book may be unquestionable, and its spirit blameless. And yet, even in the matter of morality it seems as if some "more excellent way" could be devised of teaching it, than is followed in this novel. Truth, to find a lodgment in the heart, by the means of fiction, must glide in imperceptibly, and not be pushed in bodily, in the shape of long harangues and labored discourses. We doubt also in regard to the correctness of some of the teachings of this book. For example, a Christian mother, in her last sickness, is represented as deceiving her husband and physician, and making her only daughter a party to the deception, in order that she may go herself and buy a Bible for the daughter, there being no necessity of her going, which can, in any degree justify the deception: we do not approve of such practices. The heroine too acts at times, we fear, under a mistaken idea of duty, and it certainly is not very consistent for the author of a novel to put into the mouth of the hero, who is supposed always to say what is right, the advice to his friend, never, under any circumstances, to read any *novel* of any description. Still the *Wide, Wide World* has some excellent things in it—some passages of real beauty, and some sentiments of genuine nobleness. It is a pity however, that the author has such a taste for crying. The frequent outbursts of tears are really too harrowing to one's sympathies. We never knew such incessant blubbering, not even on a crowded canal boat, when every other passenger went for half price, or nothing, being "*under* 10 years of age." Indeed, this *Wide, Wide World* is nothing but one wide, wide waste of waters, with only here and there an Ararat struggling to the surface. We hope that the next work of E. W. will contain less dry logic and more dry land. (p. 136-37)

> *A review of "The Wide, Wide World," in* Holden's Dollar Magazine, *Vol. 7, March, 1851, pp. 136-37.*

Caroline Kirkland   (essay date 1853)

[*Kirkland was an American editor, critic, and fiction*

writer. In the following excerpt, she offers a generally favorable assessment of The Wide, Wide World *and* Queechy. *Although she criticizes the structure of Warner's plots, Kirkland praises her portrayal of American life and character.*]

Novels of American life have thus far been rather picturesque than moral or "knowing." The new circumstances of our position, and the feeling that our country is too little known to other countries, have prompted a descriptive tone—both as to scenery and manners—an appearance of the attempt to give information—which has almost put them out of the pale of fiction and within that of travels. When Scott describes manners and customs, scenery, or historic characters, he does so because they are in themselves worth describing; they are curious, or quaint, or striking, or they have the points which fit them to be the components of a great picture in which the imagination shall find delight; when Mr. Cooper or Miss Sedgwick brings them forward, it is because they are American—new, unknown beyond our own borders, and because they *ought* to be interesting;—Indians, for instance, which writers *will* occasionally fancy they can *make* interesting, the true Indian, truly depicted, being about as interesting as the Patagonian or New Zealander. To teach morals has been no very direct aim of our indigenous novels. They have breathed a high and pure tone, but it has been an under-tone. Mr. Cooper, in his latter days, wrote some hard, blunt satires, under the guise of novels; but there is many a deposition that deserves the name better. Miss Sedgwick's minor fictions are parables, excellent ones, adorned with all the humane graces, and distinctly American; beaming all over with the earnest goodness of the author—her truth, her courage, her religious spirit; but hardly novels.

As our space will not allow a *catalogue raisonnée* of American novels, we must content ourselves with this mere reference to them. It is more to our present purpose to say that they have been accepted and admired at home, and not a little noticed abroad; though, on every fresh venture, there is a cry of "American! we want something American! something distinctive; something that would not be at home anywhere else; grand as your rivers; rugged as your mountains; expansive, like your great lakes," &c. There has been, at times, a perfect hubbub of this sort—a very "Omnibus row," if we may credit the critic managers of British taste:

> Folks of all sorts and of every degree;
> Snob and Snip and haughty grandee;
> Duchesses, Countesses, fresh from their tea;
> And Shopmen, who only read books for a spree,
> Halloo'd and hooted and roar'd 'cross the sea,
> "Be grand! be grand!
> Let your lines expand!
> We'll take nothing small from so monstrous a
>   land!"

(We hope the ghost of the lamented Ingoldsby will not haunt us for the liberty here taken with his rhymes.) Yet the bigger we tried to write, the more they said we stole their thunder. So, by general consent, and in happy hour, we gave up trying to write to please or instruct any body but ourselves; and lo and behold, an American literature!

If we may accept as testimony the rapturous welcome of our British neighbors, *Uncle Tom's Cabin* is in itself quite sufficient to establish our claim in that quarter—an incidental obligation which we owe to Mrs. Stowe, in addition to the great one of having flung the heaviest stone at Slavery in the United States. But besides the glory of this unique production, the past year has witnessed another triumph, in the welcome given to a new venture in the new path; a welcome less enthusiastic, of course, than that accorded to the striking and masterly delineation of a social state about which the whole curiosity of the world was a-tiptoe; but most hearty, smiling, tearful; spontaneous, national, and untinctured by the poor pride which is unsatisfied without the recognition of outsiders. **The Wide, Wide World** struck a chord that was still vibrating when **Queechy** came to prolong the thrill; and later in the day, a modest, younger sister, bearing the unlovely name of *Dollars and Cents,* touched the same note, though with a less potent finger. In treating of these three books, we must notice the third only incidentally, yet its merit is undeniable. It has the disadvantage of being third and not first, or even second; and also of having appeared too soon after its elders, which it resembles too closely to hope to excite a fresh interest.

As far as we know the early history of the **Wide, Wide World,** it was, for some time, bought to be presented to nice little girls, by parents and friends who desired to set a pleasant example of docility and self-command before those happy beginners. Elder sisters were soon found poring over the volumes, and it was very natural that mothers next should try the spell which could so enchain the more volatile spirits of the household. After this, papas were not very difficult to convert, for papas like to feel their eyes moisten, sometimes, with emotions more generous than those usually excited at the stock exchange or in the counting-room. Whether any elder brothers read, we must doubt, in the absence of direct testimony; for that class proverbially despises any thing so "slow" as pictures of domestic life; but we are much mistaken if the **Wide, Wide World,** and **Queechy,** have not been found under the pillows of sober bachelors,—pillows not unsprinkled with the sympathetic tears of those who, in broad day, manfully exult in "freedom" from the effeminate fetters of wife and children.

All this while nobody talked very loud about these simple stories. They were found on everybody's table, and lent from house to house, but they made no great figure in the newspapers or show-bills. By and by, the deliberate people who look at title-pages, noticed the magic words, "Tenth Thousand," "Twelfth Thousand," and so on; and as the publishing house was not one of those who think politic fibs profitable, inevitable conclusions began to be drawn as to the popularity of the books—conclusions to which the publisher had come long before, perhaps not without a certain surprise.

With our intuitive respect for the public fiat, we scarce feel like criticizing, in the usual terms, works which have received the unbought stamp of its hearty approval. All critical rules worth using are deduced from works thus stamped; that is to say, from works of genius; for the universal heart leaps up to none other. And as each of these must be to a certain extent original, we ought, perhaps, to consider it as instituting some new rules, of which it should itself first enjoy the advantage. We should certainly be much at a loss for any single book to which we might profitably compare these truly indigenous novels, unless we take the liberty of supposing that the *Vicar of Wakefield* may have seemed to English readers of Goldsmith's time somewhat as these do to us—a simple transcript of country life and character, depending for interest partly on the ordinary joys and sorrows of our common humanity, partly on life-like pictures of individual loveliness and virtue, which sweeten what is homely in the accessories, and brighten scenes and fortunes that might otherwise leave on the mind a too oppressive sadness. As far as we can analyze the elements of literary popularity, that of the *Vicar* and that of these world-wide stories of ours rest on a somewhat similar basis, though we are far from claiming for the American tales an equality of merit. In plot they are deficient, certainly; may almost be said to have none; and in variety they fall immeasurably behind, as every picture of common life drawn by a woman necessarily must, for want of the wide experience open only to the other sex. But, even of the *Vicar of Wakefield,* Dr. Johnson said, "I myself did not think it would have had much success;" so difficult is it at first to discern the true merit of a life-like portrait by a master of the art. A daub strikes or disgusts at once; it is only the exquisite painter who keeps us long hovering in doubt through the subtle delicacy of his handling.

Miss Warner—who can no longer expect to find shelter under her pseudonyme of "Elizabeth Wetherell,"—sets out on her task with a religious intention—as who should not? under the injunction, "WHATEVER ye do"—yet she does not write what we have been accustomed to contemplate under the title of a religious novel. Attempting, as her main point, the development of a female character from mere childhood upward, she makes religion the decisive element, as whoever would draw from nature must do, spite of convention, fortune, amiable dispositions, happy circumstances, or strange reverses. Whosoever looks below the mere surface of things, finds that when virtue, happiness, or even prosperity is in question, religion is the ultimate disposer, though the world is slow to recognize its power over "the life that now is." In our view, Miss Warner allows it no higher than its due place, and ascribes to it no wider than its real influence. She makes her young girl passionate, though amiable, in her temper; fond of admiration, although withheld by innate delicacy from seeking it unduly. She places her in circumstances of peculiar trial to her peculiar traits, and brings her, by careful gradations, to the state of self-governed and stable virtue which fits woman for her great office in the world; a fitness which would be impaired by the sacrifice of a single grace, or the loss of one sentiment of tenderness. To build such a character on any basis other than a religious one, would have been to fix a palace upon the shifting sands; and we have no quarrel with Miss Warner that she has not taken pains to hide her foundations, as some poor architects do. Let us see that the base is sufficient, that we may not be disturbed by fears as to the permanence of an edifice we are compelled to admire. Ellen and

Fleda are reared, by their truly feminine and natural experiences, into any thing but "strong-minded women," at least if we accept Mr. Dickens's notion of that dreadful order. They are both of velvet softness; of delicate, downcast beauty; of flitting but abundant smiles, and of even too many and ready tears.

> Not learned, save in gracious household ways;
> Not perfect, nay, but full of tender wants.

They live in the affections, as the true woman must; yet they cultivate and prize the understanding, and feel it to be the appointed guardian of goodness, as all wise women should. Without a touch of the Corinna, we feel that neither could ever sink to the level of Priscilla. They are conscious of having a power and place in the world, and they claim it without assumption or affectation, and fill it with a quiet self-respect, not inconsistent with modesty and due humility. Such is the ideal presented, and with such skill that we seem at times to be reading a biography. There is a sweetness in the conception and execution that makes the heart and the temper better as we read. A little gentle monitor puts our pride off its guard, and we are led away captive by goodness—even religious goodness—without resistance.

So much for the *charm* of the books. As a matter of pure judgment, we must place their pictures of American country life and character above all their other merits, since we know not where, in any language, we shall find their graphic truth excelled. When after times would seek a specimen of our Doric of this date, Aunt Fortune will stand them in stead; and no Theocritus of our time will draw a bucolical swain more true to the life than Mr. Van Brunt. Even the shadow of Didenhover is a portrait; we see him, though he never appears in the flesh, and we feel him, too, though we have never let out a farm "on shares." Captain Montgomery is another of those invisible persons with whom we are perfectly well acquainted, although not a line is given to describing him; and the "hateful" clerk who wreaks his petty spite upon Ellen's horse, is a character whose truth to nature little girls bear witness to, by the hearty indignation with which they read the scene. Nancy Vawse is a white Topsy; Barby a perfect type of the American serving-girl, at once selfish and tender, coarse and delicate; and we might swell our list of life-like characters a good deal further, if their very number did not warn us against being too particular.

But, on the other hand, we are compelled to say that such magisterial lovers as Mr. Carleton and John Humphreys are not at all to our taste, nor do we believe they would in actual presence be very fascinating to most young ladies. It is true that youthful pupils have fallen in love with their schoolmasters ere now, but if we were condemned to go masquerading after a wife, we should, relying upon observation, choose almost any other *rôle* sooner. It is hard to imagine Ellen slipping into the equality of wifehood, from the childish reverence which she is represented as feeling, to the last moment, for him who has been for years her stern and almost gloomy teacher. As for Carleton, he carries his pretentiousness into the region of melodrama—awing people with looks; entering the drawing-rooms of ladies unnoticed, so as to be present when nobody is thinking of him, and scarce descending from his stilts even to his honored mamma, though he is

> All adoration, duty, and observance

to the child Fleda, and on the point of fighting a duel about her, when she is scarce a dozen years old. This contrast between a man's natural or habitual character and manner, and that which he exhibits when in love, may be what novel-reading young ladies call "interesting;" but it is one scarcely befitting a pattern man—a Christianized hero— one to whom humility is strength, and self-renunciation the only dignity. The least *soupçon* of strut spoils such a figure. We like the hero of *Dollars and Cents*—evidently a brother of the order, Rodney Collingwood by name— much better, though he walks under such a veil of dimness in the story, as told by a little girl, that we are hardly sure we know him fully.

In each and all of the three books we are thinking of, pecuniary difficulties are made the chief means of the development of character; in real life, as it seems to us, they are more certainly the means of developing talent. Is it not assigning to money an office higher than that which really belongs to it, to make the possession or lack of it so influential in that high region where the affections, the conscience, the hope for another life, are the acknowledged arbiters? Character must spring from the heart; conduct may be, in part, the result of circumstances. The possession of riches does, indeed, sometimes seem to harden the heart and deaden the sympathies; mean and shallow minds it makes self-forgetful and irreligious, sometimes. But, on the other hand, has not the struggle with poverty its mischiefs? Even the effort to escape, not from poverty, but from mediocrity, to the dazzling heights of wealth,— that strife which we of this "happy land" see around us every day,—may well remind a looker-on of the fate of those wretched prisoners, who, after agreeing to march in procession past the only breathing place, that each might have his share of the chance for life, soon forgot, in their frantic selfishness, that the good of all was the good of each, and trod one upon another, filling the air with poison and death. Only the philosopher, and, above all, the Christian, whose philosophy has possession and command of the entire man, heart as well as intellect, finds poverty favorable to the cultivation of all the virtues. Angry discontent, if not open murmuring against Providence; if not absolute and conscious envy, at least so much of it as prevents a hearty rejoicing at the prosperity of others; such a yielding to sordid cares as shall make the imagination a mere caterer to Mammon, and so stifle the affections that our eye shall be evil to the son of our bosom as being another consumer of the diminishing store; these are some of the too common and natural evils of poverty; evils against which strength of mind offers no adequate defence, because the intellect alone makes poor and wavering battle against the passions and propensities.

Poverty is not, therefore, the ordeal to which we should choose to subject an ordinary mind and heart, with a view to their highest improvement. The trials of temper to which the little Ellen is exposed, under the iron hand of Aunt Fortune, are training indeed, and tests indeed. To profit by such blows, the heart must have had the anneal-

ing of heavenly fires, for none other would serve; to bear them without absolute injury would be above the moral strength of most children, as our painful interest in the struggles and slips of the dear little girl bears witness. Another sort of trial is the persecution of Fleda by Mr. Thorn, and the petty annoyance she experiences among the Evelyns. The entire picture of her conduct in these cases is excellently done, and offers some most salutary hints of united modesty and firmness, in positions which most young ladies would find difficult. The amiable amusement called "teazing" is well characterized; we have always felt it to be akin to that of pulling off the legs and wings of flies.

> Fleda had the greatest difficulty not to cry. The lady did not seem to see her disturbed brow; but recovering herself after a little, though not readily, she bent forward and touched her lips to it in kind fashion. Fleda did not look up, and, saying again—"I will tell him, dear Fleda!"—Mrs. Evelyn left the room. Constance, after a little laughing and condoling, neither of which Fleda attempted to answer, ran off too, to dress herself; and Fleda, after finishing her own toilette, sat down and cried heartily. She thought Mrs. Evelyn had been, perhaps unconsciously, very unkind; and to say that unkindness has not been meant, is but to shift the charge from one to another vital point in the character of a friend, and one perhaps not less grave. A moment's passionate wrong may consist with the endurance of a friendship worth having, better than the thoughtlessness of obtuse wits that can never know how to be kind. Fleda's whole frame was in a tremor from disagreeable excitement, and she had serious causes of sorrow to cry for. She was sorry she had lost what would have been a great pleasure in the ride—and her great pleasures were not often—but nothing would have been more impossible than for her to go after what Mrs. Evelyn had said; she was sorry Mr. Carleton should have asked her twice in vain; what must he think? She was exceedingly sorry that a thought should have been put into her head that never before had visited the most distant dreams of her imagination—so needlessly, so gratuitously;—she was very sorry, for she could not be free of it again, and she felt it would make her miserably hampered and constrained in mind and manner both, in any future intercourse with the person in question. And then, again, what would he think of that? Poor Fleda came to the conclusion that her best place was at home, and made up her mind to take the first good opportunity of getting there.

> She went down to dinner with no traces either of tears or of unkindness on her sweet face, but her nerves were quivering all the afternoon; she could not tell whether Mrs. Evelyn and her daughters found it out. And it was impossible for her to get back even her old degree of freedom of manner before either Mr. Carleton or Mr. Thorn. All the more because Mrs. Evelyn was every now and then bringing out some sly allusion which afforded herself intense delight, and wrought Fleda to the last degree of unquietness. Unkind—Fleda thought now it was but

half from ignorance of the mischief she was doing, the other half from the mere desire of selfish gratification. The times and ways in which Lot and Abraham were walked into the conversation were incalculable—and unintelligible except to the person who understood it only too well.

Many of the social ills and errors called "petty," are touched upon with equal acuteness and courage—we say courage, because that is a quality required for touching on American social faults. One is proved a traitor, and will go nigh to be thought one shortly, who allows, even in the rarest paroxysms of candor, that our manners might be improved. But our authoress is on impregnable ground when she takes the golden rule as her standard of manners, and she makes us feel, in various instances, that convention is a far more arbitrary and fluctuating one. As good republicans, we ought to thank her for indicating the basis whereon we may build, even in this land of equality and fluctuation, a politeness more gentle, delicate, and consistent, than ever prevailed in the court of the Grand Monarque, or any other selfish King of Diamonds whatever.

It is, perhaps, unnecessary, after what we have already said, to state formally that we think the new American novels no whit too religious. If we were inclined to cavil at all in this direction, it would be at a too minute and rather feeble mode of presenting the great subject in certain conversations, where the effort has evidently been to simplify the whole matter, and clear it of the mystical dimness and dignity which persons of more intellectual pride than self-knowledge are apt to allege against it. We do not at all agree with the critic who objects to the attempt to "make people religious by quotations from Dr. Watts's hymns;" for a hymn is sometimes to a sermon what the smooth stone of the shepherd-warrior was to the ponderous spear of the heathen giant; or the scymetar of Saladin, that would divide a flying feather, to the broadsword of Sir Kenneth, made to hack and hew by the aid of main strength. "The Word"! who shall measure its potency, or prescribe the vehicle in which it shall find its appointed mark soonest? If any thing is taught equally by Scripture and experience, it is that in spiritual matters it is impossible to say "whether shall prosper, either this or that." To use an illustration called to mind by the rural pictures in the books before us;—a mass of hay not wholly dried may long be conscious of a rising heat, yet never reaching the point of combustion, grow cold again. But, while the temperature of the heap is thus raised, it takes but an electric flash from a passing cloud to wake it into flame. Poetry is electric, and oftentimes the dull, smouldering soul, long inaccessible to influences seeming stronger, finds its tiniest spark irresistible.

We cannot so confidently defend the long arguments which here and there dilute the richer current of natural thought and lively description that flows through Miss Warner's books. We tolerate interruptions to the leading interest only when they are recommended by peculiar felicities of style; importance of subject is not sufficient passport for such interpolations. Nor can we, by any glamour of *bonhommie,* be brought to look with complacency upon

certain specimens of homeliness in diction carried further than the necessities of the case demand. Colloquialisms are racy; bad grammar and coarse expressions, however true to nature in the delineations of certain characters, are sad blemishes when they creep into the writer's own style, or into the talk of people whom she represents as well-educated and accustomed to refined society. An old country gentleman may be made to say, "Suppose you and me was to have some roast apples;" but it grates on the ear sadly when Mr. Rossitur, who has spent his life in Paris and New York, says "I will not interrupt you but a minute," and the heroine herself falls into the same inelegance. Barby may talk of "hauling" a table up to the fire, or a gentleman's "feeling about his jaws and chin," as he stands before the fire; but when the author uses such expressions in her own person, or describes an elegant young lady "reaching over after a sausage," we must be allowed to feel slightly shocked. It is easy to perceive that these errors are the result of a deliberate determination on the author's part, to be true to nature at all hazards; but we submit, that, in fiction, truth must always acknowledge the dominion of taste. There is, indeed, a large class among us, lifted by sudden fortune into positions which render their lack of early advantages painfully obvious; but we protest against the insinuation that it is common to hear, among our better classes, cacophony as salient as Lord Dubuley's, or that English people alone speak correctly our native tongue. There seems a slight lurking of prejudice, hardly consistent with the general patriotism of Miss Warner's books, in this setting up of English people as models of virtue and good-breeding, and almost a solecism in sending across the water for an immensely wealthy English husband for the sturdy little American Fleda, whose breeding of hap and hazard certainly have fitted her so admirably for making some indigenous swain happy. But this choosing of husbands for themselves, or their heroines, is a matter in which ladies have always the privilege of being a little wilful, if not whimsical.

Where, then, let us ask, in conclusion, shall we class these American novels of ours? There is very little romance about them; they have nothing of the Edgworthian didactic tone; they are not devoted to showing up the vices and weaknesses of society; nor do they take up any particular grievance, in order to probe the sluggish consciences of those who practise or tolerate it. They have no evident aim at the picturesque or grotesque newness of our green land. May we not, then, consider them as having a character of their own—humane, religious, *piquant,* natural, national? They paint human nature in its American type; they appeal to universal human sympathy, but with a special reference to the fellow-feeling of those whose peculiar social circumstances and trials fit them to be judges of the life-picture in whose background may be discerned so many familiar objects. They recognize the heart as the stronghold of character, and religion as the ruling element of life; religion—no *ism,* however specious or popular—being "of one mind with Christ;" the "faith that worketh by love;" whose fruit is obedience, and whose reward, a peace that can be attained by no other method. We know of no prototype of such books, unless we venture to claim a family likeness to the world-wide favorite mentioned some time since—a claim, however, which must not imply the relinquishment of that of originality, since there is no room for suspicion of imitation. Nothing could be easier, to be sure, than to show, that, by the side of Goldsmith's, our author's literary style is "nowhere," to use a recently popular phrase; yet we insist there is a resemblance that lies deeper than mere style. Let us hope, that, encouraged in all future efforts by the gratifying welcome accorded to these comparatively crude ventures, she may catch the style, as well as the spirit, of the great master of English prose narrative.

To us, there is something very pleasing in this welcome. Such a spontaneous popularity is interesting as an index of national character. Not that we would draw too broad conclusions from a single instance, but that we must consider so striking a fact to have some general meaning. When a story of real life—American rural life, of the homeliest—unheralded at home, unstamped by foreign approval—lacking the tempting bait of national flattery—and wholly deficient in the flash and flippancy that might attract the vulgar mind, springs at once to a currency which few books ever reach—cried to the skies by the "most sweet voices," of old and young, gentle and simple,—we cannot help feeling the verdict to be significant. To borrow a Swedenborgianism, we are what our loves are; and, although nations are perhaps as subject as individuals to be led away by clamor or sympathy into demonstrations of that which has no true vitality, there are expressions whose heartiness is their warrant. What are the grounds of the admiration, or rather love, excited by these books? The interest of both lies in a most life-like picture of the character and fate of a little girl—for we feel Ellen and Fleda to be one and the same;—a little girl such as any of our daughters may be; unfortunate in some respects, happy in others; dependent, as all little girls, whatever their station or fortune, must be, on the virtue and affection of those about them; but showing, what all little girls cannot show, a degree of character, a firmness of principle, a sweetness of disposition, by no means impossible under the circumstances, yet far enough raised above common experience and expectation, to excite the imagination and stimulate the sympathy. This little figure, set in a framework of homely circumstances, coarse dress, domestic drudgery, and uncongenial companionship, is the light of the book. All else, however excellently sketched in, is subordinate. It is of the little heart, beating at once with timidity and courage, that we think. The sweet childish face and loving ways make "a sunshine in the shady place," under the most humiliating circumstances. We care for all else only as this little piece of tender, budding womanhood is affected or influenced. When she is abused, we burn with indignation; when she is exalted, we feel that only justice is done her. When saucy and teasing things are said to her by envious people, we long to hear what she will say in reply, and when she answers well, (as she always does,) our eyes sparkle as if she were our very own. From all this, we cannot help coming to the conclusion that the author is very able, and that we are—very amiable! (pp. 111-23)

> *Caroline Kirkland, in a review of "The Wide, Wide World," and "Queechy," in* The North American Review, *Vol. LXXVI, No. CLVIII, January, 1853, pp. 104-23.*

The Athenaeum   (essay date 1856)

[*In the following excerpt, the critic unfavorably compares* The Hills of the Shatemuc *to Warner's earlier novels.*]

In **Queechy** and **The Wide, Wide World** there was an interest which carried the reader through much absurd narrative and over many improbable and impossible incidents. There was a facility of drawing character, which only needed more knowledge of the world and a better acquaintance with the ordinary customs of society to have become a sterling talent. We regret to say that all the promise contained in the earlier works of this writer appears to have evaporated [in **The Hills of the Shatemuc**],—the power of exciting the reader's interest is gone,—there is no knowledge to make up for the romance which is lost,—and there is no clearness of intention, nor truth of experience, to give value to the didactic portions. There is very little narrative; for it is absorbed in long trivial conversations, or rather dialogues, which are intended to indicate some event which has not been related; but it requires microscopic attention and unwearied patience on the part of the reader to discover it. This is a mode of treatment which the author appears to have adopted deliberately. All artists are free to work in the manner that best pleases them; but, as the reading victims, we feel equally free to enter our protest against the jerking, disjointed, uncomfortable manner, in which the design is carried out. Every character is made to speak in the same snip-snap, short, broken-off sentences, without any distinction of persons, except that one has to be proud, another friendly, another foolish, as though each had drawn his or her character upon Twelfth Night, and the same author ventriloquizes through all.

Winthrop Landholm, the hero, is represented as a masculine "Queechy," capable of helping everybody, supplying all their shortcomings, rectifying their faults, doing their business and his own too. He is intended to be the type of a strong, self-contained, determined character; he might have been made interesting, but the author has chosen to make him impossible instead. His qualities are thrown crudely together like items in an auctioneer's catalogue. The history of his progress, from a boy following the plough upon his father's farm, until he became an eminent lawyer, is wearisome and minute, without being either distinct or graphic;—neither author nor reader forms a distinct notion of him or of his fortunes. Throughout the book there is an entire absence of vitality; characters that have been much talked about suddenly fall through and disappear, and only by careful search can the reader discover any indication of what has become of them. The didactic portions are vague, and what they intend to teach we really cannot tell. The story at last fairly runs aground in an interminable conversation, and finishes because it is impossible to get it again afloat. The worst sign about this book is not, however, its dullness, but the fatal facility which is evident throughout. The author has had no difficulty in her work; it is eminently a book of words, which cost little. The author copies from herself, and seems to have become bewildered by the echo of past commendations, which she will do well to forget and set to work afresh.

A review of "The Hills of Shatemuc," in The Athenaeum, Vol. 2, No. 1508, September 20, 1856, pp. 1163-64.

The Nation (New York)   (essay date 1882)

[*In the following review of* Nobody, *the critic censures Warner's treatment of religious themes.*]

Nobody is in Miss Warner's usual style both as to plot and execution. It is mentioned here only to notice the singular mistake to which her devotion to one idea, or one form of one idea, has led her. "Nobody" is the simple country girl whom the hero, upon her first visit to the gay city world, falls in love with. He has every grace of mind and manner except what Miss Warner is accustomed to call "the Christian." They part in the spring and meet again the following autumn. "Days and weeks go by," till at Christmas time he offers himself to her, and is met by a positive refusal, because, "You know, O you know, you are not a Christian!" Upon this he tells her that during the summer he has thought and studied—and "then made open profession of his belief." So the way is smooth and that is the end of it. But it is amazing that Miss Warner does not see how she has stultified herself by her representation that this change is a matter of such vital consequence that the girl will break her heart rather than marry the man without it, and yet it is so little a thing that in all the weeks since his return she has never suspected anything of it. Her surprise at his announcement is proof of that. The answer to such a criticism would be, that she *would* have felt the difference, and that therein is Miss Warner's mistake. Either way, it is an instance of the unreality which makes most of the "religious novels" positively dangerous. One kind of mind they disaffect, another they mislead, while it is not easy for a critic to deal with them, from the difficulty of separating their false views of the truth from the truth itself, so that the condemnation of the one shall not seem irreverence to the other.

A review of "Nobody," in The Nation, New York, Vol. XXXV, No. 908, November 23, 1882, pp. 447-48.

Alexander Cowie   (essay date 1948)

[*In the following excerpt, Cowie examines* The Wide, Wide World *as an early specimen of the domestic novel.*]

The Wide, Wide World made use of many of the devices that were to be standard equipment in the domestic novel for some years to come. Ellen Montgomery is not an orphan, but she is going to be soon. In the meantime the illness of her mother and the business affairs of her father make it necessary to entrust Ellen to the keeping of Aunt Fortune Emerson in a small community in New England. Since Mr. Montgomery has been slow to pay on a loan Aunt Fortune made him, she is none too gracious toward his snip of a daughter. Ellen responds to her aunt's curt treatment by being saucy and rebellious. Yet Ellen is generally sorry at her outbursts of temper, and she keeps resolving to conquer her pride. In this endeavor she is assisted by the saintly young woman Alice Humphreys. In the

meantime there are endless illustrations of the day's work—washing dishes, running errands, mending clothes, cooking meals, etc., as well as incidental object lessons . . . in which Ellen learns why sheep need salt or how a horse can be made to leap a barrier. There are also interminable discussions of how to live the good life, especially by returning good for evil. There is hardly any "plot," but there are many crises. The deaths of mother and father Montgomery are reported. More directly affecting to the reader is the death of Alice Humphreys, who one day calmly announces her own imminent demise:

> "What is the matter, dear Alice? what are you thinking about?"
>
> "I am thinking, Ellie, how I shall tell you something that will give you pain."
>
> "Pain! you needn't be afraid of giving me pain," said Ellen fondly, throwing her arms around her;—"tell me, dear Alice; is it something I have done that is wrong? what is it?"
>
>   . . . . .
>
> "Suppose Ellie," she said at length,—"that you and I were taking a journey together—a troublesome dangerous journey—and that I had a way of getting at once safe to the end of it;—would you be willing to let me go, and you do without me for the rest of the way?"
>
> "I would rather you should take me with you," said Ellen, in a kind of maze of wonder and fear;—"why where are you going, Alice?"
>
> "I think I am going home, Ellie,—before you."
>
> "Home?" said Ellen.
>
> "Yes,—home I feel it to be; it is not a strange land; I thank God it is my *home* I am going to."

With these news, Ellen

> could hardly get home. Her blinded eyes could not see where she was stepping; and again and again her fulness of heart got the better of every thing else, and unmindful of the growing twilight she sat down on a stone by the wayside or flung herself on the ground to let sorrows have full sway.

But when Alice dies in the arms of her brother, the spectacle is wholly edifying, and

> the departing spirit had left a ray of brightness on its earthly house; there was a half smile on the sweet face, of most entire peace and satisfaction.

Shortly after this Aunt Fortune decides to cast in her lot with a droll rustic and join her farm with his. It is then up to Ellen to take the advice sent her some time since by her father, to go abroad (which she does in two sentences) to search out her relatives in Edinburgh. The remainder of the book is devoted to Ellen's becoming adjusted (pleasantly, on the whole) with her Scotch relatives. It is understood, however, that after a few years she will return to the country she loves best and to Mr. Humphreys, her adopted "brother."

This story is atypical in that Ellen who is only eight or ten at the beginning of the story is spared all adult emotions of love, for the book ends with her early adolescence. *The Wide, Wide World* is a juvenile. Yet in several respects it helped to establish norms for the whole genre, especially in its casual narrative construction and its enormous content of sentimentality. Weeping and kissing are used to the point of the morbid and the unhygienic. When for example Ellen is leaving Alice Humphreys for a short time the "parting was hard. They held each other fast a good while, and kissed each other many times without speaking." Ellen is also the victim of the osculatory attentions of almost all the other characters of the book. With all this kissing, which a modern psychologist might find objectionable in ways that would have surprised Miss Warner, one might assume that Ellen is a sweet girl. And so she was finally intended by her author to be. Actually she is an impossible prissy. She is even at the beginning, as the rustic Van Brunt says, about as good as anyone can safely be in this world, but Miss Warner hounds her with admonitions to subdue her pride and cultivate true humility. In short Miss Warner rants about religion. She is trying to sanctify a saint. The heroine of her story for modern readers would be Nancy Vawse, the "bad girl" who is used as a foil for Ellen. The recent exploitation of "bad" little girls (in books like Victoria Lincoln's *February Hill,* for example) is partly explicable, no doubt, as a reaction against the saccharine heroines of the domestic sentimentalists. Little Eva has suffered a similar fate: we now prefer Topsy. Each generation selects its own heroines. But certain it is that Ellen Montgomery fitted her own times and that the public found deep satisfaction in the tears and sentiment of *The Wide, Wide World,* for allusions to it occur throughout literature since 1850. The work is even cited as read by characters in other domestic novels. (pp. 416-18)

> *Alexander Cowie, "The Domestic Sentimentalists and Other Popular Writers," in his* The Rise of the American Novel, *American Book Company, 1948, pp. 412-46.*

Nina Baym   (essay date 1978)

[*Baym is an American educator and critic. In the following excerpt, she discusses* The Wide, Wide World, Queechy, *and* The Hills of the Shatemuc, *focusing on the attempts of Warner's protagonists to adapt to their lack of control over their own lives.*]

[*The Wide, Wide World*] opens in a New York City hotel room, where Mrs. Montgomery and her ten-year-old daughter Ellen are waiting out a cheerless November day. The mother, an invalid, dozes. The little girl, as she has been instructed to do, passes the time by looking out the window.

> Rain was falling, and made the street and everything in it look dull and gloomy. The foot-passengers plashed through the water, and horses and carriages plashed through the mud; gaiety had forsaken the side-walks, and equipages were few, and the people that were out were plainly there only because they could not help it. . . . Daylight gradually faded away,

and the street wore a more and more gloomy aspect. The rain poured, and now only an occasional carriage or footstep disturbed the sound of its steady pattering. . . . At length, in the distance, light after light began to appear; presently Ellen could see the dim figure of the lamplighter crossing the street, from side to side, with his ladder; then he drew near enough for her to watch him as he hooked his ladder on the lamp-irons, ran up and lit the lamp, then shouldered the ladder and marched off, the light glancing on his wet oil-skin hat, rough greatcoat, and lantern, and on the pavement and iron railings.

These well-turned sentences of *The Wide, Wide World,* with their direct prose, pictorial vividness, and rhythmical clauses, announce a literary talent unmarked by the alleged "feminine" excesses of overblown imagery and inflated diction. But Susan Warner's subject, and the angle from which she approaches it, are relentlessly and deliberately feminine. Turning away from the window, Ellen makes tea for herself and her mother, and the two contemplate their bleak future. Mr. Montgomery, after losing a law suit, has taken a position in Europe. Mrs. Montgomery, in failing health, has been advised to accompany him. She lacks the strength to care for Ellen, so the child must go to live with her father's sister, Miss Fortune Emerson, who lives on a farm in the country. Mother and daughter are devoted to each other and have never been separated before. Each knows, though neither expresses it except in tears, that the separation will be final. These tears, which flow throughout the novel, have exasperated male critics, who repeatedly satirize its lachrymosity; for Warner, her characters, and her readers, the freedom to express grief is one of the few freedoms permitted women, though it must generally be indulged in private.

Need we say something in defense of tears? Women do cry, and it is realism in our authors to show it. The nineteenth-century woman was not ashamed of her tears, and in woman's fiction, the heroines are encouraged to cry as therapy. It is recognized that grief may literally kill if it is not vented in tears. And other emotions—above all anger and frustration—may be safely expressed in tears when no other way can be indulged. One might theorize that the frequency of tears in a woman's fiction is proportional less to the amount of tenderness and sensibility that imbues it, than to the amount of rage and frustration that it carries. I speak of safe expression because rage and frustration may not be openly voiced by the powerless without unfortunate consequences for them. More than any of the other women, Susan Warner dealt with power and the lack of it.

At the beginning of *The Wide, Wide World,* two powerless women are struggling to accept the apparent injustice of two fathers, injustice from which they have no recourse. The earthly father, a selfish, inconsiderate, and undependable man, is more easily dealt with than the Heavenly father, for he does not need to be defended. But as a pious woman Mrs. Montgomery feels that she must justify God's ways to her daughter, even when those ways include killing the mother. The decrees of God, she insists, are invariably dictated by love even if the loving motive is not apparent to mere human understanding. Many other devout people in the novel take up this refrain, telling her that God's act of depriving her of her mother was loving and gracious. Ellen learns that the dispensation must be accepted and comes gradually to look ahead rather than back, but she never fully overcomes her childish conviction that she lives in an unjust world. Over the course of this long novel (690 pages in its first, two-volume edition) Ellen learns to take pleasure where it is found and to negotiate without being destroyed by the powerful unjust. The story would have been different, of course, could she (or her author) have broken through to gestures of defiance more pleasing to the twentieth century or, better still, to an expression of existential doubt or absurdity. But Ellen, who sees powerful unjust people in the world—she cannot even make a minor purchase for her mother without being badgered by a spiteful clerk—sees no reason to conclude from metaphysical injustice that there is no God. The reason for her struggle to believe that God is not unjust follows from her certainty that he exists. One gets along better with absolute power if one accepts it as beneficent.

Susan Warner's version of the orphan's story is different from many other authors' in that she focuses so quickly and exclusively on the issue of power and how to live without it. Although this is not a purely feminine issue by any means (it concerned Melville, for example; one might say that *Moby-Dick* is a masculine treatment of the same question) Warner handles it exclusively in a feminine iconography. The loss of a mother is not traumatic to female children alone, but only women will admit to the desolation of this particular pain, and hence the primal injustice from which Ellen's story develops seems like an injustice suffered only by women. Since God is a paternal idea, it is an injustice perpetrated on women by man.

Beyond this terrible initiating event, however, Ellen's social trials—really much less severe than those endured by many heroines—are the sort that only women are supposed to suffer, whether they be fashionable people mocking her dowdy bonnet, or Aunt Fortune dyeing all her fine white stockings dun-colored (though White-Jacket and his sartorial anguish comes to mind here). In each case of humiliation or hardship, offenses are committed by those who have "charge" of Ellen, and the child cannot respond to them without damaging herself.

And then there is an offense beyond all special examples of provocation: the assumption by those who have guardianship of the child that they "own" her. How is one to endure such situations and yet remain a self? How can one submit to being owned and still be free? However much Warner's self-imposed restrictions to the feminine, to pious orthodoxy, and to a creed of superficial compliance have dated *The Wide, Wide World* for later generations, her questions and answers made sense for the time, and unquestionably for her own purposes she did right.

Ellen is taken on the journey to Aunt Fortune's by a fashionable Mrs. Dunscombe. Her final parting from her mother has been marked by violent grief, augmented by her "sense of wrong and feeling of indignation at her father's cruelty" in not revealing the day of parting until the very morning that they separate—a typical, selfish action on his part. "A child of very high spirit and violent passions," Ellen senses of how little account she is to all except the mother from whom she has been parted, and the feeling creates rage rather than fear. When Mrs. Dunscombe's fourteen-year-old daughter laughs at her unfashionable hat, "the lightning of passion shot through every vein . . . and hurt feeling and wounded pride." Unless she can better control her feelings and behavior, Ellen will find life intolerable.

Ellen's Aunt Fortune is a middle-aged spinster who lives with her aged mother and works a comfortable property; she is not poor but she displays a mean-spiritedness that a number of women authors discerned in country people who see no life beyond the arduous routines of farmwork. She is not vicious, but she is cold, narrow-minded, and bitter, with a rivulet of cruelty in her nature that finds an outlet in petty torments, like withholding her mother's letters from Ellen until she is "good." Except for denying Ellen a formal education (after teasingly implying she might go to school) she does the child no serious harm, but her coldness, coupled with her traditional belief that bringing up a child means breaking her will, leaves Ellen increasingly dissatisfied, restless, and resentful.

Matters do not come to a head, however, because Ellen finds a guide in Alice Humphreys, a young neighbor who lives with her father, a minister. (There is a brother in this family but he is away at school until later in the action.) Alice comforts Ellen and instructs her in religion; it is Alice's love rather than her doctrine that strengthens the girl, but Christianity gets the credit for Ellen's growth in control. Alice's religious teachings are actually quite pragmatic: "Return good for evil as fast as you can, and you will soon either have nothing to complain of or be very well able to bear it." She advises Ellen to be solicitous of her neglected grandmother—not to do her Christian duty, but to develop some affection in that loveless house. And as for Aunt Fortune, "see if you cannot win her over by untiring gentleness, obedience, and meekness." Actually, Ellen's new behavior does not win the aunt over, but it disarms her; unable to aggress against the child, she leaves her alone, and Ellen finds the freedom that she would never have enjoyed if she had remained defiant.

When Aunt Fortune marries the man who manages her farm, Ellen is allowed to go live with the Humphreys. There, surrounded by books and love, Ellen is gloriously happy. The return of brother John, a minister in training, completes an idyll of domestic felicity. Alice dies, but Ellen has grown into a noble young woman under her guidance and can assume her place. The interlude is terminated by the death of Ellen's father (mother had died some time before). Now she is sent to live in Edinburgh with Scottish relatives named Elliott. Ellen does not want to go, but has no choice. She does not belong to herself but to her parents, even when they are dead, and must go wherever they decree. At the Elliotts' she meets a new kind of struggle. These elegant, accomplished, sophisticated people make it clear that they expect her submission in every detail, exactly as Aunt Fortune had, to their way of life. Ellen is to do what they do, and never think to pass judgment on them. They are deeply offended by her provincial evangelical Christianity and her continually expressed longings for the Humphreys.

"She was petted and fondled as a darling possession—a dear plaything, . . . but John's was a higher style of kindness . . . and his was a higher style of authority." Uncle Elliott takes away a book that John had given her— taking things away from children is a common means by which adults manifest their ownership and authority. "But it is mine," Ellen protests. "And you are mine," Uncle Elliott responds. From this situation there is no escape other than a fairy-tale rescue, and John soon turns up in Edinburgh to impress the Elliotts with his force of character and to wrest concessions from them for Ellen that they would not accede to when she asked for them herself. She may write to John, for example, and be allowed more latitude in her religious observances. Uncle Elliott goes so far as to accompany her to church.

But John is constrained in what he can accomplish for Ellen by a greater authority. "I have no power now to remove you from your legal guardians," he tells her, "and you have no right to choose for yourself." So Ellen must wait it out, with the promise that she may return to America when she comes of age. Her Christian-based discipline enables her to do this. "Three or four more years of Scottish discipline wrought her no ill; they did but serve to temper and beautify her Christian character; and then, to her unspeakable joy, she went back to spend her life with the friends and guardians she best loved, and to be to them, still more than she had been to her Scottish relations, the 'light of the eyes.' "

The Edinburgh section serves as a coda and recapitulation of the theme that runs through the longer, rural section of the book. In their high-toned way the Elliotts aggress against Ellen no less than had Aunt Fortune. It is, however, far less realized; Warner had depicted the countryside that she knew so well with a scrupulous fidelity to detail, an ear for speech and an eye for custom, that makes *The Wide, Wide World* a thoroughly achieved work of local color. For this, at least, it deserves a place in American literary history.

Insofar as it does not follow Ellen past her adolescence, *The Wide, Wide World* might be typed as a juvenile; it does not deal with such adult issues as self-support, love, and marriage (although we assume that eventually Ellen and John will marry). The economic theme that dominates so much woman's fiction is absent here; but the terminology of ownership clearly implies a private perception of the economic theme as applied to human relations. The absence of romance, or the absorption of romance in the larger issues of family and guardianship, expresses overtly a concern that "romance" often masks in other woman's fictions. The heroine who marries happily at the end of most woman's fiction acquires a way of life, a home, a complex of human relations. Marriage is the means of establishing a family that is not a biological unit but a community of loving adults assembled under one roof. In this group the heroine plays both a child's and an adult's role. In fact, all the adults take different roles toward one another, rectifying, so to speak, the mistakes and curing the wounds that have been inflicted on them in their real family experiences. Such a surrogate family represents allegiance to the family ideal at the same time that it embodies a bitter criticism against families as the characters (and their authors) have really known them.

The ending of *The Wide, Wide World* is different from much woman's fiction in its vision of the heroine entering a domestic situation in which she is relieved from responsibility. Warner's vision of woman's restricted power allows no space in which their hegemony might be possible, and her sense of woman's needs does not include domination over others. What she wanted was relief and release from all obligation. Given the Warners' own lives, one might say that this ideal was false to any possibility of life as Susan knew it; but it is precisely such an unfulfilled life of unremitting responsibility that might generate the fantasy of complete freedom and protection. For Susan Warner, the memory of her adolescence when she was surrounded by luxury and refinement, tutored and made much of by her father and other accomplished gentlemen, became her vision of independence. She did not accept the argument that toiling away for money to get through a cold winter could constitute independence. Even the writing of fiction, a profession that might be imagined to yield satisfaction, she considered an arduous drudgery in comparison to her earlier life of self-indulgence and self-development. The cult of domesticity did not appeal to her because it centered woman's life on others. Her ideal of independence was intransigently self-centered. She cared neither to control others nor to serve them. Freedom for her meant being left alone, protected and comfortable, to pursue one's own interests. This is the situation to which Ellen is returned at the end of *The Wide, Wide World*. . . . [As] in McIntosh's *Two Pictures,* we encounter a woman's version of the American unwillingness to grow up.

The heroine of Susan Warner's second novel, *Queechy,* Fleda Ringgen, has a character much closer to perfection at the outset than does Ellen Montgomery. Selflessly, she takes the whole burden of her family's support on her inexperienced adolescent shoulders. *Queechy* shows that a woman can do this, and that she should if she must, but not that it is fun or good for her. If her character is already perfect, she does not need trials. Susan Warner depicts suffering in abundance in *Queechy,* but she is not a masochist, for she never calls it pleasure or claims that self-sacrificing drudgery enlarges the soul.

Fleda's ordeals are caused by defective men who shirk their duties and abuse their authority in a system that gives them all the economic power and responsibility. Men shrug off the responsibility on women while retaining the power, leaving women to struggle for bare survival with no hope of achieving financial comfort or security. A fairy-tale ending and continuous celebration of the heroine's perfections do not make up for *Queechy's* mood of hopelessness; Fleda's exceptional character makes her sufferings unmerited, and the improbable finale shows how little succor the author expects from mundane reality. As usual, Susan Warner fails to generalize from her particular situation to some vision of social injustice. The heroine is so clearly better than the rest of her sex that her story does not permit wide generalization and injustice is experienced as entirely personal. The reader who identifies with Fleda will think better of herself but not consequently of other women.

Fleda's world even more than Ellen's is structured so that she can be released from the unjust dominion of one man only by the intervention of another. She must be rescued. Her destiny is to exist and toil in obscurity until her perfections inspire a man to intercede for her. When *Queechy* opens, Fleda, an orphaned child of ten, is living in rural New York with her saintly grandfather. At this age she already possesses "that fine perfection of mental and moral constitution which in its own natural necessary acting leaves nothing to be desired, in every occasion or circumstance of life." She seems "a princess's child . . . dropped in some odd corner of the kingdom," or "a flower of the wood, raising its head above the frost and snow and the rugged soil where fortune has placed it, with an air of quiet, patient endurance;—a storm wind may bring it to the ground, easily—but if its gentle nature be not broken, it will look up again, unchanged, and bide its time in unrequited beauty and sweetness to the end." The compensatory force of this fantasy of the princess in disguise was probably a double-edged weapon to millions of women. It might have bolstered morale in circumstances that provided little external gratification, and thereby helped women to cope; it might have encouraged women to anticipate rescue and made their difficult lives even less bearable. Whatever its effect, Warner offered the fantasy in no spirit of condescension, not as an opiate for the masses. It strikes with the effect of a fantasy that has given its creator immense pleasure and perhaps has helped her to survive, and in this spirit it is submitted to the reader.

We see Fleda's effect on others at the outset of the story, when she and her grandfather are visited by two young men, her cousin Rossitur and his English friend Carleton, both about twenty years old. Rossitur has come with a proposal from his wealthy parents in Paris that Fleda join their family. Carleton is so "awed" by Fleda's purity that a religious conversion is initiated; this regeneration will, in the future, be Fleda's earthly salvation. Meantime, she has a long, devious path ahead. Rossitur's invitation proves most timely, for Grandfather dies suddenly, on the eve of foreclosure and dispossession from "Queechy," his farm. The grieving Fleda is taken by Carleton to Paris and on the ship she continues the work of conversion she has innocently begun. Uncle Rossitur proves to be a goodhearted, worldly, accomplished man, an esthete and hedonist. Later we will discover that his good heart is a function of his worldly success and comfort; he has no reserves for misfortune. Aunt Rossitur is a passive satellite, in her own way also unfit for tribulation. The older son is in the army, the daughter a social butterfly. Fleda finds a kindred spirit in her sickly cousin Hugh, who is about her own age. For several years she enjoys a luxurious cultivated life in Paris and New York. They are educated privately, by tutors, a system that works better for Fleda's innately disciplined nature than for Hugh's more wayward personality. Fleda develops the external graces of a lady; inherently of finer cloth than most, she now displays her quality to the world. So far as the author is concerned, when her mind

has been enlarged, her manners polished, and her sensibilities educated, Fleda has become a woman without equal in all the world.

What destiny has Warner in mind for this paragon? Uncle Rossitur fails in business and, totally ruined, permits a friend to set him up rent-free on a small farm where he is to try to live free of debt. This farm turns out to be Queechy; so, after a dream-interlude as a fine lady, Fleda is back where she began and worse off than before. She now has memories of a better life against which to measure her present lot, and her dear grandfather has been replaced by the increasingly sour-tempered Rossitur. Rossitur cannot accept his changed life. He cannot live as a poor man. He refuses to bother with the administrative details of farming or to undertake any physical labor himself. In his own eyes, he is far above the plain rural folk and he is offended by their bluff democratic ways. He quickly alienates all his neighbors and only Fleda's tact gets help in the fields and house. More and more he sits around the house wrapped in the airs of a gentleman, making demands on his dependents. Aunt Rossitur, inept at household work, expends her failing energies in soothing and flattering her husband. All labor and responsibility devolve on Fleda and Hugh.

So Warner draws a picture of two frail adolescents supporting two idle, healthy adults. Hugh, who is not only feeble but shy, struggles nobly with such chores as chopping wood and working the mill attached to the farm. Fleda runs the house with the help of a loyal, outspoken servant, Barby. ("I don't believe the world would go now, Fleda, if it wa'n't for women," says Barby. "I never see three men yet that didn't try me more than they were worth.") She tends the vegetable garden and hires the fieldhands. With an unflinching naturalism remarkably at variance with the narcissistic fantasy of the first part of the novel as well as its ending, Warner chronicles the wearying routines and penny-pinching strategies of the children. She also sketches a series of regional portraits. As the young people labor, Rossitur becomes ever more discontented and more shameless in his irresponsibility; he projects his guilt in the form of touchy pride and petty tyrannies. Hugh's health deteriorates; Mrs. Rossitur develops debilitating headaches.

When the older son comes home on furlough, he is appalled at his father's degeneration and scolds the family for craven submission to his whims. But when he undertakes to criticize his father, he sees by the older man's rage that the fawning flattery of the dependents is a strategy to contain his anger and control his potential for making their lives even more miserable. Though Rossitur has failed his dependents, they legally belong to him. After several years of inflicting misery on his family, Rossitur goes west to look after some land investments—so he says; the family knows that he is abandoning them and is relieved rather than saddened. But his ability to cause trouble for his dependents continues. His attempt to escape some debts by forging a note becomes known, and the family faces disgrace as well as poverty. It seems too high a price for six comfortable years and a lady's education, Fleda thinks. Her last efforts to save her uncle and his family, by going to New York and interceding with the young villain who threatens to expose her uncle, only enmesh her in further difficulty.

Carleton has been hovering in the wings for some time, sending Fleda flowers, and at this point he enters the action and settles everything. Male threats require male force to subdue them. On the train, taking Fleda back to Queechy, he wraps her in his fur cloak, and her troubles are over. "The comfort of the fur cloak was curiously mixed with the feeling of something else, of which that was an emblem—a surrounding of care and strength which could effectually be exerted for her protection,— somewhat that Fleda had not known for many a long day—the making up of the old want. Fleda had it in her to cry like a baby. . . . For years she had been taking care of others; and now there was something so strange in this being cared for, that her heart was full." Fleda's starved heart can barely accept its happiness. At the end, she is lifted out of her troubled world entirely and taken to England to live on a vast estate, in an elegant mansion full of servants. This is pure fantasy, of course, but *Queechy* carries it off because it has so thoroughly depicted that kind of straitened misery from which such a fantasy is created and the tremendous need to which it ministers.

Even more than in *The Wide, Wide World, Queechy* concludes with a vision of woman fulfilled within a protected domestic enclosure, although Carleton's estate is several orders of magnitude more grandiose than the unpretending Humphrey home. The novel exposes a vision that resembles Southworth's—far from being woman's sphere, home is still in reality the man's sphere. In rural New York, Uncle Rossitur behaves just like one of Southworth's planter patriarchs. But unlike Southworth, and much like McIntosh in her later works (in fact, McIntosh's later novels postdate *Queechy*), Warner does not look forward hopefully to a time when men will have been ejected from the home and it is run as woman's sphere of influence. She imagines a sphere that is policed by men but is internally free of power politics, of dominion exercised by either sex. Fleda is profoundly weary of other people. She does not want community but privacy. Removing to the fantasy world of the English gentry, Fleda withdraws altogether from the challenges and hardships of American life. Marriage is celebrated as an escape from adulthood. Warner's fiction is especially intransigent in its rejection of the conception of woman fulfilled through relations to others, whether she rules or serves them, and in its romantic assertion of the absolute primacy of self.

In American literature, such an assertion for men usually involves running away to "the wilderness," literal or figurative, and escaping involvement with the other sex either by celibacy or Don Juanism. Warner's Paradise requires one man. But although she does fantasize one perfect male in each novel, she allows the sex in general no superiority except in physical strength. Framed by its fantasy of Carleton the rescuer, *Queechy* is a bitter indictment of all other men (one is tempted to say of all real men) for their irresponsibility toward the women who are in their power. Beyond this it indicts a world that makes glowing promises to the young which it heartlessly breaks. Warner's romanticism thus looks forward and back: back to an idyll

of woman protected and allowed to remain childlike, forward to a restless refusal to be content with crumbs from the table of the powerful.

The Hills of the Shatemuc, Susan Warner's third novel, is said to have sold 10,000 copies on the first day of publication. It marks a return to the piety of *The Wide, Wide World* and a slide into a new ideology of resignation that persists in her later novels. If she chose to suppress her anger as a means of selling more books, she made a mistake, for none of her works after this sold to the extent of her first two. *Hills* is the story of how a young woman learns to be humble and unselfish and thereby gains an ideal husband. Winthrop Landholm is a poor farm boy who, encouraged by his deeply Christian mother, works his way through college to a successful law practice. Like the hero of a morality fiction, he never neglects a single family responsibility or refuses a call on his charity, and he is immune to diversions, amusements, or the manifold possibilities of self-gratification that best attractive young men in a large city. In his self-control, diligence, morality, intelligence, and perfect serenity, he is an extraordinary (indeed, unbelievable) human being and very much unlike the heroine Elizabeth Haye. She is a spoiled rich girl, intelligent and sensitive but altogether self-absorbed. The difference between Elizabeth and Winthrop is greater than her wealth and his poverty, her selfishness and his magnanimity, her passion and his control. The greatest contrast between them lies in what is possible for them to achieve. However his attainments are accompanied by an ethos of service to others, Winthrop's is a life of self-aggrandisement and expansion of influence, while Elizabeth's is a steady contraction. The young girl imagines herself a princess or a queen. But when her father marries his flighty ward, a superficial heiress just Elizabeth's age, the daughter learns at once that she is a "nobody." Then, when he dies after squandering his young wife's fortune, Elizabeth is left to take care of this uncongenial stepmother.

Her dignity in tatters, her pretensions exposed as fatuous, Elizabeth accepts her lot as protector and servant to one she doesn't care for. Warner says it is good for her. And she proves it by making this same reluctantly supported stepmother maneuver Elizabeth and Winthrop into romantic relationship with one another. Winthrop, though he has long appreciated Elizabeth's good qualities, could never have loved her had she not transcended her early selfishness and accepted the steady contraction of her horizon with plausible grace. . . . *The Hills of the Shatemuc* says that women should not expect to make something of themselves. They should find a good man who will make something of them, and in order to do this they must make themselves into a woman whom a good man will appreciate. This message, somewhat different in emphasis from that in *The Wide, Wide World* and *Queechy,* develops the idea of woman's being rather than acting with a new stress on self-abasement as a precondition for feminine reward. No humiliation is required for Winthrop, who is permitted to esteem himself and set his sights very high. (pp. 143-57)

Nina Baym, "Susan Warner, Anna Warner, and Maria Cummins," in her Woman's Fiction: A Guide to Novels by and about Women in America, 1820-1870, *Cornell University Press, 1978,* pp. 140-74.

Jane Tompkins   (essay date 1987)

[*Tompkins is an American educator and critic. In the following essay, she discusses the ideological background of* The Wide, Wide World *and its relationship to Warner's life. For a discussion impugning Tompkins's appraisal of Warner, see the essay by D. G. Myers (1988).*]

When *The Wide, Wide World* first appeared in 1850, it caused a sensation in the literary marketplace. No novel written in the United States had ever sold so well. It went through fourteen editions in two years and became one of the best-selling novels of the nineteenth century both in this country and in England. While critics praised it in the pages of the *North American Review, The Nation,* and the *Literary World* (Henry James compared Warner's realism to Flaubert's), most of Warner's contemporaries probably shared the feelings of a man from Philadelphia who wrote in a fan letter:

> When I say that your books give me exquisite pleasure, I deny them their highest and truest praise. They have done me good. They have made me a wiser and a better man—more strengthened to duty, more reconciled to suffering.

Most twentieth-century readers do not expect novels to do them good in the sense intended by the man from Philadelphia. We want to be instructed and entertained but not, as a rule, "strengthened to duty" or "reconciled to suffering." The values that made *The Wide, Wide World* a popular and critical success in its own time have changed so much in a hundred years that one might suppose Warner's novel would have become tedious or unintelligible. Yet the book remains compulsively readable, absorbing, and provoking to an extraordinary degree, though not in the same way or for the same reasons that it was for Warner's contemporaries.

The reason the novel has the power to move readers now lies in our contradictory relationship to its heroine and the heritage she represents. *The Wide, Wide World* is the Ur-text of the nineteenth-century United States. More than any other book of its time, it embodies, uncompromisingly, the values of the Victorian era. Its ideology of duty, humility, and submission to circumstance, and its insistence on the imperative of self-sacrifice, are infuriating to some readers, for these doctrines challenge everything the twentieth century has stood for in politics, psychology, and morals. The novel's ethic of submission violates everything the feminist movement has taught women about the need for self-assertion. It negates modern psychology's emphasis on the dangers of repressed anger. It rejects totally the liberal belief in self-determination and freedom of choice, performs a strange inversion of the capitalist's faith in individual enterprise, and implicitly denies the Marxist claim that collective action to reshape economic structures can improve the lives of the exploited. In an age

in which self-development and self-realization are ultimate goals, *The Wide, Wide World* seems a bizarre throwback, almost medieval in its conception of human destiny; yet at the same time, it is impossible to put the story down. Something about it refuses to let go.

For one thing, the heroine's psycho-political situation is just as relevant today as it was in 1850. Ellen Montgomery is a vulnerable, powerless, and innocent person victimized by those in authority over her. Since we have all at one time or another been in her position, we cannot help sharing her emotional point of view. We sympathize with Ellen's loneliness in strange surroundings, share her dislike for the boring, unfamiliar tasks she is forced to do, yearn along with her for the affection and understanding she craves, and hate the petty tyrannies and downright cruelty of her masters. Even her efforts to subdue her angry feelings are absorbing, because Warner's registration of psychic turmoil is so excruciatingly precise. And though Ellen's belief in submissiveness and self-abnegation may horrify us, we cannot help siding with her in her efforts to do what she believes is right. For, and this is the point at which the essential conflict surfaces, there is always the possibility that she *is* right, that self-sacrifice *is* better than self-actualization, acceptance wiser than protest. We are, after all, the children of the nineteenth century; we, too, believe in charity and service to others.

The usefulness of *The Wide, Wide World* to a modern audience is that it forces us to recognize within our own systems of belief conflicts, such as that between Christian and Freudian versions of the self, that we have been unaccustomed to face. Indeed, Warner's novel may have more to say to a modern audience than "classic" novels of the nineteenth century. Texts like *Moby-Dick* and *The Scarlet Letter* have been domesticated for us by a critical tradition that sees moral and epistemological ambiguity as the benchmark of literary merit. Warner's text, on the other hand, intends no such ambiguities. Its moral assertions, like them or not, are crystal clear. The novel's didacticism, combined with its emotional drawing power, compels the reader to make certain choices, and thus to recognize contradictions, such as those between an ideal of service and an ideal of self-actualization, that literary modernism with its fetishization of complexity has left untouched. The conflicts that *The Wide, Wide World* produces in modern readers, however, do not all belong to the twentieth century. Some are rooted in the conditions that produced the novel itself, particularly the conditions of Susan Warner's life, which were, in the directest possible way, the inspiration for her work.

The endlessly demanding attempt to achieve self-sacrifice that is the principle of Ellen's education in *The Wide, Wide World* also governed Susan Warner's life. While self-sacrifice was certainly the universal prescription for moral development in the antebellum era, Susan Warner and her sister, Anna, had a special reason to adopt it as their own, since circumstances seemed peculiarly arranged to thwart their desires. Though born into a world of wealth and privilege, they spent most of their lives learning to cope with want and deprivation. The struggle between an imperious desire for luxury and sway and a felt obligation to submit herself to God's will is the central drama of Susan Warner's life.

The preface to Anna Warner's biography of her sister captures perfectly both the tone and content of their moral striving.

> If ever this book is printed and read, at two things, I doubt not some people will wonder. First, at our strange, exceptional life, and then that I should be willing to tell it so freely.
>
> I was *not* willing. I am by nature a terribly secretive person, and it goes hard with me to tell anybody what is nobody's business. Furthermore, our home life was so unendingly precious, that it hurts me to have it gazed at by cold and careless eyes; this also is true.
>
> But a faithful chronicler must not please himself. I could not truly set forth my sister's character, without giving the surroundings among which it took shape and strength.
>
> For the rest, I have no call to be sensitive. New England blood is never ashamed of any work that ought to be done; and no believer has cause to cover his face, in any spot where his dear Lord sees fit to bid him dwell; for work, for service, or for the mere polishing attrition.

Anna's preface, typically, places duty before self. By nature terribly secretive, Anna nevertheless reveals the Warners' home life to strangers. The act of writing the biography is a version of her whole life in miniature—and of her sister's, too—as she sees it: an act of self-abnegation. Susan and Anna are the "believers" who have had to dwell where the Lord saw fit (in a "poor-looking" house far from the society they were accustomed to), leading lives that were not their own but his, every moment given over to the Lord's service, whether actively (writing, day and night, books that would bring people to Jesus), or, in Anna's telling phrase, through "the mere polishing attrition"—simply being worn by the frustrations of daily life to greater spiritual refinement. (pp. 584-87)

The bitter circumstances that led to the writing of ***The Wide, Wide World*** contributed to the novel's phenomenal success. By reproducing her own situation in that of her heroine, Warner managed to reproduce the situation of most her contemporaries. Or rather, she mirrored the way they felt about themselves. The belief that one does not control the circumstances of one's life but must learn instead to become reconciled to them informed the outlook of many people in the antebellum era. "In popular thought of the pre-Civil War period," writes Lewis Saum [in *The Popular Mood of Pre-Civil War America*], "no theme was more pervasive or philosophically fundamental than the providential view. Simply put, that view held that, directly or indirectly, God controlled all things." Learning to resign oneself to the will of God was not regarded as cowardly or defeatist behavior but as a realistic way of meeting the facts of life. Contrary to the modern critical view that popular women's novels were escapist and unable to deal with grim facts, the strength of such novels lay precisely in showing what it is like to face facts you cannot change and live with them day by day. Ellen Montgomery says to her aunt early in the novel that if she were free to do what she wanted she would run away—and spends the rest of the novel learning to extirpate that impulse from her being. One cannot run away in the world of nineteenth-century women's fiction, any more than the Warner sisters in real life could have run away from Constitution Island. Women writers of that era, unlike their male counterparts, could not walk out the door and become Mississippi riverboat captains, go off on whaling voyages, or build themselves cabins in the woods. Escape, consequently, is the one thing their novels never offer; on the contrary, they teach their readers that the only way to overcome adversity is through overcoming the enemy within.

The fact that Ellen is not even allowed to protest against injustice, much less escape from it, but learns instead to practice humility and acceptance of the divine will, was a cause of her enormous popularity. While not everybody in the culture believed in submission rather than protest—the year that Warner began to write the novel was also the year of the first women's rights convention—, most readers found the doctrine familiar and persuasive, for it belonged to the ideology of the evangelical reform movement that had molded the consciousness of the nation in the years before the Civil War.

The conception of reality on which the reform movement was based is dramatically illustrated in the activities of the New York City Tract Society, to which the Warner sisters belonged. The purpose of the society was to help the city's poor by distributing a religious tract to every family once a month. Tract Visiters believed that the only real help one could offer another person, rich or poor, was not material but spiritual, and the Directions that guided them in their work insisted on this: "Be much in prayer," the Directions said. "Endeavor to feel habitually and deeply that all your efforts will be in vain unless accompanied by the Holy Ghost. And this blessing you can expect only in answer to prayer. Pray, therefore, without ceasing. Go from your closet to your work and from your work return again to the closet." To understand what made these Directions meaningful and effective for the people who carried them out is to understand the power of what has been labelled pejoratively, and in retrospect, "sentimental" fiction. "Sentimental" novels take place, metaphorically and literally, in the "closet." Their heroines rarely get beyond the confines of a private space—the kitchen, the parlor, the upstairs chamber—and most of what they do takes place inside the "closet" of the heart.

For what the word "sentimental" means as applied to these novels is that the arena of human action, as in the Tract Society Directions, has been defined not as the world but as the human heart. This fiction shares with the reform movement a belief that all true action is not material but spiritual, that one obtains spiritual power through prayer, and that those who know how, in the privacy of their closets, to struggle for possession of their souls will one day possess the world through the power given to them by God. This theory of power makes itself felt, in the mid-nineteenth century, not simply in the explicit assertions of religious propaganda, nor in personal declarations

Title page from an edition of The Wide, Wide World.

of faith, but as a principle of interpretation that gave form to experience itself.

One Tract Visiter, for example, records that a young woman who was dying of pulmonary consumption became concerned at the eleventh hour about the condition of her soul and asked for spiritual help:

> She was found by the Visiter, [the report reads] supplied with a number of tracts, and kindly directed to the Saviour of sinners. . . . For some time clouds hung over her mind, but they were at length dispelled by the sun of righteousness. . . . As she approached the hour which tries men's souls, her strength failed fast; her friends gathered around her; . . . and while they were engaged in a hymn her soul seemed to impart unnatural energy to her emaciated and dying body. To the astonishment of all, she said to her widowed mother, who bent anxiously over her, 'Don't weep for me, I shall soon be in the arms of my Saviour.' She prayed fervently, and fell asleep in Jesus.

The facts of this anecdote do not correspond to what a twentieth-century observer would have recorded had he or she been at the scene: the furniture of the sick room,

the kind of house the woman lived in, her neighborhood, her socio-economic background, the symptoms of her illness, its history and course of treatment. Instead of all this, the Tract Visiter sees a spiritual predicament: the women's initial "alarm," God's action on her heart, the turn from sin to righteousness. Whereas the modern observer would have structured the events in a downward spiral, as the woman's condition deteriorated from serious to critical, and ended with her death, the report reverses that progression. Its movement is upward, from "thoughtlessness" to "conviction" to "great tranquility, joy, and triumph." The events the Visiter records are structured by assumptions about the nature of reality that bear little relation to a contemporary perspective on the scene.

The story of the young woman's death from pulmonary consumption is exactly the kind of exemplary tale that had formed the consciousness of the nation in the early years of the nineteenth century. Such stories were the staple of pulpit oratory and filled the religious publications, which were distributed in astoundingly large quantities (the American Tract Society alone claims to have published thirty-seven million tracts at a time when the entire population of the country was only eleven million), and were the backbone of the McGuffey's readers and other primers on which virtually the entire nation had been schooled. They appeared in manuals of social behavior and in instructional literature of every variety, filled the pages of popular magazines, and appeared even in the daily newspapers.

When one turns from tract society reports, primers, etiquette books, journal entries, magazine stories, and pulpit homilies to the fiction of writers like Susan Warner, one finds the same assumptions at work. Her novels are motivated by the same commitments; they are hortatory and instructional in the same way, depend upon the same rhetorical conventions, and they take for granted the same relationship between the daily activities of humble people and the spiritual destiny of humankind. The popular fiction written by women of the mid-nineteenth century has been dismissed by modern critics primarily because it follows from assumptions about the shape and meaning of existence that we no longer hold. But once one understands the coherence and force of those assumptions, the literature that helped to shape the world in their image no longer seems thoughtless or trivial. Rather, novels like *The Wide, Wide World* which enunciate this vision in narrative terms lent dignity and purpose to lives that otherwise would have been impossibly narrow and stultifying. The conviction that human events are, ultimately and inevitably, shaped by secret prayer produces a view of society in which orphan girls like Ellen Montgomery, and writers like Susan Warner, can hope to change the world.

To say that Susan Warner hoped to change the world through writing fiction is misleading to the extent that it implies a desire on her part to transform political and economic structures. Although Warner believed in giving material aid to the poor and in relieving suffering, the sources of oppression and injustice, as she sees them, do not lie in social arrangements. Evil is disobedience to the will of God. Doing good, therefore, means helping human beings to become receptive to God's will, which is accomplished through religious conversion. While Warner's failure to confront questions of property and class directly leads, as we shall see, to certain contradictions within her own practice as a Christian writer, she gave herself wholly to the pursuit of her ideals as she understood them. Warner wrote novels in order to save souls and hence to save herself. When the man from Philadelphia said that the "highest and truest praise" of her books was that "they have done . . . good," he told her, in effect, that she had accomplished her purpose.

The question is, what are we to make of such an enterprise now? While it is crucially important to recognize that novels like *The Wide, Wide World* helped women—and men—in the nineteenth century to make sense of their lives, it is also necessary to ask what they can do for us. If we do not share a belief in the ultimate reality of God in Jesus Christ, or expect to become more reconciled to suffering for having read these novels, how can we enter imaginatively into their fictional world? Why should anyone in the late twentieth century *care* about the perils of a pious orphan and her masochistic ways?

The answer, I think, is that Warner's heroine cannot be dismissed because she *is* us. Although Ellen Montgomery's submissive behavior may enrage us, we follow her adventures with bated breath because we feel, or have felt at some time, our own relation to the world to be like hers. It is not only that as children we have felt powerless and overwhelmed by circumstance, but that as adults we share, or have shared, with Ellen a whole range of character traits and psychological needs. The sense that our difficulties are undeserved, our efforts to overcome them heroic, our merits exceptional, and our misfortunes unique makes it much easier than we might have supposed to inhabit the consciousness of this blameless, persecuted orphan. At one time or another we feel (or have felt) that we, too, are innocent, have only the best intentions, are insufficiently armed against the world, easily injured, unable to hide our emotions, and in need of love and attention.

The enormous amount of attention Ellen receives is one of the most seductive features of her story. People are always talking about her when she isn't present and can't take their eyes off her when she is. Alice and Mr. John continually ask her to reveal her innermost thoughts, and seize upon every tremulous word. What tasks Ellen most about Aunt Fortune is not that she makes Ellen churn butter when she would rather be learning French, it is that Ellen is not the primary focus of her aunt's thoughts. To read *The Wide, Wide World* is to experience life as if everything that happened to you, every thought that passed through your mind, every feeling you ever had, deserved the most minute consideration. Warner knows how to make a story out of anything—leaving a party early, catching a cold. Her ability to register, through Ellen's inner turmoil, the intensity and range of emotion aroused in people's daily lives by the tiniest occurrences makes the novel at times absolutely riveting.

Moreover, Ellen's predicament—subjugation to a series of authorities over which she has no control—springs from hierarchies of power that still structure most people's ex-

perience: I mean the authoritarian relationships that obtain between parents and children, men and women, teachers and pupils. What makes Ellen's situation so highly charged for modern readers is that, instead of rebelling against the injustice of her masters, she is forced by others and learns to force herself to submit to them. The whole weight of the novel, every ounce of rhetoric it contains, is calculated to drive this lesson home: "though we *must* sorrow," Ellen's mother teaches her, "we must not rebel."

The Wide, Wide World draws us irresistibly and intimately into the mind of a character who affirms and acts on beliefs that, in many respects, violate our innermost sense of what a human being can be. Indeed, it is a kind of bildungsroman in reverse. Instead of initiating her into society, the heroine's experience teaches her how to withdraw into the citadel of herself. The Christian precepts she internalizes teach her not how to succeed in the marketplace, or implement her purposes in the world, but how to become a saint who makes herself malleable to the will of others. Under the guidance of her mentors, she undergoes repeated trials in the course of mastering the principles of her vocation—which is to forget self. As the novel progresses, and the trials that befall her grow more severe, she is required to show an equanimity more unperturbed and a humility more complete. At the endpoint of the disciplinary process, the heroine does not exist for herself at all any more but only for others. Sanctified by the sacrifice of her will, Ellen becomes, like her friend Alice, "a person who supplied what was wanting everywhere; like the transparent glazing which painters use to spread over the dead color of their pictures; unknown, it was she gave life and harmony to the whole." The ideal to which the novel educates its heroine and its readers is the opposite of self-development and self-realization, it is to become empty of self, an invisible transparency that nevertheless is miraculously responsible for the life in everything.

That is why the novel provokes such powerfully conflicted reactions now. If Ellen is right, *we* are doomed, and yet we cannot write her off because she is part of us. Not only are her vulnerability, her inner turmoil, and her victimization familiar, but so are the Christian values she affirms. It is impossible not to admire Ellen's treatment of other people—her kindness to her grandmother, her patience with Nancy Vawse, her affection for Mr. Van Brunt—nor is the selflessness she strives for altogether foreign to a modern conception of ideal behavior. Ellen incarnates ideals of charity and service to others that remain integral to the Judeo-Christian tradition of our culture. We are, literally, the grandchildren of the nineteenth century, lineal descendants of people just like Ellen whose values and beliefs survive in us alongside the teachings of Nietzsche, Marx, and Freud.

In fact, it is when you look at *The Wide, Wide World* in terms of the issues that preoccupied these thinkers—the issues of power and sexuality—that the novel reveals the source of its strongest and most disturbing appeal. The love of power even when it is not our own, the love of seeing power displayed, power triumphant, crushing everything in its path, even—and perhaps especially—when what it crushes happens to be us is at the core of the

Portrait of Warner's sister, Anna.

novel's attraction. At this level, **The Wide, Wide World** is a chronicle of violence. For all its exaltation of passivity and turning the other cheek, its central situation, repeated over and over again, is the violation of one human being by another. To see ourselves as the objects of acts of domination as we read about Ellen's successive humiliations is to be in the position of master at the same time as we are identifying with the victim. Witnessing the process of subjugation, not once, but time after time, we lend ourselves, emotionally, to it even as we are horrified.

The novel's dramatization of domination and submission, moreover, is sexualized from the start. At the same time that Ellen's self-immolations are excruciatingly painful, they are also, and for the same reason, titillating. While the tears Ellen sheds on every page are tears of repressed anger, they are also tears of orgasmic release, spilling again and again in situations where she is being psychically stripped. These scenes replicate what Susan Griffin [in *Pornography and Silence*] has called the basic pornographic situation, in which one person is robbed by another of everything that makes him or her a human being and is reduced to the status of an object. The thrill of abandoning the self completely, of giving one's self over to the power of another, as when Mr. John says to Ellen "be humbled in the dust before Him—the more the better," suggests a relationship between punishment and sexual pleasure that recalls nothing so much as *The Story of O,* another education in submission in which the heroine undergoes ever more painful forms of self-effacement, until finally she

asks "permission" to die. In its ruthless suppression of Ellen's outrage and pain, *The Wide, Wide World* reenacts, as pornography does, the primal initiation of the child into a culture that denies the body and its feelings. It is the memory of that subjugation in ourselves, more than anything else, that keeps us turning the pages of Warner's book.

On the other hand, the tears that flow when Ellen is embraced by her mother and Alice Humphreys, and the physical intimacy that subsists between her and them, hint at an alternative to the brutal sexuality embodied in her male masters, Uncle Lindsay and, especially, Mr. John, whose prowess as a horse-beater is Warner's oblique acknowledgment of the sexual style he represents. The affection and closeness that women share in the sheltered spaces of domestic fiction and the homely sacraments (often the taking of food and tea) through which they offer tenderness, nourishment, and support to one another, embody an intimacy that takes the place of heterosexual love. Combining sensual delight, emotional comfort, and spiritual communion, these rituals offer moments of wholeness and fulfillment that compensate the female characters for the renunciations that are their daily portion.

Those renunciations, which guarantee the complementarity of male and female roles, also underline their similarity. As Joanne Dobson points out, Mr. John has raised Ellen to be his wife—he educates her, molds her mind, prescribes her behavior and makes her will completely malleable to his. Thus the roles of men and women in this fiction are interdigitated, he will command, she will obey. Yet at the same time, the heroine's role is not so much the antithesis of the hero's as a transformation of it. Whether one's salvation is material or spiritual, the recipe for achieving it is the same. Ellen's long journey toward sainthood imitates the traditional male model of striving for worldly success in that both are based on the Protestant idea that self-denial, discipline, and hard work will pay off eventually. Though Ellen's "success" is the extinction of her personality, and thus is the inversion of a man's, her reward, in the end, is also the same as his. All of Ellen's material losses, like Job's, are finally returned to her a hundredfold—in contemporary terms, she "has it all." According to this scenario, which amalgamates capitalist striving with Christian self-effacement, the meek really do inherit the earth.

The conflicts expressed in the novel between body and spirit, between Christian dedication to selflessness and middle-class materialism, between a woman's desire for independence and her desire for male protection, emerge most strikingly in the last chapter. In the poverty and isolation of Constitution Island, amidst unremitting efforts to trust in God's goodness, Warner dreamed of luxury and access to the world.

In the final chapter, Warner gives her heroine everything that she herself wanted and couldn't get: city living, wealth and position, relief from household cares, people who adore her, and marriage to an all-powerful protector. In the construction of this paradise, Warner's longing for old times struggles with her new-found dedication to the Lord. She yearns for the sheltered existence she led before her father lost his money, and to be free from burdens that young women of her class were neither expected nor prepared to shoulder. In fact, reinfantilization, along with luxury and ease, is Ellen's reward for years of suffering and discipline. She is entirely free of responsibility, and entirely dependent on others. Although she is married, her life still has the character of a preadolescent fantasy (sex is alluded to in embarrassed blushes and silences). Her relationship to Mr. John is still that of pupil to teacher. He will be her "pilot" as she navigates the seas of thought, and her moral preceptor, whose "eyes . . . see every spot of weakness in her composition." "You will tell me if I do anything wrong," says Ellen to her husband, "and it will be just like old times." In Mr. John's house there is no kindling to gather; there are no tables to set or dishes to wash: "I will not have your time taken up with petty details," says Mr. John. "Margery is to keep the house." Best of all, there is money to burn. The final treasure John bestows on Ellen is a drawerful of cash totally at Ellen's disposal. This is the paradise of someone who had written in her diary: "I wish one thing—that father would give each of us an allowance."

Susan Warner's desire to have a man shield her from the world is symbolized by the position of Ellen's room, which stands, as John puts it, "between mine." The inner sanctum, an emblem of Ellen herself, unites the values left over from the old New York society life with those acquired as a convert to evangelical Christianity. It is the room of a sybarite who has given herself to Jesus. Expensive works of art and other evidences of good taste symbolizing wealth and prestige serve as sacramental objects belonging to a religion in which cultivation of the intellect and imagination is felt to be identical with spiritual elevation. The opulence of the treasures Mr. John has collected— paintings, engravings, pieces of statuary, relics of antiquity, copies of the old masters—is justified by their power to awaken the higher faculties. They are "things to seize the eye and lead off the wandering thought upon some track of pleased fancy or useful research or stirring remembrance." The luxury of the room, if it is there at all, is not material but a "luxury of the mind." [The critic adds in a footnote that "Warner's insistence that Ellen prefers to keep her treasures in an upstairs room to avoid the appearance of display is a coded way of indicating her social class."]

The contradiction between Warner's commitment to a life of selfless service to the Lord and her desire for sensual and intellectual gratification, as well as for the power and position conferred by the ownership of expensive commodities, expresses itself most markedly in the discussion between Ellen and Mr. John comparing the paintings of a recumbent Magdalen and a Madonna and child which are the pièces de résistance of Ellen's room. Hanging side by side, their purpose is to illustrate the difference between physical and moral beauty. As Mr. John pontificates:

> "*There* is only the material outside . . . *here* is the immaterial soul. . . . Beauty of feature does not make the charm of *this* picture [alluding, of course, to the Madonna]—it serves but the purpose of a clear glass through which what is behind may be the more easily and perfectly

seen. . . . What makes these features so lovely but the exceeding loveliness of that which shines through them? . . . There you have the beauty that fades—the beauty of the earth; here is that which endures. Charity never faileth!"

The passage reflects Warner's anxiety about her own looks (hence the "loveliness" that "shines *through*" the physical features), her ambivalent relation to her body and its craving for pleasure (the recumbent Magdalen); the resolution (that was being forced upon her) to renounce sexual fulfillment by emulating the Virgin; and her determination, in the absence of more tangible supports, to rely on divine love. The passage also points to the contradiction between Ellen's obvious delight in owning such costly and precious objects and the lesson of those objects which is, ironically, that treasures are nothing, charity all. In using the last chapter to supply herself, in imagination, with the luxury and the protection she longed for, Warner has become aware, at some level, that the dream of wealth and comfort does not jibe with her hard-won resolve to accept the Lord's will. In turning the reward she has invented for Ellen into an elaborate rationalization of her own desire, a desire to which she had been socialized by her upbringing, Warner only makes more obvious a split she does not see and therefore cannot acknowledge within her culture and within herself. (pp. 593-603)

> *Jane Tompkins, in an afterword to* The Wide, Wide World *by Susan Warner, The Feminist Press, 1987, pp. 584-608.*

Joyce Carol Oates (essay date 1987)

[*Oates is an American fiction writer and critic who is perhaps best known for her novel* Them *(1969), which won a National Book Award in 1970. Her fiction is noted for its exhaustive presentation of realistic detail and its striking display of imagination, especially in the evocation of abnormal psychological states. As a critic, Oates has written on a remarkable diversity of authors—from Shakespeare to Herman Melville to Samuel Beckett— and is appreciated for the individuality and erudition that characterize her critical work. In the following essay, Oates examines* Diana, *emphasizing the difficulties of interpreting nineteenth-century morals and manners from a modern perspective.*]

The Lady's Vase, The Lady's Wreath, Letters to Young Ladies, The Gentle Art of Pleasing, The Lady's Guide to Perfect Gentility, The Physical Life of Woman: Advice to the Maiden, Wife, and Mother by the pious physician Dr. George N. Naphey . . . such best-selling novels as *St. Elmo* by Mrs. Augusta Jane Evans, *The Gates Ajar* by Mrs. Elizabeth Stuart Phelps Ward, *The Discarded Daughter* by Mrs. E. D. E. N. Southworth, *Tempest and Sunshine* by Mary Jane Holmes, **The Wide, Wide World** and **Diana** by Susan Warner . . . these are a few of the titles enormously popular in the second half of nineteenth-century America, when both the etiquette book (for Christian ladies anxious to please God *and* man) and the "romance" (the genre practiced by those "scribbling women" who aroused such uncharacteristic outrage and envy in Nathaniel Hawthorne) were in vogue. Reading them today is a sobering and instructive experience, not least because we really cannot *read* them, whatever our intentions. We examine them, analyze them, exclaim over them, isolate passages here and there to quote in amusement or alarm, or both—

> Dependence is in itself an easy and pleasant thing: dependence upon one we love perhaps the very sweetest thing in the world. To resign oneself totally and contentedly into the hand of another; to have no longer any need of asserting one's rights or one's personality . . . how delicious this all is. [From "A Woman's Thoughts About Women," in *Chambers' Journal,* 1857. Quoted in Jennie Calder, *Women and Marriage in Victorian Fiction*]

—but we are incapable of reading these books with the suspension of disbelief and skepticism required if we are to understand them as they were intended—emotionally. Academics approach them as "texts" (that most sinister of terms); they were written as urgent human documents.

Contemporary feminist criticism of nineteenth-century women's literature is handicapped, to a degree, by its secular and humanist perspective. Confronted with religious convictions of a traditional sort, often expressed in the most banal and shopworn of terms, the feminist is inclined to see the author as misguided, or self-deluded, or (what seems to us more attractive) *ironic:* love of God and Christ and one's fellowman, the sacrifice of the self, an elevation of duty over all human activities—are these not clever authorial strategies for the indirect expression of hostility and anger? For if *we* employed them, assuredly they would be.

Our assumptions about virtually everything have changed irrevocably since the mid- and late nineteenth century. Few of us believe that society, the strife of nations, the very phenomenon of chronological historical time itself, must be interpreted in the context of a God- or Christ-centered universe; we don't, can't, believe that suffering is finite but the bliss of Heaven infinite. That Christ died for our sins is not a notion that inspires very many contemporary writers to create complex works of fiction. We can analyze our ancestors' stated beliefs, and the philosophical, sociological, political, and psychological foundations of those beliefs, but it is virtually impossible for us to *believe:* we read their musical notations but we can't hear them. We presumably share a common language with our ancestors, but much of our vocabulary—such words as "soul," "eternity," "subservience," "dependence"—even "lady"; even "sin"—is irrevocably altered. Hamlet is our contemporary, Emma Bovary is our contemporary, even Swift's Gulliver is our contemporary, but what of the numberless heroines of the best-selling novels of 1850 to 1900? We are prone to the anthropologist's occupational hazard—the imposition of unconscious and unexamined cultural prejudices upon the subject to be studied.

Of virtually no interest to the formalist critic, the popular-sentimental romance—frequently selling in the hundreds of thousands of copies—yields its occasional riches to those with other expectations from literature. Since the plot of the typical romance, along with its numerous digressions and melodramatic reversals, appears to be a given, it is in *parts,* and rarely in structural *wholes,* that we find evidence of fresh insights and imaginative writing: descriptions of female domestic life, including conversations between women (with no men present); descriptions of church activities, quilting bees, blackberry-picking excursions; passages of rigorous self-examination and prayer. In the foreground the romances are "realistic"; in other respects they are sheer fantasy—fairy tales populated by stereotypical characters, set in a wholly recognizable America.

"There is no pleasure apart from duty . . . God's will is happiness" is the grim lesson finally absorbed by Diana Starling, one of the most independent of all the heroines of the popular-sentimental genre. The tragic curve of Susan Warner's best-selling *Diana* (1888) is its remorseless catheterizing of Diana's youthful passion: in 388 pages we witness the transformation of an impulsive, courageous, strong-willed young woman—a feminist heroine in embryo—into her temperamental opposite. Though Susan Warner seems wholly sympathetic to her heroine and well aware of the hypocrisy of many of her elders (including Diana's "ugly" meddlesome mother), it is nonetheless her intention to squeeze Diana's rebellious blood from her drop by drop until, at the novel's end, she stands before us, a minister's "selfless" wife, a portrait of Christian womanhood. Unlike Henry James's Isabel Archer—the "lady" of another, more famous nineteenth-century portrait—Diana expresses no ambivalence about her fate. The secret message of *Diana* is not that there is no pleasure apart from duty but that there is no pleasure.

Yet this is a rich, complex, psychologically satisfying novel, at least until the point at which its didactic spirit takes over and it becomes rather suddenly yet another cautionary tale or handbook for female (i.e., feminine) behavior. Warner's special gift is for the meticulous, intimate examination of inner states—the "nervous breakdown" (as we might call it) Diana suffers, and her subsequent healing. One is reminded of similar introspective passages in George Eliot and of the obsessive intensity with which D. H. Lawrence describes Ursula Brangwen's wildly fluctuating states of mind in *The Rainbow* and *Women in Love.* Warner's treatment of the aftermath of extreme psychic violence gives the novel a resonance shared by few others of its genre.

In the beginning Diana is presented as an attractive, forceful young woman driven by "nervous energy" and an uncommon "power of will"; virtually alone among the colorfully drawn inhabitants of her New England community—Pleasant Valley!—she is a religious skeptic. Told that Christianity reveals the meaning of life, Diana replies, "No, it doesn't—to me." She sees no purpose in life, or why people live, "what it amounts to." She rejects commonplace pieties about God, Christ, religion; she has no illusions about human destiny or human relations; her feeling for her widowed mother is thoroughly unsentimental.

Yet Diana has her romance, Diana loses her lover (as a consequence of melodramatic complications), Diana suffers a collapse and a "death" of sorts, sympathetically rendered. It is this destruction of Diana's romantic sensibility that constitutes the novel's heart; and when Diana convalesces, marries a good-hearted but rather pallid minister, and, over a period of years, comes finally to love him by way of her awakened love for Christ, Warner's writing becomes increasingly perfunctory and predictable. The contemporary reader "loses" Diana: where she was stubborn, doubting, even arrogant, a plain dealer in the midst of the insipid pieties of "Pleasant Valley," she becomes priggish, complacent, narrow, self-righteous. Her cynicism and anger are completely obliterated in the denial (Warner would see it as the transcendence) of the self. How ironic, for us at least, that the Christian platitudes Diana scorns in her youth turn out to be the truths of her mature life: yet more ironic is the scene in which, a married woman, she exults in condemning her former lover for his "weakness" in still loving her. For passion *is* weakness in the Christian romance, just as it is redemptive in the romances of D. H. Lawrence; denial of passion is strength. One may read Warner's message as the eunuch's scorn or as a deeply felt and altogether sincere attempt to render, in prose fiction, the experience of conversion to a selfless, in this case Christian, mode of consciousness. We lose Diana as her ostensible "modern" attitudes are revealed, in nineteenth-century terms, as merely shallow and adolescent . . . the fancies of the unconverted.

"I cannot think of anything lovelier than to see . . . faces change with the knowledge of Christ," Diana says when, at the novel's conclusion, she and her saintly husband move to a dreary mill town in order to bring the Word to both mill workers and mill owners. The novel's final vision:

> And you may think of them as happy, with both hands full of work. They live in a house just a little bit out of town, where there is plenty of room for gardens, and the air is not poisoned with smoke or vapor. Roses and honeysuckles flourish . . . banks of violets and beds of lilies, and, in the spring-time, crocuses and primroses and hyacinths and snowdrops. . . . For even Diana's flowers are not for herself alone, nor even for her children alone, whose special connection with them is to make nosegays for sick and poor people, and to cultivate garden plots in order to have more to give away. . . . It is as [Diana's husband] meant it to be, and knew it would be. It is as it always is; when the box is broken at Christ's feet, the house is filled with the odour of the ointment.

The feminist response to so painfully "happy" an ending is to view Diana as a self-deluded, broken woman, whose life really ended with her marriage; the victim of a sanctimonious partriarchal religion in which the ideal of humility, meekness, and subservience is best practiced by women—and by lowly mill workers who will learn from Christ how to accept their lot. Diana, so animated once, has now become a function, a role. The postmodernist response might be to dismiss both Diana and Susan Warner as contemptible, unworthy of our serious critical interest, for where there is no irony or ambiguity, where words lack stylistic resonance, and fiction does not alter our ways of perceiving the world but merely confirms the most tedious

of platitudes—there there *is* no literature: *Diana* falls off the map, to sink in the uncharted waters with *St. Elmo,* and *Fern Leaves from Fanny's Portfolio,* and *Haunted Hearts,* and *The Hidden Hand,* and *The Mother's Trial.*

Today, for most of us, a novel like Warner's **Diana** is examined rather than read; if we are able to contemplate its primary ethical and psychological issues at all, it is only through the clinical prismatic lens of irony. How, or why, a writer of Susan Warner's gifts would want to systematically destroy the individuality of her heroine is a mystery; and why end a work of idiosyncratic vigor with the most crushingly familiar of visions? Yet **Diana** is not a romance written for us; it is no less representative of its era than Doris Lessing's *The Golden Notebook* is of ours. The Christian romance demands the sacrifice of the self *as a liberation;* in this distant region of the soul, piety is not contrived but utterly natural.

In contemplating the heroines of nineteenth-century fiction—those who have survived, like Dorothea Casaubon of *Middlemarch;* those who have perished, like Warner's Diana—we are moved to wonder: Can irony and faith inhabit the same sensibility? Is it inevitable that one drive the other out? The anachronistic fallacy might be defined as a predilection for those who live *now* to feel automatically condescending to those who lived *then;* we imagine ourselves superior to our ancestors because they are not us. As a novelist of the 1980s my vision is postmodernist, and therefore predisposed to irony; as a woman, however, an inhabitant of the 1980s, I don't feel at all superior to these puzzling heroines of a bygone world. I simply feel different. Very different. (pp. 190-97)

Joyce Carol Oates, "Pleasure, Duty, Redemption Then and Now: Susan Warner's 'Diana',"
in (Woman) Writer: Occasions and Opportunities, E. P. Dutton, 1988, pp. 190-97.

D. G. Myers   (essay date 1988)

[*In the following essay, Myers argues that current interest in* The Wide, Wide World *owes more to the efforts of the influential critic Jane Tompkins (see essay dated 1987) than to the actual merits of Warner's work.*]

Among the many challenges to humanistic study in this country over the past several years, perhaps none has won easier acceptance than the notion that the traditional "canon" of English literature was established, in part, for the purpose of suppressing important works by women. In the face of such a contention, the usual rites of scholarly dispute—example and counter-example, criticism and self-correction—were set aside as those who leveled the charges took sole possession of the field. Lost in the general retreat, however, was an unasked question. What are these important, undiscovered works? Who are their authors?

To date the strongest candidate for enshrinement in the new counter-canon is the nineteenth-century American novelist Susan Warner. An exact contemporary of Whitman, Melville, and James Russell Lowell and a prolific author of sentimental and religious stories, Warner is the author of an 1850 novel, *The Wide, Wide World.* Although that book was published the same year as *The Scarlet Letter,* it was much more widely known than Hawthorne's in the nineteenth century. Indeed, its popularity was eclipsed only by that of *Uncle Tom's Cabin.*

In our own time, *The Wide, Wide World* was almost completely forgotten until it was rescued from oblivion by a single enterprising critic—Jane Tompkins. Since Tompkins first brought it to the attention of the English Institute in 1983, the novel has been fully rehabilitated and has begun to attract wider notice. Reissued in paperback by the Feminist Press and praised as "energetic and vivid" by James Atlas in *The New York Times Magazine,* it has even begun to appear on examination lists for the Ph.D. in American literature—the last of the three miracles prior to canonization.

In all of this, it might be fairly asked if the renewal of interest in *The Wide, Wide World* owes as much to the intrinsic merit of the book as it does to the fact of its being championed by Tompkins. Jane Tompkins, after all, is a very important person in the academic criticism of literature. She is a professor of English at Duke—the new headquarters of critical theory—and is the wife of Stanley Fish, chairman of the department there. Originally the *doyenne* of the reader-response method, Tompkins has recently moved on to become one of the leading lights of the New Historicism, the school that seeks to "re-historicize" literary texts—that is, to reconstruct their ideological backgrounds. Her study *Sensational Designs,* of which an entire chapter is devoted to Warner's novel, gives every promise of becoming the standard treatment of the new canonical works of nineteenth-century American fiction.

But the question is this: Given Tompkins's authority and renown as a critic, coupled with the fact that she is the first to have dealt with *The Wide, Wide World* at any length, which is the work that is more likely to become "canonical"—Warner's novel or Tompkins's interpretation of it? The two are far from being the same thing.

As Warner conceived it, *The Wide, Wide World* is the story of a young girl's spiritual education between the ages of about eight and thirteen. When the novel opens, Ellen Montgomery is living in New York with her mother and father. She is content with her lot, despite the fact that her mother is bedridden with illness. But Ellen's contentment is fated not to last. Her father has only recently lost a major lawsuit, and Ellen learns that he must leave America "to go soon on some government or military business to Europe." When he goes, he takes Ellen's mother with him—for her health. Ellen is abandoned to the care of her father's childless sister, Fortune Emerson, who lives a few miles outside the distant farming village of Thirlwall. Ellen never sees her parents again.

The remainder of the nearly six-hundred-page novel is taken up with Ellen's attempts to make her way in the wide, wide world, where "a little one alone . . . is in danger of being trampled upon." Ellen faces this danger time after time—Aunt Fortune resents her, odd people try to kiss her, some children plague her, old tormentors return to torment her again—but in the end she learns to meet

these "trial[s] of temper and patience" with an attitude of Christian resignation. Harder trials follow. Her mother dies ("it seemed as if Ellen's very heart was flowing away in her tears"); then her dearest friend. But Ellen is never entirely alone: a kindly stranger or an unoccupied friend is always close at hand with a bit of moral instruction, an uplifting hymn, or an apposite quotation from Scripture.

After her father's death, Ellen is packed off to Scotland. There she faces her hardest trial yet. Her Scottish relatives, afraid that Ellen is "hurting [herself] by poring over serious matters [she] is too young for," hoping to brighten the unnatural gravity of so young a child, forbid her to rise an hour before the rest of the household to say her morning prayers. It is the moment of Ellen's spiritual crisis. She retreats to her room to sing "Rock of Ages" and "a little Methodist hymn she had learned when a mere child." Her uncle, listening outside the door, is touched. He permits her an hour after breakfast for prayer; and with that, although "Ellen's principles were still now and then severely tried," her spiritual development is largely complete.

So far, Warner's novel as she wrote it. Astonishingly, out of this story of spiritual uplift Jane Tompkins spins a political tale. Although *The Wide, Wide World* is usually classified as a religious novel, Tompkins prefers to see it as representative of a genre which is "preoccupied, even obsessed, with the nature of power." Barred from self-fulfillment by men's priorities in "a Puritanical and trading nation," women in the nineteenth century, Tompkins says, discovered in sentimental and domestic novels like *The Wide, Wide World* "a counter-strategy against their worldly masters that would finally give them the upper hand." Along the way they also discovered sisterhood and solidarity.

> The fact is that American women simply could not assume a stance of open rebellion against the conditions of their lives for they lacked the material means of escape or opposition. They had to stay put and submit. And so the domestic novelists made that necessity the basis on which to build a power structure of their own. Instead of rejecting the culture's value system outright, they appropriated it for their own use, subjecting the beliefs and customs that had molded them to a series of transformations that allowed them both to fulfill and transcend their appointed roles.

Thus in Protestant religion, for example, Ellen Montgomery finds the means of "bypassing" the worldly authority of men by "merg[ing]" her own authority with God's." An actual nineteenth-century woman, forced to live in the social reality outside of novels, may have believed that through the practice of her religion she was seeking Christian salvation by means of self-mastery and submission to God's will. But this was a delusion. When "translated into social terms," Tompkins says, all salvation really means is "learning to submit to the authorities society has placed over you"—father, husband, pastor. Only in novels like *The Wide, Wide World* could women find an imaginative "design" for evasion of this tyranny; the sentimental-religious novel taught women to "internalize" God's authority and by so doing to transform "the condition of their lives."

Likewise, women in the nineteenth century were confined to the home. Forbidden to own property, to vote, or to speak at a public meeting if men were present, a woman's only "territory" and "material advantage," according to Tompkins, was the house she kept for her husband and family. Such an existence offered women few satisfactions; "in order to survive, they had to imagine their prison as the site of bliss." This was the function—or, as Tompkins calls it, the "cultural work"—performed by novels like *The Wide, Wide World.* They invested "domestic routines" with "sacramental power"; by exalting domesticity, they allowed women (imaginatively at least) to make "a successful bid for status and sway." Bound in union by their household chores, the female characters in sentimental novels find "compensat[ion] for their servitude by celebrating daily their exclusive, mutually supportive love for one another." The thousands of women who devoured these novels, Tompkins implies, must have found no less.

Of course, Tompkins realizes that "such claims are pathetic and ridiculous—the fantasies of a disenfranchised group, the line that society feeds to members whom it wants to buy off with the illusion of strength while denying them any real power." But it isn't that simple. The crucial point, Tompkins says, is that sentimental-religious novels like *The Wide, Wide World* actually did give women in the nineteenth century a sort of "real power." By helping to shape "the discourse of the age," the popular view of such matters, these novels influenced the way in which nineteenth-century Americans conceived of women, religion, the home. They bestowed upon women a sort of power by *representing* women as "all-powerful in relation to the world." Even though submission to God "looks like slavery to us" and homemaking "looks to us like deprivation," the nineteenth century looked at things quite differently—religion offered "mastery" and the home a "means of personal fulfillment." Of course they were not these. But how did nineteenth-century Americans come to think they were? Tompkins replies: by reading novels like *The Wide, Wide World.* These novels were, in other words, "attempts to redefine the social order." And this is the basis of Tompkins's claim for the importance of novels like Susan Warner's.

Two things must be said about Tompkins's treatment of *The Wide, Wide World.* First, in its political tendentiousness, it is absurdly wrongheaded. Second, and perhaps more important, Tompkins's claims are undermined by the novel's failings. The book is simply too bad for its exclusion from the canon to have been, as Tompkins insists, a "mistake." Susan Warner's intentions are more dignified and admirable than anything Jane Tompkins dreams of, but her novel simply does not realize them.

To begin with, *The Wide, Wide World* is not a novel about power. It is a religious novel; it is concerned with the problem of living in the world without compromising one's faith, and it treats this problem entirely in religious terms. The only way that Tompkins can misread *The Wide, Wide World* as a political novel is by failing to take Warner's religion as seriously as Warner herself took it. Tompkins is

apparently unable to conceive of religion as anything more than a sham—a protective, self-deluding response to a condition of powerlessness. She is capable of writing that a woman who submits to God's will is merely "merg[ing] her own authority" with His, or that salvation "means learning to submit to the authorities society has placed over you," perhaps because she has never felt a sincere religious impulse herself, or because she has never leavened her hostility toward religious belief with an effort to understand believers on their terms. In any case, she refuses even to entertain the possibility that Warner's religious feeling might have been genuine. Although Tompkins faults male critics for deriding the "triviality" of *The Wide, Wide World,* it is she who trivializes Warner.

That said, however, the point remains to be made that *The Wide, Wide World* fails utterly as a religious novel. Warner's intention is to give an exhaustive account of one child's moral development, to produce a kind of guidebook for spiritual growth. The problem is that Ellen is not very immoral to begin with. From the first, she is befriended by people who recognize her native spirituality; they shield her from those who don't. Ellen is good *in potentia* from first to last; and when she is good *in actu*—when she performs a small kindness—she acts in such a way that others will plainly see. Ellen's actions do not establish her innate goodness; that much is given; their one purpose is to identify who is good and who is not among the other characters in the novel. There are the Teachers, who explicitly dogmatize the moral lessons Ellen is to learn. And there are the Tormentors, who vex Ellen in one way or another and provide her with an occasion to learn her lessons. ("You mustn't get vexed so easily, my child," she is told. "Don't let every little untoward thing roughen your temper." This is the level on which her moral instruction takes place.) The real interest in the novel lies not in witnessing Ellen's trials of faith—we know ahead of time that she will pass all her tests—but in watching to see which characters will recognize her goodness and which will not, and whether her Tormentors will get their comeuppance.

Warner seems to have perceived that Ellen's self-evident goodness created both dramatic and religious problems for her book. But she was unable to solve them. " 'I am not good at all,' " she has Ellen protest when someone calls her so: " 'we're none of us good,' and the tears rose to her eyes,—'but the Bible will teach us how to be. . . .' " Yet the protest is feeble. "[I]f you ain't good," one character objects, "I should like to know what goodness is." And as if in acknowledgment of this character's point, Warner hastens to exhibit Ellen at her worst: she is annoyed when a naughty book is taken out of her hands! And again when she is asked to set aside her drawing in order to hold a skein of cotton for her dearest friend!

The fact is that Warner cannot *imagine* what it would mean for such a little girl as Ellen Montgomery to be totally depraved; though she accepts the doctrine of original sin on faith, Warner is incapable of giving it imaginative life. For a novel which was conceived as a Christian *Bildungsroman,* then, *The Wide, Wide World* has little religious resonance—or dramatic appeal. The spiritual theme is wholly contained in the sermons that various characters deliver to Ellen: the novel has no more of a religious dimension than that.

For Tompkins, however, the graver charge against *The Wide, Wide World* is that it is unrealistic, "divorced from actual human experience" and, more specifically, unaware of "the brute facts of political and economic oppression." Someone without Tompkins's ideological preconceptions might put the matter a bit differently. The novel's greatest flaw, the quality that keeps it from being a genuine work of literature, is its shameless sentimentality.

What is apt to strike any modern reader of *The Wide, Wide World* is the sheer amount of tears shed by little Ellen over the course of the novel. A letter-writer to the turn-of-the-century literary journal *The Critic* [see Further Reading] once skewered the book by listing the manifold phrases that Warner had come up with to describe Ellen's weeping:

> Her tears almost choked her, began to drop again, brought no relief, came faster than her words, dropped in to the water, fell faster, fell from the eyes, fell much too fast for her eyes to do their work, flowed, flowed faster than ever, followed in a flood, gushed forth, had to be wiped away, kept coming all the time, knew no measure, mingled, poured, ran down her cheeks, ran down her face and frock, ran fast again, ran fast down her face and fell into her lap, rose to her eyes, rushed to her eyes, started, streamed from her eyes, used to flow abundantly when they could unseen. . . .

Tompkins tries to defend all this by saying it is "rage" that Ellen betrays in "the deluge of [her] tears." But this is ridiculous. Ellen cries for many reasons. She cries when she is vexed and she cries when she is moved by piety—her tears "blind" her when she realizes that she loves Christ, and she falls to her knees "in a perfect agony of weeping." If truth be told, Ellen cries at the drop of a hat, and far too often for her fits of weeping to be lumped together as "rage" at a condition of powerlessness. It would be more accurate to say that the real purpose, the literary purpose, of Ellen's tears is to evoke pity in the reader. They are *cues* to the reader that compassion and tenderness are called for. This is how they act even on the other characters in the novel:

> "Mr. Van Brunt, are you one of that fold?"
>
> "What fold?"
>
> "The fold of Christ's people."
>
> "I'm afeard not, Miss Ellen," he said soberly, after a minute's pause.
>
> "Because," said Ellen, bursting into tears, "I wish you were, very much."
>
> She carried [Van Brunt's] great brown hand to her lips before she let it go. He went without saying a word. But when he got out he stopped and looked at a little tear she had left on the back of it. And he looked till one of his own fell there to keep it company.

Tompkins defends this gagging sentimentality by insisting

that the picture of life held up by such passages was conditioned by the conventions of the age—they seemed perfectly real to people at the time. "[T]he 'order of things' to which both readers and fictions belonged was itself structured by such narratives [as *The Wide, Wide World*]," she says. What she means is that the sentimental *Weltanschauung* governed how everyone within the culture conceived of genuine emotion. This seems a doubtful claim; it reduces all of human emotion to the sentimental novel's narrow, narrow world. Only an extremely ungenerous view of literature and life could allow one so severely to disparage both the emotional range of novels and the emotional capacities of those who read them.

Tompkins means to justify Warner's sentimentality, then, by assimilating it to that of her audience. But this in itself is a criticism of Warner. For another way to make much the same point is to say that Susan Warner was not in command of her material. She could be said to have been as much the victim of the cult of sentimentality as any reader addicted to the books of E. D. E. N. Southworth, Maria Cummins, Mary J. Holmes, Marion Harland, Ann Stephens, Marion McIntosh, and the myriad other sentimental novelists of the day.

But this just won't do. If all the sentimental novelists of the nineteenth century can be shown to have groaned under the yoke of the sentimental convention, why read one of them rather than another? Tompkins says that *The Wide, Wide World* represents the "entire body of work" in "its purest form." But why read any of them at all? One purpose of great literature has always been to train the affective life of man by making subtle distinctions between emotions. Sentimental literature, by contrast, blurs subtleties of feeling, confuses similar emotions, refuses to discriminate, finds in every mood a cause for tears.

Tompkins recognizes that *The Wide, Wide World* concentrates "exclusively on the emotions." But the novel would have to do a better job than it does at disciplining and ordering the emotions to qualify as genuine literature. All too typically, Warner is tongue-tied, baffled, in the face of strong emotion. In what is meant to be the most moving scene of the novel, Ellen bids farewell to her mother:

> [Ellen's mother] said not a word, but opened her arms to receive her little daughter; and with a cry of indescribable expression Ellen sprang upon the bed, and was folded in them. But then neither of them spoke or wept. What could words say? Heart met heart in that agony, for each knew all that was in the other.

Indescribable expression, each knew all that was in the other. These are not the phrases of a genuine artist, a writer who wishes to describe expression, to *make known* all that was in her characters. This is the prose of a writer who expects her readers to sense vaguely what she means and to supply the necessary feeling.

Susan Warner is of some minor importance as a historical figure, but she is almost devoid of literary value. Nevertheless, she has become important for another reason altogether: she is symbolic of attempts to redefine the meaning of literature in our time. What is too little perceived is that efforts such as Jane Tompkins's on behalf of Susan Warner involve a calculated assault on the very principle of literary and intellectual distinction. Looking back on *The Wide, Wide World,* Henry James said that, though edifying and even charming, such works can "legitimate themselves" as genuine novels only if they are the products of a first-rate mind—a mind, that is, which "is the master and not the slave of its material." Like so many critics in the university these days, Tompkins insists on seeing all writers as second-rate minds—as slaves to their age's ideology. She does not really care if new canonical texts such as *The Wide, Wide World* are bad books. In fact, the worse the better, she might say: the weaker the book, the more useful it may prove. For the weak is what can be taken advantage of. Small wonder, then, that Tompkins and critics of her kind would reorganize literary study in the university by devoting more and more classroom time to second-rate writers like Susan Warner and by teaching better writers as equally second-rate. (pp. 73-8)

> D. G. Myers, "The Canonization of Susan Warner," in The New Criterion, *Vol. VII, No. 4, December, 1988, pp. 73-8.*

FURTHER READING

Baker, Mabel. *Light in the Morning: Memories of Susan and Anna Warner.* West Point, N. Y.: Constitution Island Association Press, 1978, 144 p.

> Biography of the Warner sisters.

"A Religious Novel." *Blackwood's Edinburgh Magazine* XCIX, No. DCV (March 1866): 275-86.

> Review of *The Old Helmet* that discusses the influence of literature on manners.

Bode, Carl. "The Scribbling Women: The Domestic Novel Rules the 'Fifties." In his *The Anatomy of American Popular Culture: 1840-1861,* pp. 169-87. Berkeley: University of California Press, 1959.

> Analysis of Jungian archetypes in *The Wide, Wide World.*

Calabro, John A. "Susan Warner and Her Bible Classes." *Legacy* 4, No. 2 (Fall 1987): 45-52.

> Discusses Warner's weekly bible classes for West Point cadets, focusing on her character and religious beliefs.

"Tears, Idle Tears." *The Critic* 21, No. 538 (29 October 1892): 236-37.

> Presents "an analytical synopsis of lamentations," an alphabetically arranged list of the numerous phrases used to describe crying in *The Wide, Wide World.* The critic sarcastically suggests that Warner must have compiled a similar list and checked off each phrase while writing to ensure "so great a variety of expression."

Denman, Frank. "How to Drive the Sheriff from the Homestead Door." *The New York Times Book Review* (24 December 1944): 8.

> Examines popular reception of *The Wide, Wide World.*

Denman writes: "Today the most devout would find the excessive piety of *The Wide, Wide World* wearing. . . . And yet those characters must have taken on the substance of reality to millions of Victorian readers who shed oceans of tears over them."

Dobson, Joanne. "The Hidden Hand: Subversion of Cultural Ideology in Three Mid-Nineteenth-Century American Women's Novels." *American Quarterly* 38, No. 2 (Summer 1986): 223-42.

> Interprets various subversions of the conventions of the sentimental novel in Warner's *Wide, Wide World,* E. D. E. N. Southworth's *The Hidden Hand,* and A. D. T. Whitney's *Hitherto: A Story of Yesterdays* as a commentary on the role of women in society. Dobson concludes: "It would be a mistake to consider these novels as feminist statements. . . . Rather, these popular women writers of the last century were sharing with their readers a clear-eyed understanding of the losses and limitations imposed upon individual women by close adherence to the societal text of feminine identity."

Foster, Edward Halsey. *Susan and Anna Warner.* Boston: Twayne Publishers, 1978, 138 p.

> Critical and biographical study of the Warner sisters.

Jordan, Alice M. "Susan Warner and Her *Wide, Wide World.*" In her *From Rollo to Tom Sawyer and Other Papers,* pp. 82-91. Boston: The Horn Book, 1948.

> Revised version of an earlier essay discussing characterization and setting in *The Wide, Wide World* and *Queechy.*

Kelley, Mary. *Private Woman, Public Stage: Literary Domesticity in Nineteenth-Century America,* pp. 7ff. New York: Oxford University Press, 1984.

> Includes numerous references to Warner's life and works.

Martin, Rebecca. "Remembrance of Trash Past: Good Girls Get a Sentimental Education." *The Village Voice Literary Supplement* 34, No. 77 (August 1989): 21-2.

> An examination of *The Lamplighter* by Maria Susanna Cummins and *The Wide, Wide World* as "cultural indexes" to "the ingenuity and delusions of women coping with a narrowing sphere in a time of ever-broadening possibilities."

Mitchell, Sally. "How to Grovel." *The New York Times Book Review* (10 May 1987): 10.

> Reviews the 1987 expanded edition of *The Wide, Wide World.*

Overmyer, Grace. "Hudson River Bluestockings: The Warner Sisters of Constitution Island." *New York History* 40, No. 2 (April 1959): 137-58.

> A biographical study of the Warner sisters that includes discussion of *The Wide, Wide World* and *Queechy.*

Papashvily, Helen Waite. "All Women—All Enchained—All Enchanted" and "Keepers of the Keys to the Kingdom." In her *All the Happy Endings: A Study of the Domestic Novel,* pp. 1-14, pp. 95-109. New York: Harper & Brothers Publishers, 1956.

> The first essay discusses the early publication history and reception of *The Wide, Wide World.* The second compares the character Ellen Montgomery with the her-

oines of Maria Cummin's *The Lamplighter* and Marion Harland's *Alone*.

Pattee, Fred Lewis. "The Second Flowering of New England." In his *The Feminine Fifties,* pp. 50-67. New York: D. Appleton-Century Company, 1940.

    Studies the sudden rise in popularity after 1850 of novels written by women, citing *The Wide, Wide World* as one of the earliest examples of this phenomenon.

Reynolds, Cuyler. "The Author of *The Wide, Wide World.*" *The National Magazine* IX, No. 1 (October 1898): 73-81.

    Discusses the setting of *Queechy* in Canaan, New York, and reactions of local residents to the novel.

Sanderson, Dorothy Hurlbut. *They Wrote for a Living: A Bibliography of the Works of Susan Bogert Warner and Anna Bartlett Warner.* West Point, N. Y.: The Constitution Island Association, 1976, 44 p.

    Bibliography of primary and secondary sources.

Smith, Henry Nash. "The Scribbling Women and the Cosmic Success Story." *Critical Inquiry* 1, No. 1 (September 1974): 47-70.

    Examines submission to authority and portrayal of characters in popular fiction of the 1850s, most notably in *The Wide, Wide World*.

Tompkins, Jane. "The Other American Renaissance." In her *Sensational Designs: The Cultural Work of American Fiction 1790-1860,* pp. 147-85. New York: Oxford University Press, 1985.

    An expanded version of a 1983 essay on Warner. Tompkins argues that sentimental novels have been mistakenly excluded from the canon of American literature. Some of this material is duplicated in her afterword to the 1987 edition of *The Wide, Wide World* (see excerpt dated 1987).

Warner, Anna. *Susan Warner ("Elizabeth Wetherell"). New York: G. P. Putnam's Sons, 1909, 509 p.*

    A biography by Warner's sister that includes numerous excerpts from Warner's diaries.

Walt Whitman

1819-1892

American poet, essayist, novelist, short story writer, journalist, and editor.

The following entry presents criticism of Whitman's poetry collection *Leaves of Grass,* which was published in nine editions between 1855 and 1892. For discussion of Whitman's complete career, see *NCLC,* Volume 4.

Hailed as a masterpiece of American literature, *Leaves of Grass* pioneered a vision of humanity based on Whitman's radically egalitarian, democratic ideals and unveiled an ambitious poetic persona designed by Whitman to serve as the embodiment of America. The collection comprises poems Whitman wrote between 1855 and 1892, glorifying America through evocations of its citizenry, landscape, and history as filtered through a prophetic and extremely sensual subjectivity—the "self" of the longest and most highly regarded poem of. *Leaves of Grass,* "Song of Myself." Eschewing conventional verse forms and diction, Whitman wrote in an unrestrained and idiosyncratic style that reflected the iconoclasm of his personal outlook. The influence of *Leaves of Grass* on American literature has been pronounced and lasting; as Roy Harvey Pearce has stated, "the history of American poetry could be written as the continuing discovery and rediscovery of Whitman, an on-going affirmation of his crucial relevance to the mission of the American poet."

Before 1855, when he published the first edition of *Leaves of Grass,* Whitman wrote nothing of critical regard. He published sentimental verse in several periodicals and served for a short time as editor of the *New York Aurora* and the *Brooklyn Eagle.* His only novel, *Franklin Evans; or, The Inebriate,* published in 1842, is largely a sermon on the evils of alcohol, and he later dismissed it as "damned rot." Whitman's sudden transformation from a conventional journalist into a radical poet remains unexplained, though commentators have suggested causes ranging from Ralph Waldo Emerson's 1842 lecture "The Poet"—in which Emerson called for an American poet to capture the spirit of the burgeoning republic—to the emotional freedom resulting from Whitman's discovery of his homosexuality. Whatever the motivation, critics note that from the publication of the first edition of *Leaves of Grass,* Whitman actively promoted himself as a representative of the common people. The first edition of *Leaves of Grass,* published when Whitman was thirty-five years old, contains twelve untitled poems and no indication of its author aside from the copyright notice, in which the holder is identified as "Walt Whitman, an American, one of the roughs, a kosmos," a phrase that is echoed in one of the poems. In a preface that has come to be regarded as one of literature's most influential expositions of artistic aims, Whitman outlines the methods and concerns of a new mode of poetry: "The art of art, the glory of expression

and the sunshine of the light of letters is simplicity. Nothing is better than simplicity . . . nothing can make up for excess or for the lack of definiteness . . . [To] speak in literature with the perfect rectitude and insouciance of the movements of animals and the unimpeachableness of the sentiment of trees in the woods and grass by the roadside is the flawless triumph of art." In accordance with the preface, the poems in *Leaves of Grass* sharply break from the American verse tradition established by such poets as Henry Wadsworth Longfellow and William Cullen Bryant, employing unrhymed and unmetered lines, blending poetic and unpoetic speech, and addressing subjects that had been considered unfit for poetry, most conspicuously the body and human sexuality. Edgar Lee Masters records that America "was shocked to stupefaction" by the first poem of *Leaves of Grass,* to be called "Song of Myself" in later editions of the book. Although Whitman did attract a group of devoted disciples who viewed him as the prophet of American democracy, his contemporaries generally condemned *Leaves of Grass* as incoherent and vulgar; most of the favorable reviews were written by Whitman himself and published anonymously. Although Emerson congratulated Whitman on *Leaves of Grass* in a letter stating, "I greet you at the beginning of a great career," biographers note that he too disapproved of the sexually explicit passages in Whitman's work.

In the subsequent editions of *Leaves of Grass,* Whitman included new poems, revised and combined existing ones, added and altered titles, and shifted poems into thematic groupings. He once referred to the different editions of *Leaves of Grass* as "a succession of growths like the rings of trees." The poems Whitman incorporated into the 1856 edition include "Crossing Brooklyn Ferry," a poem described by Edwin Haviland Miller as "a hedonistic statement of faith" to quell desperation in the machine age. In the 1860 edition, Whitman added the sections "Enfans d'Adam"—later altered to its English equivalent "Children of Adam"—and "Calamus." "Children of Adam" celebrates heterosexual relationships, or what Whitman called "amativeness," and includes "From Pent-up Aching Rivers," "I Sing the Body Electric," and "I Am He that Aches with Amorous Love." "Calamus" concerns itself with homosexual relationships, or "adhesiveness." In such poems as "Scented Herbage of My Breast" and "City of Orgies," Whitman articulated his dream of democracy founded on the existence of close bonds between men. "As I Ebb'd with the Ocean of Life," another important poem that was added to *Leaves of Grass* in 1860, is filled with anxiety about writing, death, and the "self," and as is characteristic of Whitman, the "self" becomes a metaphor for humanity as a whole. Often cited as one of his most moving poems, "As I Ebb'd with the Ocean of Life" has been read as a process of confronting fears and striving to transform them into hope.

Drum-Taps was published as a separate book in 1865, and was later incorporated into *Leaves of Grass.* Derived from Whitman's experiences tending wounded Civil War soldiers, the poems in *Drum-Taps* mourn the dissolution of the United States as well as the loss of lives. *Sequel to Drum-Taps,* published later in 1865, features "When Lilacs Last in the Dooryard Bloom'd," a threnody for Lincoln that Whitman later incorporated into the "Memories of President Lincoln" section of *Leaves of Grass.* The poem is, in the words of Betsy Erkkila, "a kind of civil ritual" attempting to come to terms with the loss of the President on a collective level. Though another work occasioned by Lincoln's death, "O Captain! My Captain!", is Whitman's best-known poem, it is also the one he most regretted writing, as he felt it was too formally rigid and distant in emotion. Whitman, capable of deftly rendering such humble images as a spiderweb in "A Noiseless Patient Spider," a highly praised poem written in 1868, more often aspired to grand articulations of cosmic beauty and exultation. "Passage to India" was published in 1871 as part of a collection of the same name, and was incorporated into *Leaves of Grass* later that year. Inspired by the technological breakthroughs of the Suez Canal and the transcontinental railroad, Whitman envisioned a utopia without national borders. Whitman said of "Passage to India," "There's more of me, the essential ultimate me, in that than in any of the poems." With the writing of "Passage to India," nearly all the important poems of *Leaves of Grass* were completed.

Despite the initial negative critical judgments, *Leaves of Grass* has come to be recognized as a remarkable accomplishment. Galway Kinnell has written about Whitman's "transformation, in the world of letters, from freak to master," theorizing that except for a few perceptive minds—Emerson and Henry David Thoreau in the nineteenth century, Carl Sandburg and Vachel Lindsay in the first half of the twentieth century—mainstream critics were generally too shocked or puzzled by *Leaves of Grass* to give it a fair and thoughtful reading. By the middle of the twentieth century, however, Whitman's poetry had gained wide acceptance, due in part to more open societal attitudes towards sex. It has been the task of critics to sort out the large quantity of myths generated by Whitman's detractors, his disciples, and the poet himself. In particular, critics have sought to explain the significance of sexual imagery in his poetry, and a major trend has been the application of psychoanalytic theory to his life and works. Textual analyses continue to reveal complexities and paradoxes in Whitman's work, and such investigations contribute to an evolving appreciation of his powers as a poet.

(See also *Concise Dictionary of American Literary Biography,* 1640-1865; *Dictionary of Literary Biography,* Vols. 3 and 64; and *Something About the Author,* Vol. 20.)

Walt Whitman   (essay date 1855)

[*The following is one of three reviews of* Leaves of Grass *that Whitman published anonymously.*]

To give judgment on real poems, one needs an account of the poet himself. Very devilish to some, and very divine to some, will appear the poet of these new poems, the **Leaves of Grass;** an attempt, as they are, of a naive, masculine, affectionate, contemplative, sensual, imperious person, to cast into literature not only his own grit and arrogance, but his own flesh and form, undraped, regardless of models, regardless of modesty or law, and ignorant or slightly scornful, as at first appears, of all except his own presence and experience, and all outside the fiercely loved land of his birth and the birth of his parents, and their parents for several generations before him. Politeness this man has none, and regulation he has none. A rude child of the people!—no imitation—no foreigner—but a growth and idiom of America. No discontented—a careless slouch, enjoying today. No dilettante democrat—a man who is part-and-part with the commonalty, and with immediate life—loves the streets—loves the docks—loves the free rasping talk of men—likes to be called by his given name, and nobody at all need Mr. him—can laugh with laughers—likes the ungenteel ways of laborers—is not prejudiced one mite against the Irish—talks readily with them—talks readily with niggers—does not make a stand on being a gentleman, nor on learning or manners—eats cheap fare, likes the strong flavored coffee of the coffeestands in the market, at sunrise—likes a supper of oysters fresh from the oyster-smack—likes to make one at the crowded table among sailors and workpeople—would leave a select soirée of elegant people any time to go with tumultuous men, roughs, receive their caresses and welcome, listen to their noise, oaths, smut, fluency, laughter, repartee—and can preserve his presence perfectly among these, and the like of these. The effects he produces in his poems are no effects of artists or the arts, but effects of the original eye or arm, or the actual atmosphere, or tree, or bird. You may feel the unconscious teaching of a fine brute, but will never feel the artificial teaching of a fine writer or speaker.

Other poets celebrate great events, personages, romances, wars, loves, passions, the victories and power of their country, or some real or imagined incident—and polish their work, and come to the conclusions, and satisfy the reader. This poet celebrates natural propensities in himself; and that is the way he celebrates all. He comes to no conclusions, and does not satisfy the reader. He certainly leaves him what the serpent left the woman and the man, the taste of the Paradisaic tree of the knowledge of good and evil, never to be erased again.

What good is it to argue about egotism? There can be no two thoughts on Walt Whitman's egotism. That is avowedly what he steps out of the crowd and turns and faces them for. Mark, critics! Otherwise is not used for you the key that leads to the use of the other keys to this well-enveloped man. His whole work, his life, manners, friendships, writings, all have among their leading purposes an evident purpose to stamp a new type of character, namely his own, and indelibly fix it and publish it, not for a model but an illustration, for the present and future of American letters and American young men, for the South the same as the North, and for the Pacific and Mississippi country, and Wisconsin and Texas and Kansas and Canada and Havana and Nicaragua, just as much as New York and Boston. Whatever is needed toward this achievement he puts his hand to, and lets imputations take their time to die.

First be yourself what you would show in your poem—such seems to be this man's example and inferred rebuke to the schools of poets. He makes no allusions to books or writers; their spirits do not seem to have touched him; he has not a word to say for or against them, or their theories or ways. He never offers others; what he continually offers is the man whom our Brooklynites know so well. Of pure American breed, large and lusty—age thirty-six years (1855)—never once using medicine—never dressed in black, always dressed freely and clean in strong clothes—neck open, shirt-collar flat and broad, countenance tawny transparent red, beard well-mottled with white, hair like hay after it has been mowed in the field and lies tossed and streaked—his physiology corroborating a rugged phrenology—a person singularly beloved and looked toward, especially by young men and the illiterate—one who has firm attachments there, and associates there—one who does not associate with literary people—a man never called upon to make speeches at public dinners—never on platforms amid the crowds of clergymen, or professors, or aldermen, or congressmen—rather down in the bay with pilots in their pilot-boat—or off on a cruise with fishers in a fishing-smack—or riding on a Broadway omnibus, side by side with the driver—or with a band of loungers over the open grounds of the country—fond of New York and

Brooklyn—fond of the life of the great ferries—one whom, if you should meet, you need not expect to meet an extraordinary person—one in whom you will see the singularity which consists in no singularity—whose contact is no dazzle or fascination, nor requires any deference, but has the easy fascination of what is homely and accustomed—as of something you knew before, and was waiting for—there you have Walt Whitman, the begetter of a new offspring out of literature, taking with easy nonchalance the chances of its present reception, and, through all misunderstandings and distrusts, the chances of its future reception. (pp. 23-5)

> *Walt Whitman, in an originally unsigned review of* Leaves of Grass, *in* Critical Essays on Walt Whitman, *edited by James Woodress, G.K. Hall & Co., 1983, pp. 23-5.*

Richard Maurice Bucke   (essay date 1883)

[*Bucke was a Canadian psychiatrist and the author of* Walt Whitman, *the first book-length biography of the poet. According to scholars, Whitman himself played a significant role in the production of the biography, writing numerous passages and exerting editorial control over its contents. In the following excerpt from that work, Whitman's poetry is acclaimed for its spiritual wisdom.*]

In examining [*Leaves of Grass*], the first thing that presents itself for remark is its name, by no means the least significant part. It would indeed be impossible to select for the volume a more perfect title. Properly understood, the words express what the book contains and is. Like the grass, while old as creation, it is modern, fresh, universal, spontaneous, not following forms, taking its own form, perfectly free and unconstrained, common as the commonest things, yet its meaning inexhaustible by the greatest intellect, full of life itself, and capable of entering into and nourishing other lives, growing in the sunshine (*i.e.,* in the full, broad light of science), perfectly open and simple, yet having meanings underneath; always young, pure, delicate and beautiful to those who have hearts and eyes to feel and see, but coarse, insignificant and worthless to those who live more in the artificial, (parlors, pictures, traditions, books, dress, jewels, laces, music, decorations, money, gentility), than in the natural, (the naked and rude earth, the fresh air, the calm or stormy sea, men, women, children, birds, animals, woods, fields, and the like).

I might say here a preparatory word or two about the absence of ordinary rhyme or tune in Walt Whitman's work. The question cannot be treated without a long statement, and many premises. Readers used to the exquisite verbal melody of Tennyson and Longfellow may well wince at first entering on *Leaves of Grass.* So does the invalid or even well person used to artificial warmth and softness indoors, wince at the sea, and gale, and mountain steeps. But the rich, broad, rugged rhythm and inimitable interior music of *Leaves of Grass* need not be argued for or defended to any real tone-artist. [During] the gestation of the poems, the author was saturated for years with the rendering by the best vocalists and performers of the best operas and oratorios. Here is further testimony on this point, from a lady, a musician and art-writer, Mrs. Fanny Raymond Ritter, wife of Music-Professor Ritter of Vassar College:

> Those readers who possess a musical mind cannot fail to have been struck by a peculiar characteristic of some of Whitman's grandest poems. It is apparently, but only superficially, a contradiction. A fault that critics have most insisted upon in his poetry is its independence of, or contempt for, the canons of musico-poetical art, in its intermittent, irregular structure and flow. Yet the characteristic alluded to which always impressed me as inherent in these—especially in some of the Pindaric "Drum-Taps"—was a sense of strong rhythmical, pulsing, *musical* power. I had always accounted to myself for this contradiction, because I, of course, supposed the poet's nature to be a large one, including many opposite qualities; and that as it is impossible to conceive the Universe devoid of those divinely musical forces, Time, Movement, Order, a great poet's mind could not be thought of as an imperfect, one-sided one, devoid of any comprehension of or feeling for musical art. I knew, too, that Whitman was a sincere lover of art, though not practically formative in any other art than poetry. Therefore, on a certain memorable Olympian day at the Ritter-house, when Whitman and Burroughs visited us together, I told Whitman of my belief in the presence of an overwhelming musical pulse, behind an apparent absence of musical form in his poems. He answered with as much sincerity as geniality, that it would indeed be strange if there were no music at the heart of his poems, for more of these were actually inspired by music than he himself could remember. Moods awakened by music in the streets, the theatre, and in private, had originated poems apparently far removed in feeling from the scenes and feelings of the moment. But above all, he said, while he was yet brooding over poems still to come, he was touched and inspired by the glorious, golden, soul-smiting voice of the greatest of Italian contralto singers, Marietta Alboni. Her mellow, powerful, delicate tones, so heartfelt in their expression, so spontaneous in their utterance, had deeply penetrated his spirit, and never, as when subsequently writing of the mocking-bird or any other bird-song, on a fragrant, moonlit summer night, had he been able to free himself from the recollection of the deep emotion that had inspired and affected him while he listened to the singing of Marietta Alboni.

(pp. 155-57)

After their unquestionable birthmarks, so different from European models or from any copied or foreign type whatever, the first thing to be noticed about *Leaves of Grass* (this is what strikes nearly every one immediately upon trying to read it) is the difficulty to the ordinary, even intelligent reader, of understanding it. On this point my own experience has been as follows. About eighteen years ago, I began to read it. For many months I could see absolutely nothing in the book, and at times I was strongly inclined to believe that there was nothing in it to see. But I could not let it alone; although one day I would throw

it down in a sort of rage at its want of meaning, the next day or the day after I would take it up again with just as lively an interest as ever, persuaded that there was something there, and determined to find out what that might be. At first as I read, it seemed to me the writer was always on the point of saying something which he never actually said. Page after page seemed equally barren of any definite statement. Then after a time I found that a few lines here and there were full of suggestion and beauty. Gradually these bright spots, as I may call them, grew larger, more numerous and more brilliant, until at last the whole surface was lit up with an almost unearthly splendor.

And still I am well aware that I do not yet fully understand this book. Neither do I expect ever to understand it entirely, though I learn something more about it almost every day, and shall probably go on reading it as long as I live. I doubt whether I fully understand any part of it. For the more it is studied the more profound it is seen to be, stretching out vista beyond vista apparently interminably. Now it may seem strange that any person should go on reading a book he could not understand, and, consequently, could in the ordinary way take no interest. The explanation is that there is the same peculiar magnetism about *Leaves of Grass* as about Walt Whitman himself, so that people who once really begin to read it and get into the range of its attraction, must go on reading it whether they comprehend it or not, or until they do comprehend it. As Walt Whitman says:

> I teach straying from me, yet who can stray from
>   me?
> I follow you whoever you are from the present
>   hour,
> My words itch at your ears till you understand
>   them.

But after all, granting that this is true, is it worth while to read any book for years on the mere chance of understanding it at last? Certainly it would not be worth while with many books, but I will answer for it that no one who reads *Leaves of Grass* so as to understand it at all will ever repent the time and pains. For this is not a book that merely amuses or instructs. It does neither of these in the ordinary sense, but it does far more than amuse or instruct. It is capable of making whoever wishes to be so, wiser, happier, better; and it does these not by acting on the intellect, by telling us what is best for us, what we ought to do and avoid doing, and the like, but by acting directly on the moral nature itself, and elevating and purifying that. Why is this book so hard to understand? In the first place it is worth while to notice that the author of *Leaves of Grass* was himself well aware of this difficulty, as he says in the two following and in many other places:

> But these leaves conning you con at peril,
> For these leaves and me you will not understand,
> They will elude you at first, and still more afterward, I will certainly elude you,
> Even while you should think you had unquestionably caught me, behold!
> Already you see I have escaped from you.

Then in the lines **"To a Certain Civilian"**:

> Did you ask dulcet rhymes from me?

Did you seek the civilian's peaceful and lan-
  guishing rhymes?
Did you find what I sang erewhile so hard to follow?
Why I was not singing erewhile for you to follow, to understand—nor am I now;
(I have been born of the same as the war was
  born,
The drum-corps' rattle is ever to me sweet
  music—I love well the martial dirge,
With slow wail and convulsive throb leading the
  officer's funeral;)
What to such as you anyhow such a poet as I?
  therefore leave my works,
And go lull yourself with what you can understand, and with piano-tunes,
For I lull nobody, and you will never understand
  me.

Are we to conclude that Walt Whitman wished and intended his writings to be difficult of comprehension? I do
not think so at all. I think he would gladly have every one
comprehend him at once if possible. Must we suppose then
that he had not the ability to so write as to make himself
easily intelligible? that in fact he is deficient in the faculty
of clear expression? On the contrary I should say that
Walt Whitman is a supreme master of the art of expression. In a case like this there is some one else besides the
poet who may be to blame, and perhaps the fault may lie
with—the reader. Must we say then that ordinary men, or
even able men (for many of these have tried to read *Leaves
of Grass* and failed), have not sufficient intelligence to
comprehend the book? No, I neither say nor believe this.

The fact is, in the ordinary sense, there is nothing to understand about *Leaves of Grass* which any person of average intelligence could not comprehend with the greatest
ease. The secret of the difficulty is, that the work, different
from every popular book of poetry known, appeals almost
entirely to the moral nature, and hardly at all to the intellect—that to understand it means putting oneself in emotional, and not simply mental relation with its author—
means to thoroughly realize Walt Whitman—to be in
sympathy with the heart and mind of perhaps the most advanced nature the world has yet produced. This, of course,
is neither simple nor easy. *Leaves of Grass* is a picture of
the world as seen from the standpoint of the highest moral
elevation yet reached. It is at the same time an exposition
of this highest moral nature itself. The real difficulty is for
an ordinary person to rise to this spiritual altitude. Whoever can do so, even momentarily, or in imagination, will
never cease to thank the man by whose aid this was accomplished. It is such assistance which Walt Whitman is
destined to give to large sections of the human race, and
doubtless it is this which he refers to in the following passages:

I am he bringing help for the sick as they pant
  on their backs,
And for strong upright men I bring yet more
  needed help.

Behold, I do not give lectures or a little charity,
When I give I give myself.

I bring what you much need yet always have,

Not money, amours, dress, eating, erudition, but
  as good,
I send no agent or medium, offer no representative of value, but offer the value itself.

For I myself am not one who bestows nothing
  upon man and woman,
For I bestow upon any man or woman the entrance to all the gifts of the universe.

Now, in the mouth of any man known to history, with
very few exceptions, these claims would be ludicrous.
They would not, however, have been ludicrous if we suppose them made by such men as Siddhartha Guatama,
Confucius, Zoroaster, or Mohammed, for these men did
as far as it was possible in their times and lands what Walt
Whitman in these verses promises to do now,—that is,
they bestowed their own higher natures upon all who
came under their influence, gave them the help they most
needed, and opened to them (the best gift of all) the way
to a higher spiritual life. They made such claims, and fulfilled them. Walt Whitman too makes them. Can he fulfil
them? I say he has done so, and that he will do so throughout the future.

But let us examine this question and these claims a little
more in detail, and see what they really mean. Whoever
will consider them will see that they all amount essentially
to the same thing, which is a promise on Walt Whitman's
part to bestow upon any person who asks it, and who will
put his or her mind in full relation with the poems, moral
elevation. In other words, he will give to such person a
greater amount of faith, a greater power of affection, and
will consequently reduce in that person the liability to, and
the capacity of, fear and hate. Now, love and faith are the
elements of which happiness is composed, and hate and
fear (their opposites) are the elements of which unhappiness is composed. If, therefore, Walt Whitman can produce in us moral elevation, he will increase our true happiness, and this, to my mind, is the most valuable of all the
"gifts of the universe," so far, at all events, as we know at
present. Again: modern science has made it capable of
proof that this universe is so constructed as to justify on
our part love and faith, and not hate and fear. For this reason, the man who has in his composition the most love and
faith, and the least hate and fear, will stand (other things
being equal) in the closest relation to universal truth,—
that is, he will be the wisest man. If, then, Walt Whitman
gives us moral elevation, he will also give wisdom, which,
it seems to me, is clearly another of the chief "gifts of the
universe." Yet once more: conduct flows from moral nature. The man with a low moral nature who is full of hate
and fear, and the compounds of these, such as envy and
jealousy, cannot possibly live a beneficent and happy life.
On the other hand, it is inconceivable that the man who
is full of love and faith should, on the whole, live a bad life.
So that moral elevation, besides giving us happiness and
wisdom, gives us also the power and inclination to lead
good lives; and this, I should say, is another "gift of the
universe" really worth having, in contradistinction to
mere wealth, education, social position, or fame, which
the current standards make the main objects of existence.

Let us not forget that of all mental qualities, exceptional
moral elevation is the hardest to see. So true is this, that

in the whole history of our race, as far back as it is known, every man, without one exception, who has stood prominently in advance of and above his age by this quality, has not only not been considered exceptionally good, but has been in every instance looked upon by the majority of his contemporaries as a bad man, and has been consequently traduced, banished, burned, poisoned, or crucified.

In philosophy, science, art, religion, men's views, their ways of looking at things, are constantly altering. And it is equally plain that on the whole they are altering for the better—are constantly acquiring a more just and worthy mental attitude towards their surroundings, towards each other, and towards Nature. This progress necessitates the constant abandonment of old ideas, and the constant taking up of new intellectual and moral positions. These successive readjustments are always the cause of more or less social, political, and literary disturbance. The antagonism is naturally deeper and stronger in the case of religious and social changes than new departures in science, philosophy, or art, since in religious tenets the feelings are more deeply involved. The men who initiate such readjustments of the soul of man to its environment are the master minds of the race. These are the men Walt Whitman calls Poets. He says: "The true Poet is not the follower of beauty, but the august master of beauty." That is to say, he does not take merely the matter recognized as beautiful already and make it the theme of his verse, or amuse himself and his readers by dressing it up and admiring and praising it. This, in the language of *Leaves of Grass,* is the office of a "singer," not of a "Poet"; to do this is to be a follower of beauty. But the Poet is the master of beauty, and his mastery consists in commanding and causing things which were not before considered beautiful to become so. How does he do this? Before this question can be answered we must understand why one thing is beautiful to us and another not—why persons, combinations, etc., that are beautiful to one are often not so to another—and why one man sees so much beauty in the world, another so little. The explanation is, that beauty and love are correlatives; they are the objective and subjective aspects of the same thing. Beauty has no existence apart from love, and love has no existence apart from beauty. Beauty is the shadow of love thrown upon the outer world. We do not love a person or thing because the person or thing is beautiful, but whatever we love, that is beautiful to us, and whatever we do not love, is not beautiful. And the function of the true Poet is to love and appreciate all things, nationalities, laws, combinations, individuals. He alone illustrates the sublime reality and ideality of that verse of Genesis, how God after His entire creation looked forth, "and pronounced it *all* good." A parallel statement would be true of Faith. As that which is seen from without inwards is love, and seen from within outwards is beauty, so that which seen from without inwards is faith, is goodness when seen from within outwards.

The human race began by fearing or distrusting nearly everything, and trusting almost nothing; and this is yet the condition of savages. But from time to time, men arose who distrusted and feared less and less. These men have always been considered impious by those about them; but for all that, they have been the saviors and progressists of the race, and have been recognized as such when their views and feelings penetrated the generations succeeding them. Such evolution has always been going on, and will continue. So far, fear has been a part of every accepted religion, and it is still taught that to destroy fear is to destroy religion. But if faith is to increase, fear, its opposite, must continually decrease and at last disappear. Fear is the basis of superstition. Faith, its opposite, along with love, is the basis of religion. I know it is still said by some to-day in the name of religion, that men should hate this and that—sin for instance, and the devil, and that they should fear certain things, such as God and the Judgment. But this really is irreligion, not religion.

An important feature of *Leaves of Grass* is what I would call its continuity or endlessness. It does not teach something, and rest there. It does not make, in morals and religion, an important step in advance, and stop satisfied with that. It has unlimited vista. It clears the way ahead, with allowance and provision for new advances far, far beyond anything contained in itself. It brings no one to "a terminus," nor teaches any one to be "content and full." It is a ceaseless goad, a never-resting spur. To those to whom it speaks, it cries continually, forward! forward! and admits of no pause in the race. A second trait is its universality. There is nothing of which humanity has experience that it does not touch upon more or less directly. There must have been a deliberate intention on the part of the author to give the book this all-embracing character, and no doubt that was one reason for the catalogues of objects in a few of the poems which have so irritated the critics. I have often tried to think of something objective or subjective, material or immaterial, that was not taken cognizance of by *Leaves of Grass,* but always failed. A third feature is the manner in which the author avoids (either of set purpose, or more likely by a sure instinct) dealing specifically with any topics of mere class or ephemeral interest (though he really treats these too through the bases upon which they rest), and concerns himself solely with the elementary subjects of human life, which must necessarily have perennial interest.

Leaves of Grass is curiously a different book to each reader. To some, its merit consists in the keen thought which pierces to the kernel of things—or a perpetual and sunny cheeriness, in which respect it is the synonyme of pure air and health; to others it is chiefly valuable as being full of pictorial suggestions; to a third class of men it is a new Gospel containing fresh revelations of divine truth; to a fourth it is charged with ideas and suggestions in practical life and manners; to some its large, sweet, clear, animal physiology is its especial charm; to some, the strange abysses of its fervid emotions. Upon still others (on whom it produces its full effect), it exerts an irresistible and divine power, strengthening and elevating their lives unspeakably, driving them from all meanness and toward all good, giving them no rest, but compelling them to watch every act, word, thought, feeling—to guard their days and nights from weakness, baseness, littleness, or impurity—at the same time giving them extraordinary power to accomplish these ends.

There is still another class (altogether the most numerous

so far), who see in the book nothing of all these fine things or good uses. To them it suggests contempt for laws and social forms, appears coarse, prosaic, senseless, full of impure ideas, and as seeking the destruction of religion, and all that is decent in human life. If men were really, as theologians tell us, inclined by Nature to evil, I could imagine *Leaves of Grass* might on the whole do some serious harm. But since, as I think is certainly the case, (for who would not rather be healthy than sick? loved than hated? happy than wretched?) humanity on the whole is far more disposed to good than evil, there is no question that whatever stimulates and encourages the native growth and independent vigor of the mind, as it does, must in the final result be beneficial.

Leaves of Grass belongs to a religious era not yet reached, of which it is the revealer and herald. Toward that higher social and moral level the race was inevitably tending—and thither, even without such an avant-courier, it would still eventually have reached. This book, however, will be of incalculable assistance in the ascent. As John Burroughs has suggested, it may have to wait to be authoritatively assigned to literature's highest rank, first by the law-givers of the Old World, before America really acknowledges her own offspring in Walt Whitman's work. With the incoming moral state to which it belongs, certain cherished social and religious forms and usages are incompatible; hence the deep instinctive aversion and dread with which it is regarded by the ultra-conventional and conservative. Just so, in their far-back times, was Zoroastrianism, Buddhism, Mohammedanism, Christianity, and every new birth received. Our whole theory of property, of individual ownership (for example) is by implication condemned by the spirit of the book, and when its level is reached, our present ideas and practice in this department will seem as backward and outré as the ownership and transfer of one man by another seems to us now. So also our church-going, bible-reading, creeds, and prayers, will appear from its vantage-ground mere make-believes of religion, hollow shells whose kernels have long since imperceptibly mouldered into dust. So does one birth of Time succeed another. So is it still as ever true that the gods are devoured by their own children—that what the deepest and holiest heart-throbs of the race have brought into being, is again successively overwhelmed and destroyed by the legitimate offspring of those same spiritual impulses.

Every marked rise in the moral nature, when it has become diffused over broad sections of the race, necessitates and inspires as its accompaniment, new manners, new social forms, new politics, new philosophies, new literatures, and above all, new religious forms. For moral elevation is the mainspring of all these, and of the world's progress—the rising tide upon which float all the fleets and argosies, as well as all the driftwood and foam, the ascending sap which vitalizes all the fruit of human life. *Leaves of Grass* is the initiative of such a rise, the preface and creator of a new era. This old world has seen many such new departures, and is to see many more before it is done. They have always been begun by one man, embodying what suspends in nebulous forms through the humanity of the time, and from him have spread more or less over the earth's surface. And for their basis these movements have had invariably, since the invention of writing, and in some instances before that time, *a book,* to embody themselves and radiate from. *Leaves of Grass* is such a book. What the Vedas were to Brahmanism, the Law and the Prophets to Judaism, the Avesta and Zend to Zoroastrianism, the Kings to Confucianism and Taoism, the Pitakas to Buddhism, the Gospels and Pauline writings to Christianity, the Quràn to Mohammedanism, will *Leaves of Grass* be to the future of American civilization. Those were all Gospels; they all brought good news to man, fitting his case at the period, each in its way and degree. They were all "hard sayings" and the rankest heresy at first, just as *Leaves of Grass* is now. By and by it too will be received, and in the course of a few hundred years, more or less, do its work and become commonplace like the rest. Then new Gospels will be written upon a still higher plane.

In the mean time, *Leaves of Grass* is the bible of Democracy, containing the highest exemplar of life yet furnished, and suited to the present age and to America. Within it is folded (as the oak in the acorn, or the man in the new-born babe) a new spiritual life for myriads of men and women.

Very few people have any conception what such books are to those who first receive them—what enthusiasm and devotion they inspire—what reckless abandonment to the new feeling of spiritual exaltation they kindle—how they absorb all life, and make the old worldly interests poor and contemptible—how they light up new joys, and end by placing existence on a higher plane. As few to-day realize this, though they have heard and read of it all their lives, so no one, except those who have felt it, can realize what *Leaves of Grass* is to the first men and women who experience its power.

Then from a merely literary, technical, pictorial point of view, where else are so depicted in living words the complex storms of action in the midst of which we of the Nineteenth century live—the trains on the railways, the steam and sail ships and their cargoes, the myriads of factories, the interminable stretches of cultivated land, the towns and villages, with thousands of throbbing lives—curious flashes of the life of wildest Nature (as in **"The Man-of-War Bird"**)—the geography of the globe, the diverse races, circumstances, employments—fraternal love and fratricidal strife—the arming for the war, 1861-65, the fields of battle, victory, defeat, the heaped burial trenches, the hospitals filled with mangled and maimed, the final disbandment of the soldiers—the scenery of a Continent, its rivers, lakes, bays, prairies, mountains, forests, the crags and ravines of Colorado and California, the vast fertile spread of the Prairie States, the snows and wildernesses of the North, the warm bayous and lagoons of the South, the great cities to the East—all the shows of the sea, of the sky, of the seasons—sexual passions, religious mystery, the records of the past, the facts of the present, the hopes of the future—the splendors of life, the equal splendors of death—all the speculations and imaginations of man, all the thoughts of his composite mind, all the visions of his dreaming soul, all the beats of his great heart, all the works of his giant hands—the seething crowds, the passionate longings of men and women everywhere, their fervor and their ceaseless striving, their intense egoism and equally intense sympathy, the attractions and repulsions that sway them from moment to moment, the contradictory forces that dwell in every soul, the passion and energy of the globe. For all these—not in polished literary descriptions, but with their own life and heat and action—make up *Leaves of Grass.* Its themes and treatment, so august, so complex (yet uniform), so tremendous, how curious it is to see the book sneered at for "want of form." Criticism of it from such point of view were a senseless waste of time. Its form will be unprecedently beautiful to all who know its spirit, and to those who do not, it is a matter of no consequence. The function of first-class works is not to follow forms already instituted, but to institute new forms. "He who would achieve the greatest production of art," said Voltaire, "must be the pupil of his own genius." The language in which a book is written will never finally save or condemn it; only the soul of the book counts, nothing else is of any lasting consequence. The three first Gospels were chiefly written by quite illiterate people, and they have no pretensions at all to "style." St. Paul's epistles were written in very bad Greek, and had perhaps still less pretension to mere literary excellence. But in those books lived and through them shone the Soul of a Divine Man. How many hundred tons of classically correct poems, essays, speeches, letters, and dramas have they outlived! and how many will they still outlive! Walt Whitman will endure, not as having reached or conformed to any existing standard, but as having set one up.

Other first-class poets possess a mental scope and grandeur that dwarf ordinary humanity, and intimate existences higher than those of earth. They excite in us admiration and wonder, give us glimpses of celestial beauty and joy, but leave us intrinsically as we were—or perhaps fill us with pain at our own inherent littleness. While no reader of *Leaves of Grass* (once entering their meaning and influence) fails to absorb every piece, every page, every line, as intensely *his*—how strangely different, in their effect, the hitherto accepted poems! We revel amid the beauty, fulness, majesty and art, of the plots and personages of the *Iliad, Odyssey,* or *Æneid,* or in Shakespeare's immortal plays, or Spenser or Milton, or *La legendes des siècles,* or Goethe's masterpieces, or Tennyson's *Idyls.* With them the reader passes his time as in sumptuous dreams or feasts, far from this miserable every-day world, man's actual and vulgar experience, one's own sphere. He enjoys those incomparable works like some sweet, and deep, and beautiful intoxication. But a mortifying and meagre consciousness invariably follows. Not for *him* the stage where Achilles and Coriolanus and Lancelot so grandly tread. He himself dwindles to a mere nothing in comparison with such exceptional types of humanity. However splendid the pageant and the shows of the march, a latent humiliation brings up the rear. Was it not time one should arise to show that a few selected warriors and heroes of the past, even the gods, have not monopolized and devoured (nay, have hardly entered into) the grandeur of the universe, or of life and action, or of poems? arise to "shake out," for common readers, farmers, mechanics, laborers, "carols stronger and haughtier than have ever yet been heard upon the earth"? Well did Thoreau, after reading and visiting Walt Whitman, hit the centre of the matter by exclaiming *"He is Democracy."* For what possible service in that department so great as to practically demonstrate to each of the countless mass of common lives that its scope and sphere are as divine, as heroic, as illuminated, as "eligible," as any? As pure air, wholesome food, clear water, sunshine, pass into and become the life of the body, so do these *Leaves* interpenetrate and nourish the soul that is fitted to receive them. The others stand outside our identity; this poet comes within, and interfuses and incorporates his life with each of us. We share his health, strength, savage freedom, fierce self-assertion, fearlessness, tamelessness. We take part in his large, rugged humanity, his tender love and steadfast faith. The others are for hours of clearness and calm. He suits equally well (perhaps better) with worry, hard work, illness, and affliction. Every-day lives, common employments, become illustrious. For you, "whoever you are," the past has been, the present exists, and the future will exist.

A word, (I ought to have given it farther back) as to the curious *catalogue character,* so hesitatingly dwelt on by not a few—even by Emerson. The latter wrote to Carlyle, sending him an early *Leaves of Grass,* in 1856: "If, on reading, you think its pages the catalogue of an auctioneer, you can light your pipe with them." The book is doubtless open to a charge of the kind. Only it is as if the primary Creator were the "auctioneer," and the spirit in which the lists are made out is the *motif* of all vitality, all form. Or, a new Adam, in a modern and more complex Paradise, here gives names to everything—to mechanics' trades, tools—to our own days, and their commonest objects.

In still hours, reading the biblic poems of the ages, and entirely possessed with them, flits through the brain the phantom thought that in the impalpable atmosphere of those poems' expression and endeavor, man's ultimata are involved; and all the rest, however multitudinous, is only preparation and accessory.

I have been so occupied with the features portrayed through the preceding pages that I have said nothing on a point, or series, partly personal, by no means least in giving character to Walt Whitman and his works. His position in the history of his country is a peculiar one. Receiving the traditions of Washington from men who had seen and talked with that great chieftain—of the old Revolutionary War from those who had been part of it—as a little boy, held in the arms of Lafayette, and his childish lips warmly pressed with a kiss from the French warrior—his youth passed amid the scenes and reminiscences of the gloomy Battle of Brooklyn—the direct memories of that whole contest, of the adoption of the American Constitution, of the close of the last century, and of Jefferson, Adams, Paine, and Hamilton, saturating, as it were, his early years—he brings on and connects that receding time with the Civil War of 1861-65—with the persons and events of our own age—with Lincoln, Grant, Sherman, Lee, the Emancipation Proclamation, the fights around Richmond, and the surrender at Appomattox. Then, the Secession War over, he merges it, or at least the spirit of it, in oblivion. The brotherhood of the States re-united, now indissolubly, he chants a tender and equal sorrow for the Southern as for the Northern dead—in one of his last utterances passionately invoking the Muse, through himself, in their behalf:

> Give me exhaustless, make me a fountain,
> That I exhale love from me wherever I go, like
>   a moist perennial dew,
> For the ashes of all dead soldiers South or
>   North.

Until a long period elapses few will know what the pages of *Leaves of Grass* bestow on America. Granting all its unprecedented thrift and material power, the question arises to serious inquiry, Is the New World Republic actually a success on any but lower grounds? Is there not, to its heart-action and blood-circulation to-day, a profound danger, a pervading lack of something to be supplied, without which its richest and amplest fruits will continually turn to ashes? It is in response to such inquiry, and supply to such deficiency (or rather to suggest the means of every man supplying it within himself, and as part of himself) I consider Walt Whitman's life and poems unspeakably important. (pp. 175-90)

> *Richard Maurice Bucke, in his* Walt Whitman, *1883. Reprint by Johnson Reprint Corporation, 1970, 236 p.*

Walt Whitman   (essay date 1888)

[*In the following excerpt from the essay "A Backward Glance o'er Travel'd Roads," Whitman examines his literary career.*]

[Whitman adds in a footnote: "As there are now several editions of **L. of G.,** different texts and dates, I wish to say that I prefer and recommend the present one, complete, for future printing, if there should be any; a copy and facsimile, indeed, of the text of these 422 pages. The subsequent interval which is so important to form'd and launch'd works, books, especially, has pass'd; and waiting till fully after that, I give these concluding words."]

Perhaps the best of songs heard, or of any all true love, or life's fairest episodes, or sailors', soldiers' trying scenes on land or sea, is the *résumé* of them, or any of them, long afterwards, looking at the actualities away back past, with all their practical excitations gone. How the soul loves to float amid such reminiscences!

So here I sit gossiping in the early candle-light of old age—I and my book—casting backward glances over our travel'd road. After completing, as it were, the journey—(a varied jaunt of years, with many halts and gaps of intervals—or some lengthen'd ship-voyage, wherein more than once the last hour had apparently arrived, and we seem'd certainly going down—yet reaching port in a sufficient way through all discomfitures at last)—After completing my poems, I am curious to review them in the light of their own (at the time unconscious, or mostly unconscious) intentions, with certain unfoldings of the thirty years they seek to embody. These lines, therefore, will probably blend the weft of first purposes and speculations, with the warp of that experience afterwards, always bringing strange developments.

Result of seven or eight stages and struggles extending through nearly thirty years, (as I nigh my three-score-and-ten I live largely on memory,) I look upon *Leaves of Grass,* now finish'd to the end of its opportunities and powers, as my definitive *carte visite* to the coming generations of the New World, if I may assume to say so. That I have not gain'd the acceptance of my own time, but have fallen back on fond dreams of the future—anticipations—("still lives the song, though Regnar dies")—That from a wordly and business point of view *Leaves of Grass* has been worse than a failure—that public criticism on the book and myself as author of it yet shows mark'd anger and contempt more than anything else—("I find a solid line of enemies to you everywhere,"—letter from W. S. K., Boston, May 28, 1884)—And that solely for publishing it I have been the object of two or three pretty serious special official buffetings—is all probably no more than I ought to have expected. I had my choice when I commenc'd. I bid neither for soft eulogies, big money returns, nor the approbation of existing schools and conventions. As fulfill'd, or partially fulfill'd, the best comfort of the whole business (after a small band of the dearest friends and upholders ever vouchsafed to man or cause—doubtless all the more faithful and uncompromising—this little phalanx!—for being so few) is that, unstopp'd and unwarp'd by any influence outside the soul within me, I have had my say entirely my own way, and put it unerringly on record—the value thereof to be decided by time.

In calculating that decision, William O'Connor and Dr. Bucke are far more peremptory than I am. Behind all else that can be said, I consider *Leaves of Grass* and its theory experimental—as, in the deepest sense, I consider our American republic itself to be, with its theory. (I think I have at least enough philosophy not to be too absolutely certain of any thing, or any results.) In the second place, the volume is a *sortie*—whether to prove triumphant, and conquer its field of aim and escape and construction, nothing less than a hundred years from now can fully answer. I consider the point that I have positively gain'd a hearing, to far more than make up for any and all other lacks and withholdings. Essentially, *that* was from the first, and has remain'd throughout, the main object. Now it seems to be achiev'd, I am certainly contented to waive any otherwise momentous drawbacks, as of little account. Candidly and dispassionately reviewing all my intentions, I feel that they were creditable—and I accept the result, whatever it may be.

After continued personal ambition and effort, as a young fellow, to enter with the rest into competition for the usual rewards, business, political, literary, &c.—to take part in the great *mêlée,* both for victory's prize itself and to do some good—After years of those aims and pursuits, I found myself remaining possess'd, at the age of thirty-one to thirty-three, with a special desire and conviction. Or rather, to be quite exact, a desire that had been flitting through my previous life, or hovering on the flanks, mostly indefinite hitherto, had steadily advanced to the front, defined itself, and finally dominated everything else. This was a feeling or ambition to articulate and faithfully express in literary or poetic form, and uncompromisingly, my own physical, emotional, moral, intellectual, and æsthetic Personality, in the midst of, and tallying, the momentous spirit and facts of its immediate days, and of current America—and to exploit that Personality, identified with place and date, in a far more candid and comprehensive sense than any hitherto poem or book.

Perhaps this is in brief, or suggests, all I have sought to do. Given the Nineteenth Century, with the United States, and what they furnish as area and points of view, *Leaves of Grass* is, or seeks to be, simply a faithful and doubtless self-will'd record. In the midst of all, it gives one man's—the author's—identity, ardors, observations, faiths, and thoughts, color'd hardly at all with any decided coloring from other faiths or other identities. Plenty of songs had been sung—beautiful, matchless songs—adjusted to other lands than these—another spirit and stage of evolution; but I would sing, and leave out or put in, quite solely with reference to America and to-day. Modern science and democracy seem'd to be throwing out their challenge to poetry to put them in its statements in contradistinction to the songs and myths of the past. As I see it now (perhaps too late,) I have unwittingly taken up that challenge and made an attempt at such statements—which I certainly would not assume to do now, knowing more clearly what it means.

For grounds for *Leaves of Grass,* as a poem, I abandon'd the conventional themes, which do not appear in it: none of the stock ornamentation, or choice plots of love or war, or high, exceptional personages of Old-World song; nothing, as I may say, for beauty's sake—no legend, or myth, or romance, nor euphemism, nor rhyme. But the broadest average of humanity and its identities in the now ripening Nineteenth Century, and especially in each of their countless examples and practical occupations in the United States to-day.

One main contrast of the ideas behind every page of my verses, compared with establish'd poems, is their different relative attitude towards God, towards the objective universe, and still more (by reflection, confession, assumption, &c.) the quite changed attitude of the ego, the one chanting or talking, towards himself and towards his fellow-humanity. It is certainly time for America, above all, to begin this readjustment in the scope and basic point of view of verse; for everything else has changed. As I write, I see in an article on Wordsworth, in one of the current English magazines, the lines, "A few weeks ago an eminent French critic said that, owing to the special tendency to science and to its all-devouring force, poetry would cease to be read in fifty years." But I anticipate the very contrary. Only a firmer, vastly broader, new area begins to exist—nay, is already form'd—to which the poetic genius must emigrate. Whatever may have been the case in years gone by, the true use for the imaginative faculty of modern times is to give ultimate vivification to facts, to science, and to common lives, endowing them with the glows and glories and final illustriousness which belong to every real thing, and to real things only. Without that ultimate vivification—which the poet or other artist alone can give—reality would seem incomplete, and science, democracy, and life itself, finally in vain.

Few appreciate the moral revolutions, our age, which have

been profounder far than the material or inventive or war-produced ones. The Nineteenth Century, now well towards its close (and ripening into fruit the seeds of the two preceding centuries)—the uprisings of national masses and shiftings of boundary-lines—the historical and other prominent facts of the United States—the war of attempted Secession—the stormy rush and haste of nebulous forces—never can future years witness more excitement and din of action—never completer change of army front along the whole line, the whole civilized world. For all these new and evolutionary facts, meanings, purposes, new poetic messages, new forms and expressions, are inevitable.

My Book and I—what a period we have presumed to span! those thirty years from 1850 to '80—and America in them! Proud, proud indeed may we be, if we have cull'd enough of that period in its own spirit to worthily waft a few live breaths of it to the future! (pp. 561-65)

Without yielding an inch the working-man and working-woman were to be in my pages from first to last. The ranges of heroism and loftiness with which Greek and feudal poets endow'd their god-like or lordly born characters—indeed prouder and better based and with fuller ranges than those—I was to endow the democratic averages of America. I was to show that we, here and to-day, are eligible to the grandest and the best—more eligible now than any times of old were. I will also want my utterances (I said to myself before beginning) to be in spirit the poems of the morning. (They have been founded and mainly written in the sunny forenoon and early midday of my life.) I will want them to be the poems of women entirely as much as men. I have wish'd to put the complete Union of the States in my songs without any preference or partiality whatever. Henceforth, if they live and are read, it must be just as much South as North—just as much along the Pacific as Atlantic—in the valley of the Mississippi, in Canada, up in Maine, down in Texas, and on the shores of Puget Sound.

From another point of view *Leaves of Grass* is avowedly the song of Sex and Amativeness, and even Animality—though meanings that do not usually go along with those words are behind all, and will duly emerge; and all are sought to be lifted into a different light and atmosphere. Of this feature, intentionally palpable in a few lines, I shall only say the espousing principle of those lines so gives breath of life to my whole scheme that the bulk of the pieces might as well have been left unwritten were those lines omitted. Difficult as it will be, it has become, in my opinion, imperative to achieve a shifted attitude from superior men and women towards the thought and fact of sexuality, as an element in character, personality, the emotions, and a theme in literature. I am not going to argue the question by itself; it does not stand by itself. The vitality of it is altogether in its relations, bearings, significance—like the clef of a symphony. At last analogy the lines I allude to, and the spirit in which they are spoken, permeate all *Leaves of Grass,* and the work must stand or fall with them, as the human body and soul must remain as an entirety.

Universal as are certain facts and symptoms of communities or individuals all times, there is nothing so rare in modern conventions and poetry as their normal recognizance. Literature is always calling in the doctor for consultation and confession, and always giving evasions and swathing suppressions in place of that "heroic nudity" on which only a genuine diagnosis of serious cases can be built. And in respect to edictions of *Leaves of Grass* in time to come (if there should be such) I take occasion now to confirm those lines with the settled convictions and deliberate renewals of thirty years, and to hereby prohibit, as far as word of mine can do so, any elision of them.

Then still a purpose enclosing all, and over and beneath all. Ever since what might be call'd thought, or the budding of thought, fairly began in my youthful mind, I had had a desire to attempt some worthy record of that entire faith and acceptance ("to justify the ways of God to man" is Milton's well-known and ambitious phrase) which is the foundation of moral America. I felt it all as positively then in my young days as I do now in my old ones; to formulate a poem whose every thought or fact should directly or indirectly be or connive at an implict belief in the wisdom, health, mystery, beauty of every process, every concrete object, every human or other existence, not only consider'd from the point of view at all, but of each.

While I can not understand it or argue it out, I fully believe in a clue and purpose in Nature, entire and several; and that invisible spiritual results, just as real and definite as the visible, eventuate all concrete life and all materialism, through Time. My book ought to emanate buoyancy and gladness legitimately enough, for it was grown out of those elements, and has been the comfort of my life since it was originally commenced.

One main genesis-motive of the *Leaves* was my conviction (just as strong to-day as ever) that the crowning growth of the United States is to be spiritual and heroic. To help start and favor that growth—or even to call attention to it, or the need of it—is the beginning, middle and final purpose of the poems. (In fact, when really cipher'd out and summ'd to the last, plowing up in earnest the interminable average fellows of humanity—not "good government" merely, in the common sense—is the justification and main purpose of these United States.)

Isolated advantages in any rank or grace or fortune—the direct or indirect threads of all the poetry of the past—are in my opinion distasteful to the republican genius, and offer no foundation for its fitting verse. Establish'd poems, I know, have the very great advantage of chanting the already perform'd, so full of glories, reminiscences dear to the minds of men. But my volume is a candidate for the future. "All original art," says Taine, anyhow, "is self-regulated, and no original art can be regulated from without; it carries its own counterpoise, and does not receive it from elsewhere—lives on its own blood"—a solace to my frequent bruises and sulky vanity.

As the present is perhaps mainly an attempt at personal statement or illustration, I will allow myself as further help to extract the following anecdote from a book, *Annals of Old Painters,* conn'd by me in youth. Rubens, the Flemish painter, in one of his wanderings through the galleries of old convents, came across a singular work. After looking at it thoughtfully for a good while, and listening to the criticisms of his suite of students, he said to the latter, in answer to their questions (as to what school the work implied or belong'd,) "I do not believe the artist, unknown and perhaps no longer living, who has given the world this legacy, ever belong'd to any school, or ever painted anything but this one picture, which is a personal affair—a piece out of a man's life."

Leaves of Grass indeed (I cannot too often reiterate) has mainly been the outcropping of my own emotional and other personal nature—an attempt, from first to last, to put *a Person,* a human being (myself, in the latter half of the Nineteenth Century, in America,) freely, fully and truly on record. I could not find any similar personal record in current literature that satisfied me. But it is not on *Leaves of Grass* distinctively as *literature,* or a specimen thereof, that I feel to dwell, or advance claims. No one will get at my verses who insists upon viewing them as a literary performance, or attempt at such performance, or as aiming mainly toward art or æstheticism.

I say no land or people or circumstances ever existed so needing a race of singers and poems differing from all others, and rigidly their own, as the land and people and cir-

Whitman caricatured by Max Beerbohm.

cumstances of our United States need such singers and poems to-day, and for the future. Still further, as long as the States continue to absorb and be dominated by the poetry of the Old World, and remain unsupplied with autochthonous song, to express, vitalize and give color to and define their material and political success, and minister to them distinctively, so long will they stop short of first-class Nationality and remain defective.

In the free evening of my day I give to you, reader, the foregoing garrulous talk, thoughts, reminiscences,

> As idly drifting down the ebb,
> Such ripples, half-caught voices, echo from the
>   shore.

Concluding with two items for the imaginative genius of the West, when it worthily rises—First, what Herder taught to the young Goethe, that really great poetry is always (like the Homeric or Biblical canticles) the result of a national spirit, and not the privilege of a polish'd and select few; Second, that the strongest and sweetest songs yet remain to be sung. (pp. 571-74)

> *Walt Whitman, "A Backward Glance o'er Travel'd Roads and Prefatory Letter," in his* Leaves of Grass, *edited by Harold W. Blodgett and Sculley Bradley, 1965. Reprint by W. W. Norton & Company, Inc., 1968, pp. 559-74.*

Havelock Ellis   (essay date 1890)

[*Ellis was a pioneering sexual psychologist and a respected English man of letters. His most famous work is his seven-volume* Psychology of Sex *(1897-1928), a study containing frankly stated case histories of sex-related psychological abnormalities that was greatly responsible for changing British and American attitudes toward the hitherto forbidden subject of sexuality. In addition to his psychological writings, Ellis edited the Mermaid Series of sixteenth to eighteenth century English dramatists (1887-89) and retained an active interest in literature throughout his life. As a critic, according to Desmond MacCarthy, Ellis looked for the expression of the individuality of the author under discussion. "The first question he asked himself as a critic," wrote MacCarthy, "was 'What does this writer affirm?' The next, 'How did he come to affirm precisely that?' His statement of a writer's 'message' was always trenchant and clear, his psychological analysis of the man extremely acute, and the estimate of the value of his contribution impartial. What moved him most in literature was the sincere expression of preferences and beliefs, and the energy which springs from sincerity." In the following excerpt, Ellis examines Whitman's outlook on morality, ego, and love.*]

It is not as an artist that Whitman is chiefly interesting to us. It is true that he has written **"Out of the Cradle Endlessly Rocking," "When Lilacs Last in the Dooryard Bloomed," "This Compost,"** and other fragments from which may be gained a simple and pure æsthetic joy. Frequently, also, we come across phrases which reveal a keen perception of the strangeness and beauty of things, lines that possess a simplicity and grandeur scarcely less than

Homeric; thus, "the noiseless splash of sunrise"; or of the young men bathing, who "float on their backs, their white bellies bulge to the sun." But such results are accidental, and outside the main purpose. For that very reason they have at times something of the divine felicity, unforeseen and incalculable, of Nature; yet always, according to a rough but convenient distinction, it is the poetry of energy rather than the poetry of art. When Whitman speaks prose, the language of science, he is frequently incoherent, emotional, unbalanced, with no very just and precise sense of the meaning of words or the structure of reasoned language. It is clear that in this man the moral in its largest sense—that is to say, the personality and its personal relations—is more developed than the scientific; and that on the æsthetic side the artist is merged in the mystic, wrapt in emotional contemplation of a cosmic whole. What we see, therefore, is a manifold personality seeking expression for itself in a peculiarly flexible and responsive medium. It is a deep as well as a superficial resemblance that these changes bear to the Scriptures of the old Hebrews—as Isaiah or the Book of Job—wherein also the writer becomes an artist, and also absorbs all available science, but where his purpose is the personal expression of a moral and religious conception of life and the world. Whitman has invented a name for the person who occupies this rare and, in the highest degree, significant position; he calls him the "Answerer." It is not the function of answerers, like that of philosophers, to arrange the order and limits of ideas, for they have to settle what ideas are or are not to exist; nor is it theirs, like the singers, to celebrate the ostensible things of the world, or to seek out imaginative forms, for they are "not followers of beauty, but the august masters of beauty." The answerer is, in short, the maker of ideals.

Whitman will not minimize the importance of the answerer's mission. "I, too," he exclaims, "following many and followed by many, inaugurate a religion." If we wish to understand Walt Whitman, we must have some conception of this religion. We shall find that two great and contradictory conceptions dominate his work; although in his thoughts, as in his modes of expression, it is not possible to find any strongly marked progression.

The **"Song of Myself"** is the most complete utterance of Whitman's first great conception of life.

> I have said that the soul is not more than the
>   body,
> And I have said that the body is not more than
>   the soul;
> And nothing, not God, is greater to one than
>   one's self is.

The absolute unity of matter and spirit, and all which that unity involves, is the dominant conception of this first and most characteristic period. "If the body were not the soul," he asks, "what is the soul?" This is Whitman's naturalism; it is the re-assertion of the Greek attitude on a new and larger foundation. "Let it stand as an indubitable truth, which no inquiries can shake, that the mind of man is so entirely alienated from the righteousness of God, that he cannot conceive, desire, or design anything but what is wicked, distorted, foul, impure and iniquitous; that his heart is so thoroughly environed by sin that it can breathe out nothing but corruption and rottenness." That is the fundamental thought of Christian tradition set down in the "Institutes," clearly and logically, by the genius of Calvin. It is the polar opposite of Whitman's thought, and therefore for Whitman the moral conception of duty has ceased to exist.

> I give nothing as duties,
> What others give as duties I give as living im-
> pulses.
> (Shall I give the heart's action as a duty?)

Morality is thus the normal activity of a healthy nature, not the product either of tradition or of rationalism.

"Whatever tastes sweet to the most perfect person, that is finally right"—this, it has been said, is the maxim on which Whitman's morality is founded, and it is the morality of Aristotle. But no Greek ever asserted and illustrated it with such emphatic iteration.

From the days when the Greek spirit found its last embodiment in the brief songs, keen or sweet, of the "Anthology," the attitude which Whitman represents is the **"Song of Myself "** has never lacked representatives. Throughout the Middle Ages those strange haunting echoes to the perpetual chant of litany and psalm, the Latin student-songs, float across all Europe with their profane and gay paganism, their fresh erotic grace, their "In taberna quando sumus," their "Ludo cum Cæcilia," their "Gaudeamus igitur." In the sane and lofty sensuality of Boccaccio, as it found expression in the history of Alaciel and many another wonderful story, and in Gottfried of Strasburg's assertion of human pride and passion in *Tristan and Isolde,* the same strain changed to a stronger and nobler key. Then came the great wave of the Renaissance through Italy and France and England, filling art and philosophy with an exaltation of physical life, and again later, in the movements that center around the French Revolution, an exaltation of arrogant and independent intellectual life. But all these manifestations were sometimes partial, sometimes extravagant; they were impulses of the natural man surging up in rebellion against the dominant Christian temper; they were, for the most part consciously, of the nature of reactions. We feel that there is a fatal lack about them which Christianity would have filled; only in Goethe is the antagonism to some extent reconciled. Beneath the vast growth of Christianity, for ever exalting the unseen by the easy method of pouring contempt on the seen, and still ever producing some strange and exquisite flower of *ascêsis*—some Francis or Thereas or Fénelon—a slow force was working underground. A tendency was making itself felt to find in the theoretically despised physical—in those every-day stones which the builders of the Church had rejected—the very foundation of the mysteries of life; if not the basis for a new vision of the unseen, yet for a more assured vision of the seen.

No one in the last century expressed this tendency more impressively and thoroughly, with a certain insane energy, than William Blake—the great chained spirit whom we see looking out between the bars of his prisonhouse with those wonderful eyes. Especially in "The Marriage of Heaven and Hell," in which he seems to gaze most clearly "through narrow chinks of his cavern," he has set forth his conviction that "first the notion that man has a body distinct from his soul is to be expunged," and that "if the doors of perception were cleansed, everything would appear to man, as it is, infinite." This most extraordinary book is, in his own phraseology, the Bible of Hell.

Whitman appeared at a time when this stream of influence, grown mighty, had boldly emerged. At the time that *Leaves of Grass* sought the light Turgenev was embodying in the typical figure of Bassaroff the modern militant spirit of science, positive and audacious—a spirit marked also, as Hinton pointed out, by a new form of asceticism, which lay in the denial of emotion. Whitman, one of the very greatest emotional forces of modern times, who had grown up apart from the rigid and technical methods of science, face to face with a new world and a new civilization, which he had eagerly absorbed so far as it lay open to him, had the good inspiration to fling himself into the scientific current, and so to justify the demands of his emotional nature; to represent himself as the inhabitant of a vast and coordinated cosmos, tenoned and mortised in granite:

> All forces have been steadily employed to com-
> plete and delight me,
> Now on this spot I stand with my robust soul.

That Whitman possessed no trained scientific instinct is unquestionably true, but it is impossible to estimate his significance without understanding what he owes to science. Something, indeed, he had gained from the philosophy of Hegel—with its conception of the universe as a single process of evolution, in which vice and disease are but transient perturbations—with which he had a second-hand acquaintance that has left distinct, but not always well assimilated, marks on his work; but, above all, he was indebted to those scientific conceptions which, like Emerson, he had absorbed or divined. It is these that lie behind "Children of Adam."

This mood of sane and cheerful sensuality, rejoicing with a joy as massive and calm-eyed as Boccaccio's, a moral-fibered joy that Boccaccio never knew, in all the manifestations of the flesh and blood of the world—saying, not: "Let us eat and drink, for to-morrow we die," but, with Clifford: "Let us take hands and help, for this day we are alive together"—is certainly Whitman's most significant and impressive mood. Nothing so much reveals its depth and sincerity as his never-changing attitude towards death. We know the "fearful thing" that Claudio, in Shakespeare's play, knew as death:

> to die and go we know not where;
> To lie in cold obstruction and to rot;
> . . . . to be worse than worst
> Of those that lawless and uncertain thoughts
> Imagine howling!

And all the Elizabethans in that age of splendid and daring life—even Raleigh and Bacon—felt that same shudder at the horror and mystery of death. Always they felt behind them some vast medieval charnel-house, gloomy and awful, and the sunniest spirits of the English Renaissance quail when they think of it. There was in this horror something of the child's vast and unreasoned dread of darkness and mystery, and it scarcely survived the scientific and philosophic developments of the seventeenth century. Whitman's attitude is not the less deep-rooted and original. For he is not content to argue, haughtily indifferent, with Epicurus and Epictetus, that death can be nothing to us, because it is no evil to lose what we shall never miss. Whitman will reveal the loveliness of death. We feel constantly in *Leaves of Grass* as to some extent we feel before the *Love and Death* and some other pictures of one of the greatest of English artists. "I will show," he announces, "that nothing can happen more beautiful than death." It must not be forgotten that Whitman speaks not merely from the standpoint of the most intense and vivid delight in the actual world, but that he possessed a practical familiarity with disease and death which has perhaps never before fallen to the lot of a great writer. At the end of the **"Song of Myself"** he bequeaths himself to the dust, to grow from the grass he loves:

> If you want me again, look for me under your
>   bootsoles,
> You will hardly know who I am or what I mean,
> But I shall be good health to you nevertheless,
> And filter and fiber your blood.

And to any who find that dust but a poor immortality, he would say with Schopenhauer, "Oho! do you know, then, what dust is?" The vast chemistry of the earth, the sweetness that is rooted in what we call corruption, the life that is but the leavings of many deaths, is nobly uttered in **"This Compost,"** in which he reaches beyond the corpse that is good manure to sweet-scented roses, to the polished breasts of melons; or again, in the noble elegy, **"Pensive on Her Dead Gazing,"** on those who died during the war. In his most perfectly lyrical poem, **"Out of the Cradle Endlessly Rocking,"** Whitman has celebrated death—"that strong and delicious world"—with strange tenderness; and never has the loveliness of death been sung in a more sane and virile song than the solemn death-carol in **"When Lilacs Last in the Dooryard Bloomed"**:

> Dark mother, always gliding near with soft feet,
> Have none chanted for thee a chart of fullest
>   welcome?
> Then I chant it for thee, I glorify thee above all,
> I bring thee a song, that when thou must indeed
>   come, come unfalteringly.
>
>   . . . . .
>
> Over the tree-tops I float thee a song,
> Over the rising and sinking waves, over the myr-
>   iad fields and the prairies wide,
> Over the dense-packed cities all and the teeming
>   wharves and ways,
> I float this carol with joy, with joy to thee, O
>   Death.

Whitman's second great thought on life lies in his egoism. His intense sense of individuality was marked from the first; it is emphatically asserted in the **"Song of Myself"**—

> And nothing, not God, is greater to one than
>   one's self is—

where it lies side by side with his first great thought. But even in the **"Song of Myself"** it asserts a separate existence:

> This day before dawn I ascended a hill and
>   looked at the crowded heaven,
> And I said to my spirit, *When we become the en-*
>   *folders of those orbs, and the pleasure and*
>   *knowledge of everything in them, shall we be*
>   *filled and satisfied then?*
> And my spirit said, *No, we but level that lift to*
>   *pass and continue beyond.*

In the end he once, at least, altogether denies his first thought; he alludes to that body which he had called the equal of the soul, or even the soul itself, as excrement:

> Myself discharging my excrementitious body to
>   be burned, or reduced to powder, or buried,
> My real body doubtless left to me for other
>   spheres.

The first great utterance was naturalistic; this egoism is spiritualistic. It is the sublime apotheosis of Yankee self-reliance. "I only am he who places over you no master, owner, better, God, beyond what waits intrinsically in yourself." This became the dominant conception in Whitman's later work, and fills his universe at length. Of a God, although he sometimes uses the word to obtain emphasis, he at no time had any definite idea. Nature, also, was never a living vascular personality for him; when it is not a mere aggregate of things, it is an order, sometimes a moral order. Also he wisely refuses with unswerving consistency to admit an abstract Humanity; of "man" he has nothing to say; there is nothing anywhere in the universe for him but individuals, undying, everlastingly aggrandizing individuals. This egoism is practical, strenuous, moral; it cannot be described as religious. Whitman is lacking—and in this respect he comes nearer to Goethe than to any other great modern man—in what may be possibly the disease of "soul," the disease that was so bitterly bewailed by Heine. Whitman was congenitally deficient in "soul"; he is a kind of Titanic Undine. "I never had any particular religious experiences," he told Bucke, "never felt the need of spiritual regeneration"; and although he describes himself as "pleased with the earnest words of the sweating Methodist preacher, impressed seriously at the camp-meeting," we know what weight to give to this utterance when we read elsewhere, of animals:

> They do not sweat and whine about their condi-
>   tion,
> They do not lie awake in the dark and weep for
>   their sins,
> They do not make me sick discussing their duty
>   to God,
> Not one is dissatisfied, not one is demented with
>   the mania of owning things,
> Not one kneels to another, nor to his kind that
>   lived thousands of years ago,
> Not one is respectable or unhappy over the
>   whole earth.

We may detect this lack of "soul" in his attitude towards music; for, in its highest development, music is the special exponent of the modern soul in its complexity, its passive resignation, its restless mystical ardors. That Whitman delighted in music is clear; it is equally clear, from the testimony of his writings and of witnesses, that the music he delighted in was simple and joyous melody as in Rossini's operas; he alludes vaguely to symphonies, but

> when it is a grand opera,
> Ah! this indeed is music—this suits me.

That Whitman could have truly appreciated Beethoven, or understood Wagner's *Tannhäuser,* is not conceivable.

With Whitman's egoism is connected his strenuousness. There is a stirring sound of trumpets always among these *Leaves of Grass.* This man may have come, as he tells us, to inaugurate a new religion, but he has few or no marks upon him of that mysticism—that Eastern spirit of glad renunciation of the self in a larger self—which is of the essence of religion. He is at the head of a band of sinewy and tan-faced pioneers, with pistols in their belts and sharp-edged axes in their hands:

> And he going with me leaves peace and routine
> behind him,
> And stakes his life to be lost at any moment.

This strenuousness finds expression in the hurried jolt and bustle of the lines, always alert, unresting, ever starting afresh. Passages of sweet and peaceful flow are hard to find in *Leaves of Grass,* and the more precious when found. Whitman hardly succeeds in the expression of joy; to feel exquisitely the pulse of gladness a more passive and feminine sensibility is needed, like that we meet with in **"Towards Democracy"**; we must not come to this focus of radiant energy for repose or consolation.

This egoism, this strenuousness, reaches at the end to heights of sublime audacity. When we read certain portions of *"Leaves of Grass"* we seem to see a vast phalanx of Great Companions passing for ever along the cosmic roads, stalwart Pioneers of the Universe. There are superb young men, athletic girls, splendid and savage old men—for the weak seem to have perished by the roadside—and they radiate an infinite energy, an infinite joy. It is truly a tremendous diastole of life to which the crude and colossal extravagance of this vision bears witness; we weary soon of its strenuous vitality, and crave for the systole of life, for peace and repose. It is not strange that the immense faith of the prophet himself grows hesitant and silent at times before "all the meanness and agony without end," and doubts that it is an illusion and "that may-be identity beyond the grave a beautiful fable only." Here and again we meet this access of doubt, and even amid the faith of the **"Prayer of Columbus"** there is a tremulous, pathetic note of sadness.

Yet there is one keen sword with which Whitman is always able to cut the knot of this doubt—the sword of love. He has but to grasp love and comradeship, and he grows indifferent to the problem of identity beyond the grave. "He a-hold of my hand has completely satisfied me." He discovers at last that love and comradeship—adhesiveness—is, after all, the main thing, "base and finale, too, for all metaphysics"; deeper than religion, underneath Socrates and underneath Christ. With a sound insight he finds the roots of the most universal love in the intimate and physical love of comrades and lovers:

> I mind how once we lay, such a transparent summer morning,
> How you settled your head athwart my hips and gently turned over upon me,
> And parted the shirt from my bosom-bone, and plunged your tongue to my bare-stript heart,
> And reached till you felt my beard, and reached till you held my feet.
> Swiftly arose and spread around me the peace and knowledge that pass all the argument of the earth,
> And I know that the hand of God is the promise of my own,
> And I know that the spirit of God is the brother of my own,
> And that all the men ever born are also my brothers, and the women my sisters and lovers,
> And that a kelson of the creation is love.

This "love" of Whitman's is a very personal matter; of an abstract Man, a *solidaire* Humanity, he never speaks; it does not appear ever to have occurred to him that so extraordinary a conception can be formulated; his relations to men generally spring out of his relations to particular men. He has touched and embraced his fellows' flesh; he has felt throughout his being the mysterious reverberations of the contact:

> There is something in staying close to men and women and looking on them, and in the contact and odor of them, that pleases the soul well,
> All things please the soul, but these please the soul well.

This personal and intimate fact is the center from which the whole of Whitman's morality radiates. Of an abstract Humanity, it is true, he has never thought; he has no vision of Nature as a spiritual Presence; God is to him a word only, without vitality; to Art he is mostly indifferent; yet there remains this great moral kernel, springing from the sexual impulse, taking practical root in a singularly rich and vivid emotional nature, and bearing within it the promise of a city of lovers and friends.

This moral element is one of the central features in Whitman's attitude towards sex and the body generally. For the lover there is nothing in the loved one's body impure or unclean; a breath of passion has passed over it, and all things are sweet. For most of this influence spreads no farther; for the man of strong moral instinct it covers all human things in infinitely widening circles; his heart goes out to every creature that shares the loved one's delicious humanity; henceforth there is nothing human that he cannot touch with reverence and love. *Leaves of Grass* is penetrated by this moral element. How curiously far this attitude is from the old Christian way we realize when we turn to those days in which Christianity was at its height, and see how Saint Bernard with his mild and ardent gaze looked out into the world of Nature and saw men as "stinking spawn, sacks of dung, the food of worms."

But there is another element in Whitman's attitude—the artistic. It shows itself in a two-fold manner. Whitman came of a vigorous Dutch stock; these van Velsors from Holland have fully as large a part in him as anything his

English ancestry gave him, and his Dutch race shows itself chiefly in his artistic manner. The supreme achievement in art of the Dutch is their seventeenth-century painting. What marked those Dutch artists was the ineradicable conviction that every action, social or physiological, of the average man, woman, child, around them might be, with love and absolute faithfulness, phlegmatically set forth. In their heroic earthliness they could at no point be repulsed; color and light may aureole their work, but the most commonplace things of Nature shall have the largest nimbus. That is the temper of Dutch art throughout; no other art in the world has the same characteristics. In the art of Whitman alone do we meet with it again, impatient indeed and broken up into fragments, pierced through with shafts of light from other sources, but still constant and unmistakable. The other artistic element in Whitman's attitude is modern; it is almost the only artistic element by which, unconsciously perhaps, he allies himself to modern traditions in art instead of breaking through them by his own volcanic energy—a curious research for sexual imagery in Nature, imagery often tinged by bizarre and mystical color. Rossetti occasionally uses sexual imagery with rare felicity, as in "Nuptial Sleep":

> And as the last slow sudden drops are shed
> From sparkling eaves when all the storm has
>   fled,
> So singly flagged the pulses of each heart.

With still greater beauty and audacity Whitman, in **"I Sing the Body Electric,"** celebrates the last abandonment of love:

> Bridegroom night of love working surely and
>   softly into the prostrate dawn,
> Undulating into the willing and yielding day,
> Lost in the cleave of the clasping and sweet-
>   fleshed day.

Or, again, in the marvelously keen **"Faces"**—so realistic and so imaginative—when the "lily's face" speaks out her longing to be filled with albescent honey. This man has certainly felt the truth of that deep saying of Thoreau's, that for him to whom sex is impure there are no flowers in Nature. He cannot help speaking of man's or woman's life in terms of Nature's life, of Nature's life in terms of man's; he mingles them together with an admirably balanced rhythm, as in **"Spontaneous Me."** All the functions of man's or woman's life are sweet to him because they bear about them a savor of the things that are sweet to him anywhere in the world,

> Of the smell of apples and lemons, of the pairing
>   of birds,
> Of the wet of woods, of the lapping of waves.

Sometimes when he is on this track he seems to lose himself in mystic obscurity; and the words in which he records his impressions are mere patches of morbid color. (pp. 103-21)

Behind *Leaves of Grass* stands the personality of the man Walt Whitman; that is the charm of the book and its power. It is, in his own words, the record of a *Person*. A man has here sought to give a fresh and frank representation of his nature—physical, intellectual, moral, æsthetic—as he received it, and as it grew in the great field of the world. Sometimes there is an element in this record which, while perhaps very American, reminds one of the great Frenchman who shouted so lustily through his huge brass trumpet, seated on the apex of the universe in the Avenue d'Eylau. The noble lines to **"You Felons on Trial in Courts"** accompany **"To Him that Was Crucified."** Such rhetorical flourishes do not impair the value of this revelation. The self-revelation of a human personality is the one supremely precious and enduring thing. All art is the search for it. The strongest and most successful of religions were avowedly founded on personalities, more or less dimly seen. The intimate and candid record of personality alone gives quickening energy to books. Herein is the might of *Leaves of Grass.*

In our overstrained civilization the tendency in literature—and in life as it acts on literature and is again reacted on by it—is, on the one hand, towards an artificial mode of presentment, that is, a divorce between the actual and the alleged, a divorce which, in the language of satire, is often called hypocrisy. On the other hand, the tendency is towards a singleness of aim and ideal indeed, but a thin, narrow, superrefined ideal, at the same time rather hysterical and rather prim. In youth we cannot see through these Tartuffes and *Précieuses;* when we become grown men and women we feel a great thirst for Nature, for reality in literature, and we slake it at such fountains as this of *Leaves of Grass.* Like Antæus of old we bow down to touch the earth, to come in contact with the great primal energies of Nature, and to grow strong. We realize that the structure of the world is indeed built most gloriously on the immense pillars of Hunger and Love, and we will not seek to deny or to attenuate its foundations. Presenting a truth so abstract in fresh and living concrete language, this man, as an Adam in a new Paradise, which is the very world itself, walks again upon the earth, sometimes with calm complaisance, sometimes "deliriating" wildly:

> Behold me where I pass, hear my voice, ap-
>   proach,
> Touch me, touch the palm of your hand to my
>   body as I pass,
> Be not afraid of my body.

He has tossed "a new gladness and roughness" among men and women. He has opened a fresh channel of Nature's force into human life—the largest since Wordsworth, and more fit for human use—"the amplitude of the earth, and the coarseness and sexuality of the earth, and the great charity of the earth, and the equilibrium also." And in his vigorous masculine love, asserting his own personality he has asserted that of all—"By God! I will accept nothing which all cannot have their counterpart of on the same terms." Charging himself in every place with contentment and triumph, he embraces all men, as St. Francis in his sweet, humble, Christian way also embraced them, in the spirit of audacity, and rankness, and pride. So that all he has written is summed up in one ejaculation: "How vast, how eligible, how joyful, how real is a human being, himself or herself !" (pp. 125-27)

Havelock Ellis, "Whitman," in his The New

Spirit, 1890. Reprint by Boni and Liveright, 1921, pp. 86-127.

Louis Untermeyer (essay date 1919)

[*A poet during his early career, Untermeyer is better known as an anthologist of poetry and short fiction, an editor, and master parodist. Horace Gregory and Marya Zaturenska have noted that Untermeyer was "the first to recognize the importance of the anthology in voicing a critical survey of his chosen field." Notable among his anthologies are* Modern American Poetry *(1919),* The Book of Living Verse *(1931),* New Modern American and British Poetry *(1950), and* A Treasury of Laughter *(1946). Untermeyer was a contributing editor to* The Liberator *and the* Seven Arts, *and served as poetry editor of the* American Mercury *from 1934 to 1937. In the following essay, Untermeyer characterizes Whitman as the single most "American" poet.*]

The four days in February that did triple duty by celebrating the centenary of James Russell Lowell, the birthday of George Washington and what seemed to be an Anglo-American alliance, were not without a significant humor. Held ostensibly to honor the author of "The Vision of Sir Launfal," there were not a half a dozen American poets of note at any of the various dinners, theatre-parties and public love-feasts. Among all the tributes showered upon Lowell the diplomat, Lowell the bookman and Lowell the foe of slavery, there was no word for Lowell the recorder of homely folk or Lowell the seditious "pacifist." Scraps of his academic odes were read with unction, placid stanzas on Agassiz and Longfellow were printed with polite approbation; but scarcely anyone spoke of the first three Biglow Papers, and no one dared to quote such stanzas of flat conscientious objection as:

> Ez for war, I call it murder—
> There you hev it plain an' flat;
> I don't want to go no fuder
> Than my Testyment for that. . .
> Er you take a sword an' dror it,
> An' go stick a feller thru,
> Guv'ment ain't no answer for it,
> God'll send the bill to you.

But what was possibly the most curiously ironic feature of the celebration was the unanimity of the press in echoing the *New York Times'* estimate that "a more determined, a more thorough American than Lowell it would be hard to find." No one evidently thought of searching—or they would have found that another poet, the most truly indigenous writer we have ever produced, was born just a hundred years ago at West Hills, Long Island. Nor would the joint festivities have been any the less appropriate for, strangely enough, it was England that first discovered the authentic Americanism of Walt Whitman.

It will be interesting to observe how many of our universities and academies of arts and letters appreciate Whitman's liberating influence even to-day; May thirty-first (Whitman's birthday) will be a fresh test for those who dwelt with such emphasis on the fact that Lowell used the English language. I venture to predict that there will be no four-day chorus of lauds and magnificats. It is one thing to glorify a man who has worked industriously in the bonds of an old rhetoric and a routine romanticism; it is another thing to praise the man who struck off the bonds. And it is as a liberator, even more than as a poet, that Whitman has influenced American art. Whether we regard him as pioneer or (as Van Wyck Brooks has it [see *NCLC*, v. 4, pp. 563-64) the great precipitant, there is scarcely any strong tendency in native letters that Whitman has not somehow strengthened, clarified, impelled, democratized.

He came with a double-barreled challenge to a literary aristocracy. His was, first of all, a democracy of thought, of emotion, of theme. When the New Englanders (whose colonial poetry was not nearly as representative of New England as of old England) were going to village blacksmiths and chambered nautili for embroidered mottoes and neatly-turned maxims, he was taking his material hot from the raucous tumble of life. While most of his transatlantic contemporaries were strolling elegantly through Bulfinch's Mythology, hymning the minor amours of the major Greek divinities, Whitman was writing:

> Come, Muse, migrate from Greece and Ionia.
> Cross out, please, those immensely overpaid accounts;
> That matter of Troy and Achilles' wrath, and Æneas', Odysseus' wanderings.
> Placard "Removed" and "To Let" on the rocks of your snowy Parnassus . . .
> For know a better, fresher, busier sphere; a wider, untried domain awaits and demands you.

It was Whitman who first revealed "the glory of the commonplace"; for him ugliness was fused perfectly in a vast harmonic counterpoint. Nothing remained casual. He showed the ordinary in a blaze of color that shamed the attempted brilliance of the PreRaphaelites; his daily street-corners, ferries, bridges, were more bewildering than the lunar landscapes of Poe. His barbaric yap could be softened to express a lyric ecstasy over a blade of grass which to him was "no less than the journeywork of the stars"; his naïf wonder dwelt on the miracle of a mouse that would "stagger sextillions of infidels" and his own hairy hand, whose "narrowest hinge puts to scorn all machinery." It is this large naturalism, this affection for all that is homely and of the soil that set him apart from his fellow-craftsmen as our first American poet.

> And the cow, crunching with depressed head, surpasses any statute . . .
> And the running blackberry would adorn the parlors of heaven.

Scarcely less important than his anti-patrician thought, was his democratic speech. It was Whitman's use of the rich verbal matter that he found in the street rather than in libraries that made his influence so dominating. And, again in distinction to his scholarly compatriots, it was an American speech he was using. He even went so far as to declare that he often thought the whole of **Leaves of Grass** was only a language experiment, an effort toward a democratic (as opposed to a merely genteel) tongue. "It is," he said, "an attempt to give the spirit, the body, the man, new words, new potentialities of speech—an American, a cosmopolitan (the best of America is the best cosmopolitanism) range of self-expression. The new world, the new times, the new peoples, need a tongue according—yes, what is more, they will have such a tongue—will not be satisfied until it is evolved." He went back to this thought a score of times. One can find it amplified with a hundred suggestive phrases and variations in his **An American Primer,** a sketch for a lecture that was never delivered, a series of astonishing notes that extended over ten years. Here is an illuminating scrap:

> I like limber, lasting, fierce words. I like them applied to myself—and I like them in newspapers, courts, debates, congress.—Do you suppose the liberties and the brawn of These States have to do only with delicate lady-words? with gloved gentleman words? . . . Bad Presidents, bad judges, bad editors, owners of slaves, monopolists, infidels, castrated persons, shaved persons, supplejacks, ecclesiastics . . . cry down the use of strong, cutting, beautiful, rude words. To the manly instincts of the People they will forever be welcome.

And, here, in this half-musing, half-brusque fragment, the poet and propagandist join hands:

> What is the fitness—what the strange charm of aboriginal names?—Monongahela—It rolls with venison richness upon the palate. Among names to be revolutionized: that of the city of "Baltimore."

American writers, he prophesied, would learn to love their own land and the language that reflected it; they would show "far more freedom in the use of words. Ten thousand native idiomatic words are growing, or are already grown . . . words that would be welcomed by the nation, being of the national blood." And it was Whitman, with his prodigal energy and vulgar health, that blazed the way through a forest of pedantry and clichés.

The breadth, the jubilant acceptance, a roughshod faith in life and death—these things led a regiment of writers out of sequestered gardens and worm-eaten towers, once labelled ivory. It was a new literature that followed; it flourished in the coarse sunlight and the keen air. It had strong roots in the earth; from its seeds sprang Frost, Sandburg, Dreiser, Oppenheim, Anderson, Masters, Lindsay and a score of autocthonous others. It was not so classic a thing as a renascence; it was a slow and painful birth. And thus one looks to the last of May. In the centenary of Whitman, American letters celebrates its own birthday. (pp. 245-47)

> *Louis Untermeyer, "A Whitman Centenary,"*
> *in* The New Republic, *Vol. XVIII, No. 229,*
> *March 22, 1919, pp. 245-47.*

T. S. Eliot (essay date 1926)

[*Perhaps the most influential poet and critic to write in the English Language during the first half of the twentieth century, Eliot is closely identified with many of the qualities denoted by the term Modernism: experimentation, formal complexity, artistic and intellectual eclecticism, and a classicist's view of the artist working at an emotional distance from his or her creation. He introduced a number of terms and concepts that strongly affected critical thought in his lifetime, among them the ideas that poets must be conscious of the living tradition of literature in order for their work to have artistic and spiritual validity. In general, Eliot upheld values of traditionalism and discipline, and in 1928 he annexed Christian theology to his overall conservative world view. Of his criticism, he stated: "It is a by-product of my private poetry-workshop: or a prolongation of the thinking that went into the formation of my verse." In the following excerpt, Eliot notes philosophical and political similarities between Whitman and Alfred, Lord Tennyson.*]

[With] relation to Whitman, it must be recognized that his was a time with a character of its own, and one in which it was posible to hold certain notions, and many illusions, which are now untenable. Now Whitman was . . . a "man with a message," even if that message was sometimes badly mutilated in transmission; he was interested in what he had to say; he did not think of himself primarily as the inventor of a new technique of versification. His "message" must be reckoned with, and it is a very different message from that of Mr. Carl Sandburg.

The world of the American voyage in *Martin Chuzzlewit* is the same. Dickens knew best what it looked like, but Whitman knew what it felt like. There is another interesting parallel: **Leaves of Grass** appeared in 1856, *Les fleurs du mal* in 1857: could any age have produced more heterogeneous leaves and flowers? The contrasts should be noted. But perhaps more important than these contrasts is the similarity of Whitman to another master, one whose greatness he always recognized and whose eminence he always acknowledged generously—to Tennyson. Between the ideas of the two men, or, rather, between the relations of the ideas of each to his place and time, between the ways in which each held his ideas, there is a fundamental resemblance. Both were born laureates. Whitman, of course, fought hard against corruption, against Press servility, against slavery, against alcohol (and I dare say Tennyson would have done so under the same conditions); but essentially he was satisfied—too satisfied—with things as they are. His labourers and pioneers (at that date all Anglo-Saxon, or at least North European, labourers and pioneers) are the counterpart to Tennyson's great broad-shouldered Englishman at whom Arnold pokes fun; Whitman's horror at the monarchical tyranny of Europe is the counterpart to Tennyson's comment on the revolutions of French politics, no "graver than a schoolboy's barring out." Baudelaire, on the other hand, was a disagreeable person who was rarely satisfied with anything; *je m'ennuie en France,* he wrote, *ou tout le monde resemble à Voltaire.* ["I'm bored in France, where everyone resembles Voltaire."]

I do not mean to suggest that all discontent is divine, or that all self-righteousness is loathesome. On the contrary, both Tennyson and Whitman made satisfaction almost magnificent. It is not the best aspect of their verse; if neither of them had more, neither of them would be still a great poet. But Whitman succeeds in making America as it was, just as Tennyson made England as it was, into something grand and significant. You cannot quite say that either was deceived, and you cannot at all say that either was insincere, or the victim of popular cant. They had the faculty—Whitman perhaps more prodigiously than Tennyson—of transmuting the real into an ideal. Whitman had the ordinary desires of the flesh; for him there was no chasm between the real and the ideal, such as opened before the horrified eyes of Baudelaire. But this, and the "frankness" about sex for which he is either extolled or mildly reproved, did not spring from any particular honesty or clearness of vision: it sprang from what may be called either "idealization" or a faculty for make-believe, according as we are disposed. There is, fundamentally, no differences between the Whitman frankness and the Tennyson delicacy, except in its relation to public opinion of the time. And Tennyson liked monarchs, and Whitman liked presidents. Both were conservative, rather than reactionary or revolutionary; that is to say, they believed explicitly in progress, and believed implicitly that progress consists in things remaining much as they are.

If this were all there is to Whitman, it would still be a great deal; he would remain a great representative of America, but emphatically of an America which no longer exists. It is not the America of Mr. Scott Fitzgerald, or Mr. Dos Passos, or Mr. Hemingway—to name some of the more interesting of contemporary American writers. If I may draw still one more comparison, it is with Hugo. Beneath all the declamations there is another tone, and behind all the illusions there is another vision. When Whitman speaks of the lilacs or of the mocking-bird, his theories and beliefs drop away like a needless pretext.

> *T. S. Eliot, "Whitman and Tennyson," in* The Nation and the Athenaeum, *Vol. 40, No. 11, December 18, 1926, p. 426.*

Malcolm Cowley   (essay date 1946)

[*A prominent American critic during much of the twentieth century, Cowley made several valuable contributions with his editions of works by important American authors (Whitman, Nathaniel Hawthorne, Ernest Hemingway, William Faulkner, F. Scott Fitzgerald), his writings for the* New Republic, *and above all, with his chronicles and criticism of modern American literature. Cowley's literary criticism does not attempt a systematic philosophical view of life and art, nor is it representative of a neatly defined school of critical thought. Rather, Cowley focused on works that he considered worthy of public appreciation and that he believed personal experience qualified him to explicate, such as the works of the "lost generation" writers whom he knew. The critical approach Cowley followed is undogmatic and is characterized by a willingness to view a work from whatever perspective—social, historical, aesthetic—that the work itself seemed to demand for its illumination. In the following essay, he speculates on Whitman's abrupt transformation from a minor journalist into a major poet with the publication of* Leaves of Grass.]

There was a miracle in Whitman's life; we can find no other word for it. In his thirty-seventh year, the local politician and printer and failed editor suddenly became a world poet. No long apprenticeship; no process of growth that we can trace from year to year in his published work; not even much early promise: the poet materializes like a shape from the depths. In 1848, when we almost lose sight of him, Whitman is an editorial writer on salary, repeating day after day the opinions held in common by the younger Jacksonian Democrats, praising the people and attacking the corporations (but always within reasonable limits); stroking the American eagle's feathers and pulling the lion's tail. Hardly a word he publishes gives the impression that only Whitman could have written it. In 1855 he reveals a new character that seems to be his own creation. He writes and prefaces and helps to print and distributes and, for good measure, anonymously reviews a first book of poems, not only different from any others known at the time, but also unlike everything the poet himself had written in former years (and only faintly foreshadowed by three of his experiments in free verse that the New York *Tribune* had printed in 1850 because it liked their political sentiments). It is a short book, this first edition of *Leaves of Grass;* it contains only twelve poems, including the **"Song of Myself "**; but they summarize or suggest all his later achievements; and for other poets they are better than those achievements, because in this first book Whitman was a great explorer, whereas later he was at best a methodical exploiter and at worst a mere expounder by rote of his own discoveries.

At some point during the seven "lost years," Whitman had begun to utilize resources deep in himself that might have remained buried. He had mastered what Emerson called the "secret which every intellectual man quickly learns"—but how few make use of it!—"that beyond the energy of his possessed and conscious intellect he is capable of a new energy (as of an intellect doubled on itself), by abandonment to the nature of things; that beside his privacy of power as an individual man, there is a great public power on which he can draw, by unlocking, at all risks, his human doors, and suffering the ethereal tides to roll and circulate through him; then he is caught up into the life of the Universe, his speech is thunder, his thought is law, and his words are universally intelligible as the plants and animals." Whitman himself found other words to describe what seems to have been essentially the same phenomenon. Long afterwards he told one of his disciples, Dr. Maurice Bucke: *"Leaves of Grass* was there, though unformed, all the time, in whatever answers as the laboratory of the mind. . . . The *Democratic Review* essays and tales," published before 1848, "came from the surface of the mind and had no connection with what lay below—a great deal of which, indeed, was below consciousness. At last the time came when the concealed growth had to come to light, and the first edition of *Leaves of Grass* was published."

Whitman in these remarks was simplifying a phenomenon by which, quite evidently, he continued to be puzzled until the end. The best efforts of his biographers will never fully explain it; and a critic can only point to certain events, or probable events, that must have contributed to his sudden discovery of his own talent. The trip to New Orleans in 1848 was certainly one of them. It lasted for only four months (and not for years, as Whitman later implied), but it was his first real glimpse of the American continent, and it gave him a stock of remembered sights and sounds and emotions over which his imagination would play for the rest of his life.

A second event was connected with his interest in the pseudo-science of phrenology. The originators of this doctrine believed that the human character is determined by the development of separate facilities (of which there were twenty-six according to Gall, thirty-five according to Spurzheim, and forty-three according to the Fowler brothers in New York); that each of these faculties is localized in a definite portion of the brain; and that its strength or weakness can be ascertained from the contours of the skull. Whitman had the bumps on his head charted by L. N. Fowler in July, 1849, a year after his return from the South. In these phrenological readings of character, each of the faculties was rated on a numerical scale running from one to seven or eight. Five was good; six was the most desirable figure; seven and eight indicated that the quality was dangerously overdeveloped. Among the ratings that Whitman received for his mental faculties (and note their curious names, which reappeared in his poems), were Amativeness 6, Philoprogenitiveness 6, Adhesiveness 6, Inhabitiveness 6, Alimentiveness 6, Cautiousness 6, Self-esteem 6 to 7, Firmness 6 to 7, Benevolence 6 to 7, Sublimity 6 to 7, Ideality 5 to 6, Individuality 6 and Intuitiveness 6. It was, on the whole, a highly flattering report, and Whitman needed flattery in those days; for he hadn't made a success of his new daily, the Brooklyn *Freeman,* and no other position had been offered to its editor. Apparently the phrenological reading gave him some of the courage he needed to follow an untried course. Seven years later he had Fowler's chart of his skull reproduced in the second or 1856 edition of **Leaves of Grass.**

Another event that inspired him was his reading of Emerson's essays. Later Whitman tried to hide this indebtedness, asserting several times that he had seen nothing of Emerson's until after his own first edition had been published. But aside from the Emersonian ideas in the twelve early poems (especially the **"Song of Myself "**), there is, as evidence in the case, Whitman's prose introduction to the first edition, which is written in Emerson's style, with his characteristic rhythms, figures of speech and turns of phrase. As for the ideas Whitman expressed in that style, they are chiefly developments of what Emerson had said in "The Poet" (first of the *Essays: Second Series,* published in 1844), combined with other notions from Emerson's "Compensation." In "The Poet," Emerson had said:

> I look in vain for the poet whom I describe. . . . We have yet had no genius in America, with tyrannous eye, which knew the value of our incomparable materials, and saw, in the barbarism and materialism of the times, another carnival of the same gods whose picture he so much admires in Homer; then in the Middle Ages; then in Calvinism. . . . Our log-rolling, our stumps and their politics, our fisheries, our Negroes and Indians, our boasts and our repudiations, the wrath of rogues and the pusillanimity of honest men, the northern trade, the southern planting, the western clearing, Oregon and Texas, are yet unsung. Yet America is a poem in our eyes; its

ample geography dazzles the imagination, and it will not wait long for meters.

> . . . Doubt not, O poet, but persist. Say "It is in me, and shall out." Stand there, balked and dumb, stuttering and stammering, hissed and hooted, stand and strive, until at last rage draws out of thee that *dream*-power which every night shows thee is thine own; a power transcending all limit and privacy, and by virtue of which a man is the conductor of the whole river of electricity.

Whitman, it is clear today, determined to be the poet whom Emerson pictured; he determined to be the genius in America who recognized the value of our incomparable materials, the Northern trade, the Southern planting and the Western clearing. "The United States themselves are the greatest poem," he wrote, he echoed in his 1855 introduction, conceived as if in answer to Emerson's summons. At first balked and dumb, then later hissed and hooted, he stood there until he had drawn from himself the power he felt in his dream.

There was, however, still another event that seems to have given Whitman a new conception of his mission as a poet: it was his reading of two novels by George Sand, *The Countess of Rudolstadt* and *The Journeyman Joiner.* Both books were written during their author's socialistic period, before the revolution of 1848, and both were translated into English by one of the New England Transcendentalists. *The Countess of Rudolstadt* was the sequel to *Consuelo,* which Whitman described as "the noblest work left by George Sand—the noblest in many respects, on its own field, in all literature." Apparently he gave *Consuelo* and its sequel to his mother when they first appeared in this country, in 1847; and after her death he kept the tattered volumes on his bedside table. It was in the epilogue to *The Countess of Rudolstadt* that Whitman discovered the figure of a wandering musician who might have been taken for a Bohemian peasant except for his fine white hands; who was not only a violinist but also a bard and a prophet, expounding the new religion of Humanity; and who, falling into a trance, recited "the most magnificent poem that can be conceived," before traveling onward along the open road. . . .*The Journeyman Joiner* was also listed by Whitman among his favorite books. It is the story—to quote from Esther Shephard, who discovered his debt to both novels—"of a beautiful, Christlike young carpenter, a proletary philosopher, who dresses in a mechanic's costume but is scrupulously clean and neat. He works at carpentering with his father, but patiently takes time off whenever he wants to in order to read, or give advice on art, or share a friend's affection."

Both books helped to fix the direction of Whitman's thinking; for they summarized the revolutionary ideas that prevailed in Europe before 1848. But the principal effect of these novels was on Whitman's picture of himself. After reading them, he slowly formed the project of becoming a wandering bard and prophet, like the musician in the epilogue to *The Countess of Rudolstadt.* He stopped writing for the magazines and, according to his brother George, he refused some editorial positions that were offered him; instead he worked as a carpenter with his father, like the hero of *The Journeyman Joiner* (and also like Jesus in his youth; for Whitman was planning to found a religion). About this time there is an apparent change in his personality. Whitman as a young editor had dressed correctly, even fashionably, had trimmed his beard, had carried a light cane, had been rather retiring in his manners, had been on good but not at all intimate terms with his neighbors and had shown his dislike for their children. Now suddenly he begins dressing like a Brooklyn mechanic, with his shirt open to reveal a red-flannel undershirt and part of a hairy chest, and with a big felt hat worn loosely over his tousled hair. He lets his beard grow shaggy, he makes his voice more assured and, as he wanders about the docks and ferries, he greets his friends with bear hugs and sometimes a kiss of comradeship. It is as if he has undertaken a double task: before creating his poems, he has to create the hypothetical author of the poems. And this author bears a new name: *Walter* Whitman, as he was always known to his family and till then had been called by his friends, now suddenly becomes:

> Walt Whitman, a kosmos, of Manhattan the son,
> Turbulent, fleshy, sensual, eating, drinking and breeding.

The world is his stage, and Whitman has assumed a role which he will continue to play for the rest of his life. Sometimes, in his letters, we can see him as in a dressing-room, arranging his features to make the role convincing. In 1868, for example, he sent his London publisher a long series of directions about how his portrait should be engraved from a photograph that he rather liked. "If a faithful presentation of that photograph can be given," he said, "it will satisfy me well—of course it should be reproduced with all its shaggy, dappled, rough-skinned character, and not attempted to be smoothed and prettified . . . let the costume be kept very simple and broad, and rather kept down too, little as there is of it—preserve the effect of the sweeping lines making all that fine free angle below the chin . . . It is perhaps worth your taking special pains about, both to achieve a successful picture and likeness, something characteristic, and as certain to be a marked help to your edition of the book." There is more in the same vein, and it makes us feel that Whitman was like an actor-manager, first having his portrait painted in costume, then hanging it in the lobby to sell more tickets.

He had more than the dash of charlatanism that, according to Baudelaire, adds a spice to genius. But he had also his own sort of honesty, and he tried to live his part as well as acting it. The new character he assumed was more, far more, than a pose adopted to mislead the public. Partly it was a side of his nature that had always existed, but had been suppressed by social conventions, by life with a big family of brothers and sisters and by the struggle to earn a living. Partly it represented a real change after 1850: the self-centered young man was turning outwards, was trying to people his loneliness with living comrades. Partly it was an attempt to compensate for the absence in himself of qualities he admired in others; for we know that Whitman at heart was anything but rough, virile, athletic, savage or luxuriant, to quote a few of his favorite adjectives. Partly his new personality was an ideal picture of himself that he

tried to achieve in the flesh and came in time to approximate. You might call it a mask or, as Jung would say, a *persona* that soon had a life of its own, developing and changing with the years and almost superseding his other nature. At the end, one could hardly say that there was a "real" Whitman underneath the public figure; the man had become confused with his myth.

We might find it easier to picture the complexities of his character if we imagined that there were at least three Whitmans existing as separate persons. There was Whitman I, the printer and politician and editor, always described by his acquaintances as indolent, shy (except when making public speeches), awkward and rather conventional in his manners. He disappeared from public sight after 1850, yet he survived for thirty years or more in his intimate relations with his family. Then there was Whitman II, the *persona,* who characterized himself as "One of the roughs, large, proud, affectionate, eating, drinking and breeding, his costume manly and free, his face sunburnt and bearded, his posture strong and erect, his voice bringing hope and prophecy to the generous races of young and old." This second Whitman, ripening with age (and becoming a great deal more discreet after he moved to Washington and went to work for the government), at last emerged into the figure of the Good Gray Poet. He wrote poems too, as part of his role, but they were windy and uninspired. The real poet was still another person; let us call him Whitman III. He never appeared in public life; he was hardly more than a voice from the depths of the subconscious; but the voice was fresh, moving, candid; and it spoke in different words and in different tones not only from Whitman the editor but also from Whitman the self-styled bard of democracy. Whitman III was sometimes boastful but also tender and secret where Whitman II was bluff and lusty; he was feminine, maternal, rather than physically adventurous; at the same time he was a revolutionist by instinct where Whitman I was liberal and Whitman II merely sententious. He appeared from nowhere in 1855; he had little to say after 1860 and fell silent forever in 1873; yet during his short career he wrote (or dictated to other Whitmans) all the poems that gave **Leaves of Grass** its position in the literature of the world.

But what explains the mystery of the poet's birth? There was an apparently very ordinary fellow named Walter Whitman, who wrote editorials and book reviews and moral doggerel; then there was an extraordinary showman named Walt Whitman who peddled his personality as if it were a patent medicine; but there was also for six years, and at intervals thereafter, a poet of genius known by the same name. How did he come to exist? Was it merely because Whitman the editor visited New Orleans, had a phrenological reading, was inspired by Emerson's doctrine of the representative individual, and tried to make himself over into a character by George Sand? Is there some other cause for what we must still regard as the Whitman miracle?

The only evidence that bears on this question consists of Whitman's early notebooks and the poems themselves, which are not often a trustworthy guide. Still, they return so often to one theme that its importance in his life seems fixed beyond dispute. Whitman had apparently been slow to develop emotionally as well as intellectually. The poems suggest that, at some moment during the seven shadowy years, he had his first fully satisfying sexual experience. It may have been as early as his trip to New Orleans in 1848, to judge by what he says in a frequently quoted poem, **"Once I Passed through a Populous City,"** which, incidentally, has more biographical value in the early draft discovered by Emory Holloway than it has in the altered and expurgated version that Whitman published. Or this Louisiana episode, if real, may have been merely an introduction to his new life, and the decisive experience may have come later, during his carpenter years in Brooklyn. Whenever it occurred, the experience was so intense that it became an almost religious ecstasy, a moment of vision that wholly transformed his world. Whitman describes such a moment in the fifth section of the **"Song of Myself "**:

> Swiftly arose and spread around me the peace
>   and knowledge that pass all the argument of
>   the earth,
> And I know that the hand of God is the promise
>   of my own,
> And I know that the spirit of God is the brother
>   of my own,
> And that all the men ever born are also my
>   brothers, and the women my sisters and lov-
>   ers,
> And that a kelson of the creation is love,
> And limitless are leaves stiff or drooping in the
>   fields,
> And brown ants in the little wells beneath them,
> And mossy scabs of the worm fence, heap'd
>   stones, elder, mullein and poke-weed.

After this experience, Whitman had to revise not only his philosophical picture of the world but also his personal and private picture of himself. "I am not what you supposed," he would say in one of his 1860 poems, "but far different." The discovery of his own sexual direction must have been a shock to him at first; but soon he determined to accept himself with all his vices and "smutch'd deeds," just as he accepted everything in an imperfect universe. He wrote: "I am myself just as much evil as good, and my nation is—and I say there is in fact no evil." All his nature being good, in the larger view, he felt that all of it should be voiced in the poems that he now determined to write.

At first his revelations concerning one aspect of his nature were made obliquely, in language that could be easily understood only by others of his own type. By 1860, however, when he was preparing the third edition of his poems, the impulse to reveal himself had become so strong that he was no longer willing to speak by indirection. "Come," he said, "I am determin'd to unbare this broad breast of mine, I have long enough stifled and choked." And in the first of his "Calamus" poems, written for that edition, he proclaimed his resolve "to sing no songs today but those of manly attachment":

> I proceed for all who are or have been young
>   men,
> To tell the secret of my nights and days,
> To celebrate the need of comrades.

There has been a long argument about the meaning of the "Calamus" poems, but it is or should be clear enough from the title under which they were published. Whitman is sometimes vague and a little hard to follow in his metaphysical symbols, but his sexual symbols are as simply conceived as an African statue of Potency or Fertility. The calamus root is one of these symbols, even though Whitman disguised the fact when writing to William Michael Rossetti, his English editor, who had asked him for an explanation. " 'Calamus' is a common word here," Whitman replied: "it is the very large and aromatic grass, or root, spears three feet high—often called 'sweet flag'—grows all over the Northern and Middle States—(see Webster's Large Dictionary—Calamus—definition 2).—The recherché or ethereal sense, as used in my book, probably arises from it, Calamus presenting the biggest and hardiest spears of grass, and from its fresh, a romatic, pungent bouquet." But if Rossetti had referred to Section 24 of the **"Song of Myself,"** he would have discovered what the poet really meant. In that section, Whitman exults in his own body and describes the various parts of it in metaphors drawn from the animal and vegetable world. The calamus plays its proper part in the description:

> Root of wash'd sweet-flag! timorous pond snipe!
>   nest of guarded duplicate eggs! it shall be you!

The sweet-flag or calamus root, the "growth by the margin of pond-waters," was simply Whitman's token or symbol for the male sexual organ. "This," he said in a poem, "O this shall henceforth be the token of comrades, this calamus-root shall." The poems under this general title were poems of homosexual love, in its physical aspects and with its metaphysical lessons. They were "blades" or "spears" or "leaves" of the calamus, to use another of Whitman's favorite symbols; and, as he said in his letter to Rossetti, they were the biggest and hardiest of the grasses; in fact they were bigger and hardier than all the other leaves of grass. (pp. 385-88)

> *Malcolm Cowley, "Walt Whitman: The Miracle," in* The New Republic, *Vol. 114, No. 11, March 18, 1946, pp. 385-88.*

John Berryman   (essay date 1957)

[*Berryman is considered one of the most important modern American poets. His work developed from objective, classically controlled poetry into an esoteric, eclectic, and highly emotional expression of his personal vision. He has called poetry "the means by which the writer can shape from an experience in itself usually vague, a mere feeling or phrase, something that is coherent, directed, and intelligible." In the following essay written in 1957 but not published until 1976, Berryman explains "Song of Myself" in terms of national, religious, metaphysical, and personal issues.*]

The arbiters of current taste—Pound, Eliot, Auden, others—have generally now declared themselves in favour of Whitman; but always reluctantly and with a certain resentment or even contempt. I am not able to feel these reservations myself, but I think I understand their origins and will try presently to suggest what these are. I like or love Whitman unreservedly; he operates with great power and beauty over a very wide range, from small pieces like **"A Noiseless, Patient Spider"** and **"I Saw in Louisiana a Live-Oak Growing"** up through **"Out of the Cradle Endlessly Rocking"**—a poem in which a profound experience crucial to the poet's vocation is rendered as fully as in the Cliff passage in the First Book of *The Prelude* and nearly as fully as in "Resolution and Independence" (Wordsworth comes first to mind as being far the greatest poet of his century in England, as Whitman was here)—up through this range, I say, to **"Song of Myself,"** which seems to me easily his most important achievement and indeed the greatest poem so far written by an American. It is not by any means an easy poem to understand. It is hard, frequently, to see why the poet is saying what he is saying, and hard therefore also to see what he is saying. All I mean to do here is to construct a crude approach that may prove helpful to the discovery of answers to the questions that these difficulties inspire.

Though I wish so far as possible to avoid the paradoxes that writers on Whitman too readily indulge in, I note, as an initial problem, that this poem of fifty pages is the work of a man who agreed with Poe "that (at any rate for our occasions, our day) there can be no such thing as a long poem" ("The same thought had been haunting my mind before, but Poe's argument, though short, worked the sum and proved it to me"—this in 1888). Now "long" is a relative term, and the author of *The Faerie Queene,* for instance, may well not have considered *The Rape of Lucrece* (at 1,850 lines) a "long" poem. But clearly this is not what Whitman has in mind. What I think he does have in mind comes up sharply in another passage: "It is not on **Leaves of Grass** distinctively as *literature,* or a specimen thereof, that I feel to dwell, or advance claims. No one will get at my verses who insists upon viewing them as a literary performance, or attempt at such performance . . . " He did not, that is, think of **"Song of Myself"** as a *long* poem, because he did not think of it as a poem at all. Our problem has become a question: What then did he think of it as? The question is quite unanswerable in this form, unless we say that he thought of it as a work of *life* (as I feel sure he did), but we can get on by inquiring what it was intended to *do,* what purposes it was desired to serve. Declared purposes, first; here we have many statements from him—too many—of which I am going to take four that seem to me indefeasible. The first is national, the second religious, the third metaphysical, the fourth personal. And although *he* is talking about **Leaves of Grass,** in quoting him you will understand *me* to be referring to **"Song of Myself,"** the epitome of his book, where it stands first.

First: "One main genesis-motive of the **Leaves** was my conviction (just as strong today as ever) that the crowning growth of the United States is to be spiritual and heroic. To help start and favor that growth—or even to call attention to it, or the need of it—is the beginning, middle and final purpose of the poems." Nothing could be more comprehensible and explicit, and nothing more incomprehensible or repugnant to most cultivated readers a century later; though not, as it happens, to me. But in what way **"Song of Myself"** was designed to "favor that

growth—or . . . to call attention to . . . the need of it" is not yet clear.

For the second intention, not less fundamental than the first, I must quote rather a long passage—in which Whitman had to coin a word, "germenancy," corresponding to "growth" in the first.

> When I commenced, years ago, elaborating the plan of my poems, and continued turning over that plan, and shifting it in my mind through many years, (from the age of twenty-eight to thirty-five,) experimenting much, and writing and abandoning much, one deep purpose underlay the others, and has underlain it and its execution ever since—and that has been the Religious purpose. Amid many changes, and a formulation taking far different shape from what I at first supposed, this basic purpose has never been departed from in the composition of my verses. Not of course to exhibit itself in the old ways, as in writing hymns or psalms with an eye to the church-pew, or to express conventional pietism, or the sickly yearnings of devotees, but in new ways, and aiming at the widest sub-bases and inclusions of Humanity, and tallying the fresh air of sea and land. I will see, (said I to myself,) whether there is not, for my purposes as poet, a Religion, and a sound Religious germenancy in the average Human Race, at least in their modern development in the United States, and in the hardy common fiber and native yearnings and elements, deeper and larger, and affording more profitable returns, than all mere sects or churches—as boundless, joyous, and vital as Nature itself—A germenancy that has too long been unencouraged, unsung, almost unknown . . . With Science, the Old Theology of the East, long in its dotage, begins evidently to die and disappear. But (to my mind) Science—and may be such will prove its principal service—as evidently prepares the way for One indescribably grander—Time's young but perfect offspring—the New Theology—heir of the West—lusty and loving, and wondrous beautiful. For America, and for to-day, just the same as any day, the supreme and final Science is the Science of God—what we call science being only its minister—as Democracy is or shall be also. And a poet of America (I said) must fill himself with such thoughts, and chant his best out of them . . .

You will have observed how intense for Whitman was the despised word (but not by our political institutions) "average"—a word hardly likely to be found bearing this exalted stress in Pound or Eliot or Auden. It is clear that Whitman envisages a post-Christianity (and post-Buddhism, post-Hinduism) which will serve science and, *eventually* (a dramatic qualification, showing how little Whitman was taken in by American pretensions), egalitarianism.

Third: as of what I am calling metaphysics, a very short remark: "To the true and full estimate of the Present both the Past and the Future are main considerations." It is the second part of this that is startling, and calls in question the nature of *time;* I suppose being is either associated with, or precisely dissociated from, time, or is both; this is why I call the present intention metaphysical. We see that the optimism emotionally visible in the national and religious intentions is here intellectually asserted. But since we have come thus so close to what has really to be called doctrine, Whitman's statement having indeed a dogmatic air, it is time to point out his massive insistence upon the word "suggestiveness" in all these connections. "I round and finish little, if anything; and could not, consistently with my scheme." Again: "I think I have at least enough philosophy not to be too absolutely certain of anything, or any results." Again: "A great poem is no finish to a man or woman but rather a beginning."

It is this last quotation that brings him into conflict with current aesthetics, that of the artwork made, finished, autonomous. (Let us concede at once that *The Waste Land* winds up with various bogus instructions, and so might be thought to aim at a beginning; but except for the lines about "the awful daring of a moment's surrender," all this end of that poem is its weakest, most uneasy, crudest, least inventive, most willed part.) The conflict is absolutely equally in Whitman's formulation of the fourth or *personal* intention. *"Leaves of Grass . . ."* he says, "has mainly been the outcroppings of my own emotional and personal nature—an attempt, from first to last, to put *a Person,* a human being (myself, in the latter part of the Nineteenth Century, in America,) freely, fully and truly on record." I call your attention to an incongruity of this formulation with Eliot's amusing theory of the impersonality of the artist, and a contrast between the mere *putting-on-record* and the well-nigh universal current notion of *creation,* or making things up. You will see that, as Whitman looks more arrogant than Eliot in the Personality, he looks less pretentious in the recording—the mere recording—poet not as *maker* but as spiritual historian—only the history must be, as we'll see in a moment, of the Present—and inquirer (characteristically; Eliot's word in the *Quartets,* "explorer," is more ambitious and charged than "inquirer"). Small wonder—I finish with the arbiters—if they resent Whitman: he has sold the profession short. The poet as creator plays no part in Whitman's scheme at all.

For Whitman the poet is a *voice*. Not solely his own—let us settle this problem quickly: a poet's first personal pronoun is nearly always ambiguous, but we have the plain declaration from Whitman that "the trunk and centre whence the answer was to radiate . . . must be an identical soul and body, a personality—which personality, after many considerings and ponderings I deliberately settled should be myself—indeed could not be any other." I would sorrow over the credulity of anyone who took this account-of-the-decision-as-conscious to be historical; but I am convinced of the reality of the decision. A voice, then, for himself and others; for others *as himself*—this is the intention clearly (an underlying exhibitionism and narcissism we take for granted). What others?—Americans, man. A voice—that is, expressing (not creating)—expressing things already in existence. But what is a voice from?—a *body*. And where?—in America, but this is going to be difficult. And what is in existence? (If anyone doubts that Whitman saw the thing—his intention, his subject—in these apparently abstract but in fact quite literal terms, let him consider these expressions: in Section 23 at the center of *"Song of Myself,"* "I accept Time, ab-

solutely" and "I accept Reality, and dare not question it"; and as the initial phrase of Section 33, "Space and Time!"—all these capitalized.)

I am going to be most interested in time and existence, but first another word about voice. Other voices in Whitman are regularly metaphors for the human voice, and the voice of the *soul* in Section 5—it must be understood that the "I" in *"Song of Myself"* often refers only to the body—is metaphorical also, in the exquisite line:

> Only the lull I like, the hum of your valvèd voice.

In the light of "lull," the kind of valve here imagined must be a safety valve (compare "loose the stop from your throat" just above): the soul being that which lets the body free a little and then controls it. In the lines immediately following, incest with the soul is dramatized (*by* the body); and that this is not enough we learn from the lines straight after these,

> Swiftly arose and spread around me the peace and knowledge that pass all the argument of the earth,
> And I know that the hand of God is the promise of my own . . .

After the New Testament air of the first of these lines, it is clear that "the promise" is a theological allusion, brought over into the New Theology; and suddenly it is also clear that the Johannine *Logos* (God's self-revelation, in Christ—whose name is Word, as His Father's is I AM or Being) influenced Whitman's thought even more than his passion for grand opera, which dominates Section 26:

> The orbic flex of his mouth is pouring and filling me full.

And *when* he is full enough . . . a valve will open. This valve notion, sense of outlet, is crucial to the poem, not only in the fine line discarded in draft (it turned up revised in Section 47)—

> I am your voice—It was tied in you—In me it begins to talk

—but in the marvellous passage in Section 24:

> Through me many long dumb voices
> Voices of the interminable generations of prisoners & slaves,
> Voices of the diseas'd and despairing and of thieves & dwarfs,
> Voices of cycles of preparation & accretion,
> And of the threads that connect the stars, and of wombs and of the father-stuff,
> And of the rights of them the others are down upon,
> Of the deform'd, trivial, flat, foolish, despised,
> Fog in the air, beetles rolling balls of dung.

The poet—one would say, a mere channel, but with its own ferocious difficulties—fills with experiences, a valve opens; he speaks them. I am obliged to remark that I prefer this theory of poetry to those that have ruled the critical quarterlies since I was an undergraduate twenty-five years ago. It is as humble as, and identical with, Keats's view of the poet as having no existence, but being "forever in, for, and filling" other things.

Several things have to be said about this passionate sense of identification. In the first place, it supplies the method by which the "I" of the poem is gradually expanded, characterized, and filled with meaning; not until near the end of the poem is the "I" complete—and then it flees. In the second place, the identification is not of course a device adopted for the purposes of the poem; Whitman actually felt thus. Most newspapermen learn to despise the public; but Whitman wrote in the Brooklyn *Eagle,* shortly after he became its editor, "There is a curious kind of sympathy (haven't you ever thought of it before?) that arises in the mind of a newspaper conductor with the public he serves. He gets to *love* them." These italics are his, and I take this declaration literally and observe that one always wishes to identify oneself with the loved object. At the same time we recognize as of psychological origin the profound dissatisfaction (no doubt sexual in character) that aims at *loss of identity,* in the poem, in two ways, through these identifications and through death—this is why death is a major subject. But in the third place, I would deny that this is mystical—indeed, it is the opposite, as a writer in *PMLA* confessed (in 1955) while producing and maintaining the monstrous term "inverted mystical." I object to the word

First edition of Leaves of Grass (1855).

"mystical" in relation to Whitman altogether, as a mere grab-bag term, like "instinct," for whatever we don't happen to understand, unless it refers to the perfectly well-known phenomena described in the *Philokalia,* say, and the works of the English and Spanish mystics. I see no need for a single word to apply to the complicated phenomenon we are now studying, since none exists. In the fourth place, this process of identification has limits; it does not include God. God is envisaged as our lover, first, not very different from ourselves, except that, second, he provides for us. These roles are important, certainly, but still leave man very much on his own—though, Whitman insists, incurious and at peace with this idea. Identification is limited also within humanity: as against "myself and my neighbors, refreshing, wicked, real," in Section 42 there are people so despicable, so unreal, that the poet denies them even personal pronouns, suddenly saying:

> Here and there with dimes on the eyes walking,
> To feed the greed of the belly the brain liberally
>   spooning,
> Tickets buying, taking, selling, but in to the feast
>   never once going,
> Many sweating, ploughing, thrashing, and then
>   the chaff for payment receiving,
> A few idly owning, and they the wheat continu-
>   ally claiming.

It is clear that the allusion to the parable of the Wedding Feast in the third line has called up the participles in the next line corresponding to "wailing and gnashing of teeth," and that what the poet is thinking about is the punishment of the *self*-excluded: the living dead, the sullen, the greedy, the extortionate. These excepted, all are invited to the identification—the New Kingdom.

So much, with various questions still unanswered, by way of preamble. I think it will be easiest to speak to these questions—*how* the poem is to favour spiritual and heroic growth, what the *content* of the religious sense is, what are the natures of Time and Being in the poem—by way of a commentary on the progressive unfolding of the work. But I must say first that its form is perhaps misleading, like the form of the Hebrew poem of Job. That mysterious work—never mind the prose folktale in which we find it imbedded—has at any rate the form of a theodicy; but that form is ironic, for God's justice is never vindicated at all, solely his power is demonstrated; so that we have to call the poem a theodicy of power—that is, no theodicy at all. Now Whitman's poem has the form of a paean or exultation—"I celebrate myself"—unconditional, closed, reflexive. But this is misleading, for we do not yet know what "I" is—though in the fourth line we learn at least that it does not include the soul ("I loafe and invite my soul"), which is thus the first guest to be invited. I take the work in fact to be one of Welcome, self-*wrestling,* inquiry, and wonder—conditional, open, and astonished (not exulting as over an accomplished victory, but gradually revealing, puzzling, discovering).

The first five sections I see as the poem's first movement—let's use the musical term, since the poem is as deeply influenced by music as Eliot's poems are. It consists of a double invitation, from "I," or the human body, to the human soul and from "I," or the poet, to the reader. Each invitation is from equal to equal, and from what is already related to what it is already related to—he invents the word "entretied" and later "intertinged." The passionate hatred for hierarchy and dissociation is one of the poem's foremost motives, accounting for the ferocious lines in Section 3, first

> Showing the best and dividing it from the worst
> age vexes age.

and then the rest of the sentence about God: As God sleeps by me and withdraws, leaving me baskets,

> Shall I postpone my acceptation and realization
> and scream at my eyes,
> That they turn from gazing after and down the
> road,
> And forthwith cipher and show me to a cent,
> Exactly the value of one and exactly the value
> of two, and which is ahead?

These passages come too early in the work to be successfully entered into by the reader, but I am discussing intention and substance. What the second section is about is air, used as a prime symbol for equality and ubiquity—the earth's air and human air (symbol for life as well as singing, speech, the poem itself) coming together:

> The smoke of my own breath,
> Echoes, ripples, buzz'd whispers . . .
> The sound of the belch'd words of my voice
> loos'd to the eddies of the wind . . .

Since the second invitation, to the reader, may be rejected, the poet proves his equality by attacking poems himself and by standing indifferent,

> . . . amused, complacent, compassionating,
> idle, unitary . . .

The first invitation, to the soul, is accepted, and results in what I shall call the incest passage of Section 5 ("I mind how once we lay such a transparent summer morning") which, bringing soul and body for the first time together—I cannot avoid remarking what a deeply divided personality created this work—produces the "peace and knowledge" in two lines that I quoted earlier,

> And that a kelson of the creation is love . . .

Meanwhile, the attack upon time that characterizes all great poets has begun in Section 3:

> There was never any more inception than there
> is now,
> Nor any more youth or age than there is now,
> And will never be any more perfection than
> there is now,
> Nor any more heaven or hell than there is now.

This notion of a continuous present, which is Eastern, he may have derived from "the ancient Hindoo poems" to which he refers, or he may have invented it. How schematic it was will be clear from his statement in the 1855 preface that the poet "is to compete with the laws that pursue and follow time." What it does for Whitman—very briefly—is to enable him to disparage the past, and to contain the future (accessible, equal), and to head in the direction of the line in Section 46,

> You must habit yourself to the dazzle of the light
> and of every moment of your life.

—which takes us far into the heart of the poem's "favoring." The Kingdom will be here, and now, forever.

I pause to notice certain elements of the exquisite transition from the First Movement into the great Section 6, which begins, I think, the Second Movement. After the air (2), that which is like it, being everywhere, uniform, the grass. After the love wrestling of Body and Soul, a child speaks. After all the "knowledge" then claimed, a true instruction: the child's question, and the poet's ignorance and guessings. After the "peace" achieved—and owing to the strength of the union (between soul and body) effected—the question of their sundering, of death. With this question, and the enigmatic, magisterial consolation the poet gives, his work really begins. I want to quote this, wishing to emphasize in particular his extraordinary passage from helplessness through four stages of the jaunty to solemnity and darkest, most grievous mystery, *back* to a sort of helplessness which yet proves consonant with the most exalted and persuasive confidence.

> A child said What is the grass? fetching it to me
> with full hands,
> How could I answer the child? I do not know
> what it is any more than he.
>
> I guess it must be the flag of my disposition, out
> of hopeful green stuff woven.
>
> Or I guess it is the handkerchief of the Lord,
> A scented gift and remembrancer designedly
> dropt,
> Bearing the owner's name someway in the corners, that we may see and remark, and say
> Whose?
>
> Or I guess the grass is itself a child, the produced
> babe of the vegetation.
>
> Or I guess it is a uniform hieroglyphic,
> And it means, Sprouting alike in broad zones
> and narrow zones,
> Growing among black folks as among white,
> Kanuck, Tuckahoe, Congressman, Cuff, I give
> them the same, I receive them the same.
>
> And now it seems to me the beautiful uncut hair
> of graves.
>
> Tenderly will I use you curling grass,
> It may be you transpire from the breasts of
> young men,
> It may be if I had known them I would have
> loved them,
> It may be you are from old people, or from offspring taken soon out of their mothers' laps,
> And here you are the mothers' laps.
>
> This grass is very dark to be from the white
> heads of old mothers,
> Darker than the colorless beards of old men,
> Dark to come from under the faint red roofs of
> mouths.
>
> O I perceive after all so many uttering tongues,
> And I perceive they do not come from the roofs
> of mouths for nothing.

> I wish I could translate the hints about the dead
>   young men and women,
> And the hints about old men and mothers, and
>   the offspring taken soon out of their laps.
>
> What do you think has become of the young and
>   old men?
> And what do you think has become of the
>   women and children?
>
> They are alive and well somewhere,
> The smallest sprout shows there is really no
>   death,
> And if ever there was it led forward life, and
>   does not wait at the end to arrest it,
> And ceas'd the moment life appear'd.
>
> All goes onward and outward, nothing col-
>   lapses,
> And to die is different from what any one sup-
>   posed, and luckier.

I take the last line—which sounds surprisingly, not only in assertion but in tone, like another great poet of death, Rilke—to be anti-existential and to be *literally* true, in the following sense: the death a man considers is his own *now,* not his own *then,* when it will actually take place, to himself another man; therefore he can form no just conception of it; and besides—as of the second part of the line—always considers it as the ultimate disaster, whereas in practice for a great part of mankind it comes as the final mercy. Doctors in numbers are on record to this point: most terminal patients *want* to die.

The Second Movement of the poem runs, I should say, through Section 19 and is concerned, after this prelude of the grass and death, with the "I's" identifications *outward,* beginning

> I am the mate and companion of people, all just
>   as immoral and fathomless as myself.

The movement ends as quietly as possible, foreshadowing indeed the tone of the conclusion of the whole work:

> This hour I tell things in confidence,
> I might not tell everybody, but I will tell you.

Few poets have ever been able to sound like this, so simple and intimate; though Robert Frost has.

The Third Movement has for its theme Being—"What is a man anyhow?"—and runs from the beginning of Section 20 nearly to the end of Section 38 and contains most of what is supreme in the poem except for Section 6 and the final sections. I can't hope to do any sort of justice to the triumphant explorations of experience in this movement, but I want to distinguish two series of answers (if we can call them that) given by Whitman to the question that he has asked, what a man is: first, answers that are given as of the *Self;* second, answers that are given as *not* of the Self. Most of the famous passages occur in the first series, but the most intense reality, as a matter of fact, is experienced by him in the second series. *Both* series *become* intolerable, and have to be abandoned (he has been trying, as it were, a series of experiments on himself—two series—to see what he is). I attach importance, in connection with these failures, to his envisaging between them,

with obvious envy, an entirely different kind of being, in the animals of Section 32.

The first real answer given then is that man is: a lover. This being so, and in the light of the fact that most men do not appear to know it but think of themselves as intelligences or whatever, an impulse of revolt against ideas gathers head for some time, until he names himself as a "kosmos" and cries out, wonderfully,

> Unscrew the locks from the doors!
> Unscrew the doors themselves from the jambs!

Let no access be barred, that is: let's rip things up and get at the truth (*and* he is alluding to Paul's "Knock, and it shall be opened unto you," for in the lines following he speaks in the person of Christ—that is, a new Revelation is coming). Then we hear the staggering apostrophe to his body—". . . it shall be you! . . . it shall be you!"—wherein even the winds have genitals—written in the same year or so as "Un voyage à Cythère," such is the inscrutable variety of man's love of himself—and summed up in the ravishing line,

> I dote on myself, there is that lot of me and all
>   so luscious . . .

But at once in the next section (25) we hear:

> Dazzling and tremendous how quick the sun-
>   rise would kill me,
> If I could not now and always send sun-rise out
>   of me,

which if heard aright is thoroughly ominous; and when in 26 he settles down to listen to music,

> It sails me, I dab with bare feet, they are lick'd
>   by the indolent waves,
> I am cut by bitter and angry hail, I lose my
>   breath,
> Steep'd amid honey'd morphine, my windpipe
>   throttled in fakes of death,

the pleasure is rendered as pure pain. Section 28—a wild one—is about his senses as sentries who become *traitors,* and it takes 29, a sort of coda to all this, to stabilize the tone of the poem. So far for the reality of the Self, the core of which is absolutely *touch.*

Then, after a rapid passage demonstrating the incapacity of Time and Space to delimit his incorporations and followings, the magical interlude of the animals:

> I think I could turn and live with animals, they
>   are so placid and self-contain'd,
> I stand and look at them long and long.
> They do not sweat and whine about their condi-
>   tion,
> They do not lie awake in the dark and weep for
>   their sins,
> They do not make me sick discussing their duty
>   to God,
> Not one is dissatisfied, not one is demented with
>   the mania of owning things,
> Not one kneels to another, nor to his kind that
>   lived thousands of years ago,
> Not one is respectable or unhappy over the
>   whole earth.

(We see here, by the way, where one large aspect of Pound's tone in poetry comes from.) But what I am interested in is how little is said about the animals that is not negative—only "placid and self-contain'd," which withdraws from and criticizes the series of violent, out-tending experience just finished, and also the one to come; and "Not . . . unhappy" which comes to an affirmation. At radical points in the poem (in Sections 25 and 50), the word "happiness" is used to characterize the ultimate human reality, the goal of the New Theology, or indeed its permanent condition. Visible to us in creatures nearest to us in the natural scale, this is here the doctrinal point; and because it does not *sound* doctrinal, as in the other passages, it succeeds. I notice that Rilke also was hypnotized by animals—envy of whom expresses again, like death, a longing for escape from the human condition.

The second series begins with an exultation over Time and Space at his command, ". . . I am afoot with my vision"—here, there, then, now—"I fly those flights of a fluid and swallowing soul" (we see the perfect double sense of "swallowing," either of which would be artificial alone, but together instead of being worse seem natural and indeed pass almost unnoticed)—but increasingly in pain—

> All this I swallow, it tastes good, I like it well,
>   it becomes mine,
> I am the man, I suffer'd, I was there.

This superb last line probably includes an allusion to "Ecce homo" and so another Christ-identification, but this is incidental to its compendious report of what an artist is up to. The Self, of course, has disappeared, been put aside; the "I" is now Soul only, the imagination. As if in passing, in its perpetual present, itself assumes the functions of Time:

> Distant and dead resuscitate,
> They show as the dial or move as the hands of
>   me,
> I am the clock myself.

Then comes the land fight ("the murder of the four hundred and twelve young men," telling the poet's time), the admirable narrative of the fight at sea and its magnificent, dreadful aftermath—the poet, out of sight, coming closer and closer into the experience, which is his—I quote only the close of the brilliant sentence that is Section 36:

> Cut of cordage, dangle of rigging, slight shock
>   of the soothe of waves,
> Black and impassive guns, litter of powder-
>   parcels, strong scent,
> A few large stars overhead, silent & mournful
>   shining,
> Delicate sniffs of sea-breeze, smells of sedgy
>   grass and fields by the shore, death-messages
>   given in charge to survivors,
> The hiss of the surgeon's knife, the gnawing
>   teeth of his saw,
> Wheeze, cluck, swash of falling blood, short wild
>   scream and long, dull, tapering moan,
> These so, these irretrievable.

"Irretrievable" mediates between two facts for the poet:

that they *are* retrievable (he retrieves them) and that they are *intolerable*. So we get the lines next, opening 37:

> You laggards there on guard! look to your arms!
> In at the conquer'd doors they crowd; I am pos-
>   sess'd!

Yet still the presences that he must be come, throng, then more and more quiet, isolating, not less but more harrowing, down to

> Not a cholera patient lies at the last gasp but I
>   also lie at the last gasp,
> My face is ash-color'd, my sinews gnarl, away
>   from me people retreat.
>
> Askers embody themselves in me and I am em-
>   bodied in them,
> I project my hat, sit shame-faced, then, and beg.

This terrible, almost funny, deeply actual, final humiliation to the poet's dignity and independence brings on

> Enough! enough! enough!
> Somehow I have been stunn'd. Stand back!
> Give me a little time beyond my cuff 'd head,
>   slumbers, dreams, gaping,
> I discover myself on the verge of a usual mistake.
> . . . I remember now
> I resume the overstaied fraction . . .

He becomes, in self-defense, a Self again—he resumes his (too long in coming back, "overstaied") Body, which, like most men ("a usual mistake") he had forgotten; the Body that anchors us among the swallowings of the Soul, the predicaments of the imagination, the Body which is *also* part of his subject, a fraction of Man.

The Fourth Movement is addressed to his "Eleves"—disciples—"lovers of me, bafflers of graves." Not all, as we have seen, but all who will. The form used is a setting out, there are instructions, recapitulations, but

> Not I, not anyone else can travel that road for
>   you,
> You must travel it for yourself.

Therefore, the poet gradually withdraws. Part of this might be taken as coda, but I prefer at present to see the Fourth Movement as including everything from the salute near the end of Section 38 through 52, the final section. Little, until toward the close, is impressive in itself, but much, when read in the poem and especially the close, affects me like some of the late, great songs in *Winterreise* and above all "Leiermann." I take some lines from 49, the little, pleading Section 50, and 52, which truly sounds like the speech-back-to-us of a being already elsewhere, *in* Happiness as a place. One might be surprised that he troubles to speak back, but this is his nature.

We listen to these final sections, I think, with a peculiar intimacy of involvement—the reason being that we have been with him now so long in a personal way, unlike what happens in Lucretious, and without any intervening narrative distance such as one experiences in most long poems—an intimacy such, I say, as to make one friendly to his resistance to his work's being taken as literary; one feels what he means, and sympathizes; although it is of course a literary work—too idiosyncratic, like *Paradise*

Lost, to rank with the very first poems (I am thinking of the *Iliad,* the poem of Job, the *Oedipus Tyrannus,* the *Mahābhārata,* the *Commedia, King Lear*), but one that will do good to us so long as our language persists and the human race remains capable of interest in such things. (pp. 227-41)

> *John Berryman, " 'Song of Myself': Intention and Substance," in his* The Freedom of the Poet, *Farrar, Straus and Giroux, Inc., 1976, pp. 227-41.*

Walter Allen   (essay date 1959)

[*Allen is an English novelist of working-class life and a distinguished popular historian and critic of the novel. In the following excerpt, he discusses the difficulty of separating Whitman the poet and Whitman the person, and compares "Song of Myself" with T. S. Eliot's* The Waste Land.]

'Ain't he the damnedest simulacrum?' Whitman said of Swinburne. The trouble is, Whitman was often pretty much a simulacrum himself. Obviously Gerard Manley Hopkins, when he described him as 'a very great scoundrel' [see Further Reading], wasn't implying that Whitman was a crook: merely that he was neither an Oxford man, a Catholic nor a Tory. But there are times when the Good Gray Poet seems just a holy old faker, a phoney with a Father-Christmas beard. It is the sense of this, more than anything else perhaps, that has prevented Whitman from ever having been accepted wholeheartedly and universally as a great poet.

But ought it to matter? After all, many poets have had feet of clay, and we think none the less of their work because of it. Unfortunately, Whitman himself inextricably confused his poetry with his personality. As he said himself [see excerpt dated 1888],

> I found myself remaining possess'd, at the age of thirty-one to thirty-three, with a special desire and conviction. . . . This was a feeling or ambition to articulate and faithfully express in literary or poetic form, and uncompromisingly, my own physical, emotional, moral, intellectual, and aesthetic Personality, in the midst of, and tallying, the momentous spirit and facts of its immediate days, and of current America—and to exploit that Personality, identified with place and date, in a far more candid and comprehensive sense than any hitherto poem or book.

As soon as we begin to read Whitman, we are thrown back, whether we like it or not, on to the poet's life; and we are thrown back by the poet himself . . . [His] life was a succession of evasions, concealments and ambiguities. And in his work he remains enigmatic, for all that no poet has been more lavish than he in his use of the first person singular. We get far more hard facts about Wordsworth's life, career and personality from *The Prelude* than we do about Whitman's from all his collected poems. And at the same time, we know that it was Whitman's aim always to break down the distinctions between himself as man and himself as poet.

And of course it didn't work. It merely made confusion greater. It is impossible to get far with ***Leaves of Grass*** which, if not his greatest poem—surely that is **'When Lilacs Last in the Dooryard Bloom'd'**—is at least central to his work, without one's having to come to some sort of decision about the identity of the Walt Whitman Whitman is celebrating in it:

> Walt Whitman, a Kosmos, of Manhattan the son,
> Turbulent, fleshy, sensual, eating, drinking and breeding,
> No sentimentalist, no stander above men and women or apart from them,
> No more modest than immodest . . .

If that Walt Whitman is the actual Walt Whitman who edited the Brooklyn *Eagle* and rode the Brooklyn ferry, then one can only say that he is a very unpleasant and impertinent fellow, with his narcissism ('I dote on myself, there is that lot of me and all so luscious'), exhibitionism and voyeurism, his inability to know whether he is male or female and his readiness to become either at a moment's notice, his eagerness to adopt the role of Christ, his constant craving to merge into someone else (as Lawrence wrote in his essay on Whitman [see *NCLC,* Vol. 4, pp. 564-66], which is at once superb comic writing and magnificent literary criticism, 'If he knew that an Eskimo sat in a kyak, immediately there was Walt being little and yellow and greasy, sitting in a kyak'), above all, perhaps, his bullying insistence that he is going to love us, by force if necessary, and his demands for our love in return (and sometimes, it seems, he got it: there are few more comic episodes in literary history than the wooing of Walt across 3,000 miles of sea by Mrs Anne Gilchrist, widow of Alexander Gilchrist who wrote the life of Blake, who appears to have taken ***Leaves of Grass*** as a love-letter addressed personally to her; she proposed marriage to the poet, which was all right so long as she remained in England but very disconcerting when she turned up with her children in Philadelphia).

'This awful Whitman', in fact, as Lawrence said. Yet, when all the faults of taste have been gone over and criticism has done its worst, ***Leaves of Grass*** remains a great poem. And the clue to its greatness and to the kind of poem it is probably lies in the line 'I was the man, I suffer'd, I was there'. If one were to come to that line after reading later poetry surely more than anything else it would recall Eliot's

> And I Tiresias have foresuffered all
> Enacted on this same divan or bed;
> I who have sat by Thebes below the wall
> And walked among the lowest of the dead.

In his notes to *The Waste Land,* Eliot writes: 'Tiresias, although a mere spectator and not indeed a "character", is yet the most important personage in the poem, uniting all the rest. Just as the one-eyed merchant, seller of currants, melts into the Phoenician Sailor, and the latter is not wholly distinct from Ferdinand Prince of Naples, so all the women are one woman, and the two sexes meet in Tiresias'. **"Song of Myself"** is much less dramatised a poem than *The Waste Land;* in structure it more closely resembles a film or a radio script; but the Walt Whitman of the poem plays the part of Tiresias in Eliot's poem; he is, in fact, a Tiresias figure, the soothsayer who has been both man and woman, who can foretell the future, and who has been granted near-immortality. He is not the historical Whitman, writing the anonymous rave-notices of his own poems, at all.

Once the old Kosmos, of Manhattan the son, is seen in these terms, **"Song of Myself"** becomes assimilable and acceptable, and most of the criticisms normally made of it fall away. The function of Whitman-Tiresias is exactly that of Eliot's Tiresias: to be, in Professor Gay Wilson Allen's phrase, a time-binder. On the face of it, no two poets could have less in common than Eliot and Whitman, about whom Eliot in his time has expressed himself snootily enough; while his famous dictum that poetry is 'not the expression of personality, but an escape from personality', might have been phrased with direct reference to the nineteenth-century poet. Yet, so far as such categories are important, **"Song of Myself"** and *The Waste Land* are poems of a kind. The differences between them are glaring but can be over-stated, for in part they are differences stemming from differences in temperament and education and in the times at which the poems were composed: Whitman like Emerson, was a spokesman of that nineteenth-century American liberal optimism Eliot reacted against so vigorously; and we might expect to find in Eliot, too, the traditional Boston repugnance to the self-proclaimed 'rough' with his 'barbaric yawp'. But what the two poems share is at least as striking as their differences. Both are attempts to seize and recapitulate history in an eternal present, as *Ulysses* and *Finnegans Wake* are, too; though Whitman is here more ambitious than Eliot, taking in, as he does, the whole dark backward and abysm of geological time—

> For it the nebula cohered to an orb,
> The long slow strata piled to rest it on,
> Vast vegetables gave it sustenance,
> Monstrous sauroids transported it to their
> mouths and deposited it with care—

and penetrating to the bounds of astronomical space:

> I visit the orchards of spheres and look at the
> product,
> And look at quintillions ripen'd and look at
> quintillions green.

Both are poems of the modern city, Whitman's partly so at any rate. Technically, both proceed by what Richards, writing of the early Eliot, called a 'music of ideas':

> The ideas are of all kinds, abstract and concrete, general and particular, and, like the musician's phrases, they are arranged, not that they may tell us something, but that their effects in us may combine into a coherent whole of feeling and attitude and produce a peculiar liberation of the will. They are there to be responded to, not to be pondered or worked out.

Perhaps the best summing-up of them is that the one is as ineradicably of the nineteenth century as the other is obstinately of the twentieth, but the juxtaposition indicates how firmly rooted in American poetry Eliot's own work

is. Critics sometimes make great play with the alleged existence of two opposed traditions of American poetry, that of Poe and that of Whitman. It is doubtful whether there is much in it. For Lawrence, despite his scintillating tomahawk attack on him, Whitman was the one pioneer: 'After Whitman, nothing'. Right on his own terms, Lawrence was wrong on others. Ahead of Whitman were Pound and Eliot—and Joyce. They, more than the Sandburgs, the Wolfes, the Kerouacs and the practitioners of the Great American Novel, or even Hart Crane, are his true successors. (pp. 327-28)

> *Walter Allen, "Kosmos, of Manhattan the Son," in* New Statesman, *Vol. LVIII, No. 1487, September 12, 1959, pp. 327-28.*

James E. Miller, Jr. (essay date 1962)

[*Miller is an American educator and critic who has written extensively on American authors. In the following excerpt, he examines recurring imagery in* Leaves of Grass.]

Because *Leaves of Grass* is something more than simply a collection of miscellaneous lyric poetry written over the period of a lifetime, it offers many aesthetic gratifications to the reader who explores it as a unified whole. One of the devices that the structure makes possible, and which in turn contributes to the shaping of the structure, is the recurring image. Such images abound in *Leaves;* as they appear again and again they gather a body of meaning and a wealth of suggestion, until they develop into symbols of major significance for the poet—and the reader. Some of the most important of the recurring images are the grass, the sea, the bird, a whole cluster of celestial bodies, and others—such as the tree and the city. Any reader could compile his own list, and the diversity of the lists would simply reflect the complexity of the *Leaves* and its intricacy of design.

The dominant image in all of Whitman's work is the simple, separate leaf of grass. It is an image that gave him his title in his first edition in 1855, that served as a cluster-title in several subsequent editions, and that stuck to the end, without change, as the one single symbol that concentrated in itself the suggestion of the poet's many meanings. In the first edition *Leaves of Grass* appeared to be the title of every poem and appeared on every page as the running-title of the book.

Just how Whitman hit upon the term *leaves* in referring to blades of grass is not known. But that he was fully aware of the ambiguity and novelty of the word is clear. Throughout his book, he capitalizes on the merged meaning of the leaf as a common product of nature and as a page of his poetry. And he fuses the images or the blade of grass and the leaf of a tree, permitting himself to move from one to the other in successive poems without blurring his dominant image. In view of Whitman's theory of the suggestiveness of poetry, it would be misleading to define the symbolic meaning of the *leaves of grass* with precision. But many meanings closely related to Whitman's themes suggest themselves. Among them the most fundamental derives from the characteristic of grass to grow not only in single blades but also in clusters or clumps. The grass thus becomes a graphic representation of Whitman's central concept of democracy—individuality in balance with the mass, distinguished singleness in harmony with massive grouping.

The imagination of the reader will supply many related and supplementary meanings for the grass, especially on exploring **"Song of Myself "** as it incorporates the image in the basic foundations of its own (and the book's) structure. From the beginning of the poem, as the poet leans and loafs at his "ease observing a spear of summer grass," to the end, as he bequeaths himself to the "dirt to grow from the grass" he loves, the grass commands the poem's central position and directs its movement. It recurs not with mechanical regularity but in strategic sections where it springs to the fore with renewed life, and gathers the meaning of the poem into its slender, vital spears.

The spear of summer grass which the poet nonchalantly observes symbolizes in its simplicity the miracle of the universe. The mystery of life, of existence, of being, lies not far away in the exotic and mythical; it is in the near at hand, in the familiar and common. The spear of summer grass may therefore serve as the object of contemplation in launching the mystic journey. If the poet can apprehend the miraculous mystery of the silent, self-defined spear growing the globe around, he can then come to terms with the meaning of the universe. The one provides the key to the other: "I believe a leaf of grass is no less than the journey-work of the stars."

In a sense, then, the leaf of grass has no limits in its symbolic meaning—it means *everything, all,* the *total.* When the poet specifically explores the variety of its meanings in Section 6 of **"Song of Myself,"** he confesses his own uncertainty:

> A child said *What is the grass?* fetching it to me
> with full hands;
> How could I answer the child? I do not know
> what it is any more than he.

But the poet is willing to guess at some of the meanings. It may be the "flag" of his disposition, "out of hopeful green stuff woven." It may be the "handkerchief of the Lord," or it may itself be a child ("the produced babe of the vegetation"):

> Or I guess it is a uniform hieroglyphic,
> And it means, Sprouting alike in broad zones
> and narrow zones.

Indeed, the grass may have as many meanings as there are spears, each one significant in its own right:

> O I perceive after all so many uttering tongues,
> And I perceive they do not come from the roofs
> of mouths for nothing.

Outside **"Song of Myself,"** the grass appears and reappears, sometimes merely mentioned, sometimes presented in full portrait; but it always carries along the complex of meaning that has accrued. It is surely the floor of the renewed "garden" of the "Children of Adam" poems; it certainly appears along the **"Open Road"** which the poet takes to "afoot and light-hearted." It survives even its embracement in French in **"Our Old Feuillage."** It provides the bed for the **"Broad-Axe"** to lie upon ("Resting the grass amid and upon"), and it must provide the seat for the poet as he sits observing "By the Roadside."

In these and in other places throughout the *Leaves* the grass is glimpsed, subtly injecting its slender shape and green color. But probably the most dramatic variation in the use of the image is in the "Calamus" section. When queried about calamus by someone who did not know the plant, Whitman replied: "Calamus is the very large and aromatic grass, or rush, growing about water ponds in the valleys—spears about three feet high; often called Sweet Flag; grows all over the Northern and Middle States. The recherché or ethereal sense of the term, as used in my book, arises probably from the actual Calamus presenting the biggest and hardiest kind of spears of grass, and their fresh, aquatic, pungent bouquet." This was the symbol that the poet wished to identify with the theme of adhesiveness, or comradeship. In contrast with the common grass "that grows wherever the land is and the water is," the calamus plant grows

> In paths untrodden,
> In the growth by margins of pond-waters,
> Escaped from the life that exhibits itself.

The true calamus-relationship is rare, exceptional, uncommon. As the poet elaborates the image in such poems as **"Scented Herbage of My Breast"** and **"These I Singing in Spring,"** he exploits all the possibilities for symbolism that the strongly individualistic plant offers—"Indeed O death, I think now these leaves mean precisely the same as you mean," "And this, O this shall henceforth be the token of comrades, this calamus-root shall." Anyone familiar with the long, tapering leaves and the cylindrical flower of the calamus plant will recognize the phallic symbolism immediately. Whitman seemed to acknowledge the ambiguity of the image in **"Scented Herbage of My Breast"** when he exclaimed: "Emblematic and capricious blades I leave you, now you serve me not, / I will say what I have to say by itself." The outcry is, of course, merely a part of the poem's drama, and its ultimate consequence is to emphasize the spirituality (as suggested by the "pungent bouquet" of the calamus) of the "manly attachment" celebrated by the poet as the basis of genuine democracy.

Probably no image, not even that in the title, appears more frequently in *Leaves of Grass* than the sea and the related water-images such as rivers, lakes, and ponds. The image is established almost from the beginning as a major symbol; certainly by the time one has read through the introductory pages, he has become aware of the important role that the sea is to assume in the poetry that follows.

The third poem in "Inscriptions," **"In Cabin'd Ships at Sea,"** introduces the image—

> The boundless blue on every side expanding,
> With whistling winds and music of the waves,
> the large imperious waves. . . .

And the mariners, or voyagers, in their contemplation of the poet's "reminiscence of the land," assert that they "feel" the "ebb and flow of endless motion," "the vague and vast suggestions of the briny world, the liquid-flowing syllables." In this poem the land-ocean dichotomy, which functions symbolically (along with that point of union, the seashore) throughout *Leaves of Grass,* is vividly introduced. Although *Leaves of Grass* is "ocean's poem," it is also land's poem—it is the poem of both the body and the soul.

After the sporadic appearance of the sea image in the song section of *Leaves,* it becomes dominant in the "Sea-Drift" cluster. As the title of this section indicates, emphasis is placed on one attribute of the sea—the refuse thrown up by the waves to the shallow waters of the seashore. And of course the poet intends, as applicable to himself and to mankind, all of the connotations of the word "drift." The word suggests the quality of questioning restlessness which seems to define the poet's emotional state in the poems throughout the section. But although **"Out of the Cradle Endlessly Rocking"** (the first poem) is a "seashore" poem, the only "drift" cast up by the ocean in it is the word *death:*

> But edging near as privately for me rustling at my feet,
> Creeping thence steadily up to my ears and laving me softly all over,
> Death, death, death, death, death.

There seems to be here an enactment of the death-scene, with the sea assuming the role of death. But the sea is identified as a "cradle endlessly rocking" in the opening line of the poem, and the metaphor is repeated at the end— "old crone rocking the cradle, swathed in sweet garments, bending aside." This vivid figure is inevitably associated with the word whispered out of the sea—*death.* The poet, through the association of images, links birth with death, death with birth. Because of his realization that the two are closely linked, that death is not an end but a beginning, the poet accepts the word *death* as the "word of the sweetest song."

Although the sea is described as "the fierce old mother" who "endlessly cries for her castaways" in **"As I Ebb'd with the Ocean of Life,"** the central symbol is "The rim, the sediment that stands for all the water and all the land of the globe." As in **"In Cabin'd Ships at Sea,"** the poet utilizes both land and sea as major symbols. The seashore becomes the meeting ground for body and spirit, life and death; but it is a meeting ground ambiguous in meaning because of the "tufts of straw, sands, fragments" which are "Buoy'd hither from many moods, one contradicting another." But when the poet asserts, "I too have bubbled up, floated the measureless float, and been wash'd on your shores," he seems to acknowledge an awareness of his origin in the world of spirit and his ultimate, perhaps imminent, return.

After its full exploitation in "Sea-Drift" the sea or water image appears frequently in *Leaves of Grass.* In **"When Lilacs Last in the Dooryard Bloom'd,"** it is "Down to the shores of the water, the path by the swamp in the dimness" that the poet is finally lured by the hermit-thrush and "death's outlet song of life." And as the poet listens, the bird song "floats" "over the rising and sinking waves." In **"By Blue Ontario's Shore,"** what was once the 1855 Preface has been translated into poetry and given a seminarra-

tive framework and a setting beside a large body of water. Ontario's shore gains significance from the seashore symbolism of the "Sea-Drift" section. There is the clear suggestion that the poet's spiritual insight is related to his position by the waters of Ontario.

> Thus by blue Ontario's shore,
> While the winds fann'd me and the waves came trooping toward me,
> I thrill'd with the power's pulsations, and the charm of my theme was upon me,
> Till the tissues that held me parted their ties upon me.

The poet here dramatizes a spiritual trance; and Ontario's shore, its winds and waves, play a vital role in bestowing the vision.

The "Autumn Rivulets" section of *Leaves* incorporates the symbolic water image in its title. And the opening poem, **"As Consequent, Etc.,"** asserts that "life's evermodern rapids" are "soon to blend, / With the old streams of death":

> In you whoe'er you are my book perusing,
> In I myself, in all the world, these currents flowing,
> All, all toward the mystic ocean tending.

The "mystic ocean" is the realm of the spirit, as the reader of *Leaves* by now already knows. The poet also makes further use in this poem of the seashore symbol exploited in "Sea-Drift":

> Currents for starting a continent new,
> Overtures sent to the solid out of the liquid,
> Fusion of ocean and land, tender and pensive waves. . . .

Those "overtures" sent out of the liquid could be none other than a spiritual wooing which, in turn, seems to culminate in the "fusion" of water and earth represented by the seashore. Such a fusion is a marriage of body and soul, of the material and the spiritual, of life and death.

"Passage to India" makes full use of the ocean as symbol in the central dramatic situation of the poem, in which the poet pleads with his soul to venture forth on the voyage. Near the end the poet exclaims:

> Sail forth—steer for the deep waters only,
> Reckless O soul, exploring, I with thee, and thou with me,
> For we are bound where mariner has not yet dared to go. . . .

The place for which the poet and his soul are bound is, surely, the country of death—the realm of the spirit. Or, as the poet says a few lines later, "O daring joy, but safe! are they not all the seas of God?"

The seas throughout *Leaves of Grass* are "the seas of God." **"What Ship Puzzled at Sea"** in the "Whispers of Heavenly Death" section, utilizes the sea as symbol to dramatize the situation of an individual spiritually lost and in need of direction. The poet says, "Here, sailor! here, ship! take aboard the most perfect pilot," referring to himself and his book. In the "Songs of Parting" section, use is made of the sea-image in two poems of farewell, **"Joy,**

Shipmate, Joy!" and "Now Finalè to the Shore." And throughout the annexes, the sea maintains its position as a dominant image in Whitman's poetry. Almost the entire symbolic significance of such a slight poem as **"From Montauk Point"** (in "Sands at Seventy") is dependent on the meanings the sea accumulates throughout *Leaves*. The poet looks out and contemplates

> The tossing waves, the foam, the ships in the dis-
>   tance,
> The wild unrest, the snowy, curling caps—that
>   inbound urge and urge of waves,
> Seeking the shores forever.

Although in *Leaves* the sea and other water images invariably are associated with the soul and the world of spirituality, their contexts frequently suggest more complex meanings. Sigmund Freud, in his discussion of dream imagery [in *A General Introduction to Psycho-Analysis*], asserted that birth almost always is associated with water—either the entering of it or the emerging from it. He conjectured that the reason for this association is twofold: first, there is a racial memory, unconscious, of the evolutionary emergence of life from the sea; and second, there is a personal memory, quite likely unconscious, of an individual's emergence from the embryo stage in the amniotic liquid of the womb. Throughout *Leaves,* water is associated with death; but in Whitman's view, death is birth, a rebirth, an entry into the spiritual world comparable to the previous entry into the physical world. In **"Out of the Cradle Endlessly Rocking,"** the identification of the sea with the old crone rocking the cradle appears to associate the ocean with the amniotic fluid of the womb and is suggestive of the ocean as the evolutionary source of all life. With birth and life came also, as the old crone of the sea whispers ("hissing melodious" like the snake of the Garden of Eden)—"death, death, death, death, death." There is suggested, then, the cyclic paradox: life brings death; death brings life.

The bird image is first introduced in **"Starting from Paumanok."** The mockingbird, the thrush, and hawk—the birds Whitman writes about most frequently—all appear:

> Having studied the mocking-bird's tones and the
>   flight of the mountain-hawk,
> And heard at dawn the unrivall'd one, the her-
>   mit-thrush from the swamp-cedars,
> Solitary, singing in the West, I strike up for a
>   New World.

In the introduction the poet places emphasis on particular distinguishing details which are to have greatest significance in the dramatic roles to be played later by the birds—the song of the mockingbird, the flight of the mountain-hawk, the habitat (swamp-cedars) of the hermit-thrush. And the poet is careful to capitalize on the connotations implicit in the adjectival elements in the names of these birds—*mocking, mountain, hermit.*

Between its introduction in **"Starting from Paumanok"** and its major symbolic use in "Birds of Passage" and **"Out of the Cradle Endlessly Rocking,"** the bird-image appears only sporadically. At the end of **"Song of Myself,"** in the famous "barbaric yawp" passage, the poet identifies himself and his primitive nature with the hawk. Vivid use is made of the bird-image in a "Children of Adam" poem, **"We Two, How Long We Were Fool'd";** in these two poems, hawks symbolize the realization of the transcendent fulfillment of primitive, natural, and uninhibited sexuality. In **"Crossing Brooklyn Ferry,"** sea gulls are among the "dumb, beautiful ministers" which furnish their "parts toward eternity."

But it is not until the "Birds of Passage" section that the bird-image comes clearly to the fore. In the opening poem of the section, **"Song of the Universal,"** the "uncaught bird," ever "hovering, hovering, / High in the purer, happier air" is one of several images used to symbolize the presence of future perfection within the imperfect now. By "spiral routes" this seed of perfection will eventually reach fulfillment, as all things tend toward the ideal in "mystic evolution." All events in time are, like the flights of birds, simply happenings in the unfolding of mystic evolution; these events have significance only in "passage"—that is, only in their contribution to time's unraveling. Also, events unfold rhythmically (on "spiral routes"), just as the flights of birds are recurrent, patterned after the rhythmical rotation of the seasons.

In **"Out of the Cradle Endlessly Rocking,"** the bird is for the first time given a major dramatic role. The mockingbirds in **"Out of the Cradle Endlessly Rocking"** are "two feather'd guests from Alabama" whose domestic bliss is destroyed by the disappearance of the she-bird. As the small boy listens, the he-bird pours forth his great, sad carol of "lonesome love." Were the song no more than a lament of the bereaved lover, the poem would still be a masterpiece. But the mockingbird's outcry of bereavement has a special significance: "The aria's meaning" deposited in the soul of the boy is never explicitly stated but it is hinted at when the poet exclaims:

> The messenger there arous'd, the fire, the sweet
>   hell within,
> The unknown want, the destiny of me.

The mockingbird symbolizes the creative transfiguration brought by consuming but unfulfilled love. And when the sea sends forth its word of death as the "clew" the boy requests, the "outsetting bard" has found the theme for all his songs.

In **"When Lilacs Last in the Dooryard Bloom'd,"** the poet makes full use of the attributes of the bird chosen to play a major role in the poem:

> Solitary the thrush,
> The hermit withdrawn to himself, avoiding the
>   settlements,
> Sings by himself a song.

The bird sings, in the "secluded recesses" of the swamp, his "song of the bleeding throat." The poet quickly realizes that the bird's song will effect a reconciliation to the lamented death, but he tells the "bashful and tender" singer, "But a moment I linger, for the lustrous star has detain'd me." His grief over the death of Lincoln spent, the poet flees to the swamp to listen to and translate the thrush's song. The song turns out to be a paean in praise of "the sure-enwinding arms of cool-enfolding death," a carol of joy at the bliss of death. The insight granted the poet in **"Out of the Cradle Endlessly Rocking,"** where he fuses the bird's song and the sea's word, is in **"Lilacs"** granted by the bird's song alone. After the song of the hermit-thrush the poet is granted a mystic vision which assures him of the joy of death. In initiating this reconciliation, the thrush represents the voice of spirituality. Like the "uncaught bird" of **"Song of the Universal,"** the hermit-thrush in **"Lilacs"** is the spiritual which exists in the present imperfection (or grief), the impulse toward the ideal which is the hope in the tragedy of death.

Near the end of *Leaves of Grass,* in **"Thou Mother with Thy Equal Brood"** the poet envisions the nation itself as a bird in flight:

> As a strong bird on pinions free,
> Joyous, the amplest spaces heavenward cleaving,
> Such be the thought I'd think of thee America,
> Such be the recitative I'd bring for thee.

The figure seems apt for the view that America's promise must find its fulfillment in the future: "Shalt soar toward the fulfillment of the future, the spirit of the body and the mind, / The soul, its destinies." The figure of the bird is here again used to suggest the hidden if not secret resource of mystic evolution. America is like the hovering "uncaught bird" of **"Song of the Universal."**

In view of the various symbolic functions of the bird image in *Leaves,* the systematic introduction of the three birds—mockingbird, mountain-hawk, hermit-thrush—in **"Starting from Paumanok"** may have special significance. Later in the poem the poet cries out the greatness of another trinity:

> My comrade!
> For you to share with me two greatnesses, and
>   a third one rising inclusive and more resplendent,
> The greatness of Love and Democracy, and the
>   greatness of Religion.

Whitman's three birds seem clearly to relate to his three themes:

> Mockingbird—Love
> Mountain-hawk—Democracy
> Hermit-thrush—Religion

Poems in *Leaves of Grass* in which these birds are most fully portrayed bear out their association with particular themes: the mockingbird with love, both fulfilled and "lonesome," in **"Out of the Cradle Endlessly Rocking"**; the mountain-hawk (or eagle or sea gull with which the hawk, in its attribute of soaring flight, is associated) with democracy in **"Thou Mother with Thy Equal Brood"** (once called "As a Strong Bird on Pinions Free"); and the hermit-thrush with religion (or spirituality) in **"When Lilacs Last in the Dooryard Bloom'd."** Most frequently throughout *Leaves of Grass* the bird-image is, like the hermit-thrush in **"Lilacs,"** a "santa spirita" figure (the "light, lighter than light" in **"Chanting the Square Deific"**, reminding the poet by its presence and its notes, no matter how small or low, of the eternal in the temporal, of the spiritual beyond the material.

The earth, sun, moon, and star appear separately or, frequently, in groups in the celestial scenes of *Leaves.* For example, in **"Eidólons"**:

> All space, all time,
> (The stars, the terrible perturbations of the suns,
> Swelling, collapsing, ending, serving their longer, shorter use,)
> Fill'd with eidólons only.

A sky-scene is evoked by the very words *space* and *time,* and the gradual evolution of the celestial destiny is cited as "proof " of the existence of the spiritual (and guiding) world of eidólons. Perhaps the most impressive scene of this kind in Whitman is in **"Song of Myself "**:

> I open my scuttle at night and see the far-sprinkled systems,
> And all I see multiplied as high as I can cipher edge but the rim of the farther systems.
>
> Wider and wider they spread, expanding, always expanding,
> Outward and outward and forever outward.
>
> My sun has his sun and round him obediently wheels,
> He joins with his partners a group of superior circuit,
> And greater sets follow, making specks of the greatest inside them.

The immense, far-flung, and endless "superior circuits" serve to imply to man, in his quest for order in a chaotic world, that his disorder is part of a greater harmony. The balance and rhythm of an infinite universe are the basis for a faith in a cosmic plan in which man serves his purpose. Paradoxically, that universe which shrinks not just man but his solar system into microscopic specks by its order and complexly intricate interrelationships, makes man and his destiny supremely important in an unfolding cosmic scheme.

The earth frequently appears in *Leaves* as a great round globe sailing through the heavens. This perspective serves to project both poet and reader into the universe as cosmic observers witnessing the dramatic progression of the earth. For example—

> Earth, my likeness,
> Though you look so impassive, ample and spheric there,
> I now suspect that is not all. . . .

The *there* (end of the second line) suggests a gesture of pointing by the poet to a globe from which he has somehow cast himself adrift. Curiously enough, it is almost always this independent view of the earth that appears in *Leaves.* Some of Whitman's most interesting effects are achieved by dramatic changes in perspective involving this "spheric" earth. In **"Salut au Monde!"** for instance, the poet passes from a point of observation on the earth to one out in space and then, finally, to a position back on the earth. As the poet observes from afar the ball of earth, he seems to assume the magnitude of a deity: "I see a great round wonder rolling through space . . . /I see the shaded part on one side where the sleepers are sleeping, and the sunlit part on the other side." Such a view of the earth, reduced in size to the scale of a child's toy, results in a corresponding enlargement of the observer. As the earth comes within the grasp of the onlooker, so the individual assumes a position of greater magnitude in the universe. Such a result seems clearly the intent of the poet; in **"A Song of the Rolling Earth"** he says:

> Whoever you are! motion and reflection are especially for you,
> The divine ship sails the divine sea for you.

Because of its appearance in **"When Lilacs Last in the Dooryard Bloom'd,"** the star is perhaps the best known of the celestial images in Whitman. The drama of the dark cloud obscuring the bright star is, however, a recurring symbolic event in *Leaves.* The drama first appears in **"On the Beach at Night"**:

> Up through the darkness,
> While ravening clouds, the burial clouds, in black masses spreading,
> Lower sullen and fast athwart and down the sky,
> Amid a transparent clear belt of ether yet left in the east,
> Ascends large and calm the lord-star Jupiter. . . .

The father assures the frightened child that the "ravening clouds" obscure the stars "only in apparition." In **"When Lilacs Last in the Dooryard Bloom'd"** the same symbolic drama recurs. In the opening of the poem the poet grieves:

> O powerful western fallen star!
> O shades of night—O moody, tearful night!
> O great star disappear'd—O the black murk that hides the star!.

Later in the poem, this "harsh surrounding cloud" is identified directly with the long funeral procession bearing the President's body from east to west:

> Falling upon them all and among them all, enveloping me with the rest,
> Appear'd the cloud, appear'd the long black trail. . . .

This recurring image receives climactic treatment in one of the key poems in the latter part of *Leaves of Grass*— "Whispers of Heavenly Death":

> I see, just see skyward, great cloud-masses,
> Mournfully slowly they roll, silently swelling and mixing,
> With at times a half-dimm'd sadden'd far-off star,
> Appearing and disappearing.

It is clear that this simple but vivid celestial image signified for the poet the rebirth that is inherent in death. By their very nature—the star in its fixedness and the cloud in its transience—these heavenly objects symbolize the triumph of the eternal, the illusoriness of death.

The sun figures in a number of poems in *Leaves.* In **"Crossing Brooklyn Ferry,"** the "sun there half an hour high" becomes an important part of the dynamic setting. In Section 3, at the opening of the scene, the sun's reflection forms the "fine centrifugal spokes" of a halo for the poet as he gazes down into the water; but gradually the sun disappears, day fades, and by the end of the scene it is night. In **"Out of the Cradle Endlessly Rocking,"** the sun is the most important figure in the first, happy song of the bird: "Pour down your warmth, great sun! / While we bask, we two together." The sun in both of these poems is associated with fruitful, fulfilled life.

As some such symbol the sun receives its fullest treatment in the "Drum-Taps" poem, **"Give Me the Splendid Silent Sun"**:

> Give me the splendid silent sun with all his beams full-dazzling,
> Give me juicy autumnal fruit ripe and red from the orchard,
> Give me a field where the unmow'd grass grows,
> Give me an arbor, give me the trellis'd grape. . . .

The sun in this poem is associated with the rich fertility of the orchard, grass, fruit—with unhampered nature in all its varied abundance. But the sun is more than the symbol of fertility; it is also the symbol of the "primal sanities" of solitude and nature. The sun thus symbolizes a way of life contrasted in the poem with the crowded and noisy "life of the theatre, bar-room, huge hotel." In Section 2 of the poem, beginning with the startling "Keep your splendid silent sun," the poet asserts his preference for the life of the cities, for the life of the war itself with its human tumult and impact.

The section of *Leaves of Grass* called "From Noon to Starry Night" utilizes in its title the sun as a symbol of fertility. In the opening poem of the section, **"Thou Orb Aloft Full-Dazzling,"** the poet identifies the fruitfulness of the "hot October noon" with his own productivity as an artist; and he suggests that the poetic process, like the sun, has its "perturbations, sudden breaks and shafts of flame gigantic." But the "fructifying heat and light" of the poet must eventually dissipate, as "noon" gives way to "starry night." One of the poems in "Songs of Parting"—**"Song at Sunset"**—uses the sun as symbol in much the same way as "From Noon to Starry Night." When the poet says, "Splendor of ended day floating and filling me," he is suggesting again the sun as symbol of creativity. As the sun sets in splendor, so the poet feels the magnificence of his last creative impulses. He pledges to sing until the "last ray gleams."

There is one "picture" which recurs in *Leaves of Grass* with so little variation in detail that one wonders whether it might not originate in an experience indelibly impressed on the poet's mind. The scene is most elaborately delineated in **"Dirge for Two Veterans,"** a "Drum-Taps" poem, which describes the funeral for two soldiers, father and son. The poet meticulously avoids sentimentality by focusing not on the pathos but on the details of setting. Of these, the moon is the most prominent:

> Lo, the moon ascending,
> Up from the east the silvery round moon,
> Beautiful over the house-tops, ghastly, phantom moon,
> Immense and silent moon.

The moon serves in some mystic way to reconcile the poet

to the tragic deaths he witnesses. At one point he says that it is "Some mother's large transparent face, / In heaven brighter growing." And he exclaims, "O moon immense with your silvery face you soothe me!" The moon also seems to transfigure death and diminish its horror in another "Drum-Taps" poem, **"Look Down Fair Moon"**:

> Look down fair moon and bathe this scene,
> Pour softly down night's nimbus floods on faces
>   ghastly, swollen, purple,
> On the dead on their backs with arms toss'd
>   wide,
> Pour down your unstinted nimbus sacred moon.

Perhaps the secret of this obsessive scene is revealed in **"Old War-Dreams,"** in the "From Noon to Starry Night" section. The poet confesses, as the title suggests, that although the "carnage" through which he moved has long since passed away, now he dreams "of their forms at night." He dreams—

> Of scenes of Nature, fields and mountains,
> Of skies so beauteous after a storm, and at night
>   the moon so unearthly bright,
> Shining sweetly, shining down, where we dig the
>   trenches and gather the heaps,
> I dream, I dream, I dream.

This scene of "the dead on their backs with arms extended wide" seems almost a precise duplication of that in **"Look Down Fair Moon"**; and the moon of "unearthly brightness" shedding its soothing nimbus seems to be an image common to all of these battlefield scenes. The refrain, "I dream, I dream, I dream," suggests that the experience is so deeply imbedded in the poet's consciousness that not even the embodiment of the scene in art can purge it. If Whitman did derive the scene from some experience in the Civil War, it was a scene he was in part prepared for; for even before the war, in one of his most celebrated poems, **"Out of the Cradle Endlessly Rocking,"** he had associated the moon ("The yellow half-moon enlarged, sagging down, drooping, the face of the sea almost touching" with death. The mockingbird in the poem, in his first song, invests the sun with his own feelings of a fulfilled, happy life; and, in his second "aria," he invests the moon with his keen sense of tragic loss in death. Underlying these identifications is, of course, the common association of the day with life, the night with death.

Many additional images recur throughout the *Leaves* and gather a special significance as they appear and reappear. Each reader will carry from the book memory of particular images which made vivid impressions. Not many readers, however, will miss Whitman's individual use of the tree and the city. These by no means exhaust the memorable images of *Leaves,* but they are representative. A glance at Whitman's handling of them should reveal, therefore, much of his method in using imagery throughout the whole of *Leaves.*

The tree was at one time destined to have a larger role in *Leaves.* Whitman at first wrote many of the "Calamus" poems under the title "Live Oak, with Moss," and this tree apparently once held the symbolic position now held by the calamus plant in the "Calamus" poems. There are elements of this original plan which have survived. In **"Start-**ing from Paumanok,"** in the section which commands the reader to *see* in the poet's poems the whole varied life of the New World, Whitman says: "See, pastures and forests in my poems—see, animals wild and tame—see, beyond the Kaw, countless herds of buffalo feeding on short curly grass." In this slight reference to forests, Whitman merges them with other elements of the West to balance the "cities, solid, vast, inland, with paved streets" of the immediately succeeding line. In **"Song of Myself,"** however, it is clear that the trees have acquired a symbolic function. "Earth of the slumbering and liquid trees" is a line in the midst of a passionate passage in which the feminine earth is described as awaiting her lover, the poet. In another passage nature is described in sexual terms: "Broad muscular fields, branches of live oak, loving lounger in my winding paths, it shall be you!" There seems no doubt that the tree has become identified in these passages with the procreative processes of life.

This identification is suggested in **"I Saw in Louisiana a Live-Oak Growing,"** one of the survivors of the original series on the live-oak in the "Calamus" section. The look of the live-oak, "rude, unbending, lusty," makes the poet think of himself; and he breaks off "a twig with a certain number of leaves upon it," twines "around it a little moss," and brings it home to place in his room. Both this token and the live-oak itself ("the live-oak glistens there in Louisiana solitary in a wide flat space") seem clearly phallic symbols. The poet himself says, "Yet it remains to me a curious token, it makes me think of manly love." Like the calamus root, the tree in this case seems to be a physical symbol of a spiritual love, that love which transcends the earthly love of man and woman.

In **"Our Old Feuillage"** trees are a vivid part of the multitude of images which constitute the "divine leaves" of the poet:

> In lower latitudes in warmer air in the Carolinas
>   the large black buzzard floating slowly high
>   beyond the tree tops,
> Below, the red cedar festoon'd with tylandria,
>   the pines and cypresses growing out of the
>   white sand that spreads far and flat. . . .

And trees are inevitably included in the cast of characters in **"Song of the Broad-Axe"**: "Welcome are lands of pine and oak, / Welcome are lands of the lemon and fig. . . . " But in this poem, it is as victims that the trees fulfill their function in the progression of events: "The solid forest gives fluid utterances, / They tumble forth, they rise and form. . . . " Their destiny, like man's, is a death and rebirth; the "real" fulfillment arrives only with the rebirth.

It is, of course, as symbol of the wilderness and of the West that the trees appear in **"Song of the Broad-Axe,"** and it is as such a symbol that the tree becomes the protagonist in **"Song of the Redwood Tree,"** the only long poem devoted exclusively to this image. Whitman uses the device of the personified redwood tree, in the throes of death, to prophesy the accomplishment in the West of "the promise of thousands of years, till now deferr'd, / Promis'd to be fulfill'd, our common kind, the race." In the description of the life experienced by the dying tree, the poem becomes clearly symbolic. The tree sings:

> *Perennial hardy life of me with joys 'mid rain and*
> *   many a summer sun,*
> *And the white snows and night and the wild*
> *   winds;*
> *O the great patient rugged joys, my soul's strong*
> *   joys unreck'd by man. . . .*

The "white snows" and "wild winds" are suggestive of turbulent human emotions; and, in the context of the symbolic significance of the tree in the previous pages of *Leaves,* the description of the habitat becomes more meaningful:

> *But come from Nature's long and harmless*
> *   throes, peacefully builded thence,*
> *These virgin lands, lands of the Western shore,*
> *To the new culminating man, to you, the empire*
> *   new. . . .*

This dedication of the "virgin lands" to the "new culminating man" suggests a feminine-masculine relationship perhaps symbolized by the tree itself on the lands. Such a suggestion seems reinforced as the tree continues to sing:

> *You occult deep volitions,*
> *You average spiritual manhood, purpose of all,*
> *   pois'd on yourself, giving not taking law,*
> *You womanhood divine, mistress and sources of*
> *   all, whence life and love and ought that comes*
> *   from life and love. . . .*

The "occult deep volitions," perhaps the life-force manifested in the sex instinct, seem to be symbolized by the masculine tree, poised and independent, and by the feminine earth, mistress and source of all. The earlier identification of the live-oak as a phallic symbol appears to be exploited in the portrayal of other trees as complex symbols of the frontier West.

Unlike many romantic poets, Whitman does not place a premium on nature at the expense of the human. Whenever Whitman sketches the city image in a few brief strokes, the reader feels his sense of excitement and awe and pleasure. Perhaps the equality with which Whitman viewed both country and city may be best seen in the opening passage of **"Starting from Paumanok,"** in which the poet presents himself as a composite American born of both city and the frontier. Not only is he the "lover of populous pavements" and the "Dweller in Mannahatta" but he is also a "miner in California" and roams "Dakota's woods"—

> *. . . withdrawn to muse and meditate in some*
> *   deep recess,*
> *Far from the clank of crowds intervals passing*
> *   rapt and happy. . . .*

When Whitman ends this passage with, "Solitary, singing in the West, I strike up for a New World," the *West* is not the prairies or the Pacific coast, but all these states which make up, in their populous cities as well as their vast empty prairies, the New World.

Whitman had a genius for evoking in the fewest possible words the busy, noisy, peopled city: "populous pavements," "the clank of crowds." In the first the single detail chosen—pavements—is precisely right for the dominant visual impression of a large city. In the second the "clank" captures the dominant audio-impression. In a section of **"Song of Myself"** (beginning the "blab of the pave"), Whitman succeeds admirably in a minimum of lines in evoking the entire complex and exciting life of a city by the rapid listing, one after the other, of evocative details— the "heavy omnibus," the "snow-sleighs," the "rous'd mobs," the "curtain'd litter," the "meeting of enemies" with the "excited crowd" penetrated by the policeman:

> *The impassive stones that receive and return so*
> *   many echoes,*
> *What groans of over-fed or half-starv'd who fall*
> *   sunstruck or in fits,*
> *What exclamations of women taken suddenly*
> *   who hurry home and give birth to babes,*
> *What living and buried speech is always vibrat-*
> *   ing here, what howls restrain'd by decorum,*
> *Arrests of criminals, slights, adulterous offers*
> *   made, acceptances, rejections with convex*
> *   lips. . . .*

These images, all the "echoes" of the "impassive stones," are designed for the ear; they are also an extension of the opening image, "the blab of the pave." Through these images of sound, Whitman recreates the infinite and varied life of the city, not through an indiscriminate piling of detail on detail but rather through careful selection of details which combine to convey the essence of the immense and hurried city. And Whitman does not portray the city in order to reject it. He says, "I mind them or the show or resonance of them—I come and I depart."

Whitman was always able to evoke the turbulent and chaotic city in a few vivid words. In **"In Paths Untrodden"** he says, "Here by myself away from the clank of the world." In **"Song of the Open Road"** he says, "You flagg'd walks of the cities! you strong curbs at the edges!" In **"Song of the Broad-Axe,"** he explains that the great city is "not the place of stretch'd wharves, docks, manufactures, deposits of produce merely," but rather the city which "stands with the brawniest breed of orators and bards." **"A Broadway Pageant"** takes place when "million-footed Manhattan unpent descends to her pavements." In **"First O Songs for a Prelude,"** the opening song of "Drum-Taps," Manhattan is personified in a dramatic scene:

> *Sleepless amid her ships, her houses, her incal-*
> *   culable wealth,*
> *With her million children around her, suddenly,*
> *At dead of night, at news from the south,*
> *Incens'd struck with clinch'd hand the pave-*
> *   ment.*

In **"Give Me the Splendid Silent Sun,"** half the poem is devoted to the portrayal of the poet's beloved Manhattan, "People, endless, streaming, with strong voices, passions, pageants." In this poem Whitman's theme is his preference for the populous city over the solitude of nature.

Something of Whitman's vast affection for his native town, the city which, no doubt, served as the prototype for all the cities in *Leaves,* is embodied in **"Mannahatta"** (in "From Noon to Starry Night"), a poem unashamedly dedicated to the celebration of the metropolis:

> Trottoirs thron'd, vehicles, Broadway, the
> women, the shops and shows!
> A million people—manners free and superb—
> open voices—hospitality—the most coura-
> geous and friendly young men. . . .

If Whitman's attitude toward the city as seen in **"Give Me the Splendid Silent Sun"** was shaped by his faith in the cause of the Civil War and his belief in the necessity of mass action, so his attitude in **"Mannahatta"**—and no doubt in other poems celebrating the city—is formed in part out of his strong emotional devotion to the "Calamus" idea. Companionship, friendship, comradeship, or the potential of such relationships existent in masses of people—all were for Whitman strong attractions of the city of a million people. It is significant that the ideal delineated in "Calamus," in the poem called **"I Dream'd in a Dream,"** is, paradoxically, not an ideal of secluded nature as the "Calamus" symbol would suggest, but rather the ideal of a city—"the new city of Friends." But in addition the city attracted because it offered the full rich complexity, multiplicity, comedy, and tragedy of life.

Even in "Sands at Seventy" Whitman could envision the romance of the city with excitement:

> Could but thy flagstones, curbs, façades, tell
> their inimitable tales;
> Thy windows rich, and huge hotels—thy side-
> walks wide.

Man was, after all, the supreme fact for Whitman. The universe of *Leaves* is man-centered, even though there is full acceptance of science which paradoxically proves otherwise. It is only natural that one of Whitman's most frequently recurring images should be the populous city—the dwelling place of man en masse. And the detail which appears almost invariably—the sidewalk or pavement—suggests not man comfortably situated in his home but man in movement, energetic and creative, traveling the open, and endless, road. (pp. 114-35)

> *James E. Miller, Jr., in his* Walt Whitman,
> *Twayne Publishers, Inc., 1962, 188 p.*

Kenneth Rexroth   (essay date 1966)

[*Rexroth was one of the leading pioneers in the revival of poetry in the San Francisco area during the 1940s and 1950s. Largely self-educated, he became involved early in his career with such left-wing organizations as the John Reed Club, the Communist party, and the International Workers of the World. During World War II he was a conscientious objector, and since that time has become antipolitical in his work and writing. Rexroth's early poetry was greatly influenced by the surrealism of André Breton, but his later verse has become more traditional in style and content, though by no means less complex. However, it is as a critic and translator that Rexroth has gained prominence in American letters. As a critic, his acute intelligence and wide sympathy have allowed him to examine such varied subjects as jazz, Greek mythology, the works of D. H. Lawrence, and the Cabala. As a translator, Rexroth is largely responsible for introducing the West to both Chinese and Japanese clas-* sics. In the following essay, he expresses admiration for Whitman's vision of democracy.]

Our civilization is the only one in history whose major artists have rejected its dominant values. Baudelaire, Mallarmé, Rimbaud, Stendhal, Flaubert, Dostoevsky, Melville, Mark Twain—all are self-alienated outcasts. One nineteenth-century writer of world importance successfully refused alienation, yet still speaks significantly to us—Walt Whitman, the polar opposite of Baudelaire.

Most intellectuals of our generation think of America as the apotheosis of commercial, competitive, middle-class society. Because Whitman found within it an abundance of just those qualities that it seems today most to lack, the sophisticated read him little and are inclined to dismiss him as fraudulent or foolish. The realization of the American Dream as an apocalypse, an eschatological event which would give the life of man its ultimate significance, was an invention of Whitman's.

Other religions have been founded on the promise of the Community of Love, the Abode of Peace, the Kingdom of God. Whitman identified with his own nation-state. We excuse such ideas only when they began 3,000 years ago in the Levantine desert. In our own time we suspect them of dangerous malevolence. Yet Whitman's vision exposes and explodes all the frauds that pass for the American Way of Life. It is the last and greatest vision of the American potential.

Today, when many intellectuals and politicians hold each other in supreme contempt, few remember that America was founded by, and for three generations ruled by, intellectuals. As they were driven from power in the years before the Civil War their vision of a practicable utopia diffused out into society, went underground, surfaced again in cooperative colonies, free-love societies, labor banks, vegetarianism, feminism, Owenites, Fourierists, Saint-Simonians, anarchists, and dozens of religious communal sects. Whitman was formed in this environment. Whenever he found it convenient he spoke of himself as a Quaker and used Quaker language. Much of his strange lingo is not the stilted rhetoric of the self-taught, but simply Quaker talk. Most of his ideas were commonplaces in the radical and pietistic circles and the Abolition Movement. This was the first American Left, for whom the Civil War was a revolutionary war and who, after it was over, refused to believe that it was not a won revolution.

Unfortunately for us, as is usually the case in won revolutions, the language of the revolutionists turned into a kind of newspeak. The vocabulary of Whitman's moral epic has been debauched by a hundred years of editorials and political speeches. Still, there are two faces to the coin of newspeak—the counterfeit symbol of power and the golden face of liberty. The American Dream that is the subject of *Leaves of Grass* is again becoming believable as the predatory society that intervenes between us and Whitman passes away.

Walt Whitman's democracy is utterly different from the society of free rational contractual relationships inaugurated by the French Revolution. It is a community of men related by organic satisfactions, in work, love, play, the family, comradeship; a social order whose essence is the liberation and universalization of selfhood. *Leaves of Grass* is not a great work of art just because it has a great program, but it does offer point-by-point alternatives to the predatory society, as well as to the systematic doctrine of alienation from it that has developed from Baudelaire and Kierkegaard to the present.

In all of Whitman's many celebrations of labor, abstract relations are never mentioned. Money appears to be scorned. Sailors, carpenters, longshoremen, bookkeepers, seamstresses, engineers, artists—all seem to be working for "nothing," participants in a universal creative effort where each discovers his ultimate individuation. The day's work over, they loaf and admire the world on summer hillsides, blowing on leaves of grass, or strolling the quiet First-Day streets of Manhattan, arms about one another's broad shoulders, or making love in religious ecstasy. Unlike almost all other ideal societies, Whitman's utopia, which he calls "These States," is not a projection of the virtues of an idealized past into the future, but an attempt to extrapolate the future into the American present. His is a realized eschatology.

The Middle Ages called hope a theological virtue. They meant that, with faith and love, hope was essential to the characteristic being of mankind. Now hope is joy in the presence of the future in the present. On this joy creative effort depends, because creation relates past, present, and future in concrete acts that result in enduring objects and experiences. Beyond the consideration of time, Whitman asserts the same principle of being, the focusing of the macrocosm in the microcosm, or its reverse, which is the same thing, as the source of individuation. Again and again he identifies himself with a transfigured America, the community of work in love and love in work, this community with the meaning of the universe, the vesture of God, a great chain of being which begins, or ends, in Walt Whitman, or his reader—Adam-Kadmon who contains all things—ruled in order by love.

Whitman's philosophy may resemble that of the *Upanishads* as rewritten by Thomas Jefferson. What differentiates it is the immediacy of substantial vision, the intensity of the wedding of image and moral meaning. Although Whitman is a philosophical poet, almost always concerned with his message, he is at the same time a master of Blake's "minute particulars," one of the clearest and most dramatic imagists in literature.

Not the least element of his greatness is his extraordinary verse. He was influenced, it is true, by Isaiah, Ossian, and all the other sources discovered by scholarship. His poetry has influenced all the cadenced verse that has come after it. Yet, in fact, there has never been anything like Whitman's verse before or since. It was original and remained inimitable. It is the perfect medium for poetic homilies on the divinization of man.

Only recently it was fashionable to dismiss Whitman as foolish and dated, a believer in the myth of progress and the preacher of an absurd patriotism. Today we know that it is Whitman's vision or nothing.

Mankind, the spirit of the Earth, the paradoxical

conciliation of the element with the whole and of unity with multitude—all these are called utopian, and yet they are biologically necessary. For them to be incarnated in the world all we may need is to imagine our power of loving developing until it embraces the total of man and of the earth.

So said Teilhard de Chardin. Or, as Whitman says in the great mystical poems which are the climax of his book, contemplation is the highest form and the ultimate source of all moral activity because it views all things in their timeless aspect, through the eyes of love.

Kenneth Rexroth, "Walt Whitman," in Saturday Review, *Vol. XLIX, No. 36, September 3, 1966, p. 43.*

Jorge Luis Borges   (lecture date 1968)

[An Argentine short story writer, poet, and essayist, Borges was one of the leading figures in twentieth-century literature. His writing is often used by critics to illustrate the modern view of literature as a highly sophisticated game. Justifying this interpretation of Borges's works are his admitted respect for stories that are artificial inventions of art rather than realistic representations of life, his use of philosophical conceptions as a means of achieving literary effects, and his frequent variations on the writings of other authors. In his literary criticism, Borges is noted for his insight into the manner in which an author both represents and creates a reality with words, and the way in which those words are variously interpreted by readers. With his fiction and poetry, Borges's critical writing shares the perspective that literary creation of imaginary worlds and philosophical speculation on the world itself are parallel or identical activities. In the following transcript of a lecture on Whitman given at the University of Chicago, Borges describes the epic hero "Walt Whitman" that Whitman invented for Leaves of Grass. *Translations appearing within brackets in this excerpt were provided by the editor of the journal.]*

In the year 1855, American Literature made two experiments. The first, quite a minor one, the blending of finished music with sing-song and Red Indian folklore, was undertaken by a considerable poet and a fine scholar, Longfellow. The name of it, *Hiawatha*. I suppose it succeeded, as far as the expectations of the writer and of his readers went. Nowadays, I suppose it lingers on in the memory of childhood and survives him. Now the other is, of course, *Leaves of Grass. Leaves of Grass* is a major experiment. In fact, I think I can safely venture to say that *Leaves of Grass* is one of the most important events in the history of literature. If I speak of it as an experiment, perhaps you will think that I am implying a profanation, a desecration, and a blasphemy, since, when we speak of experiments in literature, we generally think of unsuccessful ones. For example, when we speak of experimental literature, well, we think of works that we do our best to admire and that somehow defeat us (for example, *Ulysses, Finnegans Wake,* may I add the ninety-odd *Cantos* of Ezra Pound?) because, after all, the word "experiment" is a polite word. Well, in the case of *Leaves of Grass* the experiment succeeded so splendidly that we think that it could never have failed. Somehow when something goes right—and that hardly ever happens in literature—we think it somehow inevitable. We think that **Leaves of Grass** lay there, lay unsuspected there, ready for anybody to discover and write it down.

Here, of course, we come to the old Platonic theory, the theory that somehow survives in the Latin world. Invents. "Invents" means to discover something that was there around the corner all the time. You will remember what Bacon wrote. He said, "If to learn is to remember, then to be ignorant is to have forgotten." And so, we think that **Leaves of Grass** was inevitable. In fact, we could almost kick ourselves for not having written **Leaves of Grass.** And yet, when the thing was done way back in 1855, more than a hundred years ago, the feat would have seemed impossible to anybody. For there is no doubt whatever that **Leaves of Grass** was intended to be a great book. This is perhaps beyond the tradition of most great books. Let us take a very obvious example. Now, suppose that when Cervantes thought of writing *Don Quixote* he simply thought of making a mockery of the romances of chivalry, of the romances of the Matière de Britaigne. Maybe he did not know how good his work had been until years afterwards he came to the writing of the second part. Then he was a sadder and a wiser man, and he saw all the possibilities in his work, and he wrote the second part, the second part that contradicts his own sentence, "Nunca sequnda partes fueran buenes" (No second part is ever good). It surpasses, I should say, the first part because the author is at the same time the hero. I mean to return to this later on.

There is, of course, a tradition of writing purposefully great books. And this came, I suppose, from the idea of Holy Writ, from the idea of a book being written by the Holy Ghost, from the concept of a man being no more than a secretary or a pen of the Holy Ghost. When men began to lose their faith in the sacred writings, they thought that perhaps literature might supply those writings. In fact, it was not needful that religion should die out before we came to one of the great ambitions, or perhaps will-o'-the-wisps, of literature: the idea of writing a book, a book that shall be somehow all the other books, a book of books, a book like that seashell of which Wordsworth speaks in his *Prelude.* I wonder if you remember the dream of Wordsworth. In that dream you find two stones. The two stones are also books. One of the stones is also the *Elements of Geometry* by Euclid. And the other, well, the other is not a stone. It is a seashell, but within that seashell is a voice, saying, as Wordsworth tells us, "In an unknown tongue / Which yet I understood," saying that the world will be destroyed; and, as a character in the dream, the voice informs Wordsworth that in the seashell are all the poems written in the world, amongst them, of course, the very *Prelude* of Wordsworth. It speaks in an unknown tongue. It is a passion, a music, and in that single seashell are all the books ever written, or ever to be written. And, many men have toyed with the idea, a book that should be something of a Platonic archctypc, a book of books. Then we see how Dante wrote his *Divine Comedy.* His book of the guilty, of the repentant, and of the just, shad-

owed forth under the images of Hell, of Purgatory, and of Heaven. And afterwards we find that very strange book of John Donne, *The Progress of the Soul*—the idea of a book written to outlive all books except Holy Writ. That book would be made of the many adventures of a soul wandering from one shape to another. In the beginning we find the apple of the Tree of Knowledge. And then the soul finds his way into a monkey; afterwards, in the body of Cain, the first murderer, and so on. The work was left unfinished, but it is the draft of a great book. Then we have Milton. There were so many books trying to be the absolute book. And in our days we have *Ulysses.* The idea that in a single day all things happen or may happen to a single man. The idea that between daybreak and sunset all things happen to us, Heaven and Hell and Purgatory, Glory and Shame, Hatred and Happiness and Victory. And afterwards we find the same idea in *Finnegans Wake.* Those books are doubtless failures, while **Leaves of Grass** is a success, a success so great that you could hardly imagine its being otherwise.

Now, when Walt Whitman set out to write his book, he knew what he was undertaking. He was a very ambitious man, but he had full confidence in himself. And he began with the idea of being the poet of Democracy. The word "democracy" may signify much or little to us. I do my best to believe in it, but sometimes I fail, of course. But we must remember that to Walt Whitman and to his age the word was a living one. Whitman could look back on the American Revolution. He might well think that without it there might have been no French Revolution. (I wonder if he followed our South American Wars of Independence.) But he knew that something new had come into the world. You must remember that Goethe said the same when he wrote, "Amerika, du hast es besser / Als unser Kontinent, das alte, / Hast keine verfallenen Schlösser / Und keine Basalte." ["America you are better off / Than our continent, the old one. / You have no ruined castles / And no basalts." Goethe in his theory of volcanoes relates them to basalt. The meaning here is then "there are no dangers in your continent."] That is to say, people were still looking to America's people as they might look for the light of morning. And Emerson had already written *The American Scholar,* and in *The American Scholar,* if you care to look for it, you find a prefiguration, a prophecy of Walt Whitman, when he says, "America, the geography of America, dazzles our imagination." There he speaks of the idea of the poetry of America. He knew that he was not fated to be that poet, though he could be a very fine, cool, a secretly passionate intellectual poet. And he says that if America produced a poet, all things American would find their way into his book, all things not only noble but ignoble, even such things as Charles Dickens might have written of in *Martin Chuzzlewit* or his *American Notes.* He felt, Emerson felt, that the whole of America might find its way into the pages of that book. And Emerson began with one central problem, the problem of writing a democratic poem.

For Walt Whitman, writing a poem to democracy did not mean saying, "Oh Democracy" and then going on. It meant working out a new pattern. Whitman thought of the past as being feudal. He thought of all previous poetry

Whitman's birthplace in Huntington, Long Island.

as mere feudalism. I suppose the past is more complex than Whitman thought, but that simplification was good enough for his purposes. And then he discovered, as he could not fail to discover, that in epic poetry (and he was essentially an epic poet—he says this in the very first poem of his *Leaves of Grass,* in his descriptions), he discovered that in all epic poetry there was a hero, a man standing out from the rest, a king and a conqueror. He thought of Achilles, of Hector, of Aeneas, of Beowulf, of Siegurd, of Roland, of the Cid and so on, and he felt that was the poetry of feudalism. He thought, "I will have to write a poem, a poem of democracy, that is to say, a poem where there shall be no central hero, or rather the central hero shall be everybody, Everyman," to use the old name. As Everyman, as everybody, had to be somebody, Whitman began, strangely enough, with himself.

Now Whitman, I suppose, knew all about himself. He knew more about his loneliness, about his sadness, of the fact of his not being a too happy man, more than we do. But he rejected that idea. He said, I suppose he must have said to himself, "I will take myself for the hero. But that hero shall be two men; that hero shall be myself, the Brooklyn journalist, the editor of the *Brooklyn Eagle,* the second-rate literary man, and also a magnification of myself." And when we turn from *Leaves of Grass* to any biography of Walt Whitman, say, what Traubel wrote, or even if we turn from *Leaves of Grass* to *Democratic Vis-*

tas, we feel sadly disappointed, because the picture of Walt Whitman that we get in *Leaves of Grass* is a picture of a divine vagabond, a man of a large hospitality, a man who feels that he's not able to judge other men. He has to take other men as they come. He has to accept them, as he accepts the universe. And also a man beyond good and evil, not in the sense of being a mean man or a doer of wicked things, but rather in the sense of repairing from morality, except perhaps in his own case. We think of Walt Whitman as essentially a friend; we think of him as essentially good, though not worried by any ethical scruples about right or wrong. And then once we have felt the friendship of that happy, of that divine vagabond, we turn to *Democratic Vistas,* to the biographies, and there we find somebody very different: we find a man of letters, a man who takes great care about the success of his own work, who prints, for example, Emerson's letter of encouragement for propaganda [see *NCLC,* Vol. 4, p. 535], who writes anonymous letters to the papers calling the attention of the public to that fine, though of course faulty, work just published called *Leaves of Grass.* And in the end Whitman becomes a kind of prophet, he has disciples, he takes on all the paraphernalia of being a prophet, and that has very little to do with the Walt Whitman of the poem, with the Walt Whitman of the cosmos, of Manhattan, of the sun, turbulent, fleshly sensual, eating, drinking, and breeding. We do not find that Whitman in his life, and many people have been unfair. They have thought of Whitman as being a liar.

Now this, I think, is hardly true. In fact, I think that the whole thing comes from a misconception. I think that we should conceive two Whitmans—one, the rather seedy journalist and man of letters who had read many of the great books, but who had no very fine literary judgment, who worked-in foreign words in his books, who spoke of "Camerado," who called a poem **"Salut au Monde"** instead of "Greeting to the World," and so on. And then we think of the other. We think of that semidivine hero of *Leaves of Grass.* But we have to think that they're different. We hardly need to compare one with the other. And Walt Whitman knew all about this because he was—[Robert Louis] Stevenson was the first to point this out [see *NCLC,* Vol. 4, pp. 549-51]—the most deliberate of writers, the most self-conscious of poets, although he succeeded, of course, in hiding this fact. So his poems seem to us to be mere lyric cries. He compares himself to a Spotted Hawk. He wrote, "I sound my barbaric yawp over the roofs of the world." But he knew quite well that the yawp was not barbaric. He was very self-conscious about it.

Now let us take, if my memory does not betray me, the poem **"Starting for Paumanok."** You will forgive my slips, because I have lost my sight. For the last ten years my memory has not been refreshed by reading poems. But I remember it as I read it in Geneva way back in 1916 or 1917 during the First World War. And since then I have not reread Walt Whitman. I have not reread him because Walt Whitman has become a part of myself. And besides I know that in Walt Whitman the words are less important than what lies behind the words. A German writer, Herman Bruetts, compared him to the sea. He said that words followed after words as a wave follows a wave, and that the waves were not important, for the sea was behind them. So, let us take this rather haphazard Walt Whitman I am about to offer you, and I think it will run thus:

> Starting for fishshaped Paumanok where I was born, well-begotten and raised by a perfect mother, . . .

No other writer in the world would have thought of writing "well-begotten and raised by a perfect mother."

> After roaming many lands all over populous pavements I dwell in southern savannas or in Manhattan, my city. A soldier camped with a knapsack and gun, a miner in California, my diet, meat, my drink, from the springs. A world of mighty Niagara, a world of the buffalo herds, a world of the strong, and a world of the hirsute and strong-breasted bison, hearing at dawn the rivaled one, the hermit thrush from the swamp cedars, I, in this year of the states, in perfect health, in the West I strike up for a New World.

Walt Whitman wrote those lines in a lodging house in Camden, I suppose. I don't think he'd ever been in the West. He knew quite well that he had never been a soldier or a miner. And yet at the same time he was not telling us a lie. At the same time he was essentially true. Because when Whitman wrote those verses he thought of himself, not of the mere individual Walt Whitman, but he thought of himself as of many Americans and of many men. This comes out in many of his poems. For example, in one of them, one of the most moving I should say, he says,

"These are really the thoughts of all men, in all ages and lands. They're not original with me. They're not as near, they are far. They're nothing or next to nothing. They're as much yours as mine. They're nothing or next to nothing. They're not a riddle, or the untying of the riddle, they're nothing or next to nothing. This is a grass that grows wherever the land is and the worker is. This is a common air that bathes the globe."

And here we have something extraordinary, something that had never been done before. Because all poets, or most poets—let us think of such outstanding examples as Byron or Baudelaire—tried to convince us that they have felt extraordinary thoughts, that they are writing extraordinary poetry, while Walt Whitman, as a democrat, wanted to write the poems of all men. Of course he failed in this, since only Walt Whitman could have written "These are really the thoughts of all men in all ages and lands," because we other poets who are not great poets, we can hardly speak in that way. We try to think that we are somehow different from the rest, we who are quite like everybody else. But Whitman, in a kind of divine humility, in a kind of god-like modesty, tried to think that he was Everyman, and so, he wrote those poems.

But, though in the book we have Walt Whitman, that man of letters, or the journalist, and also Walt Whitman, his magnification, Walt Whitman as he might have been had he been born in many places at once, had he led a lazier and a happier life—Walt Whitman knew that that was not sufficient for his purposes. And so he worked-in—this seems unbelievable at first, but somehow he accomplished the work—a third person. It is not enough that Walt Whitman should be the dream image of Mr. Whitman of Brooklyn *and* Mr. Whitman of Brooklyn, also. He needed something else. The book had to include all men. And so Whitman somehow found a third person, a third person to his poetic trinity. And that third person is the reader, himself. That is to say, if you take up *Leaves of Grass,* then somehow, and I don't think the trick can be explained, somehow you also are Walt Whitman. There is a relationship between the writer and his reader. Of course, all writers have been more or less conscious of this, but no one has ever tried the dramatic possibilities of this relationship with the same themes with which Walt Whitman attempted it. So that we have, first, the relationship of the reader to Whitman. And then Whitman thinks of himself as a lover of the person. He thinks of himself as a friend of the reader. And the reader, of course, need not be a contemporary of his. In fact, one of Whitman's habits is to think of himself as dead and to think of the reader as coming many centuries after him. That was imitated by a minor English poet. I cannot recall his name at the present, but the verse is written after the Whitman tradition, but with a different sort of voice: "Old friend, unborn, unseen, unknown, / Student of our sweet English tongue, / Read out my words at night alone. / I was a poet, I was young." And this is the same kind of feeling that you get in "Camerado." "This is no book, who touches this touches a man. Is it night? Are we here together, alone?" And then, "I spring from the pages into your arms. The seas hold me forth." And then, "I love you." And then we have the last appeal. We have this incomparable verse: "I was one disembodied, triumphant, dead." And if you will forgive my saying so, perhaps the trick has been worked. I do not mean the word "trick" in any normal sense, but no better one comes to my mind at this moment. The trick has been worked by the fact that the words get shorter; you heard "disembodied," then "triumphant," and then finally the word "dead." And the word "dead" kills the words that came before it, and at the same time the word "triumphant" came before it. It is an appeal, a peal of victory also. And with this Saxon monosyllable the book and the poem is ended. Whitman began by speaking to the reader, began by saying to the reader that doubtless he, the reader, was sorry, because he was looking for Whitman and Whitman had died.

Ezequiel Martínez Estrada, a very great poet, wrote a poem to Whitman. He took that same subject. I can hardly translate his verses. I will say them for the benefit of you who have Spanish.

> Perseguiré tus huellas con la ansiedad del perro
> en la tierra que plasma y en los astros que rit-
>   man,
> dondequiera que ahora reproduzcas, Walt Whit-
>   man,
> las canciones autóctonas de la Isla de Hierro.
>
> . . . en el vacío enorme del silencio y la muerte,
> recibe este saludo, que hago al azul y al viento
> con la impresión segura de abrazarte un momen-
>   to
> y el miedo lacerante de volver a perderte.
>   ["Walt Whitman," *Humoresca*, 1929]

["I will follow your footsteps with the eagerness
    of a dog,
upon the firming earth and amid the pulsing
    stars,
wherever you may now be recreating, Walt
    Whitman,
the indigenous songs of the Iron Isle.

. . . in the enormous emptiness of silence and
    death,
receive this greeting, which I give to the blue
    above and to the wind
with the certain feeling of embracing you for a
    moment
and with the gnawing fear of losing you again."]

And this is exactly what the reader feels. The reader says, "Oh, I am unhappy. I should have known Whitman. I should have been his friend. And yet he has eluded me." And yet Whitman tells him, "You who read me today, after so many centuries, wishing I could be with you and be your friend, thinking how happy you'd be if I were by your side, be not too sure but I am now with thee." So, he felt this.

Now, in this way, there is a relationship between Whitman and the reader. And sometimes the words of the poems come from the reader. For example, in that very strange poem, **"Salut au Monde,"** a poem where he speaks of the gaucho, the incomparable rider of horses with his lasso on his arm, he makes the reader speak. He makes the reader say, "What do you see, Walt Whitman?" And then Walt Whitman answers him back, "I see a great, proud wonder

whirling through space. I see day and night at the same time." And then, "What do you hear, Walt Whitman?" And then Walt Whitman hears the songs of workmen, the songs of fishermen. And then again, "What do you see, or what do you remember, Walt Whitman?" And then the poem goes on, and Walt Whitman sees the whole round world at a glance, even as if he were God. And then in the end he says, "To you, to all of you, to all of you whom I mention not but include just the same. Goodwill to you from me and America sent." And then the reader, by having words put into his mouth, and sentiments put into his mind, becomes, in a sense, Walt Whitman.

And so we have this very strange character, perhaps the most complex and daring adventurer in all literature, anywhere; and the strange idea of having a hero for an epic. And the hero is partly the writer, partly a dream image of himself, a dream of magnification of himself; and also the reader, any reader. How Whitman did it, I do not know. I know that it seems idle to analyze art, because as an American painter, Whistler, said, "Art happens, and that's all that can be said for it." Art happens, and perhaps if we had Whitman here at our side—be not too sure but that he is now with us—and if we asked him how he did it, he would hardly explain it to us. I mean, I think he would do it, but I don't think he could explain it. And besides, it does not need to be explained. The important thing is that it happened, and this is important to poetry all over the world.

Now another explanation might be sought for. Of course we critics do our best to probe into poetry to try to ferret out the inner core of poetry. We know that we shall never get at the heart of poetry. We can never "pluck out the heart of its mystery," as Hamlet said. But still we try to go a little deeper down, though we know the task is endless, and perhaps one of the beauties, one of the joys of criticism, is in knowing that you are attempting something impossible, because there is something noble, I think, in the fact of attempting impossible things. Even Satan felt that it was his dignity to fight almighty Omnipotence.

Now it might be said at once that Whitman found something that greatly helped him. And that was the surge and thunder of his verse. We might easily say that Whitman's verse came from the Bible, from the Psalms of the Bible. And yet, if we take the Bible, if we read one of the Psalms, and then if we take a poem by Walt Whitman, we see that though they both are in what is still, I suppose, called free verse, yet the sound is different. I mean, the breathing of the poem is different. When you are reading Walt Whitman, you hear Walt Whitman's voice. And, of course, the vocabulary is quite different, because in the Bible—I am thinking, of course, of the King James Bible—the words belong to a special dialect, while in Walt Whitman you get time-honored words mixed with modern slang, or the slang that was modern way back in 1855.

And here I would like to say something about the problem of free verse, because I remember what an Argentine poet, Luonis, wrote way back in 1909. He wrote about free verse. He said that free verse—he wrote of the facility of free verse—and he said that the facility of free verse was merely the facility, the easiness of prose. And I think that

Luonis was wrong, because prose is not really easier than verse. And there is one fact in history that stands out. If prose were really easier than verse, then prose should have been given to man before verse. And yet in all literatures we find verse. And there are literatures that are so primitive that we find no prose in them. Prose comes later. Let me go back to a favorite hobby of mine, Old English literature. There in Old English you can find many very passionate and very strong poems. We find the *Finnsburgh Fragment,* we find the elegies, we find some passages from *Beowulf,* and also the *Battle of Brunanburh,* and above all I should say, the epic *Fragment of Maldon* and that poem, "The Grave," so finely done into English by Longfellow. Well, Old English literature had a very fine and perhaps a rather untranslatable poetry of its own. But if we turn from poetry toward prose, if we turn from the unknown poets to King Alfred, we find a rather undistinguished prose, a prose written in a straightforward way, a prose that says what it has to say but that has no other beauty than the beauty of its meaning. So prose is not really easier than verse. And I have tried my hand at free verse and at, let's say, formal verse, or classical verse, and I find that the common forms of verse, let's say the sonnet, the ballad, and so on, are easier than free verse, because if you write, let us say, with a certain number of syllables, and if you work in certain rhymes, you have a pattern behind you to help you. While if you try your hand at free verse, then you are left to your own devices. And unless you have the spirit of Whitman or the spirit of Sandburg behind you, then you are helpless, you are merely doing something that looks like verse but is really disguised prose, and not too good prose at that. So that Whitman tried free verse, and it suited his convenience. And in doing so, he was a blessing to the world, because somehow good poets—I am thinking also of some of the best pieces of Edgar Lee Masters—have been moved to verse by the example of Whitman. I think I should remember Pablo Neruda also and perhaps the Russian poet, Mayakovski, and many others.

Since we are speaking of Whitman, I should like to say something about those verses that so shocked his contemporaries, those verses that Emerson advised him to leave out. I mean the erotic verses of "Children of Adam." I don't think anywhere in the world can be found poetry more straightforward than those erotic poems of Whitman. He says all things. I do not attempt to quote the whole initial poem, "The Children of Adam," but I remember the end.

> From what the divine husband knows, from the
>   work of fatherhood,
> From exultation, victory and relief from the bed-
>   fellow's embrace in the night . . .
> From the hour of shining stars and dropping
>   dews . . .
> (Yet a moment O tender waiter, and I
>   return,) . . .
> Celebrate you act divine and you children pre-
>   pared for,
> And you stalwart loins.
> ["Pent-up Aching Rivers," "Children of
> Adam"]

And there are other lines I dare not quote that came before

them, and in those lines we find that, perhaps, for the first time in the history of poetry, a man is talking about the act of love. He's not being bashful or daring about it. He's speaking with a kind of divine innocence, with a kind of god-like chastity, it may be said. It is as if Whitman were not speaking of himself but were speaking about the loves of gods, even as Blake did in some of his verses.

And now we come to another subject, and this is all-important, the subject of joy, because poets have always spoken of joy as of past joy. They have spoken of joy with wistfulness. All paradise has been a lost paradise to them. But in Whitman we find a paradox. Whitman speaks of joy as being present, as being around the corner. He does not think of it as something he has had and lost but as something he may be worthy of in the future. No, he speaks of joy and happiness as if they were the birthright of all men. And if we think that he was a rather unhappy man, that he had suffered from the injustices of his contemporaries, from meanness, from misfortune, and in the end I think from paralysis, we have to thank him. Of course you know that joy breeds no poetry. Joy is an end to itself, while misfortune, unhappiness, dishonor have to be transmuted into something else, and it is the poet's job to do that. And Whitman did it wonderfully. Whitman had to be all men and he wanted all men to be happy, and so he took democracy and joy as his field, and he wrote that wonderful book, a book with which we may disagree—I mean we may disagree with many of the lines but we can hardly disagree with the book itself. I think of the English poet, Lascelles Abercrombie, who wrote that Walt Whitman is one of the chief heroes in the literature of the world. We need not think of the author. Perhaps we may forget the author. That would be all to the good. I think that we should think of Walt Whitman even as we think, for example, of Hamlet, or of Don Quixote, or of Virgil and the Dante of the *Divine Comedy.*

And now there's another aspect. This I suppose will be the last. I don't want to overtax your patience. This is the subject of Walt Whitman and of America. I have lived for some time in America. Six years ago I was in Texas. I am living now in New England, and I have always loved this country ever since I was introduced to it by Huckleberry Finn when I was eight or nine years old. So, strangely enough, when I think of America, I do not think of the red buildings and the white window frames in Cambridge or the tall towers of San Francisco and New York, or of Chicago, the city of Sandburg. I think instinctively of the raft drifting down the river. I think of Huck Finn and Nigger Jim. I never heard them. I never saw the river myself. But they are somehow more real to me than the things I have seen. I suppose one might say that *Huckleberry Finn* is a book that one may reread, if one is lucky enough, in Heaven. At least it is a book that one might read in Heaven. And perhaps also Walt Whitman. And, Walt Whitman has created an image of America. Of course he had American history behind him. He has created an image, not of what America actually is—I suppose it sometimes comes short of Walt Whitman's image of it—he knew it well enough—but of the aims of America. I mean that all over the world there are people who think of America as of a friend, a child who is also a friend. That image comes to us not only through Mark Twain, through Emerson (I greatly admired Emerson), but especially through Walt Whitman. And in this sense, I suppose, we should all be grateful to Whitman.

I remember when I first read Walt Whitman, I was a neurotic young man in Geneva. I felt very unhappy. I read Russian novels. I did my best to think of myself as a character in a Russian novel, explaining my misery to the world. When, after all that bathos, all that sinking down in unhappiness, I ran across Walt Whitman, I felt blinded, and dazzled and overwhelmed by him. And then I said, "Well, this is really shameful. I am not Walt Whitman." Although I thanked Walt Whitman, for I blessed my stars that I had come across him, somehow I felt unworthy of being a reader of Walt Whitman. And this is perhaps the reason why after so many years here in America, here in Sandburg's city, I try to comfort myself by thinking that Walt Whitman was not Walt Whitman either, that Walt Whitman was a man you would have liked to be. And if Walt Whitman's ghost be around, and for all we know it may be, I would like to tell him, "You can forget men of ill will, you may forget the miseries you have undergone, you may forget your loneliness, your sickness, all the wrongs that have been piled on you. Now you are no longer those things. Now you are Walt Whitman, Walt Whitman of the *Leaves of Grass.* Now you are as one disembodied, triumphant, dead." (pp. 707-18)

Jorge Luis Borges, "Walt Whitman: Man and Myth," in Critical Inquiry, *Vol. 1, No. 4, June, 1975, pp. 707-18.*

William M. White   (essay date 1972)

[*White is an American educator, critic, and editor who has compiled numerous studies of American authors, including Whitman. In the following essay, he notes the synthesis of masculine and feminine elements in Whitman's poetic voice.*]

When Emerson wrote on July 21, 1855, his famous letter praising *Leaves of Grass* and greeting Walt Whitman "at the beginning of a great career" [see *NCLC,* Vol. 4, p. 535], he made a rather standard critical conjecture when he surmised that it was a career "which yet must have had a long foreground somewhere, for such a start". This was proclaiming a standard truism which would certainly be applicable to most poets. But because Whitman was not "most" poets, Emerson was dead wrong. Whitman's style of life, self-knowledge, and evolving attitudes did provide a seedbed for the most revolutionary breakthrough in nineteenth-century American poetry. But what was the catalyst that transformed Whitman into a poet who suddenly began to write with the freest and purest voice which America has yet produced? For it is not true that Whitman's early writings (editorials, short stories, journal entries, the temperance novel, poetry, etc.) showed significant hints of the development of a unique poet who was suddenly to emerge with a radical approach to poetic style, subject matter, and, most important, with a fused and mystical concept of the inner nature, meaning, and direction of all life.

It is easy enough in studying the early writings of Emerson, Thoreau, Poe, Hawthorne, and Melville to trace the growth of themes and styles that were to climax so richly between 1836 and 1854. It is not easy with Whitman; in fact, it is impossible. Had he died in 1854 (the year of Thoreau's *Walden*), there would be nothing to assure the critic that Whitman was an emerging genius who had not yet reached a peak in his development. For example, almost none of the earlier versions of **"Song of Myself"** have the power, the scope, the poetic majesty of the completed poem. They lack the clarity and the profound confidence of the fused vision which enable **"Song of Myself"** in the 1855 edition of *Leaves of Grass* to stand forth as the most powerfully assertive, candid, and artistically satisfying poem to appear in any first volume of poetry published in America during the nineteenth century.

The fifth section of **"Song of Myself"**, though intriguing in its erotic and mystical implications, has been stressed beyond its proper significance and has been misread by numerous Whitman buffs (from Dr. Richard Bucke to the present) as a symbolic statement of Whitman's having been "chosen" or "ordained" as a voice of the cosmic consciousness. The poet who is "afoot with my vision" proclaims in section forty-four that "I am an acme of things accomplished, and I am encloser of things to be." Although Whitman is almost deified by certain enthusiasts for his cosmic consciousness and cosmic optimism, he is also downgraded by detractors as a purely "visionary" poet for whom unbridled and untested optimism came far too easy. He suffers the same condemnation as Emerson, who gloried in the "Over-soul", while choosing to view the real (material) world and the evil of life surrounding him as mere appearance.

If Whitman can be taken instead as a poet who had unlocked (subjectively for himself) the inner reality and truth of all existence, the continuum of time, and the cyclic nature of life itself, then the reader may begin to understand Whitman's message. Unlike the Transcendentalists, by whom he was strongly influenced (compare Emerson's "The Poet" essay with the preface to the 1855 edition of *Leaves of Grass* [see *NCLC,* Vol. 4, pp. 537-39]), Whitman was chained to the physical body, to the five senses (which he fuses and elevates into a sixth sense), and to the stream of time. How compelling and constantly intriguing is the physical world to Walt Whitman! This same physical world, being merely emblematic to the Transcendentalists, was viewed by them as transient and unreal.

The long and startlingly vigorous preface to the 1855 edition speaks of affirmation, human dignity and brotherhood, freedom, the equable man, and the rôle of the poet; but it does not disclose the "why's" or "how's" (dynamics) of Whitman's cosmic view and his spontaneously flowing poetry. The preface tends to depict him as the voice "of America", or of the "common working man" or "the democratic spirit" or the "life force" (*élan vital*). While it is true that he is at times each and all of these things, they are partial aspects of the whole poet and should not be singled out for undue attention or separated from the much larger context within which he lived and wrote.

To begin with, *all* of Whitman's poems, not merely the "Children of Adam" poems and the "Calamus" poems, are "love" poems of a very special kind. An examination of the process of Whitman's bringing together what seem to be polar opposites and his synthesizing (mating) of them to form a new wholeness at a higher level can aid the reader in comprehending what often passes for mysticism in *Leaves of Grass.* Whitman's view is based on a very subjective acceptance of reality, one which necessarily gives rise to the cosmic optimism which permeates his poetry. It differs from the familiar thesis-antithesis-synthesis pattern to be found in other artists. Whitman works with identities, with cyclic patterns (existing in time, in nature, and in man), and with the almost unspeakable and joyous ecstasy of regeneration and miraculous rebirth.

As a start it is essential to list some of the apparently opposite concepts which are such an integral part of the poetry of Whitman from the 1855 through 1892 editions of *Leaves of Grass.*

GROUP I	GROUP II
arrogance	docility
activity	passivity
day	night
sun	moon
life	death
body	soul
adhesiveness	amativeness

All of the words in Group I relate to masculinity and those in Group II to femininity. The words listed in the two groups are basic and representative; the grouping does not purport to be definitive in terms of Whitman's art. Sex (procreation) is the energizing force which joins the two groups and gives birth to a total union from which arise by cyclic development a new birth and progress. Strangely, the words in the two groups are not opposites at all, as they would be with most poets; instead, they are dual aspects of the same thing and they exist as equal to each other, necessary to each other, and, even more strangely, as identical to each other within the upward spiralling continuum of time. From another view, these same two groups represent aggressiveness (assertiveness) and receptiveness (humility). These key words in the two groups are not reverse aspects of the same thing but are really overlapping and almost indistinguishable faces of the same thing.

Whitman's blatant sexuality was frightening to some of those who read and liked him and was a real bugbear to those who considered him a terrible man (Whittier and Emily Dickinson, for example) without bothering to read him. Emerson, though he had called for an outspoken and unchained voice in both "The American Scholar" and "The Poet", was doubtless thinking in spiritual rather than physical terms in both these challenging essays. The graphic sensuality of the "Children of Adam" and "Calamus" poems probably struck Emerson as being excessive and in rather bad taste; for Emerson, the intellectual rebel of his age, was at least partly classical in his temperament and ultimately moral in all of his judgments. Thoreau, who was himself indifferent to sex (if not actually afraid of it), liked Whitman as a man. He professed not to be appalled by the dominant rôle of sexuality in Whitman's poetry, but he did lament the fact that readers were not pure enough and mature enough to read without harm. When Secretary Harlan examined a copy of *Leaves of Grass* in the summer of 1865 and dismissed Whitman on June 30 from his position with the Indian Bureau (probably on the vague grounds of "moral character"), he became a living testimony to the fact that the "average" American was not pure enough to view the book as anything other than obscene.

The point is that the explicit scenes and images of the "Children of Adam" and "Calamus" poems are not really so frightening, nor do they differ essentially in their sexuality from that which permeates *all* of Whitman's poetry. **"This Compost"** would appear to be among the least sexual of Whitman's poems. Out of the cycle of nature comes life-death-new life, and out of the cycle of life comes life-death-new life. An electric sexuality (an urge toward procreation) is the force which sustains both cycles and which helps to explain them as twin aspects of the same thing. This rejuvenation or rebirth or new life is taken by Whitman as a proof of the affirmative and ascending nature of God's world and of humanity itself. Sex is not something debasing, something to be whispered about behind the hand; it is deserving of the highest celebration. The "What Chemistry!" of **"This Compost"** is a key to the sexual, cyclic pattern of all living things. At the close of the poem Whitman affirms of the earth that "it renews with such unwitting looks, its prodigal, annual, sumptuous crops." Taken in its deeper sense, **"This Compost"** is just as overtly sexual as **"A Woman Waits for Me"**, a poem of amative love, or **"Scented Herbage of My Breast"**, a poem of adhesive love.

All living things—men, animals, crops, even a blade of grass—are miracles to Whitman and are ample evidence of immortality. Whitman does not extol the beauties of cathedrals, tall buildings, portraits, or mountainsides. These are static; and he is the poet of life, constantly flowing and moving. In section thirty-one of **"Song of Myself"**, the poet proclaims:

> And the narrowest hinge in my hand puts to
> scorn all machinery,
> And the cow munching with depress'd head sur-
> passes any statue,
> And a mouse is miracle enough to stagger sextil-
> lions of infidels.

Whitman was attracted to energy—drawn by its glorious, magnetic charge. Since reproduction is the prime energizing force in the universe, it would have been inconsistent, if not impossible, for Whitman to neglect its power. In **"A Backward Glance"**, his preface to the 1888 edition [see excerpt above], Whitman reaffirms his basic belief:

> From another point of view *Leaves of Grass* is
> avowedly the song of Sex and Amativeness, and
> even Animality—though meanings that do not
> usually go along with those words are behind all,
> and will duly emerge. . . .

It was the sweating, muscular laborer, not the thin, pale bank clerk, that held his attention and love. Whitman saw the teeming force of American life as representative of the democratic ideal (the equality and brotherhood of all men), and he identified himself, the poet, as the equable or representative man. This is the image which he wished to project of himself. It is typified by the strutting and jaunty picture which he published with the 1855 edition— shirt flung open, chest exposed, hand defiantly on his hip, hat cocked at a rakish angle. It is a picture and an image which is true in several respects; but it is also one which is basically defensive (controlled by his subconscious), one which is a pose.

Despite the masculine assertiveness of his poetry, Whitman's inner nature is primarily passive and feminine. He is an "absorber" who receives and accepts all into himself, as illustrated in **"There Was a Child Went Forth"**, in **"Out of the Cradle Endlessly Rocking"**, in **"Song of Myself "**, and in dozens of other poems. He is a Cosmic Eye who searches out and seizes all, a Cosmic Sponge who absorbs and contains all. In the short poem entitled **"To a Common Prostitute"**, Whitman writes: "Not till the sun excludes you, do I exclude you." After the process of absorption is complete, the poet becomes a translator. He uses the word "translate" often. For example: "I wish I could translate the hints about the dead young men and women" (from section six of **"Song of Myself "**), or "Cautiously peering, absorbing, translating" and "Listen'd, to keep, to sing—now translating the notes" (from **"Out of the Cradle Endlessly Rocking"**). What occurs in the act of translation is that Whitman accepts the particular and concrete as symbolic or representative—"A gigantic beauty of a stallion" (from section thirty-two of **"Song of Myself "**)— and then quickly fuses the particular into a cosmic view where it is elevated and submerged in deeper meanings far beyond its own limitations.

When Whitman speaks in **"Song of Myself "** as the Cosmic *I*, as distinct from the Personal *I*, he seldom writes "I said" or "I think" or "I state". Like Emerson, he does not qualify or hedge in his statements. He asserts. Few poets who have written in the English language, perhaps none, have used the active, concrete verb with such boldness and artistic excellence. The assertions of Whitman are far too grandiose to be contained by the standard verse forms of his day or to be restricted by rhyme or regular meter. Because Whitman is "Spontaneous Me" rather than an intellectualized "me", he must "sing" or "carol" or "chant" as he rises and falls from peaks of ecstasy. His message is not intellectual; it is anti-intellectual. It is not moral; it flows beyond and beneath morality into a beautiful and loving amorality. It springs from a feeling, a fusion, an accompanying certitude that is at the very core of his being. It is made possible because he is the "reconciler" of apparent opposites, which are, when properly understood, not opposites at all.

Whitman's verse is as vitally alive as the man himself was. It is melodic and rhapsodic oral poetry which almost leaps from the printed page to enclasp the reader. The poems in *Leaves of Grass* are leaves of life which have been absorbed, fused, translated, and proclaimed. They mirror the poet in all his complexity. Accordingly, they flow outward toward mankind and speak intimately to mankind in all his complexity.

The reason that the fusion, the wellspring of his poetry, is so complete, so candid, and so persistently exciting is that both the passive (feminine) and active (masculine) components were blended and united within Whitman. It was his total acceptance and emotional extension of his own identity, with his joyous pride in its inclusiveness, which gave America the miraculous volume in 1855. Rather than a joining together of body and soul, it was a synthesis of the masculine and feminine within Whitman which caused the mystical vision which inspired his poetry. His poetry can be viewed as a child of this blending; therefore, its rhythms are necessarily sexual since the fusion itself is emotional, subjective, and sensual rather than logical.

Masculine and aggressive elements within Whitman's poetry (arrogance, activity, day, sun, life, body, and adhesiveness) all relate to Whitman as he projected his image. It was Whitman himself in his unsigned review of *Leaves of Grass* [see *NCLC*, Vol. 4, pp. 536-37] who depicted its author as "one of the roughs, large, proud, affectionate, eating, drinking and breeding". Though he was gregarious and outgoing, there was always a bit of the dandy in Whitman and a rather formidable streak of narcissism. His excessive passion for personal cleanliness and his pride in "good blood" are well-known attributes of his personality. Actually, Whitman was in love with the masculine image of himself. It was the feminine element of his being, at the very core of his make-up, which held this love.

There are numerous instances in his poetry in which Whitman tends to view himself as Christlike. In addition, the references to his background as a carpenter are part of this same pattern. In section ten of **"Song of Myself "** the poet is sheltering a runaway slave: "And brought water and fill'd a tub for his sweated body and bruis'd feet." In section forty-eight of the same poem he declares, "In the faces of men and women I see God, and in my own face in the glass." In **"A Sight in Camp in the Daybreak Grey and Dim"** the poet removes the blankets from the faces of three slain soldiers. It is the third soldier of whom the poet states: "Young man, I think I know you—I think this face of yours is the face of Christ himself." Whitman's ministering to wounded and sick soldiers during the Civil War, described in detail in *Specimen Days,* was truly Christlike. He came to these thousands of men not as wound-dresser but as a spiritual comforter. He gave unselfishly of his time, his energy, and his love. The faces of the wounded and dying would light up when he entered the hospital wards, and the soldiers were miraculously uplifted by his presence because they loved him in return. Whereas Christ was masculine in his courage, in his rebellion against the established order, and in his stoical attitude at his crucifixion, he was also feminine in his passive humility, his tender compassion, and in his ability to turn the other cheek.

Although masculine elements are visibly present in Whitman's splendid physique and in his boundless vitality, his overt masculinity is partly a projection (wish fulfillment) and partly a confusion of himself with his love object. His primary nature, largely subconscious, is feminine, absorptive, receptive. It is because of this that he becomes ecstatic when describing the muscularity of energetic young men. Typical is a line in section twelve of **"Song of Myself"** where the poet is picturing blacksmiths: "The lithe sheer of their waists plays even with their massive arms." Perhaps the fact that Whitman's love for his mother was much stronger than his respect for his stern father (as evidenced in **"There Was a Child Went Forth"** and in the correspondence with his mother) may help account for the passiveness so basic to Whitman.

That Whitman had little interest in women throughout his lifetime is a well-established fact. The mysterious "Creole lady" was a protective device on the part of Whitman enthusiasts that has never been substantiated by evidence. A contrast of the passivity of the Indian squaw described in **"The Sleepers"** with the activity of the handsome young man who drowns makes it all too obvious where Whitman's love is focused.

Women of the ultra-feminine, dainty, and charming type (what the Victorians called "young ladies") are totally absent from Whitman's verse. He was very probably deathly afraid of them. The women in Whitman's poetry are glorified for their strength rather than their delicacy; they become sinew and womb. Although Whitman had an enduring sympathy for mothers, he actually seemed to hate young women unless they were down-trodden and among the laboring classes. His deification of motherhood is apparent in section twenty-one of **"Song of Myself"**: "And I say there is nothing greater than the mother of men." This veneration for motherhood is understandable because of Whitman's warm feelings for his own mother and because motherhood is the visible evidence of procreation—the force which is vital to life and to his poetry. It was the omnibus drivers and ferry-boat pilots that Whitman knew by their first names—not the secretaries and shopgirls. Even his hospital work as spiritual healer, soother, and companion was in a rôle traditionally reserved for women. He praises older women, strong women, mothers; but he is afraid of the very feminine woman because she is a challenge to his masculinity and because she is a rival for his subconscious love object.

Whitman's relationships with Sergeant Thomas P. Sawyer and Peter Doyle are partly paternal and partly homosexual in nature. What is even clearer from Whitman's letters is that he is the passive and dependent partner in each instance. These were deeply-felt emotional attachments which literally tore Whitman apart. The letters have the same fervor as the "love" letters of Margaret Fuller to Emerson. Although all of these relationships were probably Platonic, there is no denying the depth and intensity of the love expressed.

The receptive or feminine element dominates Whitman's personality and his poetry. His poetry is an utterly candid extension of a complex personality in which he bares his bodily hungers to the reader. The feminine elements or symbols (docility, passivity, night, moon, death, soul, amativeness) were so strongly present within Whitman himself that they gave him great trouble in his poetry. These are the forces that he had to understand and accept before he could write **Leaves of Grass.** This does not mean that they did not continue to plague him throughout his life-

time. The opening line of **"This Compost"** is typical: "Something startles me where I thought I was safest." There is the difficulty of reconciling death both in **"Out of the Cradle Endlessly Rocking"** and in **"When Lilacs Last in the Dooryard Bloom'd"**. From out of the anguished sorrow and doubt of these two remarkable poems came a meaningful acceptance of death, and in **"When Lilacs Last . . ."** the calm and certain assurance that it leads to renewed or new life at a higher level. This same doubt-resolution pattern holds true in numerous other poems. In other words, the poet does not see the thing as something separate to be dealt with on its own terms (as Emily Dickinson, for example, saw death); instead he reconciles it as being the other face of the same thing. Death is the other face of life, but out of the fusion of life and death, out of their unified wholeness, emerges new life. Night, as in **"The Sleepers"**, is the other face of day, but out of their fusion comes daybreak and new life.

In most of his longer poems Whitman deals with both the active and passive elements and unites them to produce new life. This is the key to his optimism. He never needs to judge or evaluate. He accepts. What he is accepting is the mystical bisexual mixture of his own personality, which is for him, like the blade of grass, a microcosm of the benevolent intricacy ("What chemistry!") of nature herself.

What Whitman extols, explores, and glorifies most in his poetry is the masculine element in a variety of its implications—firm muscularity, heroism, and the democratic (Christian) concept of brotherly love. He is writing about that which excites him to peaks of climax and attracts him physically to the point of overwhelming him, as the excessive sensuality of his language makes obvious. All of **Leaves of Grass** may be best understood as one long love-poem. It springs from the chemistry which takes place when the passive forces in Whitman are accepting and admiring the active forces in humanity and in all of nature. It also contains the fusion and identification of seeming opposites into a union which lifts them beyond their individuality and into a higher state of perfection. In section six of **"I Sing the Body Electric"** the poet affirms:

> (All is a procession;
> The universe is a procession, with measured and
>   beautiful motion.)

Although **"Passage to India"** came closest, Whitman was unable to write his planned poem dealing with the soul and its spiritual journeyings. In truth, he was incapable of writing it. The body held him prisoner. He states in the closing two lines of **"I Sing the Body Electric"**:

> O I say, these are not the parts and poems of the
>   Body only, but of the Soul,
> O I say now these are the Soul!

Most of his poetry is based on a sensuous fusion which he felt and accepted on faith without stopping to analyze, dissect, or define. Whitman wrote not of life's limitations but of its infinite potential, and he wrote a new song in a new tongue for ears scarcely attuned to hear it. Read without proper understanding, Whitman appears as a colossally egotistical poet; read with understanding, he is as humble as the grass itself, for he is the very essence of mankind and of life in all of its myriad forms.

Sexuality is at the core of Whitman's personality and his poetry. Even in **"A Backward Glance"**, written when Whitman was almost seventy, he defends the sexual lines and images in his verse: ". . . the bulk of the pieces might as well have been left unwritten were those lines omitted." In truth, there is far more sexuality in Whitman's poetry than even he realized. **"Crossing Brooklyn Ferry"** is just as sexual as **"From Pent-up Aching Rivers"**. Sex is Whitman's basic metaphor. The ebb and flow of the tide, the beat of the pulse, the blood flow, the expansion and contraction, the reaching forth and withdrawing, the sexual rhythm—all these are one and the same. They are at the center of his poetry and the center of his being; they are the basis of the rising and falling patterns which characterize his free verse. *Leaves of Grass* is vibrantly alive, just as the single blade of grass contains life's full mystery and force. When Whitman's subjective fusion is accepted by the reader and when it is also recognized that all of Whitman's poems are love songs, an emphatic and far richer appreciation of his poetry becomes possible.

Only by accepting the fact that all things, while still retaining individual identity and dignity, are in a deeper sense symbolic representatives of the same thing, and that all things contain not only themselves but their apparent opposites, can the reader lose and then find himself in the full freedom of Whitman's cosmic vision. When one reads Whitman in this light, structure takes on new meaning. **"When Lilacs Last . . . "**, which is probably the best-structured, from a technical and analytical viewpoint, of any of Whitman's major poems, is discovered to have no tighter structure than **"Song of Myself"** or **"The Sleepers"**. There is structure to Whitman's art, but it is structure rooted in an emotional rapport rather than intellect and mere technique. His poetry progresses toward resolution and affirmation and immortality. The most meaningful structure resides in the fact that each individual poem in *Leaves of Grass* is actually a part of all the other poems, and the poet (despite his line in section fifty-one of **"Song of Myself"**: "Very well then I contradict myself") never really contradicts himself. Like the spider spinning out "filament, filament, filament", it is all a part of the same web. It all comes from the poet's integrity. It is all spiralling in the same upward direction.

Only when we realize that Whitman is not a conscious and deliberate rebel, nor a mere chauvinist, nor a naive optimist, nor a discursive egotist—only when we grasp the wholeness of the man and his love and vision—can we finally learn to feel him aright. For Whitman's poetry ranges beyond all studies and analyses; it is to be read aloud, to be sensed, to be absorbed, to be fused with—just as the poet fused the diverse elements of life and the contending elements of his own personality, accepting them in such a way as to create the most remarkable volume of poetry in nineteenth-century America.

Finally, it is necessary to be clearly aware that there is really no duality or paradox or ambiguity in the representation of the various masculine and feminine elements which are the key to Whitman's poetry. Even more important, there are no opposites. Day-man-life are not really separate from night-woman-death. They all merge to become a whole; all are of equal value; and all lead to new birth and a higher level on the life cycle within the upward-bound continuum of time. As Whitman himself affirms, "Out of the dimness opposite equals advance, always substance and increase, always sex"; or, again, the ultimate affirmation: "All goes onward and outward, nothing collapses." (pp. 347-60)

William M. White, "The Dynamics of Whitman's Poetry," in The Sewanee Review, *Vol. LXXX, No. 2, Spring, 1972, pp. 347-60.*

Galway Kinnell   (essay date 1973)

[*Kinnell is one of America's most renowned poets and the winner of both a Pulitzer Prize and an American Book Award for his* Selected Poems *(1982). In the following essay, he praises Whitman as a poet who strove to express basic truths about the self, the body, and the soul.*]

Whitman knew that in its own time *Leaves of Grass* was a failure. But he belonged to that little era which had the dream of progress, and he could believe that one day the book would come into its glory. He tells poets to come:

Portrait of Whitman from the frontispiece of the first edition of Leaves of Grass *(1855).*

> I myself write but one or two indicative words
>   for the future,
> I but advance a moment only to wheel and hurry
>   back in the darkness.
>
> I am a man who, sauntering along without fully
>   stopping, turns a casual look upon you and
>   then averts his face,
> Leaving it to you to prove and define it,
> Expecting the main things from you.

It has turned out as he hoped, but his transformation, in the world of letters, from freak to master, took a very long time. It took so long because, excepting Thoreau and Emerson, most American literati of the 19th century suffered from intense anglophilia and thought of Whitman as a queer cultist or a blethering yokel. In the 20th century this anglophilia has persisted among the New Critics and their poets. Furthermore, these critics, being true 20th century Americans—that is, of a technological cast of mind—took a very theoretical approach to poetry, and from their cerebral heights, they could only patronize this poet who lived on instinct.

A few American poets did feel attracted to Whitman—Vachel Lindsay and Carl Sandburg, and perhaps in a preverse, or reverse way, Robinson Jeffers too. But not until Hart Crane do we find an American poet who was drawn to Whitman's essential enterprise. In Crane's case, however, the temperamental differences were extreme, and also Crane was always being lectured on Whitman's faults by his literary friends, particularly Allen Tate. In the end Whitman's influence is barely visible in Crane's work; as far as I can see, except possibly in "The River" section of *The Bridge,* Crane was not even very deeply affected by that most affecting element, Whitman's musical line.

Great foreign poets, especially Lawrence and Neruda, absorbed Whitman's influence long before our own poets did, but for Pound, Eliot, Frost, and Williams, Whitman meant very little. Whitman's return to American poetry, if we can set a date, did not come until one hundred and one years after the appearance of *Leaves of Grass,* with the publication of Ginsberg's *Howl* in 1956. Other American poets were turning to Whitman about the same time, and some few, such as Tom McGrath and Robert Duncan, had begun as much as a decade earlier to retrieve Whitman's music. Only now is Whitman fully accepted as our greatest native master, the bearer of the American tradition.

In these notes I want to try to describe some of the attraction Walt Whitman holds for me—and I trust for others—to make out if I can one or two of his indicative words, to catch something of the casual gaze he turns towards us.

What first strikes me when I read Whitman is the music, what I can only call the mystic music, of his voice. There are debts to Shakespeare and the King James Bible, but Whitman was an original: no one before him had thrust his presence and actual voice so boldly onto the written page. The voice is unmistakably personal, and it is universal. It is outgoing and attaches itself to the things and creatures of the word; yet it speaks at the same time of a life far within. In this it resembles prayer. Its music is that which speech naturally seeks when given entirely to expressing inner burdens of feeling.

This music seems to flow from a source deeper even than its words. If you croon to a baby in iambs, the baby will laugh, for helpless creatures find control of nature amusing. A woman who has nursed many babies, however, croons to the infant in Whitmanesque lines, and the infant croons back also in Whitmanesque lines. They communicate perfectly, yet use no words, only that deep rhythm the words themselves will also have when their time comes. The rhythms of Whitman's line are not ornamental at all but an essential expressive element.

It is true that the nursery rhyme, which often uses countable meter, appeals to little children too, and not just because of its power to control nature. The iambic beat seems embedded in our language, and Whitman does not ignore it. His free verse speaks in iambs almost as much as do the more intense passages in Shakespeare's blank verse. Yet his iambic flow is never regular, never counted out, and connects seamlessly to surrounding passages that don't use iambs at all. D.H. Lawrence compares this music, which so profoundly affected him, to the flight of birds, now flapping, now flapping, now soaring, now gliding, as opposed to that of counted measures, which is like the plod of earthbound creatures.

Whimsical as it must strike a sensible person, I believe that long before Whitman came on the scene, ever since Milton in fact, poets writing in English unconsciously hungered for such a music as Whitman was to discover. It may have been heroic for the post-Miltonic poets, all of them brought up on the King James Bible and on Shakespeare, nevertheless to swear fealty to counted meter, in the faith that this was loyalty to poetry itself, but it is possible for me to imagine that more was lost than gained. In *Howl,* Ginsberg is an innovator; historically speaking, his revival of Whitman's line was long overdue, historically speaking, Whitman's discovery of his own line was overdue.

His music exerts a power on words. It draws from them both pre-historic and infantile resonances, these deepest sub-meanings, whereas most other 19th century poetry relies on overtones that are superficial and usually nostalgic. In Whitman's poetry, the words are spoken for the first time, while in Longfellow's or Tennyson's the great words appear to have already spent all their force: spent it already putting into the reader, in other poems, the emotions they try to elicit from him in these. Whitman knew that for the voice which loves it every word is virginal. There are "archaic" things, which may drag words along with them into the past, and there are archaic phrases, but very likely there is no such thing as an archaic word.

In the history of literary criticism, tracts have been written on practically every subject there is—as well as on many subjects there aren't—but as far as I know only Whitman has written on this primary subject, the original music of the human voice, how it rescues words and makes them fresh. Since words form in the poet's throat muscles, they can be said to come out of his very flesh. And since the reader's throat muscles also have to form the words, the words enter the reader's very flesh. Poetry goes not merely from mind to mind, but from the whole body to the whole body. Whitman understood this.

Given the great public voices of Theodore Roethke and Dylan Thomas, it is true that Whitman's specific prescriptions occasionally appear to be in error.

> Drinking brandy, gin, beer, is generally fatal to the perfection of the voice;—meanness of the mind the same;—gluttony in eating, of course the same; a thinned habit of body, or a rank habit of body—masturbation, inordinate going with women, rot the voice.

But Whitman was the first to grasp the basic truth, that the music of the voice releases the word's secret life, just as being loved makes plain people brighten.

> The charm of the beautiful pronouniation of all words, of all tongues, is in perfect flexible vocal organs, and in a developed harmonious soul.— All words, spoken from these, have deeper sweeter sounds, new meanings, impossible on any less terms.—Such meanings, such sounds, continually wait in every word that exists—in these words—perhaps slumbering through years, closed from all tympans of temples, lips, brains, until that comes which has the quality patiently waiting in the words.

Ezra Pound thought all 19th century poets used archaic language, but to my ear, except for certain passages in the *Pisan Cantos,* his own language turned brittle and old-fashioned rather quickly. Whitman's is as fresh as if spoken today—or for that matter tomorrow.

Whitman's love of words was not, as was Pound's, literary, referential, and etymological. Whitman loved words as physical entities, but entities which could only become physical through absolute attachment to reality. For it's curious with words, they can't be loved for themselves alone. Like our human lovers, words attach to a deeper life than their own, and are loved for their own particular qualities, yes, but loved supremely because in them flowers that which we more deeply love. In these few passages, picked nearly at random, it is obvious that what entrances Whitman is not words in themselves but the luminous reality. In return for his love, or his carnal knowledge, reality lays its own words freely and unasked for on his tongue.

> The brisk short crackle of the steel driven slantingly into the pine,
> The butter-color'd chips flying off in great flakes and slivers . . .
>
> . . . . .
>
> Evening—me in my room—the setting sun,
> The setting summer sun shining in my open window, showing the swarm of flies, suspended, balancing in the air in the centre of the room, darting athwart, up and down, casting swift shadows in specks on the opposite wall where the shine is . . .
>
> . . . . .
>
> I too many and many a time cross'd the river of old
> Watched the twelfth-month sea-gulls, saw them

high in the air floating with motionless wings, oscillating their bodies,
> Saw how the glistening yellow lit up parts of their bodies and left the rest in strong shadow,
> Saw the slow-wheeling circles and the gradual edging toward the south,
> Saw the reflection of the summer sky in the water,
> Had my eyes dazzled by the shimmering rack of beams,
> Look'd at the fine centrifugal spokes of light round the shape of my head in the sunlit water . . .
>
> . . . . .
>
> She sits in an armchair under the shaded porch of the farmhouse,
> The sun just shines on her old white head . . .

These examples of Whitman's novelistic virtuosity are, more than that, loving acts which evoke things and creatures and bring them alive in words, and so they rescue them from time and death.

Such adjectives as "butter-color'd," which is photographically descriptive, belong, it's true, to the realm of prose. At his best Whitman goes far beyond photographic description. His adjectives do not merely try to categorize, give colors, shapes, likenesses. They try to bring into language the luminous, nearly unspeakable presence. So his descriptions may even detach themselves completely from any visible surface.

> Hefts of the moving world at innocent gambols silently rising, freshly exuding,
> Scooting obliquely high and low.
>
> Something I cannot see puts upward libidinous prongs,
> Seas of bright juice suffuse heaven.

An energy flows between Whitman and the thing. He loves the thing; he enters it, becomes its voice, and expresses it. But to enter a thing is to open oneself to it and let the thing enter oneself, until its presence glows within oneself. Therefore, when Whitman speaks for a leaf of grass, the grass also speaks for him. The light from heaven which shines in Whitman's poetry is often a consequence of these loving unions. At the end of **"Crossing Brooklyn Ferry"** Whitman tells the appearances of things, "We use you, and do not cast you aside—we plant you permanently within us," in his off-hand way coming close to describing the resurrection of the world within us which Rilke strains his whole being to describe at the end of the Ninth Elegy.

Whitman says that in ***Leaves of Grass*** his aim was to set forth "uncompromisingly, my own physical, emotional, moral, intellectual, and aesthetic personality . . . in a far more candid and comprehensible sense than any hitherto poem or book." He doesn't quite do that. It is impossible not to feel in this man who always proclaims his health, this good gray poet who writes constantly about himself yet about whom we know very little, something unavowed, a trouble, perhaps even a sickness, at least an intense loneliness and a more than ordinary fear of sex and dread of death.

He protests too much, to begin with; no healthy person could generate that much energy merely to announce that he is healthy. Sometimes he almost suggests the nature of his troubles, the source of those wounds, still unhealed, which were inflicted on an exceptionally indulged child when it confronted the "reality principle," in this case an exceptionally puritan society.

He says, for instance:

> I keep as delicate around the bowels as around
> the head and heart.
> Copulation is no more rank to me than death is.

The explicit content is unexceptional. Yet something in the phrasing isn't quite right. The first line makes one think of people who, appalled by their own excrement, perform enemas on themselves daily. With the comparison in the second line, I can imagine Whitman trying it the other way around, "Death is no more rank to me than copulation is," before, still vaguely bothered, settling on the line as it is, even though its use, even in the negative, of "rank" to link fucking and death is still disquieting.

Whitman did not like us to see his troubled side. He wanted us to see him as he wished to be. His confessions of having experienced base emotions are concessions, claims to common humanity, which have a patronizing tone. His poems, therefore, rarely contain struggles of any kind. They begin in the same clarity in which they end. This is often their weakness; it is what spoils, for instance, **"When Lilacs Last in the Dooryard Bloomed,"** in which the grief is too thoroughly consoled before the first line is uttered. One of the exceptions is the curious **"This Compost,"** which begins with Whitman's telling us how frightened he is of the earth, since in it have been buried so many diseased carcasses.

> Something startles me where I thought I was saf-
> est,
> I withdraw from the still woods I loved,
> I will not go now on the pastures to walk,
> I will not strip the clothes from my body to meet
> my lover the sea,
> I will not touch my flesh to the earth as to other
> flesh to renew me.
>
> O how can it be that the ground itself does not
> sicken?
> How can you be alive you growths of spring?
> How can you furnish health you blood of herbs,
> roots, orchards, grain?
> Are they not continually putting distemper'd
> corpses within you?
> Is not every continent work'd over and over with
> the sour dead?
>
> Where have you disposed of their carcasses?
> Those drunkards and gluttons of so many gener-
> ations?
> Where have you drawn off all the foul liquid and
> meat?
> I do not see any of it upon you to-day, or perhaps
> I am deceiv'd.
> I will run a furrow with my plough, I will press
> my spade through the sod and turn it up un-
> derneath,
> I am sure I shall expose some of the foul meat.

At the end of the poem, of course, he comes around and blesses the earth, as healthy after all, but along the way he exhibits an ultra-fastidiousness which would strike me as hysterical if I were able to take it quite seriously.

Nevertheless, when Whitman does affirm his own health I believe him, even as I disbelieve him. The truth of prose is usually imponderable, for in prose to be persuaded one has to follow all the steps of its argument. Poetry verifies itself, telling us by the authenticity of its voice how true it is, in this respect resembling actual speech. I don't fully believe Thoreau, for example, when he says with just a touch of elegant cleverness, "we need pray for no higher heaven than the pure senses can furnish, a purely sensuous life . . . ," a skepticism which may have grounds, for Thoreau elsewhere remarks, this time in response to *Leaves of Grass:*

> There are 2 or 3 pieces in the book which are dis-
> agreeable to say the least, simply sensual. He
> does not celebrate love at all. It is as if the beasts
> spoke. I think that men have not been ashamed
> of themselves without reason.

I am able to believe in Whitman's declarations of health because, being spoken in poetry, I hear the tone in which he speaks them, I listen carefully, I note the authentic music, the energy of the language, the hum, I could say of his valvèd voice. What he says is raised to the level of truth by the aliveness of his words. Is it absurd to say that even the passages that betray his sickness are convincing statements of health?

Leaves of Grass set out not only to rescue the things and creatures of the world; it also tried, more seriously from Whitman's viewpoint, to redeem in the flesh this nineteenth century American puritan: to transform him from one who felt ill toward himself into one who exuberantly loved himself, to make him into "one of the roughs, a kosmos, disorderly, fleshy and sensual"—which, of course, in some way he must have been all along. The energy which made me feel his declarations of health to be false overflow; the surplus energy that remains in the poems gives them life; it is this surplus, this life, that convinces. I see the sickness; in the same moment I see the sickness healed. On Whitman's face, as it turns briefly towards us, there is both radiance and amazement: it is a face almost confident of its light and yet surprised by it, still trying to get used to this radiance that is all the more startling for coming from within, from an extremely unstable source.

In certain incandescent passages Whitman's poetry approaches a vision, in Norman O. Brown's sense of the phrase, of the "resurrected body." In the following passage he feels his way back into an infant's joy in the body: he fondles himself, adores himself, revels in that lot of him which is all, he discovers with his saving humor, totally luscious, that sweet fat sticking to his own bones.

> If I worship one thing more than another it shall
> be the spread of my own body, or any part of
> it,
> Translucent mold of me it shall be you!
> Shaded ledges and rests it shall be you!
> Firm masculine colter it shall be you!
> Whatever goes to the tilth of me it shall be you!

You my rich blood! your milky stream pale
   strippings of my life!
Breast that presses against other breasts it shall
   be you!
My brain it shall be your occult convolutions!
   nest of guarded duplicate eggs! it shall be you!
Mix'd tussled hay of head, beard, brawn, it shall
   be you!
Trickling sap of maple, fibre of manly wheat, it
   shall be you!
Vapors lighting and shading my face it shall be
   you!
You sweaty brooks and dews it shall be you!
Winds whose soft-tickling genitals rub against
   me it shall be you!
Broad muscular fields, branches of live oak, lov-
   ing lounger in my winding paths, it shall be
   you!
Hands I have taken, face I have kiss'd, mortal
   I have ever touch'd, it shall be you!

The infantile narcissism opens outward in the last line. In this line Whitman re-crosses the reality principle, the frontier which once damaged him so severely, re-crosses it this time with tenderest words of outgoing and freely given love.

Perhaps the supreme sexual moment in Whitman comes in the fifth section of **"Song of Myself."** The passage may be about the self and the body and the soul, but to begin with, it is about a man and his lover. If in the previous passage Whitman succeeds in transforming self-love into love for another person, here he transforms love for another person into sacred relationship with all creation. It is true, as Thoreau said, more eloquently than he knew, "It is as if the beasts spoke"; in poetry there are not many higher tributes.

Loafe with me on the grass, loose the stop from
   your throat,
Not words, not music or rhyme I want, not custom or lecture, not even the best,
Only the lull I like, the hum of your valvèd
   voice.

I mind how once we lay such a transparent summer morning,
How you settled your head athwart my hips and
   gently turn'd over upon me,
And parted the shirt from my bosom-bone, and
   plunged your tongue to my bare-stript heart,
And reach'd till you felt my beard, and reach'd
   till you held my feet.

Swiftly arose and spread around me the peace
   and knowledge that pass all the argument of
   the earth,
And I know that hand of God is the elder-hand
   of my own,
And I know that the spirit of God is the brother
   of my own,
And that all the men ever born are also my
   brothers, and the women my sisters and lovers,
And that a kelson of the creation is love,

And limitless are leaves stiff or drooping in the
   fields,
And brown ants in the little wells beneath them,

And mossy scabs of the worm fence, heap'd
   stones, elder, mullein, and poke-weed.

In this last passage Whitman climbs down the Platonic ladder. The direction is Blakean, or Rilkean—a motion from the conventionally highest downward toward union with the most ordinary and the least, the conventionally lowest, the common miracles that are the things of this world.

It is the same at the close of **"Song of Myself"** where Whitman disintegrates before us, bequeaths his flesh and spirit not to heaven but to the ground and the air of this world:

I depart as air, I shake my white locks at the runaway sun,
I effuse my flesh in eddies, and drift it in lacy
   jags.

I bequeath myself to the dirt to grow from the
   grass I love,
If you want me again look for me under your
   boot-soles.

You will hardly know who I am or what I mean,
But I shall be good health to you nevertheless,
And filter and fibre your blood.
Failing to fetch me at first keep encouraged.
Missing me one place search another,
I stop somewhere waiting for you.

Had Whitman been less secretive, it is possible he might have grown more and changed more through the rest of his life. As it was, after this re-invention and salvation of himself, he seems to have concentrated on establishing the personage perhaps only flimsily created. In this light, I know, his work can be regarded as nothing but an elaborate act of wishful thinking. But perhaps "wishful thinking" is only a disparaging term for what might be called "vision"—and the vision of glory more than the possession of it produces art. Whatever the case with Whitman, we should not ask everything of anyone, least of all of the very great, whose single gift may have been achieved at severe cost in other realms of his life and art. In Whitman's case remember also that between the appearance of *Leaves of Grass* and Whitman's first stroke, he had only eighteen years of good health, very little time compared to that given to Yeats, for instance.

I know of only one account of Whitman written by someone who knew him both before and after the publication of *Leaves of Grass.* It describes a person rather different from the rapt and garrulous hero of the poems.

Walt Whitman had a small printing office and book store on Myrtle avenue, Brooklyn, where after his return from the South he started the *Freeman* newspaper, first as a weekly, then as a daily, and continued it a year or so. He always earned his own living. I thought him a very natural person. He wore plain, cheap clothes, which were always particularly clean. Everybody knew him; everyone, almost, liked him. We all of us [referring to the other members of his family—brothers, sisters, father and mother] long before he published *Leaves of Grass,* looked upon him as a man who was to make his mark in the world. He was always a good listener, the best I ever knew—of late years, I think, he talks somewhat more. In those early years (1849-54) he talked very little indeed. When he did talk his conversation was remarkably pointed, attractive, and clear. When **Leaves of Grass** first appeared I thought it a great book, but that the man was greater than the book. His singular coolness was an especial feature. I have never seen him excited in the least degree; never heard him swear but once. He was quite gray at thirty. He had a look of age in his youth, as he now has a look of youth in his age.

It is not surprising that Whitman was a listener. Ezra Pound's silence during his last years was perhaps his own tribute, paid too late (but paid), to that one law he had overlooked—that the mother of poetry is silence. Whitman gathered the world into his own silence. His poetry is his receptive consciousness turned inside out: the listener becomes the speaker, magnetism changes to radiance, the words glow with infra-reality.

I am fascinated by that observation about Whitman's changed appearance. "We poets in our youth begin in gladness, Whereof in the end come despondency and madness." The curse is often quoted. But to achieve his exemplary self-portrait—a self-portrait which would also portray everyone—Whitman had to lift the curse. He had to set against his despondency all his gratefulness, he had to clarify his madness, find in it possibilities of joyful health—and do this, moreover, as a work of supererogation: the surplus would be the poems. *He was quite gray at thirty. He had a look of age in his youth, as he now has a look of youth in his age.* If Whitman's poetry in some sense consists of wishes, it is useful for our faith in his enterprise to know that they came true in his own flesh.

Speaking in New York in the Spring of 1972, Pablo Neruda acknowledged Whitman to be his greatest master.

He said:

> For my part, I, who am now nearing 70, discovered Walt Whitman when I was just 15, and I hold him to be my greatest creditor. I stand before you feeling that I bear with me always this great and wonderful debt which has helped me to exist.

> I must start by acknowledging myself to be the humble servant of a poet who strode the earth with long, slow paces, pausing everywhere to love, to examine, to learn, to teach and to admire. The fact of the matter is that this great man, this lyric moralist, chose a hard path for himself: he was both a torrential and a didactic singer—qualities which appear opposed, seeming also more appropriate to a leader than a writer. But what really counts is that Walt Whitman was not afraid to teach—which means to learn at the hands of life and undertake the responsibility of passing on the lesson!

Whitman not only saved himself, not only resurrected himself in his body, but, being, as Neruda says, also a teacher, he bravely undertook that most difficult role, of being a model for others to do the same for themselves.

He indicated to poets to come—and in fact to everyone—that one's poetry, and also one's life, is not to be a timid, well-made, presentable, outward construction. It is to be the consuming enterprise, leading if possible to intensified life, even to self-transfiguration. He indicated, too, that the great poem may or may not be set down on paper, but first it shall be written by the glory of this life in the flesh of a man or woman.

> This is what you shall do: love the earth and sun and the animals, despise riches, give alms to everyone that asks, stand up for the stupid and crazy, devote your income and labor to others, hate tyrants, argue not concerning God, have patience and indulgence toward the people, take off your hat to nothing known or unknown or to any man or number of men, go freely with powerful uneducated persons and with the young and with the mothers of families, re-examine all you have been told at school or church or in any book, dismiss whatever insults your own soul . . . and your very flesh shall be a great poem and have the richest fluency not only in its words but in the silent lines of its lips and face and between the lashes of your eyes and in every motion and joint of your body.

(pp. 9-11)

Galway Kinnell, "Whitman's Indicative Words," in The American Poetry Review, *Vol. 2, No. 2, March-April, 1973, pp. 9-11.*

Robert K. Martin   (essay date 1975)

[*Martin is an American critic who has said of his literary outlook: "I try to combine the best of a New Critical sensitivity to the text and the power of language with a sense of engagement and an awareness of historical context." The following is an excerpt from an essay that won the Pushcart Prize in 1975; in it, Martin affirms homosexuality as the central theme in Whitman's poetry.*]

It has become common among critics of Walt Whitman to argue that the protracted debate over the nature of the poet's sexuality, whether he may have been homosexual, heterosexual, or bisexual, is essentially beside the point. This argument has not been based on any reading of the poetry, but rather on the general modern and "liberal" tendency towards acceptance and tolerance. Acceptance and tolerance of homosexuality have not only been disastrous for the development of a homosexual consciousness; they have also led to a critical irresponsibility which seeks to equate all experience and to deny that homosexuals are "really" different from heterosexuals (to test the absurdity, substitute women and men, or blacks and whites).

Homosexuality shares a number of the general functions of all sexuality, but it bears a particular burden, given the social view of homosexuality and the virtual universality of repression of homosexual desires, at least in their most overt or public manifestations. The homosexual artist has a double need to express his sexual drives through his art because he is (or was) far less able than his heterosexual brother to give expression to these drives in his own life. In a society which attaches serious penalties to the open practice of homosexuality, the homosexual will often turn to art as a way of confronting those desires that he cannot acknowledge through action. Through the symbolism of his art he can communicate the facts of his homosexuality to his readers, knowing that those of them who are similarly homosexual will read the signs properly. Thus it was certainly with Whitman. He wrote a large part of his poetry directly out of his own sexual conflicts and fantasies, and he used his poetry to convey the news of his homosexuality to his readers. He knew that they were to be his "cameradoes," his only faithful lovers and only true readers, for all others would (Whitman predicted accurately) fail to see the "message" that would be unmistakable to some:

> This hour I tell things in confidence,
> I might not tell everybody, but I will tell you.
> **("Song of Myself,** sec. 19)

Whatever homosexual readers may have thought (and John Addington Symonds was but the first to have recognized Whitman's homosexual meanings; he has been echoed by gay writers from André Gide to Allen Ginsberg to any of a large number of young American poets all of whom take Whitman as a point of reference, exceeded by no other American gay poet with the possible exception of Hart Crane), Whitman's readers in general have made a sorry record of misreading Whitman's poems. If one is charitable, one can suggest that these readers were simply unable to see the homosexual meanings, which were so divorced from their own experiences. But I am not inclined to be charitable. The record of absolute lies and half-truths and distortions is so shameful as to amount to a deliberate attempt to alter reality to suit a particular view of normality. If Whitman is to be a great poet, then the must be straight. If the poetry shows something else, Whitman must be made to alter his own poetry, censor himself. Despite considerable concessions made by Whitman during the course of his career, and the removal of a number of passages, the rabid heterosexualists were not satisfied. Whitman's life must be betrayed, rewritten, and his poems reread in a "safe" manner. Whitman must be saved from himself. (pp. 80-1)

The history of Whitman criticism in this connection is shameful. I can think of no parallel example of the willful distortion of meaning and the willful misreading of a poet in order to suit critics' own social or moral prejudices. And it must be added that the very few critics who spoke against this tradition of distortion were generally Europeans, who perhaps did not totally share American Society's total and relentless hostility to the homosexual. It is thanks to the work of Jean Catel, Roger Asselineau, and Frederik Schyberg that Whitman finally can be seen as a poet of sexual love between men. In the last few years there has been the important work done by Edwin Haviland Miller, which has unfortunately not received the attention it deserves (despite his overly normative Freudian bias). One begins to suspect that the history of Whitman misreading is not over.

Whitman's own life was marked by the same pressures toward sexual conformity that now lead to critical distortions. He seems to have felt the need to act out a role, to hide behind the mask of the tough. And he had to learn the strategies of concealment, strategies that, until recently at least, all of us had to learn in order to succeed as homosexuals in a heterosexual world. The changing of texts, the excision of passages, these are but the most obvious of what must have been an enormously painful series of acts performed almost daily in order to conform to someone else's version of normality. And how painful they must have been to the man who was able to give another man a wedding band, who from his youth on wrote with passion only of friendship between men, who cried out in suffering "O unspeakable passionate love" (**"Song of Myself,"** sec. 21) for the love, "the secret of my nights and days," which lay hidden "in paths untrodden."

One important consequence of his homosexuality is that Whitman, unlike so many male poets, does not see women as sexual objects even in his ostensibly heterosexual poems. Freed of the need to enslave the opposite sex, the homosexual is free to see women as human beings, and thus we find in Whitman a strong sense of compassion for suffering figures of women—the mother, the prostitute, the spinster. It is not only that he does not see woman as sex object, but that he can thereby see himself as self-enjoying. Whitman's poetry is frequently auto-erotic in the sense that he takes his own body as a source of sexual pleasure much as Freud's famous polymorphously perverse child does, and derives pleasure from his own orgasm, rather than from any sense of conquest or aggression.

Whitman makes no distinction between subject and object (a distinction necessary to the position of woman as "other" and as property). All experience becomes a part of himself—"Absorbing all to myself and for this song" (sec. 13)—as the total egotism of the child is restored. The **"Song of Myself "** is the song of the world, as seer and seen, male and female become one. If Whitman's vision is regressive, it looks back to an earlier ideal of play. We need to see the sensitivity, the *finesse* of Whitman, a sensitivity which has too long been obscured by the image of him as

> Walt Whitman, A Kosmos, of Manhattan the son,
> Turbulent, fleshy, sensual, eating, drinking and breeding
> **("Song of Myself "** sec. 24)

This was what Whitman wanted to seem to be; but the poetry reveals the happy truth that he was indeed a much deeper, more sensitive person than he dared admit.

The great debate over homosexuality in Whitman's poetry has generally centered on the poems in the Calamus section or those poems which, although not actually placed in that section, seemed to belong there, by similarity of theme or imagery. But this emphasis is somewhat unfortunate for two reasons. First it tends to isolate the "homosexual" poems of Whitman into one neat category which can be labelled and then safely forgotten and put away. Second it tends to assume that Whitman's sexuality is only relevant to his most explicit and frequently didactic poems. On the (hopeful) assumption that most readers are capable of reading Calamus themselves, I have therefore preferred to center my discussion here on another mode of Whitman's poetry, which is perhaps slightly more elusive and yet which seems to me essential to an understanding of the whole body of his work. I refer to what I have called Whitman's dream-vision poems, those poems which are written in a state of the mind somewhere beneath full consciousness and which invoke the experience of the mind in that state.

"The Sleepers" has received a fair amount of attention in recent years, probably due to the general interest in stream of consciousness techniques and also to a new willingness to look more carefully at explicit sexual imagery. I do not wish to give a full reading of the poem here—one may be referred to the helpful comments of Leslie Fiedler and Edwin Haviland Miller in particular, as well as to the reading of James E. Miller—but I do want to look at it sufficiently to suggest that it is similar to **"Song of Myself"** in its sense of wavering consciousness, in its use of cosmic observation, in its shifts through time and space, and in its sexual imagery.

"The Sleepers" is explicitly about a vision, as the first line informs us, and its action is the movement of the poet within his vision,

> I wander all night in my vision,
> Stepping with light feet, swiftly and noiselessly
> stepping and stopping,
> Bending with open eyes over the shut eyes of
> sleepers,
> Wandering and confused, lost to myself, ill-
> assorted, contradictory,

Whitman with Peter Doyle, a friend and correspondent.

Pausing, gazing, bending, and stopping.

The first section of the poem is agitated, marked by continual movement. The poet uses the game metaphor to depict the atmosphere of levity which prevails as the covers are lifted and the genitals are revealed.

> wild-flapping pennants of joy!

It concludes with a remarkable depiction of orgasm, in which it becomes clear that the naked speaker who has been exposed is using his body as a metaphor for his penis and that the entire exposure motif of the poem operates on these two levels (the exposure of the poet for what he is—the fear of being revealed as a homosexual—and the exposure of the penis which may bring forth castration anxiety in a hostile world). The text is worth quoting in full, especially since Whitman later removed these lines from the 1855 edition and they are therefore not present in most of the editions regularly used.

> O hotcheeked and blushing! O foolish hectic!
> O for pity's sake, no one must see me now!. . . .
> my clothes were stolen while I was abed,
> Now I am thrust forth, where shall I run?
>
> Pier that I saw dimly last night when I looked
> from the windows
> Pier out from the main, let me catch myself with
> you and stay. . . . I will not chafe you;
> I feel ashamed to go naked about the world,
> And am curious to know where my feet
> stand. . . . and what is this flooding me,
> childhood or manhood.
> . . . . and the hunger that crosses the bridge be-
> tween.
>
> The cloth laps a first sweet eating and drinking,
> Laps life-swelling yolks. . . . laps ear of rose-
> corn, milky and just ripened:
> The white teeth stay, and the boss-tooth ad-
> vances in darkness,
> And liquor is spilled on lips and bosoms by
> touching glasses, and the best liquor after-
> ward.

Miller manages to see vaginal imagery here, but I do not see it. It seems clear to me that what is being depicted is the act known politely as fellatio—the penis protrudes from the foreskin, the balls are sucked, the penis is sucked, and finally there is ejaculation in the mouth. The sexual experience is the starting place for the poem, and the poet begins his vision with the second section, after the orgasm when "my sinews are flaccid / Perfume and youth course through me, and I am their wake." The physical experience leads toward the spiritual experience which is the dream, and which is also in its turn physical and sexual.

The third section brings a fantasy of the destruction of the "beautiful gigantic swimmer," a warning in dream terms of the dangers in the unconscious world of the sea with its "swift-running eddies." The swimmer seems to be a sexual object, but is also an ideal presentation of the self. The dream of the third section is a dream of the destruction of the self—the clue lies in Whitman's surprising line "will you kill him in the prime of his middle age?" (Whitman was 35 at the time) and in the transition to the next section through its first line, "I turn but do not extricate myself."

The poet-dreamer wants to escape from his dream, but the nightmare is not yet over. In another key passage that was omitted from later editions Whitman introduces his conflict with the Satanic through the figure of Lucifer (whom Whitman seems perhaps to have taken in his literal sense as light-bearer, for it is the coming of dawn that will destroy the dream and take away the lover, real or imaginary).

The theme of slavery is linked to the sexual by the sequence of the poem, where the poet moves from the mother's vision of the "red squaw":

> My mother looked in delight and amazement at
> 　the stranger,
> She looked at the beauty of her tallborne face
> 　and full and pliant limbs,
> The more she looked upon her she loved her

to his own identification with the black slaves. Both evoke guilt because of their (implicit) double violation of taboo: homosexuality and miscegenation are the twin crimes so feared in American thought. (And we recall that Whitman's famous letter implied that he had broken the lesser of the two, lest he be found guilty of the greater!)

Starting with section 7 there is a drastic change brought about by the poet's acceptance of the world, an acceptance which is possible through his perception of unity in space and time. The agitation of sexuality, the immediate sensation of guilt following it, and the fantasy of death and loss which accompany its completion give way to a sense of sexual calm and peace. The poet learns to accept the daytime world of disunity ("the rich running day") because it is part of the cycle which always leads back to the night and love and the Great Mother. His love of experience and diversity does not lead him to forget the world of unity and calm, but rather to accept both:

> I love the rich running day, but I do not desert
> 　her in whom I lay so long:
>
> 　　　· · · · ·
>
> I will stop only a time with the night, and rise
> 　betimes.
> I will duly pass the day O my mother and duly
> 　return to you.

Much as I am indebted to the thoughtful book of Edwin Haviland Miller (*Walt Whitman's Poetry: A Psychological Journey*), I must take issue with his particular emphasis on such a passage as evidence of Whitman's regressive patterns and what he implies to be an unresolved oedipal situation. I do not feel any *personal* maternal qualities in his poem. The mother addressed here seems to me to be a universal mother, goddess of the night, of the dream, of the vision, of all that is excluded from the daylight world of jobs, reason, and fathers. Reading the poem in terms of personal psychology seems to me to miss the essential significance of Whitman's vision, which achieves a return to a state of primal consciousness, which is pre-patriarchal, and cyclical rather than linear. His essentially matriarchal vision leads him to send the poet back to the Night-Mother (forces of darkness, mystery, and the unknown) to be reborn from her. The Mother is the death-sleep which follows upon the male striving of sexuality, but it

is also the repose that heals and out of which the fallen penis may rise again:

> Not you will yield forth the dawn again more
> 　surely than you will yield forth me again,
> Not the womb yields the babe in its time more
> 　surely than
> I shall be yielded from you in my time.

The sexual experience is revealed by this poem to be the gateway to the visionary—literally because ejaculation leads to sleep and thus to dream, but metaphorically because it is the realization of the possibility of transcending the self through sexual ecstasy which leads to an acceptance of the world. As we fall off to sleep following orgasm, we are able to see a kind of inner sense in the world, a world freed from the pressures of the day and in which we have regained a kind of repose that Freud thought found its only model in intrauterine existence. Through that vision Whitman could come to his understanding of the world and greet all men and women as sleepers, each dreaming his own dream, but each dream like the others.

Whitman's most important poem, in terms of length, and in terms of the themes broached there, is clearly his **"Song of Myself."** Critics have attempted to find an adequate way of understanding the poem's strength and sense of inner unity despite an appearance of disorder, but no one has fully explained the poem's patterns by looking at it in the light of **"The Sleepers"** as a dream-vision based on sexual experience. I would like to attempt such a reading now with the clear understanding that I am not denying any epic or mystic or democratic elements—they are clearly all there but they do not explain how the poem works, nor do they deal with any of the sexual structure.

The poem appears, at first glance, to be very unlike **"The Sleepers"** in that it seems to be the product of a wholly conscious mind which is engaged in a number of identifiable traditional poetic functions—e.g. singing, being an epic poet; debating, being a metaphysical poet. But a careful look at the poem will reveal that the poem is a monologue posing as a dialogue, or perhaps a dialogue which turns out to be a monologue. A dialogue for one speaker might be a nice way of putting it. The second role is clearly nonspeaking.

The mode of the poem seems to be a body/soul dialogue, such as those popular in the Renaissance, and known in American poetry through the example of Anne Bradstreet. But the body does most of the talking, the soul does not seem to respond, and the reader is addressed so often and so insistently as "you" that he indeed becomes a part of the poem. The poem is cast as a love poem; it involves a seduction, a growing desire which leads to final fulfillment and then to the vision which follows on sexual experience and which, as in **"The Sleepers"**, permits the poet to perceive the unity of all things. The poem also ends with a sense of contentment brought on by acceptance but not until the poet has marked the end of the night by bidding farewell to his lover.

The structure of the poem is loose, but nonetheless clear if one follows the basic themes which are developed. I can only outline a few of them here and suggest their similarity to the patterns we have already seen in **"The Sleepers."** The first section is a very brief introduction, particularly in the 1855 edition, where it consists of only five lines which provide a setting and the argument. In the second section, the process of natural intoxication has begun. The poet concludes this section by asking the you-reader to "stop this day and night with me." It is clear that, in fantasy at least, the request is granted, and the rest of the poem is an account of that day and night. At this very early stage of the poem it is clear that the poet has a sense of acceptance—"I am satisfied" he writes—and that acceptance is based on the metaphor of God as the lover who sleeps with him by night, leaving him "baskets covered with white towels bulging the house with their plenty." In the scarcely concealed sexual symbolism of this section, the genitals are hidden by white towels, not unlike the "cunning covers" of **"The Sleepers."** It is the coming of God at night which gives the poet a "bulging basket" and permits him to accept the day in the knowledge of a forthcoming night and permits him to ask whether in fact he should

> postpone by acceptation and realization and
> scream at my eyes,
> That they turn from gazing after and down the
> road,
> And forthwith cipher and show me to a cent,
> Exactly the value of one and exactly the value
> of two, and which is ahead?

In the world of nighttime vision there is no counting, one and two are the same, real and imaginary lovers are equal.

The poet continues his address to you, through the recollection of a previous sexual experience which is the source of his first knowledge of peace:

> I mind how once we lay such a transparent sum-
> mer morning,
> How you settled your head athwart my hips and
> gently turn'd upon me,
> And parted the shirt from my bosom-bone, and
> plunged your tongue to my bare-stript heart,
> And reach'd till you felt my beard, and reach'd
> till you held my feet.

From this reminder of previous love and the insights it gave, the poet turns to the beginning of a new sexual experience, which begins with undressing of the you; "undrape!" Once undraped the loved one is subject of one of the most interesting passages of this poem, section 8, which depicts the progress of life through sexual metaphor.

> The little one sleeps in its cradle,
> I lift the gauze and look a long time, and silently
> brush away flies with my hand.
>
> The youngster and the red-faced girl turn aside
> up the bushy hill,
> I peeringly view them from the top.
>
> The suicide sprawls on the bloody floor of the
> bedroom,
> I witness the corpse with its dabbled hair, I note
> where the pistol has fallen.

From childhood to adolescence to death; from birth to reproduction to death; from the "little one . . . in its cradle"

to the "bushy hill" to "the bloody floor . . . the pistol has fallen." The sight of nakedness leads in visual terms to a realization of death and suggests the ambivalent attitude toward the male genitals. But it is crucial to see that if one "cannot be shaken away" then one must accept all. He must accept the penis beneath the foreskin, the erect penis, and the penis after coitus. The acceptance of these three stages can lead to an acceptance of the same three stages of life and thereby to an acceptance of life as a whole in all its multiplicity, and so the second half of this leads to the first catalogue, and we begin to understand the meaning in Whitman's work of the catalogue—the expression of ultimate unity of things seen not on their surface but seen *sub specie aeternitatae,* a point of view that for Whitman was best arrived at through a sexual experience.

The following sections of the poem go out, literally, into the world and lead, for instance, to the celebrated section 11, where the abstract vision of section 8 is transformed into a very specific vision of masturbation.

> Twenty-eight young men bathe by the shore,
> Twenty-eight young men and all so friendly;
> Twenty-eight years of womanly life and all so
> lonesome.
>
> She owns the fine house by the rise of the bank
> She hides handsome and richly drest aft the
> blinds of the window.
>
> Which of the young men does she like the best?
> Ah the homeliest of them is beautiful to her.
>
> Where are you off to, lady? for I see you,
> You splash in the water there, yet stay stock still
> in your room
>
> Dancing and laughing along the beach came the
> twenty-ninth bather,
> The rest did not see her, but she saw them and
> loved them.
>
> The beards of the young men glisten'd with wet,
> it ran from their long hair,
> Little streams pass'd all over their bodies.
>
> An unseen hand also pass'd over their bodies,
> It descended tremblingly from their temples and
> ribs.
>
> The young men float on their backs, their white
> bellies bulge to the sun, they do not ask who
> seizes fast to them,
> They do not know who puffs and declines with
> pendant and bending arch,
> They do not think whom they souse with spray.

This poem, or part of the poem, is exquisite in its evocation of the mood of sexual arousal. As many readers have pointed out, Whitman achieves the feat here of being both subject and object, of being the woman voyeur, and also of being the men who are masturbated. Not only is this one of the loveliest sexual poems I know, it is also a clear defense of the anonymity of sexual encounter. In the dream-vision of Whitman there are no persons, but rather a general feeling of the delight of sexual experience regardless of the partner. They are totally tactile, since they take place in the dream-world of closed eyes. The experience could well be repeated in almost any steam bath of a modern large city. But the important point to see is that not asking, not knowing and not thinking are integral parts of Whitman's *democratic* vision, and anonymous sexuality is an important way-station on the path to the destruction of distinctions of age, class, beauty, *and* sex. Whitman loves all being, and will love, and be loved by, all being. It is perhaps at this juncture that the implications of Whitman's perspective become most revolutionary.

The sense of universality of experience leads to the long catalogues of the following sections, which introduce the transitional sections 21 and 22, concerned with the yearning for love. In section 21, Whitman returns to his Body/Soul division to express his desire to return to the bodily. He concludes the section with the line I have quoted earlier

> unspeakable passionate love

and then 2 lines omitted in later editions but which make the sexual male marriage metaphor clear:

> Thruster holding me tight and that I hold tight
> We hurt each other as the bridegroom and the
>   bride hurt each other.

The sense of growing desire and longing culminates in section 24, where playing gives way to direct phallic arousal, and introduction of the calamus theme. The sperm is risen up:

> You my rich blood! Your milky stream pale
>   strippings of my life.

As the poet imagines himself making love, his assertions become bolder. He refuses the stigma that society may attach: "What we do is right and what we affirm is right." The imagery becomes more violent as he asserts his right to homosexual love:

> Unscrew the locks from the doors!
> Unscrew the doors themselves from their jambs!

All that is hidden must be exposed; there must be no secrets, in this metaphor strikingly similar to the more modern "Out of the closets into the streets!" As his ire increases, the blood and sperm rise, he introduces his calamus symbol ("Root of washed sweet-flag, timorous pondsnipe, nest of guarded duplicate eggs") as a metaphor for his own genitals, and he is able to sing all of the body, with penis and sperm ("Your milky stream pale strippings of my life"). The extraordinary crescendo of section 24 is based in sexual ecstasy and reaches its culmination in a sexual climax: "Seas of bright juice suffuse heaven."

And yet suddenly the passage comes to an end with the apparent arrival of the dawn, which would destroy the night. The reference is at the same time ambiguous, since the physical dawn would end the nighttime vision, but the day-break of sexual ecstasy would show the poet the possibility of ultimate victory over the day through his sexual powers.

> Dazzling and tremendous how quick the sunrise
>   would kill me,
> If I could not now and always send sunrise out
>   of me.

> We also ascend dazzling and tremendous as the
>   sun
> We found our own my soul in the calm and cool
>   of the daybreak.

Man can make his own sunrise and thereby master the natural world and escape the necessity of the cyclical pattern—recalling the first sexual experience, section 5, which also took place in the morning. Making love in the morning seems to break the tyranny of the day.

The next few sections record the poet and his playful reluctance to give in, to let himself be brought to orgasm, a coyness which is ended by rebirth of section 28.

> Is this then a touch? quivering me to a new iden-
>   tity,
> Flames and ether making a rush for my veins,
> Treacherous tip of me reaching and crowding to
>   help them,
> My flesh and blood playing out lightning to
>   strike what is hardly different from myself,
> On all sides prurient provokers stiffening my
>   limbs,
> Straining the udder of my heart for its withheld
>   drip,
> Behaving licentious toward me, taking no deni-
>   al,
> Depriving me of my best as for a purpose,
> Unbuttoning my clothes, holding me by the bare
>   waist,
> Deluding my confusion with the calm of the sun-
>   light and pasture-fields,
> Immodestly sliding the fellow-senses away,
> They bribed to swap off with touch and go and
>   graze at the edges of me,
> No consideration, no regard for my draining
>   strength or my anger,
> Fetching the rest of the herd around to enjoy
>   them a while,
> Then all uniting to stand on a headland and
>   worry me.
> The sentries desert every other part of me,
> They have left me helpless to a red marauder,
> They all come to the headland to witness and as-
>   sist against me.
> I am given up by traitors,
> I talk wildly, I have lost my wits, I and nobody
>   else am the greatest traitor,
> I went myself first to the headland, my own
>   hands carried me there.
> You villain touch! what are you doing? my
>   breath is tight in its throat,
> Unclench your floodgates, you are too much for
>   me.

The cycle is complete, the sexual anticipation is ended through fulfillment, tension gives way to satisfaction, and the pattern we have now come to recognize is again present: the orgasm is followed by passages of philosophical summary and visionary perception of unity.

Something very similar happens a few sections further on, in section 32, when he turns to the stallion, symbol of the male lover. But the poet who in section 28 was the so-called passive partner in anal intercourse has now become the active partner as Whitman makes vivid the banal sexual metaphor of "riding" someone.

> A gigantic beauty of a stallion, fresh and responsive to my caresses,
> Head high in the forehead, wide between the ears,
> Limbs glossy and supple, tail dusting the ground,
> Eyes full of sparkling wickedness, ears finely cut, flexibly moving.
> His nostrils dilate as my heels embrace him.
> His well-built limbs tremble with pleasure as we race around and return

Thus again the sexual leads to the visionary, in this case to the famous section 33, where the poet is "afoot in my vision," recalling the first lines of **"The Sleepers."**

This vision, like those in **"The Sleepers,"** includes the negative, for the poet is not able to separate sexuality from guilt. Death images are pervasive and culminate in his vision of himself as a crucified victim, in section 38. His racial memory includes all experience, and all suffering. He becomes a sacrificial victim, taking upon himself the sins of the world, and thereby assuring the safety and the sleep of his beloved. Reborn like the resurrected Christ, he can begin his journey across the continent—"Ohio and Massachusetts and Virginia and Wisconsin and New York and New Orleans and Texas and Montreal and San Francisco and Charleston and Savannah and Mexico"—and beyond. He recognizes that his poetic mission will be carried on by his élèves, the poet's disciples, who can learn the meaning of his words only if they have followed out the sexual patterns of the poem and have in fact become the poet's lovers. He is now awake but lets the other sleep:

> Sleep—I and they keep guard all night,
> Not doubt, not decease shall dare to lay finger upon you.

He carries his message of salvation, his Christ-like role to the world and feels certain of the correctness of his mission. Thus assured, he awakens the lover in section 44. "It is time to explain myself—let us stand up." He realizes that he has escaped the trap of reality through the acceptances, including that hardest of all to accept, Death. But once he has accepted it, and acceptance was already implied in section 8, he is already out of time and out of space (to quote Poe, who sometimes seems surprisingly like Whitman). Having achieved that state of ascension, he can now say good-by to the lover, recognizing his transitoriness. The recognition of death means that no earthly love is final; that all lovers will part; and so he parts from his lover, prepared to give himself to the world rather than to any one individual. He cannot take this lover with him, but must ask him to make his own journey.

> Not I, not anyone else can travel that road for you,
> You must travel it for yourself
>
> . . . . .
>
> I kiss you a good-by kiss . . .
> Long have you timidly waded holding a plank by the shore,
> Now I will you to be a bold swimmer
> To jump off in the midst of the sea . . .

Having made love, learned about the world, and then bid the world adieu, he is calm again, he has found happiness. Characteristically Whitman's image is physical and sensual:

> Wrench'd and sweaty—calm and cool then my body becomes,
> I sleep—I sleep long.

It is only after the experience of sexual gratification, achieved through the dream, that the visionary experience becomes possible. It is the euphoria of the satisfied lover that gives rise to Whitman's poetry of vision—the poems of realization of unity. Its needs fulfilled, the body expands to encompass the world, through its physical embodiment of the lover, who in his role as "other" is the world. One can accept the death of the world only after transcending unitary death, escaping beyond the fear of the "little death" into a realization that all death brings resurrection, that the penis shall indeed rise again.

Homosexuals are a constant affront to the society, because they demand to be defined in terms of their sexuality. The homosexual has no existence as a group unless it is through sexual preferences and experiences. He cannot be wished away with the thought that such matters are of no importance, or with the piety that all human experience is basically similar. Whitman's poetry, particularly **"Song of Myself,"** shows how the poet translates his love for the world, his cosmic promiscuity, into a myth of the wandering lover seeking his partners in all places and at all times. The visionary is rooted in the sexual, and Whitman will not let his root be torn out. He remains what he is for those who will read him, despite all that has been done to him. He can be secure in the knowledge he spoke of in **"Scented Herbage of My Breast"** and which we have seen to be fundamental to his other poems as well:

> Every year shall you bloom again, out from where you retired you shall emerge again;
> O I do not know whether many passing by will discover you or inhale your faint odor, but I believe a few will;
>
> . . . . .
>
> Do not fold yourself so in your pink-ringed roots timid leaves!
> Do not remain down there so ashamed, herbage of my breast!
> Come I am determin'd to unbare this broad chest of mine, I have long enough stifled and choked;
> Emblematic and capricious blades I leave you, now you serve me not
> I will say what I have to say by itself,
> I will sound myself and comrades only, I will never again utter a call only their call,

Out of the cycle of the penis is born the cycle of the soul; out of his erections, ejaculations (the pun is crucial), and re-erections comes Whitman's faith in a cycle of the world which will comprehend and conquer death. The real sleep is the sleep of the contented lover who will not die. (pp. 83-96)

Robert K. Martin, "Whitman's Song of Myself: Homosexual Dream and Vision," in **Par-**

tisan Review, *Vol. XLII, No. 1, 1975, pp. 80-96.*

Harold Bloom   (essay date 1975)

[*Bloom is one of the most prominent of contemporary critics and literary theorists. In* The Anxiety of Influence *(1973), he formulated a controversial theory of literary creation called revisionism. Influenced strongly by Freudian theory, which states that "all men unconsciously wish to beget themselves, to be their own fathers," Bloom believes that all poets are subject to the influence of earlier poets and that, to develop their own voice, they attempt to overcome this influence through a process of misreading. By misreading, Bloom means a deliberate, personal revision of what has been said by another so that it conforms to one's own vision. In this way the poet creates a singular voice, overcoming the fear of being inferior to poetic predecessors. Bloom's later books are applications of this theory, extended in* Kabbalah and Criticism *(1974) to include the critic or reader as another deliberate misreader. In addition to his theoretical work, Bloom is one of the foremost authorities on English Romantic poetry and has written widely on the influences of Romanticism in contemporary literature. In the following excerpt, he interprets "As I Ebb'd with the Ocean of Life" as an artistically brilliant and moving reaction against the powerful influence of Ralph Waldo Emerson.*]

Whitman is at once the greatest and the most repressed of American poets. If the surmise is correct that the poets invented all of the defenses, as well as all the tropes, then more is to be learned about why the repressed cannot wholly return by reading Whitman's **"The Sleepers"** than by reading Freud's essay "Repression." Freud thought that the repressed returns through a number of processes, but particularly through displacement, condensation and conversion. Whitman is a master of all three operations, but in him they converge, not to reverse repression, but to exalt repression into the American Sublime.

I choose **"As I Ebb'd"** because it is, to me, the most moving of all Whitman's poems, and if I am to justify an antithetical mode of practical criticism, even to myself, it must help me interpret such a poem. . . . I will try to remember that the common reader cares little to be taught to notice tropes or defenses. Images must suffice, and so I will concentrate on images, but will indicate the trope or the defense when it seems to me an inevitable aid to reading.

Emerson, Whitman's precursor, wrote the motto to Whitman's poem in his 1823 Journals: "The worst is, that the ebb is certain, long and frequent, while the flow comes transiently and seldom." A seer is always undoing himself, and only a few times mounts into the Sublime. Some remarks by Anna Freud in her book on defenses are relevant here:

> The obscurity of a successful repression is only equalled by the transparency of the repressive process when the movement is reversed. . . .
>
> Repression consists in the withholding or expulsion of an idea or affect from the conscious ego.

> It is meaningless to speak of repression where the ego is still merged with the id. . . .

The first of these remarks may help illuminate the constant emblem of the American Sublime down to [Wallace] Stevens: transparency. The second may remind us that the ephebe cannot mount up into the Sublime until he has separated himself, so far as he is capable of doing, from the internalized precursor. As we begin reading **"As I Ebb'd,"** with its rather complex opening irony, another of Anna Freud's observations is useful:

> . . . reaction-formation can best be studied when such formations are in process of disintegration. In such a case the id's inroad takes the form of a reinforcement of the libidinal cathexis of the primitive instinctual impulse which the reaction-formation concealed. This enables the impulse to force its way into consciousness and, for a time, the instinctual impulse and the reaction-formation are visible within the ego side by side. . . .

In terms of figuration, that is the same as saying one thing while meaning another, the *illusio* that in disintegrating itself allows a poem to begin. Once again, it hardly matters whether one calls a defense a concealed trope a concealed defense, for this kind of concealment *is* poetry.

Whitman's poem may be divided thus: section 1, *clinamen* and *tessera;* 2, *kenosis;* 3, *daemonization;* and 4, *askesis* and *apophrades.* That is, the first section moves from images of presence and absence to part/whole representations. The second section is a radical and regressive undoing, dominated by a large image of emptiness. With the third section, imagery of a fall into lowness dominates, in a beautifully grotesque version of sublimity. The fourth and last section juxtaposes an imagistic opposition of nature and Whitman's self as outside and inside with images of lateness accepted as such, and with the present firmly negated.

This application of the map of misreading is only a broad and rough one, for the entire poem is remarkable as a version of *kenosis,* of Whitman undoing the Whitmanian bardic self of **"Song of Myself."** Yet it shows us how close Whitman is to the English Romantic crisis-poem, particularly to Shelley's "Ode to the West Wind." For Shelley's leaves Whitman substitutes "those slender windrows, / chaff, straw, splinters of wood, weeds" and the rest of his remarkable metonymic catalog. For Shelley's "trumpet of a prophecy," Whitman gives us "that blare of the cloud-trumpets," which helps give us a sense of glory as "we too lie in drifts" at the close of his poem.

Whitman's opening stanza, with its fierce swerve away from Emersonian Nature, is the poem in embryo:

> As I ebb'd with the ocean of life,
> As I wended the shores I know,
> As I walk'd where the ripples continually wash
>   you Paumanok,
> Where they rustle up hoarse and sibilant,
> Where the fierce old mother endlessly cries for
>   her castaways,
> I musing late in the autumn day, gazing off
>   southward,

> Held by this electric self out of the pride of
>   which I utter poems,
> Was seiz'd by the spirit that trails in the lines un-
>   derfoot,
> The rim, the sediment that stands for all the
>   water and all the land of the globe.

Like Shelley in a wood skirting the Arno, or Stevens confronting the auroras, Whitman muses "late in the autumn day." All three poems adopt a belated stance, with Whitman confronting the south, Shelley the west, and Stevens the north. Whitman gazes at Ferenczi's and tradition's emblem of the mother, Shelley at revolutionary change and death, Stevens at natural change and death. But Whitman, more powerfully than the others, gazes at poetic change and death also. His opening *illusio* or irony is the subtlest of the three. He says "I ebb'd" but he means that "this electric self" ebbed, for it is the pride out of which he is able to write poems, the self of **"Song of Myself,"** that is ebbing. He is dying as a poet, he rightly fears. The fear is very close to the fear of Wordsworth, Shelley and Stevens, but the irony is more pervasive, since Whitman, following Emerson, proclaims a greater monism, yet Whitman is knowingly the most severely dualistic of these poets.

Yet Whitman moves to a restituting representation far more quickly than the others, in the overt synecdoche of "The rim, the sediment that stands for all the water and all the land of the globe." The beach for him is the greatest of synecdoches, standing for ocean and for earth, for mother and for father, but most of all for himself, Whitman, as human sufferer rather than as poet. The insight our map of misreading gives us here is precisely how the part/whole image of representation directly restitutes for the absence/presence image of limitation. Whitman walks the beach as man rather than as poet, "with that electric self seeking types" but not *as* that self. What the poem most quickly returns to him is the *tikkun* of being at once closer to both his father and his mother, whereas when most the poet he is farthest away from his father (as in **"The Sleepers"** and **"Out of the Cradle Endlessly Rocking"**).

The image of emptying out the self until it is only a windrow is already present in the first section, but totally dominates the second, where the defense of undoing the poetic self is more direct than anywhere else in the language, even in Shelley:

> I too but signify at the utmost a little wash'd-up
>   drift,
> A few sands and dead leaves to gather,
> Gather, and merge myself as part of the sands
>   and drift.

Beautiful as the first two sections are, they become dwarfed by the grandeur of the Sublime rising up so strangely and indeed in so American a way in the second half of the poem. Whitman's *daemonization* is a profound humanization of the Sublime, a repression that strengthens his life, that binds him more closely and savingly to earth:

> I throw myself upon your breast my father,
> I cling to you so that you cannot unloose me,

> I hold you so firm till you answer me something.

> Kiss me my father,
> Touch me with your lips as I touch those I love,
> Breathe to me while I hold you close the secret
>   of the murmuring I envy.

Few writers reveal so well what repression truly defends against, and why repression is so close to the apotropaic function of representation, to the way in which poetry wards off destruction. What Whitman has repressed, *and goes on repressing,* now more strongly than ever, is the close association in him between the Primal Scene of Instruction (covenant with Emerson) and the Primal Scenes proper, Freud's *Urphantasie* and *Urszene* (refusal of covenant with Walter Whitman, Sr.). As the covenant with Emerson that begat the poetic self ebbs, so the rejected covenant with the actual father is accepted and made whole. Emersonian Self-Reliance freed Whitman from the totalizing afflictions of the family romance. Now the consequences of the poetic analogue of the family romance allow Whitman a reconciliation he never found while his father was alive. Imaginative loss quite literally is transformed into experiential gain, in a far more direct way than Wordsworth or Coleridge could have envisioned.

Original and life-enhancing as this is, Whitman goes beyond it in the magnificent final section of his poem. He begins with metaphor and its perspectives, yet goes beyond such dualism within six lines of his last section. The ocean of life or fierce old mother is outside him, but now she fears his touch more than he fears her, for he is one with the father. But the outside/inside relation of ocean-of-life/Whitman is too negative a knowledge to be long sustained. The astonishing last stanza of the poem is a grand scheme of transumption, troping again upon every crucial trope in the text preceding it:

> Ebb, ocean of life, (the flow will return,)
> Cease not your moaning you fierce old mother,
> Endlessly cry for your castaways, but fear not,
>   deny not me,
> Rustle not up so hoarse and angry against my
>   feet as I touch you or gather from you.

> I mean tenderly by you and all,
> I gather for myself and for this phantom looking
>   down where we lead, and following me and
>   mine.

> Me and mine, loose windrows, little corpses,
> Froth, snowy white, and bubbles,
> (See, from my dead lips the ooze exuding at last,
> See, the prismatic colors glistening and rolling,)
> Tufts of straw, sands, fragments,
> Buoy'd hither from many moods, one contra-
>   dicting another,
> From the storm, the long calm, the darkness, the
>   swell,
> Musing, pondering, a breath, a briny tear, a dab
>   of liquid or soil,
> Up just as much out of fathomless workings fer-
>   mented and thrown,
> A limp blossom or two, torn, just as much over
>   waves floating, drifting at random,
> Just as much for us that sobbing dirge of Nature,
> Just as much whence we come that blare of the
>   cloud-trumpets,

We, capricious, brought hither we know not
    whence, spread out before you,
You up there walking or sitting,
Whoever you are, we too lie in drifts at your feet.

The "just as much" repetition is the agency by which the metonymy of "Me and mine, loose windrows, little corpses" becomes the metalepsis of "We, capricious, brought hither we know not whence." As a metonymy of a metonymy, the "We, capricious" triumphantly reverses the reductive pattern of the poem, for the present time in which Whitman is cut off from his poetic self becomes a wholly negated time, and so no time at all. The poetic past is introjected, and the images of lateness become exalted:

> Just as much for us that sobbing dirge of Nature
> Just as much whence we come that blare of the
>   cloud-trumpets. . . .

If we put this in terms of the transformation of defenses, we would say that undoing has been undone by introjection, that the self has come to a rest in an identification with an earlier version of what once it was (or fantasizes itself to have been). But I would prefer to call this finally a strong or deep misreading of Emerson's *Nature*, in its apocalyptic conclusion:

> Know then that the world exists for you. For you is the phenomenon perfect. What we are, that only can we see. . . . Build therefore your own world. . . . The kingdom of man over nature, which cometh not with observation,—a dominion such as now is beyond his dream of God,—he shall enter without more wonder than the blind man feels who is gradually restored to perfect sight.

From Emerson's "for you" to Whitman's "just as much for us" is a long movement, when "for us" means "me and mine, loose windrows" and not the spirit made a giant through influx. Whitman's ultimate misprision of the seer his master is to assert that the blind man is restored to sight by the ebb, rather than the flow. (pp. 178-84)

> *Harold Bloom, "In the Shadow of Emerson,"*
> *in his* A Map of Misreading, *Oxford Universi-*
> *ty Press, Inc., 1975, pp. 177-92.*

Stephen A. Black   (essay date 1975)

[*In the following excerpt, Black examines psychoanalytically "The Sleepers" and "To Think of Time," and explains the poems of the first edition of* Leaves of Grass *as a traceable psychological progression from anxiety to a belief in immortality.*]

[In **"Song of Myself"**] Whitman creates a narcissistic world that he partly rejects as he becomes increasingly committed to his emerging vocation. His growing confidence in his poetic craftsmanship enables him to begin to discover his identity, a discovery that leads to tangible if limited relations with the external world. My qualifying words—"*partly* rejects," "*emerging* vocation," "*growing* confidence," "*begin* to discover," "*limited* relations"—indicate areas of conflict that require further defensive maneuvers on the part of Whitman's ego. Except for **"Europe"** and **"A Boston Ballad,"** the poems of the first

Leaves of Grass are addressed to sources of personal anxiety. Three of the poems—**"A Song for Occupations," "Who Learns My Lesson Complete,"** and **"Great Are the Myths"**—repeat without further exploration affirmation made in **"Song of Myself."** The remaining six poems are more complex. Of these, **"To Think of Time"** and **"The Sleepers"** have the most to tell us about the psychological patterns fundamental to Whitman's growing vocation and to the growth of *Leaves of Grass.*

One of the most undeservedly neglected poems in *Leaves of Grass,* **"To Think of Time,"** is a virtual anatomy of Whitman's morbidity and his wish to escape mortality. It is hard to imagine a more personally conceived, or more agonized, response to the "wounds" to humanity's "narcissism" that Freud once attributed to the revelations of Copernican cosmology, Darwinian biology, and psychoanalysis. Although the last of these blows had not been struck in 1855, Whitman nevertheless sensed its most desperate implications—that we cannot escape our personal past, nor separate our conscious lives from unconscious, instinctual drives, and that consciousness can do little to mitigate the facts of existential mortality. **"To Think of Time"** begins with the poet's subjective apprehension of mortality, implied by time; the poem continues with the poet's attempts to escape dying. When he fails, the poet protests that death does not mean annihilation, but as the poem ends, intimations of mortality emerge like weeds in a garden.

At the start the poet recognizes that because "retrospection" depends on time and memory, time and memory imply mortality:

> To think of time. . . . to think through the re-
>   trospection,
> To think of today . . . and the ages continued
>   henceforward.
>
> Have you guessed you yourself would not con-
>   tinue?
> Have you dreaded those earth-beetles?
> Have you feared the future would be nothing to
>   you?

The shift in line three from the impersonal infinitive (implying that the poet himself has these fears) to the second person suggests that mortal terror may be dissipated by asserting its universality. Simultaneously, Whitman seeks to diffuse his sense of self among everything he perceives, adding that unless we accept the future as *something*, the past and present are *nothing*. Whitman's dubious logic seems to mean that although he does not wish to accept mortality, he can find little basis for denying it. The defensive position he takes is probably as old as mankind: existence (*now, was*) points to future continuity, preparing man for eternity.

As if for the first time, Whitman imagines a past that did not include his consciousness, and at the same time he recognizes his current location within the present. Lines seven to nine suggest a cosmos in which individual lives seem intolerably unimportant.

> To think that the sun rose in the east. . . . that
>   men

and women were flexible and real and
    alive. . . .
that every thing was real and alive;
To think that you and I did not see feel think nor
    bear our part,
To think that we are now here and bear our part.

So long as the apprehension of death remains abstract, the
terror Whitman feels remains inexpressible. Although this
is what he seems to want, he can neither let the subject
drop nor continue to abstract it. His fantasy turns to a particular death:

> When the dull nights are over, and the dull days
>   also,
> When the soreness of lying so much in bed is
>   over,
> When the physician, after long putting off, gives
>   the silent and terrible look for an answer,
> When the children come hurried and weeping,
>   and the brothers and sisters have been sent
>   for,
> When medicines stand unused on the shelf, and
>   the camphor-smell has pervaded the rooms,
> When the faithful hand of the living does not de-
>   sert the hand of the dying,
> When the twitching lips press lightly on the fore-
>   head of the dying,
> When the breath ceases and the pulse of the
>   heart ceases,
> Then the corpse-limbs stretch on the bed, and
>   the living look upon them,
> They are palpable as the living are palpable.

The first lines of this passage take us back to the lines immediately preceding. The "dull" nights and days seem
similar to bearing "our part," the period between "ac-
couchement" and death. From the beginning of the episode the poet identifies with the dying man. Whitman unconsciously compares the tedium of bearing his part with
the high drama on which the dying man embarks, a moment when one's specialness and identity are indisputable.
Then, as at no other time since infancy, one is unmistakably in the center of his world and is the deserving recipient of all attention. Doctor and relatives alike must stand
back and proclaim: Here is a phenomenon beyond understanding, control, or sharing. But the poet's identification
takes an odd turn at the end of the scene:

> The living look upon the corpse with their eye-
>   sight,
> But without eyesight lingers a different living
>   and looks curiously on the corpse.

If Whitman intended to affirm that the soul of the recently
dead hovers above its former body and looks on curiously,
another implication exists, one in which the poet identifies
with the dying man up to the moment of death, then becomes the disembodied, detached, and "curious" witness.
As in **"Song of Myself,"** loss of identity results from continuing too long in identification. Whitman's characteristic ambivalence continues: without identity he is a voyeur
of life, incapable of relationships with other people and
things; yet he prefers lingering in painful ambivalence to
commitment one way or the other.

The man's death leads Whitman to imagine life going on
without him. He reflects on the futility of "building the

house" that serves "seventy or eighty years at most" and
of building the coffin that serves "longer than that." He
abandons this meditation and returns to the stagedriver's
funeral, during which he compulsively contemplates that
which he can neither escape nor accept. The funeral is
presented with great power and economy, but the presentation leaves an overwhelming question: in the face of
death's certainty: Does anything else matter? Why bother
with farms, crops, wages, goodness or sin? And yet, what
else can one do?

Perhaps one can renew the infantile "oceanic" feeling:

> [Sensual pleasures] flow onward to others. . . .
>   you and I flow onward;
> But in due time you and I shall take less interest
>   in them.
>
>   . . . . .
>
> The sky continues beautiful. . . . the pleasure
>   of men with women shall never be sated . . .
>   nor the pleasure of women with men . . . nor
>   the pleasure from poems;

In yet another twist of the fantasy, Whitman seems to
verge upon diagnosis of his own crisis:

> You are not thrown to the winds . . . you gather
>   certainly and safely around yourself,
> Yourself! Yourself! Yourself! forever and ever!
>
> It is not to diffuse you that you were born of your
>   mother and father—it is to identify you,
> It is not that you should be undecided, but that
>   you should be decided;
> Something long preparing and formless is ar-
>   rived and formed in you,
> You are thenceforth secure, whatever comes or
>   goes.

Whitman wanted "identity" to mean the mark of uniqueness he saw conferred by the living on the dying man, but
the concept gets out of hand. Mortality is inseparable from
identity; and mother, father, and birth are to blame for
mortality. He recalls the vague alternative that came in a
dream: "there is no life without satisfaction." But he
moves in a circle, for only immortality can grant this satisfaction: "We cannot be stopped at a given point. . . . that
is no satisfaction." The inadequacy of the dream is all too
apparent:

> If otherwise, all these things came but to ashes
>   of dung;
> If maggots and rats ended us, then suspicion and
>   treachery and death.
>
> Do you suspect death? If I were to suspect death
>   I should die now,
> Do you think I could walk pleasantly and well-
>   suited toward annihilation?

But dreaming of immortality no more makes him immortal than contemplating the "beautiful and perfect" animals makes him invulnerable to the pains of introspection.
The more emphatically Whitman "swears" his faith, the
more desperate is his uncertainty:

> I swear I see now that every thing has an eternal
>   soul!

. . . . .

> I swear I think there is nothing but immortality!
> That the exquisite scheme is for it, and the nebu-
> lous float is for it, and the cohering is for it,
> And all preparation is for it . . . and identity is
> for it . . . and life and death are for it.

The psychoanalytic theory that defense mechanisms are motivated by the inexpressibility of instinctual drives supports my contention that Whitman's affirmation of immortality, like his morbidity, is itself a defense against something else. In . . . **"Out of the Cradle"** . . . Whitman preoccupies himself with death in order to escape "the fire, the sweet hell within, / The unknown want, the destiny of me." That is, preoccupation with mortality defends against accepting latent sexual identity. **"To Think of Time"** indicates that this defense existed as early as 1855.

Deeply buried in **"To Think of Time"** are Whitman's longings to share with the dying man a central place in the world's attention and to win recognition for his uniqueness and importance. The longings emerge as prominent themes in **"The Sleepers,"** one of Whitman's most widely admired and analyzed poems. In **"The Sleepers"** the poet seems to accept from the start certain difficult facts he tried to avoid in **"Song of Myself."** Twin threats inhibit his achieving a secure sense of identity: loss of autonomy from merging with others if he should permit object relationships, and the actuality of mortal and sexual limitations that imply an end to infantile desires and fantasies. Although the anxiety created by Whitman's ambivalence energizes **"The Sleepers,"** the poet makes little progress toward resolving his dilemma. Finally, when he seeks to evade the confrontation by an act of transcendental faith, the act fails and the former doubt and ambivalence return. In the end he yields to the authority of his vision and retreats into the maternal night, with whom he seeks passive unity.

Whitman announces the problem of **"The Sleepers"** immediately: separated in his vision from those who sleep, he wanders, watching with "open eyes over the shut eyes of the sleepers." What follows suggests the tension and alienation of the watcher:

> Wandering and confused. . . . lost to
> myself. . . . ill-assorted. . . . contradictory,
> Pausing and gazing and bending and stopping.

Everyone can sleep but the poet, who emphasizes his isolation by naming the others. Though he may well have something in common with each of those he names (the "ennuyees," the drunkard, the onanist, the married couple), the something in difference is presently more important. These others seem more capable of letting go in sleep, of risking temporary "death," than he. That fear of death is fundamental to Whitman's sense of loss and confusion is suggested by the profusion of morbid things pervading the first six stanzas (not to mention the four narratives in the middle). The poet's visionary associations relentlessly lead to the puzzle of mortality early in the poem. Whitman responds by creating a mythical role that lets him merge with the sleepers and the elements:

> I go from bedside to bedside. . . . I sleep close
> with the other sleepers, each in turn;
> I dream in my dream all the dreams of the other
> dreamers,
> And I become the other dreamers.

Thus the poet deals with his fear of mortality by identifying with the sleepers. The evasion is temporarily successful enough for him to feel a moment of ecstasy:

> I am a dance. . . . Play up there! the fit is whirl-
> ing me fast.
> I am the everlaughing. . . . it is new moon and
> twilight,
> I see the hiding of douceurs. . . . I see nimble
> ghosts whichever way I look,
> Cache and cache again deep in the ground and
> sea, and where it is neither ground or sea.

The expression of ecstasy reveals the infantile sexual fantasies at the core of the poem. In fantasy the poet becomes the infant tyrant identifying with those who in reality might tyrannize him. By regressing, Whitman momentarily resolves through wishful dreaming a problem of adult mortality. Physical sexual delights no longer carry the threats that forbid their expression in reality. The infant tyrant leads his "gang" of adult "journeymen":

> Well do they do their jobs, those journeymen di-
> vine,
> Only from me can they hide nothing and would
> not if they could;
> I reckon I am their boss, and they make me a pet
> besides,
> And surround me, and lead me and run ahead
> when I walk,
> And lift their cunning covers and signify me
> with stretched arms, and resume the way;
> Onward we move, a gay gang of blackguards
> with mirthshouting music and wildflapping
> pennants of joy.

This is one of those occasions when Whitman finds sudden release from his customary anaesthesia. The sensual pleasure now available to him replicates the polymorphous sexuality of infancy, as characterized by his relation to "those journeymen divine," the "nimble ghosts" who have hidden "douceurs" from him. Whitman flees, fearing that abandonment or rejection will result from heterosexual intimacy. He seeks not homosexual love (which involves another objective person), but masturbation, the ecstatic climax of which floods him with an infantile sense of oneness. The stanzas that follow develop various aspects of the poet's uncertainty about his identity, including permutations of Oedipal conflicts. After identifying with various public roles (the "actor, the actress"), the poet becomes a woman who has a confusing autoerotic fantasy.

The woman is alone, acting out her desire in masturbation. Even in fantasy Whitman can convincingly express sexuality only in autoerotic terms. The wish for vicarious homosexual fulfillment in this passage is thwarted by the imperfection of the identification, for the poet does not identify with the woman but with the role he thinks she plays. He attributes a form to her fantasies that originates in himself and that is psychologically determined by his inability to differentiate between the feminine and the maternal. As with the first intimations of sensual gratification (the "journeymen divine"), the fantasies become regressive and finally self-destructive. In stanza twenty-two the poet feels himself falling back toward the first discovery of phallic sexuality:

> Pier that I saw dimly last night when I looked
>   from the windows,
> Pier out from the main, let me catch myself with
>   you and stay. . . . I will not chafe you;
> I feel ashamed to go naked about the world,
> And am curious to know where my feet
>   stand. . . . and what is this flooding me,
>   childhood or manhood. . . . and the hunger
>   that crosses the bridge between.

As in **"Out of the Cradle** (and as Edwin Miller has said) it is this bridge that Whitman cannot cross. Whitman often substitutes death for sex, unconsciously hoping that morbidity will drive the "unknown want, the destiny of me" from consciousness. In **"The Sleepers"** he moves from the moment of troubling discovery to the earlier period of infantile polymorphous sexuality when he confused breast with penis and the mouth with the genitals.

> The cloth laps a first sweet eating and drinking,
> Laps life-swelling yolks. . . . laps ear of rose-
>   corn, milky and just ripened:
> The white teeth stay, and the boss-tooth ad-
>   vances in darkness,
> And liquor is spilled on lips and bosoms by
>   touching glasses, and the best liquor after-
>   ward.

The regressive impulse apparently led back to the first physical gratification: nursing. Nevertheless, the poet identified less with his former infantile self than with the woman whose naked shame he discovered in stanzas twenty-one, and whose breast spilled "liquor" on "lips and bosoms." By now he is so deeply committed to his fantasy that he cannot easily withdraw. His identification with the woman continues as she is suddenly transformed into decrepitude:

> I descend my western course. . . . my sinews
>   are flacid,
> Perfume and youth course through me, and I am
>   their wake.
>
> It is my face yellow and wrinkled instead of the
>   old woman's,
> I sit low in a strawbottom chair and carefully
>   darn my grandson's stockings.
>
> It is I too. . . . the sleepless widow looking out
>   on the winter midnight,
> I see the sparkles of starshine on the icy and pal-
>   lid earth.
>
> A shroud I see—and I am the shroud. . . . I
>   wrap a body and lie in the coffin;
> It is dark here underground. . . . it is not evil
>   or pain here. . . . it is blank here, for reasons.
>
> It seems to me that everything in the light and
>   air ought to be happy;
> Whoever is not in his coffin and the dark grave,
>   let him know he has enough.

As usual, Whitman's fantasies of sexual gratification bring to the surface the morbidity that always waits just beneath. At the last moment the identification shifts from the woman to the shroud—that which envelops her in blankness. Blankness—meaninglessness—characterizes the poet's visionary state and reveals his own lack of identity, his inability to make order, to give meaning, or even to perceive. To the extent that he identifies with the woman, he escapes blankness, for her narrative has order and meaning. But the identification brings nothing resembling resolution. The poet's morbidity does not end; nor does he escape the sense of isolation that prompted this journey among the sleepers. As he complains in the last of these stanzas, he is still nothing; nor has he, at this moment, any faith in immortality. A brief symbolic glance at deadness is altogether enough.

In an effort to fill the blankness of his vision, Whitman resorts to mythmaking, the imposition of structure on certain items he discovers in his chaotic memory. Four stories of commitment, battle, destruction, and ritual sacrifice exemplify the apparent impossibility of one person's connecting with others. These myths lead at last to what he will call "the myth of heaven," which he fervently hopes will afford beautiful peace. The telling and thus the ordering of each story gives the poet a momentary insight into himself and his relation to the situation he describes, but neither catharsis nor assimilation occurs. Instead, the very activity of mythmaking objectifies the insight and enforces the poet's tendency toward stasis. Once something is perceived by means of the myth, whatever was formerly dynamic in the material becomes fixed. Although, having told the story, the poet may better understand his mother's attraction to the Indian woman, the process of mythmaking turns the living into frozen figures, as on the Grecian urn. The mythic insight becomes irrelevant as soon as it is formed; its continued existence repudiates the process by which it was made.

Telling of the "beautiful gigantic swimmer swimming naked through the eddies of the sea," the poet imparts Promethean qualities to the swimmer and simultaneously evokes the usual elemental conflict. Similarly, Whitman emphasizes his own detachment in the very act of identification. Having learned (when the woman aged and died) the penalty for too close an identification with someone else, the poet is now careful to keep his distance, to remain on the shore. The swimmer is an example to the poet, and the story is a cautionary tale: there but for sexual immobility goes Whitman's own Oedipal body. For Whitman what is horrible in the story is that the swimmer must die merely because of his impulse to swim. Should Whitman fail to identify with this man, he would fail blatantly in courage. Perhaps by mythmaking and through identification he can be both swimmer and watcher. But he cannot escape the story's grim ending, for the sea bears out of sight the "brave corpse." Morbidity as a defense against sexuality has created more problems than it has solved and now requires new defenses against itself.

The poet tells his stories from inside the confusion that dominates most of **"The Sleepers"**: "I turn but do not extricate myself; / Confused. . . . a pastreading. . . . another, but with darkness yet." In the visionary ambience, the story of the swimmer is obscure and can be seen "but with darkness yet." In fact, the mythic qualities attributed to the swimmer assure that the poet will never perceive the story clearly. Whitman tries to become more intimate, telling of a shipwreck he witnessed and the impotence of rescuers to combat the sea's icy destructiveness. All the poet can do about the death of the swimmer is to give the protagonist epic proportions. The poet's function in the story of the shipwreck is to "help pick up the dead and lay them in rows in a barn." He witnesses both disasters, sensing man's powerlessness. But the unconsciousness of Whitman's assumptions about earth, air, fire, and water cause the stories of the swimmer and the shipwreck to remain incomprehensible. The morbidity that leads him to become a voyeur of death precludes acceptance of his own mortality. Whitman places myths and rituals between nature and his vulnerable, protesting self, as if by stereotyping his reactions he can ensure that his world will no longer be lonely and separate.

Whitman's defense against morbidity directs the poet to evade the subjective. In the next two stories, he removes himself from the action. Both stories are passed to the reader as received myth; as such they are beyond scrutiny or revision. The narrative of Washington's defeat at Brooklyn comes to us as the remotest and most objectified of battles; all its actions are ritualized, none is particularized. The battle, the defeat, the deaths are given the same emotional weight as the tears on the general's face. Similarly, the story of the red squaw and Louisa Whitman is presented as if Whitman intends to distill his own feelings out of the poetic atmosphere, leaving us and himself not the distillation, but the mash: "the distillation would intoxicate me also, but I shall not let it."

Whitman's most important literary problem is to learn to permit the distillation to "intoxicate" him into regression, where he can express the discoveries of his poetic journeys and especially the feelings awakened by those discoveries. By regression unattached emotions can be integrated into a poetic structure. On the other hand, when Whitman seems least coherent, it is usually because he cannot relate his feelings to his poetic material. The outburst against Lucifer that follows seems unrelated to anything else in **"The Sleepers"**; the anger expressed has existed from the beginning of the poem—so we may infer—but its cause is by no means clear:

> Now Lucifer was not dead. . . . or if he was I
>   am his sorrowful terrible heir;
> I have been wronged. . . . I am oppressed. . . .
>   I hate him that oppresses me,
> I will either destroy him, or he shall release me.

Various tensions generated by the fantasy underlying **"The Sleepers"** cause this outburst, in which catharsis takes the form of rage rather than ecstasy. Here catharsis carries a confused latent insight. Although Lucifer, the archetypal rebel, unconsciously symbolizes the poet's aggressive id-drives, Whitman attacks what he thinks symbolizes hated qualities in his father. The "father" is both Whitman's interpretation of his real father and the poet's unconscious superego; if Whitman could destroy an uncontrollable object he might be less troubled by the uncon-

trollable inner self. With his declaration that he will either "destroy" or be released by his oppressor, Whitman's attention begins to wander:

> Damn him! how he does defile me,
> How he informs against my brother and sister
>   and takes pay for their blood,
> How he laughs when I look down the bend after
>   the steamboat that carries away my woman.
>
> Now the vast dusk bulk that is the whale's
>   bulk. . . . it seems mine,
> Warily, sportsman! though I lie so sleepy and
>   sluggish, my tap is death.

The fantasy of identification with a slave (lines 2 and 3 above) comes from one who feels too weak to compete for a woman he cannot win; to retaliate the poet becomes Moby Dick. But the narcissistic fantasy of omnipotence inhibits coping with either external or internal reality. The fantasy ensures that the poet will never have to test his actual strength against objects.

And yet, for all his fears, Whitman genuinely wants to confront the external world—a fact we learn from the four narratives. All four deal with freedom, confinement, and identity. When the swimmer lets go in his battle with the sea, he is destroyed. The shipwreck victims lose their identities as they are laid out in rows. Washington's soldiers alternate between civilian and military restraints, conventions and morality. The poet's adolescent mother falls suddenly and possessively in love with the unpossessive freedom represented by the red girl. The idea of freedom pervades the questions that cloud the problem of identity. Because freedom implies the chaos and meaninglessness of the visionary world, it may lead to paralysis: when nothing can be known for certain, no choice is better than any other. But to want freedom implies a desire for strength and autonomy. The idea of freedom leads the poet away from orderly narrative back to wandering in his vision. The shift in poetic mode from meditation to narration and back brings the poet's half-understood desires to feel ecstatically free and to imagine himself in harmony with the elements. By asserting physical and metaphysical order Whitman intends to allay the sense of chaos previously felt:

> A show of the summer softness. . . . a contact
>   of something unseen. . . . an amour of the
>   light and air;
> I am jealous and overwhelmed with friendliness,
> And will go gallivant with the light and the air
>   myself,
> And have an unseen something to be in contact
>   with them also.
>
> O love and summer! you are in the dreams and
>   in me,
> Autumn and winter are in the dreams. . . . the
>   farmer goes with his thrift,
> The droves and crops increase. . . . the barns
>   are wellfilled.
>
> Elements merge in the night. . . . ships make
>   tacks in the dreams. . . . the sailor sails. . . .
>   the exile returns home

Since the poet previously identified the light and air with

life, he now feels he can live and be free. Narrative logic abandoned, the poetry becomes meditative and associative. In the next stanzas, as the poet revisits the sleepers he witnessed at the start, he tidies up their lives with fantasies of unity and integrity. All of the sleepers become whole and even "beautiful," as the "myth of heaven" allocates to the ugliest a place in the orderly universe. Yet the images of chaos, ugliness, and disorder overwhelm the poet's assertions of peace and order.

The peace found through the "myth of heaven" encompasses the miraculous healing of injuries and deformities, the closing of gulfs between people and castes, the cessation of desire. The beauty of the sleepers is the beauty of the dead—the dead swimmer, the dead shipwreck victims, the dead soldiers, the dead woman in her grave, the mother's dead desire to be free. Only in death can there be such unity and order. Yet because death is imagined to be merely analogous to creative passivity it seems to offer escape from subsequent discoveries.

> The swelled and convulsed and congested awake
> to themselves in condition,
> They pass the invigoration of the night and the
> chemistry of the night and awake.

The "myth of heaven" leads to immortality and the cessation of fear and desire. If the objective world of slavery, insanity, prisons, consumption, and paralysis may be left behind, perhaps the poet may also escape his personal terrors. He asserts that his former fears of sleep and the night are gone, that he will sleep as peacefully as the other sleepers:

> I too pass from the night;
> I stay awhile away O night, but I return to you
> again and love you;
> Why should I be afraid to trust myself to you?
> I am not afraid. . . . I have been well brought
> forward by you;
> I love the rich running day, but I do not desert
> her in whom I lay so long:
> I know not how I came of you, and I know not
> where I go with you. . . . but I know I came
> well and shall go well.
>
> I will stop only a time with the night. . . . and
> rise betimes.
>
> I will duly pass the day O my mother and duly
> return to you;
> Not you will yield forth the dawn again more
> surely than you will yield forth me again,
> Not the womb yields the babe in its time more
> surely than I shall be yielded from you in my
> time.

The assertions that end **"The Sleepers"** are set in terms that raise more questions than they answer. When Whitman asks, "Why should I be afraid to trust myself to you?" he makes explicit a fear the reader has previously been able only to infer. If the reader can accept at face value the poet's assertion of having overcome former fears and doubts, he can accept the poem in the terms Whitman clearly intends, as proving rebirth in a narcissistic world where nature takes the place of the lost mother. But the associations that link the night to maternity—"her in

whom I lay so long," "I will duly pass the day O my mother and duly return to you," "Not the womb yields the babe in its time more surely than I shall be yielded from you in my time"—reveal that beneath the idea of transcendence lies the impossible wish to return to primary symbiosis.

The last two lines of **"The Sleepers"** (deleted after 1855) show the poet as passive as ever, as incapable of touching the other sleepers as before. Whitman's passivity indicates an openness to regressive impulses that the creative process requires, yet it also indicates one of Whitman's "usual mistakes," which is that the poet could not always be satisfied if regression yielded a poem instead of restoring the infantile security he sought. The assertion of universal order that ends **"The Sleepers"** lets the poet momentarily believe that he can be again the child he once was. Ideas of transcendental order support regressive impulses by promising that the "exquisite flexible doors" of the uterus permit both outward and inward passage; "immortality" means life before birth.

But, as we know, Whitman's scheme of order failed to provide the psychological comfort required to cope with the ebbing of visionary faith. If the sea and night become angry again, Whitman will be as devastated as he was in the past. As the poems of 1856 and 1860 show, the unconscious conflicting attitudes toward the maternal continue at full force.

The first *Leaves of Grass* evolved according to a definable psychological movement rather than according to philosophical ideas or logic. In **"Song of Myself"** Whitman sought to accommodate regressive impulses to his need to find a vocation to which he could commit himself. Whitman's search required the establishment of new psychological defenses against unresolved neurotic conflicts, defenses that were sometimes successful. His most important psychological needs and defenses (evident in **"Song of Myself," "To Think of Time,"** and **"The Sleepers"**) may be expressed as follows:

NEEDS	DEFENSES
Sexual expression	Autoerotic fantasies; masturbation; morbidity
Restoration of infantile security; justification of existence	Assertion of immortality; creation of ideal, sexually diffused reader
Justification of infantile feelings of megalomania	Creation of narcissistic fantasy world
Oral gratification	Exchange of poetry for breath and breast

Apparently Whitman's inability to satisfy his needs through ordinary "adult" relations with external objects led to intolerable anxiety, from which he sought relief by creating a narcissistic fantasy world. When, as was inevitable, regression to narcissism failed to give adequate satisfaction, Whitman looked for surrogate identities by identifying with others, hoping to avoid isolation by participating vicariously in the others' experiences. The second line of defense also failed because it jeopardized autonomy and exacerbated fears about mortality: identification led merely to another form of secondary narcissism. When the second line of defense failed, Whitman began to explore a third, which arose from his growing confidence in his poetic processes. Because regression is an inherent part of the creative process, Whitman's commitment to poetry did not conflict with the wish to restore primary symbiosis. Whitman sought to identify himself as a bard whose poems might be exchanged with external objects in return for gratification of basic needs.

The movement through these lines of defense is reflected in the placement of poems in the first *Leaves of Grass.* I suggest the following relationships and transitions between the poems.

From **"Song of Myself "** to **"A Song for Occupations."** Whitman needed to affirm the existence of his ideal reader, to justify his "occupation" as the bard.

From **"Occupations"** to **"To Think of Time."** The least secure defense achieved in **"Song of Myself "** is that against fears of mortality. Whitman's poetic method, depending on memory and a sense of time, constantly and inevitably led the poet to thoughts of death.

From **"Time"** to **"The Sleepers."** Fear of mortality almost always reminded Whitman of his lack of sexual identity; the two sources of anxiety were interwoven in the poet's Oedipal neurosis, the unconscious foundation of **"The Sleepers."**

From **"The Sleepers"** to **"I Sing the Body Electric."** From adolescence on, Whitman escaped Oedipal anxieties by imagining himself a family patriarch, as loved and honored as the eighty-year-old farmer in **"Body Electric."** Whitman's unconvincing attempt to imagine himself in heterosexual intercourse testifies to a reaction formation against fear of sexual intimacy.

From **"Body Electric"** to **"Faces."** **"Faces"** further explores the poet's fear of sexuality, especially his feeling of guilt for horrible things being as they are.

From **"Faces"** to **"Song of the Answerer."** **"Answerer"** attempts to justify being a bard in a world pervaded by injustice, sickness, deformity—the world of **"Faces."**

From **"Answerer"** to **"Europe."** One "answer" is that the bard must explain the external world and reorganize it according to his poetic vision.

From **"Europe"** to **"A Boston Ballad."** These two poems contrast the failing ideals of American democracy with revolutionary European movements toward democratic ideals.

From **"Boston"** to **"There Was a Child Went Forth."** The doubts about America expressed in **"Boston"** parallel the "doubts of daytime and the doubts of nighttime" Whitman meets in **"There Was a Child."** Whitman's uncharacteristically direct expression of childhood unhappiness

constitutes a moment of profound doubt in the midst of a clear and strongly willed movement, throughout the book, toward affirmation.

From **"There Was a Child"** to **"Who Learns My Lesson Complete."** **"Who Learns"** denies the doubts expressed in the preceding poems and affirms the poet's recently attained bardic identity by affirming Whitman's belief in the existence of an ideal reader.

From **"Who Learns"** to **"Great Are the Myths."** **"Great Are the Myths"** clearly, if unconvincingly, asserts that although there is little reason to believe in immortality, he must try to believe.

The first *Leaves of Grass* attests to the growth of Whitman's courage to explore his unconscious and to his increasing skill to speak from the deepest abysms of his soul. (pp. 119-41)

> Stephen A. Black, "The Psychological Structure of the First 'Leaves of Grass'," in his Whitman's Journeys into Chaos: A Psychoanalytic Study of the Poetic Process, *Princeton University Press, 1975, pp. 119-41.*

Allen Ginsberg   (discourse date 1980)

[*Ginsberg is one of the most celebrated poets in contemporary America. Known for his morally and aesthetically iconoclastic verse, he has been an important voice of the country's disaffected youth. He was a leading member of the Beat movement of the 1950s and a prominent figure in the counterculture movement of the 1960s. In 1972, he received the National Book Award for his collection* The Fall of America: Poems of These States, 1965-1971. *Galway Kinnell has commented, "I feel that Ginsberg is the only one to understand Whitman and to bring into the poetry of our time a comparable music." In the following transcription of an extemporaneous monologue, Ginsberg explicates many of Whitman's poems, admiring the prescience of his ideas.*]

There was a man, Walt Whitman, who lived in the nineteenth century, in America, who began to define his own person, who began to tell his own secrets, who outlined his own body, and made an outline of his own mind, so other people could see it. He was sort of the prophet of American democracy in the sense that he got to be known as the good gray poet when he got to be an old, old man because he was so honest and so truthful and at the same time so enormous-voiced and bombastic that he sounded his "barbaric yawp over the roofs of the world." As *he* said: "I sound my barbaric yawp over the roofs of the world," writing in New York City probably then, thinking of the skyline and roofs of Manhattan as it might have been in 1883 or so. He began announcing himself, and announcing person, with a big capital P, Person, self, or one's own nature, one's own original nature, what you really think when you're alone in bed, after everybody's gone home from the party or when you're looking in the mirror, shaving, or you're not shaving and you're looking in the mirror, looking at your long, white, aged beard, or if you're sitting on the toilet, or thinking to yourself "What happened to life?" "What happened to your Mommy?" or if you're just walking down the street, looking at people full of longing.

So he wrote a book called *Leaves of Grass.* [The text referred to here is the Modern Library edition: *Leaves of Grass and Selected Prose,* 1950.] And the very first inscription, at the beginning of *Leaves of Grass,* was **"One's-Self I Sing"**:

> One's-Self I sing, a simple separate person,
> Yet utter the word Democratic, the word En-
>   Masse.
> Of physiology from top to toe I sing,
> Not physiognomy alone nor brain alone is wor-
>   thy for the Muse, I say the Form complete is
>   worthier far,
> The Female equally with the Male I sing.
>
> Of Life immense in passion, pulse, and power,
> Cheerful, for freest action form'd under the laws
>   divine,
> The Modern Man I sing.

Well, that's kind of interesting. He starts with the female equally with the male, so he begins in the middle of the nineteenth century to begin saying "women's lib," actually, "The Female equally with the Male I sing." But he's going to talk about the body he says, of physiology from top to toe, so he's going to sing about the toes and the hair: modern man. This is on the very first page of his book *Leaves of Grass.*

Then, the next page, he has a little note, **"To Foreign Lands"**:

> I heard that you ask'd for something to prove
>   this puzzle the New World,
> And to define America, her athletic Democracy,
> Therefore I send you my poems that you behold
>   in them what you wanted.

An "athletic Democracy," so that was an idea. But what did he mean by that? He means people who are able to get up off their ass and get out and look up at the blue sky in the middle of the night and realize how big the universe is and how little, tiny America is, or, you know, how vast our souls are, and how small the state is, or the Capitol building, magnificent and glorious as it is, it's rendered the size of an ant's forefoot by the immensity of a cloud above it. And so, the soul that sees the cloud above the Capitol or the universe above the cloud, is the giant athletic soul, you could almost say. So, it's democracy, though, that is the key, which for him is meaning, in the long run, the love of comrades, that men will love men, women love women, men love women, women love men, but that there be a spontaneous tenderness between them as the basis of the democracy. "Athletic" probably ultimately for him means "erotic," people having sports in bed.

So he goes on, **"To the States,"** announcing:

> To the States or any one of them, or any city of
>   the States, *Resist much, obey little,*
> Once unquestioning obedience, once fully en-
>   slaved,
> Once fully enslaved, no nation, state, city of this
>   earth, ever afterward resumes its liberty.

Well, that's a warning to America, much needed later on, when as Eisenhower, once President a hundred years later, warned, "Watch out for the military-industrial complex which demands unquestioning obedience and slavery to military aggression." Fear, nuclear apocalypse, unquestioning obedience like "Don't ask, maybe they know better than you do." So this is a warning from Whitman about the difficulties of democracy. Then he, like a Bodhisattva, that is to say, someone who has taken a vow to enlighten all beings in all the directions of space and in all the three times—past, present, and future—has a little poem or song to his fellow poets that would be born after him, that, like myself, will sit in a recording studio reading his words aloud to be heard by ears through some kind of movie/television/theater: "Poets to come! orators, singers,"—that must be, "orators," now who would that be, as "Thou shalt not crucify mankind upon a cross of gold," that was William Jennings Bryan, a great political orator; "singers," that must be Bob Dylan; "musicians to come," that must be Mick Jagger; "Poets to come! orators, singers, musicians to come . . . " "orators," that must be Kerouac.

> Poets to come! orators, singers, musicians to
>   come!
> Not to-day is to justify me and answer what I am
>   for,
> But you, a new brood, native, athletic, continen-
>   tal, greater than before known,
> Arouse! for you must justify me.
>
> I myself but write one or two indicative words
>   for the future,
> I but advance a moment only to wheel and hurry
>   back in the darkness.
>
> I am a man who, sauntering along without fully
>   stopping, turns a casual look upon you and
>   then averts his face,
> Leaving it to you to prove and define it,
> Expecting the main things from you.

Ah, he wants somebody to pick him up in the street and make love to him. But he wants to give that glance, so that you know he's open, but what kind of love does he want?

He wants a democratic love, and he wants an athletic love, he wants a love from men, too, and he also wants a love in the imagination. He wants an expansiveness, he wants communication, he wants some kind of vow that everybody will cherish each other sacramentally. So he's going to make the first breakthrough, which is what he's saying. So he's got another little poem following that, **"To You"**:

> Stranger, if you passing meet me and desire to
>   speak to me, why should you not speak to me?
> And why should I not speak to you?

Well, I don't know why not except everybody's too scared to be generally walking down the street, they might get hit for being a fairy or something. Or, you know, be trying to pick you up or be a nut talking in the subway, or somebody babbling to himself walking in the street. So there's all these bag ladies and bag men, old Whitmans wandering around with dirty white beards eating out of the garbage pail wanting to talk to nobody actually. Those are the people that won't talk to anybody, they just go around mumbling to themselves, they talk to themselves. But he was willing to talk to anybody, he said. Of course he was living in a time when there weren't too many people to talk to anyway, in the sense of nineteenth-century America. Population was growing but there were still lots of farms. There was still some sense of sport in the cities. Not a total fear of being mugged by a junkie, I guess. I wonder what he would've done with a junkie going along, "Hey, Mr. Whitman, you got some smash? Got some spare change?" Or maybe he would have been the one going around asking for spare change. Well why not? Spare, he's looking for spare love, actually. Or spare affection. Or just spare openness, spare democracy. "You got any spare democracy, Mister?" Some enthusiasm, a little bit of vitality, a little bit of that hard, gem-like flame that artists burn with.

So, his major work is known as **"Song of Myself." "Song of Myself"** is a long thing, about thirty-two pages of not such big type; he wrote a lot. And this was a major statement, this was his declaration of his own nature. Now, what is a declaration of nature for a guy? In the nineteenth century, everybody was writing closed verse forms. They all went to Germany for their education, like Longfellow, they went to Heidelberg University, and they studied esoteric sociology and epistemology and linguistics and ancient Greek and they thought back on the United States romantically and wrote long poems about Hiawatha and the Indian maidens under the full moon near the Canadian lakes. Whitman actually just stated America and slugged it out with the beer carts along the Bowery and wandered up and down and sat afternoons in Pfaff's. Pfaff's was a bar he used to go to, a Bohemian hang-out, a downstairs beer hall, sort of like a German *bierstuben*. Bohemian friends used to meet there, probably like a gay gang, plus a newspaper gang, plus a theatrical gang, and the opera singers, and some of the dancers, a Broadway crowd sort of, way down, downtown though. And that was his hang-out. Probably down around the Bowery I think it was.

There he'd meet his friends, there he'd sit around and try to pick up people I guess or he'd write his articles. He was very naive at first. A young guy, he started out writing temperance novels and editing the *Brooklyn Eagle,* or some such newspaper from Brooklyn. Then, something happened to him in his thirties, about thirty-four, well, you know, crucifixion time, he realized he was going to die some day maybe, or that America was weird, or that he was weird, or maybe some kind of breakthrough of personal affection, maybe some kind of gay lib thing, anyway, he discovered his own mind and his own enthusiasm, his own expansiveness is the thing. The fact that his mind was so expansive that it was completely penetrant. That it penetrated through curiosity and inquisitiveness into every crevasse and nook, every tree, bowl, every vagina, every anus, every mouth, every flower stamen, every exhaust pipe, every horse's ear and behind that he met, penetrated through the clouds; notice he wandered, he thought a lot, he wandered in his mind and he wasn't ashamed of what he thought.

So, Whitman was probably the first person in America who was not ashamed of the fact that he thought things that were as big as the universe. Or that were equal to the universe, or that fitted the universe. He wasn't ashamed

of his mind or body. So he wrote **"Song of Myself,"** and it began tipping off where he was coming from and where he was going, saying that you, too, needn't be ashamed of your thoughts: "I celebrate myself, and sing myself [quotes Part 1] . . . with original energy," Wow, what a thing to do!

So that's nineteenth century, and he's threatening to speak Nature without check, with original energy. Well, who's willing to pick that one up? What does that mean, anyway? Means, born here from parents the same, so you can't accuse him of being un-American, he's 4th, 5th, 6th generation so he can say whatever he wants, on his own soil, on his own land, nobody can intimidate him, nobody can say "You didn't think that thought how dare you make up a thought like that and say you thought it." He just said what he actually thought.

So, Part 2 of **"Song of Myself,"** going on with his original mind that he is presenting, and then he looks out at the drawing rooms of Brooklyn and lower Manhattan and the rich of his day, and the sophisticated culture of his day, and he sees that it's pretty shallow: "Houses and rooms are full of perfumes . . . " [quotes Part 2]. So, what he's done here is he has completely possessed his own body, he's gone over and realized he's breathing, that his heart is beating, that he has roots that go from his crotch to his brain, he begins to sniff around him and extend his thought around him to the sea, to the woods, to the cities, recognizes his emotions, going all the way out to the millions of suns, then realizing that most of the time he and most everybody else is taking things second- and third-hand from television, from *Time, Newsweek, New York Times,* from the *Boulder Camera,* from the *Denver Post,* from the *Minneapolis Star,* from the *Durham Gazette,* from the *Raleigh News of the Dead,* from *Las Vegas Sporting Spectator,* from the *Manhattan Morbid Chronicle,* but who actually looks out of their own eyes and sees the revolutions in the trees in the fall or the bursting forth of tiny revolutions with each grass blade? Well, Whitman looked that way and recommended that everybody else look at the actual world around them rather than the abstract world they read about in the newspapers or saw as a pseudo-image/event, screened dots on television: "You shall listen to all sides and filter them from yourself."

So, then what is he going to do now? What is he going to say next about where we all come from, where we are going?

> I have heard what the talkers were talking, the
>   talk of the beginning and the end,
> But I do not talk of the beginning or the end.
>
> There was never any more inception than there
>   is now,
> Nor any more youth or age than there is now,
> And will never be any more perfection than
>   there is now,
> Nor any more heaven or hell than there is now.

That's a great statement, very similar to what some of the Eastern, Oriental meditators, transcendentalists, or grounded Buddhists might say. Their notion is the unborn, that is to say, everything is here already, it wasn't born a billion years ago and slowly developed, it isn't going to be dead a billion years from now and slowly undevelop, it's just here, like a flower in the air. There's never going to be any more hell than there is now and never be any more understanding of heaven than there is right now in our own minds, with our own perception. So that means you can't postpone your acceptation and realization, you can't scream at your own eyes now, you've got to look out through your own eyes as Whitman said, hear with your own ears, smell with your own nose, touch with your own touch, fingers, taste with your own tongue, and be satisfied. " . . . I see, dance, laugh, sing . . . " [reads rest of Part 3].

So he's not interested in that kind of invidious comparison and competition. In the midst of **"Song of Myself"** he does come to a statement of what is the very nature of the mind, what is the nature of the human mind, his mind as he observed it in himself and when the mind is most open, most expanded, most realized, what relation is there between human beings and between man and nature. So I'll just read these little epiphanous moments showing, for one thing, his meditative view, this is the fourth part of **"Song of Myself,"** and then an epiphany or ecstatic experience that he had. First of all, does he doubt himself? So, he says: "Trippers and askers surround me . . . " [reads Part 4]. Now that's a real classical viewpoint, the last poet to really announce that was John Keats, who said he had a little idea about what made Shakespeare great. He said that was "negative capability," quote negative capability unquote. Which is to say, the possibility of seeing contending parties, seeing the Communists and Capitalists scream at each other, or the Buddhists and non-Buddhists, or the Muslims and Christians, or the Jews and the Arabs, or the self and the not-self, or your mommy and daddy, or yourself and your wife, or your baby and yourself. You can see them all screaming at each other, and you can see as a kind of comedic drama that you don't get tangled and lost in it, you don't enter into the daydream fantasy of being right and being one side or the other so completely that you go out and chop somebody's head off. Instead you just sort of watch yourself, you watch them in and out of the game at the same time, both in and out of the game, watching and wondering at it. That is to say, the ability to have contrary ideas in your head at the same time without it freaking out, without "an irritable reaching out after fact" or conclusions. Without an irritable reaching out. Naturally, you reach out and want to know more, but you don't get mad, crazed, say "I gotta know the answer, there is one answer and I, me, I have to have the one answer, me, my answer, me, answer answer." Well, you don't have to go through all that. Because maybe you don't know the answer, maybe there is no answer, maybe the question has no answer, maybe there is not even a question, though there may be perturbation and conflict. So, you could apply that, say, to the present Cold War situation where everyone wants to destroy the world in order to win victory over the Wrong (either side). Here, "apart from the pulling and hauling stands what I am," which is actually what we are, in the sense of nobody really believes all the stuff they talk, you know, you say it to hear what it sounds like most of the time. Even Whitman, I think, is just saying to hear what it sounds like because it's sort of the sound you might make when you're talking more frankly

to yourself, or to friends. "Apart from the pulling and hauling stands what I am / Stands amused, complacent, compassionating," compassionating because both sides are right, and they don't even know it, both sides are wrong and they don't even know it. "Idle," he's not going to act on it, he's going to observe it, maybe go fry an egg. "Unitary," unitary is one thing, it is not divided up into this half of me is right and this half of me is wrong. "Looks down," well, you have to be looking down. "Is erect," straightens up, "bends an arm on an impalpable certain rest," maybe puts his arm down on the library desk, and thinks a little bit more, or spaces out. "Looking with sidecurved head curious what will come next," come next out of his own mind he means, or who will come into the door of the library. What plane, or when Mt. St. Helens will explode. Both in and out of the game, watching and wondering at it which is the best we can do actually. The best thing we can do is wonder at everything, it's so amazing. So, then what happens? If you take that attitude and open yourself up and allow yourself to admit everything, to hear everything, not to exclude, just be like the moon in the old Japanese haiku: "The autumn moon / shines kindly / on the flower-thief," or like Whitman's sun which shines on the common prostitute in his poem **"To A Common Prostitute"**—"Not till the sun excludes you do I exclude you." His mind is there, he's aware of her, she's aware of him and everybody's sitting around and internally scratching their head. So there is an epiphany out of this, or a rise, or a kind of exquisite awareness that intensifies.

Part 5 of **"Song of Myself"**: "I believe in you my soul . . . " [reads Part 5]. So just out of that one experience of a touch with another person, of complete acceptance, his awareness spread throughout the space around him and he realized that that friendly touch, that friendly awareness was what bound the entire universe together and held everything suspended in gravity.

So given that, where could he go from here? Well, a long survey of America, which he did in **"Song of Myself,"** in which he extended his own awareness to cover the entire basic spiritual awareness of America, trying to make an ideal America which would be an America of comradely awareness, acknowledgment of tenderness, acknowledgment of gentleness, acknowledgement of comradeship, acknowledgment of what he called adhesiveness. Because what he said was that if this country did not have some glue to keep people together, to bind them together, adhesiveness, some emotional bond, there was no possibility of democracy working, and we'd just be a lot of separate people fighting for advantage, military advantage, commercial advantage, iron advantage, coal advantage, silver advantage, gold, hunting up some kind of monopoly on molybdenum. On the other hand, there was a total democracy of feeling around, so in Part 11 of **"Song of Myself"**: "Twenty-eight young men bathe by the shore . . . " [reads Part 11].

Well, so he pointed out the longing for closeness; erotic tenderness is of course implicit here, his own as well as in empathy, the spinster lady behind her curtains looking at the naked bathers. He pointed to that as basic to our bodies, basic to our minds, basic to our community, basic to our sociability, basic to our society, therefore basic to our politics. If that quality of compassion, erotic longing, tenderness, gentleness, was squelched, repressed, pushed back, denied, insulted, mocked, seen cynically, then the entire operation of democracy would be squelched, debased, mocked, seen cynically, advantaged, poorly made into a paranoid, mechano-megalopolis congregation of freaks afeard of each other. Because that may have been the very nature of the industrial civilization, that by the very roboting of work and homogenization of talk and imagery, unlike Whitman, people not speaking for themselves but talking falsely, as if they represented anything but themselves, like as if a President could represent anybody but his own mind, then there was going to be trouble. So, at one point he says human society is kind of messed up; so, Part 32 of **"Song of Myself,"**

> I think I could turn, and live with animals, they
>   are so placid and self-contain'd,
> I stand and look at them long and long.
>
> They do not sweat and whine about their condition,
> They do not lie awake in the dark and weep for
>   their sins,
> They do not make me sick discussing their duty
>   to God,
> Not one is dissatisfied, not one is demented with
>   the mania of owning things,
> Not one kneels to another, nor to his kind that
>   lived thousands of years ago,
> Not one is respectable or unhappy over the
>   whole earth.

Not one animal is respectable, in all of creation. All these human beings want to be respectable, but he's pointing out that not one elephant in Africa would ever dream of considering himself respectable. So, they ". . . show their relations to me and I accept them, / They bring me tokens of myself, they evince them plainly in their possession."

Then, what does he do in the city? He's lonesome, so there's a little one-line description of himself in the city, "Looking in at the shop-windows of Broadway the whole forenoon, flatting the flesh of my nose on the thick plateglass." But then, also he can get out in his mind: "I go hunting polar furs and the seal, leaping chasms with a pike-pointed staff, clinging to topples of brittle and blue." He empathizes with everybody: "I am an old artillerist, I tell of my fort's bombardment, / I am there again." And in Part 34: "Now I tell what I knew in Texas in my early youth," and then he goes on with a long anecdote. Or, Part 35: "Would you hear of an old-time sea-fight," and he went on and on to that, telling about old-time sea-fights, and "Toward twelve there in the beams of the moon they surrender to us,"—the moony imagination. Then, maybe he's a sea fighter, or he's an Arctic explorer, or maybe he's a jerk. Part 37: "You laggards there on guard! look to your arms! / In at the conquer'd doors they crowd! I am possess'd!" He wasn't afraid of that, see: "Askers embody themselves in me and I am embodied in them, / I project my hat, sit shame-faced, and beg." That's like Bob Dylan in his film *Renaldo and Clara,* walking down the street and all of a sudden the camera catches him and stares him in the eye and he stares the camera in the eye and all of

a sudden he shivers and puts out his right hand held by his left palm out, "Some change? Spare change of love? Spare change?" And so you have, "Enough! enough! enough! / Somehow I have been stunn'd. Stand back! . . . That I could look with a separate look on my own crucifixion and bloody crowning." Ah, so he has suffered a bit here, he does empathize with all the beggars, the monstrous convicts with sweat twitching on their lips, but his point here is that everybody so suffers, everybody is everybody else, in the sense of having experienced in imagination or in real life all of the non-respectable emotions of the elephants and the ants. So he says, "It is time to explain myself—let us stand up . . . " [reads Part 44], and "I am an acme . . . Now on this spot I stand with my robust soul." So that's great, so he's here, he recognizes he's here:

> My rendezvous is appointed, it is certain,
> The Lord will be there and wait till I come on
>   perfect terms,
> The great Camerado, the lover true for whom I
>   pine will be there.

So he says:

> I have no chair, no church, no philosophy,
> I lead no man to a dinner-table, library, exchange,
> But each man and each woman of you I lead
>   upon a knoll,
> My left hand hooking you round the waist,
> My right hand pointing to landscapes of continents and the public road.
>
> Not I, not any one else can travel the road for
>   you,
> You must travel it for yourself.
>
> It is not far, it is within reach,
> Perhaps you have been on it since you were born
>   and did not know,
> Perhaps it is everywhere on water and on land.
>
> Shoulder your duds dear son, and I will mine,
>   and let us hasten forth,
> Wonderful cities and free nations we shall fetch
>   as we go.
>
> If you tire, give me both burdens, and rest the
>   chuff of your hand on my hip,
> And in due time you shall repay the same service
>   to me,
> For after we start we never lie by again.

On the road, Walt Whitman, 1883 probably, prophesying what would happen to America 100 years later.

So he comes to his conclusions at the end of the poem. He wants to tell finally what he can get out of it all. Part 50 of **"Song of Myself,"** approaching the end of the poem: "There is that in me—I do not know what it is—but I know it is in me . . . It is not chaos or death—it is form, union, plan—it is eternal life—it is Happiness." And Part 51: "The past and present wilt— . . . " [reads Part 51]. Finally, Part 52, the last section, he'll make his last prophecy, dissolve himself into you the listener, the reader, and his poem will become a part of your consciousness: "The spotted hawk swoops by . . . [reads Part 52] . . . I stop somewhere waiting for you." That's a very tearful, deep promise, "I stop somewhere waiting for you," so he's going to wait a long, long, long time, and have to go through a great deal of his own loves and fears before he actually finds a companion. What kind of companion does he want, what does he look for? "The expression of the face balks account . . . " and this is in the poem called **"I Sing the Body Electric,"** in which he begins to describe his own body and other peoples' bodies in an intimate way, numbering all the parts, numbering all the emotions, and naming them and actually attempting to account, and give an accounting and itemization of all men. There is a little four or five lines of, just about, well, what does he look for?

> The expression of the face balks account,
> But the expression of a well-made man appears
> not only in his face,
> It is in his limbs and joints also, it is curiously
> in the joints of his hips and wrists,
> It is in his walk, the carriage of his neck, the flex
> of his waist and knees, dress does not hide
> him,
> The strong sweet quality he has strikes through
> the cotton and broadcloth,
> To see him pass conveys as much as the best
> poem, perhaps more,
> You linger to see his back, and the back of his
> neck and shoulder-side.

Well, everybody's done that, man or woman to each other, who is interesting, who's got something going there. "Spontaneous me," he says, and so he keeps walking around, "has native moments."

Finally he has a little short poem, **"Native Moments,"** actually, defining what they are, when some authentic flash comes to him: "Native moments—when you come upon me— . . . " [reads **"Native Moments"**]. Well he is really declaring himself, declaring his own feelings, he's not scared of them, like born for the first time in the world, recognizing his own nature, recognizing the world. The last of the poems in the first part of *Leaves of Grass* is **"As Adam Early in the Morning"**:

> As Adam early in the morning,
> Walking forth from the bower refresh'd with
> sleep,
> Behold me where I pass, hear my voice, approach,
> Touch me, touch the palm of your hand to my
> body as I pass,
> Be not afraid of my body.

Well, there is some false note there I guess, he really wants someone to love him, and he's not quite able to say it right. Still he does want to make democracy something that hangs together using the force of Eros, so, **"For You O Democracy,"** in the "Calamus" section of *Leaves of Grass:* "Come, I will make the continent indissoluble . . . [reads] . . . With the life-long love of comrades," Beatles, Rolling Stones, beatniks, the life-long love of comrades, "I will plant companionship as thick as trees . . . [reads the rest of **"For You O Democracy"**] . . . For you, for you, I am trilling these songs." Well, that's his statement of politics, actually, and, however, you never can tell, maybe he's just a big fairy egotist.

So he's got a little poem **"Are You the New Person Drawn toward Me?"** in the "Calamus" section of *Leaves of Grass,* "Calamus," that is a section of *Leaves of Grass;* calamus has a forked root, oddly enough, it is a marsh plant, calamus grows, lives in marshes in the northeast, around Manhattan, in the old days on Long Island up near Cherry Valley where I live in the bogs. It has a somewhat manlike forked root, and its root is said to contain elements of LSD according to the *Encyclopedia of Hallucinogens* by Humphrey Osmond and Abraham Hoffer, the standard encyclopedia scholarly work in the subject. Odd title, "Calamus."

The "Calamus" section of *Leaves of Grass* was that describing erotic pleasure and parts of the body, which when Whitman sent them to Ralph Waldo Emerson shocked the elder American prophet Emerson a bit, and he suggested that Whitman leave it out when he published the book because it was perhaps that people were not ready for it, America was not ready for it. Whitman, however, persisted and felt that that was an integral part of his message that if he was going to talk about honesty and frankness and openness and comradeship he did have to say the unsayable, did have to talk about people's bodies, did have to describe them with beauty and Greek levity and healthiness and heroism. So he did have to make heroes out of our private parts. So "Calamus" does include that but it's actually, nowadays reading, very tame. However, because he was so intent on his purpose, he was a little worried. So: "Are you the new person drawn toward me? . . . " [reads **"Are You the New Person Drawn toward Me?"**]. I guess he's talking to himself. However, he's willing to trust his senses. So he says, "Behold this swarthy face . . . " [reads **"Behold This Swarthy Face"**]. Okay, so he's proposing that the dear love of comrades and the unabashed affection between citizens be acknowledged as it stands rather than mocked. And then, of course, not to get people upset, so: "I hear it was charged against me . . . " [reads **"I Hear It Was Charged against Me"**]. And that includes like the prairie grass everyone equal, so that there are " . . . those that look carelessly in the faces of Presidents and governors, as to say *Who are you?*," that's a little line from a poem called **"The Prairie-Grass Dividing."** So what's the big thrill like our big thrill nowadays? Well, here's my big thrill, here's Whitman's big thrill:

> A glimpse through an interstice caught,
> Of a crowd of workmen and drivers in a bar-
> room around the stove late of a winter night,
> and I unremark'd seated in a corner,
> Of a youth who loves me and whom I love, si-
> lently approaching and seating himself near,
> that he may hold me by the hand,
> A long while amid the noises coming and going,
> of drinking and oath and smutty jest,
> There we two, content, happy in being together,
> speaking little, perhaps not a word.

So that's a recognizable emotion between friends.

But there may be things that he doesn't want to say even, so he says: "Earth, my likeness . . . " [reads from **"Earth, My Likeness"**]. So there's more to come and it'll come out of Whitman as he goes forward in his life, renouncing all formulas " . . . O bat-eyed and materialistic priests," (that's from **"Song of the Open Road"**).

So his next long poem is called **"Salut au Monde!,"** saying, 'Come on, let's go out, let's explore life, let's find out what's going on here. Let's look at the tents of the Kalmucks and the Baskirs, let's go out and see the African and Asiatic towns, go to the Ganges, let's go to the groves of Mona where the Druids walked and see the bodies of the gods and wait at Liverpool and Glasgow and Dublin and Marseilles, wait at Valparaiso, Panama, sail on the waters of Hindustan, the China Sea, all the way around the world, on the road.' So it began: "O take my hand Walt Whitman! / Such gliding wonders! . . . "—he's going to guide everybody around the world, spiritual trip around the work, like fuck in bed, but it will be in the spirit.

Then there's this very famous poem where he realizes, yeah, sure, but all that's transitory, it's going, there's not much, you know, like 20 years, 50 years, 70 years, then zap it's gone. So there is this great poem, in the middle of Manhattan looking over at Brooklyn on the Brooklyn ferry, called **"Crossing Brooklyn Ferry,"** realizing, okay, he's had these feelings, everybody has these kinds of feelings, everybody rarely has the chance to experience them, much less say them aloud, much less propose them as politics, much less offer to save the nation with feeling and at the same time it's in the appearances of life even though it was very rare for people to understand that, except that at the deepest moment of their life they do understand that. And, looking at the vast apparition of Manhattan and the masts of ships around it and the sunset and the seagulls, what more does he have to ask than the immensity of universe around him and the river on which he's riding and the feelings which he's aware of and the ability he has to call these feelings out to other people from his time to the future. He says:

> We understand then do we not?
> What I promis'd without mentioning it, have
>   you not accepted?
> What the study could not teach—what the
>   preaching could not accomplish is accom-
>   plish'd, is it not?

[Reads from first half of Part 9.] That's very subtle, you see from the sunshine halo, aureole, aura around the hair in the sunshine reflected in the water. He's even noticing, his noticing is so exquisite and ethereal and fine that he's got massive masts of the aureole of the light of the sun reflected shining in water and reflected in people's hair around him. [Reads second half of Part 9.]

So, he needs from that, after **"Crossing Brooklyn Ferry,"** he needs someone to answer him, so his next long poem is **"Song of the Answerer,"** in which he imagines the answerer, he is the answerer, what can be answered he answers and what cannot be answered he shows how it cannot be answered and that goes on and on and on and praises the words of true poems of the true poets which do not merely please: "The true poets are not followers of beauty, but the august masters of beauty. . . ."

Well, he'll go on and then there's a great tragedy coming up ahead. He's passed through California and he's written about lonesome Kansas and he's written about birds of passage and a song of the rolling earth and he's written about the ocean and then back to his birthplace in Long Island looking at the city, a vision of birth continuous and death continuous. Again, sort of an ecstatic acknowledgment of the continuity of feeling from generation to generation as the continuity of birth that no matter what the appearances, there always is a rebirth of delight, of feeling of acknowledgment, of the spaciousness of glittery sunlight on the ocean. And that's the famous poem **"Out of the Cradle Endlessly Rocking"** [reads first stanza]. Of course, the form there is a classical form: "Of Man's First Disobedience, and the Fruit / Of that Forbidden Tree, whose mortal taste / Brought Death into the World, and all our woe . . . Sing Heav'nly Muse," that's John Milton's opening of *Paradise Lost*. Or the opening of Homer's *Iliad*: "Sing O Goddess of the wrath of Achilles, Peleus' son, the ruinous wrath that brought down countless woes upon the heads of the Achaeans and sent many brave souls hurring down to Hades and many a hero left for prey to dogs and vultures . . . " or something like that. Again, in that same long, long, long breath of realization that ends with an accomplished trumpet call, almost to sing the personal, I mean, " . . . a reminiscence sing," and then it's a reminiscence of a whisper of death, when he was young at the oceanside. "Sea-Drift," **"Tears," "On the Beach at Night Alone," "The World Below the Brine," "Song for All Seas, All Ships,"** those are some of the titles of the poems of that era—that was up until about 1854. Then, a few prophecies of the presidents, and some patriotic songs, and more awareness of the problems of America as it was going into the Civil War. Then, in the Civil War he himself following his instincts, followed the soldiers, went to Washington, worked in hospitals, took care of dying men, was out on the battlefields as a nurse and then in the hospitals in Washington, D.C. as a nurse, saw a link in walking around Washington likely enough at 4 A.M.; as Whitman was walking around on his own mission of mercy or mercies of mission, he wrote a lot of poems, like **"A Sight in Camp in the Daybreak Gray and Dim"**—this is a little, say, a snapshot, the same theme of human divinity in the midst of the degradation of horror and war: [reads from **"A Sight in Camp in the Daybreak Gray and Dim"**].

So, he worked as a wound-dresser, taking care of the wounds of the injured and the dying in the Civil War. Having the same delicate, emotional relationships with the people he met as:

> O tan-faced prairie-boy,
> Before you came to camp came many a welcome
>   gift,
> Praises and presents came and nourishing food,
>   till at last among the recruits,
> You came, taciturn, with nothing to give—we
>   but look'd on each other,
> When lo! more than all the gifts of the world you
>   gave me.

Funny, his idea of America, "tan-faced prairie-boy," full of feeling and awareness, not at all a stereotyped television Barbie doll.

Then, in the midst of the tragedies of the war and the visions of death he had, the actual dying, memories of President Lincoln who was shot, and so his great old elegy for Lincoln, which most every kid in America knew back in the 20s and 30s, with its very beautiful description of the passing of Lincoln's coffin on railroad through lanes and streets, through the cities and through the states and with processions, seas of silence, seas of faces and unbared heads, the coffin of Lincoln mourned and in the middle of this poem a recognition of death in a way that had not been proposed in America before. Just as he had accepted the feelings of life, there was the appearance and feelings of death, the awareness of death that he had to tally finally. So there's this great italicized song in Part 14 of **"When Lilacs Last in the Dooryard Bloom'd,"** from "Memories of President Lincoln."

Actually, the whole of **"When Lilacs Last in the Dooryard Bloom'd"** is so beautiful that it would be worth reading, but it's so long that I can't do it and also it's so beautiful that I'm afraid I'll cry if I read it. **"When Lilacs Last in the Dooryard Bloom'd,"**—which is a very interesting title because I visited Whitman's house in Camden, New Jersey, and in the back yard in the old brick house on Mickle Street where he lived the last years of his life, though not likely where he wrote this poem, there were lilacs blooming in the back yard, blooming by the outhouse which was right outside the back door in the garden. "When lilacs last in the dooryard bloom'd . . . " [reads Parts 1, 2, 3, 5, 6 & **"Hymn to Death"** in Part 14].

Then Whitman grew older, traveled, extended his imagination to blue Ontario shore, began to see the declining of his own physical body in a series of poems called "Autumn Rivulets." He wrote about the compost, as Peter Orlovsky did a hundred years later. So Whitman wrote:

> Behold this compost! behold it well!
> Perhaps every mite has once form'd part of a
>   sick person—yet behold!
> The grass of spring covers the prairies,
> The bean bursts noiselessly through the mould
>   in the garden,
> The delicate spear of the onion pierces
>   upward, . . .

So, after the carol to death there is a realization of the recycling in the compost, the recycling of soul, the recycling of body, the inevitability of passage, transitoriness, of things entering the earth and emerging from the earth, and he wrote poems about the city dead-house, too. So these were all autumn rivulets. He wrote his poem to the singer in prison, and **"Outlines for a Tomb."**

Incidentally, he took his own tomb at that point, made up a little drawing of a tomb for himself which he took from the opening page of William Blake's last great prophetic book *Jerusalem,* of a man entering a stone, open door, stone pillars on each side, stone floor, stone arch, a triangular arch on top with a great stone door opened, a man carrying a great globe of light. A consciousness entering into this dark, he can't see what's in it, he's going in like passing through with a big black cat. Whitman designed this tomb for himself, which is now standing in Camden, New Jersey, in exactly the same image as the Blake. He

wrote little poems to his own tomb then and to the negative and began to consider the negative, how do you recompost the negative?

So, the line I was quoting from **"To a Common Prostitute,"** that line occurs here: "Be composed—be at ease with me—I am Walt Whitman, liberal and lusty as Nature, / Not till the sun excludes you do I exclude you . . . " [reads all of **"To a Common Prostitute"**]. That's a good way to be kind to your neighbor, and to acknowledge the varying vocations.

He took a trip out to Kansas and wrote funny little poems about the encroaching civilization that was beginning to cover the prairies. There is a little tiny poem that I've quoted, **"The Prairie States"**:

> A newer garden of creation, no primal solitude,
> Dense, joyous, modern, populous millions, cities
>   and farms,
> With iron interlaced, composite, tied, many in
>   one,
> By all the world contributed—freedom's and
>   law's and thrift's society,
> The crown and teeming paradise, so far, of
>   time's accumulations,
> To justify the past.

So, that was ambitious and hopeful thought, he might have had some change of mind if he saw Kansas during the Vietnam War, with army bases and airplane bases and "iron interlaced" above the plains there, horrific iron.

He wrote a great poem now beginning to go into a recognition of the Orient and recognition of the ancient wisdoms of death that were understood there, that is, the acceptance of death as well as the acceptance of life, seeing an identity between his own extended empathy and sympathy and compassion, and the ancient empathies and sympathies and compassions of the meditators of the Himalayas.

There's a very interesting section in **"Passage to India,"** interesting to those of us who already made that passage ourselves, either mentally or physically. Remember, in the nineteenth century lots and lots of poets and philosophers in America were interested in transcendentalism and oriental wisdom and Brahma and the Hindus and the romantic, glamorous wisdom of the East, the Brook Farm experiment, many people and Bronson Alcott were interested in Western gnosticism, and Bronson Alcott went to England to buy up the neo-Platonic and hermetic translations of Thomas Taylor, the Platonist, translations which were from Greek Orphic mysteries and Dionysian mysteries, that were also read by the great British transcendental mystic poets like Coleridge, Shelley, William Blake, those same books were brought to Brook Farm and then translations by Thomas Taylor of ancient hermetic Greek texts were circulated by Bronson Alcott to Emerson and to Thoreau and Hawthorne. So there was this movement of transcendentalism and a recognition of the exotic East, there was the opening of Japan around that time. There was Lafcadio Hearn, maybe thirty years later, going to Japan and making great collections of Japanese art to bring to Boston to impress the New Englanders in the second wave of Oriental understanding thirty years later, but even in Europe at that time, Japanese prints by Hiroshige were circulating and were eyed by Gauguin and van Gogh, who began imitating their flat surfaces and their bright colors. So, a whole new calligraphy of the mind was beginning to be discovered by the West—in the same time that the West was peddling opium in China, oddly enough, that was the trade exchange, opium for meditation.

However, Whitman reflected that in **"Passage to India"**: "Lo soul, the retrospect brought forward . . . " [reads next 15 lines of Part 6]. So he acknowledged that transcendent, and like D. H. Lawrence a hundred years later, wrote about the great ship of death that goes forward to explore: "O we can wait no longer, / We too take ship O soul, . . . " Talking about going through the soul as well as going through the world.

However he sees that most of the world is asleep. Alas, so there's this long poem **"The Sleepers."** This is like middle age now, it's really getting deeper on him now and death is coming a bit into his mind as he gets into his 50s and 60s. Also the fact that most of the living on the world are the living dead or the sleepers:

> I wander all night in my vision,
> Stepping with light feet, swiftly and noiselessly
>   stepping and stopping,
> Bending with open eyes over the shut eyes of
>   sleepers,
> Wandering and confused, lost to myself, ill-
>   assorted, contradictory,
> Pausing, gazing, bending, and stopping.
> How solemn they look there, stretch'd and still,
> How quiet they breathe, the little children in
>   their cradles. . . .

Well, they all sleep, so he moves on, and says at the end of all these sleepers, "I too pass from the night . . . " [reads conclusion of **"The Sleepers"**]. So he's now beginning to think of the future, what's going to happen to him.

Then the next set of poems in *Leaves of Grass* is called "Whispers of Heavenly Death," very interesting, beginning to get more and more close to the grand subject of all poetry. **"Quicksand Years"** is a very charming little statement on that. Now he's beginning to doubt himself a little bit:

> Quicksand years that whirl me I know not
>   whither,
> Your schemes, politics, fail, lines give way, sub-
>   stances mock and elude me,
> Only the theme I sing, the great and strong-
>   possess'd soul, eludes not,
> One's-self must never give way—that is the final
>   substance—that out of all is sure,
> Out of politics, triumphs, battles, life, what at
>   last finally remains?
> When shows break up what but One's-Self is
>   sure?

Well, how does he know that? That one's self is even sure, well, he's going to get older, we'll see what happens next.

That's an interesting thing, because now he realized that it is the notion of an unconquerable self or soul that all along has sustained him, but that, too, will dissolve and as a great poet he's going to let it dissolve. He has a few

thoughts about the dissolution, also, incidentally, just as of his soul, of the soul of the nation, the dissolution of democracy, and in those days, of public opinion. Well, here's what he's got to say, "Thoughts," he's not going to give it a title, you know. It's all about Watergate basically: "Of public opinion . . . " [reads from **"Thoughts"**]. So that prophesied way in advance, even the President of the United States someday must stand naked, by Bob Dylan.

"So long!" finally he says to all these thoughts. It's toward the end of *Leaves of Grass,* in fact, I think it's the last great poem in *Leaves of Grass,* salutation and farewell and summary, conclusion, triumph, disillusion, giving up, taking it all on, giving it all over to you who are listening. **"So Long!"**: "To conclude, I announce what comes after me . . . " [reads **"So Long!"**].

But he wasn't dead yet, actually, he was only 70. So now he's got to go through the actual dying, so how does he do that? How does he take that? What has he got to say about that? Well, there are some really interesting "Sands at Seventy" thoughts, giving out, he was quite ill and old in his 70s, in the sense of old in the body, gallstones, paralysis, uremia probably, emphysema, great many of his heart difficulties. I think his autopsy, according to a poem by Jonathan Williams I once read, showed him to have been universal in his illnesses near death as he was in his healths in life. So, little poems, then, just whatever he could write now, his great major work over, and yet the little trickle drops of wisdom of a man of 70 are exquisite and curious.

> As I sit writing here, sick and grown old,
> Not my least burden is that dulness of the years,
>   querilities,
> Ungracious glooms, aches, lethargy, constipa-
>   tion, whimpering *ennui,*
> May filter in my daily songs.

And he's got a little poem to his canary bird, he's stuck in his little bedroom up in Camden, on Mickle Street, in a little house with low ceilings, visited by many people including Edward Carpenter, the tutor to Queen Victoria's children who abandoned his official role and went out as one of the first six revolutionists, humanists, visited Walt Whitman and Whitman told him to go to India. He studied, probably with Ramakrishna or one of the other sages. Edward Carpenter left behind a testament of his sleeping with Whitman, in the form of a conversation with Gavin Arthur, one of the gentlemen of the old school, the grandson of President Chester A. Arthur, who was living in San Francisco, and told me one day the story of his sleeping with Edward Carpenter, and Carpenter's account of his sleeping with Whitman, so I asked Gavin before he died to write me an account of that which he did, which was published in *Gay Sunshine Interviews* [Vol. I, 1978, p. 126]. And since the later Whitmanic hero Neal Cassady slept with Edward Carpenter, there is a straight transmission from Whitman on down through the present day.

So, he's sitting there talking to his canary bird, "Did we count great, O soul, to penetrate the themes of mighty books . . . ?" Then **"Queries to My Seventieth Year"**: "Approaching, nearing, curious, / Thou dim, uncertain spectre—bringest thou life or death?" Well, everything wasn't bad, he had his first dandelion, springtime:

> Simple and fresh and fair from winter's close
>   emerging,
> As if no artifice of fashion, business, politics, had
>   ever been,
> Forth from its sunny nook of shelter'd grass—
>   innocent, golden, calm as the dawn,
> The spring's first dandelion shows its trustful
>   face.

So he had that same witty awareness, even lying in his sickbed.

Then people began exploring the North Pole, and he was amazed at that: **"Of That Blithe Throat of Thine . . . "** [reads this poem]. Well, that's what wisdom brings, he's no longer dependent on that youthful self, in fact the self is dissolving as it will in these last poems. **"To Get the Final Lilt of Songs,"** he says in "Sands at Seventy": "To get the final lilt of songs, / To penetrate the inmost lore of poets—to know the mighty ones / . . . Old age, and what it brings from all its past experience." So, you need that, otherwise you ain't gonna learn nuttin' if you don't grow old and die, you just know what you have in your mind when you think you've got the world by the crotch.

So, an odd lament for the aborigines, an Iroquois term **"Yonnondio,"** the sense of the word is *lament for the aborigines,* Whitman has a little note here, " . . . an Iroquois term; and has been used for a personal name." It's an odd little political poem at the end, warning us of Black Mesa, of the Four Corners, of the civilization's destruction of the land and the original natives there. "A song, a poem of itself . . . " [reads from **"Yonnondio"**]. So he's also saying as he dies, so may all the machinery of the civilization, so there's nothing for anybody to get too high and mighty about.

But he's got to give thanks in old age. For what? [Reads **"Thanks in Old Age."**] But there is also **"Stronger Lessons"**—is everything thanks for the memories and thanks for the good times, and thanks for the gifts and thanks for the loves? **"Stronger Lessons"**:

> Have you learn'd lessons only of those who ad-
>   mired you, and were tender with you, and
>   stood aside for you?
> Have you not learn'd great lessons from those
>   who reject you, and brace themselves against
>   you? or who treat you with
> contempt, or dispute the passage with you?

That's a good piece of advice of how to alchemize fear to bliss, how to alchemize contrariety to harmony, how to ride with the punches, so to speak. But what is it all about? So he's got finally, twilight, not quite sure about that old self. **"Twilight"**:

> The soft voluptuous opiate shades,
> The sun just gone, the eager light dispell'd—(I
>   too will soon be gone, dispell'd,)
> A haze—nirwana—rest and night—oblivion.

But there are still a few thoughts left in his mind before he goes off into that rest and night. [Reads from **"You Lingering Sparse Leaves of Me."**] Well, what has he done,

he wonders, with his life? So he says farewell to all of his earlier poems. [Reads from **"Now Precedent Songs, Farewell."**] Then, having summed up his life, well, just waiting around, **"An Evening Lull"**:

> After a week of physical anguish,
> Unrest and pain, and feverish heat,
> Toward the ending day a calm and lull comes
>   on,
> Three hours of peace and soothing rest of brain.

Then, **"After the Supper and Talk"** is the last of the poems of "Sands at Seventy," and perhaps his last. [Reads from **"After the Supper and Talk."**] So, that was goodbye my fancy, but that wasn't his last word, no, because he lived on. So he's got, what, **"Good-Bye My Fancy,"** "Second Annex," "Preface Note to the Second Annex," where he says:

> Reader, you must allow a little fun here—for
> one reason there are too many of the following
> poemets about death, &c., and for another the
> passing hours (July 5, 1890) are so sunny-fine.
> And old as I am I feel to-day almost a part of
> some frolicsome wave, or for sporting yet like a
> kid or kitten— . . .

Still there are a couple of little last poems. [Reads **"My 71st Year."**] Then at last he'll have another comment on his work: **"Long, Long Hence"**:

> After a long, long course, hundreds of years, de-
>   nials,
> Accumulations, rous'd love and joy and
>   thought,
> Hopes, wishes, aspirations, ponderings, victo-
>   ries, myriads of readers,
> Coating, compassing, covering—after ages' and
>   ages' encrustations,
> Then only may these songs reach fruition.

Well, that's actually what happened to him in the sense that his work was little famous, not much read and a bit put down in the years after his death, to the point of . . . or to the situation that when I went to Columbia College in 1945, between '44 and '49, by scholars and academic poets and by professors and their ilk and by the Cold War soldiers and warriors of those days, Whitman was considered some lonesome, foolish crank who'd lived in poverty and likely Bohemian dis-splendor, having cantankerous affairs with jerks of all nations, in his mind. Not to be considered a major personage like the witty dimwits of midtown Manhattan who worked for *Time, Life,* CIA, *Newsweek,* and their own egos.

Whitman, still clinging on, recognized what it was that was his victory, the commonplace, ordinary mind, as it is known around the world. [Reads **"The Commonplace."**] So he knew what the basis was where everybody could stand, which was where we all actually are, and was recognizable in our own bodies in our own thoughts in our own work in our own nation, in our own local particulars. A wisdom that was inherited by Ezra Pound and William Carlos Williams and whole generations of poets after Walt Whitman who had discovered that common ground of self and dissolution of self, common ground of his own mind and the common ground of city pavement he walked on with his fellow citizens and the common ground of their emotions between them.

At the end, there is a rounded catalogue complete, he says, [reads **"The Rounded Catalogue Divine Complete."**] Okay, so he says, finally, in the **"Purport"** to *Leaves of Grass,* his entire book, "Not to exclude or demarcate, or pick out evils from their formidable masses (even to expose them,) / But add, fuse, complete, extend—and celebrate the immortal and the good. . . . " So what was there unexpressed, actually, in his life? He has a little poem, almost his last here, **"The Unexpress'd"**: "How dare one say it? . . . Still something not yet told in poesy's voice or print—something lacking, / (Who knows? the best yet unexpress'd and lacking.)"

So, if there is yet unexpressed form, there'll be unseen buds for the future. His next-to-the-last poem: **"Unseen Buds"**: "Unseen buds, infinite . . . " of course he's garrulous to the very last, as he's said, "Unseen buds, infinite, hidden well . . . " [reads rest of **"Unseen Buds"**].

So he can with good conscience say farewell to his part, to his own fancy, to his own imagination, to his own life's work, to his own life, **"Good-Bye My Fancy!"**: "Goodbye my Fancy! / Farewell dear mate, dear love! . . . " [reads from the rest of **"Good-Bye My Fancy!"**]. And that's counted as almost his last poem, but then he didn't die, he had to go on, there's more. He had to keep going, poor fellow, thinking, putting it all out, *Old Age Echoes.* To be at all, he's amazed at it, and he's there, so what can you do? Remember all the dirty deeds he did? **"Of Many a Smutch'd Deed Reminiscent"**:

> Full of wickedness, I—of many a smutch'd deed
> reminiscent—of worse deeds capable,
> Yet I look composedly upon nature, drink day
> and night the joys of life, and await death with
> perfect equanimity,
> Because of my tender and boundless love for him
> I love and because of his boundless love for
> me.

Well, that's something fine to figure on, but his actual last poem after writing something about death's valley, and there are poems about death's valley and **"Nay Tell Me Not Today the Publish'd Shame,"** he's got an account of the horrible politics going on there as he was dying. Last: **"A Thought of Columbus,"** it's a forward-looking thing about exploration, navigation, going on into worlds unknown, unconquered, etc. **"A Thought of Columbus,"** not his most moving poem, not his greatest poem, but on the other hand his last poem as listed, and so maybe his last thoughts: "The mystery of mysteries . . . " [reads from **"A Thought of Columbus"**].

So, he ended on a heroical historic note, congratulating the explorer, himself really, or the Columbus in himself, and the Columbus in all of us for seeking outward in our spiritual journey looking for not even truth, because it wasn't truth he was proposing, except the truth of the fact that we are here with our lusts and delights, our givings up and grabbings, growings into trouble and marriage and birth and growings into coffins and earth and unbirth. Good character, all in all, the kind of character that if a nation were composed of such liberal, large-minded gen-

tlemen of the old school or young, large-bodied persons with free emotions and funny thoughts and tender looks, there might be the possibility of this nation and other nations surviving on the planet, but to survive, we'd have to take on some of that large magnanimity that Whitman yawped over the roof tops of the world. (pp. 231-54)

Allen Ginsberg, "Allen Ginsberg on Walt Whitman: Composed on the Tongue," in Walt Whitman: The Measure of His Song, *Jim Perlman, Ed Folsom, Dan Campion, eds., Holy Cow! Press, 1981, pp. 231-54.*

Howard Moss (essay date 1981)

[*Moss is an American poet, dramatist, and critic whose writings frequently appear in the* New Yorker. *In the following review of Justin Kaplan's* Walt Whitman: A Life *(cited in Further Reading), he emphasizes Whitman's stature in American history.*]

Certain writers belong not only to the history of literature but to History itself, and Whitman is one of them. He was crucially positioned: The American colonies declared their independence exactly forty-three years before his birth, in 1819, and the Revolution was still a vivid event in the minds of the adults around him. Psychically, his life stretched from the Revolution through the Civil War to the era of the robber barons. Truly an American poet of change, Whitman tends toward the heroic, the mythological. One of the great virtues of Justin Kaplan's *Walt Whitman: A Life* is its ability to rescue the man from the giant without diminishing his stature. Whitman was several men in one: Brahmin, bohemian, spokesman for a new democratic society, dandy, creator of an original kind of American poetry—a self-educated and self-intoxicated peasant of the ecstatic. Even the photographs in this volume—many of them unfamiliar—reinforce the kaleidoscopic sense of an ever-shifting personality. Mr. Kaplan, letting the various Whitmans speak, allowing for ambiguities, comes to no ringing conclusions.

A child of Long Island's "bare unfrequented shore," Whitman became, in time, a printer, newspaperman, teacher, and editor. He was the son of a dour housebuilder of English stock and a Quaker mother of Dutch descent, and his childhood was marred by instability. The record of insanity, intemperance, and failure in the Whitman family makes dismal reading. Living in the country provided no roots; the Whitmans moved from West Hills to Brooklyn and back. At the age of eleven, the poet stayed behind in Brooklyn, as a printer's apprentice, on his own. Mr. Kaplan estimates that by that time "Walt had lived in about a dozen different houses." In Brooklyn and in Manhattan, "the blab of the pave" mingled with the "Howler and scooper of storms, capricious and dainty sea" to become strands in an original verbal amalgam that makes **"Song of Myself "**—the key poem of *Leaves of Grass"*—remarkable.

The first, 1855 edition of that book bore no author's name; an engraved daguerreotype of a gypsylike workman—one of Whitman's guises—adorned the frontispiece. Its poems untitled, the book opened with what is now **"Song of My-**

self." In truth a song of everyone *but* myself—"Of every hue and caste am I, of every rank and religion"—it speaks for a consciousness beyond any individual ego: one made up of many. Whitman's ability to be androgynous and anonymous, his gifts of identification and sympathy are those of a great poet. They developed into an uneasy egotism later in life, as if the many characters of a literary work had filtered into the person who created them. Whitman's notion of himself *as* America, at first the mark of a passive generosity of spirit, grew overbearing, and narrowed into mere ambition. Empathy in the artist was reduced to role-playing in the man; the mythmaker and the self-server became interchangeable.

Whitman's homosexuality complicated his role as an American spokesman, just as his "mysticism" added an eerie note to his social views—those of a freethinker brought up on Quakerism, Carlyle, George Sand, and Margaret Fuller. Divorced from any traditional faith, his spiritual illuminations are closer to the sutras of the Oriental contemplative religions than to the visions of Christian saints. Denial and excoriation—the desert and the hair shirt—were alien to him. Divine irrationality—the kind we associate with Blake, Christopher Smart, and Rimbaud—is nearer the mark. These illuminations had to be accommodated to a nineteenth-century notion of progress. Queen Victoria and Whitman were born in the same year. Mr. Kaplan writes that "sex was a major disorder," and Whitman, the only writer of nineteenth-century America completely at odds with Puritanism, was—in his trust in an expansive commercialism, his "pursuit of health as the supreme good"—a true product of the Victorian age. No matter how original his thought, it wove in and out of commonly held beliefs. Phrenology, for instance, was accepted by the science of Whitman's time—Horace Mann, Henry Ward Beecher, Ralph Waldo Emerson, Edgar Allan Poe, and Daniel Webster all believed in it—and so was "animal magnetism." "I sing the body electric" was more a literal than a figurative reference. Life was seen as voltage and wattage. People were little wireless posts at the mercy of internal shocks and outgoing currents. Mr. Kaplan sums it up: "Whitman was a sort of storage battery or accumulator for charged particles of the contemporary."

In **"Song of Myself,"** we hear for the first time Whitman's unique blend of Biblical cadence (particularly the Psalms), primitive chant, and the ongoing catalogue: devices eventually to be at the service of a cosmic universe made up of American particularities—a secular Bible of sorts, full of contradictions and oddities. No other major poem I know sets itself such contrary tasks: to reveal the oneness of things, to praise the freedom of the individual, to celebrate the multitude in song. The over-all title **Leaves of Grass** is brilliantly fitting: the mass individuated in the unique leaf, the leaf one with the general green. The musical side of the poem sprang from Whitman's love of voices. Aroused as a youth by fiery preachers and professional orators, he savored, as his taste matured, the delights of the theatre. Italian opera became a passion. The works and the singers opened up—were exemplars of—a whole hidden emotional life. Opera introduced Whitman to the fusion of sound and action, the projection of emotion

through virtuosity. Thematic repetition in Whitman is conscious but has a characteristic sounding board. Many of the poems are best approached as long arias; even when Whitman is trying to transcribe the natural music of bird song, it has the calculated effect of a musical motif entering a score.

In 1848, Whitman, now editor of the Brooklyn *Eagle,* was fired after a political squabble with its owners. Invited to edit the New Orleans *Crescent,* he made with his brother Jeff a two-week journey south and west by train, stage-coach, and steamboat. Whitman's only reference points had been Long Island, Brooklyn, and Manhattan. Words had been his only form of travel. New Orleans, with its French and Spanish heritage, was sensuous and fruitful. "By the time he returned to Brooklyn," Mr. Kaplan writes, "he had travelled five thousand miles and seen democratic vistas of city and wilderness, river and lake, mountain and plain." The cosmic intentions of **Leaves of Grass** were accumulating a continental underpinning.

In his notebook, Whitman kept clarifying his thoughts, perfecting his design: "Make no quotations and no references to other writers. Take no illustration whatsoever from the ancients or classics. . . . Make no mention or allusion to them whatever, except as they relate . . . to American character or interests." Again, "[Make] the poems of emotions, as they pass or stay, the poems of freedom, and the exposé of personality—singing in high tones democracy and the New World of it through These States." The words after the dash are the kind of sentiments that put many readers off by their air of fake grandiosity. The grandeur was partly temperamental, partly defensive. Mr. Kaplan says, "There were hints that a less robust spirit had once prevailed, a spirit covert, hesitant, perturbed, lonely, and always unrequited. ('It is I you hold and who holds you,' he addressed his reader, becoming his own book, 'I spring from the pages into your arms.')" Whitman was "cautious" and "artful," and told Edward Carpenter, one of his many English admirers, "I think there are truths which it is necessary to envelop or wrap up."

One of them was obvious—but to some not obvious enough. After the publication of the "Calamus" poems, Whitman found himself in a position for which he had no taste: that of an international advocate of homosexual love. John Addington Symonds was relentless in his pursuit of explications. What Symonds really wanted was for Whitman to declare himself. (There was a side to Whitman which Symonds could never have imagined. Referring to an essay by Symonds called "Democratic Art, with Special Reference to Walt Whitman," Whitman said, "I doubt whether he has gripped 'democratic art' by the nuts, or L[eaves] of G[rass] either.") A whole colony of English homosexuals trooped to Whitman's flag. His brother George could never understand why Oscar Wilde would travel all the way to Camden, hardly a pleasure spot, just to see "Walt." It was in a letter replying to Symonds that Whitman first mentioned his six illegitimate children. A "mulatto mistress" was a later embellishment. This story was taken seriously by scholars for years, even though no one ever came forward to claim the famous name and the possibly lucrative literary rights.

Whitman was attracted to ferry hands, drivers, and mechanics, enjoying their naturalness, their savvy, their lingo. Peter Doyle, a horsecar conductor whom he met in his Washington days, was the most satisfactory companion of his life. But even here he pressed too far:

> Give up absolutely, & for good, from this present hour, this feverish, fluctuating, useless undignified pursuit of 16.4—too long (much too long) persevered in—so humiliating.

In Whitman's notebooks, 16 stands for "P" and 4 for "D"—the cryptography of a child. It becomes clear from Mr. Kaplan's book that Whitman's intense emotional affairs were all with men. Ellen O'Connor, the wife of Whitman's friend and critic William O'Connor, fell madly in love with him, and Anne Gilchrist, an English widow, wrote him passionate letters offering her hand in marriage. Whitman tried to put her off, to no avail. She came over and lived in America with her children for several years, only to return to England, in the end, disappointed. Not quite able to deny any form of idolatry, Whitman welcomed women cautiously, proffering them his person in place of his love. He became a familiar figure in the O'Connor household in Washington and in the Gilchrist ménage in Philadelphia. In fact, he liked nothing better than to "join" an already established domestic circle, adopting and being adopted by one family after another. In these establishments, he was the overgrown prodigal son come home to roost, or that friendly but remote familiar the genius uncle.

Leaves of Grass went through nine editions in Whitman's lifetime, its author striving in each successive recasting for the proper arrangement of the poems—readjusting sections and shifting sequences to accommodate additions to an ever-expanding work. It grew from the twelve poems of the 1855 edition to the more than three hundred and eighty poems of the so-called "Deathbed" edition, which bears Whitman's imprimatur. Lines and phrases were always being revised and stanzas tightened. As new poems were added, old ones were jettisoned to make room for them. Juvenile outpourings were discarded.

Leaves of Grass was full of prescriptions for the future. Emerson's clever description of it as "a singular blend of the Bhagvat Ghita and the New York Herald," meant as a put-down, would today be considered a compliment—but only because *Leaves of Grass* is already in place to show the way. Emerson's comment was a far cry from his first, spontaneous reaction to the poem, emblazoned forever in a famous letter: "I am not blind to the worth of the wonderful gift of *Leaves of Grass.* I find it the most extraordinary piece of wit and wisdom that America has yet contributed. . . . I find incomparable things said incomparably well. . . . I greet you at the beginning of a great career"—the most generous unsolicited response of one writer to another in the history of American letters. Without it, the poem, which had few takers, might have been lost forever. Whitman sent the letter to the New York *Tribune* and incorporated it into the second edition of *Leaves of Grass,* without permission from Emerson—two acts

of insensitivity in Whitman's long career of self-advertisement. A poet, prophet, and public-relations man, he wrote three anonymous reviews of his own book, modestly characterizing it in one as "the most glorious of triumphs, in the known history of literature."

The true miracle of *Leaves of Grass* is that, for all its excesses, its extravagant claims, its endless catalogues, it is, at its very best, a poem of pure feeling—feeling that seeps through phrase after phrase, poem after poem. The transformation of its emotions into words on so vast a scale is astonishing. A long love affair with the future, broken in speech sometimes, eloquent beyond anything one remembers, remarkable in the minting of its language, it is a sad poem, a love poem to some "you" never found, some "you" not only personal, intimate, and sexual but connected with an epic largeness of democratic vistas, as if the poet were in love with Americans not yet born or always yet to come. No one, including Mr. Kaplan—and certainly not Whitman—has yet explained where it sprang from. Whitman encouraged the view of the "transformation miracle"—the "journalist-loafer" turned into the great poet and prophet, as if at the touch of a wand. His followers, sodden with worship, helped the idea along. Actually, Whitman worked on it for years. It was *almost* a miracle—a flawed one, for there is always the problem in Whitman of the false prophecy, the naïve dream, the wished-for fulfillment seen as accomplished fact. *Leaves of Grass* did more than change opinions; it altered the intellectual climate of the world. (And the moral climate, too. "Free love?" Whitman once asked. "Is there any other kind?") Van Gogh, working on *The Starry Night* in Arles, was affected by it; Gerard Manley Hopkins took it to heart; La-Forgue translated the "Children of Adam" poems; it was crucial to D. H. Lawrence and Hart Crane and García Lorca. People as wildly different as Thomas Eakins and Tennyson, Gertrude Stein and Henry James felt its impact. In our time, the Black Mountain School, the Beats, and the New York School of poets emerged from it.

When the Civil War started, *Leaves of Grass* had been through three editions. **"Out of the Cradle Endlessly Rocking,"** the "Children of Adam" poems, and the "Calamus" poems had all been added. Its message of brotherly love became literal. Just as one brother, Jeff, had been party to Whitman's expanding conception of America, it was concern for another, George, that led Whitman to the battlefields of the South. In a garbled casualty report, Whitman learned that George had been wounded. No news followed. Whitman left Washington for Virginia in search of him, found him, and saw at first hand what the war was really like. He dealt with it the only way he knew—as a healer. He returned to Washington to become a "wound-dresser" at Armory Square Hospital. Whitman came into the wards, according to Mr. Kaplan, like "a rich old sea captain, he was so red-faced and patriarchal-looking and big." He entertained the wounded, recited Shakespeare and Scott, told stories, wrote letters for the illiterate and the disabled, attended the feverish young, assisted at grisly amputations, and comforted the dying. The suffering was indescribable: "By the end of the war Whitman figured he had made over six hundred hospital visits and tours, often lasting several days and nights, and in some degree had ministered to nearly a hundred thousand of the sick and wounded of both sides." Yet there were compensations: the alleviation of pain; the sense of being part of a great design, of contributing. Paternal concern, brotherly companionship, mothering compassion were mixed up with emotions sometimes dangerously close to obsession. In the end, he was undone not only by the physical and mental suffering of the patients and the fatigue of the work but by his barely controllable feelings. Here is a letter from Whitman to Thomas P. Sawyer, one of the soldiers:

> Dear comrade, you must not forget me, for I never shall you. My love you have in life or death forever. I don't know how you feel about it, but it is the wish of my heart to have your friendship, and also that if you should come safe out of this war, we should come together again in some place where we could make our living, and be true comrades and never be separated while life lasts. . . . My soul could never be entirely happy, even in the world to come without you, dear comrade. . . . Good bye, my darling comrade, my dear darling brother, for so I will call you, and wish you to call me the same.

Here is Sawyer's reply:

> I fully reciprocate your friendship as expressed in your letter and it will afford me great pleasure to meet you after the war will have terminated or sooner if circumstances will permit.

The generalized "you," the beloved addressed in Whitman's poems, had, like a Platonic universal, an idealized counterpart in President Lincoln. As a poet of the body, Whitman believed "The scent of these armpits [is] aroma finer than prayer / This head more than churches, Bibles, and all the creeds;" but as a poet of the soul, having eschewed Christianity, he needed a god of his own. Mr. Kaplan writes that Lincoln became "his personal agent of redemption, a symbolic figure who transcended politics, leadership, and victory." His mother was the only other person in Whitman's life who had this idealized aura. The "Drum-Taps" poems came out of the war and were dutifully added to *Leaves of Grass.* Their price was high: "The perfect health Whitman was so proud of broke in the hospitals along with a delicate structure of denial and sublimation. Love became irreversibly linked with disease, mutilation, death, absence." In 1865, Lincoln was assassinated; in 1873, Whitman's mother died. Long before, he had written a line that now seemed perfectly appropriate: "Agonies are one of my changes of garments."

The year Whitman's mother died, he became partially paralyzed. Strokes were to cripple him the rest of his life. After living with the family of his brother George, in Camden, for several years, he bought a small house of his own. Some of Mr. Kaplan's most charming pages are devoted to Whitman's last years. Confined more or less to an upper front bedroom-workroom, he recovered, only to be laid back by another bout of illness. "It was not until old age that Whitman's presence and ambience became fully achieved"—Kaplan is using John Burroughs, the naturalist, who knew Whitman for more than twenty years, as a source. "He created an overall impression of sunniness,

equanimity, and contemplative leisure." Whitman, still fiddling with *Leaves of Grass,* stirred the mass of papers at his feet with his cane. Everything natural, found, or man-made was source material for the mesmeric catalogues of the poem. The house had the air of a ship's cabin—landlocked, and foundering in debris, in spite of the efforts of a sailor's widow who kept house for him. Whitman was a collector of people and things, but in both cases the choices had nothing to do with market values or current fashion. Like a bird building a nest, he knew exactly what was required (not much) for his comfort, and what he had to have (everything) for his poem. Whitman needed help to get around and always found it; he was surrounded by people who revered him to the point of idolatry. In 1893, he was finally laid to rest in the elaborate tomb in Harleigh Cemetery that had cost him more than the Camden house. By the time the reader comes to Whitman's death, he can almost take "My foothold is tenoned and mortised in granite / I laugh at what you call dissolution" as the literal truth.

Whitman's life is enigmatic not only by virtue of genius; it is steeped in the deliberately muddied waters of destroyed evidence and manipulated fact. Putting a coherent Whitman together is an exercise in conjecture; the more insistent the claim, the more suspicious its truth. Mr. Kaplan never insists; he merely presents. If he is sometimes long on Freud and short on philosophy, his is still the best all-around portrait we have of a man whose influence can only increase. Whitman bears a relation to Lincoln not unlike Shakespeare's to Elizabeth I and Michelangelo's to the Medici. In each instance, as the years pass the more obvious it becomes that the representative figure of the age, like a negative gradually developing in time, is not the ruler but the artist. (pp. 184-99)

Howard Moss, "A Candidate for the Future," in The New Yorker, *Vol. LVII, No. 30,* September 14, 1981, pp. 184, 190-94, 197-99.

Ezra Greenspan (essay date 1990)

[In the following excerpt, Greenspan discusses Whitman's relation to his audience.]

Whitman's relations with the reading public had never been smooth, even before the war, either in theory or in actuality. He had never been able to sort out the paradox surrounding his, the self-proclaimed national poet's, failure to reach the "democratic masses." That problem continued to follow Whitman in the years after the Civil War, even as he receded from the creative edge of 1855-60 to a position closer to respectability. The "good, gray poet" of the postwar era who could turn out **"O Captain! My Captain!"** or recite, on the few occasions when he read publicly, from a reading book stocked with his own and others' traditional verse knew very well how to please conventional taste and occasionally even condescended to do so. By 1867, he was prepared to present a new face to the public: "The author of *Leaves of Grass* is in no sense or sort whatever the 'rough,' the 'eccentric,' 'vagabond' or queer person, that the commentators . . . persist in making him. [He is] never defiant even to the conventions, always bodily sweet and fresh, dressed plainly and cleanly . . . using only moderate words . . . All really refined persons, and the women more than the men, take to Walt Whitman. The most delicate and even conventional lady only needs to know him to love him."

From "rough" to graybeard, revolutionary to patriarch within a dozen years—so Whitman was to recast himself in his unrelenting desire for broad acceptance. Likewise, he intensified his effort to make over his early poems in his self-image of later years by putting them through a ceaseless process of editorial revision. Slang was toned down, rough edges were smoothened, a more "aesthetic" tack was taken, and tamer new poems were added. Toward the end of his life, wondering how far this process had actually gone, Whitman would find himself asking whether his old-age writings were still "consonant" with the spirit of the original *Leaves of Grass.* On the other hand, he refused to forswear his earlier poetry or the principles upon which it had been based.

His persistence in going on with his poetry and attempting to create his reading audience for it, despite all the old problems now compounded by the paralysis and other physical disabilities which intensified his isolation, was remarkable. The story of Whitman the literary professional during the three remaining decades of his life, during which time most of his contemporaries, major and minor, either died or ceased to write for the public, is in most respects a continuation of that of the pre-Civil War years. It is a story of troubled relations with printers and publishers, of resort to private publication when commercial publication was impossible, of small editions and small sales, of accusations of piracy and of nonpayment of royalties, of reviews often hostile and uncomprehending mixed with occasional praise and eulogy, of various promotional campaigns managed by himself or by his few but loyal followers. Whitman would pass into, and usually just as quickly out of, publishing agreements in this period with such respectable publishers as the Roberts Brothers and Osgood of Boston and the Bunces of New York; attempts to place his works with such major publishers as George Carleton of New York, James Fields of Boston, and J. B. Lippincott of Philadelphia would fail. Fields, who was not unsympathetic to Whitman, expressed the hesitations of nineteenth-century publishers generally in explaining his own reluctance to publish Whitman: "From mere considerations of policy, I wouldn't put our names to a first edition of Byron or even the Bible. When Walt Whitman has become a standard book like them, as I suppose he will, any firm will be glad to publish him." For the most part, Whitman was a self-publisher during the 1860s and 1870s, overseeing and selling his own works on either a small-scale mail order or subscription basis. Finally in 1882, he was able to make a permanent arrangement with the young Philadelphia publisher David McKay, then only at the very beginning of his distinguished career, for bringing out the works of his last decade.

Even through years of genuine suffering, Whitman staunchly refused to accept the kind of commonsensical conclusion put forth by John Stuart Mill in his *Autobiography* that "the writings by which one can live are not the writings which themselves live, and are never those in which the writer does his best." Despite his best efforts, Whitman was never to become a "standard" or even a widely accepted author during his lifetime; his failure to become so hurt him deeply. Not even the homage paid him in Camden by distinguished visitors from overseas or the plaudits from foreign critics could compensate him for his sense of public failure. In recoil, he began in the late 1860s to fabricate the myth that he was completely ignored, even conspired against, by the American literary establishment. Blaming the establishment, of course, was easier than blaming the people, something which Whitman was unable and unwilling to do. In truth, however, it was never with Whitman, as Melville feared it would be with himself, "Down goes his body and up flies his name." Whitman's name and his poems, articles, and squibs were to appear in American papers and magazines far more often in the postwar period than previously; and the question of his popularity was to become so much a public issue that one contemporary newspaper was to state the matter aptly in 1878 in calling Whitman "one of the most renowned unknowns living." Or as another contemporary newspaper was to claim in a review of the well-publicized Osgood edition of *Leaves of Grass,* "The celebrity of this phenomenal poet bears a curious disproportion to the circulation of his works."

The credit for making the issue of Whitman's reputation into a national, even an international, cause belonged in large part to him and to his loyal band of followers, acting with or without his direction but always with his blessing. They stood guard over his name so relentlessly before his critics that the phenomenon of Whitmaniacs became recognized even during the last decades of their master's life. Their persistent, often exorbitant efforts on his behalf were to goad Bayard Taylor, speaking in 1876 during the *West Jersey Press* affair, to state the belief common among many of Whitman's detractors that "no man in this country has ever been so constantly and skillfully advertised by his disciples as Walt Whitman." Even a reasonable, fair-minded man such as Edmund Stedman, who admired Whitman's poetry, was appalled by the ferocity and extravagance of Whitman's and his followers' promotional efforts. Likewise, the normally equable William Dean Howells was to confess to Stedman that he was "tired of the whole Whitman business." But the Whitman business did not go away; it only intensified during the poet's life. As a result of his and his supporters' combined efforts, aided also by the diminishing shock of his originality and changing patterns of thinking and taste, Whitman's position gradually improved during the last several decades of his life. By the time of his death, his critical reputation was approaching a point of solidification.

But the great breakthrough with the general reading public for which he never entirely ceased to hope was not to come in the nineteenth century. Emerson, Thoreau, Burroughs, Gosse, Wilde, Swinburne, W. Rossetti, Symonds, Buchanan, Dowden, and Carpenter might have read him with excitement, pleasure, even awe; but his more general acceptance remained elusive. An American Pushkin he was never to be. This phenomenon was well analyzed by a writer in the November 5, 1881, issue of the *Critic,* a periodical sympathetic to him, in the course of a review of the newly issued Osgood edition of *Leaves of Grass:*

> One great anomaly of Whitman's case has been that while he is an aggressive champion of democracy and of the working-man, in a broad sense of the term working-man, his admirers have been almost exclusively of a class the furthest possibly removed from that which labors for daily bread by manual work. Whitman has always been truly caviare to the multitude. It was only those that knew much of poetry and loved it greatly who penetrated the singular shell of his verses and rejoiced in the rich, pulpy kernel.

> . . . As he stands complete in *Leaves of Grass,* in spite of all the things that regard for the decencies of drawing-rooms and families may wish away, he certainly represents, as no other writer in the world, the struggling, blundering, soundhearted, somewhat coarse, but still magnificent vanguard of Western civilization that is encamped in the United States of America. He avoids the cultured few. He wants to represent, and does in his own strange way represent, the lower middle stratum of humanity. But, so far, it is not evident that his chosen constituency cares for, or has even recognized him. Wide readers are beginning to guess his proportions.

A similar observation was to be drawn by numerous other contemporary writers, some far less close or charitable to him; and Whitman himself, as he could not otherwise have been, was acutely aware of the phenomenon. He had proclaimed himself so often and volubly to be the national poet as to have left himself vulnerable to the incongruity between his claims and his public reception. But more than the public inconsistency, the private frustration was difficult to bear. His very breeding and temperament, not to mention the efforts and ambitions of years of work, protested against his failure; and he must have needed all of what he once called his "immense bufferism" to have held himself up against it. Little wonder that he spent so much time in inglorious pursuit of scapegoats. And little wonder that he reacted so strongly to his reviews, which he read, clipped, and kept scattered around him in his room to his dying day in loose piles and scrapbooks. For a writer who had invested so deeply and inventively in the ideal of reader reception, popular or otherwise, those reviews were to have been the proof that his country had "absorbed" him fittingly.

How did Whitman react in his later years to his failure? His response was as complicated and self-contradictory as was his personality. On the one hand, he courted the good favor of people, such as Tennyson, whom he would earlier have dismissed simply as "dudes of literature." Whitman had always had a deeply ingrained mixture of feelings of inferiority and superiority toward men of learning and cultivation greater than his own, an ambivalence which normally put him on his guard in addressing them. He never overcame this mix of attitudes, which accounts in part for the gaping inconsistency in his formal evaluations of their merits; but his own drift toward respectability led him increasingly in his later years to a public flirtation

with them. A visit from Wilde, a greeting from Tennyson, a phrase from Ruskin became endorsements to be used in his ongoing, self-publicizing campaign. On the other hand, he continued to long for a more visceral reception by the common man and woman, even though his post-1860 poetry shows a declining preoccupation with the cultivation of this relationship.

Despite all his disappointments, his instincts for patronage by the many, rather than by the few, remained strong. He never retreated completely from his earlier insights into the changing nature of patronage in his time or from the realization that his own career would be a test case for the status of the American writer as democrat. Horace Greeley, with whom Whitman was compared as often as with any of his contemporaries, once wrote something on this subject which, to my mind, bears interestingly on the issue of Whitman's status as a democratic writer. He noted that the writer's dedication to his patron was no longer in the nineteenth century the essential act it had once been:

> And thus it chanced that the *dedication* of books, now so absurd and unmeaning, had once a real force and significance . . . The Dedication, then, was the author's public and formal acknowledgment of his obligation to his patron,—his avowal that the credit of the work ought to be divided between them,—just as today the inventor of a mechanical improvement, and the capitalist who supplies the money wherewith to perfect and secure it, often take out a patent jointly. But the Art of Printing, and the general diffusion of knowledge and literary appetite, have abolished patrons, by abolishing the necessity which evoked them: so that there is now but one real patron, The Public, and nearly all dedications to particular individuals are affected, antiquated, and unmeaning.

Greeley, whose own rise from the farm nearly to the White House was a by-product of the printing revolution he was here talking about, was basically correct in the main line of his thinking. But dedications were not yet dead. Instead of being directed to an individual patron, they were increasingly directed to the democratic public, the new patron of American letters. In this regard, I think of Hawthorne's continuing string of Prefaces addressed to the reader or of Melville's various invocations in his novels as profoundly difficult, creative attempts by the nineteenth-century writer, in Hawthorne's words, to "stand in some true relation with his audience."

Whitman, of course, had been drawing the communicatory lines between writer and reader in his original way ever since the 1855 *Leaves of Grass.* In his earliest editions, he had taken the question of readership so far . . . as to have incorporated it into his new poetics, treating reader-writer relations as simultaneously a literary and an extraliterary phenomenon. By the late 1850s, however, he had begun to retreat from this reader-in-the-text strategy, and this retreat continued for the remainder of his career. In the last three decades of his career, making poetry out of the idea of persona and reader as "two souls interchanging" became an increasingly uncommon practice; moreover, in numerous instances he would subsequently edit out such passages from his early poems.

Just the same, he continued to invest a considerable portion of his energies after 1860 in pursuit of the reader. If less went into the poems themselves, more went into the external means of their presentation and into the advocacy of their reception. For purposes of self-promotion, the old fascination with the photographic process served Whitman particularly well in his later years. In the period after the Civil War, Whitman began the practice of sending out his picture to friends and readers, often in combination with, and as an extension of, his printed book. "My work is extremely personal," he told an 1876 interviewer, "rightly considered so—and on the fly-leaf of each volume I have put my photograph with my own hand." The selection of protraits for later editions of *Leaves of Grass* remained, as ever, a major creative decision, a key, in his mind, to the manner of his self-presentation. A new strategy of a similar sort was his policy of sending out his later editions with his autograph appended: "as, first, I here and now, / Signing for Soul and Body, set to them my name, / Walt Whitman." Mailings of reviews, articles, poems, pictures, and other forms of memorabilia became the common reward of friends and supporters on the Whitman mailing list.

His most ambitious attempts to define his relations with the public, however, were in the various prefatory pieces he continued to attach to later editions of *Leaves of Grass.* With Whitman, the preface was designed to explain the purpose of his writing both to himself and to his reader; the logic of his authorial position had normally presupposed the mutuality of self-discovery. It was here, therefore, that Whitman was most particularly intent to put or keep the reader in the text, treating him or her to the one-to-one address he had used in his early poems. Often, the most important thoughts of his prefaces were those which could not have been expressed except as addresses to the reader reading: "The reader will always have his or her part to do, just as much as I have had mine. I seek less to state or display any theme or thought, and more to bring you, reader, into the atmosphere of the theme or thought—there to pursue your own flight."

He was to work away on and off throughout the rest of his life on the formulation of the supreme statement of his poetic purpose in *Leaves of Grass* but with particular urgency during the 1860s, by which time, the years of his most intense creativity already behind him, he was looking to define his achievement. The most sustained product of this ambition was the series of musings, alternately in prose and verse, which he unsuccessfully attempted over the course of the decade to cohere into the final preface to *Leaves of Grass.* The manuscripts in which he worked over these musings, one of the most revealing batches of his papers as to his method of work, offer an unobstructed view of Whitman's manner of thinking and composing at this stage of his life. One can see in them how the same thoughts and ideas, expressed in lines and stanzas which changed little except for their order or phraseology, were worked over and over in Whitman's mind for years, as Whitman punctiliously recombined parts in the search for

the perfect whole. He appropriately thought of this preface as his "Inscription: To the Reader at the Entrance of Leaves of Grass," with himself stationed at the meeting point between life and literature, waiting to recieve the reader with opened arms. This final address to the American reader became the "Inscription" to the fourth edition of *Leaves of Grass:*

> Small is the theme of the following Chant, yet
>   the greatest—namely,
> ONE'S SELF—that wondrous thing, a simple, sep-
>   arate person.
> That, for the use of the New World, I sing.
> Man's physiology complete, from top to toe, I
>   sing. Not physiognomy alone, nor brain alone,
>   is worthy for the muse;—I say the Form com-
>   plete is worthier far. The female equally with
>   the male, I sing.
> Nor cease at the theme of One's-Self. I speak the
>   word of the modern, the word EN-MASSE.
> My Days I sing, and the Lands—with interstice
>   I knew of helpless War.
> O friend, whoe'er you are, at last arriving hither
>   to commence, I feel through every leaf the
>   pressure of your hand, which I return. And
>   thus upon our journey link'd together let us
>   go.

The familiar Whitman motifs are all there: the individual and the collective, man and woman, body and soul, art and America. And so, too, is the familiar Whitman ploy of communicating these themes through reader involvement. But even the appearance of this statement in print did not satisfy Whitman, who eventually condensed this inscription into the short programmatic poem, **"One's-Self I Sing,"** which was to become the lead poem to all later editions of *Leaves of Grass.* Slim as it was, it contained the kernel of his thinking about the dichotomy in his society between the individual (the "simple separate person") and the democratic whole (the "En-masse").

From its beginning, his *Leaves of Grass* career had been a continuous attempt to provide a creative answer to this duality, to locate the individual—himself—in the national collective. One of his most ambitious attempts to provide an answer was the series of essays he worked on separately during the late—1860s before publishing them collectively in 1870 as *Democratic Vistas.* Even in the book's final form, the formal and intellectual division in Whitman's mind between "democracy" and "personalism" was still evident. So, too, were his accordant fears for the nation and for the individual. Of the former he was to say in that book with great truth, "The fear of conflicting and irreconcilable interiors, and the lack of a common skeleton, knitting all close, continually haunts me." No doubt, the Civil War vividly demonstrated to him the living danger of that thought, although in truth his instincts long antedated the lessons taught by the war. As for the modern individual, he also feared the danger, if taken too far, of the "centripetal isolation of a human being in himself."

Even against the changing context of postwar America with its booming economy, sprawling vitality, and rampant corruption, Whitman was still prescribing the same recipe he had for years prescribed for the national ills: literature. This was the third variable in his thinking, and it naturally became the subject of the third and concluding part of his *Vistas.* Not since the 1855 Preface had he spoken so forcefully about the redeeming force of a national literature. But unlike in 1855, the time for such talk, even by his peers, was past. Contemporary writers had abandoned the national camp and were moving to more regional subjects or more overtly realistic modes of writing, and Whitman was left the rare writer who kept to the old nationalist territory and rationale. If there was a transformation in Whitman, it was primarily that he adhered to the old ideas and themes with an ever-stiffening faith and that he chose to state his position more frequently in prose than in verse.

With his country changing and writers going off in new directions, Whitman remained staunchly what he had been in the fifties: the writer in search of connection. The very cast of his imagination shows the impress of this idea: his constant imagining of himself standing at the center of the crowd, his love of the ferry, his fascination with the strand of beach between land and sea, his enthusiasm for the transcontinental railroad and the transatlantic telegraph cable, his longing for a **"Passage to India."** This quest for connection he was to describe best in a poem of the 1860s which I understand as a model of his conception of the creative artist:

> A noiseless patient spider,
> I mark'd where on a little promontory it stood isolated,
> Mark'd how to explore the vacant vast surrounding,
> It launch'd forth filament, filament, filament, out of itself,
> Ever unreeling them, ever tirelessly speeding them.
>
> And you O my soul where you stand,
> Surrounded, detached, in measureless oceans of space,
> Ceaselessly musing, venturing, throwing, seeking the spheres to connect them,
> Till the bridge you will need be form'd, till the ductile anchor hold,
> Till the gossamer thread you fling catch somewhere, O my soul.
> ("A Noiseless Patient Spider")

Whitman was that irreducibly singular, sphere-leaping soul, dropping himself into the void held only by the ceaseless "filament, filament, filament" of his art. He had begun his *Leaves of Grass* career by throwing out his filament to the nation of readers he presupposed, and that remained the common thread of his thinking about his poetry throughout the entirety of his life.

Now, it is one thing to speak of Whitman as the poet of connection; it is quite another to unravel the complexities, at times even the contradictions, surrounding his theory and practice of poetry as communication. I can most vividly explain what I mean by retelling the story of Whitman's relations with Anne Gilchrist, the widow of the Blake biographer Alexander Gilchrist. Upon coming across *Leaves of Grass* for the first time in 1870, Gilchrist was as close an approximation to Whitman's ideal reader as he was ever to have. She read him closely, actively, and

enthusiastically—too much so for his comfort. To the pressure of his flesh-become-the-word literary strategy, she applied the counterpressure of her own. When Whitman was foolish enough to send her a ring, she responded by reversing one of his favorite figures: "O the precious letter, bearing to me the living touch of your hand vibrating through and through me as I feel the pressure of the ring that pressed your flesh and now will press mine so long as I draw breath . . . Perhaps it will yet be given us to see each other, to brave the last stage of this journey side by side, hand in hand."

The shock with which Whitman responded when Gilchrist offered him her hand, as it were, from over the Atlantic is one of the most amusing incidents in the Whitman record; and it is also one of the most revealing, separating as nothing else apparently could the man from the persona. Being the poet of connection was one thing; subjecting himself to the marriage tie was quite another. Her offer of love shocked him to a degree of self-understanding he was not always capable of reaching: the "actual" Walt Whitman, he tried to persuade her, was not the persona of the poems. "Dear friend," he had felt compelled the previous year to write her, "let me warn you somewhat about myself—and yourself also. You must not construct such an unauthorized and imaginary ideal Figure, and call it W. W. and so devotedly invest your loving nature in it. The actual W. W. is a very plain personage, and entirely unworthy such devotion." (pp. 216-25)

I hope the point is clear: Whitman "coming personally to you" in life and in poetry was two separate, if related, phenomena. We know as much as we are ever likely to know about those to whom the poet came—or did not come—in real life. But to whom did Whitman come in his art? Who was the "you" of Whitman's poems? It is never simple or easy, if it is possible at all, to identify the addressee of a poem; but in the case of Whitman, the question is too fundamental to go unexamined. Was he addressing an audience of men or women, of young or old, of the working or the middle class—to mention some of the categorizations which typically came to his mind? Given Whitman's desire to make his poetry inclusive as poetry had never been before by making it encompass all demographic as well as all geographical sectors of the country, it is not surprising that there are occasional addresses to each of these groups dutifully scattered through his poetry. But in all likelihood, Whitman never paid any of these groups, not even the young men of the working class, with whom he felt a special rapport, anything but an incidental regard when he composed the vast majority of his poems.

A more significant question about the identity of Whitman's "you" is this: Was Whitman addressing an audience which he conceived of as singular or plural? Unlike the previous question, this one can be answered with some assurance that Whitman himself addressed it with clear and serious artistic thought. At times, to be judged by the reflexive pronoun which occasionally followed it, "you," in Whitman's mind, was singular, which was as his thinking about the unqualified individuality of the reading experience would lead one to expect. And this was in harmony with the dynamics of a typical Whitman poem, which works toward a position of increasing intimacy with its audience of a kind one would naturally assume as being possible only with a single reader. But these things notwithstanding, one is more often than not unsure in reading most or all of a Whitman poem whether Whitman is addressing a singular or a plural audience. This was not by chance; it was the result, rather, of careful forethought and strategizing.

As an English-language writer, Whitman faced the dilemma unknown to writers in other European languages of addressing a "you" whose number was normally indeterminate. Whitman was not only aware of this problem but he was also able, as C. Carroll Hollis has pointed out [see Further Reading], to turn a potential dead spot in the language deftly into a source of resonance, playing on this indeterminacy in his poems so as to harmonize what would otherwise have been a dissonance between the individual reader and the nation of readers. For a writer as concerned as was Whitman about the loosening of the organic tie between the individual and society, the indeterminacy of the addressee could be turned into an extremely valuable poetic asset, one which Whitman worked with considerable ability, especially in his early editions. In such poems as **"Song of Myself," "A Song for Occupations," "To Think of Time," "Crossing Brooklyn Ferry,"** and **"Song of the Open Road,"** to mention only a few of the many early poems for which the generalization holds, not only can one not easily pin down the addressee as being a singular or a plural figuration but one is under no obligation to do so, since the underlying logic of the audience address of these poems is all for one and one for all. The "you" he was addressing in such poems was typically an absorptive rather than a specified "you," one which, rather like the catalogues, could take into itself any number of individuals or groups. So that when Whitman invites his "you" to partake of the fullness of art and life, he can include simultaneously in this invitation both the individual and the national collective, of which each individual is the potential center. Not every poet would know how to plant a single kiss, as did Whitman, on a thousand brows.

What allowed him to work this strategy as well as he did was the abstract character of his addressee; names, faces, specific details were not only unnecessary but counterproductive. In fact, the single most intriguing hint as to his thinking and imagining about the identity of his "you" is to be found in the apposition he often tacked on afterwards: "you whoever you are." Whitman's "you," in all likelihood, was "whoever you are." The paradox becomes immediately clear: the poet coming personally to "you," the poet saving his kiss especially for "you," the poet inviting "you" to join him on the open road was addressing an unknown, untouchable, hypothesized "you." This was, of course, as the limitations of print and audience, or more exactly, of modern print and modern audience, necessarily dictated. In fact, Whitman, the ex-printer who claimed to "pass so poorly" through the medium of print, was one of the most extreme overreachers of such limitations that the print world has ever seen. Although he had been quick to foresee the revolutionary changes coming with the new printing technology and the changing character of his society and keen to plan his advance upon the American

public through the agency of the new technology, there was a contradiction between the personalized poetic relations he was cultivating in his poems and the realities of modern print culture. True, a writer of Whitman's time could reach a larger and more broadly based audience than could writers of previous generations, but he could do so only by communicating across the increasing distance between himself and his readers as their society grew in size and heterogeneity. In these cultural circumstances, Whitman's odd-sounding "you whoever you are" struck just the right note; with its peculiar combination of the intimate and the remote, it captured in a phrase the paradoxical task of Whitman's poetry, one which only a writer of the finest rhetorical skills could have hoped to carry off convincingly: to personalize an impersonal audience. Ironically, none but the most unsuccessful or private author, he most unable or unwilling to reach the broad reading public, could afford to self-publish and orient his writing to a specific "you."

One more time, let the too eager biographical reader of Whitman's poems beware: He who would hunt for a specific lover or personality in or behind Whitman's "you" looks in vain. In evaluating Whitman's manner of address, one should never underestimate the extent of Whitman's own personal caginess and elusiveness. To read the drafts of his poems and letters is to become aware of how manipulated was the degree of intimacy Whitman worked into and out of his literary and epistolary addresses. Judged by the number of times he worked over his address to the reader in his notebooks and trial drafts, it was often a subject for negotiations between Whitman and himself, negotiations which continued into and through the various editions of the printed texts. And even in the finality of print, it is seldom clear what degree of intimacy he wished to establish between himself and his reader. But one thing is certain: People who confused the relations of the poetry for the relations of real life were to be held firmly away at arm's length. In Anne Gilchrist's case, only the distance of the Atlantic Ocean would have sufficed, had Whitman had his choice. And what was her mistake, after all, but doing what one of his most insinuating poems insisted that its reader do: Touch this book and touch a man. Little did she know that Whitman would shrink from such real life contact.

In short, Whitman's "you" is best understood as what, in fact, it could only have been: a hard-worked literary device; I know of no writer who ever worked it any harder than did Whitman. And thus it is, finally, in his poetry and with his pen that Whitman did his speaking and his coming personally to "you." This is another way of stating Harold Bloom's proposition about the meeting of persona and reader in Whitman's poetry: "The poetry of the 'real Me,' intricate and forlorn, is addressed to the 'real Me' of the American reader." Private personalities cast aside, Whitman felt freest to express himself to the reader and did so most ingeniously in his poems. It is here that one is to find Whitman at his greatest; and it is here, in the end, that one must come to evaluate the magnitude and limitations, successes and failures, of his achievement.

In assessing that achievement, I would like to pursue

Whitman's own thinking in considering his poems—their ideas, their content, even their conception of the reading process—as inseparable from the context of democracy. In this regard, F. O. Matthiessen's term for describing the literary undertaking of Whitman and his co-workers at a distance as being the creation, in two senses, of a "literature for democracy" seems as appropriate today as it was in Matthiessen's own day. This idea was absolutely central to Whitman's thinking about poetry. For him, "democracy" and "America" were, as he once said, "convertible terms"; and whether taken separately or together, they were key operational terms in his conceptual vocabulary of poetry.

The free convertibility of these terms and the tendency to identify them with his own poetry often led Whitman into a circle of logical reasoning, but before I explain what I mean by this, I would like to juxtapose Whitman's thinking about democracy and literature with that of Alexis de Tocqueville, whose analysis of midnineteenth-century America defined with unusual clarity the territory occupied by Whitman and the writers of his time. In a key chapter of *Democracy in America,* Tocqueville identified the idea of "individualism" as a novel phenomenon accompanying the advent of democracy: "Individualism is a mature and calm feeling, which disposes each member of the community to sever himself from the mass of his fellows and to draw apart with his family and his friends, so that after he has formed a little circle of his own, he willingly leaves society at large to itself." The result, for Tocqueville, was an unhealthy swing of authority from the society to the individual: "Thus not only does democracy make every man forget his ancestors, but it hides his descendants and separates his contemporaries from him; it throws him back forever upon himself alone and threatens in the end to confine him entirely within the solitude of his own heart."

This was a situation which a more self-sufficient writer, such as Emily Dickinson, might have been able to tolerate; for Whitman, however, it was unacceptable. Unwilling to restrict his range to the "centripetal isolation of a human being in himself," he had reached out to the nation through the mediacy of his newspapers in the 1840s and thereafter, once his thinking had matured, through that of his poems. Aloof and elusive as he was by nature, he had devoted his finest artistic thoughts and powers to expressing his individuality in such a way as to write himself—his own name, personality, and ambitions—at large into America. But the script of *Leaves of Grass* was written not exclusively for one but more often for two actors, one a richly fictionalized version of Walt Whitman and the other a no less richly fictionalized personality lacking face or features other than the vague lineaments of modern man or woman. Of that fictional "you whoever you are" he asked and promised no less than he did of "Walt Whitman," stating his proposition perhaps most boldly in **"By Blue Ontario's Shore"**: "The whole theory of the universe is directed to one single individual—namely, to You." Under Whitman's dispensation, the world was his and his readers' simply for the taking.

Such a formulation, put into practice in his poems, placed unavoidably heavy demands upon their presupposed readers, and there are signs that Whitman and his circle were at least intermittently aware of this. John Burroughs, for one, often spoke this view: "Whitman always aimed to make his reader an active partner with him in his poetic enterprise." Or again: "He makes extraordinary demands upon the reader, undoubtedly; he tries him as no other modern poet does or dares." And as Whitman himself was to tell Traubel in one of his numerous remarks of the sort on the subject, "All my poems require to be read again and again—three, four, five, six times—before they enter into the reader, are grasped—filter their way to the undersoil." Whatever the critical insight of these statements, they fail to state the price that such a view would entail for a poet of Whitman's nationalist aspirations: a poetry which was not only difficult but immensely challenging for its readers. No less than Melville with his pose of conviviality, Whitman with his pose of camaraderie was making the most extreme demands upon his readers, asking of them no less than that they rethink their existence with him.

Had he been thinking objectively and dispassionately, of course, he would have known that this was anything but a reliable formula for popularity. But then again, not only did such thinking lie remote from the sources of Whitman's creative imagining but Whitman was far from being able to see the circularity involved in his thinking about his relations with his readers and his country. That thinking went like this: His writing had been called out by the conditions of American democracy, it transformed those conditions into acts of poetry, and those resultant poems, in turn, were to be "absorbed" by the new generation of American readers. This was the logic underlying the concluding statement of his 1855 Preface that "the proof of a poet is that his country absorbs him as affectionately as he has absorbed it." If that statement was also a personal prediction, as I can only suppose it was, it was the most problematic one he made in his career.

The proof should have been before his eyes. A history of scattered sales, few readers, and frequently hostile or obtuse reviews was an indication of how specious his reasoning had been. That reasoning was weakest precisely where it touched upon the relations between writers and readers. Whitman had never scrupulously questioned his assumptions in this regard, which is why he seems never to have appreciated, early or late, how complicated and difficult might be the task of the American writer. Tocqueville had foreseen otherwise, and what he predicted had important implications for Whitman. For if his analysis of the consequences of equality and individuality for democratic culture was correct and the democratic writer was forced to write from a position of a diminishing number of shared themes, concepts, and myths and from a narrowing basis of community, then what was to be the basis of shared assumptions between a democratic writer with nationalist aspirations, such as Whitman, and his reading audience? The young Whitman of the pre-*Leaves of Grass* years had felt in his bones the force of the cultural situation Tocqueville was talking about and was ready and waiting in 1855 with the poetic answer: "And what I assume you shall assume." But attempts to draw freely on that statement were inevitably to lead him to complications.

In truth, Whitman was far less able to draw on a body of shared assumptions than he commonly believed. To a certain extent, this was simply a matter of personalities; how many Americans of his time were willing to give over their hearts and souls to a man of Whitman's unconventional personality, views, and ideas? If Whitman felt himself unbearably cramped while sitting in the parlors of middle-class homes, how would their residents have felt being yanked out of comfortable circumstances and led out onto Whitman's open road? On a deeper cultural level, though, Whitman was finding himself in the situation that Tocqueville had predicted of a diminishing number of shared symbols and themes available to writers in a decentralized culture. No less than other contemporary writers, Whitman failed badly in his attempts to make direct poetic use of the public realm. His occasional and patriotic poems were as bad as any poems he ever wrote in his maturity; it is a real shock to hear a poet who could sound so like a master of poetic voice in poems such as **"Song of Myself"** and **"Crossing Brooklyn Ferry"** sound so like a charlatan in his declaredly public poems. Only the purest self-deception could have led Whitman to believe that he could be the singer of the Civil War, the American Institute, the Centennial Exposition, or any other public gathering or national event.

The public sphere never sat quite as neatly on the private sphere as Whitman, or at least as Whitman the national poet, had theorized. In truth, the inexact fit between the private and the public was always to put Whitman at his unease; but it was also one of the factors which drove him to some of his most inspired creative thinking and imagining about the meeting in his time between the individual and society. Unable to meet his readers on the parade grounds of his society, Whitman plotted to meet them on the more tenable grounds of the public made private (and then remade public) in his audience-address poems. If the reader could not come to it, Whitman would have the public sphere come to the reader:

> The President is up there in the White House for
>   you. . . . it is not you who are here for him,
> The Secretaries act in their bureaus for
>   you. . . . not you here for them,
> The Congress convenes every December for you,
> Laws, courts, the forming of states, the charters
>   of cities, the going and coming of commerce
>   and mails are all for you.
>   **("A Song for Occupations")**

For a poet unable to take anything as fixed fact, this was a far more effective and viable way than would have been provided by any more conventional technique for bringing about the merge between the private and the public. But such thinking and strategizing had its price.

The price—the considerable price, I would emphasize—of this view was its devaluation of the objective and the traditional in favor of a radically subjective view of life and culture. In its search for at least common denominator which sacrificed nothing of the dignity or intelligence of "the average man of to-day," Whitman's poetry made that individual, with himself and sometimes through himself, the final arbiter of value and taste. Lest this view degenerate into some form of solipsism, Whitman had insisted on the representativeness of his "I" and "you," the abstractions upon which he balanced his poems. In truth, such thinking made Whitman perform a delicate balancing act in his poems, so slim was their fulcrum and so weighty the burden he placed upon it. But given the cultural circumstances of his society, this was the only way Whitman could make his poetry into the instrumentality he desired for affecting his readers and his society in fundamental ways.

He applied his finest powers to this task; and his achievement, in my opinion, was to have made his poetry into what Harry Levin once called, in a different context, "the richest and most sensitive of human institutions—not a two-dimensional page in a book, but a rounded organism embracing the people by and for whom it was created." **Leaves of Grass** is an American institution in this sense; but it is one which, with its sharply anti-institutional, anti-nomian edges, could exist only in a complicated relation to its society. There was a frailty of connection inherent in the terms of its conception which reflected Whitman's own tenuous connection to his polity and people. The artist swinging freely through time and space held only by the filament of his art was a figure of the most extreme looseness, as was the conception of the reader free to rethink for himself or herself any and all of the basic conventions of the society.

The most it allowed Whitman to hope for, in a manner of speaking, was to effect a situation for readers parallel to the one he imagined for children in **"There Was a Child Went Forth"**: a myriad of separate instances of readers going forth into the pages of **Leaves of Grass,** each to discover individually his or her separate identity. This was what he meant when he wrote in a self-review of 1860 about the role his poems were meant to perform: "The egotistical outset, 'I celebrate myself,' and which runs in spirit through so much of the volume, speaks for him or her reading it precisely the same as for the author, and is invariably to be so applied. Thus the book is a gospel of self-assertion and self-reliance for every American reader—which is the same as saying it is the gospel of Democracy." But Whitman's gospel of democracy, unlike the only other gospel of which he could have conceived for purposes of comparison, rested on no commonly accepted authority, only on that assumed by its simple separate author. Resting on so narrow a base of support and posed in such highly individualized terms, Whitman's bible could do no more than assert a position for each reader, in Richard Fein's term, of his or her "shared separateness."

We do not readily grant any creative writer entry to the category of gospel, not even gospel made over in Whitman's kind of modern, secularized terms. But what do we grant our writers, and what do we expect their works to *do?* I suppose that the answer to that question is necessarily grounded in the cultural circumstances of the responder. Whitman, living in an age of general literacy when the written word had no cultural rivals for domestic, leisure-time activity, was no doubt justified in answering that question more liberally than would poets and readers in America today. I would not wish to claim that Whitman's poems ever effected national purposes or solved national problems; I do believe, however, that they fulfilled his own ambition "to articulate and faithfully express in literary or poetic form, and uncompromisingly, my own physical, emotional, moral, intellectual, and aesthetic Personality, in the midst of, and tallying, the momentous spirit and facts of its immediate days, and of current America—and to exploit that Personality, identified with place and date, in a far more candid and comprehensive sense than any hitherto poem or book." To have done that much, to have done it with unrivaled artistic vision and power, and to have offered that achievement, printed and bound, to his public was already enough for an American to be considered a national poet. (pp. 228-36)

Ezra Greenspan, in his Walt Whitman and the American Reader, *Cambridge University Press, 1990, 267 p.*

FURTHER READING

Anderson, Quentin. "Consciousness and Form in Whitman" and "The World in the Body." In his *The Imperial Self: An Essay in American Literary and Cultural History,* pp. 88-118, pp. 119-65. New York: Alfred A. Knopf, 1971.
> Analyzes Whitman as a phenomenon of cultural history, arguing that the poet revolutionized concepts of the self and the artist.

Anderson, Sherwood. "Walt Whitman." In *Leaves of Grass,* by Walt Whitman, pp. v-vii. New York: Thomas Y. Crowell, 1933.
> Introduction to *Leaves of Grass* stating, "Whitman is in the bones and blood of America."

Aspiz, Harold. *Walt Whitman and the Body Beautiful.* Urbana: University of Illinois Press, 1980, 290 p.
> Study of Whitman's ideas about the body in relation to the scientific knowledge and moral climate of the time.

Bauerlein, Mark. "Whitman's Language of the Self." *American Imago* 44, No. 2 (Summer 1987): 129-48.
> Psychological analysis of Whitman's concept of "self" in "Song of Myself." "Some of Whitman's self-amplifications," Bauerlein observes, "actually undermine the centrality of his identity."

Bergman, Herbert. "Ezra Pound and Walt Whitman." *American Literature* XXVII, No. 1 (March 1955): 56-61.
> Sampling of comments made by Pound about Whitman including a previously unpublished essay, "What I Feel about Walt Whitman" from 1909.

Bové, Paul A. "*Leaves of Grass* and the Center: Free Play or Transcendence." In his *Destructive Poetics: Heidegger and Modern American Poetry,* pp. 131-79. New York: Columbia University Press, 1980.
> Argues that Whitman's poems "are deconstructive yet, almost simultaneously, entrapped within a tradition marked by the possibilities of transcendence and of centered discourse."

Brown, Clarence A. "Walt Whitman and the 'New Poetry'." *American Literature* 33, No. 1 (March 1961): 33-45.
> Reviews critical reactions to Whitman's poetry by American poets of the early twentieth century.

Byers, Thomas B. "Walt Whitman: The Word Made Flesh, The Flesh Made Word." In his *What I Cannot Say: Self, Word, and World in Whitman, Stevens, and Merwin,* pp. 15-42. Urbana: University of Illinois Press, 1989.
> Attempts to "map the Whitmanian self and cosmos."

Carlisle, E. Fred. *The Uncertain Self: Whitman's Drama of Identity.* East Lansing: Michigan State University Press, 1973, 207 p.
> Depicts the act of writing poetry as a self-absorbing task for Whitman.

Cather, Willa. "Whitman." In *The Kingdom of Art: Willa Cather's First Principles and Critical Statements, 1893-1896,* edited by Bernice Slote, pp. 350-53. Lincoln: University of Nebraska Press, 1966.
> An 1896 letter in which Cather states, "However ridiculous Whitman may be there is a primitive elemental force about him."

Cavitch, David. "Whitman's Mystery." *Studies in Romanticism* 17, No. 2 (Spring 1978): 105-28.
> Studies the poetic ramifications of Whitman's belief that his soul was divided in two.

Colum, Padraic. "The Poetry of Walt Whitman." *The New Republic* XIX, No. 241 (14 June 1919): 213-15.
> Views Whitman as an innovator of form and language.

Crawley, Thomas Edward. *The Structure of "Leaves of Grass."* Austin: University of Texas Press, 1970, 256 p.
> Contends that while *Leaves of Grass* lacks a perfectly ordered structure, several themes unify the work.

Creeley, Robert. "Introduction to Penguin *Selected Whitman.*" In his *Was That a Real Poem, & Other Essays,* pp. 61-73. Bolinas, Calif.: Four Seasons Foundation, 1979.
> Discloses ways in which praise for Whitman from the poets Allen Ginsberg, Robert Duncan, and Louis Zukofsky helped the critic to comprehend the importance and relevance of Whitman's innovations.

Erkkila, Betsy. *Whitman the Political Poet.* New York: Oxford University Press, 1989, 360 p.
> Addresses Whitman's "overtly political postures and designs," as well as "the more subtle and less conscious" undertones in his poetry.

Foerster, Norman. "Whitman and the Cult of Confusion." *North American Review* CCXIII, No. 787 (June 1921): 799-812.
> Describes Whitman's glorification of the dichotomy between "an impersonal pure reason or spirit in man and the personal life of the temperament."

Fredrickson, Robert S. "Public Onanism: Whitman's Song of Himself." *Modern Language Quarterly* 46, No. 2 (June 1985): 143-60.
> Discusses the autoerotic element in "Song of Myself."

Hesse, Hermann. "Walt Whitman: *Leaves of Grass.*" In his *My Belief: Essays on Life and Art,* pp. 312-13. New York: Farrar, Straus and Giroux, 1974.
> Brief essay dated 1904 that claims, "The author of

Leaves of Grass is not the most literarily gifted but he is humanly the greatest of all American poets."

Hindus, Milton, ed. *"Leaves of Grass": One Hundred Years After*. Stanford: Stanford University Press, 1955, 144 p.
Highly regarded selection of essays on *Leaves of Grass*.

Hollis, C. Carroll. *Language and Style in "Leaves of Grass."* Baton Rouge: Louisiana State University Press, 1983, 277 p.
Explication of Whitman's poetry based on late-twentieth-century theories of rhetoric.

Hopkins, Gerard Manley. "XC." In *The Letters of Gerard Manley Hopkins to Robert Bridges,* edited by Claude Colleer Abbott, pp. 154-58. London: Oxford University Press, 1935.
Letter dated 18 October 1882 in which Hopkins maintains, "I always knew in my heart Walt Whitman's mind to be more like my own than any other man's living. As he is a very great scoundrel this is not a pleasant confession."

Hughes, Langston. "The Ceaseless Rings of Walt Whitman." In *I Hear the People Singing: Selected Poems of Walt Whitman,* by Walt Whitman, pp. 7-10. New York: Young World Books, 1946.
Introduction to a children's volume of Whitman calling him "one of literature's great faithholders in human freedom."

Hutchinson, George B. *The Ecstatic Whitman: Literary Shamanism & the Crisis of the Union.* Columbus: Ohio State University Press, 1986, 231 p.
Devises a "shamanistic model of prophetic role-playing" to explain Whitman's poetry in an attempt to reconcile "various interpretations of the poet's religious orientation, his visionary ecstasies, and his psychological make-up."

Kaplan, Justin. *Walt Whitman: A Life.* New York: Simon and Schuster, 1980, 429 p.
Critical biography of Whitman.

Keller, Karl. "The Puritan Perverse." *Texas Studies in Literature and Language* 25, No. 1 (Spring 1983): 139-64.
Examines the significance of a meeting between Whitman and Ralph Waldo Emerson in 1860, in which Emerson unsuccessfully argued for the deletion of the erotic poems in *Leaves of Grass*.

Krieg, Joann P., ed. *Walt Whitman: Here and Now.* Westport, Conn.: Greenwood Press, 1985, 248 p.
Collects the lectures given at a Walt Whitman conference at Hofstra University in April 1980.

Larson, Kerry C. *Whitman's Drama of Consensus.* Chicago: University of Chicago Press, 1988, 269 p.
Describes the tone of *Leaves of Grass* as both indeterminate and vehement, and explores the consequences of this paradox.

Loving, Jerome. *Emerson, Whitman, and the American Muse.* Chapel Hill: University of North Carolina Press, 1982, 220 p.
Inquiry into the intellectual relationship between Whitman and Ralph Waldo Emerson.

Marki, Ivan. *The Trial of the Poet: An Interpretation of the First Edition of "Leaves of Grass."* New York: Columbia University Press, 1976, 301 p.
Discusses the 1855 edition of *Leaves of Grass*.

Metzger, Charles R. *Thoreau and Whitman: A Study of Their Esthetics*. Seattle: University of Washington Press, 1961, 113 p.
Compares Whitman and Henry David Thoreau as mystics and transcendentalists.

Miller, Edwin Haviland. *Walt Whitman's "Song of Myself": A Mosaic of Interpretations*. Iowa City: University of Iowa Press, 1989, 179 p.
Assembles the responses of prominent critics to "Song of Myself" in a line-by-line format.

Miller, Henry. "Letter to Pierre Lesdain." In his *The Books in My Life,* 196-263. London: Peter Owen, 1961.
Comparison of the philosophies and aesthetics of Whitman and Fyodor Dostoevsky.

Miller, James E., Jr. "Whitman's *Leaves* and the American 'Lyric-Epic.'" In *Poems in Their Place,* edited by Neil Fraistat, pp. 289-307. Chapel Hill: University of North Carolina Press, 1986.
Views *Leaves of Grass* as a precursor to a tradition of long poems.

Nathanson, Tenney. "Whitman's Tropes of Light and Flood: Language and Representation in the Early Editions of *Leaves of Grass.*" *ESQ* 31, No. 2 (1985): 116-34.
Explores patterns of imagery in *Leaves of Grass,* suggesting that "Whitman's images of light and flood are . . . part of a pervasive imaginative reversal . . . that seeks to displace the notion of representation from words onto things and invest language and the poet's voice with direct, performative power."

Pearce, Roy Harvey. "Whitman and Our Hope for Poetry." In his *Historicism Once More: Problems & Occasions for the American Scholar,* pp. 327-50. Princeton, N.J.: Princeton University Press, 1969.
Argues that the "history of American poetry could be written as the continuing discovery and rediscovery of Whitman, an on-going affirmation of his crucial relevance to the mission of the American poet."

Perlman, Jim; Folsom, Ed; and Campion, Dan, eds. *Walt Whitman: The Measure of His Song.* Minneapolis: Holy Cow! Press, 1981, 394 p.
Reprints poems and essays by poets who have recorded their responses to Whitman.

Rajasekharaiah, T. R. *The Roots of Whitman's Grass.* Rutherford, N. J.: Fairleigh Dickinson University Press, 1970, 522 p.
Comparative study of *Leaves of Grass* and Indian literature.

Renner, Dennis K. "Tradition for a Time of Crisis." In *Poetic Prophecy in Western Literature,* edited by Jan Wojcik and Raymond-Jean Frontain, pp. 119-30. Rutherford, N.J.: Fairleigh Dickinson University Press, 1984.
Argues for a reading of *Leaves of Grass* "as a prophetic appeal," based on the critic's observations of "situational and generic parallels to Hebraic prophecy."

Salska, Agnieszka. *Walt Whitman and Emily Dickinson.* Philadelphia: University of Pennsylvania Press, 1985, 220 p.
Comparison between the poetry of Whitman and Dickinson, focusing on aesthetics, worldview, and language.

Sánchez-Eppler, Karen. "To Stand Between: A Political Perspective on Whitman's Poetics of Merger and Embodiment." *ELH* 56, No. 4 (Winter 1989): 923-49.

Examines Whitman's notebooks in a reassessment of "the political sources and implications of his corporeal poetry."

"Walt Whitman." *The Saturday Review* (London) 41, No. 1,064 (18 March 1876): 360-61.

An extremely negative assessment of Whitman's poetry.

Thomas, M. Wynn. *The Lunar Light of Whitman's Poetry.* Cambridge, Mass.: Harvard University Press, 1987, 313 p.

Considers Whitman's poetry as a product of and a response to historical circumstances.

Updike, John. "Whitman's Egotheism." In his *Hugging the Shore: Essays and Criticism,* pp. 106-17. New York: Vintage Books, 1983.

Defines Whitman's egocentric metaphysics.

Warren, James Perrin. *Walt Whitman's Language Experiment.* University Park: The Pennsylvania State University Press, 1990, 217 p.

Exploration of Whitman's "theory of language and how it relates to his poetic practice."

Waskow, Howard J. *Whitman: Explorations in Form.* Chicago: University of Chicago Press, 1966, 279 p.

Critical work attempting "to define Whitman's formal range by demonstrating how each of his forms works."

Wiegman, Robyn. "Writing the Male Body: Naked Patriarchy and Whitmanian Democracy." *Literature and Psychology* 33, Nos. 3 and 4 (1987): 16-26.

Contends that in Whitman's poetry there is not, as most critics believe, "a radical challenge to repressive sexual mores," but rather an affirmation of "the phallocentric origins of American democratic rhetoric."

Woodress, James, ed. *Critical Essays on Walt Whitman.* Boston: G. K. Hall, 1983, 338 p.

Anthology of important Whitman criticism, including assessments by William Dean Howells, William James, and Ezra Pound.

Zweig, Paul. *Walt Whitman: The Making of the Poet.* New York: Basic Books, 1984, 372 p.

Investigates Whitman's transformation from a journalist to a poet.

Nineteenth-Century Literature Criticism

Cumulative Indexes
Volumes 1-31

This Index Includes References
to Entries in These Gale Series

Contemporary Literary Criticism presents excerpts of criticism on the works of novelists, poets, dramatists, short story writers, scriptwriters, and other creative writers who are now living or who have died since 1960.

Twentieth-Century Literary Criticism contains critical excerpts by the most significant commentators on poets, novelists, short story writers, dramatists, and philosophers who died between 1900 and 1960.

Nineteenth-Century Literature Criticism offers significant passages from criticism on authors who died between 1800 and 1899.

Literature Criticism from 1400 to 1800 compiles significant passages from the most noteworthy criticism on authors of the fifteenth through the eighteenth centuries.

Classical and Medieval Literature Criticism offers excerpts of criticism on the works of world authors from classical antiquity through the fourteenth century.

Short Story Criticism combines excerpts of criticism on short fiction by writers of all eras and nationalities.

Poetry Criticism presents excerpts of criticism on the works of poets from all eras, movements, and nationalities.

Children's Literature Review includes excerpts from reviews, criticism, and commentary on works of authors and illustrators who create books for children.

Contemporary Authors Series encompasses five related series. *Contemporary Authors* provides biographical and bibliographical information on more than 97,000 writers of fiction and nonfiction. *Contemporary Authors New Revision Series* provides completely updated information on authors covered in *CA*. Only entries requiring significant change are revised for *CA New Revision Series*. *Contemporary Authors Permanent Series* consists of listings for deceased and inactive authors. *Contemporary Authors Autobiography Series* presents specially commissioned autobiographies by leading contemporary writers. *Contemporary Authors Bibliographical Series* contains primary and secondary bibliographies as well as analytical bibliographical essays by authorities on major modern authors.

Dictionary of Literary Biography encompasses three related series. *Dictionary of Literary Biography* furnishes illustrated overviews of authors' lives and works. *Dictionary of Literary Biography Documentary Series* illuminates the careers of major figures through a selection of literary documents, including letters, interviews, and photographs. *Dictionary of Literary Biography Yearbook* summarizes the past year's literary activity and includes updated entries on individual authors. A cumulative index to authors and articles is included in each new volume. *Concise Dictionary of Literary Biography,* a six-volume series, collects revised and updated sketches on major American authors that were originally presented in *Dictionary of Literary Biography*.

Something about the Author Series encompasses three related series. *Something about the Author* contains illustrated biographical sketches on authors and illustrators of juvenile and young adult literature from all eras. *Something about the Author Autobiography Series* presents specially commissioned autobiographies by prominent authors and illustrators of books for children and young adults. *Authors and Artists for Young Adults* provides high school and junior high school students with profiles of their favorite creative artists.

Yesterday's Authors of Books for Children contains heavily illustrated entries on children's writers who died before 1961. Complete in two volumes.

Literary Criticism Series
Cumulative Author Index

This index lists all author entries in the Gale Literary Criticism Series and includes cross-references to other Gale sources. References in the index are identified as follows:

AAYA: *Authors & Artists for Young Adults,* Volumes 1-6
CAAS: *Contemporary Authors Autobiography Series,* Volumes 1-13
CA: *Contemporary Authors* (original series), Volumes 1-132
CABS: *Contemporary Authors Bibliographical Series,* Volumes 1-3
CANR: *Contemporary Authors New Revision Series,* Volumes 1-33
CAP: *Contemporary Authors Permanent Series,* Volumes 1-2
CA-R: *Contemporary Authors* (revised editions), Volumes 1-44
CDALB: *Concise Dictionary of American Literary Biography,* Volumes 1-6
CLC: *Contemporary Literary Criticism,* Volumes 1-65
CLR: *Children's Literature Review,* Volumes 1-24
CMLC: *Classical and Medieval Literature Criticism,* Volumes 1-6
DC: *Drama Criticism,* Volume 1
DLB: *Dictionary of Literary Biography,* Volumes 1-104
DLB-DS: *Dictionary of Literary Biography Documentary Series,* Volumes 1-8
DLB-Y: *Dictionary of Literary Biography Yearbook,* Volumes 1980-1988
LC: *Literature Criticism from 1400 to 1800,* Volumes 1-16
NCLC: *Nineteenth-Century Literature Criticism,* Volumes 1-31
PC: *Poetry Criticism,* Volumes 2-2
SAAS: *Something about the Author Autobiography Series,* Volumes 1-12
SATA: *Something about the Author,* Volumes 1-64
SSC: *Short Story Criticism,* Volumes 1-7
TCLC: *Twentieth-Century Literary Criticism,* Volumes 1-40
YABC: *Yesterday's Authors of Books for Children,* Volumes 1-2

Aiken, Conrad (Potter)
1889-1973 . . . . **CLC 1, 3, 5, 10, 52**
See also CANR 4; CA 5-8R;
obituary CA 45-48; SATA 3, 30; DLB 9,
45

Aiken, Joan (Delano) 1924- . . . . **CLC 35**
See also CLR 1, 19; CANR 4; CA 9-12R;
SAAS 1; SATA 2, 30

Ainsworth, William Harrison
1805-1882 . . . . **NCLC 13**
See also SATA 24; DLB 21

Ajar, Emile 1914-1980
See Gary, Romain

Akhmadulina, Bella (Akhatovna)
1937- . . . . **CLC 53**
See also CA 65-68

Akhmatova, Anna
1888-1966 . . . . **CLC 11, 25, 64; PC 2**
See also CAP 1; CA 19-20;
obituary CA 25-28R

Aksakov, Sergei Timofeyvich
1791-1859 . . . . **NCLC 2**

Aksenov, Vassily (Pavlovich) 1932-
See Aksyonov, Vasily (Pavlovich)

Aksyonov, Vasily (Pavlovich)
1932- . . . . **CLC 22, 37**
See also CANR 12; CA 53-56

Akutagawa Ryunosuke
1892-1927 . . . . **TCLC 16**
See also CA 117

Alain-Fournier 1886-1914 . . . . **TCLC 6**
See also Fournier, Henri Alban
See also DLB 65

Alarcon, Pedro Antonio de
1833-1891 . . . . **NCLC 1**

Alas (y Urena), Leopoldo (Enrique Garcia)
1852-1901 . . . . **TCLC 29**
See also CA 113

Albee, Edward (Franklin III)
1928- . . . **CLC 1, 2, 3, 5, 9, 11, 13, 25, 53**
See also CANR 8; CA 5-8R; DLB 7;
CDALB 1941-1968

Alberti, Rafael 1902- . . . . **CLC 7**
See also CA 85-88

Alcott, Amos Bronson 1799-1888 . . **NCLC 1**
See also DLB 1

Alcott, Louisa May 1832-1888 . . . . **NCLC 6**
See also CLR 1; YABC 1; DLB 1, 42, 79;
CDALB 1865-1917

Aldanov, Mark 1887-1957 . . . . **TCLC 23**
See also CA 118

Aldington, Richard 1892-1962 . . . . . . **CLC 49**
See also CA 85-88; DLB 20, 36

Aldiss, Brian W(ilson)
1925- . . . . **CLC 5, 14, 40**
See also CAAS 2; CANR 5; CA 5-8R;
SATA 34; DLB 14

Alegria, Fernando 1918- . . . . **CLC 57**
See also CANR 5; CA 11-12R

Aleixandre, Vicente 1898-1984 . . . **CLC 9, 36**
See also CANR 26; CA 85-88;
obituary CA 114

Alepoudelis, Odysseus 1911-
See Elytis, Odysseus

Aleshkovsky, Yuz 1929- . . . . **CLC 44**
See also CA 121, 128

Alexander, Lloyd (Chudley) 1924- . . **CLC 35**
See also CLR 1, 5; CANR 1; CA 1-4R;
SATA 3, 49; DLB 52

Alger, Horatio, Jr. 1832-1899 . . . . . **NCLC 8**
See also SATA 16; DLB 42

Algren, Nelson 1909-1981 . . . . **CLC 4, 10, 33**
See also CANR 20; CA 13-16R;
obituary CA 103; DLB 9; DLB-Y 81, 82;
CDALB 1941-1968

Alighieri, Dante 1265-1321 . . . . **CMLC 3**

Allard, Janet 1975- . . . . **CLC 59**

Allen, Edward 1948- . . . . **CLC 59**

Allen, Roland 1939-
See Ayckbourn, Alan

Allen, Woody 1935- . . . . **CLC 16, 52**
See also CANR 27; CA 33-36R; DLB 44

Allende, Isabel 1942- . . . . **CLC 39, 57**
See also CA 125

Alleyne, Carla D. 1975?- . . . . **CLC 65**

Allingham, Margery (Louise)
1904-1966 . . . . **CLC 19**
See also CANR 4; CA 5-8R;
obituary CA 25-28R; DLB 77

Allingham, William 1824-1889 . . . **NCLC 25**
See also DLB 35

Allston, Washington 1779-1843 . . . . **NCLC 2**
See also DLB 1

Almedingen, E. M. 1898-1971 . . . . . . **CLC 12**
See also Almedingen, Martha Edith von
See also SATA 3

Almedingen, Martha Edith von 1898-1971
See Almedingen, E. M.
See also CANR 1; CA 1-4R

Alonso, Damaso 1898- . . . . **CLC 14**
See also CA 110; obituary CA 130

Alta 1942- . . . . **CLC 19**
See also CA 57-60

Alter, Robert B(ernard) 1935- . . . . . . **CLC 34**
See also CANR 1; CA 49-52

Alther, Lisa 1944- . . . . **CLC 7, 41**
See also CANR 12; CA 65-68

Altman, Robert 1925- . . . . **CLC 16**
See also CA 73-76

Alvarez, A(lfred) 1929- . . . . **CLC 5, 13**
See also CANR 3; CA 1-4R; DLB 14, 40

Alvarez, Alejandro Rodriguez 1903-1965
See Casona, Alejandro
See also obituary CA 93-96

Amado, Jorge 1912- . . . . **CLC 13, 40**
See also CA 77-80

Ambler, Eric 1909- . . . . **CLC 4, 6, 9**
See also CANR 7; CA 9-12R; DLB 77

Amichai, Yehuda 1924- . . . . . . **CLC 9, 22, 57**
See also CA 85-88

Amiel, Henri Frederic 1821-1881 . . **NCLC 4**

Amis, Kingsley (William)
1922- . . . . . . **CLC 1, 2, 3, 5, 8, 13, 40, 44**
See also CANR 8; CA 9-12R; DLB 15, 27

Amis, Martin 1949- . . . . **CLC 4, 9, 38, 62**
See also CANR 8, 27; CA 65-68; DLB 14

Ammons, A(rchie) R(andolph)
1926- . . . . **CLC 2, 3, 5, 8, 9, 25, 57**
See also CANR 6; CA 9-12R; DLB 5

Anand, Mulk Raj 1905- . . . . **CLC 23**
See also CA 65-68

Anaya, Rudolfo A(lfonso) 1937- . . . . **CLC 23**
See also CAAS 4; CANR 1; CA 45-48;
DLB 82

Andersen, Hans Christian
1805-1875 . . . . **NCLC 7; SSC 6**
See also CLR 6; YABC 1, 1

Anderson, Jessica (Margaret Queale)
19??- . . . . **CLC 37**
See also CANR 4; CA 9-12R

Anderson, Jon (Victor) 1940- . . . . **CLC 9**
See also CANR 20; CA 25-28R

Anderson, Lindsay 1923- . . . . **CLC 20**
See also CA 125

Anderson, Maxwell 1888-1959 . . . . . **TCLC 2**
See also CA 105; DLB 7

Anderson, Poul (William) 1926- . . . . **CLC 15**
See also CAAS 2; CANR 2, 15; CA 1-4R;
SATA 39; DLB 8

Anderson, Robert (Woodruff)
1917- . . . . **CLC 23**
See also CA 21-24R; DLB 7

Anderson, Roberta Joan 1943-
See Mitchell, Joni

Anderson, Sherwood
1876-1941 . . . . . . **TCLC 1, 10, 24; SSC 1**
See also CAAS 3; CA 104, 121; DLB 4, 9;
DLB-DS 1

Andrade, Carlos Drummond de
1902-1987 . . . . **CLC 18**
See also CA 123

Andrewes, Lancelot 1555-1626 . . . . **LC 5**

Andrews, Cicily Fairfield 1892-1983
See West, Rebecca

Andreyev, Leonid (Nikolaevich)
1871-1919 . . . . **TCLC 3**
See also CA 104

Andrezel, Pierre 1885-1962
See Dinesen, Isak; Blixen, Karen
(Christentze Dinesen)

Andric, Ivo 1892-1975 . . . . **CLC 8**
See also CA 81-84; obituary CA 57-60

Angelique, Pierre 1897-1962
See Bataille, Georges

Angell, Roger 1920- . . . . **CLC 26**
See also CANR 13; CA 57-60

Angelou, Maya 1928- . . . . **CLC 12, 35, 64**
See also CANR 19; CA 65-68; SATA 49;
DLB 38

Annensky, Innokenty 1856-1909 . . . **TCLC 14**
See also CA 110

Anouilh, Jean (Marie Lucien Pierre)
1910-1987 . . . . . . **CLC 1, 3, 8, 13, 40, 50**
See also CA 17-20R; obituary CA 123

Anthony, Florence 1947-
See Ai

Anthony (Jacob), Piers 1934- . . . . . . **CLC 35**
See also Jacob, Piers A(nthony)
D(illingham)
See also DLB 8

Browning, Robert
     1812-1889 . . . . NCLC 19; PC 2
     See also YABC 1; DLB 32

Browning, Tod   1882-1962 . . . . CLC 16
     See also obituary CA 117

Bruccoli, Matthew J(oseph)   1931- . . CLC 34
     See also CANR 7; CA 9-12R

Bruce, Lenny   1925-1966 . . . . CLC 21
     See also Schneider, Leonard Alfred

Brunner, John (Kilian Houston)
     1934- . . . . CLC 8, 10
     See also CAAS 8; CANR 2; CA 1-4R

Brutus, Dennis   1924- . . . . CLC 43
     See also CANR 2; CA 49-52

Bryan, C(ourtlandt) D(ixon) B(arnes)
     1936- . . . . CLC 29
     See also CANR 13; CA 73-76

Bryant, William Cullen
     1794-1878 . . . . NCLC 6
     See also DLB 3, 43, 59; CDALB 1640-1865

Bryusov, Valery (Yakovlevich)
     1873-1924 . . . . TCLC 10
     See also CA 107

Buchanan, George   1506-1582 . . . . LC 4

Buchheim, Lothar-Gunther   1918- . . . . CLC 6
     See also CA 85-88

Buchner, (Karl) Georg
     1813-1837 . . . . NCLC 26

Buchwald, Art(hur)   1925- . . . . CLC 33
     See also CANR 21; CA 5-8R; SATA 10

Buck, Pearl S(ydenstricker)
     1892-1973 . . . . CLC 7, 11, 18
     See also CANR 1; CA 1-4R;
        obituary CA 41-44R; SATA 1, 25; DLB 9

Buckler, Ernest   1908-1984. . . . . CLC 13
     See also CAP 1; CA 11-12;
        obituary CA 114; SATA 47

Buckley, Vincent (Thomas)
     1925-1988 . . . . CLC 57
     See also CA 101

Buckley, William F(rank), Jr.
     1925- . . . . CLC 7, 18, 37
     See also CANR 1, 24; CA 1-4R; DLB-Y 80

Buechner, (Carl) Frederick
     1926- . . . . CLC 2, 4, 6, 9
     See also CANR 11; CA 13-16R; DLB-Y 80

Buell, John (Edward)   1927- . . . . CLC 10
     See also CA 1-4R; DLB 53

Buero Vallejo, Antonio   1916- . . . CLC 15, 46
     See also CANR 24; CA 106

Bukowski, Charles   1920- . . . . CLC 2, 5, 9, 41
     See also CA 17-20R; DLB 5

Bulgakov, Mikhail (Afanas'evich)
     1891-1940 . . . . TCLC 2, 16
     See also CA 105

Bullins, Ed   1935- . . . . CLC 1, 5, 7
     See also CANR 24; CA 49-52; DLB 7, 38

Bulwer-Lytton, (Lord) Edward (George Earle
     Lytton)   1803-1873 . . . . NCLC 1
     See also Lytton, Edward Bulwer
     See also DLB 21

Bunin, Ivan (Alexeyevich)
     1870-1953 . . . . TCLC 6; SSC 5
     See also CA 104

Bunting, Basil   1900-1985. . . . CLC 10, 39, 47
     See also CANR 7; CA 53-56;
        obituary CA 115; DLB 20

Bunuel, Luis   1900-1983 . . . . CLC 16
     See also CA 101; obituary CA 110

Bunyan, John   1628-1688 . . . . LC 4
     See also DLB 39

Burgess (Wilson, John) Anthony
     1917- . . . . . CLC 1, 2, 4, 5, 8, 10, 13, 15,
                                          22, 40, 62
     See also Wilson, John (Anthony) Burgess
     See also DLB 14

Burke, Edmund   1729-1797. . . . . LC 7

Burke, Kenneth (Duva)   1897- . . . . CLC 2, 24
     See also CA 5-8R; DLB 45, 63

Burney, Fanny   1752-1840 . . . . NCLC 12
     See also DLB 39

Burns, Robert   1759-1796 . . . . LC 3

Burns, Tex   1908?-
     See L'Amour, Louis (Dearborn)

Burnshaw, Stanley   1906- . . . . . CLC 3, 13, 44
     See also CA 9-12R; DLB 48

Burr, Anne   1937- . . . . CLC 6
     See also CA 25-28R

Burroughs, Edgar Rice
     1875-1950 . . . . TCLC 2, 32
     See also CA 104; SATA 41; DLB 8

Burroughs, William S(eward)
     1914- . . . . CLC 1, 2, 5, 15, 22, 42
     See also CANR 20; CA 9-12R; DLB 2, 8,
        16; DLB-Y 81

Busch, Frederick   1941- . . . CLC 7, 10, 18, 47
     See also CAAS 1; CA 33-36R; DLB 6

Bush, Ronald   19??- . . . . CLC 34

Butler, Octavia E(stelle)   1947- . . . . . CLC 38
     See also CANR 12, 24; CA 73-76; DLB 33

Butler, Samuel   1612-1680 . . . . LC 16
     See also DLB 101

Butler, Samuel   1835-1902 . . . . . . TCLC 1, 33
     See also CA 104; DLB 18, 57

Butor, Michel (Marie Francois)
     1926- . . . . CLC 1, 3, 8, 11, 15
     See also CA 9-12R

Buzo, Alexander   1944- . . . . CLC 61
     See also CANR 17; CA 97-100

Buzzati, Dino   1906-1972 . . . . CLC 36
     See also obituary CA 33-36R

Byars, Betsy   1928- . . . . CLC 35
     See also CLR 1, 16; CANR 18; CA 33-36R;
        SAAS 1; SATA 4, 46; DLB 52

Byatt, A(ntonia) S(usan Drabble)
     1936- . . . . CLC 19, 65
     See also CANR 13, 33; CA 13-16R;
        DLB 14

Byrne, David   1953?- . . . . CLC 26

Byrne, John Keyes   1926-
     See Leonard, Hugh
     See also CA 102

Byron, George Gordon (Noel), Lord Byron
     1788-1824 . . . . NCLC 2, 12

Caballero, Fernan   1796-1877. . . . . NCLC 10

Cabell, James Branch   1879-1958 . . . TCLC 6
     See also CA 105; DLB 9, 78

Cable, George Washington
     1844-1925 . . . . TCLC 4; SSC 4
     See also CA 104; DLB 12, 74

Cabrera Infante, G(uillermo)
     1929- . . . . CLC 5, 25, 45
     See also CANR 29; CA 85-88

Cage, John (Milton, Jr.)   1912- . . . . . CLC 41
     See also CANR 9; CA 13-16R

Cain, G.   1929-
     See Cabrera Infante, G(uillermo)

Cain, James M(allahan)
     1892-1977 . . . . CLC 3, 11, 28
     See also CANR 8; CA 17-20R;
        obituary CA 73-76

Caldwell, Erskine (Preston)
     1903-1987 . . . . CLC 1, 8, 14, 50, 60
     See also CAAS 1; CANR 2; CA 1-4R;
        obituary CA 121; DLB 9, 86

Caldwell, (Janet Miriam) Taylor (Holland)
     1900-1985 . . . . CLC 2, 28, 39
     See also CANR 5; CA 5-8R;
        obituary CA 116

Calhoun, John Caldwell
     1782-1850 . . . . NCLC 15
     See also DLB 3

Calisher, Hortense   1911- . . . . CLC 2, 4, 8, 38
     See also CANR 1, 22; CA 1-4R; DLB 2

Callaghan, Morley (Edward)
     1903-1990 . . . . CLC 3, 14, 41, 65
     See also CANR 33; CA 9-12R;
        obituary CA 132; DLB 68

Calvino, Italo
     1923-1985 . . . . CLC 5, 8, 11, 22, 33, 39;
                                           SSC 3
     See also CANR 23; CA 85-88;
        obituary CA 116

Cameron, Carey   1952- . . . . CLC 59

Cameron, Peter   1959- . . . . CLC 44
     See also CA 125

Campana, Dino   1885-1932 . . . . TCLC 20
     See also CA 117

Campbell, John W(ood), Jr.
     1910-1971 . . . . CLC 32
     See also CAP 2; CA 21-22;
        obituary CA 29-32R; DLB 8

Campbell, (John) Ramsey   1946- . . . . CLC 42
     See also CANR 7; CA 57-60

Campbell, (Ignatius) Roy (Dunnachie)
     1901-1957 . . . . TCLC 5
     See also CA 104; DLB 20

Campbell, Thomas   1777-1844 . . . . NCLC 19

Campbell, (William) Wilfred
     1861-1918 . . . . TCLC 9
     See also CA 106

Camus, Albert
     1913-1960 . . . CLC 1, 2, 4, 9, 11, 14, 32,
                                             63
     See also CA 89-92; DLB 72

Canby, Vincent   1924- . . . . CLC 13
     See also CA 81-84

Canetti, Elias   1905- . . . . CLC 3, 14, 25
     See also CANR 23; CA 21-24R; DLB 85

Canin, Ethan   1960- . . . . CLC 55

Cape, Judith   1916-
     See Page, P(atricia) K(athleen)

Author Index

Author Index

Drummond de Andrade, Carlos 1902-1987
See Andrade, Carlos Drummond de

Drury, Allen (Stuart) 1918-........ CLC 37
See also CANR 18; CA 57-60

Dryden, John 1631-1700 .... LC 3

Duberman, Martin 1930-.......... CLC 8
See also CANR 2; CA 1-4R

Dubie, Norman (Evans, Jr.) 1945- .. CLC 36
See also CANR 12; CA 69-72

Du Bois, W(illiam) E(dward) B(urghardt)
1868-1963 .... CLC 1, 2, 13, 64
See also CA 85-88; SATA 42; DLB 47, 50,
91; CDALB 1865-1917

Dubus, Andre 1936- .... CLC 13, 36
See also CANR 17; CA 21-24R

Ducasse, Isidore Lucien 1846-1870
See Lautreamont, Comte de

Duclos, Charles Pinot 1704-1772 ..... LC 1

Dudek, Louis 1918- .... CLC 11, 19
See also CANR 1; CA 45-48; DLB 88

Dudevant, Amandine Aurore Lucile Dupin
1804-1876
See Sand, George

Duerrenmatt, Friedrich
1921- .... CLC 1, 4, 8, 11, 15, 43
See also CA 17-20R; DLB 69

Duffy, Bruce 19??- .... CLC 50

Duffy, Maureen 1933- .... CLC 37
See also CA 25-28R; DLB 14

Dugan, Alan 1923- .... CLC 2, 6
See also CA 81-84; DLB 5

Duhamel, Georges 1884-1966 .... CLC 8
See also CA 81-84; obituary CA 25-28R;
DLB 65

Dujardin, Edouard (Emile Louis)
1861-1949 .... TCLC 13
See also CA 109

Duke, Raoul 1939-
See Thompson, Hunter S(tockton)

Dumas, Alexandre (Davy de la Pailleterie)
(pere) 1802-1870........... NCLC 11
See also SATA 18

Dumas, Alexandre (fils)
1824-1895 .... NCLC 9; DC 1

Dumas, Henry 1918-1968 .... CLC 62

Dumas, Henry (L.) 1934-1968....... CLC 6
See also CA 85-88; DLB 41

Du Maurier, Daphne 1907- ... CLC 6, 11, 59
See also CANR 6; CA 5-8R;
obituary CA 128; SATA 27

Dunbar, Paul Laurence
1872-1906 .... TCLC 2, 12
See also CA 104, 124; SATA 34; DLB 50,
54, 78; CDALB 1865-1917

Duncan (Steinmetz Arquette), Lois
1934- .... CLC 26
See also Arquette, Lois S(teinmetz)
See also CANR 2; CA 1-4R; SAAS 2;
SATA 1, 36

Duncan, Robert (Edward)
1919-1988 ... CLC 1, 2, 4, 7, 15, 41, 55;
PC 2
See also CANR 28; CA 9-12R;
obituary CA 124; DLB 5, 16

Dunlap, William 1766-1839 .... NCLC 2
See also DLB 30, 37, 59

Dunn, Douglas (Eaglesham)
1942- .... CLC 6, 40
See also CANR 2; CA 45-48; DLB 40

Dunn, Elsie 1893-1963
See Scott, Evelyn

Dunn, Stephen 1939- .... CLC 36
See also CANR 12; CA 33-36R

Dunne, Finley Peter 1867-1936.... TCLC 28
See also CA 108; DLB 11, 23

Dunne, John Gregory 1932-........ CLC 28
See also CANR 14; CA 25-28R; DLB-Y 80

Dunsany, Lord (Edward John Moreton Drax
Plunkett) 1878-1957......... TCLC 2
See also CA 104; DLB 10

Durang, Christopher (Ferdinand)
1949- .... CLC 27, 38
See also CA 105

Duras, Marguerite
1914- .... CLC 3, 6, 11, 20, 34, 40
See also CA 25-28R; DLB 83

Durban, Pam 1947-................ CLC 39
See also CA 123

Durcan, Paul 1944-................ CLC 43

Durrell, Lawrence (George)
1912-1990 .... CLC 1, 4, 6, 8, 13, 27, 41
See also CA 9-12R; DLB 15, 27

Durrenmatt, Friedrich
1921- .... CLC 1, 4, 8, 11, 15, 43
See also Duerrenmatt, Friedrich
See also DLB 69

Dutt, Toru 1856-1877.......... NCLC 29

Dwight, Timothy 1752-1817...... NCLC 13
See also DLB 37

Dworkin, Andrea 1946- .... CLC 43
See also CANR 16; CA 77-80

Dylan, Bob 1941- .... CLC 3, 4, 6, 12
See also CA 41-44R; DLB 16

Eagleton, Terry 1943-............. CLC 63

East, Michael 1916-
See West, Morris L.

Eastlake, William (Derry) 1917-..... CLC 8
See also CAAS 1; CANR 5; CA 5-8R;
DLB 6

Eberhart, Richard 1904-... CLC 3, 11, 19, 56
See also CANR 2; CA 1-4R; DLB 48;
CDALB 1941-1968

Eberstadt, Fernanda 1960-......... CLC 39

Echegaray (y Eizaguirre), Jose (Maria Waldo)
1832-1916 .... TCLC 4
See also CA 104

Echeverria, (Jose) Esteban (Antonino)
1805-1851 .... NCLC 18

Eckert, Allan W. 1931- .... CLC 17
See also CANR 14; CA 13-16R; SATA 27,
29

Eco, Umberto 1932-........... CLC 28, 60
See also CANR 12; CA 77-80

Eddison, E(ric) R(ucker)
1882-1945 .... TCLC 15
See also CA 109

Edel, Leon (Joseph) 1907-...... CLC 29, 34
See also CANR 1, 22; CA 1-4R

Eden, Emily 1797-1869 .... NCLC 10

Edgar, David 1948-............... CLC 42
See also CANR 12; CA 57-60; DLB 13

Edgerton, Clyde 1944- .... CLC 39
See also CA 118

Edgeworth, Maria 1767-1849...... NCLC 1
See also SATA 21

Edmonds, Helen (Woods) 1904-1968
See Kavan, Anna
See also CA 5-8R; obituary CA 25-28R

Edmonds, Walter D(umaux) 1903- .. CLC 35
See also CANR 2; CA 5-8R; SAAS 4;
SATA 1, 27; DLB 9

Edson, Russell 1905- .... CLC 13
See also CA 33-36R

Edwards, G(erald) B(asil)
1899-1976 .... CLC 25
See also obituary CA 110

Edwards, Gus 1939-.............. CLC 43
See also CA 108

Edwards, Jonathan 1703-1758........ LC 7
See also DLB 24

Ehle, John (Marsden, Jr.) 1925-.... CLC 27
See also CA 9-12R

Ehrenburg, Ilya (Grigoryevich)
1891-1967 .... CLC 18, 34, 62
See also CA 102; obituary CA 25-28R

Eich, Guenter 1907-1971
See also CA 111; obituary CA 93-96

Eich, Gunter 1907-1971........... CLC 15
See also Eich, Guenter
See also DLB 69

Eichendorff, Joseph Freiherr von
1788-1857 .... NCLC 8
See also DLB 90

Eigner, Larry 1927- .... CLC 9
See also Eigner, Laurence (Joel)
See also DLB 5

Eigner, Laurence (Joel) 1927-
See Eigner, Larry
See also CANR 6; CA 9-12R

Eiseley, Loren (Corey) 1907-1977.... CLC 7
See also CANR 6; CA 1-4R;
obituary CA 73-76

Eisenstadt, Jill 1963- .... CLC 50

Ekeloef, Gunnar (Bengt) 1907-1968
See Ekelof, Gunnar (Bengt)
See also obituary CA 25-28R

Ekelof, Gunnar (Bengt) 1907-1968 .. CLC 27
See also Ekeloef, Gunnar (Bengt)

Ekwensi, Cyprian (Odiatu Duaka)
1921- .... CLC 4
See also CANR 18; CA 29-32R

Eliade, Mircea 1907-1986 .... CLC 19
See also CA 65-68; obituary CA 119

Eliot, George 1819-1880.... NCLC 4, 13, 23
See also DLB 21, 35, 55

Eliot, John 1604-1690 .... LC 5
See also DLB 24

Federspiel, J(urg) F. 1931-........ **CLC 42**

Feiffer, Jules 1929-.......... **CLC 2, 8, 64**
See also CANR 30; CA 17-20R; SATA 8,
   61; DLB 7, 44; AAYA 3

Feinberg, David B. 1956-.......... **CLC 59**

Feinstein, Elaine 1930-............ **CLC 36**
See also CAAS 1; CA 69-72; DLB 14, 40

Feke, Gilbert David 1976?-......... **CLC 65**

Feldman, Irving (Mordecai) 1928-.... **CLC 7**
See also CANR 1; CA 1-4R

Fellini, Federico 1920-............ **CLC 16**
See also CA 65-68

Felsen, Gregor 1916-
See Felsen, Henry Gregor

Felsen, Henry Gregor 1916- .... **CLC 17**
See also CANR 1; CA 1-4R; SAAS 2;
   SATA 1

Fenton, James (Martin) 1949-...... **CLC 32**
See also CA 102; DLB 40

Ferber, Edna 1887-1968........... **CLC 18**
See also CA 5-8R; obituary CA 25-28R;
   SATA 7; DLB 9, 28, 86

Ferlinghetti, Lawrence (Monsanto)
   1919?- .... **CLC 2, 6, 10, 27; PC 1**
See also CANR 3; CA 5-8R; DLB 5, 16;
   CDALB 1941-1968

Ferrier, Susan (Edmonstone)
   1782-1854 .... **NCLC 8**

Ferrigno, Robert 19??-............ **CLC 65**

Feuchtwanger, Lion 1884-1958 ..... **TCLC 3**
See also CA 104; DLB 66

Feydeau, Georges 1862-1921...... **TCLC 22**
See also CA 113

Ficino, Marsilio 1433-1499 .... **LC 12**

Fiedler, Leslie A(aron)
   1917- .... **CLC 4, 13, 24**
See also CANR 7; CA 9-12R; DLB 28, 67

Field, Andrew 1938-.............. **CLC 44**
See also CANR 25; CA 97-100

Field, Eugene 1850-1895 .... **NCLC 3**
See also SATA 16; DLB 21, 23, 42

Fielding, Henry 1707-1754 .... **LC 1**
See also DLB 39, 84

Fielding, Sarah 1710-1768 .... **LC 1**
See also DLB 39

Fierstein, Harvey 1954-........... **CLC 33**
See also CA 123, 129

Figes, Eva 1932-................. **CLC 31**
See also CANR 4; CA 53-56; DLB 14

Finch, Robert (Duer Claydon)
   1900- .... **CLC 18**
See also CANR 9, 24; CA 57-60; DLB 88

Findley, Timothy 1930- .... **CLC 27**
See also CANR 12; CA 25-28R; DLB 53

Fink, Janis 1951-
See Ian, Janis

Firbank, Louis 1944-
See Reed, Lou
See also CA 117

Firbank, (Arthur Annesley) Ronald
   1886-1926 .... **TCLC 1**
See also CA 104; DLB 36

Fisher, Roy 1930-................ **CLC 25**
See also CANR 16; CA 81-84; DLB 40

Fisher, Rudolph 1897-1934 .... **TCLC 11**
See also CA 107; DLB 51

Fisher, Vardis (Alvero) 1895-1968.... **CLC 7**
See also CA 5-8R; obituary CA 25-28R;
   DLB 9

FitzGerald, Edward 1809-1883 .... **NCLC 9**
See also DLB 32

Fitzgerald, F(rancis) Scott (Key)
   1896-1940 .... **TCLC 1, 6, 14, 28; SSC 6**
See also CA 110, 123; DLB 4, 9, 86;
   DLB-Y 81; DLB-DS 1;
   CDALB 1917-1929

Fitzgerald, Penelope 1916-... **CLC 19, 51, 61**
See also CAAS 10; CA 85-88,; DLB 14

Fitzgerald, Robert (Stuart)
   1910-1985 .... **CLC 39**
See also CANR 1; CA 2R;
   obituary CA 114; DLB-Y 80

FitzGerald, Robert D(avid) 1902-... **CLC 19**
See also CA 17-20R

Flanagan, Thomas (James Bonner)
   1923-.................... **CLC 25, 52**
See also CA 108; DLB-Y 80

Flaubert, Gustave
   1821-1880 .... **NCLC 2, 10, 19**

Fleming, Ian (Lancaster)
   1908-1964 .... **CLC 3, 30**
See also CA 5-8R; SATA 9; DLB 87

Fleming, Thomas J(ames) 1927- .... **CLC 37**
See also CANR 10; CA 5-8R; SATA 8

Fletcher, John Gould 1886-1950 ... **TCLC 35**
See also CA 107; DLB 4, 45

Flieg, Hellmuth
See Heym, Stefan

Flying Officer X 1905-1974
See Bates, H(erbert) E(rnest)

Fo, Dario 1929-.................. **CLC 32**
See also CA 116

Follett, Ken(neth Martin) 1949- .... **CLC 18**
See also CANR 13; CA 81-84; DLB-Y 81

Fontane, Theodor 1819-1898..... **NCLC 26**

Foote, Horton 1916-.............. **CLC 51**
See also CA 73-76; DLB 26

Forbes, Esther 1891-1967.......... **CLC 12**
See also CAP 1; CA 13-14;
   obituary CA 25-28R; SATA 2; DLB 22

Forche, Carolyn 1950-............ **CLC 25**
See also CA 109, 117; DLB 5

Ford, Ford Madox
   1873-1939 .... **TCLC 1, 15, 39**
See also CA 104; DLB 34

Ford, John 1895-1973............. **CLC 16**
See also obituary CA 45-48

Ford, Richard 1944-.............. **CLC 46**
See also CANR 11; CA 69-72

Foreman, Richard 1937-.......... **CLC 50**
See also CA 65-68

Forester, C(ecil) S(cott)
   1899-1966 .... **CLC 35**
See also CA 73-76; obituary CA 25-28R;
   SATA 13

Forman, James D(ouglas) 1932- .... **CLC 21**
See also CANR 4, 19; CA 9-12R; SATA 8,
   21

Fornes, Maria Irene 1930-...... **CLC 39, 61**
See also CANR 28; CA 25-28R; DLB 7

Forrest, Leon 1937- .... **CLC 4**
See also CAAS 7; CA 89-92; DLB 33

Forster, E(dward) M(organ)
   1879-1970 .... **CLC 1, 2, 3, 4, 9, 10, 13,**
                                      15, 22, 45
See also CAP 1; CA 13-14;
   obituary CA 25-28R; SATA 57; DLB 34

Forster, John 1812-1876 .... **NCLC 11**

Forsyth, Frederick 1938-...... **CLC 2, 5, 36**
See also CA 85-88; DLB 87

Forten (Grimke), Charlotte L(ottie)
   1837-1914 .... **TCLC 16**
See also Grimke, Charlotte L(ottie) Forten
See also DLB 50

Foscolo, Ugo 1778-1827.......... **NCLC 8**

Fosse, Bob 1925-1987............. **CLC 20**
See also Fosse, Robert Louis

Fosse, Robert Louis 1925-1987
See Bob Fosse
See also CA 110, 123

Foster, Stephen Collins
   1826-1864 .... **NCLC 26**

Foucault, Michel 1926-1984 .... **CLC 31, 34**
See also CANR 23; CA 105;
   obituary CA 113

Fouque, Friedrich (Heinrich Karl) de La
   Motte** 1777-1843 .... **NCLC 2**

Fournier, Henri Alban 1886-1914
See Alain-Fournier
See also CA 104

Fournier, Pierre 1916-............ **CLC 11**
See also Gascar, Pierre
See also CANR 16; CA 89-92

Fowles, John (Robert)
   1926- .... **CLC 1, 2, 3, 4, 6, 9, 10, 15, 33**
See also CANR 25; CA 5-8R; SATA 22;
   DLB 14

Fox, Paula 1923-................. **CLC 2, 8**
See also CLR 1; CANR 20; CA 73-76;
   SATA 17; DLB 52

Fox, William Price (Jr.) 1926- ..... **CLC 22**
See also CANR 11; CA 17-20R; DLB 2;
   DLB-Y 81

Foxe, John 1516?-1587............. **LC 14**

Frame (Clutha), Janet (Paterson)
   1924- .... **CLC 2, 3, 6, 22**
See also Clutha, Janet Paterson Frame

France, Anatole 1844-1924 .... **TCLC 9**
See also Thibault, Jacques Anatole Francois

Francis, Claude 19??-............. **CLC 50**

Francis, Dick 1920- .... **CLC 2, 22, 42**
See also CANR 9; CA 5-8R; DLB 87

Francis, Robert (Churchill)
   1901-1987 .... **CLC 15**
See also CANR 1; CA 1-4R;
   obituary CA 123

Frank, Anne 1929-1945 .... **TCLC 17**
See also CA 113; SATA 42

Gordon, Adam Lindsay
1833-1870 . . . . NCLC 21

Gordon, Caroline
1895-1981 . . . . CLC 6, 13, 29
See also CAP 1; CA 11-12;
obituary CA 103; DLB 4, 9; DLB-Y 81

Gordon, Charles William 1860-1937
See Conner, Ralph
See also CA 109

Gordon, Mary (Catherine)
1949- . . . . CLC 13, 22
See also CA 102; DLB 6; DLB-Y 81

Gordon, Sol 1923- . . . . CLC 26
See also CANR 4; CA 53-56; SATA 11

Gordone, Charles 1925- . . . . CLC 1, 4
See also CA 93-96; DLB 7

Gorenko, Anna Andreyevna 1889?-1966
See Akhmatova, Anna

Gorky, Maxim 1868-1936 . . . . TCLC 8
See also Peshkov, Alexei Maximovich

Goryan, Sirak 1908-1981
See Saroyan, William

Gosse, Edmund (William)
1849-1928 . . . . TCLC 28
See also CA 117; DLB 57

Gotlieb, Phyllis (Fay Bloom)
1926- . . . . CLC 18
See also CANR 7; CA 13-16R; DLB 88

Gould, Lois 1938?- . . . . CLC 4, 10
See also CA 77-80

Gourmont, Remy de 1858-1915 . . . . TCLC 17
See also CA 109

Govier, Katherine 1948- . . . . CLC 51
See also CANR 18; CA 101

Goyen, (Charles) William
1915-1983 . . . . CLC 5, 8, 14, 40
See also CANR 6; CA 5-8R;
obituary CA 110; DLB 2; DLB-Y 83

Goytisolo, Juan 1931- . . . . CLC 5, 10, 23
See also CA 85-88

Gozzi, (Conte) Carlo 1720-1806 . . NCLC 23

Grabbe, Christian Dietrich
1801-1836 . . . . NCLC 2

Grace, Patricia 1937- . . . . CLC 56

Gracian y Morales, Baltasar
1601-1658 . . . . LC 15

Gracq, Julien 1910- . . . . CLC 11, 48
See also Poirier, Louis
See also DLB 83

Grade, Chaim 1910-1982 . . . . CLC 10
See also CA 93-96; obituary CA 107

Graham, Jorie 1951- . . . . CLC 48
See also CA 111

Graham, R(obert) B(ontine) Cunninghame
1852-1936 . . . . TCLC 19

Graham, W(illiam) S(ydney)
1918-1986 . . . . CLC 29
See also CA 73-76; obituary CA 118;
DLB 20

Graham, Winston (Mawdsley)
1910- . . . . CLC 23
See also CANR 2, 22; CA 49-52;
obituary CA 118

Granville-Barker, Harley
1877-1946 . . . . TCLC 2
See also CA 104

Grass, Gunter (Wilhelm)
1927- . . CLC 1, 2, 4, 6, 11, 15, 22, 32, 49
See also CANR 20; CA 13-16R; DLB 75

Grau, Shirley Ann 1929- . . . . CLC 4, 9
See also CANR 22; CA 89-92; DLB 2

Graves, Richard Perceval 1945- . . . . CLC 44
See also CANR 9, 26; CA 65-68

Graves, Robert (von Ranke)
1895-1985 . . . CLC 1, 2, 6, 11, 39, 44, 45
See also CANR 5; CA 5-8R;
obituary CA 117; SATA 45; DLB 20;
DLB-Y 85

Gray, Alasdair 1934- . . . . CLC 41
See also CA 123

Gray, Amlin 1946- . . . . CLC 29

Gray, Francine du Plessix 1930- . . . . CLC 22
See also CAAS 2; CANR 11; CA 61-64

Gray, John (Henry) 1866-1934 . . . . TCLC 19
See also CA 119

Gray, Simon (James Holliday)
1936- . . . . CLC 9, 14, 36
See also CAAS 3; CA 21-24R; DLB 13

Gray, Spalding 1941- . . . . CLC 49

Gray, Thomas 1716-1771 . . . . LC 4; PC 2

Grayson, Richard (A.) 1951- . . . . CLC 38
See also CANR 14; CA 85-88

Greeley, Andrew M(oran) 1928- . . . . CLC 28
See also CAAS 7; CANR 7; CA 5-8R

Green, Hannah 1932- . . . . CLC 3, 7, 30
See also Greenberg, Joanne
See also CA 73-76

Green, Henry 1905-1974 . . . . CLC 2, 13
See also Yorke, Henry Vincent
See also DLB 15

Green, Julien (Hartridge) 1900- . . CLC 3, 11
See also CA 21-24R; DLB 4, 72

Green, Paul (Eliot) 1894-1981 . . . . . . CLC 25
See also CANR 3; CA 5-8R;
obituary CA 103; DLB 7, 9; DLB-Y 81

Greenberg, Ivan 1908-1973
See Rahv, Philip
See also CA 85-88

Greenberg, Joanne (Goldenberg)
1932- . . . . CLC 3, 7, 30
See also Green, Hannah
See also CANR 14; CA 5-8R; SATA 25

Greenberg, Richard 1959?- . . . . CLC 57

Greene, Bette 1934- . . . . CLC 30
See also CLR 2; CANR 4; CA 53-56;
SATA 8

Greene, Gael 19??- . . . . CLC 8
See also CANR 10; CA 13-16R

Greene, Graham (Henry)
1904- . . . . . CLC 1, 3, 6, 9, 14, 18, 27, 37
See also CA 13-16R; SATA 20; DLB 13, 15;
DLB-Y 85

Gregor, Arthur 1923- . . . . CLC 9
See also CANR 11; CA 25-28R; SATA 36

Gregory, Lady (Isabella Augusta Persse)
1852-1932 . . . . TCLC 1
See also CA 104; DLB 10

Grendon, Stephen 1909-1971
See Derleth, August (William)

Grenville, Kate 1950- . . . . CLC 61
See also CA 118

Greve, Felix Paul Berthold Friedrich
1879-1948
See Grove, Frederick Philip
See also CA 104

Grey, (Pearl) Zane 1872?-1939 . . . . . TCLC 6
See also CA 104; DLB 9

Grieg, (Johan) Nordahl (Brun)
1902-1943 . . . . TCLC 10
See also CA 107

Grieve, C(hristopher) M(urray) 1892-1978
See MacDiarmid, Hugh
See also CA 5-8R; obituary CA 85-88

Griffin, Gerald 1803-1840 . . . . NCLC 7

Griffin, Peter 1942- . . . . CLC 39

Griffiths, Trevor 1935- . . . . CLC 13, 52
See also CA 97-100; DLB 13

Grigson, Geoffrey (Edward Harvey)
1905-1985 . . . . CLC 7, 39
See also CANR 20; CA 25-28R;
obituary CA 118; DLB 27

Grillparzer, Franz 1791-1872 . . . . . . NCLC 1

Grimke, Charlotte L(ottie) Forten 1837-1914
See Forten (Grimke), Charlotte L(ottie)
See also CA 117, 124

Grimm, Jakob (Ludwig) Karl
1785-1863 . . . . NCLC 3
See also SATA 22; DLB 90

Grimm, Wilhelm Karl 1786-1859 . . NCLC 3
See also SATA 22; DLB 90

Grimmelshausen, Johann Jakob Christoffel
von 1621-1676 . . . . LC 6

Grindel, Eugene 1895-1952
See also CA 104

Grossman, Vasily (Semenovich)
1905-1964 . . . . CLC 41
See also CA 124, 130

Grove, Frederick Philip
1879-1948 . . . . TCLC 4
See also Greve, Felix Paul Berthold
Friedrich

Grumbach, Doris (Isaac)
1918- . . . . CLC 13, 22, 64
See also CAAS 2; CANR 9; CA 5-8R

Grundtvig, Nicolai Frederik Severin
1783-1872 . . . . NCLC 1

Grunwald, Lisa 1959- . . . . CLC 44
See also CA 120

Guare, John 1938- . . . . CLC 8, 14, 29
See also CANR 21; CA 73-76; DLB 7

Gudjonsson, Halldor Kiljan 1902-
See Laxness, Halldor (Kiljan)
See also CA 103

Guest, Barbara 1920- . . . . CLC 34
See also CANR 11; CA 25-28R; DLB 5

Guest, Judith (Ann) 1936- . . . . CLC 8, 30
See also CANR 15; CA 77-80

Guild, Nicholas M. 1944- . . . . CLC 33
See also CA 93-96

Guillen, Jorge 1893-1984 . . . . CLC 11
See also CA 89-92; obituary CA 112

Guillen, Nicolas 1902-1989 . . . . **CLC 48**
See also CA 116, 125; obituary CA 129

Guillevic, (Eugene) 1907- . . . . **CLC 33**
See also CA 93-96

Guiraldes, Ricardo 1886-1927 . . . . . **TCLC 39**

Gunn, Bill 1934-1989 . . . . **CLC 5**
See also Gunn, William Harrison
See also DLB 38

Gunn, Thom(son William)
1929- . . . . **CLC 3, 6, 18, 32**
See also CANR 9; CA 17-20R; DLB 27

Gunn, William Harrison 1934-1989
See Gunn, Bill
See also CANR 12, 25; CA 13-16R;
obituary CA 128

Gurney, A(lbert) R(amsdell), Jr.
1930- . . . . **CLC 32, 50, 54**
See also CA 77-80

Gurney, Ivor (Bertie) 1890-1937 . . . **TCLC 33**

Gustafson, Ralph (Barker) 1909- . . . . **CLC 36**
See also CANR 8; CA 21-24R; DLB 88

Guthrie, A(lfred) B(ertram), Jr.
1901- . . . . **CLC 23**
See also CA 57-60; DLB 6

Guthrie, Woodrow Wilson 1912-1967
See Guthrie, Woody
See also CA 113; obituary CA 93-96

Guthrie, Woody 1912-1967 . . . . **CLC 35**
See also Guthrie, Woodrow Wilson

Guy, Rosa (Cuthbert) 1928- . . . . **CLC 26**
See also CLR 13; CANR 14; CA 17-20R;
SATA 14; DLB 33

Haavikko, Paavo (Juhani)
1931- . . . . **CLC 18, 34**
See also CA 106

Hacker, Marilyn 1942- . . . . **CLC 5, 9, 23**
See also CA 77-80

Haggard, (Sir) H(enry) Rider
1856-1925 . . . . **TCLC 11**
See also CA 108; SATA 16; DLB 70

Haig-Brown, Roderick L(angmere)
1908-1976 . . . . **CLC 21**
See also CANR 4; CA 5-8R;
obituary CA 69-72; SATA 12; DLB 88

Hailey, Arthur 1920- . . . . **CLC 5**
See also CANR 2; CA 1-4R; DLB-Y 82

Hailey, Elizabeth Forsythe 1938- . . . **CLC 40**
See also CAAS 1; CANR 15; CA 93-96

Haines, John 1924- . . . . **CLC 58**
See also CANR 13; CA 19-20R; DLB 5

Haldeman, Joe 1943- . . . . **CLC 61**
See also CA 53-56; DLB 8

Haley, Alex (Palmer) 1921- . . . . . . **CLC 8, 12**
See also CA 77-80; DLB 38

Haliburton, Thomas Chandler
1796-1865 . . . . **NCLC 15**
See also DLB 11

Hall, Donald (Andrew, Jr.)
1928- . . . . **CLC 1, 13, 37, 59**
See also CAAS 7; CANR 2; CA 5-8R;
SATA 23; DLB 5

Hall, James Norman 1887-1951 . . . **TCLC 23**
See also CA 123; SATA 21

Hall, (Marguerite) Radclyffe
1886-1943 . . . . **TCLC 12**
See also CA 110

Hall, Rodney 1935- . . . . **CLC 51**
See also CA 109

Halpern, Daniel 1945- . . . . **CLC 14**
See also CA 33-36R

Hamburger, Michael (Peter Leopold)
1924- . . . . **CLC 5, 14**
See also CAAS 4; CANR 2; CA 5-8R;
DLB 27

Hamill, Pete 1935- . . . . **CLC 10**
See also CANR 18; CA 25-28R

Hamilton, Edmond 1904-1977 . . . . **CLC 1**
See also CANR 3; CA 1-4R; DLB 8

Hamilton, Gail 1911-
See Corcoran, Barbara

Hamilton, Ian 1938- . . . . **CLC 55**
See also CA 106; DLB 40

Hamilton, Mollie 1909?-
See Kaye, M(ary) M(argaret)

Hamilton, (Anthony Walter) Patrick
1904-1962 . . . . **CLC 51**
See also obituary CA 113; DLB 10

Hamilton, Virginia (Esther) 1936- . . . **CLC 26**
See also CLR 1, 11; CANR 20; CA 25-28R;
SATA 4; DLB 33, 52

Hammett, (Samuel) Dashiell
1894-1961 . . . . **CLC 3, 5, 10, 19, 47**
See also CA 81-84; DLB-DS 6

Hammon, Jupiter 1711?-1800? . . . . **NCLC 5**
See also DLB 31, 50

Hamner, Earl (Henry), Jr. 1923- . . . **CLC 12**
See also CA 73-76; DLB 6

Hampton, Christopher (James)
1946- . . . . **CLC 4**
See also CA 25-28R; DLB 13

Hamsun, Knut 1859-1952 . . . . . . **TCLC 2, 14**
See also Pedersen, Knut

Handke, Peter 1942- . . **CLC 5, 8, 10, 15, 38**
See also CA 77-80; DLB 85

Hanley, James 1901-1985 . . . **CLC 3, 5, 8, 13**
See also CA 73-76; obituary CA 117

Hannah, Barry 1942- . . . . **CLC 23, 38**
See also CA 108, 110; DLB 6

Hansberry, Lorraine (Vivian)
1930-1965 . . . . **CLC 17, 62**
See also CA 109; obituary CA 25-28R;
CABS 3; DLB 7, 38; CDALB 1941-1968

Hansen, Joseph 1923- . . . . **CLC 38**
See also CANR 16; CA 29-32R

Hansen, Martin 1909-1955 . . . . **TCLC 32**

Hanson, Kenneth O(stlin) 1922- . . . . **CLC 13**
See also CANR 7; CA 53-56

Hardenberg, Friedrich (Leopold Freiherr) von
1772-1801
See Novalis

Hardwick, Elizabeth 1916- . . . . **CLC 13**
See also CANR 3; CA 5-8R; DLB 6

Hardy, Thomas
1840-1928 . . . **TCLC 4, 10, 18, 32; SSC 2**
See also CA 104, 123; SATA 25; DLB 18,
19

Hare, David 1947- . . . . **CLC 29, 58**
See also CA 97-100; DLB 13

Harlan, Louis R(udolph) 1922- . . . . . **CLC 34**
See also CANR 25; CA 21-24R

Harling, Robert 1951?- . . . . **CLC 53**

Harmon, William (Ruth) 1938- . . . . . **CLC 38**
See also CANR 14; CA 33-36R

Harper, Frances Ellen Watkins
1825-1911 . . . . **TCLC 14**
See also CA 111, 125; DLB 50

Harper, Michael S(teven) 1938- . . **CLC 7, 22**
See also CANR 24; CA 33-36R; DLB 41

Harris, Christie (Lucy Irwin)
1907- . . . . **CLC 12**
See also CANR 6; CA 5-8R; SATA 6;
DLB 88

Harris, Frank 1856-1931 . . . . **TCLC 24**
See also CAAS 1; CA 109

Harris, George Washington
1814-1869 . . . . **NCLC 23**
See also DLB 3, 11

Harris, Joel Chandler 1848-1908 . . . **TCLC 2**
See also YABC 1; CA 104; DLB 11, 23, 42,
78, 91

Harris, John (Wyndham Parkes Lucas)
Beynon 1903-1969 . . . . **CLC 19**
See also Wyndham, John
See also CA 102; obituary CA 89-92

Harris, MacDonald 1921- . . . . **CLC 9**
See also Heiney, Donald (William)

Harris, Mark 1922- . . . . **CLC 19**
See also CAAS 3; CANR 2; CA 5-8R;
DLB 2; DLB-Y 80

Harris, (Theodore) Wilson 1921- . . . . **CLC 25**
See also CANR 11, 27; CA 65-68

Harrison, Harry (Max) 1925- . . . . . . **CLC 42**
See also CANR 5, 21; CA 1-4R; SATA 4;
DLB 8

Harrison, James (Thomas) 1937-
See Harrison, Jim
See also CANR 8; CA 13-16R

Harrison, Jim 1937- . . . . **CLC 6, 14, 33**
See also Harrison, James (Thomas)
See also DLB-Y 82

Harrison, Tony 1937- . . . . **CLC 43**
See also CA 65-68; DLB 40

Harriss, Will(ard Irvin) 1922- . . . . . . **CLC 34**
See also CA 111

Harte, (Francis) Bret(t)
1836?-1902 . . . . **TCLC 1, 25**
See also CA 104; SATA 26; DLB 12, 64,
74, 79; CDALB 1865-1917

Hartley, L(eslie) P(oles)
1895-1972 . . . . **CLC 2, 22**
See also CA 45-48; obituary CA 37-40R;
DLB 15

Hartman, Geoffrey H. 1929- . . . . **CLC 27**
See also CA 117, 125; DLB 67

Haruf, Kent 19??- . . . . **CLC 34**

Harwood, Ronald 1934- . . . . **CLC 32**
See also CANR 4; CA 1-4R; DLB 13

Hasek, Jaroslav (Matej Frantisek)
1883-1923 . . . . **TCLC 4**
See also CA 104, 129

Hass, Robert 1941-............ **CLC 18, 39**
See also CANR 30; CA 111

Hastings, Selina 19??- .... **CLC 44**

Hauptmann, Gerhart (Johann Robert)
1862-1946 .... **TCLC 4**
See also CA 104; DLB 66

Havel, Vaclav 1936-........ **CLC 25, 58, 65**
See also CA 104

Haviaras, Stratis 1935- .... **CLC 33**
See also CA 105

Hawkes, John (Clendennin Burne, Jr.)
1925- ...... **CLC 1, 2, 3, 4, 7, 9, 14, 15,
27, 49**
See also CANR 2; CA 1-4R; DLB 2, 7;
DLB-Y 80

Hawking, Stephen (William)
1948- .... **CLC 63**
See also CA 126, 129

Hawthorne, Julian 1846-1934 ..... **TCLC 25**

Hawthorne, Nathaniel
1804-1864 ... **NCLC 2, 10, 17, 23; SSC 3**
See also YABC 2; DLB 1, 74;
CDALB 1640-1865

Hayashi Fumiko 1904-1951...... **TCLC 27**

Haycraft, Anna 19??-
See Ellis, Alice Thomas
See also CA 122

Hayden, Robert (Earl)
1913-1980 .... **CLC 5, 9, 14, 37**
See also CANR 24; CA 69-72;
obituary CA 97-100; CABS 2; SATA 19;
obituary SATA 26; DLB 5, 76;
CDALB 1941-1968

Hayman, Ronald 1932-............ **CLC 44**
See also CANR 18; CA 25-28R

Haywood, Eliza (Fowler) 1693?-1756.. **LC 1**
See also DLB 39

Hazlitt, William 1778-1830 ...... **NCLC 29**

Hazzard, Shirley 1931- .... **CLC 18**
See also CANR 4; CA 9-12R; DLB-Y 82

H(ilda) D(oolittle)
1886-1961 .... **CLC 3, 8, 14, 31, 34**
See also Doolittle, Hilda

Head, Bessie 1937-1986........... **CLC 25**
See also CANR 25; CA 29-32R;
obituary CA 119

Headon, (Nicky) Topper 1956?- .... **CLC 30**
See also The Clash

Heaney, Seamus (Justin)
1939- .... **CLC 5, 7, 14, 25, 37**
See also CANR 25; CA 85-88; DLB 40

Hearn, (Patricio) Lafcadio (Tessima Carlos)
1850-1904 .... **TCLC 9**
See also CA 105; DLB 12, 78

Hearne, Vicki 1946-.............. **CLC 56**

Hearon, Shelby 1931-............. **CLC 63**
See also CANR 18; CA 25-28

Heat Moon, William Least 1939-... **CLC 29**

Hebert, Anne 1916- .... **CLC 4, 13, 29**
See also CA 85-88; DLB 68

Hecht, Anthony (Evan)
1923- .... **CLC 8, 13, 19**
See also CANR 6; CA 9-12R; DLB 5

Hecht, Ben 1894-1964 .... **CLC 8**
See also CA 85-88; DLB 7, 9, 25, 26, 28, 86

Hedayat, Sadeq 1903-1951....... **TCLC 21**
See also CA 120

Heidegger, Martin 1889-1976 ...... **CLC 24**
See also CA 81-84; obituary CA 65-68

Heidenstam, (Karl Gustaf) Verner von
1859-1940 .... **TCLC 5**
See also CA 104

Heifner, Jack 1946-.............. **CLC 11**
See also CA 105

Heijermans, Herman 1864-1924 ... **TCLC 24**
See also CA 123

Heilbrun, Carolyn G(old) 1926-..... **CLC 25**
See also CANR 1, 28; CA 45-48

Heine, Harry 1797-1856
See Heine, Heinrich

Heine, Heinrich 1797-1856 .... **NCLC 4**
See also DLB 90

Heinemann, Larry C(urtiss) 1944- .. **CLC 50**
See also CA 110

Heiney, Donald (William) 1921-..... **CLC 9**
See also Harris, MacDonald
See also CANR 3; CA 1-4R

Heinlein, Robert A(nson)
1907-1988 ...... **CLC 1, 3, 8, 14, 26, 55**
See also CANR 1, 20; CA 1-4R;
obituary CA 125; SATA 9, 56; DLB 8

Heller, Joseph
1923- .... **CLC 1, 3, 5, 8, 11, 36, 63**
See also CANR 8; CA 5-8R; CABS 1;
DLB 2, 28; DLB-Y 80

Hellman, Lillian (Florence)
1905?-1984..... **CLC 2, 4, 8, 14, 18, 34,
44, 52; DC 1**
See also CA 13-16R; obituary CA 112;
DLB 7; DLB-Y 84

Helprin, Mark 1947- ..... **CLC 7, 10, 22, 32**
See also CA 81-84; DLB-Y 85

Hemans, Felicia 1793-1835 ...... **NCLC 29**

Hemingway, Ernest (Miller)
1899-1961 ... **CLC 1, 3, 6, 8, 10, 13, 19,
30, 34, 39, 41, 44, 50, 61; SSC 1**
See also CA 77-80; DLB 4, 9; DLB-Y 81,
87; DLB-DS 1; CDALB 1917-1929

Hempel, Amy 1951-.............. **CLC 39**
See also CA 118

Henley, Beth 1952-.............. **CLC 23**
See also Henley, Elizabeth Becker
See also CABS 3; DLB-Y 86

Henley, Elizabeth Becker 1952-
See Henley, Beth
See also CA 107

Henley, William Ernest
1849-1903 .... **TCLC 8**
See also CA 105; DLB 19

Hennissart, Martha
See Lathen, Emma
See also CA 85-88

Henry, O. 1862-1910 ... **TCLC 1, 19; SSC 5**
See also Porter, William Sydney
See also YABC 2; CA 104; DLB 12, 78, 79;
CDALB 1865-1917

Henry VIII 1491-1547............ **LC 10**

Hentoff, Nat(han Irving) 1925-..... **CLC 26**
See also CLR 1; CAAS 6; CANR 5, 25;
CA 1-4R; SATA 27, 42; AAYA 4

Heppenstall, (John) Rayner
1911-1981 .... **CLC 10**
See also CANR 29; CA 1-4R;
obituary CA 103

Herbert, Frank (Patrick)
1920-1986 .... **CLC 12, 23, 35, 44**
See also CANR 5; CA 53-56;
obituary CA 118; SATA 9, 37, 47; DLB 8

Herbert, Zbigniew 1924- .... **CLC 9, 43**
See also CA 89-92

Herbst, Josephine 1897-1969....... **CLC 34**
See also CA 5-8R; obituary CA 25-28R;
DLB 9

Herder, Johann Gottfried von
1744-1803 .... **NCLC 8**

Hergesheimer, Joseph
1880-1954 .... **TCLC 11**
See also CA 109; DLB 9

Herlagnez, Pablo de 1844-1896
See Verlaine, Paul (Marie)

Herlihy, James Leo 1927-.......... **CLC 6**
See also CANR 2; CA 1-4R

Hermogenes fl.c. 175-............ **CMLC 6**

Hernandez, Jose 1834-1886...... **NCLC 17**

Herrick, Robert 1591-1674 .... **LC 13**

Herriot, James 1916-............. **CLC 12**
See also Wight, James Alfred
See also AAYA 1

Herrmann, Dorothy 1941-......... **CLC 44**
See also CA 107

Hersey, John (Richard)
1914- .... **CLC 1, 2, 7, 9, 40**
See also CA 17-20R; SATA 25; DLB 6

Herzen, Aleksandr Ivanovich
1812-1870 .... **NCLC 10**

Herzl, Theodor 1860-1904........ **TCLC 36**

Herzog, Werner 1942-............. **CLC 16**
See also CA 89-92

Hesiod c. 8th Century B.C.- ...... **CMLC 5**

Hesse, Hermann
1877-1962 .... **CLC 1, 2, 3, 6, 11, 17, 25**
See also CAP 2; CA 17-18; SATA 50;
DLB 66

Heyen, William 1940- .... **CLC 13, 18**
See also CAAS 9; CA 33-36R; DLB 5

Heyerdahl, Thor 1914-............ **CLC 26**
See also CANR 5, 22; CA 5-8R; SATA 2,
52

Heym, Georg (Theodor Franz Arthur)
1887-1912 .... **TCLC 9**
See also CA 106

Heym, Stefan 1913-.............. **CLC 41**
See also CANR 4; CA 9-12R; DLB 69

Heyse, Paul (Johann Ludwig von)
1830-1914 .... **TCLC 8**
See also CA 104

Hibbert, Eleanor (Burford) 1906-.... **CLC 7**
See also CANR 9, 28; CA 17-20R; SATA 2

Killigrew, Anne 1660-1685.......... LC 4

Kincaid, Jamaica 1949?- .... CLC 43
See also CA 125

King, Francis (Henry) 1923- ..... CLC 8, 53
See also CANR 1; CA 1-4R; DLB 15

King, Stephen (Edwin)
1947- .... CLC 12, 26, 37, 61
See also CANR 1, 30; CA 61-64; SATA 9,
55; DLB-Y 80; AAYA 1

Kingman, (Mary) Lee 1919-........ CLC 17
See also Natti, (Mary) Lee
See also CA 5-8R; SAAS 3; SATA 1

Kingsley, Sidney 1906-........... CLC 44
See also CA 85-88; DLB 7

Kingsolver, Barbara 1955-........ CLC 55
See also CA 129

Kingston, Maxine Hong
1940- .... CLC 12, 19, 58
See also CANR 13; CA 69-72; SATA 53;
DLB-Y 80

Kinnell, Galway
1927- .... CLC 1, 2, 3, 5, 13, 29
See also CANR 10; CA 9-12R; DLB 5;
DLB-Y 87

Kinsella, Thomas 1928- ...... CLC 4, 19, 43
See also CANR 15; CA 17-20R; DLB 27

Kinsella, W(illiam) P(atrick)
1935- .... CLC 27, 43
See also CAAS 7; CANR 21; CA 97-100

Kipling, (Joseph) Rudyard
1865-1936 .... TCLC 8, 17; SSC 5
See also YABC 2; CA 105, 120; DLB 19, 34

Kirkup, James 1918- .... CLC 1
See also CAAS 4; CANR 2; CA 1-4R;
SATA 12; DLB 27

Kirkwood, James 1930-1989 .... CLC 9
See also CANR 6; CA 1-4R;
obituary CA 128

Kis, Danilo 1935-1989 .... CLC 57
See also CA 118, 129; brief entry CA 109

Kivi, Aleksis 1834-1872 .... NCLC 30

Kizer, Carolyn (Ashley) 1925-... CLC 15, 39
See also CAAS 5; CANR 24; CA 65-68;
DLB 5

Klappert, Peter 1942-............. CLC 57
See also CA 33-36R; DLB 5

Klausner, Amos 1939-
See Oz, Amos

Klein, A(braham) M(oses)
1909-1972 .... CLC 19
See also CA 101; obituary CA 37-40R;
DLB 68

Klein, Norma 1938-1989 .... CLC 30
See also CLR 2, 19; CANR 15; CA 41-44R;
obituary CA 128; SAAS 1; SATA 7, 57;
AAYA 2

Klein, T.E.D. 19??-............... CLC 34
See also CA 119

Kleist, Heinrich von 1777-1811.... NCLC 2
See also DLB 90

Klima, Ivan 1931-............... CLC 56
See also CANR 17; CA 25-28R

Klimentev, Andrei Platonovich 1899-1951
See Platonov, Andrei (Platonovich)
See also CA 108

Klinger, Friedrich Maximilian von
1752-1831 .... NCLC 1

Klopstock, Friedrich Gottlieb
1724-1803 .... NCLC 11

Knebel, Fletcher 1911-............ CLC 14
See also CAAS 3; CANR 1; CA 1-4R;
SATA 36

Knight, Etheridge 1931-........... CLC 40
See also CANR 23; CA 21-24R; DLB 41

Knight, Sarah Kemble 1666-1727 ..... LC 7
See also DLB 24

Knowles, John 1926- ...... CLC 1, 4, 10, 26
See also CA 17-20R; SATA 8; DLB 6;
CDALB 1968-1987

Koch, C(hristopher) J(ohn) 1932- ... CLC 42
See also CA 127

Koch, Kenneth 1925- .... CLC 5, 8, 44
See also CANR 6; CA 1-4R; DLB 5

Kochanowski, Jan 1530-1584........ LC 10

Kock, Charles Paul de
1794-1871 .... NCLC 16

Koestler, Arthur
1905-1983 .... CLC 1, 3, 6, 8, 15, 33
See also CANR 1; CA 1-4R;
obituary CA 109; DLB-Y 83

Kohout, Pavel 1928-............. CLC 13
See also CANR 3; CA 45-48

Kolmar, Gertrud 1894-1943....... TCLC 40

Konigsberg, Allen Stewart 1935-
See Allen, Woody

Konrad, Gyorgy 1933-.......... CLC 4, 10
See also CA 85-88

Konwicki, Tadeusz 1926-..... CLC 8, 28, 54
See also CAAS 9; CA 101

Kopit, Arthur (Lee) 1937- .... CLC 1, 18, 33
See also CA 81-84; CABS 3; DLB 7

Kops, Bernard 1926-.............. CLC 4
See also CA 5-8R; DLB 13

Kornbluth, C(yril) M. 1923-1958.... TCLC 8
See also CA 105; DLB 8

Korolenko, Vladimir (Galaktionovich)
1853-1921 .... TCLC 22
See also CA 121

Kosinski, Jerzy (Nikodem)
1933- .... CLC 1, 2, 3, 6, 10, 15, 53
See also CANR 9; CA 17-20R; DLB 2;
DLB-Y 82

Kostelanetz, Richard (Cory) 1940- .. CLC 28
See also CAAS 8; CA 13-16R

Kostrowitzki, Wilhelm Apollinaris de
1880-1918
See Apollinaire, Guillaume
See also CA 104

Kotlowitz, Robert 1924-........... CLC 4
See also CA 33-36R

Kotzebue, August (Friedrich Ferdinand) von
1761-1819 .... NCLC 25

Kotzwinkle, William 1938- ... CLC 5, 14, 35
See also CLR 6; CANR 3; CA 45-48;
SATA 24

Kozol, Jonathan 1936-............ CLC 17
See also CANR 16; CA 61-64

Kozoll, Michael 1940?-........... CLC 35

Kramer, Kathryn 19??-........... CLC 34

Kramer, Larry 1935- .... CLC 42
See also CA 124, 126

Krasicki, Ignacy 1735-1801...... NCLC 8

Krasinski, Zygmunt 1812-1859 .... NCLC 4

Kraus, Karl 1874-1936............ TCLC 5
See also CA 104

Kreve, Vincas 1882-1954 .... TCLC 27

Kristofferson, Kris 1936-.......... CLC 26
See also CA 104

Krizanc, John 1956-.............. CLC 57

Krleza, Miroslav 1893-1981........ CLC 8
See also CA 97-100; obituary CA 105

Kroetsch, Robert (Paul)
1927- .... CLC 5, 23, 57
See also CANR 8; CA 17-20R; DLB 53

Kroetz, Franz Xaver 1946- .... CLC 41
See also CA 130

Kropotkin, Peter 1842-1921....... TCLC 36
See also CA 119

Krotkov, Yuri 1917-.............. CLC 19
See also CA 102

Krumgold, Joseph (Quincy)
1908-1980 .... CLC 12
See also CANR 7; CA 9-12R;
obituary CA 101; SATA 1, 48;
obituary SATA 23

Krutch, Joseph Wood 1893-1970.... CLC 24
See also CANR 4; CA 1-4R;
obituary CA 25-28R; DLB 63

Krylov, Ivan Andreevich
1768?-1844.................. NCLC 1

Kubin, Alfred 1877-1959 .... TCLC 23
See also CA 112; DLB 81

Kubrick, Stanley 1928-............ CLC 16
See also CA 81-84; DLB 26

Kumin, Maxine (Winokur)
1925- .... CLC 5, 13, 28
See also CAAS 8; CANR 1, 21; CA 1-4R;
SATA 12; DLB 5

Kundera, Milan 1929- ..... CLC 4, 9, 19, 32
See also CANR 19; CA 85-88; AAYA 2

Kunitz, Stanley J(asspon)
1905- .... CLC 6, 11, 14
See also CANR 26; CA 41-44R; DLB 48

Kunze, Reiner 1933-............. CLC 10
See also CA 93-96; DLB 75

Kuprin, Aleksandr (Ivanovich)
1870-1938 .... TCLC 5
See also CA 104

Kureishi, Hanif 1954-............. CLC 64

Kurosawa, Akira 1910-............ CLC 16
See also CA 101

Kuttner, Henry 1915-1958........ TCLC 10
See also CA 107; DLB 8

Kuzma, Greg 1944-............... CLC 7
See also CA 33-36R

Kuzmin, Mikhail 1872?-1936...... TCLC 40

Labrunie, Gerard 1808-1855
See Nerval, Gerard de

Laclos, Pierre Ambroise Francois Choderlos de 1741-1803 . . . . **NCLC 4**

La Fayette, Marie (Madelaine Pioche de la Vergne, Comtesse) de 1634-1693 . . . . **LC 2**

Lafayette, Rene
See Hubbard, L(afayette) Ron(ald)

Laforgue, Jules 1860-1887 . . . . **NCLC 5**

Lagerkvist, Par (Fabian) 1891-1974 . . . . **CLC 7, 10, 13, 54**
See also CA 85-88; obituary CA 49-52

Lagerlof, Selma (Ottiliana Lovisa) 1858-1940 . . . . **TCLC 4, 36**
See also CLR 7; CA 108; SATA 15

La Guma, (Justin) Alex(ander) 1925-1985 . . . . **CLC 19**
See also CANR 25; CA 49-52; obituary CA 118

Lamartine, Alphonse (Marie Louis Prat) de 1790-1869 . . . . **NCLC 11**

Lamb, Charles 1775-1834 . . . . **NCLC 10**
See also SATA 17

Lamming, George (William) 1927- . . . . **CLC 2, 4**
See also CANR 26; CA 85-88

LaMoore, Louis Dearborn 1908?-
See L'Amour, Louis (Dearborn)

L'Amour, Louis (Dearborn) 1908-1988 . . . . **CLC 25, 55**
See also CANR 3, 25; CA 1-4R; obituary CA 125; DLB-Y 80

Lampedusa, (Prince) Giuseppe (Maria Fabrizio) Tomasi di 1896-1957 . . . . **TCLC 13**
See also CA 111

Lampman, Archibald 1861-1899 . . **NCLC 25**
See also DLB 92

Lancaster, Bruce 1896-1963 . . . . **CLC 36**
See also CAP 1; CA 9-12; SATA 9

Landis, John (David) 1950- . . . . **CLC 26**
See also CA 112, 122

Landolfi, Tommaso 1908-1979 . . . **CLC 11, 49**
See also CA 127; obituary CA 117

Landon, Letitia Elizabeth 1802-1838 . . . . **NCLC 15**

Landor, Walter Savage 1775-1864 . . . . **NCLC 14**

Landwirth, Heinz 1927-
See Lind, Jakov
See also CANR 7; CA 11-12R

Lane, Patrick 1939- . . . . **CLC 25**
See also CA 97-100; DLB 53

Lang, Andrew 1844-1912 . . . . **TCLC 16**
See also CA 114; SATA 16

Lang, Fritz 1890-1976 . . . . **CLC 20**
See also CANR 30; CA 77-80; obituary CA 69-72

Langer, Elinor 1939- . . . . **CLC 34**
See also CA 121

Lanier, Sidney 1842-1881 . . . . **NCLC 6**
See also SATA 18; DLB 64

Lanyer, Aemilia 1569-1645 . . . . **LC 10**

Lapine, James 1949- . . . . **CLC 39**
See also CA 123, 130

Larbaud, Valery 1881-1957 . . . . **TCLC 9**
See also CA 106

Lardner, Ring(gold Wilmer) 1885-1933 . . . . **TCLC 2, 14**
See also CA 104; DLB 11, 25, 86; CDALB 1917-1929

Larkin, Philip (Arthur) 1922-1985 . . . **CLC 3, 5, 8, 9, 13, 18, 33, 39, 64**
See also CANR 24; CA 5-8R; obituary CA 117; DLB 27

Larra (y Sanchez de Castro), Mariano Jose de 1809-1837 . . . . **NCLC 17**

Larsen, Eric 1941- . . . . **CLC 55**

Larsen, Nella 1891-1964 . . . . **CLC 37**
See also CA 125; DLB 51

Larson, Charles R(aymond) 1938- . . . **CLC 31**
See also CANR 4; CA 53-56

Latham, Jean Lee 1902- . . . . **CLC 12**
See also CANR 7; CA 5-8R; SATA 2

Lathen, Emma . . . . **CLC 2**
See also Hennissart, Martha; Latsis, Mary J(ane)

Latsis, Mary J(ane) . . . . **CLC 2**
See also Lathen, Emma
See also CA 85-88

Lattimore, Richmond (Alexander) 1906-1984 . . . . **CLC 3**
See also CANR 1; CA 1-4R; obituary CA 112

Laughlin, James 1914- . . . . **CLC 49**
See also CANR 9; CA 21-24R; DLB 48

Laurence, (Jean) Margaret (Wemyss) 1926-1987 . . **CLC 3, 6, 13, 50, 62; SSC 7**
See also CA 5-8R; obituary CA 121; SATA 50; DLB 53

Laurent, Antoine 1952- . . . . **CLC 50**

Lautreamont, Comte de 1846-1870 . . . . **NCLC 12**

Lavin, Mary 1912- . . . . . . **CLC 4, 18; SSC 4**
See also CA 9-12R; DLB 15

Lawler, Raymond (Evenor) 1922- . . . **CLC 58**
See also CA 103

Lawrence, D(avid) H(erbert) 1885-1930 . . . . **TCLC 2, 9, 16, 33; SSC 4**
See also CA 104, 121; DLB 10, 19, 36

Lawrence, T(homas) E(dward) 1888-1935 . . . . **TCLC 18**
See also CA 115

Lawson, Henry (Archibald Hertzberg) 1867-1922 . . . . **TCLC 27**
See also CA 120

Laxness, Halldor (Kiljan) 1902- . . . . **CLC 25**
See also Gudjonsson, Halldor Kiljan

Laye, Camara 1928-1980 . . . . **CLC 4, 38**
See also CANR 25; CA 85-88; obituary CA 97-100

Layton, Irving (Peter) 1912- . . . . . **CLC 2, 15**
See also CANR 2; CA 1-4R; DLB 88

Lazarus, Emma 1849-1887 . . . . **NCLC 8**

Leacock, Stephen (Butler) 1869-1944 . . . . **TCLC 2**
See also CA 104; DLB 92

Lear, Edward 1812-1888 . . . . . . **NCLC 3**
See also CLR 1; SATA 18; DLB 32

Lear, Norman (Milton) 1922- . . . . . . **CLC 12**
See also CA 73-76

Leavis, F(rank) R(aymond) 1895-1978 . . . . **CLC 24**
See also CA 21-24R; obituary CA 77-80

Leavitt, David 1961?- . . . . **CLC 34**
See also CA 116, 122

Lebowitz, Fran(ces Ann) 1951?- . . . . **CLC 11, 36**
See also CANR 14; CA 81-84

Le Carre, John 1931- . . . **CLC 3, 5, 9, 15, 28**
See also Cornwell, David (John Moore)
See also DLB 87

Le Clezio, J(ean) M(arie) G(ustave) 1940- . . . . **CLC 31**
See also CA 116, 128; DLB 83

Leconte de Lisle, Charles-Marie-Rene 1818-1894 . . . . **NCLC 29**

Leduc, Violette 1907-1972 . . . . **CLC 22**
See also CAP 1; CA 13-14; obituary CA 33-36R

Ledwidge, Francis 1887-1917 . . . . . . **TCLC 23**
See also CA 123; DLB 20

Lee, Andrea 1953- . . . . **CLC 36**
See also CA 125

Lee, Andrew 1917-
See Auchincloss, Louis (Stanton)

Lee, Don L. 1942- . . . . **CLC 2**
See also Madhubuti, Haki R.
See also CA 73-76

Lee, George Washington 1894-1976 . . . . **CLC 52**
See also CA 125; DLB 51

Lee, (Nelle) Harper 1926- . . . . . . **CLC 12, 60**
See also CA 13-16R; SATA 11; DLB 6; CDALB 1941-1968

Lee, Lawrence 1903- . . . . **CLC 34**
See also CA 25-28R

Lee, Manfred B(ennington) 1905-1971 . . . . **CLC 11**
See also Queen, Ellery
See also CANR 2; CA 1-4R; obituary CA 29-32R

Lee, Stan 1922- . . . . **CLC 17**
See also CA 108, 111

Lee, Tanith 1947- . . . . **CLC 46**
See also CA 37-40R; SATA 8

Lee, Vernon 1856-1935 . . . . **TCLC 5**
See also Paget, Violet
See also DLB 57

Lee-Hamilton, Eugene (Jacob) 1845-1907 . . . . **TCLC 22**
See also CA 117

Leet, Judith 1935- . . . . **CLC 11**

Le Fanu, Joseph Sheridan 1814-1873 . . . . **NCLC 9**
See also DLB 21, 70

Leffland, Ella 1931- . . . . **CLC 19**
See also CA 29-32R; DLB-Y 84

Mead, Margaret 1901-1978 .... CLC 37
  See also CANR 4; CA 1-4R;
    obituary CA 81-84; SATA 20

Meaker, M. J. 1927-
  See Kerr, M. E.; Meaker, Marijane

Meaker, Marijane 1927-
  See Kerr, M. E.
  See also CA 107; SATA 20

Medoff, Mark (Howard) 1940- ... CLC 6, 23
  See also CANR 5; CA 53-56; DLB 7

Megged, Aharon 1920-............ CLC 9
  See also CANR 1; CA 49-52

Mehta, Ved (Parkash) 1934-....... CLC 37
  See also CANR 2, 23; CA 1-4R

Mellor, John 1953?-
  See The Clash

Meltzer, Milton 1915-............ CLC 26
  See also CLR 13; CA 13-16R; SAAS 1;
    SATA 1, 50; DLB 61

Melville, Herman
  1819-1891 ...... NCLC 3, 12, 29; SSC 1
  See also SATA 59; DLB 3, 74;
    CDALB 1640-1865

Membreno, Alejandro 1972- .... CLC 59

Mencken, H(enry) L(ouis)
  1880-1956 .... TCLC 13
  See also CA 105, 125; DLB 11, 29, 63;
    CDALB 1917-1929

Mercer, David 1928-1980.......... CLC 5
  See also CANR 23; CA 9-12R;
    obituary CA 102; DLB 13

Meredith, George 1828-1909...... TCLC 17
  See also CA 117; DLB 18, 35, 57

Meredith, William (Morris)
  1919-.............. CLC 4, 13, 22, 55
  See also CANR 6; CA 9-12R; DLB 5

Merezhkovsky, Dmitri
  1865-1941 .... TCLC 29

Merimee, Prosper
  1803-1870 .... NCLC 6; SSC 7

Merkin, Daphne 1954-............ CLC 44
  See also CANR 123

Merrill, James (Ingram)
  1926- .... CLC 2, 3, 6, 8, 13, 18, 34
  See also CANR 10; CA 13-16R; DLB 5;
    DLB-Y 85

Merton, Thomas (James)
  1915-1968 .... CLC 1, 3, 11, 34
  See also CANR 22; CA 5-8R;
    obituary CA 25-28R; DLB 48; DLB-Y 81

Merwin, W(illiam) S(tanley)
  1927- ...... CLC 1, 2, 3, 5, 8, 13, 18, 45
  See also CANR 15; CA 13-16R; DLB 5

Metcalf, John 1938-.............. CLC 37
  See also CA 113; DLB 60

Mew, Charlotte (Mary)
  1870-1928 .... TCLC 8
  See also CA 105; DLB 19

Mewshaw, Michael 1943-.......... CLC 9
  See also CANR 7; CA 53-56; DLB-Y 80

Meyer-Meyrink, Gustav 1868-1932
  See Meyrink, Gustav
  See also CA 117

Meyers, Jeffrey 1939- .... CLC 39
  See also CA 73-76

Meynell, Alice (Christiana Gertrude
  Thompson) 1847-1922 .... TCLC 6
  See also CA 104; DLB 19

Meyrink, Gustav 1868-1932...... TCLC 21
  See also Meyer-Meyrink, Gustav

Michaels, Leonard 1933-........ CLC 6, 25
  See also CANR 21; CA 61-64

Michaux, Henri 1899-1984 ...... CLC 8, 19
  See also CA 85-88; obituary CA 114

Michelangelo 1475-1564........... LC 12

Michelet, Jules 1798-1874....... NCLC 31

Michener, James A(lbert)
  1907-............ CLC 1, 5, 11, 29, 60
  See also CANR 21; CA 5-8R; DLB 6

Mickiewicz, Adam 1798-1855 ..... NCLC 3

Middleton, Christopher 1926-...... CLC 13
  See also CANR 29; CA 13-16R; DLB 40

Middleton, Stanley 1919-........ CLC 7, 38
  See also CANR 21; CA 25-28R; DLB 14

Migueis, Jose Rodrigues 1901-..... CLC 10

Mikszath, Kalman 1847-1910 ..... TCLC 31

Miles, Josephine (Louise)
  1911-1985 .... CLC 1, 2, 14, 34, 39
  See also CANR 2; CA 1-4R;
    obituary CA 116; DLB 48

Mill, John Stuart 1806-1873..... NCLC 11
  See also DLB 55

Millar, Kenneth 1915-1983 .... CLC 14
  See also Macdonald, Ross
  See also CANR 16; CA 9-12R;
    obituary CA 110; DLB 2; DLB-Y 83;
    DLB-DS 6

Millay, Edna St. Vincent
  1892-1950 .... TCLC 4
  See also CA 103; DLB 45;
    CDALB 1917-1929

Miller, Arthur
  1915- ...... CLC 1, 2, 6, 10, 15, 26, 47;
                     DC 1
  See also CANR 2, 30; CA 1-4R; CABS 3;
    DLB 7; CDALB 1941-1968

Miller, Henry (Valentine)
  1891-1980 .... CLC 1, 2, 4, 9, 14, 43
  See also CA 9-12R; obituary CA 97-100;
    DLB 4, 9; DLB-Y 80; CDALB 1929-1941

Miller, Jason 1939?-.............. CLC 2
  See also CA 73-76; DLB 7

Miller, Sue 19??-................. CLC 44

Miller, Walter M(ichael), Jr.
  1923- .... CLC 4, 30
  See also CA 85-88; DLB 8

Millhauser, Steven 1943-....... CLC 21, 54
  See also CA 108, 110, 111; DLB 2

Millin, Sarah Gertrude 1889-1968 .. CLC 49
  See also CA 102; obituary CA 93-96

Milne, A(lan) A(lexander)
  1882-1956 .... TCLC 6
  See also CLR 1; YABC 1; CA 104;
    DLB 10, 77

Milner, Ron(ald) 1938-............ CLC 56
  See also CANR 24; CA 73-76; DLB 38

Milosz Czeslaw
  1911-........... CLC 5, 11, 22, 31, 56
  See also CANR 23; CA 81-84

Milton, John 1608-1674............. LC 9

Miner, Valerie (Jane) 1947-....... CLC 40
  See also CA 97-100

Minot, Susan 1956- .... CLC 44

Minus, Ed 1938-................. CLC 39

Miro (Ferrer), Gabriel (Francisco Victor)
  1879-1930 .... TCLC 5
  See also CA 104

Mishima, Yukio
  1925-1970 .... CLC 2, 4, 6, 9, 27; DC 1;
                     SSC 4
  See also Hiraoka, Kimitake

Mistral, Gabriela 1889-1957 .... TCLC 2
  See also CA 104

Mitchell, James Leslie 1901-1935
  See Gibbon, Lewis Grassic
  See also CA 104; DLB 15

Mitchell, Joni 1943-.............. CLC 12
  See also CA 112

Mitchell (Marsh), Margaret (Munnerlyn)
  1900-1949 .... TCLC 11
  See also CA 109, 125; DLB 9

Mitchell, S. Weir 1829-1914...... TCLC 36

Mitchell, W(illiam) O(rmond)
  1914- .... CLC 25
  See also CANR 15; CA 77-80; DLB 88

Mitford, Mary Russell 1787-1855.. NCLC 4

Mitford, Nancy 1904-1973........ CLC 44
  See also CA 9-12R

Miyamoto Yuriko 1899-1951...... TCLC 37

Mo, Timothy 1950-.............. CLC 46
  See also CA 117

Modarressi, Taghi 1931- .... CLC 44
  See also CA 121

Modiano, Patrick (Jean) 1945-..... CLC 18
  See also CANR 17; CA 85-88; DLB 83

Mofolo, Thomas (Mokopu)
  1876-1948 .... TCLC 22
  See also CA 121

Mohr, Nicholasa 1935-............ CLC 12
  See also CLR 22; CANR 1; CA 49-52;
    SAAS 8; SATA 8

Mojtabai, A(nn) G(race)
  1938-................ CLC 5, 9, 15, 29
  See also CA 85-88

Moliere 1622-1673 .... LC 10

Molnar, Ferenc 1878-1952........ TCLC 20
  See also CA 109

Momaday, N(avarre) Scott
  1934- .... CLC 2, 19
  See also CANR 14; CA 25-28R; SATA 30,
    48

Monroe, Harriet 1860-1936....... TCLC 12
  See also CA 109; DLB 54, 91

Montagu, Elizabeth 1720-1800 .... NCLC 7

Montagu, Lady Mary (Pierrepont) Wortley
  1689-1762 .... LC 9

Montague, John (Patrick)
  1929-.................... CLC 13, 46
  See also CANR 9; CA 9-12R; DLB 40

Montaigne, Michel (Eyquem) de
1533-1592 . . . . LC 8

Montale, Eugenio   1896-1981 . . . CLC 7, 9, 18
See also CANR 30; CA 17-20R;
obituary CA 104

Montgomery, Marion (H., Jr.)
1925- . . . . CLC 7
See also CANR 3; CA 1-4R; DLB 6

Montgomery, Robert Bruce   1921-1978
See Crispin, Edmund
See also CA 104

Montherlant, Henri (Milon) de
1896-1972 . . . . CLC 8, 19
See also CA 85-88; obituary CA 37-40R;
DLB 72

Montisquieu, Charles-Louis de Secondat
1689-1755 . . . . LC 7

Monty Python . . . . CLC 21

Moodie, Susanna (Strickland)
1803-1885 . . . . NCLC 14

Mooney, Ted   1951- . . . . CLC 25

Moorcock, Michael (John)
1939- . . . . CLC 5, 27, 58
See also CAAS 5; CANR 2, 17; CA 45-48;
DLB 14

Moore, Brian
1921- . . . . CLC 1, 3, 5, 7, 8, 19, 32
See also CANR 1, 25; CA 1-4R

Moore, George (Augustus)
1852-1933 . . . . TCLC 7
See also CA 104; DLB 10, 18, 57

Moore, Lorrie   1957- . . . . CLC 39, 45
See also Moore, Marie Lorena

Moore, Marianne (Craig)
1887-1972 . . . CLC 1, 2, 4, 8, 10, 13, 19,
47
See also CANR 3; CA 1-4R;
obituary CA 33-36R; SATA 20; DLB 45;
CDALB 1929-1941

Moore, Marie Lorena   1957-
See Moore, Lorrie
See also CA 116

Moore, Thomas   1779-1852 . . . . NCLC 6

Morand, Paul   1888-1976 . . . . CLC 41
See also obituary CA 69-72; DLB 65

Morante, Elsa   1918-1985 . . . . CLC 8, 47
See also CA 85-88; obituary CA 117

Moravia, Alberto
1907- . . . . CLC 2, 7, 11, 18, 27, 46
See also Pincherle, Alberto

More, Hannah   1745-1833 . . . . NCLC 27

More, Henry   1614-1687 . . . . LC 9

More, (Sir) Thomas   1478-1535 . . . . . . LC 10

Moreas, Jean   1856-1910 . . . . TCLC 18

Morgan, Berry   1919- . . . . CLC 6
See also CA 49-52; DLB 6

Morgan, Edwin (George)   1920- . . . . . CLC 31
See also CANR 3; CA 7-8R; DLB 27

Morgan, (George) Frederick
1922- . . . . CLC 23
See also CANR 21; CA 17-20R

Morgan, Janet   1945- . . . . CLC 39
See also CA 65-68

Morgan, Lady   1776?-1859 . . . . NCLC 29

Morgan, Robin   1941- . . . . CLC 2
See also CA 69-72

Morgan, Seth   1949-1990 . . . . CLC 65
See also CA 132

Morgenstern, Christian (Otto Josef Wolfgang)
1871-1914 . . . . TCLC 8
See also CA 105

Moricz, Zsigmond   1879-1942 . . . . . TCLC 33

Morike, Eduard (Friedrich)
1804-1875 . . . . NCLC 10

Mori Ogai   1862-1922 . . . . TCLC 14
See also Mori Rintaro

Mori Rintaro   1862-1922
See Mori Ogai
See also CA 110

Moritz, Karl Philipp   1756-1793 . . . . . . LC 2

Morris, Julian   1916-
See West, Morris L.

Morris, Steveland Judkins   1950-
See Wonder, Stevie
See also CA 111

Morris, William   1834-1896 . . . . NCLC 4
See also DLB 18, 35, 57

Morris, Wright (Marion)
1910- . . . . CLC 1, 3, 7, 18, 37
See also CANR 21; CA 9-12R; DLB 2;
DLB-Y 81

Morrison, James Douglas   1943-1971
See Morrison, Jim
See also CA 73-76

Morrison, Jim   1943-1971 . . . . CLC 17
See also Morrison, James Douglas

Morrison, Toni   1931- . . . . . CLC 4, 10, 22, 55
See also CANR 27; CA 29-32R; DLB 6, 33;
DLB-Y 81; CDALB 1968-1987; AAYA 1

Morrison, Van   1945- . . . . CLC 21
See also CA 116

Mortimer, John (Clifford)
1923- . . . . CLC 28, 43
See also CANR 21; CA 13-16R; DLB 13

Mortimer, Penelope (Ruth)   1918- . . . . CLC 5
See also CA 57-60

Mosher, Howard Frank   19??- . . . . . . CLC 62

Mosley, Nicholas   1923- . . . . CLC 43
See also CA 69-72; DLB 14

Moss, Howard
1922-1987 . . . . CLC 7, 14, 45, 50
See also CANR 1; CA 1-4R;
obituary CA 123; DLB 5

Motion, Andrew (Peter)   1952- . . . . . . CLC 47
See also DLB 40

Motley, Willard (Francis)
1912-1965 . . . . CLC 18
See also CA 117; obituary CA 106; DLB 76

Mott, Michael (Charles Alston)
1930- . . . . CLC 15, 34
See also CAAS 7; CANR 7, 29; CA 5-8R

Mowat, Farley (McGill)   1921- . . . . . CLC 26
See also CLR 20; CANR 4, 24; CA 1-4R;
SATA 3, 55; DLB 68; AAYA 1

Mphahlele, Es'kia   1919-
See Mphahlele, Ezekiel

Mphahlele, Ezekiel   1919- . . . . CLC 25
See also CA 81-84

Mqhayi, S(amuel) E(dward) K(rune Loliwe)
1875-1945 . . . . TCLC 25

Mrozek, Slawomir   1930- . . . . CLC 3, 13
See also CAAS 10; CANR 29; CA 13-16R

Mtwa, Percy   19??- . . . . CLC 47

Mueller, Lisel   1924- . . . . CLC 13, 51
See also CA 93-96

Muir, Edwin   1887-1959 . . . . TCLC 2
See also CA 104; DLB 20

Muir, John   1838-1914 . . . . TCLC 28

Mujica Lainez, Manuel
1910-1984 . . . . CLC 31
See also CA 81-84; obituary CA 112

Mukherjee, Bharati   1940- . . . . CLC 53
See also CA 107; DLB 60

Muldoon, Paul   1951- . . . . CLC 32
See also CA 113, 129; DLB 40

Mulisch, Harry (Kurt Victor)
1927- . . . . CLC 42
See also CANR 6, 26; CA 9-12R

Mull, Martin   1943- . . . . CLC 17
See also CA 105

Munford, Robert   1737?-1783 . . . . LC 5
See also DLB 31

Munro, Alice (Laidlaw)
1931- . . . . CLC 6, 10, 19, 50; SSC 3
See also CA 33-36R; SATA 29; DLB 53

Munro, H(ector) H(ugh)   1870-1916
See Saki
See also CA 104; DLB 34

Murasaki, Lady   c. 11th century- . . . CMLC 1

Murdoch, (Jean) Iris
1919- . . . . . . CLC 1, 2, 3, 4, 6, 8, 11, 15,
22, 31, 51
See also CANR 8; CA 13-16R; DLB 14

Murphy, Richard   1927- . . . . CLC 41
See also CA 29-32R; DLB 40

Murphy, Sylvia   19??- . . . . CLC 34

Murphy, Thomas (Bernard)   1935- . . . CLC 51
See also CA 101

Murray, Les(lie) A(llan)   1938- . . . . . CLC 40
See also CANR 11, 27; CA 21-24R

Murry, John Middleton
1889-1957 . . . . TCLC 16
See also CA 118

Musgrave, Susan   1951- . . . . CLC 13, 54
See also CA 69-72

Musil, Robert (Edler von)
1880-1942 . . . . TCLC 12
See also CA 109; DLB 81

Musset, (Louis Charles) Alfred de
1810-1857 . . . . NCLC 7

Myers, Walter Dean   1937- . . . . CLC 35
See also CLR 4, 16; CANR 20; CA 33-36R;
SAAS 2; SATA 27, 41; DLB 33; AAYA 4

Nabokov, Vladimir (Vladimirovich)
1899-1977 . . . . CLC 1, 2, 3, 6, 8, 11, 15,
23, 44, 46, 64
See also CANR 20; CA 5-8R;
obituary CA 69-72; DLB 2; DLB-Y 80;
DLB-DS 3; CDALB 1941-1968

Obstfelder, Sigbjorn   1866-1900.... TCLC 23
See also CA 123

O'Casey, Sean
1880-1964 .... CLC 1, 5, 9, 11, 15
See also CA 89-92; DLB 10

Ochs, Phil   1940-1976............. CLC 17
See also obituary CA 65-68

O'Connor, Edwin (Greene)
1918-1968 .... CLC 14
See also CA 93-96; obituary CA 25-28R

O'Connor, (Mary) Flannery
1925-1964 ... CLC 1, 2, 3, 6, 10, 13, 15,
21; SSC 1
See also CANR 3; CA 1-4R; DLB 2;
DLB-Y 80; CDALB 1941-1968

O'Connor, Frank
1903-1966 .... CLC 14, 23; SSC 5
See also O'Donovan, Michael (John)
See also CA 93-96

O'Dell, Scott   1903-............. CLC 30
See also CLR 1, 16; CANR 12; CA 61-64;
SATA 12; DLB 52

Odets, Clifford   1906-1963 .... CLC 2, 28
See also CA 85-88; DLB 7, 26

O'Donovan, Michael (John)
1903-1966 .... CLC 14
See also O'Connor, Frank
See also CA 93-96

Oe, Kenzaburo   1935-.......... CLC 10, 36
See also CA 97-100

O'Faolain, Julia   1932-....... CLC 6, 19, 47
See also CAAS 2; CANR 12; CA 81-84;
DLB 14

O'Faolain, Sean   1900- ..... CLC 1, 7, 14, 32
See also CANR 12; CA 61-64; DLB 15

O'Flaherty, Liam
1896-1984 .... CLC 5, 34; SSC 6
See also CA 101; obituary CA 113; DLB 36;
DLB-Y 84

O'Grady, Standish (James)
1846-1928 .... TCLC 5
See also CA 104

O'Grady, Timothy   1951-.......... CLC 59

O'Hara, Frank   1926-1966 ..... CLC 2, 5, 13
See also CA 9-12R; obituary CA 25-28R;
DLB 5, 16; CDALB 1929-1941

O'Hara, John (Henry)
1905-1970 ...... CLC 1, 2, 3, 6, 11, 42
See also CA 5-8R; obituary CA 25-28R;
DLB 9; DLB-DS 2; CDALB 1929-1941

O'Hara Family
See Banim, John and Banim, Michael

O'Hehir, Diana   1922-............. CLC 41
See also CA 93-96

Okigbo, Christopher (Ifenayichukwu)
1932-1967 .... CLC 25
See also CA 77-80

Olds, Sharon   1942-............ CLC 32, 39
See also CANR 18; CA 101

Olesha, Yuri (Karlovich)
1899-1960 .... CLC 8
See also CA 85-88

Oliphant, Margaret (Oliphant Wilson)
1828-1897 .... NCLC 11
See also DLB 18

Oliver, Mary   1935-............ CLC 19, 34
See also CANR 9; CA 21-24R; DLB 5

Olivier, (Baron) Laurence (Kerr)
1907- .... CLC 20
See also CA 111, 129

Olsen, Tillie   1913- .... CLC 4, 13
See also CANR 1; CA 1-4R; DLB 28;
DLB-Y 80

Olson, Charles (John)
1910-1970 ..... CLC 1, 2, 5, 6, 9, 11, 29
See also CAP 1; CA 15-16;
obituary CA 25-28R; CABS 2; DLB 5, 16

Olson, Theodore   1937-
See Olson, Toby

Olson, Toby   1937- .... CLC 28
See also CANR 9; CA 65-68

Ondaatje, (Philip) Michael
1943- .... CLC 14, 29, 51
See also CA 77-80; DLB 60

Oneal, Elizabeth   1934-............. CLC 30
See also Oneal, Zibby
See also CLR 13; CA 106; SATA 30

Oneal, Zibby   1934-................ CLC 30
See also Oneal, Elizabeth

O'Neill, Eugene (Gladstone)
1888-1953 .... TCLC 1, 6, 27
See also CA 110; DLB 7;
CDALB 1929-1941

Onetti, Juan Carlos   1909-....... CLC 7, 10
See also CA 85-88

O'Nolan, Brian   1911-1966
See O'Brien, Flann

O Nuallain, Brian   1911-1966
See O'Brien, Flann
See also CAP 2; CA 21-22;
obituary CA 25-28R

Oppen, George   1908-1984 .... CLC 7, 13, 34
See also CANR 8; CA 13-16R;
obituary CA 113; DLB 5

Orlovitz, Gil   1918-1973 .... CLC 22
See also CA 77-80; obituary CA 45-48;
DLB 2, 5

Ortega y Gasset, Jose   1883-1955 ... TCLC 9
See also CA 106, 130

Ortiz, Simon J.   1941-............. CLC 45

Orton, Joe   1933?-1967 .... CLC 4, 13, 43
See also Orton, John Kingsley
See also DLB 13

Orton, John Kingsley   1933?-1967
See Orton, Joe
See also CA 85-88

Orwell, George
1903-1950 .... TCLC 2, 6, 15, 31
See also Blair, Eric Arthur
See also DLB 15

Osborne, John (James)
1929- .... CLC 1, 2, 5, 11, 45
See also CANR 21; CA 13-16R; DLB 13

Osborne, Lawrence   1958- .... CLC 50

Osceola   1885-1962
See Dinesen, Isak; Blixen, Karen
(Christentze Dinesen)

Oshima, Nagisa   1932- .... CLC 20
See also CA 116

Oskison, John M.   1874-1947...... TCLC 35

Ossoli, Sarah Margaret (Fuller marchesa d')
1810-1850
See Fuller, (Sarah) Margaret
See also SATA 25

Ostrovsky, Alexander
1823-1886 .... NCLC 30

Otero, Blas de   1916- .... CLC 11
See also CA 89-92

Ovid   43 B.C.-c. 18 A.D. .... PC 2

Owen, Wilfred (Edward Salter)
1893-1918 .... TCLC 5, 27
See also CA 104; DLB 20

Owens, Rochelle   1936-............. CLC 8
See also CAAS 2; CA 17-20R

Owl, Sebastian   1939-
See Thompson, Hunter S(tockton)

Oz, Amos   1939- ... CLC 5, 8, 11, 27, 33, 54
See also CANR 27; CA 53-56

Ozick, Cynthia   1928-...... CLC 3, 7, 28, 62
See also CANR 23; CA 17-20R; DLB 28;
DLB-Y 82

Ozu, Yasujiro   1903-1963 .... CLC 16
See also CA 112

Pa Chin   1904-.................... CLC 18
See also Li Fei-kan

Pack, Robert   1929-................ CLC 13
See also CANR 3; CA 1-4R; DLB 5

Padgett, Lewis   1915-1958
See Kuttner, Henry

Padilla, Heberto   1932-............. CLC 38
See also CA 123

Page, Jimmy   1944-................ CLC 12

Page, Louise   1955-................ CLC 40

Page, P(atricia) K(athleen)
1916- .... CLC 7, 18
See also CANR 4, 22; CA 53-56; DLB 68

Paget, Violet   1856-1935
See Lee, Vernon
See also CA 104

Palamas, Kostes   1859-1943 .... TCLC 5
See also CA 105

Palazzeschi, Aldo   1885-1974 .... CLC 11
See also CA 89-92; obituary CA 53-56

Paley, Grace   1922-........... CLC 4, 6, 37
See also CANR 13; CA 25-28R; DLB 28

Palin, Michael   1943- .... CLC 21
See also Monty Python
See also CA 107

Palliser, Charles   1948?-........... CLC 65

Palma, Ricardo   1833-1919........ TCLC 29
See also CANR 123

Pancake, Breece Dexter   1952-1979
See Pancake, Breece D'J

Pancake, Breece D'J   1952-1979 .... CLC 29
See also obituary CA 109

Papadiamantis, Alexandros
1851-1911 .... TCLC 29

Papini, Giovanni   1881-1956....... TCLC 22
See also CA 121

Paracelsus   1493-1541.............. LC 14

Author Index

Queneau, Raymond
   1903-1976 . . . . CLC 2, 5, 10, 42
  See also CA 77-80; obituary CA 69-72;
  DLB 72

Quin, Ann (Marie) 1936-1973 . . . . CLC 6
  See also CA 9-12R; obituary CA 45-48;
  DLB 14

Quinn, Simon 1942-
  See Smith, Martin Cruz
  See also CANR 6, 23; CA 85-88

Quiroga, Horacio (Sylvestre)
   1878-1937 . . . . TCLC 20
  See also CA 117

Quoirez, Francoise 1935-
  See Sagan, Francoise
  See also CANR 6; CA 49-52

Rabe, David (William) 1940- . . . CLC 4, 8, 33
  See also CA 85-88; CABS 3; DLB 7

Rabelais, Francois 1494?-1553 . . . . LC 5

Rabinovitch, Sholem 1859-1916
  See Aleichem, Sholom
  See also CA 104

Rachen, Kurt von 1911-1986
  See Hubbard, L(afayette) Ron(ald)

Radcliffe, Ann (Ward) 1764-1823 . . NCLC 6
  See also DLB 39

Radiguet, Raymond 1903-1923 . . . . TCLC 29
  See also DLB 65

Radnoti, Miklos 1909-1944 . . . . . . TCLC 16
  See also CA 118

Rado, James 1939- . . . . CLC 17
  See also CA 105

Radomski, James 1932-
  See Rado, James

Radvanyi, Netty Reiling 1900-1983
  See Seghers, Anna
  See also CA 85-88; obituary CA 110

Rae, Ben 1935-
  See Griffiths, Trevor

Raeburn, John 1941- . . . . CLC 34
  See also CA 57-60

Ragni, Gerome 1942- . . . . CLC 17
  See also CA 105

Rahv, Philip 1908-1973 . . . . CLC 24
  See also Greenberg, Ivan

Raine, Craig 1944- . . . . CLC 32
  See also CANR 29; CA 108; DLB 40

Raine, Kathleen (Jessie) 1908- . . . CLC 7, 45
  See also CA 85-88; DLB 20

Rainis, Janis 1865-1929 . . . . TCLC 29

Rakosi, Carl 1903- . . . . CLC 47
  See also Rawley, Callman
  See also CAAS 5

Ramos, Graciliano 1892-1953 . . . . . TCLC 32

Rampersad, Arnold 19??- . . . . CLC 44

Ramuz, Charles-Ferdinand
   1878-1947 . . . . TCLC 33

Rand, Ayn 1905-1982 . . . . CLC 3, 30, 44
  See also CANR 27; CA 13-16R;
  obituary CA 105

Randall, Dudley (Felker) 1914- . . . . . . CLC 1
  See also CANR 23; CA 25-28R; DLB 41

Ransom, John Crowe
   1888-1974 . . . . CLC 2, 4, 5, 11, 24
  See also CANR 6; CA 5-8R;
  obituary CA 49-52; DLB 45, 63

Rao, Raja 1909- . . . . CLC 25, 56
  See also CA 73-76

Raphael, Frederic (Michael)
   1931- . . . . CLC 2, 14
  See also CANR 1; CA 1-4R; DLB 14

Rathbone, Julian 1935- . . . . CLC 41
  See also CA 101

Rattigan, Terence (Mervyn)
   1911-1977 . . . . CLC 7
  See also CA 85-88; obituary CA 73-76;
  DLB 13

Ratushinskaya, Irina 1954- . . . . CLC 54
  See also CA 129

Raven, Simon (Arthur Noel)
   1927- . . . . CLC 14
  See also CA 81-84

Rawley, Callman 1903-
  See Rakosi, Carl
  See also CANR 12; CA 21-24R

Rawlings, Marjorie Kinnan
   1896-1953 . . . . TCLC 4
  See also YABC 1; CA 104; DLB 9, 22

Ray, Satyajit 1921- . . . . CLC 16
  See also CA 114

Read, Herbert (Edward) 1893-1968 . . CLC 4
  See also CA 85-88; obituary CA 25-28R;
  DLB 20

Read, Piers Paul 1941- . . . . . . CLC 4, 10, 25
  See also CA 21-24R; SATA 21; DLB 14

Reade, Charles 1814-1884 . . . . NCLC 2
  See also DLB 21

Reade, Hamish 1936-
  See Gray, Simon (James Holliday)

Reading, Peter 1946- . . . . CLC 47
  See also CA 103; DLB 40

Reaney, James 1926- . . . . CLC 13
  See also CA 41-44R; SATA 43; DLB 68

Rebreanu, Liviu 1885-1944 . . . . TCLC 28

Rechy, John (Francisco)
   1934- . . . . CLC 1, 7, 14, 18
  See also CAAS 4; CANR 6; CA 5-8R;
  DLB-Y 82

Redcam, Tom 1870-1933 . . . . TCLC 25

Redgrove, Peter (William)
   1932- . . . . CLC 6, 41
  See also CANR 3; CA 1-4R; DLB 40

Redmon (Nightingale), Anne
   1943- . . . . CLC 22
  See also Nightingale, Anne Redmon
  See also DLB-Y 86

Reed, Ishmael
   1938- . . . . CLC 2, 3, 5, 6, 13, 32, 60
  See also CANR 25; CA 21-24R; DLB 2, 5,
  33

Reed, John (Silas) 1887-1920 . . . . . TCLC 9
  See also CA 106

Reed, Lou 1944- . . . . CLC 21

Reeve, Clara 1729-1807 . . . . NCLC 19
  See also DLB 39

Reid, Christopher 1949- . . . . CLC 33
  See also DLB 40

Reid Banks, Lynne 1929-
  See Banks, Lynne Reid
  See also CANR 6, 22; CA 1-4R; SATA 22

Reiner, Max 1900-
  See Caldwell, (Janet Miriam) Taylor
  (Holland)

Reizenstein, Elmer Leopold 1892-1967
  See Rice, Elmer

Remark, Erich Paul 1898-1970
  See Remarque, Erich Maria

Remarque, Erich Maria
   1898-1970 . . . . CLC 21
  See also CA 77-80; obituary CA 29-32R;
  DLB 56

Remizov, Alexey (Mikhailovich)
   1877-1957 . . . . TCLC 27
  See also CA 125

Renan, Joseph Ernest
   1823-1892 . . . . NCLC 26

Renard, Jules 1864-1910 . . . . TCLC 17
  See also CA 117

Renault, Mary 1905-1983 . . . . CLC 3, 11, 17
  See also Challans, Mary
  See also DLB-Y 83

Rendell, Ruth 1930- . . . . CLC 28, 48
  See also Vine, Barbara
  See also CA 109; DLB 87

Renoir, Jean 1894-1979 . . . . CLC 20
  See also CA 129; obituary CA 85-88

Resnais, Alain 1922- . . . . CLC 16

Reverdy, Pierre 1889-1960 . . . . CLC 53
  See also CA 97-100; obituary CA 89-92

Rexroth, Kenneth
   1905-1982 . . . . . . CLC 1, 2, 6, 11, 22, 49
  See also CANR 14; CA 5-8R;
  obituary CA 107; DLB 16, 48; DLB-Y 82;
  CDALB 1941-1968

Reyes, Alfonso 1889-1959 . . . . TCLC 33

Reyes y Basoalto, Ricardo Eliecer Neftali
   1904-1973
  See Neruda, Pablo

Reymont, Wladyslaw Stanislaw
   1867-1925 . . . . TCLC 5
  See also CA 104

Reynolds, Jonathan 1942?- . . . . . . CLC 6, 38
  See also CANR 28; CA 65-68

Reynolds, (Sir) Joshua 1723-1792 . . . . LC 15

Reynolds, Michael (Shane) 1937- . . . CLC 44
  See also CANR 9; CA 65-68

Reznikoff, Charles 1894-1976 . . . . CLC 9
  See also CAP 2; CA 33-36;
  obituary CA 61-64; DLB 28, 45

Rezzori, Gregor von 1914- . . . . CLC 25
  See also CA 122

Rhys, Jean
   1890-1979 . . . . . . CLC 2, 4, 6, 14, 19, 51
  See also CA 25-28R; obituary CA 85-88;
  DLB 36

Ribeiro, Darcy 1922- . . . . CLC 34
  See also CA 33-36R

Rossetti, Gabriel Charles Dante 1828-1882
See Rossetti, Dante Gabriel

Rossner, Judith (Perelman)
1935- .... CLC 6, 9, 29
See also CANR 18; CA 17-20R; DLB 6

Rostand, Edmond (Eugene Alexis)
1868-1918 .... TCLC 6, 37
See also CA 104, 126

Roth, Henry 1906- .... CLC 2, 6, 11
See also CAP 1; CA 11-12; DLB 28

Roth, Joseph 1894-1939 .... TCLC 33
See also DLB 85

Roth, Philip (Milton)
1933- ...... CLC 1, 2, 3, 4, 6, 9, 15, 22,
31, 47
See also CANR 1, 22; CA 1-4R; DLB 2, 28;
DLB-Y 82

Rothenberg, James 1931- .... CLC 57

Rothenberg, Jerome 1931- .... CLC 6, 57
See also CANR 1; CA 45-48; DLB 5

Roumain, Jacques 1907-1944 ...... TCLC 19
See also CA 117

Rourke, Constance (Mayfield)
1885-1941 .... TCLC 12
See also YABC 1; CA 107

Rousseau, Jean-Baptiste 1671-1741 ... LC 9

Rousseau, Jean-Jacques 1712-1778 ... LC 14

Roussel, Raymond 1877-1933 ..... TCLC 20
See also CA 117

Rovit, Earl (Herbert) 1927- .... CLC 7
See also CANR 12; CA 5-8R

Rowe, Nicholas 1674-1718 .... LC 8

Rowson, Susanna Haswell
1762-1824 .... NCLC 5
See also DLB 37

Roy, Gabrielle 1909-1983 ...... CLC 10, 14
See also CANR 5; CA 53-56;
obituary CA 110; DLB 68

Rozewicz, Tadeusz 1921- .... CLC 9, 23
See also CA 108

Ruark, Gibbons 1941- .... CLC 3
See also CANR 14; CA 33-36R

Rubens, Bernice 192?- .... CLC 19, 31
See also CA 25-28R; DLB 14

Rudkin, (James) David 1936- ...... CLC 14
See also CA 89-92; DLB 13

Rudnik, Raphael 1933- .... CLC 7
See also CA 29-32R

Ruiz, Jose Martinez 1874-1967
See Azorin

Rukeyser, Muriel
1913-1980 .... CLC 6, 10, 15, 27
See also CANR 26; CA 5-8R;
obituary CA 93-96; obituary SATA 22;
DLB 48

Rule, Jane (Vance) 1931- .... CLC 27
See also CANR 12; CA 25-28R; DLB 60

Rulfo, Juan 1918-1986 .... CLC 8
See also CANR 26; CA 85-88;
obituary CA 118

Runyon, (Alfred) Damon
1880-1946 .... TCLC 10
See also CA 107; DLB 11

Rush, Norman 1933- .... CLC 44
See also CA 121, 126

Rushdie, (Ahmed) Salman
1947- .... CLC 23, 31, 55, 59
See also CA 108, 111

Rushforth, Peter (Scott) 1945- ..... CLC 19
See also CA 101

Ruskin, John 1819-1900 .... TCLC 20
See also CA 114; SATA 24; DLB 55

Russ, Joanna 1937- .... CLC 15
See also CANR 11; CA 25-28R; DLB 8

Russell, George William 1867-1935
See A. E.
See also CA 104

Russell, (Henry) Ken(neth Alfred)
1927- .... CLC 16
See also CA 105

Russell, Willy 1947- .... CLC 60

Rutherford, Mark 1831-1913 ...... TCLC 25
See also CA 121; DLB 18

Ruyslinck, Ward 1929- .... CLC 14

Ryan, Cornelius (John) 1920-1974 ... CLC 7
See also CA 69-72; obituary CA 53-56

Ryan, Michael 1946- .... CLC 65
See also CA 49-52; DLB-Y 82

Rybakov, Anatoli 1911?- .... CLC 23, 53
See also CA 126

Ryder, Jonathan 1927-
See Ludlum, Robert

Ryga, George 1932- .... CLC 14
See also CA 101; obituary CA 124; DLB 60

**Séviné, Marquise de Marie de
Rabutin-Chantal** 1626-1696 ..... LC 11

Saba, Umberto 1883-1957 .... TCLC 33

Sabato, Ernesto 1911- .... CLC 10, 23
See also CA 97-100

Sacher-Masoch, Leopold von
1836?-1895 .... NCLC 31

Sachs, Marilyn (Stickle) 1927- ..... CLC 35
See also CLR 2; CANR 13; CA 17-20R;
SAAS 2; SATA 3, 52

Sachs, Nelly 1891-1970 .... CLC 14
See also CAP 2; CA 17-18;
obituary CA 25-28R

Sackler, Howard (Oliver)
1929-1982 .... CLC 14
See also CA 61-64; obituary CA 108; DLB 7

Sade, Donatien Alphonse Francois, Comte de
1740-1814 .... NCLC 3

Sadoff, Ira 1945- .... CLC 9
See also CANR 5, 21; CA 53-56

Safire, William 1929- .... CLC 10
See also CA 17-20R

Sagan, Carl (Edward) 1934- .... CLC 30
See also CANR 11; CA 25-28R; SATA 58

Sagan, Francoise
1935- .... CLC 3, 6, 9, 17, 36
See also Quoirez, Francoise
See also CANR 6; DLB 83

Sahgal, Nayantara (Pandit) 1927- ... CLC 41
See also CANR 11; CA 9-12R

Saint, H(arry) F. 1941- .... CLC 50

Sainte-Beuve, Charles Augustin
1804-1869 .... NCLC 5

Sainte-Marie, Beverly 1941-1972?
See Sainte-Marie, Buffy
See also CA 107

Sainte-Marie, Buffy 1941- .... CLC 17
See also Sainte-Marie, Beverly

**Saint-Exupery, Antoine (Jean Baptiste Marie
Roger) de** 1900-1944 .... TCLC 2
See also CLR 10; CA 108; SATA 20;
DLB 72

Saintsbury, George 1845-1933 ..... TCLC 31
See also DLB 57

Sait Faik (Abasiyanik)
1906-1954 .... TCLC 23

Saki 1870-1916 .... TCLC 3
See also Munro, H(ector) H(ugh)
See also CA 104

Salama, Hannu 1936- .... CLC 18

Salamanca, J(ack) R(ichard)
1922- .... CLC 4, 15
See also CA 25-28R

Salinas, Pedro 1891-1951 .... TCLC 17
See also CA 117

Salinger, J(erome) D(avid)
1919- .... CLC 1, 3, 8, 12, 56; SSC 2
See also CA 5-8R; DLB 2;
CDALB 1941-1968

Salter, James 1925- .... CLC 7, 52, 59
See also CA 73-76

Saltus, Edgar (Everston)
1855-1921 .... TCLC 8
See also CA 105

Saltykov, Mikhail Evgrafovich
1826-1889 .... NCLC 16

Samarakis, Antonis 1919- .... CLC 5
See also CA 25-28R

Sanchez, Florencio 1875-1910 ..... TCLC 37

Sanchez, Luis Rafael 1936- .... CLC 23

Sanchez, Sonia 1934- .... CLC 5
See also CANR 24; CA 33-36R; SATA 22;
DLB 41

Sand, George 1804-1876 .... NCLC 2

Sandburg, Carl (August)
1878-1967 ... CLC 1, 4, 10, 15, 35; PC 2
See also CA 5-8R; obituary CA 25-28R;
SATA 8; DLB 17, 54; CDALB 1865-1917

Sandburg, Charles August 1878-1967
See Sandburg, Carl (August)

Sanders, (James) Ed(ward) 1939- ... CLC 53
See also CANR 13; CA 15-16R, 103;
DLB 16

Sanders, Lawrence 1920- .... CLC 41
See also CA 81-84

Sandoz, Mari (Susette) 1896-1966 .. CLC 28
See also CANR 17; CA 1-4R;
obituary CA 25-28R; SATA 5; DLB 9

Saner, Reg(inald Anthony) 1931- .... CLC 9
See also CA 65-68

Sannazaro, Jacopo 1456?-1530 .... LC 8

Sansom, William 1912-1976 .... CLC 2, 6
See also CA 5-8R; obituary CA 65-68

Santayana, George 1863-1952 ..... TCLC 40
See also CA 115; DLB 54, 71

Santiago, Danny 1911-............ CLC 33
See also CA 125

Santmyer, Helen Hooven
1895-1986 .... CLC 33
See also CANR 15; CA 1-4R;
obituary CA 118; DLB-Y 84

Santos, Bienvenido N(uqui) 1911-... CLC 22
See also CANR 19; CA 101

Sappho c. 6th-century B.C.-....... CMLC 3

Sarduy, Severo 1937-.............. CLC 6
See also CA 89-92

Sargeson, Frank 1903-1982 .... CLC 31
See also CA 106, 25-28R; obituary CA 106

Sarmiento, Felix Ruben Garcia 1867-1916
See Dario, Ruben
See also CA 104

Saroyan, William
1908-1981 ..... CLC 1, 8, 10, 29, 34, 56
See also CA 5-8R; obituary CA 103;
SATA 23; obituary SATA 24; DLB 7, 9;
DLB-Y 81

Sarraute, Nathalie
1902-.......... CLC 1, 2, 4, 8, 10, 31
See also CANR 23; CA 9-12R; DLB 83

Sarton, Eleanore Marie 1912-
See Sarton, (Eleanor) May

Sarton, (Eleanor) May
1912- .... CLC 4, 14, 49
See also CANR 1; CA 1-4R; SATA 36;
DLB 48; DLB-Y 81

Sartre, Jean-Paul (Charles Aymard)
1905-1980 ... CLC 1, 4, 7, 9, 13, 18, 24,
44, 50, 52
See also CANR 21; CA 9-12R;
obituary CA 97-100; DLB 72

Sassoon, Siegfried (Lorraine)
1886-1967 .... CLC 36
See also CA 104; obituary CA 25-28R;
DLB 20

Saul, John (W. III) 1942- .... CLC 46
See also CANR 16; CA 81-84

Saura, Carlos 1932- .... CLC 20
See also CA 114

Sauser-Hall, Frederic-Louis
1887-1961 .... CLC 18
See Cendrars, Blaise
See also CA 102; obituary CA 93-96

Savage, Thomas 1915- .... CLC 40
See also CA 126

Savan, Glenn 19??-.............. CLC 50

Sayers, Dorothy L(eigh)
1893-1957 .... TCLC 2, 15
See also CA 104, 119; DLB 10, 36, 77

Sayers, Valerie 19??- .... CLC 50

Sayles, John (Thomas)
1950- .... CLC 7, 10, 14
See also CA 57-60; DLB 44

Scammell, Michael 19??-.......... CLC 34

Scannell, Vernon 1922- .... CLC 49
See also CANR 8; CA 5-8R; DLB 27

Schaeffer, Susan Fromberg
1941- .... CLC 6, 11, 22
See also CANR 18; CA 49-52; SATA 22;
DLB 28

Schell, Jonathan 1943-........... CLC 35
See also CANR 12; CA 73-76

Schelling, Friedrich Wilhelm Joseph von
1775-1854 .... NCLC 30
See also DLB 90

Scherer, Jean-Marie Maurice 1920-
See Rohmer, Eric
See also CA 110

Schevill, James (Erwin) 1920-...... CLC 7
See also CA 5-8R

Schisgal, Murray (Joseph) 1926-..... CLC 6
See also CA 21-24R

Schlee, Ann 1934-................ CLC 35
See also CA 101; SATA 36, 44

Schlegel, August Wilhelm von
1767-1845 .... NCLC 15

Schlegel, Johann Elias (von)
1719?-1749................... LC 5

Schmidt, Arno 1914-1979......... CLC 56
See also obituary CA 109; DLB 69

Schmitz, Ettore 1861-1928
See Svevo, Italo
See also CA 104, 122

Schnackenberg, Gjertrud 1953-..... CLC 40
See also CA 116

Schneider, Leonard Alfred 1925-1966
See Bruce, Lenny
See also CA 89-92

Schnitzler, Arthur 1862-1931 ...... TCLC 4
See also CA 104; DLB 81

Schor, Sandra 1932?-1990 .... CLC 65
See also CA 132

Schorer, Mark 1908-1977 .... CLC 9
See also CANR 7; CA 5-8R;
obituary CA 73-76

Schrader, Paul (Joseph) 1946-...... CLC 26
See also CA 37-40R; DLB 44

Schreiner (Cronwright), Olive (Emilie
Albertina) 1855-1920 .... TCLC 9
See also CA 105; DLB 18

Schulberg, Budd (Wilson)
1914- .... CLC 7, 48
See also CANR 19; CA 25-28R; DLB 6, 26,
28; DLB-Y 81

Schulz, Bruno 1892-1942.......... TCLC 5
See also CA 115, 123

Schulz, Charles M(onroe) 1922- .... CLC 12
See also CANR 6; CA 9-12R; SATA 10

Schuyler, James (Marcus)
1923- .... CLC 5, 23
See also CA 101; DLB 5

Schwartz, Delmore
1913-1966 .... CLC 2, 4, 10, 45
See also CAP 2; CA 17-18;
obituary CA 25-28R; DLB 28, 48

Schwartz, John Burnham 1925- .... CLC 59

Schwartz, Lynne Sharon 1939-..... CLC 31
See also CA 103

Schwarz-Bart, Andre 1928-....... CLC 2, 4
See also CA 89-92

Schwarz-Bart, Simone 1938-........ CLC 7
See also CA 97-100

Schwob, (Mayer Andre) Marcel
1867-1905 .... TCLC 20
See also CA 117

Sciascia, Leonardo
1921-1989 .... CLC 8, 9, 41
See also CA 85-88

Scoppettone, Sandra 1936-......... CLC 26
See also CA 5-8R; SATA 9

Scorsese, Martin 1942- .... CLC 20
See also CA 110, 114

Scotland, Jay 1932-
See Jakes, John (William)

Scott, Duncan Campbell
1862-1947 .... TCLC 6
See also CA 104; DLB 92

Scott, Evelyn 1893-1963.......... CLC 43
See also CA 104; obituary CA 112; DLB 9,
48

Scott, F(rancis) R(eginald)
1899-1985 .... CLC 22
See also CA 101; obituary CA 114; DLB 88

Scott, Joanna 19??-............... CLC 50
See also CA 126

Scott, Paul (Mark) 1920-1978.... CLC 9, 60
See also CA 81-84; obituary CA 77-80;
DLB 14

Scott, Sir Walter 1771-1832 ..... NCLC 15
See also YABC 2

Scribe, (Augustin) Eugene
1791-1861 .... NCLC 16

Scudery, Madeleine de 1607-1701..... LC 2

Sealy, I. Allan 1951- .... CLC 55

Seare, Nicholas 1925-
See Trevanian; Whitaker, Rodney

Sebestyen, Igen 1924-
See Sebestyen, Ouida

Sebestyen, Ouida 1924-........... CLC 30
See also CLR 17; CA 107; SATA 39

Sedgwick, Catharine Maria
1789-1867 .... NCLC 19
See also DLB 1, 74

Seelye, John 1931-................ CLC 7
See also CA 97-100

Seferiades, Giorgos Stylianou 1900-1971
See Seferis, George
See also CANR 5; CA 5-8R;
obituary CA 33-36R

Seferis, George 1900-1971....... CLC 5, 11
See also Seferiades, Giorgos Stylianou

Segal, Erich (Wolf) 1937- .... CLC 3, 10
See also CANR 20; CA 25-28R; DLB-Y 86

Seger, Bob 1945-................. CLC 35

Seger, Robert Clark 1945-
See Seger, Bob

Seghers, Anna 1900-1983....... CLC 7, 110
See also Radvanyi, Netty Reiling
See also DLB 69

Seidel, Frederick (Lewis) 1936-..... CLC 18
See also CANR 8; CA 13-16R; DLB-Y 84

Seifert, Jaroslav 1901-1986 ..... CLC 34, 44
See also CA 127

Trevanian 1925- .... CLC 29
See also CA 108

Trevor, William 1928- ..... CLC 7, 9, 14, 25
See also Cox, William Trevor
See also DLB 14

Trifonov, Yuri (Valentinovich)
1925-1981 .... CLC 45
See also obituary CA 103, 126

Trilling, Lionel 1905-1975 .... CLC 9, 11, 24
See also CANR 10; CA 9-12R;
obituary CA 61-64; DLB 28, 63

Trogdon, William 1939-
See Heat Moon, William Least
See also CA 115, 119

Trollope, Anthony 1815-1882 ..... NCLC 6
See also SATA 22; DLB 21, 57

Trollope, Frances 1780-1863 ..... NCLC 30
See also DLB 21

Trotsky, Leon (Davidovich)
1879-1940 .... TCLC 22
See also CA 118

Trotter (Cockburn), Catharine
1679-1749 .... LC 8
See also DLB 84

Trow, George W. S. 1943- .... CLC 52
See also CA 126

Troyat, Henri 1911- .... CLC 23
See also CANR 2; CA 45-48

Trudeau, G(arretson) B(eekman) 1948-
See Trudeau, Garry
See also CA 81-84; SATA 35

Trudeau, Garry 1948- .... CLC 12
See also Trudeau, G(arretson) B(eekman)

Truffaut, Francois 1932-1984 .... CLC 20
See also CA 81-84; obituary CA 113

Trumbo, Dalton 1905-1976 .... CLC 19
See also CANR 10; CA 21-24R;
obituary CA 69-72; DLB 26

Trumbull, John 1750-1831 .... NCLC 30
See also DLB 31

Tryon, Thomas 1926- .... CLC 3, 11
See also CA 29-32R

Ts'ao Hsueh-ch'in 1715?-1763 .... LC 1

Tsushima Shuji 1909-1948
See Dazai Osamu
See also CA 107

Tsvetaeva (Efron), Marina (Ivanovna)
1892-1941 .... TCLC 7, 35
See also CA 104, 128

Tunis, John R(oberts) 1889-1975 ... CLC 12
See also CA 61-64; SATA 30, 37; DLB 22

Tuohy, Frank 1925- .... CLC 37
See also DLB 14

Tuohy, John Francis 1925-
See Tuohy, Frank
See also CANR 3; CA 5-8R

Turco, Lewis (Putnam) 1934- ... CLC 11, 63
See also CANR 24; CA 13-16R; DLB-Y 84

Turgenev, Ivan
1818-1883 .... NCLC 21; SSC 7

Turner, Frederick 1943- .... CLC 48
See also CANR 12; CA 73-76; DLB 40

Tutuola, Amos 1920- .... CLC 5, 14, 29
See also CA 9-12R

Twain, Mark
1835-1910 ... TCLC 6, 12, 19, 36; SSC 6
See also Clemens, Samuel Langhorne
See also YABC 2; DLB 11, 12, 23, 64, 74

Tyler, Anne
1941- .... CLC 7, 11, 18, 28, 44, 59
See also CANR 11; CA 9-12R; SATA 7;
DLB 6; DLB-Y 82

Tyler, Royall 1757-1826 .... NCLC 3
See also DLB 37

Tynan (Hinkson), Katharine
1861-1931 .... TCLC 3
See also CA 104

Tytell, John 1939- .... CLC 50
See also CA 29-32R

Tzara, Tristan 1896-1963 .... CLC 47
See also Rosenfeld, Samuel

Uhry, Alfred 1947?- .... CLC 55
See also CA 127

Unamuno (y Jugo), Miguel de
1864-1936 .... TCLC 2, 9
See also CA 104

Underwood, Miles 1909-1981
See Glassco, John

Undset, Sigrid 1882-1949 .... TCLC 3
See also CA 104

Ungaretti, Giuseppe
1888-1970 .... CLC 7, 11, 15
See also CAP 2; CA 19-20;
obituary CA 25-28R

Unger, Douglas 1952- .... CLC 34
See also CA 130

Unger, Eva 1932-
See Figes, Eva

Updike, John (Hoyer)
1932- ...... CLC 1, 2, 3, 5, 7, 9, 13, 15,
23, 34, 43
See also CANR 4; CA 1-4R; CABS 2;
DLB 2, 5; DLB-Y 80, 82; DLB-DS 3

Urdang, Constance (Henriette)
1922- .... CLC 47
See also CANR 9, 24; CA 21-24R

Uris, Leon (Marcus) 1924- .... CLC 7, 32
See also CANR 1; CA 1-4R; SATA 49

Ustinov, Peter (Alexander) 1921- .... CLC 1
See also CANR 25; CA 13-16R; DLB 13

Vaculik, Ludvik 1926- .... CLC 7
See also CA 53-56

Valenzuela, Luisa 1938- .... CLC 31
See also CA 101

Valera (y Acala-Galiano), Juan
1824-1905 .... TCLC 10
See also CA 106

Valery, Paul (Ambroise Toussaint Jules)
1871-1945 .... TCLC 4, 15
See also CA 104, 122

Valle-Inclan (y Montenegro), Ramon (Maria)
del 1866-1936 .... TCLC 5
See also CA 106

Vallejo, Cesar (Abraham)
1892-1938 .... TCLC 3
See also CA 105

Van Ash, Cay 1918- .... CLC 34

Vance, Jack 1916?- .... CLC 35
See also DLB 8

Vance, John Holbrook 1916?-
See Vance, Jack
See also CANR 17; CA 29-32R

Van Den Bogarde, Derek (Jules Gaspard
Ulric) Niven 1921-
See Bogarde, Dirk
See also CA 77-80

Vandenburgh, Jane 19??- .... CLC 59

Vanderhaeghe, Guy 1951- .... CLC 41
See also CA 113

Van der Post, Laurens (Jan) 1906- ... CLC 5
See also CA 5-8R

Van de Wetering, Janwillem
1931- .... CLC 47
See also CANR 4; CA 49-52

Van Dine, S. S. 1888-1939 .... TCLC 23

Van Doren, Carl (Clinton)
1885-1950 .... TCLC 18
See also CA 111

Van Doren, Mark 1894-1972 ..... CLC 6, 10
See also CANR 3; CA 1-4R;
obituary CA 37-40R; DLB 45

Van Druten, John (William)
1901-1957 .... TCLC 2
See also CA 104; DLB 10

Van Duyn, Mona 1921- .... CLC 3, 7, 63
See also CANR 7; CA 9-12R; DLB 5

Van Itallie, Jean-Claude 1936- ...... CLC 3
See also CAAS 2; CANR 1; CA 45-48;
DLB 7

Van Ostaijen, Paul 1896-1928 ..... TCLC 33

Van Peebles, Melvin 1932- ...... CLC 2, 20
See also CA 85-88

Vansittart, Peter 1920- .... CLC 42
See also CANR 3; CA 1-4R

Van Vechten, Carl 1880-1964 ...... CLC 33
See also obituary CA 89-92; DLB 4, 9, 51

Van Vogt, A(lfred) E(lton) 1912- ..... CLC 1
See also CANR 28; CA 21-24R; SATA 14;
DLB 8

Varda, Agnes 1928- .... CLC 16
See also CA 116, 122

Vargas Llosa, (Jorge) Mario (Pedro)
1936- .... CLC 3, 6, 9, 10, 15, 31, 42
See also CANR 18; CA 73-76

Vassilikos, Vassilis 1933- .... CLC 4, 8
See also CA 81-84

Vaughn, Stephanie 19??- .... CLC 62

Vazov, Ivan 1850-1921 .... TCLC 25
See also CA 121

Veblen, Thorstein Bunde
1857-1929 .... TCLC 31
See also CA 115

Verga, Giovanni 1840-1922 .... TCLC 3
See also CA 104, 123

Verhaeren, Emile (Adolphe Gustave)
1855-1916 .... TCLC 12
See also CA 109

Verlaine, Paul (Marie)
1844-1896 .... NCLC 2; PC 2

Watkins, Vernon (Phillips)
1906-1967 .... CLC 43
See also CAP 1; CA 9-10;
obituary CA 25-28R; DLB 20

Waugh, Auberon (Alexander) 1939-.. CLC 7
See also CANR 6, 22; CA 45-48; DLB 14

Waugh, Evelyn (Arthur St. John)
1903-1966 ... CLC 1, 3, 8, 13, 19, 27, 44
See also CANR 22; CA 85-88;
obituary CA 25-28R; DLB 15

Waugh, Harriet 1944- .... CLC 6
See also CANR 22; CA 85-88

Webb, Beatrice (Potter)
1858-1943 .... TCLC 22
See also CA 117

Webb, Charles (Richard) 1939-...... CLC 7
See also CA 25-28R

Webb, James H(enry), Jr. 1946-.... CLC 22
See also CA 81-84

Webb, Mary (Gladys Meredith)
1881-1927 .... TCLC 24
See also CA 123; DLB 34

Webb, Phyllis 1927-.............. CLC 18
See also CANR 23; CA 104; DLB 53

Webb, Sidney (James)
1859-1947 .... TCLC 22
See also CA 117

Webber, Andrew Lloyd 1948-...... CLC 21

Weber, Lenora Mattingly
1895-1971 .... CLC 12
See also CAP 1; CA 19-20;
obituary CA 29-32R; SATA 2;
obituary SATA 26

Webster, Noah 1758-1843 .... NCLC 30
See also DLB 1, 37, 42, 43, 73

Wedekind, (Benjamin) Frank(lin)
1864-1918 .... TCLC 7
See also CA 104

Weidman, Jerome 1913-............ CLC 7
See also CANR 1; CA 1-4R; DLB 28

Weil, Simone 1909-1943......... TCLC 23
See also CA 117

Weinstein, Nathan Wallenstein 1903?-1940
See West, Nathanael
See also CA 104

Weir, Peter 1944-................ CLC 20
See also CA 113, 123

Weiss, Peter (Ulrich)
1916-1982 .... CLC 3, 15, 51
See also CANR 3; CA 45-48;
obituary CA 106; DLB 69

Weiss, Theodore (Russell)
1916- .... CLC 3, 8, 14
See also CAAS 2; CA 9-12R; DLB 5

Welch, (Maurice) Denton
1915-1948 .... TCLC 22
See also CA 121

Welch, James 1940-......... CLC 6, 14, 52
See also CA 85-88

Weldon, Fay
1933-........ CLC 6, 9, 11, 19, 36, 59
See also CANR 16; CA 21-24R; DLB 14

Wellek, Rene 1903- .... CLC 28
See also CAAS 7; CANR 8; CA 5-8R;
DLB 63

Weller, Michael 1942-......... CLC 10, 53
See also CA 85-88

Weller, Paul 1958-............. CLC 26

Wellershoff, Dieter 1925-.......... CLC 46
See also CANR 16; CA 89-92

Welles, (George) Orson
1915-1985 .... CLC 20
See also CA 93-96; obituary CA 117

Wellman, Mac 1945- .... CLC 65

Wellman, Manly Wade 1903-1986 .. CLC 49
See also CANR 6, 16; CA 1-4R;
obituary CA 118; SATA 6, 47

Wells, Carolyn 1862-1942 .... TCLC 35
See also CA 113; DLB 11

Wells, H(erbert) G(eorge)
1866-1946 ...... TCLC 6, 12, 19; SSC 6
See also CA 110, 121; SATA 20; DLB 34,
70

Wells, Rosemary 1943-............ CLC 12
See also CLR 16; CA 85-88; SAAS 1;
SATA 18

Welty, Eudora (Alice)
1909- .... CLC 1, 2, 5, 14, 22, 33; SSC 1
See also CA 9-12R; CABS 1; DLB 2;
DLB-Y 87; CDALB 1941-1968

Wen I-to 1899-1946 .... TCLC 28

Werfel, Franz (V.) 1890-1945 ...... TCLC 8
See also CA 104; DLB 81

Wergeland, Henrik Arnold
1808-1845 .... NCLC 5

Wersba, Barbara 1932-............ CLC 30
See also CLR 3; CANR 16; CA 29-32R;
SAAS 2; SATA 1, 58; DLB 52

Wertmuller, Lina 1928-............ CLC 16
See also CA 97-100

Wescott, Glenway 1901-1987....... CLC 13
See also CANR 23; CA 13-16R;
obituary CA 121; DLB 4, 9

Wesker, Arnold 1932- .... CLC 3, 5, 42
See also CAAS 7; CANR 1; CA 1-4R;
DLB 13

Wesley, Richard (Errol) 1945-....... CLC 7
See also CA 57-60; DLB 38

Wessel, Johan Herman 1742-1785 .... LC 7

West, Anthony (Panther)
1914-1987 .... CLC 50
See also CANR 3, 19; CA 45-48; DLB 15

West, Jessamyn 1907-1984 ...... CLC 7, 17
See also CA 9-12R; obituary CA 112;
obituary SATA 37; DLB 6; DLB-Y 84

West, Morris L(anglo) 1916-..... CLC 6, 33
See also CA 5-8R; obituary CA 124

West, Nathanael 1903?-1940 .... TCLC 1, 14
See also Weinstein, Nathan Wallenstein
See also CA 125, 140; DLB 4, 9, 28

West, Paul 1930-............... CLC 7, 14
See also CAAS 7; CANR 22; CA 13-16R;
DLB 14

West, Rebecca 1892-1983 .. CLC 7, 9, 31, 50
See also CANR 19; CA 5-8R;
obituary CA 109; DLB 36; DLB-Y 83

Westall, Robert (Atkinson) 1929-... CLC 17
See also CLR 13; CANR 18; CA 69-72;
SAAS 2; SATA 23

Westlake, Donald E(dwin)
1933-..................... CLC 7, 33
See also CANR 16; CA 17-20R

Westmacott, Mary 1890-1976
See Christie, (Dame) Agatha (Mary
Clarissa)

Whalen, Philip 1923-........... CLC 6, 29
See also CANR 5; CA 9-12R; DLB 16

Wharton, Edith (Newbold Jones)
1862-1937 .... TCLC 3, 9, 27; SSC 6
See also CA 104; DLB 4, 9, 12, 78;
CDALB 1865-1917

Wharton, William 1925-........ CLC 18, 37
See also CA 93-96; DLB-Y 80

Wheatley (Peters), Phillis
1753?-1784...................... LC 3
See also DLB 31, 50; CDALB 1640-1865

Wheelock, John Hall 1886-1978.... CLC 14
See also CANR 14; CA 13-16R;
obituary CA 77-80; DLB 45

Whelan, John 1900-
See O'Faolain, Sean

Whitaker, Rodney 1925-
See Trevanian

White, E(lwyn) B(rooks)
1899-1985 .... CLC 10, 34, 39
See also CLR 1; CANR 16; CA 13-16R;
obituary CA 116; SATA 2, 29, 44;
obituary SATA 44; DLB 11, 22

White, Edmund III 1940-......... CLC 27
See also CANR 3, 19; CA 45-48

White, Patrick (Victor Martindale)
1912-1990 ..... CLC 3, 4, 5, 7, 9, 18, 65
See also CA 81-84; obituary CA 132

White, T(erence) H(anbury)
1906-1964 .... CLC 30
See also CA 73-76; SATA 12

White, Terence de Vere 1912-...... CLC 49
See also CANR 3; CA 49-52

White, Walter (Francis)
1893-1955 .... TCLC 15
See also CA 115, 124; DLB 51

White, William Hale 1831-1913
See Rutherford, Mark
See also CA 121

Whitehead, E(dward) A(nthony)
1933-....................... CLC 5
See also CA 65-68

Whitemore, Hugh 1936-........... CLC 37

Whitman, Sarah Helen
1803-1878 .... NCLC 19
See also DLB 1

Whitman, Walt 1819-1892..... NCLC 4, 31
See also SATA 20; DLB 3, 64;
CDALB 1640-1865

Whitney, Phyllis A(yame) 1903-.... CLC 42
See also CANR 3, 25; CA 1-4R; SATA 1,
30

Whittemore, (Edward) Reed (Jr.)
1919-....................... CLC 4
See also CAAS 8; CANR 4; CA 9-12R;
DLB 5

Whittier, John Greenleaf
1807-1892 .... NCLC 8
See also DLB 1; CDALB 1640-1865

Author Index

Literary Criticism Series
Cumulative Topic Index

This index lists all topic entries in the Gale Literary Criticism Series *Contemporary Literary Criticism, Literature Criticism from 1400 to 1800, Nineteenth-Century Literature Criticism,* and *Twentieth-Century Literary Criticism.*

NCLC Cumulative Nationality Index

Dostoevski, Fedor Mikhailovich   **2, 7, 21**
Gogol, Nikolai   **5, 15, 31**
Goncharov, Ivan Alexandrovich   **1**
Herzen, Aleksandr Ivanovich   **10**
Karamzin, Nikolai Mikhailovich   **3**
Krylov, Ivan Andreevich   **1**
Lermontov, Mikhail Yuryevich   **5**
Leskov, Nikolai Semyonovich   **25**
Nekrasov, Nikolai   **11**
Ostrovsky, Alexander   **30**
Pisarev, Dmitry Ivanovich   **25**
Pushkin, Alexander   **3, 27**
Saltykov, Mikhail Evgrafovich   **16**
Smolenskin, Peretz   **30**
Turgenev, Ivan   **21**

SCOTTISH
Baillie, Joanna   **2**
Beattie, James   **25**
Campbell, Thomas   **19**
Ferrier, Susan   **8**
Galt, John   **1**
Hogg, James   **4**
Lockhart, John Gibson   **6**
Oliphant, Margaret   **11**
Scott, Sir Walter   **15**
Stevenson, Robert Louis   **5, 14**
Thomson, James   **18**
Wilson, John   **5**

SPANISH
Alarcón, Pedro Antonio de   **1**
Caballero, Fernán   **10**
Castro, Rosalía de   **3**
Larra, Mariano José de   **17**
Tamayo y Baus, Manuel   **1**
Zorrilla y Moral, José   **6**

SWEDISH
Bremer, Fredrika   **11**
Tegnér, Esias   **2**

SWISS
Amiel, Henri Frédéric   **4**
Keller, Gottfried   **2**
Wyss, Johann David   **10**

Nationality Index

Title Index to Volume 31

Title Index